THE CAMBRIDGE HISTORY OF MEDIEVAL
POLITICAL THOUGHT

c. 350–c. 1450

THE CAMBRIDGE
HISTORY OF MEDIEVAL
POLITICAL THOUGHT
c. 350–c. 1450

EDITED BY

J.H. BURNS

*Emeritus Professor of the
History of Political Thought,
University of London*

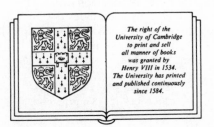

The right of the
University of Cambridge
to print and sell
all manner of books
was granted by
Henry VIII in 1534.
The University has printed
and published continuously
since 1584.

CAMBRIDGE UNIVERSITY PRESS

CAMBRIDGE

NEW YORK   PORT CHESTER

MELBOURNE   SYDNEY

Published by the Press Syndicate of the University of Cambridge
The Pitt Building, Trumpington Street, Cambridge CB2 1RP
40 West 20th Street, New York, NY 10011-4211, USA
10 Stamford Road, Oakleigh, Melbourne 3166, Australia

First published 1988
First paperback edition 1991

Printed in Great Britain at the University Press, Cambridge

British Library cataloguing in publication data
The Cambridge history of medieval political
thought c. 350–c. 1450.
1. Political science – History
I. Burns, J.H.
320.9182′1   JA82

Library of Congress cataloguing in publication data
The Ca nbridge history of medieval political thought c. 350–c. 1450.
Bibliography.
Includes index.
1. Political science – History.   I. Burns, J.H.
(James Henderson)
JA82.C27   1987   320′.01   87-6601

ISBN 0 521 24324 6 hardback
ISBN 0 521 42388 0 paperback

CONTENTS

ABBREVIATIONS

CC	*Corpus Christianorum*
CSEL	*Corpus Scriptorum Ecclesiasticorum Latinorum*
JE	*Regesta Pontificum Romanorum ab condita Ecclesia ad annum post Christum*
JK	*natum MCXCVIII*, ed. P. Jaffé, 2nd edn, rev. by W. Wattenbach, 2 vols.,
JL	contrib. P. Ewald, F. Kaltenbrunner and S. Loewenfeld, Veit, 1885–8
LTK	*Lexicon für Theologie und Kirche*
MGH	*Monumenta Germaniae Historica*
AA	*Auctores Antiquissimi*
Cap.	*Capitularia regum Francorum*
Conc.	*Concilia*
Const.	*Constitutiones*
DD	*Diplomata Karolinorum*
Epp.	*Epistolae*
Form.	*Formulae merovingici et karolini aevi*
Leges	*Leges nationum Germanicarum*
Libelli	*Libelli de Lite*
Poetae	*Poetae Latini Medii Aevi*
SS	*Scriptores*
PG	J.P. Migne, *Patrologia Graeca*
PL	J.P. Migne, *Patrologia Latina*

INTRODUCTION

The character of 'medieval political thought' is problematic. Its very existence, as an identifiable entity or subject, may be questioned, and has been denied. Yet such doubts and denials seem less than plausible in the light of the sustained and fruitful scholarly investigation and exposition that the subject – though not always under this title – has received for the best part of a century. Some aspects of that historiography will be considered in a moment. First, however, something needs to be said more directly about the nature of the subject itself. It is no doubt true that if certain definitions of 'political thought' are accepted it will be hard to find such thought in the period surveyed in this book. For most medieval thinkers the analysis, whether conceptual or institutional, of 'politics' in its original Greek sense was neither relevant nor possible. Even after the so-called 'Aristotelian revolution' of the thirteenth century this is still substantially true. Concepts and terminology derived from Aristotle's *Politics* then indeed became common intellectual currency; and yet there is no medieval work challenging even distant comparison with that massive treatise. The influence of Platonic or neo-Platonic ideas was no doubt more continuous, though the light it shed was refracted; but there is no medieval text of the character, let alone the calibre, of Plato's *Republic*. Ideas, whether Platonic or Aristotelian, rooted in the life of the *polis* or city-state had at best a limited application in most medieval societies.

If, on the other hand, 'political thought' is understood in terms of 'the state' as it has been experienced and analysed in the post-medieval western world, we shall again encounter a concept largely inappropriate in the medieval context. There is certainly room for argument both for and against the view that some kind of 'state' emerged, both in fact and in idea, in medieval Europe. This is a recurrent issue in the chapters that follow. Even if that question is resolved in an affirmative sense, however, it remains a hazardous enterprise to credit any medieval writer with a 'theory of the state' in what has been, at least for one tradition, the classic modern sense of the term.

In comparison, it may seem, medieval thinkers were concerned with issues much less distinctively 'political'. Walter Ullmann argued that the medieval outlook in general was characterised by a 'wholeness point of view'.[1] By this he intended to discriminate between that outlook and one in which, as in modern thinking, separate spheres are distinguished for what is 'moral', what is 'religious', and so on – including, specifically and emphatically, a sphere of 'the political'. It is certainly the case that this kind of division and specialisation of disciplines has been a characteristic and important modern development. It is not, however, the case that the alternative 'wholeness point of view' has been peculiarly or exclusively medieval. It is surely a viewpoint of that kind that makes Plato's *Republic*, for instance, so much more than a 'theory of the state'. As for Aristotle, just because the *polis* was for him a society uniquely capable of making possible a 'good life' in comprehensive terms, its analysis could not be narrowly 'political'. Thus a theory of the household forms an integral part of Aristotle's 'political theory'; and his account of political systems as such cannot dispense with such ethical concepts as 'friendship' and 'justice'. Theories of 'the modern state' have likewise transcended the restrictions of the explicitly 'political'. There are 'sociological' dimensions in the thought of Bodin or Montesquieu. Again, vitally important political thinking in the modern period has developed within the matrix of jurisprudence or of the 'political economy' which emerged from the moral philosophy of the seventeenth and eighteenth centuries. As for explicit modern variants of the 'wholeness point of view', it may suffice to cite the influential case of Hegel, for whom 'the strictly political state' is far from exhausting the content of the term 'state' itself.[2]

The credentials of 'medieval political thought', then, are not impugned by the recognition that its subject-matter extends to themes which, in other periods or for some thinkers, might seem alien to strictly political discourse. Nor is it necessary, in the defence of those credentials, to have recourse to a definition of politics as nothing less than (in Michael Oakeshott's phrase) 'the activity of attending to the general arrangements' of a society.[3] It is sufficient to recognise that issues seemingly *prima facie* 'social', 'economic',

---

1. Cf., e.g., Ullmann 1975a, pp. 16ff.
2. Cf. translator's note to § 267, *Hegel's Philosophy of Right*, translated with notes by T.M. Knox, Clarendon Press, 1942, pp. 364–5. For the phrase 'strictly political state' see § 267 (p. 163); and cf. 'the state as a political entity', §§ 273, 176, (pp. 276, 179).
3. M. Oakeshott, *Rationalism in Political and Other Essays*, Methuen, 1962, p. 122: 'Politics I take to be the activity of attending to the general arrangements of a set of people whom chance or choice have brought together.'

'ecclesiastical' or even 'spiritual' arise here because of their bearing upon questions of *authority* and *jurisdiction*. Thus the theory of *dominium* expounded by John of Paris at the turn of the thirteenth and fourteenth centuries has a great deal to do with problems arising from changing economic conditions,[4] but it is expounded deliberately in the context of an argument – a *political* argument, we may properly say – about royal and papal *power*. Again, the theoretical issues raised by the conciliar movement of the fifteenth century were largely theological issues regarding the nature of the church as a spiritual society; but – setting aside the overtly political conflicts in the context of which the movement developed – those issues were, for some writers at least, concerned with the consequences of treating the church as a particular instance of the genus comprising *political* societies as such.

There are various ways, accordingly, in which the genuinely political character of 'medieval political thought' can be established. Yet it remains, also, *medieval*; and nothing said here is intended to deny that there are specifically 'medieval' characteristics to be considered and particular problems in the historical interpretation of this body of ideas. For one thing, medieval society was theocentric and even, for some of its leading figures, theocratic. Necessarily, therefore, an account of medieval political thinking will include more theology and ecclesiology than would be expected in a modern sequel. Chapters 11 and 14 below, for example, would be hard to parallel in a history of modern political thought, whereas the ecclesiastical and theological issues with which they deal are central here. Again the relative dearth, especially in the earlier phases, of explicit political theorising in medieval society means that historians must concern themselves to a very considerable extent with ideas that are implicit in institutions and procedures, including (an important element in the evidence) ritual and ceremonial. The exploration of ideas and attitudes embedded in governmental and social structures means, moreover, that the history of medieval political thought must frequently merge into the historical analysis of medieval society itself. This demonstrates the advantage – indeed the necessity – of, for instance, the account in chapter 9 of 'Government, law and society' in the period from the mid-eighth to the mid-twelfth century. There is also, however, a more general question about the approach to the subject adopted here, which may itself be approached by way of some brief comments on earlier historiography.

4. Cf. pp. 638–40 below.

It is possible, and not necessarily unrewarding, to write the history of political thought in this as in other periods as, essentially, the history of political thinkers. Medieval thinkers can indeed be given places among 'the masters of political thought'.[5] 'The medieval contribution to political thought', again, can be assessed by reference to the work of outstanding figures – Aquinas, Marsilius, Hooker.[6] Yet whatever the merits and disadvantages of this kind of history may be for other periods, it can hardly fail to yield an imperfect and distorted picture of political ideas in the medieval centuries. For reasons already stated, few writers in that period can be meaningfully identified as 'political thinkers' at all; and very few indeed can be regarded as having made a major individual contribution to the subject. Even if the net is cast more widely and the definition of a 'political thinker' made more flexible, so much of the evidence will be lost as to leave the resulting 'history' unacceptably spasmodic and patchy. Whole tracts of time, indeed, would virtually disappear if the record were restricted to the work of individual thinkers. Yet without an understanding of, in particular, the earlier medieval centuries, our perspectives on the later period, with its revival of explicit political discussion and analysis carried out by more readily identifiable 'political thinkers', must be misleadingly foreshortened. To see these later medieval political ideas, in some sense no doubt ideas reflecting a more sophisticated culture, in the context of the earlier sources upon which their exponents continued to draw is, for one thing, to gain a degree of security against the risk of distortion when what is 'medieval' is viewed and assessed in terms of its supposed anticipation of what is regarded as 'modern'.

Thus a more thematic or conceptual approach must potentially be, and has been in fact, more fruitful in the history of medieval political thought. The point may be illustrated by a brief consideration of three major contributions to the historiography of the subject since the late nineteenth century. There is first the dominant figure of Otto von Gierke and the three volumes (published between 1868 and 1881) of *Das deutsche Genossenschaftsrecht*. Gierke's monumental and magisterial work was of course concerned with more than the strictly medieval period; and particular importance here, especially for English-speaking scholars, attaches to that part of the third volume which was translated by F.W. Maitland and published in 1900 under the significant title of *Political Theories of the Middle Age*. Gierke was indeed concerned with 'political

---

5. M.B. Foster, *Plato to Machiavelli*, vol. 1 in E.McC. Sait (ed.), *The Masters of Political Thought*, Harrap, 1942.   6. Passerin d'Entrèves 1939.

theories', and his concern was expressed through the deployment of formidable learning in an immense body of source-material. It was, however, for all its range, a concern of a rather specific kind. Not only is Gierke's work explicitly directed to 'the law of associations' (*Genossenschaftsrecht*): it seeks and finds in that law an 'ideal type' or model of fellowship and group personality. The ideal, moreover, is essentially and avowedly Germanic, even if both Gierke and those influenced by him saw it as a source of more generally applicable principles for a modern world suffering from excessive 'individualism'. In this powerful perspective, medieval political thought reveals above all the principles of a group or corporate life generating in those who share it morally valuable qualities of loyalty and brotherhood which transcend even the political division between rulers and ruled. It is a thesis which can be and has increasingly been questioned;[7] but it cannot be doubted that Gierke's work opened up, effectively for the first time, much of the buried wealth of medieval thinking about society.

Shortly after the publication of Maitland's important translation from Gierke, R.W. and A.J. Carlyle produced the first of what eventually amounted to the six volumes of *A History of Mediaeval Political Theory in the West*. Reprinted as recently as 1970, this remains an invaluable contribution to the subject, not least on account of its copious provision of quotations from the sources in the original languages. What calls for comment here, however, is the structure and method adopted by Carlyle (the singular form seeming warranted in view of the fact that the work was preponderantly written by A.J. Carlyle, with some contributions by the brother who predeceased him). Within a broadly chronological framework, the approach is essentially thematic, with relatively little attempt to give sustained and systematic attention even to major individual thinkers.[8] A particularly characteristic feature is the recurrence in successive sections and volumes of the work of chapter-headings which Carlyle clearly regarded as identifying the principal themes to be explored: 'The source of law'; 'The source and nature of the authority of the ruler'; 'The theory of the divine right'; 'Representative institutions', and so on. Even more striking and important, however, is the clear conviction that it is possible to identify certain 'great political conceptions of the Middle Ages': these are listed as 'the supremacy

---

7. Cf. pp. 588–9 below; also Black 1984, as index, esp. pp. 210–17.
8. Exceptionally, separate chapters are devoted in vol. IV to John of Salisbury and Gerhoh of Reichersberg (Part IV, chaps. II, III); but these deal only with the two authors' views on the relationship between the spiritual and temporal powers.

of law, the authority of the community, the contractual relation between ruler and subject'.[9] Here again we have a view – with its corollary, that 'the theory of the absolute Divine authority of the King . . . had little importance in the Middle Ages'[10] – which has exercised a good deal of influence but which would now be regarded as too restricted and one-sided for anything like unqualified acceptance.

The Carlyle view would, in terms of a third important and influential approach to medieval political thought, be seen as an emphatic – indeed over-emphatic – assertion of an 'ascending', in contradistinction from a 'descending', conception of political authority. Walter Ullmann's familiar formulation recognised indeed the presence and the importance of both views in medieval thought; but he argued that throughout the long period between the Christianisation of the Germanic peoples of northern and western Europe and the late thirteenth century, it was the descending theory – in which political power comes by delegation from God, to whom alone the ruler is accountable – that overwhelmingly preponderated. Even so, Ullmann claimed, 'The history of political ideas in the Middle Ages is to a very large extent a history of the conflicts between these two theories of government.'[11] Here yet again, no doubt, we have an illuminating and fruitful hypothesis which is nevertheless open to question and debate and which would certainly not be universally accepted as a sufficient framework for a thorough exploration of the subject. In any case it is of course by no means the only important general concept to have emerged from Ullmann's massive and wide-ranging scholarship. His insistence on the medieval 'wholeness point of view' has already been mentioned. Even more important, arguably, is Ullmann's concern to convince his readers that for most of the medieval period our investigation is concerned with 'governmental' rather than strictly 'political' ideas – with ideas essentially about the exercise of authority in *gubernatio*, which in turn was seen as being indissolubly connected with *jurisdictio*, 'laying down the law'.[12] It followed from this that legal and juristic sources had for Ullmann an importance which had assuredly not been overlooked by other historians but which for him meant that the medieval view of society and authority 'found its most conspicuous expression in the law and in . . . jurisprudence'.[13]

The present volume cannot, as a work of co-operative scholarship, offer

9. Vol. IV, p. vii.
10. Vol. VI, pp. 185, 191. This however is not entirely consistent with views expressed elsewhere by Carlyle: cf. vol. III, pp. 115–24 on the eleventh and twelfth centuries, and, perhaps especially, vol. I, pp. 215ff, on ninth-century writers and the influence of Gregory the Great.
11. Ullmann 1975a, p. 13.   12. *Ibid.*, pp. 17–18.   13. Ullmann 1975b, p. 12.

anything like the single magisterial view to be found in a Gierke, a Carlyle, or an Ullmann. Its aim is, rather, to present a conspectus, as comprehensive as is possible within prescribed limits of space, of the present state of historical scholarship in the field surveyed. Such a conspectus need not be, nor is it here, so neutral as to preclude critical assessment. The judgements of the authors concerned have been brought to bear upon the issues arising in scholarly debate; and since the division between one chapter and another cannot be absolute and rigid, there is room for differences of emphasis and approach in the handling of topics that are relevant to more than one chapter. It is hoped that such differences do not amount to contradictions and that their presence may yield a degree of cross-fertilisation rather than confusion. This is applicable not only to topics but to texts and their authors; for the formula adopted has meant that even major thinkers have not, as individuals, been regarded as the preserve of any one contributor. The reader who is for the time being concerned with, let us say, Aquinas or Marsilius, should be able, with the help of the index, to bring together the views of several scholars approaching the ideas in question from a diversity of angles.

The political thought discussed here is predominantly that of Latin Christendom, of 'the West'. However, besides the brief introductory sketches of Christian, classical and Roman-law 'foundations', there is a substantial chapter on the political ideas of Byzantium, which are examined over the whole period down to the final eclipse of the eastern empire in the middle of the fifteenth century. This has been included because of the persistent significance for political development in the Latin West, especially during the first half of the millennium here surveyed, of both the fact and the idea of the Byzantine imperial system. Similarly, though less elaborately and systematically, space has been found, especially in chapter 12, for some attention to ideas derived from non-Christian cultures either on the frontiers of or within Latin Christendom. The political ideas of Jewish and Islamic thinkers could obviously have received much fuller treatment; but to have provided this would have extended the scope of the book beyond what the available space could have sustained.

For the rest, the various chapters may be left to speak for themselves with the further clarification provided in the introductory chapters to parts III, IV and V respectively. A word about the apparatus may suffice to conclude this brief general introduction. The abbreviated 'author and date' references which are, with very few exceptions, employed in the footnotes, can be elucidated by reference to the relevant section of the Bibliography, which in turn is intended primarily to serve this specific purpose. It is not, of course, claimed that the listing of primary and secondary works cited in the body of the book constitutes a comprehensive bibliography of the subject as a whole. It is hoped, however, that, subdivided as it is, the Bibliography may go some considerable way towards providing rapid access to details of much of the relevant material. So far as the biographical (in some cases necessarily quasi-biographical) notes are concerned, their function is limited to that of ready reference – to locate authors chronologically and in some measure bibliographically in respect of their principal writings.

I
FOUNDATIONS

I
CHRISTIAN DOCTRINE

The early Christians understood the Church to which they adhered to consist of a community called out to serve God as his people and focused on Jesus of Nazareth as model for the disciples' filial relation to God. At first entirely Jewish both in composition and in conception, the community was transformed by St Paul into a body of universal extension. In the apostle's conviction God, through Jesus the Messiah and his society, had at last disclosed his eternal plan: that is, to call men and women of all races and conditions in faith and obedience to a Master who acted out and embodied the redeeming love of God for his fallen creation. The huge success of the Gentile mission, led by this Jew of the Dispersion with Roman citizenship, changed the Church from being an ethnic minority group which could hope for easy toleration within an empire generally ready to allow tribal religion, even when it diverged from the official religion of the government. Romans believed that empire had been bestowed not only by their own gods, but also by the gods of the conquered peoples; the latter deities could therefore be taken over. The Jews, whose Maccabaean resistance to assimilation made them respected but little loved in Greco-Roman society, were unmolested in their cultic practices which 'though very peculiar, were at least ancestral' (Celsus). But alarm was generated by the Christians dividing families and recruiting from all races and classes: mixing slaves and free; treating 'brothers and sisters' within the community as equal (Gal. 3:28; Col. 3:11); above all refusing to accord divine honour to the emperor or to swear by his genius.

Under Nero at Rome in 64 Christians were made the scapegoat for a catastrophic fire and were branded as criminals. Evidently they were already unpopular in society. Thereafter for two and a half centuries they were periodically liable to varying levels of harassment, ranging from local riots to officially sponsored efforts to search out and destroy. The occasions often arose from belief that their ignoring of the gods and emptying of the temples were responsible for poor crops or civil wars or some other uncontrollable disaster. The experience of persecution produced a kind of schizophrenia in Christian attitudes to government which may be seen as a highly acute version of the common human sense of ambivalence towards all governmental authority – as being on the one hand, an instrument by which one class or group in society dominates the majority in ways they do not like; on the other hand, a beneficent provision of order and justice, with centralised control of defence, refuse disposal, public health (baths and lavatories) and roads. Ancient postal services were for government use only. In one group of early Christian texts the persecuting government seems the very instrument of the Devil, the scarlet woman of Babylon drunk with the blood of the saints (Rev. 17). Moreover the Christians had from the start a strong sense of radical dualism between the people of God and 'the world', *kosmos* or *saeculum*, whose essential business consists in power, honour, sex and wealth. The Christians were sharply conscious that no large proportion of money can be called wholly clean; that avarice is insatiable (almost irresistible to parents ambitious for their children), for as needs are satisfied they increase; that in human nature there is an inherent conflict between physical appetite and man's higher or more psychic aspirations, and total dedication to God may entail a calling to a single life; above all, that power is corrupting to its possessor to the degree to which it lacks checks and restraints, and honour breeds ridiculous vanity and pride. The Beatitudes flatly contradict the accepted values of a society in which, by means of conflict, power is sought for the sake of domination, comfort, pleasure, and prestige.

On the other hand, the Christians were commanded by their Master to obey the requirements of legitimate government: 'Render to Caesar the things that are Caesar's and to God the things that are God's.' St Paul bids his congregations pray for those in authority. He assures the Christians in Rome (a community evidently sensitive on the point) that 'the powers that be are ordained by God'. Irenaeus, bishop of Lyon c. 180, opposes those who take 'the powers' to be superhuman and demonic, and explains that the Devil was being deceitful when in the Temptation of Jesus he claimed to have the kingdoms of this world in his gift (*Adversus Haereses* V 22–4). The Christians, for whom theft was forbidden and fidelity in marriage enjoined, were expected to be good citizens. It would be a reasonable gloss on Romans 13 to say that government, without whose laws and sanctions of ultimate enforcement, even by recourse to violence, society will not cohere, has some positive role in the divinely intended order of creation, even though it may never be a grand reflection of cosmic harmony and justice. It is certain from St Paul's words that 'the magistrate does not bear the sword to no purpose', that, because of the cupidity and pride in the heart of fallen man, a power of coercion is an indispensable restraint. The magistrate will get no one to heaven, but may yet do something to fence the broad road to the hell of anarchy which, as Thucydides first observed with disturbing eloquence, brings out the full human capacity for depravity.

Between the positive and the negative attitudes to government there lay a middle way of relativism, almost indifference. The first Christians did not expect the world to last long. They soon came to make their own an old Greek distinction between possession and use: one should use what one possesses with detachment lest one be possessed by it. St Paul applied the maxim both to wealth and to sex in marriage (1 Cor. 7:29–31). The adoption of indifference towards earthly authority produced very varied reactions, ranging from the positive relativism of St Paul to an almost anarchic antinomianism for which the prescriptions of the secular world counted for nothing. The proconsul of Africa, Saturninus, in 180 was confronted by a Christian of Scilli named Speratus who declared himself a ready taxpayer not because of the 'imperium' of this world which he did not recognise, but because of the sovereignty of the King of Kings. Speratus and his companions were executed.

Another form of the middle way could produce less drastic consequences. It was one of the merits of possessing a strong sense of the transhuman power of evil that the antithetical attitudes could be intellectually reconciled by the hypothesis that persecutions resulted more from an external demonic prompting than from something inherently diabolical in the very nature of governmental authority. Likewise the politically awkward fact that Jesus had been crucified under Pontius Pilate was mitigated by a very early tendency to exonerate the Roman people and to transfer moral, if not legal, responsibility for the judicial murder onto the Sadducees.

In the eyes of observant and devout Jews the Roman government, sadly polluted by idolatry and polytheism, was resented, above all when the emperor Caligula attempted in 41 to set up his own statue in the Temple at Jerusalem; the ferment of agitation which this satanic act generated left its mark in the New Testament (Mark 13:14; 2 Thess. 2:3ff). In one rabbinic text the Roman Empire is pictured as presenting an apologia for the excellence of its administration to the divine Judge: Rome has stimulated trade, built roads, and imposed law and order simply that devout Israelites may be undisturbed in the study of the Mosaic Law. But the Judge rejects the plea: you did it all solely for your own gain. Much of the Jewish Zealots' antipathy to Roman rule was shared by the Christians. Nevertheless in AD 66 they dissociated themselves from the violent revolution of the Zealots. They fled to the mountains (Matt. 24:15–22). The tradition of Jesus' sayings included instruction to pay taxes and to eschew all violence: 'Those who take the sword shall perish with the sword.' The Gentile Christians were told to be politically submissive even under persecution (1 Peter 2:13–14; Titus 3:1). 'Let none of you suffer as a murderer or thief or sorcerer or agitator' (1 Peter 4:15).

Despite St Paul's positive evaluation of the functions of government, he tells the Corinthian Christians not to take disputes to the lawcourts but to have them settled by arbitration within the community, since magistrates 'count for nothing in the Church' (1 Cor. 6:4; cf. Matt. 18:15–17). This instruction came in time to impose a heavy social burden on bishops who had to spend Monday mornings trying to reconcile quarrelling members. Arbitration was particularly embarrassing if the dissension were between rich and poor since, in cases where the wealthy Christian had all justice on his side, the bishop might well judge that charity must prevail over strict equity, and that the rights of private property (which the Christians defended, in the sense that they were much against theft) could not be absolute. Property is held by human law, but not by divine law. Augustine thought it unjustly held if unjustly used (*Sermo* 50, 2.4).

The original apostolic band kept a bag of money for necessaries, and the circle of Jesus' followers included persons of substance. St Paul had to tell his converts that Christians earn their bread to have means to give alms, and should not presume on richer fellow-Christians (2 Thess. 3:10; 4:11). The pursuit and possession of material wealth and property are treated in the gospel tradition as at least potentially hazardous to the soul whose priorities must lie in the kingdom of God and in support to the needy. Possessions are precarious and transitory. 'The love of money is a root of all evils' (1 Tim. 3:8; 6:9–10). The moral issue is seen to lie in use, not in (a necessarily ephemeral) possession. Where it is retained, the rich have a duty to share their abundance with the destitute who are of equal care to God (so the Shepherd of Hermas, *Sim.* ii, 5–10, and the second-century *Preaching of Peter*). Both Irenaeus (IV, 30,1–3) and Origen (*In Rom.* ix. 25) write of property as being a necessary evil because of bodily needs. To the ascetic Origen the evil lies in distracting the soul from higher things. But Lactantius (*Inst.* v, 14, 19–20) makes it a Christian criticism of secular society that the disparity between rich and poor is grossly unjust, and is exacerbated by the insolence of the propertied classes. 'Private affluence and public squalor' was characteristic of Roman society long after Sallust so described it. Lactantius draws back from communism, however, which could do nothing for moral virtue (*Inst.* iii, 21–2). The ideal which many early Christian writers express is one of simplicity and frugality, any surplus being devoted to generous alms which should not be confined to church members. Thereby the Church created a haven at least for some victims of a stormy and ruthless world. Augustine complained that the rich 'benefactors' of late Roman cities were far too concerned to get honour to themselves by paying for public games and saw no advantage or credit in providing welfare for the destitute, begging outside the church door (*Sermo* 32, 30), and sometimes finding even Augustine's congregation reluctant to provide (*Sermo* 123, 5; esp. 61, 12–13).

The poor were vulnerable to the high interest rates demanded by money-lenders. The consequent bankruptcies, which Jerome regarded as lying at the root of much urban rioting, led to such destitution that the Church took a hard line against all usury (e.g. Clement of Alexandria, *Paed.* i, 95; Tertullian, *Marc.* iv, 17). But it does not appear that objection was seriously taken to loan capital for commerce, and there is considerable evidence of the clergy providing a banking service for their congregations.

Slaves and the majority of women did not enjoy an enviable status in ancient society. Christian ethical attitudes and principles did something for the interests of both without, however, pressing for changes in their legal rights. The Church had enough trouble repelling the charge of sedition without giving the accusation this degree of plausibility. The ancient world could hardly imagine a society without slaves, except in a Utopian golden age or in small religious communities like the Essenes by the Dead Sea or the nearby Therapeutae in Egypt. St Paul expressly lays down that, while within the Christian family all are equal to their heavenly Father, the Church makes no change in the civil status of slaves (1 Cor. 7:21). The epistle to Philemon does not in principle ask for the emancipation of the delinquent, now believing slave Onesimus. But it is fundamental that the discipline of an erring slave in a Christian household shall be of paternal mildness. A slave in a good household was much better cared for than a free labourer (Aug. *Sermo* 159, 5). It was not uncommon for poor parents with too many children in hard times to sell superfluous offspring; not unknown for husbands to sell their wives if they valued the cash more.

Church funds could be used for the manumission of Christians. An emancipated slave rose to be Pope (Callistus) in the third century. But under the Christian empire care had to be taken not to prejudice the property rights of owners by the ordination of unemancipated slaves. After Constantine had conferred the powers of civil magistrates on bishops, a Christian householder could come to the church family to manumit his slave before the bishop, *Gestis episcopalibus*, with the proceedings formally recorded by lawyers, and this counted as a meritorious act. Slave-trading was not regarded as an acceptable occupation for a believer (Aug. *En.Ps.* 127, 11), and Augustine viewed the system with sad resignation as a consequence of man's fallen estate (*De Genesi ad litteram* xi, 50; *De civ. Dei* xix, 15–17). Nevertheless providence can turn even this evil to a good purpose in helping to give order to society; and it will be of benefit to the individual slave if the Christian owner duly educates the servants in Christian faith and practice and treats them never as chattels, but always with love (*De Virgin.* 9; *De Sermone Dom. in monte* i, 59). Augustine was sure that at the last judgement many slaves would appear among the sheep, many masters among the goats (*En.Ps.* 124, 8).

If the 'secular' city churches did not break the system, the monastic movement did so. The monks' calling was to live the angelic life now, to realise the perfect society where the ethic of the sermon on the mount could be acted out, as it could hardly be in the secular world. It was felt permissible for city churches to own slaves to work the land given to them by benefactors for the sake of the endowments and for the maintenance of the poor on the church roll. But deep disapproval attached to monasteries that tried to act in this way (e.g. Theodore of Studium's will, *PG* 99, 1817).

The married woman in ancient society was often not much more than a highly privileged chattel-slave (privileged to the degree that her children alone counted as legitimate, not to the extent that her husband would keep his hands off the slave-girls). Within the Church, by contrast, her status and her right to ask equal fidelity of her husband were strongly emphasised. The Genesis narrative of Eve's derivation from Adam's rib and succumbing to the serpent's blandishment seemed to many early Christian writers to provide a 'myth' or rationale for resisting feminine emancipation. Augustine observes that in mind and intelligence woman is equal to the male and that it is her biological sexual role which makes her subordinate (*Confessions* xiii, 32, 47). But elsewhere he remarks that in respect of sexual intercourse a wife's rights are equal to those of the husband, *par potestas*; it is outside the bed that her social role is to support and to obey (e.g. *c.Faustum* xxii, 31). Again the monastic movement became the principal engine for emancipation, making it possible to live in communities without male domination, recognised to be of equal standing with monasteries for men, so that the abbess (often a well-connected lady) came to enjoy high social status and power. However, the ascetic followers of Priscillian, bishop of Avila 381–5, alarmed the socially conservative Spanish churches of the fourth century by giving women an active role in their charismatic movement. A similarly hostile reaction met the contemporary Messalians in Syria and Asia Minor.

Reconciliation and peace are words occurring frequently in early Christian texts. In God's family brothers and sisters must not bite and devour one another (Gal. 5:14). But the Pauline tradition freely employed military metaphors for the Christian struggle against evil (1 Thess. 5:8; 1 Cor. 9:7; 2 Cor. 11:8; Phil. 2:25; Eph. vi, 12–18 etc.). Timothy is to endure as a good soldier of Christ (2 Tim, 2:3). By the third century Latin-speaking Christians had come to describe the unbaptised as 'pagani', the soldiers' slang for civilians, uninvolved in the conflict with evil powers.

Melito, bishop of Sardis c. 170, regarded it as a special providence that Augustus had established peace in the empire at the time when Christ's gospel of peace was proclaimed. He accepted a providential role for the empire in the purposes of God. But could an individual Christian fight to maintain this peace? Origen, who echoes Melito's view (*c.Cels.* ii, 30), explains that Christians may not take up arms to fight, but offer earnest prayers for the just defenders of the realm (viii, 73). Surviving fragments of early liturgies include prayers for the emperor and for the army, that they 'may subdue all barbarian nations for our perpetual peace'. (See the Solemn Prayers for Good Friday in the Roman Missal, which probably go back to the fourth century.) The pagan Celsus (c. 180) exhorts the Christians to accept public office and serve in the army. The evidence shows that during the third century the Christians followed his advice, and the more they did so the more alarm they caused to the pagans. As soldiers were converted, the question was asked if they could continue in the army after baptism. Tertullian thought not (*De Corona* 11); Clement of Alexandria thought soldiering no exception to the Pauline rule that Christians should remain in the state in which they were at the time of their being 'called' (*Paed.* i, 12; *Strom.* iv, 61–2). The impetus for the great persecution of Diocletian in 303 came when Christian army officers of high rank made the sign of the cross during some sacrifices, and the augurers felt that the lack of omens and signs was attributable to their presence. The story underlines a point made by Origen, that idolatry is one reason which keeps Christians out of the legions. But Origen also thought bloodshed wrong in principle for a Christian. The council of Arles (314) ruled against Christians in time of peace abandoning military service as a matter of conscience; in other words, their 'policing' role is acceptable, but not killing. In the 370s Basil of Caesarea similarly allows for the possibility of just war, but even then a soldier who takes life is excommunicate subject to penance (*Ep.* 188, 13).

The attitude to capital punishment is similarly almost uniformly negative among the Church Fathers. In the second century Athenagoras declares the death penalty intolerable even when prescribed by law (*Leg.* 35). Hippolytus' *Apostolic Tradition* (16, 17) forbids any Christian magistrate to order an execution. Lactantius (*Inst.* vi, 20, 15–20) rules that no Christian may cause death whether in war or by accusing anyone of a capital offence or by exposing an unwanted child. However, the excommunication of Christian governors passing a death sentence became a mark of the ultra-rigorous Novatianist sect. Ambrose was content to advise a governor against it, for 'even pagan governors commonly boast of having never executed a man' (*Ep.* 25; cf. Libanius, *Or.* 45, 27). Augustine does not forbid it in all conceivable circumstances, but felt that a wise justice would forgo the use of this sanction which shares with torture (to which Augustine also objected) the demerit that a mistake is hard to rectify, and that on a remedial theory of punishment it is indefensible. Once it had been admitted that there could be just war, it was hard in logic to reject in absolute terms the possibility of capital punishment for murderous atrocities.

The conversion of Constantine and the consequent accession of a Christian emperor marks no great divide in the development of Christian thinking about government, power, coercion, and war. Long after Constantine's time Christians continued to talk as if, despite all the public responsibilities thrust upon bishops and despite the conversion of the majority of the population to Christianity, they were still a relatively small minority group standing for peace and thereby doing something to mitigate if not to eliminate conflict. Long before his time they had recognised that in this fallen world peace will not be maintained without the threat of the possibility of war, and therefore that the army, like the magistrate in Romans 13, performed a necessary service. In the gospels centurions are well spoken of. In Justin a century later the mystery of the cross is discerned even in the shape of the Roman army's standards.

Yet the conversion of Constantine was an event of catalytic significance for the conversion of Europe. His panegyrist, the historian Eusebius bishop of Caesarea, saw his conversion and reign as the breaking in on the world of that final kingdom of righteousness to which the prophets had looked forward: his victory in driving the opposition into the Tiber at the battle of the Milvian Bridge in 312 is prefigured in the drowning of the Egyptians in the Red Sea at the Exodus. Even so western a writer as Ambrose, for whom the dualism of church and state and the superiority of priesthood over kingship are prominent themes, regarded Theodosius' wars against the Goths as fulfilling the Johannine prophecy of conflict between God's people and Gog and Magog (Rev. 20:8). This exegesis, for all his reverence for Ambrose, Augustine expressly rejects: the city of God has as much room for Goths as for Romans (*De civ. Dei* xx, 11). Augustine has the utmost reserve before the application of the Biblical eschatology to legitimate the imperial Christian monarchy. Thereby he set in motion the restoration of its authentic religious power to the eschatological language, and reduced to a modest pitch human confidence in the capacity of government, whether pagan or Christian, to realise a regime of true justice in this corrupt world. But relative peace is worth striving for (*Tr.Joh.* 34, 10).

The early Christians were not like Epicureans, indolently apathetic towards the political life of the empire or the local government of the cities and provinces in which they lived. They influenced subsequent political theories, into the twentieth century, by holding a religious position which entailed a relativism about the use of power in this world. Some, like Eusebius of Caesarea, affirm strongly positive evaluations of the providential role of the empire under the specifically Christian rule of the devout autocrat, whose earthly monarchy mirrors that of God in heaven. (Eusebius had to cancel the pagan panegyrists' legitimation of Diocletian's tetrarchy as a reflection of the fourness which the winds, seasons, elements, etc., show to be inherent in the nature of things.) At the opposite extreme stood those, like the African Donatists and some ascetics in Syria, for whom a Christian emperor was a contradiction in terms, the office being one inherently lying in the arms of Satan. But between the two extremes there lay a passionately religious indifference to political power for which government, though not diabolical, is essentially concerned with short-term problems and the abrasions of administrative difficulty, not with those things which will get men and women to heaven. Before the awful ultimacy of heaven, hell, and the last judgement, conflicts in this life about power, wealth, honour, comfort, and sex are not merely ephemeral but trivial tinsel. The daily realities of life forced many who were in principle indifferentist to accept the truth that the nature and the exercise of worldly power are not matters so secular as to be of no concern to the people of God. Even if the Church thinks in centuries while politicians are content to get through the coming week, the Christians come to see that politics cannot be exempt from moral judgements, and indeed has to be treated as a branch of ethics. Hence the force of Augustine's cannonade in the *City of God* (iv, 4): 'If justice is removed, what are kingdoms but large-scale brigandage?' The early Christians did not launch any particular political theory upon the Roman world. They simply ensured that subsequent political thought would be controlled by a greater debate, namely about the nature and destiny of man; that no one should long suppose man capable of living by bread alone; that religion itself is abused if its function becomes that of providing an ultimate legitimation for whatever be the current order; and that, since individuals matter to God, they are objects of his care in this world and the next, and therefore have rights now meriting deep respect.

2

GREEK AND ROMAN POLITICAL THEORY

Philosophers: metaphysics, ethics and political theory

European political philosophy had its first home in Greece, in a society made up of numerous small city-states, each with its own laws, customs and constitution. The term 'politics' in fact derives from '*polis*', the Greek noun for 'city-state'. The sheer variety of constitutions known in Greece – Aristotle and his school were to produce monographs on no less than 158 of them – meant that it was hardly possible there, as it may well have been in Egypt or Mesopotamia, to assume that there is only one way in which to run a society. Varied as the Greek states were, and subject to further variation by reform or revolution, they fell into three main classes – *monarchy* or rule by one man, described approvingly as 'kingship' or disapprovingly as 'tyranny'; *oligarchy* or rule by a few, politely called 'aristocracy' or rule by the best; and *democracy* or rule by the entire adult male citizen body, known to later detractors as 'ochlocracy' or mob-rule. Their respective merits were hotly discussed from the time of Herodotus (3.80–2) onwards, even if some states, notably Sparta, a totalitarian society much admired for its discipline, stability and prowess in war, fell into none of these categories.

Different societies, it was observed, tend to produce different kinds of people. Democratically ruled Athenians, for instance, had a different character from oligarchically ruled Corinthians. Such observations, abundantly reinforced by a growing familiarity with the customs of foreign peoples, brought home the importance of social factors, of '*nomos*', a term which meant not only 'law' but 'convention'. Moreover, the fact that laws vary, that what is right and proper in one country may be wrong in another, led to questions about the validity of *nomos* altogether. By the end of the fifth century BC it had come to be contrasted with '*physis*' or uncontaminated 'nature', an authority no less ambiguous. The contrast served numerous political and moral theories.[1] Some argued that what is worthwhile in life is due entirely to *nomos* and civilisation;[2] others, with

1. Sinclair 1951, pp. 48–51, 75–7.
2. E.g. the anonymous writer 'On Laws' preserved in Demosthenes 25.15–35, 86–91, 93–6.

nature as their standard, could reach widely differing conclusions, one of them condemning slavery on the ground that 'God has left all men free, nature made none a slave',[3] another claiming that it is in fact a 'law of nature' for the strong to enslave the weak,[4] while Cynic philosophers of the fourth century BC and later turned their backs on society and its conventions altogether, in favour of the 'life according to nature'. But it was commoner, after Plato (427–347 BC), for thinkers to reconcile the claims of Law and Nature, arguing that man is, in Aristotle's phrase (*Pol.* 1252a3), 'a political animal', that he needs a regulated society such as the *polis*.

   The shortcomings of existing states in the fifth and fourth centuries BC led, further, to speculations as to how a state should ideally be organised, and so to the most famous of all political writings by a classical philosopher. Plato's *Republic*, a vast dialogue on justice, contains, amongst other things, a sketch of how states come into existence, a blueprint for an ideally just society (a totalitarian state governed by philosophers) and a highly suggestive account of how existing imperfect forms of government develop into each other. But the dialogue is a work of metaphysics as well as of politics. It expounds Plato's central metaphysical doctrine of Forms or Ideas, eternal transcendent realities apprehended by thought, which underlie and account for the transient phenomena of the empirical world. This metaphysical doctrine is fundamental to the political doctrine of the *Republic*. For what justifies the claim there (473cd) that philosophers should govern is their insight, laboriously acquired, into the eternal nature of things, their knowledge of what Justice itself is. To use a later terminology, what entitles them to govern, to make and unmake *positive* laws, is their understanding of *natural* law. In somewhat divergent ways, the same principle underlies two later works by Plato to do with politics. The *Laws*, an immensely long and detailed work of legislation for a community somewhat more practical than that prescribed in the *Republic*, speaks in an untranslatable pun of 'law' (*nomos*) as the 'distribution' (*dianome*) of immortal reason (*nous*) within us (713e); its legislation is an attempt to apply divine reason to the details of social life. The *Politicus* puts the emphasis on the philosophical statesman, arguing that the best would be for supreme power to lie not in laws, which are all too often inflexible, but in the 'kingly man with practical wisdom' (294a), whose expertise and intelligence raise him above convention and written enactments. For the rest of antiquity, that was probably Plato's most seminal pronouncement on politics.

---

3. Alcidamas, quoted by Aristotle, *Rhetoric* 1373b18.   4. Callicles at Plato, *Gorgias* 483e.

Plato's interests in political theory were continued, from a more empirical standpoint, by his erstwhile pupil Aristotle (384–322 BC). The *Politics*, a somewhat disorganised assemblage of writings based on considerable historical research, presents Aristotle's own model of an ideal state, along with criticisms of previous models. But its central books (III–VI) are concerned, more pragmatically, with existing varieties, good and bad, of democracy, oligarchy and monarchy, with the reasons for their instability and with remedies for it. Most valuably of all, the work discusses certain fundamental questions of political theory: the nature and function of the state, the meaning of citizenship and whether to be a good citizen is the same thing as to be a good man, the elements of a constitution – executive, legislative, judiciary – and their relation to one another. These discussions were to exercise considerable influence on European political thinking, after the thirteenth century. But not till then.

Aristotle saw politics as a prime concern for the moral philosopher, since he believed that only in a political community can a fully human life be realised. Subsequent philosophers had far less time for political questions. In their view, the supreme goal in life is some state of mind – pleasure, for instance, or 'harmony with nature' – which individuals have to attain on their own. Politics ranked at best as a minor branch of ethics. Epicurus (341– 270 BC) indeed advised his disciples to keep out of public life. He denied that human beings are naturally sociable or that justice is established in the nature of things, defining 'natural justice' as a 'pledge of expediency' made by men at a certain stage of human evolution, 'with a view to not harming each other or being harmed' (*Principal Doctrines* 31), and binding only when it is advantageous to all concerned. (In other words, Epicurus approached the question of justice by way of a historical analysis, as Plato had done in *Republic* II, and as Hobbes and Rousseau were to do 2,000 years later.) His principal opponents, the Stoics, did preach participation in public life and did derive justice from nature. They could speak, like Aristotle, of man as a 'political animal' or, more vaguely as a 'reasonable, sociable and affectionate animal' (*Stoicorum Veterum Fragmenta* III. 314, 686). But the school offered little, if anything, by way of a political programme; and its adherents could associate themselves with a wide range of political figures and causes. Zeno of Citium (335–263 BC), its founder, had in his youth, perhaps in reply to Plato, written a *Republic* portraying an ideal community of the good and wise, in which laws and lawcourts, money and temples, marriage and distinctions in dress between men and women were all abolished (Diogenes Laertius 7.32–3). But this recognisably Cynic utopia, was not a blueprint for social reform – in the way that Plato's ideal states possibly were – so much as a paradigm of what the world might be, if all men were virtuous.[5] Zeno and his followers were concerned primarily with personal ethics; and the language of politics, as they used it, tended to be metaphorical. Epictetus (c. 55–c. 135), an ex-slave himself, has much to say about 'inner' servitude; he is silent on slavery as an institution. The Stoa saw men first and foremost as 'rational animals', members of a species, not as products of a social environment. Indeed, its aim was to free the individual from the corrupting pressure of society. Its emphasis on the unity of mankind (*Stoicorum Veterum Fragmenta* III. 340–8), its picture of the universe as a single commonwealth of gods and men (*Stoicorum Veterum Fragmenta* III, 333, 338, 339), was profoundly apolitical, an attempt to counteract the loyalties felt towards Rome, Athens or any other real political community. Similarly, the Stoic idea of 'natural law' as 'right reason commanding what should be done and forbidding the opposite' (Cicero *Laws* I, 33) applied, in the first instance, to ethics. It dramatised the claim that human beings have a natural awareness of things which should and of things which should not be done, especially in their dealings with one another. This concept of moral principles which all men intuitively accept provided individual Stoics with a bastion against coercion from tyrants, from public opinion and even from written laws. But it also provided Roman jurists with a basis for developing their own positive law; and their concern was primarily with the public good. At their hands, the doctrine took on a distinctly 'collectivist' colouring. Theft and murder may be 'against nature'; but if you accept, as Cicero (106–43 BC) does, that what is most in accord with nature is human society, this belief may justify the killing of a tyrant for the good of the state or robbery from a worthless man so as to preserve the life of a brave, wise and good man (*De Officiis* 3.19, 33). This 'corporate' interpretation of natural law was what Ambrose and Augustine passed on to the Middle Ages.[6]

Under the Roman Empire, philosophy became increasingly theological. The dominant school was now a revived Platonism, enriched with Aristotelian and Stoic teachings. It devoted little attention to Plato's political teachings. Neoplatonist philosophers concentrated on his metaphysics, elaborating his original dichotomy between sensibles and intelligibles, into ever more numerous levels of Being, each somehow reflecting or emanating from that prior to it. The hierarchical pattern of such metaphysics had a parallel in the heavily hierarchical ordering of late

5. Long 1974, pp. 110, 205.   6. Watson 1971, pp. 231–6.

Roman society, and could doubtless have served to justify it. But there was no need to justify it; and philosophers, anyway, had their minds on higher things. When Themistius (c. 317–c. 388), a distinguished commentator on Aristotle, placed his service at the disposal of the emperor, on the grounds that 'philosophers capable of doing good to individuals can do good to the many as well' (*Orat.* 22.265c), he was bitterly satirised for preferring a silver orb to the orb of heaven (*Anthologia Palatina.* 11.292).

Ideals of kingship

The distaste of most philosophers after Aristotle for political questions has a ready historical explanation. The scope of political theorists was no longer what it had been. 'Politics' meant properly the study of things to do with the *polis*, a city-state small enough, as Aristotle had pointed out (*Pol.* 1276a27–30, 1325b33–1326b27), for its citizens to be acquainted with each other. Only in communities of that size, given the fact that no satisfactory means of representative government had been devised, could the raw materials of Greek political theory, the numerous varieties of democracy, oligarchy and so forth, have come into being. But Aristotle died in the same year (323 BC) as Alexander, whose conquest of the Persian Empire transformed the political map of the Greek world. States like Athens found themselves dwarfed by the empires of his successors, by the powers of Macedon, of Egypt, of the Seleucids and, finally, of Rome. In war and diplomacy they were outclassed; attempts at federation had only a limited success; and traditional politics sank to the level of a local activity. For the large empires, the one bearable form of government was monarchy. On an imperial scale, anything else, any form of government with regular competition for office, was just too destructive, as the last century of the Roman Republic showed all too clearly. After Alexander, Greek political history is largely one of kingdoms; and Greek political theory came to concentrate on questions to do with kingship.

The Greek world had a tradition of thought about kingship, which went back to Homer. Isocrates (436–338 BC) had expressed views, in the *Nicocles* and *Evagoras*, on what a monarch should be. So had Xenophon (428–354 BC), above all in his *Education of Cyrus*. Under the Hellenistic kings, Greek thinking fused with foreign traditions[7] – Egyptian, Mesopotamian and Persian – to produce a remarkably long-lived synthesis. Rehearsed in one

---

7. See Dvornik 1966, vol. 1, pp. 1–131, and Hadot 1971, 556–64.

loyal panegyric after another and in a long series of works *On Kingship*, the
royal ideology remained static in its main features from the third century BC
to the fourth century AD and later. Our clearest introduction into what was
expected of a Hellenistic monarch comes in two fragments, of very
uncertain date, purportedly by the Pythagorean philosopher Diotogenes.[8]
We learn there that the king has three functions – to fight wars well, to
dispense justice, to serve the gods (71.3–72.5). In his triple capacity of
general, judge and priest, he requires three peculiar virtues: he must be
'dread' (*deinos*), 'graciously good' (*chrestos*) and 'majestic' (*semnos*). The titles
of Hellenistic and later monarchs, their assertions on inscriptions and coins,
refer again and again to these three aspects of royalty.[9]

The first of the royal functions was the most basic and obviously
important: 'the role of the king and general is to save those at risk in war'
(72.7–8). To survive at all, a king had to hold his kingdom together against
external and also internal enemies. If successful in doing so, he might very
well preen himself with the title of *Soter* or 'Saviour'. To be a 'fearsome,
invincible' foe and a 'high-souled, confident' ally (74.2–4), he must,
according to Diotogenes, be capable of inspiring dread, by his severity and
swiftness in punishing the wicked, by his experience and skill in ruling
(75.13–124).

His loyal subjects, on the other hand, expect two things from a gracious
monarch. He must show the qualities necessary for establishing 'law and
order' (*eunomia*) – namely, 'justice' which holds the community together,
'reasonableness' (*epieikeia*) to take the edge off his justice, together with a
certain 'indulgence' towards offenders. He should also be 'disposed to help'
(*boethos*), 'grateful' for honours accorded to him, and 'easy-going',
particularly towards the poor (74.20–75.13). Here, no less than on the
battlefield, he is watching over his subjects, exercising *pronoia, providentia*,
on their behalf. Moreover, as the dispenser of justice, the king is 'living
law' (*nomos empsychos, lex animata*).[10] This concept ranked by the first
century AD as an 'ancient' doctrine; Clement of Alexandria detected it in
Plato's *Politicus*; later, it found its way into the Code of Justinian, and so to
the medieval West.[11] 'Living law' and similar phrases derived their force
from their contrast with ordinary written laws. To be at all effective as an
expression of justice, a statute must be enforced; Aristotle, accordingly,

8. The fragments of Diotogenes and Ecphantus are cited by page and line of their latest edition:
   Thesleff 1965.
9. See Schubart 1937 and Charlesworth 1937.   10. See Steinwenter 1946 and Aalders 1969.
11. Musonius p. 37.1 Hense, Clement *Stromata* 2.18.4, Justinian *Novellae* CV.ii.4.

could speak of a juror as '*animate justice*' (*Nicomachean Ethics* 1132a22). Laws merely written can be disobeyed and thus fail to do good; but a good ruler can detect disobedience and punish it, thus ranking for Xenophon as 'law with sight' (*Cyrop.* VIII.1.22). Furthermore, a law on the statute-book may prove to be quite inadequate for complex changing circumstances; that was why Plato expressed a preference for the kingly statesman with practical wisdom. The commonest application, in fact, of the principle that the king is animate law is that he can make exceptions to the law as it stands. Above all, he can exercise clemency, the supreme royal prerogative, thereby demonstrating his *philanthropia*, his *benignitas*. (In practice, a Hellenistic monarch, in control of numerous cities each with its own different laws, might well have to override these on occasion.) What the principle was not supposed to mean was that the king can do as he pleases. Unlike the tyrant, the king is a 'lawful' ruler, governing his willing subjects for their own benefit[12] – though the law which he follows need not be anything on the statute-book. 'Who, then, shall rule the ruler?', asks Plutarch, '"Law, the king of all"', not written in books or on tablets outside him, but animate reason within, abiding with him always and watching over him . . . Rulers serve God for the care and preservation of men' (*Moralia* 780cd). The function of the good king in his every act of government is to establish within the social order a justice that mirrors the perfect unchanging cosmic order. He is the human exponent of natural law, and his role is to imitate God's rule of the universe.

'Accountable to no one, himself, himself a living law', says Diotogenes, the king is a manifestation of God among men (72.22–3). As such, he must be awesome, majestic; and the purpose of court ritual was to hedge him with an aura of divinity. But he had not only to imitate God in appearance and action; he had also to mediate with God, since the continued existence of his kingdom depended on divine favour. As well as being general and judge, the king is thus a priest, responsible for the religious wellbeing of his subjects and answerable to the deity for their transgressions. In this thoroughly Hellenistic spirit, the Indian king Asoka could claim in a bilingual inscription to have converted his subjects from eating meat and from showing disrespect to their parents![13] The monarch could act as mediator because of his position in the state: 'it is fitting that the best should be honoured by the best: God is best in the universe, and the king is best among men' (72.16–19). Theologically, his status might be uncertain.

---

12. See Xenophon *Memorabilia* IV.6.12, Plato *Politicus* 291e, Aristotle *Politics*, 1285a24–9, Polybius VI.4.2, Dio Chrysostom 1.66–84, etc.   13. Festugière 1951.

Hellenistic monarchs, and also Roman provincial governors, received divine honours; but that meant little more than homage, an expression of gratitude without theological implications. Some texts do speak of the king as a 'diviner being, fashioned by the King of the gods in his own image',[14] as a being intermediate between gods and mortals. It was also possible to describe the monarch, more modestly but no less effectively, as the supreme God's viceregent on earth. Pliny (c. 61–c. 112) and Dio Chrysostom (c. 40–c. 112) both speak in this way of Trajan.[15] And the concept could serve, without more ado, a Christian account of a Christian emperor.

Greece, Rome and absolute monarchy

Political theory after Aristotle was not, however, concerned exclusively with the ideology of kingship, any more than the political history of the ancient world after Alexander was exclusively a story of kingdoms. Under the shadow of the great monarchies, Greek city-states survived and in fact multiplied. Retaining considerable local autonomy, they provided scope for politics of a traditional kind, long after the Hellenistic monarchies had been absorbed by the Roman Empire. In its heyday, the empire was a patchwork of urban territories, surrounded by a garrisoned frontier. Democracies in name, its provincial cities were in fact aristocracies; and local politics, pursued with cantankerous vigour, attracted the attention of Plutarch (c. 50–c. 120), Dio Chrysostom and other writers. Works like Plutarch's *Precepts on Statesmanship* or Dio's second *Tarsian Oration* offer advice on the proper conduct of civic affairs under Roman suzerainty, on relations with the provincial governor and with other cities in the province, on how to control the populace at home and on the vital need to maintain 'concord' within the local ruling class.[16]

More importantly, Rome itself was a state which Greeks could recognise as a *polis* similar to their own. A need to explain the rise of Rome to an educated Greek public led to some of the most striking political literature of the last two centuries BC. The historian Polybius (c. 200–118 BC) found the explanation in the excellence of the Roman constitution. His account of it reflected earlier theories, commonly associated with Aristotle's pupil Dicaearchus (fr.71 Wehrli), about a 'mixed' constitution, an ideal compound (perhaps inspired by Sparta) of monarchy, oligarchy and demo-

14. Ecphantus 80.3–4: Thesleff 1965. See Kantorowicz 1952, p. 172.
15. Pliny *Panegyricus* 80.5, Dio 1.11 (quoting Homer *Iliad* 2.205–6).
16. See Jones 1971, pp. 110–21, and 1978, pp. 75–81.

cracy. In Polybius' judgement, the Roman Republic, with its balance of monarchy in the power of the consuls, of aristocracy in that of the Senate and of democracy in that of the people, was a supreme embodiment, pragmatically evolved, of this ideal. He attempted, further, to put his political views on a scientific basis with a theory of constitutional cycles which goes back to Plato. According to this theory, kingship degenerates into tyranny, which is then supplanted by an aristocracy degenerating into mere oligarchy, which in its turn is followed by democracy, which collapses into mob-rule; the virtue of the mixed constitution is to slow down, even if it cannot completely halt, the process of change and degeneration.[17] In the following century, Cicero's *De Republica* praised the 'old constitution' of Rome, on the same Dicaearchan lines, for its even distribution of *potestas* to the magistrates, *auctoritas* to the Senate and *libertas* to the people. Without some such balance of rights, duties and functions, Cicero argued, the state cannot be safe from revolution (2.57). Indeed, it cannot strictly be called a *res publica* or 'common weal' at all. For what that term means is *res populi*, the 'weal' of the whole people and not just one section of it. Since, further, *populus* means properly an association of people in a partnership of rights and interests,[18] a *res publica* without justice is a contradiction in terms, a point which Augustine was to take up for polemical purposes in the *City of God* (ii.21, xix.21). But justice implies more than legality. Cicero turned therefore to a Stoic concept of primal unalterable 'natural Law' as a basis for legislation. Realising, too, that the laws can be disregarded and are not enough on their own to ensure good government, he emphasised, in a very Roman way, the importance of personal moral authority, talking of the *princeps* or 'leading citizen' in such a manner as to suggest – to some modern scholars, at least – that he was anticipating Augustus' principate.

Attempts to explain Rome in terms of Greek constitutional theory were of limited use. What counted in Roman politics were factors which had little to do with constitutions, factors such as personal patronage and personal *auctoritas* or influence.[19] It was by sheer *auctoritas* that Q.Caecilius Metellus Celer, while still consul designate and as yet without *potestas* or 'legal power', was able to stop the performance of games legally ordered by a tribune in defiance of the Senate (Cicero, *In Pisonem* 8). And it was by its *auctoritas*, rather than by any statutory powers, that the Senate controlled

17. Walbank 1957, pp. 643–8.
18. Note Cicero's opening definition, *Rep.* i.xxvi.39: 'Est igitur . . . res publica res populi, populus autem non omnis hominum coetus quoquo modo congregatus, sed coetus multitudinis iuris consensu et utilitatis communione sociatus.'
19. Sinclair 1951, p. 280. See Crawford 1978, pp. 30–7.

the magistrates and the state. In theory, the people may have been sovereign at Rome, but they did not actively exercise power, as they would have done in a Greek democracy. In practice, power was in the hands of annually elected consuls whose obligation was to consult the Senate. Domestic politics were a matter of competition among members of the senatorial aristocracy for office and standing, while externally, Rome's imperial power rested very much on the establishment of like-minded aristocracies in her allies and subject states. But the Roman Republic was even more opposed to kingship than to democracy. The tritest fact about Rome was that it was no longer a kingdom. By expelling their kings, the Romans had gained their *libertas*, their civic rights; and what assured its continuance was a system of checks and balances, above all, the fact that the consuls, the successors of the kings, were elected for only a year and in pairs. To brand an opponent as a would-be monarch was to justify his assassination. But the ideology of the Roman Republic was notably flexible. Its catch-words – *libertas, dignitas, concordia*, and so forth – could be invoked to very different effect by would-be reformers and by their conservative opponents. This flexibility permitted and even encouraged the justification in traditional terms of actions which were in fact revolutionary.[20] It meant that, when the republican order had visibly broken down, when competition between its leading members had led to unparalleled devastation, when it had become clear that some kind of monarchy was indispensable, Octavian could present his settlement as a 'restoration' of the Republic.

The success of Octavian's settlement was due largely to its ambiguity. He was careful to respect the republican forms of government. He reformed the Senate, sharing with it, if not power, at least the labour and proceeds of government. (The Senate in fact was to survive the end of the Roman Empire in the West by nearly 130 years.) The title which he chose for himself was '*princeps*' or 'first citizen', an honorific term suggesting something more than an ordinary citizen but less than a king, just as in religious terms 'Augustus', the title decreed to him by the Senate in 27 BC, implied a compromise between a god and a mere mortal. In a much discussed sentence, he claimed that, after his settlement, he 'surpassed all men in authority, but held no more power than any of his colleagues in any given magistracy'.[21] That may have been true, in the sense that the magistracies which he now held were collegiate, annual and ordinary. But

20. Crawford 1978, p. 13.
21. *Monumentum Ancyranum* 34.3: 'Post id tempus auctoritate omnibus praestiti, potestatis autem nihilo amplius habui quam ceteri qui mihi quoque in magistratu conlegae fuerunt.'

the prerogatives which he accumulated – his proconsular command of the armies, and so forth – were neither annual nor collegiate. They were uncontrollable, and he held them for life. Still more importantly, his surpassing *auctoritas*, only possible because he was permanently in power, established him in the pre-eminence which had formerly belonged to the Senate, enabling him to perform functions for which strictly he had no legal warrant. Moreover, as his use of the phrase '*me principe*' ('when I was *princeps*') makes clear, he regarded the principate as an office. And he left the office to one of his own family.[22]

If the principate of Augustus and his successors was, in Gibbon's phrase, 'an absolute monarchy disguised by the forms of a commonwealth', it was up to the *princeps* himself to maintain the disguise. There was nothing to prevent his becoming an out and out despot. His decisions had the force of law; the *lex regia*, the enabling act at the start of his reign, was 'a legitimate title to virtual absolutism'.[23] The old system of checks and balances was gone. The two centuries after Augustus did see a number of 'good' emperors who kept to the style, the *civilitas*, of a republican magistrate, who got on well with the Senate and lived, or claimed to live, by the same laws as other citizens. But that was only because they saw fit to do so. There was nothing that anyone could do about a bad emperor, a Nero or Domitian, short of assassinating him – to make way for some more promising *princeps*. A genuine restoration of republican government was out of the question. The one guarantee that the emperor would not be corrupted by power, and corrupt those around him by fear, lay in his and their personal characters. In the absence of constitutional safeguards, moral considerations became paramount. It was still possible to remind the *princeps*, constrained though he might be by no positive laws, of his duty towards the unwritten law of morality. Indeed it might well be preferable to invoke his royal virtues – his *clementia, benignitas, humanitas, beneficentia* – instead of demanding justice from him. It might be better, in short, to treat him, not as a 'first citizen', but unashamedly as a Hellenistic monarch. That was Seneca's approach to Nero in the *De Clementia*. Its theoretical implications clashed with the concept of the *princeps* as the holder of power vested in him from below, by Senate and people. The Hellenistic ruler derived his legitimation from above, as the delegate or even the incarnation of God on earth. But that, more and more, was the style which the emperor adopted, as his power increased and the role of the Senate declined. From being a *princeps* greeted with *salutatio* by

---

22. See Wirszubski 1950, pp. 109–23, Ste Croix 1981, pp. 383–92, or (better still) E. Gibbon *The Decline and Fall of the Roman Empire*, ch. 3.   23. Wirszubski 1950, p. 133.

his fellow-citizens, he became increasingly the *dominus*, hedged with divinity and approached by his subjects with *adoratio*, a ceremony of Persian origin. The transformation was complete by the time of Constantine, whose portrait in the *Panegyric* to him by Eusebius of Caesarea (260–340) is recognisably indebted to Hellenistic treatises on kingship.[24] Like the king portrayed by the Pythagoreans Diotogenes and Ecphantus, Constantine is God's image – most of the *Panegyric* goes to elaborating and varying that one theme. The 'friend' of God's only-begotten Word (2.1, 2, 3, 4), he resembles his archetype above all in his *philanthropia* (2.5). Like the monarch depicted by Ecphantus, he has a redemptive role. The shepherd of his people, he offers as a sacrifice to God the souls of the rational beings in his care, having 'cleansed all the filth of godless error from his kingdom on earth' (2.5). In Eusebius' laudation, the Hellenistic monarch reappears in aggressively Christian guise; notably absent, since quite unnecessary, is any attempt to disguise Constantine's absolute monarchy with the 'forms of a commonwealth'.

Controversy after Constantine

In the Middle Ages, Constantine was to rank as the paragon of a Christian monarch; to his contemporaries, his conversion to Christianity may have meant less, in social and political terms, than his foundation of Constantinople. The presence of an imperial capital in the Eastern half of the empire exacerbated the tensions there between provincial cities and central government, between the rival attractions for the ambitious of the local city council and the imperial court. Moreover, the existence of two imperial capitals, Rome and Constantinople, endorsed the fateful decision, long in the making, between the two halves of the empire. In political controversies of the fourth century, the dividing-lines were not just between pagans and Christians (who preferred, anyway, to quarrel among themselves); they were also between the provinces and the capital, between the Greek East and the Latin West; while the points at issue concerned the three traditional areas of royal activity – warfare abroad, government at home, religion.

As regent on earth of the one God, the Roman emperor ought logically to have been ruler of the whole world. The monotheism of Constantine and his successors, if anything, strengthened the universalist claims of the Roman Empire. But these claims, as the fourth century proceeded, became

24. See Baynes 1955, pp. 168–72, and Barnes 1981, pp. 253–5.

increasingly hard to maintain. Pressure increased on all frontiers, and the question of what to do with barbarian invaders became urgent. Should they be crushed or assimilated? The traditional answer was straightforward and uncompromising: 'expel what is alien from body and state alike', as Synesius (c. 370–413) put it (*De Regno* 1089d). On this view, the empire was a confederation of cities, protected by the emperor and his armies; he himself was primarily a soldier, and his place was on the frontier; 'the king is an expert in wars, just as the cobbler is an expert in shoes' (1076b). Different advice came from Themistius:[25] instead of staging expensive wars, the emperor should stay in his capital and govern, winning a far more popular victory over the tax-collectors (*Orat.* 8.114c–115a). The loss of individual provinces was a minor matter compared with the preservation of Constantinople, 'the second eye of the whole world' (6.83c). Allowed to settle on imperial territory, barbarians would in time become civilised; 'taking leave of Ares, they will turn in prayer to Demeter and Dionysus' (16.211b). Such, certainly, would be the more philanthropic course (10.132bc). On this view, it was still possible for Rome to carry out her world mission as a civilising force, controlling the barbarians by diplomacy where force was not possible. Without realising it, Themistius pointed forward to what in fact came about in Eastern Europe – a 'Byzantine Commonwealth' of kingdoms, united by a common religion and shared principles of law, conceding – at least, tacitly – to the emperor at Constantinople a measure of authority over the whole of Orthodox Christendom, and deriving from his empire their standards of literature, art and scholarship.[26]

Within the empire, the main political questions concerned the emperor's right to rule and his duties as a ruler. The ambiguities of the principate were never wholly resolved. Constitutionally, the emperor remained a successor to the republican magistrates, exercising a sovereignty voluntarily surrendered to him by the people. He could also be seen – and more plausibly, since he had usually reached the throne through hazards of inheritance or military action – as God's choice, acclaimed as such by army, Senate and populace. To present an appearance of legitimacy, he needed the backing of God and man alike – to have been elected, like Valentian I, by the civilian and military powers with divine prompting, or vice versa.[27] Moreover, the two factors, divine and human, which gave the emperor his right to rule could also justify a revolt against him. As the elect of God and the people, he

25. See Dagron 1968, pp. 85–120.   26. Obolensky 1971, p. 13.
27. See Karayannopoulos 1956, pp. 374–7.

had duties towards both; if he failed in his duties towards either, he forfeited his claims to God's favour and could legitimately be removed. The one proof that revolt against him was in fact willed by God, and hence legitimate, lay in its success.[28] There was no other way to resist an unsatisfactory monarch.

The duty of the emperor towards his people was to watch over their welfare and to maintain justice within the empire. But that could mean more than one thing. On the conservative, legalist view, voiced at its severest by Libanius of Antioch (314–c. 393), the function of emperor and his officials is to defend the laws, as they have been handed down. It is not his business to interfere with them even on grounds of humanity. The well-being of the state depends on a time-honoured order of rights and duties, embracing gods and men alike and assigning to each his due. Administrative decision and new legislation must follow the principles of that order. This attitude found expression memorably in a plea by Symmachus (c. 340–402) to the Christian emperor Gratian for the restoration of a pagan Altar of Victory: 'you rule all, but preserve for each his due; justice counts more with you than untrammelled power'. Ambrose expressed the opposite view no less memorably: the duty of the emperor as God's regent on earth is to impose God's will; 'injury is done to no one, if God almighty is given priority over him'.[29] What is required of the ruler, and what in fact preserves the state, is not conformity to law, but rather the right religious and moral attitude. He is perfectly entitled to override the law, especially in the interests of clemency; and the duty of his officials is simply to carry out his will, to be his image as he is God's image. This concept of royal prerogative was not confined to Christians. Its most consistent exponent was the pagan Themistius.[30]

As the controversy between Ambrose and Symmachus showed, questions of law were intimately connected with questions of religion. In the fourth century, the monarch's duties towards God assumed an unprecedented seriousness. Roman emperors from Augustus onwards had held the office of *pontifex maximus*. But Roman state religion was primarily a matter of cult; and the principle of *deorum iniuriae dis curae* made for widespread religious tolerance. Persecution of Christians and others had been sporadic and local, a political move against groups suspected of subversion. In the

---

28. *Ibid.*, pp. 381–2.
29. Symmachus *Relatio* 3.18: 'Omnia regitis, sed suum cuique servatis, plusque apud vos iustitia quam licentia valet.' Ambrose *Epistle* 17.7: 'Nullius iniuria est, cui deus omnipotens antefertur.' The texts in this dispute are assembled with German translation, introduction and commentary by Klein 1972. See also Dihle 1973.   30. See Dagron 1968, pp. 127–44.

third century, however, the disasters besetting the empire were interpreted as a punishment by the gods for sacrilege; Christians under Decius and Diocletian were persecuted throughout the empire. More positively, attempts were made to bolster the empire by the promotion of a state religion. It was to that end that Aurelian instituted the cult of *Sol invictus* and Constantine later adopted Christianity. He and his successors saw their duty as the encouragement of true religion, lending it theological as well as material assistance. Religious belief had come to be as important, for the state, as religious practice. Constantine was, amongst other things, a 'teacher of knowledge about God' (Eusebius *Paneg.* 58). The unity of a threatened empire was seen to depend on a unity of religious belief among its subjects. The result was a mounting intolerance, punctuated only by changes in the state religion, with persecution of Christians under Diocletian followed by Constantine's adoption of Christianity and a period of religious tolerance dwindling under Constantius, a brief renewal of paganism under Julian, followed by the comparatively tolerant Christianity of Valentinian and Valens and the far less tolerant orthodoxy of Theodosius. Pleas by Themistius (*Orat.* 5) and Symmachus for religious pluralism had little effect.

The extent to which an emperor could take a personal hand in the religious life of his subjects was demonstrated, ironically, by the man who became a symbol of reaction against the policies of Constantine and his Christian successors. The revival of paganism in Julian's short reign (361–3) was not a return to the easy-going past. Like Aurelian and Constantine before him, Julian was promoting a state cult with the political function of uniting the empire; 'One God, one Julian', said his votive inscriptions. But he was doing so now in direct competition with an established and highly developed state religion. In answer to Christianity, Julian tried to organise a state church with a regulated clergy and even its own charitable institutions. He himself was to be its head. Nor were his efforts confined to the organisation of his church. He was also its principal theologian, polemical and dogmatic. Attacking Christianity, Cynicism and even heterodox Platonism, he expounded his own dogmatic synthesis of Greek religion and oriental mystery cult, applying the principles of Neoplatonism to the relations between, say, Sol-Mithra and Apollo, in much the manner of a contemporary Christian theologian at work on the Persons of the Trinity. Here Julian very much anticipated a fully-fledged Byzantine emperor, carrying out functions which in the West were to be the business of the Pope.

In other fields, too, Julian combined 'reactionary' aspirations[31] with uncomfortably 'modern' thinking. In his youth, he voiced the idea of a prince who owes his position to virtue rather than birth; but he was deeply conscious of ruling by divine favour, and developed a positively mystical concept of his own dynasty as the elect of Helios the Sun-god. Subscribing to the 'old-fashioned' view that the legal traditions of a nation are the true embodiment of divine law, and that the role of the monarch is to obey, guard and interpret them,[32] he was also prepared, from the start, to override them in favour of clemency, and his manner of government became increasingly high-handed. Steeped in the political works of Plato and Aristotle, he could briefly adopt (*Discourse* 6.261b) Aristotle's critique of absolute monarchy – and yet go on to anticipate, more than any other fourth-century emperor, the totalitarian attitude to faith and civilisation, church and state, of a Byzantine autocrat. His notorious edict on education which forbade Christians to teach the classics, had its counterpart later in Justinian's prohibition of pagan teachers.

The irony of Julian's progress towards 'Caesaropapism' reflected a broader irony. The tradition of political theory on which he drew had arisen in response to the sheer diversity of political practice in Greece. It had been enriched with the observations, analyses and speculations of statesmen, historians and philosophers. By Julian's time, however, it had long been submerged in questions to do with one form of political organisation, the monarchy required by the Roman empire; and its principal legacy to the centuries which followed the dismemberment of that empire was an ideology of absolute kingship.

31. See Dvornik 1955.   32. *Epistle* 89a, 253b. See Athanassiadi-Fowden 1981, p. 175.

3
ROMAN LAW

Knowledge of Roman law was transmitted to later ages through two main bodies of material, first the so-called barbarian codes, collections of materials made by Gothic and Burgundian kings at the beginning of the sixth century for application to their Roman subjects, and secondly, the *Corpus Iuris* of the Emperor Justinian, enacted in the 530s. Very few texts survived except by incorporation in these collections, and they did not become known until the sixteenth century or later. The legal material in the sixth-century collections is the product of a thousand years of legal development, and is in various forms, partly legislation and partly discussion by legal experts. It is concerned with private law, governing the relations between private individuals, rather than public law, governing the organs of the state, which was relatively undeveloped until the Byzantine period.

Technically Roman law reached its peak in the first two centuries AD, known as the classical period, but the seeds of the classical law can already be discerned in the tribal law of the small city state of the fifth century BC. On the establishment of the Republic in 509 BC, the law was a set of unwritten customary rules regarded as part of the way of life of the Roman people. Its application was confined to Roman citizens (*ius civile*, law for *cives*, citizens). In matters of doubt, the interpretation of the pontiffs, a body of patrician aristocrats, was decisive both as to the law and to the ritual forms for enforcing it. As a result, it is said, of agitation by the disadvantaged plebeians, many disputed points of customary law were settled in a comprehensive set of written laws (*leges*), enacted by the popular assembly in 451–0, and known as the Twelve Tables.

During the remainder of the Republic, however, there was little popular legislation affecting private law and development was achieved rather through the control of legal remedies. A legal action was divided into two stages. The first, held before an annually elected magistrate, the praetor, settled what in legal terms was the issue between the parties. In the second, a private citizen chosen by the parties (the *iudex*) heard evidence and decided the issue refered to him by the praetor. As Rome's territories expanded, she was faced with the problems of dealing with numerous non-citizens (*peregrini*), and a special praetor was elected to deal with cases involving them. Since the *ius civile* and its forms did not apply to non-citizens, this 'peregrine praetor' allowed the parties to express their claims informally. If these claims disclosed a proper legal issue, he set it out in a written document, the formula, which told the *iudex* in what circumstances he was to condemn the defendant and in what circumstances he should absolve him. In deciding whether to grant a remedy, the praetor took into account those rules which were considered to be part of the laws of all civilised peoples, the *ius gentium*, law of nations (the sense of 'the law governing the relations between nation states' did not exist in antiquity).

In the second half of the second century BC, the formulary procedure became available to citizens and non-citizens alike, and institutions of the *ius gentium* were fused with those of the *ius civile*. On taking up office, each praetor issued an edict listing the circumstances in which he would grant an action or a defence. A praetor would usually take over most of the remedies promised in his predecessor's edict, but he was entitled to give a remedy for which there was no precedent. He had no power to legislate in the sense of making new rules of civil law, but by his control of remedies, he could in effect create new rights. He could not make someone an heir who was not an heir at civil law, but he could give him control of the deceased's goods. The law which owed its origin to such magisterial innovation was known as *ius honorarium*, in contrast with *ius civile* in the narrower sense of law derived from custom and *leges*.

The odd feature of Roman administration of justice was that neither praetor nor *iudex* nor even the advocates who represented the parties before them were lawyers. From the third century BC, however, there was a class of legal experts, the jurists, who, although they had no formal role to play in the legal drama, provided any advice that was required, so replacing the pontiffs as guardians of the law. Their concern was with particular problems submitted to them. They not only explained the law but also helped to adapt it to new social conditions, for example, by suggesting to a praetor that a new action or defence should be included in his edict. The jurists collected and published their opinions, the authority attributed to them being dependent on the reputation of the author.

When the Republic gave way to the Empire, *leges* in the sense of enactments of the popular assemblies, which after the Twelve Tables had never been a prominent source of private law, soon ceased. However, *senatusconsulta*, resolutions of the senate, a body composed largely of ex-magistrates, which had not been legally binding in the Republic, acquired the force of *lex* in their place, and were a source of law in the first and second centuries AD. The praetorian edict was codified in permanent form by the jurist Julian under the Emperor Hadrian (117–38). Gradually through the principate, the emperor assumed legislative powers, which he expressed through imperial constitutions. He could and did legislate directly by edict, but his influence on the law was most frequent through rescripts, written answers prepared by the imperial chancery to questions or petitions sent to him either by officials, such as provincial governors, or by private citizens. By the time of Hadrian the most prominent jurists were members of the emperor's council. The vast majority of rescripts were drafted by them and were in substance jurist-law, although in form imperial constitutions. Normally, such rescripts clarified the existing law. In regard to private law the emperors showed no inclination to make substantial changes.

The largest agency of legal development until the third century AD was the writings of the jurists, whether members of the imperial council or not. They continued to collect their opinions given as answers to problems (*responsa* or *quaestiones*), which sometimes arose in practice but which increasingly were invented by the jurists themselves. The jurists of the first century were divided into two schools, or sects, the Proculians and the Sabinians, whose disputes contributed to the vitality of the classical law. In general, the Proculians favoured strict interpretation of any legal text, whether statute, contract or last will, and saw the law as a coherent system of logically interrelated rules. The Sabinians put more emphasis on justice in the individual case and relied on practice and authority rather than logic.

The jurists also wrote commentaries, both on the civil law in the sense of law derived from custom and *lex*, and on the praetorian edict. In the early third century, the ideas of the earlier writers were synthesised in the work of three great jurists: Papinian, praetorian prefect (the highest imperial official) under Septimius Severus, who specialised in the analysis of individual cases, and Paul and Ulpian, who both served as assessors to Papinian. Paul and Ulpian each wrote commentaries on the praetorian edict and on the civil law (*ad Sabinum*), Ulpian's work in particular covering every aspect of the law and giving full references to the views of earlier authorities. After his death in 223, juristic writing of quality became very rare, although the constitutions of the Emperor Diocletian at the end of the century show that his chancery was still staffed by knowledgeable lawyers concerned to maintain the classical law.

In the fourth and fifth centuries there was a dramatic decline in the level of legal science. Amid the social upheavals and breakdown of stable government a sophisticated legal system could not be maintained and the best brains were attracted away from the law to theology. The edict of Caracalla, or *Constitutio Antoniniana*, of 212 had made virtually all the inhabitants of the Empire Roman citizens, but the rules of Roman law were no longer applied uniformly throughout the Empire and were modified in practice to suit the local conditions of the various provinces. It was now recognised that the emperor was an absolute ruler and the abandonment of the lingering theory that he shared power with the senate was symbolised by the replacement of the term *princeps* by that of *dominus*. The imperial bureaucracy grew, the Empire was divided into two parts for administrative purposes, West and East, the main capital was transferred by Constantine to Byzantium. The fact that Christianity became the official religion of the Empire had little substantial effect on the body of the law, although some emperors attempted to enforce orthodox beliefs by legislation.

There were corresponding changes in legal procedure. The formulary system gave way to the *cognitio* procedure in which a state-appointed professional judge presided over the whole case, deciding questions both of law and of fact, and giving judgements which, unlike those of the earlier *iudex*, could be the subject of appeal through the judicial hierarchy up to the emperor himself. The procedure was taken over by the courts of the Church and was the basis of the medieval Romano-canonical procedure. The writings of the classical jurists were simplified and edited to fit what is now called 'vulgar law' (by analogy with vulgar Latin). For example, the classical notion of ownership as an absolute entitlement quite distinct from possession was modified by the recognition of various forms of limited ownership which foreshadowed feudal notions. The distinction between contract and conveyance of property was blurred and ownership could be passed merely by the contract for sale.

Imperial constitutions, now known as *leges*, continued to be published apace and were more frequently *leges generales*, normative rules of general application, than hitherto. The problem for the unlearned lawyers was to cope with this flow of *leges* and with the confusing mass of juristic literature, collectively known as *ius*. The Law of Citations enacted by Theodosius II in 426 identified five primary authorities among the jurists, Papinian, Paul, Ulpian, Modestinus (a pupil of Ulpian, who was included as the very last of the classical jurists) and Gaius, a second-century law teacher, little regarded in his own time, who achieved posthumous fame through the clarity of his exposition. In 438, the Theodosian *Code*, an official collection of those imperial constitutions intended to have general effect, enacted since the time of Constantine, was published. The constitutions were arranged in chronological order in titles, each title being devoted to a particular legal topic, and the titles were collected into sixteen books.

In the later fifth century imperial authority in the western part of the Empire collapsed and barbarian tribes, which for the most part had long been settled within the frontiers of the Empire, set up independent kingdoms. Following the personal principle in law, which the Romans themselves had followed in the early Republic, they considered their own Germanic laws to be applicable only to themselves and continued to apply (vulgar) Roman law to their Romanised subjects. The most important of the barbarian codes of Roman law was the *Lex Romana Visigothorum*, enacted in 506 by Alaric II, king of the Visigoths in Spain and south-western Gaul. It was the standard source of knowledge of Roman law in the West before the study of Justinian's compilation began in the eleventh century and consists of selections from imperial *leges* and the more popular juristic writings. About one sixth of the constitutions in the Theodosian *Code* are included, as well as some more recent *novels* (*novellae constitutiones*); but *ius* is represented merely by an epitome of Gaius' *Institutes*, a popular students' manual, some extracts from a much adapted text of the *Sententiae* ('Opinions') attributed to Paul and a single fragment of Papinian. Although these extracts were accompanied by explanatory paraphrases, there was practically no discussion of legal theory.

Officially this compilation was abrogated in the seventh century when the Visigothic kings acknowledged the fusion of the Visigothic and Romanised populations in Spain by applying the same law to both. In practice it maintained its authority, particularly in the Frankish kingdom which had been established in northern Gaul at the end of the fifth century and later incorporated both the Burgundian kingdom in eastern Gaul and most of Visigothic Gaul. The Franks applied the *Lex Romana Visigothorum* together with the *Lex Romana Burgundionum*, enacted by King Gunobad some time after 517 for the Romans in the Burgundian kingdom. It consists of extracts of *lex* and *ius*, set out as an organic code without attribution to their source. Such was the lack of knowledge of earlier law that this Burgundian code was thought to be a continuation of the fragment of Papinian with which the Visigothic code ended, and so was itself sometimes referred to by the corruption *Papianus*.

Justinian's codification

The Roman Empire in the East, now largely Greek-speaking, continued until 1453. In 527 Justinian became Emperor and immediately initiated a programme designed to restore the ancient glory of the Roman Empire, through military campaigns in the West, which were for a time remarkably successful, through architecture, through the enforcement of religious orthodoxy and through the revival of the Roman law of the classical period. He was fortunate in having as the executant of his legal policy Tribonian, a lawyer of great ability and organising power. In the fifth century there had been a revival of legal science in the law schools of Beirut and Constantinople, and he could call on lawyers with sufficient academic preparation for the task.

The most ambitious part of Justinian's codification is the *Digest* (or *Pandects*), an anthology of extracts from the writings of thirty-nine classical jurists but over one third of them taken from the works of Ulpian and one sixth from those of Paul. They are collected into titles, each title being devoted to a particular topic and the titles arranged in fifty books. According to Justinian the excerpts represent one twentieth of the mass of writings used by the compilers. The order of the titles is the traditional order of the commentaries on the edict. Within each title there is no attempt to arrange the fragments in any sort of order. Only in the nineteenth century was it shown that the compilers must have divided themselves into three sub-committees, each of which worked through a group (or 'mass') of classical works, since the excerpts from the works in each mass regularly appear in the same order, although the masses themselves do not appear in the same order in each title. The compilers were instructed to choose what they considered best and to attribute every fragment to its original source with an inscription giving author, title of work and number of book. But at the same time they were to ensure that the *Digest* included nothing out of date, no contradictions and no repetitions, and they were given powers to make such alterations as were necessary to achieve these ends. Such alterations, formerly known as *emblemata Triboniani* and now as interpolations, were probably made mainly for the purpose of abbreviation, but their extent has been a major problem for scholars since the sixteenth century. In the Middle Ages the *Digest* was divided into three parts: *Digestum vetus* (up to the end of *Dig.* 24.2); *Infortiatum* (from *Dig.* 24.3 to the end of Book 38) and *Novum* (from *Dig.* 39.1 to the end of Book 50). This curious division was thought to be derived from the order in which the parts were discovered.

Since the *Digest* was too difficult for students, it was supplemented by the *Institutes*, an introductory textbook in four books subdivided into titles, based on the manual of Gaius. After an introduction on sources of law it divides the whole of private law into persons, things and actions. The category of things is subdivided into physical things and their acquisition, inheritances and obligations.

The third part of what came (in the sixteenth century) to be called the *Corpus Iuris Civilis* is the *Code*. This is a collection of imperial constitutions based on the Theodosian *Code* and (for pre-Constantine constitutions) two earlier private collections but with much post-Theodosian legislation. It includes many constitutions enacted by Justinian himself to settle outstanding disputes which the work on the *Digest* had brought to light. The *Code* is in twelve Books, subdivided into titles (usually much shorter than those of the *Digest*), the constitutions within each title being arranged in chronological order. Book 1 deals with questions of faith and the position of the Church, sources of law and duties of officials, Books 2 to 8 with private law, Book 9 with criminal law and Books 10–12 (known in the Middle Ages as the *Tres Libri* and copied separately from the rest of the *Code*) with Byzantine administrative law.

With the publication of the *Code* in 534, the codification of the old law was complete, but it made little immediate impact, being largely inaccessible in the Latin-speaking West, and unintelligible in the Greek-speaking East (although a Greek version, the Basilica, appeared in the ninth century). Apart from its language, the whole tone of the codification was dictated by the aim of reviving the classical law of three centuries earlier. There were few hints of the vulgar law and insufficient concessions to Byzantine practice for use in the Byzantine courts. Justinian continued to legislate until his death in 565, some of his *Novels*, such as those dealing with the law of succession, being far-reaching. But, whereas the *Digest*, *Institutes* and *Code* looked backwards to the law of the classical period, the *Novels* were more Byzantine in character, and mostly written in Greek. Two collections were known in the Middle Ages, the *Epitome Iuliani*, which contains an abridged Latin version of 124 *Novels*, and the *Authenticum*, which contains 134 constitutions, the Latin in the original and the Greek in a poor translation, arranged by the medieval doctors in nine *Collationes*. The *Novels* too came to be regarded as part of the *Corpus Iuris Civilis*.

By his codification Justinian reduced the whole of the law, whether of juristic or imperial origin, to a series of his own enactments. All parts (even the *Institutes*) were henceforth to have the same force of law. No reference was to be made to the earlier authorities on which the compilation was based and commentaries were forbidden. As Justinian says in the constitution introducing the *Digest* (*Deo Auctore*, 6), 'we rightly make it all our own, since all its authority derives from us, for one who amends what is not done exactly deserves more praise than the original writer'.[1] Thus no part of the codification was to have more authority than any other, and its form discouraged any qualitative comparison of passages in the different parts. It had to be assumed that there were no contradictions.

In general the sources which Justinian's compilers used contained little speculation about the theoretical foundations of law. The commentaries of the jurists and the rescripts of the emperors concentrated on the casuistic elucidation of the law. Scattered among the texts were some desultory comments on the nature of law, mostly taken from Greek philosophy, which the compilers collected together in the introductory titles of the *Digest*, *Institutes* and *Code*, but without indicating the relation between them.

The opening title of the *Digest*, 'On justice and law', contains a number of explanations of terms. *Ius civile* in the general sense is the law peculiar to a particular legal system by contrast with the *ius gentium* which is the sum of the rules common to all legal systems. Since the *Constitutio Antoniniana* there were no *peregrini*, but the jurists were interested in whether a particular institution of Roman law belonged to the Roman *ius civile* alone or was the common law of all men. Thinking about why some institutions were recognised equally by all people, they doubtless recalled Aristotle's distinction (which became a Stoic commonplace) between law that was common because it was natural, and so universally observed, and law that was man-made (*Nichomachean Ethics*, 5.7.1; *Rhetorica*, 1.13.2). In many texts in which the jurists referred a legal rule to nature they meant that it was rooted in the facts of social life and so required no further justification. 'It stands to reason' that what nature dictates must be so. The Sabinians were particularly fond of relying on argument from nature when combating a view based on the allegedly peculiar ultra-legal character of Roman civil law, urged by the Proculians. In a famous text Gaius says that some rules are universal because *naturalis ratio* dictates them (*Dig.* 1.1.9, cf. *Inst.* 1.2.1). This phrase came to mean a somewhat technical 'natural reason', but for the classical jurists it meant little more than 'common sense'. When discussing rules of Roman law which were common to all systems, they generally used *ius gentium* and *ius naturale* interchangeably. Although one passage of the

---

1 'Omnia enim merito nostra facimus, quia ex nobis omnis eis impertietur auctoritas. Nam qui non suptiliter factum emendat, laudabilior est eo qui primus invenit.'

Institutes (1.2.11) echoes Cicero's notion of natural law as eternal and unchanging, nowhere in the codification is it suggested that a rule of civil law which contravenes natural law is any less valid on that account. Indeed in one instance even an institution of the *ius gentium*, slavery, was recognised to be contrary to the natural law (*Inst.* 1.2.2), but its validity was unaffected. There is one passage, ascribed to Ulpian, which identifies the law of nature with the instincts that men share with animals, such as mating and procreation (*Dig.* 1.1.1, repeated in *Inst.* 1.2pr.), but it is an isolated view which is not taken up elsewhere. Generally natural law meant the law suggested by the natural reason common to all men, and the civil law neither wholly deviates from it nor follows it in everything (Ulpian, *Dig.* 1.1.6pr.).

Roman law was further divided, following a Greek model, into *ius scriptum*, written law, and *ius non scriptum*, unwritten law. In earlier law the contrast intended was probably between law stated in a fixed authoritative text, as in a *lex*, the praetorian edict or an imperial constitution, and the law which 'without being written down existed in the interpretation of the jurists alone' (*Dig.* 1.2.2.5). By Justinian's time, however, written law included any statement of the law in writing, including juristic opinions, by contrast with local custom. The principal text which justifies regarding custom as law (apparently in the provinces) is *Dig.* 1.3.32.1, ascribed to Julian:

Since *leges* themselves bind us only because they have been accepted by decision of the people, it is right that what the people has approved without any writing shall be binding on all. For what does it matter whether the people declare its will by vote or by actual behaviour? Consequently, it is also rightly accepted that *leges* may be repealed not only by vote of the legislature but also by the tacit agreement of all through their disuse.[2]

Other texts seem to contradict the last sentence (which may be a post-Julian addition), especially *Cod.* 8.52.2, which says that custom is only authoritative when not contrary to *lex* or to reason, but in general they confirm that unwritten custom should be followed as law, because it has received popular approval.

In contrast with the idea of popular sovereignty expressed in Julian's text stand the texts which appear to justify the unlimited power of the emperor

---

2 'Nam cum ipsae leges nulla alia ex causa nos teneant, quam quod iudicio populi receptae sunt, merito et ea quae sine ullo scripto populus probavit, tenebunt omnes: nam quid interest suffragio populus voluntatem suam declaret an rebus ipsis et factis? Quare rectissime etiam illud receptum est, ut leges non solum suffragio legis latoris, sed etiam tacito consensu omnium per desuetudinem abrogentur.'

to legislate. This was the result of a gradual acceptance. The earliest emperors held themselves to be bound by the laws, unless the senate dispensed them from the operation of a particular rule. Later emperors took to dispensing themselves from laws, and if they acted contrary to a particular rule, they were assumed to have dispensed themselves from it. It is to this practice that Ulpian refers in the famous text which describes the emperor as 'released from the laws', *legibus solutus* (*Dig.* 1.3.31). In another much cited text (*Dig.* 1.4.1pr., cf. *Inst.* 1.2.6), Ulpian says that what the emperor has decided (*quod principi placuit*) has the force of a *lex*. Ulpian probably meant that where the law was doubtful, it was the view favoured by the emperor which must prevail. He explains this statement by citing the *lex de imperio* of the popular assembly, passed at the beginning of each emperor's reign, which formally gave him power to do everything necessary for the benefit of the state. In the time of Augustus this referred to executive power, but it was used by later jurists to justify the accomplished fact of the emperor's power of legislation. The implication that in some sense the emperor, when legislating, was the delegate of the people was supported by such texts as *Cod.* 1.14.4 (*digna vox*), a constitution of Theodosius II in 429, which states that the emperor should declare himself bound by the laws, for his authority depends on that of the laws.

The texts derived from the classical period and some post-classical constitutions tended to suggest that the emperor's legislative power was limited both by the need to respect the traditional law and to depart from it only in cases of justified necessity and by the need for popular approval of any change. Yet some statements, such as those of Ulpian in *Dig.* 1.3.31 and 1.4.1pr., could easily be read as attributing absolute power to the emperor. Justinian himself was unequivocal in asserting the latter view, particularly in ecclesiastical matters. In a letter to one of Justinian's predecessors, Anastasius, in 494, Pope Gelasius I had put forward the view that the world is governed by two separate authorities, that of the pope in matters spiritual and that of the emperor in matters temporal, both being subordinated to the lordship of Christ. Justinian rejected this view and saw the emperor as uniting in himself not only the supreme temporal power (*imperium*) but also the highest spiritual power (*sacerdotium*). In the opening fragment of the *Code* (1.1.1, *cunctos populos*), he declares his will that all peoples under his benevolent sway should practise the orthodox faith which St Peter had transmitted to the Romans, and in the preface to *Novel* 6 (*Auth. Coll.* I.6pr.), he speaks of his great concern to ensure both sound doctrines in the Church and good behaviour in its clergy. Most of the first book of the *Code* consists of his own pronouncements on issues of dogma, promulgated 'that no one should dare publicly to challenge the catholic faith', and he clearly considered it to be his function to enforce them with vigour.

Even the introductory titles of Justinian's codification, which purported to deal with such matters, did not present a clear view of where legislative power lay, some texts attributing unlimited power to the emperor, others suggesting that ultimately power resided in the people. But the codification was presented as a single whole and scattered among the titles devoted to private law were a number of phrases, which, when taken out of their context, could be used in debates on political issues. For example, the famous maxim 'what touches all should be approved by all' (*quod omnes tangit*), was declared in a constitution of Justinian dealing with the relationship of guardian and ward (*Cod.* 5.59.5.2). Where there are several guardians looking after the interests of the same ward, certain acts must be agreed by all of them, since they must all give approval to what affects them all. The compilers of the *Digest* themselves gathered over 200 such maxims, many dealing with the ways in which laws should be interpreted, into the concluding title, 50.17. For example, *Dig.* 50.17.3, 'he who can consent is in a position to refuse', was taken from a discussion of the position of an heir, nominated in a will, who was deciding whether or not to accept the inheritance. By including it in the title on maxims, the compilers, without altering the wording, gave it a general application.

Like the Bible, Justinian's *Corpus Iuris* was a vast quarry from which principles and maxims of different kinds could be extracted. Despite the emperor's assurances to the contrary, it contained contradictory statements which could not be reconciled, least of all by readers who were not familiar with the original context in which they were made. Yet they were presented as all of equal authority and treated with a veneration similar to that accorded to Holy Scripture. Those arguing for totally opposed political views could find support among its texts. Throughout the codification, however, there is consistent emphasis on the moral character of the law as the 'science of the good and the fair' (*ars boni et aequi, Dig.* 1.1.1), on its relationship with justice in the sense of assigning to each individual what is his right (*ius suum cuique, Dig.* 1.1.10; *Inst.* 1.1pr.) and on the high calling of those who make it their profession.

II
BYZANTIUM

4
BYZANTINE POLITICAL THOUGHT

The Byzantine Empire, or the Byzantinisation of the Roman Empire, began with the conversion to Christianity of Constantine and his foundation of Constantinople on the site of the ancient Greek city of Byzantium. At once the main elements of Byzantine political thought are gathered together in one sentence. For Byzantine civilisation was an amalgam of three ingredients: Greek, Roman and Christian. Its political theory derived from the first two of those ingredients, which were tempered to accommodate the third. Its originators and its first apologists were the first Christian Emperor, Constantine, and the first historian of the Christian Church, Eusebius of Caesarea. The sincerity of Constantine's conversion has often been questioned, but his own writings leave little room for doubt that he saw himself as the servant and representative on earth of the Christian God.[1] None of the Christians in his empire thought otherwise. The majority of his subjects were still pagan. They were shocked and offended that their emperor had seen fit to embrace a minority religion. But their pagan theorists, such as Themistius, were able to mitigate the shock by appealing to the Hellenistic theories of kingship. Here was common ground where pagan and Christian could meet on the subject of monarchy.

Themistius regarded earthly monarchy as a copy of the kingship of Zeus, the supreme emperor (*basileus*). The kingdom of this world would be a reflection, a replica of that higher model. The king must possess and display a whole catalogue of virtues.[2] Such notions can be traced back to the political theorists of Greek antiquity. But they were elaborated most fully by the apologists of the monarchs of the Hellenistic kingdoms in the third and second centuries BC who were pleased to be reassured of their divinity as gods among men. These theories were part of the stock in trade of Greek political thinkers by the time of Constantine. Eusebius neatly accommodated them to the new phenomenon of a Christian Roman Empire with a Christian monarch.

---

1. Dvornik 1966, vol. II, pp. 634ff, 650.   2. *Ibid.*, pp. 623–4.

Eusebius was perhaps not so close a confidant of Constantine as has
sometimes been supposed.[3] But he was of one mind with his emperor on the
proper interpretation of Constantine's vision and its consequences. As a
scholar, chronicler and historian of the Christian Church, he could see that
Constantine's reign was a culminating point in the history of mankind, the
fulfilment of prophecies in the Old Testament. Isaiah in particular could be
said to have foretold the downfall of the persecutors of the Christians and
the establishment of a Christian Roman Empire.[4] But it was Eusebius who
adapted to the changed circumstances the Hellenistic theory of the monarch
as God's image. The adaptation can best be seen in the oration which he
delivered in 335–6 in celebration of the thirteenth year of Constantine's
reign.[5]

Here the thought is expressed that the empire of Constantine is the
earthly reflection (*mimesis*) of the Kingdom of Heaven. As there is but one
God so there is but one emperor (*basileus*). Thus, in imitation of the divine
monarchy, Constantine has established himself as sole ruler.[6] The pagan
Roman emperor had been *dominus et deus*. The Christian emperor was lord
but not God. Nevertheless, it is from God that all imperial power derives;
and Eusebius declared that Constantine had a special relationship with God
through the Divine Word, the Logos. He is the friend of God, the
interpreter of the Word; his eyes are ever turned to receive the message from
on high; he prepares his subjects for the heavenly kingdom and aspires to
recall the whole human race to the knowledge of God by proclaiming the
laws of truth and godliness to all men. In Hellenistic theory the king had
been guided by the Logos of philosophy and the reason of the law. In
Eusebian theory the Christian emperor was guided by the Logos of God. In
short, he was God's vicegerent or viceroy on earth presiding over a
monarchy that reflected the higher and more perfect order of heaven.

He was also endowed with or exhorted to cultivate the catalogue of
virtues that had been recommended for the Hellenistic kings. They were
after all virtues which could be recommended as well in a Christian as in a
pagan context – wisdom, goodness, justice, courage and in particular the
qualities of philanthropy and piety or *eusebeia*. Eusebius praised Constantine
for imitating the divine philanthropy and reflecting as in a mirror the
radiance of God's virtues.[7] But he also emphasised Constantine's personal,

3. Barnes 1981, pp. 265–6.   4. *Ibid.*, p. 249.
5. Eusebius, *Triakontaeterikos* (*Tricennelia*), ed. Heikel, *Eusebius Werke*, vol. I (1902), I–X, XI–XVIII.
6. *Ibid.*, IV.2: . . . τῷ τῆς κατὰ γῆν βασιλείας μιμήματι τὴν οὐράνιον ἐκτυπούμενος, ἐφ' ἣν καὶ σπεύδειν τὸ
πᾶν τῶν ἀνθρώπων παρορμᾷ γένος, ἀγαθὴν ἐλπίδα ταύτην προβεβλημένος.
7. *Ibid.*, V.1–2: ἀτὰρ δὴ καὶ βασιλεὺς ἀληθεῖ λόγῳ χρηματίσειεν < ἂν > οὗτος ὁ τῆς ἐπέκεινα βασιλείας τὸ
μίμημα βασιλικαῖς ἀρεταῖς τῇ ψυχῇ μεμορφωμένος.

familiar and direct relationship with God as one who had often experienced
the divine presence in visions and in dreams. It was a belief that the emperor
himself shared. Eusebius' oration was nicely calculated to encourage the
Christians in his audience without giving offence to the pagans. The name
of Christ is not mentioned. But so far as his central theme was concerned all
were in agreement. Monarchy was the best form of government; and since
there was only one God, one Supreme Being, there could be only one
emperor.

It is not certain that any of Constantine's successors made a point of
reading the works of Eusebius. But they were assuredly read by the church
fathers and historians, in the west as well as the east; and it was through them
that he exerted his enormous influence. Eusebius had once and for all
established the new way to interpret history; and his followers, from
Socrates and Sozomen down to Nicephorus Callistus Xanthopoulos in the
fourteenth century, applied the same philosophy. In this if in no other sense
Eusebius was the founder of Byzantine political theory. It was a theory that
went almost unchallenged in its essentials for over 1000 years.

A no less potent factor in the formulation of Byzantine political thought
was the foundation of the city of Constantinople. It was in every sense a new
city, though built on the site of old Byzantium. And it was the first
predominantly Christian city in the world. It thus had a symbolic
significance as the religious centre of the new imperial faith, a significance
that was quickly enshrined in the legends that grew up about its foundation.
It was near Byzantium that Constantine had defeated his last rival for the
throne, Licinius; and it was there, by a stroke of genius, that he elected to
build the second capital of the empire which he now ruled as sole emperor.
He personally marked out its limits on 8 November 324. It was formally
inaugurated on 11 May 330. That date may be taken as the official birthday
of what it has become convenient to call the Byzantine Empire. The
adjective would have seemed strange to the inhabitants of that empire.
From the start until the end of the fifteenth century they thought of
themselves as Romans. Some of their more pedantic writers, ever given to
archaising, called the city Byzantion. But most knew it as the City of
Constantine, or simply the City (*polis*); and it was soon known as the New
Rome. Its boundaries encompassed seven hills and fourteen districts
(*regiones*). It had its imperial palace, its hippodrome, senate house, forum
and milestone from which all roads radiated. Only its temples were
different, for they were Christian. Constantine's church of St Eirene was the
new Rome's answer to Old Rome's *Ara Pacis*, the Altar of Peace of
Augustus. But the central religious building was dedicated to St Sophia, the

Holy Wisdom of God which guided the emperor's hand. This was the shrine in which he communed with the only being greater than himself, whose earthly deputy he was.

Constantine seems to have preferred to call his city the Second rather than the New Rome. He could not and would not dare to question the supremacy of the original capital of the Roman Empire. Nor could he afford to alienate its people by flouting their hallowed traditions. Constantinople had as yet no traditions. It was the city of the future. The thought was illustrated on the coins minted for its inauguration. Constantinople is represented as the bust of a female figure bearing on her shoulder the orb, the globe of the world, set on the Cross of Christ. The elder Rome on the other hand is shown simply as the allegorical female figure of *Urbs Roma*, the embodiment of all the pagan past.[8] The office of tutelary deity of the New Rome was soon to be assumed by the Virgin Mother of God. The idea of the Roman monarchy being explained in Hellenistic terms was probably more acceptable in the Greek-speaking parts of the empire. But it is doubtful if its christianisation would have gone so smoothly if Constantine had selected Antioch, Alexandria or even Nicomedia as the site of his New Rome. It suited his plans that Byzantium had no great past and no rooted traditions. It was an ideal site for the defence and the commerce of the empire in the east. But it was also an ideal setting for applying the new political theory of the empire as a whole; and its phenomenal success and expansion assured that the theory would mature and be carried to the bounds of the *oecumene* and beyond in succeeding centuries. The unique role of the Queen of Cities, the 'New Jerusalem', of Constantinople, inspired a new genre of rhetorical literature, the *Laudes Constantinopolitanae*.[9]

Christians in the age of the persecutions cannot have drawn much comfort from the thought that the Christian religion and the Roman Empire were founded at the same moment in time. After Constantine the coincidence seemed to be providential. Eusebius had made this point. The one empire founded by Augustus had done away with the polyarchy of earlier generations; and at the same point in history the knowledge of one God and one religion had been imparted to all men by Christ. 'Together, as from one starting point, two great powers came forth to civilise and unite the whole world, the monarchy of the Roman Empire and the teaching of Christ.'[10] Jupiter's promise to Augustus – '*imperium sine fine dedi*' – was

---

8. Alföldi 1948, pp. 116–18.   9. Fenster 1968.

10. Eusebius, *Triak.*, XIV.4: ἀλλὰ γὰρ ἀθρόως ἅπαντα ὥσπερ ἀπὸ νύσσης μιᾶς δύο μεγάλαι προελθοῦσαι δυνάμεις ἡμέρωσάν τε καὶ εἰς φιλίαν συνήγαγον, ἥ τε Ῥωμαίων ἀρχὴ μόναρχος ἐξ ἐκείνου φανθεῖσα καὶ ἡ τοῦ Χριστοῦ διδασκαλία . . .

echoed by Eusebius: 'The Roman Empire, . . . eager to bring the whole human race together in one unity and concord, has already united most of the diverse peoples [of the earth], and is destined to reach all those not yet [included] up to the very limits of the inhabited world.'[11] The same idea was later to be independently expressed by many others;[12] and in the time of Justinian it was majestically propounded by the sailor Cosmas Indicopleustes:

While Christ was still in the womb the Roman Empire received its authority from God as the agent of the dispensation which Christ introduced, since at that very time began the never-ending line of the successors of Augustus. The Empire of the Romans thus participated in the majesty of the Kingdom of Christ, for it transcends, so far as an earthly realm can, every other power; and it will remain unconquered until the final consummation.[13]

Constantine the Great held the throne of the world longer than any other emperor since Augustus. God had given him time to change the mould of history. It has been well observed that the account of his funeral ceremony in 337 vividly illustrates the nature of the change.[14] The emperor was dead. The Christian Church, into which he had only just been baptised, took over the funeral rites as soon as the secular and pagan ritual had been performed. As a *dominus et deus* the emperor should have joined his peers among the gods; and for the pagans he did. But the Christians could not deify him. They therefore made him a saint, as the equal of the Apostles (*isapostolos*), the Thirteenth Apostle. It was a nice compromise. But it was never repeated. Later emperors might be styled *isapostoloi*. But Constantine was the only Byzantine emperor ever to be canonised as a saint of the church universal.[15]

Byzantine society after the fourth century produced little in the way of political theorising. Indeed it has been argued that there was none.[16] Men had no need of it. The empire in which they lived was planned by God. Its government by a God-protected emperor was preordained and there was

---

11. *Ibid.*, XVI.6: ἡ δὲ Ῥωμαίων ἀρχή, ὡς ἂν προκαθηρημένων τῶν τῆς πολυαρχίας αἰτιῶν, τὰς ὁρωμένας ἐχειροῦτο, εἰς μίαν ἕνωσιν καὶ συμφωνίαν τὸ πᾶν γένος συνάπτειν σπεύδουσα, καὶ τὰ πολλὰ μὲν παντοίων ἐθνῶν συναγαγοῦσα, μέλλουσα δὲ ὅσον οὔπω καὶ αὐτῶν ἄχρι τῶν ἄκρων τῆς οἰκουμένης ἐφάπτεσθαι . . .   12. Dvornik 1966, vol. II, pp. 725–6.
13. Cosmas Indicopleustes, *Topographie Chrétienne*, II.74, 75: Τοῦ γὰρ Χριστοῦ ἔτι κυοφορουμένου, κράτος ἐδέξατο παρὰ Θεοῦ ἡ τῶν Ῥωμαίων βασιλεία, ὡς ὑπηρέτις οὖσα τῶν τοῦ Χριστοῦ οἰκονομιῶν· ἐν αὐτῷ γὰρ τῷ καιρῷ καὶ αἰώνιοι Αὔγουστοι προσηγορεύθησαν . . . Μετέχει οὖν ἡ βασιλεία τῶν Ῥωμαίων τῶν ἀξιωμάτων τῆς βασιλείας τοῦ Δεσπότου Χριστοῦ, πάσας ὑπεραίρουσα ὅσον ἐνδέχεται κατὰ τὸν βίον τοῦτον, ἀήττητος διαμένουσα μέχρι τῆς συντελείας.
14. Moss 1966, p. 1; McCormack 1981, pp. 115–32.
15. The Emperor John III Vatatzes (died 1254) came to be venerated, but only as a local saint in Asia Minor; Heisenberg 1905.
16. Ensslin 1967, p. 18: 'The Byzantines themselves accepted the Empire as *sui generis*, because it was sent from God, and any idea of theorising about it never entered their minds.'

no sense in speculating on alternative forms of society. Numerous abstract treatises on kingship or 'Mirrors for Princes' were addressed to their rulers by Byzantine writers over the centuries. But one would not expect them to betray evidence of any original political thought. Like so many other exercises in Byzantine literature they were set pieces, designed partly to flatter the recipient, partly to display their authors' rhetorical expertise and erudition. One of the earliest is that composed for Justinian by the deacon Agapetus, a set of seventy-two precepts derived from Christian and pre-Christian sources.[17] Among the most interesting is the letter of the Patriarch Photius to the newly converted Boris of Bulgaria on the duties of a Christian prince – a work which, in its studied sophistication, contrasts unfavourably with the more practical and down-to-earth advice given to the same ruler by Pope Nicholas I.[18] It was a genre of literature rather than of thought that persisted to the very end of the empire. Notable examples from the later period are the *Paideia Basilike* (or *Institutio Regia*) of Theophylact, Archbishop of Ochrida, addressed to his pupil Constantine, son of Michael VII, about 1088–9;[19] the advice to the emperor of the veteran soldier Cecaumenus;[20] the *Andrias Basilikos* (Statue of a King) of Nicephorus Blemmydes, addressed to his pupil Theodore II Lascaris, emperor in exile at Nicaea after the Fourth Crusade;[21] and the letter of John Apocaucus, Bishop of Naupactus, addressed to the rival claimant to the empire in Greece about 1224.[22] From the fourteenth century come the speeches of Thomas Magister on the Duties of a King and of his subjects, which contain some practical advice about defence and administration, but also a plea for more attention to be paid to learning and to the cultivation of the archaising rhetoric that makes these works so unoriginal.[23] The last and in many ways the most interesting of such productions is the celebrated letter of the Patriarch Antony IV to Basil I of Moscow in 1393. This will be discussed below; but it is worth noting here that it is a document somewhat more attuned to the realities of the age than most of its predecessors in this form of Byzantine literature.

The most realistic of all such pieces of advice and the most illustrative of the facts of Byzantine political thought is surely the *De Administrando*

17. Agapetus: text in *PG* 86, 1:1164–86. Selections translated in Barker 1957, pp. 54–61.
18. Photius, ep. 8, *PG* 102, 628–96. *Responsa Nicolai ad consulta Bulgarorum*, *PL* 119, 978–1016.
19. Theophylact: text in *PG* 126, 253–86. Selections translated in Barker 1957, pp. 146–9.
20. Cecaumenus: text in ed. Wassiliewsky and Jernstedt 1896. Barker 1957, pp. 125–9.
21. Blemmydes: text in ed. Emminger 1906. Barker 1957, pp. 154–9.
22. Apocaucus: text in ed. Vasilievskij 1896, p. 286.
23. Thomas Magister: texts in *PG* 145, 488–96, 496–548.

Imperio compiled by Constantine Porphyrogenitus.[24] This is a manual on kingcraft rather than kingship addressed by the emperor to his son and heir apparent Romanus II. The fact that it was confidential and not for general publication permitted its author to descend from the heights of rhetorical, archaising abstraction to what he calls 'the plain and beaten track of speech'.[25] The treatise thus clearly shows how Byzantine political theory was translated into practice, especially in matters of foreign policy and diplomacy. The 'nations' beyond the bounds of the empire, insatiate in their greed, were to be dazzled and intimidated by the divinity of the successors of Constantine, by their sacred vestments and diadems and by the religious ceremonial of their court. The chosen people of Byzantium were so exclusive that it was unthinkable that one of their emperors should ever marry a foreigner, a barbarian or a gentile. The only exception allowed by Constantine Porphyrogenitus was in favour of the Franks, 'for the holy Constantine drew his origin from those parts, and there is much relationship and converse between Franks and Romans'.[26]

This was certainly not the reason why the Franks were a most-favoured nation in Byzantine eyes. Constantine did not hail from the Kingdom of the Franks. But it was not the whole story. The Byzantine superiority complex made it embarrassing for them to treat foreigners on equal terms. The military, political or commercial treaties which they made with foreign powers were not contracts between equal partners. They were considered to be privileges and favours graciously conferred by their emperors in the form of chrysobulls or charters sealed with the imperial golden bull. Not until the thirteenth century were they forced to admit that such advertisements of their universal autocracy were no longer realistic or acceptable.[27] But in the tenth century, in the great days of Constantine Porphyrogenitus, they still had a face-saving device for accommodating the growing political aspirations of their awkward neighbours. They invented the conceit of a hierarchical world order of rulers, or a family of kings, presided over by its *paterfamilias*, the one true Emperor of the Romans in Constantinople. He and he alone could graciously associate them with his *imperium* by bestowing upon them honorary degrees of affinity to his sacred person. In this manner had Charlemagne been designated as a 'spiritual

24. *Constantine Porphyrogenitus De Administrando Imperio.*
25. *Ibid.* I: . . . σαφεῖ καὶ κατημαξευμένῳ λόγῳ . . .
26. *Ibid.* 13 (ll.117–19): τούτους γὰρ μόνους ὑπεξείλετο ὁ μέγας ἐκεῖνος ἀνήρ, Κωνσταντῖνος ὁ ἅγιος. ὅτι καὶ αὐτὸς τὴν γένεσιν ἀπὸ τῶν τοιούτων ἔσχε μερῶν, ὡς συγγενείας καὶ ἐπιμιξίας πολλῆς τυγχανούσης Φράγγοις τε καὶ Ῥωμαίοις.
27. Dölger and Karayannopoulos 1968, pp. 97–100.

brother' of the Emperor Michael I in 812. It was for this reason that the Franks were regarded as being barbarians with a difference by Constantine Porphyrogenitus 130 years later.[28]

The coronation of Charlemagne in 800 was indeed the most serious affront to the Byzantine idea of the way the world was ordered. Their emperors still clung to the belief that the single, universal *imperium Romanum* of east and west would one day be restored. Justinian had made the last great effort to act on that belief with his reconquest of North Africa, Italy and parts of Spain in the sixth century. God had allowed infidels and barbarians to undo that achievement, doubtless because of the sins of the Christian people. But in his own good time God would find another imperial agent of his will to re-enact the *restauratio imperii*. The emergence of Charlemagne on the western scene, and more particularly his coronation as emperor, struck at the very root of Byzantine political exclusiveness; for it denied the principle that there could only be one emperor, one viceroy of God, in the world. The event worried the Byzantines, but it did not cause them to modify their ideology. In 812, by the exercise of a little 'economy', they agreed to recognise Charlemagne as 'emperor' in an abstract sense, though not as Emperor of the Romans. It was a purely personal honour; and it was meant to be more qualified than enhanced by the gracious nomination of Charlemagne as a 'spiritual brother' of the true emperor in Constantinople. It is instructive, however, that the emperors in Constantinople, who had formerly described themselves with the simple Greek title of *basileus*, seldom missed an occasion after 812 to employ their full title of Emperor of the Romans.

Byzantine political theory was soon to receive other rude shocks. Still greater 'economy' had to be exercised to satisfy the pride of Symeon of Bulgaria, a nearer and more threatening enemy than Charlemagne. Symeon's ambition was to set up an empire that would include Bulgaria, with himself as its emperor at Tsargrad or Constantinople. In 913 he came near to fulfilling it. The Patriarch Nicholas Mysticus who was regent at the time, took the unprecedented step of inviting Symeon into the city and crowning him as 'Emperor of Bulgaria'. Byzantine *amour propre* was satisfied by the story later put about that the patriarch had fooled the barbarian Bulgar by putting a bogus crown on his head;[29] and in due course, though not before he had done much further damage, Symeon was

28. Dölger 1940; Ostrogorsky 1956.
29. Leo Grammaticus, ed. Bekker 1842, p. 292: ἀντὶ στέμματος τὸ ἑαυτοῦ ἐπιρριπτάριον τῇ ἑαυτοῦ ἐπέθηκεν κεφαλῇ. Theophanes Continuatus, ed. Bekker 1938, VI.5.

struck down and made to answer for his presumption at the seat of judgement in 927.[30]

The same problem arose in still more acute form a generation later when Otto I was crowned as emperor in the west in 962. Otto and his heirs were firmly convinced of the *romanitas* of their status. They were not to be fobbed off with Byzantine acknowledgement of their claim to an abstract title of emperor, nor fooled by the gift of a special place in the family of kings. The awful truth slowly dawned on the Byzantines that there was a rival claimant to the universal *imperium* and that this time he and his heirs had come to stay. They resorted to increasingly urgent statements and justifications of the claim of their own emperors to be the successors of Augustus and of Constantine. The fiction of the *translatio imperii* was elaborated. The first Christian emperor, it was said, had deliberately abandoned his capital in Italy and transferred the seat of empire from the Old Rome to the New Rome of Constantinople. When Liudprand of Cremona went to Constantinople as ambassador of Otto I in 968 he was treated to an early version of the tale. Pope John XIII had seen fit to write to the Emperor Nicephorus Phocas as 'Emperor of the Greeks' instead of Emperor of the Romans. It was no doubt a calculated solecism. Liudprand was informed that 'The stupid, silly pope has failed to realise that St Constantine transferred to this city [of Constantinople] the sceptres of imperial power together with the whole senate and the whole Roman army, leaving at Rome nothing but villeins such as fishermen, cooks, fowlers, bastards, plebeians and slaves.'[31]

In the twelfth century Anna Comnena expressed a generally held conviction when she declared that imperial authority had long since been 'transferred from [Rome] to here, to our land and to our Queen of Cities, together with the senate and the whole administration', not to mention the senior archbishopric of the church.[32] A generation later the imperial secretary and historian John Cinnamus confessed that he was reduced to tears by the impertinence of western rulers who dared to suggest that the imperial office of Byzantium was somehow inferior to that at Rome. Everyone knew that the imperial title had disappeared from Rome with

30. Obolensky, 1971, pp. 106–15; Browning 1975, pp. 56–67.
31. Liudprand of Cremona, *Legatio*, 51: 'papa fatuus, insulsus, ignorat Constantinum sanctum imperialia sceptra huc transvexisse, senatum omnen cunctamque Romanam militiam, Romae vero vilia mancipia, piscatores scilicet, cupedinarios, aucupes, nothos, plebeios, servos tantummodo dimisisse'.
32. Anna Comnena, *Alexiad*, I.13: μεταπεπτωκότων γὰρ τῶν σκήπτρων ἐκεῖθεν ἐνθάδε εἰς τὴν ἡμεδαπήν τε καὶ ἡμετέραν βασιλίδα πόλιν καὶ δὴ καὶ τῆς συγκλήτου καὶ ἅμα πάσης τῆς τάξεως μεταπέπτωκε καὶ ἡ τῶν θρόνων ἀρχιερατικὴ τάξις.

Romulus Augustulus in 476 and that after that date the one legitimate *basileus* resided in Constantinople. Only he could bestow titles such as king (*rex*) on lesser princes.[33] The myth of the *translatio imperii* was still an article of Byzantine faith in the fourteenth century. The Patriarch Philotheos, writing in 1352, stated it in these words:

The great and wonderful Empire of the Romans was transferred from Italy to the east when Constantine the Great, by divine command, was converted from Hellenism to faith in Christ and transformed the city of Byzantium into the present great city, which he called by his own name. It was he who built here a palace and moved the council and the senate over from Old Rome to make this, the New Rome, leader in authority over all other cities . . . The situation now is that those of the New Rome, that is to say all of us who belong to the universal church and are subjects of the Roman Empire and therefore continue to call ourselves Romaioi, differ so greatly from those of the Old Rome and all the various principalities of that now divided nation that very few of them recognise the fact that they too were once Romans and of the same nation and empire and that the cause of their present detachment from the church as from the empire is their own shortsightedness and folly.[34]

The ideology of the emperors themselves, or of their secretaries and civil servants, is abundantly revealed in the *prooimia* or preludes to their imperial charters and documents.[35] In these the epithets and qualities accorded to the emperor include all those recommended for the Hellenistic monarchs of antiquity and many more besides. But one looks in vain for any startlingly new developments of thought about the theory or the practice of kingship. It is the same with the numerous encomia, panegyrics and funeral orations for emperors that survive. The panegyrist or orator performed a well-known and well-tried ritual, which also had its roots in antiquity.[36] He disguised his feelings, real or feigned, in a Greek literary form that had been set long before the Byzantine era began. His audience would expect the familiar style. To have inserted any new thought, to have expressed any new idea, would have been bad taste and possibly dangerous.

A different undercurrent of thought can sometimes be glimpsed in what might be called the literature of Byzantine protest, or satire. The portrait of Justinian presented by Procopius in his *Secret History* is scarcely that which the great man himself presented to the world. Procopius depicts Justinian and Theodora as fiends in human shape, arch-destroyers of well-established

---

33. John Cinnamus, *Epitome rerum* . . ., v.7: . . . ἀλλ' ἤδη καὶ τὴν ἐν Βυζαντίῳ βασιλείαν ἑτέραν παρὰ τὴν ἐν ῾Ρώμῃ ἀποφαίνειν τολμῶσιν ἅπερ ἐμοὶ διασκοπουμένῳ πολλάκις ἤδη καὶ δακρῦσαι ἐπῆλθεν.
34. Philotheos Kokkinos, *Logos Istorikos* . . . ed. Psevtongas 1981, pp. 243–4.
35. Hunger 1964.   36. Hunger 1978, pp. 2, 120–45.

institutions.[37] But why he did so remains obscure. Later Byzantine historians were not above criticising or even lampooning the persons or the policies of deceased emperors. But none went so far as Procopius. The satirists modelled themselves on Lucian.[38] The tenth-century work known as the *Philopatris* (*The Patriot*) is directed against the two evils of the day: the unseemly revival of pagan Greek studies, and the prophets of doom who undermine the achievements of the soldier–emperor Nicephorus Phocas.[39] The works known as the *Timarion* and the *Descent of Mazaris into Hell*, of the twelfth and fifteenth centuries respectively, are also both based on Lucian.[40] Finally, there is the *Dialogue between the Rich and the Poor* written by Alexios Makrembolites about 1343, in which the exploitation of the poor by the rich is denounced as a major cause of the empire's evident decline.[41] None of these productions, however, reveals much original thought or proposes any alternative order of government or society. The message of the *Philopatris* is that the emperor will provide. 'Poor though I am', says its author, 'it suffices for my children that the emperor should live; for then wealth will not fail us, nor any race terrify us.'[42] The message of Makrembolites is that the world can only be saved by a return to Orthodox Christian standards and a respect for the divine order of things. The so-called Zealot revolution in Thessalonica in the 1340s did, for a few years, produce a unique and alternative form of government in that city. But no political manifesto of the Zealots, if such existed, has been preserved; and though they have been credited, not least by Marxist historians, with a programme of political and social reform which would have required some thought, there is no documentary or circumstantial evidence to prove it. The government by commune which they seem to have introduced was contemptuously denounced by writers of the time as *ochlokratia* or the rule of the mob; and it was put down in 1350 without inspiring any political commentator or theorist to draw conclusions from it.[43]

On the whole then there was a general consensus that, so long as there was an emperor on his throne, the divine order of the Christian world would be maintained. Doubts were only expressed when it was felt necessary to adjust the workings of a political system which everyone agreed was immutable.

37. Procopius, *Anecdota*, vi.21: . . . ἅπαντα δὲ νεοχμοῦν ἐς ἀεὶ ἤθελε, καὶ, τὸ ξύμπαν εἰπεῖν, μέγιστος δὴ οὗτος ἦν διαφθορεὺς τῶν εὖ καθεστώτων.
38. Tinnefeld 1971.   39. *Philopatris*, ed. Macleod 1967.
40. Timarion, ed. Romano 1974; Mazaris, ed. Barry *et al.* 1975.
41. Alexios Makrembolites, *Dialogue*, ed. Ševčenko 1960.
42. *Philopatris*, p. 464: τοῦτο ἀρκεῖ τοῖς παισίν, αἱ ἡμέραι τοῦ αὐτοκράτορος· πλοῦτος γὰρ ἡμᾶς οὐκ ἐκλείψει καὶ ἔθνος ἡμᾶς οὐ καταπτοήσει.
43. Bibliography on the Zealots in Nicol 1979, p. 20.

Occasions for such adjustment were most often given in two matters: that of the emperor's position with regard to the law, and that of his powers with respect to the church. The Byzantines were not fond of making binding definitions. Their empire had no written constitution. They recognised that they were the heirs to and the guardians of the whole corpus of Roman law. This required reinterpretation from time to time as well as adjustment to meet the style of a Christian society and changing circumstances. They were content to set the laws of the church among those of the empire, since the two institutions were coterminous and were indeed in many ways one and the same. They were content too, and for the same reasons, to recognise their emperor as the visible head of the church on earth and arbiter of its councils. For them the empire, the *basileia*, was the church on earth. They had no Greek word for Christendom or *christianitas*. But there was sometimes room for doubt or disagreement about the limit of the emperor's authority over the bodies and souls of the faithful.

On the other hand, the Byzantines had a horror of 'novelty' or innovation. Stability and order (*taxis*), the *pax Byzantina*, were personified in the institution of the emperor. Questioning of that order could lead to *ataxia*, confusion and disturbance. In the preface to his work on the ceremonies of the court, Constantine Porphyrogenitus declared that 'the imperial power should be exercised with due rhythm and order', and that 'the empire represented the harmony and motion of the universe as it comes from its Creator'.[44] Neither the emperor nor the patriarch, however, claimed an infallible knowledge of how that order must be kept. Gradual adaptations to changing circumstances could be permitted by the practice of compromise or economy (*oikonomia*). But abrupt changes or drastic modifications of the existing order were likely to produce *ataxia*. In the ninth century, Basil I, writing to Louis II, seems to have raised as one capital objection to the western use of the imperial title the fact that it was a 'novelty'. In other words, it disturbed the divine order and was therefore illegitimate.[45] It is significant that one of the normal Byzantine words for 'heresy' was 'novelty' or innovation (*kainotomia*). The Emperor Alexius I Comnenus, seeing the breakdown of the divine order on several fronts at the start of his reign, took stern measures to suppress the religious heresy of the Bogomils and the intellectual heresy of John Italus and his followers.

44. Constantine Porphyrogenitus, *De cerimoniis*, proem.: . . . ὑφ' ὧν τοῦ βασιλείου κράτους ῥυθμῷ καὶ τάξει φερομένου, εἰκονίζοι μὲν τοῦ δημιουργοῦ τὴν περὶ τόδε τὸ πᾶν ἁρμονίαν καὶ κίνησιν . . . .
45. Louis II's reply to Basil I in *MGH, Epistolae Karolini aevi*, VII, 386–94. See Grierson 1981, pp. 890–7.

Such 'novelties' were no less dangerous to order than the attacks on the empire of the Normans, the Pechenegs and the Turks.

The emperor was the elect of God. He did not come by his powers through hereditary right. The Byzantinised Roman Empire upheld the ancient tradition that the monarchy was elective. In theory each and every emperor was elected by the senate, the army and the people. Their choice and their acclamation revealed and implemented the will of God and the Holy Spirit. It made no difference that the senate was a moribund institution, nor that the acclamation of the people became a ritualised invocation. Nor was the theory shaken by the fact that most emperors strove to perpetuate their power and their name by founding or maintaining a dynasty. There were nine such dynasties in the years between Heraclius in 610 and Constantine XI in 1453. Only for thirty of those 843 years was the empire ruled by men who were not the heirs by blood or by kinship of their predecessors. Theoretically, however, the *imperium* remained a *carrière ouverte aux talents*. The point was proved by Basil I, the palace groom, who murdered his way to the throne in 867 and went on to establish the longest of all Byzantine dynasties. Such practice was legitimised by the principle of co-option, whereby the emperor had the right to appoint his heir as co-emperor. The right was tempered, but only in theory, by the requirement of obtaining the acclamation of the co-emperor by the people. Basil I made sure of the future of his line by co-opting three of his sons in this manner.

The constitutional position of the emperor was thus assured by adherence to Roman tradition. For a time even the ancient ceremony of raising the new emperor on a shield was continued. But from the fifth century a new element was introduced. In 457 Leo I received his crown from the Patriarch of Constantinople. All succeeding emperors, save for the very last of them, were crowned by their patriarchs. The significance of this ceremony was not at first apparent; and the religious rite of coronation was not held to be a constitutive act in the making of an emperor. Nor was it thought to signify any hold of the church over the state. But inevitably the act became one of consecration of the duly elected ruler and the patriarch required a profession of faith from the emperor before he would perform it.[46] In the thirteenth century, when the church's authority had almost outstripped that of the emperor, the coronation rite assumed a deeper religious significance. To the

46. Christophilopoulou 1956. Nelson 1976.

ceremony of anointing with oil was added that of Chrismation with the holy chrism of baptism, implying, as Symeon of Thessalonica explained in the fifteenth century, that the patriarch 'set the seal of the Holy Spirit' on the emperor.[47]

Once duly elected and crowned, the emperor was always hedged about with much divinity. Whatever his antecedents or his past record, he was transmuted to a higher estate. Every occasion of his waking life was ritualised by ceremonial procedure, vividly described by Constantine Porphyrogenitus in the tenth century and by Pseudo-Codinus in the fourteenth.[48] The ceremonial dramas, hallowed by antiquity and reflecting the order of the universe, were in themselves a guarantee of continuity and a safeguard against abrupt innovation. It was, however, always within the power of an emperor's electors to demote him to his former state if he proved unworthy or unacceptable. Forty-three of the Byzantine emperors were violently removed from office or obliged to abdicate. There were also various impediments to candidature for the throne. Blindness was customarily held to be a disqualification. The blinding of usurpers, potential or actual, was thus quite common. But an aspiring emperor could also be refused recognition by his patriarch until he had done penance for his past crimes, as was the case with John Tzimiskes in 969. The patriarch could even excommunicate the emperor. Nicholas Mysticus closed the doors of St Sophia to Leo VI on Christmas Day 906; the Patriarch Arsenius quite properly anathematised Michael VIII for his crimes in 1261. Such instances publicly demonstrated that the emperor was not above the law.

Yet he was the embodiment of the law. Another of the concepts of Hellenistic thought adopted by Byzantium was that of the monarch as 'the living law' (*lex animata, nomos empsychos*). Eusebius fought shy of it; but Themistius carried it forward in his speech in praise of his Emperor Theodosius I: 'For he is the animate law, not merely a law laid down in permanent and unchangeable terms . . . God sent kings on earth to serve men as a refuge from an immovable law to the safety of the animate and living law.'[49] The idea was enshrined by Justinian in one of his Novels: 'The imperial station, however, shall not be subject to the rules which we have

47. *Symeonis Thessalonicensis Archiepiscopi Opera Omnia*, in PG 155, 353: . . . τῷ μὲν μύρῳ σφραγίζων αὐτόν. Nicol 1976.
48. Constantine Porphyrogenitus, *De cerimoniis*. Pseudo-Codinos, ed. Verpeaux 1966.
49. *Themistii Orationes Quae Supersunt*, ed. Schenkl and Downey 1965, 1971, I, Or. 19: 'Ἐπὶ τῇ φιλανθρωπίᾳ τοῦ αὐτοκράτορος Θεοδοσίου. (p. 331: Teubner): . . . Βασιλείαν ἐκ τοῦ οὐρανοῦ κατέπεμψεν εἰς τὴν γῆν ὁ Θεός, ὅπως ἂν εἴη καταφυγὴ τῷ ἀνθρώπῳ ἀπὸ τοῦ νόμου τοῦ ἀκινήτου ἐπὶ τὸν ἔμπνουν καὶ ζῶντα.

just formulated, for to the emperor God has subjected the laws themselves by sending him to men as the living law.'[50] In one sense this was a survival of the ancient Roman claim that the emperor was above the law (*princeps legibus solutus*). Some later theorists and some later emperors took this view. The eleventh-century soldier and author Cecaumenus agreed that the emperor was not subject to the law. The emperor *is* law, provided that he acts on this principle in a correct manner.[51] In another sense, however, the idea of the emperor as 'living law' gave him the scope to exercise his required virtue of philanthropy by tempering the otherwise inflexible law with his prerogative of mercy. Thus it was possible for Leo III to claim that his *Ecloga* or selection of the laws was a revision of the Code of Justinian 'with a view to greater humanity'.[52]

It was clearly within the emperor's powers to revise the laws and several such revisions were made. But he could also add Novels (*Novellae*), new laws or constitutions. The Byzantines, living as they did in a theocratic society, found it hard to be sure where things temporal ended and things spiritual began. Thus the laws of their state frequently incorporated legal rulings of the church. Where a necessary qualification for citizenship was Orthodoxy in religious belief, it was natural that the canons of the church councils which had defined that belief should also be the law of the land. Justinian had decreed that 'the canons of the first four councils of the church, at Nicaea, Constantinople, Ephesus and Chalcedon, should have the status of law. For we accept as holy writ the dogmas of those councils and guard their canons as laws.'[53]

The church could add to and interpret those canons. One version of the law indeed laid down that only the patriarch had the right to interpret the rulings of the Fathers and the canons of the councils.[54] But some emperors thought themselves empowered to do likewise and to legislate on ecclesiastical or even doctrinal matters. Hence there came into existence the collections known as *nomocanones* in which the laws of the church and the laws of the state were set down side by side and compared, though the

50. Justinian, Nov. 105. 2, 4: 'Omnibus enim a nobis dictis imperatoris excipiatur fortuna, cui et ipsas deus leges subiecit, legem animatam eum mittens hominibus.' Steinwenter 1946, pp. 250–1.
51. Cecaumenus, ed. Wassiliewsky and Jernstedt 1896, p. 93: 'Ἐπεὶ λέγουσί τινες ὅτι ὁ βασιλεὺς νόμῳ οὐχ ὑπόκειται, ἀλλὰ νόμος ἐστί, τὸ αὐτὸ κἀγω λέγω· πλήν ὅσα ἂν ποιῇ καὶ νομοθετῇ καλῶς ποιεῖ καὶ πειθόμεθα τούτῳ . . .
52. *Ecloga*, ed. Zepos 1931, p. 11: ἐπιδιόρθωσις εἰς τὸ φιλανθρωπότερον ἐκτεθεῖσα . . .
53. Justinian, Nov. 131. 1: 'Sancimus igitur vicem legum obtinere sanctas ecclesiasticas regulas, quae a sanctis quattor conciliis expositae sunt aut firmatae . . . Praedictarum enim quattuor synodorum dogmata sicut sanctas scripturas accipimus et regulas sicut leges servamus.'
54. *Epanagoge* 3.5: Τὰ παρὰ τῶν παλαιῶν κανονισθέντα καὶ παρὰ τῶν ἁγίων πατέρων ὁρισθέντα καὶ παρὰ τῶν ἁγίων συνόδων ἐκτιθέντα τὸν πατριάρχην μόνον δεῖ ἑρμηνεύειν.

former always precede the latter. The *Nomocanon in Fourteen Titles*, compiled in the seventh century, was the best known of such collections. But the greatest canonists, such as Theodore Balsamon, Patriarch of Antioch in the twelfth century, and Demetrios Chomatianos, Archbishop of Ochrida in the thirteenth century, never set themselves to produce a *Corpus juris canonici*. They preferred to work piecemeal from heterogeneous collections of legal rulings derived from the canons of the oecumenical councils, the so-called apostolic canons, the decisions of local synods and excerpts from the Scriptures and the Fathers. The uncharted territory between the secular law (*nomos*) of the emperor and the church law (*canon*) of the patriarch and his synod gave them great scope for the setting of one text against another and arriving at various opinions by interpretation and adaptation.

The *nomocanones* and the commentaries of the canonists advertised the fact that church and state went together. The two were interdependent and it was generally believed that the one could not exist without the other. The monks of Constantinople, when being persecuted for their faith by the Latinophile Emperor Michael VIII in the thirteenth century, counted the days till they should be rid not of their emperor but of their miseries; for, they said, they could no more live without an emperor than a body can live without a heart.[55] Yet the monks, throughout the empire's history, were usually the first to complain about an emperor's interference in the affairs of the church. It was in this realm of thought that the Byzantines found most room for debate. Here again the tone was set by Constantine. As the first Christian emperor he saw it as his imperial duty to regularise the affairs of his Christian subjects, to incorporate their society within the framework of empire. They must be made to arrive at a uniformly and universally agreed form of their creed. Either Arius was right or he was wrong. The only way to find out was to convene the Bishops of the church and seek the guidance of the Holy Spirit in common council. The Council of Nicaea in 325 was summoned by Constantine and presided over by him. Its procedure and protocol were modelled on that of the Roman senate. The emperor presided as *princeps*; the deputy of the Bishop of Rome, still the capital of the empire, took the place of the *princeps senatus*.

Such was the model for all subsequent councils of the church in the Byzantine world. The last was the council in Constantinople in 1351, summoned by the Emperor John VI Cantacuzene, at which the theology of

---

55. George Pachymeres, ed. Bekker 1835, VI.24:I, p. 490: . . . ἀβασιλεύτοις γὰρ οὐδὲ ξυνήνεγκε ζῆν, ὡς σώματι μὴ καρδίαν ἔχοντι . . . .

the Hesychasts was found to be Orthodox; though no papal legate was present on that occasion and no one could pretend that it was a fully oecumenical council. The decrees of such assemblies had to be signed by the emperor. Without his signature they could not become law, since he was the source of law human and divine. The signing of the decree of Union at the Council of Florence in 1439 provoked much argument, since the emperor claimed the right to put his signature before that of the pope.[56] How far an emperor could intervene in debates and determine the course of discussions was for him to decide. Different emperors held different views, knowing that Constantine's intervention at Nicaea had been decisive. But everyone accepted that he could direct the proceedings as the supreme upholder of the right belief that was Orthodoxy, not simply as the defender of the faith, but as its embodiment.

After Constantine the position of the emperor with regard to the church was firmly established, if somewhat ill-defined. Theodosius the Great set the seal on the triumph of Christianity.[57] It was he who coined the word Orthodoxy. Heterodoxy or heresy was declared to be a criminal offence. The ancient pagan religions were proscribed and their adherents were persecuted. The oracle at Delphi, the games at Olympia and the mysteries at Eleusis were banned and their shrines destroyed. The privilege of Roman citizenship was reserved for those who professed the true faith as it had been defined at the Councils of Nicaea in 325 and of Constantinople in 381. The policy of Theodosius was followed and brought to its final uncompromising form by Justinian. Justinian was convinced that the propagation of Orthodox Christianity was part of his mission to restore the boundaries of the Roman Empire. The lost provinces in the west must be rescued from the Arian heretics who tyrannised them. He was the defender of the faith and the terror of its enemies, but also its organiser and director. The last elements of paganism, and with them the last champions of religious tolerance, were hunted down. The Platonic Academy in Athens was closed in 529. But Christianity was favoured by more imperial attention than ever before. Every aspect of the life of the church was covered by Justinian's legislation; and though on occasions he treated popes and patriarchs as if they were his servants, the church was on the whole grateful and not resentful. It regarded the emperor's concern not as interference but as proper solicitude.

The Byzantine emperors have often been accused of 'Caesaropapism'. It is now generally agreed that the term is not apt. No emperor before or after

---

56. Sylvester Syropoulos, ed. Laurent 1971, X.4 (p. 478).   57. Dvornik 1966, vol. II, p. 764.

Justinian exercised such unlimited authority over his church. Yet he was the
first to propose a legal distinction between empire and priesthood, between
imperium and *sacerdotium*. He confessed that he found the distinction to be
slight.[58] But he felt that it should be stated. He therefore declared that

> The greatest of the gifts of God to men, granted by the heavenly mercy, are the
> priesthood and the imperial authority: the one serves divine ends, the other rules
> over and cares for human affairs; and each of these springs from one and the same
> source and each adorns the life of man . . . For if the priesthood be blameless in
> every respect and full of faith before God, and if the imperial authority duly and
> rightly adorn the state which is entrusted to it, then there will result a fair harmony
> which will furnish every good thing to the human race. We are therefore
> concerned in the highest degree for the true doctrines inspired by God and for the
> integrity of the priesthood.[59]

The ideal thus postulated of harmony and co-operation between
emperor and patriarch, between church and state, remained the guiding
principle thereafter. It was also accepted that it was the emperor's divine
obligation to concern himself with the true doctrines of the church, even
though those doctrines could only be defined or amended in a council of all
its leading bishops. Some canonists such as Balsamon gave it as their private
opinion that the emperor was above the canons of the church as he was
above the laws.[60] Some emperors behaved as if they were. But the idea was
never openly accepted. The harmony between emperor and patriarch was
most often upset by two eventualities: when the emperor was thought to
have trespassed too far into the field of doctrine, or when he was thought to
have overreached himself in restricting the freedom of monks and clergy to
manage their own affairs. The iconoclast emperors of the eighth and ninth
centuries were guilty on both counts. Not only did they presume to decree
that the traditional veneration of icons or religious images was uncanonical;
they also penalised and persecuted those churchmen and monks who
disagreed with them. They had of course a large body of clerical opinion
behind them. But their opponents were given much opportunity to remind

---

58. Justinian, Nov. 7.2: 'cum nec multo differant ab alterutro sacerdotium et imperium, et sacrae res a
communibus et publicis'.
59. Justinian, Nov. 6, praef.: 'Maxima quidem in hominibus sunt dona dei a superna collata clementia
sacerdotium et imperium, illud quidam divinis ministrans, hoc autem humanis praesidens ac
diligentiam exhibens; ex uno eodemque principio utraque procedentia humanam exornant vitam
. . . Nam si hoc quidem inculpabile sit undique et apud deum fiducia plenum, imperium autem
recte et competenter exornet traditam sibi rempublicam, erit consonantia quaedam bona, omne
quicquid utile est humano conferens generi. Nos igitur maximam habemus sollicitudinem circa
vera dei dogmata et circa sacerdotum honestatem.'
60. Theodore Balsamon, ed. Rhalles and Potles 1853, vol. III, pp. 349, 350: ὁ βασιλεὺς οὔτε νόμοις οὔτε
κανόσιν ὑπόκειται . . . ὁ βασιλεὺς ὁ μὴ ἀναγκαζόμενος ἀκολουθεῖν τοῖς κανόσι.

them of the limits of imperial authority. St John of Damascus, who lived beyond the reach of the emperor's wrath, could in these circumstances write: 'It appertains not to kings to make laws for the church. Kings have not preached the word to you, but apostles and prophets, pastors and doctors. Political welfare is the concern of kings: the ecclesiastical system is a matter for pastors and doctors. I cannot be persuaded that the church is governed by imperial edicts.'[61]

St Theodore of Studius and his fellow victims of imperial displeasure put the matter less politely:

The issue does not turn on secular and carnal affairs, in which the emperor has the power of judgement and [jurisdiction in] the secular court. It is an issue that concerns divine and heavenly doctrines, and this is a thing entrusted only to those to whom the Word of God has himself spoken . . . To kings and rulers it appertains [only] to lend their aid, to join in attesting doctrines, and to reconcile differences in respect of secular affairs. Nothing else has ever been given them by God, in the matter of divine doctrines; nothing else, should it ever come to pass, will endure.[62]

So far as iconoclasm was concerned this statement was prophetic. But when the storm of that famous controversy had blown over, the Patriarch Photius re-enunciated the earlier ideal in the *Epanagoge*, the introduction to the projected new collection of the laws proposed by Basil I. 'As the constitution of the state consists, like man, of parts and members, the greatest and most necessary parts are the emperor and the patriarch. Wherefore the peace and felicity of subjects in body and soul depend upon the agreement and concord of the kingship and the priesthood in all things.'[63]

The Emperor John Tzimiskes, whose patriarch had made him do public penance for his implication in the murder of his predecessor in 969, is reported as saying that he knew of two powers here on earth, 'the power of the priesthood and that of the kingship, the one entrusted by the Creator with the cure of souls and the other with the government of bodies'.[64] Some 200 years later Theodore Balsamon was inclined to allow the emperor a larger share in the concord between kingship and priesthood: 'The service

61. John of Damascus, *PG* 94, 1295. Translated in Barker 1957, p. 86.
62. Theodore of Studius, *PG* 99, 1417. Translated in Barker 1957, p. 88.
63. *Epanagoge, Jus graeco-romanum* 2, tit. III. . . 8: Τῆς πολιτείας ἐκ μερῶν καὶ μορίων ἀναλόγως τῷ ἀνθρώπῳ συνισταμένης, τὰ μέγιστα καὶ ἀναγκαιότατα μέρη βασιλεύς ἐστι καὶ πατριάρχης. Διὸ καὶ ἡ κατὰ ψυχὴν καὶ σῶμα τῶν ὑπηκόων εἰρήνη καὶ εὐδαιμονία βασιλείας ἐστι καὶ ἀρχιερωσύνης ἐν πᾶσιν ὁμοφροσύνη καὶ συμφωνία. Translated in Barker 1957, p. 92.
64. Leo Diaconus, *History* VI.7: δύο δὲ τὰς ἐν τῷ τῷδε βίῳ γινώσκω καὶ τῇ κάτω περιφορᾷ, ἱερωσύνην καὶ βασιλείαν, ὧν τῇ μὲν τὴν τῶν ψυχῶν ἐπιμέλειαν, τῇ δὲ τῶν σωμάτων κυβέρνησιν ἐνεχείρισεν ὁ δημιουργός.

of the emperors includes the enlightenment and strengthening both of soul and body: the dignity of the patriarchs is limited to the benefit of souls, and to that only (for they have little concern with bodily well-being).'[65] Yet another and rather different view was expressed by the Patriarch Athanasius I in the early fourteenth century: 'Priesthood was not granted to Christian people for the sake of empire, but empire for the sake of priesthood so that if the empire in a manner pleasing to God supported the church with the secular arm and honoured and protected her, the empire in turn would be supported and protected and increased by God.'[66] All of these opinions, and examples could be multiplied, might have been variations on the classic statement of St John Chrysostom that 'the government and the priesthood have each their own boundaries, though the priesthood is the greater of the two'.[67]

The true boundary between *imperium* and *sacerdotium* was revealed in the fact that the emperor was not a priest. His encomiasts might address him as 'the new David', the 'new Solomon', or compare him with Moses or Melchizedeck. The biblical figure of the priest-king was familiar in Byzantine art and literature. Constantine and his early successors retained the pagan title of Pontifex Maximus, christianised for a time as Pontifex Inclitus by Marcian and Anastasius. The bishops in Constantinople in 448 hailed Marcian as 'the high-priestly emperor' or imperial bishop. At the Council of Chalcedon in 451 they hailed him as 'priest and emperor'.[68] Constantine had once described himself as 'Bishop of those (or of the things) outside the church ($\tau \hat{\omega} \nu$ $\dot{\epsilon} \kappa \tau \acute{o} s$)'.[69] This curious phrase has been variously construed, to mean Bishop of the pagans who were not members of the church;[70] or Bishop of all affairs external to the church;[71] or as a mere witticism cast forth when the emperor was entertaining some bishops to dinner.[72] It remains that the emperor proposed some claim to the title of bishop. The claim could clearly only have been made at a time when there was still no ruling, however vague, on the respective qualities or estates of priesthood and kingship. The emperor's person was sacred; he was acclaimed as *hagios* (holy); he was the equal of the Apostles; and he was

---

65. Theodore Balsamon, PG 138, 1017: ... $\tau \hat{\omega} \nu$ $\mu \grave{\epsilon} \nu$ $\alpha \mathring{\upsilon} \tau o \kappa \rho \alpha \tau \acute{o} \rho \omega \nu$ $\mathring{\eta}$ $\grave{\alpha} \rho \omega \gamma \grave{\eta}$ $\pi \rho \grave{o} s$ $\phi \omega \tau \iota \sigma \mu \grave{o} \nu$ $\kappa \alpha \grave{\iota}$ $\sigma \acute{\upsilon} \sigma \tau \alpha \sigma \iota \nu$ $\dot{\epsilon} \pi \epsilon \kappa \tau \epsilon \acute{\iota} \nu \epsilon \tau \alpha \iota$ $\psi \upsilon \chi \hat{\eta} s$ $\tau \epsilon$ $\kappa \alpha \grave{\iota}$ $\sigma \acute{\omega} \mu \alpha \tau o s$, $\tau \grave{o}$ $\delta \grave{\epsilon}$ $\mu \epsilon \gamma \alpha \lambda \epsilon \hat{\iota} o \nu$ $\tau \hat{\omega} \nu$ $\pi \alpha \tau \rho \iota \alpha \rho \chi \hat{\omega} \nu$ $\epsilon \grave{\iota} s$ $\mu \acute{o} \nu \eta \nu$ $\psi \upsilon \chi \iota \kappa \grave{\eta} \nu$ $\dot{\epsilon} \sigma \tau \epsilon \nu o \chi \acute{\omega} \rho \eta \tau \alpha \iota$ $\lambda \upsilon \sigma \iota \tau \epsilon \lambda \epsilon \acute{\iota} \alpha \nu$ ($\dot{o} \lambda \acute{\iota} \gamma \eta$ $\gamma \grave{\alpha} \rho$ $\tau o \acute{\upsilon} \tau o \iota s$ $\dot{\epsilon} \sigma \tau \grave{\iota}$ $\phi \rho o \nu \tau \grave{\iota} s$ $\epsilon \mathring{\upsilon} \pi \alpha \theta \epsilon \acute{\iota} \alpha s$ $\sigma \omega \mu \alpha \tau \iota \kappa \hat{\eta} s$).
66. Athanasius I, *Correspondence*, ed. Talbot 1975, no. 104, p. 264.
67. John Chrysostom, *Ad populum Antiochenum*, Hom. III, PG 56, 50.　68. Bréhier 1948.
69. *Vita Constantini*, IV. 24, ed. Winkelmann 1975, *Eusebius Werke*, vol. I, p. 126: $\grave{\alpha} \lambda \lambda$' $\mathring{\eta} \mu \epsilon \hat{\iota} s$ $\mu \grave{\epsilon} \nu$ $\tau \hat{\omega} \nu$ $\epsilon \mathring{\iota} \sigma \omega$ $\tau \hat{\eta} s$ $\dot{\epsilon} \kappa \kappa \lambda \eta \sigma \acute{\iota} \alpha s$, $\dot{\epsilon} \gamma \grave{\omega}$ $\delta \grave{\epsilon}$ $\tau \hat{\omega} \nu$ $\dot{\epsilon} \kappa \tau \grave{o} s$ $\mathring{\upsilon} \pi \grave{o}$ $\theta \epsilon o \hat{\upsilon}$ $\kappa \alpha \theta \epsilon \sigma \tau \alpha \mu \acute{\epsilon} \nu o s$ $\dot{\epsilon} \pi \acute{\iota} \sigma \kappa o \pi o s$ $\mathring{\alpha} \nu$ $\epsilon \mathring{\iota} \eta \nu$.
70. So, most recently, De Decker and Dupuis-Masay 1980.
71. Dvornik 1966, vol. II. pp. 752–4.　72. Barnes 1981, p. 270.

surrounded by a numinous aura enhanced by ceremony and ritual. But he was never an ordained priest, let alone a bishop. He and he alone of the laity was allowed to enter the sanctuary and to take communion in the manner of a priest or deacon.[73] But the order of priesthood was denied him, and would indeed have disqualified him from being emperor. The iconoclast Emperor Leo III once indignantly informed the pope that he was priest as well as emperor (*hiereus kai basileus*). The pope was aware that Constantine, Theodosius and Justinian had been called the same. But he refused to gratify the vanity of an iconoclast.[74]

Some of the canonists employed the technical term *epistemonarches* to describe the emperor's ecclesiastical status. It implied that he was 'the wise defender of the faith and regulator of order in the church'. But it permitted no suggestion that he was himself a priest or bishop even of honorary rank. Demetrios Chomatianos in the thirteenth century summarised the emperor's ecclesiastical prerogatives in these words: 'The emperor is as the general *epistemonarches* of the churches. He defends the decrees of the councils and regulates the hierarchy of the church. With the single exception of the sacramental office, all the other privileges of a bishop are clearly represented by the emperor, and he performs them legally and canonically.'[75] Even the ascetic and monkish Patriarch Athanasius I accorded the title of *epistemonarches* to his emperor, for all that he put a slightly different emphasis on the balance between *sacerdotium* and *imperium*.[76]

Not until some seventy years before the fall of Constantinople were the constitutional rights of the emperor in ecclesiastical matters clearly and definitively committed to writing. About 1380 a document was issued with the agreement of the Emperor John V and his patriarch.[77] It contained nine clauses. The emperor, in accordance with custom, nominated metropolitan bishops by choosing from three names submitted to him by the patriarch; he had the exclusive right to create, promote or demote bishoprics, to amalgamate them, or to transfer their incumbents; he must sanction all nominations to the highest and senior offices in the church; it was for him to ensure that the boundaries of dioceses were respected as he had established

---

73. Constantine Porphyrogenitus, *De cerimoniis* 1, ch. 10.   74. Mansi 1759–98, vol. XII, p. 975.
75. Demetrios Chomatianos, *Analecta*, ed. Pitra 1891, pp. 631–2: ὁ βασιλεὺς γάρ, οἷα κοινὸς τῶν ἐκκλησιῶν ἐπιστημονάρχης, καὶ ὢν καὶ ὀνομαζόμενος, καὶ συνοδικαῖς γνώμαις ἐπιστατεῖ . . . καὶ ἐκκλησιαστικὰς τάξεις ῥυθμίζει . . . . καὶ ὡς ἔπος εἰπεῖν, πλὴν μόνου τοῦ ἱερουργεῖν, τὰ λοιπὰ ἀρχιερατικὰ προνόμια σαφῶς εἰκονίζει ὁ βασιλεύς, ἐφ' οἷς πράττει νομίμως καὶ κανονικῶς.
76. Athanasius I, *Correspondence*, ed. Talbot 1975, no. 61, p. 142, no. 95, p. 248.
77. Laurent 1955.

them, during and after the lifetimes of their bishops; neither the emperor nor his senators and ministers could be excommunicated by the patriarch, whose power in such cases was limited to admonition, for the emperor is the defender of the church and the canons; the emperor and not the patriarch had the last word as to whether bishops should stay in Constantinople on important business or be sent back to their sees; every bishop must take an oath of allegiance to him and to the empire when appointed; every bishop must sign acts passed by a synod or a council; every bishop must observe the rulings here laid down and refuse his support to any candidate for office in the church who is not a loyal friend of the emperor. This document at long last clarified the emperors' practical jurisdiction over the church. But it still failed to clear the air with regard to his unique relationship with God. The special mystique of the imperial office could not so easily be defined.

The last pronouncement on the matter was made by the Patriarch Antony IV in 1393. At the time the city of Constantinople was isolated by the Ottoman Turks. Little else was left of the empire. It seemed that the end might come at any moment. The Grand Duke of Moscow, Basil I, who had cause to resent Byzantine interference in his own domain, instructed his bishop to cease commemorating the emperor's name. His reason for so doing was that, though the Byzantine church appeared to be surviving, there was not much sign of the emperor's continuing ability to lead society. The news of Basil's action stirred the Patriarch Antony to compose his well-known letter to Moscow, restating the ancient Byzantine theory of the harmony between church and state in lucid and forceful terms.

The patriarch wrote to his spiritual son Basil as 'the universal teacher of all Christians', a title which the last patriarchs of Constantinople were fond of adopting. Philotheos, one of Antony's predecessors, had deemed himself to be 'appointed by God as pastor and teacher of all the universe'. Antony himself elsewhere had claimed to be 'father and spiritual lord by God appointed over all Christians in the universe', and 'judge general of the *oecumene* to whom every Christian could appeal to have his wrongs righted'.[78] Such claims, almost papal in their phraseology, advertised the fact that the church in Byzantium had indeed greater powers of survival than the empire. When the patriarchs appeared to have taken over as vicegerents of God on earth, the Prince of Moscow might be forgiven for supposing that the emperor had become a nonentity. The Patriarch Antony

---

78. Philotheos to the Metropolitan of Kiev (1371): Miklosich and Müller 1860–90, vol. I, p. 582. Antony IV to the Bishop of Novgorod (1393): *ibid.*, vol. II, pp. 182, 187.

was quick to put him right and to remind him of the eternal verities of Byzantine political theory.

'The holy emperor', he wrote,

has a great place in the church. He is not to be compared with other rulers and local princes. For from the beginning the emperors established and confirmed the true faith in all the *oecumene*. The emperors convened the oecumenical councils. They ratified and made legally binding the decrees of the sacred and holy canons concerning correct doctrines and the government of Christian citizens . . . If, by God's will, the nations [the Turks] have encircled the seat of imperial government, still the emperor to this day retains the same approval from the church, the same status and the same prayers. He is still anointed with the holy chrism and elected *basileus* and *autokrator* of the Romans, that is of all Christians; and the name of the emperor is still commemorated by all patriarchs, metropolitans and bishops in every place where men call themselves Christians. No other ruler or local prince has ever had such privileges . . .

Therefore, my son, it is not proper for you to say that we have a church but no emperor. It is not possible for Christians to have a church and not to have an emperor. For the church and the empire have a great unity and communion. The one cannot be separated from the other. The only emperors whom Christians reject are those heretics who attacked the church and introduced into it corrupt dogmas contrary to the teaching of the apostles and the fathers. Our [present] mighty and holy emperor, however, is, by the grace of God, most Orthodox, most true to the faith. He is a champion of the church, its defender and vindicator; and it is impossible for a bishop not to commemorate his name. Listen to what Peter, the prince of the apostles, said in the first of his general epistles: 'Fear God, honour the king'. He did not say 'the kings', so that no one could suspect him of referring to those who are called kings here and there among the 'nations'. He said 'the king', thereby demonstrating that the universal king is one . . . For if others among the Christians have assumed for themselves the name of Emperor, they have done so by tyranny and violence and their actions are unnatural and illegal.[79]

Forty years after this letter was written it was to be dramatically and sadly proved that a church without an emperor was not an impossibility; and yet there was still an emperor of a kind. When the Turks took Constantinople on 29 May 1453, the last Christian Emperor, Constantine XI Palaeologus, died fighting at the walls of his city. But the conquering Sultan Mehmed II saw how the Christian Church could serve his purpose. He picked on the scholar and monk Gennadius to be the first Patriarch of Constantinople under the new dispensation. He was to be held responsible for the conduct of all the Christian 'nation' within the Ottoman Empire. It was the Sultan,

79. Text in Miklosich and Müller 1860–90, vol. II, pp. 188–92. Partial translation in Barker 1957, pp. 194–6.

or as some Greeks called him the 'Sultan-Basileus', who acted the part of emperor by investing the new patriarch with the insignia of his office before he was consecrated in the traditional manner. Thus, after more than 1000 years, a definition was at last imposed upon the issue which the Byzantines had never clearly resolved. The church was henceforth answerable to the state.

In the last and apparently hopeless years of the empire's existence, there were various schools of thought about what had gone wrong. By far the most prevalent explanation was that God was punishing the people for their sins. This was a favourite theme of sermons in the fourteenth and fifteenth centuries. The victorious Turks had been sent as God's agents to chastise the wicked Christians. A patriarchal document of 1350 expressed the idea in these words:

It is through the divine anger at [our] wickedness that we are visited by these plagues, famines, earthquakes, tidal waves, floods and conflagrations, and that we have to witness the murder of Christians by each other in civil war, the Black Death, and the great and terrible enslavement and diaspora of the Christian nation by their impious, godless and barbarian enemies'.[80]

The only hope of salvation lay in a return to the faith and practice of the pure, unadulterated Orthodox faith. The Patriarch Athanasius had already preached the same message fifty years earlier.

Inasmuch as the empire sincerely keeps the holy commandments of Christ together with the Orthodox faith, prosperity will last as long as the empire, 'until the end of the world', as it has been proclaimed. If, on the other hand, the empire rejects both faith and works, it will in direct proportion be deprived of his succour.[81]

Some people took comfort in magic and astrology; others in eschatology. The prophets foretold that the end of the world was nigh in any case. This was hardly political thought. Some intellectuals, however, were stirred to reconsider at least some of the ideology of the past. In the fourteenth century it was inevitable that Byzantium should be washed by the tide of new ideas from the western world. It was a slow process and there was a difficulty of communication. Not many Greeks felt inclined to learn Latin, and they tended to judge western culture by the behaviour of the Italian merchants and sailors in Constantinople. Demetrius Cydones, a minister of state for many years in the fourteenth century, was one of the few exceptions. But the knowledge of Latin that he acquired led him to

80. Text in *ibid.*, vol. I, pp. 303–4.
81. Athanasius I, *Correspondence*, ed. Talbot 1975, no. 110, p. 272.

theology rather than to politics. He remained a faithful servant of his emperor while at the same time hoping to bridge the cultural gap between east and west by bringing together the churches of Rome and Constantinople. He translated the *Summa contra Gentiles* of Aquinas into Greek in the belief that others would be as impressed as he was by the clarity of Latin theology. In due course Cydones was converted to the Roman faith, and his influence had much to do with the later conversions of Bessarion of Nicaea and Isidore of Kiev, both of whom were made Cardinals after the Council of Florence in 1439. But these men were not political thinkers. They embraced with some relief a western ideology which seemed at the time to promise more hope for the future than that into which they had been born.

The germ of some new ideas, or some new doubts and perplexities, can be discerned in the writings of Theodore Metochites, the Grand Logothete of the Emperor Andronicus II, who died in 1332. Metochites was a polymath steeped in classical Greek learning, a prodigious author and a leading light in the revival of scholarship patronised by his emperor. Like all educated Byzantines, he found it hard to express his thoughts except in the terms set by the ancient Greek writers and philosophers whom he so much admired. His political thought, such as it was, is mainly to be found in his Essays. In the preface to them he admits that his studies have left him with the discouraging feeling that the great men of the past have said everything to perfection, leaving nothing left to say.[82] His essays on Democracy and Monarchy inevitably conclude that the rule of a king, or an emperor, is the best possible constitution. 'Moreover, under a single person, the divine laws of our Christian religion, which includes in its perfect wisdom both things divine and things human, will also best keep their place and their effective power . . . .'.[83]

Metochites was an intellectual snob. He despised his fellow Byzantines for their lack of culture. But he knew that he and they alike were living in an age of decadence of other kinds, economic, military, political and even religious. He heartily disapproved of the more extreme forms of monasticism so dear to the Byzantine tradition. He believed and said that the attainment of Christian perfection was more likely to be helped than hindered by involvement in social life and public affairs. Man was a political

82. *Theodori Metochitae Miscellanea philosophica et historica*, ed. Müller and Kiessling 1821. His first essay is entitled: προοίμιον, ἐν ᾧ καὶ ὅτι οὐκ ἔστι νῦν λέγειν.
83. *Ibid.*, p. 626: Καὶ μὴν ἔτι μάλιστ' ἂν ἕνι χώραν ἔχοιεν ἴσως καὶ κράτος ἀνύσιμον καὶ θεῖοι καθ' ἡμᾶς νόμοι τῆς χριστιανικῆς θεοσεβείας, καὶ τὰ θεῖα καὶ τἀνθρώπινα πανσόφως ἐχούσης . . . .

animal; and the hermit's rush to the desert was a form of escapism 'far from the Christian ordinances' and 'contrary to nature'.[84] These were unusual views for an Orthodox Christian. Still more unusual was his suggestion that the evident decline and fall of the empire was a matter of chance and had little to do with divine dispensation. Other empires had in the past come and gone. That of the Romans, even in its finest hour, had in fact never been universal; nor was it any more eternal than the others. *Tyche* (Fortuna) and fate or destiny were the dominant factors in the lives of men and of societies. Metochites was in love with Plutarch among many other ancient writers who would have shared these sentiments. He was a man who thought deeply; and perhaps these reflections are something more than mere *jeux d'esprit* or thoughts plucked from his reading. But in his Poems he reverts to the more familar theme that the empire is in trouble because of its morals. It is about 'to be destroyed by God because of the innumerable sins of its people'.[85] His most lasting and most beautiful memorial remains the monastery church of the Chora (Kariye Djami) in Constantinople, where he ended his days as a monk.

The City of Constantinople, the New Rome, the Queen of Cities, remained to the end one of the anchors of Byzantine political thought. For men like Metochites who lived, worked and worshipped there, it was almost impossible to think their way beyond or outside its traditions and associations. It is perhaps no accident that the most original thinker that the dying Byzantine world produced lived most of his life not in the capital but in Mistra in the Peloponnese. Mistra, on a spur of Mount Taygetos overlooking the plain of Sparta, had since 1349 been the military and administrative centre of the Byzantine enclave in the south of Greece, the Despotate of the Morea. It had flourished and grown, though it was never a large city. By 1400 it had become a hive of cultural, intellectual and artistic activity, housing within its walls numerous churches, monasteries, palaces and libraries. Writers, philosophers and artists settled there to escape from the stresses and strains of the beleaguered city of Constantinople; and it was especially favoured and endowed by the last emperors, whose families provided its rulers or Despots. Among the residents of Mistra in the first half of the fifteenth century were Isidore of Kiev, Bessarion of Nicaea and George Scholarios who, as the monk Gennadius, was to become the first Patriarch of Constantinople after the Turkish conquest.

It was a place where new ideas might grow and new hopes be born. It was

84. *Ibid.*, p. 486: πόρρω γὰρ δὴ τοῦτο πάνυ τι τῆς χριστιανικῆς νομοθεσίας, καὶ τῶν καθ᾽ ἡμᾶς, ὡς οὐκ ἄλλο τι, καθάπαξ ἀλλοτριώτατον.　　85. Guilland 1959, pp. 201–2.

here that George Gemistos, known as Plethon, settled about 1407. He was already nearly fifty years of age and celebrated as a Platonist and teacher in Constantinople. Apart from a visit to Italy to attend the Council of Ferrara–Florence in 1438–9, he lived the rest of his long life at Mistra. Plethon was the first, some would say the only, Byzantine philosopher to break his way out of the traditional cast of thought. He was in some sense the intellectual heir of Theodore Metochites; but he allowed his thoughts to roam wider than any of his predecessors had dared. He probably knew no Latin. But his reading of the ancient Greek philosophers and historians encouraged him to develop the idea or the fancy that the people of the Peloponnese were the direct descendants of the Hellenes of the past. The idea was not wholly new. Some Byzantines, proud of their exclusive possession and understanding of the literary and philosophical legacy of ancient Greece, had taken to calling themselves 'Hellenes'. But Plethon was the first to see in this idea the possibilities for regeneration. Hellenism as a political and philosophical system could be recreated on the Hellenic soil of the Peloponnese. Not for nothing did Mistra look down on ancient Sparta.

In 1415 and 1418 Plethon elaborated his theme in two long memoranda addressed to the Emperor Manuel II and his son Theodore who was then Despot at Mistra.[86] Plethon implicitly rejected the Byzantine concept of a universal empire. His advice to the emperor was to make the most of the little principality which already existed in Greece. The Peloponnese, he emphasised, was both an island and a continent, secure, self-contained and an ideal testing ground for new political theories. Its people were, he claimed, of pure Hellenic stock. The Hellenic spirit lay dormant within them waiting to be revived. This would require leadership. Plethon therefore proposed a new form of constitution. At its head there must be a strongly centralised monarchy, for monarchy was the best of all systems of government. The monarch, or the Despot of Mistra, would have as his advisers a small body of educated men of moderate means and of the middle class of citizens. The army must be reorganised. It must be a professional, standing army composed not of mercenaries but of native Greeks, a privileged order of society with no duties other than defence and warfare. As such it would be supported by the other social order, the taxpayers, who would be exempt from military service and would be designated, Spartan fashion, as Helots. Taxes would be paid in kind from the produce of the land. All land would become common property which any citizen could

86. George Gemistos Plethon, ed. Lambros 1926, 1930, *Παλαιολόγεια καὶ Πελοποννησιακά*, vol. III, pp. 246–65; vol. IV, pp. 114–35.

cultivate or build on; and the cultivation of waste or virgin land was to be particularly encouraged. But no land was to be private and every farmer of the tax-paying class must render one third of his produce to the common funds.

Trade was to be carefully regulated with a view to protecting and stimulating the home market. The use of coinage as currency should be limited. Necessary imports like iron and weapons could be acquired by exchanging them for the locally made silk; and there was no need to go on importing wool, flax or cotton for clothing when such commodities could be produced at home. Crime in this new society was to be deterred and punished not, as was the Byzantine custom, by mutilation, which Plethon considered to be barbaric and 'un-Hellenic'. The death penalty could be kept; but the best form of punishment would be to set criminals to work in chain gangs on repair of the defences and such like hard labour. This would relieve the soldiers of one unpalatable task and benefit the whole country. Homosexuals, however, and other sexual deviants must be burnt at the stake. Plethon's social and political ideas were much indebted to Plato's *Republic*. Indeed he saw himself in the part that Plato had enacted at the court of the tyrant Dionysius II in Syracuse.

Plethon's proposals were meant to be comprehensive. But the one element to which he gave least attention was religion. Mistra in his day was alive with churches and monasteries proclaiming not Platonist Hellenism but the Orthodox Christianity of Byzantium. It is clear that Plethon disliked monasticism even more than Metochites had done. 'Those who profess to pursue philosophy [i.e. monks] render no service to the common good.'[87] The religious life which he advocated in his advice to his emperor depended upon a vaguely expressed belief in three principles: that there is a Supreme Being; that this divinity has a concern for mankind; and that it orders all things rightly and justly according to its own judgement without being influenced or deterred by men's gifts or flattery.[88] One sees here the germ of the ideas which were later to cause Plethon's condemnation by the church.

The emperor and his son listened politely to the great man's advice for the restructuring of society in Greece. No attempt was made to put his thoughts into practice, and indeed, although they were highly original, they were hardly practicable. But Plethon's ideas on religion, when he finally put them in writing, could not be so politely received, for they were original to

87. Plethon, ed. Lambros 1926, vol. III, p. 257.   88. Plethon, ed. Lambros 1930, vol. IV, p. 125.

the point of being blasphemous and sacrilegious. Towards the end of his long life he completed his treatise entitled *On the Laws* (*Nomon Syngraphe*).[89] It was a curious hotch-potch of neoplatonism with a dash of Zoroastrianism, badly arranged and perhaps never properly finished. It was not a work of political thought. It aimed to provide the moral and metaphysical sanction for his new constitution of society with a new 'Hellenic' religion worthy of the credence of his regenerated Hellenes. The God of the Christians is replaced by a Supreme Being to whom he gives the name of Zeus. Other members of the ancient pantheon of Olympian gods are allotted their places in the divine scheme. A new Hellenic theology was laboriously contrived, with hymns and prayers for the edification of its presiding deities. Only fragments of this bizarre work survive. After Plethon's death in 1452 the manuscript came into the hands of his former friend, the new Patriarch Gennadius. He was so horrified by its contents that he committed it to the flames. No patriarch, especially in the circumstances after 1453, could allow such a total rejection of Christian doctrine and Byzantine tradition to circulate and poison the minds of the faithful.

One modern Greek scholar has labelled George Gemistos Plethon as 'the last Byzantine and the first Hellene'. Another applied the same title to the Patriarch Gennadius.[90] Plethon's religious ideas were somewhat absurd and would surely have been foolishness to the Greeks. His political theories could only have been applicable to the microcosm of the Peloponnese. In one sense he was the most original Greek thinker since Eusebius. In another sense, however, he was not an exponent of *Byzantine* political thought, for he had ceased to think like a Byzantine. He was a prophet without honour in his own country. Even his mortal remains were later to be disinterred and taken to Italy, where his fame as a Platonist eclipsed all his other activities. The Patriarch Gennadius who had condemned his works to perdition was the true spokesman of the Byzantine conscience and tradition in the hour of crisis. It was thanks to him and his like that the Byzantine church survived during the long years of the Ottoman Empire, perpetuating the saving myth that Orthodox Christians still lived under a special divine dispensation. They belonged to a theocratic society, whose political structure was ordained by God and therefore not to be questioned.

---

89. Plethon, *Traité des Lois*, ed. Alexandre. 1858.
90. C. Sathas, *Documents inédits relatifs a l'histoire de la Grèce au moyen âge*, 9 vols., Maisonneuve et Cie, 1833, vol. IV, p. vii: 'Gennadius Scholarius . . . peut être regardé comme le dernier des Byzantins et le premier des Hellènes.' Zakythinos 1953, 1975, p. 350: 'Pléthon mérite d'être considéré comme le dernier des Byzantins et le premier des Néo-hellènes'.

III
BEGINNINGS: c. 350–c. 750

5
INTRODUCTION: THE WEST

The world of the Christian fathers from Ambrose to Isidore of Seville had come to differ profoundly from the world of the early Apologists, of Origen and Tertullian. The transformations which produced these differences came in two great waves: the first, sweeping across the whole of the Roman world, is the crisis of the third century from which Roman society was to emerge into a new stability in the fourth, a stability won through extensive re-organisation and accompanied by far-reaching changes not only in the administrative and social structure of the Empire, but also in its traditional culture and religion. These changes, though their incidence differed from region to region, affected the Empire everywhere. The second wave rolled mainly over the Western provinces: the Germanic invaders who settled within imperial frontiers came to create their own, eventually independent, kingdoms on what had been Roman soil. Both waves radically altered the social and political structures of Western Europe, and also the cultural conditions in which reflection on those structures could take place.

The later Roman Empire

The reforms of the emperors at the end of the third century, continued by Constantine in the fourth, secured the Empire from anarchy, from military, economic and social collapse. The means employed, emergency measures which gradually turned into a system, created a novel kind of political reality: a centralised, bureaucratic state very different from the Empire as it had been in the time of the Antonine or even the Severan dynasty. Much of the municipal self-government previously carried on by local urban aristocracies was taken over by an elaborately organised administration and a hierarchy of officials. The emperor who stood at the head of this hierarchy had come to be a figure very different from Augustus and his successors down to the third century. The military crises of the third century brought new kinds of men to the imperial office, soldiers who often had little respect for the traditions of Roman public life. The idea of government shared by emperor and Senate, always and increasingly something of a fiction, finally dissolved in the third century in the hands of the military autocrats who came to the throne and excluded the Roman Senate from government. Traditional notions of public life and public office, rooted in the ideals of the Roman Republic and Principate, found little reflection in the new political realities. In so far as they survived, they did so as romantic fictions nursed in literary circles or among aristocratic groups opposed to the new style of monarchy and self-consciously dedicated to the maintenance of older traditions. The shifts in political attitudes, the increased value set on *disciplina* as against *concordia*, the shifts in attitudes to private and public life and office-holding, to municipal beneficence and responsibility, are large themes beyond the scope of this book. They are, however, among the conditions which helped to determine the shape of fourth- and fifth-century Romans' thought about their society.

That the figure of the emperor and the idea of the Empire came to hold a much larger place in such thought in comparison with earlier periods is the result as much of the eclipse of traditional political ideals, so often rooted in the language and the thought-world of republican Rome, as of the change in the nature of the imperial office. There is a close, though by no means simple, relationship between the image of the emperor in the thought of late Roman thinkers, writers and preachers, and that image as it was presented in the official 'propaganda' contained in court ritual and protocol, on imperial coinage and the monuments of imperial art and in the public ceremonial surrounding the autocratic late Roman emperor, larger than life, over-shadowing his ordinary subjects. The change in the nature of the office itself, with its ritual and symbolic trappings, is among the most important determinants of the ways in which political thought came to conceive the ruler and his relation to his subjects.

The major writers whose thought on political questions is discussed here are, of course, all Christians. There had been learned converts to Christianity from the second century, and gradually educated Christians were becoming common in the churches, especially in the Greek-speaking world. In the course of the third century Christianity had made great headway among all classes of Roman society. In many places by the end of the century the cross-section of Christian groups would probably have been a fairly good reflection of the composition of Roman society at large. The appeal of Christianity was a consequence of its own readiness to adopt many of the forms which were acceptable to the literate, learned, urban and governing classes of the Empire, and enhanced by the loosening of the religious and cultural conservatism which, in earlier times, had checked the advance of many minority religions originating in distant provinces. The atrophy of Roman religious conservatism and the diminishing power of classical traditions in so many areas of Roman life contributed to the great advances made by Christianity even in the period before Constantine.

Constantine's conversion to Christianity in 312 gave added momentum to a process well under way by then. The emperor's adoption of Christianity gave the Church added prestige, new wealth and public standing, reflected in prestigious architecture, and a new confidence. Imperial patronage and the vastly increased scope given it by the mobility in late Roman society ensured a flow of converts from all classes. That the traditional education of the Roman urban classes should be generally adopted in Christian circles – the Christian Church had never devised its own alternative system of schooling – is only to be expected. So long as the public schools of the Roman world survived, Christian bishops, clergy and laymen received the same education as their pagan contemporaries. The fathers of the fourth century moved in a culture which was the common property of educated Romans, whether pagan or Christian.

The attitudes of Christians towards this shared secular culture were, however, far from uniform. Earlier hesitations about the propriety of Christians assimilating pagan secular culture had been largely overcome by the middle of the fourth century, and the attitude of sharp opposition, such as had been voiced by Tertullian in particularly vehement form, was wholly anachronistic now. The pagan revival under the emperor Julian (d.363), though too short-lived to arrest the Christians' appropriation of classical learning, awakened ancient suspicions. The conflicts between the Christian court and the pagan aristocracy in the West in the following generation renewed distrust and hostility towards secular culture among Christians. The age of Ambrose, Jerome and Augustine spanned these conflicts which coloured their attitudes towards pagan learning, thought and culture; but it was not long after their generation that such conflicts ceased. The descendants of the educated pagan aristocrats who had interested them-selves in the preservation and transmission of secular Roman culture were by the 430s almost all Christians. With their conversion a continued interest in secular thought and letters among Christians was to be assured. When in many provinces such as Gaul in the fifth and sixth centuries public education was largely superseded by education in private households, especially the households of Christian bishops descended, as they so often were, from aristocratic families (see below, pp. 89–90), a certain degree of continuity in the transmission of classical learning was thus ensured.

The christianisation of the Empire during the century following Constantine's conversion gave added impetus to the assimilation of classical learning by the Christian Church. In another respect it brought a more far-reaching change in the position of the Church in the Empire which has led many historians to speak of a 'Constantinian revolution'. Christianity, subject to persecution on the very eve of Constantine's establishing control over the Western provinces in 312, became, by the end of the century, the legally enforced religion of the Empire. If this amounted to a revolution, it had not been unprepared and was only slowly completed. It is impossible to trace the changing balance of public opinion, or to assess the impact of imperial legislation enforcing Christianity and repressing paganism and heresy. The social pressures of conformity, increased prestige, respectability and influence certainly had their importance. The mixed reaction accorded to Julian's attempt to revive paganism and the reports of Christian mob violence in widely scattered cities in the last quarter of the fourth century at any rate suggest a heavy swing towards Christianity in many towns.

By the end of the reign of Theodosius I (d.395) Christianity was not only the majority religion, but also enforced as the official religion of the Empire. The gradual transformation of a persecuted minority into a dominant majority is, perhaps, the most fundamental transformation that Christianity underwent in the course of its history, its dramatic character disguised only by the time-span it took to achieve. For Christian thinkers concerned with the nature of man's existence in politically organised society, the change in the Church's status raised fundamental questions. Earlier Christian ways of thinking were generally rooted in the experience of a (sporadically) persecuted elite; some of the sharpest Christian conflicts of the fourth century sprang from the need to adjust attitudes to the experience of having emerged as a dominant elite. Judaeo-Christian thinking about politically organised society had always stressed God's initiative and action in bringing about the only truly just society. In relation to His Kingdom men were subjects rather than agents; in respect to all other, earthly, kingdoms they were in some degree aliens, temporary residents, exiles from their true home. In the fourth century a whole tradition of political thinking (see chapter 1 above) rooted in the need for Christians to adjust themselves to a society radically alienated from the one ultimately acceptable social order had to be abandoned or re-thought. The imagery of exile running through Old and New Testaments, rabbinic and patristic writings, could continue to serve to represent all human life on earth; but it needed re-interpreting in a society governed by Christian emperors and officials, in which Christian bishops wielded extensive public influence and, increasingly, supreme local municipal authority.

The revolution in the Christian Church's mode of existence was only one facet of the varied and complex changes brought by our first 'wave', the transformation of the Roman world in the third and fourth centuries into its characteristically 'late Roman' shape. In helping to bring about a re-direction of Christian political thought it was, however, unquestionably the major factor at work in the minds of the Christian writers of the fourth and fifth, and indeed subsequent, centuries, perceptible in Christian thinking about society even in modern times. The second wave of change, the invasions and settlement of Germanic barbarians in Roman provinces, affected the conditions for political thinking no less profoundly, though less directly, and over a more drawn-out period.

The Germanic settlements

In the Greco-Roman political tradition the barbarian was the outsider. Rational human order was embodied in Greek or Roman society. The rhetorical commonplaces inspired by this image of Roman and barbarian had a powerful hold on educated Romans' minds, and survived long after the outsiders had come to live in their midst. Small bodies of barbarians had, from time to time, been settled on Roman territory. From the last quarter of the fourth century, however, whole Germanic peoples, Visigoths and later others, were allowed to settle within the Roman frontiers. Some seized Roman provinces by conquest: the Vandals in North Africa, the English in Britain. Sometimes such seizures were recognised by the government in formal treaties of partition or cession. In some of the most significant settlements, however, such as those of the Visigoths and the Burgundians in Gaul and the Ostrogoths in Italy, lands were assigned in a different manner. Roman sovereignty was here maintained over the area in question; the barbarian settlers, as 'allies' (*foederati*) of the Romans, were assimilated in juridical status to that of Roman armies. They lived under their own traditional laws, subject to the authority of their own leaders, and maintained, to an extent and for periods which vary from case to case, their own ethnic cultures, institutions and religion. According to Roman constitutional fiction, however, these settlements were not autonomous kingdoms, but government-arranged quarterings of Roman armies.

Constitutional theory held firmly to the notion of uninterrupted Roman sovereignty over the areas of settlement, and sometimes Roman administration continued to function in barbarian-occupied territory. This fiction of two superimposed sovereignties and the continuity of Roman authority helped to disguise the gradual emergence of independent kingdoms in what had been Roman provinces.

It was not until the middle of the sixth century that it became common for historians to speak with hindsight of the Western Roman Empire as having come to an end at one or another time in the later fifth century. By then the Western provinces had come for the most part under barbarian control, though the Empire had secured partial and precarious reconquests in North Africa, Italy and Spain. By the end of the period dealt with in part III the outlines of what were to become the kingdoms of Western Europe had crystallised. The Empire retained control of parts of the Italian peninsula, principally in the South. The rest of Western Europe was a mosaic of German kingdoms, with the Moslem conquests spreading across North Africa and Spain. Byzantine official protocol continued, for a time, to represent barbarian rulers as imperial officials; in reality, however, the Empire had shrunk to its Eastern remnant, and was seen, from the West, as a foreign neighbour. Increasingly hazy memories of its reality long continued to colour the political language and imagination of Western writers. Political fragmentation, however, became the reality they had to recognise. Only at the end of this period did idealised images of a re-unified Western Empire begin to approach the realm of political reality.

The contrast between the Germanic West and the surviving imperial East, from the sixth century appropriately referred to as 'Byzantine', has often been overdrawn. Contacts, influences and, especially, a shared antique cultural heritage restricted the extent to which the two worlds came to diverge. Nevertheless, the Latin West (with the exception of Sicily and enclaves in Italy) and the Greek, and non-Greek, East can be seen to be developing along their own separate lines. If the Germanic settlements did not begin this divergence, they certainly accentuated it. Looked at from the point of view of the Roman *oikoumene* the growth of an increasingly homogeneous and increasingly ecclesiastical Latin culture in the West, distinct from the Byzantine Greek, is only one facet of a 'regionalism', signs of which have been detected in many parts of the Roman world as early as the third and fourth centuries. The emergence of regional groupings among the ruling aristocracies, of local or native cultures, of increasingly cohesive local societies has been observed in distant provinces as far apart as Syria and

Britain as well as in central areas such as Italy, Gaul and North Africa. In this perspective the creation of independent Germanic kingdoms appears as the climax of a process of fragmentation whose roots reach far back in Roman history. The loss of political unity and the narrowing of horizons in Western Europe, fundamental though they are in its historical development, are no sudden break with its past.

Moreover, the blending of Roman with Germanic elements in the institutions and the social mix of the kingdoms of Western Europe also helped to secure some degree of continuity. Remnants of Roman administration often survived. Romans generally continued to live according to their own law at least for some time. Barbarian rulers were commonly assisted by advisers or officials of Roman origin and educated in traditional ways. Clergy were to play a crucial part in royal courts and government. A shared Latin, ecclesiastical culture was widely diffused. Germanic law codes were written down in Latin, influenced by the language and concepts of the vulgarised versions of Roman law current in the Western provinces. To a degree which varied from place to place, Roman personnel, Roman legal and institutional traditions, Roman administrative geography and the survival of a more or less romanised native population everywhere gave the new western kingdoms some continuity with the Roman past.

Education and letters

Education in the Roman world had been based on the Hellenistic legacy. In late antiquity this continued to provide the framework for the education provided in the public schools. The conservative, strongly literary and rhetorically orientated culture encouraged by the traditions of Roman education left their mark on most of the literary products – even those of the greatest originality – of late antiquity. From the later fifth century onwards, the public provision of education ceased, along with much else of municipal life. Although Justinian sought to re-establish (554) some regular public education in Italy, very little is known about any schools that might have existed in Rome or elsewhere. Nevertheless, some literary and legal education could still be acquired, especially in Rome and Ravenna. In the more romanised parts of Frankish Gaul and Visigothic Spain, too, written documents continued to play a part both in government and in private commercial life. It is likely that for the most part the notarial staff required for this kind of activity received their training in practice rather than in formally established schools. Royal courts, too – especially the Visigothic court at Toledo – often patronised learning; but in the absence of public schools private households came to assume a growing importance in education. Aristocratic families with inherited libraries had a crucial part in maintaining some degree of educational continuity, until, as in Frankish Gaul, they finally conformed with the less literary tastes of their Frankish counterparts. Bishops being very often of aristocratic descent, episcopal households could become significant centres of education. The most important centres of learning from the sixth century until the eighth (and beyond), however, were monastic communities. During the early centuries of the Germanic kingdoms Latin grammar and rhetoric and some of the classics of Latin literature continued to be studied; but the general development of education in this period led to its impoverishment and to an increasing degree of clericalisation and biblical orientation. The revival which is observable in some Italian towns in the eighth century, in the British Isles from the end of the seventh century and in much of Frankish Europe later in the eighth century was not to leave its mark on political thought until the Carolingian period (see part IV).

Political thought in the Latin West, c. 350–c. 750

Political thought in this period was deeply affected by the changes both in the culture within which it was carried on and in the nature of its objects, the social relationships and political structures with which it was concerned. The disappearance of the Roman Empire in Western Europe did not bring with it the eclipse of the imperial theme in political reflection. Many of its assumptions and images remained firmly embedded in the language of Western writers and were to find new application when a Western Empire once again became a real political possibility. The change in the objects of political thinking was rather that while surviving imperial imagery and concepts were losing their foothold in reality from the sixth century onwards, new political entities and institutions previously absent or peripheral now assumed central interest. Foremost among these was the institution of kingship. The christianisation of society also brought new questions to the fore: the relationship between sacred and secular power, the problems of religious freedom and coercion, the nature and distribution of ecclesiastical authority, all became central themes. Moreover, for a millennium the concepts concerning the relations between men and their fellows, their rulers, their obligations and rights had to be formulated within an intellectual structure based on principles furnished by the Bible and Christian theology.

This was the most fundamental of the conditions among those which shaped the development of political thought from the fourth century. One of its consequences is that political treatises such as were known in classical antiquity – those of Plato, Aristotle or Cicero – are entirely lacking in our period. Political thought has to be disentangled from theological treatises, biblical commentaries and sermons. A rich deposit of political ideas is often buried in the conventions of official, especially papal, correspondence. Materials of this kind are far from homogeneous. Students of most of the major figures considered in chapter 6 – St Ambrose, St Augustine, St Gregory the Great (Isidore of Seville is discussed in chapter 7) – have detected in their work and their personalities various strands and tensions, often unresolved, sometimes unrecognised. They were not 'political' thinkers in the sense that Aristotle or Hobbes were; they did not generally work out the implications of such 'political' ideas as are contained in their writings. The modern historian of political thought must often build on hints and mere seeds of ideas, and he has to by-pass the complexity of attitudes produced by the interplay of theory and practice, principles and daily political realities, theology and pastoral pressures.

The material which forms the subject of chapter 7 is even less overtly 'political thought', but in a scattered and often only implicit form it contains political ideas of fundamental significance in our period: law codes, official formulae of royal acts and the like. The symbolism of public ceremonies and liturgical rituals and formulae provide another rich seam to be quarried. A special group of writings, lying somewhere between these two – the overt theological reflections of Christian writers on their societies and the scattered concepts and images to be found in laws, formulae and a variety of such documents – is the work of Roman writers who worked under barbarian kings, sometimes as their advisers or officials, sometimes only as reflective subjects. Writers such as Sidonius Apollinaris, Avitus, Ennodius and, above all, Cassiodorus provide a good deal of material revealing the ways in which educated Romans saw barbarian societies and their kings. The work of historians such as Jordanes or Gregory of Tours also belongs in this intermediate group. In so far as these touch on important and fundamental questions of political thought, they are dealt with in chapter 7.

6

THE LATIN FATHERS

The problem of the Christian Empire: 'Imperium' and 'Sacerdotium'

Two traditions shaped the political thought of Western Christendom in the later fourth and the early fifth centuries, the age of St Ambrose and St Augustine. The first was the collection of ideas about human society which the Christian fathers of the fourth century inherited from the pre-Constantinian period. This included, of course, the hints on these subjects contained in the New Testament writings as well as ideas elaborated by Christians of the second and third centuries, in large part but not entirely in their reflection on the New Testament hints and their implications (see part I, chapter I above). The second set of ideas consisted of those engendered by the Christian response to the conversion of Constantine and to the progressive christianisation of the Roman Empire culminating, during the years which spanned the careers of Ambrose of Milan and Augustine of Hippo, in the official establishment of Christianity as the legally enforced religion of the Empire. Christians have always been apt to see the conversion of Constantine as a watershed between the age of a persecuted church and the age of a triumphant established Christianity. Whatever the appropriateness of such a view may be to the historical development (see Introduction to part III, above pp. 86–7), it does only partial justice to the political ideas rooted in the two different sets of circumstances, and to their overlap in the post-Constantine age. Some Christian political ideas distinctive of the age of the persecutions showed an obstinate ability to survive the Constantinian revolution, and to receive new infusions of life repeatedly. Conversely, some ideas more at home in the christianised Empire had their origins in the second and third centuries. The interplay between these two sets of ideas remained important to the generation of Ambrose and Augustine. The relationship of Roman political structures, and by implication of human societies in general, to the Christian Church, to man's salvation and to God's providence was the central problem in this period.

The vision of a christianised Roman Empire had been dimly foreshadowed in earlier writers (see above, chapter 1, p. 17; chapter 4, pp. 51–2); but with the conversion of Constantine Eusebius' interpretation of that vision came to dominate the minds of many fourth-century Christians. They saw the whole course of their history changed in consequence of the miracle which had brought about the conversion of the first Christian emperor, and they saw God's hand at work in the christianisation of the Empire under his successors. The images in which Eusebius had represented the Christian Empire and its emperor received wide currency. Church and Empire were both reflections of a heavenly kingdom; the monarchy of Constantine brought that kingdom to men, and with his conversion the earthly city became the city of God. Hellenistic and biblical ideas blended to produce an image of the emperor as entrusted with representing God's authority among men. The notion of the Empire as the vehicle of the Christian religion, embodying God's providential plan for the salvation of mankind, became a literary commonplace and was to be frequently heard from Christian pulpits. Christianity and the Empire became indissolubly united: Christianity was the Empire's religion and the Empire its proper, divinely intended, setting.

The frequency of the clichés and images of this way of thinking attests the ease with which the ideas of 'Roman' and 'Christian' tended to merge, even to the point of identification, in the minds of many Christians of the later fourth and fifth centuries. This fusion of the two, previously distinct, spheres raised one of the central problems for political thought during this period, and one which remained central so long as the Roman Empire – or any other political structure – was instinctively identified with the 'Christian society': who exercised ultimate authority in such a society? Who was God's accredited representative and wielded his supreme authority over those who acknowledged the lordship of Christ? In what ways, if any, was his authority limited in relation to other bearers of authority, perhaps also divinely sanctioned?

It was not until the time of Ambrose of Milan that the Eusebian assumptions began to be questioned. Under Constantine himself and during the reign of his son Constantius II (337–59) the emperor continued to be seen as God's representative in the Christian Empire, as the 'bishop of bishops' endowed with an authority sacred in its source and embracing the sacred in its scope. Already in the time of Constantine, however, dissident groups had questioned the emperor's authority in ecclesiastical affairs. Donatist schismatics, ready as they had been to resort to the emperor's judgement, were later said to have raised the question: 'What have Christians to do with kings, bishops with the imperial palace?'[1] Such heart-searchings, in language reminiscent of the rhetoric of Tertullian, seemed to revive ancient feelings of hostility. They were also expressed by adherents of Nicene orthodoxy against the arianising views of Constantius. Protests against imperial interventions in the Church's affairs multiplied in the 350s and sometimes, notably in the writings of Lucifer, bishop of Caralis, reached an apocalyptic pitch of denunciation. The text of Matthew 22:21 ('Render therefore unto Caesar the things which are Caesar's; and unto God the things that are God's') and its synoptic parallels were occasionally cited to give scriptural authority to the dissenters' – the orthodox Nicene – rejection of the emperor's authority over the Church. There is little doubt, however, that such protests were directed not against the Eusebian–Constantinian conception of the imperial office so much as against the misuse of an imperial authority by emperors regarded as heretical or godless. Behind the protests there is a shared body of assumptions about the nature of properly Christian imperial authority. In the writings of Athanasius of Alexandria, Ossius of Cordova, Hilary of Arles and even Lucifer of Caralis the divide runs between 'Christian', orthodox emperors and godless, heretical tyrants; not between two spheres we might label as 'lay' and 'clerical' or 'sacred' and 'profane'.[2]

Donatist and Nicene dissent from the official orthodoxy of the court had kept alive the language and attitudes of a persecuted elite in the Empire of Constantine and Constantius. Ambrose of Milan made use of its resources to express the confident self-consciousness of a Christian elite emerging to dominate Roman society in the 380s and 390s. Like many of his contemporaries, Ambrose was apt to identify 'Roman' and 'Christian' almost instinctively: unbecoming conduct in a heretical priest was 'as abhorrent to Roman manners' as it was 'sacrilegious'.[3] He was still inclined to think of the Empire as the embodiment of God's providence and to identify the *pax Augusta* with the *pax Christi*.[4] The survival of such clichés in

1. Optatus, *De schismate* 1.22.
2. See the important study by K.M. Girardet, 'Kaiser Konstantin II. als "episcopus episcoporum" und das Herrscherbild des kirchlichen Widerstandes', *Historia* 26 (1977), pp. 95–128.
3. *Ep.* 10.9. 4. *In Ps.* 45 *Enarr.* 21; cf. *In Ps.* 61 *Enarr.* 20.

his writings is a testimony to their wide currency; but it is significant that despite his strong Roman patriotism and universalism[5] which tended to encourage the equation of 'Roman' with 'Christian', Ambrose sometimes went out of his way to avoid or to qualify the Eusebian image of the Empire.[6] His view of the role of Christian emperors in the Church owed as much to the Nicene opponents of Constantius II as to the Constantinian–Eusebian tradition. The continuity with the former appears most clearly in the conflict between Ambrose and the court of Milan over the basilicas in 385–6, when the court was claiming the right to take over some of the city's churches for Arian use. In this conflict Ambrose was defending the Church's right to its places of worship and repudiating the court's claim to the right of appropriation. This conflict raised no new principles, but it gave Ambrose an occasion for questioning the all-embracing autocratic power claimed by the emperor. His statements fall into the mould made familiar by his 'dissenting' predecessors: 'divine things are not subject to the imperial power'.[7]

This incident gave Ambrose an opportunity to treat the emperor as a 'son of the Church'. This principle came to guide him in his rebuke to Theodosius I in 390 for the massacre the emperor had ordered in Thessalonica as a reprisal for the murder of a Gothic officer in the Roman army. Ambrose's success in exacting penance from the emperor for that precipitate act of inhumanity quickly became the classic example of a bishop treating an emperor as a *filius ecclesiae*, vindicating the normal claims of Christian morality and a bishop's authority in punishing breaches of it. So dramatic a demonstration that the emperor was in the Church, not above it, certainly played an important part in defining the model for the Christian ruler: the idea of the humble prince, ready for penitence and willing to heed the admonition of his bishop recurs in Ambrose's preaching and writing[8] and quickly established itself in the repertory of 'mirrors for princes'.

Incidents of this kind served to establish the principle that rulers as individual Christians were subject to ecclesiastical censure. Ambrose, like most of his contemporaries, failed to draw a clear distinction between the emperor as a private Christian and the imperial office as an institution. He was well placed and able to exercise influence over the Christian court, and he saw that exercise in terms of his pastoral responsibilities, not in terms of

5. E.g. *Exp. Ev. Luc.* x.10; *De Tob.* 15.61.   6. *Exp. Ev. Luc.* ii.36–7; *In Ps.* 118 *Sermo* 20.49.
7. *Ep.* 20.8; cf. *ibid.*, 19; *Ep.* 21.4; *Sermo C. Aux.* 18; 30–7.
8. *Apol. proph. David* 2.6; 6.29; *In Ps.* 37 *Enarr.* 1; *De ob. Theod.* 28, 34; *De of. min.* ii.7.32–5.

establishing the right relationship between 'Church' and 'state'. Two other well-known incidents, however, have more far-reaching implications and throw some light on Ambrose's assumptions about the public nature of the office which might well have influenced his pastoral practice.

In the controversy over the pagan senators' appeal for the restoration of the Altar of Victory in the Senate house and of the endowments and revenues for the support of public pagan cults, both the pagan senators and Ambrose opposing their spokesman, Symmachus, seem clear about the crucial issue involved. What was at stake was the nature of the religious basis of the Roman state. Symmachus had made a clear distinction between the personal religion of the emperor and the public religion of the Empire: Constantius, he said, though he followed his own (Christian) religion, had maintained that of the Empire.[9] Ambrose's intervention against the petition was an appeal to Valentinian's personal piety: he should have no truck with heathen cults and give them no encouragement. But Ambrose was equally aware that the crucial issue was the question of revenues and stipends: to restore these would amount to nothing less than an endorsement of the public adhesion of the Empire – whatever the private religion of the emperor – to the traditional pagan cults.[10] This has sometimes been seen as a call for the 'secularisation' of the Roman state. Some twenty years later, however, the Christian poet Prudentius saw it as something quite different. In his *Contra Symmachum*, recapitulating the conflict, he represented it as heralding the final triumph of Christianity in the Roman Empire – indeed, in the world.

Ambrose's own attitude seems to have been more in line with the way Prudentius thought than with the way it is represented by those who want to see it as a demand for official neutrality in religion. This is suggested by another much-discussed episode in his dealings with Christian emperors: the affair of Callinicum a few years later. When the bishop of this town had been ordered to restore Jewish property and to rebuild a synagogue destroyed by Christians in a riot apparently instigated by the bishop, Ambrose insisted that as a Christian, Theodosius must rescind the order. This dealt a severe blow to traditional notions about the government's duty to maintain public order and safeguard property rights. 'Which is more important: the show of discipline or the cause of religion?'[11] The notion of a neutral, secular Roman state – anachronistic anyway – is scarcely compatible with Ambrose's conduct in this matter, or with his approval of

9. *Rel.* 3.6–7.   10. *Ep.* 18.11–13; *Ep.* 57.2.   11. *Ep.* 40.11.

Theodosius' anti-heretical and anti-pagan legislation.[12] All this suggests that, beyond wanting to set up moral standards for the personal conduct of Christian emperors, Ambrose envisaged the Roman Empire as a society which was, or should be, a radically Christian society and the Church as called upon to mould its public life and institutions.

This is much clearer in Ambrose's episcopal actions and admonitions than in any systematic exposition, for which we look in vain in his writings. There are some hints with a bearing on the nature of society or political authority to be found; always, however, in the context of discussions directed to other ends. Two of these raised problems of a political kind, though only incidentally: the discussion of men's duties towards their fellows, and the exposition of the biblical narratives of the Creation and Fall of man.

Ambrose's crowning work on Christian morality is the professional handbook addressed to clergy, *De officiis ministrorum*. Here he drew together the threads of his thought on Christian living, much as Cicero had drawn together his reflection on public conduct in his *De officiis*, the work Ambrose took as his literary model. Cicero had set himself the task of re-interpreting the best of Greek philosophy, especially the ethical teaching of Panaetius, for a Roman public. Ambrose re-interpreted Ciceronian Stoicism for a Christian public. In doing so he found himself compelled to modify, sometimes so profoundly that his debt to Cicero has been seen as literary rather than philosophical, the Stoic concepts he found in Cicero's (and perhaps other philosophical) writings. Some central moral concepts required fundamental re-interpretation in a Christian sense. Thus the notion of the virtuous life in accordance with reason or nature constituting man's supreme good had to be given a more theocentric orientation, but placed within a Christian perspective it continued to serve Ambrose as a basic moral principle.[13] The Stoic morality of reason and nature thus remained embedded in Ambrose's, as in many other Christian moralists', ethics. Of the cardinal virtues justice was the bond of society. Ambrose adopted Cicero's statement that 'the foundation of justice is faith (*fides*)';[14] but he gave a new meaning to the concept of 'faith'. Cicero's 'good faith' is turned into 'trust in Christ'. A society based on 'faith' thus understood could not be the same as Cicero's. Stoic teaching on the brotherhood of man – present in Cicero's version though somewhat eclipsed by the competitive orientation of his society – was given a new twist, and Cicero's ideas

12. *De ob. Theod.* 38.   13. E.g. *Ep.* 73.2; *Iac.* 6.   14. *De off. min.* 1.29.142; *De off.* 1.7.23.

underwent drastic modification in a God-centred direction.[15] The body
and its members, Cicero's simile for the solidarity of human society, is for
Ambrose no longer a simile: it is the Body of Christ.[16] The *res publica* has
been transformed into the Christian community.

Stoic concepts were thus carried over, re-interpreted in varying degrees,
into Ambrose's Christian moral system. Similarly, in his theological
interpretation of the biblical stories of Creation and Adam's Fall, he
inherited a long Christian exegetical tradition, but here, too, the
contributory influence of classical ideas is noticeable. The traditional
Christian teaching concerning man's paradisal state of innocence, at
harmony with himself and with God's creation, traced the tension,
disharmony, conflict, inequality and force in human affairs to man's
alienation from his original state through Adam's Fall. This teaching had a
great deal in common with classical imagery of a Golden Age and
subsequent decline, which often furnished political writers with utopian
images of an ideal society. Their trace appears clearly in Ambrose's
exposition of the book of Genesis. In his exegesis he follows in the footsteps
of St Basil of Caesarea. The Fall is the key to man's present condition.
Ambrose is clearest in this respect in his discussions of property and slavery;
both subjects on which Stoic views helped him to formulate his own.

Following Cicero's principle that nothing is private by nature,[17]
Ambrose held that private ownership was not an institution of nature but
the result of 'usurpation'.[18] It must therefore be used for the common good
and the support of others.[19] He was concerned to preach the virtues of
poverty and generous giving, not to reject the right to property. This right
he disputed no more than it had been disputed in the mainstream of the
tradition according to which property, like other forms of inequality, was
rooted in man's sinful state. Ambrose's views on slavery are all of a piece
with this. He did not question the institution, but held that it belonged to
man's sinful state after the Fall, not to his nature as intended by God. A long
letter (*Ep.* 37) is largely devoted to arguing that slavery and freedom, as the
Stoics had taught, are not fundamental realities of human nature. True
freedom is wisdom, true slavery folly and wickedness. Although he says
that subjection of the stupid to the wise was intended by God for the
subject's own good,[20] he sees the institution as inextricably bound up with
the loss of equality brought in its train by the fall from innocence.

Ambrose is much less clear concerning the effects of this fall on the

15. Hill 1979, pp. 196–7.   16. *De off. min.* iii.3.19; *De off.* iii.5.21–2.   17. *De off.* i.7.21.
18. *De off. min.* i.28.132.   19. *Ibid.* 135; cf. *In Ps.* 118 *Sermo* 8.22.   20. *Ep.* 37.7–8; cf. *Ep.* 77.6.

government of human societies. With the help of Virgilian images of the societies of birds and bees he sketched his notions of a rightly ordered society, one in accordance with nature. The contrast he drew between a 'republic' based on full equality such as is found among the cranes, and a 'monarchy' such as the bees have, suggests that in some way the former is superior to the latter; perhaps Ambrose intends it to portray the natural, the paradisal form of social organisation from which others represent a decline. Both forms, however, are given as instances of 'natural' types of constitution. A monarchical form of government, like the cranes' 'free city',[21] is a fully natural form of social organisation in which ruler and ruled are singled out for their place and tasks by nature; they collaborate for the common and indeed for their own individual good.[22] On the other hand he also asserts men's equality by nature[23] and holds that inequality and subjection are the result of greed and lust for power.[24] It is not at all clear from all this whether he regarded all subjection of men to other men, or only imperfect forms of subjection, as bound up with man's sinful condition.[25]

Ambrose never resolved the ambiguity in his views about government. Problems of this kind did not interest him greatly. He was more concerned to use classical imagery, philosophy and the biblical stories for the purpose of moral exhortation than for the philosophical analysis of human nature and social relationships. These problems were to receive much more systematic attention from later Christian thinkers, not least from his younger contemporary, Augustine of Hippo.

An unknown contemporary commentator on the Pauline letters known since Erasmus as the Ambrosiaster, who was beyond much doubt the author also of a set of Questions on the Old and New Testaments, is notable among fourth-century writers for his strong legal interests. He owed much to Stoic philosophy and to Roman legal traditions and shared some of Ambrose's approach to this subject. Like Ambrose,[26] he founded all law on the 'law of nature'; but he grounded this concept more firmly in Pauline than in Stoic thought. The idea of a law inscribed into the structure of the world by its creator, which is the norm for men and accessible to them, being 'written on

---

21. Hex. v.15.52.   22. Ibid. 21.68–72.   23. Ep. 37.9.

24. Hex. v.15.52; Exp. Ev. Luc. IV.29.

25. It has been suggested that Ambrose's main concern in this discussion is quite different: to give the Empire as respectable a justification in 'nature' as the Republic had been given: see J. Béranger, Principatus. Etudes de notions et d'histoire politiques dans l'Antiquité gréco-romaine, Droz, 1973, pp. 303–30.   26. E.g. De fuga III.15; Abr. 1.2.8; cf. above, pp. 98–9.

their hearts' (Rom. 2.15), is fundamental to the Ambrosiaster's thought about the various kinds of written law. St Paul's long discussion of the Law (of the Old Covenant) in his letter to the Romans furnished the Ambrosiaster with the key notions for the relations between the law of nature and all other laws.[27] The Law of the Old Testament, and secondarily other written law, is imposed to remedy man's failure to follow the natural law. Roman law and 'ecclesiastical' law – a concept which was coming into use in the later fourth century and generally used to refer to the Church's power to bind and to loose[28] – are drawn, along with the Jewish law, into the framework of this schematisation of natural and written law.

A lively interest in the administration of Roman law and in legal procedure prompted the Ambrosiaster to give some thought to the ruler's function in society. Here again Pauline teaching gave the main impulse: commenting on Rom. 13.1 the Ambrosiaster defines the subject's obligation to obey the ruler very firmly: 'the law of heavenly justice' must be obeyed, and those who administer the law – which has God as its author – are ordained by God; men must obey them.[29] Political obligation is grounded in the law of God and nature. The ruler bears God's authority in repressing wickedness.[30] Even pagan rulers must be honoured and obeyed, since they enforce God's order.[31] In his estimate of the ruler's position the Ambrosiaster goes far beyond Pauline teaching in the exalted hierarchical status he ascribes to the ruler. Subordination to the Emperor's authority is analogous to the body's subjection to rational control by the mind;[32] the imperial officials (*comites*) stand to the emperor – as in much Christian iconography – as the angels to God.[33] The emperor receives *adoratio* on earth as God's vicar, just as Christ will be adored 'in heaven and on earth' after the fulfilment of the 'vicarial' dispensation.[34] This pronounced monarchical streak in the Ambrosiaster's concept of the ruler leaves little room for any restriction of the sphere of secular authority as against ecclesiastical. In fact there seems to be no trace in these writings of any interest in problems such as those Ambrose had encountered in this respect. The Ambrosiaster's hints on the obscure notion of 'vicarial' authority seems to point in another direction altogether. Repeatedly he asserts that the ruler has the image of God, whereas the bishop has that of Christ.[35] This distinction is apparently related to the notion that ruling is the essential

27. *Comm. in Ep. ad Rom.*, c.7 passim, 5.13; cf. *ad I Tim.* 1.11.
28. Heggelbacher 1959, p. 100.   29. *Comm. in Ep. ad Rom.*, 13.1.
30. *Ibid.* 13.3.   31. *Q. vet. et novi test.* 35; cf. ibid., 110.6.   32. *Ibid.* 115.35, 40.
33. *Ibid.* 45.1; 114.2, 9.   34. *Ibid.* 91.8.   35. *Ibid.* 35; 106.17; 127.36.

constituent of having the image of God, the ruler of all; derivatively, man is also the image of God in so far as he is set over woman whom he rules; woman, lacking rule, lacks the image of God.[36] The ruler is God's *vicarius* in representing and mediating God's rule over men; the 'vicariate' of Christ held by bishops and their ministers appears to consist in carrying out prayer, offering and sacramental action among the people.[37] This 'incomplete' political theory[38] needs far more study than it has so far received, having been unduly neglected in comparison with the wealth of work devoted to the problem of the relations of clerical and lay power in this period.

The Ambrosiaster had little interest in this problem, and Ambrose's interest, as we have seen (see above, pp. 97–9), was worked out in pastoral practice rather than on the level of political theory. Ambrose did, however, leave a rich legacy to be exploited by later thinkers. In the course of the hundred years following his demonstration that emperors could be treated as sons of the Church, his lead was taken up by a series of popes. The development of papal thinking during this century was dominated by two closely linked efforts: to set limits to the scope for lay, especially imperial, intervention in ecclesiastical affairs, and to lay the foundations for the special authority the popes were claiming for the see of Rome. Ambrose had not given the Roman see any special authority among the other bishoprics; on the contrary, he denied that Peter's primacy involved any precedence in honour or jurisdiction.[39] At the hands of the popes who developed the concepts of lay and clerical authority, however, the assertion of the supremacy of spiritual over secular power involved upholding the supremacy of the Roman over the other churches. Ambrose's somewhat pragmatic attempt to set limits to the right of the secular authorities to intervene in ecclesiastical affairs and to influence the conduct of emperors was absorbed into a grander design for the right distribution of authority in the Christian world.

The christianisation of Roman society – largely achieved by the middle of the fifth century – prompted the equation of the *plebs romana* with the *plebs Dei*. Pope Leo I in the middle years of the century could take this identification for granted. Echoing the old providential view of the Empire as God's instrument for establishing a *pax christiana* in the world, Leo depicted the Empire as now reborn into a new, Christian society. The

36. *Ibid.* 106.17; 45.3.   37. *Ibid.* 127.36.
38. The description is from Heggelbacher 1959, p. 31.
39. See Ullmann 1981, pp. 19–20, referring to *De inc. sacr.* 4.32.

foundation of Romulus and Remus was renewed by the apostles Peter and Paul. Rome was reborn as a 'holy nation, an elect people, a priestly and royal City'.[40] The debates of this period over spiritual and secular authority spring from the assumption that what is at stake is the right distribution of authority within this Christian Roman society. It was in this context that a succession of popes – Innocent I, Boniface I, Celestine I, Leo himself, Simplicius and, finally, Gelasius I, put together the ideas of a Roman *principatus* and the distinction of functions within the Church. The unifying hierarchical principle was Ambrose's distinction of functions: teaching and learning.[41] In matters of religion laymen are subject to clergy, bishops to their metropolitan, and these to the pope. It was Gelasius who rounded off this grand scheme of subordination, at much the same time as an unknown Greek monk gave classic expression to a more mystical version of such a vision of hierarchical order. Gelasius' more modest, though momentous, contribution was to define the role of the secular ruler in the Church. In his letter to the emperor Anastasius in 494 Gelasius spoke of the emperor's duty to submit to the bishops in religious matters, while they must recognise the laws he makes for the maintenance of public order.[42] These are the respective functions of the 'sacred authority of bishops' (*auctoritas sacrata pontificum*) and the 'royal power' (*regalis potestas*). Whatever the implications of this much-debated vocabulary, which Gelasius was anyway not consistent in using,[43] the main thrust of his argument is clear: the sacral character of the imperial office, the idea of a priest-king, must be abjured by Christian rulers. Their role is confined to dealing with outward necessities and public order among the Christian people committed to their care. Gelasius' language left much imprecise, and his views could be developed in either of two different directions: to assert the separateness of two co-ordinate and complementary powers, or, alternatively, to assert the ultimate supremacy of the clerical over the lay power, the latter being represented as its agent and servant in mundane matters.

The development of this line of thinking between Ambrose and Gelasius presupposed the equation of 'Christian' with 'Roman' and the consequent need to define the distinct functions and the mutual subordination of authorities in the single politico-religious structure. The only thinker to question this underlying assumption and to reject the implicit equation of 'Roman' with 'Christian' was Augustine of Hippo.

40. *Sermo* 83.1–2.
41. Ambrose's use of *discere/docere*; *Ep*. 21.4. For references to papal applications, see Ullmann 1981, pp. 46, 52, 57, 114, 148, 174. A particularly revealing application of the doublet is to be found in pope Hilarus *Ep*. 17.1 (Thiel).   42. *Ep*. 12.2 (Thiel).
43. In *Tract*. IV.11 (Thiel) he speaks of two 'powers'.

St Augustine: a radical alternative

Augustine's surviving writings span a period of over forty years. Many of them were called forth by controversy or served the needs of his congregation. All are the product of a restless mind, perpetually on the move. Any attempt to distil his political ideas from his writings must reckon with changes of mind, not only on matters of detail or particular questions, but also in the intellectual perspectives in which he came to approach his questions. Several of the subjects to which Augustine devoted serious thought are directly related to problems of political life. Most important among these for our purpose are his views on (i) the Roman Empire, its place in the divine plan of salvation and its relationship to Christianity; (ii) human nature and relationships in society, and the effect of the Fall upon them; and (iii) the Church in relation to the secular world. Two notes are added on themes less fundamental to his preoccupations, but of considerable importance for the future development of political ideas: (iv) religious coercion; and (v) the just war.

i. *The Roman Empire and the two cities*

For a long time Augustine did not question the view of the Roman Empire widely current among fourth-century Christians (above, p. 93).[44] He accepted the notion that the Empire was God's providentially intended instrument for the establishment of Christianity in the world. In the years around 400 views of this kind were almost universally held among Christians. The official enforcement of Christianity under Theodosius I in the 390s, the legislation to repress heresy and paganism and Theodosius' victory over the pagan opposition (392–4) produced a sense of elation among Christians. In the Empire of Theodosius and his sons they saw the fulfilment of God's plan for mankind: in subjection to Rome the peoples of the world were united in an idealised, universal Christian Empire. The rule of Rome was now the reign of Christ in the world. This sense of Christian triumph was most fully voiced in the poetry of Prudentius. In the late 390s and the opening years of the fifth century Augustine shared this euphoric vision of a Christian Empire realised under his very eyes. The ancient prophecies about the conversion of the heathen were now being fulfilled: secular rulers have come to save Christ and through them God himself was destroying the idols of the heathen. 'The whole world has become a choir praising Christ.'[45] For many Romans, pagan as well as Christian, these years

44. For a fuller exposition containing further references both to texts and to other discussions, see Markus 1970, pp. 22–71.   45. *Enarr. in Ps.* 149.7.

of Theodosius and his sons were the 'Christian times' *par excellence*.

The calamities which hit the Western Roman provinces from 406, the barbarian raids culminating in the sack of Rome by the Goths in 410, gave a severe jolt to the confident assurance of the Theodosian age. Old conflicts rekindled in this time of general dismay, and many pagan Romans turned against the 'Christian times'. In their eyes those times became an age of disaster and decay directly linked with the Empire's betrayal of its religious traditions. It was to answer pagans who were blaming the troubles on the adoption of the new cult in place of the old, and to give comfort and hope to Christians baffled by a providence which permitted such reverses to the fortunes of an Empire which Christ had made his own, that Augustine wrote his *City of God*. The work occupied him (along with other tasks) during the years 413–27. Much of it, especially the first ten of its twenty-two Books, is primarily polemical in intent and directed against pagan jibes. But the work also represents the maturing of a plan Augustine had in mind for a treatise devoted to the opposition of holiness and impiety in the drama of human history: a subject he had already given some thought to early in his career as a writer. The later Books of the *City of God* contain the long-planned constructive exposition of his theological understanding of history. The work as a whole is thus a fusion of polemical argument and a personal meditation – carried out over fourteen years and fully matured only in its later parts – on human history and on the Roman Empire and Christianity in the perspective of divine providence.

By the time Augustine embarked on this 'huge work', he had already moved away from the views he had held in the years around 400 about the Christian Roman Empire. The elation he felt over the Theodosian 'establishment' of Christianity became noticeably less pronounced and vanished almost without trace from his preaching and writing from about 405. The *City of God*, especially in its last eight Books, is the result and the record of his rethinking of the place of the Roman Empire in the divine scheme of redemption forced upon him by his disenchantment with the collective mirage of the Theodosian epoch. He had come to see the idea of a fully realised Christian Empire fulfilling the ancient prophecies as a delusion. He now turned his back on the whole tradition of Christian thought represented by Eusebius, and hardly questioned among his contemporaries, according to which the historical destiny of Rome was achieved in a fully christianised Roman society. He was now in no doubt that there was no scriptural warrant for the prophetic interpretation of contemporary history. Any attempt to be assured about the future course of

Roman history was sheer guesswork and could claim no prophetic insight.[46] Augustine rejected both the assurance of his Christian contemporaries and the bewildered despair it was turning into by discarding the assumptions from which both sprang. By adopting an agnostic attitude to history Augustine emptied the idea of Rome of what had been its universally accepted religious significance. For him the Empire is neither the indispensable instrument of salvation in the divine plan, nor an obstacle to its realisation, an alien and hostile power in the midst of which the Christian Church was set as God's chosen elite. In a religious perspective the Empire was, ultimately, neutral. Rome became an ambivalent symbol. Augustine could speak of it with moving patriotism, and genuine admiration for Roman achievement, Roman virtue and glory.[47] At the same time he insistently rejected any identification of 'Roman' with 'Christian'. The contrast between 'theirs' and 'ours' – between Roman heroes, thinkers, writers, and their Christian counterparts – a contrast with a strong flavour of the age of persecutions, recurs constantly in the pages of the *City of God*. The Roman Empire (and, by implication, any earthly society) is of itself neither holy nor diabolical. Like all human work, its ultimate value is determined by the ultimate allegiances of its creators: their piety or impiety.[48]

Augustine defined this indeterminateness of human society in the image of two 'Cities', the City of God and the earthly City. Both are abstract. He defined them in several ways, evidently intended to be equivalent: as the societies of the saints and the unjust,[49] the proud and the humble,[50] the pious and the impious,[51] the elect and the reprobate, those destined for salvation or damnation.[52] His fullest version traces the two 'Cities' to the opposition of two kinds of 'love':

These two loves [the perverse love 'which isolates the mind swollen with pride from the blessed society of others' and its opposite, 'charity which seeketh not its own': contrasted in the preceding paragraph] of which the one is holy, the other impure; the one sociable, the other self-centred (*privatus*); the one concerned for the common good for the sake of heavenly society, the other subordinating the common good to self-interest for the sake of a proud lust for power.

These two loves (Augustine's catalogue of their contrasts continues) 'have brought about the distinction among mankind of the two cities . . . the one of the just, the other of the unjust'.[53] This is Augustine's favoured

46. *De civ. Dei* XVIII.53.1, 52.1.   47. *Ibid.* II.29, V.15.
48. *Ibid.* II.29.1   49. *De cat. rud.* 19.31.   50. *Ibid.*
51. *De vera rel.* 27.50.   52. *De civ. Dei* XV.I.I.   53. *De Gen. ad litt.* XI.15.20.

formulation. In the *City of God* he adopts it at the outset of his sketch of the historical careers of the two 'cities': 'two loves have built the two cities: self-love in contempt of God the earthly city, love of God in contempt of self the heavenly'.[54]

The two 'cities' are the outcome of divergent fundamental human motivations. They are radically opposed and mutually exclusive; no individual can belong to both and each belongs to one or the other. It follows that no human group can be unmixed. Augustine insists that on earth in any actual or possible society the two 'cities' are bound to overlap and melt into one another. Their boundaries are invisible. Any society must necessarily cut across them: 'in this world the two cities are inextricably interwoven and mingled with each other, until they shall be separated in the last judgement'.[55] As actual, discernible societies the two 'cities' have a separate identity only eschatologically. They are inextricably interwoven in the Roman Empire as in the Christian Church or indeed in any social group. In this image Augustine represented the course of human history in terms of a dramatic conflict of forces which will appear in their naked reality only beyond history, while actual temporal societies must always remain radically ambiguous. A theology of the primordial forces at work in human will and action has become an interpretation both of history and of social existence.

Augustine's mature reflection on political life and institutions took shape within this framework. A political society is irretrievably mixed. This is the reason for his rejection of Cicero's definition of a 'commonwealth' (*res publica*). The definition involved identifying a human group (*populus*) as a 'multitude joined together by one consent of law and their common good'.[56] Augustine poured into Cicero's *ius* far more than it had been intended to contain: he made it mean 'justice', 'righteousness' in a very full-blooded sense. He thus drew from Cicero's premiss the conclusion that in the absence of true justice there can be no *res publica*.[57] On Cicero's definition thus construed there could only be one genuine commonwealth, the one society in which true justice was perfectly realised; all others are in greater or lesser degree 'dens of robbers'.[58] Augustine therefore rejected this definition of a *res publica* as inapplicable to any actual state. In its stead he adopted a neutral definition in which he tried to define a group in pragmatic, value-free terms as 'a multitude of rational beings united in

54. *De civ. Dei* XIV.28.　　55. *Ibid.* I.35.
56. 'Coetus iuris consensu et utilitatis communione sociatus': *ibid.* II.21.2, XIX.21.1.
57. *Ibid.* XIX.21.1, II.21.2–3.　　58. *Ibid.* IV.4.

agreement over the things they love'.[59] On this definition the values to which members of a group are committed will be immaterial to the question as to whether they constitute a group which may be politically structured (a *res publica*). Any common bond of allegiance is enough to constitute a society which, given political shape, will rank as a *res publica*.

Augustine's re-definition of the *res publica* in terms of the 'loves' of its members is designed to bring it into relation with his distinction between the two 'cities' (above, pp. 105–6). These are defined by their members' ultimate 'loves', the fundamental orientation of their wills. But not all 'loves' are ultimate: we love many things for the sake of others, some for their own sake, some modestly on a scale of graded goods, appreciated more or less on the scale of our valuations, some supremely, some not at all. Human excellence is attained in achieving a balanced perspective over the whole range of these 'loves' placed in a rightly graded hierarchy of values. 'Things are loved well when the right order is kept in loving, badly when it is upset.'[60] Thus there will be many lesser, intermediate goods which members of the two 'cities' can and are bound to agree in 'loving', conditionally, with reference to something else which forms the object of their ultimate 'love' or supreme allegiance. The two 'cities' are bound to be in radical opposition in their ultimate 'loves', by definition; but their members' intermediate 'loves' will coincide over a wide area, thus constituting a web of values generally acknowledged in the group. It is this realm of shared intermediate values which defines a society and in Augustine's view it is within this area that its political institutions function. The discussion in Book XIX of the *City of God* of the relations between the two 'cities' in actual societies is based upon the possibility of coincident decisions springing from fundamentally divergent structures of motivation. Thus the satisfaction of material needs, security from attack and orderly social intercourse are valued by citizens both of the earthly and the heavenly 'cities'.[61] This is what Augustine calls the 'earthly peace'. It is everybody's concern to maintain it, though people are bound to wish to maintain it for the sake of different ultimate objectives. For the members of the heavenly city within the society the 'earthly peace' will be referred 'to the enjoyment of eternal peace'.[62] Augustine thus came to see secular societies as intermediate provisions, forms of social organisation on which the 'heavenly city', transcending them all, was temporarily contained while on its pilgrimage to its final goal:

59. *Ibid.* XIX.24.   60. *Ibid.* XV.22. Cf. *De doctr. chr.* 1.27.28 on *ordinata dilectio*.
61. *De civ. Dei* XIX.17.   62. *Ibid.* XIX.14.

The heavenly city, while on its earthly pilgrimage, calls forth its citizens from every nation, and assembles a multilingual band of pilgrims; not caring about any diversity of customs, laws, or institutions whereby they severally make provision for the achievement and the maintenance of earthly peace. All these provisions are intended, in their various ways among the different nations, to secure the aim of earthly peace. The heavenly city does not repeal or abolish any of them, provided that they do not impede the religion whereby the one supreme God is taught to be worshipped.

So the heavenly city, too, uses the earthly peace in the course of its earthly pilgrimage. It cherishes and desires, as far as it may without compromising its faith and devotion, the orderly coherence of men's wills concerning the things which pertain to the mortal nature of man; and this earthly peace it refers to the attainment of the heavenly peace.[63]

ii. *Nature, Fall and society*

Reflecting on the destiny of Rome in relation to the ultimates of salvation and damnation Augustine arrived at a discovery of a place for the intermediate and the ambivalent: the realm of secular social life and institutions. The close bonds which had linked the Roman Empire to Christianity were severed; its – and any state's – sacral pretensions drastically deflated. His thought on social relationships was also, however, linked to another context, that of the Fall and its effect on human nature. In this respect, too, his mind was subject to important changes in perspective over the years.

In his earliest writings Augustine stood closer to a Greco-Roman than to a Judaeo-Christian attutude towards human society (see above, pp. 86–7).[64] In the years following 385–6, when Augustine heard Ambrose preach sermons soaked with a Platonic interpretation of Christianity and read the 'books of the Platonists' circulating among his neo-Platonic acquaintances in Milan, 'order' (*ordo*) was the keynote of his thought. Society was not, at this time, a subject central to his interests. In so far as it entered the subject matter of his reflection, however, it did so as an element of the all-embracing order which he saw, with the Platonic tradition, running through the universe. Society was part of the ordered hierarchy of the world and a stage of man's itinerary for his journey towards his final goal. 'Order', at this stage of Augustine's intellectual career, was 'that which if we follow it in our lives, will lead us to God'.[65] The social order had its place within the cosmic order. The order of earthly society is the reflection of a higher, intelligible order, and is among the means whereby that order is

63. *Ibid.* XIX.19.   64. For this section, Markus 1970, pp. 72–104.   65. *De ord.* I.9.27.

brought into human affairs.[66] In principle the over-arching world order was accessible to rational and educated human beings. The vital link which anchored social institutions in the rational order of the universe was the ruler. He must be a wise man, able to resist the appeal of things which distract other men from seeking their true good. He must remain firm in bringing true rational order into the society he governs; thus will its members be led to their final self-realisation and their ultimate happiness.[67] This was Augustine's youthful vision of a 'rational myth of the state', founded on a conception of a cosmic order akin to and accessible to reason and a human destiny which could be achieved by human intellectual and moral resources.

At this early stage of his intellectual development this, essentially Greco-Roman, perspective could accommodate the biblical ways of thinking which Augustine was beginning to make his own. It was not until later that he came to see the tensions between the two modes of thought. Now he still found it easy to identify Christ's kingdom which 'is not of this world' (John 18:36) with the intelligible world of the Platonic forms.[68] This was a characteristic, but precarious assimilation of two essentially disparate bodies of thought. It was not until much later that Augustine came to perceive the gulf between the Platonic and the biblical discourses.[69] The strains began to show well before the time when Augustine repudiated his early belief in human self-determination as illusory in his *Confessions*, written around 400.[70]

What undermined Augustine's youthful confidence in the ordered rationality of the world and the real possibility of attaining a rational order in human life, individual and social, was his reading of St Paul in the 390s. This gave him a vivid sense of the power of sin over men's lives, men's inability to free themselves from it unaided and the impossibility of realising the harmony of order in this world. The order which led to God was not to be found, now, in human affairs, and the hope that it might be established through the rule of wise men or men perfectly dedicated to God was revealed as illusory.[71] Since Adam's fall, the harmony of human life was lost. Neither the tensions which threaten the wholeness of the self from within, nor the conflicts in society at large are capable of resolution, except eschatologically. Here, they are permanent features of existence. Disenchanted with the notion of an ordered harmony attainable in human life and

---

66. *Ibid.* II.4.12.   67. *Ibid.* II.8.25, 5.14.   68. *Ibid.* I.11.32.   69. *Retr.* I.3.2.
70. On this development, see Cranz 1954, where the evidence is marshalled.
71. *De Trin.* III.4.9.

affairs Augustine thus re-entered that mainstream of earlier Christian thought which saw conflict, inequality, subjection and violence in society as the product and the punishment of sin. Augustine continued to regard man as social by nature; but he ceased to think he was also political by nature. Life in politically organised societies, in subjection to rulers and coercive institutions is – like slavery and other forms of inequality – the result of man's sinful state, and its object is to deal with the conflict and disorder attendant upon it. On this view the institutions of government are concerned, not to help men to achieve the right order, but to minimise disorder.[72]

The business of government is not the promotion of the good life, or virtue, or perfection, but the more modest task of cancelling out at least some of the effects of sin. Its function, summarily stated, is to resolve some of the tensions in society and to contain those that cannot be resolved. In the condition of radical insecurity – 'this hell on earth'[73] – political authority exists 'to safeguard security and sufficiency' (*securitatem et sufficientiam vitae*).[74] All the institutions of political and judicial authority and their administrative and coercive agencies serve this object: that the wicked be held in check and the good given a space to live in innocence.[75] Thus by another route, from neo-Platonism through St Paul, Augustine was travelling towards the view he would expound fully, a few years later, in the *City of God*. The convergence is manifest in the very terms he now uses to commend the value of the 'order of the state (*rei publicae*)': 'it controls the wicked within the bonds of a certain earthly peace'.[76] This is an anticipation of the 'temporal peace' which in the *City of God* forms the shared concern of both the earthly and the heavenly Cities (see above, pp. 107–8). It embraces the whole sphere of material needs and security, as well as subtler and more positive means of bringing some harmony into disordered social relationships: 'the fostering of a certain coherence of men's wills'.[77] The obligations laid on men by membership of a society are serious and not to be escaped. They demand unremitting dedication, even though men's best efforts to procure justice and order in society are doomed to frustration.[78]

The sombre realism of Augustine's later views on political existence was born of his disenchantment with the idea of an order accessible to men and capable of realisation through their intellectual and moral resources. He

---

72. For detailed justification of this interpretation against attempts to assimilate Augustine's views to the Thomist-Aristotelian tradition, see Markus 1965.
73. *De civ. Dei* XXII.22.4.   74. *Ibid.*   75. *Ep.* 153.6.16; *De Gen. ad litt.* IX.5.9.
76. *De Gen. ad litt.* IX.9.14.   77. *De civ. Dei* XIX.17.   78. *Ibid.* XIX.6.

continued, however, to speak of a political 'order'[79] and to hold that the state was part of an order. *Ordinata est res publica*, he once said remonstrating with a congregation which had been involved in lynching a local officer.[80] The order, however, to which political authority belongs is no longer the rational cosmic order as envisaged on Platonic lines earlier in his career. Now it is the mysterious order of God's unfathomable providence and hidden purposes. Augustine had to rethink his early ideas on law in the light of this drastic change in perspective. He had at first conceived human law as a reflection of the rational order pervading all things. Like many others he thought of this universal law as imprinted by the creator upon all his creatures and 'written in the heart of man' (see above, pp. 98–9). Temporal laws, to be valid, had to be derived from this eternal law, to be its public embodiment: 'for it is just that all things should be perfectly ordered'.[81] This conception of law could not survive the collapse of his notion of a rational order accessible to men and capable of being realised in their societies; and in the late 390s Augustine had to revise his views on law. His new ideas are worked out in his *Contra Faustum*, where he came to adopt systematically a new formula: 'the eternal law is divine reason, or the will of God, which orders (*iubet*) the preservation of the natural order and prohibits its transgression'.[82] The 'natural law' is now separated from the divine; no longer its reflection or impression, it is now commanded to be observed by it. This new language belongs to a careful rethinking that Augustine undertook at about this time of his views on God's providence. He now saw it as operating through two distinct channels: through created natures, and through the acts of wills and the trains of events in which these issue. The two streams of divine providence generate two distinct kinds of order in the world: the order of nature, subject to its own law, and the order expressed in human choices, actions and their consequences. Such order as men could produce in their social existence through their laws is no longer part of a natural order, but runs alongside it; both are subject, though in different ways, to God's providence. Human law is no longer directly related to natural law nor, through it, to the cosmic order. It takes its place among the institutions of political society. As human work, it is infected with sin; as God's providence, it is intended to cope with the results of sin, to be a remedy for the disorder and conflict endemic in man's fallen condition.

---

79. See n. 76 above.   80. *Sermo* 302.13; cf. *C. Gaudent.* 19.20.   81. *De lib. arbit.* 1.6.15, 5.11.
82. *C. Faust.* xxII.27; cf. *ibid.*, 28, 30, 43, 61, 73, 78, etc.

iii. *The Church and the world*

Both Augustine's pastoral work as a bishop and the controversies in which he was involved throughout his life prompted him to devote much thought to the nature of the Church. Most of this, though crucially important in the history of ecclesiology and of the theology of the sacraments and the ministry, is of no direct interest for his political ideas. Questions about the distribution of authority within the Church, though occasionally touched on, did not interest Augustine greatly. Problems about the relationship between secular and ecclesiastical authority, in so far as they were more than pastoral, were peripheral to his thought. In one important respect, however, his views on the nature of the Church and its relations to the world are of importance for a discussion of his political thought, in so far as they are linked with the central themes discussed in sections (i) and (ii) of this chapter.

Augustine formulated his views on the Church mainly in the course of the controversy with the Donatists. This schismatic movement dating back to the time of Constantine continued to create anxiety for Augustine throughout his career.[83] The Donatists upheld a view of the Church as the lineal descendant of a persecuted elite. For them it was a Church of the gathered faithful, holy and unspotted, alien to the hostile world of secular society around it. The Catholics they regarded as the apostate Church – the Church which had compromised with the secular authorities in the time of persecution and which now, since Constantine, depended on secular support. For the Donatists the Catholic Church was a permanent betrayal of the ancient African tradition of Cyprian, Tertullian and the martyrs. Augustine had much in common with their view of the Church. Once he had come to turn his back on the Theodosian 'establishment' of Christianity (see above, pp. 104–5), the tenacity of the old African tradition reasserted itself in his mind. Although he felt himself wholly identified with the 'universal' Church and therefore committed to communion with the churches 'across the sea' which in Donatist eyes had apostatised from true Christianity, he could nevertheless endorse the 'established' Christianity of the Theodosian or Constantinian Empire no more than could his Donatist opponents. Significantly, it was an outstanding Donatist writer, eventually disowned by his own sect, the shadowy Tyconius, from whom Augustine adopted some of the central ideas which went into the making of his

83. For this section see Markus 1970, pp. 105–32. On Donatism also the survey in Markus 1972b.

ecclesiology as well as his concept of the two 'cities'. The crucial insight which Augustine received from Tyconius was that the actual community of Christians which constitutes the visible Church is a mixed body, containing the holy and wicked side by side. It was not an elite of the chosen set in the midst of an alien profane world, either persecuted by it or, later, called to dominate it. This was the insight which led Augustine to elaborate his views on the two 'cities' and their necessary presence in any human group (see above, pp. 105–6).

The stark antithesis between righteousness and iniquity could not be expressed in sociological categories. Hence, as we have seen, the two 'cities' are only eschatologically separable within any social group. Nevertheless, the Church can be identified with the City of God, and not only in the rhetorical manner in which the Roman Empire could be identified with the earthly City. In this respect there is a lack of parallelism between the Church and the Empire, despite the fact that they are both mixed bodies containing both the elect and the reprobate. The Empire, and any secular society, is neutrally 'open' to both 'cities'; the Church is not, but is, in some profound sense, sacramentally identical with the eschatological community of the redeemed. Here and now it contains many who shall not be with her at the end; but the essential continuity between the Church 'as it now is' with the Church 'as it then will be'[84] creates an asymmetry between Church and Empire in the way the language of the two 'cities' applies to them. The Church *is* the City of God here and now in a sense in which no state or group *is* the earthly City. Like the Donatists, Augustine rejected a sacred conception of the Empire; like them, he affirmed the holiness of the Church; but unlike them he rejected – with Tyconius – the dichotomy of sacred and profane as distinct spheres each contained within its own sociological milieu. There can be no clear frontiers between Church and world, the old opposition especially dear to African ecclesiological language of 'inside' and 'outside' has lost its applicability. The conflict between sin and holiness cuts into the substance of all human groups, the Church not excluded.

iv. *Religious coercion: a note*

As a provincial bishop Augustine was deeply involved in the coercive regime of Theodosius and his successors.[85] He has been called the father of the Inquisition and the prince of persecutors. Soon after the publication of the

---

84. E.g. *De civ. Dei* xx.9.1.   85. See especially Brown 1964.

Edict of Unity (405), having held out against his fellow-bishops, he consented to their wishes and endorsed the government's measures against Donatists. This seems surprising in a man who was, at about this time, coming to view the Empire as a neutral secular institution, not directly concerned with enforcing matters concerned with ultimate choices. Around 400 he would have had no reason for hesitation about measures against paganism (pagans were, however, not forced to become Catholics, only forbidden to continue their own worship). In 408 he wrote his famous letter to Vincentius (*Ep.* 93) to justify the forcible conversion of Donatists and the view he adopted there remained substantially unchanged in his mind thereafter, throughout the period of the gestation and the writing of the *City of God*. The paradox calls for some comment.[86]

Augustine had always envisaged the recourse to pastoral 'severity' as a last resort to curb sinners. God had used *disciplina* to teach his people to keep his law; men still needed the discipline of externally applied force to bend their wills to the pursuit of their good. This was the principle Augustine appealed to: 'We see many who have renounced their former blindness; how could I begrudge them their salvation, by dissuading my colleagues [fellow-bishops] from exercising their fatherly care, by which this has been brought about?'[87] Coercion is like medicine administered to an unwilling patient for his own good;[88] how can we doubt that people should be compelled to embrace their own salvation when we read that the master commanded all who could be found to be compelled to come in to the wedding-feast?[89] The application of external pressure for pastoral ends, to procure the salvation of souls, remained Augustine's principle to justify religious coercion.[90]

Augustine did not notice the strain thus introduced into the view of the functions of government towards which he had been moving. With growing clarity he saw its sphere as confined to outward needs, public order and security (see above, p. 107); but he failed to see how hard it was to reconcile religious coercion with that conception. He was helped to conceal this conflict from himself by his habit of thinking (like Ambrose and many others) of Christian rulers and public officials as members of the Church rather than as officials of an institution charged with carrying out specific public functions. As individual Christians it was their duty to use whatever power they had at their disposal for the good of souls. The idea of a 'state'

---

86. On this section see Markus 1970, pp. 133–53. For an important discussion since the publication of this, see Lamirande 1975.   87. *Ep.* 93.1.1, 5.19.   88. *Ibid.* 1.3.
89. *Ibid.* 2.5, referring to Luke 14.23.   90. E.g. *C. Gaudent.* 24.27–25.28.

with its distinctive and restricted function, just emerging in Augustine's mature thought, thus remained liable to dissolve. 'When you act', he once wrote to a high African official, 'it is the Church that acts, for whose sake and as whose son you act.'[91] He regarded religious coercion primarily as a function not of the civil authorities, but of the Church.[92] Through Christian rulers it is the Church that 'uses power'.[93] This tendency to allow the Church to absorb the state has been seen as Augustine's most distinctive legacy to the political thought of the Middle Ages.[94] Nevertheless, this 'political Augustinianism' was no part of what is distinctive of Augustine's own mature reflection on the nature of society and politics.

v. *The just war: a note*

Questions about the morality of warfare, though linked with the fundamental themes of Augustine's political thought, were also on the edges of his interest. His views on war were, however, often quoted by later writers and were to play an important part in the development of the theory of the 'just war'. In essence, Augustine's views on war are a simple affirmation that warfare, for all the misery, suffering and almost unavoidable wickedness that it involves, may in some circumstances be justifiable and that it may be a Christian's duty to take part in it. Augustine never defined the conditions under which a war may be just with the systematic care which was later to be given to the question.[95] It is clear from his scattered statements that relatively few wars, especially few wars which were not defensive, would have qualified. To be legitimate a war had to be either defensive or fought to remedy some grave injustice perpetrated by the enemy; it had to be carried out under the command of a properly constituted public authority, not as private vengeance; and its conduct had to be confined within some bounds of human decency, to be waged without the sins which are its almost inevitable companions: violence, cruelty, savagery, lust for power, and the like.[96]

Augustine justified warfare on exactly the same lines as he justified recourse to force in society in general: as a necessary evil which had its part to play in the maintenance of order. The order in question was, as we have seen (above, pp. 108–11) differently conceived at different times. At first it was

---

91. *Ep.* 134.4.   92. *Ep.* 185.6.23, 2.11.   93. *Ep.* 173.10.   94. Arquillière 1934, p. 4.

95. For one of the important problems not fully resolved by Augustine see Hartigan 1966.

96. For details, the best full account is Deane 1963, pp. 154–71. Russell 1975, though mainly devoted to the medieval tradition, gives a perceptive and balanced, though brief, assessment of Augustine (pp. 16–26). For a fuller account of Augustine's views in the context of the development of his political ideas, see Markus 1983a.

the rational order of the universe of which the social order was a part. Later it was the 'earthly peace', that minimal condition of security and public order required for the maintenance of civilised life, between nations as well as within them. War is among the tragic necessities laid upon men in their conflict-ridden fallen state. Pre-Constantinian Christianity had not been entirely unanimous in the way it regarded warfare. Augustine could not return to the 'pacifist' tendencies predominant in it, upheld as late as the age of Constantine by Lactantius. Though killing was still often viewed with disapproval even in a justified war, the 'pacifist' thread in the early Christian tradition had been largely eroded during the fourth century by the willingness of Christians to identify themselves with the Roman Empire. Augustine's attitude to war, especially in his later years when he had come to reject this identification, was a much less positive and more reluctant and limited endorsement than could be found in many fourth-century Christian writers before him. Far from throwing the weight of his authority into the scales against the Christian 'pacifism' of the first three centuries, Augustine brought back something of that reserve into the wholly changed world of the Christian Empire of Theodosius and his successors.

Gregory the Great: towards new forms of community

During the 200 years between Augustine and Gregory the Great Europe had changed dramatically. Of Western Europe only Gregory's Italy remained under imperial control, and even here the Lombards had been advancing for some twenty years before his accession to the pontificate and were settling in large parts of the peninsula. Since about 540 Italian society had been profoundly dislocated by the long-drawn-out wars against the Goths, by plague and depopulation, by the collapse of the old aristocracy and the rise of new classes, mainly military and clerical, to positions of power in a society increasingly localised and restricted in its horizons. In a more than geographical sense Gregory lived on the edges of two overlapping worlds: that of the post-Justinianic Empire and that of Germanic Europe.[97]

Gregory's political consciousness was shaped both by his dealings with the Germanic *regna* and his daily experience of the *imperium*. He had been in contact with the imperial court at Constantinople; the imperial representative in Italy, the Exarch at Ravenna, maintained an extensive administra-

---

97. This is the form of the classic presentation in Caspar 1933, pp. 306–514.

tion. The contacts of bishops with the civil administration had become closer than ever since Justinian's time. Churchmen now had public functions of unprecedented scope, and with them came increased exposure of the Church to imperial interest and legislation. The imperial Church after Justinian, Gregory's Church, was so closely integrated into the administrative structure of the Empire and this dispensation was so readily accepted by its bishops and popes that questions such as those that had agitated the age of Gelasius (see above, p. 102) could now scarcely arise. If conflict arose between Gregory and the emperor, as sometimes happened over particular ecclesiastical measures enacted by the government (as well as over some questions of secular politics in Italy), the conflict was formulated in personal rather than institutional terms. The pope, even when bitterly opposed to particular instances of the exercise of imperial power over ecclesiastical affairs, remonstrated with the emperor but did not dispute his right to legislate in ecclesiastical matters.[98] In general, Gregory's official correspondence and particularly the traditional formulae of its preambles suggests that he never questioned the provisions Justinian had laid down for the imperial Church, but took them for granted as the normal framework of his activities. Even in his dealings with the now independent kings of Western Europe, Gregory tended to see them within the perspective of Byzantine constitutional fictions.[99]

Gregory inherited many of the basic assumptions about the Byzantine regime for the Church and about the Christian Empire, which he accepted as a necessary part of the world order. There are, however, two other important sources for Gregory's ideas about society. The first was his wide reading of the works of previous Christian writers, the Latin fathers, especially Augustine, and Greek writers (in Latin translations). The second was his acquaintance with various traditions of monastic life, his admiration for one of its towering figures, St Benedict, and his own attachment to monastic ideals. Gregory was not a speculative thinker such as Augustine or the Greek fathers. There is no trace in his writings of any sustained attempt to integrate into a theoretical whole disparate ideas from such a variety of sources, or even to reconcile them with some of the inherited political assumptions which still had a powerful grip on his mind. Nevertheless, there are clear traces in his work of new ideas on Christian social living, taking form gradually. He made use of his reading, especially of Augustine, to help him give shape to these ideas. He used Augustine's language to

98. E.g. *Epp.* III.61, 64, VIII.10. See Fischer 1950.
99. Markus 1981. The following summarises Markus 1985.

express thoughts sometimes very different from their original content. Two overriding needs in his mind dominated the way in which he appropriated ideas from earlier writers: the need to represent all rule and authority in terms of service – itself an old Christian idea – and the need to find a way of integrating the active and the contemplative lives in the life and work of the ruler.[100]

His allusion to Augustine's two 'cities' reveals the direction of the reorientation that such ideas underwent in his mind. In a characteristic section of his commentary on the Book of Job (*Mor.* XVIII.43.69–70), one full of echoes of Augustine, the tension between citizenship of Jerusalem and Babylon – Augustine's types of the two 'cities' – is transformed into the tension between the contemplative and the active lives. Augustine had used the image of the two 'cities' to evaluate in a Christian perspective a whole political and cultural tradition rooted in the pagan past of Rome and charged with pagan associations. Much of this tradition was still alive in the culture and the institutions of his society; and he wished to give the sphere of secular institutions its proper place, emptied of the religious significance it had carried. This need had vanished from Gregory's world. The secular traditions of pagan Rome no longer offered a real intellectual or moral option and its social and ceremonial expressions claimed no allegiance, even of the kind that the Lupercalia had commanded among some Christian senators as late as the end of the fifth century. The secular past had drained away from Rome and Gregory's Italy. Christianity had absorbed such of its traditional institutions and culture as remained. Gregory's *Dialogues* present an image of an Italy where the pagan past appears only in the remote haze of folklore and which is being drawn, through the *patres Italici*, into a Christian ecclesial community.

Gregory's historical consciousness was shaped by a sense of the crumbling away of the secular institutions and the profane traditions rooted in Rome's past. The result is clearly visible in his views both on Roman secular society and on the Church. The expectation of an imminent end, a sense of doom and the dissolution of the established order hangs over much of his work.[101] At the same time, Gregory viewed the future of the Church with a calm assurance of peace and secure progress which contrasts as sharply with Augustine's agnosticism about the vicissitudes in store for it as does his apocalyptic imagination with Augustine's concern and hope for the regeneration of Rome.[102] The eschatological tension of Augustine's two

---

100. An early instance of the two themes in combination: *Mor.* V.11.18–19.
101. *Hom. in Ez.* II.6.22, I.9.9; *Ep.* III.29; *Dial.* II.15.3.   102. Dagens 1970.

'cities' interwoven in all secular institutions as well as in the Church on earth is relaxed by Gregory, transformed into another tension: that between the active and the contemplative forms of life. His image of the Church of his own time is that of a community which has absorbed earthly powers into its own being, and he can envisage no reversal of this condition until the final persecution in the last days preceding the end. Until then her life and mission are secure; even the rhinoceros of earthly power which had raised its horn against the Church now humbly bends his neck to the plough by ministering to the preaching of the holy faith.[103]

Gregory and the Christians he was preaching to or writing for had come to define their identity in religious terms. They thought of themselves as belonging to groups centred on holy men, on bishops or clergy. Gregory's ideas about authority assume the radically religious basis of the group in which authority is wielded as well as the essentially religious nature of the authority itself. His favourite word for those who bore authority was *rector*. In his *Moralia* he had used it often, both as a general word for 'ruler' and as a synonym for 'those who are at the head of' (*qui praesunt, praepositi*, etc.) Christian congregations, bishops and others. He had found the term in one of his most important sources, in Gregory of Nazianzus' *Apologeticus*.[104] Here it was embedded in a wealth of political imagery of hierarchy and subordination, of ruler and ruled, higher and lower. The word had sometimes been used in reference to bishops before him; its more common meaning, however, was quite general: 'ruler', 'superior', anyone in a position of authority. In Gregory's time it was also the official title of the Church's agents in charge of its estates. Gregory's constant dealing with these men makes it all the more striking that when he came to write a handbook for bishops, at the outset of his own pontificate, he chose *rector* as his normal term for their office. Gregory's use of the vocabulary of government in the formulation of his own ideal of ecclesiastical office appears, at first sight, to offer a sharp contrast with Ambrose's title for his treatise on the same subject: *De officiis ministrorum*. In fact one of the threads running through Gregory's *Regula pastoralis* is the insistence that the exercise of power must be a mission of service to those subject to it, and humility its indispensable condition. The contrast with Ambrose's vocabulary of office as ministry is therefore not one of substance; but it reveals a

103. *Mor.* XXXI.4.4.
104. *Apol.* 3, in the translation by Rufinus, discussed in Markus 1986. This study now seems to me inadequate and both the lexicography of the word and its use by Gregory require further study. See also G. Folliet, 'Les trois catégories de chrétiens. Survie d'un thème augustinien', *L'Année théologique augustinienne* 14 (1954), 81–96.

fundamental shift in the perception of authority. Gregory chose a word encrusted with strong overtones of government and hierarchy. These overtones were precisely the associations he set about to dissipate. The result is a model for the ecclesiastical superior formulated in the language of government; but as the language was borrowed from that of secular government, the ideal it was used to sketch could be taken over by secular *rectores*. There was no radical distinction to be drawn between ruling in the two spheres. The ruler merges into the spiritual guide.

Gregory was well aware – the point is especially clear in his correspondence – that ecclesiastical and civil administration remained distinct, though overlapping. In his political vocabulary, however, he was moving towards a world in which sacred and secular were apt to melt into each other. In his desecularised world the language of secular politics acquired a religious dimension and could be used to speak of ecclesiastical office, while, conversely, secular authority was envisaged within a religious setting. The *cura regiminis* was synonymous with the *cura pastoralis*,[105] secular governing was as much a *ministerium* as ecclesiastical rule,[106] bishop, priest and king could all be symbolised by the image of the shepherd.

Gregory's ideas on the exercise of authority had been anticipated in St Benedict's image of the abbot. Like Gregory's *rector*, the abbot had to know how to profit (*prodesse*) rather than to 'be over' (*praeesse*) those subject to him.[107] This 'paternalist' view of authority had deep roots in a long tradition of thought, Greek as well as Christian, and could be found in Augustine's *City of God* in a chapter (XIX.14) echoed in one of Gregory's crucial passages on the *rector* (*Regula pastoralis* II.6). This is one of those dense chapters which distils years of thought, reading and personal experience; and Gregory allows us to see the threads of his thought as they are being woven together. He had long ago absorbed Augustine's teaching on how anyone in authority should conduct himself towards his subordinates. Like Augustine, he insisted that authority must be exercised with compassionate care (*consulendo*) not with lust for power and pride (*dominandi cupiditate*; *dominando*).[108] Gregory's ideal coincides with Augustine's, even, to a noticeable extent, verbally. Despite the identity of their ideals, there is, however, a profound difference between Gregory and Augustine.

Augustine had gone on in his immediately following chapter (XIX.15; on

105. E.g. *Reg. past.* I.4.   106. E.g. *Mor.* XXVI.26.45.

107. Benedict, *Regula monachorum* 64. Gregory's source for the doublet *praeesse/prodesse* in *Reg. past.* II.6 is however more likely to have been Augustine, *De civ. Dei* XIX.19; cf. *Sermo* 340.1.

108. *Mor.* XXIV.25.52 contains some of the clearest allusions to Augustine, *De civ. Dei* XIX.14; the idea occurs in his works too frequently to multiply references.

it see above, pp. 110–11) to state his views on the origins and the nature of authority and subjection. It contains his classic exposition of his theology of the original equality of men by nature and the loss of equality with the loss of innocence. Gregory knew the chapter well. He borrowed heavily from it in a passage of his *Moralia* (xxi.15.22) to which he refers in the *Regula pastoralis* (ii.6). Yet he failed to notice the change in Augustine's argument between the two chapters: the subject of the first was the ideal ruler's conduct; in the second Augustine moved on to the origin and nature of authority and subjection. Gregory was so little interested in the second theme that he not only failed to notice it, going on to use Augustine's views in his own exposition of his ideal for the ruler to follow; but he misunderstood its central point. Augustine had traced inequality, especially servitude, to sin, not nature (*culpa meruit non natura*). Gregory took the 'sin' to refer to the personal faults of individuals.[109] In contrast with Augustine, who thought of Adam's sin as the source for the dislocation of nature which runs through man's whole historical existence, Gregory traced the inequality among men and their subjection to others to the uneven distribution of merit among them, and to the mysterious operation of God's providence.[110] Those placed in authority must merit their position by virtue. God will often permit the unworthy, the proud or the foolish to wield power; but the wise will know how to profit from the rule of the fool and the sinner will receive in it his just punishment.[111] There is a strong streak of egalitarianism in Gregory's *omnes natura aequales sumus*: whereas Augustine pushed this equality back into primordial origins to explain its evident absence from our present world, Gregory made it a moral demand here and now.[112] This was one of the more far-reaching consequences of his failure to understand Augustine. The *rector*, especially, must always remember men's fundamental equality and act in accordance with that knowledge.[113]

Deeply as Gregory was influenced by the writings of the fathers and particularly Augustine, whose phrases he often reproduces (perhaps from memory), this divergence between them, at a point where Gregory is borrowing particularly freely from Augustine, reveals the fundamentally different orientations of their thought. Augustine's concern to trace universal features of the human condition, the nature of power and social institutions had no interest for Gregory. His bent was pastoral and

109. Reydellet 1981, pp. 465–6.
110. *Mor.* xxvi.26.44–8, xxv.16.34.   111. *Mor.* xx.24.52, xxv.16.34–41.
112. Reydellet 1981, p. 465.   113. *Mor.* xxvi.26.46, xxiv.25.52.

contemplative rather than speculative; but, more important, the problems raised by the society he lived in were different. Gregory saw it in terms of groups defined in religious terms, and he wished to uphold an ideal – a thoroughly Pauline and ancient ideal – for all rulers, lay or clerical, in which power was understood as ministry. How to promote holiness among men: that was his overriding concern. He had seen the power of the Spirit at work in the holy men of the Italian countryside, drawing it into the orbit of a radically christianised society. He wished his fellow-bishops and his clergy to become foci of Christian living like them; to be *praedicatores*, channels for the power of the Gospel, rooted in God's world by a life in which the painful tensions between action and contemplation were held in a fine equilibrium. His *Regula pastoralis*, a classic equally of 'spiritual' and of 'political' literature, created a model in which not only the active and the contemplative ideals but also the acquired status of the Italian *viri Dei* of the *Dialogues* and the bestowed status of the *rector* were integrated.

The grand simplification of Gregory's model had more influence on medieval political thought than the complexities of Augustine's theology of social living. The Aristotelian revolution of the thirteenth century swept Augustine's theology of society aside, to substitute for it a fundamentally different account of political institutions;[114] but it left Gregory's ideal intact.

114. See n.72, p. 110 above.

7

THE BARBARIAN KINGDOMS

For all the tribulations and transformations experienced by the Roman empire in the third and fourth centuries, the territorial configuration of its western half in 400 was not significantly different from that of 200 years before. Just a lifetime later imperial power was extinct in the west, which lay parcelled out among an assortment of kings and other warlords, predominantly Germans. *Ex uno plura*. The political map was to be redrawn time and again in the years ahead as new barbarian powers asserted themselves, as the empire strove to re-impose its control, as Islam expanded its dominion. Not one of the Germanic kingdoms of 750 had arisen at the direct expense of the fifth-century empire: the Anglo-Saxons had descended in force upon an already abandoned Britain; the origins of the huge *regnum Francorum* lay with Clovis (c. 481–511); the Lombards had entered Italy only in 568. But, as all this demonstrates, the west had continued to know political fragmentation. Indeed, it has known it ever since. If the unitary ideal, among the most potent of Rome's legion legacies, has never been far from the forefront of the western European consciousness, it is the political plurality bequeathed by the fifth-century collapse which in practice has always prevailed.

To multiplicity of polities corresponded diversity of ethos and inner form. That Germanism, *Romanitas* and Christianity worked as shaping influences upon all the barbarian kingdoms may be granted. But the generalisation conceals a host of variables. The Germans were no undifferentiated mass, and the nature of their contribution varied from kingdom to kingdom. So did the degree of its significance, much greater in the north; and so again – a closely related matter – did both the form and the extent of the influence exerted by *Romanitas*. By and large, it is true, the Germans respected and had an interest in preserving what they found. But not all of them valued everything in Roman civilisation; nor was will to preserve always matched by ability; nor again was what they found everywhere the same. Even Christianity was no constant, for while the indigenous population was staunchly orthodox, certain of the barbarian peoples adhered, sometimes obdurately, to heretical Arianism. Numerous further matters, such as the circumstances in which kingdoms arose and native reaction to German rule (or German perception of this), made for variety, while change over time within kingdoms goes without saying.

There was also diversity in political thought, naturally. But what here requires emphasis is rather, first, the constancy and ubiquity of certain fundamental principles, second, the absence of contribution by those concepts normally considered characteristically Germanic (see pp. 149ff) and, third, the general dependence upon sources and attitudes current in the late Roman west. This is not so say that thought stood still; simply, development and new growth drew their sustenance from old roots. What may be termed the Roman-imperial tradition formed one mass of these, a tangled cluster indeed, while a second comprised the ideas implicit or explicit in the writings of Christians and in the bible itself, the role of which as the ultimate determinant of Christian political thought followed naturally from its perception as the written expression of God's will. These two conceptual complexes were extensively intermeshed, however, and not solely by reason of Constantine's conversion and Christianity's consequential dominance. The faith originated and spread on imperial soil, and its adherents, as inhabitants of the empire, perforce shared in many contemporary assumptions about government and society; unsurprisingly, their writings frequently reflected these, as did already the New Testament. The Old Testament, too, often revealed viewpoints expressive of a general eastern *Weltanschauung* which itself contributed to the Roman-imperial tradition. The very Latinisation of the bible, moreover, involved its profound Romanisation; indeed, the significance of the Vulgate in the transmission of Roman concepts to the medieval west can scarcely be overestimated.[1]

The concepts of empire and emperor current c. 400 reveal this interpenetration of Roman and Christian thinking particularly clearly. The singleness of the empire (*imperium*) was a fundamental constitutional doctrine, maintained despite the normality of simultaneous rule by two emperors (*imperatores*), each possessed of sovereign authority (also *imperium*) within his realm, itself sometimes called an 'empire'. More than this, however, it was a conceptual necessity. Inseparable from the empire's very existence was its universalist ideology, sired centuries before out of Stoic thought by the reality of the Republic's political and military power. The empire was traditionally conceived of as the political and cultural

1. Essential and detailed is Ullmann 1963.

expression of the single community which was all mankind worthy of the name. The civilised world – the world *tout court* to a Roman – and the empire were coterminous, so that what prevailed beyond the frontiers was by definition barbarism, characterised by irrationality, savagery, perfidy and everything else antithetical to what Rome represented. The buttressing and sublimation of this ideology by no less universalist Christianity, begun already in the third century with the view that the empire's peace and immensity were divinely ordained to ensure the widest possible transmission of the faith, gained in both pace and intensity during the fourth; it is the progressive Christianisation of the concept of empire no less than of the empire itself which explains, and was acknowledged by, Theodosius' establishment of the faith as the official religion of the *res publica*. Both universality and the related notion of eternality were given biblical sanction – the second in necessarily modified form – by an exegesis of Daniel which identified Rome as the fourth of his world-monarchies and, in an interpretation popularised by Jerome, understood him to foretell its endurance until Christ's second coming.[2] The currency of these various ideas in the late Roman west is abundantly attested.[3]

The emperor himself had long since shrugged off the last threadbare tatters of the cloak of theoretical republicanism draping his earlier predecessors, to stand exposed in the nakedness of absolutism. If he recognised a duty to govern in the public interest and to obey the laws, this was a matter of choice, not of constitutional obligation. Behind him stood that strongest of ideological supports, the sanction of religion; to pagans and Christians alike he was the divinely chosen ruler. This did not, however, imply plenipotence in religious matters in the view of many Christians in the west, where sentiment, influenced by disillusionment with imperial policies during the Arian controversies and exposed to nascent papal ideology, was also shaped by a traditional predilection for envisaging the ideal emperor as a *princeps*, a first citizen.[4] Eloquently reflective of this 'republican' tendency is the address which Claudian, writing in 398, has Theodosius deliver to his son. Emphasised here are the virtues of self-knowledge and self-rule, concern for the general good, self-subjection to the laws, mercifulness and openness. Honorius must lead by example, showing himself no less a citizen than a father; Trajan, 'gentle to his country', should be his model.[5] Like Ammianus Marcellinus, very similar

2. Stengel 1965, pp. 18ff. For the prophecies, Daniel 2.31–45 and 7.3–27.
3. Many references in Teillet 1984, pp. 62ff.   4. Reydellet 1981, pp. 7ff.
5. *De Quarto Consulatu Honorii* 214–352, 396–418 (*MGH AA* x, 158ff).

in his viewpoint, Claudian was a pagan, albeit no zealot; but everything he wrote here was consonant with Christian ideals. Indeed, several of the same qualities appeared a little later in a brief 'mirror of the prince' in Augustine's *City of God* (v.24). They had a long and worthy career ahead of them.

We are ill-informed concerning Roman conceptions of the barbarian kingship established in the west from the 410s. Neither Orosius' awesome catalogue of the world's calamities, the *Histories Against the Pagans* (418), nor Salvian's fulminatory *On the Government of God* (c. 440) is enlightening, and it is only with Sidonius Apollinaris (c. 430–c. 480), Gallo-Roman aristocrat, *littérateur* and, eventually, bishop, that we encounter valuable testimony. Sidonius was every inch a Roman. He did not care for barbarians, and there was much more to his dislike than the distaste of a polished *grand seigneur* for the unwashed, as his valiant resistance to Visigothic expansion in the 470s demonstrates. To make him some sort of propagandist, inspired by the vision of a Romano-Gothic nation,[6] is wholly to misconceive him. But Sidonius entertained an elevated conception of kingship (if rarely of individual kings), seeing this as a dignity to which certain qualities were proper and high esteem potentially due. It is the clearest index of the respectability which kingship enjoyed in his eyes that his laudatory, even enthusiastic, picture (*Ep.* 1.2) of the Visigoth, Theoderic II (453–66), should have presented the king as an approximation to that model of the citizen-emperor cherished by westerners, including Sidonius himself. Theoderic is marked by *civilitas*, a propensity to conduct befitting the *civis*; 'he fears to be feared'; he is modest, self-controlled in his private pursuits (dwelt on by Sidonius, who thus underlines the king's humanness) and responsible in discharging the cares of government; he has an appropriate sense of the dignity of a ruler, showing *regia gravitas*, *disciplina* and *severitas*.

Sidonius' appraisal testifies to the fullness of the rehabilitation undergone by the figure of the *rex* since Rome's early days and to the immense advantage accruing to the fifth-century barbarian king therefrom. Proscription of the name and office of king had not in fact prevented the acceptance still in Republican times (partly under Greek influence, partly through the association of *rex* with *recte*, 'rightly', and *regere*, 'to rule') of regality as a concept expressive of moral nobility. By the later fourth century traditional repugnance had so far waned that *regnum*, 'dominion',

6. Teillet 1984, p. 189.

long used of an emperor's rule, appeared as a designation for the territorial empire and *rex* for the emperor. The exaltation of Christ the King in contemporary art and literature and the bible's abundant 'royal' terminology help to explain the emergence and spread of these usages.[7] Possession of the name of *rex* in common with the emperor and Christ Himself could not but have enhanced the status of the barbarian ruler enormously. One suspects, indeed, that the terminological phenomenon, working upon men's minds to blur old distinctions, may have contributed vitally towards easing the barbarians' path to domination.

Sidonius' was an outsider's view. Of ideas of kingship within contemporary *Gothia* we know almost nothing, and the same darkness enshrouds all the *regna* save the independent Vandal kingdom, illuminated chiefly by Victor of Vita's *History of the Persecution* (484). It is a sovereign monarchy, Roman and Christian in its bases, which is revealed.[8] There is no trace of a popular assembly, of any other constitutional curb on the exercise of the king's will, of any area of activity exempt from royal control. As the emperor wielded authority in religious matters, calling councils, deciding which creed his subjects should follow, persecuting dissidents – for what could be more germane to the public welfare than God's propitiation by correct worship? – so did the Arian Vandal king. Geiseric (d. 477) even established a permanent rule of succession, vesting the crown in his house; here he went further than any emperor chose, or dared, to do. A throne and the purple, witnessed for the 530s, will assuredly have appeared earlier, as had the diadem. The king described himself, in traditional imperial nomenclature, as 'Our Piety' and 'Our Clemency', held himself to possess 'majesty' and was addressed in the reverential language customarily employed of the emperor.[9] Instances of *imitatio imperii* could easily be multiplied. Most significant, the ruler considered heavenly authority to be the source of his own. God Himself had conceded his dominions to him, said Huniric (d. 484); he held them 'by divine favour'.[10]

The Vandal picture anticipates that eventually yielded by all the *regna* in numerous respects. But Huniric's statements merit especial note as the vanguard of a formidable army of testimony to the currency in the

---

7. For the above Suerbaum 1977, pp. 89–90, 285ff, Reydellet 1981, pp. 27ff.
8. On the following Courtois 1964, pp. 233–51, Diesner 1966, pp. 111–17.
9. Thrasamund was even eulogised as 'Imperiale decus . . . gloria mundi' by Florentinus (cit. Courcelle 1964, p. 363).
10. Victor, *Hist.* II.39: 'provinciis a deo nobis concessis' and III.14: 'terris et regionibus . . . quae propitia divinitate imperii nostri regimine possidentur'. Cf. Jordanes, *Getica* 169 (of Geiseric): 'a divinitate, ut fertur, accepta auctoritate'.

kingdoms of the belief that the ruler was such by God's *fiat*. At its roots lay the most fundamental of principles, that all that existed or occurred terrestrially was ultimately traceable to the celestial will, not to the intrinsic merits or unaided efforts of men. One need only state the doctrine, encapsulated in 1 Corinthians 15.10 and John 3.27, to glimpse the immensity of its implications. It affected all spheres of life, underlay numerous medieval institutions (like the ordeal) and attitudes (like the disinclination to search for physical laws) and engendered both fatalism – for if God disposed why should man bother even to propose? – and a remarkable adventurousness by those confident in His alliance. Like anything else, political power existed by God's will; and those who wielded it occupied their positions by His favour. By Christ's own witness (John 19.11), Pilate's power against Him derived 'from above', and Paul's statement in Romans 13.1 was unequivocal: 'There is no power but of God; the powers that be are ordained of God.' When orthodox bishops declared that 'divine favour' had 'provided' Theoderic (d. 526) – an Arian! – to govern Italy, or a seventh-century Frankish formula attributed elevation to kingship to 'divine mercy', or Ine of Wessex (d. 725) called himself king 'mid Godes gife',[11] they were operating with precisely the same notion expressed in the celebrated formula 'king by the grace of God' which was to become part of the Carolingian royal *intitulatio*, for *gratia*, 'grace', meant simply 'favour'. Indeed, already the Lombard, Agilulf (590–616), was 'king by the grace of God' and the Visigoth, Svinthila (621–31), brought to kingship 'by divine grace'.[12] Nicely illustrative of the root-concept was Boniface's designation of Æthelbald of Mercia (d. 757) as 'you whom not your own merits but God's abundant mercy constituted king and prince of many'.[13] The implications, necessary or possible, of the notion of the ruler's divine institution were numerous and of crucial significance for centuries to come in determining the shape of political thinking. Just three may briefly be mentioned here. First, God gives power for a purpose, namely the well-being of the people committed to the ruler's charge; rulership signifies responsibility. Second, the ruler stands supreme in his God-given authority;

---

11. *MGH AA* xii, 249: 'scientes divinitate propitia regere dominum, quem ad Italiae gubernacula ipsa providerit'; *MGH Form.*, p. 53: 'divina pietas'; Haddan and Stubbs 1871, p. 214. Hundreds of further examples could be given.

12. For Agilulf, see Bognetti, Gian Piero, *L'Età Longobarda*, vol. iii, Giuffrè, 1967, pp. 521–7, with a convincing defence of the authenticity of an inscription (p. 525) beginning: ' + AGILULF GRAT DI VIR GLOR REX TOTIUS ITAL . . .'. For Svinthila, Isidore, *Hist.* 62.

13. Rau 1968, p. 218: 'tu, quem non propria merita, sed larga pietas Dei regem ac principem multorum constituit'; cf., though idiosyncratically, Vollrath-Reichelt 1971, pp. 31ff. Similar language in a charter of Æthelbald: Haddan and Stubbs 1871, p. 386.

his charge embraces not a part of the people but the whole, not certain aspects of the direction of society but all. Third, he is answerable to God alone; however gross his failure to fulfil the obligations divinely laid upon him, he remains God's appointee and must not be resisted. Responsible government, sovereign authority, earthly unaccountability: all also found direct biblical support and corresponded to Roman ideas.

What disappeared from the west during the fifth century was the reality of imperial power and, with the murder of Julius Nepos in 480, the distinct western emperorship. Imperial authority survived inasmuch as certain kings, though *de facto* independent, regarded their lands as constituting part of the empire and secured imperial sanction for their rule. The Burgundian kings Gundobad (d. 516) and Sigismund (d. 524) were both patricians and masters of soldiers, and Sigismund's lieutenancy is laid bare in an effusive letter to the emperor: 'My people is yours . . . we consider ourselves nothing other than your soldiers . . . through us you administer the expanses of distant regions . . . I strive to know if there be something you deign to command.'[14] For Clovis the evidence is far from clear-cut. But status as an imperial officer, which would certainly help to explain much in his remarkable career, is perhaps implied by the terminology of an early letter (*Ep. Aust.* 2), while another letter (see p. 133) suggests that his lands were considered part of the empire. It may be, therefore, that the emperor's conferment upon Clovis in 508 of an honorary consulate, a patriciate and regalia was not a new diplomatic initiative but the culminating expression of regard for a ruler long formally dependent and seen as winning an 'imperial' victory in his recent Visigothic campaign. Clovis took the honours bestowed at Tours seriously and thereafter, allegedly, was acclaimed as 'consul' or 'Augustus'.[15] In several ways he did act the Augustus in his remaining years: he established a capital, at Paris, produced a law-code and not only convoked an ecclesiastical council but dictated part of the agenda.[16] It is not impossible, in fact, that Clovis was elevated in 508 to a vice-imperial kingship such as Theoderic enjoyed in Italy.

That Italy, under both Odovacer and the Ostrogoths, was considered part of the empire is amply evidenced, apparent indications to the contrary

14. Avitus, *Ep.* LXXXXIII: 'Vester quidem est populus meus . . . non aliud nos quam milites vestros credimus . . . Per nos administratis remotarum spatia regionum . . . ambio, si quid sit, quod iubere dignemini.'
15. For this and the honours Gregory of Tours, *Hist.* II.38 (with chapter-heading), a much debated text.
16. Wallace-Hadrill 1962, pp. 177ff. Note Remigius' 'imperial' terminology in *Ep. Aust.* 3 (of 512): 'Regionum praesul, custus patriae, gentium triumphator.'

finding explanation in the fact that Italy, like the earlier west as a whole, was a realm within a realm. The question of the constitutional standing of Odovacer and Theoderic can only be touched on here.[17] But everything argues that the basis of the authority Theoderic wielded, far fuller than that of any established figure in the Roman hierarchy, was kingship, granted a legitimate place within the imperial constitutional framework. Recalling the federate kingdoms, we might envisage some earlier move in this direction; new circumstances necessitate constitutional departures. By what authority, one wonders, had the Visigoth, Theoderic I, legislated on a matter – the division of lands – gravely affecting the Romans of his region? Noteworthy is the territorial designation 'king of *Gothia*' bestowed upon Theoderic's son, Thorismund (d. 453); similarly, Odovacer was 'king of Italy'.[18] As for Theoderic, whom the emperor sent to Italy in 488 to overthrow Odovacer, fallen from favour, we know that he soon requested 'royal attire'; refused, he had another embassy already in the east when in 493 the Goths, deciding not to wait for Anastasius' 'command', themselves declared Theoderic king. The kingship in question was assuredly territorial; Theoderic already enjoyed kingship over the Goths, and had the declaration of 493, as is often claimed, served simply to extend this to those in his host not already acknowledging it, the matter would have been of little moment to Constantinople. As it was, Theoderic evidently saw the kingship he sought as *de iure* the emperor's to give; correspondingly, Anastasius was evidently angered by what is called the 'arrogation of the kingship' for he recognised the *fait accompli*, on conditions, only in 497.[19] It is significant that, whereas the formal titles of the barbarian rulers normally presented them as kings of specified *gentes*, or peoples, Theoderic's *intitulatio* lacked this gentile element.[20] He is termed *rex Italiae* only in later sources; but *rector Italiae*, a contemporary usage, is probably equivalent.[21]

Our view of the Ostrogothic kingdom is largely conditioned by the evidence of the *Variae*, an extensive collection of official papers drafted by Cassiodorus. Too much has been made of this loyally undiscriminating minister as an independent political thinker. Whatever his motives for serving the Ostrogothic regime, he wrote as a government functionary and in accordance with what he knew was expected of him. To grasp what this

17. Claude 1978, pp. 42ff, cites many of the relevant texts.
18. Sidonius, *Ep.* VII.12.3; Victor of Vita, *Hist.* I.14.
19. Basic is Anonymous Valesianus 53, 57, 64 ('praesumptione regni'). Imperial recognition is particularly clear in Hormisdas, *Ep.* 12 (Thiel 1867) of 516, where Anastasius, writing to 'his' senate in Rome (but referring also to 'both commonwealths'), calls Theoderic 'excelsum regem, cui regendi vos potestas et sollicitudo commissa est'. 20. Wolfram 1967, pp. 55–6, 76ff.
21. Ennodius, *Panegyricus* 92 (cf. *ibid.* 14, where the emperor is 'illarum rector partium'), Avitus, *Ep.* LXXXXIII. Teillet 1984, p. 279 n. 57, remarks the tendency to use *ductor* for *dux* in this period.

was in Theoderic's day we must understand that to the king and his barbarians, a dominant but alien minority living on appropriated estates, the world was a threatening place. The dangers of imperial aggression and of internal disaffection had both to be reckoned with. To ensure the perpetuation of his control Theoderic saw it as imperative that the Goths remain distinctive and separate rather than be swallowed up into the mass of the population. What resulted, in contrast to the 'open' society of the kingdom of the Franks, whose situation was quite different, was a dualist state, one built upon the principle of the separate development of its two peoples. There was nothing exceptional in the existence of distinct legal regimes,[22] true; the rule of gentile law was a general feature of the barbarian kingdoms (see p. 138). The prohibition of Roman–barbarian marriage was another matter; how better to prevent the fusion of peoples than to forbid that of persons? To legal and social separation was added religious; Goths were Arians, Romans Catholics, and Theoderic, for all his reputation for toleration, was determined that they should so remain. Finally, there was a functional segregation, the army being the exclusive preserve of the barbarians.

All this on the one side; but on the other Theoderic's sense of insecurity made him anxious to present himself and his regime in such a way as would not feed Roman resentment at barbarian domination or otherwise provoke hostility. Although this was by no means the only reason for his commitment to the maintenance of *Romanitas*, it was an important one. The papers of the *Variae* belong within this context. Their immediate, administrative purpose apart, they served the government's interests by conveying a reassuring message of continuity, intrinsic to which was their presentation of Theoderic as an emperor in all but title; in this respect they constituted the written ideological counterparts to the king's determined display of an imperial image through building activity, patronage of the arts and so forth. 'Roman prince' is one designation; past emperors are 'our predecessors'; *imperium* is used of Theoderic's rule and realm.[23] Devoted to the cares of the *res publica*, to *libertas*, to *civilitas* (here meaning primarily respect for the laws), the king appears as the very incarnation of the magistrate-emperor.[24] Cassiodorus cannot pretend that nothing has changed; indeed, the separateness of Goths and Romans is emphasised. But

---

22. The so-called *Edictum Theoderici* is now widely thought not to have been Theoderician; some lit. in King 1972, p. 7 n. 4.
23. *Var.* III.16.3: 'Romanum principem' (precisely the phrase used of Anastasius by Gelasius in the celebrated *Ep.* 12 (Thiel 1867)); v.14.7: 'maiores . . . nostri'; 1.18.2: 'Italiae . . . imperium' (and see Index to the edn).
24. Reydellet 1981, pp. 214ff: 'Il n'est pas une seule vertu traditionelle de l'empereur que Cassiodore n'ait reconnue à Théodoric' (p. 218).

on the one hand it is presented as a virtue; the two peoples complement each other. And on the other its potential dangers are countered by urging concord, collaboration and the singleness of the community which they form under the single king. There is some skilful packaging; the barbarians' military monopoly, for example, in reality the guarantee of their domination, is portrayed as a burden selflessly undertaken in the general interest: 'Romans, you ought to love the Goths . . . who defend the whole commonwealth by war.'[25] In two other works, one, his *Chronicle*, commissioned by Theoderic's heir, the second, a history of the Goths – now lost, but accessible in some measure through its summarisation in Jordanes' *Getica* – prompted by Theoderic himself, Cassiodorus deals extensively (and imaginatively) with the Gothic past, and his message is unmistakable: ancient, courageous and worthy, the Goths are a people to be proud of. More than the reconciliation of Romans to barbarian rule is here the objective; he seeks to cultivate a positive appreciation of the especial merit of the Romano-Gothic polity which has come to exist. Cassiodorus, in short, was a professional royal propagandist – and, it should be said, an outstandingly successful one; the image of Theoderic 'the Great' which flourishes still today is in the greatest measure his creation.

To a lesser degree it is that of the deacon Ennodius. The view that in his *Panegyric* (506) and earlier *Life of Epiphanius* Ennodius sought to restore the Romans' courage and faith in the force of their tradition is distinctly uncompelling.[26] One need not be a cynic to see, rather, a careerist's calculation in the choice of subjects – and its reward in his eventual elevation to Epiphanius' old see, Pavia, an important royal city. But if Ennodius writes to no ideological purpose, he remains of considerable interest in his revelation of a mental world – a reflection of the real one – in which emperors and kings are essentially equals. Thus, Euric, the Visigothic ruler, is 'stupendous prince of the earth', his dominion an *imperium*, his relationship with the emperor Nepos one between *reges*.[27] Thus too Theoderic, though regularly 'my king' in the *Panegyric*, is portrayed in a thoroughly imperial light and associated with the old themes, both with a long future before them, of Rome as mistress of the world and of Rome's regeneration.[28] Theoderic is the 'venerable prince', the embodiment of the

25. *Var.* VII.3.3; cf. XII.5.4 (of 535/6).   26. The view is that of Reydellet 1981, pp. 141ff.
27. *Vita Epiph.* 86 ('stupende terrarum princeps' and 'fines imperii'), 81 ('inter reges').
28. E.g., *Pan.* 30 ('te orbis domina ad status sui reparationem Roma poscebat') and 56 ('ipsa mater civitatum Roma iuveniscit'). In *Libellus pro Synodo* 74 Ennodius does call Theoderic *imperator*; cf. *ibid.* 73 ('imperialia . . . scripta') and *Vita Epiph.* 187 ('boni imperatoris est . . .'). For 'Augustus' in inscriptions Claude 1978, p. 53.

state; the emperor may bear the titles but Theoderic's are the verities without which these are bare, pompous words. 'You show yourself by strength, by vigilance, by success a *princeps*, by gentleness a priest.'[29] In calling Theoderic a 'born king' Ennodius means primarily to say that he is one of nature's rulers;[30] unlike Cassiodorus he is uninterested in the royal lineage or, indeed, in the Goths. *Gothi* and *Romani* are words rare in his writings; he thinks in terms of the geopolitical singleness of the *imperium* or *regnum* of Italy, not in those of its duality of peoples.[31]

Ennodius seems to have been totally unperturbed by the Goths' Arianism: not so Avitus of Vienne (d. 518) by the Burgundians'. A man of much deeper religious sentiment, Avitus was vitally concerned with conversion. He succeeded in winning over Sigismund, though not Gundobad, and his response to the baptism of Clovis, the very first barbarian king to embrace orthodoxy, was exultant. No longer, he wrote to the Frankish king, was *Graecia* alone in meriting the benefit of a Catholic *princeps*; 'your world also is illuminated by its own brightness, and in the form of a king the light of a splendour which is not new bathes the western parts'.[32] If 'a splendour which is not new' meant orthodox rulership, Avitus was here presenting Clovis as the moral counterpart not only of the existing emperor in Constantinople but also of the earlier, Catholic, Augusti who had ruled 'the western parts'. There was a lesson for Gundobad in this, nor was it the only one in the letter, assuredly drafted with one eye to influencing the Burgundian king. Clovis was praised, for example, for not allowing ancestral custom to prevent him from following his judgement 'as many are wont to do'. Gundobad was among these 'many',[33] and Gregory of Tours reports Avitus' reproof: Gundobad was the head of the people, not the people his head; as he led and the people followed in war, so he should lead the way also to the truth.[34] Avitus knew full well that the key to the conversion of masses was that of monarchs; Constantine had shown that, and now Clovis was demonstrating it anew: 'in choosing for yourself, you judge for all . . . through you God will make your entire people His'.[35]

29. *Pan.* 1 ('princeps venerabilis'), 5 ('status reipublicae'), 80 ('Exhibes robore vigilantia prosperitate principem, mansuetudine sacerdotem').
30. *Pan.* 13: 'rex genitus'; see Reydellet 1981, pp. 166–9.   31. Teillet 1984, pp. 275, 279–80.
32. *Ep.* XXXXVI: 'Illustrat tuum quoque orbem claritas sua, et occiduis partibus in rege non novi iubaris lumen effulgurat.' Translations have varied considerably.
33. Avitus, *Ep.* VI (p. 34, *ad fin.*).
34. *Hist.* II.34: 'Tu enim es capud populi, non populus capud tuum.' Remigius calls Clovis 'Populorum caput' in *Ep. Aust.* I.
35. *Ep.* XXXXVI: 'Dum vobis eligitis, omnibus iudicatis . . . deus gentem vestram per vos ex toto suam faciet.'

Avitus did not call Clovis 'new Constantine', though he will certainly have had the great emperor in mind, but Gregory of Tours was to do so, and John of Biclar was to write similarly, and for the same reason, of Reccared at the Third Council of Toledo.[36] Not only Franks would benefit from Clovis' baptism, however, Avitus hoped, for the king was urged to carry the faith to the pagans beyond the Rhine. The initiative is noteworthy, such missionary concern being almost unprecedented. Avitus' vision, 'imperial' in complexion, of a multigentile dominion bound together by a single faith under a single *princeps* was prophetic.

To the emperors, the barbarians controlling the west at best held by precarious tenure, at worst were squatters. Theoderic had proved an untrustworthy bailiff, but Justinian (527–65) carried through evictions on a grand scale, and his successors clung as tenaciously as the dire circumstances of their times allowed to what had been repossessed. There was an imperial presence in Spain till the 620s, in North Africa till c. 700, in Italy till beyond the close of our period. From the 530s, this is to say, it was no distant power with which the *regna* had to reckon; the empire was close at hand, its impact and influence direct. Admired, albeit grudgingly, as in some measure an exemplar of what could be achieved, it was also disliked and feared. As will be seen later, its re-establishment in the west not only had a profound effect upon political thought in the Visigothic kingdom but also, paradoxically, worked to the general detriment of the emperor's claim to universal authority.

That authority was already denied by Theodebert I (533–47), Clovis' grandson, when, first among Germanic kings, he issued gold coins bearing his own name, titles and so forth;[37] such a breach of imperial prerogative was tantamount to a declaration of equality. Monarch of an enormous realm, Theodebert looks to have been an outstanding ruler. Certainly he left a high reputation, as Gregory of Tours, some half-century later, reveals: 'He showed himself great and distinguished in all goodness. For he ruled his kingdom justly, venerated his bishops, enriched the churches, succoured the poor, and with pious and most loving intent rendered many benefits to many people.'[38] The passage is a classic statement of the qualities which

36. Gregory of Tours, *Hist.* II.31; John, *Chron.* 590? 1. Gregory I presents Constantine as the model for Æthelberht in *Ep.* XI.37 (cit. Bede, *Hist.* I.32). But cf. Ewig 1956b, pp. 26–9.

37. Recently on Theodebert, Roger Collins in Wormald *et al.* 1983, pp. 7ff (with pp. 27–30 on the coins).

38. *Hist.* III.25: 'magnum se atque in omni bonitate praecipuum reddidit. Erat enim regnum cum iustitia regens, sacerdotes venerans, eclesias munerans, pauperes relevans et multa multis beneficia pia et dulcissima accommodans voluntate.'

Gregory thought a true king should display, as is also, *e converso*, his portrayal (*Hist.* VI.46) of Chilperic, 'the Nero and Herod of our time'. They do not surprise; indeed, justice, deference to the episcopate and aid for the disadvantaged had all been enjoined upon Clovis, when still a youthful pagan, by Remigius of Rheims in a brief letter (*Ep. Aust.* 2), first in a centuries-long line of hortatory writings directed at western kings, which reflects Roman ideals – particularly clear in the recommendations to consult and to be accessible – no less than Christian. With these royal desiderata may be compared those catalogued by Aurelian, of unknown see, in an extravagant missive to Theodebert himself. [39] Of the most important virtues appearing here – mercy, justice, concord, mildness, generosity and humility – only the last had no roots in secular Roman as well as Christian thinking. *Humilitas*, as unthinkable an ideal imperial virtue as *superbia* to a Roman of old but applauded in emperors by both Ambrose and Augustine, had been associated with Clovis in Remigius' and Avitus' letters to him; its importance to Avitus is elsewhere demonstrated by his presentation of David, humble in his greatness, as the model for the *princeps Christianus*.[40] Broadly, it signified acknowledgement of God's power and submissiveness to His commands; but it implied too that respect towards His bishops which Remigius and Gregory looked for. Emphasised by Aurelian was the theme of the Day of Judgement, popular with Gelasius and Caesarius of Arles among others, and present too, despite Clovis' paganism, in Remigius' letter. Of particular interest here is Aurelian's assertion that the ruler must answer *qua* ruler to God. The more he has received, the more he owes; the greater his *regnum*, the greater his peril at the settlement. 'It is an inestimable account which the Christian prince has to render to God.'[41] Aurelian will have had Hebrews 13.17 somewhere in mind, and perhaps Romans 13.4–6, for the linking of power from God with responsibility to Him implies a view of rulership as an office, a ministry, exercised in the divine name.

The notion of royal accountability points the way forward. To move from Aurelian's letter to the edict issued by another of Clovis' grandsons, Guntram, in 585 is to leave a thought-world still recognisably Roman in certain of its features and enter one of overwhelmingly Christian complexion. The king knows, he declares, that to please God he must maintain *iustitia* but knows also, thanks to his 'watchful solicitude', that

---

39. *Ep. Aust.* 10; note, e.g., 'ad praesentiam sacratae mentis' and 'sacratissime praesul'.
40. *Homil.* VII (p. 117).
41. *Ep. Aust.* 10: 'tantum eris magis debitor, quantum copiosius accepisti, et tantum erit reddenda ratione magis periculum, quantum amplius regnum. A christiano principe inestimabilis ratio Deo reddenda est.'

wrongdoing is everywhere. Hence earthly calamities for society; hence damnation for the offenders, even those ignorant of their faults; hence too, should he and his clergy not act, their own mortal peril, for 'we too, to whom the authority of the celestial king has committed the function of ruling, cannot avoid His anger if we do not have solicitude for the subject people'. The answer lies in preaching and correction by the clergy – to aid whom Sunday observance is decreed – and, should this fail, the severity of the law, canon or secular. 'It is no lesser *pietas* to crush the shameless than to relieve the distressed.' The goal is to bring all to love *iustitia* and live honestly so that God's favour may concede tranquillity on earth and salvation in the hereafter.[42] This could have been a capitulary of Charlemagne. *Iustitia* is Christian righteousness, *pietas* Christian mercifulness, society Christian society, to be governed in accordance with Christian norms and in the pursuit of Christian ends by a king appointed by God and – fearsome prospect! – answerable to Him for the care devoted to the task.

Christian themes dominate ideas of rulership and government in the later Merovingian kingdom, as they do those in contemporary England.[43] One mark of this is the frequency of recourse to biblical exemplars and citations. Already in a poem of 566 Venantius Fortunatus had compared Charibert with David for his gentleness and *patientia*, with Solomon for his justice and wisdom,[44] and both models reappear; Chlotar II (d. 629) is likened to David at the council of Clichy in 626/7 and Dagobert (d. 639) to Solomon in an early eighth-century source.[45] David and Solomon are also held up as paradigms to Chlotar II in a most interesting exhortatory letter, an excellent advertisement for the earnestness of contemporary Christian sentiment.[46] The author's very first injunction is that the king should study the scriptures often, so that he may learn from the examples of the old kings how to please God – for instance, by heeding the priests. *Humilitas* it was which gave David his victories. A family model is Chlotar I, a ruler of such *benignitas* as to have been 'like a priest' ('quasi sacerdos'). This is not the first time that the sacerdotal comparison – lacking sacramental implications, naturally – has

---

42. *MGH Cap.* I, no. 5: 'sollicitudine pervigili . . . nec nos, quibus facultatem regnandi superni regis commisit auctoritas, iram eius evadere possumus, si de subiecto populo sollicitudinem non habemus . . . nec minor est pietas protervos conteri quam relevare compressos.'
43. On England and Bede, left aside here, see particularly Wallace-Hadrill 1971, pp. 59–97.
44. And with Trajan and Fabius also: *Carm.* VI.2.77–84. On Fortunatus, Reydellet 1981, pp. 297–344, who sees a greater unity in his thought than can I.
45. *MGH Conc.* I, 196; Wolfram 1982, p. 364 (*Lib. Hist. Franc.* 42). Fredegar notes Chlotar's *pietas* and *patientia* and Dagobert's devotion to *iustitia*, beloved of God: *Chron.* IV.42, 58.
46. *MGH Epp.* III, 457–60; cf. Anton 1968, pp. 51–4.

been considered appropriate for a Frankish king.[47] Studded with biblical quotations, the letter also contains the earliest specific reference to a king as a *minister Dei*. Pointing out, after citing John 3.27, that God's gift of power lays an obligation upon its recipient, the writer continues: 'You should know that you are a minister of God, constituted by Him for this purpose, that those who do good may have you as their kindly helper, that those who commit evil may recognise in you a mighty avenger, so that, before they act, they may fear you.'[48] If the bible is rarely cited in the late seventh-century Marculfian formulary, itself a rich ideological repository, especially as regards kingship, its influence is pervasive. Liturgical evidence elaborates the picture of the Christian king and suggests parallels between the Franks and Israel.[49] Much in Carolingian ideology had Merovingian antecedents.

Mention of the Frankish–Israelite connection raises the important matter of gentilism. The term *gens* was used by contemporaries in about as many ways as is 'people' nowadays. It did not necessarily signify a political community or even a social or cultural one. Nor did it imply an ethnic entity, in the sense of a group united in consciousness of common blood and heritage. 'National' histories like Paul the Deacon's for the Lombards testify to pride in the ancientness of peoples, and a degree of continuity between some *gentes* and peoples living in Germania centuries before is assured. Nonetheless, the *gentes* which took over the west were regularly ethnic commixtures, aggregations of diverse elements clustered around a core grouping, the name and traditions of which extended to the *gens* as a whole. Composition and size fluctuated with the fortunes of war. It was not even necessary, though it was certainly normal, that the king of a *gens* stem from the core grouping. Unusually, the Franks had no ethnic kernel; they were a federative people composed of tribes which retained their distinct identities while sharing the *nom de guerre* first witnessed in the third century. In the seventh their lack of ancient provenance was met by the invention of a Trojan origin, satisfyingly assertive of parity with the Romans. By the eighth 'Frank' designated any inhabitant of central northern Gaul; such gentile territorialisation, also observable elsewhere, compounds the difficulties of generalising about the *gentes*.

47. *MGH Conc.* I, 2: 'sacerdotalis mentis' (of Clovis); Venantius Fortunatus, *Carm.* II.10.21: 'Melchisedech noster merito rex atque sacerdos' (of Childebert I); Gregory of Tours, *Hist.* IX.21: 'rex acsi bonus sacerdos' (of Guntram).
48. 'Ministrum te Dei esse scias ad hoc constitutum ab ipso, ut, quicumque bona faciunt, te habeant misericordem adiutorem, vindicem fortem te cognoscant hi, qui faciunt mala, ut, antequam faciant, te timeant' (p. 460).   49. Ewig 1956a, pp. 23–4.

Though no defining feature, a distinctive law was a normal characteristic of a *gens*. This law governed all its members, so that to reject it was to reject the people itself,[50] and only them. But it ruled wherever they might be within the *regnum*; they carried their law with them, so to speak. The prevailing principle was therefore that of the personality rather than territoriality of law.[51] Much contemporary law was put into writing and survives. Particularly copious is the legacy from the Visigothic kingdom, where at least twelve rulers legislated and only the work of the first, Theoderic I, is wholly lost. It was Theoderic's son, Euric, who in c. 476 produced the earliest code of which anything (though it is not much) survives. The next half-century saw the publication of Clovis' Frankish code, *Lex Salica*, separate compilations for the Burgundians and the Roman inhabitants of their kingdom (see p. 41), an Ostrogothic edict, not preserved, and the first of three complete codes extant from the Visigothic kingdom, the Breviary (see p. 41). Further recensions of *Lex Salica* and codes for Ripuarian Franks, Alamans and Bavarians are attributable to Frankish kings before Charlemagne.[52] Compilations were also produced in England, with Æthelberht (d. 616) the pioneer; for some reason these were in the vernacular rather than the otherwise universal Latin. In the Lombard kingdom, finally, the Edict of Rothari (643) initiated a series of legislative monuments, most important in the history of Italian law, which formed an accumulative code.

Even when the Roman codes are ignored, this mass of law poses numerous problems, and much remains obscure, disputed or unexplored. In part this is because scholars have often approached the codes as a giant quarry, to be picked over for the material from which the chimerical edifice of 'Germanic law' might be fabricated, rather than as the individual products of gentile singularity which they were. Borrowings there certainly were, but the variety which comparison of rulings on given topics reveals – and which remains even when legislation on which Roman influence was profound (Visigothic) or marked (Burgundian and later Lombard) is excluded – is striking and extends also to such matters as lucidity and sophistication of expression and underlying thought, organisation and range.[53] Generalisation is, however, admissible to this extent: all the codes represent a mixture of gentile tradition and innovation

---

50. Paul the Deacon, *Hist.* III.6, on the Saxons, is instructive.
51. Against the alleged territoriality of Visigothic law, King 1980.
52. Wormald 1977, pp. 108–9. Wormald's article is most valuable, and I follow him in several respects in this section.   53. A quite different picture in Wallace-Hadrill 1971, pp. 33ff, esp. 37.

and all owe their existence to the will of the ruler. The old thesis of a distinction between *Volksrecht* and *Königsrecht*, between the *Leges*, seen as repositories of popular custom, unchangeable except by popular consent, and capitulary-like enactments, seen as royal responses to problems not catered for in the *Leges*, does not hold water. The question of royal motivation admits of less obvious answers than might be assumed, for while some codes were certainly or very probably intended to serve the interests of society by providing a full statement of the law – the Lombard and Visigothic collections belong in this category – others are far less comprehensive. The principles determining what went into these 'selective' codes and what did not elude identification. Whatever they were, it seems likely that the fact of a code's appearance often mattered rather more than the form of its contents.

For the promulgation of a code was of high political and ideological significance. First, it served to affirm gentile identity, certifying this, so to speak, through the concrete and permanent medium of the written word. Important enough for this reason to a ruler's own people, it will perhaps have had greater significance still to a subject *gens*, as a reassuring acknowledgement of his intention that it should retain its distinctiveness. Second, it both asserted authority over the *gens* by demonstrating royal control over a fundamental manifestation of its individuality and offered the prospect of consolidating and enhancing that authority by bringing gentile sentiment to focus more sharply than before on the king. Third, it declared that the king was a true ruler, devoted to justice, that the recipient *gens* was a civilised people and that he and it stood in the company of rulers and peoples of the highest lustre. What was the bible but the *lex scripta* of the heavenly king-legislator? What was to be found early in the Old Testament but the gentile law-codes of the Israelites? Were not the Romans celebrated for their written law and the Theodosian and Justinianean collections the clearest evidence that eminent rulers gave codes? The preface to the Bavarian code lists the world's great law-givers, beginning with Moses; Bede reports that Æthelberht produced his compilation 'after the example of the Romans'; it is in the prologue to *Lex Salica* that Frankish self-esteem is most triumphantly proclaimed.[54]

Law-codes occupy pride of place among the sources for the kingdom boasting the most sophisticated civilisation and most mature political

---

54. *MGH Leges* v/ii, 198ff; Bede, *Hist.* ii.5 ('iuxta exempla Romanorum'); *MGH Leges* iv/ii, 2ff.

ideology of the seventh-century west: the Visigothic. Its ethos stood in striking contrast with that which had earlier prevailed. Entering the empire in 376, the Visigoths had long remained divided in attitude towards it, the dichotomy of viewpoint finding expression in an alleged declaration of Athaulf (d. 415) that his first aim had been to replace *Romania* with *Gothia* but that Gothic inability to obey the laws, 'without which a *res publica* is not a *res publica*', had made him resolve instead to become the 'author of Roman restoration'.[55] Euric's seizure of power by the murder of the Romanophil Theodoric II in 466 marked the victory of the 'independence' party, and the autonomous kingdom which resulted was characterised, like Ostrogothic Italy, by internal barriers between Arian Goths and orthodox Romans. Many of the reverses and *malaises* of the first two-thirds of the sixth century may fairly be traced to the policy of 'separateness'.

With Leovigild (568/9–86), however, the kingdom came to be directed onto a new path, with unity, centred on the monarchy, the beckoning goal. The inspiration and model was unquestionably the empire, now embracing south-eastern Spain. While Leovigild's military exploits, including the conquest of the Sueves, were of the highest importance, he also acted to enhance the status of the monarchy by assuming royal garb, introducing (or reintroducing) a throne, issuing an independent coinage and publishing a revised edition of Euric's law-code; and he removed the ban on intermarriage. Religious unification, unavailingly sought by Leovigild on the basis of a modified Arianism, came about in 589 under Reccared, his son, when the Goths and the Sueves adopted orthodoxy. In the 620s the expulsion of the Byzantines signified the extension of royal authority to virtually the entire peninsula. And in 643/4 Chindasvind demolished the last formal obstacle to internal unity, the system of separate legal regimes; although his territorial code has not survived, both Reccesvind's revised version of 654(?) and Ervig's fuller code of 681 have.[56] These developments reflected, as they fostered, the distinctively proud, self-confident, unitary ethos of thought in the later Visigothic kingdom. Some scholars have seen 'Spanish nationalism' or at least 'Spanish national sentiment' at work, citing particularly the association in Isidore's *History of the Goths*, especially the rhapsodic *In Praise of Spain* which serves as its prologue, of enthusiasm for the Goths with a fervent patriotism.[57] Isidore, living through most of the time of transform-

---

55. Orosius, *Hist.* VII.43.5–7.
56. Further on the foregoing, with lit., King 1972, ch. 1, and for Chindasvind's introduction of territoriality (an unorthodox view), *idem* in James 1980, pp. 131ff.
57. Teillet 1984, pp. 3ff, gives the views.

ation, was certainly inspired by its spirit, as the *History*, markedly pro-Gothic and anti-imperial in its tone and often distorted presentation of events, clearly reveals. 'Nationalism', however, indissociable from modern political doctrines, is a wholly inappropriate concept to unearth in the seventh century, and even talk of 'national sentiment', while arguably strictly justified, is better renounced as likely to mislead.

Isidore, the brightest luminary of Visigothic civilisation and probably the most read author of the early Middle Ages, was not a thinker of anything approaching the first rank. But there was a good deal more to him than has been allowed by those who have represented him – principally on the evidence of his *Etymologies* – as merely an encyclopaedic collector of other men's wisdom; and his influence on medieval thought was to be considerable and enduring. His vast, eclectic erudition sometimes produced incoherence. There seems confusion in his treatment of natural law, which he distinguishes from *ius gentium* and *ius civile*, both defined broadly in accordance with the Roman lawyers.[58] *Ius naturale* is 'common to all peoples and what is everywhere held, not by some constitution or other but by the urging of nature'.[59] Yet in noting as institutions of this law on the one hand universal freedom and 'communis omnium possessio', on the other the repulsion of violence by force and the restitution of deposits and loans, Isidore appears to be operating with two differing concepts of nature, the one, common to Stoic and patristic tradition, of nature as man's original, ideal, state, the other, rooted in experience of generally observed ethical rules, of nature as the condition of man as he actually is. There is an obvious problem, moreover, in reconciling 'common possession of everything' with rights in deposits and loans.[60] Elsewhere Isidore shows his adherence to the doctrine of 'ideal' nature in tracing the origin of slavery and government to the Fall; dominion is both the penalty for Adam's sin and the merciful remedy for its consequences. Yet he is at pains to declare that baptismal grace removes original sin; why it is nevertheless the act of an equitable God to constitute some men masters, others slaves, is not at all clear, especially since Isidore manifestly rejects any correlation between the possession of dominion and that of greater merit.[61]

The thrust of Isidore's thought is clear, however. Its basis lies in the two intimately related concepts of Christ as eternal king and priest and of the

---

58. *Etym.* v.4–6; cf. Carlyle 1903–36, vol. I, pp. 42–3, 106–10.
59. *Etym.* v.4.1: 'Ius autem naturale est, aut civile, aut gentium. Ius naturale est commune omnium nationum, et quod ubique instinctu naturae, non constitutione aliqua habetur.'
60. But cf. Carlyle 1903–36, vol. I, pp. 142–4.
61. *Sent.* III.47.1 and 3. Reydellet 1981, pp. 569ff, engages the problem.

church as His body, in and through which His kingship and priesthood are perpetuated and made manifest.[62] As Christ is king of the church, *rex ecclesiae*,[63] so the church forms a single *regnum*, bound together by faith and embracing a single people,[64] incorporation into which comes with baptism, at which the Christian is imprinted with the mark of his heavenly king.[65] But the singleness of this kingdom implies no argument for singleness of terrestrial political authority to Isidore, who, inhabiting a world of Christian *gentes*, sees in the congregation of these the one people of God which is the church.[66] Indeed, far from offering support for traditional imperial universalist ideology, Isidore clearly believes, like Julian of Toledo after him, that Daniel had foretold the survival of the universal sway of the (Roman) 'kingdom of iron' until Christ's first, not second, coming.[67] While Isidore accepts the primacy of the pope among the *sacerdotes* of Christ's universal kingdom,[68] nothing suggests that he attributes even a paramountcy of honour among its *principes* to the emperor.[69]

Within the worldly *regna* which constitute, so to speak, the material cells of the body of the church Isidore envisages the complementary operation of clerical and lay authority. Thus, he deems the *principes* subject to religious discipline and bound by the faith but also considers the church divinely entrusted to their power and warns them of their obligation to render account for it before God.[70] His concept of the princely role is emphatically teleological. *Principatus* is a gift from God to the end that the ruler should profit the ruled; to Isidore, *praeesse*, 'to be above', and *prodesse*, 'to be of benefit', are so far from standing in their traditional antithesis that the second is the very *raison d'être* of the first.[71] The divinely imposed duty of service means above all the furtherance of ecclesiastical discipline and peace:

---

62. *De Ecc. Off.* II.26.2, *Alleg.* 142, *Quaest. in Vet. Test.* 'In Genesin' 11.8 and 'In Esdram' 1.2, etc. On the concept of Christ's royalty, Reydellet 1981, pp. 557ff.
63. *Quaest. in Vet. Test.* 'In Genesin' 28.8.
64. *De Fid. Cath.* II.1.3, where Isidore glosses Psalms 102.22: 'In unum utique, id est, in unum regem, ut qui . . . regna multa, et populi multi dicebantur, in unam conveniendo fidem, unus Dei populus, unumque regnum vocetur.'
65. *De Ecc. Off.* II.25.10: 'character est enim regis mei'.
66. *De Fid. Cath.* II.1.3–4: 'Hujus populi congregatio ex gentibus ipsa est Ecclesia' (c. 4).
67. I follow Löwe 1973, pp. 42ff (cf. Stengel 1965, p. 19), rather than Ewig 1956a, pp. 30–1. Particularly important are *Alleg.* 227, *De Fid. Cath.* 1.58.1–3 and *Etym.* VI.2.25. For Tertullian's influence, Suerbaum 1977, p. 242 n. 37.   68. Cf. King 1972, p. 123, with texts and lit.
69. Against Erdmann 1951, pp. 16–17, and Folz 1953, p. 15, see Löwe 1973, pp. 45 n. 50, 46 n. 56.
70. *Sent.* III.51.3 and 6.
71. Cf. *ibid.* III.49.3: 'Dedit Deus principibus praesulatum pro regimine populorum, illis eos praeesse voluit, cum quibus una est eis nascendi moriendique conditio. Prodesse ergo debet populis principatus, non nocere; nec dominando premere, sed condescendendo consulere, ut vere sit utile hoc potestatis insigne, et dono Dei pro tutione utantur membrorum Christi.'

the prince should prevent evil by his 'terror', preach the faith and impose 'right living' by his laws, set a personal example of righteousness and so forth.[72] Isidore sees the ruler's cardinal virtues as justice and mercifulness, with the latter the more praiseworthy since 'justice in itself is severe'.[73] Here, as sometimes elsewhere, *iustitia* signifies exaction of what is strictly due,[74] but often it expresses the much fuller concept of righteousness; thus the just ruler is humble, emulating David, and obeys the laws.[75] Isidore's profoundly ethical conception of rulership is exemplified in a celebrated etymologisation: the very name of *rex* is dependent upon right behaviour.[76] The constraint upon the king to act rightly is solely moral, however; so convinced is Isidore that the evil ruler, or tyrant, whom he sees as the product of a wicked people,[77] must be endured, since possessed of God-given power, that he is at pains to explain away Hosea 8.4, seemingly contradictive of Romans 13.1.[78]

Isidore's thought, reflecting secular Roman as well as biblical and patristic, especially Augustinian and Gregorian, ideas, was immensely influential within the Visigothic kingdom, both in his own day – as witness king Sisebut's *Life of Desiderius*[79] and the canons of the Fourth Council of Toledo (633) – and after. Law-codes and the *acta* of the numerous councils held at Toledo, the capital, and elsewhere are the principal sources exposing this kingdom's ideological world. Its multifacetedness can be done no justice here, where attention must be confined to the governing themes.[80] The king appears as the predestined appointee of God, set at the summit of society as the head is set over the body and for the same purpose, to rule the 'subject members'. As the metaphor implies, royal power was considered to be granted for the benefit of those ruled. The king was the *minister Dei*; he held the kingdom 'by vicariate authority' ('jure vicario'); God worked through him. His essential instrument in the pursuit of the well-being of society (*salus populi, utilitas publica*) was law, by which he might implement

72. *Ibid.* iii.47.1, 48.5, 50.6, 51.3–6.   73. *Etym.* ix.3.5.
74. Cf., e.g., *Sent.* iii.49.2 and 50.3. In *MGH Epp.* iii, 196, Desiderius of Cahors cites James 2.13 in writing to Dagobert: 'Iuditium quoque misericordia comitetur.' Cf. Psalms 112.4 for God as 'misericors . . . et justus'.
75. *Sent.* iii.48.1, 49.1–2 (humility), *ibid.* iii.50.4, 51.1–2 (laws: cf. Reydellet 1981, pp. 594–5). General definitions in *Diff.* ii.156, 158.
76. *Etym.* ix.3.4: 'Reges a regendo vocati . . . Non autem regit, qui non corrigit. Recte igitur faciendo regis nomen tenetur, peccando amittitur. Unde et apud veteres tale erat proverbium: "Rex eris, si recte facias: si non facias, non eris".' Cf. *Sent.* iii.48.7 and Anton 1968, pp. 57–8.
77. Reydellet 1981, pp. 578–84, with reference to Augustine and Gregory I. For the term and the different Greek usage *Etym.* ix.3.19–20. *Tyrannus* in late Roman and early medieval texts usually means 'usurper'.   78. *Sent.* iii.48.10–11. Cf. *ibid.* 39.5–6 and Diesner 1978, p. 52.
79. See Jacques Fontaine in James 1980, pp. 99, 107–8, 126.
80. For the following, with texts and literature, King 1972, ch. 2 and pp. 122ff.

and inculcate *iustitia*, which God had ordered mankind to embrace – which *was* God, indeed. On the one hand law appeared as the medicine with which the king countered what he diagnosed as noxious within the body he headed; its coercive and deterrent roles were stressed. On the other it was identified, as the 'messenger of justice' ('iustitiae nuntia'), with that body's soul ('anima totius corporis popularis'). The notion that law might serve the private rather than the public interest was expressly rejected.

Nothing lay outside the purview of the king. Far from there being an autonomous body, 'the church', authority over which belonged to others, society and the church were conceptually equated. It was precisely because fact did not correspond to idea that such savage action was taken against the Jews, whose presence within the territorial but beyond the ideological confines of the kingdom affronted the Christian, unitary premisses of the Visigothic standpoint. The king's authority over clerics and religious matters, inherent in his God-given responsibility for the health of society, was fully accepted by the *sacerdotium* itself. Kings nominated bishops, judged metropolitans, summoned councils, established agenda and confirmed rulings. They even provided excommunication as a legal penalty. The bishops laid down the norms of behaviour which the good king ought to follow and did their best to ensure that these were observed by involving themselves in royal elections and requiring the swearing of pre-accession oaths. But they never talked of deposition, and it was the fiction of abdication to which they resorted when Svinthila was in fact toppled by revolt. The introduction of the Old Testament rite of royal anointing, perhaps in 631 to make it visibly and ceremonially clear that Svinthila's usurping successor ruled by God's favour, confirmed and buttressed the loftiness of the monarchical status. Perhaps the clerics would eventually have made capital out of the constitutive unction evidenced later in the century. As it was, in 711 the Arabs crossed the straits and snuffed out the life of this most remarkable of the barbarian kingdoms.

In denying political universalism Isidore may appear to have been expressing the common viewpoint of the post-Justinianean barbarian west, where no writer testifies to the currency of the old ideology. Though this was still maintained by imperial subjects, it could not have carried its earlier conviction. It had been the closeness of correspondence between universalist ideality and political, cultural and religious reality which had endowed the former with the great strength of its grasp upon men's minds. That correspondence was now lacking, as Jordanes, writing in 551, acknowledged. To him, the *res publica* (destined on Daniel's authority to last until the end of the world) still indeed held what it had once subjected ('almost the entire earth'); but it did so, when not actually, then – the word is an exquisite choice – 'imaginarie'.[81] Time served only to widen the gap which had opened up. It is not clear that any western *regnum* recognised imperial authority after Justinian, while the incongruity of identifying the Christian world and the empire grew ever more patent. The calamitous reverses suffered by the seventh-century empire at Muslim and pagan hands made matters worse. Moreover, westerners were deeply alienated by the character, real or perceived, of the contemporary empire. Fear and hostility on the political and military fronts played a role, while in imperial Italy resentment at high taxation and inadequate defence fuelled animosity towards what was seen as a foreign regime. Throughout the west as a whole, indeed, the empire was regarded as essentially a Greek affair – a characterisation which came the more naturally in view of the prevalence of gentile thinking – and suffered accordingly, for the traditional contempt and antipathy towards easterners had survived. Closely related was enmity in the theological sphere; the age was full of controversies which confirmed the widespread – and again traditional – western distrust of easterners as intellectual conjurors, given to unorthodoxy. In turn the theological disputes were bound up with the fundamental papal–imperial conflict, usually latent but occasionally exploding into violent life; this and its concomitants, including the ill-treatment of some popes by some emperors, brought further hostility.

Yet none of this argues for repudiation of the political universalist *ideal*; and the fact is that outside Spain this was not denied, even implicitly. Of no significance in this regard is the employment by Bede and others of the term *imperium* to denote the dominion of Anglo-Saxon kings.[82] This usage has perhaps attracted greater attention than it merits, for it is not peculiarly insular; numerous authors, before and after the barbarian take-over, used *imperium* of the authority or territories of non-Roman rulers, as did the bible also.[83] More noteworthy is Adamnan's affirmation in the 680s that Oswald, the Northumbrian king, 'was constituted by God emperor of all Britain'.[84] But it is no more material; moreover, it is not an unprecedented instance of

---

81. *Romana, Praef.* and 84.
82. Most recently on the usage Wormald in *idem et al.* 1983, pp. 105–10, with literature.
83. For Tacitus, Justin, Orosius and Jordanes, see Suerbaum 1977, pp. 97ff, 129ff, 237ff, 276–7; generally, *ibid.*, pp. 293ff. For Ennodius and the Vandals, above, in text or notes. Further, Gregory of Tours, *Hist.* v.39, Isidore, *Hist.* 1c and 52, and Erdmann 1951, p. 18 (liturgy). For the bible, 2 Chronicles 28.5, Esther 1.20, Daniel 6.26 etc.
84. See, fully if idiosyncratically, Stengel 1965, pp. 301–9, from whom (p. 304) I take the text: 'totius Britanniae imperator a Deo ordinatus est'.

the designation as *imperator* of a ruler who was on no showing a Roman emperor.[85] Much suggests that in fact there persisted within the western consciousness a sentiment that as Christians knew unity in the one body of Christ which was the universal *ecclesia*, so ideally they should know it also in one body politic, a universal *res publica*. If one reason why this did not find expression was the concrete reality of western political multiplicity, another was the impossibility of conceiving of any polity but the Roman empire as having a legitimate claim to universality yet the impossibility also of recognising in the empire as it actually existed the universal *res publica* of the western vision. This was a deadlock which could be broken only if the Roman empire were recast in a satisfactory western mould. The speed and strength with which the imperial idea came to be reasserted once western circumstances were propitious to such a recasting are themselves the strongest argument that it had never been banished but had simply lain dormant. Two things were necessary for its reinvigoration and realisation: first, the emergence of a western *Grossreich* providing the geopolitical realities by which it was naturally prompted and without which its entertainment would have been wholly utopian; second, the inclusion within this polity of Rome.

The importance of the latter cannot be overestimated. Back in the fifth century a combination of matters – most importantly, the popes' steadfast residence in the old capital, the absence of rival western apostolic sees, the inherent strength of papal ideology and the work of Leo the Great – had served to bring about a shift of emphasis in perceptions of Rome as westerners came to see there rather the city of St Peter and his heirs than that of Augustus and his. 'Rome, the see of Peter', sang a contemporary poet, '. . . holds with religion what may not be possessed by arms.'[86] Notwithstanding the great strains imposed upon western loyalties by some popes and the tenuousness of Rome's relationship with much of the west, the statement continued to hold good. As the barbarian peoples adopted orthodoxy, so too they came to share in a measure of veneration for St Peter, his vicar and his city. True, this was conspicuously lacking, despite Isidore, from the later Visigothic kingdom. But the Visigoths were put paid

85. John of Biclar, *Chron.* 590? 2, Gregory of Tours, *Hist.* IV.40, and Fredegar, *Chron.* IV.9, all use it of the Persian ruler, to whom it is also applied on its sole biblical appearance in Esther 3.2. I pass over Theoderic (above, p. 132 n. 28) and the late fifth-century Moorish potentate and self-styled *imperator* Masties, the extent of whose pretension is unknown; on him, Courtois 1964, pp. 337–9, 382 (inscription no. 132).

86. Prosper, *Carmen de Ingratis* 40–2 (*PL*, LI, 97): 'Sedes Roma Petri . . . quidquid non possidet armis, Relligione tenet.'

to by the Muslims, whose irruption into the west served also to strengthen there the sense of Christian unity, of which the pope was the natural focus. The concept of community is strikingly witnessed in a mid-eighth-century Spanish chronicler's designation of the troops who, under Charles Martel, defeated the Muslims at Poitiers in 732 as 'Europeans', seemingly a georeligious term, like the 'Europa' of which Charlemagne was to be called 'father' or 'head', and meaning 'Christian westerners'.[87] Precisely at this time Anglo-Saxon missionaries were active on the continent, where, exporting to those among whom they worked their own devotion to St Peter, they repaid with abundant interest the (somewhat meagre) capital invested in the conversion of England by Gregory I and some of his successors. The reverential attitude which they encouraged among the Franks was not the least of the several circumstances which at length brought the papacy, albeit with many a wistful backward glance, to abandon Constantinople and throw in its lot with the west, a decision upon which the final, momentous, seal was to be set in St Peter's on Christmas Day 800.

There remains an issue the thornier for the learned myths which thicket it about, that of 'Germanic political thought'. Two fundamental assumptions have determined the shape of much of the mountainous literature on this topic: first, that the Germans were possessed of a common and distinctive identity, manifest in a basic uniformity of attitudes, practices and so forth, that there existed a sort of Germanic analogue to *Romanitas*; second, that where unequivocal evidence of the amendment or abandonment of these *echtgermanisch* characteristics is lacking, they perdured, unchanged, over centuries. The use of sources scattered over a millennium and more in order to construct the image of a homogeneous *Germanentum*, the practice of filling gaps in knowledge of particular peoples by attributing to them supposedly *gemeingermanisch* concepts and institutions, the readiness to discover quintessential Germanic features lurking concealed in apparently innocent data – all depend upon these postulates, astonishingly tenacious of life. It is high time that they were consigned once and for all to the historiographical curiosity shop, to join other nineteenth-century relics. Germanic diversity is what comparative history suggests, common sense demands and the evidence demonstrates. There was change over time; the attractions and pressures of external exemplars and the necessity of

---

87. *MGH AA*, xi, 362: 'Europenses'.

adjustment as peoples expanded, migrated, absorbed others and so forth were only the most important reasons for that. There is the gravest methodological impropriety in lumping together the evidence of authors from Caesar to Ammianus Marcellinus, 450 years later, in order to create a collective picture, as if the Germanic world were somehow static, frozen in time; and it should be self-evident that what the *Life of Lebuin* tells us about the eighth-century continental Saxons, or the *Life of Anskar* about the ninth-century Danes, or even later sources about even later Saxons or Scandinavians permits few conclusions, if any, about these peoples' predecessors, and none whatsoever about the Germans *in toto*. For there was also diversity over space; indeed, since the forces making for change over time will never have been equally felt, we can be sure, even granting the notion of a uniform *Germanentum* in the very remotest past, that already by the time the Germans move mistily into our ken they were of heterogeneous composition.

The postulate of Germanic homogeneity would seem to rest partly on wishful thinking, partly on the perceived implication of the common name 'German', partly on the practice of Caesar, Tacitus and others in writing in apparently general terms of the *Germani*. As regards this last matter, we should not be misled; they no more offer true generalisations than does many a more recent author in writing of 'Africans' or North American 'Indians'. Caesar, whose brief observations appear in *The Gallic War* (VI.21ff), knew only the western periphery of Germania, and some whom he held to be Germans were not so on any criterion of definition save the geographical. Tacitus is more fruitful, despite tendentiousness; nevertheless 'Germans' in his celebrated *Germania* certainly does not mean all Germans and probably does not mean most. Indeed, Tacitus' works reveal with full clarity that the peoples of Germania were far from homogeneous, politically, socially, economically or religiously. His report (*Germ.* 2) that the *Germani* were divided into three geographical groupings, each named after and regarding as its founder a different grandson of a single deity, Tuisto, shows, if trustworthy, Germanic awareness of a common origin. But this does not imply a sense of unity, let alone homogeneity; Tuisto, remarkably, is otherwise unknown; and not all Germans fell into Tacitus' categories. Language apart, it is in fact extraordinarily difficult to establish any definitional features of the German. The name *Germani* itself was originally that of a single tribe; it was the Gauls who then employed it as a general designation for those across the Rhine. Tacitus' statement (*Germ.* 2) that the Germans then applied it to themselves is uncorroborated. Not only is hard evidence of Pan-Germanic sentiment wholly lacking but the Germans were frequently at each other's throats. To say all this is by no means to assert that the Germans of Caesar's day or of Tacitus' had no institutions or habits of mind in common; very probably, though quite undemonstrably, they had. But there is nothing distinctively Germanic about bloodfeud, kindredship and those other features likely to have been shared.

Mined the more assiduously for its sparseness, Caesar's and, particularly, Tacitus' evidence has constituted the basic building-material of numerous scholarly constructs of 'Germanic political thought', and this supposed body of ideas has been widely taken, thanks to the 'continuity' postulate, still to have ruled the Germans on their entry to the empire. Modern specialists, more alive to the limitations of this evidence and more willing to acknowledge variety and development, nevertheless often display a predilection towards generalisation or at least schematisation, especially in the categorisation of Germanic rulers,[88] with the frequent starting-point a problematical Tacitean statement that the Germans 'take kings for their nobility, war-leaders for their prowess'.[89] The fact is that this and the other early evidence, of limited value for its own day, is of none at all for the period of barbarian take-over of the west, later by several murky centuries of upheaval, movement and exposure to Roman influence, and that we are deeply ignorant of political organisation, institutions and thinking among the pre-entry Germans. Even of the fourth-century Visigoths, about whom we are best informed,[90] that is true. The material cannot be examined here but in the writer's judgement, for all the perspicacity shown by scholars in its investigation, does not yield legitimate and significant conclusions as to the character of political thought within any people, let alone suggest the existence of a stock of common or at least characteristic political concepts.

What are these concepts supposed to have been? Judgements have varied enormously, but most scholars over the years have maintained their essentially populist character. At the heart of the populist thesis lies the notion that ultimate authority resided in the people and that royal power was therefore limited. Characteristically, the king has been alleged to have been subject to the law and to the will of the popular assembly; were he to overstep the bounds of the powers conferred upon him or otherwise prove unjust or incapable, he might legitimately be resisted. While election or at least acclamation has normally been regarded as making him king, many

---

88. E.g., Schlesinger 1956.   89. *Germ.* 7: 'Reges ex nobilitate, duces ex virtute sumunt.'
90. See Thompson 1966, Claude 1971, ch. 2.

scholars have emphasised the importance of legitimism; in their view election meant the singling out of a particular individual belonging to a ruling dynasty, a *stirps regia*, whose members were exclusively but equally possessed of a right to be considered. Closely associated with the thesis of blood-right has been that of sacrality, still much in vogue. Discussion of this is made none the easier by the different senses in which the term is used, sometimes by the same author, but is is fair to say that most of its exponents consider the sacral king to have been a ruler who, in pagan-German eyes, partook in some way of the divine essence, usually through descent from a god.

Only the most cursory of observations upon these viewpoints are possible here. As regards populism, Tacitus offers explicit evidence of limited kingship – if also of royal absolutism.[91] But there is no trace of the currency of populist ideas in the western kingdoms (though it must be said that many have thought otherwise). None of the *regna* yields evidence of constitutional, as opposed to moral or practical, restrictions upon the king's exercise of his rule. Neither the authoritative Tacitean folk-assembly nor any other sort of gathering possessing jurisdictional or governmental powers independent of the royal will is witnessed. Certainly kings called councils. But the purpose of these was to air matters of general significance, gain advice, win consent, endow deeds or decisions with greater solemnity, and so forth. Absolutists more accomplished and secure by far than the kings of this period have recognised the value of such consultative and confirmative exercises, reflective of political utility not constitutional necessity. The occasional association of subjects in the publication of law was a similarly pragmatic device; this law was no less the king's (see p. 139). As for the famed Germanic right of resistance, this is a fiction. Indubitably, resistance, which was frequent, was sometimes grounded in a principled conviction that the king was failing to act as a true ruler should; a classic case in point is provided by the Ostrogoths' abandonment of Theodahad in 536. But a recent exhaustive study reveals but a single text, concerning the pre-Christian Burgundians (see pp. 151–2), which suggests the justification of resistance in terms of an objective legal order.[92]

If populist notions were indeed current among the pre-entry Germans, it is not difficult to account for their disappearance. Which of the barbarian leaders could have failed to feel a quickening of the monarchical pulse in face of the resplendent and comprehensive authority marking the Roman

91. Compare *Germ.* 7 and 11 with 44 (and cf. 42 and 43).
92. Bund 1979 (an admirable work), esp. pp. 132–8, 143, 787ff.

emperor and to be drawn towards his emulation? As for their followers, the dissolvent effect upon traditional attitudes of the upheavals of migration and settlement, the shifting composition of the *gentes*, the necessary reliance in sink-or-swim times upon strength and singleness of command, and Roman influence, including respect for regality, must all be borne in mind. Further, and crucially, there was Christianity, offering the most powerful support for what Walter Ullmann was fond of calling a 'descending' ideology of government.[93] For whatever reasons particular groupings of Germans may have adopted Christianity, once adopted it exposed them to assumptions and injunctions about rulership which contrasted starkly with populist ideas and had behind them, moreover, divine sanction. It is not to make irreligious *politiques* of the barbarian kings to believe them the readier to lead their peoples to Christianity precisely because its teaching on government accorded so satisfyingly with their own monarchical yearnings.

It would be both foolhardy and impractical to grapple here with the subject of king-making in the *regna*, complex enough to swallow a large tome. Let it simply be said that the picture is one of remarkable diversity, both within and between kingdoms, and that there is no case for the notion that election from within the ranks of a *stirps regia* was customary.[94] Nor, it may be added, does the pre-entry material sustain that idea, the origin of which, one suspects, lies in nothing more compelling than Tacitus' already cited observation that the Germans 'take kings for their nobility', with 'take' read as 'elect' and *nobilitas* interpreted to mean 'membership of the *stirps regia*'. Election itself is unwitnessed in certain of the kingdoms. The notion, finally, that the Germans brought with them to the *regna*, and in some measure maintained, a pagan-sacral conception of kingship lacks convincing evidentiary support.[95] Neither Caesar nor Tacitus so much as hints at the existence of such a conception, and the earliest citable testimony is Ammianus' statement that the (late fourth-century) Burgundian king 'by ancient custom, having laid down his power, is removed if under him the fortune of war has faltered or the earth denied a full harvest'.[96] There is certainly no case for seeing physical sacrifice here, as some have maintained. Nor, however, need the Burgundian practice attest a belief that the king

93. See, e.g., Ullmann 1978, pp. 20ff.
94. Grierson 1941 shows this for the Lombards, Visigoths and Ostrogoths, and the Burgundian, Frankish and Vandal evidence yields the same picture. I have not scrutinised the Anglo-Saxon material.
95. Wallace-Hadrill 1971, pp. 8ff, himself supporting, surveys much of the evidence. For literature, Bund 1979, pp. 146–7.
96. *Rer. Gest.* XXVIII.5.14 (Loeb, p. 168): 'ritu veteri potestate deposita removetur, si sub eo fortuna titubaverit belli, vel segetum copiam negaverit terra'.

possessed a sacral, or magical, quality which worldly misfortune proved he had lost; viewed without sacralist preconceptions, it seems simply to reflect the commonplace notion that earthly calamity flowed from divine displeasure and to represent an attempt at propitiation by requiring the king, whether as scapegoat or as offender, to abdicate. Since 'ancient custom' was involved, we may reasonably think that a true *right* of resistance existed in the event of refusal.

As regards the Ostrogoths, Jordanes reports that in the first century a great (and imaginary) victory against the Romans had led the Goths to acclaim the leaders 'by whose *fortuna*, as it were, they conquered, not mere men but demigods, that is Anses'.[97] These leaders were the forefathers of the Amals – Theodoric's house – and Jordanes names as first of the line Gapt, whom scholars often identify with Gaut, the deity. But before the mid-fourth century just one of Gapt's alleged descendants appears among the several Gothic rulers known;[98] moreover, the Visigoths, a separate grouping only from the third century, held the Amals in no particular regard. These circumstances are hardly reconcilable with a Gothic conviction that the Amals partook in divinity through their blood – a conviction in fact witnessed neither in Jordanes nor elsewhere but simply assumed. That the Anglo-Saxons saw their kings as having something god-like in them by virtue of their claimed descent from Woden – whom there are actually good grounds to think a mortal, subsequently deified[99] – is similarly an unsupported assumption. For the Franks, it is alleged that the Merovingians' long hair was symbolic of their sacrality – that it even, so to speak, *contained* that sacrality; in fact, nothing argues it to have been other than a badge of legitimism, 'a kind of recognition mark and special privilege', as Agathias put it.[100] Legitimism does not imply sacrality; blood carries its own charisma, claims its own loyalty. Again, the Frankish association of healing powers with Guntram supposedly betrays belief in his pagan-sacral nature; but Gregory of Tours, our source, himself accepts the genuineness of the powers, which he sets within the context of the king's Christian holiness (*Hist.* IX.21). Fredegar's cock-and-bull story – the phrase is peculiarly apt – that some considered Merovech, Clovis' grandfather, the

---

97. *Getica* 78: 'proceres suos, quorum quasi fortuna vincebant, non puros homines, sed semideos id est Ansis vocaverunt'.   98. Grierson 1941, p. 5.

99. See Kenneth Harrison, 'Woden', in Gerald Bonner, ed., *Famulus Christi*, Society for the Promotion of Christian Knowledge, 1976, pp. 351–6, and note particularly Bede, *Hist.* I.15, Paul the Deacon, *Hist.* I.8–9, and Æthelweard, cit. Chaney 1970, p. 39. Scandinavian evidence suggests Woden to have been a late, imported, addition to the pantheon.

100. *Hist.* I.3 (transl. by Averil Cameron in *Annali della Scuola Normale Superiore di Pisa* 37 (1968), 106).

offspring of a sea-beast seems etymologically inspired.[101] The Lombard evidence, derisorily thin, can be passed over, and neither the Vandal kingdom nor, despite its extensive source-material, the Visigothic offers grist for the mill. Much more could be said, especially in connection with the conversion to Christianity, on the question of Germanic sacral rulership, but there it must be left.[102]

101. *Chron.*, III.9. See Graus 1965, pp. 319–20.
102. It ought to be said, however, that to deny a Germanic conception of sacral rulership is not, of course, pace Höfler 1956, p. 75, to deny Germanic religiosity.

IV
FORMATION: c. 750–c. 1150

8
INTRODUCTION: THE FORMATION OF POLITICAL THOUGHT IN THE WEST

Western Europe during the four centuries that precede the establishment of the Carolingian monarchy in 751 saw the conversion to Catholic Christianity of the barbarian successor kingdoms within the limits of the western empire and their progressive withdrawal from Byzantium's sphere of influence. Within a short period of about fifty years the Carolingian Franks became masters of all western Christendom excluding the British Isles. With the imperial coronation of Charlemagne in Rome in 800 and with the experience of personal rule on an apparently universal scale the barbarian phase of European history reaches its zenith.

The empire of Charlemagne, the 'father of Europe', did not retain its fullest size or its unity for long but it left an enduring memory to the later generations. Its lands were divided in 843 among different members of the Carolingian dynasty although one of the family always carried an imperial title until 924. The ninth century experienced the irruption into northwestern Europe of the pagan Vikings, while central Europe became destabilised following invasions by the Magyars until the battle of Lechfeld in 955. The collapse of the Carolingian state in west Francia made way for regional or territorial principalities whose rulers around 900 attempted to exercise the functions nominally still belonging to the Carolingian king. When the last such king died in 987, and Hugh Capet secured election to the throne, there was no hint that the Capetian house would ever come to rule on more than a small local scale. In the tenth century, as the west Frankish provinces disintegrated, effective rulership passed often to individual castle lords governing a few square kilometres with the aid of some knights. By contrast, among the east Franks in the tenth and eleventh centuries a succession of strong Saxon and Salian kings controlled the duchies which constituted the German kingdom, dominated the Slavs and Hungarians, and entered into Italian politics. All of them were crowned as emperors after 962. England too became a united kingdom in the tenth century under the most centralised government to be found in the west at the time.

Europe under the last Carolingians, and afterwards too, presents a picture of contrasts. On the one hand large unitary kingdoms were liable to collapse rapidly into a multiplicity of purely local units of rule, while on the other segmentary states might succumb to the rule of an expanding neighbour and form part of an enlarged power bloc. The twentieth-century inclination to view large-scale feudal monarchies as instruments of progress in the Middle Ages, and to question private rights and other obstacles to the development of sovereignty, should be kept in check. Small-scale, virtually independent lordships were not anarchic if they supplied a need for government when monarchy was ineffective or absent. Dispersed authorities, be they bishops or manorial lords, were to most of their subjects the only power that mattered most of the time. We must be cautious of imposing our ideas of what is a normal unit of government on societies that still only vaguely suggested the outlines of a later system of national kingdoms. Strong centralising monarchs such as Henry IV of Germany or Barbarossa or the Anglo-Norman kings of England were viewed by many as subversive tyrants.

By the twelfth century many parts of Europe were experiencing a revival of the arts of government. This did not everywhere result in the strengthening of monarchy. In north Italy urban communes broke up the old kingdom of Lombardy by resisting the claims of the German kings to wear the Lombard crown and by establishing their own city-states. But in the Anglo-Norman world from 1066 to 1135 vigorous king-dukes created remarkable wealth for their loyal supporters and entrusted the administration of justice and finance to professional officials wholly subordinate to themselves. The same is true of the contemporary Norman rulers of Sicily and south Italy who created a new kingdom out of their conquests in 1130. In France King Louis VI (1108–37), although he did not often impose his will outside his personal demesne, at least established secure control of a large area centred on Paris which provided a firm basis for the wider government sought by his Capetian successors. Yet there continued to be dramatic failures. The kingdom of the Germans was racked by revolts and civil war between 1076 and 1152. When Count Charles the Good was assassinated in 1127 Flanders was suddenly reduced to anarchy. The Anglo-Norman realm was disunited and disordered from 1135 to 1153 following the disputed royal succession of Stephen.

Nonetheless western Europe by the middle of the twelfth century had expanded and was changing fast. Within its boundaries areas that were traditionally thinly peopled were now being newly colonised. For centuries Franks had emigrated to Spain as Muslim power receded. In the twelfth century the emigration of Flemings and others eastwards to the southern coasts of the Baltic Sea appears to have been considerable in scale. Flanders, the Rhineland and north Italy became urbanised and industrialised to a degree barely imaginable even in the middle of the eleventh century. By the mid-twelfth century therefore Latin Christians were found beyond the furthest limits reached by Carolingian arms; they had established new colonies and kingdoms in lands long subject to other non-Christian regimes. Muslim Spain had largely fallen to Frankish conquerors. The western islands of the Mediterranean had all been wrested back from the Saracens. Italian, Catalan and Provençal seamen traded profitably in the ports of Africa, the Levant and the Aegean Sea. The Crusades resulted in the creation and maintenance of the Latin kingdom of Jerusalem. Scandinavia had begun to enter the orbit of Latin Christendom. German and Flemish merchants had acquired a commercial and naval supremacy throughout much of the Baltic world. The kingdoms of Hungary, Bohemia and Poland had all come into being and looked to papal Rome rather than to Constantinople. Scotland, Wales and Ireland, as well as England after 1066, were increasingly linked with Continental Europe. An impression of cultural and religious unity throughout the west can plausibly be entertained. Scholars still looked to the legacy of ancient thought and learning but they had learned to formulate distinctive answers to questions about political principles and their reasonings found an audience, including both supporters and critics, across the length and breadth of Europe.

Feudalism

So many changes took place in western society during these four centuries that no single term such as feudalism or feudal government suffices to characterise the bonds of society or the nature of rulership. The attempt to define feudal government carries with it the risk of simplification, but without at least a provisional description the meaning of the terminology associated with feudalism cannot be discussed further. Feudal government is the exercise of power by kings or lords with the support of a military class (*comitatus*) of horse-borne knights who were bound to their lords, as these might be to the king, by oaths of fealty in permanent vassalage, and who were economically sustained by serfs who constituted an unfree, largely agricultural, working class. Feudalism is merely a highly general and abstract label of convenience, and it has often been remarked that, like the term Middle Ages, it was only invented after the medieval period had ended and did not exist in anyone's mind at the time itself. Nonetheless, when every qualification has been made as to the many varieties of contractual dependence that were evolved and also as to the ambiguous and variable vocabulary that was used to describe it, fealty and vassalage were important and typical features of many relationships between men of power in this period.

Vassalage is the tie that binds a warrior to a lord when the former, the vassal, does homage and swears an oath of fealty to the latter. Vassalage basically was meant to be a mutual and life-long bond between a lord and his man. The Carolingian Franks gave vassalage considerable importance by using vassals to create a large army of warriors and to attach leading men to the king. Enduring personal loyalty (*commendatio*) of a warrior to his lord is the central feature of vassalage. Only when the vassal is rewarded with a grant (*beneficium*) of lands known as a fee or fief does such vassalage become feudal vassalage. The fief, however, is usually only granted on account of the service due from the vassal (*servitium debitum*). Later in the Middle Ages fiefs often took the form of money – money fiefs – or other kinds of reward, although tenurial feudalism remained the prevalent form. Vassals themselves were able to create their own vassals by the same means, so chain relationships developed (e.g. suzerain – vassals or tenants-in-chief – rear-vassals or sub-tenants).

The key element in the relationship between unequal holders of power in a vassalic situation was, then, the oath of personal allegiance. This was a sworn contract obliging both vassal and lord to be mutually faithful. In many situations the link cemented existing bonds of kinship. The obligations created thereby were permanent but nonetheless conditional; resistance was legitimate if fidelity was breached (*diffidatio*) by one of the parties. Feudal courts might be convened to adjudge a dispute between a lord and his vassal. A famous example is the court of nobles held at Worms in 1179 where the charges made by the Emperor Frederick Barbarossa against his subject Henry the Lion, Duke of Saxony, were examined. As a result of failure to appear before the court, Henry was convicted of contumacy and in 1180 deprived of his duchy. Another example is the summons issued to King John of England in 1202 to appear at Paris before the court of King Philip II to answer complaints presented to Philip by the Lusignan family. John, having failed to answer the summons, was adjudged contumacious. Philip thereupon 'defied' his vassal as a traitor and proceeded by force to remove Normandy from John.

The role of the overlord in the feudal system was variable. He might be merely a suzerain, as were the earliest Capetian kings of France. To these the holders of the greatest fiefs theoretically owed homage, but they had their own vassals in whose affairs and disputes the suzerain was unable, and was not expected, to intervene. The overlord might, however, also acquire sovereignty as William I revealed when, at Salisbury in 1086, he received oaths of fealty to himself not only from his tenants-in-chief, who held their lands directly of the Crown, but also from their vassals, who thereby recognised their own accountability to the king. The steps of the feudal ladder leading up from the humblest feudatory to the king at the apex were in practice seldom complete; even without a king vassals might be created and changes of allegiance could also alter the scope of rulership. Much of the fluidity of medieval society at the time of the Spanish Reconquest, of the Norman Conquests of England and of Sicily, and of the Crusades reflects the willingness of men to create new vassalic systems for their own local or immediate needs. The vassalage system thereby lent itself as easily to the development of monarchy as to the development of the petty sovereignties of remote provincial rulers.

Nobility and community

A vassal was a freeman; he was not a serf but a noble, however insignificant his degree of nobility. But what constituted nobility and what qualities were required to obtain or to exercise lordship? The origins and attributes of the medieval nobility in the Carolingian period and after are still much debated, largely because of the difficulty of constructing genealogies and thereby defining the noble class. The importance of blood, of distinguished ancestors, was everywhere recognised, but it is difficult to establish to what extent nobility, after the collapse of Carolingian power, remained essentially the prerogative of the older-established families, and to what extent a new nobility fought its way to preeminence in disturbed conditions. For example, the role of the Norman or Northman element in the rise of the duchy of Normandy is not at all clear. This question of the nature of nobility is of some importance in understanding the perceived basis of lordship in this period. Violence was sometimes so endemic that dynastic continuities were not maintained. The peace movements that appear from the late tenth century onwards in many parts of the Continent took the form not only of brotherhoods of fighting men who agreed to restrict warfare among themselves, but also of new associations, for example of townsmen, which lay at the basis of new kinds of collective lordship. These peace movements also underlay the attempts made by churchmen and others to define anew the conditions under which Christian nobles and knights might justly engage in warfare, e.g. on crusades.

Medieval societies rested therefore largely on a diffuse network of agreements between privileged individuals within groups. Such agreements to provide mutual aid and protection reflected changing circumstances and tended to be based on oaths binding in the sight of God. Roman law ignored oaths, but they became in medieval times the ordinary basis of many kinds of association and contract. Kings made a profession on coming to the throne. Alliances, contracts, treaties, guilds, judicial ordeals were also formalised with oath-takings. The associations of peace were constituted by collective oaths. Such sworn confederations could seem dangerous, for *conjuratio* might be close to *conspiratio*. Rulers sought to control or to prevent them. They underlay protest movements, both urban and rural, and they lay too at the basis of communes or corporations which were founded to provide collective self-government in towns, especially in France and northern Italy. At the folk level too the rural community of neighbours was to some degree collectively organised for the use of arable fields, woods and pastures. The regulation of agricultural and pastoral life was not simply imposed on unfree serfs by powerful manorial lords; it required some consent and co-operation, admitted of much variation and witnessed increasingly the granting of 'liberties' to village communes. Urban communes were not a complete novelty in the eleventh century; already in the tenth some settlements, though small, had urban features and distinctive laws and customs agreed by local assemblies which administered common funds and regulated common privileges. Representation occurred through leading men or through a guild. More formal and more complete municipal self-government followed from the eleventh century as towns became larger and wealthier. Towns were not the only custodians of communal values, but rather the developers of such values. The occasional insurrectionary outbreak of republicanism does not obscure the deeply rooted sense of communal responsibility even in a society ruled by lords. Relationships in societies were thus not always 'vertical', i.e. personal and feudal relationships between lords and subjects. Many relationships were 'horizontal' and collective and such relationships did not all arise from reactions against seignorial oppression. There was never any rush out of serfdom, although periodically the legal status of the serf was exchanged for that of personal independence and periodically serfs might be released from their tie to the soil and enter town life. Urban communes may seem the antithesis of rustic feudalism but they also reflect older forms of sworn associations among groups which included feudal lords, their clans and their followers.[1]

Associationist tendencies constitute a powerful current of thought even when the personal prerogatives and responsibilities of individual rulers were loudly proclaimed. How medieval communities came into being after the barbarian invasions may be as mysterious as the formation of the galaxies but at the start of the Middle Ages such communities were defined by common descent, custom and language or at least dialect. The identity of communities was more often explained in historical terms than in territorial or governmental terms. Descent myths traced the origins and progress of different peoples (*gentes, populi, nationes*) from Noah or from Troy or Scandinavia. Such origin stories were very general from the sixth century onwards and outlived the Middle Ages. They reflect the wish of different peoples to find honourable beginnings for themselves and also to make sense of history by using the only historical records of earlier peoples they had. Such stories assumed that peoples were biologically united, on-going communities; they thereby reinforced a sense of national or tribal solidarity. From the tenth century they gained an enhanced importance because then the solidarities of supposed common descent and custom came to coincide more closely with the solidarities of kingdoms; they were not weakened by the advances of centralised law and jurisdiction.

Kingship and law

Kingship rested on the consent of a king's subjects. There could be no succession to kingship, even in the context of usurped rule, without some recognition of the king's fitness to rule or an election by parts of the community or the making of promises to uphold law and custom. In general any important exercise of government involved consultation. The king was subject to the authority of law and custom, and the dependence of custom on the community that adhered to it meant that government was contractual and collective, at least implicitly, and representative too, because consultation and consent were frequently required long before theories of representation were articulated. A king who acted tyrannically or a king who was negligent or ineffective could find his authority questioned. Horizontal relationships and collective processes of deliberation

---

1. Michaud-Quantin 1970, pp. 233–45; also 129–33.

have an importance therefore that should qualify the concomitant importance of the vertical relationship of kingship, lordship and subjection.

The responsibility of a ruler to provide laws was a variable aspect of his duty to uphold the received laws and customs of his people. The wide ranging Carolingian capitularies represented an extreme of hopeful reform promulgated by the king with the consent of assemblies. The law-giving traditions of the Anglo-Saxon kings were also exceptional. Continental rulers usually lacked the advisers to frame much new law as well as officials to apply it effectively at a local level. Custom, therefore – unwritten law – was highly important, as were *ad hoc* judgements or particular privileges; law might be announced or changed in a charter or in a letter of purely local or individual importance. A revival of law making occurs in the twelfth century. The first Capetian *ordonnances* applying to the whole of the kingdom of France appear under Louis VI. Roger II of Sicily issued assizes for all his kingdom in 1140. The number of decretal letters sent by successive popes to all parts of Christendom grew by leaps and bounds during the twelfth century and caused collectors of decretals to gather such as announced significant points of law into compilations for the benefit of students of the developing canon law. After the mid-twelfth century decretalist scholars take over from the decretists such as Ivo of Chartres and Gratian of Bologna who had monumentally assembled the earlier canonical materials. Such new papal law was often the adaptation of the old canons to changing circumstance. However, law was often presented as a new commitment to writing of previously unwritten customs; Henry II of England issued the Constitutions of Clarendon (1164) in this way and thereby highlights an important shift in the outlook of government in his time from the use of memory to the written record. The change was more than merely technological as it reflects the growing recognition by governments of the uses of literacy. Clerks educated in the schools of theology and law and experienced in princely or episcopal service were anxious, especially in the twelfth century, to develop formal and consistent procedures in the workings of the law. In Carolingian times too learned men, the products of the teaching of Alcuin and his colleagues, had been the authors of capitularies. These enactments have a strongly religious and moral content as do the didactic writings of the churchmen who were dominant in Carolingian politics. A measure of change is, however, provided by the mention of the treatises produced in or for the English royal court in the early twelfth century. The authors of the *Leges Henrici primi* and the *Constitutio domus regis*, like their successors who prepared the

Dialogus de scaccario and the common law treatise known as Glanvill, provided manuals for professional lawyers and bureaucrats; they go beyond the task not only of edification but also of reliance on custom, practice and memory.

Empire

Kingship was throughout the period an important focus of loyalty, but the nature of the kingdoms over which kings ruled varied considerably, as did the vocabulary which was used to denote them. Bede had described the English people as a single *gens* speaking a common language but divided into separate kingdoms such as those of Mercia and Northumbria; the work of unification was to be slow but enduring. However, the kingdom of the Franks included many peoples – Bretons, for example – who did not consider themselves to be Franks. When kings acquired control over neighbouring peoples or neighbouring kingdoms they tended to be acclaimed as emperors on account of their supra-national hegemony. The Frankish empire in the ninth century rested on this fact; emperorship was by no means always necessarily viewed in Roman or in universal terms, but frequently as rulership over many different peoples. The kings of León from the tenth century onwards were called emperors on account of their achievements in uniting Christian Spain against the Moors, and the Anglo-Saxon kings who exercised sway over all Britain were also entitled *imperator*, *basileus* and *casere*. For them emperorship was a prestigious, honorific, supra-national reinforcement of their kingship. But the memory of the empire of ancient Rome could also be readily invoked. The *Carmen de Hastingae praelio* hails the victory of William the Conqueror – 'Iulius' – over Harold as a repetition of Caesar's invasion and conquest of Britain. The city of Pisa, when flushed with success in clearing the Tyrrhenian sea of rival shipping and in achieving naval and commercial dominance in many parts of the twelfth-century Mediterranean, naturally proclaimed its compara-bility with ancient Rome. Claims to wield the legitimate imperial authority that was claimed by Byzantium were made by the Carolingian emperors and their German successors in the west, who tended to imitate Byzantine emperorship. Near the opening of this period there was a renewal or restoration of the idea of the Christian Roman empire of Constantine under Charles the Great (*renovatio imperii romani*), and the ideology of Roman imperial restoration and renovation continues to find champions on many subsequent occasions in the northern and Frankish world. One of the younger poets at Charlemagne's court, Modoin or Muaduuinus who was nicknamed Naso (Ovid) had proclaimed the resurrection of ancient Rome in an oft-quoted line: 'Golden Rome renewed is once more reborn to the world' ('Aurea Roma iterum renovata renascitur orbi'). The mirage of the *renovatio imperii romani* reinforced the unity and the distinctiveness of the Latin west in and after the ninth century. In a famous letter written in 865 Pope Nicholas I questioned the right of the Byzantines to have a Roman Caesar who no longer spoke Latin but Greek and who was no longer the ruler of Rome itself. This imperial renewal was repeated after 962, but now with less impact among the western Franks, under Saxon and then Salian emperors. In 962 Otto I of Germany inaugurated, by his imperial coronation in Rome, a second *renovatio imperii* and headed a series of emperors in the west that was uninterrupted until the death of Frederick II in 1250. As Gerbert of Aurillac proclaimed in 997 to Otto III: 'The Roman empire is ours; it is ours!'; the empire properly belonged to the actual ruler of Rome, not to the Greek *basileus* in Constantinople. The period ends with a further great renewal of Roman imperial ideals following the accession of the Staufen family to the Crowns of Germany, Lombardy and Rome. The Staufen emperors expected other national kingdoms to acknowledge their superior authority. However, the movement towards the unity of a universal empire was more than balanced by movements towards the separation and division of independent states or kingdoms.

Priestly kingship

The Carolingian empire constituted an example of a state in which Catholic Christianity was a compulsory religion. Among the principal tasks of a Carolingian monarch were the convening of church councils, the nomination of bishops, the maintenance of clerical discipline and public morality, and the promulgation of sound religious doctrine. Carolingian monarchy was theocratic; it intervened extensively in church affairs. Throughout the Carolingian kingdom many churches were the property of lords, established by them and served by their clerical nominees. Out of this situation developed a practice which has come to be called *lay investiture* – the conferment by a lay patron of a benefice on a cleric. The most famous case is the conferment of the papacy by German kings on their nominees from 963 (the *Ottonianum*) to 1059. On the other hand all kings owed something to the church. The Carolingians owed their royal title to papal recognition, and they and other monarchies depended heavily upon the practical support given them by the bishops and abbots. Royal and secular patronage over the church continued in the post-Carolingian world to be a powerful instrument of government.

The ecclesiastical complexion of kingship is developed to the fullest in this period. With the anointing of Pepin as King at Soissons in 751, and again at St Denis along with his sons Carloman and Charles in 754, the old magical power of the long hair of the former Merovingian kings was replaced by a sacrament whereby the Carolingian kings became *Christi*. The Carolingian image of kingship was shaped by the Old Testament models of holy kings such as David and Solomon or Melchizedek who was both king and priest. Otto I's imperial crown publicly displayed his authority as king and as high priest; it was both a royal crown and a bishop's mitre. He was at once *rex et sacerdos*, like Melchizedek and also like Christ. By the tenth century both in Germany and in France a king entered upon his office and fulfilled his duties by means of rites that were very similar to those used for the making of bishops. Kingship became the *typus Christi* and imitated priesthood as well as imitating antiquity and Byzantium. Kings became canons of cathedrals and abbots of monasteries and not in a merely titular way. To the question whether the king was a layman or a cleric the answer often was that he was a cleric.

The old principle, laid down by Pope Gelasius I in his famous letter to the emperor Anastasius in 494, that there are two powers by which the world is ruled, the sacred authority (*auctoritas sacrata*) of pontiffs and the power (*potestas*) of kings, remained important. Both spiritual and temporal rulers derive their function from God. But the two kinds of rule now increasingly overlapped, so much so that considerable debate is found on the nature of the differences between them.

Hierocracy

At the same time as Carolingian kingship acquired a greater ecclesiastical role, and as the king appeared more and more to be an ecclesiastical person, voices were raised on behalf of the Frankish bishops who asserted that kingship was an office within the church, accountable to the priesthood. The removal from office of the emperor Louis the Pious at Compiègne in 833 provided an opportunity to develop such themes. Whatever the effective reasons and causes underlying Louis' deposition, bishops were predominant in the assembly at Compiègne. They represented their role as penitential: Louis' power had been wrested from him by God because of his incapacity and the bishops now had to impose public penance.

Pope Stephen II's anointing of Pepin as the first Carolingian king of the

Franks in 754, Pope Leo III's coronation of Charlemagne as emperor, and subsequent imperial and royal coronations encouraged the idea that emperorship and kingship should be exercised by apostolic favour. Roman ideas of papal primacy and magistracy over the whole church found powerful exponents in the ninth century. Among them were in particular Anastasius the papal librarian, c. 860 and Pope Nicholas I (858–67).

When in the eleventh century the reforming popes from Leo IX onwards set about the work of eliminating the practice of simony – simony being the inclusion within the grant of an ecclesiastical office of a temporal or material obligation to the patron – they were confident of the rightness of their claims to primacy over all the bishops and to dominion over all secular powers. The growth of papal government resulted in a series of notable universal councils (Lateran Councils I–IV, 1123–1215) which displayed papal supremacy over the whole Latin church. The papal curia became a much used supreme court of appeal. The development of the canon law served to differentiate the clerical order from the laity since it was the law applied by the clergy to spiritual affairs.

The first time a pope was to depose a king was when Pope Gregory VII on 7 March 1080 excommunicated and deposed Henry IV. The doctrine on which he based his action had been slowly built up in earlier centuries: kings and emperors were members of the church; their first duty was to provide for the spiritual needs of themselves and their subjects; it was the responsibility of bishops and especially of the successor of St Peter to judge the spiritual fitness of the souls committed to their charge. In his second letter to Hermann, bishop of Metz, Gregory VII argued that the emperor occupies within the church a place lower than that occupied even by the lowest of the orders of clergy, that of exorcist.

Just as kings had increasingly appeared to be quasi-pontifical and quasi-sacerdotal figures so too bishops, abbots and popes appeared to imitate and to possess the features and functions of temporal rulers. Priesthood imitated kingship, and the papacy imitated empire, as much as kingship and empire imitated priesthood. The *ecclesia* was itself a *res publica*, a spiritual counterpart to a secular *res publica*, the imitation of the heavenly kingdom on earth, a house of God with many parts and ruled by many different ranks, a hierarchy modelled on the celestial ranks of angels who are equal by nature but differentiated according to their office. The kingship, even the emperorship, of Christ was emphasised. The Virgin Mary was regarded as a queen or empress. The model of imperial Rome under the Christian Emperor Constantine was used by the Roman papacy to the point where in the eleventh century the *pontifex Romanus* or Roman pontiff was represented as a Caesar and the College of Cardinals was remodelled after the ancient Senate. Nor was this a merely metaphorical resurrection of archaic attributes. The forged *Donation of Constantine* had ostensibly endowed the papacy with empire in the west. Especially in the eleventh century the papal court began to acquire the features of a *palatium* or palace and a *curia* or court such as a secular ruler might have; officials such as a chamberlain, institutions such as a *militia* and vassalage, features such as banners appeared in the papal court as they did in courts of other kinds. Papal ceremonial, e.g. for papal coronations, developed fast in the late eleventh century. Proposition 8 of the *Dictatus papae* of Pope Gregory VII (1075) asserted the exclusive right of the pope to use the imperial *insignia*. A Lateran inscription of 1125 proclaimed the pope to be *regalis sacerdos* and *imperialis episcopus* – a royal priest and an imperial bishop. He was able to send crowns to those whom he honoured with royal titles and to depose emperors (*Dictatus papae*, 12).

The sources and the character of political thought to the twelfth century

Throughout this period political philosophy was recognised as one of the disciplines of study. Although Aristotle's *Politics* was not available, his division of philosophy into theoretical and practical branches and his division of practical philosophy into three disciplines, ethics, economics and politics, were known through Boethius, *In Porphyrium dialogi*, i.iii, Isidore, *Etymologiae*, ii.xxiv.16, and Cassiodorus, *Institutiones*, ii.iii.7. Politics was defined as the study of the government of republics or as public, civil science.[2] But this science was not given any time in curricula of teaching, no doubt because throughout the period the necessary text books or authorities – Plato's *Republic*, Cicero's *Republic*, Aristotle's *Politics* – were not available to attract commentators.

For the most part the political ideas of this period have to be recovered from theological treatises, from sermons and biblical commentaries, from official decrees and capitularies, and from public correspondence. Much also is conveyed in feudal custom and in the symbolism and formulae of coronation and liturgical rituals, in official titles, in the iconography of art and architecture, in seals, bulls and crowns. That is true for other periods of medieval history as well. However, the most important sources of political

2. See, for example, the texts printed by Grabmann 1911, vol. ii, pp. 37 and 45 n. 1. Also Hugh of St Victor, *Didascalicon*, ii.xix.

thought were those already well known in the previous period – the Old
Testament and the New Testament above all, Roman law before Justinian's
codification (Justinian's *Corpus* was only studied in the west from the late
eleventh century although the Emperor Henry II left a copy of the *Corpus*
which is now in Bamberg) and the writings of the Fathers, especially
Ambrose, Augustine and Gregory. In addition there already existed a body
of writings devoted to the duties of the clergy and the bishops, including
particularly Pope Gregory the Great's *Regula pastoralis*. Nonetheless after
750 there do appear writers who are prepared to use these given materials
and sources to write expressly and for the first time about the nature of
kingship and laity. The genre of 'mirrors of princes' literature was born.
Such specialised writings are particularly numerous in the Carolingian
renaissance of the ninth century and during the church reform and the new
renaissance which began in the mid-eleventh century and continued into
the twelfth. Finally in 1159 John of Salisbury completed his highly
influential *Policraticus* or *Statesman's Book*.

The appearance of formal works of political thought – and these writings
were political in the context of their day – justifies the description of this
period as one of formation, formation, that is, of a medieval tradition of
exposition and of debate over the nature of government, church and
society. If most such works do not warrant being called works of political
philosophy, the political theology and the ecclesiology they contain are
nonetheless contributions to thought about the government of society as it
then was and as it might be. We see the preoccupations of the earliest
thinkers, all clerics, in some of the titles of their works: the *Via regia* or *The
Royal Way* of Smaragdus (813), the *Institutio laicalis* and *Institutio regia* or
The Lay and *The Royal Institution* of Jonas of Orleans (818 and 831/4), the
letters of Agobard of Lyons, the *De regis persona* or *The Person of the King* and
the *De ordine palatii* or *The Ordering of the Palace* (882) of Hincmar of
Rheims, the *De rectoribus christianis* or *Christian Rulers* of Sedulius Scottus.
Such works do not contain coherent and systematic political philosophy.
Their authors largely provide admonishments to kings to be just and
dutiful. But these authors were also keenly interested in many practical
matters which are the concerns of the political theorist – the source and
nature of authority and law, the relationship of kingship to law, the
relationship of pope and bishops to the secular prince. There are only
fragments of speculation, all borrowed from earlier writers, on the origins
of society. But in their fundamental principles – such as that the institutions
of government or property or servitude are ultimately mere convention

and not part of nature – they restate the common positions of the Church Fathers and the Roman Stoics. In this same Carolingian period appear the great forgeries, the *Donation of Constantine* and the *Decretals* of the Pseudo-Isidore. The latter work was by far the more influential through the support the author gave to the idea of the universality of papal jurisdiction and of the immunity of the clergy.

In the eleventh century the church reform, the conflict between papacy and empire, the disturbances in Germany following the Saxon revolt against Henry IV in 1073, were accompanied by a spate of scholarly, polemical writing concerned especially with the relationship between *regnum* and *sacerdotium*, with the function of kingship and with the place of the Roman papacy within Christian society. Many of these are aptly called *libelli de lite* – because they are pamphlets on *the* struggle or contest – by the editors of the *Monumenta Germaniae Historica*. Canon law collections were made increasingly frequently; the *Decretum* of Burchard of Worms (c. 1000) did not sufficiently serve the needs of those engaged in the struggle in favour of papal primacy. One of the major collections of the Gregorian age of papal reform, *Diversorum patrum sententiae* (c. 1074–6), demonstrates the consistency of papal teaching across the centuries, as 250 of its 315 *capitula* are drawn from the work of Pseudo-Isidore and strongly emphasise papal jurisdiction; its first *sententia* is *De primatu romane ecclesie* (*On the Primacy of the Roman Church*). Pope Gregory VII's claims to excommunicate and to depose Henry IV and to absolve subjects from their allegiance to an excommunicated king, as well as the reformers' attack on the practises of simony and lay investiture, dominate the struggles between the papacy and the empire. Not less important is the struggle against simony outside the empire and the progress made by reforming popes to give practical shape to the idea of papal primacy over the episcopate at large. In the new order of society the popes themselves were universal monarchs using the trappings of imperial and feudal authority, raising troops, declaring war and crusade and creating vassals. In the course of argument ultimate questions were raised about the origin of rulership, the distinction between kingship and tyranny, the nature of consent, the idea of liberty and of equality. *Regnum* and *sacerdotium* still appeared to be contained within the church; their relationship seemed essentially to call for a definition of their respective limits of jurisdiction. The concept that the state might be an autonomous body was not developed. Freedom was defined, following St Paul, as the freedom of the man who is justified by the grace of God. Kingship was also a gift conferred by divine grace, and priests were the mediators of such grace.

But within a large area of common agreement there were sharp differences between the champions of the papacy and hierocracy and the supporters of the traditional prerogatives of kings and emperors, particularly since the former maintained that, the king's function being the maintenance of justice, one who does not behave justly is no true king. As examples of writers who supported papal and hierocratic claims we should mention Peter Damian, Anselm of Lucca, Cardinal Humbert, Pope Gregory VII, Manegold of Lautenbach, Bernold of St Blasien, Bernard of Constance, Cardinal Deusdedit, Bonizo of Sutri and Honorius Augustodunensis. On the imperialist side writers tended to uphold the accountability of a king as king to God alone, not to the priesthood. They included Peter Crassus, Guy of Osnabruck, Gregory of Cattino, Sigebert of Gembloux, Guy of Ferrara, Wenrich of Trier, the anonymous monk of Hersfeld who wrote *De unitate ecclesiae conservanda*. The tensions between lay and spiritual power were reflected outside the lands of the empire as reforming popes extended the range of their supervision. In the Anglo–Norman world Hugh of Fleury (c. 1102) dedicated a work called *Tractatus de regia potestate et sacerdotali dignitate* (*A Treatise on Royal Power and on Priestly Dignity*) to King Henry I of England and the remarkable Norman Anonymous advanced a radical thesis in favour of the autonomy of the state, so radical that it gained no obvious support.

The appearance in the twelfth century of notable works of theology and canon law confirms the new order of Christian society under active papal leadership. Hugh of St Victor, Bernard of Clairvaux, Gerhoh of Reichersberg and John of Salisbury vigorously extolled the papal *plenitudo potestatis* or fullness of power, while Gratian of Bologna in his *Concordia discordantium canonum* (c. 1140) put a seal upon the rapid development of canon law studies since the time in particular of Ivo of Chartres (d. 1116) by providing an enduring work of synthesis. On the other hand the rediscovery of Justinian's *Corpus* of civil law stimulated a series of commentators and teachers, including Irnerius and Azo. The civil law sometimes led imperialists to proclaim the emperor's sovereignty in spite of papal and hierocratic arguments.

Throughout the period from the ninth to the twelfth century we find continuity of thought as well as new beginnings, especially in the eleventh and twelfth centuries which R.W. and A.J. Carlyle characterised as 'the great formative period of the Middle Ages'.[3] It is not, any more than any

---

3. Carlyle 1903–36, vol. III, p. 115.

other period of history, watertight or self-contained, but it is distinguishable from the later period beginning in the thirteenth century when, as the
Carlyles wrote,[4] Aristotle's *Politics* was recovered and the great schoolmen
began to reduce the world of ideas and theories to a systematic form; until
then men had

in the writings of the Christian Fathers a great body of theories and principles which
had a constant influence upon them, while their habit of life and feeling was
grounded in the traditions of the new Teutonic societies, but in neither of these had
they an ordered and articulated system of political thought, but rather a body of
principles, significant indeed and profound, but not always easily to be reconciled
with each other.[5]

The judgement of the Carlyles is only to be qualified by the success with
which writers before the twelfth century clarified profound differences of
principle.

4. *Ibid.*, pp. 1–2.   5. *Ibid.*, p. 2.

9
GOVERNMENT, LAW AND SOCIETY

The student of political action and thought from the Carolingian age to the 'renaissance of the twelfth century' will naturally concentrate on the development of monarchy and of feudalism. It is, after all, in this period that the 'feudal monarchy' – to use a phrase given wide circulation by Petit-Dutaillis' classic work – is said to have flourished.[1] The first part of this chapter will therefore seek to unravel the main lines of development in the monarchy built by the Carolingians in the eighth and ninth centuries. This underwent an eclipse verging on total collapse during the tenth and eleventh centuries, and was followed in the twelfth by a number of successors, the direct ancestors of the national states of modern Europe. The second and third parts of what follows will deal with manorialism and feudalism respectively, with the aim of establishing their role and importance in this period.

Monarchical government

The Carolingian Empire and its disintegration

The starting point of the analysis is the historic fact that the Carolingians founded a great multiracial state which comprised all western Christendom except the British Isles and gave its mainly Romanic and Germanic peoples a period of political stability and peace such as they had not known since before the days of the Germanic invasions. This *pax Francorum*[2] was the result of an original mixture of Germanic and Mediterranean elements, strongly influenced by Christian ideas and based on the prestige of the house of Charlemagne. It was a real state (the term, of course, was used in the phrase *status regni*, not only in the time of the Franks but also by eleventh-century authors who deplored the fall of the *status* of former days).[3] By this

1. Petit-Dutaillis 1933. The term 'feudal monarchy' had also been used in La Monte 1932. See the remarks in Bisson 1978, p. 461.
2. Poly 1976, p. 1, uses this phrase in the title of Part I of this book: 'De la paix des Francs à l'anarchie féodale.' As to the phrase 'feudal anarchy', see below, p. 199.
3. The phrase *status regni* occurs in Louis the Pious' famous *ordinatio imperii* of AD 817, *Capitularia regum Francorum* 1883, 1, no. 136, p. 271. For the term 'state' and its historical development see *inter alia*

is meant that the empire of Charlemagne and his immediate successors disposed of the necessary central organs of government and local officials to ensure that minimum of security, administration, adjudication and legislation which we associate with the very concept of a state. This political experience was never forgotten by later generations, particularly when suffering most from the disappearance of public authority on any but the smallest scale and trying to return to a political order inspired by Rome or the Franks.

For some time, under Charlemagne and Louis the Pious, it looked as though Rome had been reborn:[4] the western nations had restored the old, the normal *ordo*. That *ordo* was Roman and imperial (Louis the Pious in contrast with his father used only this title in his diplomas); it was the western equivalent of the East-Roman Empire; and it united a great variety of peoples under the aegis of one monarchy and one Church.

Whatever hopes or illusions the leaders and thinkers of this great Christian empire had about its stability and permanence, it proved to be transient and was soon subject to a series of disruptions. These were twofold: there was not only the break-up of the empire as a political unit and its division into several successor kingdoms, but also the internal weakening or even disintegration of public authority within these new formations. These two phenomena are connected but not identical and must therefore be studied separately. The wars and treaties that led to the emergence of such kingdoms as France, Germany and (northern) Italy[5] were only the first stage in a long process of dissolution. Indeed, soon after the kingdom of the western Franks (in other words France) had been established, a second phase of disintegration set in which led to the break-up of that kingdom into a number of regional states, usually referred to as the territorial principalities, ruled by powerful families exercising the political authority which should normally have been in the king's hands. Most of these principalities were founded by descendants of royal officials, the counts of the *pagi*, who had thrown off their subjection to the crown and taken power into their own hands. In the case of Normandy, however, an alien war-leader had obtained a portion of French territory for himself and his followers and turned it into a separate dukedom. The main reason for this development, which set in about AD 900, was the weakness of the

Meyer 1950, Suerbaum 1961 and Weinacht 1968. For the eleventh century see Duby 1978, p. 43, and the texts of Bonnaud-Delamare 1957, pp. 145–57, 165–88.

4. See the verse – 'Aurea Roma iterum renovata renascitur orbi' – of one of the younger poets at Charlemagne's court, Modoin Naso, who became bishop of Autun (quoted in Ladner 1982, p. 3).

5. See Halphen 1947, pp. 305–496; Ganshof 1970, pp. 56–77; Folz 1972, 375–499; Hoyt and Chodorow 1976, pp. 181–209.

crown: it could not guarantee the safety of its subjects, who found protection (*inter alia* against the Vikings) in the leadership of powerful local figures. Finally the kings of France themselves, although they always remained the nominal heads of the whole country and received the royal anointing from the Church, became in fact one regional dynasty among many others, ruling over the area around Paris and Orleans, first as (Robertinian) dukes of *Francia* (in its most restricted sense) and then as Capetian kings of France.

It has been suggested that old ethnic allegiances played a role in the rise of these territorial states, but it has been pointed out against this theory that they arose precisely when the old ethnic feeling was so weakened that the personal element gave way to the territorial in the administration of the law.[6] Furthermore, in the case of the county of Flanders, one of the classic examples of these principalities, there was no ethnic basis at all. Its inhabitants had never belonged to one single Germanic tribe and were even bilingual, the southern part Romanic- and the northern Germanic-speaking.[7] The German *Stammesherzogtümer* or stem-duchies, on the other hand, reflected old ethnic allegiances to a considerable degree; but they never eclipsed royal authority as the principalities did in France. There the king was in fact a provincial ruler, and how much the counts and dukes, nominally his subjects and vassals, bothered about him depended on his usefulness as an ally in the power game of the moment.

Political decomposition did not stop there: a third and ultimate phase was to follow. The first phase had seen, in the ninth century, the break-up of the Frankish empire; the second, in the tenth, the division of the kingdom of France into territorial principalities. The third, mainly in the eleventh century, brought for several (though not all) of these regional states another, ultimate collapse. This resulted in the establishment of tiny castellanies as the basic political units, each acting autonomously, with a castle as its centre, whence an area of a few miles around was controlled and ruled by the castellan and his small band of knightly vassals. Here the authority of the post-Carolingian counts and dukes underwent the collapse from which they themselves had profited a century before, and they became the helpless witnesses of the rise of independent castellans. Not all principalities suffered this fate – Flanders and, most notably, Normandy

6. Guterman 1972 for a recent survey of the passage from personal to territorial law. Dhondt 1948, the classic study of the principalities, attaching great importance to the ethnic element, was rightly criticised by Poly and Bournazel 1980, p. 342.

7. For criticism of Lemarignier 1970, p. 112 (following Dhondt with some reservations), see Van Caenegem in *Legal History Review* (1973) 41: 209.

were exceptions, where the old regional dynasties firmly held the reins of power in their respective 'fatherlands' (although even they went through some critical moments).[8] However, the majority of the French principalities fell victim to the final phase of decomposition – which Bournazel has called *la poussée châtelaine*. In Anjou and Maine, counts who previously administered a single *pagus* in the Carolingian tradition, established themselves as autonomous political leaders:[9] the terrible count of Anjou, Foulque Nerra (d. 1040) was one of the great castle-builders of his time.[10] In eastern France there were several regions – southern Champagne, Burgundy, Forez and Beaujolais – where the counts' authority did not survive the eleventh century: some of them even gave up their old titles and merged with the mass of the 'lords of castles'. The reason was that their *comitatus* offered them no more power or rights than the castellans enjoyed.[11] The duchy of *Francia* itself, which became the *domaine direct* of the Capetian kings, did not avoid this internal dismemberment. At this stage political life had become amazingly small scale.[12] The mass of the population lived in miniature states controlled by knightly castellans who recognised no authority above themselves but were kept in some kind of order by arbitration, by the balance of (vassalitic) allegiances and by the threat of excommunication and hell-fire if they broke their engagements to observe some truce or peace – most notably the Truce or Peace of God (about which more later). Small wonder that the epic songs in which those warriors liked to join 'often ridiculed the powerlessness of the sovereigns and exalted the deeds of the lords'.[13]

The internal decadence of the state

The break-up of the great empire of the Franks was accompanied by a decline in the exercise of authority by the state and its organs. Numerous public functions diminished to the point of extinction or were taken over by landowners who, in modern eyes, had no public status at all. That this process of internal degradation or destructuration coincided with the loss of Frankish political unity is a historic fact. What is, however, open to

8. For Normandy and the victory of the young William the Bastard, the later Conqueror, over rebellion, see Yver 1969, p. 330; and for Flanders, under Arnulf II (965–88), see Dhondt 1943, pp. 47–52, and Ganshof 1944, pp. 23–6.
9. Bournazel 1975, p. 12. Lemarignier 1970, pp. 113.
10. Fourquin 1970, p. 87.   11. Richard 1968, p. 170.
12. How small the judicial and administrative areas had become can be gathered, for example, from the decision of the court of the viscount of Thouars in 1055–93 discussed by Strayer 1965, no. 20, pp. 109–10, who rightly says that this document 'illustrates the extreme fragmentation of rights of government in the eleventh century'.   13. Duby 1967, p. 58.

discussion is the causal nexus between the two phenomena. It may be argued that the break-up of a great state can naturally be expected to lead to a loss of quality in the public service it used to provide. It may also be argued that a small political unit, such as a castellany, simply could not afford to run an efficient administration and that in a country divided into numerous small areas justice could hardly transcend the village level, since the castellans were not subjected to any higher authority (only the mass of the peasants, the *homines de potestate*, were real 'subjects'). On the other hand it can be pointed out that there is no intrinsic reason why small provincial states – such as the great counties and duchies of the tenth century – could not provide good administration, continuing Carolingian precedents. And it can be argued that small-scale government has advantages in terms of familiarity with the real needs and wishes of the population. In fact, even in Normandy, where the duke kept firm political control and enforced respect for many of the traditional *regalia*, the exercise of public authority in terms of legislation and the use of written documents could in the tenth and eleventh centuries only be called abysmal; and everywhere in France public affairs were run by amateurs, operating in an atmosphere of extreme rustic simplicity.[14] Under Diocletian the Roman Empire had reached a zenith of bureaucratisation: the reaction against that heavy machine which had started at the end of Antiquity reached a dialectical extreme in the post-Carolingian era, when not even the king disposed of a proper writing office and had recourse to his chaplain if there was a need for a royal document which was not (as was the normal practice) being drawn up by the beneficiary.

The fragmentation of public authority and its passing from the rulers and their officials into the hands of landholders, large or small, is so often described as the 'privatisation of public rights' (which are said to have been 'usurped') that it may be useful to try to clarify some current notions and terms in this context.[15] There is a real danger of anachronism here, of projecting a modern notion on to the Middle Ages and particularly on to this period.[16] This modern (and Roman-law) notion makes an absolute distinction between *jus publicum* and *jus privatum*: there are public rights,

---

14. Strayer 1965, pp. 62–3.
15. For various phrases and formulations see the following: Bisson 1978, p. 465; Duby 1953, p. 258; Evergates 1975, p. 138; Fourquin 1970, p. 32; Garaud 1964, p. 29; Herlihy 1970, p. 78; Lemarignier 1970, p. 120; Poly 1976, p. 125; Strayer 1965, p. 12; Strayer 1967, p. 71. Cf. also ch. 10 below, pp. 219–26. On the eighteenth-century idea that aristocratic government was based on usurpation in the ninth and tenth centuries, see Sprandel 1975, p. 11, and, for discussion of the classic view (Waitz and Brunner) of 'feudal dominance' being associated with 'illegitime, unstaatliche Privatherrschaft', p. 13; and cf. Werner 1968, p. 194.   16. See on this particular point Herlihy 1970, p. 79.

which belong exclusively to the state and its agents, and there are private rights, enjoyed by the citizens; a private citizen who exercises public rights without being appointed by the state and thereby becoming a public figure, is a usurper. Underlying this is the idea that all legitimate power belongs to the central state agencies and those organs and persons whom they appoint: it is the idea of concentration of power. These notions and terms are, however, less than helpful for an analysis of realities which stemmed from the fundamental notion of the dispersion of authority throughout society and its legitimate exercise by numerous corporations and persons in their respective spheres. Of course, royal authority was supreme (and deserved the adjective *publicus*, which simply meant 'royal'), but the authority of a lord over his vassals, a landowner over the peasants on his manors, the governors of a guild over its members or the father over his children were no less real and legitimate. In this view the Norman kingdom of England, for example, consisted of numerous 'honours', held by greater and lesser barons, whereas the greatest and most eminent honour, that of the crown, was the kingdom itself, which comprehended and surpassed the others, whose model it was.[17] If, after the collapse of a great empire, a new political order is established in which regional and local dynasties of warriors rule their respective areas and offer them security, ought we to call those rulers usurpers? Can we really maintain that the dukes of Normandy or Aquitaine or the counts of Flanders and Anjou, or even the castellans of the Mâconnais were usurpers? Only if one operates with the Roman-law ideas which the legists of King Philip IV of France later used so successfully and which have become familiar to modern lawyers. To operate with notions of public and private right and discuss the state of affairs in post-Carolingian Europe in terms of 'usurpation' may obscure the real nature both of its institutions and of their underlying ideas.[18] Whatever our own approach may be, it certainly is in itself interesting to find Europe going through a phase when social life went on without the state. It is now necessary to consider what this meant in the spheres of security, justice, legislation and administration.

In the early eleventh century the breakdown of public order had reached a point where only the peasant population was subjected to discipline, that of the lord and his manor. All others, the members of the free landowning

17. Well explained by Stenton 1932, p. 66.
18. Another term often encountered in this context is the 'patrimonialisation' of public rights – closely connected with the idea of the latter being turned into private rights and thus treated like other elements in a private person's estate.

class, all those who boasted of a castle of their own, behaved as they liked and recognised no power above them. They were the 'masters of peace and war', 'knights who lived without restraint, without knowing anyone in the world who might have punished them'.[19] Suger, a staunch supporter of the monarchy, called them 'tyrants' and was proud that the king neutralised their 'audacity'. They were constantly involved in warfare, which corresponded to their knightly way of life, and often had great fun – of the sort described in Huizinga's *Homo Ludens* and hardly distinguishable from our modern sports, although tales of grim mutilation should warn us against undue nostalgia.[20] This anarchy was tempered by the fear of revenge, which could be exercised by one's lord, fellow vassals or kinsmen. It was also tempered by the desperate attempt of the Church to step into the shoes of the state and to organise public safety by the proclamation of the Peace of God. Some eleventh-century authors pinpointed this nadir of public disorder. Thus the Chronicle of Saint-Hubert, which deplores the lack of vigour of 'public' law, i.e. of royal authority, indicates a worsening of the situation after the middle of the eleventh century, referring to the years 1044–8 as a time when 'justice of royal law was still in vigour'.[21] The old Adalbero, who had been chancellor in 974 of the Carolingian King Lothair of France and was bishop of Laon from 977 to 1030, cherished the memory of the *pax Francorum* and, in a poem dedicated between 1015 and 1030 to King Robert the Pious, gave vent to his anger at the ruin of the state, expressing his conviction that as long as the Carolingian order had prevailed the world had lived in peace, but now the law had collapsed peace was gone and moral values were turned upside down, as also was the right order of things.[22]

These extremes of anarchy and self-help were, of course, linked to the decadence of the administration of justice. No one except the rustics was really subjected to the authority of law courts. The *comes palatii*, the court of the *pagus* presided over by the *comes*, the *missi dominici* – all these instruments of Carolingian justice were gone. Freemen gathered in the court of their feudal overlord to be judged by their equals, but even then they only went to court if they were willing to do so. The proceedings usually ended in a compromise rather than a clear judgement, whose execution would in any

19. Duby, 1978, p. 189. Duby 1953, p. 569: 'Les chevaliers avaient vécu sans frein, sans connaître personne au monde qui fût capable de les punir.'
20. Bournazel 1975, p. 172. See on all this Garaud 1964, p. 101; and cf. the *index verborum* in Orderic Vitalis, ed. Chibnall 1980, vol. I, s.v. *bellum, castellum, castrum, miles, militaris, militia.*
21. Genicot 1982, p. 26: 'adhuc eo tempore vigente publici juris justitia'; and cf. p. 12.
22. Lemarignier 1965, pp. 78–80. See also on Adalbero, Duby 1978, p. 151, and cf. Carozzi ed. 1979.

case have been problematic. The wrongdoer always got away with something and arbitration was really the best one could hope for.[23] This went so far that even the king of France, in a conflict with one of his vassals, accepted arbitration by another of his vassals: thus in 1022 Robert the Pious actually submitted his quarrel with Odo II of Blois to Duke Richard II of Normandy, who summoned both parties to his court (Halphen 1950). And all this same King Robert could do against those who refused to appear in *his* court was to ask the bishops to be so good as to excommunicate them.[24]

Charlemagne's ambitions and Roman-inspired plans to put in writing and even to unify the laws of his subjects met, as is well known, with very limited success. Nevertheless the Carolingians did legislate on a considerable scale, and their capitularies (whether intended as supplements to the old tribal laws or not) covered, albeit unsystematically, a great variety of topics. The end of this great legislative effort – by AD 898 in Italy and 884 in France[25] – ushered in a period of more than two centuries in which the European Continent lived without legislation. Neither kings nor princes – nor popes for that matter[26] – issued laws, edicts or constitutions containing new legal norms for their subjects. At most one could mention some formal statements in the form of a judicial pronouncement, i.e. a *Weistum*, or a very exceptional injunction such as that on feudal inheritance issued by the Emperor Conrad II while besieging the city of Milan in 1037.[27] The reasons for this eclipse are not far to seek. It was a direct consequence of the feebleness of the authority that should have legislated. The power base for the promulgation and introduction of new rules simply was not there, neither the central offices to make the laws, nor the local machinery to make them known nor the royal emissaries to check their implementation. One also has the feeling that the minimum of political stability was lacking: when the whole political structure was in flux, who could believe that new laws would last and be observed? It is not surprising therefore that the revival of legislation had to wait for the rebuilding of solid monarchies in the twelfth century. There were also certain ideas about the very nature of the law which stood in the way of true, innovative legislation. These concerned particularly the notion that the law was a God-given ancestral

---

23. Bongert 1949, pp. 37–78. See also Boussard 1964, p. 172; Duby 1953, pp. 161, 164; Garaud 1964, pp. 11, 95, 105–8; Poly 1976, p. 55.

24. Lemarignier 1965, p. 163.   25. Ganshof 1958b, pp. 102–3.

26. There were no papal decretals between the end of the ninth and the middle of the eleventh centuries.

27. Herlihy 1970, no. 22, pp. 107–9.

treasure which man could not manipulate but at the most 'find', i.e. declare or define. The law was something fixed and eternal like the stars, not made by man or to be altered to suit his whim, but to be preserved with reverence. This was the conservative sentiment that made Charlemagne conform to the 'patrimonial' tradition of dividing the realm among the sons of the ruler by proceeding to the *divisio regnorum* of 806, several years after he became emperor. It also inspired the resistance of an important group of Frankish leaders to the innovation of the *ordinatio imperii* of 817, which broke that tradition by preserving the unity of the empire.[28] The same sentiment led Bishop Arnulph of Orleans, in or around the year 1000, to write about the eternal authority of the sacred canons and to ask the rhetorical question whether some new instruction could reverse the canons and the decretals of the first popes, and what established laws were good for if everything was subjected to the caprice of a single person.[29]

The reality of such sentiments about legal immobility in the backward and agricultural Europe of those days should not blind us, however, to the fact that legal change was taking place, and taking place all the time. It took the form of a change in the customs of everyday life, a less perceptible and therefore less provocative process than the promulgation of a new edict. The repeated demands for new payments or services which knightly landlords made upon their peasants quickly turned into legal dues based on custom: the hated *consuetudines* – an old word with a new meaning, i.e. of seignorial rights – which appear in the texts around AD 1000 and for whose reduction the peasants would fight with a good deal of success in the twelfth century. The abolition of 'bad customs' by the king was one of the first signs of the rebirth of royal legislation in France (Olivier-Martin 1938, Lemarignier 1951, Bongert 1970). Nor should we forget that such venerable usages of the period under review as the royal investiture of bishops started by Louis the Pious, or the *Reichskirche*-system started by Otto I, were not ready-made institutions introduced by imperial decree, but resulted from individual practical measures of administration that were repeated and thus became customary and lawful. The holiness of custom was invoked by the imperial party when the Gregorian reformers attempted to ban those practices and institutions hallowed by the usage of centuries, and it is not surprising that custom as a source of law drew

28. Krause 1965 has counted twenty 'laws' in the 226 years between the accession of Conrad I (911) and the death of Lothar (1137), eighteen of which were certainly or probably destined only for Italy, where Roman ideas had not entirely died out. On the question of the divisibility of the realm see further ch. 10 below, pp. 232–3, 243–4.   29. Poly and Bournazel 1980, p. 252.

particularly sarcastic remarks from Pope Gregory VII, who was a believer in legislation and convinced that custom did not turn injustice into justice (Ladner 1956).

As they had no writing-office, the kings, dukes and counts could hardly have disposed of a central administration. The king of France stopped appointing local officials in his kingdom and stayed away from the greatest part of it. Coinage, always a sign of sovereignty, also slipped out of the king's hands and gave rise to the proliferation of coins issued by greater and lesser barons (the *monnaies féodales*). Typically, in the better organised principalities such as Normandy and Flanders, the dukes and counts managed to keep coinage in their own hands.[30] Care of roads and bridges was also turned over to local lords who, however, were more interested in raising revenue from harassed travellers than keeping the means of communication in good order.[31] As a result of the general intellectual decline and the collapse of administration no more written orders or notifications were issued by the national or regional rulers. These adminis-trative documents – called *indiculi* – had been widely used by the Frankish kings to summon witnesses, mobilise troops, announce a holiday for the birth of a royal baby and for many other acts of government.[32] They went out of use on the Continent about the time when their English equivalent, the royal writs, were devised (Harmer 1952) and reappeared in French royal government in a very modest way around 1100 in the form of the *mandamenta*.[33] Nor was this the only difference between the Continent and England.

Anglo-Saxon England: a distinct destiny

As the Franks of the eighth and ninth centuries tried, in vain, to unite the peoples of the western Continent in one neo-Roman superstate, the tribes of the *gens Anglorum* were being gathered in one nation-state. This more modest undertaking was successful and when the Roman-Frankish Empire was only a souvenir of the past and the French were not even united under one king, the English solidly and permanently built their own unified state. This was achieved in the very century, the tenth, when the disintegration of

30. For Normandy see Lemarignier 1970, p. 123, and Yver 1969, pp. 341–3; for Flanders see the texts in Espinas 1943, vol. III, no. 622, art. 14, p. 298 and no. 623, art. 18, p. 305.
31. Garaud 1964, p. 129; Richard 1968, p. 170.
32. Ephemeral in their very nature, these documents were not preserved: we know them almost exclusively from models in the formularies (texts in Zeumer 1886).
33. Lemarignier 1965, pp. 159–63; Van Caenegem and Ganshof 1978, pp. 73–4.

France was fast moving to its nadir. This English nation-state stood up to the dramas and disasters under Aethelred the Unready, the union with Denmark and even the Norman Conquest: the foundations of the national monarchy appeared indestructible. This political phenomenon was accompanied by a corresponding internal development, i.e. the building of a solid network of institutions, guided by a monarchy whose writ ran nation-wide. To a certain extent Carolingian influence can be detected here – the ceremony of anointing is of continental origin, *indiculi* may have influenced the writs (although there are considerable external differences), the capitularies were not unnoticed across the Channel and the Frankish *denarius* inspired the reform of the currency under King Offa.[34] The fact remains however that in this period the Anglo-Saxons founded the most solid and best administered kingdom of the western world. Their kings were great law-givers and this tradition was in no way diminished after legislation had lapsed on the Continent. On the contrary, the voluminous and numerous dooms (some of which are unfortunately lost) of Ine, Offa, Alfred the Great, Edward the Elder, Athelstan, Edmund, Edgar, Aethelred the Unready and Canute form a collection of texts unique in Europe, bearing witness to an equally unique tradition of royal, national law-giving in England right through the Anglo-Saxon period (Liebermann 1898–1916).

The nation-wide administration of justice was equally impressive. There was a network of hundred and shire courts, topped by the *witenagemot* and receiving decisive impulses from the crown, *inter alia* by means of the writs, which were often addressed to such local gatherings.[35] There were also franchisal courts belonging to lords, to be considered later. Finally the comparative excellence of royal administration should be mentioned. England enjoyed a high measure of internal peace and order (staving off enemies from overseas was another matter): private warfare and adulterine castles (of which there were a few under the Confessor, built by Norman knights) were practically unheard of, and practices such as tithing and frankpledge guaranteed a measure of public safety that must have astounded people on the other side of the Channel.[36] The efficiency of the royal writing-office has already been mentioned. Equally efficient was the new network of local royal officials, the sheriffs, who had no equals on the Continent. These 'counts of the shire' had nothing to do with hereditary regional princes, but were real appointees of the crown.[37] The royal mint was also one of the wonders of Europe because of its monopolistic position,

34. Finberg 1974, p. 102; Fisher 1973, p. 194.   35. Lyon 1980, pp. 59–68.
36. *Ibid.*, pp. 80–1.   37. *Ibid.*, pp. 63–6.

its efficiency and its enormous output.[38] National defence was centrally directed and general military service, in the local and the national *fyrd*, was never abandoned in favour of the feudal formula of the army of professional knights: the disaster of October 1066 should not obscure the fact that English armies had successfully resisted the Danes in the ninth and tenth centuries and that King Harold had, a few weeks before Hastings, destroyed a powerful army led by the king of Norway. The foundation of a solid national monarchy was a notable Anglo-Saxon achievement and its consequences were far reaching. When in the twelfth century the rebirth of the state became a general European phenomenon, the existence of these Anglo-Saxon antecedents gave Norman and Angevin England an advantage which goes a long way towards explaining England's pioneering role in this European development.[39]

Rebirth of the state

After the downward spiral had reached bottom in the eleventh century, the opposite movement, towards strengthening the monarchy and the role of central government, got under way all over Europe. Its geographical framework varied from national kingdoms, such as France or Denmark, to regional kingdoms, such as León or Castile, and regional dukedoms, counties and prince-bishoprics. These regional principalities were liable to be brought together by a personal union, such as that between the countries of Provence and Barcelona, or that most famous example of a 'political multi-national', the 'Angevin Empire'. Whether these states were national or regional, kingdoms or counties, made little difference to their internal structure. The term *regnum*, for example, was used for the county of Flanders,[40] and states were sometimes promoted from one title to another: the princes of Bohemia began to style themselves kings under Vratislaw II and Vladislaw II and the title became hereditary in 1198 under Ottokar I (always within the framework of the empire, of which the kings of Bohemia became electors in the thirteenth century). The essential point is that the inhabitants looked upon these states, large or small, as their fatherland (*patria*). Several of these regional states were in the course of time absorbed by the great national monarchies. Thus the French crown took over Normandy and Toulouse with their existing administrative structures,

---

38. Wormald 1978, p. 65.   39. See Campbell 1975; Wormald 1978.
40. Galbert of Bruges, ed. Pirenne 1891, cc. 9, 20 and *passim*: the count is the father (cc. 23, 29) and rules as the *naturalis dominus et princeps* (Prol.). Bruges is the *regni sedes*, situated *in medio patriae* (c. 37) and Galbert calls the count's house there *regalem aulam* and *thesaurum regni* (c. 38).

the only difference being that the duke and the count disappeared and these
territories were ruled from Paris and the local officials henceforth were the
king's *baillis* or *sénéchaux*. In Germany the opposite movement took place
and the territorial states, whether lay or ecclesiastical, far from being
absorbed by the crown became more and more independent, so that
institutional modernisation in Germany took place at the regional rather
than the national level. In Italy three zones are to be distinguished: the south,
where a strong monarchy originated under Norman rule; the centre, where
the papal state modernised its structures *inter alia* by borrowing from the
feudal monarchies; and the north, the *regnum Italiae*, where the power of the
German kings (who ruled over both Germany and northern Italy) was
undermined by the Investiture Struggle and the communal movement.
The attempts of Frederick I and Frederick II to turn their Italian kingdom
into a modern bureaucratic monarchy failed for political reasons and as a
consequence the old Lombard kingdom broke up into a number of
autonomous city-states. The Roman Empire of the German kings never
stood a chance of being a true European superstate wielding effective power
in or above the kingdoms: the empire did not have any institutions, let alone
military or fiscal possibilities of its own. This was in sharp contrast with the
Latin Church, which, except in the military field, came to dispose of every
institutional advantage: a centralised government, an advanced bureaucracy, strong discipline, an excellent judicial and fiscal organisation and
legislative organs. Yet, although the pope pretended to direct and dominate
the kings, not even the Church ever thought of becoming a European
government that would direct all Christians in their everyday lives and
make the kings redundant.

Throughout European history the size of political units has varied
considerably and it is useful to visualise this in the perspective of a long-term
dialectical movement. In late Antiquity the situation was clear and
straightforward. People led their political lives on two levels, the local *polis*,
municipium or *civitas*, and the universal empire, which embraced them all
under one law, one emperor and one Roman peace. From the beginning of
the Middle Ages until our own time, however, things have never been so
easy again and Europe has oscillated and hesitated between several
possibilities, without ever coming to a definite resting point. The empire
gave way, in the west, to tribal and then to territorial kingdoms. Under
Charlemagne and Louis the Pious attempts were made to go back to the
'normal' situation – Antiquity being medieval man's great model and
inspiration – but this neo-Roman Empire failed and a return to the level of

the kingdom took place. In the case of France not even that framework persisted and political life there became regional or even local. The late Middle Ages witnessed in most of Europe the triumph of large or small national kingdoms, but Germany and Italy, which had unsuccessfully clung to the imperial dimension, stayed outside this main stream and fell back upon regional and local states or city-states. Modern Europe saw the triumph of the nation-state and it is only in our own time that attempts have been made to build supranational European structures. Having placed this political aspect in its proper diachronic perspective, we shall now turn to the institutional developments and analyse their starting point and chronology.

The starting point for the revival of the state was dissatisfaction with the disorders of the eleventh century, i.e. a deep-seated revulsion against the lawlessness and oppression of those days. The *harmonie sauvage de la liberté aristocratique*[41] was more savage than harmonious. So helpless, however, were the lay authorities to remedy this state of affairs that it was at first left to the Peace of God, a Church-inspired mass movement, to launch a crusade against violence and oppression. Its success was considerable and the enthusiasm of the masses, including many knights, betrayed their deep-seated need and anxiety. Also it was fortunate that religious belief was so strong that purely ecclesiastical sanctions – there were hardly any others left – proved not totally inadequate. The movement started in France and had its greatest success there, as one could expect in the country where public authority had suffered most. It reached Germany belatedly and in spite of the resistance of those who held that keeping the peace was the business of kings and not of enthusiastic masses led by monks. It never penetrated into England, where the crown, as we have seen, was strong enough to maintain public order.[42] Already in the course of the eleventh century it became clear that the movement, although it inspired great enthusiasm, was not really adequate for keeping peace and organising society: only a return to strong monarchic rule could bring the required stability, but what sort of monarchy? It certainly had to be religiously inspired, for this gave the king the one element that the regional rulers lacked, the prestige of the wonder-working anointed of the Lord. However, society did not need monarchs like Robert the Pious who cared only for his collection of saints' relics, or Edward the Confessor who dreamt only of his great abbey at Westminster,

41. Poly 1976, p. 75.
42. See, besides the well-known surveys by Bonnaud-Delamare 1957 and Hoffmann 1964a, the remarks in Duby 1953, pp. 199–200; Lemarignier 1965, p. 64; Richard 1968, p. 172; Poly and Bournazel 1980, pp. 234–50.

it needed monarchs who combined this religious halo with fighting and organising qualities. Such were the Anglo-Norman kings, who exploited the prestige of English kingship to the full, but were also down-to-earth administrators and war-leaders of their barons. Such also was King Louis VI, Suger's great hero, who spent a lifetime fighting the robber barons of the Ile de France. This was the sort of monarchy the people wanted and their support explains the sustained expansion of royal government from the early years of the twelfth century. At a later stage Roman-law ideas about the majesty of the state would play a role, but at first it was the old notion of the Christian monarchy that was the real source of inspiration: not Justinian but Charlemagne. Hence the theme of the return to the *stirps Carolinorum* and the revival of the Carolingian mystique in chronicles and epic poems (Werner 1952).

Since the national monarchies were the bases of the new states, it is clear that the older monarchies which were functioning adequately around AD 1100 were at an advantage. Hence the precociousness of the Anglo-Norman complex in twelfth-century Europe, hence also the precociousness of Christian Spain, where certain traditions of Visigothic kingship or Carolingian rule (Catalonia) had never disappeared and where the permanent tension with Moslem Spain made strong leadership indispensable (Grassotti 1969). It is indeed useful to have a look at the geography and the chronology of this *Intensivierung des Staatsbetriebes* (intensification of state activity), which though general did not occur everywhere at the same time. We mentioned already the old monarchic traditions in England and Spain. Modernisation also came early to old and strong territorial principalities such as Flanders and Normandy. The latter produced another early example of the new state in Sicily, promoted to a kingdom in 1130. In France the *domaine direct* followed in their footsteps and royal control and administration progressed under Louis VI; its pace was somewhat slowed down under Louis VII, but resumed vigorously under Philip II Augustus. German attempts, notably under English and French influence, at modernising national government were foiled by political developments. Eventually modernisation reached the German territories and also the states on Germany's eastern borders, but it came rather late and sometimes under the influence of western dynasties, such as the house of Anjou in Hungary.

State and administration in twelfth-century Europe

The 'rebirth of the state' demands more detailed analysis; but such a vast and complex process can be illustrated here only by a few examples. It was a movement in which much that had been done in previous centuries had to be undone, while much that had been neglected had to be achieved. A good deal of what the Carolingians had striven for was now realised, and this time with lasting results. This was done within more confined political boundaries than those of the Carolingian Franks and also with superior means. The European rulers of the later Middle Ages had at their disposal both material and intellectual resources, in terms of fiscal revenue and of ideas and university-trained officials, vastly superior to anything Charlemagne had been able to muster.

The twelfth century saw the reintroduction of real officialdom (at least on the Continent, for it had never disappeared in England). By this is meant that there was a regular staff appointed to execute specific administrative tasks and thus to carry out the ruler's political intentions in the daily running of public affairs. This personnel was freely appointed, revocable and salaried, did not hold office in fief and operated at the national as well as the local level. A central writing-office (later generally called 'chancery') had existed in England ever since Anglo-Saxon times, and the Norman rulers, who before 1066 had not had one of their own, continued the practice. Already in the twelfth century the output of the English royal chancery, *inter alia* of ephemeral writs on fiscal, judicial and other governmental business, was very considerable and on its staff some forty-eight scribes have been identified for the reigns of Henry I, Stephen and Henry II.[43] In Flanders in 1089 the provost of the chapter of St Donatian in Bruges was appointed as the count's perpetual chancellor, receiver of his revenues and head of all the *notarii*, chaplains and clerks in the *curia comitis*.[44] Nevertheless all through the twelfth century the practice of having the count's charters drawn up by the beneficiaries continued to a considerable extent. In France there was a royal chancellor, but he was more a political than an administrative figure, and one, Etienne de Garlande, appointed in 1105 or 1106, was deposed in 1127 for his overbearing conduct; the office was repeatedly left vacant for long periods. Here too the practice of having royal charters drawn up by the beneficiaries and merely sealed by the king's seal bearer continued to a considerable extent right through the twelfth century,

43. For the varying numbers of scribes at work at any given time, from one in Stephen's last years or two at the accession of Henry I to four or five before the middle of Henry I's reign, at Stephen's accession, and for most of Henry II's reign, with a peak of ten in 1155 and at least sixteen scribes employed at various times between then and 1158, see Bishop 1961, pp. 1, 30.
44. Vercauteren 1938, nr 9, pp. 23–32.

after having reigned supreme in the eleventh. To speak of the 'anaemia' of the French royal chancery in those days is not to use too strong a word. Not until Philip Augustus and Louis IX do large numbers of charters with a uniform style and language prove the existence of a permanent service staffed by specialised officials.[45]

In central fiscal administration too England was far in advance. The treasury at Winchester certainly dates from before 1066, and about the middle of Henry I's reign its successor, the exchequer, began to function as the central accounting office. Its yearly records, the Pipe Rolls (oldest extant from 1130, continuous series from 1155 onwards) are an impressive testimony to its early development, as is the treatise on its organisation (Richard fitz Nigel's *Dialogue of the Exchequer*, 1177–9). The county of Flanders also had an advanced fiscal administration, both central and local: there is a fragment of a comital account conserved from 1140 and the first complete *Grote Brief* from the year 1187.[46] Capetian finance, on the other hand, was slower to develop; and real progress in France came only under Philip Augustus (oldest surviving fragment: a royal account for 1202–3).

In local administration also England was exceptional because the Norman kings carefully preserved the office of sheriff from Anglo-Saxon times and prevented it being feudalised, unlike so much else. In Flanders the count's local representatives in the castellanies (*castellani, burggraven*), although true comital administrators, were more independent, since they held their office and land in fief, i.e. hereditarily. Gradually, from Count Philip of Alsace (1157–91) onwards, they gave way to officials of a modern type, the non-heritable and non-feudal comital bailiffs, who operated in the towns and in the countryside. Their origin has been traced to the *notarii*, reeves and other receivers of the comital domain (De Gryse 1976), which is comparable to that of the Anglo-Saxon sheriff. In France too the *prévôts* or reeves of the royal domain are the earliest local officials and there also – at least in the north – the *baillis* became the foremost local representatives of the crown, at first travelling, later resident in their respective *bailliages*.[47] According to Lemarignier the *baillis*, although they were preceded by the *prévôts*, did not descend from them, but rather from Anglo-Norman models and were originally intended to supervise the *prévôts*.[48]

45. Tessier 1962, pp. 125–49.
46. Lyon and Verhulst 1967, pp. 84, 86. See also Verhulst and Gysseling 1962; Pacaut 1964, pp. 149–60; Van Caenegem and Ganshof 1978, pp. 109–11.
47. Lot and Fawtier 1958, pp. 99–182; Pacaut 1964, pp. 149ff; Werner 1968, p. 211.
48. Lemarignier 1970, p. 338.

In the dispensation of justice also the central element was enhanced in the twelfth century and consequently the power of local notables reduced. This strengthening of the monarchical element was a widespread phenomenon and took several forms. The foremost example is again England, where a network of royal courts with a considerable competence in first instance gave birth to a national law, common to the whole kingdom (a unique feat in medieval Europe). This expansion of royal justice was not achieved by abolishing feudal and manorial, shire and hundred courts: it happened slowly and imperceptibly. The competence of the local franchise-holders was reduced by giving a more stringent and extended meaning to the old *placita coronae* or crown pleas (the Norman *plez de l'espée*), whose continental equivalents were the *causae majores* or *cas réservés*. The status of the local courts was also reduced by the extended possibility of transferring cases up the hierarchical ladder by means of the procedures of *tolt* (from a seignorial to the county court) and *pone* (from the county to the common pleas). The royal itinerant judges or 'justices in eyre' also played a considerable role, for they were sent out by the king to travel in well-defined circuits all over the country to exert royal justice at the local level, without being hampered by existing franchises: they had a nation-wide and direct impact on the observance of the law. This practice, which can be traced to the late eleventh century, became important and systematic under Henry II. Under Henry I and Stephen and in the early years of Henry II there had been an interesting experiment, later discontinued, with permanent local justiciars, who were possibly a threat to the old sheriff. They had, nevertheless, made their mark on legal history by exerting the prosecution *ex officio* of crime, a function that was taken over by the jury of presentment (Van Caenegem 1976). The greatest expansion of royal jurisdiction certainly took place through the rise and development of the common law applied in the king's court. It meant that for increasing numbers of complaints royal writs were devised and made 'of course', i.e. giving automatic access to the central courts to plaintiffs in first instance. The possibility for all free men and women – the unfree were ignored – of starting an action in the king's court, even against some powerful local personage, and of obtaining a judgement invested with all the authority of the crown meant a considerable curb on the lords and created a special and direct link between the people and the monarchy. The curbing of the power of the unruly feudal aristocracy had similarly been the task of Count Charles the Good in Flanders: when Borsiard oppressed the peasants around Bruges by violence and robbery and they went and complained to the count, 'begging him for his customary paternal help', he did not hesitate and had Borsiard condemned and his stronghold burnt down.[49] It is well known that Louis VI of France launched royal justice on its road to recovery by relentlessly compelling lawless knights to appear in his court and/or to undergo its judgement, which often necessitated a little war and the siege of a defiant castle.[50] The kingdom of Sicily also, founded and ruled by Norman knights and kept in continuous contact with Anglo–Norman ruling circles, could boast one of the most modern administrations of the time. The 'systematization of the state'[51] really got under way after 1140, when the newly crowned King Roger began to operate with royal justiciars centrally as well as locally. Here too the reservation of serious cases for royal jurisdiction (oldest text 1093) was expanded and that of the king's vassals limited and controlled: one peculiar example was the practice of submitting a case in a franchisal court where proof was problematical to royal justiciars, who conducted an inquest to discover the culprit.[52] This development gained particular momentum from 1144 onwards and was related to the foundation of the *dohana de secretis*, a new style fiscal organisation, whose Arabic name is but one indication of the multifarious influence of Arabic civilisation. William II (1166–89) expanded the activity of the royal bailiffs (*baiuli*), who were lower judicial officers.[53]

New laws formally issued by the prince (and his council) for the whole country were still very rare in twelfth-century Europe. Few of the old imperial traditions were so thoroughly lost as the publication of constitutions and rescripts – only the Church (some 2,000 decretals from Alexander III to Gregory IX) had revived the practice to any extent. To many people this intervention dictated from above amounted to unacceptable interference with the law. And the prevailing feudal ideas visualised the king as a party to a contract with the nation's leading class, with whom he was expected to negotiate, rather than as a majestic legislator who issued decrees according to his 'pleasure' and whose *placitum* had the force of law. All this explains not only why formal legislation by way of ordinances, 'assizes', statutes or 'establishments' was slow to emerge, but also why other forms were so popular, viz. coronation oaths and borough charters, 'liberties' and other privileges granted to urban or rural communities. Hence also we find

49. Galbert of Bruges, ed. Pirenne 1891, c. 10, p. 16: 'obsecrantes paternum et consuetum ab eo auxilium'. 50. Lemarignier 1965, p. 165.
51. Caravale 1966, p. 159. 52. *Ibid.*, p. 319. 53. *Ibid.*, pp. 298, 311.

legislation under the guise of a written statement of the customs of the good old days.[54] Even in England the great tradition of the royal dooms came to an end. The Norman kings, who so carefully preserved so many Anglo-Saxon institutions, gave this one up: efforts were made by clerics to describe the old English laws for the new Norman generations, but this in no way amounted to the promulgation of great national codes. Royal legislation was revived in a more humble, sporadic, even shame-faced way. It was incidental and dealt merely with a few very specific points; it was sometimes introduced for a limited period only and often orally, as no appropriate diplomatic forms had yet been devised. Often enough such texts have only been preserved in narrative sources. William the Conqueror replaced the death penalty, which he found too lenient, by blinding and emasculation, but Henry restored it. This king also made a change in the laws of wreck, giving it to any one of the vessel who escaped the disaster instead of to the crown or a franchise-holder. With his death, however, the old law was deemed to have revived, since the king had acted without the counsel of his barons.[55] Henry II's decrees, often called assizes and several of which are lost, dealt with crime, conflicts of jurisdiction and ecclesiastical and military matters. Because of the dearth of contemporary texts the true importance of ducal legislation in Normandy has only recently come to light. Thus we know Henry I's ordinance on the Truce of God of AD 1135 and we know of a dozen Norman ordinances of Henry II and of nine others (probably by Henry II): traces may be detected in the *Très Ancien Coutumier de Normandie* (Yver 1971). They concerned ecclesiastical, procedural, feudal, jurisdictional, military and fiscal matters – some had only passing but some had permanent effect. None of this, however, was comparable to the same prince's legislation in England. In neighbouring Brittany a famous assize was issued in 1185 by Count Geoffrey, a son of the English King Henry II, concerning the indivisibility of fiefs (Planiol 1887). The kingdom of Sicily produced an impressive series of legislative acts, beginning with the Assizes of Ariano of AD 1140[56] and culminating, less than a century later, in Frederick II's *Liber Augustalis* of AD 1231.[57] Right from the start these documents used an imperious and indeed imperial style. Already at Ariano the tone was set with the words: 'we will and order that you shall receive these sanctions . . .', i.e. the king proclaims his will, the vassals and other

---

54. Constitutions of Clarendon of 1164; Stubbs 1913, pp. 161–7.   55. Bigelow 1879, pp. 143–6.
56. Text in Brandileone 1884, pp. 94–118, Monti 1940; commentary and discussion in Schminck 1969, Ménager 1969, Zecchino 1980.
57. Text: Dilcher 1973; translation: Powell 1971; commentary: Dilcher 1975.

subjects receive it and obey.[58] Criminal, fiscal and feudal (inheritance) matters were the main concerns in the earlier stages, the range was expanded later on.[59]

What prompted all this legislation and which ideas influenced the law-givers? They certainly were under great social pressure, for people were looking to the kings and other rulers and hoping for a better and more secure society. The monarchy was expected to put right things which had indeed gone badly wrong, not merely by abolishing *malae consuetudines*, but by positive innovation. Much, no doubt, could be done without expressly issuing new laws – very little legislation went into the piecemeal foundation of the writ process of the common law in England – but not everything in all circumstances. The establishment *coram populo* of new rules had obvious advantages of clarity and certainty, where customs could be obscure or conflicting. Legislation was also politically important as an affirmation of the ruler's supreme position, which is exactly what was called for in the twelfth century. Since the monarchy was expected to offer more security and had to dispose of the necessary financial means to do it, it is not surprising that criminal and fiscal matters occupy pride of place in the laws of the period. Two other important fields were feudal law (protection of rightful tenant and heir) and questions of jurisdiction. This again is not surprising, since in many countries the leading people held their land in fee and since the increasing impact of royal justice necessarily created problems for the existing courts of the Church and the landowners. If however the social and political trend of the age clearly demanded legislation, this does not mean that extraneous ideas and models were without importance. The ever-present example of legislation by Church councils and popes must have been an encouragement and a source of inspiration for the states. And so, demonstrably, was Roman law, either via Byzantium – in Sicily in the early stages, or – all over Europe – via the school of Bologna. The doctors had defined the *regalia* at Roncaglia in AD 1158, explaining that all jurisdiction belonged to the emperor and stressing the emperor's position as law-giver, and Archbishop Hubert of Milan had said in so many words to Barbarossa that his will was the law.[60] Glanvill, the first treatise on the common law, echoing the *Corpus Iuris Civilis*, explains that *regia potestas* must be furnished with laws as well as arms.[61] All this was decided and

---

58. Caravale 1966, p. 96: 'Volumus igitur et iubemus ut sanctiones . . . fideliter et alacriter recipiatis.' A charter of 1145 speaks of the 'regalia nostrae Majestatis' (*ibid.*, p. 298).

59. On the Sicilian monarchy, besides the works cited in nn. 35–7, see Ménager 1959; Marongiu 1964; Jamison 1968; Bellomo 1977, pp. 75–134; Ullmann 1979 (with special reference to the contacts with England). For a comprehensive and detailed survey of medieval legislation in Europe see Wolf 1973.

60. Ullmann 1979; Benson 1982, pp. 364–9.   61. Ed. Hall 1965, pp. xxxvi, 1.

thought out at the highest level in the Church, the states and the universities; but the historian should not be concerned only with the thoughts and actions of the leading circles: the repercussions of the political and institutional changes on the life of ordinary people deserve no less attention and it is to the everyday life of the peasant communities that the discussion must now turn.

Lords and manors

In the centuries under review most of the peasantry lived in manors which were not only agricultural communities, but separate legal units: the landowners were no mere 'private' rent-collectors, they were lords, ruling over their peasants and exerting 'public' rights in matters of discipline, taxation, justice and defence. The inhabitants of their estates – free as well as unfree – were not only their tenants, but their subjects. This coincidence of ownership and lordship, this subjection of the peasantry reached a peak in the eleventh century and was reversed from the twelfth onwards. It was a European phenomenon, just as widespread in England (before and after 1066) as on the Continent. Historians have analysed various mechanisms in the long process which turned the *seigneurie foncière* into a *seigneurie banale* (so called because the landowner exerted the *bannum*, i.e. the right to command) or *justicière* (so called because the landowner was responsible for the administration of justice).[62] They have pointed to the grant of immunities, i.e. franchises, by Frankish kings to great landowners – *potentes* or churches who were freed from the interference of royal agents and from paying royal taxes. The latter were granted to the *immunistes*, who organised police, justice (except probably the gravest of crimes) and taxation for the inhabitants of their lands (Ganshof 1958a). They have pointed to the grant of court-fines by English kings to landowners, leading naturally to the latter's control over the courts themselves: express royal grants of old communal jurisdictions such as the Anglo-Saxon hundred courts are well documented and some may have been intended to secure the independence of the Church as well as to provide additional income.[63]

---

62. For the variations in terminology see Genicot 1982, p. vi. To call an owner a *seigneur* is not very helpful but this confusion between ownership and lordship is widespread. In Rome too *dominus* meant both 'lord' and 'owner'; and the 'lord' of a medieval lordship is of course quite different from a modern 'landlord'. The French term *seigneurie* is often used in English works, in such forms as 'seignory' and 'seignorial' systems, although 'lordly estate', 'patrimonial lordship', or 'lord's manor' seem better terms, since *senior* or *seigneur* can also refer to a vassal's lord.
63. For various forms of grant between the late seventh century and the eleventh, see Fisher 1973, pp. 123–32; Finberg 1974, p. 230; Lyon 1980, pp. 76–80.

Besides these legal transfers of jurisdiction there was a good deal of sheer oppression and arbitrary appropriation of the *bannum*: landowners were powerful and it was not surprising that they turned people who depended on them economically into their subjects, particularly in times of great insecurity. Thus it is understandable that the introduction of 'bad customs', i.e. arbitrary demands for labour and money, was a particular grievance in the eleventh century, when in France the traditional political order broke down. Nor should we forget that – besides this oppression – in times of unrest and anxiety people were spontaneously driven to place themselves and their goods under the protection and control of those powerful enough to offer them some degree of peace. Thus there are figures to show that in the Chartres area the percentage of freeholds (*allodia*) fell from 80% in the period 940–1030 to a mere 8% in the years from 1090 to 1130; while in Catalonia the percentage of allodial lands fell from 80% at the end of the tenth century to 25% in the last quarter of the eleventh.[64] By the early twelfth century large areas of western Europe were practically without free peasants and freeholds and this had, of course, much to do with the prevalent institutional weakness. In England, insecurity was also partly to blame for the spread of manorialism; for although the monarchy maintained internal order to a remarkable degree, the country experienced grave external threats and heavy fighting in the ninth, tenth and eleventh centuries.

Grants, oppression and insecurity all, no doubt, played a part in creating manorial lordship; but it seems likely that the origins of the familiar lordly estates of the eleventh and twelfth centuries can be traced back further into the early medieval period. The Frankish and Anglo-Saxon war-leaders occupied land on which they settled their followers under their lordly direction in communities called after them (place-names formed by combining a personal name with the element *ing* or *heim*): ownership and leadership went hand in hand.[65] It seems too that permanent settlement in fixed and ordered communities was an aspect of the evolution of the Germanic newcomers from a semi-nomadic to a sedentary way of life. It has been observed earlier that the distinction between the public and private spheres had little relevance in this period. The king who ruled over his kingdom was also deemed to own it as if it were a family asset, and the owner who was master of the land easily came to be considered the master of its inhabitants. Manorialism also fitted well into a pattern where, as we

64. Poly and Bournazel 1980, p. 92.   65. Fisher 1973, p. 128; Finberg 1974, p. 71.

have already seen, diffusion rather than concentration of power was characteristic.

On the Continent the rise of the *seigneurie* led to the amalgamation of the distinct Carolingian classes of freemen and bondmen into one class of villeins or 'men in somebody else's power' (*hommes de poesté*): since they were all their lord's tenants, all owed him services and payments, and all lived under his jurisdiction, it was only natural that they all came to enjoy the same low legal status.[66] Their situation improved from the twelfth century onwards, when many village communities obtained – by 'charters of franchises' or otherwise – the curbing of their lords' arbitrary power. This was a consequence of greater royal control over the knights and also of the rise of the towns. The peasants had never really been able to fight and stand up to their masters who were professional warriors, and the sole resistance open to them was running away.[67] But it was only with the revival of urban life and the occupation of new lands in the east and in Spain that there were effective and copious possibilities for runaway villeins easily to find new agricultural and other outlets. In England manorialism was widespread long before 1066 – few historians nowadays believe in the Stubbsian peasant democracy of Anglo-Saxon times – and it was continued by the Norman conquerors and exploiters, whom it suited very well. There the distinction between free and unfree peasants continued longer than across the Channel, which may have something to do with England's semi-colonial situation. The area of Danish settlement in north-eastern England was exceptional in that a free peasantry was and remained important there.

There is a good deal of terminological confusion about many medieval institutions, but the worst cacophony can be heard when manorialism and feudalism – *seigneurie* and *féodalité* – are confused.[68] Yet there is no reason why they should be: the lordship of a landowner over his peasants is quite different from the vassalic bond between a warrior and the lord to whom he

66. Carabie 1943, p. 218; Duby 1953, pp. 230–62; Garaud 1964, p. 170; Evergates 1975, p. 138 ('after c. 1120 there were in the *bailliage* of Troyes neither *servi* nor "free" men: except for the *domini* and *milites*, all rural inhabitants were *homines de corpore* and subjected to the private justice of a landlord') and pp. 142–3; Poly and Bournazel 1980, pp. 194–6, 212–17; Genicot 1982, pp. 207–52.

67. Sprandel 1975, p. 128, quotes the example of the abbot of St Pantaleon in Cologne who, in 1141, gave up various rights and incomes in favour of the *pauperes* of two manors, who had threatened to leave their ancestral homestead. On franchises resulting from widespread rural migration see Evergates 1975, p. 138.

68. Duby 1978, p. 189, rightly points out that 'mieux vaut ne pas l'appeler féodal . . . mais seigneurial', but still discusses the rise of seignorial power in the chapter, under the heading 'La révolution féodale'. It is well known that already during the Ancien Régime some learned authors maintained that fiefs and seignory had nothing in common, whilst others asserted that they were one and the same thing (Critchley 1978, p. 58).

has done homage (and from whom he may hold a fief). Thus we find in Anglo-Saxon England a society without feudalism but with widespread manorialism, and in Germany a *Grundherrschaft* existed on allodial land which its lord did not hold from anyone.[69] In France on the other hand – as in England after 1066 – it was common for lords to be mediate or immediate vassals of the king and to hold their estates in fief. In modern times this feudal connection has led to the wholesale condemnation of numerous agricultural charges and taxes of diverse origins as 'feudal' and to the attachment of the 'feudal' label to seignorial dues that had strictly nothing to do with homage, vassalic service, relief, feudal inheritance and other institutions that are properly called feudal; Church tithes too were encompassed in this attack on 'feudalism', although their nature and origin were quite different again. All this eighteenth-century confusion should be no reason for modern medievalists to go on mixing up different institutions that are not inherently connected.[70] What feudalism exactly meant and what role it really played in European society from the days of Charlemagne to those of Barbarossa, Henry II and Philip Augustus must now be considered.

Feudalism

'Feudal' is derived from *feodalis* and concerns fiefs; fiefs were usually held from lords by vassals: so 'feudalism', properly understood, relates to lords, vassals and fiefs.[71] It would be superfluous to state such an obvious truth, were it not for the fact that the term 'feudal' has been applied to various social phenomena that have no intrinsic connection with fiefs and vassals, such as backward agricultural techniques, warlordism, peasant oppression and irrational or 'primitive' modes of thinking which occur in many periods and countries where fiefs and vassals are unknown.[72] Like

69. Strayer 1965, p. 36; Fourquin 1970, pp. 6–8; Herlihy 1970, p. xviii; Slicher van Bath 1974, pp. 233–7; Van de Kieft 1974, pp. 203–4; Lyon 1980, p. 88. Critchley 1978, p. 82, writes: 'territorial warlords feature in the political decline of other states [than the Frankish], feudal or otherwise'.
70. See, among others, Boutruche 1968, vol. I, who (like Fourquin 1970) carefully chose the title *Seigneurie et Féodalité* to differentiate between the two institutions, and discusses (pp. 11–25) the use and abuse of the term 'feudal'. Cf. Bloch 1939, vol. I, pp. 1–8; Fourquin 1970, p. 6; Herlihy 1970, p. xv; Brown 1974; Critchley 1978, p. 159.
71. The literature on feudalism is immense. See in particular Mitteis 1933; Bloch 1939–40 (English translation 1961); Strayer 1965; Boutruche 1968–70; Fourquin 1970; Herlihy 1970; Poly and Bournazel 1980; Ganshof 1982 (most recent English translation 1964). Select bibliography: Ganshof and Van Caenegem 1972.
72. To a medieval jurist such as Alvarottus (d. 1453), author of a *De feudis*, feudalism was about the law of fiefs, the *feudalis scientia* (for treatises on feudal law see Kelley 1964). For Adam Smith – the first to

'medieval' the term 'feudal' has even been used for everything modern man considers an abuse, such as absolute monarchy, the exaggerated power of political parties and trade unions or the farmers' lobby in France.[73] Even when this sort of confusion is avoided, however, there is still room for considerable uncertainty as to the historical significance of feudalism. Some authors use 'feudal' as a synonym for 'anarchic': for them feudalism is equated with the collapse of public order and the destruction of peace and of the state. One famous medievalist talks dramatically of 'Europe cut to pieces by feudalism'.[74] Others, on the contrary, praise feudalism as the sound basis upon which the late medieval state was built, and maintain that 'the regions of Europe which were the most thoroughly feudalised (by any definition) were the regions that eventually developed the governments which became the models for all other European states'.[75] The contradiction between these views seems to have escaped some authors' notice altogether. Thus one excellent legal historian explains how Charlemagne used vassalage as a means to strengthen the bond between him and his subjects, and yet describes these *réseaux de vassaux* as *anarchiques*.[76] Other historians are content to point out, in some puzzlement, that 'the same institution led in some countries to centralisation and a strong monarchy, and in others to the latter's ruin'.[77] It is evident that conceptual clarification is called for.

In the most general terms and in its early stages vassalage was concerned with the personal and life-long bonds between *vassi* or *homines* and their *domini*, i.e. with poor but free warriors who commended themselves in loyal service to war-leaders, who had the means to provide for their livelihood. These personal relationships between lords and followers were known in Anglo-Saxon England and in the kingdom of the Merovingians and owed much to the way of life in the Germanic tribes. This early, rather fluid vassalage, whose institutional significance was limited, was elevated by the Carolingians into a distinct system and given considerable military and political importance. They used royal vassalage to create an army of professional warriors on horseback and to attach them and other leading

use the term 'feudal system' in English – it meant a low-yielding mode of production using servile labour (Herlihy 1970, p. xv). For a recent survey of feudalism as 'un système socio-économique, surtout agraire, aux forces productives médiocres' see Kula 1970; and for critical analysis of all this, Brown 1974.   73. Boutruche 1968, vol. I, pp. 20–5.
74. Duby 1967, p. 19: 'L'empire est le mythe où l'Occident, que la féodalité met en pièces, retrouve l'unité foncière dont il rêve . . .'. For the old tradition, assimilating the feudal age to political anarchy, see Tabacco 1960, p. 398.
75. Strayer 1971, pp. 64–5.   76. Lemarignier 1970, p. 92.
77. Conrad 1962, p. 254: 'So führte die Entwicklung des Lehnrechtes in Deutschland zum Territorialfürstentum und zum Partikularismus, in England und Frankreich zum Zentralismus und zur Stärkung der Königsmacht.'

men personally to the king. This gave vassalage a social eminence and a
political and military significance it had not known before. The Carolingians
also granted tenures of land (*beneficia*; later *feoda*) to some of their vassals
(*vassi, homines, fideles*) to be held till the end of the vassalic bond and
specifically designed to ensure that the vassal could maintain himself: a
specific fee served to enable the holder to perform a specific service. From
that moment it is correct to speak of the 'vassalic-feudal' or the 'feudal-
vassalic' system, though it is convenient to use the less cumbersome and
more usual term 'feudalism'. Many of these early fiefs consisted of Church
land, which the king had mobilised for the defence of the realm without
being able to grant it away in full property, but only as a temporary
'benefice' for the duration of the vassal's service, i.e. for life. Soon not only
land but public functions, in state and Church, were granted in fee to such
royal vassals, who used the same formula to create their own feudal
following.[78]

The aims of the Carolingians were manifold. They wanted to strengthen
the cohesion of their expanding multiracial state through the personal
sworn commendation of the top figures in all their lands: to most people this
personal link and oath of loyalty in the hands of the king must have meant
more than abstract allegiance to the empire and subjection to its laws. As less
important persons were thus linked to the leading notables and these in their
turn to the king or emperor himself, the feudal chain was meant to create
order and establish an hierarchy of which the monarch was the apex.
Feudalism also provided a new military organisation different from the
traditional infantry of armed peasants and consisting of a professional army
of horsemen who were set free by the produce of their 'benefices' to give all
their time to their military task and able to cover the heavy expenses of a
cavalryman. In other countries too warriors lived from the produce of land
received from kings, but it was land which was given away by perpetual and
irrevocable grant (the Merovingians had done this on a large scale and the
Anglo-Saxon kings did the same). The feudal grants of the Carolingians
merely put the land at a man's disposal for the duration of his vassalage:
afterwards the 'benefice' reverted to the lord, who could bestow it on
someone else.

This Carolingian system was anything but anarchic: it was so well
adapted to material and mental circumstances as to endow the Frankish
empire with an adequate military and political organisation. In fact this

78. Ganshof 1982, pp. 35–104.

grand scheme came to ruin because of the collapse of the keystone of the whole structure, the monarchy, and not because of the part played by feudalism: it has been clearly established, for example, that in Lazio the *crisi dell' autorità* preceded feudalism.[79] In France especially nothing held the warlords together: all went their own way and dragged their vassals with them. Some of these new rulers, such as the counts of Flanders, could mobilise 1,000 knights, but there were many 'sovereign' castellans who mustered no more than five or six. All this was a consequence of the political collapse analysed above and it meant that everyone was trying to find someone more powerful to depend on. Everyone depended on a lord – the warrior class by vassalage and fief-holding, the peasant class by living under the rule and on the land of the warriors – both classes had often given up their ancient freeholds and turned them into fiefs or peasant tenements. As a class, feudal warriors were distinguished by their fiefs and they developed their own rules about homage, service and the acquisition and inheritance of fiefs and also their own feudal courts, where rules were discussed and applied. Their feudal relationships were no longer props of the monarchy, but a mere technique for concluding formal alliances and finding patronage or knights in the ever-changing and uncontrolled power game: even warring knights needed some leadership and formal contact – and they needed fiefs! How little this had to do with order and hierarchy was dramatically shown when the king of France himself did not hesitate to become the vassal of his own vassals, if that was the price for obtaining some interesting fief (like a strategic area with castles). As the regional ruler in the Ile de France, he was only playing the same game as the other territorial princes. But as a king he was committing the worst possible betrayal of the original concept of feudalism and it was natural that as soon as the monarchy recovered, Suger, Louis VI's guide, protested that a king could hold other people's fiefs, but could not become their vassal: the monarchy stood high above such arrangements and bonds of dependence, and the king of France had to extricate himself from the feudal system in which he was enmeshed.[80] This royal betrayal was itself connected with another element of corruption that had crept into the original scheme, namely that the fief,

---

79. Tabacco 1960, p. 399; Toubert 1973, p. 1096.
80. The oldest texts date from 1124, in connection with Louis VI's position as a vassal of the abbey of St Denis for the county of Vexin, for which, according to Suger, the king acknowledged that he would have been obliged to do homage 'si rex non esset' (Halphen 1950b, pp. 267–8). The first explicit formulation of the rule came in 1185, when Philip Augustus held the county of Amiens in fee from the cathedral there, but did not do homage 'cum utique nemini facere debeamus hominium vel possimus' (*ibid.*, p. 268).

the material element, had become more important than the personal
element, i.e. the vassalic bond: the means had become more important than
the aim and vassals became known as 'feudatories'.[81] There is thus solid
historical justification for the modern use of 'feudalism' instead of
'vassalage', for from the later Middle Ages onwards the system was mainly a
peculiar form of land-holding. Of this there are several indications. Fiefs
had become or were becoming hereditary: the chronology of this
development was varied and is not always clear, but the fact itself is not in
dispute,[82] nor is its meaning: fiefs were entering into the family patrimony
irrespective of the personal qualifications of their holders. For the same
reason, by the twelfth century, fiefs were regularly inherited by women,
who could not render the military service that was the *raison d'être* of most
fiefs and had to find men to represent them.[83] This 'patrimonialisation', or
rather commercialisation of fiefs manifested itself even more strikingly
when vassals began trading them, i.e. selling or donating them or giving
them in gage. At first this could only be done with the lord's consent and via
a new investiture and homage by the new feudatory. In the course of the
twelfth century at the latest, this requirement was given up and the express
or even tacit agreement of the lord was deemed enough. It is well known
that the statute *Quia emptores* of 1290 granted the tenant the freedom to
transfer his land to another. What was left of the old personal bond if the
lord could find himself landed with a vassal he did not know or did not
approve of?[84] It also became possible for fiefs to be held by one man from
several lords, some of whom might be his own vassals, and each of whom he
was supposed to serve with the loyalty of a lifetime.[85] This made a mockery
of the old idea of the free and unconditional loyalty unto death of a man to
his lord. Attempts to remedy this abuse by introducing the category of the
main lord (*dominus ligius*), who had priority in case of conflict of loyalties,
could not hide the fact that fief-hunger had become the overriding impulse.

81. Lemarignier 1965, p. 174.
82. For an early, though temporary, indication, in 877, see Ganshof 1982, p. 84. In France heredity was
    general by the end of the eleventh century, though there were then still some feudal grants for life
    (Poly and Bournazel 1980, p. 132). In England, the Norman aristocracy after 1066 'was already
    accustomed to inheritance' (Holt 1972, p. 5; and cf. DeAragon 1982, p. 381). In the empire, Conrad
    II's Italian decision in favour of vassals' hereditary rights in 1037 has been noted (p. 181 above and n.
    27); but in Germany this development was much slower. In Spain fiefs were not only not hereditary,
    they were not even for life: vassalage could easily be terminated by either lord or vassal
    (Valdeavellano 1963, pp. 251–3; Sánchez Albornoz 1969, p. 26; Grassotti 1969, p. 629).
83. Ganshof 1982, pp. 222–4.   84. *Ibid.*, pp. 225–32.
85. The count of Champagne in the early thirteenth century, for example, held fiefs not only from the
    king of France and the emperor, but also from the duke of Burgundy, the archbishops or bishops of
    Rheims, Sens, Autun, Auxerre, Châlons-sur-Marne and Langres, and from the abbot of St Denis,
    who were themselves his vassals for various lands (Halphen 1950b, pp. 266–7).

Feudalism was now concerned with fiefs: personal loyalty and various traditional military and judicial duties had turned into more or less cumbersome charges, annexes of the fief, which the *feodatarius* had to accept if he wanted to acquire and keep feudal land. The land-hunger of these fief-collecting knights was a political factor in its own right, for they put pressure upon their leaders to provide them with ever more manors, which often meant foreign conquest and, if the king's foreign policy failed and resulted in loss of land, revolt – as in England in 1215. The logical outcome of the ascendancy of the fief over homage was reached in the twelfth century. We find fiefs to which no service was attached but only a vague obligation to appear at the lord's court, which implied only a vague right to his sympathy; and since the failure to fulfil even the minimal vassalic duty carried no sanction, it is clear that we are in the presence of a form of possession that is almost undistinguishable from Roman ownership or the Germanic allod.[86] Even more remote from the classic feudal scheme of things were the peasant holdings which were called *fehu, feudo, fevum, feudum condicionale* or *terra feovalis* and for which we even find serfs doing homage and being called *fevales, feodales* or *feodatarii*. The real fiefs were then called *honorata* or *franca*, to distinguish them from peasant tenures with which they had only the name in common.[87] The basic attitudes and terms of feudalism fitted the most diverse realities and suited all classes of people, because the bond of man to man and the holding of land from someone else were as widespread and fundamental in medieval Europe as subjection to the state and free ownership of capital in later centuries.

In the eleventh and twelfth centuries feudalism was a truly European phenomenon and had even been exported to the Holy Land,[88] but the pattern varied from country to country. The ingredients were the same but their combination and respective importance were not. Two points call for special attention here: connection between vassalage and fief and the degree of monarchical control.

In southern France, where the uncontrolled variety was fully established until the middle of the twelfth century (when the house of Barcelona took

---

86. For instances in northern Italy see Rippe 1975 and Rippe 1979; also Brancoli-Busdraghi 1965. For France see Duby 1953, pp. 365–6; some moral obligation often remained after all material duties had been eliminated.
87. Petot 1927; Carabie 1943, p. 284; Duby 1953, p. 562; Grassotti 1969, p. 575; Fourquin 1970, p. 130; Rippe 1975, p. 198; Poly 1976, pp. 163–4; Rippe 1979, pp. 694–5; Poly and Bournazel 1980, pp. 135–6; Giordanengo 1981, pp. 3, 8, 39.
88. Grandclaude 1923; La Monte 1932; Prawer 1969, pp. 463–503.

Provence in hand), the connection between vassalage and fief was never the rule: some people became vassals without holding fiefs[89] and others who had nothing to do with the warrior class held tenures which were styled fiefs.[90]

In Spain feudalism developed along very distinct lines, except in Catalonia, where the European model, going back directly to the Frankish *marca hispanica*, prevailed. The north Spanish Christian kingdoms produced a system of their own, where fiefs and homage certainly had a role and were clearly influenced by Frankish and afterwards French models, particularly in the eleventh and twelfth centuries; but Visigothic traditions and the need for strong monarchic leadership in the struggle against Islam were responsible for a fighting feudalism of the controlled variety. The kings kept their vassals, who had learned to dread the *ira regis*,[91] and their fiefs well in hand and the notion of public offence was never lost, so that, as one authority put it, although Spain knew vassalage, benefice and immunity, it was never feudalised.[92] Nor were vassalage – the term *vasallos* is rare in the tenth century, more usual, under French influence, in the eleventh[93] – and fiefs – sometimes temporary, sometimes for life, but never hereditary – regularly linked together.[94] The Spanish variety of the *feodum*, the *prestimonio*, was current in the twelfth century.[95] Because of the proximity of the wealthy Arabic world the Spanish monarchs disposed of large amounts of money and very soon resorted to paying stipends to their knights instead of granting them land – a point for further consideration later.[96]

In marked contrast to Asturias, León, Castile and Aragon, we find the western feudal system being imported wholesale by the great abbeys in Lazio from 1060 onwards (*equites cum fegis, milites cum beneficio*). The initiative was meant to establish a solid military control by dependent and dependable knights. After being applied by the great abbeys, this feudalism was adopted by the central government of the papal state from 1130–40 onwards; the papacy, as one leading authority put it, by turning feudalism into the keystone of the state structure gave it the public dimension which it

89. Magnou 1964, p. 148; Magnou-Nortier 1968, pp. 130–4; Poly 1976, p. 170; Giordanengo 1981, pp. 3, 50.
90. Garaud 1964, p. 231; Magnou 1964, p. 150; Poly and Bournazel 1980, pp. 105–27, 135–6; Giordanengo 1981, pp. 3–8, 39.
91. Valdeavellano 1963, p. 254; Grassotti 1969, pp. 927–36; Sánchez Albornoz 1969, p. 23.
92. Valdeavellano 1963, p. 232, cf. also pp. 233–5; Bisson 1978, pp. 464–8.
93. Grassotti 1969, p. 33.
94. Valdeavellano 1963, pp. 234–43; Grassotti 1969, p. 678.
95. Valdeavellano 1963, pp. 265–6. For some rare thirteenth-century Castilian *feudos* which were hereditary after the European model, see Grassotti 1969, p. 655.
96. Valdeavellano 1963, p. 248; Grassotti 1969, pp. 721–895; Sánchez Albornoz 1969, p. 25.

had so far lacked.[97] We have already seen what happened to fiefs in northern Italy, where homage was disappearing in the eleventh century; as to the south, it produced the feudal monarchy of Norman origin whose importance was emphasised above.

A similar introduction of an 'adult' feudal organisation by a strong monarch took place, on a much larger scale, in England after 1066. Here too vassalage and fiefs were closely linked and the whole organisation firmly controlled from the top. Its continental, Norman origin is obvious, although it betrays in England an almost mathematical systematisation which it had not known in the duchy (this was caused by the special conditions of the regime of conquest and military occupation imposed on England).[98] After serving himself abundantly, the Conqueror bestowed huge areas of land (and their peasant population) on his continental tenants, lay and ecclesiastical, who owed him fixed quotas of knights for those fiefs: these *tenentes in capite* recruited their own vassals and in course of time provided them also with fiefs. This closely knit group of warriors formed a true feudal pyramid. They did not, however, replace the political framework of the Anglo-Saxon state, but only added a dimension to it and organised it into a war machine such as the country had never seen. If Norman and Angevin England was such a success, it was because the new rulers had preserved the solid foundations of their English predecessors. As soon as the monarchy weakened, as in the days of Stephen and Matilda, the disruptive potential of warlordism and regional state-building by military leaders disposing of castles and vassals became apparent. This is illustrated, for example, by the treaty concluded in the years 1148–53 between Earl Ranulf of Chester and Earl Robert of Leicester, defining their spheres of local interest and the conditions under which either might make war upon the other. According to the commentator of this remarkable agreement, it would be hard to find another English document which demonstrates so clearly the tendencies of a feudal society emancipated from royal control.[99]

97. Toubert 1973, p. 1128: 'La papauté . . . faisant de la féodalité une pièce maîtresse de l'édifice étatique lui a donné la dimension publique qui lui manquait encore.' In a thorough survey of this development (pp. 1135–90) Toubert also draws attention to the fact that in Lazio feudalism was introduced belatedly as 'un système déjà adulte', whereas in Catalonia, southern France and northern Italy it had already existed for a long time. In Lazio, *inter alia*, this meant a constant link between vassalage and fief, while firm papal control had by the end of the twelfth century established universal *ligantia* in favour of the pope.
98. For the controversy as to the native or Norman character of English feudalism see, among others, Hollister 1968 and Brown 1973. On Norman feudalism before 1066 see Tabuteau 1982.
99. Stenton 1932, p. 253; text *ibid.* nr 48, pp. 285–8.

Henry II understandably treated the whole disgraceful interlude under Stephen as a non-event, studiously omitted even mentioning it and systematically restored the crown to the position it occupied under Henry I, sparing neither the Church nor the barons who had profited from the crisis of the monarchy.

It is well known that in England after 1066 the feudalisation of land was complete, in the sense that freehold, allod and property were unknown and all land – whether knight's fee, Church almoign or peasant holding – was held from someone higher up the tenurial ladder and finally from the crown. However striking, this situation was not so different from many regions in France – the uniqueness in the case of England lies in the fact that this feudal stage was preserved there in later centuries, when property, *inter alia* because of Roman law influence, was re-established elsewhere. In many parts of France the old *allodium* or *alleu* was in the eleventh and twelfth centuries turned either into a feudal tenure held by a knight or into a rent-paying peasant holding: in Normandy and Brittany,[100] around Beauvais[101] and around Chartres,[102] in Poitou[103] and southern France generally.[104] The old term *allodium* might persist, but with the new meaning of a hereditary tenure, synonymous with *feudum*![105]

In Germany, where this development was much slower, *allodia*, particularly those owned by the nobility, never disappeared and the crown was never considered the highest feudal suzerain of the soil. German feudalism went, of course, straight back to Frankish times and the German kings always understood its centripetal potential – the 'stem-dukes' and the bishops and abbots of the *Reichskirche* were royal vassals. Nevertheless it was given a new lease of life by Frederick Barbarossa who, through the *Heerschildordnung* sought to create a feudal pyramid with hierarchical ramifications from the crown and the *Fürsten* down to the simple knights. His attempt was a failure because, once again, the monarchy itself was utterly weakened and during the *interregnum* the throne was even left vacant for twenty-three years (1250–73). It is noteworthy that at the same time the king of France was using with great success the old feudal ties with the territorial princes to facilitate and justify their elimination and the unification of his kingdom – but he, of course, was acting from a position of strength. This, incidentally, shows again that feudalism was a hollow form,

---

100. Ganshof 1982, p. 204.   101. *Ibid.*
102. Poly and Bournazel 1980, p. 92.   103. Garaud 1964, pp. 231, 257.
104. Poly and Bournazel 1980, pp. 210–12.   105. Carabie 1943, pp. 232–7.

a mere technique that could serve for the most diverse purposes, according to circumstances and men strong enough to manipulate it.

In the course of the twelfth century there were unmistakable signs of the decline of feudalism, not only the 'uncontrolled' variety in France, which was being tamed by the invigorated monarchy, but the 'controlled' Anglo-Norman type which would soon also be a spent force. Everywhere modern forms of political organisation were breaking through and the old feudal arrangements appeared as irrelevant, if not positively harmful. These new style kingdoms were based less on the personal tie binding the leading men to the sovereign than on the allegiance of the nation to 'the crown'. It is in connection with the Second Crusade and the absence of King Louis VII that we find, for the first time in a royal charter of 1147, the crown (*corona regni*) not as a precious and symbolic headgear, but as an abstract notion: henceforth all subjects owed loyalty to 'the crown', even in the absence of the king. Suger, who was a staunch supporter of the monarchy and believed that the king and the law shared the same majesty in their command, had previously always written about the person of the king and it was only in his last writings that the crown appears as an entity distinct from the physical person of the king, yet clothed in the same dignity.[106] This crown proceeded to organise a national administration and began, before the end of the twelfth century, to create the national political assemblies representing a wide spectrum of subjects, which eventually led to our modern parliaments.[107] The fief-holding fighting knights, without whom feudalism was rather meaningless, were fast losing their importance, for the kings found other and more adequate defence arrangements. They employed (foreign) mercenaries, recreated the ancient non-professional peasant armies,[108] and discovered the usefulness and fighting qualities of the urban militia. Thus, although the decline of the knightly army based on the feudal quotas was gradual, it was real: the last summons of the English feudal levy took place in 1385 (Lewis 1958; Palmer 1968). What remained after feudalism was stripped of its institutional and military significance was a peculiar form of possession of land, not essentially different from ownership

106. Bournazel 1975, p. 172; and cf. p. 173 for a charter of 1156 for the church of Soissons extolling *regiam majestatem et dignitatem coronae.*
107. E.g. the *cortes* (*curia*) of León held in 1188 by Alfonso IX, which consisted of bishops, lay magnates and elected citizens, by whose counsel the king was to be bound in questions of war and peace (Grassotti 1982, p. 358).
108. Assize of Arms of Henry II of 1181, text: Stubbs 1913, pp. 181–4.

but not quite the same, and distinguished, *inter alia*, by peculiar inheritance laws such as primogeniture (which went back to the days when the fief had to be kept intact to allow the heir to do the service for a knight's fee). The causes of this 'decline and fall' (Cam 1940) were numerous, but they were all connected and flowed fundamentally from the emergence of a more advanced form of civilisation. The intellectual climate was changing: Roman law and Aristotelian philosophy provided new tools of social analysis and a new approach to politics (Benson and Constable 1982). The nation was a *res publica* and the *princeps* was its first magistrate, to whom the people had (long ago and irrevocably) granted their sovereign rights, not a king who administered the realm as his family's patrimony and headed a clientele of barons. John of Salisbury was well placed to give an early expression to these new ideas. He was a cosmopolitan Englishman who, after a spell at the Roman curia, ended his career as bishop of Chartres. He 'showed a growing awareness of the transpersonal, public character of the *res publica*; on the basis of Roman law he styled the prince a *persona publica*, a *potestas publica*'.[109] In his *Policraticus* (1159), 'a monograph which was the first to call upon the Roman law as the backbone of an argumentation in the service of the science of government',[110] John of Salisbury, who found it 'the apotheosis of order',[111] 'leant heavily on Roman law, because he clearly realised that only with its help could the monarchic form of rulership persuasively and plausibly be advocated'.[112] Social reality also was changing fast: the relative importance of the rural nobility and knighthood was reduced by the emergence of urban power. In this new phase European society consisted not only of peasants and knights, but also of wealthy and educated burgesses and a small but expanding bureaucracy. The economic picture was also changing fast and with direct consequences for the feudal world. The abundance of money and the expanding produce of taxation meant that the grant of land was becoming obsolete as a technique of rewarding soldiers. Mercenaries were easier to handle, to recruit and to dismiss and if this form of recruitment was felt to be demeaning for knights attached to traditional forms, the money fief offered the perfect solution. The recipient was a vassal in the traditional style, but instead of a landed fief he received a regular stipend. This 'fief' was, however, not alienable and admitted no subinfeudation, nor was it hereditary, so that the device offered greater flexibility to the monarchy and secured greater dependency of the tenants, since cutting off payment was easier than dislodging a knight from

109. Kantorowicz 1961, p. 97. 110. Ullmann 1978, p. 520.
111. *Ibid.*, p. 535. 112. *Ibid.*, p. 520.

his tenement (Lyon 1951). The very first beginnings of the money fief can be traced to the end of the eleventh century,[113] but the technique only became usual in the thirteenth and fourteenth centuries.

It might seem paradoxical that the rules of feudalism were only put in writing in the very century, the twelfth, when its decline became apparent, but in fact this is not so surprising. Not only were the preceding two centuries altogether poor in learning and writing, legal or otherwise, but the nature of feudal law did not lend itself easily to written formulation: it was customary and almost totally ignored legislation or the recording of judgements. It is understandable therefore that the first compilation of feudal laws was made, some four centuries after their foundation, in northern Italy, where legal studies, *inter alia* of Lombard law, had never disappeared and where the revival of Roman law took place. The various parts of the *Libri feudorum* (text: Lehmann 1896) are not easy to date, comprising as they do miscellaneous laws, opinions, precedents and customs from northern Italy. The little treatise formed by the first six chapters of book I goes back to the eleventh century. The main part, the work of Obertus de Orto, a well-known Milanese judge who had studied at Bologna, was written in the middle of the twelfth century in the form of two letters to his son Anselm, who was a student there. It was based on the feudal custom of Milan. The compilation was completed in the second half of the twelfth century with the texts of imperial constitutions. Fiefs are here envisaged as property liable to specific services and subject to peculiar – and in the eyes of civilians odd – rules of creation, conveyance, inheritance and forfeiture. The glossators gave their early attention to feudal institutions and made interesting attempts to reduce these oddities to the universal standards of Roman law. For Irnerius, for example, the fief is a public office which, by reference to the *curiales*, meant the exclusion of women. His method of studying feudal law in the light of Roman-law teaching found a wide following, and, quite naturally, the *Libri feudorum* found their own glossators, the earliest being Pillius Medicinensis (d. c. 1207), who was also the author of a *Summa feudorum*, possibly written in the 1180s.[114] Outside Italy the *Libri feudorum* had some importance in Spain, where their influence has been traced in the laws of Alfonso X in the middle of the thirteenth century.[115]

---

113. For an instance in Flanders in 1087 see Fourquin 1970, p. 133; and for French cases in the reign of Louis VI (1108–37), Poly and Bournazel 1980, p. 281.
114. Critchley 1978, pp. 11–19; Giordanengo 1981, pp. 129–39.
115. Grassotti 1969, pp. 627–8, 655.

If, for feudal law, we can turn to the *Libri feudorum* (and later to work on customary law such as Eike von Repgau for treatises on *Lehnrecht*), there is nothing similar for feudal political thought. That the people involved with feudalism had ideas about the state and its organisation and the wielding of power is beyond doubt, but we shall find no treatises where they are set forth and spelt out. The feudal milieu was more concerned with values and a code of conduct than with abstract conceptions and deductions from them. Thus the famous letter which Bishop Fulbert of Chartres wrote in 1020 to Duke William of Aquitaine merely contains a list of the obligations of vasssals to their lords. The bishop explains in the first place what a good vassal should avoid doing, but points out that it is not for doing this alone that he deserves his benefice and that positive action is required also. The author also explains what the lord's duties are towards his men: failing to fulfil them the lord will rightfully be regarded as guilty of bad faith.[116] That personal loyalty to the lord was absolutely central appears from such diverse sources as epic literature and criminal law. The most heinous crime imaginable was felony, i.e. betraying one's lord, and it is typical that in English criminal law this became the term for all the worst offences, including those that had nothing to do with the personal disloyalty of a man to his lord; nevertheless the lands of such a criminal escheated to his lord and were not forfeited to the crown, as were his chattels.[117]

The modern state has eliminated most of the feudal norms and values, but in the political institutions of our present world one element has survived that can be directly traced to feudal origins: the notion that the relation between rulers and citizens is based on a mutual contract, which means that governments have duties as well as rights and that resistance to unlawful rulers who break that contract is legitimate. Indeed, the king, however majestic and anointed, was also a feudal lord who had a contractual relationship with his men and, by extension, with the nation. These feudal convictions were opposed to and a hindrance to royal absolutism, which never completely overcame them, and they were the historic starting point of the limitation of the monarchy and the constitutional form of government, whose fundamental idea is that governments as well as individuals ought to act under the law.[118]

116. Herlihy 1970, nr 14, pp. 96–7.   117. Milsom 1981, p. 355.
118. On this often neglected truth see Ullmann 1966, pp. 53–79, and Ullmann 1967, pp. 63–98.

I0

KINGSHIP AND EMPIRE

For ideas of kingship, the period c. 750 to c. 1150 was no longer one of beginnings but of consolidation.[1] It saw the formation of a single culture in an expanded Latin Christendom. It began with the incorporation of significant Spanish and insular contributions into the mainstream of western political thought, and it ended with new contributions from as far afield as Bohemia and Denmark.[2] The history of the period was dominated first by the Frankish Empire, then by states that succeeded to or were profoundly influenced by it. Its creation strengthened in the short run the traditional elements in barbarian kingship, successful leadership of the people (*gens*) in wars of conquest and plunder bringing Frankish domination of other *gentes*. Hence the hegemonial idea of empire, of the emperor ruling many peoples and realms, arose directly from the political experience of the eighth-century West. In the longer run power devolved to kingdoms that proved durable, without a gentile identity or an economic base in plunder and tribute. This brought new formulations of the realm as a territorial and sociological entity, the aristocracy sharing power and responsibility with the king. The idea of empire detached from its gentile anchorage acquired Roman-Christian universality.

In the eighth century the Frankish kings Pippin and Charlemagne successfully mobilised two elites, the higher clergy of the Frankish Church and the Frankish aristocracy. Power-sharing was built into the fabric of the Carolingian Empire though it was masked at first by a community of interest that evoked a chorus of praise for rulers evidently possessed of

1. A general note on bibliography for this chapter: most of the secondary literature is in German, but English-readers will find invaluable the comprehensive survey, with many translated extracts from primary texts, in Carlyle and Carlyle 1903–36, vols. I-III. A useful survey of the sources, though brief and with curious omissions, is Ullmann 1975b. Ullmann 1975a and Morrall 1971 have little for the period before the eleventh century, while the excellent Lewis 1954 and Tierney 1964 unfortunately do not cover it. McIlwain 1932 remains valuable but mainly for the later Middle Ages.
2. Contributions from Spain and the British Isles: Anton 1968, pp. 55–74, 103–7; Bohemia: below, p. 251; Denmark: Strand 1980. Important developments in Italy: Keller 1976. The present chapter was completed before the appearance of Reynolds 1984, of which chapters 1 and 8 especially illuminate kingship in this period.

divine approval. Second thoughts were voiced in the ninth century when the stabilising of internal and external frontiers engendered fiercer competition for power within kingdoms. Some churchmen now clarified and qualified the terms of their support for kings and emperors, while aristocratic groupings formed by and around royal regimes recalled ideas of rights and of consent which could justify restraints on, and even resistance to, royal power.

In the latter part of the period, more intensive economic exploitation made possible new concentrations of resources in the hands of magnates, lay and clerical, and also of kings. The religious fervour of the Gregorian age was accompanied by a revived apocalypticism which could assign new and positive roles to kings and especially to emperors: this, more even than re-reading of Roman law, accounts for the enthusiastic tone of much twelfth-century writing on divinely ordained rulership. Few ecclesiastical reformers, save in some areas of Italy, could part company with kings for long, though a richer, better-served post-Gregorian papacy could sometimes underwrite clerical protest against royal oppression. But it was the reaction of lay aristocrats against 'tyranny' that stimulated the clearer, more widespread articulation of ideas of collective resistance and of representation of political communities. The period 750–1150 is therefore doubly crucial: in the legitimisation of kingship and empire, and in the working-out of critiques of power. Theocracy thrived: but so did the seeds of constitutionalism.

The relationship of ideas to reality is a general problem in the history of political thought. Peculiar to the earlier Middle Ages however is the difficulty with so much of the material of answering such basic questions as: who wrote it and for what audience? Is it a public work in the sense of expressing the 'official line' of the regime? Or is it a private work revealing the opinions of an individual or coterie? To take an example: the Donation of Constantine is an eighth-century forgery that purports to convey the transfer of imperial power and privileges to the pope and his entourage. Assessment of its significance in terms of its contemporary impact depends on whether it is identified as a papal document produced in 753 to justify Pope Stephen II's summoning of the Franks into Italy to protect the lands of St Peter, in disregard of Byzantine claims to authority,[3] or alternatively as a 'literary *divertissement*' produced in the late 750s or 760s by a Lateran cleric[4] to elevate Rome at the expense of Ravenna. Further, the circumstances of its

---

3. Ullmann 1962, p. 58–61, 74–86.   4. Ourliac 1980, p. 790. See also below, pp. 230–1.

production, whatever these were, have to be distinguished from the motives of the Frankish clergy who in the ninth century incorporated the text into a collection of canons designed to buttress ecclesiastical property-rights. Ideological content may vary with context. The fact that medieval writers, often with polemic purpose, used and re-used 'authorities' like the Donation with blithe unconsciousness of anachronism makes it especially important – and difficult – for modern historians to avoid this pitfall. Finally there is the problem of assessing how far a writer's view or concept was shared by his or her contemporaries. For instance, Agobard of Lyons' suggestion that the Emperor Louis the Pious should impose one law on all the peoples of his empire is interesting but quite unrepresentative[5] (as well as impractical!). It has seemed best in a general survey to concentrate mainly on texts that have a normative character or seem to present some fairly widely-held viewpoint for their period. But it has to be admitted that sheer scarcity of evidence sometimes makes representativeness hard to gauge.

Carolingian kingship

In tracing the development of ideas about kingship, 750 is a more defensible starting-point than most periodisations of history. In that year envoys were sent from Francia

> to Pope Zacharias to ask him whether or not it was good that there should be kings in Francia at that time who lacked royal power. Pope Zacharias told Pippin that it would be better to call king the man who had power than the man who was still there without royal power. So that order might not be disturbed, he ordered through apostolic authority that Pippin be made king.

Thus the Royal Frankish Annals produced at the court of Pippin's son Charlemagne some forty years after these events.[6] A strictly contemporary writer, Pippin's own uncle, simply notes that 'an embassy was sent to the apostolic see' and that 'on receipt of the pope's official reply', Pippin 'by the election of all the Franks to the throne of the kingdom, by the consecration of bishops and by the subjection of the lay magnates, together with the

---

5. Nelson 1977c, p. 63. For the general problem of ideas and contexts: Staubach 1983, pp. 7–8.
6. *Annales regni Francorum* s.a. 749, p. 8: 'Burghardus Wirzeburgensis episcopus et Folradus capellanus missi fuerunt ad Zachariam papam, interrogando de regibus in Francia, qui illis temporibus non habentes regalem potestatem, si bene fuisset an non. Et Zacharias papa mandavit Pippino, ut melius esset illum regem vocari, qui potestatem haberet, quam illum, qui sine regali potestate manebat; ut non conturbaretur ordo per auctoritatem apostolicam iussit Pippinum regem fieri.' There is an English translation: Scholz 1970. But here and elsewhere in this chapter, all translations are the author's own, unless otherwise indicated.

queen Bertrada, as the rules of ancient tradition require was elevated into the kingdom'.[7] Whatever form previous royal inaugurations had taken, the novelty here was certainly the 'consecration', the anointing of Pippin by bishops – a novelty which it is obviously tempting to link with the pope's 'reply'.[8] Fritz Kern, probably the most influential of modern commentators on medieval political thought, did make this link, and drew far-reaching conclusions from these events. Hitherto, he inferred, the Franks' 'primitive beliefs', their 'superstitious aversion . . . from parting with a phantom-like dynasty', had permitted Merovingian kings without power to succeed one another for over a century. The appeal to the pope in 750 meant the replacement of Germanic kin-right by 'Christian principles', of supernatural sanctification drawn from 'old pagan mythical roots' by an equally supernatural but Christian sanctification. Pippin's anointing, for Kern, signified a 'great revolution'.[9] For Henri Pirenne, it signalled the transition from the late-antique to the medieval world, from a still basically secular Merovingian kingship to the ecclesiastically conditioned rule of Carolingians 'by the grace of God'.[10]

There is too much evidence of the christianisation of Merovingian kingship and of the Frankish aristocracy in the seventh and early eighth centuries[11] for Kern's 'revolution' to carry conviction. What is really striking about 750/1 is the coincidence of Frankish clerical and lay aristocratic interests and of those with the papacy's. Pippin invoked papal approval 'with the consent of the Franks'. There was no question of alternative or competing types of legitimation when the pope approved what the Franks, with Pippin, had in fact already decided.[12] Pippin's installation as king demonstrated what dissension amongst the Franks had been obscuring for some time before 750: the gentile basis of Frankish kingship. Pippin's constituency was the *gens francorum*, already in the generation before 750 learning to see themselves as a chosen people, a new Israel.[13] Their thought-world was shaped by the Old Testament Books of Exodus and Deuteronomy. The Children of Israel had had a special relationship with the Almighty, who had promised them that their kings,

7. Continuator of Fredegar, ed. Wallace-Hadrill 1960, c. 33. p. 102: 'Praecelsus Pippinus electione totius Francorum in sedem regni cum consecratione episcoporum et subiectione principum una cum regina Bertradane, ut antiquitus ordo deposcit, sublimatur in regno.'
8. Jarnut 1982, pp. 54–7.
9. Kern 1954, pp. 20–2, 25, 66–7. Quotations in text are from the translation by Chrimes 1939, pp. 13, 16, 21, 35.
10. Pirenne 1939, pp. 265–74. See also Arquillière 1955, p. 43. For the title *rex dei gratia*: Wolfram 1967, pp. 213–17.   11. Ewig 1956; Riché 1972; Werner 1976.
12. Affeldt 1980, esp. pp. 178ff; *idem* 1972.   13. Ewig 1956, pp. 42–5.

when they got them, would be chosen by Him 'out of the number of your brothers' (Deut. 17:15). Only in the light of this identification with Israel was it apposite for Frankish priests to be anointed like Aaron (as they were already some decades before 750) or for a Frankish king to be anointed as Samuel anointed David.[14] The religious legitimation of Pippin depended on a prior and equally religious legitimation of the Franks. This theme, rather than their own individual consecrations, was what Pippin and Charlemagne sought to cultivate and played on in the years after 750. Pippin's reissue of *Lex Salica*, the law of the *gens*, was accompanied by a paean of praise to the God-beloved Franks.[15] The Royal Frankish Annals report the victories not of Charlemagne alone but of 'the Franks, with God's help',[16] and the oaths of the conquered Saxons 'to maintain christianity and faithfulness to King Charles and his sons and the Franks'.[17] Liturgical acclamations for Charlemagne and his family, the *Laudes regiae*, also have invocations for 'all the judges and the whole army of the Franks'.[18]

The new intimacy of this linking of the Franks with their ruling dynasty emerges equally clearly from the papal correspondence of the period. In a letter of 747 to Pippin, Mayor of the Palace, and 'all the magnates (*principes*) in the region of the Franks', Pope Zacharias acknowledged that in Francia, as in contemporary Rome, a warrior aristocracy held the key to the Church's well-being.[19] The form of Zacharias' response in 751 may have been influenced by Augustinian notions of cosmic order,[20] but its substance was a shrewd assessment of the realities of power in Francia and their relevance to papal interests. Zacharias' successor Stephen II invoked 'the utility of your patron St Peter' when he appealed to all the chiefs (*duces*) of the Frankish *gens* to help King Pippin.[21] This papal utilitarianism meant the mobilising of not only Frankish kingship but Frankish consent. When the needs of St Peter – that is, the need to defend claims to territory in central Italy – drove Stephen II to cross the Alps in winter to seek Frankish aid, he forged links not only (through a new consecration) between himself and Pippin and his sons, but between St Peter and the Frankish aristocracy. To

---

14. Nelson 1977b, pp. 56–8.   15. *Lex Salica. 100-Titel Text*, pp, 6–8.

16. E.g. *Annales Regni Francorum* s.a. 775, 776, 783, pp. 40–2, 44, 64. Compare Haselbach 1970, pp. 146–52. For some qualifications: Hannig 1982, pp. 139–40.

17. *Annales Regni Francorum* s.a. 777, p. 48.   18. Kantorowicz 1958, pp. 15, 43.

19. *Codex Carolinus* no. 3, p. 480: 'Principes et seculares homines atque bellatores convenit curam habere . . . et provintiae defensionem, praesulibus vero sacerdotibus . . . pertinet salutaribus consiliis et oracionibus vacare, ut nobis orantibus et illis bellantibus, Deo praestante, provincia salva persistat.' See Patlagean 1974.   20. Büttner 1956, pp. 160–1.

21. *Codex Carolinus* no. 5, p. 488: 'utilitas fautoris vestri, beati apostolorum principis Petri'.

them as well as to the royal family, 'St Peter' appealed as his 'adoptive sons'. Just as God called the Israelites 'his peculiar people', so Stephen's successor Paul I (757–67) enrolled the Franks as 'St Peter's peculiar people', calling them, in words St Peter himself was believed to have used for the Christian community, 'a holy tribe, a royal priesthood'.[22]

Less dominant in papal appeals, but no less resonant in Frankish ears, were the notes of lordship and patronage. Paul I reminded Pippin of 'the faithful kings [of Israel] who in days of old pleased God'.[23] Pippin too was cast as a faithful king who would please his patron St Peter. Faithfulness for the Franks immediately evoked the service of the youth (*puer, vassus*) to the older man (*senior*), a service first and foremost military. Physical power was the prime qualification for those who served. Again, Frankish and papal views coincided. Annals written c. 805 to glorify the Carolingians castigated the fecklessness (*desidia*) of the Merovingians and praised the toughness and stamina (*strenuitas*) of the new leaders under whom the Franks had reestablished their power over other peoples.[24] In the 830s Einhard, Charlemagne's biographer, drew a dramatic (and perhaps ironic) contrast between the symbolic senescence of the last Merovingian and the youthful vitality of Charles Martel and Pippin.[25] Also c. 830 a historian of the Franks imagined a conversation at the Frankish court between the last Merovingian and Pope Stephen II (*sic!*) in which the king explained his inability to give military help: ' "Don't you see, Father, that I lack both the power and the dignity of a king?" The pope agreed . . . and turning to Prince Pippin said: "On St Peter's authority I order you to tonsure this man and send him into a monastery. How can he hold a land? He is useful neither to himself nor to others!" ' In context, this is clearly a usefulness gauged in terms of benefits to king, Franks and St Peter alike.[26]

Though they were aware that past societies, including ancient Israel and until recently the Saxons, had managed with the rule of judges or nobles,[27]

22. *Codex Carolinus* nos. 10, p. 501, 39, p. 552: 'Et vos quidem, carissimi, "gens sancta, regale sacerdotium, populus adquisitionis" [1 Peter 2:9], cui benedixit dominus Deus Israhel, gaudete et exultate, quia nomina vestra regumque vestrorum exarata sunt in celis.' See Angenendt 1980, pp. 40–63, idem 1982, pp. 109–10. Historical context: Noble 1984, chs. 2 and 3.

23. *Codex Carolinus* no. 42, p. 555: 'divinae gratiae lumine et oleo sanctificationis inter fideles reges qui olim Deo placuerunt, unctus connumeratus conprobaris . . . et ideo oleo sancto unxit te [Deus]'.

24. The so-called *Annales Mettenses*: Haselbach 1970, pp. 171–2, 178–9.

25. Einhard, ed. Holder-Egger 1911, c. 1, p. 3 (English translation Thorpe 1969): the Merovingian had only the *inane regis vocabulum*, Charles Martel and Pippin had *et opes et potentia regni*.

26. Erchanbert, ed. Pertz 1829, p. 328: 'Tunc rex: "Videsne", inquit, "Papa, quod dignitatis regiae ac potestatis non fungor? Quomodo possum horum aliquid agere?" "Vere", inquit Papa, "hoc iuste convenit, quia non es dignus tali honore". Reversusque ad principem Pipinum aiebat: "Ex auctoritate Sancti Petri tibi praecipio: tonde hunc et destina in monasterium; ut quid terram occupat? nec sibi nec aliis utilis est".' See Peters 1970, pp. 53–4; Affeldt 1980, p. 187 n. 337.

27. *Vita Lebuini antiqua* cc. 4–6, pp. 793–4.

Carolingian writers of contemporary history saw kingship as the basic political form in their own world. Christianity was no necessary qualification. The emir of Cordoba was a king, so were the Muslim ruler of Barcelona and the Bulgar khan.[28] Archbishop Hincmar of Rheims in a learned treatise distinguished between kings and tyrants, between legitimate and illegitimate ways of assuming power, between rulers directly instituted by God to promote justice and 'usurpers' permitted by God to punish sin – while insisting, with St Paul, that all power was divinely authorised and hence to be obeyed.[29] Wearing another hat, as annalist, Hincmar recognised that the sustained support of a sizeable faction of the aristocracy in a particular region was what in fact made a king, both in the sense of installing him and of supplying him with the means to rule.[30] Other annalists reflect a similar contemporary pragmatism. When two rivals for the kingship of the Wilzi brought their case before a Frankish assembly, Louis the Pious had no difficulty in recognising as king the man favoured by the 'will of the people' (*voluntas gentis*), that is, with greater support among the leading men of the Wilzi.[31] Horic 'king of the Danes' was the man to whom Carolingian kings could appeal to make a wayward Danish warlord (*dux*) disgorge what he had plundered from the Franks.[32] When the Colodici were beaten by the Franks and their king killed, another king had to be 'hurriedly made' so that the Franks could take from him 'oaths, hostages and much of their land'.[33]

A royal blessing-prayer, *Prospice* ('Look down'), provides an epitome of Frankish expectations of their king in the time of Charlemagne when the prayer was used, and probably composed.[34] It also sets out ideas of kingship which were to remain standard throughout the Middle Ages and beyond, for the prayer was incorporated into the rite of royal consecration early in the Carolingian period and thence passed into general use in the kingdoms of the Latin West.[35]

Look down, Omnipotent God, with serene eyes on this most glorious king. As Thou didst bless Abraham, Isaac and Jacob, so deign to irrigate and bathe him by Thy potency with abundant blessings of spiritual grace with all its fullness. Grant him from the dew of heaven and the fatness of earth abundance of corn, wine and oil and a wealth of all fruits from the generous store of divine gifts, through long

---

28. *Annales Bertiniani* s.a. 847, p. 53; Ermold, *In Honorem Hludowici*, l. 638, p. 50; *Annales Bertiniani* s.a. 866, p. 133.
29. Hincmar, *De Divortio* col. 758, and *De Regis Persona* cols. 834–6. See Anton 1968, pp. 295ff.
30. *Annales Bertiniani* s.a. 873, pp. 189–90. 31. *Annales Regni Francorum* s.a. 823, p. 160.
32. *Annales Bertiniani* s.a. 847, pp. 54–5. Compare *MGH Cap.* II, no. 204, p. 70.
33. *Annales Bertiniani* s.a. 839, p. 35. 34. Bouman 1957, pp. 7, 40, 90–4; Ewig 1956, p. 45.
35. Dewick 1899, cols. 23–4; Bouman 1957, pp. 90, 107–8; Nelson 1982, pp. 120, 125–7. 'Prospice' was also included in imperial consecration-rites from the mid-tenth century: below, p. 245.

years; so that, while he is reigning, there may be healthiness of bodies in the fatherland, and peace may be unbroken in the realm, and the glorious dignity of the royal palace may shine before the eyes of all with the greatest splendour of royal power and be seen to be glittering and bright as if filled with the utmost splendour by the greatest light.

Grant him, Omnipotent God, to be a most mighty protector of the fatherland, and a comforter of churches and holy monasteries with the greatest piety of royal munificence, and to be the mightiest of kings, triumphing over his enemies so as to crush rebels and heathen nations; and may he be very terrible to his enemies with the utmost strength of royal potency.

Also may he be generous and loveable and pious to the magnates and the outstanding leaders and the faithful men of his realm, that he may be feared and loved by all.

Also may kings come forth from his loins through successions of future times to rule this whole realm. And after glorious and happy times in this present life, may he be worthy to have eternal joys in perpetual blessedness.[36]

The repeated use of the terms *potentia* and *potestas* here shows that the invocation of divine omnipotence to sustain royal potency is no mere liturgical cliché but conveys the central political idea of the Carolingian period: power came from God. The king acted as his deputy in securing justice and peace for the Christian people. Authors of *Mirrors of Princes*, treatises of royal instruction, concentrated not on the gap between incumbent and office, between merely human ruler and God, but on the bridging of that gap through divine grace. Few scriptural tags were oftener quoted than Proverbs 21:1 – 'The heart of the king is in the hand of the Lord.'[37] 'Prospice' stressed the effects of divine action confidently asserted

---

36. 'Prospice omnipotens deus hunc gloriosissimum regem serenis obtutibus, sicut benedixisti Abraham, Isaac et Iacob, sic illum largis benedictionibus spiritalis gratiae cum omni plenitudine potentia irrigare atque perfundere dignare. Tribue ei de rore caeli et de pinguedine terrae abundantiam frumenti, vini et olei et omnium frugum opulentia ex largitate muneris divini longa per tempora, ut illo regnante sit sanitas corporum in patria et pax inviolata sit in regno, et dignitas gloriosa regalis palatii maximae splendore regiae potestatis oculis omnium fulgeat luce clarissima coruscare atque splendere quasi splendissima fulgora maximo perfusa lumine videantur. Tribue ei, omnipotens deus, ut sit fortissimus protector patriae et consolator ecclesiarum atque coenobiorum sanctorum maxima cum pietate regalis munificentiae, atque ut sit fortissimus regum, triumphator hostium ad opprimendum rebelles et paganas nationes, sitque inimicis suis satis terribilis proxima fortitudine regalis potentiae. Optimatibus quoque atque praecelsis proceribusque ac fidelibus sui regni sit munificus et amabilis et pius, ut ab omnibus timeatur atque diligatur. Reges quoque de lumbis eius per successiones temporum futurorum egrediantur hoc regnum regere totum. Et post gloriosa tempora atque felicia praesentis vitae, gaudia sempiterna in perpetua beatitudine habere mereatur.' Text in *Benedictionals of Freising* 'B', ed. Amiet 1974, p. 101. Compare Bouman 1957, p. 91. The Old Testament references are to Gen. 27:28 and Ps. 4:8.
37. Anton 1968, pp. 357–62. Compare Pippin's diploma of 762, *MGH DD* I, no. 16, p. 22: 'divina nobis providentia in solium regni unxisse manifestum est . . . et . . . reges ex Deo regnant nobisque gentes

to ensue – the outpouring of blessings – rather than priestly mediation. Just as God had acted through the patriarchs to give Israel food, health and peace, so he would act through the consecrated king of the Franks. Other regal benedictions invoke a series of Old Testament judges and kings renowned for their success in war and wisdom in judgement. David and Solomon were favourite models in *Mirrors of Princes*.[38]

The Frankish realm can be classed as in Weber's sense a patrimonial regime in which power legitimised as divinely ordained was exercised as the ruler's personal authority like a father's over his household.[39] The Frankish kingdom was a family concern, in which royal kin had a special stake.[40] They resided with the king, his wife and children in a palace that was also home and school for young aristocrats, a great household which regularly expanded when assemblies gathered there, to embrace the political realm as it were in a single huge family. Frankish writers, all too aware of the tensions in close kinship, were especially attracted by the image of the court as a place of peace where 'all dissensions and discords were to be suppressed'.[41] *Prospice* highlights the splendour of the palace – a sacred space likened by poets to Solomon's Temple and seen as prefiguring the heavenly Jerusalem.[42] One Carolingian court poet, Ermold, described an Easter Day procession at the palace:

> Each in his rank hastens to obey the royal commands.
> One man runs, another stays: one goes this way, another that . . .
> Preceded by the elders, followed by the younger man,
> With magnates surrounding you, you come, revered king.
> . . . As the sun illuminates the earth with his rays . . .
> Signalling joy to trees, crops, sailors,
> So the king in his coming brings joy to his people.[43]

Royal biographers chose to locate their heroes in the setting of the household, where arrangements for the hunt or the dining-table symbolised

---

et regna pro sua misericordia ad gubernandum commisit'. See Fichtenau 1957, p. 143. Divine grace: Kantorowicz 1952; Cristiani 1978, pp. 104–23.

38. Wallace-Hadrill 1965; Anton 1968, pp. 419–36; Eberhardt 1977, pp. 560–9. Regal benedictions: Bouman 1957, pp. 191–2. Ullmann 1964, pp. 81–2 takes reference to priestly mediation out of context; compare idem 1969, pp. 105–8. *Mirrors of Princes* in general: Eberhardt 1977, pp. 267–311.

39. Weber 1978, vol. I, pp. 231–41, vol. II, pp. 1006–110. See also Eberhardt 1977, pp. 453–4, and esp. Fried 1982.

40. Dhuoda, ed. Riché 1975, III, c. 8, pp. 166–70. See Nelson 1985, pp. 269ff.

41. Council of Paris (829), c. 91, *MGH Conc.* II, p. 678: 'Ubi igitur omnes dissensiones et discordiae dirimendae et omnis malitia imperiali auctoritate est comprimenda, necesse est ut quod in aliis corrigere decernit, in ea [i.e. sacra domu] minime reperitur.' Peace as cosmic order: Bonnaud-Delamare 1939. *Familiaritas* at assemblies: Nelson 1983a, p. 220.

42. Wolfram 1963, pp. 135–6; Riché 1976, pp. 167–9. Compare Kolb 1971.

43. Ermold, *Carmen in honorem Pippini regis*, I, ll. 18–32, p. 204.

their authority.[44] It was thought essential that the ruler maintain right relations within the royal family itself. The divine injunction in Deuteronomy 14:17, 'Let [the king] not have more than one wife', quoted by learned churchmen to Charlemagne and Louis the Pious,[45] had special relevance when all politics were 'palace, even family politics',[46] and the ambitions of successive royal wives and their offspring could throw kingdoms into confusion. Archbishop Agobard of Lyons justified the rebellion of his patron Lothar against his father the emperor by invoking his duty to restore and purify the palace that evildoers had made a brothel.[47] The programme of rectification (*correctio*) proposed by ecclesiastical reformers and eagerly taken up by Charlemagne and his successors was in effect a transposition to the realm as a whole of the ruler's personal and domestic good order. It was the more necessary for Lothar II, whose domestic affairs were notoriously *dis*ordered, to be advised that a good king did the job of ruling (*regendi ministerium*) in three ways: 'by ruling first himself, second his own wife and children and the members of his household, third the people committed to him'.[48]

Carolingian clerical theorists used the Church as a model of an ordered society: in this sense the realm, and the king's job, were contained within the Church.[49] But in terms of practical politics, the Church was part of the realm, and the king's obligation to safeguard it an essential part of his patrimonial role. The clergy and monks, unarmed, were like widows and orphans in need of protection.[50] The Carolingians involved the resources and personnel of the Church much more closely in their regime than any previous medieval rulers had done.[51] The author of *Prospice* observed the rewards of 'royal munificence'. But the king believed his power to depend on the Church's preservation of the Faith.[52] When the papacy itself seemed to waver in its response to the Byzantine court's excessive veneration of icons, Charlemagne had his leading theologian Theodulf in the *Libri Carolini* remind the pope of the orthodoxy Rome stood for. Justifying his

---

44. Ermold, *In Honorem Hludowici*, ll. 2338–503, pp. 178–90; Notker, ed. Haefele 1959, I, c. 11, p. 16, c. 30, p. 41, II, c. 6, pp. 54–7, c. 8, pp. 59–61 (English translation Thorpe 1969). See Goetz 1981, pp. 23–36, 85–97.

45. Cathwulf, *MGH Epp.* IV, p. 503; Council of Paris (829), c. 55, *MGH Conc.* II, p. 649.

46. Stafford 1983, ch. 4.   47. Agobard, ed. Waitz 1887, p. 275.

48. Sedulius Scottus, ed. Hellmann 1906, c. 5, p. 34: 'primo se ipsum . . . secundo uxorem propriam et liberos suosque domesticos, tertio populum sibi commissum'. Carolingian *correctio* and *rectitudo*: Fleckenstein 1953.   49. Fried 1982, pp. 18–27. Compare pp. 226–7 below.

50. Pseudo-Cyprian, ed. Hellmann 1910, c. 9, p. 51: 'justitia regis est . . . advenis et pupillis et viduis defensorem esse . . . ecclesias defendere, pauperes elemosynis alere'. See Devisse 1975–6, vol. I, pp. 500ff; Duby 1978, p. 224.

51. Ganshof 1960 (English translation Ganshof 1971, ch. 11); Prinz 1971.   52. Waas 1966.

implied rebuke, Charlemagne told the pope that the Church had been 'committed to us for ruling'.[53] In 747 Pope Zacharias had set out in a letter to the Franks and their leader a division of labour between those who fought and the clergy who prayed for their victory.[54] In 796, Alcuin on Charlemagne's behalf quoted this back at Pope Leo III: 'Our job is the defence of the Church and the fortification of the Faith; yours to aid our warfare by prayer.'[55] But the Church owed more than prayer alone. In bracketing royal 'comfort of churches and monasteries' with royal triumph over rebels and heathens, *Prospice* hinted at the military service owed, and faithfully performed, by the Church to the Carolingians.[56]

The model of Christian rulership elaborated in *Mirrors of Princes* was projected mainly for kings themselves. But the evangelising Carolingian Church aimed at the minds (as well as the souls) of the laity at large. It preached lordship, using the same language for political and religious obligation. 'Faith' (*fides*) meant both Christian belief and the bond between lord and man.[57] The Book of Psalms, the text-book of Carolingian spirituality, could be read as a manifesto of divine Lordship. Christ was presented as lord of a warrior-retinue.[58] Fidelity in political contexts acquired strong Christian overtones. In addressing his documents, Pippin identified his own faithful men with God's: *fideles dei et regis*.[59] Charlemagne hammered the point home when he imposed faithfulness in both kinds on the conquered Saxons.[60] In the mid-ninth century the Frankish noblewoman Dhuoda urged both on her son as he joined the king's military retinue.[61]

The great household as an image of order and purity, and the ordered hierarchy of personal service within it, were political ideas that corresponded to social realities and were constantly reinforced by experience.

53. *MGH Conc.* II, Supplement, p. 2: 'nobis [i.e. Charlemagne, using the royal 'we'] quibus in huius saeculi procellosis fluctibus [ecclesia] ad regendum commissa est'. See Dahlhaus-Berg 1975, pp. 186–90; Wallace-Hadrill 1983, pp. 219–22. 54. Above p. 215 n. 19.
55. *Codex Carolinus* no. 93, pp. 137–8: 'Nostrum est secundum auxilium divinae pietatis sanctam undique Christi ecclesiam ab incursu paganorum et ab infidelium devastatione armis defendere foris, et intus catholicae fidei agnitione munire. Vestrum est, sanctissime pater, elevatis ad Deum cum Moyse manibus nostram adiuvare militiam, quatenus vobis intercedentibus . . . populus christianus super inimicos . . . semper habeat victoriam.' See Scheibe 1959, p. 190–3.
56. Nelson 1983b.
57. Graus 1959. The stress of Schlesinger 1963, pp. 296–334, on the Germanic background is compatible with Graus' insistence on the ideological role of the Carolingian Church. Compare Green 1965, pp. 216–32.
58. By Otfrid of Weissenburg, writing probably for nobles inside as well as outside monasteries and episcopal households. See below pp. 235–6 and n. 131.
59. Helbig 1951. 60. *MGH Cap.* I, no. 26, pp. 68–70.
61. Dhuoda, ed. Riché 1975, III, cc. 4, 5, pp. 148–59.

Peasants who journeyed to palaces to seek royal protection against lordly violence[62] perceived the king as a mighty overlord who could uphold the free status of the humble. Enthroned, flanked by his counsellors and warrior-retinue, in a hall adorned with depictions of his ancestors' achievements, the Carolingian ruler was a commanding yet approachable figure.[63] The aristocracy who sustained his regime were in regular contact with the court. Dhuoda, familiar with both palace and noble household, saw parallels between them. Much could be learned, she told her son as he went off to the palace, from the discussions that go on 'in a big house such as that one'. 'When you are grown-up, organise your own household in lawful ranks, and effectively. And [meanwhile] . . . carry out all your tasks in public affairs in due order, and faithfully'.[64] Faithfulness, which bound the faithful man to his lord, provided Dhuoda with a model for the relationship of wife to husband, of child to father – and of those who served to the king.[65]

When the author of *Prospice* mentioned royal 'piety', in precisely this context, he had in mind a political as well as a moral virtue, manifested, with 'generosity' and 'lovableness', in the distribution of wealth and the delegation of power over men. This piety was the return for faithful service.[66] Charlemagne, like his Merovingian predecessors, wanted all the men in his realm to swear fidelity to him. In 802 he added to the oath the phrase: '[faithful] as a man ought in right (*per drictum*) to be faithful to his lord'.[67] This heralded no constitutional change, no shift (as sometimes alleged) from 'sovereignty' to 'contractual' authority, no watering-down of 'subjects' obligations'.[68] Classical, or modern, legal categories imposed on the early Middle Ages can mislead. The relationship between Frankish king and aristocracy had been based all along on mutual, personal, service

62. Tessier 1943–55, II, no. 228, pp. 7–9. Compare Levillain 1926, no. XII, pp. 44–7; Wickham 1982, pp. 109–12.

63. Ermold, *In Honorem Hludowici*, ll. 2148–63, p. 164, describes the *gesta paterna* depicted at Ingelheim. See Lammers 1973. Throne-image in Carolingian ruler-iconography: Schramm and Mütherich 1983, plates 21–3, 36, 38, 40–1, 45. It is uncertain how far reality was designed to correspond to manuscript-image, and how far genre-bound image reflected contemporary (as distinct from late antique) ideology: Bak 1973, pp. 53–63; Bullough 1975, pp. 252–3.

64. Dhuoda, ed. Riché 1975, III, c. 9, p. 170, X, c. 3, pp. 346–8: 'Cum, auxiliante Deo, ad perfectum perveneris tempus, domum tuam per legitimos gradus utiliter disponas et . . . in re publica cuncta ordinabili cursu fidenter perage.'

65. Wollasch 1957, pp. 179, 187; Riché 1975, pp. 24–7. A priest's oath of fidelity to his bishop: Schmidt-Wiegand 1977, pp. 72–3.   66. Schieffer 1982. See also Haselbach 1970, pp. 153–8.

67. *MGH Cap.* I, no. 34, p. 101: 'sicut per drictum debet esse homo domino suo'.

68. Brunner 1928, vol. II, p. 82; Ganshof 1971, pp. 117–18. Compare Magnou-Nortier 1976, pp. 35–57; Brunner 1979, pp. 56–9. Useful on historiography but over-legalistic on oath-formulae: Odegaard 1941; *idem* 1945.

and mutual advantage: there was no break here with Merovingian tradition. With the words 'in right', Charlemagne signalled faithfulness as deep-rooted in contemporaries' values.[69] He invoked it, not through conceptual muddle – the king was a lord like no other – but to clarify and intensify for each of his people a sense of what was owed to the king. Entirely apt therefore was the usual collective designation of the Carolingian aristocracy: the *fideles*, the faithful men. By contrast, the notion of the subject was never really at home in Carolingian political thought.[70] It practically never occurs in the capitularies that record the deliberations of king and aristocracy in assemblies. Similarly the Roman law concept of treason (*laesa majestas, lèse majesté*) was a learned gloss sometimes imposed on individual acts of faithlessness.[71] The near-contemporary account of the Royal Frankish Annals has Tassilo duke of the Bavarians condemned in 788 as 'not having kept his faith', but the revised text of the Annals presents this, a generation later, as treason. Tassilo's faithlessness had taken two forms: he had seduced away the loyalty of others among the king's vassals, and he had instructed his own men to swear Charlemagne false oaths.[72] The king's piety towards the faithful required the turning of wrath on Tassilo. The face of the king, now familiar now terrible, resembled the face of the Lord.

Few medieval writers cared to recall that the Lord had not originally planned for Israel to be ruled by kings. Many noted the Lord's preference, once Israel's kingship had been set up, for hereditary succession. Only such wicked kings as Jeroboam and Ahab had been divinely punished by the extinction of their lines. Pippin clearly intended to found a dynasty, for his wife, apparently unlike Merovingian queens, received some form of consecration alongside her husband.[73] This ritual practice, later adopted

---

69. Köbler 1971, pp. 18–19; Niermeyer 1976, s.v. *directum*. Merovingian background to *fidelitas*: Lemosse 1946, pp. 13–16.

70. Verbs denoting 'being subject' (less often the noun) appear as borrowings from scriptural or patristic texts: e.g. Rom. 13; Gregory the Great, *Moralia* xxi, 23, *PL* 76, col. 203, or as echoes of Roman law, canon law or liturgy. Isidore's notion of *subjectis prodesse*: Anton 1968, p. 365 n. 40. Compare Pseudo-Cyprian, ed. Hellmann 1910, c. 9, p. 51: 'Nomen . . . regis intellectualiter hoc retinet, ut subjectis omnibus rectoris officium procuret.' 71. Lemosse 1946, pp. 16ff.

72. *Annales Regni Francorum* s.a. 788, p. 80: 'Coeperunt fideles Baioarii dicere quod Tassilo fidem suam salvam non haberet . . . et Tassilo . . . confessus est . . . vassos supradicti domni regis ad se adortasse . . . et homines suos quando iurabant iubebat ut aliter in mente retinerent et sub dolo iurarent'. Compare the revised text of the *Annales*, p. 81: 'Crimine maiestatis a Baioariis accusatus est', and omitting the next passage.

73. Above, p. 214 n. 7, where 'ancient tradition' refers to 'elevation' (enthronement), not to the queen's participation in it: Nelson 1977b, pp. 53, 57–8. But *Codex Carolinus* no. 11, p. 505, implies a consecration of Bertrada in 754, even if the so-called *Clausula de unctione Pippini* cannot be accepted as near-contemporary evidence for either 754 or 751: Stoclet 1980, esp. p. 34. The final section of 'Prospice', above, p. 218, stresses hereditary succession.

elsewhere in Latin Christendom, can probably be linked with a preference for filial, rather than fraternal, succession.[74] But though eldest sons often received a preferential share, the Carolingian king, like his Merovingian predecessors, partitioned his realm between the queen's sons. In the eighth century, as already in the seventh, such divisions were far from arbitrary, however, for the building-blocks, the *regna*, from which composite 'imperial realms' were constructed were not themselves divisible. Paternal acquisitions meant shares for more sons: Charlemagne provided for two sons in this way. But his eldest son by Queen Hildigard was designated to inherit the whole patrimony of Francia[75] – a plan that probably resulted from a combination of the eldest son's ambitions with the interest of some Frankish magnates in keeping their patrimonies as far as possible under a single royal lord. In the next generation, rival fraternal ambitions were supported by nobles who gave priority to their interests in particular regions: in 843 a three-way division of Francia created the cores of three kingdoms at the Treaty of Verdun.[76]

These partitions, treating the realm as the personal property of the ruler and his heirs, have been seen as characteristic of patrimonial authority. Though Hincmar of Rheims was familiar with seventh-century Spanish legislation in which the resources of the Crown had been clearly distinguished from the ruler's private holdings,[77] he never made any such distinction in the Carolingians' case. If the term *res publica* could be used by ninth-century writers to denote simply the fisc,[78] then arguably it lacked its classical meaning of the state. It has been argued, further, that a 'true' concept of office is equally elusive in the Carolingian period.[79] Where the Visigoths had defined monarchy as an institution in terms borrowed from late Roman law, a whiff of the household clung to the Carolingian notion of 'ministry' (*ministerium*), royal or otherwise, as personal service. In the absence of a clear distinction between office and incumbent, a king could be judged only as an individual, as father or lord. This was what happened to Louis the Pious, deprived of power by rebellious sons and their supporters in 833. The rebels' propagandist, Agobard, could only pronounce this a divine judgement and Louis a confessed sinner on whom public penance could be imposed.[80] Conversely Rabanus Maurus who remained loyal to Louis, countered with appeals to filial duty and Scriptural precept: 'The powers that be are ordained of God' (Rom. 13: 1).[81] Subsequent

---

74. Stafford 1981, pp. 10–12, 16–18.   75. Classen 1972 (1983); Ewig 1981.
76. Classen 1963 (1983); Nelson 1985.   77. Cf. Nelson 1977a, p. 254 n. 1.
78. Wehlen 1970, pp. 52–5, 94–5; Fried 1982, pp. 11–16.   79. Fried 1982, pp. 29–33.
80. Nelson 1977a, pp. 243–4.   81. *MGH Epp.* v, pp. 406–7.

Carolingian conflicts evoked similar appeals, as when Hincmar reminded Louis the German, invading his brother's kingdom in 858: 'Thou shalt not touch the Lord's anointed' (Ps. 104: 15).[82]

Another major limitation of Carolingian political thought has been identified in the concept of law as an individual 'subjective' possession, for this too allegedly forestalled any awareness of the *res publica*, the state, transcending private interests. When Charles the Bald in 843 stated his willingness 'to keep for each his due law', he abdicated, on this view, the prime function of the state in defining the law. Kern, for instance, posed stark alternatives: on the one hand, strong central government making and enforcing unified 'objective' statute law, on the other, a multiplicity of 'subjective' rights tending towards anarchy.[83] Since Charles the Bald has often been blamed for the Carolingian Empire's lurch to the bad, it is worth noting that Charlemagne too had wished to keep for each his law, and promised to 'make amends' to anyone against whose law royal agents had taken action.[84] But this only underlines the point that the notion of law as right was important throughout the Carolingian period. A man was entitled to judgement according to customary procedures with due account taken of individual rank and status.

The limitations of Carolingian political thought, its hesitations, inconsistencies and shortcomings of expression, are very obvious. Yet to deny the ninth century any idea of the state or of public office is to throw out the baby with the bathwater. Political thought is embodied not only in theories but in contemporaries' *ad hoc* responses to political problems and to perceived discrepancies between ideals and realities. From the ninth century, such responses are preserved in the capitularies produced by Carolingian rulers and those who gave them counsel. So, for instance, the careful delineation of frontiers in ninth-century partitions shows that kingdoms were thought of as possessing territorial definitions and integrity. Royal control over the coinage and over fortifications was asserted throughout the whole territory. Rulers threatened, and sometimes imposed, sanctions on recalcitrant or rebellious nobles: public humiliation, withdrawal of high office,

---

82. *MGH Cap.* II, no. 297, p. 440.
83. Kern 1919, pp. 58–60 (Kern 1954, pp. 192–4); Fried 1982, p. 17 with n. 66. Charles the Bald's statement in 843: *MGH Cap.* II, no. 254, p. 255: 'Legem vero unicuique competentem . . . in omni dignitate et ordine favente Deo me observaturum perdono.' Magnou-Nortier 1976, pp. 103–8, is a valuable corrective to some earlier views. See also Nelson 1977a, p. 255; *idem* 1977c, p. 64.
84. *MGH Cap.* I, no. 25, p. 67: 'Explicare debent ipsi missi qualiter domni regi dictum est, quod multi se conplangunt legem non habere conservatam, et quia omnino voluntas domni regis est ut unusquisque homo suam legem pleniter habeat conservata; et si alicui contra legem factum est, non est voluntas nec sua iussio.'

confiscation not only of benefices but of patrimonies or allods. In the exercise of criminal justice, the king claimed the right to send agents into areas under landlords' jurisdiction (immunities) to apprehend malefactors, and all faithful men had to swear to aid in such action. This oath signalled and reinforced the free man's obligations but did not create them. 'All, without any excuse, must come to the defence of the fatherland.'[85] That liability arose, not from the holding of a benefice, or from personal commitment to the royal lord, but from residence in the realm.[86] Even if central power was mediated in practice through the aristocracy, it was exercised through institutions – courts, musters of the host – vested with public authority. The Carolingian regime rested on regalian rights and its own capacity to maintain public order. The Church's prayer that 'peace may be unbroken in the realm' was combined with a realistic perception that this outcome depended on royal 'abundance' and 'wealth'.

It is often claimed that royal authority failed in the ninth century because external attacks could only be met effectively by local resistance and this forced a devolution of power into the hands of the aristocracy.[87] Further, this political shift was allegedly reflected in ideas of consensus and of constraints on rulers, for instance through a new stress on the elective basis of kingship.[88] In such reconstructions, neither the history nor the history of thought is wholly convincing. External challenge evoked, on the whole, more vigorous exercise of central authority.[89] Ideas of consensus were not new but traditional, not anti-royal but linked to specific expectations of kingship. If these ideas and expectations were articulated more clearly in the ninth century, this was in part a response to a new, potentially oppressive, royal vigour.

Hincmar of Rheims, the leading elaborator and recorder of West Frankish royal consecration-rites in the ninth century, set down the functions of kingship in a promise required of the king before his consecration.[90] Given the clear parallel with episcopal ordination, and the

---

85. Some examples from the capitularies of Charles the Bald: *MGH Cap.* II, no. 251, pp. 193–5 (division of 870); no. 273 (Pîtres 869), cc. 8–24, pp. 314–29 (coinage), section C, c. 1, p. 328 (fortifications), c. 21, p. 319 (public humiliation), c. 18, p. 317 (royal agents empowered to enter immunities), c. 27, p. 322 (defence of fatherland); no. 260 (Servais 854), c. 13, p. 274 (oaths to denounce criminals); no. 242 (Coblenz 860), p. 158 (withdrawal of high office, confiscation of allods); no. 274 (Tusey 865), c. 13, p. 331 (summons to host). These capitularies draw on those of Charlemagne and especially of Louis the Pious, but also contain significant additions. General comments: Nelson 1983a.
86. Kaiser 1983, pp. 58–60. Compare Bisson 1978, pp. 464–5, 467–9, 477–8.
87. Bloch 1939–40, vol. II, pp. 173–5 (English translation 1961, pp. 395–6); Dhondt 1948, pp. 38–9.
88. Ganshof 1958b, pp. 30ff; Schlesinger 1963, pp. 132–8; Magnou-Nortier 1976, pp. 98ff.
89. Jäschke 1975; Campbell 1980, pp. 128–30.
90. David 1954, pp. 120–30; Morrison 1964, pp. 201–6; Nelson 1977a.

availability of Pope Gelasius' statements on the divine dispensation of a 'two-fold ruling of the world', it became possible for Hincmar both to model an idea of kingly office on a pre-existent idea of episcopal office and to link the bishops' role as consecrators with their superior dignity in terms of Gelasius' distiction between royal power and priestly authority. Hence, just as the bishop undertook before his ordination to keep the canons of the Church, so the king before his inauguration had to promise 'to keep the laws and statutes for the people committed by God's mercy to me to rule'. The form and context of this royal promise implied that human agents would be able to guarantee the king's fulfilment of this commitment by checking on his conformity to law. Moreover, where previous clerical theorists had been unable to project the Church's authority beyond spiritual responsibility for the king as an individual Christian, Hincmar could assert the bishops' jurisdiction over the king's conduct of an office to which they had consecrated him. These ideas, infrequently and hesitantly as Hincmar expressed them – he never explicitly claimed the competence to depose a king – are nevertheless remarkable attempts at an effective critique of secular rulership. No less remarkable is the insistence of the ageing Hincmar, dealing now with young and inexperienced kings, that the realm be ruled through counsel with the leading men, lay and clerical: only through consensus thus maintained could faction be avoided.[91]

The layman Nithard, writing his *Histories* between 841 and 843, showed similar concerns though his emphasis was on the role of the lay aristocracy. The public good should take priority over private interests. Nithard denounced those who misused public resources for personal advantage; he also recorded with approval an episcopal denunciation of a ruler (Lothar) who lacked both 'knowledge of how to govern the commonweal' (*scientia gubernandi rem publicam*) and 'good will in his government' (*bona voluntas in sua gubernatione*).[92] Through detailed description of contemporary politics, Nithard showed how the Franks could help their kings keep the 'royal road'. Shared counsels produced a collective judgement as to what was both fair and feasible. By following such counsels, a king could assure his faithful men's support. But they in turn had a sanction against a king who reneged on such an agreed course of action. At Strasbourg in 842 the two Carolingian kings Charles the Bald and Louis the German promised each other to maintain a common front against their brother Lothar until he

91. Nelson 1983a.
92. Nithard, ed. Lauer 1926, IV, 1, p. 118. Compare *ibid.*, I, 3, III, 2, IV, 6, pp. 10, 84, 142. Wehlen 1970, pp. 69–77; Nelson 1985.

should come to terms. Their oaths were sworn before their faithful men – 'in your sight'. Each king in pursuit 'of the common advantage' summoned his men to act as guarantors of the royal commitment: 'If I foreswear this oath I swear to my brother. I release each and every one of you from the oath you have sworn to me.' Further to underscore this point, the faithful men themselves took an oath: 'If my lord breaks his oath, while his brother keeps his . . . I shall give him no aid against his brother.'[93] Though the releasing from oath would be on an individual basis, the assumption clearly was that all the faithful men would coincide in their judgements on the king's conduct, hence would undertake *concerted* action to check the king. The significance of this was not that faithfulness was conditional – it had always been so – but that the faithful men of each kingdom were being treated as a collectivity and were committed to uphold a specific condition on which the common interest depended.

Other near-contemporary evidence from the West Frankish kingdom as it emerged from the Treaty of Verdun shows efforts being made to find appropriate terms to express the group-consciousness of the faithful men. The meeting at Coulaines in November 843 had West Frankish magnates, lay and ecclesistical, coming together 'into one thing' (*in unum*) and making an agreement (*convenientia*) to which the king then lent his backing. At Meersen in 851, the *convenientia* was said to be made by the three brother-kings and their faithful men; any individual of either category who breached the agreement was to be forced into conformity by all the rest, kings and faithful men alike. In 856 the word *pactum* was used of the similar understanding between Charles the Bald and his faithful men. If one of the latter violated the agreement, he was to be subject to a series of penalties culminating in exile from 'our collective association' (*a nostra omnium societate*). If the king breached the agreement in respect of any individual, he was to be brought back into accord with 'right reason' by the faithful men, lay and ecclesiastical together, 'none abandoning his peer'. What touched one by implication touched all the faithful men. In 857 the group was identified by a new collective noun: *bar(o)natus*.[94]

---

93. Nithard, ed. Lauer 1926, III, 5, pp. 102–8. Nithard uses the classical terms *plebs* and *populus*. Compare *Annales Bertiniani* s.a. 842, p. 40: 'Fideles populi partis utriusque pari se iuramento constrinxerunt ut, uter eorundem fratrum adversus alterum sinistri quippiam moliretur, relicto prorsus auctore discidii, omnes sese ad servatorem fraternitatis amicitiaeque converterent.' Vernacular language of the oaths: Schmidt-Wiegand 1977, pp. 62ff; Wright 1982, pp. 122–6.

94. *MGH Cap.* II, no. 254, 254; no. 205, c. 8, pp. 73–4; no. 262, c. 10, p. 281; 'ut nullus suum parem dimittat ut contra suam legem et rectam rationem et iustum iudicium, etiamsi voluerit, quod absit, rex noster alicui facere non possit'; no. 268, p. 295 (*adnuntiatio Karoli*).

Almost exactly contemporary is the appeal of West Frankish rebels to the East Frankish King Louis to come and 'liberate them from the tyranny' of Charles. Louis, as a Carolingian and Charles' elder brother, was termed 'legitimate lord'. Charles was said to 'rage against his own people', his promises and oaths no longer to command any trust. The appeal was brought by envoys claiming to speak for the 'people'.[95] Faithful men might unite to reject their king on other grounds than tyranny: withdrawal of fidelity was justified if a king neglected the functions of his rank and title (*honor et nomen*). Military and political failure could cause a Carolingian to be abandoned as 'useless'.[96]

In all these cases from the mid-ninth century, literate men seem to be striving to articulate the relationship between the king and his constituency. Classical terms jostle with the language of fidelity. The outcome is close to contract theory and a right of resistance. This burst of creativity arose from efforts to resolve an unusual prolonged period of tension in the West Frankish kingdom. It was possible only because political thought for laymen as well as clergy was on the agenda of Carolingian reformers. Thus contestation took place against a background of collaboration between king and aristocracy at an ideological as well as a practical level. In *The Government of the Palace*, Hincmar described the shaping of counsel at assemblies where the king met with 'the generality of the aristocracy as a whole' (*generalitas universorum maiorum*).[97] The reality of consensus politics was expressed in the capitularies' invocations of consent, consultation, counsel and aid, and in references to common welfare and public utility as the ends in view. The co-operation of king and faithful men in law-making and judgement-finding was grounded in shared convictions as to what constituted justice, reasonable treatment and fair dues, as well as in shared interest in social order. Participation in power at the centre, not just in the localities, made faithful men, laymen and higher clergy alike, more self-conscious political actors and keepers of the peace. Their *societas* foreshadowed the community of the realm.

95. *Annales Fuldenses* s.a. 858, pp. 49–50.
96. *Annales Bertiniani* s.a. 848, p. 55: Pippin II of Aquitaine abandoned for *desidia* and *inertia*; s.a. 862, p. 87: Charles of Provence abandoned (but not definitively) as *inutilis* and *inconveniens regio honore et nomini*. These and other instances: Bund 1979, pp. 435–6, 444–6, 478–89, 514–47. See also Peters 1970, pp. 47–80.
97. Hincmar, ed. Gross and Schieffer 1980, c. 29, pp. 84–5. Hannig 1982, p. 199: '*Consensus fidelium* is, so to speak, the "complementary concept" to the Christian ideal of kingship' ('der "Komplementärbegriff" zum christlichen Königsideal').

Ideas of empire in the Carolingian period

The Roman Empire contained many dependent *regna*: this was enough of a commonplace to be included in Isidore's *Etymologies*.[98] C. 700, the author of a little treatise on official posts excised romanity from this hegemonial conception, defining an emperor as a ruler over kings. Carl Erdmann termed this a 'Rome-free' imperial idea.[99] For Alcuin the word empire (*imperium*) could mean overlordship of a number of different *gentes* 'divided by language and separated by race according to their ancestors' names'. Alcuin was impressed by the capacity to impose peace of hegemons (past and present) in Britain.[100] The Frankish author of the early ninth-century *Paderborn Epic* was just as impressed by Charlemagne: 'a king [who] excelled kings on the summit of empire'.[101] Universality had been the hallmark of the Roman Empire, and then also of the Christian Church that grew within it. When imperial power lapsed in the West, learned men came to terms with barbarian regimes, and elaborated conceptions of Christian kingship.[102] But the equation of romanity with Christendom remained fossilised in the Church's liturgy: 'Have mercy, O God, on the sins of thy people, . . . that the secure liberty of the Roman name may always exult in thy devotion'. In the eighth century Frankish clergy substituted 'Frankish' for 'Roman' in this and similar prayers.[103] The Continuator of Fredegar imagined the pope contemplating secession from the authority of the emperor in Constantinople and turning instead to the Franks.[104] No less imaginatively, a Roman cleric c. 760, drawing on the hagiographical legend of Pope Silvester, concocted the Donation of Constantine in which the fourth-century emperor transferred his authority and privileges in the West to the pope, who, in baptising him, had also cured him of leprosy. Though

98. Isidore, *Etymologies* IX, 3, 2, echoing Augustine, *City of God* XVIII, 2, on the two great *regna* of the Assyrians, then the Romans: Reydellet 1981, p. 515. The best surveys of ideas of empire from the ninth to the twelfth century are Folz 1953 (English translation 1969) and now Werner 1980b. Still useful: Barraclough 1950.

99. Dating and genre: Schramm 1968, vol. I, pp. 120–7. 'Rome-free' idea of empire: Erdmann 1951.

100. Alcuin, ed. Godman 1982, pp. 42–3, and Godman's comments *ibid.*, pp. lxxxviii–xciii. See also Ganshof 1949 (1971); Wormald 1983.

101. *MGH Poetae* I, l. 86, p. 368: 'imperii . . . rex culmine reges/excellit'. This poem is also known as *Karolus Magnus et Leo Papa*. Schaller 1976 suggests Einhard wrote it, c. 806.

102. Reydellet 1981.

103. *Gelasian Sacramentary*, no. 1503, p. 217: 'Populi tui, quaesumus, omnipotens deus, propitiare peccatis . . . ut romani nominis secura libertas in tua devocione semper exultet'; and *ibid.*, nos. 1480, 1488 and 1496, pp. 214–16. Compare *Missale Francorum*, pp. 20–1, altering to 'regni Francorum nominis', etc. See Tellenbach 1934/5, p. 61 and comments pp. 20–2.

104. Continuator of Fredegar, ed. Wallace-Hadrill 1960, c. 22, p. 96.

echoes of the Constantine legend occasionally resounded in papal letters, the Donation itself was not used, and had almost certainly never been conceived, as documentary support for papal imperialism in the later eighth century. (Only by a quirk of fate, having got into a Frankish canon law collection in the ninth century as a proof-text for the inviolability of ecclesiastical property against lay encroachment, did the Donation return with this collection to Rome in the eleventh century, to be put to new uses by Gregorian reformers.)[105] The Donation may have scored points in the centuries-old rivalry between Rome and Ravenna. But it was not designed to meet the papacy's increasingly desperate need for an ideological as well as a practical solution to the problem of political order in and around Rome. The eighth-century Republic of St Peter was a bold but abortive experiment.[106] Charlemagne's patriciate of the Romans turned out not to commit him to act effectively to protect the pope. *Faute de mieux*, Leo III would have to call into being a new, western, Roman empire when the old one failed him.

On Christmas Day 800 the two ideas of empire, Rome-free and Rome-centred, briefly intersected in the coronation of Charlemagne by Leo III in Rome. According to Einhard, Charlemagne used to say that 'if he had known beforehand the pope's plan, he would never have entered the church'.[107] Leo's plan was to provide himself and his Roman clergy and people with a replica of the too-distant empire in Constantinople: hence the imitation of Byzantine ritual.[108] The Franks had other ideas. For them Charlemagne was an emperor but not a specifically Roman one; he owed his title not to papal coronation but to an acknowledgement of his power by the peoples he ruled. A Frankish annalist wrote that he 'assumed the title of Empire in accordance with the will of God and at the request of all his Christian people'.[109] Charlemagne's imperial seal was inscribed *Renovatio romani imperii*, but this was a renovation that could be conducted far from the city of Rome itself. The *rex francorum* fought shy of the pope's attempt to involve him in a similarly personal relationship with the people of Rome.

105. Exemplary edition (as *Constitutum Constantini*), origin and early history: Fuhrmann 1959, 1966; later incorporation in the Pseudo-Isidorian collection and subsequent use: *idem* 1972–4; English translation: Ehler and Morrall 1954, pp. 16–27. See also pp. 245–6 below.
106. Noble 1984.
107. Einhard, ed. Holder-Egger 1911, c. 28, p. 32: 'Quo tempore imperatoris et augusti nomen accepit. Quod primo in tantum aversatus est ut adfirmaret se eo die . . . ecclesiam non intraturum si pontificis consilium praescire potuisset.' 108. Schramm 1968, vol. I, pp. 215–63.
109. *Annales Laureshamenses*, p. 37: 'iustum eis [i.e. the assembled clergy and Frankish aristocracy] esse videbatur ut ipse cum deo adiutorio et universo christiano populo petente ipsum nomen [i.e. imperatoris] haberet'.

Charlemagne never used the title 'emperor of the Romans': instead he 'steered the Rome Empire' from Aachen.[110]

In 806, when Charlemagne took counsel with the Franks and envisaged the succession of his son Charles to an undivided patrimony of Francia, with his two younger sons Pippin and Louis retaining the acquired realms (which they had ruled nominally since 781) of Italy and Aquitane, he made a breach with Frankish royal custom which corresponded to the new-found role of the Franks as an imperial people and of Francia as the seat of empire.[111] The young Charles had probably been destined to succeed to the imperial title; but he and Pippin predeceased their father. In 813 at Aachen, only four months before his own death, Charlemagne named and crowned Louis co-emperor. The inscription on Louis' seal, *renovatio regni francorum*, highlighted the Frankish basis of this imperial realm, and the succession project agreed between Louis and his sons in 817 preserved, as in 806, the unity of Francia, with Louis' eldest son Lothar being crowned co-emperor with the approval of the Franks. The drafter(s) of the document specifying these arrangements put a new stress on the religious legitimacy of the empire, adducing a divine preference for unity which chimed well with Louis' concern to inhibit divisive aristocratic factionalism focusing around Lothar.[112] Growing tension between the co-emperors in the early 820s was eased in the short run when Louis sent Lothar to make an imperial kingdom of Italy. This enabled the pope to reassert the reference of the imperial title to the protectorship of Rome: Paschal I recrowned Lothar as emperor and sought renewed guarantees for papal security.[113] For the next century or so, the imperial title swung between a specific, local meaning (Lothar's heir Louis II was known to contemporary West Franks as 'emperor of Italy')[114] and a wider connotation recalling Charlemagne and the Frankish-imperial tradition. The resumption in 843 of royal custom in the division of Francia between Louis the Pious' sons, the territorial limitations of emperors' powers, and the papacy's consistent pursuit of its local interests resulted in an empire confined *de facto* to Italy. Papal efforts to recast emperorship as a papal

---

110. Classen 1951 (1983). Charlemagne's seal: Schramm 1968, vol. I, pp. 274–84. See also Beumann 1958; Folz 1964 (English translation 1974).

111. Classen 1972. Further dimensions of the 806 text: Schlesinger 1958 (1963). Text translated in Loyn and Percival 1975, pp. 91–6.

112. Religious aspects of imperial ideals of Louis and his advisers: Schieffer 1957; Noble 1976. Classen 1972, argues for continuity between 806 and 817; Hägermann 1975, tries unsuccessfully to rebut this. Political context of 817: Werner 1959, p. 168 and n. 89; Brunner 1979, pp. 96–9. Partial French translation of 817 *Ordinatio imperii*: Riché and Tate 1974, vol. II, pp. 369–70.

113. *Annales Regni Francorum* s.a. 823, pp. 160–1.

114. *Annales Bertiniani* s.a. 860, p. 83, 863, pp. 96, 97.

gift[115] foundered with the collapse of papal power in Rome in the late ninth century. Churchmen tended to be preoccupied with politics at the level of the kingdom, and the idea of empire, like the collective responsibility of Carolingian brother-kings for the one Church, came to mean little to the aged Hincmar.[116] It had been resurrected to legitimise Frankish imperialism. Frankish divisions made it hard to sustain. For its substance had always been the oneness of the Frankish people: there were many *regna* and several kings, but only one *regnum francorum*. In 881, Hincmar felt himself to be in a kingdom that was only a 'small bit' (*particula*) of that *regnum*.[117]

Yet two other dimensions of the Carolingian imperial revival ensured that the idea of empire survived the divisions of the ninth century. First, the Franks' political success brought to the spokesmen of Latin Christendom a new sense of separateness from the world of the Greeks, Byzantium. The *Libri Carolini* denied authority in the West to those 'kings' in Constantinople who had usurped the imperial title that belonged to Christ alone.[118] Charlemagne once having become (somewhat inconsistently) an emperor himself claimed parity with his 'brother' in the East and gained Byzantine recognition of his title in 812. Later, parity was no longer enough. Ermold turned against Constantinople the very symbol of cultural superiority she had once directed to the West: the organ. Constantine V had sent one to Pippin in 757 and much impressed the Franks. Seventy years later Louis the Pious had one made for him at Aachen, thereby, according to Ermold, taking away from Constantinople her 'chief glory': 'Maybe it will be a sign that they [the Greeks] should bow their necks to the Franks.'[119] In 871 a letter written on behalf of the Emperor Louis II told the emperor in Constantinople that the 'Greeks' had lost the empire of the Romans because of their heretical opinions: that empire had been transferred to the Franks 'by virtue of our orthodoxy'.[120] A Frankish court, to which came embassies and gifts from subordinate peoples and from the East, was an apt vantage-

---

115. John VIII's pontificate's significance here: Ullmann 1962, pp. 219–25.
116. Penndorf 1974, pp. 77–90.
117. Council of St Macre, Fismes, c. 8, *PL* 125, col. 1085. Plurality of *regna*: Werner 1981, pp. 176–80. *Regnum francorum*: Classen 1981, pp. 209–12.
118. *MGH Conc.* II, Supplement, pp. 3, 5, 16–17.
119. Ermold, *In Honorem Hludowici*, ll. 2520–9, p. 192: 'Organa quin etiam, quae numquam Francia crevit,/ Unde Pelasga tument regna superba nimis/ Et quis te solis, Caesar, superasse putabat/ Constantinopolis, nunc Aquis aula tenet./ Fors erit indicium quod Francis colla remittant,/ Cum sibi praecipuum tollitur inde decus./ Francia plaude, decet; Hludowico fer, pia, grates/ Cuius virtute munera tanta capis./ Det Deus omnipotens, caeli terraeque repertor,/ Saecla per ampla suum nomen in orbe sonet.' Arrival of Byzantine organ: *Annales Regni Francorum* s.a. 757, p. 14.
120. *MGH Epp.* VII, p. 385. Partial English translation: Folz 1969, pp. 181–3. Context: Grierson 1981, pp. 891–7.

point for the spatial dimension of the Latin-Christian idea of empire.

For the second dimension, that of time, the vantage-point was the monastery. At St Gall, Notker the Stammerer pondered Daniel's prophecy of the four monarchies and concluded that the contemporary Frankish Empire, reunited as Notker wrote under Charles the Fat, was the last of these and destined to last till the end of time.[121] Notker's faith could overcome such obstacles as Charles the Fat's personal failings or the fragmentation of the empire in 888. Similarly in the tenth century, when that fragmentation had become permanent, Adso of Montierender affirmed the continuance of the Roman Empire under 'the kings of the Franks' whose efforts held off the coming of Antichrist.[122] Both Notker and Adso were monks writing for rulers. 'The Christian idea of empire . . . was a powerful force in the middle ages, influential in the minds and actions of many kings and emperors', wrote Geoffrey Barraclough, '. . . But we shall simply pile up confusion if we attempt to identify it with the historical empire in the west, or indeed with any other empire of this world.'[123] Because eschatology shaped the monastic world-view and because monks shaped so much of recorded medieval thought, it was the eschatological dimension that gave the idea of empire its extraordinary capacity to withstand the repeated shocks of confrontation with dissonant political realities.

Carolingian legacies

i. *The West Frankish realm*

The rapid weakening of West Frankish kingship towards the close of the ninth century led to a reinforcing of the theocratic central prop of Carolingian political thought. Hincmar's successor Fulk of Rheims flirted with elective kingship, arguing in the disputed succession of 888 that his candidate, as a tried warleader, was more 'suitable' than a nine-year-old claimant.[124] But there were risks in putting too much stress on meritocratic criteria. The problem diagnosed by the historian Regino of Prüm was not shortage but excess of quality among the Frankish magnates leading to

---

121. Goetz 1981, pp. 69–85.   122. Schneidmüller 1979, pp. 61–4. See also Goez 1958, pp. 74–6.
123. Barraclough 1950, p. 26.
124. Flodoard, ed. Heller and Waitz 1881, IV, 5, p. 563: 'Karolus adhuc admodum corpore simul et scientia parvulus existebat nec regni gubernaculis idoneus erat.'

'emulation and mutual ruin'.[125] Hence a heavy reinvestment by church-men in the rights of heirship and blood when royal authority seemed to offer the only defence against the privatisation of ecclesiastical resources. Though the see of Rheims suffered more than most from this threat in the tenth century, its claim to possess the holy oil brought from heaven for Clovis' baptism became a powerful myth legitimising both West Frankish kingship and Rheims prerogatives.[126] From Hincmar's time onwards, consecration was indispensable for West Frankish kings in the sense that none dispensed with it.[127] The drawing of a parallel between the king and Christ the Anointed One was encouraged by the 'uncompromisingly Christocentric' monastic piety of the period.[128] A West Frankish royal *Ordo* of c. 900 invoked 'Christ anointed by the oil of exultation above His fellows.' The same rite's coronation prayer enjoined that the king 'believe himself to bear the name and deputyship of Christ', while at the enthronement, Christ was requested as 'mediator of God and man' to 'strengthen on this throne of the realm [the king] as mediator of clergy and people'.[129] These prayers should not be pressed for a precise legalistic meaning: they assert the Church's traditional view of the divine origin, and responsibilities, of kingship. The apt ritual complement to anointing and coronation is the bishop's girding-on of the king's sword for use 'in ejecting the Church's enemies and caring for the realm and protecting the fortresses of God'.[130]

As in liturgy so in vernacular literature the late ninth century was notably productive. Even if only indirectly, lay attitudes to kingship seem to be reflected here. The monk Otfrid probably wrote for lay aristocrats as well as fellow-monks when he presented Christ as a warleader dying to save his

125. Regino of Prüm, ed. Kurze 1890, s.a. 888, p. 129: '[Wars arose] non quia principes Francorum deessent, qui nobilitate, fortitudine et sapientia regnis imperare possent, sed quia inter ipsos aequalitas generositatis, dignitatis ac potentiae discordiam augebat, nemine tantum ceteros precellente, ut eius dominio relinqui se submittere dignarentur. Multos enim idoneos principes ad regni gubernacula moderanda Francia genuisset, nisi fortuna eos aemulatione virtutis in pernitiem mutuam armasset.' Despite classical echoes, the idea of suitability here is clearly contemporary.
126. Hincmar first made the claim, in 869: *MGH Cap.* II, no. 276, p. 340.
127. Schramm 1960, pp. 62ff, 145ff. 128. Kantorowicz 1957, pp. 61, 78.
129. Seven-Forms *Ordo*: Erdmann 1951, pp. 87–9. Crowning-prayer: '[Christus] cuius nomen vicemque gestare rex crederis'; sword-prayer: '[Salvator] cuius typum geris in nomine'; enthronement-prayer: 'quatinus mediator Dei et hominum te mediatorem cleri et plebis in hoc regni solio confirmet et in regnum eternum secum regnare faciat'. Co-rulership in heaven: Schramm 1968, vol. I, pp. 79–85; imitation of Christ as moral requirement: Dürig 1958; compare the image of ruler as servant: Deshman 1980.
130. 'Erdmann' *Ordo*: Schramm 1968, vol. II, p. 218.

faithful men, hence snatching victory from death.[131] The *Ludwigslied*
written in 881 to celebrate the victory of a West Frankish king over the
Vikings in that year was perhaps a learned monastic pastiche of a living oral
tradition of secular poetry, but could surely have been relished outside as
well as inside the 'fortresses of God'. It establishes King Louis' credentials:

> The Lord gave him manhood, a lordly following,
> A throne in Francia – long may he hold it!

Before battle is joined Louis promises his men:

> Who here in hero's strength does God's will
> I shall reward if he comes away safe:
> If he dies in battle I shall reward his kin . . .
> Song was sung, battle begun.
> Blood shone in cheeks as the Franks played.

And the poem ends:

> Wellbeing to you Louis, king blessed in war![132]

The *chansons de geste* survive only from two centuries later, but since they
took shape around episodes in Carolingian history are arguably another
part of this Carolingian legacy.[133] The *Song of Roland* in its extant form of
c.1100 stressed royal warleadership all the more fervently for being able to
blend it with the crusading theme of Christian warfare against Muslims.
But the ruler who fights God's battles under his orders bears the true
Carolingian stamp. His is also a traditional authority in another sense. The
Song of Roland first depicts the silver-bearded Charlemagne not on the
battlefield but in an orchard surrounded by noble peers sitting on white
carpets. The politics of counsel and consent are playing out in this setting:

> Beneath a pine straightway the king is gone
> And calls his barons to council thereupon:
> By French advice what'er he does is done.[134]

What is striking in the main *chanson* tradition is the continued centripetal
pull of kingship for the aristocracy: here, faithfulness though owed in
principle to *any* lord was focused overwhelmingly on the king. The word

---

131. McKitterick 1977, pp. 198–203; Rexroth 1978, pp. 292–4; Wallace-Hadrill 1983, pp. 385–7: one
copy of Otfrid's work was addressed to Louis the German.
132. *Ludwigslied*, ll. 5–6, 39–41, 48–9, 57, pp. 25–7: 'Gab her imo dugidi, Fronisc githigini,/ Stual hier in
Vrankon. So bruche her es lango.'/ . . . "So uuer so hier in ellian Giduot godes uuillion/ Quimit he
gisund uz, Ih gilonon imoz;/ Bilibit her thar inne, Sinemo kunnie"./ . . . Sang uuas gisungan, Uuig
uuas bigunnan./ Bluot skein in uuangon: Spilodun ther Vrankon./ . . . Uuolar abur Hluduig,
Kuning euuin salig!' The poem as pastiche: Louis 1946, vol. II, p. 107. Political context: Werner
1979, pp. 431–7. 133. Louis 1956. 134. Translated Sayers 1957, p. 57.

'betrayal' (*trahison*) acquired the sense of a uniquely heinous crime against the king or his officers. 'Treason was a dominant, even compulsory, motif in the *chansons*.'[135] Hence though *Roland*'s Charlemagne is an archetypical patrimonial figure, he is also representative of a public power whose claims override those of private vengeance. If there are clear continuities with Carolingian ideas of royal responsibility for the peace of the realm, there are also parallels with the Roman law concept of *majestas* invoked by learned men from the early eleventh century onwards to defend royal or princely authority.

Given the role of the *chansons* as a medium of cultural values in the tenth, eleventh and early twelfth centuries, it becomes unsurprising that the diminishing scope of royal power left kingship unimpugned as a source of legitimation for the power of others. The idea that all authority, and specifically high justice, depended ultimately on delegation from the king was nurtured by magnates whose own position was often threatened from below.[136] The princes of the West Frankish kingdom might not have recognised themselves in R.W. Southern's thumbnail sketch as 'shockingly unconsecrated and dumb'.[137] For they symbolically claimed their share in the king's consecration by linking their power to his, whether through participating in his ritual inauguration, or else by using titles that proclaimed them still the 'ministers' of the king, offerers of faith and counsel, sharers in royal virtues.[138] As Carolingian traditions were cultivated equally assiduously by the later Carolingian kings and by their Robertian rivals in the century following 888, the idea of the West Frankish realm became detached from a particular dynasty.[139] Further, it could be plausibly reconstructed as an imperial realm once territorial princes had laid claim to provincial authority in Normandy, Aquitaine, Gothia, Burgundy.[140] The Rheims cleric Richer at the close of the tenth century described the 'princes of the Gauls' assembled in 987 to choose between a Carolingian claimant, Charles of Lorraine, and Hugh Capet, duke of Francia. Hugh was the choice of 'Gauls, Bretons, Danes, Aquitainians, Goths, Spaniards and Gascons'[141] – wishful thinking on Richer's part since

---

135. Jones 1982, pp. 93–6. Compare a similarly 'centripetal' theme in the *Ruodlieb*: Bosl 1974.
136. Werner 1968 (English translation, Reuter 1979); Poly and Bournazel 1980, ch. VI.
137. Southern 1953, p. 99.   138. Werner 1968; compare Brunner 1973, pp. 179–214.
139. Ehlers 1978; Schneidmüller 1979.   140. Werner 1965; Schneidmüller 1979, pp. 185–93.
141. Richer, ed, Waitz 1877, IV, cc. 11–12, pp. 132–3: once the *principes Galliarum* are assembled, 'dux [Hugo] omnium consensu in regnum promovetur . . ., Gallis, Brittannis, Dahis, Aquitanis, Gothis, Hispanis, Wasconibus rex . . . prerogatur. Stipatus itaque regnorum principibus, more regio decreta fecit legesque condidit, felici successu omnia ordinans atque distribuens.'

only northern princes were in fact involved, but clearly an attempt to make
Hugh's 'empire' coextensive with the old West Frankish realm. Equally
revealing is the reason given for the princes' rejection of the Carolingian
claimant: 'he had not been horrified to serve a foreign king', that is, Otto III.
What is being asserted here is the separate identity of 'Gaul' as against the
Ottonian realm 'across the Rhine'. For Richer as for other contemporaries,
the continuance of twin Frankish kingdoms, eastern and western, had
become an anachronism. Around the turn of the tenth/eleventh centuries,
the westerners came to monopolise the 'Frankish' label for their own
kingdom.[142] A final significant point is made when Richer says that the
princes rejected Charles of Lorraine because 'he had married a wife who,
being of the knightly class, was not his equal'. Here is the reflection of the
high nobility's consciousness of themselves as 'peers' who could intermarry
with and rule with the king's family.[143] It was this group whom Richer
referred to as the 'princes' or 'primates' that in fact as well as in theory
underwrote the nascent French kingdom.

The weak early Capetian kings could gain little mileage from Carolingian traditions of royal warleadership. The monk Helgaud of the royally
patronised house of Fleury made a virtue of necessity when he presented in
his *Life* of Robert the Pious a pacific, protective royal father and almsgiver:
and an image of royal sanctity.[144] When Bishop Adalbero of Laon urged
Robert to restore law and order by collaborating with his bishops, he
recommended the skills of the *orator*, exploiting that word's double
meaning of pray-er and public-speaker.[145] Robert, swaying God and man,
might have been cast as a perfect mediator. A century later, with Capetian
kings becoming more active and more powerful, Abbot Suger of St Denis
could fuse the full range of Carolingian traditions with contemporary
themes, presenting Louis VI as a paladin of Christian warfare, defending the
Church against tyrannical castellans and his realm against an aggressor from
across the Rhine.[146] At his royal inauguration, the young Louis, 'his sword of
secular knighthood put aside, had girded on him an ecclesiastical sword, to

142. *Ibid.*, p. 133: Archbishop Adalbero of Rheims sways the assembly against the Carolingian Charles
of Lorraine: 'Quid dignum Karolo conferri potest, quem fides non regit, torpor enervat, postremo
qui tanta capitis imminutione hebuit, ut externo regi servire non horruerit?' *Francia* as the western
Frankish realm, hence France: Werner 1965, pp. 10–13; Ehlers 1976, pp. 224–7.
143. Richer, ed. Waitz 1877, IV, c. 11, p. 133: 'uxorem de militari ordine sibi imparem duxerit'. See Van
Winter 1967.   144. Carozzi 1981 with Werner's comments *ibid.*, pp. 430–1.
145. Duby 1978, pp. 64–5 (English translation 1980, p. 46); Carozzi 1978, pp. 698–700; Adalbero of
Laon, ed. Carozzi 1979, pp. lxxvff.
146. Suger, ed. Waquet 1949, pp. 218–30; Duby 1978, pp. 277–81.

wreak vengeance on malefactors'.[147] In avenging the murder of his vassal the Flemish count, Louis shed blood by which Flanders was 'washed white as if rebaptised': again a christocentric image beloved of monastic writers but appealing at the same time to the audience of the *chansons* (a genre also cultivated at St Denis).[148] In Suger's hands, the cult of monarchy was depersonalised and the Crown was on the way to becoming the symbol of the 'realm of France' – a consummation devoutly wished by the monks of St Denis, custodians of the regalia but not of Clovis' heaven-sent oil.

ii. *The Anglo-Saxon and Anglo-Norman realms*

In political ideas, as in institutions and royal ritual, English developments were influenced by Carolingian models, yet retained some traits of their own. In his version of St Augustine's *Soliloquies*, King Alfred characteristically 'took off' from his source's likening of the power of wisdom to that of the sun, and produced this memorable image of patrimonial kingship:

Consider now, in the case of men who came to the king's estate where he is then in his residence, or to his assembly, or to his army, whether it seems tó you that they all come there by the same route. I think, rather, that they arrive by very many routes . . . And yet they are all coming to the one lord . . . They neither come there with a similar ease, nor are they similarly at ease when they get there. Some are received with greater reverence and greater familiarity than others, some with less; some with virtually none, except for the one fact, that he loves them all. So it is with respect to wisdom: everyone who desires it and is eager for it may come to it and dwell in its household and live in its company; nevertheless, some are close to it, some farther away. It is likewise with the estates of every king: some men are in the chamber, some in the hall, some on the threshing floor, some in prison, and yet all of them live through the one lord's favour, just as all men live under the one sun and by its light see everything that they see.[149]

The dependence of 'all' on a personal relationship to the one royal lord could hardly be more vividly expressed.

Equally king-centred is Alfred's precocious version of the three orders:

A man cannot work on any enterprise without resources. In the case of the king, the resources and tools with which to rule are that he have his land fully manned: he must have praying men, fighting men and working men . . . [and] he must have the

---

147. Suger, ed. Waquet 1949, p. 86: 'Senonensis igitur archiepiscopus . . . abjectoque secularis militie gladio ecclesiastico ad vindictam malefactorum accingens, diademate regni gratanter coronavit.'
148. *Ibid.*, p. 250: 'His ergo et diversis ultionum modis et sanguinis multi effusione lota et quasi rebaptizata Flandria . . . rex in Franciam, Deo auxiliante, victor remeavit.' See also Spiegel 1975; Hallam 1982.
149. Quoted from the translation in Keynes and Lapidge 1983, pp. 143–4. *Tun* here rendered 'estate' can be understood as 'royal residence' or 'palace'.

means of support for his tools, the three classes of men. These, then, are their means of support: land to live on, gifts, weapons, food, ale, clothing, and whatever else is necessary for these three classes of men.

This passage is reminiscent of Asser's account in his *Life of Alfred* of the king's three-way division of his revenues for secular affairs between fighting men, craftsmen (*operatores*) 'skilled in all kinds of earthly constructing' and foreign guests.[150] Where the earliest Continental views of trifunctionality are sociological, Alfred's is political: he is talking about the use of power. It is self-justificatory ('possession of earthly power never pleased me overmuch'); it is extremely practical (Alfred forgets neither benefices nor beer); and it is firmly centred on the royal household. Alfred's 'workmen' are not labouring peasants (a warrior-king took those for granted) but craftsmen who build the king's works or make precious things for royal gift-giving. The Alfred jewel survives from a world in which a bishop could call the king 'his ring-giver' and 'the greatest treasure-giver of all the kings he has ever heard tell of'.[151]

A century later, the *Polity* of Archbishop Wulfstan of York shows the influence of Carolingian images of kingship:

> For the Christian king
> It is very fitting
> That he be in the place of a father
> For the Christian people.
> And in watching over and warding them
> Be Christ's representative,
> As he is called . . .
> And it is fitting
> That he bring to peace and reconciliation
> All Christian people
> With righteous laws.[152]

Given his Continental contacts, Wulfstan's version of the three orders is unsurprisingly like that of his contemporaries abroad. But his insistence on royal peace-bringing through law has its distinctive English context: Wulfstan himself drafted laws for Aethelred and Cnut.[153] As important as those links with the West Frankish realm were Ottonian contacts. Old insular ideas of imperial kingship gained new impetus not only from the extension of West Saxon power in Britain but also from Englishmen's

---

150. *Ibid.*, p. 132 (Alfred) and pp. 106–7 (Asser). (The idea of dividing revenues could well be modelled on the practice prescribed for bishops.)
151. Bishop Wulfsige's poem-preface to the translation of Gregory I's *Dialogues, ibid.*, pp. 187–8.
152. Wulfstan of York, ed. Jost 1959, pp. 40, 42. 153. Duby 1978, pp. 135–7.

acquaintance with Ottonian and Salian courts. Assemblies at Quedlinburg when the *gentes* acknowledged the 'king of kings' had their analogues in Edgar's durbars at Bath and Chester (973) when Celtic and Norse as well as English princes recognised the ruler of Britain.[154] The ritual splendour of a king-making at Mainz was imitated in a new, more elaborate English *ordo*.[155]

The Norman Conquest brought few changes in the ideal or practice of English rulership: rather these could strengthen the Conqueror's authority in face of an alternative Norman tradition of aristocratic freedom. Hence the paradox of Anglo-Norman development of crown-wearings and *laudes regiae* on the one hand, and on the other, royal burials that remained 'low-key affairs'.[156] It was no coincidence that a Norman cleric, the so-called Anonymous of Rouen (c. 1100) wishing to exalt royal authority took as his proof-text an Anglo-Saxon royal consecration-*ordo*. His reaffirmation of the dual personality of the king – 'by nature an individual man, by grace [through consecration] a *christus*, that is, a God-man' – was inspired by the wording of the liturgy.[157] But it was thoroughly in line with contemporary royalist sentiment: far from being outmoded, the Anonymous' political ideas were as avant-garde as his scholastic method.[158] Yet there was no break with Carolingian traditions. It was easier to challenge those in Rome than in Rouen. In the Anglo-Norman realm as in France, the Investiture Contest evoked from pro-royal polemicists a successful reassertion of royal theocracy. In both realms, competing claims began to be made by court clergy that kings had hereditary powers to cure scrofula, 'the king's evil'.[159] William of Malmesbury (c. 1120) insisted that Edward the Confessor's miracles were done through his sanctity, his own achievement, and not through his royal descent.[160] But in the end, courtiers and reformers could compromise on sacral powers conferred through the king's inauguration-rite, through priestly hands: the anointing made the *christus domini* – in the later Middle Ages as in the earlier.

---

154. Nelson 1977b, pp. 68–70; Leyser 1983, pp. 90–1.   155. Nelson 1982.
156. Cowdrey 1981; Hallam 1982, p. 359.
157. Norman Anonymous, ed. Pellens 1966, p. 130: 'Itaque in unoquoque gemina intelligitur fuisse persona: una ex natura, altera ex gratia . . . In una quippe erat naturaliter individuus homo, in altera per gratiam christus, id est, deus-homo.' See Kantorowicz 1957, pp. 42–61.
158. Some of his detailed inferences from the royal *ordo* were however idiosyncratic: Nelson 1975, p. 50. Scholastic method: Hartmann 1975. Allegedly 'outmoded' ideas: Southern 1953, pp. 97–8; Kantorowicz 1957, pp. 60–1.
159. Bloch 1924; but compare now Barlow 1980. Poly and Bournazel 1980, pp. 471–81, see in 'royauté magique' 'la pénétration des structures mentales de la paysannerie'.
160. William of Malmesbury, ed. Stubbs 1887, vol. I, p. 273.

Another equally insistent theme of Carolingian political ideas was sounded in the historical writing of the Anglo-Norman period: aristocratic consensus remained the counterpoint to kingship. Though Geoffrey of Monmouth wrote in Latin, his work brought his noble readers close to the world of *Roland* with Arthur, like Charlemagne in the *chanson*, surrounded by his knights and gaining their approval for his wars.[161] The author of the *Gesta Stephani* could find no stronger defence of his hero than that he had gained his throne by the choice of his great men and ruled by their counsels. Not Stephen but wicked magnates acted tyrannously in breaking the peace and flouting the law.[162] With such private tyrants, we are back to a thoroughly Augustinian insistence on individual will and action underlying institutions and offices of the state. As revealing of Anglo-Norman political ideas as the scholastic theorising of the Rouen Anonymous are two stories that have, deservedly, entered English political mythology: the cake-burning Alfred is a model of Christian humility for whom a woman's scolding conveys divine reproach,[163] while the foot-soaked Canute demonstrates to his courtiers the vanity of royal power compared with that of 'Him at whose nod land and sea obey eternal laws'.[164] Artists have left for us a potent image of Christ-centred kingship and Christ-like royal majesty. But we misread the message if we neglect the strenuous moral exercise of self-correction and self-control that, for medieval observers, was at the heart of the king's imitation of Christ.

ii. *The East Frankish realm*

The Ottonians' kingdom was a direct heir of the Carolingian Empire and its image was constructed by men steeped in Carolingian traditions. Widukind writing his *Deeds of the Saxons* in the late 960s in the royal abbey of Korvey, linked the Ottonians with the Saxon *gens* just as Einhard had linked the Carolingians with the destiny of the Franks. Otto I, like Charlemagne, was an overlord of *gentes*. It was the dukes as leaders of the *gentes* who symbolically sustained Otto by serving him at his coronation feast. Widukind saw no incongruity in describing, first, Otto's enthronement outside the church by 'dukes and warriors', second, his consecration inside by bishops.[165] The *virtus* Widukind saw in the Ottonians could be

161. Geoffrey of Monmouth, ed. Griscom 1929, IX, 1, 12, pp. 432–3, 451–5.
162. *Gesta Stephani*, pp. 6, 10, 170, 180, 188. See Gransden 1974, pp. 190–1.
163. Keynes and Lapidge 1983, pp. 197–202.
164. Henry of Huntingdon, ed. Arnold 1879, pp. 188–9. See Deshman 1976, pp. 404–5.
165. Widukind, ed. Hirsch and Lohmann 1935, II, c. 1, pp. 54–5. Einhard, ed. Holder-Egger 1911, c. 7, saw Franks and Saxons united as one *populus* in Christianity. Widukind, I, c. 25, called this same union one *gens*.

appreciated by warriors and bishops alike. It impressed the learned monk as a kind of muscular Christianity: there is nothing that need suggest ancient Germanic notions of sacred kingship.[166] The first Ottonian, Henry I, sacrificed territory to acquire the potent relic of the Holy Lance.[167] He may have (though Widukind does not say so) declined anointing by the archbishop of Mainz on the grounds that 'it was enough to be designated and declared king', that is, designated by his predecessor and declared by aristocratic support.[168] Henry's preference has more to do with Carolingian traditionalism (ninth-century East Frankish Carolingians were not anointed) than with resisting Christian charisma in the name of Germanic *Heil*.[169] By c. 960 some East Frankish liturgist(s), probably at Mainz, conflated an earlier East Frankish rite with a West Frankish one to produce the most splendid royal *ordo* of the early Middle Ages.[170] Here the king was said to become a 'sharer in the ministry' of his consecrators. They were 'pastors and rectors of souls *in interioribus*', he was 'strenuous defender of the Church against its enemies *in exterioribus*':[171] a partnership in the Gelasian tradition.

The court artists of the later Ottonians and Salians, like those of the Carolingians in the generations after Charlemagne, increasingly stressed the king's majesty and nearness to God.[172] Ritual linked him more publicly with the aristocracy of the *gentes* when, following his inauguration, he rode around the component *regna* of the realm to receive their recognition.[173] For the king's sacrality, as Karl Leyser has pointed out, was an evolving thing, a function of aristocratic as well as of royal needs. The king's judging – his allocation of wealth and power, reward and punishment, peace and wrath – was the 'force of cohesion' that kept the realm together.[174] Hence the extended itineraries of the later Ottonians had political as well as symbolic significance.

Some German historians have claimed that 'a principle of the indivisibility of the realm' came into being in the tenth century.[175] Though this is only an inference from a sequence of undivided successions resulting from dynastic accident, the fact that in 1024 when the Ottonian line ended Conrad II was elected to an undivided realm suggests at least a preference (if not a principle) on the part of the electors, that is, the bishops and lay

166. Leyser 1979, pp. 77–82. 167. *Ibid.*, p. 88.
168. *Vita Udalrici, MGH SS* IV, p. 389, a late tenth-century text. See Bloch 1924, pp. 472–3 (English translation 1973, pp. 270–1). 169. Schlesinger 1963, p. 160.
170. *Pontificale Romano-Germanicum*, I, pp. 246–59. 171. Coronation-prayer, *ibid.*, p. 257.
172. Kantorowicz 1957, pp. 61–78; Deshman 1976. 173. Schmidt 1961.
174. Leyser 1979, pp. 104–5; *idem* 1981 (1982), pp. 94–6.
175. Tellenbach 1941; Beumann 1981b, pp. 43–7. But compare Gillingham 1971, pp. 9–10.

magnates. From this a political idea could emerge. In his *Deeds of Conrad*, Wipo, one of Conrad's chaplains, described the dangers that in 1024 beset the commonwealth (*res publica*): it was the dowager empress and 'eminent men', clerical and lay, who steered the fatherland (*patria*) safely into harbour.[176] Like Carolingian scholars in similar circumstances, Wipo drew on his classical reading to voice anew a 'transpersonal idea of the state'. When the citizens of Pavia, hearing of Henry II's death, destroyed the royal palace there, on the grounds that there was no longer a king who owned it, Conrad countered their argument by distinguishing between 'the house of the king' and 'a royal house': 'Even if the king is dead, the kingdom has remained.'[177] The appeal to public laws may have made sense to an Italian audience. North of the Alps the 'transpersonal idea' needed another anchorage. But it was not yet associated with nationhood. Conrad's *regnum* consisted of several *regna*, and its 'archthrone' was at Aachen. Wipo quoted a saying: 'The saddle of Conrad has the stirrup of Charles.' The tendency of those whom Wipo called the 'Latin Franks' to monopolise the label 'Frankish' did not provoke Wipo to seek a new label for Conrad's kingdom.[178] Kings were, as ever, conservative in their titulature. But later in the eleventh century the term *regnum teutonicorum* appeared more often in annalists' work. Significantly, it suggests language as a defining characteristic. It had first been used by Italians, apparently to express hostility to 'foreign' rule. Later it could express Gregorians' determination to confine the Salian kings north of the Alps. German historians, eager to find the origins of Germany, have taken it as evidence of nascent national consciousness on the part of the 'German' aristocracy, noting that it is used by the same writers who seem convinced that 'responsibility for the realm is borne not by the king alone but by the magnates along with the king'.[179] The conviction itself was not new: gentile identities were giving ground before a sense of the realm as a territory, but that too continued Carolingian political traditions.

Again as in Charlemagne's time, the hegemonial character of Ottonian kingship evoked a revived Rome-free idea of empire. According to Widukind, Henry I was an 'emperor of many peoples', while Otto I was acclaimed emperor after his victory at the Lechfeld (his later coronation by

176. Wipo, ed. Bresslau 1915, c. 1, p. 9; English translation, Mommsen and Morrison 1962, p. 57–8.
177. *Ibid.*, c. 7, p. 30: '"Si rex periit, regnum remansit . . . Aedes publicae fuerant, non privatae".' 'Transpersonal idea': Beumann 1956. The idea was evidently not shared by the Pavians.
178. Wipo, ed. Bresslau 1915, cc. 1, 6, pp. 12, 28–9 (translation, Mommsen and Morrison 1962, p. 60, 72.)
179. Müller-Mertens 1970, pp. 145–327; Keller 1982, p. 124.

the pope was unmentioned by Widukind).[180] At Mainz c. 960 clergy copied out an imperial consecration-rite entirely derived from royal *ordines* (hence including the prayer 'Prospice'): an imperial realm was an empire *secundum occidentales*.[181] Then Otto followed Charlemagne in extending his authority into Italy. This brought him to Rome, where Otto, like Charlemagne, was crowned by the pope. But the Ottonians' empire became more firmly Rome-bound than Charlemagne's. Bishop Liutprand of Cremona saw Otto in the line of Constantine and Justinian, appointed by God to establish peace in this world. Returning from an embassy to Constantinople in 968, Liutprand denounced the ritual technology of the 'Greeks' as empty form: the substance of true Roman emperorship now lay in the West.[182] Otto, legislating in Italy 'as a holy emperor' (*ut imperator sanctus*) gave colour to Liutprand's claim.[183] In the *Ottonianum*, he confirmed the privileges of the Roman Church under his imperial protectorship.

Otto's grandson Otto III, while using these themes, promoted a strikingly original conception of 'the renewal of the Roman Empire'.[184] His palace and court, based in Rome, were designed to replicate and supersede those of Constantinople. He created a rival version of the Byzantine family of kings:[185] he sent a crown to King Stephen of Hungary; according to Polish tradition a century later, he made the Polish duke Boleslaw 'brother and co-operator of the empire', briefly taking the imperial crown from his own head and placing it on Boleslaw's 'as a pledge of their friendship', and giving him 'instead of a triumphal standard, a nail from the cross of the Lord'.[186] The Poles could conceive of their land as autonomous within the *imperium christianum*. The language of brotherhood was appropriate for an emperor who called himself, as St Paul had done, 'the slave of Jesus Christ'. Otto transposed political and religious universalism. In his legislation he evoked Justinian.[187] Denouncing the Donation of

---

180. Widukind, ed. Hirsch and Lohmann 1935, I, cc. 25, 39, pp. 33, 50; III, c. 49, p. 109. See Beumann 1981a, pp. 568–9.
181. *Ordines coronationis Imperialis*, pp. 3–6: 'Benedictio ad ordinandum imperatorem secundum occidentales.' 'Prospice' here, p. 4, and many subsequent appearances in imperial *ordines*.
182. Liutprand, ed. Becker 1915, cc. 9, 10, 28. (English translation, Wright 1930, pp. 240–1, 251.)
183. Werner 1980b, pp. 160–1.
184. *Renovatio Imperii Romanorum*: Schramm and Mütherich 1983, plate 101b and p. 199.
185. See Nicol in this volume, pp. 57–8.
186. Gallus Anonymus, ed. Maleczyński 1952, I, c. 6, pp. 19–20: 'Pro vexillo triumphali clavum [imperator] ei de cruce Domini cum lancea sancti sancti Mauritii dono dedit . . . [et] eum fratrem et cooperatorem imperii constituit.' The lance was a replica: Dvornik 1949, pp. 145–6; Vlasto 1970, pp. 124–8.
187. Werner 1980b, pp. 161–2.

Constantine as the product of papal arrogance,[188] Otto 'slave of the Apostles' stole the clothes of papal humility. Otto died young and his successor Henry II preferred to stay north of the Alps. But Otto's imperial vision never entirely faded. His successors perpetuated it in their symbols of state. Henry II's mantle, still to be seen at Bamberg, is embroidered with the stars of heaven in imitation of Byzantine imperial claims to cosmic authority.[189] More importantly, Otto had forged the bond between the *regnum* and the empire so strongly that it would not be broken even by rulers like Henry II with little interest in a Roman power-base. Conrad I, once elected king, was already an emperor-elect and the East Frankish realm only one of the *regna* he would rule. His son Henry III immediately on Conrad's death took the title, no longer of 'king of the Franks' but 'king of the Romans'. When, later, there was a German kingdom, its ruler was never officially entitled 'king of the Germans'. German kingship had become inseparable from Roman emperorship.[190]

It had often been argued that just as the kingdom of Germany was politically undermined by the Investiture Contest because kings could no longer control the German Church, so the Gregorians' desacralisation of kingship destroyed the ideological foundations of royal theocracy. If power came from God 'through the hands of priests', then *regnum* depended on *sacerdotium*. All the papacy had to do was translate this dependence into terms of jurisdiction and the royalist case was lost from the outset. Hence, according to Walter Ullmann, the 'hierocratic challenge' was unanswerable.[191] It was, in fact, answered by appeals not only to tradition but to scripture and in particular to Romans 13. Some historians have claimed that another and equally dangerous line of attack was the theory of 'popular sovereignty' allegedly put forward by Manegold of Lautenbach, a learned Augustinian canon and passionate supporter of Gregory VII in south-west Germany. Certainly, Manegold wrote of a 'pact' by virtue of which an emperor or king was set up, and concluded that a ruler who breached it thereby released the people from their obligation of obedience to him. But the term 'pact' is not used here in a legal sense; rather it alludes to Isidore's definition of royal virtues, and hence by implication to the loss of those virtues as a definition of tyranny.[192] This was an idea of kingship as office (Manegold was a good Augustinian) but it was not one over which the people had any control. Just how far Manegold was from any idea of

188. *MGH DD* II, no. 389, p. 819 (English translation in Folz 1969, pp. 186–8).
189. Schramm and Mütherich 1962, p. 163 and plate 130.   190. Beumann 1981b.
191. Ullmann 1962, pp. 413–14. See also Kern 1954, pp. 97–8 (translation 1939, p. 54); Leyser 1965 (1982), p. 52.   192. Fuhrmann 1975.

covenant between king and people is clear from his analogue for kingly failure: 'If you drive away with insults and no pay a swineherd who doesn't look after your pigs properly, how much the more justifiable is it that power and honour be removed from someone who leads men into sin, instead of ruling them?'[193] According to Manegold, though the people might regret oaths sworn to a ruler who then lapsed into unrighteousness, the oaths had nevertheless to be kept unless and until the pope released men bound by them.[194]

Given the fundamental importance of fidelity in the political system, this claim that the pope could release from its obligations might seem the most dangerous part of the hierocratic challenge to kingship. It was here that the royalist Anonymous of Hersfeld concentrated his defence, refuting as false history the alleged precedent of a pope's releasing the Franks from their oaths to the last Merovingian in 750.[195] The Anonymous argued, of course, that there was no parallel between the worthy Henry IV and the useless Merovingian. But his point was that it had not been the pope but the princes of the Franks who had decided to reject the useless king.[196] Here history and theory coincided with the realities of eleventh-century politics as described by the contemporary annalist and fierce critic of Henry IV, Lampert of Hersfeld. The Saxons' sworn faith (*fides*) to Henry IV was to last only so long as the king 'would govern affairs legitimately in the way of his ancestors and if he would allow each to have his rank and status and laws inviolably kept'.[197] These last words were clarified in the specific demand that the king should satisfy according to their rightful claims (*jurisdictio*) those Saxon magnates whose lands he had taken without lawful consultation. Such royal misconduct in itself released faithful men from their obligations. In the circumstances of the 1060s and 1070s, such statements had practical relevance. Law, in the sense used in ninth-century capitularies, provided both the yardstick for judging royal action and the justification for resistance. Outraged faithful men had the means to resist. The Gregorians pragmatically hitched their wagon to the rebels' cause – but then the rebels' military failure and eventual accommodation with Henry stranded the Gregorians in political impotence and exposed two weaknesses

193. Manegold of Lautenbach, ed. Francke 1891, c. 20, p. 365. (The free translation above compresses a rather longer passage.)   194. *Ibid.*, c. 48, p. 392.   195. Affeldt 1969b.

196. *Liber de unitate ecclesiae conservanda*, cc. 2–3, pp. 2–7, esp. p. 6: Zacharias only gave his consent to the 'communis legatio principum de regno Francorum'.

197. Lampert of Hersfeld, ed. Holder-Egger 1894, s.a. 1073, p. 152: the Saxons claimed 'sacramento se ei fidem dixisse . . . si iuste, si legittime, si more maiorum rebus moderetur; si suum cuique ordinem, suam dignitatem, suas leges tutas inviolatasque manere pateretur'. Compare the Saxons' demand, *ibid.*, p. 151: 'ut [rex] principibus Saxoniae quibus sine legittima discussione bona sua ademerat, secundum principum suorum iurisdictionem satisfaceret'. See Robinson 1978a, pp. 128–9, 133.

in their case. First, as Gregory VII's own hesitations already implied, there was a theoretical difficulty in constructing a papal claim to depose a king whom the pope had not consecrated. If control over the distant Italian church was German kingship's Achilles heel, the papacy's was its distance from German king-makings. It was the Rhineland archbishops, not the pope, who in the twelfth century and later could pick up Hincmar's argument: 'We invested him because he was worthy; why do we not divest him now that he is unworthy?'[198] Second, although pro-Gregorian theorists concentrated on papal authority to release faithful men from their oaths, such papal licence was strictly superfluous for the German rebels if, as Lampert suggests, they could justify opposition to Henry IV on the thoroughly traditional grounds that he had violated law and justice.

The impact of the Investiture Contest on political ideas as on political realities in Germany was therefore marginal and short-lived. There as in France, exponents of royal theocracy neglected the true Augustinian pessimism of Gregory VII's famous, but even for him untypical, assertion that kingship was rooted in sin, for a more congenial, revisionist, 'Augustinisme politique' which affirmed the divine origin of kingship in positive terms. Henry IV's successor could still claim to act as a minister of God, responsible for God's people.[199] Honorius Augustodunensis might denounce as 'blethers and madmen' those who maintained that the king was not a layman because he was anointed like a priest.[200] But kings continued to be consecrated and, at the very close of our period, Otto of Freising was still drawing the old conclusion: Frederick Barbarossa was consecrated king on the same day, in the same church and by the same bishops as another Frederick was consecrated bishop of Münster, 'so it was believed that the Highest King and Priest was actually participating in the present rejoicing . . . the two persons sacramentally anointed . . . [being] rightly called the anointed of Christ the Lord'.[201]

---

198. Helmold of Bosau, ed. Schmeidler 1937, I, c. 32, p. 62, presents the archbishop of Mainz addressing his episcopal colleagues in 1105 to urge Henry IV's deposition: ' " Nonne officii nostri est regem consecrare, consecratum investire? . . . Quem meritum investivimus, inmeritum quare non divestiamus?" ' Helmold imagines the sequel: 'Statimque accepto conamine regem aggressi sunt [pontifices] eique coronam de capite abruperunt'. Helmold writes nearly fifty years after the event and this is myth, not history. But the political ideas here are significant for the future as well as echoing the past.

199. Morrison, in Mommsen and Morrison 1962, pp. 31–2. See also Struve 1978, pp. 110–15.

200. Honorius Augustodunensis, ed. Dieterich 1897, c. 9, p. 69.

201. Otto of Freising, ed. Schmale 1965, II, c. 3, p. 105: two Fredericks, king and bishop, were consecrated on the same day in the same church 'ut revera summus rex et sacerdos presenti iocunditate hoc quasi prognostico interesse crederetur, qua in una aecclesia una dies duarum personarum, quae solae novi ac veteris instrumenti institutione sacramentaliter unguntur et christi Domini rite dicuntur, vidit unctionem'.

In the early twelfth century also, there were two developments that lent new allure to ideas of universal empire. One was the revival of Roman law studies, which enabled Barbarossa to play the role of a new Justinian, God's deputy as universal law-giver and peace-maker, ruler of a 'Holy Empire'.[202] The second was the popularity of eschatological speculation which enabled Otto of Freising in pessimistic mood to portray the empire of his own day as the final manifestation, before the coming of Antichrist, of the Roman Empire that had been transferred successively from Romans to Greeks, from Greeks to Franks – 'all human power had its origin in the East but is coming to an end in the West' – or in optimistic mood, to look forward to Barbarossa's reign as ushering in a new age of harmonious co-operation between priesthood and empire within a single universal Church.[203] Otto's Augustinism could be espoused by the politiques of Barbarossa's court: it supported claims to superiority over all the *regna* of Christendom which, like the empire, were seen as mere 'marginal phenomena, not the representatives of universal history'.[204] Barbarossa used the imperial title during the three years between his consecration as king at Aachen and his coronation as emperor at Rome, thus indicating its independence of any papal concession: it was already at Aachen that he assumed the throne of Charlemagne.

The contemporary *Kaiserchronik* offers an interesting comparison with Otto's work. An epic poem in the vernacular aimed at a wide lay public, it presented some thoroughly conventional examples of rulership, making no differentiation of virtue or function between kings and emperors, or even between pagan and Christian rulers.[205] Both Trajan and 'King Louis' the Pious are praised for their just judgements and ruthless punishment of criminals. The importance of counsel and consent is stressed. Rulers are shown as responsible for defending Christendom against the heathen (the Second Crusade led by Conrad III made this an especially appealing theme for a German audience), and maintaining the laws (*die pfahte*) of the empire ranging from the prescriptions of the Old Testament to regulations for running the ruler's household and for maintaining careful distinctions between the ranks of society (a matter of concern to the poet's audience). There are significant differences between the poet's idea of

202. Ullmann 1975b, pp. 92–6; Werner 1980b, p. 183; Benson 1982, pp. 360–9.
203. Different moods of Otto's *Historia de Duabus Civitatibus* and his *Gesta Friderici*: Classen 1982 (1983), pp. 361–5. The quotation is from *Historia* v, prologue, p. 227. (Compare the translation of Mierow 1928, p. 322.) See also Bloch 1967, pp. 24–7.
204. Classen 1982 (1983), p. 363. See also Appelt 1967, pp. 25–7; Töpfer 1974; Leyser 1975 (1982), pp. 215–40. 205. Gellinek 1971; Myers 1971, and *idem*, 1982, pp. 255–68.

empire and Otto's. In place of Otto's continuous sequence of transfers of empire derived ultimately through Augustine from the Book of Daniel, the poet signals two disjunctions, first when with Constantine's departure the papacy is left with authority in Rome, and again, when Constantine's empire is renewed in Charlemagne's. Where Otto worried about conflict between empire and papacy, the *Kaiserchronik* presents in Constantine and Silvester a model of collaboration reproduced by Charlemagne and Leo, and unsullied by reference to recent problems. Indeed the poet makes Leo Charlemagne's brother, thus expressing symbolically their identity of interest and making the transfer of empire here a kind of family arrangement. This in turn allows a new emphasis on the German character of the renewed empire: the poet produced 'a national verse history . . . in the form of a history of the emperors'.[206] The contrasting later fortunes of the *Kaiserchronik* and Otto's *History*, the former often copied, the latter virtually neglected, as well as the former's likely oral transmission, suggest that the poet's 'Middle High German best-seller'[207] both expressed and influenced German ideas of empire in the later Middle Ages more than the 'theoretical reflection'[208] of the historian.

Frederick Barbarossa exploited but could not monopolise the hegemonial idea of empire. It persisted and spread, outside Germany and Rome-free, because it expressed the political reality of composite realms and could be adapted to such imperial kingship. This happened in England and France, and perhaps most clearly of all in Spain in the reign of Alfonso VII.[209] Claims to universal authority were challenged from another quarter: the Roman law exploited by imperialist supporters of Henry IV and Barbarossa could also be pressed into royal service. The king too could claim to be prince (*princeps*) or emperor in his own kingdom.[210] Barbarossa's reign, coinciding with the increasingly firm establishment of these rival monarchic regimes in much of Latin Christendom, and of autonomous city-states in Italy, proved to be the swan-song of the universal empire. Though its echoes would seduce idealistic souls, most later medieval political thinkers would be concerned with the new realities. These realities included not only royal regimes but increasingly articulate political communities.[211] The political thought of the earlier Middle Ages carried into the later period a potent ideal of Christian rulership but at the same time a clear recognition of its potential excesses and shortcomings.

206. Van Caenegem and Ganshof 1978, p. 40.   207. Gellinek 1971, p. 18.
208. Classen 1982 (1983), p. 363.   209. Folz 1969, pp. 53–8. See also Schramm 1950, pp. 93–115.
210. Ullmann 1975b, pp. 96ff.   211. Reynolds 1984, ch. 8.

The political practice of the earlier Middle Ages, because rulers in fact shared power with aristocracy and Church, constantly pursued an accommodation of interests (peace) through consultation and consent. In the early twelfth century the Czech annalist Cosmas of Prague described the Emperor Henry III's attempt to increase unilaterally the tribute paid by the Bohemians. When they resisted the violation of their 'law', meaning custom with the extra legitimation of a Carolingian's authority, they were brusquely told by Henry: 'The law has a nose of wax, as they say in the vulgar, and the king has an iron hand and a long reach, and can bend it whichever way he likes!'[212] What they said in the vulgar conveyed a shrewd political idea: law was only as strong as the power behind it. But in fact the outcome of this confrontation was not, as Henry threatened, a forcing of the Bohemians to obey his will, but negotiations and a compromise. A faithful people, like faithful men elsewhere, could limit the bending-power of the royal hand.

212. Cosmas of Prague, ed. Bretholz 1923, II, c. 8, pp. 93–4: 'Sclavi inquiunt: "Semper salvo tenore nostre legis fuimus et hodie sumus sub imperio Karoli regis et eius successoribus, nostra gens numquam extitit rebellis et tibi in omnibus bellis mansit et semper manebit fidelis, si iustitiam tantum nobis facere velis. Talem enim nobis legem istituit Pippinus, magni Karoli regis filius, ut annuatim imperatorum successoribus CXX boves electos et D marcas solvamus . . . At si aliquo praeter solitum legis iugo nos aggravare volueris, mori potius sumus quam insuetum ferre onus". Ad hec imperator respondit: "Regibus hic mos est semper aliquid novi legi addere anteriori, neque enim omnis lex est constituta tempore in uno, sed per successores regum crevit series legum. Nam qui regunt leges non reguntur legibus, quia lex, ut aiunt vulgo, cereum habet nasum et rex ferream manum et longam ut eam flectere queat quo sibi placeat".' Historical background: Dvornik 1949, p. 232.

II

CHURCH AND PAPACY

The Church and the ordo clericorum

Images of the Church

The period 750–1150 produced no treatise *de ecclesia*, nor did it witness ecclesiological speculation of the type familiar in the later Middle Ages. The intellectuals of these four centuries possessed not so much a 'concept of the Church' (*Kirchenbegriff*) as an 'image of the Church' (*Kirchenbild*)[1] – or rather, multiple images, drawn from Holy Scripture. Trained, as most learned men of this period were, in the contemplative approach of the *lectio divina*, they knew that the whole Bible speaks of Christ and his Church 'in spiritual similitudes . . . as through a glass darkly'.[2] Reading the sacred page *allegorice*, the student would find as much ecclesiological as christological material. 'The Church . . . is called by many names in Scripture, such as the kingdom of heaven, the woman, the bride, the wife, the dove, the beloved, the vine, the sheep, the sheepfold, the city, the tower, the pillar, the firmament, the house, the temple, the body of Christ, the net, the supper and others which the reader can perhaps find.'[3] The anonymous twelfth-century encyclopaedia of biblical typology, *Allegoriae in universam sacram Scripturam*, identifies eighty allegories of holy Church in the Old and New Testaments.[4] Some of these *allegoriae* are more than metaphors: they are fully developed ecclesiological ideas of great power and complexity. In four of these allegories in particular – 'the body of Christ', 'the ship', 'the bride' and 'the mother' – the ecclesiology of the period 750–1150 can be traced.

---

1. Mayer-Pfannholz 1941, pp. 22ff; Congar 1968a, pp. 98–9.
2. Bernard of Clairvaux, *Sermones in Cantica* XLI.3, *PL* 183, 986.
3. Hincmar of Rheims, *Explanatio in ferculum Salomonis*, *PL* 125, 817B: 'Ecclesiam . . . multis in Scriptura vocatur nominibus, ut est regnum coelorum, mulier, sponsa, uxor, columba, dilecta, vinea, ovis, ovile, civitas, turris, columna, firmamentum, domus, templum, corpus Christi, sagena, coena, et aliis quae lector forte poterit invenire.'
4. [Ps.-] Rabanus Maurus, *Allegoriae in universam sacram Scripturam*, *PL* 112, 849–1088. On the authorship of this work see A. Wilmart 1920, pp. 47ff.

Corpus Christi. 'The Catholic Church is [Christ's] body, in which we desire through good works to be made members.'[5] The image of the Church as the single indivisible *corpus Christi* appears frequently in Carolingian public documents, especially in the appeals for unity in the reign of Louis the Pious, when the empire was threatened by civil war.[6] In the writings of the Carolingian theologians, *corpus Christi* is used in a double sense. It is at once the body of Christ present in the Eucharist and the Church of Christ, in which all believers are held together by the sacramental functions of the priesthood.[7] 'This bread . . ., the body of Christ, which is sanctified by many priests throughout the whole world . . . makes one body of Christ: . . . all who worthily eat of it are one body of Christ.'[8] The sacerdotal order, elected by God to 'dispense sacraments to the peoples',[9] was, therefore, the source of the unity of the Church. The fact that only the priests could administer the sacraments on which Christian society depended set them apart from the rest – the legal aspects of this separation appear in Carolingian legislation[10] – and exalted them above the laity. So Agobard of Lyons, in a treatise attacking the subservient status of the priesthood in Carolingian society in the 820s, argued that 'even unrighteous priests can administer the sacraments in which the salvation of the people consists, which righteous laymen cannot do'. Therefore laymen must submit to priests, rather than treating them as menials.[11]

While the image of the Church as *corpus Christi* in Carolingian tradition focused on the *corpus mysticum* of the Eucharist, the image developed in the eleventh and twelfth centuries in the form of the exegesis of the Pauline text 1 Cor. 12, 12–27, 'For just as the body is one and has many members, . . . so it is with Christ . . .'.[12] The Pauline image of *corpus/membra* was invaluable to

5. Louis the Pious, *Praeceptum ad Hetti archiepiscopum* (819), *MGH Cap.* 1, 356: 'catholicae ecclesiae, quae est corpus eius in qua et nos membrum ipsius per bona opera effici cupimus'.
6. Notably Agobard of Lyons, *Adversus legem Gundobadi* 2–4, PL 104, 113ff.
7. Cf. Lubac 1949, pp. 32ff.
8. Haimo [of Auxerre?], *Expositio in I Corinthios* x.17, PL 117, 564: 'panis qui consecratur in Ecclesia, unum corpus Christi . . . quod a multis sacerdotibus per universum orbem sanctificatur et facit unum corpus Christi esse'. Cf. Morrison 1964, pp. 37ff.
9. Rabanus Maurus, *De clericorum institutione* 1.2, PL 107, 297C: 'Iste autem ordo praeponitur in Ecclesia, quia iure in sanctis deservit et sacramenta populis dispensat.'
10. Conquered Saxony presents an extreme example: *Capitulatio de partibus Saxoniae*, *MGH Cap.* 1, 68ff. Cf. *ibid.* 1, 367; 2, 429.
11. Agobard, *De privilegio et iure sacerdotii* 7, PL 104, 134B: 'tamen sacramenta in quibus salus populi consistit agere possunt iniusti sacerdotes, quod non possunt iusti populares'.
12. Cf. Struve 1978, pp. 98ff.

the eleventh-century reformers who sought to express the dominant role of the *sacerdotium* in the body of Christ. 'The clerical order is foremost in the Church', wrote Cardinal Humbert of Silva Candida, 'like the eyes in the head . . . The lay power is like the breast and the arms to obey and defend the Church.'[13] In the Investiture Contest the polemicists of the papal and imperial parties vied with each other in the physiological elaboration of the body of Christ. For imperial polemicists the *caput* was the temporal authority. 'Holy Church has a head, which is the *regnum*, and a heart, which is the *sacerdotium* . . . The priesthood is understood to be both heart and stomach, because the whole people is ruled by them in spiritual matters.'[14] The encyclopaedist and populariser of 'Gregorian' ideas, Honorius Augustodunensis, provided a detailed proof that the *sacerdotium* was the head of the Church: 'the eyes are the teachers, namely the apostles; the ears are the obedient, namely the monks; the nostrils are the discreet, namely the masters; the mouth, those who speak good words, namely the priests'.[15]

The most influential version of the image to emerge from the struggles of the reform papacy – a version borrowed from papal letters of the fifth century[16] – was that the Roman church was the head of the *corpus Christi*. Cardinal Humbert argued in his treatise *De sancta Romana ecclesia* that if the papal head of the Church was unhealthy, the member churches could never be sound: an urgent appeal for the continuance of the papal reform movement.[17] Peter Damian, hermit and reforming cardinal, wrote of the Roman church as 'head of the whole Christian religion' in his treatise of 1059 rebuking the church of Milan for her rebellion against the reform papacy.[18] For Pope Gregory VII likewise, Rome was *caput*, the other churches, *membra*.[19] A further development of the Pauline image as an expression of the primacy of the Roman church is found in the writings of Bernard of Clairvaux. Reproving the Romans for their desertion of his

13. Humbert, *Adversus simoniacos* III.29, *MGH Libelli* 1, 235: 'Est enim clericalis ordo in ecclesia praecipuus tanquam in capite oculi . . . Est et laicalis potestas tanquam pectus et brachia ad obediendum et defendendum ecclesiam.'

14. *Orthodoxa defensio imperialis* 3, *ibid.* 2, 536: 'Habet autem sancta ecclesia caput quod est regnum, habet cor quod est sacerdotium . . . Cor autem et stomachus intelligitur sacerdotium, quia in rebus spiritualibus per eos totus populus gubernatur.'

15. Honorius Augustodunensis, *Expositio in Cantica Canticorum* I.1, *PL* 172, 361C: 'ut puta oculi sunt doctores ut apostoli, aures obedientes ut monachi, nares discreti ut magistri, os bona loquentes ut presbyteri'.   16. Cf. Ullmann 1970, pp. 6–7.

17. Humbert, *De sancta Romana ecclesia*, fragment A, ed. Schramm 1962, 2, pp. 128–9. Humbert would have found in the Pseudo-Isidorean Decretals the statement that the apostolic see is *cardo et caput omnium ecclesiarum* (Pseudo-Anacletus, *Epistola* III.34), but the crucial reference, 1 Cor. 12, 12–27, is absent from Pseudo-Isidore.

18. Peter Damian, *Opusculum* v (*Actus Mediolani*), *PL* 145, 89C: 'caput totius Christianae religionis'.

19. Gregory VII, *Registrum* IV.16, IX.29.

protégé, Pope Eugenius III in 1146, Bernard wrote: 'There is pain in the head and therefore pain cannot be a stranger to even the least and most distant parts of the body . . . Because the head is in pain, the body – of which I myself am a member – cannot escape suffering. So, foolish Romans . . . you disfigure your head and the head of all men.'[20] In this precise exegesis of 1 Cor. 12, 27, 'you are the body of Christ and individually members of it', Bernard substituted for the Gregorian image of Rome as *caput* and the other churches as *membra*, the more intimate relationship of pope as head and the individual Christians as members. The Gregorians understood the image of *Roma caput* to signify a disciplinary and coercive control over the whole Church. Bernard understood it to mean the papal stewardship: 'Surrender possession and dominion to [Christ]: keep for yourself the guardianship (*cura*) . . . The steward does not own the farm; nor is the tutor lord of his [charge and] master.'[21]

Navis (*Navicula*). The numerous references in the Gospels to Christ on board ship (for example, Matt. 8, 23–7, Mark 4, 35–40; 6, 45–52; Luke 8, 22–5; John 6, 16–21; 21, 1–13) were invariably understood to refer to the Church. Bruno of Segni's exposition of the storm on the sea of Galilee (Matt. 8, 23–4) summarises the patristic and Carolingian exegetical tradition. 'What is this boat, if not the Church? What is the sea, if not the world? What are the waves of the sea, if not the raging anger of persecutors and tyrants?'[22] This scene of the storm at sea and the anxious disciples waking the sleeping Lord inspired some striking illustrations in Ottonian Gospel books. It is likely that the artists realised that they were depicting *allegorice* 'the Church distressed by tribulations'.[23] One detail of the image of the Church as a ship especially preoccupied medieval authors: who was the steersman (*gubernator*) of the *navis ecclesiae*?[24] Carolingian theologians often stated the

---

20. Bernard, *Epistola* CCXLIII.2, 3, *PL* 182, 438CD, 439B: 'Dolor nempe in capite est, ac per hoc minime alienus ne a minimis quidem vel extremis quibusque corporis partibus . . . quia cum sit capitis, non potest non esse et corporis, cuius membrum sum ego . . . Sic fatui Romani . . . caput vestrum atque omnium, quod in vobis est, deturpatis.'
21. Bernard, *De consideratione* III.1, 2, *PL* 182, 759AB: 'Possessionem et dominium cede huic: tu curam illius habe . . . Numquid non et villa villico et parvus dominus subiectus est paedagogo?'
22. Bruno of Segni, *Commentaria in Matthaeum* II.27, *PL* 165, 144C: 'Quid enim navicula, nisi Ecclesia? Quid mare, nisi mundus? Quid motus maris, nisi persecutorum et tyrannorum saeviens indignatio?'
23. E.g. the early eleventh-century 'Hitda codex' from Cologne, now Darmstadt, Hessische Landesbibliothek Codex 1640, fol. 117r. Another example is found in the evangelistary of Otto III painted in Reichenau c. 990, now in the cathedral treasury of Aachen.
24. Cf. Rahner 1947, pp. 1ff; Morrison 1964, pp. 239ff.

traditional view that Christ was *gubernator* of holy Church.[25] Occasionally, however, Carolingian documents identify a human steersman. In the *Libri Carolini* Charlemagne is said to have been given the helm (*gubernacula*) of the Church by Christ;[26] but this seems to be the only Carolingian reference to the king as steersman. An increasingly familiar theme in the ninth century was that the episcopate was, if not the *gubernator* of the Church, at least directly responsible to the *gubernator*, Christ. This version of the *navis* image reflects the weakening of imperial control over the Church and the bishops' assumption of the leading role in Christian society. In the synodal legislation of the 840s, for example, the bishops call upon Christ, their steersman, to give them direction.[27] In the Pseudo-Isidorean Decretals bishops figure both as the steersman's right-hand men, the *proretae* ('lookout men' or 'under-pilots') and as steersmen themselves. Pseudo-Clement I, likening the Church to a great ship, identified the shipowner as God, the steersman as Christ, the *proretae* as bishops, the sailors as priests, the quartermasters as deacons. Pseudo-Alexander I urged bishops to 'steer [Christ's] ship rightly, lest those who dwell in her should sink and be drowned': the bishops are here clearly promoted to be *gubernatores*.[28]

The *navis* image was used by the adherents of the reform papacy in the form 'the ship of Peter', that is, the Roman church. 'Through the floods and storms, bring me back to the harbour of peace', wrote Peter Damian in a prayer to St Peter.[29] This image appears frequently in the writings of Peter Damian and sometimes in the form of *sagena Petri*, 'the net of Peter', which the great reformer used as a synonym for *navis Petri*.[30] The term *sagena* is also used in this sense in the crucial document of the early reform papacy, the Papal Election Decree of 1059, which speaks of the threatened shipwreck of 'the boat of the chief fisherman'.[31] The staunch Gregorian Bishop Anselm II of Lucca used the image of the *navis Petri* to emphasise the supremacy of the Roman church. He wrote that a storm had again blown up on the sea –

25. E.g. Remigius of Auxerre, *Homiliae* IX, *PL* 131, 916B. Cf. Rabanus Maurus, *De universo* XX.39, *ibid.* III, 554CD.
26. *Libri Carolini, praefatio, MGH Concilia* 2: Supplementum, p. 2.
27. Synod of Thionville, October 844; Cologne, November 843, *MGH Capitularia* 2, 113, 253.
28. Pseudo-Clement I, *Epistola* 1.14, ed. Hinschius 1863, p. 34: 'Similis namque est omnis status Ecclesiae magnae navi . . . Sit ergo navis huius dominus ipse omnipotens Deus, gubernator vero sit Christus. Tum deinde proretae officium episcopus impleat; presbyteri nautarum, diaconi dispensatorum locum teneant.' Pseudo-Alexander I, *Epistola* II.15, ed. Hinschius 1863, p. 103: 'iuste gubernant navem eius ne cohabitantes in ea demergantur aut suffocentur'.
29. Peter Damian, *Carmina* CXLV, *De sancto Petro, PL* 145, 961C: 'Fluctibus et spretis portum mihi redde quietis.'   30. Cf. Woody 1970, p. 36.
31. *Decretum de ordinando papa* (1059) cap. 2, *MGH Const.* 1, 539: 'sagena summi piscatoris procellis intumescentibus cogeretur in naufragii profunda submergi'.

so representing the conflict between Pope Gregory VII and King Henry IV of Germany as a recurrence of the storm on the sea of Galilee of Matt. 8, 24 – but that Peter, secure in his ship, feared neither wind nor waves, but cast his net and drew into the ship an abundant multitude. Woe to those who were not drawn on board, 'for the faith of Peter is unavailing outside the Church . . . He who does not agree with the Roman church is not a catholic.'[32] This image of the Catholic Church as the *navis Petri* became classical in the formulation of Bernard of Clairvaux, as part of his exposition of papal supremacy in the treatise *De consideratione*, addressed to Eugenius III. The starting-point of his exposition is John 21, 7, the account of Peter's leaping from his boat to meet the risen Lord on the shore.

What does this mean? It is surely a sign of the unique pontificate of Peter; that while the others had each his own ship, he received not one ship to steer, but rather the whole world to govern . . . To you is committed the greatest ship, made up of all the others, the universal Church, spread through all the world.[33]

The *navis Petri* had become the Church universal. In Bernard's exposition all bishops, as the successors of the apostles, are *gubernatores* of their own churches; but the pope has been given the whole Catholic Church 'to steer' (*gubernandum*).

Sponsa. The most widely diffused image of the Church in the Carolingian period was that of the Bride,[34] disseminated especially in commentaries on the Song of Solomon.[35] Alcuin's exposition is characteristic: Solomon composed the book 'which contains the excellent poems of the Bridegroom and the Bride, singing the praises of the Church and Christ'.[36] In the Canticle commentaries the Bridegroom of the Church is Christ; but elsewhere his identity changes. In a letter to the king, Alcuin could refer in the space of only two sentences to the Church as the Bride of God and as the Bride of Charlemagne.[37] The more conventional usage in the Carolingian period, however, identified the bishop as the *sponsus* of his church. This idea had been current since the fourth century,[38] prompted by

---

32. *Sermo Anselmi episcopi de caritate*, ed. Pásztor 1965, p. 99: 'quoniam extra Ecclesiam Petri fides inanis est . . . Constat catholicum non esse qui non concordat Romanae Ecclesiae.'

33. Bernard, *De consideratione* II.8, 752BC: 'Quid istud? Nempe signum singularis pontificii Petri, per quod non navem unam, ut ceteri quique suam, sed saeculum ipsum susceperit gubernandum . . . tibi una commissa est grandissima navis, facta ex omnibus ipsa universalis Ecclesia, toto orbe diffusa.' 34. Cf. Congar 1968a, pp. 77ff. 35. Cf. Riedlinger 1958; Ohly 1958.

36. Alcuin, *Compendium in Canticum Canticorum*, Carmen (*prologus*), PL 100, 641–2: 'Hunc cecinit Salomon mira dulcedine librum, / Qui tenet egregias Sponsi Sponsaeque camenas, / Ecclesiae et Christi laudes hinc inde canentes.'

37. Alcuin, *Epistola* CXLVIII, *MGH Epp.* 4, 241: 'Surge, vir a Deo electe . . . et defende sponsam domini Dei tui. Cogita de sponsa tua.' 38. Fuchs 1930, p. 83.

the apostle's description of the bishop as 'the husband of one wife' (1, Tim. 3, 2). The idea was elaborated in canon law, especially in the context of the translation of bishops from one see to another.[39] The episcopal ring, symbolising the bishop's marriage to his church, is first mentioned in a seventh-century text of Isidore of Seville.[40] The significance of the symbol was to be expounded by the early twelfth-century encyclopaedist Honorius Augustodunensis: 'The bishop wears a ring so that he may recognise himself to be the bridegroom of the Church and, like Christ, may lay down his life for her, if necessary.'[41] The encyclopaedist was vaguely aware in this definition of two distinct interpretations of the *sponsus ecclesiae*: the scriptural idea of Christ as Bridegroom and the canon law idea of the bishop as *sponsus*. Some Carolingian authors had also seen a contradiction here and had resolved it by bringing in more of the dramatis personae of the Song of Solomon: the bishops were 'the friends of the Bridegroom' (*amici sponsi*, Canticum 5, 1), who was Christ himself.[42]

In the age of ecclesiastical reform the image of the bishop as *sponsus* was preferred;[43] and reformers intensified the image by supposing a church to be 'widowed' by the death of her bishop.[44] It was their acute consciousness of the image of the bishop as bridegroom of his church which gave the edge to the reformers' attacks on simony and nicholaitism: a simoniac bishop became in their eyes a bawd; an unchaste bishop, an adulterer. The exploitation of this theme in reforming polemic occurs first in the work of Atto of Vercelli.[45] In the letters of Gregory VII both Christ and the bishops appear in the role of *sponsus*. What principally concerned the great reforming pope was that the simoniacs and schismatics failed to treat the Church according to her dignity of *sponsa* but instead bought and used her 'like a cheap female slave'.[46] Gregory VII represented his struggle against lay domination of the Church in this favourite terminology: 'I have been

---

39. The canonical material is summarised by Master Gratian of Bologna, *Decretum* C.7 q.1 c.1–49.
40. Isidore of Seville, *De ecclesiasticis officiis* II.5, 12, *PL* 83, 784A. Cf. H. Leclercq, 'Anneaux', *Dictionnaire d'archéologie chrétienne et de liturgie*, ed. F. Cabrol and H. Leclercq, Paris, 1924– , vol. I, pp. 2182–3.
41. Honorius Augustodunensis, *Gemma animae* I.216, *PL* 172, 609D: 'Pontifex ergo annulum portat, ut se sponsum Ecclesiae agnoscat, ac pro illa animam, si necesse fuerit, sicut Christus, ponat.'
42. E.g. Agobard of Lyons, *De cavendo convictu*, *PL* 104, 110; *idem*, *Epistola II ad clericos Lugdunenses*, *MGH Epp* 5, 154–5; Pope Nicholas I, *JE* 2819, *ibid.* 6, 519.
43. E.g. Gerbert of Rheims at the Council of Mouzon (995), Mansi, *Concilia* 19, 195AB; Pope Clement II, *JL* 4149, *PL* 142, 588.
44. E.g. Abbo of Fleury, *Epistola* xv, *PL* 139, 460C: 'Romana ecclesia . . . viduata'; Gregory VII, *Registrum* II.38: 'viduatae ecclesiae' (Fermo).
45. Atto of Vercelli, *De pressuris ecclesiasticis* 2, *PL* 134, 71.
46. Gregory VII, *Registrum* I.15: 'quasi vilem ancillam presumpsit emere'; *ibid.* I.42, IV.3, VIII.13.

concerned above all that holy Church, the Bride of God, . . . should return to her proper dignity and remain free, chaste and catholic.'[47]

The Gregorians did not devise an interpretation of the *sponsa* image which reflected their preoccupation with papal supremacy over the Church; but this omission was made good by that ardent ideologue of the Roman primacy, Bernard of Clairvaux. Steeped as he was in the language and imagery of the Song of Solomon, Bernard's most frequent image for the Church was inevitably *sponsa*.[48] The Bridegroom of the Church is Christ; and 'the friend of the Bridegroom' reappears, sometimes signifying the episcopate, as in Carolingian writings, but also in a novel sense. 'The Bride of Christ is committed to you, O friend of the Bridegroom', wrote Bernard to Pope Innocent II.[49] *Amicus sponsi* was one of Bernard's terms for the pope,[50] intended to convey the saint's complex conception of the papal office, at once episcopal and more than episcopal in character. The image appears in Bernard's analysis of the papal office in *De consideratione*, a principal source of the ecclesiology of the later Middle Ages: 'you are not the lord of the bishops, but one of them, . . . the friend of the Bridegroom, the bridesman (*sponsae paranymphum*) . . . the vicar of Christ'.[51]

Mater. The chaste and fertile maternity of the Church is a favourite theme of patristic writings[52] and of Carolingian theologians. The preface of the *Libri Carolini* summarises the traditional image: 'The Church . . . is a holy mother, spotless, beautiful, unspoiled, fertile; who cannot lose her virginity and does not cease to produce sons.'[53] While the Fathers had generally presented the Church as the mother of all the faithful, Pope Gelasius I had conceived rather of the *Roman* church as mother of all Christians;[54] and it was this version of the *mater* image – *ecclesia Romana mater* – which was taken up by the vigorous popes of the ninth century and by the reform papacy of the eleventh century. Pope Nicholas I informed the Emperor Michael III that the Roman church

---

47. Gregory VII, *JL* 5271, ed. Cowdrey 1972, p. 132: 'summopere procuravi ut sancta ecclesia, sponsa Dei, . . . ad proprium rediens decus libera, casta et catholica permaneret.'
48. Cf. Congar 1955, pp. 76ff.
49. Bernard, *Epistola* CXCI.2, 358B: 'Tibi commissa est sponsa Christi, amice sponsi.'
50. Bernard, *Epistolae* CCCXXX, CCCXLVIII.3 (to Innocent II); CCCLVIII (to Celestine II); CCXXXVIII.2 (to Eugenius III).
51. Bernard, *De consideratione* IV.7, 788: 'te vero non dominum episcoporum, sed unum ex ipsis . . . amicum Sponsi, Sponsae paranymphum . . . vicarium Christi'.
52. Cf. Beumer 1953, pp. 40ff.
53. *Libri Carolini, praefatio*, pp. 1–2: 'Ecclesia . . . est enim sancta mater, est immaculata, est praeclara, est incorrupta, est et fecunda, quae et virginitatem amittere nescit et filios generare non desinit.'
54. Gelasius I, *Epistola* 14.9, ed. Thiel 1868, p. 367.

was his mother.[55] Pope John VIII urged the Bulgarian khan to abandon the Greeks and 'return to your holy mother, the Roman church, who bore you in her religious womb, . . . who holds dominion over all the peoples and to whom flock the nations of the whole world, as to their one mother and one head'.[56] This fusion of the concepts of maternity and headship especially recommended itself to the adherents of the reform papacy.[57] Gregory VII characteristically reinterpreted the maternal image as a disciplinary control over the churches of Christendom: 'the holy Roman church, mother and mistress (*magistra*) of all the churches'.[58] Bernard of Clairvaux, equally characteristically, expunged the idea of dominance and produced an image of benevolent maternity: 'you should consider above all that the holy Roman church is the mother – not the mistress – of the churches'.[59]

In these four images of the Church – *corpus Christi, navis, sponsa, mater* – and in their changing emphases, the development of ecclesiology from the beginning of the Carolingian period to the mid-twelfth century is written. Authority in the Church was at first wielded by 'the king and priest' Charlemagne, *gubernator ecclesiae, sponsus ecclesiae*. When imperial authority was rendered ineffective by the political disorders of the ninth century, the episcopate laid claim to the *gubernatio* of the Church. The papal reform movement of the eleventh century achieved a radical revision of ideas of authority in the Church, creating out of traditional materials an innovatory papal *principatus* over the Church. In the new spiritual climate of the early twelfth century Bernard of Clairvaux modified the Gregorian view of papal government, attributing to the pope stewardship rather than dominion. However, Bernard, like other early twelfth-century reformers, had a most exalted idea of the papal office. Like his contemporary, Hugh of St Victor,[60] he held the pope to be the vicar of Christ. The expressions of reverence for the papacy of both these monastic theologians would provide valuable *auctoritates* for later generations of polemicists bent on defending the papal monarchy over the Church.[61]

55. Nicholas I, *JE* 2813, 2819, *MGH Epp.* 6, 508, 530.
56. John VIII, *JE* 3265, *ibid.* 7, 159: 'Revertere . . . ad sanctam matrem tuam Romanam ecclesiam, quae te religioso utero genuit . . . et quae omnium gentium retinet principatum et ad quam totius mundi quasi ad unam matrem et unum caput conveniunt nationes.'
57. E.g. Peter Damian, *Opusculum* V (*Actus Mediolani*), 91CD; *idem, Disceptatio synodalis, MGH Libelli* 1, 78.
58. Gregory VII, *JL* 5271, ed. Cowdrey 1972, p. 134: 'sanctam Romanam ecclesiam omnium ecclesiarum matrem et magistram'. Cf. Gregory VII, *Registrum* 1.64, VI.13.
59. Bernard, *De consideratione* IV.7, 788A: 'Consideres ante omnia sanctam Romanam ecclesiam . . . ecclesiarum matrem esse, non dominam.'
60. Hugh of St Victor, *De officiis ecclesiasticis* 1.43, *PL* 177, 402: 'Papa vicem et locum Christi tenet.'
61. The most famous examples being Boniface VIII, in *Corpus Iuris Canonici* 1879–81, vol. II, pp. 1245–6; John of Paris, *Tractatus de potestate regia et papali*, ed. Leclercq 1942, pp. 183–4.

Ordo clericorum

Men were created, wrote Hincmar of Rheims in 860 – borrowing the idea from St Gregory[62] – so that they might eventually fill the place in heaven left vacant by the fallen angels.[63] The true *patria* of mankind, therefore, is heaven; and it follows that heaven should be the model for the institutions of Christian society. So, for example, John Scotus Erigena wrote c. 860 to the West Frankish king Charles the Bald about the works of Dionysius Areopagiticus: 'His second [book] is entitled "The Ecclesiastical Hierarchy" and describes the unity of human nature, redeemed by the blood of our Saviour, ordered in the likeness of the heavenly priesthood, as far as that is possible for mortals.'[64] The translation of Pseudo-Dionysius into Latin (the ninth-century version of John Scotus Erigena proving to be the most influential)[65] served to reinforce this idea of the terrestrial order as a *similitudo* of the heavenly one. 'The ancient father and venerable doctor'[66] added his authority to the vision of a Church 'consisting of angels and men; of which a part belongs to the company of angels . . . and the other part . . . still endures the pilgrimage on earth and sighs for the company above.'[67] This Church both on earth and in heaven participated in a single liturgy and celebrated together the same sacraments.[68] It followed, therefore, that the celebrants in the terrestrial Church, the only mediators between earth and heaven – Christ's ambassadors in the Church, as Pseudo-Isidore called them[69] – should be regarded as 'rulers of the Church' on earth. Priests were 'ministers of the kingdom of God and rulers of the Christian people, preservers and defenders of divine religion and ecclesiastical sanctity'.[70]

'Rulers of the Christian people' by virtue of their sacramental office,

---

62. E.g. Gregory I, *Homiliae in evangelia* XXI.2, XXXIV.3, 6–7, 11, *PL* 76, 1171A, 1247, 1250C, 1252.
63. Hincmar, *Epistola* XXI, *PL* 126, 126BC. Cf. *idem. Opusculum LV capitulorum* XII, *ibid.*, 326AB.
64. John Scotus Erigena, *Epistola, MGH Epp.* 6, 160: 'Secundus vero, cui est inscriptio de ecclesiastica ierarchia, humanae naturae salvatoris nostri sanguine redemptae unitatem denuntiat, ad similitudinem videlicet caelestis sacerdotii, quantum possibile est mortalibus, adhuc ordinatam.'
65. Cf. Théry 1933, pp. 185ff; Théry 1932–7.
66. Gregory I, *Homiliae in evangelia* II.34, 12. Cf. Nicholas I, *JE* 2796, p. 466; Hincmar, *Opusculum LV capitulorum* XII, *PL* 126, 325D; Humbert of Silva Candida, *Adversus simoniacos* III.3, *MGH Libelli* I, 201.
67. Hincmar, *Opusculum LV capitulorum* XI, *PL* 126, 325A: 'Sancta quippe Ecclesia . . . ex angelis et hominibus constat. Quae partim ex hominibus societate angelica in ordinibus distinctis perfruens . . . partim vero in ordinibus distinctis adhuc peregrinatur in terra, et ad supernam societatem suspirat.' Cf. Odo of Cluny, *Sermo I. In cathedra Sancti Petri*, *PL* 133, 709D–10D.
68. Cf. Remigius of Auxerre, *De celebratione missae*, *PL* 101, 1262D (wrongly attributed to Alcuin); Paschasius Radbert, *De corpore et sanguine Domini* VIII.1–6, *ibid.* 120, 1286–92.
69. *Decretales Pseudo-Isidorianae* ed. Hinschius 1863, p. 230: 'Christi vicarii sacerdotes sunt, qui vice Christi legatione funguntur in ecclesia.'
70. Hincmar, *De coercendo, PL* 125, 1018B: 'religiose regni Dei constitutos ministros et populi Christiani rectores et divinae religionis atque ecclesiasticae sanctitatis conservatores ac defensores'.

priests were also *rectores ecclesiae* by virtue of the office of preaching. This favourite theme of St Gregory and of Bede[71] is very frequent in Carolingian authors. Alcuin's advice to the clergy of Canterbury – 'doctors and masters of holy Scripture, let there be no lack among you of the Word of God or of those who can rule the people of God'[72] – was echoed in synodal legislation.[73] This theme of *praedicatio* was disseminated above all by medieval commentaries on the Song of Solomon: for 'the tower of David' (Canticum 4, 4) signified *praedicatores*. 'Preachers and doctors are compared to the tower of David, because they are always at war, fighting for the defence of holy Church.'[74] As for those who were ruled by the *rectores ecclesiae*, the *populus*, their function was to obey. 'It is the duty of laymen to obey preaching, to be just and merciful.'[75] The key pronouncement in this context was that of Pope Celestine I in 429: 'The people is to be taught, not to be followed.'[76] The *auctoritas* of Celestine I was useful alike to Carolingian eulogists of the *sacerdotium*[77] and to defenders of the reform programme of the eleventh-century papacy.[78] Absorbed into the Pseudo-Isidorean collection,[79] the *auctoritas* was to figure in many canonical collections.[80]

It was therefore the duty of the *clericalis ordo* to teach; that of the *laicalis ordo* to be taught. This term *ordo* had been central to political and ecclesiastical thought in the West since the middle of the eighth century, when Pope Zacharias had acknowledged the Arnulfing warlord Pippin III as king of the Franks 'so that *ordo* may not be confounded'.[81] The new royal dynasty of the Carolingians showed itself worthy of the papacy's confidence by establishing *ordo* in the Frankish Church. *Ordo* in this sense

---

71. Cf. Congar 1968a, p. 72, with nn. 57, 58.
72. Alcuin, *Epistola* CXXIX, p. 191: 'doctores et magistros sanctae scripturae, ne sit apud vos inopia verbi Dei, aut vobis desint qui populum Dei regere valeant'. Cf. *Epistola* CCLV, p. 413.
73. E.g. Council of Attigny (822) cap. 2; Aachen (836) cap. 29, *MGH Conc.* 2, 471, 711–12.
74. Haimo of Auxerre, *Enarratio in Cantica Canticorum*, PL 117, 317D: 'praedicatores et doctores turri David comparantur, quia semper quasi in bello sunt, pro defensione sanctae Ecclesiae pugnantes'. Cf. Alcuin, *Compendium in Canticum Canticorum*, PL 100, 651C; Angelom of Luxeuil, *Enarrationes in Cantica Canticorum* IV, ibid. 115, 607C; Robert of Tombelaine, *Super Cantica Canticorum Expositio*, ibid. 79, 509AB (wrongly attributed to Gregory I); Bruno of Segni, *Expositio in Cantica Canticorum*. ibid. 164, 1257AB.
75. Alcuin, *Epistola* CCXI, p. 351: 'Laicorum est obedire praedicatione, iustos esse et misericordes.' Cf. *Epistola* XVII, p. 48.
76. Celestine I, *Epistola* V.3 (JK 371), Mansi, *Concilia* 4, 469: 'Docendus est populus, non sequendus.'
77. E.g. Alcuin, *Epistola* CXXXII, p. 199. Cf. *Epistola* XVII, p. 46.
78. E.g. Humbert of Silva Candida, *Adversus simoniacos* III.21, *MGH Libelli* 1, 226; Deusdedit, *Libellus contra invasores et symoniacos* 1.8, *MGH Libelli* 2, 307.
79. *Decretales Pseudo-Isidorianae*, ed. Hinschius 1863, p. 561.
80. E.g. Deusdedit, *Collectio canonum* IV.44; Ivo of Chartres, *Decretum* XVI.14; Gratian, *Decretum* D.62 c.2.
81. *Annales regni Francorum* a.749, *MGH SS* 1, 136: 'ut non conturbaretur ordo'.

meant the religious life regulated by the ancient canons or by the *Rule* of St Benedict.[82] Pope Zacharias' use of the term *ordo*, approving the installation of a new dynasty in the kingdom of the Franks, suggests the broader meaning of 'social and political order'.[83] An explanation of the term is found in a sermon sometimes attributed to the missionary Winfrid-Boniface, as part of an exposition of the image of *corpus* and *membra* in 1 Cor. 12, 12–17.

So in the Church there is one faith . . . but different dignities having their own services. For there is one *ordo* of rulers, another of subjects; one of rich, another of poor men; one of old, another of young men; each person making his own rules of conduct, just as each member has its own office in the body.[84]

An *ordo*, therefore, is a social group with a special function (*officium* or *ministerium*). This definition of the *ordines* within the Church was supported by St Paul's assurance that 'there are varieties of service, but the same Lord' (1 Cor. 12, 5) and also by the parable of the talents (Matt. 25, 14–30). Alcuin used the latter text in his exposition to the treasurer Megenfried of the workings of Christian society: 'It was not only to bishops and priests that the Lord gave his money to be multiplied: he also gave the talents of good works to every dignity and status, so that they may strive to administer faithfully the grace bestowed on them.'[85]

The religious concept of *ordo* was, therefore, extended by Carolingian authors to the whole of Christian society, absorbing the laity into the clerical vision of the world. Some authors conceived of two parallel *ordines*, clerical and lay, the *officia* of the ecclesiastical hierarchy having exact counterparts in the secular hierarchy. Pope and emperor were equivalent ranks, as were patriarchs and *patricii*, archbishops and kings, metropolitans and dukes, bishops and counts, down to the lowest levels of the two hierarchies.[86] The symmetry of this vision of Christian society appealed in

---

82. E.g. *Concilium Vernense* (755) cap. 11, *MGH Cap.* 1, 35: 'placuit ut in monasterio sint sub ordine regulari aut sub manu episcopi sub ordine canonica.'

83. See his letter to Pippin III, *JE* 2277, *MGH Epp.* 3, 480: 'ut nobis [praesulibus, sacerdotibus] orantibus et illis bellantibus, Deo praestante, provincia salva persistat'. Cf. Congar 1968a, p. 91 n. 54.

84. Boniface (?), *Sermo* ix, *PL* 89, 860BC: 'Sic in Ecclesia una est fides . . . sed diversae dignitates proprias habentes ministrationes. Nam alius ordo praepositorum est, alius subditorum; alius divitum, alius pauperum; alius senum, alius iuvenum; et unaquaeque persona habens sua propria praecepta, sicut unumquodque membrum habet suum proprium in corpore officium.'

85. Alcuin, *Epistola* cxi, p. 160: 'Non enim solis episcopis vel presbyteris pecuniam suam tradidit Dominus ad multiplicandum, sed omni dignitati et gradu talenta bonae operationis tradidit, ut datam sibi gratiam fideliter amministrare studeat'.

86. So Walafrid Strabo, *Walafridi Strabonis liber de exordiis et incrementis quarundam in observationibus ecclesiasticis rerum*, ed. A. Knöpfler, 2nd edn (Veröffentlichungen aus dem Kirchenhistorischen Seminar, München, Reihe 1, Nr. 1), Ludwig-Maximilians University, Munich, 1899, pp. 99–100. Cf. Jonas of Orleans, *De institutione regia* ix, ed. Reviron 1930, p. 159.

the twelfth century to Honorius Augustodunensis[87] and Hugh of St Victor,[88] as well as to anonymous illuminators of manuscripts.[89] More frequent among Carolingian authors, however, than this bipartite model of society was a tripartite model. 'The lay *ordo* should serve justice and defend with arms the peace of holy Church; the monastic *ordo* should love quiet and devote itself to prayer . . . The episcopal *ordo* should oversee all the others.'[90] This threefold division of society – laity, monks, secular clergy – had been elaborated by Augustine and by Gregory the Great from the text Ezekiel 14, 14, which speaks of the three just men, Noah, Daniel and Job. These represent the three *ordines* among Christians: the preachers, the continent and the 'virtuous married people'.[91] This tripartite model continued to be acceptable to monastic theologians: it reappears in the writings of Bernard of Clairvaux,[92] Rupert of Deutz [93] and Gerhoch of Reichersberg.[94]

Another tripartite model – that of *oratores, bellatores, laboratores* – became current in the eleventh century.[95] This division, stressing social and political function rather than spiritual condition, did not meet the ideological requirements of the papal reform movement. Reformers preferred the simple classification, *clericalis* and *laicalis ordo*. The transition to this bipartite model of society in reforming terminology is visible in descriptions of ecclesiastical councils. While reforming synods in the early eleventh century would be attended by 'a multitude of the diverse *ordines* of Christians',[96] at the end of the century they were attended by 'a multitude of the diverse clerical and lay *ordines*'.[97] The principal aim of the reformers was to exalt the *clericalis ordo* above the *laicalis ordo*. Gregory VII's reforming programme was described precisely in these terms by a faithful adherent: 'He wished that the ecclesiastical *ordo* should not be in the hands of laymen, but rather should rise above them by virtue of the holiness of their conduct

87. Honorius Augustodunensis, *Gemma animae* 1.73, 566D–567B.
88. Hugh of St Victor, *De sacramentis Christianae fidei* II.2–4, PL 176, 417B–418C.
89. E.g. Plumpe 1943, pp. 84–5.
90. Jonas of Orleans, *Historia translationis Sancti Huberti episcopi Tungrensis* I, PL 106, 389D: 'laicus ordo iustitiae deserviret atque armis pacem sanctae Ecclesiae defenderet; monasticus ordo quietem diligeret, orationi vacaret . . . Episcopalis autem ordo ut his omnibus superintenderet'.
91. Cf. Folliet 1954, pp. 82ff.   92. Bernard, *Sermones* XXXV.1, XL.9, PL 183, 634, 652.
93. Rupert, *De Trinitate et operibus eius. In Reges III, 10*; *In Ezechiel* II.23, PL 167, 1150–1, 1483–4.
94. Gerhoh, *De investigatione Antichristi* 1.10, MGH Libelli 3, 318.
95. Cf. Duby 1980.
96. E.g. Council of Poitiers (1030), Mansi, *Concilia* 19, 498: 'multitudo diversorum ordinum christianorum'.
97. E.g. Roman synod of Lent 1078, Gregory VII, *Registrum* v.14a: 'diversorum ordinum clericorum et laicorum innumerabilis multitudo'.

and the dignity of their *ordo*.'[98] Gregory VII's mentor, Cardinal Humbert of Silva Candida had propounded similar aims in a polemic of c. 1060: 'As clerks are separate from laymen in their habit and profession, so they should also be separate in behaviour and conversation . . . For just as clerks are separated from laymen in their places and offices within the walls of the basilicas, so they should remain in their occupations outside the walls.'[99] The reformers found support for this attitude in the Pseudo-Isidorean Decretals which (being concerned above all to protect bishops against trial and deposition by laymen) likewise accentuated the distinction of the two *ordines* of Christian society and the supremacy of the clergy.[100] The work of differentiating the two *ordines* involved the eleventh-century reformers in a campaign against simony and clerical marriage – the 'heresies' which blurred the distinctions between clergy and laity. *Saecularia* and *ecclesiastica* had become inextricably mixed in Ottonian times (so reformers believed),[101] with the consequence that simony flourished. It was necessary to eradicate the evil customs which overlaid the usages of the primitive Church. Hence the key word in the reformers' vocabulary was *restituere*: to restore the freedom enjoyed by the *clericalis ordo* in the early Church, as illustrated by the Pseudo-Isidorean Decretals. Gregory VII's great objective was 'to snatch [the Church] from servile oppression, or rather tyrannical slavery, and restore her to her ancient freedom'.[102] The synodal legislation of the reform party – most importantly, the decrees against lay investiture – sought to extend this same *libertas* to ecclesiastical property and appointments.

'After the great tempest' of the Investiture Contest, 'peace was made' at the First Lateran Council of 1123.[103] The conciliar canons summarise the synodal legislation of the reform papacy but omit the most contentious items, notably the prohibition of lay investiture.[104] Nevertheless, the essential reform programme of the eleventh-century papacy – the separation of the clergy from the laity 'by virtue of the holiness of their

98. Bernold of Constance, *Chronicon* a.1085, *MGH SS* 5, 444: 'Noluit sane, ut ecclesiasticus ordo manibus laicorum subiaceret, sed eisdem et morum sanctitate et ordinis dignitate praemineret'.
99. Humbert, *Adversus simoniacos* III.9, *MGH Libelli* 1, 208: 'Et quemadmodum clerici a laicis habitu et professione, sic discreti debent esse actu et conversatione . . . Nam sicut clerici a laicis etiam intra parietes basilicarum locis et officiis, sic et extra separari et cognosci debent negotiis.'
100. E.g. *Decretales Pseudo-Isidorianae*, ed. Hinschius 1863, pp. 118–19, 230.
101. Humbert, *Adversus simoniacos* III.7, *MGH Libelli* 1, 206; Gregory VII, *In die resurrectionis* (liturgical text), ed. Morin 1901, p. 179.
102. Gregory VII, *Registrum* VIII.12: 'eam de servili oppressione immo tyrannica servitute eripere et priscae libertati restituere'.
103. Gerhoh of Reichersberg, *Commentarius aureus in psalmos. Psalmum CXXXIII*, PL 194, 890C: 'post tempestatem magnam . . . pax facta est'. 104. Cf. Schieffer 1981, p. 2.

conduct and the dignity of their *ordo*' – survived undiluted. The papacy and the episcopate continued to campaign against the adoption of lay 'behaviour and conversation' by the clergy; and the *clericalis ordo* continued to demand special status and the enjoyment of its own laws from secular governments.[105] Two twelfth-century résumés of this crucial Gregorian doctrine, one theological, the other canonical, ensured its continuing influence. The former was written by Hugh of St Victor:

There are two ways of life, one earthly, the other heavenly . . . and according to these two ways of life there are two peoples and in the two peoples two powers . . ., one inferior, the other superior . . . As the spiritual life is more worthy than the earthly life . . ., so the spiritual power is superior to the earthly or secular power in honour and dignity.[106]

This statement of the superiority of the *clericalis ordo* was a prominent *auctoritas* in the writings of later medieval polemicists.[107] Equally influential was the canonical statement of Master Gratian of Bologna. Gratian attributed it to Jerome, but its origin remains mysterious.[108] 'There are two kinds of Christians', clergy and laity. The *genus clericorum* wears a tonsure, as a crown. 'For they are kings; that is, they rule themselves and others by their virtues and so they have a kingdom in God.'[109]

Canon law

The compilers of canon law collections in these four centuries sought to quarry from the ancient traditions of the Church a set of rules of right conduct. 'The Greek word "canon" is called in Latin "rule" (*regula*). A rule is so called because it leads to what is right . . . or because it shows a pattern of righteous living (*norma recte vivendi*).'[110] The canonist was both researcher and publicist, seeking general recognition for the rules which he had adduced, as the 'Common law of the Church'.[111] The researcher sought ever farther afield for these canons. The canonical collections

---

105. Cf. Cheney 1956, pp. 104ff.

106. Hugh of St Victor, *De sacramentis Christianae fidei* II.2, 4, *PL* 176, 418: 'Duo quippe vitae sunt: una terrena, altera caelestis . . . Duas esse vitas et secundum duas vitas duos populos; et in duobus populis duas potestates . . . Quanto autem vita spiritualis dignior est quam terrena et spiritus quam corpus, tanto spiritualis potestas terrenam sive secularem potestatem honore ac dignitate praecedit.' 107. See below, pp. 299–300. 108. Cf. Prosdocimi 1965, pp. 105ff.

109. Gratian, *Decretum* C.12 q.1 c.7: 'Duo sunt genera Christianorum . . . Hi namque sunt reges, id est se et alios regentes in virtutibus et ita in Deo regnum habent.'

110. Isidorus Mercator, *Praefatio* 3, ed. Hinschius 1863, p. 17, quoting from the *Hispana*: 'Canon autem graece, latine regula nuncupatur. Regula autem dicta quod recto ducit . . . vel quod normam recte vivendi praebeat.' 111. Cf. Kuttner 1947, p. 391.

inherited by eighth-century Western Christendom – the *Dionysio-Hadriana*, the *Hispana* and *Quesnelliana* – largely contained conciliar canons.[112] In the eighth-century collection *Hibernensis* the writings of the Fathers are cited, apparently for the first time in the West, as equivalent in legal authority to conciliar canons.[113] In the late ninth-century *Collectio Anselmo dedicata* Roman law is absorbed into the canons;[114] and in the eleventh-century Gregorian collections the Bible and *gesta*, Christian history, furnish canonical materials.[115] To weld all these heterogeneous materials into a universally accepted body of Church law a legitimising source of *auctoritas* was urgently needed. The solution adopted by canonists – that the assent of Rome validates the canons – was prompted by two crucial texts. Pseudo-Isidore, drawing on a well-established authentic tradition,[116] taught that no council was valid unless it was summoned or approved by the pope.[117] A much older text, the *Decretum Gelasianum de recipiendis et non recipiendis libris*,[118] cataloguing the writings held by the Roman church to be canonical, suggested that no work could enter Christian tradition without papal sanction. It was on this basis that the Gregorian canonists formulated their theory of 'consonance': canon law is that which does not contradict the decrees of the popes.[119] Master Gratian of Bologna summarised their arguments in his *dictum*, 'The holy Roman church confers right and authority on the sacred canons.'[120]

Canon law studies had been initiated in the mid-eighth century by the papacy, the educator of Western Christendom in all things Roman. Pope Zacharias in 747 sent to the Frankish mayor of the palace, Pippin III, a collection of canons drawn from the *Dionysiana*.[121] The complete *Dionysio-Hadriana* was presented by Pope Hadrian I to Charlemagne on his visit to Rome in 774, the king promising never to depart from that law. Thereafter knowledge of the great collections of canon law of the early Church was disseminated in Francia as part of Charlemagne's programme of reforming

112. Cf. Wurm 1939; Munier 1966, pp. 400ff.; Fournier and Le Bras 1931, vol. i, 24ff, 68ff, 94–5.
113. Munier 1957, pp. 7, 25ff, 95.
114. Besse 1959, pp. 207ff; Mor 1935, pp. 281ff.
115. See e.g., Fournier 1920, pp. 336, 350–1.
116. Cf. Kuttner 1947, p. 392 n. 20.
117. Isidorus Mercator, *Praefatio* 8; Pseudo-Marcellus, *Epistola* i.2, ii.10; Pseudo-Julius, *Epistola* ii.5, 13; Pseudo-Athanasius, *Epistola* 2; Pseudo-Damasus, *Epistola* 9; Pelagius II, *Epistola* 1, ed. Hinschius 1863, pp. 19, 224, 228, 459, 471, 479, 503, 721.
118. *Decretum quod dicitur Gelasianum*, ed. Dobschütz 1912.
119. E.g. Bernold of Constance, *De excommunicatis vitandis*, MGH *Libelli* 2, 135. Cf. Kuttner 1947, p. 135.
120. Gratian, *Decretum* c.25 q.1 *dictum post* c. 16: 'Sacrosancta Romana ecclesia ius et auctoritatem sacris canonibus impertitur.'   121. *Codex Carolinus* 3, MGH *Epp.* 3, 479ff.

and disciplining the Church.[122] The royal capitulary of 789, *Admonitio generalis*, urging the clergy to be diligent in observing the canons, has as an appendix a canonical collection including sixty texts from the *Dionysio-Hadriana*.[123] At the council of Aachen in 802, according to the 'Annals of Lorsch', Charlemagne commanded that 'all the canons' and 'the decrees of the popes' be observed by all the clergy.[124] (It is not clear which canonical collections are here intended: in Carolingian church councils from the mid-eighth century bishops consulted the *Quesnelliana*, the *Dionysio-Hadriana*, the *Vetus Gallica* and the *Hispana*, regarding no collection as more authoritative or 'official' than another.)[125] As it was the king's duty to render to each man his right,[126] so Charlemagne in his capitularies guaranteed to the clergy the unrestricted enjoyment of their own laws.[127] 'In that time, at the instigation of the lord Charles, wisdom began to prevail and, at the command of the said Charles, the most glorious king of the Franks, canonical authority began to be investigated in detail.' So wrote the historian of the church of le Mans, thinking in particular of the practice of trial by synod for accused clergy.[128] The *sacerdotium*, therefore, enjoyed the privileges of canon law at the king's command – an arrangement which demanded for its success the active co-operation of a king as powerful as Charlemagne.

After Charlemagne's death a series of Frankish reforming councils – Paris (829), Aachen (836), Meaux-Paris (845/6) – assumed the role of champion of the clerical right to the *canones*.[129] These councils failed, however, to deal with the threats to the *sacerdotium* caused by increasing political disorder. Laymen encroached upon the administration and property of the Church; the secular power deposed bishops and tried clergy for criminal offences without recourse to a synod. It was especially the latter affront to clerical independence which inspired the compilation of the Pseudo-Isidorean Decretals. Who was responsible for the forging of this immensely influential canonical collection remains controversial. The most recent investigation locates the forgers among the supporters of the deposed

---

122. Cf. Clercq 1936, p. 171.   123. *Admonitio generalis, MGH Cap.* 1, 52ff.
124. *Annales Laureshamenses* a.802, *MGH SS* 1, 39: 'fecit episcopos cum presbyteris seu diaconibus relegi universos canones, quas sanctus synodus recepit et decreta pontificum et pleniter iussit eos tradi coram omnibus episcopis, presbyteris et diaconibus'.
125. Cf. Fuhrmann 1972–4, vol. 1, p. 143.   126. *Codex Iustinianus, Institutiones* 1.1, 3.
127. E.g. *Karoli Magni Capitulare primum* (769), *MGH Cap.* 1, 44ff. Cf. Morrison 1964, pp. 31ff.
128. *Gesta episcoporum Cenomannensium* 17, ed. Mabillon 1723, p. 288: 'Sed illo in tempore iam sapientia ordinante atque instigante domno Carolo, pollere coeperet et canonica auctoritas, praecipiente iam dicto Carolo gloriosissimo Francorum rege, enucleatim perscrutari.'
129. Cf. Ladner 1968, p. 45.

Archbishop Ebo of Rheims and the opponents of his successor, Hincmar – himself ironically one of the earliest users of the compilation.[130] The purpose of the forgery is more easily determined. Pseudo-Isidore was above all concerned with the rights of bishops, 'the eyes of the Lord', 'pillars of the Church', 'the chief priests', 'servants of God', 'throne of God', 'gods', 'saints'.[131] Bishops, according to Pseudo-Isidore, are 'the keys' of the Church, to whom is given the power of binding and loosing.[132] The main concern of the decretals is to protect suffragan bishops from the control of their metropolitans, of provincial synods and of the secular power; especially to inhibit criminal proceedings against bishops and to prevent the possibility of their deposition. The decretals, therefore, severely limit the right of accusation of bishops. No one known to be hostile to a bishop may accuse him in a secular court. No layman, no foreigner, no freedman may accuse a bishop; nor can he be accused by an inferior. If proceedings are initiated against a bishop, the accused must first be restored to all his rights and property. He cannot be condemned without the testimony of seventy-two trustworthy witnesses. At any moment of the trial the bishop may suspend proceedings by appealing to the superior authority of the primate or the pope.[133]

It was in this context that papal authority was important to Isidorus Mercator. To be sure, Pseudo-Isidore exalted the authority of the pope. His 115 forged and 125 falsified papal letters represent the Church as ruled from its earliest days, even to the minute details of her existence, by papal decree. Pseudo-Isidore made the validity of councils dependent on papal approval and referred the judgement of accused bishops to Rome.[134] But it was in the interests of protecting the episcopate that the jurisdiction of the papacy was so greatly extended by the False Decretals. Rome was the beneficiary of Pseudo-Isidore's concern to defend the independence of the suffragan bishops: he gave the pope the right to judge bishops, so as to deny that right to the more dangerous local authorities of the metropolitan and the king.

The history of canon law from the late ninth to the mid-twelfth century is often the history of the Pseudo-Isidorean Decretals. Successive generations of canonists borrowed from the False Decretals *auctoritates* for their own systematic collections – culminating in the 400 texts of Pseudo-Isidore which came by various routes into the *Decretum* of Master Gratian of Bologna.[135] These excerptors would not necessarily share the priorities of

130. Fuhrmann 1972–4, vol. I, pp. 195ff, 211ff.   131. *Ibid.*, p. 146.
132. Cf. *Decretales Pseudo-Isidorianae* ed. Hinschius 1863, pp. 41, 243.
133. Cf. Feine 1964, pp. 394, 435; Fuhrmann 1972–4, vol. I, pp. 41ff.   134. See below, pp. 285–6.
135. *Corpus Iuris Canonici* 1879–81, vol. I, *Prolegomena* pp. xxvff; Fuhrmann 1972–4, vol. I, pp. 566ff.

Pseudo-Isidore; so that the great forger would become – especially in the later eleventh century – the champion of causes very different from (and sometimes diametrically opposed to) those which the decretals were intended to promote. Only one of the important systematic collections of our period sympathised entirely with Pseudo-Isidore's outlook and made excerpts from the decretals without distorting their sense: the *Decretum* of Bishop Burchard of Worms (1000–25), the most widely disseminated repository of Pseudo-Isidorean materials for most of the eleventh century.[136] At first sight Burchard's sympathy with the attitude of Pseudo-Isidore is unexpected: the latter was concerned to defend bishops against the encroachments of the secular power; Burchard acquiesced in the 'Ottonian system'. He was a characteristic product of that 'system', trained in the imperial chapel, enjoying the favour of the Emperor Henry II, entrusted with the work of government and the execution of imperial policy.[137] Yet though he would not attack royal rights over the Church, Burchard was a defender of the *ordo episcopalis*. He took from Pseudo-Isidore those passages which defined the authority of suffragan bishops and hedged them about with procedural defences against their accusers.[138] In this context Burchard dealt with the role of the papacy. His few texts referring to the papacy are concerned, not with the position of Rome relative to the other churches of Christendom, but with Rome as a court of appeal for accused bishops.

Burchard was not interested in Pseudo-Isidore's account of the papal *plenitudo potestatis*; and this is surprising, because one of his *fontes formales* was particularly interested in that subject. Burchard drew some of his Pseudo-Isidorean material, not directly from his copy of the False Decretals, but from earlier systematic collections, notably the *Collectio Anselmo dedicata*, dedicated to Archbishop Anselm II of Milan (882–96).[139] Here he found an author full of reverence for the Roman church,[140] whose excerpts from Pseudo-Isidore were chosen to corroborate his idea of the Roman primacy. This anonymous canonist began most of the twelve books of his collection with papal decretals, especially those of Pseudo-Isidore, in order to mark his special respect for papal decretals before other sources of canon law. For the same reason he cited in all 514 texts from Pseudo-Isidore and 268 from Pope Gregory I. The passages which he excerpted from the False Decretals emphasised in particular the Roman primacy founded by Christ and the

---

136. Cf. Fournier 1911, pp. 451ff; Meyer 1935, pp. 141ff.
137. Cf. Fleckenstein 1966, pp. 88–9, 114ff.   138. Cf. Fuhrmann 1972–4, vol. i, pp. 480ff.
139. Cf. Fournier and Le Bras 1931, vol. i. p. 375.
140. Cf. Fournier 1911, pp. 475ff; Besse 1961/2, pp. 67ff.

junior role of Constantinople and all other churches.[141] The author of the *Collectio Anselmo dedicata*, by citing Pseudo-Isidore's statements concerning the papacy out of their Pseudo-Isidorean context – the protection of bishops – created an abbreviated version of the False Decretals concerned with Rome's supremacy in the constitution of the Church. *Anselmo dedicata*'s version of Pseudo-Isidore anticipates that of the Gregorian canonists.

The main concern of the canonists of the eleventh-century papal reform movement was the definition of the *privilegium Romanae ecclesiae*. The interest of Hildebrand-Gregory VII in the canons was indeed confined to this theme, as he indicated as early as 1059, when he requested from Peter Damian a treatise demonstrating 'how great is the privilege of the Roman church in ecclesiastical cases'.[142] The canonists whom contemporaries regarded as the *discipuli* of Gregory VII[143] placed the greatest emphasis on this *privilegium* in their collections. Bishop Anselm II of Lucca – whose collection is described in the twelfth-century Barberini codex as 'completed at the command and according to the direction' of Gregory VII[144] – devoted books I and II of his *Collectio canonum* (comprising 171 *capitula*) to the primacy of Rome.[145] Here the canonist ascribed to the Roman church a jurisdiction extending not only over the whole Church, as a tribunal before which the *causae maiores* must be brought and where the appeals from all the churches are heard; but also over emperors and kings. The *Collectio* was well described by Anselm's anonymous biographer as an *apologeticus* 'by which he defended the judgement of the lord pope [Gregory VII] and all his actions and commands with canonical arguments and confirmed them with orthodox authorities'.[146] Anselm was indeed concerned to justify Gregory VII's conception of the primacy, which based the unity of the Catholic Church on the single principle of obedience to Rome.[147] This was likewise the intention of his contemporary, Cardinal Deusdedit, expressed in the prologue of his canonical collection (addressed to Pope Victor III): 'desiring to reveal to the ignorant the privilege of authority by which [the Roman

141. E.g. *Collectio Anselmo dedicata* 1.7–8 (Christ's commission of the primacy to Peter and Clement), 118 (Constantinople is *iunior* to Rome). Cf. Fuhrmann 1972–4, vol. I, p. 432.
142. Peter Damian, *Opusculum* v (*Actus Mediolani*), 89B; 'Privilegium Romanae ecclesiae . . . quantumque vigorem ad disponendam ecclesiastici status contineat disciplinam.'
143. *Cardinalium schismaticorum scripta* III.13, *MGH Libelli* 2, 399.
144. Fournier 1901, p. 451: 'facta tempore VII Gregorii sanctissimi papae a beatissimo Anselmo Lucensi episcopo . . . cuius iussione et praecepto desiderantis consummavit hoc opus'.
145. Cf. Fournier 1920, pp. 271ff.
146. *Vita sancti Anselmi episcopi Lucensis* 26, *MGH SS* 12, 21: 'Apologeticum unum . . . compilavit, quibus domni papae sententiam et universa eius facta atque praecepta canonicis defenderet rationibus et approbaret orthodoxis auctoribus.' 147. Cf. Miccoli 1966, pp. 187ff.

church] is pre-eminent in the Christian world . . . I have brought together in one place whatever is most important among the various authorities of the holy Fathers and the Christian princes.'[148] The subject-matter of Deusdedit's collection, therefore, was not the whole field of ecclesiastical legislation but its most vital aspect, the *privilegium auctoritatis Romanae ecclesiae*. By means of 'authorities of the holy Fathers' he would define the nature of this privilege; while 'authorities of the Christian princes' would demonstrate that the privilege was universally recognised throughout Christendom.

A generation ago it was a commonplace of historians that these Gregorian canonists derived their exalted view of the papal primacy from Pseudo-Isidore.[149] It is true that Pseudo-Isidore was the principal *fons formalis* of the canonical collections compiled by the adherents of the reform papacy. It is not true, however – as the exhaustive researches of Horst Fuhrmann have shown – that the supporters of the reform papacy 'rediscovered' Pseudo-Isidore or that they drew their conception of the Roman primacy directly from the pages of the False Decretals. 'It was not Pseudo-Isidore but the Church that was rediscovered' by the reformers,[150] who took from Pseudo-Isidore only what agreed with their view of the constitution of the Church. Their reinterpretation of Pseudo-Isidore is apparent as early as 1053, when Pope Leo IX intervened in the African Church to settle the primatial dispute in favour of Carthage. In the two papal letters concerning this dispute (probably composed by Cardinal Humbert of Silva Candida)[151] Pseudo-Isidore is cited in defence of the supremacy of the Roman bishop, which enables him to settle the differences of other churches. Here the Pseudo-Isidorean statement of the papal primacy is cited, not as a protection for the other bishops, but as a definition of the position of the papacy vis-à-vis the whole Church. The rank of Carthage as *prima sedes* in Africa was assured by the African councils and 'what is greater still, by the decrees of our venerable predecessors the Roman bishops'.[152] What was of secondary interest to Pseudo-Isidore, therefore, was made of primary importance in the reformers' quotations

---

148. *Die Kanonessammlung des Kardinals Deusdedit*, ed. Wolf von Glanvell 1905, pp. 2–3: 'Itaque ego auctoritatis ipsius privilegium, quo omni Christiano orbi preminent, ignorantibus patefacere cupiens . . . ex variis sanctorum patrum et Christianorum principum auctoritatibus potioribus quibusque in unum congestis . . . defloravi.'

149. E.g. Michel 1943; Michel 1947, pp. 65ff; Jordan 1958, pp. 125–6; Haller 1962, p. 232.

150. Fuhrmann 1972–4, vol. I, pp. 289ff, 339ff.   151. So Michel 1943, pp. 185ff (Exkurs I).

152. Leo IX, *JL* 4305, *PL* 143, 729D: 'quod maius est, ex venerabilium praedecessorum nostrorum Romanorum praesulum decretis'. Cf. Fuhrmann 1972–4, pp. 343ff.

from the False Decretals. Pseudo-Isidore's main concern – to defend bishops faced with judicial proceedings and to inhibit their accusers – came to seem irrelevant, even dangerous, to the eleventh-century reformers. Peter Damian addressed to Pope Alexander II between 1065 and 1071 a treatise attacking the immunity from accusation granted to bishops by the letters of Pseudo-Fabian and Pseudo-Anacletus.

> The statement, 'It is not permissible for a son of any church to bring charges against his own bishop . . . before a greater church' is too incongruous and utterly contrary to ecclesiastical discipline . . . See what is claimed: 'I am a bishop, a pastor of the Church, and I must not suffer the annoyance of accusations from the flock committed to me: for the sake of the faith it is right that I should be borne with equanimity, even if I am of evil character.' . . . Let this cunning subterfuge be abolished, so that . . . [no one] may enjoy immunity for the sins which he has committed. Let free access be permitted to just grievances and complaints made at the primatial see.[153]

Gregory VII came to see the Pseudo-Isidorean immunity of bishops as a major obstacle to reform.[154]

It is not surprising, therefore, to find that the Gregorian canonists interpreted and reworked their Pseudo-Isidorean material, often in a sense quite opposite to that intended by the author. Their approach can be illustrated from the earliest reform manual, the *Collection in Seventy-Four Titles*. The collection contains 148 fragments from Pseudo-Isidore among its 315 canons; and it has not unreasonably, therefore, been claimed that the canonist's idea of the Church, and especially of the status of the papacy, was derived from the False Decretals.[155] However, closer examination of the collection reveals that the canonist imposed his own view of Church and papacy upon his Pseudo-Isidorean material. His first section, 'On the primacy of the Roman church', contains a chapter attributed to Anacletus:

> The holy Roman and apostolic church . . . obtained the primacy from the Lord our Saviour himself . . . Therefore this apostolic see was made the hinge and head of all the churches by the Lord and by no other; and just as the door is ruled by the hinge, so all the churches, as ordered by the Lord, are ruled by the authority of this holy

---

153. Peter Damian, *Epistolae* I.12, *PL* 144, 215D, 217C, 218C: 'Illud etiam, quod dicitur: "Non licere cuiuslibet ecclesiae filium ad maiorem ecclesiam proprii reatus episcopi . . . deferre", nimis absonum et prorsus ecclesiasticae disciplinae probatur adversum. . . . Sed ecce dicitur: Ego sum episcopus, ego sum pastor ecclesiae, non debeo a commissis ovibus accusationum patere molestiis; etenim in causa fidei dignus sum etiam in pravis moribus aequanimiter ferri . . . Tollatur haec subterfugii versuta calliditas: ut is . . . immunitatem commissi piaculi non lucretur. Iustis ergo querelis liber pateat aditus, liceat apud primatem ecclesiam conqueri.' Peter Damian here refers to Pseudo-Fabian, *Epistola* II.22; Pseudo-Anacletus, *Epistola* III.39, ed. Hinschius 1863, pp. 165, 85. Cf. Ryan 1956, p. 129. 154. Cf. Robinson 1978a, pp. 103ff. 155. E.g. Michel 1953, pp. 83ff.

see. Therefore, refer to the summit of this holy see, as your head, the more difficult cases which arise among you.[156]

This chapter creates from three disparate sentences from the third letter of Pseudo-Anacletus, linked together by the interpolated adverbs *ergo* and *igitur*, a justification of the supreme judicial authority of the papacy. It was this canonist's practice to substitute for the term *canones* in his Pseudo-Isidorean texts the interpolation *decreta praesulum Romanorum*, so making papal decrees the canonical norm.[157] Elsewhere the canonist altered the sense of the text of Pseudo-Fabian prohibiting the expulsion of bishops from their sees by adding the words 'without the authority of the Roman pontiff';[158] and by a similar interpolation made the translation of bishops dependent on 'the authority and permission of the holy Roman see'.[159] Not only did the canonist amend the False Decretals in the interests of subordinating the episcopate to the papacy. He also departed from Pseudo-Isidore's intention of giving a special status to bishops by extending to the whole clergy the safeguards which Pseudo-Isidore devised for the episcopate alone (*episcopus* is amended to *pastor vel rector ecclesiae*)[160] and by ascribing to monasteries the privileges intended by Pseudo-Isidore for episcopal churches (*monasteria* and *abbas* are interpolated in the Pseudo-Isidorean text).[161] These drastic revisions of Pseudo-Isidore's view of the Church were transmitted by the *Collection in Seventy-Four Titles* to later reform collections, to the *Panormia* of Ivo of Chartres (which succeeded Burchard's *Decretum* as the most influential compilation before Gratian) and to Master Gratian's *Decretum*.[162]

In the Gregorian canonical collections the papal authority absorbs all other authority in the Church; so that, for example, the Pseudo-Isidorean

---

156. *Collectio in LXXIV titulos digesta* 2, ed. Gilchrist 1973, p. 20: 'Sacrosancta Romana et apostolica ecclesia . . . ab ipso Domino salvatore nostro primatum obtinuit . . . Ergo haec apostolica sedes cardo et caput omnium ecclesiarum a Domino et non ab alio est constituta, et sicut cardine ostium regitur, sic huius sanctae sedis auctoritate omnes ecclesiae Domino disponente reguntur. Igitur si quae causae difficiliores inter vos ortae fuerint, ad huius sanctae sedis apicem eas quasi ad caput referte.' (Pseudo-Anacletus, *Epistola* III.30, 34, ed. Hinschius 1863, pp. 83–4) Cf. Fuhrmann 1972–4, vol. I, pp. 492ff. 157. *Collectio in LXXIV titulos* 291, 307.

158. *Ibid.*, 91: 'sine auctoritate Romani pontificis'. Cf. Pseudo-Fabian, *Epistola* II.19, 20, ed. Hinschius 1863, p. 165.

159. *Collectio in LXXIV titulos* 188: 'sine sacrosanctae Romanae sedis auctoritate et licentia'. Cf. Pseudo-Anterius, *Epistola* I.2, 4, ed. Hinschius 1863, pp. 152–3.

160. *Collectio in LXXIV titulos* 86. Cf. Pseudo-Felix II, *Epistola* I.12, ed. Hinschius 1863, p. 488. See also *Collectio in LXXIV titulos* 80.

161. *Collectio in LXXIV titulos* 24. Cf. Pseudo-Anacletus, *Epistola* I.15. See also *Collectio in LXXIV titulos* 301.

162. E.g. Anselm of Lucca, *Collectio canonum* III.40, 48, 76, 89; VI.90; XII.2; Ivo of Chartres, *Panormia* III.69; Gratian, *Decretum* C.23 q.1 c.2; C.7 q.1 c.34; C.25 q.1 c.11.

expression *apostolica et synodali auctoritate* becomes in the *Collectio canonum* of Anselm of Lucca simply *apostolica auctoritate*.[163] Pseudo-Fabian's declaration that an heretical bishop should be 'accused either to his primate or to the apostolic see' was amended by Anselm of Lucca to read 'accused by his primate to the apostolic see', so sweeping aside the rival authority of the metropolitan.[164] This Roman centralism sprang from the conviction that obedience to the papacy could alone guarantee the unity of the Church. The idea is developed in the rubrics of book I of Anselm's collection. The Church must unite around the successor of Peter, from whom the ecclesiastical order derives its origin. Whoever has grieved the pope does not receive Christ: therefore we must not speak to one to whom the pope does not speak. We must never depart from the edicts of the Roman church: to do so incurs great danger.[165] The safety of the Catholic faith and the assurance of salvation depend on *obedientia*: the obedience owed by the whole *clericalis ordo* and by the whole *societas christiana* to the pope. Failure to obey is not simply a breach of ecclesiastical discipline, but heresy. This doctrine – 'the sacred canons brand as heretics those who do not agree with the Roman church' – was stated by Peter Damian in the context of the two crises of disobedience which assailed the early reform papacy: the resistance of Milan and the schism of the antipope Cadalus of Parma (1062–4).[166] The doctrine was adopted by Gregory VII as a weapon to wield against disobedient bishops;[167] and entered canon law.[168] This equation of disobedience with heresy inspired the major innovation in the Gregorian canonical collections: the devising of measures to deal with the *haeretici* and *schismatici*. In the late 1070s the *Collection in Seventy-Four Titles* was given an appendix *De excommunicatione* (probably by Bernold of Constance);[169] and the Gregorian canonists of the following decade included a section *De iusta persecutione* in their collections.[170] From the writings of Augustine against the Donatists and those of Gregory I against the Lombards Anselm of Lucca drew a justification of 'righteous persecution'. The Church has the power of coercion, to correct the wicked and to bring schismatics back to obedience.

163. Anselm of Lucca, *Collectio canonum* XII.8. Cf. Fuhrmann 1972–4, vol. I, pp. 520ff.
164. Anselm, *Collectio canonum* III.31: 'a primate suo ad sedem apostolicam'. Cf. Pseudo-Fabian, *Epistola* II.23, ed. Hinschius 1863, p. 166. This text is cited in the *Collectio in LXXIV titulos* 78 without emendation.
165. Anselm, *Collectio canonum* I.2, 5, 6, 11, 12, 16, 62. Cf. Fliche 1946, pp. 348ff.
166. Peter Damian, *Opusculum* V (*Actus Mediolani*) (1059); *Epistolae* I.20 (1062): 'eos sacri canones hereticos notant qui cum Romana ecclesia non concordant'. Cf. Ryan 1956, pp. 63ff, 78ff.
167. Gregory VII, *Registrum* VII.24; Odo of Ostia, letter to Bishop Udo of Hildesheim, *MGH Die Briefe der deutschen Kaiserzeit* 5, 26. Cf. Gregory VII, *Registrum* II.55a, no. 26.
168. Deusdedit, *Collectio canonum* I.167. Cf. Hofmann 1933, pp. 63–4.
169. So Autenrieth 1958, pp. 375ff.   170. Cf. Erdmann 1935, pp. 225ff.

The Church 'can persecute her enemies', having recourse to the powers of this world for the purpose.[171]

The Gregorian doctrine of 'righteous persecution' was absorbed into *Causa* 23 of the *Decretum* of Master Gratian of Bologna.[172] There it contributed to the canonist's vision of Christendom as an orthodox society, presided over by the priesthood. 'Every Christian who is excommunicated by the priests is given up to Satan. Why? – because the devil is outside the Church, just as Christ is within the Church.'[173] Those who are within the Church – those belonging to *ius nostrum*, a term which is sometimes used in the *Decretum* as the equivalent of *ecclesia* – are subject to the *disciplina* of the ecclesiastical hierarchy.[174] The integrity of this *ius Christianum* depends on the acceptance of right religion; and this integrity must be preserved, if necessary, by force. Gratian expressed this idea in his *dicta* concerning Jewish converts. 'Jews must not be forced into the faith; but if they accept it – albeit unwillingly – they must be forced to keep it . . . so as not to blaspheme against the name of the Lord.'[175] The compulsory society of the *Decretum*, held together by a coercive *disciplina* for the correction of the wicked and the persecution of heretics and schismatics, is the lineal descendant of Gregory VII's *societas christiana*.[176] As in the Gregorian collections, so also in the *Decretum* obedience to Rome is the touchstone of orthodoxy. 'The faith of the Roman church has destroyed every heresy'; 'the Roman church has the zeal of the Christian religion before all others'. Therefore 'it is not permitted to think or teach other than the Roman church thinks and teaches'.[177] 'It is fitting that whatever is decreed by the Roman pontiff should be observed by everyone.' For 'the holy Roman church confers right and authority on the sacred canons, but she is not herself bound by them'.[178]

---

171. Anselm, *Collectio canonum* XII.53: 'De hereticis per seculares potestates coercendis'; XIII.14: 'Quod ecclesia persecutionem possit facere.' Cf. Erdmann 1935, p. 226. (These *capitula* do not appear in the incomplete edition of Thaner 1906–15: they are here cited from the *codex Vaticanus latinus* 1363.)

172. E.g. Gratian, *Decretum* C.23 q.1 c.3 (Anselm, *Collectio canonum* XIII.4); C.23 q.7 c.3 (*ibid.* XII.57); C.23 q.8 c.17–18 (*ibid.* XIII.6, 8).

173. Gratian, *Decretum* C.11 q.3 c.32: 'Omnis Christianus . . . qui a sacerdotibus excommunicatur, satanae traditur: quomodo? scilicet, quia extra ecclesiam diabolus est, sicut in ecclesia Christus.' Cf. Chodorow 1972, pp. 65ff.   174. Gratian, *Decretum* C.11 q.3 c.32.

175. *Ibid.* D.45 *dictum post* c.4, c.5: 'Iudaei non sunt cogendi ad fidem, quam tamen si inviti susceperint, cogendi sunt retinere . . . ne nomen Domini blasphemetur.'

176. Gregory VII, *Registrum* VI.6. Cf. Ullmann 1970, p. 271.

177. Gratian, *Decretum* C.24 q.1 c.10–15: 'Fides Romanae ecclesiae omnem heresim destruit . . .; Christianae religionis zelum Romana ecclesia prae ceteris habuit; Aliud quam Romana ecclesia neque sentire neque docere permittitur.'

178. *Ibid.* C.25 q.1 *dictum post* c.16: 'ea quae a Romanis pontificibus decreta sunt, ab omnibus observari convenit . . . Sacrosancta Romana ecclesia ius et auctoritatem sacris canonibus impertitur, sed non eis alligatur.'

'Only the Roman church is able, on her own authority, to judge in all matters; but no one is permitted to judge her.'[179] In the juridical community of the Church – *ius nostrum* – the source of juridical authority, keeper and *conditor* of the canons is the pope.

In the rubrics and *dicta* of the canonists, in their truncation and mutilation of their texts, the history of the Church is written as surely as in more accessible documents. So in the canonical collections of 750–1150 it is possible to identify the transitions in the ecclesiology of these centuries. The royal domination over the Church in the age of Charlemagne gives way to the episcopal domination of the age of Pseudo-Isidore. The papal domination promoted by the eleventh-century reformers becomes the cornerstone of Master Gratian's edifice. Of these developments the most decisive was the reformers' representation of the Church as a *regnum* with the pope as monarch. It is in the sphere of canon law that the Gregorian reform strikes the reader as unmistakably revolutionary.

Papal authority

Rome was *prima sedes*, 'the first see': the threshold of the apostle Peter, to whose care the nascent Church had been committed by the Lord himself in words familiar to the faithful (Matt. 16, 18–9; John 21, 15–17), whose guardianship guaranteed the inerrancy of the Catholic faith (Luke 22, 31–2).[180] Pope Leo I developed a far-reaching conception of this primacy as a *principatus*, using the image of *caput* and *membra* to define the relations of the Roman church with the other churches of Christendom.[181] That conception, confirmed and elaborated by subsequent popes, was from the eighth century regularly and urgently communicated to the West. The education of Western Christendom in the details of the primacy is a major theme of papal history in the early and central Middle Ages; but not all of this instruction came from Rome. A vital contribution to the development and dissemination of ideas of the papal primacy was made by gifted authors north of the Alps: St Boniface, Abbo of Fleury, Humbert of Moyenmoutier, Bernold of Constance, Bernard of Clairvaux.

Boniface-Winfrid, who called himself 'servant of the apostolic see', announced that his purpose in Germany was 'to summon and incline' all his

---

179. *Ibid.* c.9 q.3 *dictum post* c.9: 'Sola enim Romana ecclesia sua auctoritate valet iudicare de omnibus; de ea vero nulli iudicare permittitur.'
180. Cf. Maccarrone 1960, pp. 633ff.   181. Cf. Ullmann 1960, pp. 25ff.

'hearers and disciples' 'to the obedience of the apostolic see'.[182] Boniface signified his own obedience to the papacy by being the first non-Italian bishop to make his confession of faith and to swear obedience to the pope. This event on 30 November 722 – the attribution to a northern bishop of the status of a bishop of suburbican Italy – marks the beginning of the papacy's implementation of the claim of Leo I, that the Roman church was the head and the other churches, members.[183] This implementation had not progressed much further when Abbot Abbo of Fleury (d. 1004) restated that claim in his polemics against the enemies of monastic reform. In the interests of protecting the monks and restraining their episcopal opponents, Abbo invoked the help of the papacy: 'The Roman church grants authority to all [churches] as her members throughout the four corners of the world. Whoever, therefore, opposes the Roman church, withdraws himself from her members and throws in his lot with the enemies of Christ.'[184] The Lotharingian monk Humbert, subsequently cardinal bishop of Silva Candida, applied these same ideas to the papal negotiations with the church of Constantinople in the early 1050s, which ended in the schism of 1054. In his letters to the patriarch of Constantinople, Humbert developed the idea of a papal monarchy over the Church: his theme was 'the earthly and heavenly *imperium* of the royal priesthood of the holy Roman see'.[185] This monarchical image of papal authority appealed also to Bernold of Constance, the first German scholar to take up the defence of Gregory VII's reform programme.[186] Bernold wrote that the pope 'has divided up his charge (*cura*) among the individual bishops, but yet has in no way deprived himself of his universal and ruling power; just as the king does not diminish his royal power, although he has divided up his *regnum* among different dukes, counts and officials'.[187] Half a century later such an analogy with secular dominion would be most objectionable to Bernard of Clairvaux. 'The voice of the Lord in the Gospel says: "The kings of the Gentiles have

182. Boniface, *Epistola* 50, *MGH Epp.* 3, 299: 'quantoscumque audientes vel discipulos in ista legatione mihi Deus donaverit, ad obedientiam apostolicae sedis invitare et inclinare non cesso'.
183. Cf. Marot 1965, pp. 23–4; Congar 1968a, p. 197.
184. Abbo of Fleury, *Epistola* 5, *PL* 139, 423D: 'Romana ecclesia auctoritatem tribuat omnibus quasi suis membris, quae sunt per quatuor climata totius orbis. Qui ergo Romanae ecclesiae contradicit, quid aliud quam se a membris eius subtrahit ut fiat portio adversariorum Christi?'
185. Leo IX, *Epistola I ad Cerullarium*, ed. Will 1861, p. 68: 'de terreno et caelesti imperio de regali sacerdotio sanctae Romanae sedis'. On the authorship of this letter see Michel 1924, pp. 45ff.
186. Cf. Robinson 1978b, pp. 51ff; Robinson 1978c, pp. 795ff.
187. Bernold, *Apologeticus* 23, *MGH Libelli* 2, 88: 'praesul apostolicus, qui licet curam suam in singulos episcopos diviserit, nullomodo tamen se ipsum sua universali et principali potestate privavit, sicut nec rex suam regalem potentiam diminuit, licet regnum suum in diversos duces, comites sive iudices diviserit'.

dominion over them, and they that have authority over them are called benefactors" and he adds: "But you are not so." It is clear: dominion is forbidden to apostles.'[188] For the authority given to the pope is far greater than mere *dominatus*. To him is committed 'not the people of this city or this region or this kingdom', 'not one people but all people', 'the universal Church spread throughout the world, made up of all the churches'.[189]

Principatus. Popes from the eighth to the eleventh century urged their authority upon their correspondents by insisting on the continued presence of St Peter in Rome. This idea predominates in the papal letters preserved in the *Codex Carolinus*, urgently requesting the aid of the Arnulfing warlords Charles Martel, Carloman and Pippin III. In the culminating appeal (756) St Peter himself addresses Pippin III and his sons, reminding them of the Gospel *auctoritates* for his commission and summoning them as his 'adoptive sons' to defend 'this Roman city and people committed to me by God and the home where I rest according to the flesh'.[190] So also Pope Nicholas I informed the Bulgarians that 'St Peter . . . lives and presides in my see';[191] and likewise Pope Gregory VII always insisted on his special relationship with the saint, summoning one correspondent to pray at his threshold and sending another a relic of his chains.[192] The obedience owed to St Peter as the key-bearer (*claviger*) of the kingdom of heaven was owed also to 'his vicar . . . who now lives in the flesh', the pope.[193]

The most effective Roman elaboration of the authority of the *vicarius Petri* in the early Middle Ages was that of Nicholas I in 865, insisting that 'the city of the Romans alone, where the bodily presence of the apostle Peter is diligently venerated . . . has received and contains in herself what God commanded the universal Church to receive and contain'. Peter alone was commanded in a vision to kill and eat animals of all kinds (Acts 10, 12); he

---

188. Bernard, *De consideratione* ii.6.10: 'vox Domini est in Evangelio: "Reges gentium dominantur eorum, et qui potestatem habent super eos, benefici vocantur" et infert: "Vos autem non sic" [Luke 22:25]. Planum est: apostolis interdicitur dominatus.'

189. *Ibid.*, ii.8, 15, 16: 'Quas? illius vel illius populos civitatis aut regionis aut certi regni? . . . non uni populo, sed cunctis praeesse deberet . . . facta ex omnibus ipsa universalis Ecclesia, toto orbe diffusa.'

190. *Codex Carolinus* 10, Stephen II, *JE* 2327, *MGH Epp.* 3, 501: 'ego, apostolus Dei Petrus, qui vos adoptivos habeo filios, ad defendendum . . . hanc Romanam civitatem et populum mihi a Deo commissum seu et domum, ubi secundum carnem requiesco'.

191. Nicholas I, *JE* 2812, *MGH Epp.* 6, 599: 'beatus Petrus, qui in sede sua vivit et praesidet'.

192. Gregory VII, *Registrum* i.19 (to Duke Rudolf of Swabia); vii.6 (to King Alfonso VI of León-Castile).

193. *Ibid.*, ix.3: 'fidelis ero . . . beato Petro apostolo eiusque vicario papae Gregorio, qui nunc in carne vivit'.

alone was commanded by the Lord to haul the net ashore (John 21, 10).[194] What is significant here is the repetition of the adjective *solus, sola*, 'alone'. It is to be understood in the light of the conviction of Carolingian authors that the power of binding and loosing was conferred on the whole *sacerdotalis ordo*, represented by St Peter – the interpretation of Matt. 16, 19 given by Cyprian and transmitted to the Carolingians by Bede.[195] 'It must not be thought that this power was given only to St Peter, but rather he as one replied on behalf of all . . . so all in one heard, "Whatever you bind on earth shall be bound in heaven" . . .'.[196] Hence Carolingian bishops were called in public *acta* 'vicars of Christ and key-bearers of the kingdom of heaven'.[197] In the Pseudo-Isidorean Decretals there is ambiguity concerning the interpretation of Matt. 16, 19. Pseudo-Anacletus considered that the power of the keys was given to all the apostles; while Pseudo-Clement claimed that St Peter and his successors alone received the keys.[198] Both opinions entered medieval canon law.[199] In Rome the theory of St Peter's exclusive power of binding and loosing was promoted by the title *princeps apostolorum*, attributed to St Peter especially by Gregory the Great.[200] Papal letters spoke of 'the *principatus* over all the peoples' held by the Roman church;[201] and this terminology was adopted by the partisans of the papal primacy north of the Alps. Abbo of Fleury, for example, thought of St Peter as 'prince of the whole Church' and 'the key-bearer of the heavenly kingdom' who 'holds the *principatus* of apostolic power'.[202] The reform papacy was particularly anxious to disseminate the idea that 'God gave to St Peter *principaliter* the power of binding and loosing in heaven and on earth'.[203]

194. Nicholas I, *JE* 2796, pp. 477–8: 'ipsa sola Romanorum urbs, apud quam eiusdem apostoli corporalis praesentia sedule veneratur . . . suscepit . . . ac continet in se . . . quod Deus universalem ecclesiam suscipere ac continere praecepit . . . Sane intuendum est, quia et hic vas, in quo omnia genera erant animantium, Petro specialiter ostensum est et, ut ea mactaret et manducaret, illi soli iussum est. Et post resurrectionem, ut rete plenum diversis piscibus ad littus traheret, a Domino ipsi proprie soli praeceptum est.' Cf. Congar 1968a, p. 207.   195. Congar 1968a, pp. 138ff.

196. Haimo of Auxerre, *Homiliae de sanctis* III, *PL* 118, 762D–763A: 'Nec tamen putandum est quod solum beato Petro haec potestas data est, sed sicut unus pro omnibus respondit . . . ita et in uno omnes audierunt "Quocumque ligaveris . . .".'

197. *Relatio episcoporum de poenitentia quam Hludowicus imperator professus est* (833), *MGH Capitularia* 2, 51–2: 'episcoporum quos constat esse vicarios Christi et clavigeros regni caelorum'.

198. *Decretales Pseudo-Isidorianae*, ed. Hinschius 1863, pp. 79, 31.

199. E.g. Ivo of Chartres, *Panormia* V.77; Gratian, *Decretum* D.21 c.2.

200. Cf. Batiffol 1938, pp. 194–5.

201. E.g. John VIII, *JE* 3265, *MGH Epp.* 7, 159: 'quae omnium gentium retinet principatum'.

202. Abbo of Fleury, *Apologeticus*, *PL* 139, 465D: 'princeps est totius ecclesiae'; *Epistola* 5, 423D: 'sicut claviger regni caelestis obtinet principatum apostolici culminis'.

203. Gregory VII, *Registrum* IV.2: 'Deus beato Petro principaliter dedit potestatem ligandi et solvendi in caelo et in terra.'

To anyone sceptical of the principate of St Peter's vicar, the eleventh-century reformers could reply: 'read the edict of the Emperor Constantine, in which he establishes the *principatus* of the apostolic see above all the churches in the world'.[204] This appeal was to the *Constitutum Constantini*, 'the Donation of Constantine', the forged privilege of the early eighth century. The purpose of the *Constitutum* had been to corroborate the papal claim to the Patrimony of St Peter against Byzantine claims to ownership. The forger also developed the monarchical image of the pope, 'more elevated than all the priests in the world and their *princeps*', with power over the Western territories and the right to use the imperial insignia 'in imitation of the empire'.[205] This monarchical conception recurs in ninth-century papal letters: Rome is 'the head of the nations', 'head of the world', 'a priestly and royal city by virtue of the holy see of St Peter'.[206] However, it was the reform papacy of the eleventh century which exploited most fully the monarchical conception of the *Constitutum Constantini*. Leo IX informed the patriarch of Constantinople that 'the most prudent prince Constantine' endowed the papacy with 'the imperial power and dignity', 'thinking it unworthy that they whom the divine majesty has placed in authority over the heavenly empire should be subject to the earthly empire'.[207] The papal *imitatio imperii* encouraged by the Donation of Constantine culminated in the claims of Gregory VII that the pope 'alone can use the imperial insignia';[208] that 'the law of the Roman pontiffs has taken possession of more lands than that of the Roman emperors'; [209] and that faithful allies of the pope desire 'to have only St Peter as their lord and emperor after God'.[210]

---

204. Peter Damian, *Disceptatio synodalis, MGH Libelli* 1, 80: 'lege Constantini imperatoris edictum, ubi sedis apostolicae constituit super omnes in orbe terrarum ecclesias principatum'.

205. *Constitutum Constantini* 12, 13, 16, 17, *MGH Fontes iuris Germanici Antiqui* 10, 83, 85–6, 93: 'celsior et princeps cunctis sacerdotibus totius mundi'. Cf. Fuhrmann 1959, pp. 523ff; Ullmann 1970, pp. 74ff.

206. John VIII, *JE* 3121, p. 74: 'caput nationum . . . caput orbis . . . civitas sacerdotalis et regia per sacram beati Petri sedem'.

207. Leo IX, *Epistola ad Cerullarium*, ed. Will 1861, p. 68: 'prudentissimus terrenae monarchiae princeps Constantinus . . . eidem apostolo in Romana sede pontifices . . . imperiali potestate et dignitate . . . valde indignum fore arbitratus terreno imperio subdi quos divina maiestas praefecit caelesti'. On the authorship of this letter see above, n. 185.

208. Gregory VII, *Registrum* II.55a: *Dictatus papae* 8: 'Quod solus possit uti imperialibus insigniis.' Cf. Schramm 1947, pp. 413–14.

209. Gregory VII, *Registrum* II.75: 'Plus enim terrarum lex Romanorum pontificum quam imperatorum obtinuit.'

210. *Ibid.* III.15: 'beato Petro, quem solummodo dominum et imperatorem post Deum habere desiderant'.

Plenitudo potestatis. The crucial terminology of papal authority derived from a letter of Pope Leo I concerning the status of the papal vicar in Thessalonica: 'you are called to take a share of the responsibilities (*in partem sollicitudinis*), not to have the fullness of power (*plenitudinem potestatis*)'.[211] Pseudo-Isidore extended the formula *in partem sollicitudinis* to all bishops in the exercise of their pastoral duties: the pope 'entrusted to the other churches his duties so that they are called to take a share of the responsibilities, not to have the fullness of power'.[212] This text of Pseudo-Vigilius was to be cited in defence of the papal primacy by the Gregorian canonist Bernold of Constance[213] and by Master Gratian of Bologna.[214] Pseudo-Isidore's interpretation of the relation of papal to episcopal authority was rigorously applied by the Gregorian papacy. Gregory VII declared that a bishop might exercise the *vicem* of the apostolic see at the behest of the pope, but that 'after some time . . . the power and authority ceased and the apostolic see granted her *vicem* to what others she pleased'.[215] It was Bernard of Clairvaux who provided the classic formulation of the papal *plenitudo potestatis*, summarising the Pseudo-Isidorean and Gregorian conceptions. 'According to your canons, some are called to a share of the responsibilities, but you are called to the fullness of power. The power of others is confined within definite limits, but your power extends even over those who have received power over others.'[216] By virtue of his *plena potestas*, the pope can judge any bishop or any of the faithful; he can create bishops, ordain them, give them a worthier see, depose them.[217]

In disseminating the Roman conception of the papal *plenitudo potestatis* throughout Western Christendom the key instrument was the papal legate. Until the Iconoclastic crisis, the popes had kept standing legates (*apocrisarii* or *responsores*) at the imperial court in Constantinople and with the exarch in Ravenna, to represent the interests of the Roman church. After 750 similar functionaries were kept at the Carolingian court.[218] Legates were also

211. Leo I, *Epistola* XIV.1 (*JK* 411), *PL* 54, 671B: 'in partem sis vocatus sollicitudinis, non in plenitudinem potestatis'. Cf. Rivière 1925, pp. 210ff.
212. Pseudo-Vigilius, *Epistola* 7, ed. Hinschius 1863, p. 712: 'reliquis ecclesiis vices suas credidit largiendas, ut in parte sint vocatae sollicitudinis, non in plenitudine potestatis'. This chapter is an interpolation in a genuine letter of Vigilius.   213. Bernold, *Apologeticus* 23, pp. 87–8.
214. Gratian, *Decretum* C.2 q.6 c.11–12. Cf. C.9 q.3 *dictum ante* c.1 (Leo I).
215. Gregory VII, *Registrum* VI.2: 'post aliqua tempora . . . potestas et auctoritas cessavit et suam vicem aliis quibus placuit sedes apostolica concessit'.
216. Bernard, *De consideratione* II.8.16: 'Ergo, iuxta canones tuos, alii in partem sollicitudinis, tu in plenitudinem potestatis vocatus es. Aliorum potestas certis arctatur limitibus: tua extenditur et in ipsos, qui potestatem super alios acceperunt.'
217. E.g. Bernard, *Epistola* CXXXI, CCXXXIX, 286–7, 431–2. Cf. Congar 1955, pp. 85ff.
218. Cf. Feine 1972, p. 327.

employed on missions to the heathen; and a legate like Boniface-Winfrid was also a disseminator of the principle of obedience to the apostolic see.[219] A principal function of the legates of the reform papacy was to secure this same obedience, beginning with Cardinal Humbert's momentous legation to Constantinople in 1054 and continuing with a series of legations to Milan intended to teach that rebellious church that Rome was 'the head of all churches'.[220] The early career of Hildebrand-Gregory VII was principally that of a legate, devoted to promoting the primacy of St Peter. As pope he upheld the principle 'that [the pope's] legate presides over all the bishops in a council even though he is of inferior rank and he can pass sentence of excommunication against them'.[221] This principle, which passed into the Gregorian canonical collections,[222] was a particular source of bitterness in the relations of the reform papacy with the episcopate of Western Europe.[223]

The supremacy of the pope in the *causae fidei* was undisputed in this period. 'The holy Roman, catholic and apostolic church, set above the other churches in matters of the faith', state the *Libri Carolini*, 'must be consulted when a question arises.'[224] Charlemagne's gift to Pope Hadrian I, a decorated Psalter, carried in its dedication the statement that the pope rules the Church by means of dogma.[225] The key *auctoritas* was Luke 22, 32: Christ's promise to Peter that his faith would not fail and his command that Peter should strengthen his brethren. Pseudo-Isidore's statement of the inerrancy of the Roman church – 'in the beginning she took possession of the norm of the apostolic faith' – appears as a comment on Luke 22, 32.[226] This Pseudo-Isidorean definition was cited by the Gregorian canonists and was perhaps also the source of Gregory VII's dictum, 'the Roman church has never erred, nor will she err to all eternity, as Scripture bears witness'.[227] The reform papacy was much preoccupied with the heresy of Berengar of Tours, condemned in Roman synods in 1059 and 1078.[228] Bernold of

219. See above, p. 278.
220. Peter Damian, *Opusculum* v (*Actus Mediolani*), 91CD: 'ipso summo omnium ecclesiarum capite'.
221. Gregory VII, *Registrum* II.55a: *Dictatus papae* 4: 'Quod legatus eius omnibus episcopis praesit in concilio etiam inferioris gradus et adversus eos sententiam depositionis possit dare.'
222. E.g. Anselm of Lucca, *Collectio canonum* 1.25; Deusdedit, *Collectio canonum* 1.206.
223. Cf. Robinson 1978a, pp. 125ff.
224. *Libri Carolini* 1.6, p. 20: 'Quod sancta Romana, catholica et apostolica ecclesia ceteris ecclesiis praelata pro causis fidei, cum quaestio surgit, omnino sit consulenda.'
225. *MGH Poetae* 1, 92: 'Ecclesiamque Dei dogmatis arte regas.'
226. Pseudo-Lucius, *Epistola* 8, ed. Hinschius 1863, p. 179: 'in exordio normam fidei apostolicae percepit'.
227. Gregory VII, *Registrum* II.55a: *Dictatus papae* 22: 'Quod Romana ecclesia numquam erravit nec in perpetuum, scriptura testante, errabit.' Cf. Anselm of Lucca, *Collectio canonum* 1.13, 35; Deusdedit, *Collectio canonum* 1.78. 228. Gregory VII, *Registrum* VI.17a.

Constance, in his polemic against Berengar, saw the main issue as not so much the latter's Eucharistic heresy, as his rebellion against papal authority: 'it is agreed . . . that whoever disagrees with the holy Roman church in the doctrine of the faith, is a heretic'.[229] The growth of popular heresies in the first half of the twelfth century provoked more frequent papal interventions in defence of the faith. Calixtus II at the Council of Toulouse in 1119, Innocent II at the Council of Pisa in 1135, Eugenius III at the Council of Rheims in 1148 condemned heretics and legislated against anti-sacerdotal practices.[230]

As with the definition of the faith, so also with the liturgy: the propagation of the Roman idea of the primacy was accompanied by the dissemination throughout Western Christendom of the Roman (that is, the Romano-Frankish) liturgy. The English synod of Clovesho in 747 ordered liturgical practice 'according to the exemplar which we have from the Roman church', 'according to the custom and rite of the Roman church'.[231] Charlemagne also received an 'exemplar . . . from the Roman church': the *Sacramentarium Gregorianum*, the liturgical book in use in Rome, sent between 784 and 791 by Pope Hadrian I.[232] In the eleventh century the great struggle between Rome and Milan involved a papal attempt to replace the Ambrosian liturgy with the Roman *ordo*.[233] *Micrologus*, the liturgical treatise of Bernold of Constance, is a polemic advocating throughout Christendom the establishment of liturgical correctness 'according to the Roman *ordo*', 'according to Roman authority'.[234] The reforming councils of Gregory VII and his legates sought to enforce this correctness.[235] In Gregory VII's councils likewise the pope began to assert control over the canonisation of saints.[236] 'It is the custom of the Roman church to canonise the saints of God in a general council.' This was the principle stated in the pontificate of Innocent II.[237] However, this principle could still be ignored by Pope Eugenius III in 1146, acting on his

---

229. Bernold, *De veritate corporis et sanguinis Domini*, ed. Weisweiler 1937, pp. 58ff: 'quemlibet hereticum esse constat, quicumque in fidei doctrina sancta Romana ecclesia discordat'.
230. Mansi, *Concilia* 21, 225, 718; *Actus pontificum Cenomannis in urbe degentium*, ed. Busson 1901, pp. 437–8; *Continuatio Sigeberti Chronici* a.1148, *MGH SS* 6, 390.
231. Synod of Clovesho, cap. 13, 15, 16, ed. Haddan and Stubbs 1871, p. 367: 'iuxta exemplar videlicet quod scriptum de Romana habemus ecclesia; quod Romanae ecclesiae consuetudo permittet; iuxta ritum Romanae ecclesiae'.
232. Cf. H. Leclercq, 'Sacrementaires', *Dictionnaire d'archéologie chrétienne et de liturgie*, ed. F. Cabrol and H. Leclerq, Paris, 1924– , vol. xv, p. 247. 233. Cf. Cowdrey 1968, pp. 25ff.
234. Bernold, *Micrologus*, PL 151, 977–1022: 'iuxta Romanum ordinem; secundum Romanam auctoritatem'.
235. E.g. Gregory VII, *Registrum* vi.5b, cap. 8, 13; Synod of Quedlinburg (1085), *MGH SS* 5, 443.
236. Cf. Erdmann 1935, p. 198; Kemp 1948, p. 66.
237. In the case of the canonisation of Godehard of Hildesheim, *MGH SS* 12, 641: 'cum consuetudo sit Romanae ecclesiae in generali concilio sanctos Dei canonizare'.

own authority when requested by the church of Bamberg to canonise the Emperor Henry II: 'although a petition of this kind is usually not admitted except in general councils, nevertheless by virtue of the authority of the holy Roman church, which is the chief support of all councils, we agree to your petitions'.[238]

While the papal authority in respect of the *causae fidei* was generally acknowledged in the West from an early date, the papal judicial authority had more modest origins and developed more gradually. Before the mid-eleventh century the popes not infrequently held provincial councils to deal with the affairs of the Roman church; but these councils were usually attended only by the bishops of suburbican Italy. It was the papal reform movement which changed the character of these councils, just as it reinterpreted the authority of the popes who presided over them. From 1049 onwards, papal synods held at Easter or at the beginning of Lent (later also in the autumn) dealt, not with the concerns of the diocese of Rome, but with the struggle against simony and clerical marriage throughout the West; and these synods were attended by non-Italian bishops.[239] The councils of the reforming popes – culminating in the First Lateran Council of 1123 – were the main forum for Church reform and reforming legislation, in which 'the impious are restrained from their endeavours and the Christian religion is strengthened in that freedom and peace in which it was founded'.[240] The canonical basis of this development was the principle that a council derived its legality from the fact that the pope convoked it. This principle, stated most vigorously by Pope Nicholas I[241] and by Pseudo-Isidore,[242] elaborated the earlier Roman tradition that the pope must *confirm* the decisions of a council.[243] These statements inspired the Gregorian canonists with the theory of papal judicial authority over the Church. 'We read that no councils are valid if they are not supported by apostolic authority . . . For the bishop of that see is judge of the whole Church.'[244]

238. Eugenius III, *JL* 8882, *PL* 180, 1118–19: 'tametsi huiusmodi petitio nisi in generalibus conciliis admitti non soleat, auctoritate tamen sanctae Romanae ecclesiae, quae omnium conciliorum firmamentum est, petitionibus vestris acquiescimus'.   239. Cf. Feine 1972, p. 329.

240. Gregory VII, *Registrum* II.42: 'impii a suis conatibus arceantur et christiana religio in ea, qua primum fundata est, libertate et pace roboretur'.

241. Nicholas I, *JE* 2682, 2691, 2764, 2784, 2796, pp. 433ff, 447ff, 295ff, 389ff, 454ff.

242. Pseudo-Isidore, *Praefatio* 8; Pseudo-Marcellus, *Epistola* I.2, 11.10; Pseudo-Julius, *Epistola* 5, 6, 11, 13; Pseudo-Felix II, *Epistola* 2; Pseudo-Damasus, *Epistola* 9; Pseudo-Pelagius II, *Epistola* I, ed. Hinschius 1863, pp. 19, 224, 228, 459, 465, 471, 479, 503, 721.

243. Cf. Congar 1968a, pp. 133ff.

244. Bernold of Constance, *De excommunicatis vitandis*, *MGH Libelli* 2, 126: 'Nam nulla concilia rata leguntur, quae apostolica auctoritate fulta non fuerint . . . Nam illius sedis episcopus iudex est totius ecclesiae.' Cf. Gregory VII, *Registrum* II.55a, *Dictatus papae* 16; Anselm of Lucca, *Collectio canonum* I.52.

The idea of the pope as *iudex totius ecclesiae* was promoted by a number of other canonical traditions inherited and exploited by the reform papacy. The principle found in the spurious *constitutum* of Pope Silvester I, 'No one will judge the first see',[245] absorbed into the False Decretals[246] and corroborated by Pope Nicholas I,[247] became established in canon law.[248] It was accompanied by the analogous principle that no one may appeal against a papal decision, stated in the fifth century[249] and strongly restated by Nicholas I – 'no one is permitted to judge concerning the judgement of the apostolic see or to retract her sentence'[250] – whose version was readily quoted by the Gregorians.[251] Master Gratian of Bologna summarised the resultant judicial supremacy of the papacy: 'the Roman church alone is able by virtue of her authority to judge concerning all men; but no one is permitted to make judgement concerning her'.[252] The court of this supreme judge must be the supreme court of appeals in the Church; therefore 'the greater causes' (*causae maiores*) must be reserved for the judgement of the pope. This development had been promoted above all by Pseudo-Isidore. In the interests of protecting diocesan bishops from the judicial authority of their metropolitans and of the secular power – his abiding preoccupation – Pseudo-Isidore emphasised the bishops' right of appeal to the apostolic see and the principle that 'the greater questions of the Church must always be referred to the head'.[253] In effect, Pseudo-Isidore extended to the whole episcopate the judicial role which the papacy traditionally exercised only over the suburbican bishops, for whom in the time of Gregory the Great the pope was the metropolitan.[254] The Pseudo-Isidorean insistence on the freedom of appeal and on the referring of the *causae maiores* to Rome was readily absorbed into the conception of the

---

245. *Constitutum Silvestri* (*JK ante* + 174) cap. 27, ed. Coustant 1721, appendix 52A: 'Nemo iudicabit primam sedem.'   246. Pseudo-Silvester I, *Epistola*, ed. Hinschius 1863, p. 449.
247. Nicholas I, *JE* 2796, *MGH Epp.* 6, 466.
248. Gregory VII, *Registrum* II.55a: *Dictatus papae* 19; *Collectio in LXXIV titulos* 8; Anselm of Lucca, *Collectio canonum* 1.19; Ivo of Chartres, *Panormia* IV.5; Gratian, *Decretum* C.9 q.3 c.13.
249. Boniface I, *JK* 365, *PL* 20, 779ff; Gelasius I, *Epistola* XXVI.2 (*JK* 664), *ibid.* 59, 61ff.
250. Nicholas I, *JE* 2879, p. 606: 'nemini sit de sedis apostolicae iudicio iudicare aut illius sententiam retractare permissum'.
251. Gregory VII, *Registrum* II.55a: *Dictatus papae* 18; *Collectio in LXXIV titulos* 17; Anselm of Lucca, *Collectio canonum* 1.21. Cf. Gratian, *Decretum* C.17. q.4, c.30.
252. Gratian, *Decretum* C.9 q.3 *dictum post* c.9: 'Sola enim Romana ecclesia sua auctoritate valet de omnibus iudicare; de ea vero nulli iudicare permittitur.'
253. Pseudo-Vigilius, *Epistola* 7, ed. Hinschius 1863, p. 712: 'maiores ecclesiarum quaestiones quasi ad caput semper referendae sunt'.
254. E.g. Pseudo-Anacletus, *Epistola* 1.17; III.34; Pseudo-Eleutherius, *Epistola* 2; Pseudo-Zepherinus, *Epistola* 6; Pseudo-Melchiades, *Epistola* 3, ed. Hinschius 1863, pp. 74, 84, 125, 132, 243.

Gregorians[255] and of Master Gratian[256] of the pope as supreme judge of the Church. In particular the pope was the only judge of bishops. This principle had again been developed by Pseudo-Isidore as a safeguard for the episcopate;[257] and it was transformed by the reform papacy into an aspect of the papal magistracy over the Church. The fact 'that [the pope] alone can depose or reconcile bishops'[258] confirmed the Gregorian opinion that bishops, 'called to take a share of the responsibilities, not to have the fullness of power', were agents of the papacy, owing obedience to the pope.[259]

This concentration of judicial authority in the papacy meant in effect that papal authority in relation to the law was different in kind from that of other bishops. Master Gratian expressed this by comparing the universal judicial authority of the Roman church (which 'alone is able by virtue of her authority to judge concerning all men') with the limited authority of the metropolitan, who may not intervene in the diocesan affairs of his suffragan without seeking the latter's advice.[260] The pope is not bound by laws because he makes the laws. This principle had gradually developed against the grain of tradition. For, according to the formula of the mid-seventh century *Liber Diurnus*, a newly elected pope must swear 'to diminish or change nothing of the tradition of my most virtuous predecessors nor to admit any novelty'.[261] However, Pope Nicholas I suggested an amendment of this inflexible rule: 'we do not deny that the judgement of this [Roman] see can be changed for the better'.[262] This concession was seized upon by the Gregorian canonist Bonizo of Sutri as a statement of the pope's legislative power: 'as the blessed Nicholas . . . says, it was lawful and always will be lawful for Roman pontiffs to make new canons and to change old ones, according to the needs of the times'.[263] Gregorian scholars were convinced that the papal primacy included the right to 'order the churches of the whole world not only with the ancient regulations (*instituta*) but also

255. Gregory VII, *Registrum* II.55a: *Dictatus papae* 20–1; *Collectio in LXXIV titulos* 10–12; Anselm of Lucca, *Collectio canonum* I.9, 24; II.16, 18.
256. Gratian, *Decretum* C.2 q.6 *dictum ante* c.1, *dictum post* c.10.
257. E.g. Pseudo-Anacletus, *Epistola* 1.17, ed. Hinschius 1863, p. 74.
258. Gregory VII, *Registrum* II.55a: *Dictatus papae* 3: 'Quod ille solus possit deponere episcopos vel reconciliare'. Cf. no. 25.   259. Cf. Robinson 1978a, pp. 109ff.
260. Gratian, *Decretum* C.9 q.3 *dictum post* c.9; C.9 q.3 c.8 (rubric).
261. *Liber Diurnus Romanorum Pontificum. Ex unico codice Vaticano* ed. T. von Sickel (Österreichische Akademie der Wissenschaften, Vienna, 1889), p. 92: 'Nihil de traditione quae a probatissimis praedecessoribus meis servatum repperi, diminuere vel mutare aut aliquam novitatem admittere.'
262. Nicholas I, *JE* 2796, p. 481: 'non negamus eiusdem sedis sententiam posse in melius commutari'.
263. Bonizo, *Liber de vita christiana* 1.44, ed. Perels 1930, p. 33: 'ut enim beatus Nicolaus . . . ait, licuit semperque licebit Romanis pontificibus novos canones cudere et veteres pro consideratione temporum immutare'.

with new ones'.[264] This legislative authority incorporated the power of _dispensatio_: 'since the pontiffs of this see made the canons, it belongs to them to moderate them by a useful dispensation, if necessity impels'.[265] The pope also possessed the power to cancel existing privileges.[266] Hence, from the pontificate of Celestine II (1143–4) onwards, the papal curia issued privileges with the clause 'saving the authority of the apostolic see'.[267]

Master Gratian summed up the ideological progress of the late eleventh and early twelfth centuries. 'The holy Roman church confers right and authority on the sacred canons, but she herself is not bound by them, because she has the right of making the canons.'[268] The papacy had outgrown the profession of faith of the _Liber Diurnus_: 'to diminish or change nothing of the tradition of my most virtuous predecessors nor to admit any _novitas_'. The limited role of defender of Christian tradition was inappropriate to an institution on which had been thrust the urgent task of reforming the Church. It was 'far better to re-establish divine justice by means of new counsels, than to allow the souls of men to perish along with the laws which they have neglected'.[269] As Bernard of Clairvaux told Pope Eugenius III, the canons were the pope's.[270] The pope was not only the guardian of Christian _ius_, he was the maker of _ius_, creating 'the pattern of righteous living' for Christian society.

Regnum _and_ sacerdotium

Duo sunt

The political theology of the Middle Ages was dominated by a single _sententia_, the passage of the letter of Pope Gelasius I to the Emperor Anastasius I of 494, in which he wrote:

The world is chiefly governed by these two: the sacred authority of bishops and the royal power. Of these the burden of the priests is greater in so far as they will answer

---

264. Bernold of Constance, _Apologeticus_ 21, p. 86: 'ut totius mundi ecclesias non solum antiquis institutis sed etiam novis disponat'.
265. Calixtus II (1123), according to Hugo Cantor, _History of the Four Archbishops of York_, in _The Historians of the Church of York and its Archbishops_, vol. II, ed. J. Raine (Rerum Britannicarum medii aevi Scriptores: Rolls Series, London, 1886), p. 203: 'quoniam sedis huius pontifices canones fecerunt et ipsorum est eos urgente necessitate vel utili dispensatione moderari'. Cf. Bernold, _De excommunicatis vitandis_, pp. 116–17; Gratian, _Decretum_ D.14 c.2.
266. Gregory VII, _Registrum_ VI.2.
267. Cf. Feine 1972, p. 333: 'salva sedis apostolicae auctoritate'.
268. Gratian, _Decretum_ C.25 q.1 _dictum post_ c.16: 'Sacrosancta Romana ecclesia ius et auctoritatem sacris canonibus impertit, sed non eis alligatur. Habet enim ius condendi canones.'
269. Gregory VII, _Registrum_ II.45: 'melius nobis videtur iustitiam Dei vel novis reaedificare consiliis, quam animas hominum una cum legibus deperire neglectis'.
270. Bernard, _De consideratione_ II.8.16.

to the Lord for the kings of men themselves at the divine judgement. For you know, most merciful son, that although you rule over the human race in dignity, you nevertheless devoutly bow the neck to those who are placed in charge of religious matters and seek from them the means of your salvation; and you understand that, according to the order of religion, in what concerns the receiving and correct administering of the heavenly sacraments you must be subject rather than in command.[271]

According to Gelasius I, the emperor is subject to the bishops for the *res divinae* – matters touching his salvation; but this does not mean that the imperial *potestas* is subject to the episcopal *auctoritas* in other matters.[272] Zealous though he was for the freedom of the Church from secular control, Gelasius' definition of the relations of *imperium* and *sacerdotium* reflects the situation of the patristic age. The *auctoritas pontificum* and *regalis potestas* comprised a duality, divinely ordained to govern the world side by side. It was the emperor's task to 'rule over the human race'; but in matters of the faith he must regard himself as a faithful son of the Church. Gelasius emphasised the distinctness of the functions of the two powers in a statement of 496: 'Christ . . . separated the offices of both powers according to their proper activities and their special dignities . . . so that Christian emperors would have need of bishops in order to attain eternal life and bishops would have recourse to imperial direction in the conduct of temporal affairs.'[273]

Transmitted in the authoritative canonical collections of the *Quesnelliana* and the *Hadriana*,[274] the Gelasian sentence *Duo sunt* communicated to the Carolingian age the idea of a single Christian society governed by two powers with different roles. Alcuin faithfully echoed this doctrine. 'The secular and the spiritual power are separated; the former bears the sword of death in its hand, the latter bears the key of life in its tongue', he wrote to Archbishop Aethelheard of Canterbury in 793, teaching him how to face the persecution inflicted by the Vikings. 'Secular

271. Gelasius I, *Epistola* XII (*JK* 632), ed. Thiel 1868, p. 350: 'Duo quippe sunt . . . quibus principaliter mundus hic regitur: auctoritas sacra [sacrata] pontificum et regalis potestas. In quibus tanto gravius est pondus sacerdotum, quanto etiam pro ipsis regibus [hominum] Domino in divino reddituri sunt examine rationem. Nosti etenim, fili clementissime, quod licet praesideas humano generi dignitate, rerum tamen praesulibus divinarum devotus colla submittis, atque ab eis causas tuae salutis expetis [exspectas], inque sumendis caelestibus sacramentis, eisque, ut competit, disponendis, subdi te debere cognoscis religionis ordine potius quam praeesse.' On the influence of this *sententia* see Knabe 1936.
272. Cf. Ziegler 1941–2, pp. 412ff; Ensslin 1955, pp. 661ff; Martini 1963, pp. 7ff; Ullmann 1981, pp. 198ff.
273. Gelasius I, *Tractatus* IV.11, ed. Thiel 1868, p. 567: 'Christus . . . actionibus propriis dignitatibusque distinctis officia potestatis utriusque discrevit, ut et christiani imperatores pro aeterna vita pontificibus indigerent et pontifices pro temporalium cursu rerum imperialibus dispositionibus uterentur.'   274. Maassen 1870, p. 280.

men are your defenders, you are their intercessors, so that there may be one flock under one God, with Christ as their shepherd.'[275] Alcuin repeated this teaching to the same correspondent nine years later. 'The priestly and the royal power are divided. The former bears in its tongue the key of the heavenly kingdom, the latter bears the sword of revenge upon evildoers.'[276] The strict separation of the royal and the sacerdotal power is a frequent theme among Carolingian authors. The *Life* of Abbot Wala of Corbie (perhaps by Paschasius Radbert), attributed to Wala a defence of the freedom of ecclesiastical property from secular encroachment, in which Church and *regnum* are presented as two independent *res publicae*. 'Let the king have the *res publica*, so that he may freely dispose of its resources to his army; and let Christ have the property of the churches, as another *res publica*, committed to his faithful ministers, at the disposal of all the needy and of those who serve him.'[277] Hincmar of Rheims likewise asserted the autonomous character of the *ordo ecclesiasticus* and 'the *res publica* which belongs to kings',[278] his writings offering the most extensive Carolingian commentary on Gelasius' dualism.[279]

The happy union and co-operation of the two independent powers is the constant theme of the public records of the Carolingians.[280] 'I desire an inviolable treaty of faith and charity with your blessedness', wrote Charlemagne to Pope Leo III in 796;[281] while his capitularies commanded: 'the bishops are to stand by the counts and the counts to stand by the bishops, so that both may perform their duties fully'.[282] In the troubled reign of Charlemagne's successor, Louis the Pious, the tone of the capitularies becomes more urgent: 'the bishops and the counts are to live together in harmony . . . and they are to give each other help in the performance of

---

275. Alcuin, *Epistola* XVII, *MGH Epp.* 4, 48: 'Divisa est potestas saecularis et potestas spiritalis: illa portat gladium mortis in manu, haec clavem vitae in lingua . . . Illi sint, id est saeculares, defensores vestri, vos intercessores illorum; ut sit unus grex sub uno Deo, Christo pastore.'

276. *Ibid.* CCLV, p. 413: 'Divisa est sacerdotalis atque regalis potentia. Illa portat clavem in lingua caelestis regni, iste gladium ad vindictam reorum.'

277. *Vita Walae abbatis Corbeiensis* II.2, *MGH SS* 2, 548: 'Habeat igitur rex rempublicam libere in usibus militiae suae ad dispensandum, habeat et Christus res ecclesiarum, quasi alteram rempublicam, omnium indigentium et sibi servientium usibus, suis commissam ministris fidelibus.'

278. Hincmar, *Epistola* XXVII, *PL* 126, 181A: 'sui antecessores ecclesiasticum ordinem quod suum est, et non rempublicam quod regum est, disposuerunt'.

279. E.g. *De divortio Lotharii et Tetbergae, quaestio* 7, *PL* 125, 769C; *De fide Carolo regi servanda* 39, *ibid.*, 982C; *Admonitio ad episcopos regni* 1, *ibid.*, 1007C; *Pro Ecclesiae libertatum defensione, ibid.*, 1049A. See below, p. 297.   280. Cf. Eichmann 1909, pp. 6ff; Eichmann 1912, pp. 50ff.

281. Alcuin, *Epistola* 93, p. 137: 'cum beatitudine vestra eiusdem fidei et caritatis inviolabile foedus statuere desidero'.

282. *Capitulare Baiwaricum* (810?) cap. 4, *MGH Cap.* 1, 158: 'Ut episcopi cum comitibus stent et comites cum episcopis, ut uterque pleniter suum ministerium peragere possint.'

their duties. We say again to all, that they must live in charity and peace together.'[283] Church councils echoed the commands of the secular legislation. 'Let there be harmony everywhere and agreement between kings and bishops, churchmen and laymen and all the Christian people, so that there may be unity everywhere in the churches of God and lasting peace in one Church, one faith, hope and charity, having one head who is Christ, whose members must help each other and love each other in mutual charity.'[284]

The Gelasian definition of the functions of the two powers continued to be cited by tenth-century authors, again emphasising the co-operation of *regnum* and *sacerdotium*. Leo, bishop of Vercelli – who liked to call himself 'bishop of the empire'[285] – assured Pope Gregory V in 998 that the co-operation of pope and emperor would restore the Roman church to her ancient probity and renew the empire of the Romans.[286] Ottonian authors stressed this theme of partnership: the Carolingian theme of the separation of the two powers they could not assert with conviction. For the Ottonian kings greatly increased the administrative and military duties of their bishops and treated their clergy in much the same manner as their faithful lay followers.[287] The Ottonian episcopate became a 'royal priesthood' (*regale sacerdotium*), possessing 'both priestly religion and royal strength',[288] yet exercising both at the nod of the king who had invested them with their pastoral staff, saying, 'Receive the church.'[289] The 'Ottonian system' needed to be defended against criticisms that it departed from the Gelasian ideal. 'Perhaps some men, ignorant of the divine dispensation, may ask why a bishop should handle the government of the people or face the dangers of war, when he has received only the cure of souls . . . But it was neither new nor unusual for the rulers of the holy Church of God to possess the

283. *Admonitio ad omnes regni ordines* (823–5), cap. 12–13, *ibid.*, p. 305: 'Episcopi vero vel comites ad invicem . . . concorditer vivant et ad sua ministeria peragenda vicissim sibi adiutorium ferant. Omnibus etiam generaliter dicimus et caritatem ut pacem ad invicem habeatis.'
284. *Synodus quae facta est in Anglorum Saxonia* (786) cap. 14, in *Alcuini Epistolae* 3, p. 25: 'Sic concordia ubique et unanimitas inter reges et episcopos, ecclesiasticos et laicos, omnemque populum christianum, ut sit unitas ubique ecclesiarum Dei et pax in una ecclesia, in una fide, spe et caritate permanens, unum caput habens quod est Christus, cuius membra se invicem adiuvare, mutuaque caritate diligere debeant.' Cf. *Constitutiones Odonis* 8 (941–6), in *Councils and Synods* 1, 73.
285. In a diploma of April 1001: see Manitius 1923, vol. II, pp. 514, 516.
286. Leo of Vercelli, *Rhythmus de Gregorio papa et Ottone augusto*, MGH *Poetae* 5, 477ff.
287. Cf. Fleckenstein 1966.
288. Ruotger, *Vita sancti Brunonis archiepiscopi Coloniensis* 20, in *Lebensbeschreibungen einiger Bischöfe* 1973, p. 206: 'In te namque et sacerdotalis religio et regia pollet fortitudo.'
289. Peter Damian, *Epistolae* I.13, 221A: 'Accipe ecclesiam.'

government of this world.'[290] The eleventh-century reformers regarded as traitors to the cause of *libertas ecclesiae* those bishops who 'prostitute themselves obscenely in the service of secular rulers, like slaves'[291] and recalled them to the Gelasian model of ecclesiastical independence.[292] Their opponents claimed in turn to be following the true Gelasian model of co-operation between the two powers.[293]

Concerning certain fundamental functions of the two powers, however, intellectuals were always in agreement. The definition given by Paulinus of Aquileia at the Council of Frankfurt in 794 continued to be valid. 'We must beseech our most tranquil prince to fight for us against visible enemies for the love of Christ and with the Lord's help and let us fight for him with spiritual arms against invisible enemies, praying for the Lord's power.'[294] This division of labour was the theme of Charlemagne's famous letter to Pope Leo III on his election in 796. The king's duty was 'to defend holy Church outwardly from the attack of pagans and from devastation by the arms of infidels and to fortify her inwardly through [the enforcement of] the acceptance of the catholic faith'. The pope's duty was 'to raise your hands to God like Moses [Exod. 17:11–12] . . . so that the Christian people may always have the victory everywhere'.[295] Carolingian and Ottonian liturgical texts contained appropriate prayers 'for our most Christian emperor, that God may make all the barbarian nations subject to him, for our perpetual peace'[296] – a standing reproach to any emperor who neglected his duty.[297]

This duty consisted of *dilatatio* and *defensio*, the propagation and the

---

290. Ruotger, *Vita Brunonis* 23, p. 212: 'Causantur forte aliqui divinae dispensationis ignari, quare episcopus rem populi et pericula belli tractaverit, cum animarum tantummodo curam susceperit. . . . Nec vero nova fuit huius mundi gubernatio aut sanctae Dei ecclesiae rectoribus antea inusitata.'

291. Peter Damian, *Opusculum* XXII (*Contra clericos aulicos*), PL 145, 463B: 'in clientelam potentium tanquam servos se dediticios obscoene substernunt'.

292. E.g. Peter Damian, *Epistolae* III.6, IV.9, VII.3, PL 144, 294C, 314D, 440AB; *Disceptatio synodalis*, MGH *Libelli* 1, 93.

293. E.g. Henry IV, *Epistola* 13, MGH *Kritische Studientexte* 1, 19; *Liber de unitate ecclesiae conservanda*, MGH *Libelli* 2, 230–1, 248.

294. *Concilium Francofurtense* (794): *Libellus sacrosyllabus episcoporum Italiae*, MGH *Conc.* 2, 142: 'Unde supplicandus est tranquillissimus princeps noster, ut ille pro nobis contra visibiles hostes pro Christi amore Domino opitulante dimicet, et nos pro illo contra invisibiles hostes, Domini imprecantes potentiam, spiritalibus armis pugnemus.'

295. Alcuin, *Epistola* 93, pp. 137–8: 'elevatis ad Deum cum Moyse manibus . . . quatenus . . . populus christianus . . . ubique semper habeat victoriam'.

296. Mohlberg and Baumstark 1927, p. 24: 'Oremus et pro christianissimo imperatore nostro, ut Deus et Dominus noster subdita illi faciat omnes barbaras nationes ad nostram perpetuam pacem.' Cf. Erdmann 1932, pp. 129ff.

297. E.g. Agobard of Lyons, *Apologeticus pro filiis Ludovici*, MGH SS 15.1, 275–6.

defence of the faith. The imperial mission of extending the boundaries of Christendom had been defined by St Augustine and St Gregory. War was to be waged 'for the sake of enlarging the *res publica* within which we see God worshipped . . . so that the name of Christ will travel among the subject peoples through the preaching of the faith'.[298] Charlemagne fulfilled this duty by his victories over the Saxons and the Avars;[299] the Ottonians by their wars against the Slavs on their frontier. Hence Otto III was acclaimed in the intitulatio of a diploma of 1001 (written by Leo of Vercelli) as 'most devout and most faithful *dilatator* of holy churches'.[300] His successor, Emperor Henry II, was reminded of his duty by Bruno of Querfurt, the missionary to the Slavs (and martyr) in 1008. 'Is it not a great honour and a great source of salvation for a king to expand the Church and win the name of apostle before God; to labour for the baptism of the pagan and to give peace to the Christians who help you in this enterprise?'[301] A generation later in 1044/5 Abbot Bern of Reichenau applauded the conduct of King Henry III of Germany, 'most glorious propagator of the orthodox faith', who gave thanks for a victory barefoot, intoning the Kyrie.[302] Holy wars were the characteristic business of kings and emperors until the intellectual revolution of the Investiture Contest. Then polemicists would apply the term 'just war' to rebellion against the divinely ordained ruler of the Christian empire: 'a *iustum bellum*, as against the barbarian enemy and an oppressor of Christianity';[303] and the papacy would claim the direction of holy wars *ad Dei cultum dilatandum*. The most famous medieval crusading epic, the Oxford text of *The Song of Roland*, is concerned with the holy war of Emperor Charlemagne in Spain. The poet still conceived of holy war in the traditional manner as an imperial duty; but his poem is full of topical references to the First Crusade, the alternative holy war initiated by Pope Urban II in 1095.[304]

298. Gregory I, *Registrum* 1.73: 'dilatandae causa rei publicae, in qua Deum coli conspicimus'. Cf. Erdmann 1935, pp. 5ff. See also Augustine, *De civitate Dei* v.24: 'ad Dei cultum maxime dilatandum'.

299. Alcuin, *Epistola* cx, p. 157: 'christianitatis regnum atque agnitionem veri Dei dilatavit'; *Epistola* ccii, p. 336: 'armis imperium christianum fortiter dilatare'.

300. *Diplomata Ottonis III* 388 (18 January 1001), *MGH Diplomata* 2, 818: 'sanctarumque ecclesiarum devotissimus et fidelissimus dilatator.' Cf. Schramm 1929, vol. I, p. 157.

301. Von Giesebrecht 1881, 2, 702ff: 'Nonne magnus honor magnaque salus regis esset, ut ecclesiam augeret et apostolicum nomen coram Deo inveniret, hoc laborare, ut baptizaretur paganus, pacemque donare adiuvantibus se ad hoc christianis?' Cf. Kahl 1955, pp. 161ff, 360ff.

302. Franz-Josef Schmale (ed.), *Die Briefe des Abtes Bern von Reichenau* (Veröffentlichungen der Kommission für geschichtliche Landeskunde. Reihe A: Quellen, 6), Kohlhammer, 1961, no. 27.

303. Lampert of Hersfeld, *Annales* a.1073, *MGH SS rerum germanicarum in usum scholarum* 38, 152: 'quasi cum barbaro hoste et christiani nominis oppressore iustum . . . bellum'.

304. Cf. le Gentil 1969, pp. 16ff.

Closely linked with the duty of *dilatatio* was the imperial duty to defend the Church. *Defensio* was the crucial factor which in the early Middle Ages could make a royal or imperial dynasty out of a parvenu warrior family. It was through their defence of *regnum* and *sacerdotium* that first the Arnulfings and later the Liudolfings became kings, and through their defence of the papacy that they became emperors. The title *defensor ecclesiae* is attributed to Charlemagne in his earliest capitularies: 'ruler of the kingdom of the Franks and devout defender of holy Church and her helper in all things'.[305] Charlemagne inherited this function of 'defender of the Church' from his Arnulfing predecessors, under whose *patrocinium* the English missionaries evangelised Frisia, Hessen and Thuringia,[306] and who convoked synods to determine 'how the law of God and ecclesiastical religion might be revived'.[307] It was the Arnulfings' role as defenders of the Frankish Church which recommended them to the papacy.[308] In Rome, however, the term *defensor ecclesiae* had a more specific meaning than in Francia: it denoted an imperial officer detailed to protect the pope and subject to his orders.[309] In the collection of letters concerning papal–Arnulfing relations preserved in the *Codex Carolinus*, the popes are found exhorting the Arnulfing warlords to assume the duties of the Roman *defensor ecclesiae*. The traditional papal protector, the Byzantine emperor, had ceased to be a 'true Christian emperor' by his adoption of the policy of iconoclasm and had shown contempt for the Gelasian duality by meddling with dogma, 'which does not belong to emperors but to pontiffs'.[310] The break with Constantinople was corroborated (and backdated more than four centuries) by the forging of the *Constitutum Constantini* (Donation of Constantine). A radical version of the Gelasian separation of the two powers was envisaged in Constantine's fictitious reason for removing his capital from Rome. 'Where the chief of priests and the head of the Christian religion has been established by the heavenly emperor, it is not right that there the earthly emperor should exercise power.'[311] To make good the Italian territorial claims contained in

---

305. *Karoli Magni Capitulare primum* (769), *MGH Capitularia* 1, 44: 'regnique Francorum rector et devotus sanctae ecclesiae defensor atque adiutor in omnibus'. Cf. *Admonitio generalis* (789), *ibid.*, p. 53.

306. Boniface, *Epistola* LXIII, *MGH Epp.* 3, 329: 'patrocinio principis Francorum'. Cf. *ibid.* LVII, p. 313.

307. *Karlmanni principis Capitulare* (742), *MGH Cap.* 1, 25: 'quomodo lex Dei et ecclesiastica religio recuperetur'.

308. *Codex Carolinus* 3, Zacharias *JE* 2277, *MGH Epp.* 3, 479.

309. Fischer 1934, pp. 443ff; Ullmann 1970, pp. 69–70; Richards 1979, pp. 292ff.

310. Gregory II, *JE* 2180, in Caspar 1933, p. 86. Latin translation, *PL* 89, 518A: 'Scis, imperator, sanctae Ecclesiae dogmata non imperatorum esse, sed pontificum.'

311. *Constitutum Constantini* 18, pp. 94–5: 'ubi principatus sacerdotum et christianae religionis caput ab imperatore caelesti constitutum est, iustum non est, ut illic imperator terrenus habeat potestatem'.

the *Constitutum* and to defend Rome against the Lombards, the papacy sought a secular power more docile than the Byzantine emperor. The Arnulfing warlord Pippin III was raised from *subregulus*[312] to king of the Franks by papal advice – by papal *command*, according to the Arnulfing family chronicle[313] – and consecrated by Pope Stephen II in 754 'after [the letter] received from King Pippin the promise of defence for the Roman church'.[314] The title of *patricius Romanorum* which was now conferred on the king accentuated the obligation to defend the pope.[315]

The theme of *defensio* is equally prominent in the account of the imperial coronation of Charlemagne in 800 given in the official biography of Pope Leo III. 'All the faithful Romans, seeing how great was the defence which he gave and the love which he bore the holy Roman church and her vicar, cried out unanimously . . .: "Life and victory to Charles, most pious Augustus, crowned by God, great and peaceable emperor!" . . . and all designated him emperor of the Romans.'[316] The papal biographer believed that the *patricius Romanorum* had been transformed into an *imperator Romanorum*:[317] a promotion which he owed to his loyalty and effectiveness as defender of the pope. On the occasion of the imperial coronation of Louis the Pious performed by Pope Stephen IV in Rheims in 816, the emperor promised to 'defend the cause of St Peter . . . as [his] own'.[318] The papal theory that the imperial coronation was a constitutive act, intended to create a papal defender, was repeatedly exemplified in the emperor-making of the later ninth and early tenth centuries. The pope 'elected and constituted [the emperor] by holy unction . . . to be a protector and defender'.[319] The papal choice must promote 'the honour and the exaltation of the holy Roman church and the security of the Christian people':[320] the successful imperial

312. *Codex Carolinus* 1, 2 (Gregory III to Charles Martel, 739–40), pp. 476ff.
313. *Annales regni Francorum* a.749, *MGH SS* 1, 136.
314. *Annales regni Francorum*, revised version, a.754, p. 139: 'postquam a rege Pippino ecclesiae Romanae defensionis firmitatem accepit'.
315. Ullmann 1970, pp. 66ff.; Schramm 1929, vol. 1, pp. 59ff.
316. *Le Liber pontificalis*, ed. L. Duchesne, 2 vols., 2nd series, Bibliothèque des Ecoles Françaises d'Athènes et de Rome, 1886–92, vol. II, p. 7: 'Tunc universi fideles Romani videntes tanta defensione et dilectione quam erga sanctam Romanam ecclesiam et eius vicarium habuit, unanimiter . . . exclamaverunt: Karolo, piissimo Augusto, a Deo coronato, magno et pacifico imperatori, vita et victoria! . . . et ab omnibus constitutus est imperator Romanorum.'
317. For this title see Classen 1965, pp. 587ff.
318. Paschal I, *JE* 2550 (to Louis the Pious, c. 818), *MGH Epp.* 5, 68: 'causas sancti Petri . . . velut proprias defende'.
319. *Synodus Pontigonensis* (876), *MGH Cap.* 2, 348: 'elegit atque sacra unctione constituit . . . domnum imperatorem . . . sibi protectorem ac defensorem esse'.
320. John VIII, *JE* 3019 (fragment), *MGH Epp.* 7, 311: 'ad honorem et exaltationem sanctae Romanae ecclesiae et ad securitatem populi christiani'.

candidate must be 'an unconquered protector, a powerful defender and strenuous helper . . . of the Church in all its needs'.[321] It was in accordance with this theory that Pope John XII, threatened by the *tyrannis* of the Italian princes, called in 960 for the aid of the German king, Otto I, in language similar to that in which the eighth-century popes had appealed to the Arnulfings.[322] John 'received him [in Rome] with paternal affection and anointed him emperor with the blessing of St Peter, for the sake of the defence of the holy Church of God'.[323]

The imperial coronation of Otto I in 962, however, ushered in a century of imperial domination (albeit intermittent) over the papacy. The flaw in the papal theory of the relations of *papatus* and *imperium* was that no pope could ever find an emperor who would accept the subordinate role devised for him. An imperial candidate anxious to be crowned by the pope might imitate the subservient conduct attributed to the emperor in the Donation of Constantine:[324] once crowned, he could prove a tyrant.[325] An emperor chosen to be the defender of Rome might fulfil this function for political motives quite distinct from the papal ideology of *defensio*. It appears, for example, from the will of Charlemagne that the great *defensor ecclesiae* thought of Rome simply as the first metropolitan see of his empire, no different in kind from the rest.[326] The conduct of the Ottonians suggests a similar attitude. Otto I made subject to himself the lands which the pope regarded as belonging to the Roman church.[327] When John XII repented of his emperor-making, Otto I had him deposed. The polemical historian Liutprand of Cremona represents the emperor as demanding from the Romans an oath 'that they would never elect or ordain a pope without the consent and election of the lord emperor Otto'.[328] The extant version of

---

321. John VIII, *JE* 3093, p. 46: 'patronum invictum, defensorem potentem et strenuum adiutorem . . . in omnibus ecclesiasticis utilitatibus'.

322. Cf. Liutprand of Cremona, *De rebus gestis Ottonis* in *Liudprandi Opera, MGH SS rerum Germanicarum in usum scholarum* 41, p. 159.

323. John XII, *JL* 3690, *PL* 133, 1028B: 'quem paterno affectu suscipientes ob defensionem sanctae Dei Ecclesiae in imperatorem cum beati Petri benedictione unximus'. Cf. Erdmann 1951, p. 44 n.1.

324. The *officium stratoris* (*Constitutum Constantini* 16, p. 92) was performed by King Pippin III (*Liber pontificalis* 1, 447) and by Emperor Louis II (*ibid.* 2, 152). For a later example, see *Urbani II et Conradi regis conventus* (1095), *MGH Const.* 1, 564.

325. E.g. *Annales Bertiniani* a.864, *MGH SS rerum Germanicarum in usum scholarum* 67–8.

326. Einhard, *Vita Karoli Magni* cap. 33, *ibid.*, pp. 38–9.

327. Liutprand, *De rebus gestis Ottonis*, in *Liutprandi Opera, MGH SS rerum Germanicarum in usum scholarum* 41, p. 164.

328. *Ibid.*: 'firmiter iurantes, numquam se papam electuros aut ordinaturos praeter consensum et electionem domni imperatoris Ottonis'.

Otto's compact of 962 with the papacy, the *Ottonianum* – a falsification in the imperial interest[329] – required an oath of the pope elect to the imperial envoys before his consecration.

The idea of an Ottonian protectorate over the Roman church was given its clearest expression in the diploma which Otto III issued for Silvester II, the pope whom he had 'elected . . . ordained and created'. In this diploma of January 1001 the emperor dismissed the Donation of Constantine as a fabrication and 'from our own liberality we give to St Peter that which is ours, not what is his', the eight counties of the Pentapolis.[330] The emperor, 'servant of the apostles', 'created' the pope and endowed him *ex nostra liberalitate*. This diploma was drafted by Leo of Vercelli, who had written to Pope Gregory V that the papal duty was to cleanse the world *under* the power of Caesar.[331] A similar idea of an imperial protectorate over the Roman church preoccupied the clerical supporters of the Salian emperors Henry III and Henry IV. 'The pope is consecrated at the command of Caesar.' 'It belongs to your imperial power . . . to govern this holy apostolic church with the arm of defence, so that it suffers no harm.'[332] *Defensio* entailed, in the emperor's view, not the submissive service of the papal ideology, but *gubernatio*. The *defensor* of the pope was also his *creator*, the Salians basing their right to appoint the pope on their office of *patricius*[333] – that title which in the eighth-century papal ideology had denoted an officer of the pope, dedicated to his defence.

Critics of the secular domination of the Church and imperial hegemony over the Roman church had always taken as the starting-point of their criticism the clause of Gelasius I's letter to Anastasius which stated that the *pondus* of the priests was greater than that of secular rulers. The commentary of Hincmar of Rheims on this clause illustrates ninth-century reforming opinion.

The dignity of pontiffs is greater than that of kings, in that kings are consecrated to the summit of royalty by pontiffs, but pontiffs cannot be consecrated by kings: the charge of kings in human affairs is weightier than that of priests, in that the King of

---

329. Cf. Ullmann 1953, pp. 114ff.
330. *Diplomata Ottonis III* 389, p. 820: 'nostra liberalitate sancto Petro donamus quae nostra sunt, non sibi quae sua sunt'. Cf. Schramm 1929, vol. I, pp. 161ff.
331. Leo of Vercelli, *Rhythmus de Gregorio et Ottone augusto*; Schramm 1929, vol. I, pp. 119ff.
332. Benzo of Alba, *Libri ad Heinricum IV* VI.6, VII.2, *MGH SS* 11, 666, 671: 'Caesare praecipiente, papa benedicitur . . . Pertinet quippe ad vestram imperialem potentiam . . . hanc sanctam apostolicam ecclesiam, ne in aliquo detrimentum patiatur, brachio defensionis gubernare.'
333. Cf. Vollrath 1974, pp. 11ff.

kings has laid upon them the duty of promulgating laws and fighting for the honour, defence and peace of holy Church.[334]

The *sacerdotium* possessed a *dignitas*: a *cura* was imposed on the *regnum* for the sake of the Church and at the behest of her bishops. This was the teaching of the Frankish bishops who imposed a penance on Louis the Pious at the Council of Attigny in 822 and of the bishops at the Council of Paris in 829, whose description of the royal *ministerium* and the *sacerdotalis auctoritas* was again an extended gloss on the Gelasian sentence.[335] It was likewise the teaching of the bishops at Savonnières in 859. 'Bishops, according to their ministry and their sacred authority, are to be united and by mutual aid and counsel are to rule and correct kings, the magnates of their kingdoms and the people committed to them.'[336]

Such a view of the relations of the two powers occurs also in the Pseudo-Isidorean Decretals. According to Pseudo-Clement I, the Lord commanded all the princes of the earth and all men to obey the bishops to submit to them and be their helpers, so that all alike might show themselves faithful 'fellow-workers in God's law'.[337] The later Carolingian reformers, therefore, bequeathed a definition of the relations of the two powers radically different from that of the patristic age. It entailed a significant modification of the Gelasian formula. In the *acta* of the Council of Paris of 829, and increasingly in ecclesiastical records of the ninth century, the sentence of Gelasius is quoted in the form: '*the church* is principally divided into two excellent persons, the sacerdotal and the royal'[338] – not *hic mundus* but *ecclesia*. No longer is the Church in the empire, as in patristic thought: the empire is *in ecclesia*.[339] The two powers now appear as the separate functions of a single institution, 'the rule of souls, which is the pontifical power, being greater than the imperial power, which is temporal'.[340]

---

334. Hincmar, *Admonitio ad episcopos regni* 2, *PL* 125, 1009A: 'tanto est dignitas pontificum maior quam regum, quia reges in culmen regium sacrantur a pontificibus, pontifices autem a regibus consecrari non possunt: et tanto in humanis rebus regum cura est propensior quam sacerdotum, quanto pro honore et defensione et quiete sanctae Ecclesiae . . . a Rege regum est eis curae onus impositum'.
335. *Concilium Parisiense* (829), I.3, II.2, III.7, 8, *MGH Conc.* 2, 610, 651, 673.
336. *Synodus apud Saponarias habita* (859) cap. 2, *MGH Cap.* 2, 447: 'Episcopi namque secundum illorum ministerium ac sacram auctoritatem uniti sint et mutuo consilio atque auxilio reges regnorumque primores atque populum sibi commissum in Domino regnant et corrigant.'
337. Pseudo-Clement I, *Epistola* 1.39, ed. Hinschius 1863, p. 43: 'cooperatores legis Dei'.
338. *Relatio episcoporum ad Hludowicum imperatorem* (829) cap. 3, *MGH Cap.* 2, 29: 'Quod eiusdem ecclesiae corpus in duabus principaliter dividatur eximiis personis.' Cf. *Concilium Parisiense* (829), I.3, p. 610; Jonas of Orleans, *De institutione regia* I, ed. Reviron 1930, p. 134.
339. Cf. Congar 1968a, pp. 256ff.
340. Gregory IV, *JE* 2578, *MGH Epp.* 5, 228: 'maius esse regimen animarum, quod est pontificale, quam imperiale, quod est temporale'.

It was in this sense that the Gregorian reformers in the eleventh century interpreted the Gelasian sentence, adding a further modification. The influential canon law manual, the *Collection in Seventy-Four Titles*, in citing the sentence omits the clause which makes it clear that the emperor's submission to the bishops refers only to the sacraments, so implying a general submission to the *sacerdotium*.[341] A more tendentious omission occurs in Pope Gregory VII's use of the sentence in his doctrinal letter of 1081, justifying the excommunication of Henry IV of Germany. Omitting the statement that the emperor 'rules over the human race' and that he is subject to the priestly power only for the *res divinae*, Gregory brought the Gelasian sentence into line with the main contention of his polemic: 'that the priests of Christ are to be considered the fathers and masters of kings and princes and of all the faithful'.[342] 'The world is ruled by the authority of bishops and by the power of kings; and nevertheless the royal power ought to be subject to bishops' ran the rubric which Anselm of Lucca gave to the sentence in his *Collectio canonum*.[343] The Gregorians' reinterpretation of Gelasius was authoritatively refuted by their most learned opponent, the Anonymous of Hersfeld. 'See how Hildebrand and his bishops . . ., resisting God's ordination, uproot and bring to nothing these two principal powers by which the world is ruled, desiring all other bishops to be like themselves, who are not truly bishops, and desiring to have kings whom they themselves can command with royal licence.'[344]

It was, however, the Gregorian version of Gelasius which became a permanent part of medieval canon law. The inscription, *item Gelasius papa Anastasio imperatori* in Master Gratian's *Decretum*, *Distinctio 96*, introduces the sentence as given in Gregory VII's letter of 1081. The preceding canon is an extract from the same letter, with the rubric: 'Priests are considered the fathers and masters of kings and princes.'[345] As in twelfth-century canon law, so also in theology: the Gregorian belief in the inherent superiority of the spiritual over the temporal power was enshrined in the influential treatise of Hugh of St Victor, *De sacramentis Christianae fidei* (c. 1134). Hugh wrote: 'As the spiritual life is more worthy than the earthly and the spirit is

---

341. *Collectio in LXXIV titulos* 227, ed. Gilchrist 1973, p. 142.
342. Gregory VII, *Registrum* VIII.21: 'Quis dubitet sacerdotes Christi regum et principum omniumque fidelium patres et magistros censeri?'
343. Anselm of Lucca, *Collectio canonum* I.71.
344. *Liber de unitate ecclesiae conservanda* II.15, MGH *Libelli* 2, 231: 'videte quomodo Hildebrant et episcopi eius . . . resistentes . . . Dei ordinationi, haec duo principalia, quibus regitur mundus, extirpare et ad nihilum ducere; cupientes etiam alios omnes episcopos tales esse, sicut sunt ipsi, qui vere non sunt episcopi, et reges eiusmodi habere, quibus ipsi regia licentia possint imperare.'
345. Gratian, *Decretum* D.96 c.9–10: 'Regum et principum patres et magistri sacerdotes esse censentur.'

more worthy than the body, so the spiritual power is superior to the earthly or secular power in honour and dignity. For the spiritual power must establish the earthly power in order that it may exist and must judge it if it has not been good.'[346] Hugh never specified what was meant by this superiority of the spiritual power. Believing as he did that *spiritualia* alone were committed to the clergy, he could hardly have accepted a full-blown Gregorian supervision of temporal matters. Yet it was in this sense that Hugh was interpreted by later medieval polemicists, who quoted him in support of their contention that the vicar of Christ should have dominion over secular affairs.[347]

The two swords

When the eleventh-century reformers considered the functions of the *regnum*, they were bound to focus on that *auctoritas* fundamental to the political speculation of the early Middle Ages, Romans 13, 1–7. Early medieval commentators underlined the apostle's insistence on the Christian's duty of submission to the divinely ordained secular power, placing particular emphasis on St Paul's warning: 'those who resist incur damnation.' So, for example, Atto of Vercelli wrote c. 940 that it was sacrilegious to resist the *regnum*, even if the ruler was an enemy of the Christian faith. A *mala potestas* was imposed by God 'so that the good may be tested in the virtue of patience': hence the word of Job 34, 30, 'He makes the hypocrite reign because of the sins of the people.'[348] The eleventh-century reformers concentrated in their interpretation of the Pauline text not on the impossibility of resistance to the king, but rather on the description of kingship as a *ministerium*. From the king's role of *minister* they were able to deduce that a *mala potestas* could after all be resisted. The argument is first found in a letter of Peter Damian of 1065, instructing King Henry IV of Germany in his duties. The king 'bears the sword in vain' if he does not punish those who resist God; he is not 'the servant of God to execute his wrath on the evildoer' if he does not punish the enemies of the Church. A

---

346. Hugh of St Victor, *De sacramentis Christianae fidei* II.2, 4, *PL* 176, 418: 'Quanto autem vita spiritualis dignior est quam terrena, et spiritus quam corpus, tanto spiritualis potestas terrenam sive saecularem potestatem honore, ac dignitati praecedit. Nam spiritualis potestas terrenam potestatem et instituere habet, ut sit, et iudicare habet si bona non fuerit.'

347. E.g. Giles of Rome, *De ecclesiastica potestate* I.4, ed. Scholz 1929, p. 11; John of Paris, *Tractatus de potestate regia et papali*, ed. Leclercq 1942, pp. 183–4.

348. Atto of Vercelli, *Expositio Epistolarum sancti Pauli*, *PL* 134, 258B–259A: 'datae sunt potestates etiam malae, ut boni patientiae virtute probarentur'. Cf. Affeldt 1969a, pp. 129ff.

king who shows by his protection of the Church that he reveres God must be obeyed: a king who opposes the divine commandments is no *minister Dei* and is held in contempt by his subjects.[349]

This was the attitude to kingship which determined the actions of Gregory VII. He would countenance only 'a suitable king for the honour of holy church', 'a fitting defender and ruler': 'unless he is obedient, humbly devoted and useful to holy Church, as a Christian king ought to be . . . then without a doubt holy Church will not only not favour him, but will oppose him'. Ideally the king should be the vassal (*fidelis*) of St Peter and of his vicar, the pope.[350] Gregory VII gave lectures on Christian kingship to the rulers of the 'new' kingdoms on the edge of Christendom;[351] he sat in judgement on the conduct of the rulers of the older kingdoms, summoning their vassals to enforce his decisions.[352] If a king did not prove 'useful to holy Church', he was to be excommunicated and deposed, and replaced by a more suitable candidate. The removal of the last Merovingian and the installation of the Arnulfing mayor of the palace as king of the Franks in 751 provided Gregory VII with his most important *exemplum*.

Very many pontiffs have excommunicated kings or emperors . . . A Roman pontiff deposed a king of the Franks from the kingship not so much for his iniquities as for the fact that he was not useful enough to hold such great power, and put Pippin, father of the Emperor Charlemagne in his place and absolved all the Franks from the oath of fidelity which they had sworn to him.[353]

The papal claim 'to absolve subjects from fealty to the wicked',[354] based on the Petrine power of binding and loosing, provoked fierce controversy during the Investiture Contest.

Hitherto knights were bound by the covenant of the oath . . . and it seemed equal to sacrilege if they rebelled against their vassal-duty. Now on the contrary knights are armed against their lords, children rise against their parents, subjects are set in

---

349. Peter Damian, *Epistolae* VII.3.
350. Gregory VII, *Registrum* IX.3: 'ad honorem sanctae ecclesiae rex provideatur idoneus . . . defensorem et rectorem, sicut eam decet . . . Nisi enim ita oboediens et sanctae ecclesiae humiliter devotus ac utilis, quemadmodum christianum regem oportet . . . procul dubio ei non modo sancta ecclesia non favebit, sed etiam contradicet.'
351. *Ibid*, II.51, V.10, VI.13, VII.21, IX.14.   352. Cf. Robinson 1979, pp. 750ff.
353. Gregory VII, *Registrum* VIII.21: 'plerique pontificum alii reges alii imperatores excommunicaverunt . . . Alius Romanus pontifex regem Francorum non tam pro suis iniquitatibus quam pro eo, quod tantae potestati non erat utilis, a regno deposuit et Pippinum Caroli Magni imperatoris patrem in eius loco substituit omnesque Francigenas a iuramento fidelitatis, quam illi fecerant, absolvit.' Cf. *Registrum* IV.2.
354. *Ibid.*, II.55a: *Dictatus papae* 27: 'Quod a fidelitate iniquorum subiectos potest absolvere.'

motion against kings, right and wrong are confused, the sanctity of the oath is violated.[355]

The Anonymous of Hersfeld denied that the binding and loosing power included the right to absolve subjects from their *fidelitas*: 'it is certainly true that the Lord gave the right of binding and loosing to St Peter and in him to holy Church, but only in respect of the bonds of sin, not to loosen oaths on the Holy Scriptures or to undo the word of God'.[356] The alleged papal deposition of the last Merovingian king of the Franks in 751 was a particular preoccupation of the Anonymous,[357] who, alone among eleventh-century polemicists, contributed a historical perspective to the long debate concerning the deposition of kings.[358] Nevertheless it was the Gregorian version of the *exemplum* of 751, together with the papal claim to depose kings and to release their subjects from their *fidelitas*, which was to be enshrined in medieval canon law. Master Gratian cited the *exemplum* in Gregory VII's own words.[359] Although Gratian devoted relatively little space in his compilation to the relations of *regnum* and *sacerdotium*, his few remarks on the subject have a Gregorian ring. Reverence must be shown to secular rulers[360] – provided, however, that they do not intrude into ecclesiastical affairs[361] and provided that they defend the Church. 'The duty of defending the churches is laid upon the holders of secular dignities. If they scorn to do so, they are to be excluded from communion.'[362]

Just as the New Testament *auctoritas* Romans 13, 1–7 defined the functions of the king, so Luke 22, 38 – 'Lord, here are two swords' – defined the relations of *regnum* and *sacerdotium*: the image of the two swords, secular and spiritual, became a political theory.[363] In patristic writings the term *gladius* signifies, as in the Vulgate or in Roman Law, the coercive and punitive power of the State. It was among Carolingian authors that the

---

355. Wido of Ferrara, *De scismate Hildebrandi* I.7, *MGH Libelli* I, 539–40: 'Hactenus milites sacramenti foedere tenebantur . . . et par sacrilegio videbatur, si in honorem quippiam molirentur. Nunc autem versa vice milites armantur in dominos, insurgunt filii in parentes, subditi commoventur in reges, fas nefasque confunditur, sacramenti religio violatur.' According to Panzer 1880, pp. 10ff, 57ff, this passage is a quotation from a lost polemic of Wibert of Ravenna (antipope Clement III).

356. *Liber de unitate ecclesiae conservanda* I.4, p. 189: 'Verum etiam certum est, quod Dominus beato Petro et in ipso sanctae ecclesiae dederit ius ligandi atque solvendi, sed vincula peccatorum, non ut solveret sacramenta divinarum scripturarum, neque ut ligaret Dei verbum.'

357. *Ibid.* I.3–4, 16; II.15, pp. 188–9, 208–9, 229. Cf. Affeldt 1969a, pp. 313ff.

358. Cf. Robinson 1978b, pp. 103ff; Robinson 1982, pp. 54ff.

359. Gratian, *Decretum* C.15 q.6 c.3, citing Gregory VII, *Registrum* IV.2.

360. Gratian, *Decretum* C.23 q.5 *dictum post* c.23.

361. *Ibid.* D.96 *dictum ante* c.1; D.97 *dictum ante* c.1.

362. *Ibid.* C.23 q.5 *dictum post* c.25: 'saecularium dignitatum administratoribus defendendarum ecclesiarum necessitas incumbit. Quod si facere contempserint, a communione sunt repellendi'.

363. Cf. Arquillière 1947, pp. 501ff; Stickler 1951, pp. 414ff; Hoffmann 1964b, pp. 78ff.

same term began to be applied to the spiritual power. For Paschasius Radbert, for example, the two swords were the word of life and the sanction of excommunication.[364] Alcuin imagined Charlemagne armed with two swords for the defence of the Church *intrinsecus* against heretics and *forinsecus* against pagans.[365] The classic interpretation of the two swords as the material sword of secular coercion and the spiritual sword of excommunication appears in papal letters of the ninth century.[366] Before the Investiture Contest the image of the two swords was intended to suggest harmonious co-operation. 'I have in my hand the sword of Constantine; you hold that of Peter', wrote King Edgar to Archbishop Dunstan of Canterbury and his colleagues in 967: 'let us join our right hands; let us join sword to sword, so that the sanctuary of God may be cleansed.'[367]

It was this harmony that Pope Gregory VII was alleged to have destroyed by unlawfully seizing the secular sword. The royal chaplain and anti-papal polemicist Gottschalk of Aachen denounced Gregory for having

usurped *regnum* and *sacerdotium* and thereby shown contempt for the ordination of God, who wished government to consist principally not in one but in two . . . as the Saviour himself at the time of his passion made clear through the allegory of the two swords. When they said to him: 'Lord, here are two swords', he replied: 'It is enough', signifying by this sufficient duality that the spiritual and the carnal sword should be wielded in the Church . . .; the priestly sword to enforce obedience to the king after God, the royal sword to attack the enemies of Christ without and enforce obedience to the teaching of the priesthood within.[368]

Gottschalk's interpretation of Luke 22, 38 thus drew on the Gelasian language of *dualitas*: both *auctoritates* seemed to corroborate the customs of the 'Ottonian–Salian Church system' and to refute the claims of Gregory VII. The Gregorians responded with a different interpretation of Luke 22, 38, of which the first extant appearance is in the Canticle commentary of John of Mantua. 'The place of the sword is the righteous power which is not divided from the authority of Peter.'[369] Gregory VII had not usurped the

364. Paschasius Radbert, *Expositio in Matthaeum* XII.26, PL 120, 916D.
365. Alcuin, *Epistola* 171, p. 282.
366. E.g. John VIII, *JE* 3089, 3307, pp. 39, 218.
367. *Oratio Edgari regis*, PL 138, 515D–516A: 'Ego Constantini, vos Petri gladium habetis in manibus; iungamus dexteras, gladium gladio copulemus, ut purgetur sanctuarium Dei.'
368. Henry IV, *Epistola* 13, p. 19: 'regnum et sacerdotium . . . sibi usurpavit. In quo piam Dei ordinationem contempsit, quae non in uno, sed in duobus . . . principaliter consistere coluit, sicut ipse Salvator in passione sua de duorum gladiorum sufficientia typica intelligi innuit. Cui cum diceretur: "Domine, ecce duo gladii hic", respondit: "satis est", significans hac sufficienti dualitate spiritualem et carnalem gladium in ecclesia esse gerendum . . .; videlicet sacerdotali ad oboedientiam regis pro Deo, regali vero gladio ad expellendos Christi inimicos exterius et ad oboedientiam sacerdotii interius omnem hominem docens fore constringendum.'
369. *Johannis Mantuani in Cantica Canticorum Tractatus* ed. Bischoff and Taeger 1973, p. 52.

secular sword, therefore, because both swords, secular and spiritual, were rightfully under papal control.[370] Hence Gregory VII tended to regard kings less as ministers of God than as ministers of St Peter, bound to respond 'if your holy mother, the Roman church has need of your aid, in the form of knights and the material sword against the profane and the enemies of God'.[371]

The Gregorian idea that the pope controlled the *materialis gladius* was given practical application in the crusade under papal direction; and it was in the context of the crusade that the theory of the two swords received its classical formulation. Bernard of Clairvaux summoned Pope Eugenius III to launch a new crusade in 1150 with the words: 'Put forth both swords, now that Christ is suffering again where he suffered before. Who save you should do so? Both are Peter's, the one to be unsheathed at his nod, the other by his hand, whenever necessary.'[372] A fuller exposition appears in *De consideratione*.

If [the material sword] did not belong to you, when the apostles said: 'Behold, here are two swords', the Lord would not have replied: 'It is enough', but 'It is too much.' Therefore both the spiritual and the material sword belong to the Church; but while the former is unsheathed by the Church, the latter is unsheathed for the Church.[373]

This distinction *pro ecclesia, ab ecclesia* may have been intended as a reproof for Eugenius III, who had led his own troops into action.[374]

Bernard's prohibition on the direct use of armed force by the papacy was the culmination of a century of criticism of the warfare of the reform papacy.[375] Critics of papal warfare – for example, Bishop Bruno of Segni – declared that the pope must not himself lead troops 'but only send an army for the defence of righteousness'.[376] If the pope himself unsheathed the

---

370. Nicholas I had once claimed that the material sword and the spiritual sword were both in the hands of St Peter (*JE* 2787): *Nicolai I papae Epistolae* no. 123, ed. E. Perels, *MGH Epp.* 6:641.

371. Gregory VII, *Registrum* II.51 (to King Sven II of Denmark): 'si sancta Romana mater ecclesia contra profanos et inimicos Dei tuo auxilio in militibus et materiali gladio opus habuerit'.

372. Bernard, *Epistola* CCLVI.1, 463D–464A: 'Exserendus est nunc uterque gladius in passione Domini, Christo denuo patiente, ubi et altera vice passus est. Per quem autem nisi per vos? Petri uterque est, alter suo nutu, alter sua manu, quoties necesse est, evaginandus.'

373. Bernard, *De consideratione* IV.3, 7 (776C): 'Alioquin si nullo modo ad te pertineret et is, dicentibus apostolis "Ecce gladii duo hic", non respondisset Dominus "Satis est", sed "Nimis est". Uterque ergo Ecclesiae et spiritualis scilicet gladius et materialis; sed is quidem pro Ecclesia, ille vero et ab Ecclesia exserendus.'

374. Cf. Jordan 1921, pp. 312–13.   375. Cf. Erdmann 1935, pp. 112, 131–2, 212ff.

376. Bruno of Segni, *Libellus de symoniacis* 5, *MGH Libelli* 2, 550 (concerning Pope Leo IX's campaign against the Normans in 1053): 'utinam non ipse per se illuc isset, sed solummodo illuc exercitum pro iusticia defendenda misisset!'

material sword, the secular power would be left without a function. 'If we were all monks and priests, the Church would easily be crushed by Saracens and thieves. Hence the apostle commands us to pray for kings and all who are in high places and says that the more contemptible members are the more necessary (I Cor. 12, 22–3).'[377] This refinement of the Gregorian idea of the relations of the two powers assumed the inferiority of the *regnum* to the *sacerdotium*. The pope himself may not exercise the functions of the secular power, but yet these functions are exercised, in St Bernard's phrase: 'at the nod' of St Peter. Bernard put the theory into practice when, on 27 December 1146 at the altar of the cathedral of Speyer, he placed in the hand of the German king Conrad III the banner of St Peter, signifying the king's participation in the Second Crusade.[378]

---

377. Bruno of Segni, *Expositio in Exodum* XXVI, PL 164, 320C: 'quoniam si monachi et sacerdotes omnes essemus, facile a Saracenis et latronibus Ecclesia conculcaretur. Unde pro regibus et ceteris qui in sublimitate positi sunt, orare apostolus iubet, et membra contemptibilia magis necessaria esse dicit.'
378. *Vita Bernardi* VI, *MGH SS* 26, 126.

12

THE TWELFTH-CENTURY RENAISSANCE

The epoch of the earliest Crusades, of vigorous new development in urban life, in bureaucratic methods of government and in higher education in the schools, some of which were shortly to become the earliest universities, has many claims to be viewed as a period of renaissance or renewal, a period in which learning revived with important consequences for European systems of law, for scholastic philosophy and for the importation of new knowledge from Greek and Arabic sources. C.H. Haskins in his classic study, *The Renaissance of the Twelfth Century*, emphasised the influence of Rome, the ancient Rome of rulers and lawyers as well as of philosophers and writers. The revival of jurisprudence occurred in conjunction with the full recovery of the corpus of Roman law in the late eleventh and twelfth centuries and then touched other bodies of law as well, the canon law of the church first and then feudal and local customs and the new law of the English royal court. The Roman tradition of rulership and law grew stronger in the twelfth century; Frederick Barbarossa restored the ideal of Empire and inserted his Roncaglian decrees into the *Corpus iuris civilis* while on the other hand one of his victims, Arnold of Brescia, promoted the Roman Senate as an instrument of popular rule. Above all, there was much sharp comment on new developments, as in Gerhoh of Reichersberg's *Letter to Pope Adrian on the Novelties of the Day*.

Nonetheless, Haskins found the twelfth century a slack period in the history of political theory. The pamphlet literature dealing with the relationship between 'church and state' had spent its force during the controversy over investiture, and more systematic thought awaited the translation of Aristotle's *Politics* c. 1260. There was, Haskins maintained, no literary reflection upon the striking revival of the arts of government that took place in England, Sicily, Aragon and elsewhere. The theory of politics lagged behind its practice. Perhaps the most notable attempts to provide something in the way of theory were the *Policraticus* or *Statesman's Book* of John of Salisbury (1159) and Bernard of Clairvaux's letter to Pope Eugenius III in five books, the *De consideratione* (1145–52/3). But John scarcely mentions the papal curia or that of Henry II, of which he had wide experience; his examples are chiefly taken from the Old Testament and from ancient Rome. And Bernard is more concerned with the Pope's relationships with God and with the world in his charge.

If it is arguable then that by the twelfth century we have passed beyond a period in which political thought had developed remarkably, it is nevertheless true that the twelfth century was a time when horizons were extended and some new ideas emerged that were eventually to provide a backcloth to political thought in the thirteenth century, and even play a part in it directly.

The states of life

In the twelfth century much attention was given to the growing number of institutions or orders or states of life which bound men and women to defined obligations. Through reflection on the specific functions of these groups, attempts were made to clarify the differences between them as well as to determine the degree of superiority or inferiority they merited in relation to each other.[1] A traditional, Carolingian model of society, upheld, for example, by Adalbero of Laon[2] and Gerard of Cambrai,[3] envisaged three groups under the ruler: the military, the people who prayed and the labourers in the fields. Another three-tiered model of society, derived from St Jerome and other Church Fathers, and continuing to commend itself, placed married people in the bottom grade, the celibates above them and prelates at the top.[4] The recent struggles for church reform had sharpened the distinctions between the spiritual and the temporal groups. As Gratian of Bologna wrote c. 1140, there were two kinds of Christians: first, the clergy who are truly kings and who cannot be compelled to action of any kind by any temporal power; secondly, the laity who cultivate the earth, who give in marriage and whom the clergy lead towards the truth.[5] But the problem was not simply one of asserting or rebutting clerical superiority over the lay order because the orders, whether in a bipartite or in a tripartite model, were composed of an increasing number of parts. Hugh of St Victor in his *Commentary* (written after 1130) on *The Celestial Hierarchy* of Denis the Pseudo-Areopagite amplified the visions of Adalbero and Gerard as

---

1. Duby 1980.   2. Adalbero of Laon *Carmen ad Rotbertum regem*.
3. Gerard of Cambrai *Gesta episcoporum cameracensium*, III.52 (written in 1024 or 1025).
4. Jerome *Adversus Jovinianum*, I.
5. Gratian of Bologna *Concordia discordantium canonum*, Causa 12, qu. 1, c. 7.

well as Jerome's distinctions of merit: society on earth should conform to the organisation of the nine orders of angels in heaven in order to facilitate its absorption into eternity in the society of heaven. Later in the century Alan of Lille went beyond Hugh's elucidation of the correspondence between *potestas humana*, *potestas angelica* and *potestas divinitatis*: in his *Hierarchia* and in other writings he drew more detailed distinctions between actual social classes and professions. His world was peopled by teachers, preachers and rulers above whom were set the masters of the Sacred Page and contemplatives. Each of these groups, he writes, receives influences from and will eventually join a corresponding order of angels.

The formation of new religious orders and of new urban communes, the multiplication of different kinds of producers and traders as well as of specialised administrative officials, led to enlargement and reworking of the received 'pictures' of the channels of power and of the relative importance and distinction of roles in society. In one of several commonplace classifications of social groups Honorius Augustodunensis, in his *Elucidarium* (written before 1101), hints at a growing diversity when he lists in addition to the prince, knights and peasants a fourth class of laymen; these are the townsmen and include merchants, artisans and entertainers.[6] Towns in many parts of Europe, both northern and southern, developed features of autonomous government in the eleventh and twelfth centuries; in northern Italy in the mid-twelfth century the term *commune* became the normal designation of the legal and factual personality claimed by cities such as Milan, Bologna and Pisa in the course of their struggles against the claims of the emperor Frederick Barbarossa.[7] In the church too diversity of organisation had become more marked. The *Libellus de diversis ordinibus et professionibus qui sunt in aecclesia*, written after 1121 by a certain canon R, accounted for the different types of religious profession (which gained innumerable adherents in his day) in the light of divergent tendencies towards strictness, moderation and laxity in Christian observances. His survey embraced hermits, recluses, Cluniacs, Cistercians, Premonstratensians, Victorines, secular canons, *licoisi* and *licoisae* who led a less organised form of religious life, nuns and canonesses.

There were increasingly subtle tensions between the competing tendencies in favour of sacralisation and secularisation in the definitions of ranks and functions. In particular, the ideal of knighthood was now pulled in both

---

6. Honorius Augustodunensis *Elucidarium*, II, esp. 18, *De variis laicorum statibus*, PL 172, 1148–9. Cf. Honorius *Speculum ecclesiae* (written before 1105): lords, knights, rich, poor, merchants, peasants and married couples, PL 172, 861–70. 7. Michaud-Quantin 1970, pp. 153–6.

directions, as the development of chivalric consecration rituals shows well. In his history of the First Crusade written about 1110, Guibert of Nogent, who was joyous over the successful recovery of Jerusalem from the Arabs by western knights, proclaimed the nobility of warfare conducted in the name of God. By contrast the wars of the Old Testament Jews had been wars of greed.[8] He declares that the preaching of the Crusade has provided knights, who could once only hope for salvation by abandoning their arms, with a new dispensation: 'in our time God has instituted holy warfare so that the knightly order (*ordo equestris*) and the unsettled populace, who used to be engaged like the pagans of old in slaughtering one another, should find a new way of deserving salvation. No longer are they obliged to leave the world and choose a monastic way of life.'[9] Bernard of Clairvaux, in his treatise written for the new military-religious Order of the Temple, *In Praise of the New Knighthood* (1128–36), celebrated the inclusion of crusader knights within the order of regular canons. On the other hand, the quarrel between Becket and Henry II sharply revealed the antagonisms that set lay knights in England against the clergy; in his *Policraticus* (1159) John of Salisbury tried to counteract secularising tendencies with lengthy, oblique moral criticisms of the *curiales* or the courtly class, and he wrote of the holiness of the knight's vocation.

More down-to-earth is the evidence provided by the authors of a new type of manual, first produced about 1080, which set forth the rules of letter writing. These *artes dictaminis* placed great emphasis on the opening salutation, and gave in detail the forms of address suited to different social ranks. They reveal the proliferation of social distinctions that were accounted for not by the unequal distribution of divine grace or angelic guidance but by such human factors as power, dignity, office and birth. The terms they used for the upper order imply greatness and superiority (*sublimis, maior, summus, altior, superior, supremus, gravis, excellens, eximius*) while those used for the lower order suggest weakness and inferiority (*exilis, tenuis, minor, humilis, inferior, infimus, extenuatus*). In the middle order were the *mediocres*. But the *dictatores* differed in their attempts to fit particular groups – townsmen, merchants, clergy, masters, for example – into the

---

8. 'De his itaque spirituali solum desiderio coeptis patratisque praeliis, divina, quae a saeculo numquam acciderit, tempora moderna insigniri virtute laetemur; nec Israelis carnalia pro ventrium plenitudine bella miremur', Guibert of Nogent *Gesta Dei per Francos*, VII, p. 221.

9. '. . . instituit nostro tempore praelia sancta Deus, ut ordo equestris et vulgus oberrans, qui vetustae paganitatis exemplo in mutuas versebantur caedes, novum repperirent salutis promerendae genus; ut nec funditus electa (uti fieri assolet) monastica conversatione, seu religiosa qualibet professione, saeculum relinquere cogerentur, sed sub consueta licentia et habitu, ex suo ipsorum officio, Dei aliquatenus gratiam consequerentur', Guibert of Nogent *Gesta Dei per Francos*, I, p. 124.

appropriate orders and in their attempts to subdivide the orders.[10]
Moreover, the model of a calibrated society of orders sometimes provoked
criticism and rejection – for example, in favour of a utopian vision of
freedom from seigneurial domination. The formation of urban communes,
which was marked by the taking of common oaths and by the manumission
of serfs, and the capture of Jerusalem by crusaders in 1099, sometimes
fostered idyllic expectations of an egalitarian society.

The diversification of the orders and institutions in society is, then, a
factor to be considered when examining the political thought of the twelfth
century. The growth of urban schools as well as the multiplication of
monastic foundations provided increased scope for discussion of the
available writings of the authorities – the *auctores* or *auctoritates*. In the Bible,
in the works of the Church Fathers and in the classical writings of the
pagans, there was a wealth of reflection on the goal of human life and on the
government of society; and this legacy of thought was vigorously
disseminated to a wider and more literate audience.[11]

The moral and political legacy of Rome

Ancient and medieval education was consistently concerned not only with
the training of the mind but also with behaviour. It was therefore the
business of the schools, at least at an elementary level, to fit the educated man
for heaven and, *a fortiori*, to help him to live that good life on earth which is
the concern of the political thinker as well as of the pastoral theologian.[12]
Until at least the end of the twelfth century medieval scholars habitually
thought about right and wrong in human action in this double arena, the
earthly adjacent, as it were, and leading on to the heavenly. The 'good life' is
first of all the virtuous life and only secondly (although in the end
inseparably) the happy and satisfactory life which comes to be the primary
concern of later political thinkers. The good man's life is lived in loving
God, and in loving his neighbour as himself. That is the spring and direction
of social intercourse and the key to good behaviour as subject or citizen.

Secular authors were studied at two levels: at an elementary stage where
they were used simply as exercise-books, texts from which Latin might be
learned; and at a more advanced stage for reading by those scholars who

10. Constable 1977, pp. 253–67.
11. For a brief introduction to the schools in the twelfth century see Delhaye 1947.
12. On moral education in the twelfth century see Delhaye 1948, pp. 29–44, 1949, 1958; Luscombe, in
    Abelard 1971, pp. xv–xxiv.

were able to approach them with critical appreciation, and to extract from them, among other things, such moral instruction as they seemed to furnish. The *Distichs* of Cato, the fables of Avianus, and a rendering of Aesop's Fables, were found to lend themselves very well to the needs of young beginners. At a more advanced stage Cicero provided a fund of high-minded ideas about friendship and duty which provoked widespread discussion and adaptation to a Christian context. Contemporary readers found in Cicero's *De officiis* a view of the relationship between duty and virtue. Duties may be classified into those which are absolute and relate to the highest good and those lowlier duties which are concerned with the practical rules by which daily life is regulated (*De officiis* I.iii.7), a division not far from the monastic Christian notion of *vita contemplativa* and *activa*. Cicero also adopts the division of the virtues into wisdom, justice, fortitude, temperance, which was familiar to Christian thinkers. Of these, Cicero's discussion of justice is perhaps the most significant for its influence on political ideas. He defines justice as that which maintains the 'common bonds' of society (*De officiis* I.vii.20). Its first 'office' is to keep one man from doing harm to another unless he is provoked by wrongs done to himself; its second 'office' is to encourage men to use the common possessions of the community for the common interest, private property for their own (*De officiis* I.vii.20). Cicero extends his reflections under this heading to the *iura belli*: we must resort to force only if discussion fails; we must show consideration to those we conquer; we must ensure that those who lay down their arms are protected (*De officiis* I.xi.34ff). The main drift of what he has to say is that we are not born for ourselves alone (*De officiis* I.vii.22): the Christian would speak in terms of the love of God and our neighbour; Cicero speaks in terms of a duty to friends and country. The *De officiis* was principally used along with the other moralist writings of Cicero and Seneca as a source of wise sayings. But at least one adaptation of the whole work survives in the *Moralium dogma philosophorum*, which takes among others the themes of honesty, prudence and justice from the *De officiis*.

In the *De Senectute* of Cicero, the twelfth-century reader found confirmation of the view that a man should live for his friends and for the community, again with an emphasis upon the community as the ultimate point of reference. Seneca too was widely admired in the twelfth century as a morally edifying philosopher, although his teachings gave less encouragement to engage in public life.[13] In his *De Otio* he looks at the notion of a

13. See Nothdurft 1963.

'retirement' (*otium*) which consists in giving oneself to the society of the best men and selecting a model to live by, something which, he argues, can only be done *in otio*, at leisure (*De otio* 1.28). The comparison with the twelfth-century idea of monastic life suggests itself at once. Seneca compares the man who engages in public life but is always distraught (*semper inquietus*) and never gives himself time to look about him at earth or heaven, with the man who employs his leisure in unbroken contemplation, his tranquillity undisturbed by action (*De otio* v.6).

Cicero, Seneca and other classical authors were characteristically used as a source of saws and sayings rather than for their extended reflections. This method of selective borrowing undoubtedly did a good deal to avoid the difficulty of confrontation between Christian and pagan values and to bring out their points of similarity and agreement. The ideal of the virtuous life set forth in the classical writers was both private and public; indeed, the individual could not be truly virtuous unless he was also a good citizen. This notion was not entirely at odds with the Christian ideal, but it fitted it strictly only if the citizenship in question was the citizenship of heaven, that is, if the individual was regarded as a member of the Body of Christ. The virtuous act of the Christian individual was an act of love towards his neighbour and of obedience to the second of Christ's two commandments of love. Virtue of this kind could be practised in a religious retreat. Indeed, it was so strongly felt to be possible to be a good Christian and a hermit that the eremitical idea developed a fresh attraction in the West during this period; and for the hermit love of neighbour and commitment to the community meant mainly a spiritual commitment to membership of the body of Christ. Hermits, whether they were recluses, wandering preachers or members of religious communities, were numerous in many parts of Europe in the eleventh and twelfth centuries; they were sometimes much sought after by people who presented them with their problems and with their gifts.[14]

However, a revival of city life also occurred, particularly in northern Italy where urban agglomerations became *civitates* or sovereign communities, governing themselves in the light of *ius civile* or civil law established and applied within the city itself. In his *De officiis* Cicero had presented man as a naturally social and civic being; man's possession of reason and speech leads naturally to a kind of association or community (I.xvi). So human association is in accordance with nature (III.v) and, although not every

14. See *L'Eremetismo in occidente nei secoli XI e XII* 1965.

human association constitutes a people, where there is consent to law and an agreement as to the advantages of association, a people (*populus*) is constituted (*De republica* I.xxv). Such ideas were known not least because Augustine and Isidore had discussed them.[15] When Aristotle's teaching on the naturalness of the *polis* became available in the West in the thirteenth century, it served to reinforce a position already familiar through Cicero and the Roman law. The Augustinian tradition that viewed the state of original innocence as the only really natural state was counter-balanced by the surviving Stoic insistence that men and things continue to be regulated by natural law. This found favour in the twelfth century among those who defined *civitates* as unions of persons possessing a common view of justice. Adelard of Bath observed that men by their own good sense put aside the life led without the support of law and were drawn to the life of the *civitas* and to acceptance of communal justice. Civil consents, as Adelard terms them, underlie the practice of the honest life, while the unreasonableness of modern tyrants is checked by the impulse of men to combine in humane society.[16] In the twelfth century there were many writers who emphasised points common to both ancient pagan philosophy and Christian doctrine. Peter Abelard, in particular, claimed that the ancient philosophers' teaching about the *rei publicae status*, and about the conduct of the citizens living within it, was, like the philosophers' moral teaching, almost completely in accord with the Gospel. Evangelical moral precepts were tantamount to a reform of the natural law followed by the philosophers; their teaching on the active life, that is, the right way of ruling and living in cities, was as wholesome as their teaching on the virtuous life. Moreover, Abelard believed that the philosophers had enjoined the rulers of cities to establish communal ownership in the manner observed in the Acts of the Apostles 4:32, and upheld subsequently by Christian monks. He interpreted Plato's teaching in the *Timaeus* (18c–d) as a plea in favour of the communal life, including even the sharing of wives which Abelard contrasts with the

15. Augustine *De civitate Dei*, II.xxi, also xix.21. Isidore of Seville *Etymologiae*, IX.iv.5–6. Isidore (*ibid.*) defines the *populus* as *tota civitas* or *universi cives*. In *Etymologiae*, XV.ii.1, Isidore links *civitas* to *urbs*: 'civitas est hominum multitudo societatis vinculo adunata, dicta a civibus, id est, ab ipsis incolis urbis . . . Nam urbs ipsa moenia sunt, civitas autem non saxa, sed habitatores vocantur.' Compare also *Etymologiae*, IX.ii.1 ('Gens est multitudo ab uno principio orta sive ab alia natione secundum propriam collectionem distincta, ut Graeciae, Asiae') and *Etymologiae*, IX.iv.2 ('Cives vocati, quod in unum coeuntes vivant, ut vita communis et ornatior fiat et tutior').

16. '. . . ut illi, qui prius indiscrete et sine legali iure vivebant, in civitatem communemque iustitiam tam potenti admonitione tracti sint. Quare quicquid universae honestatis ex civilibus consensibus ortum est, huic ascribendum esse diiudico. Deinde cui dubium est, qua vi modernos tyrannos ab irrationabili impetu adhibita refrenet, cum primo mortales omni feritate rigidos in humanitatem coetumque compulerit?', Adelard of Bath *De eodem et diverso*, p. 19.

practice condemned by Jerome in his *Adversus Iovinianum*, 1.49, of using wives as objects of private pleasure. Likewise, the government of a *res publica* should tend towards the *communis utilitas*, and the rulers of a true *civitas* should follow the law of love. Abelard cited Cicero's definition of the *civitas* as a *concilium* or *coetus hominum iure sociatus*, and he looked back to Plato to find encouragement for rulers to love and to serve their people.[17] Thus civic life, civic humanism even, became an object of reflection before the entry of Aristotle.

The doctrine of natural law was familiar not only from Cicero, as reported by Lactantius[18] but also from St Paul in his Epistle to the Romans, 2.12–16, the first chapter of the *Digest* and the fifth book of the *Etymologies* of Isidore of Seville. After the revival of the study of Roman law in the late eleventh century the definitions given in the *Digest* were discussed and compared. In the introductory distinctions of the *Concordia discordantium canonum* Gratian followed Isidore in defining natural law as the law common to all nations (by virtue of being found in all nations because of the unchanging natural instinct of men rather than because of any positive enactment).[19] But Gratian went further than the Roman lawyers in adapting the natural law to the basic precept of divine law regarding neighbourly love: 'Mankind is ruled by two things: Natural law and custom. Natural law is that which is contained in the Law of the Gospel where everyone is commanded to do to another as he would be done by and forbidden to do to another what he does not wish to have done to himself.'[20] Gratian's definition thus represents an integration of classical into Christian doctrine.

Classical moralists and philosophers inculcated ideals of personal and social behaviour; the facts and legends concerning ancient history offered an inspiration to political reform and restoration.[21] Between 1144 and 1155 the Roman Commune invoked the classical past directly by seeking to restore the governmental model of ancient Rome. Much earlier, the greatness of ancient Rome had inspired the poet Alfanus, archbishop of Salerno from 1058 to 1085, to advance the claim of the papacy to the throne

---

17. Peter Abelard *Theologia Christiana*, II.43–56. Cf. Cicero *In Somnium Scipionis*, 1.8. On medieval attitudes to the *Timaeus* and to marital communism see Kuttner 1976. On the term *civitas* see Michaud-Quantin 1970, pp. 111–27.

18. Lactantius *Divinarum institutionum lib.* VI, 8; Cicero *De republica*, III, xxii, 33. Cf. Cicero *De legibus*, I, xii, 33.

19. Gratian *Concordia discordantium canonum*, D.1.7; Isidore *Etymologiae*, V.4.

20. 'Gratianus: Humanum genus duobus regitur, naturali videlicet iure et moribus. Ius naturae est, quod in lege et evangelio continetur, quo quisque iubetur alii facere, quod sibi vult fieri, et prohibetur alii inferre, quod sibi nolit fieri', Gratian *Concordia discordantium canonum*, D.1.

21. On the following see especially Benson 1982, pp. 339–86; Bloch 1982, pp. 615–36.

of the Roman empire by likening archdeacon Hildebrand to illustrious Roman pagans such as Marius, Julius Caesar and the Scipios.[22] Now, in reaction against papal domination, the Roman Senate was re-established and the Commune was defined as *senatus populusque Romanus*. In 1149 the Senate offered to crown King Conrad III of the Germans as emperor in replacement of the customary (post-Carolingian) coronation by the pope; in 1152 the Senate decided to choose for itself and constitute a new emperor. The mystique of ancient Rome found further expression in the first half of 1155 in the compilation of the *Description of the Golden City of Rome* (*Graphia Aureae Urbis Romae*), which reflected the heightening of contemporary reverence for, and interest in, Rome's glorious past, as well as the Capitoline and other ancient monuments, and also the traditions and ceremonial of the ancient imperial court. The Roman Commune had only a brief existence, but its illusions reflect a more than local readiness to revive the model of the ancient Roman empire in the early to mid-twelfth century. The reconstruction of the German monarchy after the investiture struggle also entailed a determined attempt to reinforce the Romanness of the empire, especially in areas of German domination in Italy. Frederick Barbarossa aimed at the start of his reign to achieve a *reformatio* of the Roman empire, no longer only *imperium Romanum* but now *sacrum imperium*, a sacralised empire independent of the papacy and ruled according to the law code of Justinian as well as German custom.[23] The bulls of the German kings through the twelfth century proclaimed Rome as the world's capital: ROMA CAPVT MVNDI TENET ORBIS FRENA ROTVNDI.[24] As an emperor ruling in Italy Barbarossa proclaimed his legislative authority by virtue of the *lex regia*, not by virtue of imperial coronation or of the papacy. He inserted his laws into Justinian's code; he cited Constantine, Theodosius and Justinian as well as Charlemagne and Louis the Pious as his predecessors. Otto of Freising (c. 1112–58) produced in his *Chronicle* a continuous list of the Roman emperors from Augustus to the mid-twelfth century, noting only that with Charlemagne the empire had been transferred to the Franks and with Otto I to the Germans.[25]

The rediscovery of Justinian's *Digest* in c. AD 1070 – perhaps in the library

---

22. Alfanus of Salerno 1974, no. 22, pp. 155–7. Szövérffy 1957 has shown how the numerous hymns composed in honour of Rome and St Peter before the investiture conflict had tended to proclaim the nobility of the city and the veneration due to Peter's relics and the scene of his martyrdom, but, following the papal reform in the eleventh century, such hymns become more concerned to proclaim Rome as the centre of world government with Peter as the supreme ruler providing laws for all peoples. 23. Benson 1982, pp. 363–5, 370–1. 24. Schramm 1957, pp. 203–4.
25. Otto of Freising *Chronica*, 7 post c. 35, pp. 374–85. In parallel columns Otto also lists the Roman pontiffs from St Peter to his own time. On the doctrine of *translatio imperii* – on Charlemagne's becoming emperor in 800 – see Goez 1958.

of the abbey of Montecassino in central Italy – aided a revival of the study and the practice of the Roman civil law. The texts of Justinian's *Corpus iuris civilis* rested ultimately on the authority of imperial Rome, just as the texts of the canon law rested ultimately on the authority of apostolic and papal Rome. The civilian glossators of the *Digest* who followed Irnerius in Bologna recreated the rational science of law. In the twelfth century the imperial chancery (which used Roman legal terminology), royal chanceries, Glanvill, continental notaries, all propagated the new jurisprudence to meet the practical needs of judges and advocates. In 1158 the emperor Frederick Barbarossa recognised the Bolognese *studia* through his *Authentica 'Habita'*. The new learning found its way into the laws of the church and of different countries; it was promoted both by lay and by imperial officials as well as by canonists such as the papal chancellor Aimeric (1123–41) and by Master Gratian of Bologna (c. 1140). The church became thereby a principal agent for promoting the laws of ancient Rome.

The renewal of Biblical studies

The twelfth century saw the construction of a commentary on the whole Bible, put together by a series of scholars amongst whom one of the principal instigators seems to have been the Anselm who was (with his brother Ralph) master of the school at Laon in the late eleventh and early twelfth centuries. The gloss remained an elementary aid, but this *Glossa Ordinaria* marked a new period in the evolution of Biblical criticism.[26] In the monasteries of the earlier medieval centuries, *lectio divina* had always held an important place, but now the Bible began to be studied outside the monasteries in a businesslike search for texts that might settle questions of speculative theology and moral reform. Reaction against the polemics of the Investiture Contest set in: the contest itself was stilled with the Concordat of Worms in 1122 and the masters of the Sacred Page were not generally concerned with political theory until the schism of 1159. The schools of Laon and of St Victor, of Peter Abelard and Gilbert of Poitiers, promoted Biblical study but had little to say on the relationship between *regnum* and *sacerdotium*.

By mid-century, however, Biblical scholarship was again being applied to subjects of political thought. St Paul in Romans 13.1–7 had provided the most important Biblical statement of the duty of Christians to submit to secular power, for the ruler is instituted by God. This doctrine was in no

26. Smalley 1983.

way doubted. To resist the ruler was to display *superbia* or pride and it was the responsibility of the ruler to punish wickedness as well as to promote righteousness. It was traditionally accepted that the duty of obedience did not extend to obeying commands to deny faith; instead a Christian should offer passive resistance or even prepare for martyrdom.[27] But Robert of Melun, a respected teacher in the schools of Paris and Melun until 1160 when he became bishop of Hereford, taught in his *Quaestiones* concerning the Epistles of St Paul (c. 1157 or earlier) that royal power does not excuse tyranny and should be distinguished from the person holding royal power who, if he acts tyrannically, acts (as it were) impotently.[28] Robert interpreted *potestas* as lawful power. An explicit resistance theory did not emerge, but the Biblical scholars of Robert's day were asking new questions about the source of a tyrant's power and about the difference between *mala potestas* and the *potestas malorum*.

Political allegory – a way of explaining Scripture for a political purpose by finding a deeper, spiritual but still politically relevant meaning beyond the literal sense – had developed within the framework of traditional moral and allegorical interpretation during the eleventh-century 'Gregorian' reform. The most influential of these political metaphors was the patristic interpretation of the two swords – brandished by the apostles in defence of Christ when his arrest was imminent (Luke 22.38) – as signifying respectively spiritual and temporal, or ecclesiastical and lay, power. The sword was one of many customary symbols of rulership. Ecclesiastical power was depicted by a range of motifs such as the Word, the Cross, the Keys of St Peter, the Mitre and the Staff. Secular princes often received a sword from the king as an emblem of their rank and power. The association of rulership and the sword was made by St Paul (Romans 13.4). But the image of the sword as spiritual power was also Biblical; St Paul enjoined the

---

27. Affeldt 1969a.
28. Robert of Melun *Quaestiones de epistolis Pauli* at Rom. 13.1–3 (ed. Martin 1938, pp. 152–4): '*Non enim est potestas nisi a Deo.* Hic vocat potestatem, *illam Dei ordinationem* ex qua quidam aliis habent preesse, *non ipsas personas*, ut quidam dicunt, cum ipsis non sit obsequendum in his in quibus ipsi perverse agunt. In illis vero omnibus *que ad potestatem pertinent* eis obediendum est . . . Item, *non haberes in me potestatem, nisi tibi desuper datum fuisset* . . . Sed cum ex regia potestate potest aliquis exercere tyrannidem, eo quod occasione inde sumpta et sub specie potestatis ordinate in subditos saevire potest, nec tamen regia potestate est tyrannidem exercere. Nam posse Christum crucifigere, tyrannidem exercere, inpotentia est, non potestas . . . Videtur eciam Apostolus nomine potestatis ipsos praelatos, *reges* scilicet et *principes* designare, quibus *sive sint boni sive mali* obsequendum est *in his que ad potestatem pertinent*, sicut *Glossa* dicit.
    Illud quoque caute intelligas quod dicit *Glossa: Videri malam potestatem a Deo praefectam.* Nam recipiendum non est quod malum praelatum Deus prefecerit, vel quod malus habeat esse a Deo prelatus sed potius a diabolo.'

Ephesians to put on God's armour, to carry the shield of faith and to receive the word of God to use as a sword.[29] By the eleventh century the imagery had developed to the point where bishops were conventionally described as the bearers of spiritual arms while secular princes wielded their material sword in order to coerce those who did not respond to the preaching of the Word. At the time of the struggle against simony and lay investiture a passage in the Gospel of St Luke acquired a political connotation: ' "Lord", [the Apostles] said, "there are two swords here now". He said to them, "That is enough!" . . . "Lord, shall we use our swords?" And one of them struck out at the high priest's servant, and cut off his right ear. But at this Jesus spoke. "Leave off!" he said "That will do!" '[30] John of Mantua was one early writer who introduced the notion that the two swords represented respectively spiritual and temporal power into the commentary on the Song of Songs that he wrote in 1081/3 for the Countess Matilda of Tuscany.[31] The sword of temporal or material power could not be wielded by the clergy because that seemed to be the sword that Christ (according to the Gospel of John) had commanded Peter to sheath.[32] Argument turned on the question whether the prince receives a temporal sword from the successor to St Peter in order to wield it on behalf of the latter. Cardinal Humbert of Silva Candida affirmed in his *Libri tres adversus simoniacos* (written between 1054 and 1058) that princes receive their sword from the priesthood in order to defend the church.[33] But it was not always clear whether it was being claimed that the priesthood was the unique grantor of the right to use physical coercion in a Christian society. The line between the view that catholic princes should use their swords in support of the priesthood and the view that they owed their swords to the priesthood was not always drawn.[34] Many voices in the course of the reform struggles of the eleventh century declared that the two swords signified two separate

---

29. Ephesians 6.13–17.
30. 'At illi dixerunt: Domine, ecce duo gladii hic. At ille dixit eis: Satis est . . . dixerunt ei: Domine, si percutimus in gladio? Et percussit unus ex illis servum principis sacerdotum, et amputavit auriculam eius dexteram. Respondens autem Iesus ait: Sinite usque huc', Luke 22.38, 49–51.
31. John of Mantua *In Cantica Canticorum*, pp. 51–2.
32. 'Simon ergo Petrus habens gladium eduxit eum: et percussit pontificis servum: et abscidit auriculam eius dexteram. Erat autem nomen servo Malchus. Dixit ergo Iesus Petro: Mitte gladium tuum in vaginam', John 18.10–11.
33. 'Ad hoc enim gladium a Christi sacerdotibus accipiunt, ad hoc inunguntur [*scil.* principes], ut pro ecclesiarum Dei defensione militent et, ubicunque opus est, pugnent', Humbert *Adversus simoniacos*, III.15.
34. For full documentation see Levison 1951 and Hoffmann 1964b as well as articles by Stickler 1947a and by Arquillière 1947. For a brief review of modern interpretations see especially Congar 1970, pp. 142–5.

spheres or species of rulership, spiritual and temporal, both sanctioned by God; for the priesthood to appropriate both swords was to destroy a duality that was supported by a Biblical allegory and, in effect also, to reduce two swords to one.[35] In about 1100 the Norman Anonymous questioned whether the allegory was plausible: since Christ had ordered Peter to put back into his scabbard the sword he had used to cut off the ear of Malchus, and since Christ had also promised death to any who take a sword, it did not appear that the church should have a sword at all.[36]

In the mid-twelfth century the two swords became topical again. Robert Pullen, a master in the Paris schools, discussed the theory in his *Sentences* (1142–4),[37] and Bernard of Clairvaux gave it prominence in writing to Pope Eugenius III, c. 1149. He laid stress on Christ's remark to Peter: 'Put *your* sword back in its scabbard' (John 18.11) which suggested to him that the two swords belonged to the church. The church should not wield the temporal sword but it should be used on its behalf by the temporal power.[38] The stimulus to debate was provided by the problem whether the spiritual power could require the temporal power to use physical force on its behalf, e.g. when a spiritual sanction such as excommunication had proved ineffective or when an insurrection threatened ecclesiastical life and land.

35. Cf. Gottschalk of Aachen, writing in 1076 and 1082 against Pope Gregory VII in the name of the emperor Henry IV after Henry's deposition and excommunication: 'Piam dei ordinationem contempsit, quae non in uno, sed in duobus, duo, id est regnum et sacerdotium, principaliter consistere voluit, sicut ipse salvator in passione sua de duorum gladiorum sufficientia typica intelligi innuit. Cui cum diceretur: "domine, ecce duo gladii hic", respondit: "satis est", significans hac sufficienti dualitate spiritualem et carnalem gladium in ecclesia esse gerendum, quibus omne nocivum foret amputandum, videlicet sacerdotali ad obedientiam regis pro deo, regali vero gladio ad expellendos Christi inimicos exterius et ad oboedientiam sacerdotii interius omnem hominem docens fore constringendum.' Also: 'Deus non unum, sed duos gladios satis esse dixit. Ipse [Gregory] vero unum fieri intendit, dum nos destituere contendit', ed. Erdmann 1937, p. 19, no. 13, and p. 25, no. 17.
36. 'Sed cum ipse a Christo redargutus sit dicente: Mitte gladium tuum in vaginam [John 18.11]! Omnis enim, qui acceperit gladium, gladio peribit [Matthew 26.52], quomodo significare potuit, in aecclesia esse debere gladium, quem quicunque acceperit gladio peribit? Non ergo conveniens est allegoria . . . fortasse aliqua secretiora in his latent, quae in sanctorum commentariis quaeri debent', ed. Pellens 1966, pp. 108–10.
37. Robert Pullen *Sentences*, vi, 56 (*PL* 186, 905–6): 'Gladiorum alter deputatur clericis, alter laicis . . . Nam Petrus uno aurem Malchi abscindens, alterum ad se nihil aestimavit pertinere. Sacerdotalis ergo dignitas, saecularisque potestas, hos inter se duos dividant gladios. Haec sibi corpus, illa spiritum propriae ditioni subjugare arbitretur.'
38. 'Uterque ergo Ecclesiae, et spiritualis scilicet gladius, et materialis, sed is quidem pro Ecclesia, ille vero et ab Ecclesia exserendus: ille sacerdotis, is militis manu, sed sane ad nutum sacerdotis et iussum imperatoris', *De consideratione*, iv.iii.7, p. 454. Cf. *Epistola* 256.1 (to Eugenius III): 'Petri uterque est, alter suo notu, alter sua manu, quoties necesse est, evaginandus. Et quidem de quo minus videbatur, de ipso ad Petrum dictum est: *Converte gladium tuum in vaginam* [John 18.11]. Ergo suus erat et ille, sed non sua manu utique educendus.' Bernard's fellow Cistercian Nicholas of Clairvaux also invoked the two swords allegory in the Sermon 69 that was for long attributed to Peter Damian, see Ryan 1947.

There was a further problem too: should the clergy rely solely on spiritual weapons if the temporal ruler acts tyrannically and oppresses the church? In general writers propound the view that material power exists to minister to the needs of spiritual power. But a dilemma was emerging since a 'dualist' position (spiritual and temporal power are separate but interdependent) coexisted with a hierocratic one (temporal power is bestowed by spiritual power). In the case of the emperor the hierocratic view was expressed with less inhibition: he received his imperial authority directly from the pope in order to defend Rome. Both the schism of 1159 and the Becket conflict provoked polemic in which scholars turned again to political allegory.[39] In Becket's circle the two swords allegory was sometimes used to show that temporal rulers receive the temporal sword from the clergy and also that the clergy may not receive punishment from the temporal power. A direct link with the schools of Paris can be established here. Becket relied on Herbert of Bosham as his 'Master of the Sacred Page' and Herbert was a Biblical scholar who had been trained in Peter Lombard's school. After Becket's death Herbert was to complete Peter Lombard's *Great Gloss* on the *Psalms* and on the *Epistles* of St Paul, and thereby concluded the *Gloss* begun at Laon and expanded at Paris for use in the schools. Herbert guided Becket at the time of his rejection of the Constitutions of Clarendon and fervently urged Pope Alexander III in 1166 to wield his sword against the other sword of steel.[40]

Clause 3 of the Constitutions (1164) required a clerk accused of felony in a secular court, if he is unfrocked after trial and conviction in the church court, to lose the protection of the church and thereby to become liable to punishment in the king's court as a layman. Dr Smalley has shown that, whatever views on criminous clerks may have been derived from the canons of the church in Becket's lifetime,[41] Becket himself most firmly based his objection to *traditio curiae* on the Septuagint version of a Biblical text: 'God will not judge twice for the same offence' (Nahum 1.9). Theologians had already used this text in debating the question whether condemned felons need also perform spiritual penance and thereby make satisfaction to the church as well as pay for their sin by their life. According to Edward Grim's account, Becket adduced the example of King Solomon who deposed the priest Abiathar on account of his disobedience but who respected Abiathar's priesthood by not punishing him further or physi-

---

39. On the following see Smalley 1973.
40. Herbert of Bosham *Epistola* CLVI in *Materials* v (1881), pp. 285–94, here pp. 291–2.
41. Henry's case had some basis in canon law; see Duggan 1962, pp. 1–28.

cally.[42] This Biblical example had been debated during the Gregorian reform and now came aptly to hand again in the polemic. Herbert of Bosham, in his *Life* of Becket (written in 1184–6), tells us that Henry II presented to Becket the example of the Levites of the Old Testament who were subject to the physical penalties of the Law of Moses like everyone else; indeed the higher a person's rank or order, the stiffer was the punishment.[43] John of Salisbury counter-attacked:

Assuredly, as one reads in the Book of Numbers, God decreed that the tribe of Levi, as the image of the priesthood, should be exempt from public duties and lie at the sole disposal of the high priest. Abiathar also, who had resisted the Holy Spirit when David disposed of his kingdom, was removed from the priesthood; yet he escaped sentence of death just because he had carried the ark, and waited in safety for death to come protected by the privilege of his former office. But if the clergy are not the successors to the privileges of the tribe of Levi, then is the Apostle mere wind and all interpreters of scripture deceitful.[44]

The movements of the post-Hildebrandine age to reintroduce a life of apostolic poverty and simplicity were generally informed by spiritual and Biblical ideals; on the whole they lacked political or antifeudal tendencies. But polemical reaction against the visible wealth of merchants and clergy generated some conflict with established authority, secular as well as ecclesiastical. Henry of Lausanne, who had a long career from 1116 to at least 1145 as an influential evangelical preacher in France, rejected the sacramental role of the clergy.[45] Likewise Arnold of Brescia, according to the account of Otto of Freising in his *Gesta Friderici*, found the solution to the problem of wealth in the ideal of the apostolic life: no cleric who held property, no bishop with *regalia*, no monk with possession, could be saved.[46] The Waldensians too hoped to relive the shared poverty and communism idealised in the *Acts of the Apostles*; such hopes may have encouraged guild corporatism among lay critics of orthodox clergy.

One further area of political exposition of Scripture was the use of interpretations which pointed forward to the end of the world. The place

---

42. Edward Grim *Vita Sancti Thomae*, p. 388.
43. Herbert of Bosham *Vita Sancti Thomae*, p. 267.
44. 'Sed profecto in figuram sacerdocii Deus tribum Leuiticam a publicis functionibus, sicut in Numeris legitur, immunem esse decreuit et summi tantum pontificis dispositionibus subiacere. Abiathar quoque, qui Spiritui Sancto restiterat in dispositione David, amotus a sacerdocio ea ratione sententiam mortis euasit quia archam portauerat, et praecedentis officii priuilegii tutus diem expectauit fatalem. Quod si clerus in priuilegia tribus Leuiticae non succedit, et apostolus uanus est et fallaces omnes interpretes scripturarum', John of Salisbury *Letter* 187, 1955–79, vol. II, pp. 234–7.
45. On Henry see Moore 1977, pp. 82–114.   46. Otto of Freising *Gesta Friderici*, II, XXVIII.

occupied by the present in the history of the world from Biblical times to its end was, for many, a matter of pressing interest and importance. Modern history was seen as a continuation of Bible history, and thus it fell within the province of exegesis of Scripture. Gerhoh of Reichersberg (1098–1169), like Rupert of Deutz (c. 1070–1129) and Hildegard of Bingen (1098–1179), saw decline rather than progress in the church since its early days and viewed the reign of Emperor Henry IV (1056–1106) in apocalyptical terms, the Second Coming and the Last Judgement being perhaps already very close. Ralph of Flaix, a monk whose twenty books on Leviticus (completed in 1157) were widely admired, interpreted Leviticus 24.10 as prophecy of the imminent coming of Antichrist.[47] He applied the prophecies of the beasts in Apocalypse 17.7 and in Daniel 7.1–8 to the contemporary world to show that the Roman empire was divided up into many parts and effectively non-existent, at least to an exegete writing outside Germany and the old Middle Kingdom and before the papal schism of 1159. The fact of division and the indifference of its contemporaries to the coming of Antichrist led Ralph to issue his warning. Joachim of Fiore (c. 1130–1202) was to develop spectacularly the notion that the end of the present age inaugurated by the New Testament was now coming and that judgement by the Spirit was imminent.

The study of Scripture in the schools at the end of the twelfth century underlay a further series of debates concerning other aspects of legal reform. The reformers were Biblical scholars with a progressive moral outlook. For example, the Parisian theologian Peter the Chanter attacked the practice of judgement by ordeal. Peter regarded the use of ordeals not only as empirically unreliable but also as unlawful by the light of the Old and New Testaments: 'Thou shall not tempt the Lord thy God' (Deut. 6:16 and Matt. 4:7). Ordeals constituted for Peter a flagrant *demand* for a miraculous intervention, for a *judicium Dei*; canon 18 of the Lateran Council of 1215, by renewing the censures of earlier church councils against clerical involvement in ordeals, reflected both the powerful influence of the teaching of Peter and a wider movement towards more rational legal procedures. Peter believed that a return to pure Scripture would eliminate bad customs; these included the use of capital punishment for simple theft and for heresy, practices against which Peter marshalled passages from Scripture as well as from the Church Fathers, but which persisted in spite of his protests.[48]

47. Cf. Smalley 1981, pp. 53–6.
48. On the social views of Peter the Chanter and his circle see Baldwin 1970. Peter's critique of capital punishment and of ordeals is examined by Baldwin 1970, vol. I, pp. 318–32, with full references to

The study of the Church Fathers

Next to the Bible in authority were the Fathers and amongst them Augustine was by far the most widely read and influential in the Latin West. Augustine's *City of God* contains much that has nothing to do with politics or political thought; the main drive of its argument concerns the problem of how the providential working out of God's purposes was to be seen to unfold in the fall of a Roman empire which was also a Christian empire. Augustine in the end rejected the notion that a Christian empire was the sacral fulfilment of the destiny of Rome. By putting forward an abstract division between two mutually exclusive 'cities' (a heavenly city which is both here and in the world to come and which contains all the elect, and an earthly city which is also of both worlds but which contains all the unjust) Augustine encouraged his medieval successors to envisage human society as a mixture of people belonging both to the supernatural world and to the present time and place in which its citizens live on earth.

Augustine's scheme was far from fully worked out in the *City of God*. It was given more coherent treatment by Orosius in his *History Against the Pagans* which he submitted to Augustine, as the compliment of a grateful pupil. Orosius wrote a universal history divided into a formal time-scheme of four monarchies. He transmitted the idea that the fall of the Roman empire would be the beginning of the age of antichrist. These were additions to Augustine's division of world history into six ages which correspond to the ages of man and to the six days of creation. (The time from Adam to Noah was the infancy of the world; from Noah to Abraham was its childhood; Abraham to David its youth; David to the Babylonian captivity its manhood; the Babylonian captivity to John the Baptist its middle age; the time between the First and Second Comings of Christ its old age.) The struggle between the two cities could, on this interpretation, be seen to work itself out in history. This historiographical complexion was more important than any application of Augustine's theory to the understanding of the form and function of political structures, because it provided later students with a key to the events of their own day, and, as it seemed to them, a means of calculating when the world would end.

The *History of the Two Cities* written between 1143 and 1145 by Otto of

Peter's writings in vol. II, pp. 212–20. For an earlier objection to the practice of ordeals in the course of a Biblical commentary see also Robert of Melun *Quaestiones de epistolis Pauli* at Heb. 6.16 (ed. Martin 1938, p. 302): 'haec iudicia non sunt Ecclesiae. Unde et rei multociens inde absolvuntur, et non rei quandoque iudicantur. Quod nequaquam fieret, si mater Ecclesia haec haberet. Unde in quibusdam locis potius haec tolerat quam commendet.'

Freising, the uncle of Frederick Barbarossa, made much use of the thinking of Augustine and Orosius. Otto had studied at Paris, was briefly a Cistercian monk, then abbot of Morimond and finally bishop of Freising. He set out to bring Orosius up to date and to tidy up the scheme Augustine had proposed, using the system of six ages and four monarchies. He firmly identified the City of God with the institutional church, as Augustine had not done because he believed that there were many, ostensibly members of the church, who, unknown even to themselves, were really members of the Devil's 'city'. In the twelfth century, the matter seemed to Otto of Freising to resolve itself into a conflict between spiritual and temporal. As a monk, he wanted readers to turn their backs on the *civitas mundi* and to commit themselves to the *civitas dei*; as a bishop, he believed the separation to be necessary on other grounds as well. This comes close to identifying the two cities with church and state; the Investiture Contest was still fresh in men's minds, and the church's possession of temporal power a burning issue. Otto felt it proper to justify the church's possession of temporal power on the basis of Constantine's supposed grant in the Donation, although the Cistercian in him suspected that God may have been better pleased by the humble status of the church in former times than by its present 'exaltation'. On the whole he preferred to regard the 'two swords' of temporal and spiritual power as distinct in their spheres of jurisdiction (Prologue to Book IV). However, Otto's reworking of the doctrine of the two cities seems to have been an independent effort; the manuscript tradition suggests that his work had little circulation outside Germany. The notion of the 'two swords' captured contemporary imagination more strongly.[49]

Bernard of Clairvaux has been described as the last of the Fathers of the Church. However, his political thinking was also, like almost all his reflections, the product of his efforts to find a way to a solution of contemporary practical difficulties. In the early 1130s he involved himself in the settling of the papal schism and from then onwards he was never free for long from political responsibility in areas (large or small) where the rights of the church seemed to him to be threatened. In 1145, on the election to the papacy of Eugenius III, who was a Cistercian monk, Bernard voiced his anxiety in his letters. He feared that Eugenius would prove unequal to the office as he thought it should be filled: by a man able to be hard-headed and authoritative in asserting the church's rightful position and at the same time humble at heart, remaining a monk within. This is exactly the paradoxical

49. The occurrence of the 'two swords' motif in poems written in Germanic lands has been noted by Szövérffy 1954, pp. 308–9.

ideal drawn by Gregory the Great in his *Regula pastoralis* and his letters. This balancing of the inward and outward life of the Christian, the contemplative and the active, had been a constant theme in the writings of Gregory the Great, himself a monk turned pope. His *Regula pastoralis* opened with a call to *consideratio*. Bernard, in a letter to Eugenius, developed Gregory's notion and gave Eugenius practical advice on the selection of cases to hear personally from the welter of litigation which was brought to the papal court and was taking up a disproportionate amount of Eugenius' time. This letter, which became the first book of the *De consideratione*, was followed after the failure of the Second Crusade by four more books, written over a period of nearly a decade. Bernard examines the pope's relations, not only with himself (Book 1), but also with those beneath him in this world and those around him, and finally with the heavenly realm above him. The claim he puts forward consistently – and in a nutshell in the discussion of the Gelasian theory of the two swords – is that the pope is the supreme authority in the world. The secular power is subordinate to the spiritual. This so caught the spirit of the assertions of the Hildebrandine papacy of a few generations earlier that it became a highly influential statement of the papal claim to plenitude of power. But it is not perhaps misreading Bernard's intention to see in the *De consideratione* a distant echo also of Augustine's talk of the two cities. Augustine's two cities cannot be identified neatly with the interior and exterior worlds in which the Christian lives on earth, but the essential duality of the Christian life is emphasised here too, the perpetual awareness of another frame of reference from which the Christian cannot entirely remove himself in this life, but where he cannot and must not allow himself to belong. Eugenius is instructed book by book to examine this relationship between two worlds from every vantage-point.

John of Salisbury

One of the most learned men to use classical sources to provide examples of virtue and vice was John of Salisbury, especially in his longest work, the *Policraticus* or *Statesman's Book* (1159). John, as well as being one of the most widely read men of his time, accumulated an unrivalled experience of politics, diplomacy and administration in many courts in several countries on both sides of the Alps, and he wrote about his experience and activities in his *Historia Pontificalis* and in his letters. In the *Policraticus* John cites classical authors on well over a thousand occasions, slightly more frequently even than he cites the Bible and much more often than he cites the Fathers. His readers were impressed by such vast learning, so much so that Vitalis de Furno in his *Speculum morale* (finished in 1305) assumed that the *Policraticus* had been written in classical antiquity and that in it St Augustine had found the famous story of the pirate and king Alexander.[50] John resembles many other contemporary officials and courtiers who were scholarly clerics and who wrote didactic treatises, mirrors of princes, pamphlets and letters in the course of discharging their professional duties: Arnulph of Lisieux, Gerald of Wales, Peter of Blois and Walter Map offer points of comparison. But John's achievement is greater than theirs in the formation of medieval political thought, and it is reflected in the recognition he won. His writings were extensively studied and repeatedly pillaged by jurists, preachers, reforming barons and humanists in the later Middle Ages.

The *Policraticus* is a vast, rambling treatise that has given rise to a number of differing interpretations. It is far more than a mirror of princes and contains extensive criticisms of the lives of courtiers. It has been said to offer a theory of the state and to be a literary-historical encyclopaedia as well as a didactic work of philosophy and a dissertation on the relationship between law and nature. It is, in fact, like John's *Metalogicon*, *sui generis* in an age when there was much experimenting with literary *genres*. Because John presents the 'state' as a straightforwardly social phenomenon, a part of the natural order as well as an organism susceptible to disease (such as tyranny), and because he appeals so extensively to classical political and moral teaching and history, he has been held responsible for secularising medieval political thought and for abandoning traditional political theology. His 'organic analogy' – in which the republic is compared to the human body – seems to derive in part from Plato as studied by John's master, William of Conches, in his glosses on Macrobius' commentary on the *Dream of Scipio* and on Plato's *Timaeus*.[51] In his reflections on the microcosm and the macrocosm and on natural and positive law John echoes both the pagan transmitters of Platonic philosophy and also Roman law.

Modern critics debate the question whether John sought refuge in the world of classical mythology and history and in the stories of the Old Testament because of an inability to write directly about the *Realpolitik* of the king he knew best, Henry II of England. Reasons of prudence may have caused him to concentrate his attacks on typical, not specific, targets and to veil his strictures on contemporary *curiales*. At the time when John

---

50. Cf. Smalley 1960, pp. 241–2.
51. John of Salisbury *Policraticus*, v and vi; William of Conches *Glosae super Platonem*, p. 75. Cf. Kerner 1977, p. 177.

completed his *Policraticus*, Henry was not yet the tyrant he was later seen to be; John hoped, in sending the work to Thomas Becket, that Becket might be an influence for good in the royal court. In his later letters John wrote more freely and openly about controversial issues in which he was involved, but in the *Policraticus* his concern was less with the objective features and workings of contemporary government or its institutions, such as the Exchequer, than with the personal behaviour and morality of courtiers. John would not have seen his own recourse to the Bible and to classical antiquity as a distraction from the present but as a natural and even indispensable means of holding up a mirror to rulers and their servants, of correcting moral shortcomings through philosophical instructions and of providing examples of *iustitia*. In his concern with men's behaviour rather than with the impersonal facts of government John undoubtedly addressed himself to what was most important in the Angevin world of government where the ruler's *vis et voluntas* – or his *ira et malevolentia* – were the principal facts in a system of personal rule[52] and where courts provided opportunities to acquire the favours, the pleasures and the advantages which were the bases of power in a world co-ordinated by patronage.

In his earlier poetic *Entheticus* John had accused the *curiales* of being epicureans and lovers of *nugae* or trifles. He had also attacked the servants of King Stephen who secured important positions under Henry II. He urged Becket to prevent Henry II from following in Stephen's path; cover names taken from Terence and Juvenal hid the identity of the objects of John's attacks – Hyrcanus for Stephen, Antipater for Richard de Lucy, for example. The *Policraticus* is a later collection of essays written at different times and then brought together in 1159; the lack of firm organisation in the completed work as well as its numerous digressions reflect the multifarious process of its composition. Book 7 of the *Policraticus* apparently began as a rhetorical exercise in the second half of 1156 when John was disgraced by Henry. He took Boethius' image of Fortune's wheel as his theme; he surveyed the major teachers of philosophy in antiquity, Pythagoras, Epicurus, Socrates, Plato and Aristotle, and he inquired into their views regarding happiness and virtue in what became Books 7 and 8. The space devoted to the problem of tyranny in these books (chiefly Book 8, chapters 17–23) is comparatively little. Books 1 and 2 were drafted in the summer of 1157 and deal with magic, astrology, superstition and the interpretation of dreams; they were addressed to Becket. Books 3–6 were started later; these books are a lengthy 'mirror of princes' into which are woven criticisms of

52. Cf. Joliffe 1963.

courtly parasites (*adversus Gnatonicos, Gnatho* – the parasite – being the title of one of Terence's plays). John completed the *Policraticus* in the summer of 1159 and, in gathering the books together and examining them, he united hitherto separate treatises dealing with courts and rulers and with moral philosophy under the title of *Courtier's Trifles and Philosophers' Remains (De nugis curialium et vestigiis philosophorum)*. The completed work was sent to Thomas Becket at Toulouse in July 1159 and to Brito, subprior at Canterbury, after John returned there in the same year. Only after this did John provide the title *Policraticus* or *Statesman's Book*. The rhetorical manner in which John uses *exempla*, parades pluckings from his sources and provides many learned digressions shows his ethical and literary intentions. John's unwillingness to analyse the concrete workings of government is to be explained by the fact that the *Policraticus* was not intended to be strictly or solely a political tract but to offer a wide-ranging, unsystematic, moral and philosophical programme to guide courtiers and their rulers towards a correct knowledge of letters, philosophy and law, and away from false and particularly from epicurean ways of life.

In the *Policraticus*, then, John reveals the considerable tensions and strains between English clergy trained in the French schools and the holders of English castles; between educated philosophers and courtiers; between clerical ideologists versed in law, letters and theology, and the servants of the great tyrants, chief among them the *teutonicus tyrannus*, Barbarossa, the enemy of Popes Adrian IV and Alexander III, but including also Roger II of Sicily, Stephen of Blois who imprisoned bishops, Eustace who pillaged the abbey at Bury St Edmund's, and eventually Henry II who promulgated the Constitutions of Clarendon and martyred Becket.

The problem of tyranny looms large therefore in the *Policraticus* as well as in many of John's letters, and John has sometimes been presented as a reviver of Roman republican values through his justification of tyrannicide. In *Policraticus* III.15 he refers to Cicero as well as to the Gospel of Matthew 26.52 in defence of the killing of a tyrant; in *Policraticus* IV.1 he makes a distinction between lordship and tyranny; in *Policraticus* VIII.17 he again urges tyrannicide (*tirannus plerumque occidendus*) though his concern here is mostly with the spiritual tyranny of the ruler who fails to be the image of the Godhead; in *Policraticus* VIII.20 and 21 he mentions a book he claims to be writing under the title *De exitu tirannorum*, and he lists some contemporary examples of tyrannical princes – among them King Stephen's son Eustace, Geoffrey de Mandeville and Ranulf of Chester – who had recently met an unedifying or miserable death. In reality, John's exhortations to tyrannicide are more a matter of principles than of practical politics, and are progressively qualified. John proposes no concrete plan of action nor does he seem to want the slaughter of any particular tyrant. Rather he suggests that God will punish. The justification of tyrannicide in *Policraticus* III.15 is couched in general terms, and in *Policraticus* VIII.18 tyrannicide is presented as a last resort. In *Policraticus* VIII.20 the safest and most effective means available to the tyrant slayer (who is *minister Dei*) is revealed to be prayer. Nor should anyone kill the tyrant who is bound by an oath of fealty or who would lose honour thereby; the use of poison is also prohibited. While the figure of the tyrant no doubt reflects some contemporary facts, John uses it as a literary foil and counterbalance to throw into relief by contrast the figure of the good prince, the model of justice.

Muslims and Jews

The extension of the political boundaries of Latin Christendom during the age of Crusades, to embrace peoples who were not all Catholics or Latins, made European society both more complex and more unified. In the Mediterranean world in the twelfth century as never before Greek, Islamic, Jewish and Latin currents of thought intermingled; Latin conquests brought Europeans into closer contact with Muslims in Spain, Sicily and in the Holy Land. The Muslim *Falāsifa* or philosophers possessed a wide range of the works of Aristotle and of his commentators, as well as of Plato and Galen, all in Arabic versions. Their own thought cannot be overlooked in an account of European political thought in the Middle Ages, not least because in Andalusia in the twelfth century, under the leadership of Ibn Rushd, a major revival of Aristotelianism took place. Already in the century and especially in Spain Latin scholars were developing a considerable interest in Arabic learning, and the intellectual life of the Latin West was deeply affected by the arrival in the twelfth and thirteenth centuries of successive consignments of translations into Latin of philosophical and scientific writings of Muslim, Jewish and Greek origin. In earlier centuries that part of ancient Greek and Roman thought which was known had become naturalised in the Christian West, but the range of available writings was greatly extended in the twelfth and thirteenth centuries by the new translations; in addition Arabic writings and commentaries were eagerly studied in the West in Latin versions.

Arabic writings on philosophy and science were important influences in their own right and did not merely serve as a quarry for searchers after classical Greek or Roman thought on man and the world. Nonetheless, whereas, at the beginning of the twelfth century, only two of Aristotle's logical writings (the *Categories* and *On Interpretation*) were available in Latin in the West, many other works of Aristotle were translated out of Arabic as well as Greek in the twelfth and thirteenth centuries and these were to be a very dominant influence in the reshaping of the scholastic philosophy of the university masters in the thirteenth century.[53] Aristotle's *Politics* was not translated into Latin until c. 1260 and then out of Greek, but his *Nicomachean Ethics* began to circulate in Latin in the twelfth century, and other works by him on natural philosophy and logic also arrived before the thirteenth century. In addition, commentaries on Aristotle's works written by his greatest Muslim interpreter, Ibn Rushd, were also translated from the 1220s and 1230s.

To summarise the situation of Islamic culture solely in the light of the contributions it made to the broadening of Aristotelian culture in the Latin West would, however, be misleading. It was certainly important for the survival of Aristotle that his works were introduced into the Arabic-speaking world from the eighth century at a time when the Abbasids of Baghdad were receptive to Hellenistic and Jewish influences. But it is possible that the *Politics* of Aristotle was never translated into Arabic, whereas by the tenth century full Arabic translations of Plato's *Timaeus*, *Republic*, and *Laws* had been made. The political thinking of the *Falāsifa* after Al-Fārābī (d. 950) was more Platonist than Aristotelian. Muslims turned to Aristotle for logic, metaphysics, psychology and ethics but they turned to Plato for thought about human society and law. During the classical period of Islamic philosophy – from the tenth to the twelfth centuries – political philosophy was not a marginal activity but a predominant one; the *Falāsifa* assimilated Plato's idea of the philosopher-king and lawgiver into the Muslim idea of the prophet in an ideal religious state. Islamic thinkers therefore encountered Greek political ideas and transformed them into an integral part of their own general teaching.

The leading Islamic interpreter of the thought of Plato and Aristotle before Ibn Rushd in the twelfth century was Al-Fārābī who spent much of his life in Baghdad and in Syria. He organised the branches of learning into a framework of prophetic philosophy; in addition to summarising the philosophy of Plato and of Aristotle, he attempted to make it meaningful in the context of the revealed religion of Islam. In particular, he wrote a

---

53. On the history of Latin translations of Aristotle's writings see d'Alverny 1982, pp. 435–7, and Dod 1982, pp. 45–79.

commentary upon Plato's *Republic* and possibly also upon the *Laws*. Al-Fārābī saw the subject-matter of what we call political science in terms of the characterisation of the different kinds of states and rulers and in terms of the investigation of the causes of happiness and of the ways to attain it through the exercise of virtuous (as distinct from ignorant) rulership over the city or nation. He investigated the elements that made up the Islamic community – the rulers, the law, the different kinds of states – and held that the functions of prophecy, lawgiving, philosophy and rulership did not differ and should be linked in one person, an ideal Caliph, who is both prophet-lawgiver-*imam* and (under the inspiration of Plato) philosopher-king. Thus he created a political theology in which religion and philosophy met and which allowed of methodical inquiry. He also emphasised the active role that philosophers should play in legal and political affairs and he dreamed, as Dante was to do, of a world-wide society based upon a common faith and organised under one ruler, a philosopher-prophet. There was much in Al-Fārābī's writings, particularly in *The Virtuous City*, *The Political Regime*, *the Enumeration of the Sciences*, *The Attainment of Happiness*, *Plato's Philosophy* and *Plato's Laws*, that was potentially important to the central and continuing concerns of medieval Christian and Jewish political thought: Al-Fārābī explored fundamental questions about the relationship and the harmony between philosophy, revelation and human law; he established the place of political science in societies which have a prophetically revealed religion and spiritual objectives; he surveyed the philosophy and the political thought of ancient Greece, especially that of Plato. He reflected upon the *jihād* or holy war; he proposed the analogy between the state and the human body. But Latin translations of Al-Fārābī's works were less widely available than Hebrew versions in medieval Europe. Although Dominic Gundissalinus (Gondisalvi), perhaps in collaboration with Ibn Dawud (Iohannes Avendauth), translated about half of the *Enumeration of the Sciences* after c. 1150 and although Gerard of Cremona made a complete translation in Toledo in c. 1175, Al-Fārābī's contribution to the development of Latin political thought was almost nil.

Muslim thinkers after Al-Fārābī did not fully share his conviction that a philosopher should try to lead the citizens of nations towards union with spiritual beings and supreme happiness. Ibn Sina (Avicenna, AD 980–1037), who owed much to Al-Fārābī and who was to exert a strong influence on Islamic, Judaic and Christian speculation, discussed the ideal state in the tenth part of his *Metaphysics*; this was translated into Latin after c. 1150. In addition to this, in his treatise on *Prophecy*, he assigned to the prophet the double task of providing political rule and philosophy. Political philosophy has two parts, one of which is concerned with kingship, the other with prophecy and with man's need for divine law. But for all his admiration of Plato's treatment in the *Laws* of both prophecy and law, Ibn Sina stopped short of identifying the prophet with the philosopher-king. Among Spanish Muslim philosophers, Ibn Bajja of Saragossa (Avempace, d. AD 1138) concluded from his study of Plato that the ideal city is unrealisable; it would only exist if every citizen first achieved the fullness of human existence. Philosophers, faced with the problem of life in an imperfect state, would only find happiness in solitude and self-government after withdrawal from public life and after dispensing with the need for physicians and judges. Ibn Ṭufail of Cadiz (1100–1184/5) likewise held that the philosopher's way of life was incompatible with the life of the multitude, but the work for which Ibn Ṭufail was to become most famous, *Ḥayy ibn Yagzān*, was first translated into Hebrew by Moses of Narbonne only in the fourteenth century and into Latin in the seventeenth century by E. Pocock.

The Jewish thinker Moses Maimonides, who was born in Cordova in 1135 and who died in 1204, was also a disciple in political theory of Al-Fārābī and of Plato. Man, he believed, needed the state for his perfection and happiness; in a society living according to a revealed religion the prophet assumes a political function as a ruler and a giver of law. The Biblical prophets may be seen as philosophers endowed with special qualities of imagination, and the religious community may be regarded as an ideal state. Like Al-Fārābī Maimonides includes the study of prophecy and of religious legislation in the list of the sciences. In his *Millot ha-Higgayon* xiv, having distinguished (like Aristotle) theoretical and practical philosophy, Maimonides outlines the scope of the study of ethics, economics and politics; he paraphrases some of Aristotle's general statements of which he had a vague knowledge. Maimonides also introduces a fourth class of practical philosophy which he calls 'the government of the great religion or of the other religions'; this corresponds to religious law, both Muslim and Jewish.[54] Western Arabic philosophers, writing in Spain and in the Maghrib, whether they were Jews (like Maimonides) or Muslims, generally put a high value upon Aristotle's writings. For Maimonides in particular Aristotle represented 'the extreme of human intellect, if we except those who have received divine inspiration'.[55] To understand Aristotle should be the highest ambition of a reasoning man. In his chief philosophical work,

---

54. Wolfson 1973a, pp. 493–550; Wolfson 1973b, pp. 551–60.
55. *Letter to Samuel ibn Tibbon*, ed. Marx 1934–5, p. 380. Here (p. 379) Maimonides also praises Al-Fārābī's *Principles* (his treatise on the *Political Regime*) as 'pure flour'.

the *Moreh Neḥukim* or *Guide of the Perplexed* Maimonides aimed to show that Scripture and the Talmud, correctly interpreted, are in full conformity with the metaphysical and ethical teachings of Aristotle. This respect for Aristotle proved important to Latin thinkers after the twelfth century; when they encountered the writings of Maimonides, they were impressed, not by his debt to Al-Fārābī in political or practical philosophy but by his adherence to Aristotelian philosophy.

The strongest Muslim influence upon the ways in which Aristotle was studied in the Latin West after the twelfth century was Ibn Rushd of Cordova (Averroes) who lived for most of his life (1126–98) in Spain under the Almohads and in Marakesh. The influence of his monumental attempt to restore Aristotelian philosophy in its authentic form was shortlived in Islam; on his death the philosophical tradition founded by Al-Fārābī came to an end and few copies of the original Arabic versions of Ibn Rushd's works are known. But Ibn Rushd's commentaries on Aristotle fared better in Hebrew and in Latin translations and became an important part of Judaeo-Christian culture. However, like Maimonides, Ibn Rushd was a follower of Plato in political thought: he studied sympathetically Plato's ideal state with the qualification that for him the ideal state was Islamic and originated with the prophet-lawgiver. He wrote a commentary upon Plato's *Republic* in c. 1177 in which he included observations on contemporary Muslim institutions as well as applied Plato's account of political decline to the case of his native city of Cordova. Although Aristotle's *Politics* was not available to him, he commented upon the *Nichomachean Ethics* and his middle commentary on this work was translated into Latin in 1240. The Latin scholastics of the thirteenth century, thanks to the initiative undertaken by Michael Scot, possessed translations of most of Ibn Rushd's commentaries on Aristotle by about 1250. But his commentary on the *Republic* did not circulate widely; it was first translated into Hebrew only in the early fourteenth century by Samuel ben Yehuda of Marseilles and was not translated into Latin until 1491. Moreover, when they encountered Ibn Rushd's commentaries on Aristotle in the thirteenth century, the Latins were more interested in his work on natural philosophy, physics and metaphysics, than in his ethics. The scholastics, therefore, when they created a Latin brand of Averroism, failed to appreciate Ibn Rushd's place in the history of political thought, as well as failing to understand the richness of Islamic political thought in general or to gain access in particular to its Platonic inheritance. As a result Latin political thought developed along lines very different from those taken in Islam.

Islamic political thought on the eve of the arrival in the Christian West of

Aristotle's *Politics* was, therefore, more interesting than Latin western Christians realised in the twelfth and thirteenth centuries. In the writings of Al-Fārābī the Latins could have studied an extensive political philosophy that was indirectly meaningful to Christian states; they were certainly made aware by these writings of the existence of Aristotle's treatises on *Politics* and *Ethics*. But Al-Fārābī's own contributions to political thought did not excite curiosity in the Latin world. Latin translations of the writings of Maimonides, Avicenna and Averroes were to exert an incalculably wide and deep influence on the scholastics; they found the imprint of Aristotle's teaching in them but they seem to have overlooked the imprint of Plato's *Republic*. Aristotle's triumphant entry into the Latin West, the discovery that Aristotle was not merely a logician but also a natural and moral philosopher, was initially due to the Arabs. It has been argued that the development of Aristotle's reputation in the West initially came about not so much because of a growing curiosity about his natural philosophy as because translations into Latin of Arabic astrological works generated an interest in other scientific writings available in Arabic versions in Spain. Hence, perhaps, the Latin failure to discover Islamic and Platonic political thought, even to discover Plato's dialogues or to suspect the extent to which Islam had preserved the most important ancient works of political thought. In the event it was not in Islam that the Latins found the text of Aristotle's *Politics* or his *Ethics*.

The western background to the reception of Aristotle's natural philosophy

The arrival in the thirteenth century of Latin translations of Greek texts of Aristotle's *Ethics* and *Politics* occurred after new ideas about natural philosophy had begun to be current in the West.[56] Even before Aristotle's writings on natural philosophy became widely available in Latin translations made from the mid-twelfth century onwards, theologians and lawyers viewed nature as a normative power.[57] Some writers in the twelfth century constructed philosophies in which the workings of natural forces and the natural law played a large role. The many Latin translations made in the twelfth century of works on medicine, astrology, magic and alchemy written by authors such as Ptolemy, Galen, Albumasar, Ibn Sina, Al-Fārābī, Alfarghani, and others who were anonymous or pseudonymous, represent

56. On the following see in particular Gregory 1958, 1966, pp. 27–65, and 1975a, pp. 193–218.
57. Seneca's adage – *propositum nostrum est secundum naturam vivere* – was quoted by writers as different as Abelard and William of St Thierry. Cf. Nothdurft 1963.

a remarkable surge of curiosity about such matters which was nevertheless rational in its objectives. The search for physical or natural causes of things did not first reappear in the lifetime of John of Salisbury or of his tutor William of Conches, although they and others gave a new impetus to such studies, nor was the order of nature seen in terms of contrast, still less of conflict, with the divine plan. *Natura* was often a synonym for *Deus* and, as we have seen, Gratian of Bologna equated natural with divine law.[58] But William of Conches was particularly emphatic that the works of creation – he was thinking of the composition of the microcosm and the macrocosm – should be explained by reason and by natural causes, not miraculously or allegorically. Order rules the world, and by order William meant the order of nature established by God.[59] Moreover, the rationality of nature was not emphasised only by writers with a scientific cast of mind. William of Malmesbury, the monastic scholar and historian, (c. 1080–1142) in his account of the speech of Stephen Harding prior to the establishment of the order of Cistercian monks, explains the rule of St Benedict as a means of regulating the vagaries (*fluxum*) of nature by reason: 'By reason the Supreme Author of things has made all things; by reason he rules all things; by reason the fabric of the heaven is rotated; by reason even the stars that are called wandering [i.e. the planets] are turned; by reason the elements are moved, by reason and equilibrium our nature subsists.'[60]

In the Stoic writers of antiquity was found the idea that nature was a purposeful, creative power.[61] The stress laid by John of Salisbury upon the natural or organic character of the commonwealth, in which individual members are subject to the direction of the head, reflects these trends in natural philosophy. The study of magic and astrology contributed to the

---

58. Gratian *Concordia discordantium canonum*, D.I. On 'the interplay between theology, philosophy and jurisprudence that was of such decisive importance in shaping medieval conceptions of law and government' and on the assimilation of classical ideas of nature and the natural law before the arrival of the new Aristotle, see especially Tierney 1963, pp. 307–22.

59. '*Non tam vero certus ordo etc.* Probat hoc idem scilicet Deum mundum gubernare per ordinem naturae, et est ordo naturae quod similia nascantur ex similibus ut homines ex hominibus etc.' William of Conches, glosses on the *Consolation of Philosophy* by Boethius, ed. Parent 1938, p. 131. On William see further Gregory 1955.

60. '*Ratione supremus rerum Auctor omnia fecit, ratione omnia regit; ratione rotatur poli fabrica, ratione ipsa etiam quae dicuntur errantia torquentur sidera, ratione moventur elementa; ratione et aequilibritate debet nostra subsistere natura. Sed quia per desidiam saepe a ratione decidit, leges quondam multae latae; novissime per beatum Benedictum regula divinitus processit quae fluxum naturae ad rationem revocaret.*' William of Malmesbury *De gestis regum Anglorum*, IV.334. The reference and the English translation are taken from Constable 1982, p. 61 and note.

61. Some key terms and phrases used by twelfth-century writers are: *ignis artifex* ('creative fire'); *potentia rebus naturalibus indita ex similibus procreans similia* ('a power imparted to natural things to procreate like from like'); *virtus agitativa* ('an agitating force'): *ordinata collectio creaturarum* ('an orderly collection of creatures').

understanding of the place of man, the human scale, in the universe. From Macrobius, Plato and *Asclepius* came an interest in man as a microcosm that reflects the structure of the macrocosm. The figure of Hermes was in vogue – the prototype of the wise man, magician, astrologer, prophet, who experiments with and investigates reality in order to master it. The capacity of men to control nature became better appreciated as techniques of agriculture, building, warfare, navigation and commerce evolved. John of Salisbury in *Policraticus* VI.9 was one of those who saw the value of the mechanical arts as a means whereby man improved his natural environment and his own condition and dignity. The view that law is a human instrument for shaping society was linked in the twelfth century with the idea that man and nature co-operate to embellish and to regulate the world.

In legal thought the distinction between *ius naturale* and *ius positivum* derived from Calcidius' translation and commentary on Plato's *Timaeus*; it was first advanced by scholars in France such as William of Conches, Hugh of St Victor and Peter Abelard as well as by French canonists of the twelfth century.[62] Whereas Gratian of Bologna, for example, distinguished natural law (*ius naturale*) from custom (both written and unwritten),[63] the distinction between *ius naturale* and *ius positivum* pointed a little away from the consideration of law in terms of a relationship between God and human custom and towards the view that much law comes into being through positive enactment. The word *positiva* is related to the verb to put, *ponere* – *legem ponere*, *lex posita*, *lex positiva*. That laws are made by conscious decision was more readily acceptable at a time when Justinian's collection of Roman laws was fully available for study and when fresh legislation, both ecclesiastical and secular, was fast becoming a more common activity than it had been for several centuries.

Reasonable all this may have been. Nevertheless, elements of myth blended with elements of rational inquiry: Plato's *Timaeus* – part of which was virtually the only writing by Plato which was accessible as yet in the

---

62. On this Gagnér 1960, pp. 210–40; Kuttner 1936. Calcidius spoke of *positiva* and *naturalis iustitia* and *aequitas* (ed. Waszink 1962, p. 59, ll.19–20). William of Conches in his commentary on Plato's *Timaeus* (in Calcidius' version) writes: 'Et est positiva [iustitia] quae est ab hominibus inventa ut suspensio latronis etc. Naturalis vero quae non est homine inventa ut parentum dilectio et similia.' Hugh of St Victor *Didascalicon*, I, iii, 2: 'Plato . . . libros multos de republica secundum utramque iustitiam, naturalem scilicet et positivam, conscripsit'. Abelard *Collationes* or *Dialogus inter Philosophum, Iudaeum et Christianum*, pp. 124–5: 'Ius quippe aliud naturale, aliud positivum dicitur . . . Positivae autem iustitiae illud est, quod ab hominibus institutum.' Likewise the *Summa Reverentia sacrorum canonum* (written by 1192): 'hoc apud platonem in thimeo ius positivum dicitur' (cited by Gagnér 1960, p. 212, and by Kuttner 1937, p. 176).
63. Gratian of Bologna *Concordia discordantium canonum*, D.I.

Latin world – was a key text underlying a fashion for philosophical poetry that extolled the *ornatus mundi*, the embellishment of the world, and the dignity of man. The central idea of the *Cosmographia* of Bernard Silvestris of Tours (*fl.* c. 1150) is that man is the microcosm of the elements, principles and forces in the world. Bernard makes Providence praise man's infinite potential: 'He shall behold clearly principles shrouded in darkness, so that Nature may keep nothing undisclosed . . . I have established him as ruler and high priest of creation, that he may subordinate all to himself, rule on earth and govern the universe.'[64] Alan of Lille, like Bernard Silvester a philosophical poet, also offered richly evocative visions. Both saw the material world as having been originally in chaos, lacking dignity and awaiting form. But Nature splendidly fashions and informs the world of matter. In an early work, *De planctu naturae* (composed in the 1160s) Alan eulogises *Natura*. She is queen of the universe; her own crown is the starry sky which is composed of the twelve precious stones of the zodiac surrounded by seven moving stones which correspond to the planets. The garments of Lady Nature are ornamented with all living beings as well as plants and flowers. Lady Nature is an instrument of providence, the vicar of God on earth, charged with the production of living things. She is a book in which it may be read that man has been fashioned in the likeness of the world, and the world is a machine created in working order by the divine reason. Alan's image of the cosmos is one of magnificent unity in obedience to God, stretching from heaven to earth, with Nature as its mediator with God. Nature appears too in Alan's famous epic, *Anticlaudianus*, which was composed by 1184. The work brings together the theme of the relationship between knowledge of the created world and knowledge of the divine realm, and the theme of Nature's recreation of mankind. Nature on earth creates a body from the four elements, and from the union of this body with a perfect soul procured from heaven is born a New Man. Here Alan blends Christian and Platonic imagery, but it has been argued that his work looks forward in a millenarian way to the messianic rule of Philip, later Augustus, King of France (from 1180 to 1220), who is to be the new and perfect man ushering in an age of universal peace, leisure and prosperity.[65]

---

64. 'Viderit in lucem mersas caligine causas,
     Ut Natura nichil occuluisse queat . . .
   Omnia subiiciat, terras regat, imperet orbi:
     Primatem rebus pontificemque dedi.'
   Bernard Silvestris *Cosmographia, Microcosmus*, x.
65. Cf. Wilks 1977, pp. 137–57; also Walsh 1977, pp. 117–35, and Marshall 1979, pp. 77–94.

With the close of the twelfth century therefore the philosophy of nature is on the advance. Although such philosophy was bound up with the study and practice of myth, magic and astrology, Aristotle's writings on natural philosophy were soon to enter the West. They provided, at a propitious time, a much more systematic basis for speculation on the idea of nature in the context of political thought as well as in that of metaphysics and science.

V
DEVELOPMENT: c. 1150–c. 1450

13
INTRODUCTION: POLITICS, INSTITUTIONS AND IDEAS

The thirteenth century marked the great turning-point in medieval political thought: an idea of the state was clearly acquired and located within an overtly political and this-worldly dimension. This development had its roots in the twelfth century and was the product of the assimilation of ideas derived from the study of Aristotle and Roman law in universities. Theocratic, hierocratic and feudal conceptions continued nevertheless to exist in parallel with these new ideas and the result was dialogue, interaction and confrontation. Political thought thus became more complicated and variegated in the late Middle Ages, as it mirrored the development of medieval society. A new world was emerging in which territorial states made the universalist claims of the empire anachronistic, while increasing urbanisation and commercial activity contributed to the decay of feudalism. The preoccupations which had dominated political thought in the high Middle Ages suffered a prolonged sea-change and new concerns joined them.

The political context

Relations between the papacy and secular rulers

The main preoccupation of political thought in the high Middle Ages was clearly the relationship between the church and secular rulers, and in particular that between the papacy and the empire. The history of conflict between the popes and the emperors continued after 1150, and indeed the reign of Frederick I Barbarossa (1152–90) saw a major confrontation with pope Alexander III. Frederick sought to apply in practice the universalist conception of Roman emperorship found in the *Corpus Iuris Civilis*, the study of which he favoured at Bologna. He thus saw himself as 'lord of the world' (*dominus mundi*). Frederick's idea of his imperial office involved direct rule over the whole of Italy including Rome, the seat of empire, and a rejection of any papal claims to ultimate secular authority in any sense.

Frederick's Italian campaigns to make his claims real brought about warfare with the city-communes of the north and centre of the peninsula and with the papacy which made common cause with the cities. Frederick lost the war, which was ended by the Treaty of Venice with Alexander III in 1177 whereby the emperor agreed to recognise Alexander and to restore all papal estates and lands; but Frederick salvaged something from his defeat because by the Peace of Constance of 1183 the Lombard cities accepted his ultimate sovereignty over them in return for his granting to them regalian rights and self-government. Furthermore he was able in his last years to begin to rebuild his power in Italy. However the crisis of *Outremer* after the defeat at Hattin led him to respond to Gregory VIII's calling of the Third Crusade; but having threatened to capture Constantinople and destroy the eastern empire he bypassed the city only to meet his death by drowning in the river Saleph in Asia Minor. But his demise did not end the papacy's problems with the house of Hohenstaufen. His son, Henry VI (1190–7), proved to have an even more grandiose conception of Roman emperorship and through combining in his person the imperial and Sicilian crowns faced the papacy with encirclement in Italy. Henry also, considering his Roman emperorship to be unique and universal, definitely planned to conquer the eastern empire which he held to be ruled by a Greek usurper. His early death in 1197 prevented the fulfilment of his designs and removed the immediate threat to the papacy.

Henry left an infant son, the future Frederick II, whom pope Innocent III (1198–1216) made his ward. Because of Frederick's extreme youth an interregnum occurred in the empire. Conflict arose between two contenders for imperial power in Germany: Philip of Swabia who, claiming to be the protector of Frederick's rights, supported Hohenstaufen interests, and Otto of Brunswick. The Hohenstaufen party amongst the princes maintained that through their election Philip had a right to be crowned emperor by the pope. Innocent, who favoured Otto, in the decretal *Venerabilem* (X.1.6.34) elaborated the papal view that since the Roman emperorship was a papal creation the pope had the right to examine and if necessary reject a candidate elected by the princes. Philip he found wanting. In the event Philip was assassinated in 1208 for a reason unconnected with his conflict with Otto. Innocent then, however, found that Otto reneged on his own promises to protect the church, and therefore excommunicated him. The pope turned instead to the young Frederick, who had been crowned *Rex Romanorum* in 1212, and supported him in his warfare with Otto. Frederick was victorious and at the Fourth

Lateran Council of 1215 Innocent declared Otto deposed and Frederick confirmed in his election. The pope had high hopes of his former ward.

In the event Frederick II turned out to be the worst enemy that the papacy faced in the Middle Ages. As emperor he sought to dominate the whole of Italy including the papal patrimony, and thus became embroiled in protracted warfare with the papacy under Gregory IX and Innocent IV. This papal–imperial conflict was marked by an even greater level of bitterness than had previously existed, and by a more complete immersion of the popes in the political affairs of the peninsula. Personal vituperation on both sides reached new depths. Frederick called for a general council of the church to judge his papal opponents, a foretaste of things to come. When a general council did, however, meet at Lyon in 1245, Innocent IV used it to renew the excommunication of Frederick and depose him. Frederick died unreconciled in 1250. There was a brief resurgence of Hohenstaufen power in Italy under Frederick's illegitimate son, Manfred, but he died on the battlefield of Benevento in 1266, defeated by Charles of Anjou whom the papacy supported for the crown of Sicily. The end of the house of Hohenstaufen came when the pathetic figure of Conradin (Frederick's grandson) was executed in 1268 at the age of sixteen after his defeat at Tagliacozzo. The papacy appeared to have been victorious in its conflict with the empire, which indeed never again rose to the level of power which the Hohenstaufen had enjoyed.

Nevertheless the basic problem concerning the relationship between papacy and empire remained unresolved, and conflict flared up again in the early fourteenth century. The emperor Henry VII was initially encouraged by the first Avignon pope Clement V to invade Italy to balance the power of the Angevin king Robert of Naples, and was crowned emperor by the pope's representative in 1312. Henry however developed an imperial policy and considered that the whole of Italy came under his sovereignty. He thus felt able to declare Robert of Naples deposed on grounds of high treason for refusing to stand trial at the imperial court. Alarmed by Henry's imperial pretensions, the papacy made common cause with Robert and confirmed that his kingdom was outside the empire and subject to the church. Robert and the papacy were saved by Henry's death in 1313 and the destruction of his army by malaria.

The last medieval conflict between pope and emperor followed swiftly. In 1314 a double election for the crown took place in Germany: the Habsburg faction chose Frederick of Austria, the Luxemburg party Lewis of Bavaria. Lewis finally emerged victorious from civil war with Frederick at the battle of Mühldorf in 1322. Pope John XXII maintained the traditional papal view that the papacy created the emperor, and thus declared that the empire was vacant during this conflict and that the pope exercised the powers of imperial vicar in Italy. John refused to recognise Lewis as ruler of Germany, summoned him to appear at Avignon, and on the grounds that he as pope could accept or reject any candidate for the empire ordered him not to reassume royal authority until he had received papal confirmation. Lewis was unable to accept these terms and was excommunicated on 23 March 1324. He invaded Italy in 1327 to gain the imperial crown. Having insufficient troops, he was largely ineffective in reestablishing imperial power but in 1328 temporarily gained control of Rome and the papal patrimony declaring John deposed for heresy. In a unique ceremony Lewis was crowned emperor by the city prefect, Sciarra Colonna, and anointed by the excommunicate bishop of Venice. Lewis, however, clearly had doubts about this procedure because he later had his anti-pope, Nicholas V, repeat the coronation in the traditional manner.

Thereafter papal claims to confer the imperial office were increasingly ignored in Germany. At the Diet of Rhens in 1338 it was declared that the king of the Romans was elected by a majority of the princely electors, and that full imperial authority was possessed by the king through this election and without papal approbation. In *Licet iuris* Lewis then declared that election by the princes alone conferred the title of emperor.

Charles IV (grandson of Henry VII) inherited this situation. In the context of increasing princely power he did not follow a strongly imperial policy but rather one of family aggrandisement. He did, however, undertake an expedition to Italy in 1355 to obtain the imperial title. But this journey was not so much a genuine attempt to reassert imperial sovereignty as a money-making expedition devoted to selling privileges confirming their liberties and constitutions to city-republics, and vicariates to *signori*. Although those accepting these grants acknowledged thereby the ultimate sovereignty of the emperor, they knew that he would shortly leave Italy and thus enjoy no direct or tangible power over them. No domination of Rome was involved because Charles had to agree to make only a day-visit to the city at his coronation. On his return to Germany in 1356 Charles issued the Golden Bull which consolidated the developments marked by the Diet of Rhens. The Golden Bull recognised the sovereignty of the electoral princes and declared that the only necessary stage in the choice of the emperor-elect should be that he be chosen by the princely electors. The papacy's claims were simply ignored. The constitutional position in Germany now was that the person elected king of the Romans by the electors had full imperial powers of government and that papal coronation conferred nothing but the imperial title. Two subsequent medieval kings of the Romans obtained the imperial title (Sigismund and Frederick III); the three others did not (Wenceslas, Rupert and Albert II).

The emperorship had in effect largely lost its universal dimension and had become almost a purely German affair. There were, however, some signs of the survival of a wider vision. The emperors continued to grant vicariates in Italy and indeed Wenceslas made Giangaleazzo Visconti the imperial duke of Milan in 1395, an action which contributed to Wenceslas' loss of power in 1400 on the grounds of dilapidation of the empire. Giangaleazzo's courtiers hailed this grant of a dukedom as a resurrection of the empire from the dead. Furthermore Sigismund imitated the emperors of antiquity by summoning the Council of Constance to solve the Great Schism. Overall, however, the emperors were enmeshed in German affairs and their own dynastic concerns.

The papacy did not accept this brushing aside of its claims over the empire, but any protests it made had no effect. The papal view remained enshrined in the *Corpus Iuris Canonici* and the works of papal apologists and canonists. But the world had moved on. The issues involved in the medieval papal–imperial conflict were never solved: the dispute itself withered away as times changed. This is a truly classic example of the way in which problems that appear insoluble because of the entrenched positions of both sides disappear with changing historical conditions.

In general this history of endemic conflict did not mark the relationships between the papacy and other secular rulers. The empire was a special obsession for the popes because they maintained that they created Roman emperors and because of the recurrent imperial pretensions to domination in Italy. With other rulers the popes established a *modus vivendi* which rarely broke down. Modern scholars dispute the extent to which individual popes held fully hierocratic or nuanced dualist views concerning the relationship between spiritual and secular power, but whatever ideas a particular pope might hold rulers tended to be left with considerable practical control over the churches in their own territories. The papacy did indeed try to extend its power by creating papal vassals, a policy followed especially by Innocent III. But papal vassalage did not entail any real subjection to the papacy. Thus the king of Sicily, although he held his kingdom as a papal fief, enjoyed complete practical sovereignty. Furthermore King John of England accepted papal vassalage only to extricate himself from the political crisis attending his dispute with Innocent III over the appointment of Stephen Langton as Archbishop of Canterbury, and thereupon succeeded in manipulating his vassal status to enlist the pope's aid against his political enemies. In the thirteenth century both in France and England the norm was effective royal control over the church. Because of its conflicts with the emperors the papacy needed the support of the French monarchs, and to some extent that of the English as well, and was normally unwilling to endanger good relations with them. Thus in the thirteenth century the papacy acquiesced in both monarchs' practice of taxing the clergy.

The great crisis came in the reign of Pope Boniface VIII (1294–1303) who sought to put the clock back by applying the Fourth Lateran Council's prohibition against lay taxation of the clergy without papal consent. Boniface took a strictly hierocratic view of the relationship between ecclesiastical and temporal power, and attempted to apply it to the French monarch, Philip IV. The kings of France and England were involved in war against each other. The English clergy were already opposed to this war, and Boniface considered that it was scandalous that clerical taxes should be used for war between Christian rulers who would be better employed going on crusade to recover the Holy Land, the last foothold in which had been lost by the Franks with the fall of Acre in 1291. Boniface rapidly lost this first dispute with Philip IV when the latter forbade the export of gold and silver from France, thus damaging papal revenues, and thereby forced the pope to back down. The second dispute was more serious and concerned Philip's claim to try bishop Saisset of Pamiers on charges including treason. Boniface was unable to accept this because according to canon law a bishop could not be tried in a lay court. In the conflict which ensued Philip's councillors manipulated Parisian public opinion on the king's side and called for a general council of the church to judge Boniface for heresy. The pope's policy lay in ruins when he died a few weeks after being briefly imprisoned by the French king's agent Nogaret at Anagni. Under the French threat of a posthumous trial of Boniface at a general council, Clement V annulled all Boniface's measures against Philip. The significance of this dispute is that the papacy had sought to apply hierocratic policies against the monarchy of an emergent nation state and had failed: Philip and his advisers considered that Boniface's arguments were irrelevant against the French crown. Two opposing views confronted each other. The French king considered that his sovereignty was called into issue: how could he be truly sovereign if he could not tax his clergy in a national emergency or try a French bishop for treason against the crown? For Boniface the liberty of the church was at stake: how could it be preserved if laymen could tax clergy at will and bishops be judged in royal courts? The issue was solved by force: as the royal apologist Pierre Flotte said of papal claims in this dispute, 'Your power is verbal, ours however is real.'

The papacy's policy under Boniface VIII was atypical of its normal attitude to monarchs in practice, but was nevertheless an application of traditional papal hierocratic theory which had usually been directed against the Roman emperors. Boniface's view on the relationship between papal and secular jurisdiction was expressed in lapidary form in *Unam sanctam*. But there were to be no further attempts in the remainder of the Middle Ages to apply hierocratic theory to kings in this manner. The Avignon papacy limited itself to attempts at diplomacy in the Hundred Years War and was in this endeavour undermined by suspicions of partiality towards the French. The Great Schism (1378–1417) in which support in Europe for rival popes was divided along national lines served only to weaken the popes in their relations with secular rulers. After the Schism the popes acted primarily as Renaissance princes by concentrating on rebuilding their control in the papal states, and under the threat of the extreme conciliarism of Basel were concerned not to dominate secular monarchs but to enlist their support by means of concordats which confirmed the rulers' control over their national churches: the papacy presented conciliarism as a common danger to monarchy both secular and ecclesiastical. But some ideas die hard, and it was as a throw-back to the age of Boniface VIII, if not of Gregory VII, that Pius V in 1570 in *Regnans in excelsis* declared Elizabeth I deposed and her subjects freed from their allegiance.

The papacy as a governmental institution

From the mid-twelfth century the papacy was characterised above all by its development as a legal and governmental institution. In following this path and thus continuing the work of the reform period, the papacy pursued a policy of centralisation by means of the extension of its jurisdiction. This was the context in which theories of papal power were developed and reactions against them emerged.

The main instrument which the popes employed was the canon law. In the period after Gratian the papacy dominated canon law through the production of decretals, authoritative letters containing papal statements deciding points of controversy. In the second half of the twelfth century the sheer volume of these grew very greatly. The pontificate of Alexander III is particularly noteworthy in this respect. Indeed the twelfth, thirteenth and early fourteenth centuries were dominated by lawyer-popes who kept up the flood of decretals: a sure sign of the extent to which the papacy was considered to be a legal office. Because of the recognition given to the canons of general councils it would not be quite true to say that the papacy monopolised canon law, but it was almost the case, especially since the papacy confirmed the decrees of such councils, which in canon law were legitimate only if called by the pope. The sheer volume of decretal production necessitated official codification on the part of the papacy. Innocent III published the first official collection (*Compilatio tertia,* 1209/10) but this only contained a selection from the decretals issued in the first twelve years of his pontificate, and was followed in 1225 by the second official collection, the *Compilatio quinta* of Honorius III. The chief codifications of the canon law were those of Gregory IX (*Liber extra,* 1234), Boniface VIII (*Liber sextus,* 1298) and Clement V (*Clementinae,* published by John XXII in 1317) which comprised the *Corpus Iuris Canonici,* which remained the law of the Catholic Church until 1918 when it was superseded by the *Codex Iuris Canonici.*

This growth in a papally dominated canon law was intimately related to the development of the papal governmental machine centred round the papal court, the curia. This exercised judicial, administrative, financial and executive functions and was in the twelfth century the most advanced such body in Latin Europe. It was the bureaucratic means whereby the papal policy of centralisation was put into effect. An increasing number of judicial appeals to Rome were made, and from the thirteenth century the papacy supplemented papal tithes and crusading taxes with the imposition of regular general taxation of the clergy. The papacy ate away at the autonomy of local dioceses most notably through the system of provisions and reservations of benefices. Gradually from the pontificate of Celestine III (1191–8) onwards the papacy took over the right to appoint to major ecclesiastical offices. The use of these methods increased considerably in the second half of the thirteenth century and in 1305 Clement V fixed the rule that the disposal of all patriarchates, archbishoprics and bishoprics was reserved to the Holy See. These measures were also a source of revenue, and John XXII, for instance, relied on them heavily to help finance his unsuccessful warfare to regain the papal possessions in Italy. Many prelates benefited individually from papal policy, but overall the process of papal centralisation and financial exploitation tended to produce some animosity at the episcopal level, and there were in the thirteenth century spasmodic national complaints against papal provisions and taxation – by the English at the First Council of Lyon in 1245, and by the French in the *Gravamina ecclesiae gallicanae* of 1247 (also known as the 'Protestation of St Louis'). In England this anti-papal feeling culminated in the statutes of *Provisors* and *Praemunire* of 1351–3.

In addition to their role in purely ecclesiastical government, the popes also operated as rulers in the papal patrimony in central Italy. Their claim to rule there was ancient and was supported by the forged Donation of Constantine. Papal history in the early and high Middle Ages bears witness to the vicissitudes of the popes' attempts to dominate Rome and the centre of the peninsula. Innocent III, however, through his policy of recuperations began a new era of papal control of these lands and there emerged what may be called a papal state. The popes clearly considered that control of such a state was necessary for their security, a view which had been reinforced by their endemic difficulty in ruling the city itself, by the imperial invasions and by the frequent periods of papal exile from Rome. The implications, however, of this development of a papal state were enormous. In order to protect it the popes were increasingly burdened with the preoccupations of temporal rulers: they were drawn into politics and warfare to secure their state. This was the case in their campaigns against Frederick II. Furthermore, in favouring the Angevin cause in Italy against the Ghibelline in the second half of the thirteenth century they preached crusades against their political opponents. In the 1350s Cardinal Albornoz waged war to reestablish a measure of papal power in the patrimony, and the reassertion of the papacy's power in Italy in the 1370s led it into war with its traditional supporters, Florence and Perugia. This political involvement reached its height after the Great Schism and led the secular concerns of the papacy to obscure its spiritual mission. The harvest of the papal obsession with the security of the papal state was loss of respect for the institution of the papacy and a legacy of bitterness in Italy.

Territorial states

In the period after the mid-twelfth century a great development occurred in the ordering and government of medieval society: territorial states began to emerge, and the contrast with the position earlier in the Middle Ages became increasingly marked. Indeed, the growth of the papal state itself may be seen as part of this phenomenon. Thus by the second half of the fourteenth century Latin Europe was divided into a plurality of sovereign states.

It is very difficult to trace the process whereby states in a proper sense of the word began to appear in medieval Europe, because it all depends on how rigorous one wishes to be in applying the term. Although states in a modern sense did not emerge in the Middle Ages, there is a usefulness in employing the term 'state' in an analysis of medieval political organisation from the twelfth century onwards, so long as the limitations involved in this usage are recognised. Furthermore, the process of political development was a gradual one and varied greatly in different parts of Europe. What can be discerned is the emergence of politically organised communities (or peoples) with specific and defined territories within which the internal and external sovereignty of rulers or governments was developed. Crucial to this process was the growth in the number of professionally trained personnel required for the expansion of legal and judicial activity and of government: this training was provided by the blossoming universities from the twelfth century. In a modern state the sovereign authority has a monopoly of law-making and all its citizens are subject to the law of the land. In medieval political communities the government was faced with competing jurisdictions, those of feudataries and the church. In order to establish its authority the supreme secular authority within a territory had to subordinate to itself any feudal jurisdiction and to seek to control the church in so far as ecclesiastical jurisdiction appeared to infringe the proper concerns of secular power. The immunities of the church were indeed to some extent whittled away: in general secular authorities did tend to establish a considerable measure of control over the church in their territories, but this process of attrition was never complete. The extent to which ecclesiastical jurisdiction retained a measure of autonomy in the late Middle Ages prevented the emergence of fully modern states in which either the church would be completely under the control of secular authority or ecclesiastical jurisdiction would be no more than a private set of rules for the church.

If one operates with this limited and specifically medieval concept of the state, it appears reasonable to consider England a state from the reign of Henry II, and because of its precocious administrative development, the twelfth-century Norman kingdom of Sicily would also seem to qualify. The case of France is more difficult because of the problems faced by Louis VI and Louis VII in maintaining royal authority. However, the achievements of Philip Augustus and the consolidation of the French monarchy in the thirteenth century certainly produced a French state, although the particularism of the *pays* was to remain a constant threat to the centralising policy of the crown. Indeed, the success of the last Capetians in consolidating the French state largely disappeared in the fragmentation of France in the Hundred Years War, and it was left to Charles VII and Louis XI to rebuild the state in the fifteenth century. In north and central Italy the situation was completely different. City-states developed with a republican form of government: their beginnings can be traced to the late eleventh century but the hey-day of their growth was the twelfth. This phenomenon occurred both in the lands of the empire (*terrae imperii*) and those of the church (*terrae ecclesiae*). In law these cities were subject to the ultimate sovereignty of the emperor or the pope respectively. But the reality of this subjection depended on whether it could be enforced. As we have seen, in the case of the emperor the realisation of his theoretical suzerainty was merely fitful and finally non-existent, and in that of the popes their overlordship could not be implemented for lengthy periods. Given the political impotence of their nominal overlord, these cities could turn their powers of local self-government into genuine sovereignty. Because, however, the emperor's or the pope's claims to ultimate sovereignty remained valid in law, these cities should be seen as existing within a peculiarly medieval hierarchy of sovereignty in which ultimate and legitimising authority lay with their legal overlord. It is in this context that we should understand the practical sovereignty of such cities as fourteenth-century Florence, Lucca and Perugia (before it lost its independence). Similarly the development of signorial states in Italy from the thirteenth century was in no way undermined by the system of grants of imperial or papal vicariates. In Germany the situation was different again. The emperors failed to develop proper state institutions and state-building as such was confined to the specific lands directly ruled by individual emperors and to those of individual princes. Thus Germany increasingly became a collection of princely states. The Golden Bull of 1356, as we have seen, recognised the sovereignty of the electoral princes, and further facilitated the growth of other sovereign princely states within the empire.

The above areas provide examples of the variety of state development in the period from the mid-twelfth century; they also underwent different experiences of an associated phenomenon: the growth of national feeling. The sense of nationhood emerged in the late Middle Ages, but at no time was it comparable to modern nationalism. The sense of being Italian as opposed to German under the impact of the 'Teutonic fury' (*furor teutonicus*) of the imperial invasions can be traced back to the time of Barbarossa; but with the political fragmentation of the peninsula no feeling of national loyalty developed. Love of one's city and self-definition as its citizen took the place of nationalism throughout the remainder of the Middle Ages. In the thirteenth century clear evidence for some idea of nationality is found in the organisation of the archetypal universities of Bologna and Paris into nations, although this was done primarily according to geographical criteria. However, when discussing the late fourteenth and fifteenth centuries one can with more confidence discern national feeling. During the Great Schism western Christendom divided along national lines, and the Council of Constance itself was organised into nations. The differences between the English and the French in this period were fuelled by the Hundred Years War, and there was undoubtedly a growing sense of being English or French especially in the fifteenth century, and most notably with the resurgence of French fortunes from the time of Joan of Arc. Likewise the Hussite revolt in Bohemia was in great measure a movement of Czech nationalism against German influence. The beginnings of German national-ism can be discerned in anti-papal feeling reflected in the 'complaints' (*gravamina*) of the German nation and in early German humanism, although the political fragmentation of Germany did not permit any political expression of national sentiment. In Europe in the period up to 1450 a genuine relationship between the nation and the state can be found only in England, France and Bohemia.

Overall the emergence of territorial states was a major characteristic of the period after 1150. Given the minimum requirements indicated above for the existence of a state, it is arguably misleading to employ the term in describing any period in the Middle Ages earlier than the mid-twelfth century: a certain level of political organisation and governmental sophistication was required. The emergence of a plurality of territorially sovereign states can indeed be contrasted with the demise of the universalist claims of the Roman emperor; but too much should not be made of this view, since there never was much reality behind such claims. The French crown consistently rejected such pretensions of the German monarchs; the German princes and the Italian cities and *signori* successfully sought their own independence; and the papacy, disappointed in the emperors, abandoned its earlier creation of universal emperorship and espoused the cause of territorial monarchy.

Representative institutions

A further great political development occurred in the later Middle Ages: the growth of representative institutions. These were the product both of the increasingly sophisticated structure of town life and of the element of consent inherent in feudal relationships. Whether the origin of such representation was urban or feudal or a combination of both varied from place to place. Whatever the case, the context was provided for the development of differing ideas of representation ranging from participation in government by the community of the realm to government by the people in sovereign city-republics. Furthermore, during the Great Schism and its aftermath the conciliar movement sought to change the constitution of the church through the implementation of ideas of representation (see below, chapter 17.II).

The urban environment for the development of political representation produced its most far-reaching results in north and central Italy. As the emerging communes grew into city-states they evolved increasingly complicated republican constitutions. Although the details of constitutional arrangements varied from city to city there can be discerned a fundamental process common to all of them. When the commune was small enough ultimate authority lay with a general assembly of the people to which the officers of the commune were answerable. As communes grew in size, however, this arrangement was clearly inadequate, and a structure of councils representing the people emerged. The number of such councils, the method of their election and the qualifications for membership varied from city to city and changed within individual cities. Meetings of the general assembly tended to become rarer and rarer. Ultimate sovereignty lay with the people which was represented by its councils and officers, who were either organised in councils themselves or worked in and with them. These councils had specialised legislative, executive and judicial functions and were also supplemented by *ad hoc* committees (*balìe*). Although such Italian city-republics produced the most thorough-going medieval expression of popular sovereignty they should not be thought of as being in any sense democracies. They were all oligarchies to a greater or lesser degree. Only a very small percentage of their populations had full political rights entailing some form of participation in the process of government and legislation. There were thus grades of citizens: all had the legal status of citizens; only a relatively few had full political citizenship. Even so, in medieval terms the level of direct representation which these cities achieved was a very high one and was made possible by their small size when compared with kingdoms.

The above is of course only a schematic treatment. Venice, for instance, indeed had a conciliar structure but was a unique kind of republic, dominated from 1297 by a fixed and hereditary mercantile nobility. Florence also remained in form a republic despite the Medicean manipulation of the constitution in the fifteenth century. Although from the second half of the thirteenth century onwards the number of republican regimes declined with the rise of the *signori*, enough survived in the fourteenth to provide the models for Italian political theories of popular sovereignty, and in the fifteenth Florence was the home for the theme of republican liberty. In Italy feudalism showed a renewed vigour in the late Middle Ages: many of the *signori* came from the feudal nobility and popes and emperors dignified them with feudal titles. Feudalism thus consolidated rule by one man. Elsewhere in Europe, however, the feudal element in kingdoms could facilitate the development of representative forms of government. The prime examples were to be found in England and the lands of the Crown of Aragon (Aragon, Catalonia and Valencia). The element of mutual consent, the essence of the feudal relationship, became enshrined in parliamentary institutions representing the community of the realm. In both areas this development was well established in the fourteenth century. However, the *Cortes* of the lands of the Aragonese monarchy were more independent of the crown than was the English parliament, although both through their control over taxation had gained an acknowledged part in the legislative process. The urban drive towards political participation also contributed to the development of parliamentary institutions in both England and the Aragonese lands: burgesses represented their communities in these assemblies.

The history of France was very different in the late Middle Ages. Effective representative institutions did not emerge. Although it is debatable whether the assembly of the three estates (clergy, nobility and burgesses) called by Philip IV in 1302 was truly an Estates General, meetings of the estates were called from time to time thereafter. Only the Estates General of 1357 attempted to gain a major part in government through the 'Great Ordinance'. This was issued at the time of the weakness of the French monarchy after the battle of Poitiers when John II was in English captivity. The success of the Estates General proved ephemeral, and royal authority was reestablished under Charles V. The Estates General failed to become an integral part of government: it did not gain either any control over taxation or any participation in legislation, which remained the preserve of the king. In the latter stages of the Hundred Years War, after the turmoil of civil war and defeat in the reign of Charles VI, a strong French monarchy emerged under Charles VII, who established taxation without consent and a standing army. Thus the background to French political thought in the period of the war is one of the growth of monarchy at the expense of representative institutions. The Estates General embodied the aspirations to representation felt by the feudal nobility and townsmen, but with no permanent effect. Indeed, Charles VII only called one meeting of the Estates General (1428), and thereafter consulted provincial estates; thus, for the rest of his reign, such representation as there was existed in local assemblies in the provinces of France. Charles preferred to cope with the desire for representation piecemeal rather than be faced with any national assembly of the estates which might tend to undermine his theocratic monarchy.

It remains, however, to mention one further monarchy in order to complete the picture of the range of possibilities for representation in late medieval kingdoms. In the thirteenth century the kingdom of Jerusalem was the mere rump of the realm which had been destroyed by Saladin in the aftermath of the battle of Hattin (1187), but it was notable for the extreme form of its feudal constitution as presented in the codification of the *Assises de Jérusalem*. In this kingdom the nobility as represented in the *Haute Cour* totally controlled the monarchy.

The main trends in late medieval political thought

In the period after the mid-twelfth century the sheer volume of writings which may be considered to have contributed to political thought increased markedly. Overwhelmingly these works were the products of men trained or teaching in universities or friars' schools (such as those of Cologne in the thirteenth century). Indeed the rapid development of higher education, itself partly the result of the quickening pace of urbanisation and economic growth, provided the background and forum for the elaboration of political ideas.

In the period between the 1120s and the 1270s the process of translating the whole of Aristotle into Latin was completed with the exception of the *Eudemian Ethics*, of which only partial translations survive, the *Poetics*, which was translated by William of Moerbeke in 1278 but remained unknown, and the *Rhetorica ad Alexandrum*, which was probably translated in the fourteenth century. The process of assimilation of the new Aristotle at the universities of Paris and Oxford was very slow. There is evidence that lectures on the 'new logic' and some of the works on natural philosophy were being given in both universities in the first decade of the thirteenth century. Indeed in 1210 Aristotle's works on natural philosophy were proscribed at Paris. It was, however, only in the 1240s and 1250s that the real flowering of Aristotelian studies at Oxford and Paris occurred. As far as political thought was concerned the translation of Aristotle's *Politics* and *Nicomachean Ethics* was crucial. William of Moerbeke translated the *Politics* into Latin in about 1260. Latin translations of parts of the *Ethics* were made in the twelfth and early thirteenth centuries, but the version of Robert Grosseteste (c. 1246–7) and its anonymous revision (1250–60) became the prevalent ones. Aristotle's naturalistic political conceptions had the greatest influence thenceforth on medieval political thought, but throughout the rest of the Middle Ages they also provoked intense opposition. The main problem concerned the relationship between Aristotelian ideas and Christian revelation. Scholars in the mid-thirteenth century expressed a wide variety of views ranging from the synthesis of Thomas Aquinas to the 'Averroist' distinction between the truths of theology and those of philosophy. The reaction against the study of Aristotelian and Arabian philosophy culminated in the condemnations of 1277 at Paris and Oxford. Not only 'Averroist' but also some Thomist propositions were proscribed. In terms of political thought the late thirteenth and early fourteenth centuries saw both works which relied heavily on an ultimately Aristotelian view of politics and others which elaborated a traditional papal hierocratic thesis. Discourse One of Marsilius of Padua's *Defender of Peace* would be a prime example of the first kind, and Augustinus Triumphus' *Summa de potestate ecclesiastica* of the second. In his career Giles of Rome (Aegidius Romanus) espoused both view-points. His earlier work for Philip IV of France, *De regimine principum*, was thoroughly Aristotelian, whereas his later treatise, *De ecclesiastica potestate*, written in 1302 at the height of the king's conflict with Boniface VIII, was completely hierocratic in argument.

The growth of legal studies in universities was as important as Aristotelian scholarship for the development of political thought. As regards the study of Roman law the school of the Glossators reached its maturity in the late twelfth and early thirteenth centuries with the work of the Bolognese jurist, Azo. His *Summa Codicis* (1208–10) and *Summa Institutionum* had immense influence. Indeed, his work was a major source for Accursius whose *Glossa ordinaria* on all parts of the *Corpus Iuris Civilis* was the culmination of the scholarship of the whole school of Glossators and remained the standard juristic gloss for the rest of the Middle Ages: it was still printed in editions of the Roman law in the seventeenth century. Because Accursius' Gloss was the fundamental text for the scholastic theory and practice of law during this period a very large number of manuscripts and printed editions of it survive.

Towards the end of the thirteenth century there emerged the school of the Commentators (or Postglossators). These jurists produced commentaries which applied developed Aristotelian logical method and were thus the jurisprudential expression of mature scholasticism. The chief characteristic of the Commentators was that they sought to accommodate the Roman law to contemporary social and political reality. They were thus involved not in the purely academic study of the *Corpus Iuris Civilis* but in the creative interpretation and application of it as a living law for their own times. This attitude, but in a less developed form, was also to be found in the Glossatorial school, especially in its mature period, and amongst post-Accursian jurists who were not Commentators: Odofredus (d. 1265) would be a case in point. Feudal relationships, for instance, were unknown to classical antiquity but the *Libri feudorum* became part of the curriculum in Roman law. Glosses on the feudal law were written in the twelfth century, but the first full-scale Bolognese Gloss was that of Pilius composed in the early years of the thirteenth. The final or Vulgate version of the *Libri feudorum* was produced about 1220, and was the basis for Accursius' apparatus (finished in about 1250). The major commentary on the feudal law produced by a Commentator was that of Baldus de Ubaldis (written in the 1390s). In many ways, however, the aim of the Commentators to accommodate the law to contemporary reality was best shown in the large number of legal opinions (*consilia*) which they produced for specific legal cases or questions. These *consilia* treated all topics and relationships covered by law.

The beginnings of the school of the Commentators can properly be seen in the work of jurists at the university of Orleans in the late thirteenth century. Jacobus de Ravannis (Jacques de Révigny) and Petrus de Bellapertica (Pierre de Belleperche) in particular applied the 'new logic' of Aristotle to jurisprudence. This development occurred at Orleans and not Paris because the study of Roman law was forbidden at Paris by the papacy from 1219. This advanced use of dialectic facilitated deeper and more sophisticated treatment of legal questions. The example of Orleans was followed at the universities of Montpellier and Toulouse, where the work of Guilelmus de Cuneo (Guillaume de Cunh) was particularly notable. The

Italian jurist, Cynus de Pistoia (d. 1336/7), studied in France and brought back the new ultramontane method to Italy. The two greatest luminaries of the school of the Commentators, Bartolus of Sassoferrato (d. 1357) and Baldus de Ubaldis (d. 1400), developed the technique further. A form of apostolic succession was established: Cynus taught Bartolus who in turn taught Baldus. In terms of political ideas Bartolus and Baldus rank with the most important thinkers of the Middle Ages, and their influence can be discerned into the seventeenth century. There were important Commentators in the fifteenth and early sixteenth centuries, such as Alexander Tartagnus (d. 1477), Jason de Maino (d. 1519) and Philip Decius (d. c. 1536), but the great age was the fourteenth century.

The Neapolitan school of jurists merits special attention because of its contribution to the development of the theory of monarchy. Its views reflected the claims of the kings of Sicily to independence from the empire. Of particular importance were the works of Marinus de Caramanico (d. 1288) on Frederick II's *Constitutiones regni Siciliae*, Andreas de Isernia's (d. c. 1316) commentary on the *Libri feudorum* and Lucas de Penna's (d. c. 1390) commentary on the last three books of the *Codex*. The school had a tradition of its own but was in the fourteenth century increasingly part of that of the Commentators.

Canonist scholarship developed in tandem with civilian because the study of canon law benefited from the advances in method made in civilian jurisprudence. It was no accident that Bologna was the university where the science of canon law flourished *par excellence* from the middle of the twelfth century. There was an increasing coming-together of civilian and canonist studies, as is shown by the growing number of scholars with degrees *in utroque iure* from the mid-thirteenth century. There were, however, important differences between Roman and canon law. The authoritative text of the Roman law was fixed in the sixth century with the small exception of the few additions made by medieval emperors to the *Authenticum*. The canon law in contrast was a living law continually being augmented by the papacy. As a result the text of the law could respond to contemporary requirements. Furthermore, there was direct interplay between canonist scholarship and the actual development of the canon law itself through papal decretal output. As we have seen, in the twelfth and thirteenth centuries the papacy was occupied by a series of lawyer-popes who reflected their own legal training in the decretals they issued, and indeed Innocent IV was an important canonist in his own right. Also the papal curia was increasingly staffed by men trained in the law. Thus canonist scholarship played a crucial role in determining to a considerable extent the way in which the canon law grew. In this process the university of Bologna exercised a dominant influence. As far as the canonists' impact on political thought was concerned their contribution was great indeed: it covered a wide spectrum of issues – in particular the role of the papacy and ecclesiastical jurisdiction, the relationships between secular and ecclesiastical authority, the nature of law, representation, corporational concepts and the territorial sovereignty of kings.

The work of Gratian was the turning-point in the development of canonist scholarship. In 1139/40 he produced at Bologna his *Concordantia discordantium canonum* which became known as the *Decretum*. This was a handbook which sought to resolve the mass of contradictions in the unsystematised body of canon law. To achieve this Gratian employed Abelardian dialectical method with great success. He was indeed fortunate in the time and place at which he produced his work, because it fulfilled a felt need so exactly that it became the indispensable foundation for all subsequent canonist scholarship. There emerged a school of canonists known as the Decretists whose work was the elucidation of the *Decretum*; amongst these Huguccio (d. 1210) was preeminent. The collections of papal decretals from c. 1190 onwards provided the texts for the later school of canonists, the Decretalists. Their work, especially in the period up to c. 1350, represented the most flourishing period of medieval canon law studies. Innocent IV in his very influential commentary on the *Liber extra* (written c. 1251) produced the most highly developed exposition of the papal hierocratic theme. He was rivalled only by Hostiensis himself (d. 1271). The *glossa ordinaria* on the *Liber extra* was written by Bernard of Parma (d. 1266). In the fourteenth century the commentaries of the lay canonist, Johannes Andreae (d. 1348) were of the first rank. Modern scholarly consensus is that the period from c. 1350 to 1500 saw less creativity in canonist studies. Nevertheless from the point of view of political thought three writers stand out. Baldus himself at the end of his life (late 1390s) in his lengthy commentary on the *Liber extra* produced major contributions to a very wide range of political and legal questions. Franciscus Zabarella (d. 1417), a major participant at the Council of Constance, wrote large commentaries on the *Liber extra* and the *Clementinae*. Panormitanus (Nicholas de Tudeschis, d. 1445), the most important canonist of his era, commented voluminously on the whole of the *Corpus Iuris Canonici* and became a conciliarist at Basel.

Although Aristotelian studies and legal science dominated the development of late medieval political thought, they did not provide the whole story, as the variety of sources referred to in chapters 14–19 below makes clear. A discrete mass of source material is relevant: for instance, mirrors of kings and princes, coronation orders, tracts on all manner of political subjects and eclectic publicistic literature summoned forth by conflicts such as those between Philip IV and Boniface VIII, and between Lewis IV and John XXII and Benedict XII. In the latter case the political writings of William of Ockham pose peculiar difficulties, and the relationship between his political thought and his theological and philosophical ideas remains a matter for debate. Clearly in the great mass of late medieval literature relevant to political thought ideas which were not the product of Aristotelian or legal studies were drawn on. As we have seen, there was a determined restatement of what may be termed 'Augustinian' ways of thought. Furthermore the work of Franciscans and their sympathisers was most important and particularly crucial for the political implications of the poverty debate (see below, chapter 19). Despite all these provisos, however, the eclectic nature of much of late medieval political thought meant that writers, precisely because of their education, time and again had recourse to Aristotelian and juristic ideas.

The idea of the state

The chief innovation of late medieval political thought was the development of the idea of the secular state as a product of man's political nature. This concept was acquired through the rediscovery of Aristotle's *Politics* and *Ethics*. Aristotle provided a ready-made theory of politics and the state as existing within a purely natural and this-worldly dimension. Indeed the very idea of political science as an autonomous discipline and the notion of the political as a distinct category of human activity and relationships were the product of this new view, and were to be found in Brunetto Latini's *Li livres dou tresor* (completed in the 1260s) and the early commentaries on William of Moerbeke's translation of the *Politics*: those of Albertus Magnus (c. 1265), Thomas Aquinas (on Books I–III,6, c. 1269–72) and his continuator Peter of Auvergne (c. 1274–90). Although ideas of nature and natural law were prevalent before the influx of Aristotelian works from the mid-twelfth century onwards, this rediscovery of Aristotle injected a new conception of nature into medieval philosophy: above all it provided an apparently complete and systematic naturalistic view of the world, the heavens and man's life and purpose. Indeed man's nature was defined as being specifically political. Previously, nature had been seen in terms of divine creation, which had facilitated Gratian's identification of natural law with divine law. Aristotle presented a view of nature which did not depend on creation by God.

A full-scale Aristotelian naturalism did not, however, emerge in late medieval political thought: God remained in the background as the creator of the natural world. The adoption of Aristotelian concepts did, however, permit the different aspects of man's life to be treated in specific categories. Thus political life could for all practical purposes be considered within a purely natural political dimension. The only possible exception was Marsilius of Padua who, it can be argued, adopted an 'Averroist' and thus purely naturalistic approach in Discourse One of the *Defender of Peace*.

There was, nevertheless, another source available for ideas of the state: the *Corpus Iuris Civilis*. The whole structure of the civil law was divided between *ius publicum* and *ius privatum*, thus providing an articulated language for the public and thus political dimension of human life. Although the emperor was described as deriving his power from God, much of the material concerning government in the Roman law was this-worldly in tone. Thus in D.1.1.5 the *ius gentium* was described as the basis of ordered communities, and the references to the *lex regia* present the Roman people as the historical source of imperial authority. A characteristic of medieval civilian scholarship was its this-worldly approach, which became accentuated with the Commentators. Bartolus and Baldus certainly operated with the idea of the state; indeed, Baldus is notable for his combination of Roman law concepts and the ultimately Aristotelian conception of natural, political man. Furthermore, through the application of corporation theory these two jurists were able to make important advances in the development of the idea of the state as an abstract entity (see below, chapter 15.II).

Church and state

The adoption of the ultimately Aristotelian idea of a natural political dimension facilitated a clear distinction between church and state. It was now possible to view the state as a purely natural product distinct from any ecclesiastical structure. Previously in the Middle Ages in so far as rulership was perceived in a Christian context and understood to derive from God it was not possible to make such a distinction with any clarity. The boundaries between the secular and the spiritual were blurred, which accounted for so many of the disputes between ecclesiastical and lay powers. In its theocratic aspect rulership in the high Middle Ages could accurately be described as operating within the church conceived as the body of Christians: popes, emperors and kings all performed their functional governmental roles within the one Christian community.

The distinction between church and state led to varying conclusions about the position of the church. Both Aquinas and John of Paris, for instance, accepted the essentially spiritual nature of the church in contrast to the political nature of the state, but still acknowledged a valid role for ecclesiastical jurisdiction. In so far as the church was understood as a form of governmental institution, ecclesiastical jurisdiction could be legitimate. But emphasis on the church as a mystical body of believers united in spiritual communion could lead to a denial that the church needed government and hence jurisdiction. This was the step which Marsilius of Padua took: he considered that only the state authorities possessed jurisdiction in any meaningful sense. The whole structure of canon law and clerical privileges was thus swept away. As far as the state was concerned clergy were citizens, and the public aspect of religion – that is, religion in so far as it affected the state – was under state control. Thus, for instance, excommunication had to be in the hands of the lay sovereign not of clerics, because of its effects on secular life. Although Marsilius' view of the state was in this sense essentially secular, it was still late medieval in that for him the 'corporation of citizens' (*universitas civium*) would in fact be a 'corporation of the faithful' (*universitas fidelium*).

It was paradoxical that Marsilius in his denial of ecclesiastical jurisdiction was also influenced by a movement which had little respect for Aristotle. In the late thirteenth and early fourteenth centuries the poverty movement inspired by the Spiritual Franciscans brought into question the whole structure of ecclesiastical, and especially papal, jurisdiction. The Spirituals were suppressed under John XXII, but the idea of a purely spiritual church remained strong for the rest of the Middle Ages, surfacing for instance in the fifteenth-century Hussite revolt.

The case of Marsilius, the most radical medieval employer of Aristotelian political ideas, illustrates that, despite the availability of the distinction between church and state, what may be termed a modern idea of the state did not develop in the late Middle Ages. The problem was the role attributed to religion. A thoroughly secular view of man's life in organised society did not emerge. Thus the idea of the divine source of rulership coexisted with naturalistic ideas of the state; the theoretical duty of the ruler to ensure godly government persisted; and for many writers the claims of ecclesiastical jurisdiction still limited the exercise of secular sovereignty.

Territorial sovereignty

From the late twelfth century onwards canonists and civilians developed ideas of territorial sovereignty, thus reflecting trends in contemporary government. Jurists first applied such ideas to the rule of kings. Two famous formulae were used: that the king was emperor in his kingdom (*rex in regno suo est imperator regni sui*), and that he did not recognise a superior (*rex qui superiorem non recognoscit*). These were in origin distinct although they often came to be combined: the *rex–imperator* idea maintained that the king possessed within his territory the same powers which the emperor enjoyed within the empire as a whole; whereas 'non-recognition of a superior' indicated active non-subordination to the emperor. The *rex–imperator* idea emerged in canonist writings in the last decade of the twelfth century, and also in a *quaestio* by Azo produced at the beginning of the thirteenth. The juristic elaboration of the theme, *rex qui superiorem non recognoscit*, derived from a phrase in Innocent III's decretal, *Per venerabilem* (X.4.17.13) of 1202: 'since the king himself [i.e. of the French] does not recognise a superior in temporal matters' (*quum rex ipse [Francorum] superiorem in temporalibus minime recognoscat*). Innocent himself appears to have been reiterating phraseology used by Philip Augustus in his petition to the pope of 2 November 1201. Canonists differed as to whether *Per venerabilem* indicated the French king's *de iure* or his *de facto* independence from the emperor. French and Neapolitan civilians, however, developed the *rex–imperator* idea and the theme of the non-recognition of a superior into a thesis of royal territorial sovereignty. It was Bartolus' achievement to apply the same reasoning to independent cities: the city which did not recognise a superior (*civitas quae superiorem non recognoscit*) was its own emperor (*civitas sibi princeps*). Thus, as can be seen below in chapter 15, a juristic theory of the territorial sovereignty of cities was produced, and when this was linked to corporational concepts a full-scale theory of the territorial state emerged.

The survival of universalist ideas

Although the development of theories of territorial sovereignty was of prime importance in late medieval political thought, ideas of universal authority were still articulated. These universalist ideas were indeed less in tune with the way in which society was evolving but they were highly sophisticated and elaborated for specific reasons. As we have noticed there was a recrudescence of papal hierocratic theory in the early fourteenth century when the papacy's pretensions of this kind were in practice in ruins: as well as Giles of Rome and Augustinus Triumphus, Alvarus Pelagius with his *De planctu ecclesiae* made a major contribution to the thesis of universal papal monarchy. But in the same period there was also an upsurge in pro-imperial argument. In his *Monarchia* Dante Alighieri put forward an involved scholastic justification of the universal sovereignty of the emperor. He was led to this out of desperation at the faction-ridden condition of Italy: he considered that only strong imperial authority could rectify the situation and bring peace. The high hopes he entertained of Henry VII were not justified in the event. Engelbert of Admont (d. 1331) in his *De ortu et fine Romani imperii* rejected territorially sovereign kingdoms and advocated the resurrection of the Roman empire. Marsilius of Padua held that the peace of Italy had been shattered by the illegitimate jurisdictional pretensions of the papacy. When in exile at the court of Lewis IV he espoused the imperial cause against John XXII and Benedict XII, and in his late work, the *Defensor minor*, argued in support of imperial universalist claims.

Government by the people

The survival of universalist ideas demonstrates continuity between the high and late Middle Ages. There was, however, an area of virtual discontinuity: the late medieval development of full-blown theories of government by the people. Properly speaking, this was a phenomenon of the period after about 1250. Previously monarchy justified by divine sanction was the norm of government. As we have seen, such rulership was moderated by feudal relationships, and a form of representation emerged notably in thirteenth- and fourteenth-century England in the shape of the theory and reality of the participation by the community of the realm in legislation, taxation and to some extent government. But a fully articulated thesis of popular sovereignty did not develop from feudal principles.

The recovery of Aristotelian political theory introduced the concept of participatory citizenship within independent, self-governing city-states. The marked similarities between ancient Greek city-states and thirteenth-century Italian city-republics facilitated the assimilation of such Aristotelian political ideas by Italian theorists. The similarities included size, relationship to the city's subject territories, governmental organisation and political problems such as faction. Thus the Aristotelian concept of valid rule by the many could be applied to Italian republics: in both cases only a relatively restricted citizen-body would be envisaged. Nevertheless, the theoretical basis for a thesis of government by the people now existed. There is some evidence for such a theory in the works of Aquinas although he preferred limited monarchy; the populist thesis was, however, fully enunciated by Marsilius of Padua in Discourse One of the *Defender of Peace*. This part of his book can best be understood as an application of Aristotelian political concepts to early fourteenth-century Italian city-republics: the Padua of his youth would be an example. According to Marsilius the people or corporation of citizens was the source of authority; but governmental power could be delegated to one, few or many. Marsilius' theory was, however, more flexible than might at first sight appear. In the *Defensor minor* he expressly applied the political model, described in Discourse One of the *Defender of Peace*, to account for imperial power: all subject peoples had given their authority to the Roman people; the Roman people in turn had given its authority to the emperor through the *lex regia*; and thus the human legislator, which was identified with the corporation of citizens, could also be identified with the emperor. There were indeed indications of this view in the *Defender of Peace* itself.

A theory of government by the people was also articulated in juristic terms, and was the product of civilian scholarship: it formed part of Bartolus' thesis of the sovereign city-republic and was further developed by Baldus. Bartolus' argument was an elaboration of the theme of consent, as chapter 15 below shows. Neither jurist utilised the *lex regia* in constructing this thesis. Earlier Commentators had speculated as to whether the *lex regia* had been revocable or irrevocable: if it were revocable then the contemporary Roman people could regain its original sovereignty. Both Bartolus and Baldus applied the *lex regia* strictly to the question of the origin of imperial power. Bartolus considered that the *lex regia* had been originally revocable, but had become irrevocable with time; Baldus held that it had been irrevocable from the start. It was for them irrelevant to the question of the power of the people in sovereign Italian city-republics.

The idea that the people was the source of authority was also expressed in an ecclesiological setting by the conciliar movement during the Great Schism and its aftermath. As chapter 17.II below shows, there was a considerable variety of views expressed by conciliarists, but the basic idea that ultimate authority in the Christian community lay with the body of the faithful as represented by a general council of the church informed all conciliarist thinking. Conciliarist ideas involved a rejection of the papal hierocratic theme by subjecting the pope to the authority of such councils. The office of the papacy was retained but the pope was seen as a constitutional monarch to be hedged round by a permanent structure of conciliar authority. Conciliarist ideas can validly be seen as contributions to political thought because conciliarist thinkers used arguments from existing political discourse, and expressed ideas of general relevance to political theory; furthermore, because of the position which the church held in late medieval society any treatment of its governmental structure had political relevance. Conciliar thinkers drew on a very wide range of political, juristic and theological sources: within the vast corpus of their works virtually all the material available for the construction of theses of representative government was exploited. But the forms of representation espoused did not involve election by those who were represented. Thus although conciliarism was a theory of representation based upon the ultimate authority of the Christian people, it was clearly in no sense a genuine expression of the idea of government by the people: there was no delegation of power by that people to the fathers of Constance or Basel. Conciliarism remained a clerical movement: the exclusion of the laity from the government of the church laid up trouble for Catholicism in the sixteenth century.

There was, however, another school of thought which expressed ideas of government by the people: the republican tradition of Italian humanism. Humanism may most conveniently be defined as a group of disciplines based on the study of the literature of the ancient world and concentrating on grammar, rhetoric, history and moral philosophy. Humanism properly speaking was imported into Italy from France in the second half of the thirteenth century. Its relationship with the earlier tradition of the *ars dictaminis* is a matter of debate. Humanist-inspired defences of republican liberty emerged in the later thirteenth century in the works of Brunetto Latini, Bonvesin della Riva and Alberto Mussato. The full-scale development of republican ideas by the humanists of early *quattrocento* Florence is outside the scope of this volume as is the debate about the concept of 'civic humanism'. But as Quentin Skinner has shown there is a connection between those Florentine humanists and the earlier rhetorical tradition.[1]

The relationship between Italian humanism and scholasticism in the fifteenth century illustrates that there is no clear dividing line between what may be termed late medieval political thought and that of the Renaissance. The Italian humanists of the early Renaissance rejected the scholastic approach and were particularly contemptuous of the work of the Glossators and Commentators. But a balanced interpretation reveals that scholasticism and humanism existed side-by-side in Renaissance Italy. Indeed, European political thought in general into the early seventeenth century was much indebted to the political and juristic science of the late Middle Ages.

1. Skinner 1978, esp. vol. I, chs. 2 and 4.

I 4
SPIRITUAL AND TEMPORAL POWERS

Towards the end of his classic six-volume scrutiny of medieval political thought in the west, A.J. Carlyle pronounced that

To the Western Church it was in the main clear that there were two great authorities in the world, not one, that the Spiritual Power was in its own sphere independent of the temporal, while it did not doubt that the Temporal Power was also independent and supreme in its sphere . . . This conception of the two autonomous authorities existing in human society, each supreme, each obedient, is the principle of society which the Fathers handed down to the Middle Ages, not any conception of a unity founded upon the supremacy of one or other of the powers.[1]

In one important way, Carlyle was right. That Christ himself had separated the functions of king and priest was one of the axioms of medieval politics. And Boniface VIII's much-publicised burst of irritation at a French insinuation that he was unaware of that fact symbolises the western Church's adherence to the principle of dualism.[2] Nor was that headstrong champion of the *libertas ecclesiae* any less doubtful than his predecessors that it was also axiomatic that the spiritual power was independent of the temporal. But a pope who claimed the papacy's right to institute the lay power 'that it may be' (*ut sit*), to judge it if it acted unethically, even to depose a lay ruler for serious, persistent political misconduct? This was surely to doubt the independence and supremacy of the temporal power in its own sphere, to reject the concept of an autonomous lay authority and to go on, by way of the 'two swords' allegory, to assert a unity of the powers founded on the supremacy of the spiritual. The argument that *Unam sanctam* was atypical and to be set aside as a serious misinterpretation of conventional papal theory before and after the pontificate of Boniface VIII cannot be taken seriously.

Dualism in fact meant different things to different types of ruler. The papacy accepted a principle of dualism but it was so fundamentally

---

1. Carlyle 1903–36, vol. v, pp. 254, 255.
2. 'Quadraginta anni sunt quod nos sumus experti in iure et scimus quod due sunt potestates ordinate a Deo. Quis ergo debet credere, vel potest, quod tanta fatuitas, tanta insipientia sit vel fuerit in capite nostro?' Dupuy 1655, p. 77; Muldoon 1971.

conditioned by another axiom, the superiority of the spiritual power, that it was in effect replaced by a unitary view of the two powers. Emperors and kings, in the name of dualism, challenged and rejected this hierocratic logic. This chapter will seek to identify three main areas within which debate focused on the significance of dualism. It will begin with the papal position since this was the earliest to be systematically articulated, was the one urged, with all the weight of the Church's *magisterium*, on the politicians and intellectuals of Christendom, and gave substance and direction to the policies adopted in that hurly-burly of international politics in which the papacy was such an enthusiastic participant. The evolution of the theory was inseparable from both the actual events of papal politics and the forms of political discussion developed in the schools. In turn, papal theory and practice formed the anvil on which the lay powers hammered out their own particular readings of the principle of dualism. The most important single stimulus to the development of hierocratic theory was the papacy's special relationship with the Holy Roman Empire. Imperialists provided an alternative view of that relationship. Other challenges to the papacy's own concept of its political authority came from national kings. Those mounted by the kings of France and England, for the purposes of a short discussion, may be considered representative of the attitudes of medieval Christian kingship generally.

I

At the very beginning of our period, the nearest approach to a full articulation of the hierocratic logic in its simplest form is to be found in the *De sacramentis christianae fidei* of Hugh of St Victor. It was to prove very influential and, with its inclusion in *Unam sanctam*, achieve classical status. Typically, the context of Hugh's analysis of the relations of the powers was the section of his treatise concerned with the nature of the Church. Thus the premise of his analysis is the reality of the one corporate society of all Christians: one Lord, one faith, one baptism – in the one body of Christ. Certainly this society knew an essential dualism: two orders, lay and clerical, formed the two walls or the two sides of the one body. Each order had its own distinctive way of life. Two peoples, therefore, and two powers, each with its own appropriate grades and orders of rank. Lay and clerical orders, corporal and spiritual, earthly and heavenly, spiritual and temporal: duality within the *multitudo fidelium*, the *universitas Christianorum*, the Church.[3] The logic advances: just as the spiritual life is worthier than the temporal and the spirit than the body, just so much must the spiritual power be considered to excel in honour and dignity the earthly or secular power.[4] A simple honorific precedence, without practical implications in the sphere of government? Certainly not. The superiority of the spiritual translated immediately into severely juridical terms. The spiritual power has both to establish the temporal power and to judge it if it fails to do good. The spiritual power is judged by God alone.[5]

This is a far from complete exposition of the hierocratic theme. Hugh of St Victor had made his points far too laconically for the commentator to be able to define with certainty all its implications. But within his short compass he had revealed much of how dualism could be tempered by being situated within the unitary context of the congregation of all the faithful. Royal power came into being in that congregation which Hugh expanded to include the people of Israel, God's first chosen people, prefiguration of those chosen in baptism.[6] The greater importance of the spiritual life with its corollary, the precedence of the clergy, was interpreted to mean a power to coerce that lay power which it had brought into being. Hugh of St Victor left those principles understated and underdeveloped. There was much to come from canonists, theologians and popes themselves in the way the superiority of the spiritual was elaborated and expanded. But he had gone far towards formulating the essence of hierocratic thought: the lay power enjoys no autonomy; the powers are a unity founded upon the supremacy of the spiritual.

Hugh of St Victor had found no ready formula to blend the different axioms which medieval theory postulated about the relations of the powers: that they were two, that the spiritual power was superior, that the powers were meant to be joined in mutual support and co-operation. Theorists of different persuasions had for some time been feeling their way towards just

3. 'Quid est ergo ecclesia nisi multitudo fidelium, universitas christianorum? . . . Universitas autem haec duos ordines complectitur, laicos et clericos, quasi duo latera corporis unius . . . Duas esse vitas, et secundum duas vitas duos populos; et in duobus populis duas potestates et in utraque diversos gradus et ordines dignitatum; et unam inferiorem, alteram superiorem . . . Due quippe vitae sunt: una terrena, altera coelestis; altera corporea, altera spiritualis.' *De sacramentis*, II.II.2, 3, 4.
4. 'Quanto autem vita spiritualis dignior est quam terrena, et spiritus quam corpus, tanto spiritualis potestas terrenam sive saecularem potestatem honore ac dignitate praecedit.' *Ibid.*, c.4.
5. 'Nam spiritualis potestas terrenam potestatem et instituere habet ut sit et iudicare habet si bona non fuerit. Ipsa vero a Deo primum instituta est, et cum deviat, a solo Deo iudicari potest, sicut scriptum est: *Spiritualis diiudicat omnia, et ipse a nemine iudicatur* [1 Cor. 2.15].' *Ibid.*
6. 'Quod autem spiritualis potestas, quantum ad divinam institutionem spectat, et prior sit tempore et maior dignitate; in illo antiquo veteris instrumenti populo manifeste declaratur, ubi primum a Deo sacerdotium institutum est; postea vero per sacerdotium iubente deo regalis potestas ordinata.' *Ibid.*

such a formula. They looked for it particularly in the allegory of the 'two swords'.

In Chapter 22 of his Gospel, St Luke recounted the events of the Last Supper and began his history of Christ's passion. Having foretold that Peter would deny him and subsequently repent, Jesus warned the apostles that what the scriptures had said of him was about to be fulfilled and his arrest was imminent. They reacted with thoughts of physical resistance: 'But they said: Lord, behold here are two swords.' Jesus replied enigmatically: 'And he said to them: It is enough.'

Modern commentary reads this reply as an abrupt dismissal, perhaps ironic, perhaps sad, of a reaction to his warning of the crisis at hand which Christ found imperceptive and inappropriate. The misunderstanding shown by the apostles achieved its full expression shortly afterwards when 'one of them struck the servant of the high priest and cut off his right ear' (Luke 22.50) only for the action to be rejected by Jesus and the servant healed by him. Peter was ordered to 'Put up thy sword into the scabbard' (John 18.11, cf. Matt. 26.52). The transformation of the two swords literally shown to Jesus by the apostles into an allegory of the two powers, spiritual and temporal, ecclesiastical and lay, was possible only by the medieval approach to the Bible, rejected by modern exegetes. Medieval commentators were far from indifferent to the literal sense but, following the example and instruction of the Latin fathers, moved quickly beyond 'the letter's veil'[7] to elucidate any teaching the text might be communicating 'mystically', by allegory. That two swords had been shown in fact to Jesus was one thing. The significance of the event was another: the figurative meaning of two swords, of Jesus' assertion that they sufficed and his command that the wielded sword should be sheathed was yet another. One of the earliest medieval allegorical interpretations of Luke 22.38 which was also one of the best known because it passed into the *glossa ordinaria* read one sword as the Old Testament, the other as the New, weapons with which the devil was to be combated. They were 'enough', for he who was armed with the doctrine of both Testaments lacked nothing he needed for spiritual warfare.[8] The allegory was apt, dovetailing neatly with St Paul's likening of the 'word of God' to 'the sword of the spirit' (Eph. 6.17). It took no great imaginative leap to understand the clerical function of preaching the word

---

7. Smalley 1952, p. 1.
8. '*Ecce gladii duo* . . . unus noui, alter veteris testamenti, quibus adversarius diaboli munimur insidias. Et dicitur *Satis est* quia nihil deest ei, quem utriusque testamenti doctrina munierit.' *Glossa ord. ad Luc.* XXII.38.

as the exercise of the spiritual sword: 'the priestly sword of the divine word' as Gregory VII put it.[9]

Nor did it strain language to use the word *gladius* in another specifically clerical context. The spiritual sword was the instrument which cut off diseased members from the body of the Church: the sword of excommunication, of anathema, of due canonical retribution, of apostolic indignation: 'the anger of God and the sword of St Peter', in another of Gregory VII's characteristic expressions.[10] The spiritual sword was thus not merely the image of the ecclesiastical pastoral function of preaching the faith. It was also the image of the exercise of ecclesiastical jurisdiction itself. Such had become the ordinary usage of the papal chancery by the pontificate of Gregory VII.[11]

It also used the term 'material sword' for the exercise of the function of kingship. Again, the image came into the papal vocabulary ready-made from scripture itself. St Paul had decreed the duty of Christians to submit themselves to the civil authority and provided, incidentally, a definition of the role of that authority: 'For he is God's minister to thee, for good. But if thou do which is evil, fear: for he beareth not the sword in vain. For he is God's minister: an avenger to execute wrath upon him that doth evil' (Rom. 13.4). St Peter echoed the substance of this teaching though without specific use of the word 'sword': the civil authority established 'for the punishment of evildoers and for the praise of the good' (*ad vindictam malefactorum et ad laudem bonorum*, 1 Pet. 2.14). This language of the apostles, expressing the divine origin of the temporal power and the ministerial function of monarchy, was the substance of the symbolism of the conferring of a sword in royal coronation ceremonies from their beginnings. Thus the two swords, spiritual and material, were the weapons of Christian warfare: 'the priest fights, as the Apostle says, with the sword of the word . . . the king fights with the material sword, since he is the Lord's minister, avenger in wrath on those who act with evil'.[12] The swords image conveyed in shorthand form two basic principles: God had established two powers and he meant them to co-operate. Together, 'under him and for him', they promote the common welfare of the Christian people. Such were the unexceptionable basics of the relationship of the two powers.

If the two swords image symbolised nothing more than the distinction

---

9. *Registrum* III, 4: 'gladius sacerdotalis divini verbi'.
10. *Reg.* II, 31: 'ira Dei et gladium sancti Petri'.   11. Levison 1952, pp. 22–3.
12. 'Pugnet sacerdos iuxta apostolum gladio verbi . . . Pugnet rex gladio materiali, quoniam Domini minister est et vindex in iram his, qui male agunt.' Deusdedit, *Libellus contra invasores*, 2.300.

and necessary concord of the powers it would not have found a major role in any account of medieval political thinking. What gives the doctrine of the two swords its especial significance springs from what it tried to say about the relative superiority and inferiority of one to other. No one denied that in some sense the spiritual power was the superior. But what had the image of two swords to express concerning the nature of that superiority? The matter was debated for at least a century and a half, sometimes in all the acrimony of empire–papacy controversy, more frequently, more coolly, among academics in the schools. Such discussions go far to reveal to the historian how medieval men analysed the basic principles of the relationship of the powers, or if one will, of Church and State.

The period of debate began in 1076 with a broadside from Henry IV (or from his ghost writer, Gottschalk of Aachen) against what he called the *Hildebrandica insania*. Pope Gregory VII's madness had been to excommunicate the king and threaten his throne. Thereby, the royal propaganda urged, the pope was holding in contempt that divine decree, demonstrated in Luke 22.38, that there were two powers. The two swords signified a dualism (*dualitas*) of the powers. Dualism meant the autonomy of the lay power; the pope had no power over the emperor. Two swords doctrine taught the co-operation of the powers, not the jurisdictional superiority of the spiritual power.[13] This principle, which we may very properly call dualistic, since that was Henry IV's own word, continued to be asserted and justified by Frederick Barbarossa, Frederick II, the polemists of Philip the Fair, and Dante, champion of Henry VII. Its echoes rumbled on in the later middle ages, occasionally, as with the pen of William of Ockham, finding a new burst of vitality.

The direct answer to dualism was to be that the pope held both swords. It was not given, in those terms, by Gregory VII to Henry IV. His justification of his alleged authority to depose kings did not employ two swords imagery. The assertion that the pope held both swords did not in fact emerge during the Investiture Contest. When it did, it was not in any context of empire–papacy confrontation. It was in the didactic letters addressed by St Bernard to Pope Eugenius III. In 1150 he told him, by way of Luke 22.38 and John 18.11, that in a critical period of threat to the Christian position in the Holy Land,

The time has now come when the swords spoken of in the Lord's passion must be drawn, for Christ is suffering anew where he suffered formerly. But by whom, if not by you? Both swords are Peter's: one is unsheathed at his sign, the other by his

13. *MGH Legum sectio.* IV. *Const.* I, pp. 112–13; Ullmann 1955, pp. 345–8.

own hand, as often as is necessary. Peter was told concerning the sword which seemed less his: 'Put up thy sword into the scabbard.' Thus that sword was undoubtedly his, but it was not to be drawn by him.[14]

St Bernard returned to the theme, spelling out the same doctrine in more detail:

Why should you try to usurp the sword which you were once ordered to replace in its scabbard? Yet he who would deny that the sheathed sword is yours seems to me not to have paid enough attention to what the Lord is saying when he says, 'Put up thy sword into the scabbard.' Therefore this sword is also yours and is to be drawn at your command although not by your hand. Otherwise, if that sword did not belong to you in some way, the Lord, when the apostles said to him: 'Behold, here are two swords', would not have said: 'It is enough', but 'It is too much.' Both swords, spiritual and material, then, belong to the church; the one exercised on behalf of the church, the other by the church: the one by the hand of the priest, the other by the hand of the soldier, but clearly at the bidding of the priest (*ad nutum sacerdotis*) and the order of the emperor.[15]

St Bernard was urging, persuading, preaching, appealing to the pope's feelings as well as to his mind, not writing a political treatise about the relations of the powers. In turning the two swords image to his own immediate purposes, he did not elaborate his understanding of it beyond these two passages. Much, then, is left unsaid. We would not be entitled, for instance, to deduce from them that St Bernard would have agreed with a contemporary such as Hugh of St Victor who argued that it was for the ecclesiastical power, that it was for the priesthood, to institute the temporal power into being (*instituere ut sit*). He would, however, no doubt have agreed with John of Salisbury that the prince was, in a way, *sacerdotii minister*.[16] The transition from being God's minister, as St Paul taught, to the pope's minister was not a difficult one for a theologian like St Bernard who

14. 'Exserendus est nunc uterque gladius in passione Domini, Christo denuo patiente, ubi et altera vice passus est. Per quem autem, nisi per vos? Petri uterque est, alter suo nutu, alter sua manu, quoties necesse est, evaginandus. Et quidem de quo minus videbatur, de ipso ad Petrum dictum est: "Converte gladium tuum in vaginam." Ergo suus erat et ille, sed non sua manu utique educendus.' *Ep.* CCLVI, *Opera* VIII, p. 163.

15. 'Quid tu denuo usurpare tentes, quem semel iussus es reponere in vaginam? Quem tamen qui tuum negat, non satis mihi videtur attendere verbum Domini dicentis sic: "Converte gladium tuum in vaginam". Tuus ergo et ipse, tuo forsitan nutu, etsi non tua manu, evaginandus. Alioquin, si nullo modo ad te pertineret et eis, dicentibus Apostolis: "Ecce gladii duo hic", non respondisset Dominus: "Satis est", sed: "Nimis est". Uterque ergo Ecclesiae, et spiritualis scilicet gladius, et materialis, sed is quidem pro Ecclesia, ille vero et ab Ecclesia exserendus: ille sacerdotis, is militis manu, sed sane ad nutum sacerdotis et iussum imperatoris.' *De consideratione* IV, III, 7, *Opera* III, p. 454. For arguments that in this context Bernard was arguing that 'le glaive temporel n'est pas le symbole du pouvoir civil de l'Etat, mais le symbole du pouvoir coactif de la force armée', Jacqueline 1953, p. 197, following Stickler 1951. See also Kennan 1967, pp. 101–4; Congar 1970, pp. 143–4.

16. *Policraticus* iv.3.

believed that the pope was vicar of Christ. What is unquestionable, however, is that St Bernard had fashioned phraseology that became classic. The lay power must act, at need, *ad nutum sacerdotis*. This was to be the language of such major theologians of the thirteenth century as Aquinas and Pierre de Tarentaise (the future Innocent V) and came to form an important argument in Boniface VIII's *Unam sanctam*. The word *nutus*, in classical Latin, meant 'a nod of command'. In twelfth-century usage it tended to mean 'sign' or 'order'. In any translation it must include the idea of command. Thus the expression must be read as the principle that the co-operation of the civil power could have its services commanded by the ecclesiastical power. No churchman, incidentally, thought that the ecclesiastical power could be commanded by the civil power. But what if the spiritual power issued a command and the lay power refused to obey?

St Bernard's writings provide no clear answer. But there is present in them a strong hint of the way the two swords logic was tending. The ministerial view of rulership – that the prince was God's minister for good and, by extension, the clergy's subordinate agent – readily implied coercion for non-compliance with the divinely ordained ground rules. St Bernard put it rather guardedly:

> The lord of the kings of the earth has established you as ruler so that under him and on his behalf you protect the good, coerce the evil, defend the poor, do justice to those suffering injury. If you do this, you do the work of a ruler . . . if you do not then you should fear lest what you seem to hold of honour and power might be taken from you.[17]

This admonition or threat did not state explicitly that the ecclesiastical power had the authority to take away the sword of a ruler if he was bearing it in vain. The deposition of rulers for non-fulfilment of their duty was the *ne plus ultra* of sacerdotal imperialism. Gregory VII's deposition of Henry IV was the actualisation of all the potential that lay in the claim that the pope held both swords.

II

It was in the rapidly expanding world of ecclesiastical jurisprudence, with its close contacts with the papal curia and its sensitivity to contemporary

17. 'Ad hoc te constituit principem super terram "Princeps regum terrae" [Apoc. 1.5], ut sub eo et pro eo bonos foveas, malos coerceas, pauperes defendas, facias "iudicium iniuriam patientibus" (Ps. 145.7). Si haec facis, opus Principis facis, et spes est ut tuum Deus dilatare et roborare debeat principatum. Si non, timendum tibi, ne hoc ipsum quod videris habere honoris vi maioris potestatis, auferatur, quod absit, a te.' *Ep.* CCLXXIX, *Opera* VIII, p. 191.

political developments, that the theory of the two powers received the fullest attention in the second half of the twelfth century. It was the canonists who after the death of St Bernard did most to fashion the doctrine of the two swords into the formula which came as near as any one formula could to welding a variety of particular political principles and experiences into a general analysis of the basic principles of the relations of the ecclesiastical and civil authorities. They did this within the established dialectical methodology of the newly restructured and invigorated schools of twelfth-century Europe. They shaped the allegory of Luke 22.38 into a *quaestio* of conventional scholarship, to make of it the most important single guide to hierocratic logic for a century after the appearance of Gratian's *Decretum*.

It was Gratian who brought the dialectical method pioneered by Abelard to the service of canon law. His own title for his compilation reveals his intention: he was to harmonise discordant canons. His *Concordia discordantium canonum* (c. 1140) aimed to reconcile the differences, often considerable, between the teachings of different authorities on the same subject. Further he grouped his texts on a new plan, itself with a strong dialectical emphasis, for the discussion and resolution of problems. Gratian himself offered his own solutions in the numerous *dicta* which punctuate his work. His whole method invited further discussion. That spirit of dialectic which he did so much to foster in the medieval schools, when applied to two swords doctrine, produced no less than four discussions of it in the *glossa ordinaria* of the *Decretum*[18] and, in turn, provoked two more in the *glossa ordinaria* on the *Decretales*.[19]

Gratian himself produced no pronounced political interpretation of the swords imagery. The spiritual sword was the word of God; by Christ's command to Peter after he had cut off the ear of Malchus, priests are forbidden the use of the material sword. This usage is for the prince, who 'beareth not the sword in vain' and to whom all are commanded to be subject.[20] But if his own view was cautiously dualist[21] he had assembled such a range of politically viable material that more elaborate and very different consequences could be drawn. The *Decretum* contained an amalgam of ethico-political doctrine and terminology and political history which it was the work of its commentators to bring to concord. The *quaestio* concerning the two swords was one of their more important processes of reconciling discordant canons. By and large, the twelfth-century canonists

18. *Decretum Gratiani* 1561, D.10 c.8, s.v. *discrevit*; D.22 c.1, s.v. *celestis*; D.96 c.6, s.v. *usurpavit*; D.96 c.11, s.v. *divinitus*. 19. *Decretales* 2.1.13 s.v. *iurisdictionem nostram*; 4.17.7 s.v. *ad regem*.
20. *Decretum* 23 q.8 *Grat. I Pars* and *dict. p.c.6*. 21. Stickler 1948, pp. 108–11.

were conservative about attributing two swords to the pope. When, after half a century or so of vigorous debate, Huguccio, the most distinguished of them, wrote his comprehensive survey of the discussion, he came down on the side of those who maintained that 'the emperor had the power of the sword and the imperial dignity through election by the princes and people, not from the pope'[22] and produced a strong case to prove his point. But the most lucid review of this type came with a development in the technical literature, when canonists started to produce collections of *questiones*, separate from marginal glosses in the *Decretum*. Freed from the cumbersome task of repeating the same material through different parts of the *Decretum*, canonists could dispose of the argument in a single context. Easily the best of the twelfth-century *questiones* concerning the two swords was that of Ricardus Anglicus, written about the turn of the century, exemplary in its thorough coverage of basic texts and of decretist commentary. It allows a comprehensive over-view of the nature, evolution and content of the decretist discussion of the relations of the two powers subsumed under the question 'whether or not the pope has both material and spiritual swords'.

Ricardus followed classical *quaestio* procedure. He produced arguments for and against the proposition that the pope possessed the power of both swords, a third section replied to the *pro* arguments and a fourth, for and against a compromise solution. He concluded by giving his personal opinion but, very fairly, left the very last word with those who disagreed with him. His discussion involved all the major texts of decretist analysis of the relations of the powers, was conducted with full knowledge of the play of opinion and was presented with that lucid succinctness that only the very best decretist writing could achieve.

The arguments adduced in support of papal possession of both swords constituted the most trenchant of the papacy's political claims. At the head of the list stood a politically extreme reading of Matthew 16.18: to Peter had been given the rights of both heavenly and earthly empires. This was to read literally Peter Damian's rhetorical paraphrase of Christ's conferring on

22. 'Ego autem credo quod imperator potestatem gladii et dignitatem imperialem habet non ab apostolico, set a principibus et populo per elecionem, ut di. xciii. legimus [D.93 c.24]; ante enim fuit imperator quam papa, ante imperium quam papatus. Item in figura huius rei quod diuise et discrete sint ille due potestates scilicet imperialis et apostolica, dictum fuit: "ecce duo gladii hic".' D.96 c.6 s.v. *officia* (Lincoln Cath. MS 2). The whole of this important gloss has been printed by Mochi Onory 1951, pp. 148–50. Huguccio was far from alone among twelfth-century decretists in favouring a dualist interpretation of Luke 22.38. Cf., e.g., Simon of Bisignano: 'imperator uero habet potestatem gladii; distincte enim sunt he potestates nec una pendet ex altera, unde in huius rei figuram dictum fuit "ecce gladii duo hic".' D.96 c.6 s.v. *propriis actibus* (Lambeth Palace MS 411). On Huguccio, see especially Stickler 1947.

Peter, with the commission of the keys of the kingdom of heaven, of power to bind and loose in heaven and earth. If the pope controlled both these 'empires', ran the argument, the emperor received his imperial authority from the pope and, likewise, other rulers. That the emperor swore an oath of fidelity to the pope at the coronation was to be construed as an acknowledgement of the papal source of the empire. Then following the logic of the deposing power: if popes could depose kings not so much for their evil deeds as for their uselessness, as Pope Zachary had done (it was argued) in the case of King Childeric, then it should be deduced that the pope was taking away what he had bestowed. The same deduction followed another lesson of history. When Emperor Constantine transferred the seat of empire to Constantinople, his concession of the city of Rome and the Western Empire to Pope Sylvester was an acknowledgement that he held the empire from him. When later on Pope Adrian removed the empire from the Greeks and conferred it on Charlemagne, there was a further demonstration that the pope has both swords and the emperor holds from him. Ricardus' last argument in this section took him back to his starting-point: the nature of the papal office as such. God had meant it to be omnicompetent, a refuge for all the oppressed, as much for its lay as its clerical subjects. It followed, then, that appeal lay from the civil judge to the ecclesiastical: this is what St Paul meant when he wrote: 'Know you not that the saints shall judge this world? And if the world shall be judged by you, are you unworthy to judge the smallest matters?' (1 Cor. 6.2.)[23]

These are extremist arguments and no twelfth-century decretist was prepared to press the canons quite so hard. But the arguments of the deposing power and the translation of the empire, with the view of the

---

23. 'Quod videtur posse probari: utriusque enim imperii, scilicet celestis et terreni ei iura concessa sunt, ut xxii di. c.i. [*Decretum* D.22 c.1]. Si ergo habet utrumque imperium, ab eo habet imperator potestatem quam habet, et eodem modo alii principes. Item fidelitatem facit ei imperator tanquam domino, ut di. lxiii, tibi domino [D.63 c.33]. Item legitur quod papa reges deposuit, puta Zacarias regem francorum, non tam pro suis iniquitatibus quam pro eo qui tante potestatis erat inutilis ut xv. q. vi. alius [15 q.6 c.3]; si ergo regi potuit auferre potestatem, videtur quod eo habuerit. Unde a simili videtur hodie quod si imperator abutitur potestate sua, ille possit auferre imperium et alium principatum. Hoc idem potest probari alio exemplo: Constantinus enim postquam urbem romanam et partes occidentales beato Silvestro concesserat, ad partes orientales imperium et regiam potestatem transtulit et constantinopoli sedem constituit imperii, ut di. xcvi, constantinus [D.96 c.14 *palea*]. Sic itaque aliquando fuit imperium apud grecos; postea vero ab Adriano papa Carolo est concessum, et eis ablatum est ut lxiii. di., adrianus. Ex his ergo videtur quod utrumque habeat [papa] gladium et imperator ab eo. Item romana ecclesia potestatem habet de omnibus iudicare ut ix. q. iii cuncta [9 q.3 c.18]. Item alibi dicitur quod omnis oppressus libere sacerdotis vocem appellet iudicium ut ii. q. vi. omnis [2 q.6 c.3]. Ex hoc videtur quod a iudice civili possit appellari ad ecclesiasticum, maxime cum causas privatorum apostolus iussit deferri ad ecclesiam, ut xi. q. i. placuit [11 q.1 c.43; cf. 1 Cor. 6].' *Summa Quaestionum*, Zwettl MS 162, fols. 147va–148vb collated with the text published by Stickler 1953, pp. 610–12.

nature of papal power which lay behind them, were common opinion among later twelfth-century canonists. These were the arguments developed especially by Popes Innocent III (1198–1216) and Innocent IV (1243–54) with whom the papal theory of the Holy Roman Empire was to be brought to completion.

It was not difficult to find support in the *Decretum* for a contrary position. Gratian's texts, or a selection of them, readily yielded up a dualist position. Popes of the early middle ages, concerned to halt imperial intervention in ecclesiastical affairs, had emphasised God's division of the powers and his will that neither power should usurp what was proper to the other's sphere. Gratian, sensitive to the need to conserve *libertas ecclesiae*, had reproduced many of the classic papal dualist texts of the early centuries, the texts which Carlyle had especially in mind when forming the judgement cited at the beginning of this chapter. For Ricardus Anglicus, the dualist principles formulated by popes in the period from the fifth to the ninth century had been powerfully reinforced by Alexander III in his own time. A very important ruling of this pope stated quite categorically that appeal did not lie from a civil judge to the pope in a temporal matter; a clear indication to Ricardus that the emperor did not receive his authority from the pope, for if if it were so, appeal from secular to ecclesiastical judge would be permissible. He also confirmed that Alexander III's position about the autonomy of secular jurisdiction was the established teaching of the canons. Ricardus Anglicus argued further (anticipating Robert Grosseteste and John Wyclif) that it was Christ's wish that bishops should not be involved as judges in secular courts. He deduced that the Lord was thus intimating that ecclesiastics had no authority to confer power in civil affairs on temporal rulers. Finally in this *contra* section of the *quaestio*, Ricardus posited the view that since historically there had been kings before there were priests and they had the same authority now as they did formerly, it should be concluded (as Huguccio had) that their power came not from the pope but from God.[24] An argument that was left to Dante to make the most of.

24. 'Econtra videtur quod [papa] non habet utrumque: distincte enim potestates sunt, quia *nec imperator iura pontificis nec pontifex iura imperatoris usurpare* potest, ut di. xcvi. c. cum ad verum [D.96 C.6]. Item a Deo consecuta est potestas imperatoris ut di. xcvi. c. si imperator [D.96 C.11]. Idem dicitur xxiii. q. iv. quesitum [23 q.4 c.45] ubi dicitur quod *meminerint homines has potestates a Deo fuisse concessas.* Si ergo a iudice civili ad summum pontificem appelletur, non tenetur appellatio ut in ex. alexandri iii, denique [2.28.7§1]. Ex hoc ergo manifeste potest colligi quod imperator a summo pontifice non habet imperium, quod si haberet ab eo, ad illum posset appellari. Idem potest confirmari auctoritate illius capituli, ii. q. vi. omnis oppressus [2 q.6 c.3], ubi dicitur de illo qui appellat quod coram patricio deberent ventilari secularia negocia, coram ecclesiastico ecclesiastica. Item secularium negociorum prohibetur esse cognitor apostolicus, ut xi. q. i. te quidem [11 q.1 c.29]. Videtur ergo quod nullum

The two sides of the argument thus summarised, Ricardus observed that different writers drew different conclusions from these texts. There were those who were convinced that the emperor had his power from God alone and in support of their case, proffered counter-arguments to those advanced from the other side. Thus 'the rights of heavenly and earthly empires' of the gloss on Matthew 16.18, they read simply as spiritual power over both clergy and laity. The imperial oath of fidelity was an acknowledgement by the emperor not that he held his authority from the pope but that he was subject to him spiritually. Pope Zachary could be said to have deposed Childeric because he excommunicated him and so ordered the king's subjects to withdraw their obedience from him because subjects should not obey an excommunicate lord; this was to degrade the king *per consequentiam*. Finally, when the canons stated that the pope had power to judge in all types of case, this was to be understood as referring specifically to judgements in ecclesiastical cases.[25]

Ricardus then proceeded to examine what some commentators considered to be an acceptable compromise solution. It ran along the same lines as that adopted by St Bernard in his reading of the two swords allegory. Their view was first formulated by Rufinus and argued that the pope had the authority of both swords: one to be exercised, the other not. Those canons which said that the emperor had his power from God alone should be interpreted as meaning that he had his power from God *principaliter*, since all power comes from God. But he has it too from the pope, *secundario*. However to this solution, Ricardus offered the objection that it left the pope with ultimate responsibility for the imposition of capital punishment, though the clergy were forbidden to shed blood. Further, if it were by his authority that the emperor had cognisance in a *causa sanguinis*, it followed

ius habeat cognoscendi super causis secularibus vel committendi cognitionem secularium aliquibus. Item antequam essent summi pontifices erant imperatores, et idem ius et eamdem potestatem habebant quam nunc habent. Unde videtur quod non ab isto nacti hanc potestatem fuerint set a Deo.'

25. 'Ad premissa diversi diverso modo respondeunt: sunt enim qui dicunt quod imperator a solo Deo habet potestatem suam et hoc auctoritate premissorum capitulorum. Qui autem dicit quod utrumque imperium est ei concessum ita exponit id est, tam super laicos quam super clericos habet quoad spiritualia ut si quem ligaverit in terra, sit ligatus et in celis. Si autem obiciatur quod fidelitatem facit imperator, dicunt hoc non contingere ratione alicuius potestatis quam accipiat ab eo, sed illud facit ut sciatur quod illi subiectus est in spiritualibus nec hoc est facere fidelitatem quam fideles faciunt dominis, ut ex illo capitulo colligi potest, Tibi domino [D.63 c.33]. Item si dicatur quod Zacarias deposuit regem hoc factum est set ideo deposuisse dicitur quia pro contumacia sua excommunicatus est et ita subditos ab eius obedientia subtraxit, quia subditi domino excommunicato non tenentur obedire, ut xv. q. vi. iuratos [15 q.6 c.5]. Et hoc fuit regem degradare per consequentiam. Quod autem dicitur quod potestatem habet in omnibus causis iudicare restringi debet ut tantummodo restringatur potestas illa ad causas clericorum.'

that appeal lay from emperor to pope in a case involving loss of life. But such appeals had been forbidden by Pope Alexander III in the decretal already cited.[26]

Ricardus Anglicus concluded his 'two swords' review by giving it as his own opinion that it seemed safer and therefore preferable to agree that the emperor had his power from God alone. He concluded by drawing attention to the fact that those who took the other view agreed that the pope must delegate the material sword to the civil power.[27]

The trace of this early decretist caution about attributing both swords to the pope remained in the *glossa ordinaria* on the *Decretum*, the work of Johannes Teutonicus (c. 1216). But the canonist common opinion, as expressed by Bernard of Parma in the *glossa ordinaria* on the *Decretales* (1241–63) came to accept that the pope held both swords.[28] The theologians came into line. Aquinas' adoption of the Bernardine formula in his *Commentary on the Sentences* against the Lombard's view that the Church 'non habet gladium nisi spiritualem' is sufficient evidence of that.[29] The 'safer' view, as Ricardus Anglicus had put it, however, continued to be

26. 'Sunt alii qui dicunt quod utrumque gladium habet summus pontifex, alterum auctoritate et amministratione, reliquum auctoritate absque amministratione. Capitula que dicunt quod a solo Deo habet imperator potestatem sic exponuntur: a Deo habet principaliter, quia omnis potestas a domino Deo est; a summo pontifice tamen secundario. Sic tamen dicentibus potest obici: si enim potestatem habet a summo pontifice imperator, eius ergo auctoritate cognoscit in iudicio sanguinis. Item aliter dicitur *eripe eum qui ducitur ad mortem* [Prov. 24.11], xxiii. q. iii. non in inferenda [23 q.3 c.7]. Si ergo tenetur reos sanguinis defendere ecclesia, non eius auctoritate ultima debet punire suplicio. Item si eius auctoritate debet imperator cognoscere in causa sanguinis ergo ab imperatore potest ad papam appellari, quod manifeste negatur in decretali Alexandri iii. denique. Item si appelletur ad ipsum, quod faciet in causa sanguinis, ipse siquidem cognoscere non potest, quia nec agitare iudicium sanguinis, ut xxiii. q. viii. sepe, his a quibus [23 q.8 cc.29, 30].'
27. 'Propter has et consimiles rationes videtur nobis securior via eorum qui dicunt quod imperator a solo Deo habet potestatem. Qui tamen aliam tenent sententiam dicunt quod eam deligare debet iudici civili.'
28. '*Ad regem (pertinet non ad ecclesiam de talibus possessionibus iudicare)*. Et sic patet quod iurisdictio spiritualis et temporalis distincta est et diuisa, de cons. dist. iii. celebritatem, in fine, et in authen. de fi. instrum. circa princ. per unam columnam, et sic papa non habet utramque iurisdictionem, argu. supra eod. lator [4.17.5] et xxiii. q. iiii. regum [*Decretum* 23 q.5 c.23] et viii. dist. quo iure [D.8 c.1] et xxxiii. q. ii. inter haec, in fine [33 q.2 c.6] et xxiii. q. iiii quesitum. argu. quod papa intromittit se de hereditate. Argumentum contra, supra eod. ca. i. [4.17.1] et xx. q. iii. presens, in fine [20 q.3 c.4], xv. q. vi. alius [15 q.6 c.3], et xxiiii. q. i. loquitur [24 q.1 c.18]. Huguccio dixit quod imperator a solo Deo habet potestatem in temporalibus, papa vero in spiritualibus, et sic diuisa est iurisdictio, prius enim fuit imperator quam coronam reciperet a papa, et gladium ab altari, xciii. dist. legimus [D.93 c.24], quia ante fuit imperium quam apostolatus. Sed Alanus et Tancredus dixerunt quod imperator, licet imperium a solo Deo dicatur processisse, executionem gladii temporalis recepit ab ecclesia. Ecclesia enim est unum corpus, ergo unum solum caput debet habere. Item Deus utroque gladio usus est, ut notatur de iudic. nouit [2.1.13], hic adde quod ibi dicitur. Item Moyses utrumque gladium habuit, cuius successor est papa. Preterea papa ipsum confirmat et consecrat et coronat, et eum deponit, supra de elect. venerabilem [1.6.34], et xv. q. vi. alius. Hoc ultimum verius credo'. *Glossa ordinaria ad Qui filii sint legitimi c. Causam* (4.17.7). 29. *In IV Sent.*, d. 37, exp. text.

widely publicised in the standard commentaries as the dialectical spirit of canonist scholarship kept its vitality in the thirteenth century. A canonist-fashioned dualism lay handily in the literature for those able to appreciate its value in opposition to the hierocratic logic.

That logic, however, had been much strengthened by Innocent III's detailed and trenchant reconsideration of the relationship between pope and emperor occasioned by the prolonged succession crisis following the death of Henry VI in 1197. Two lines of thought developed in this context proved especially influential. One had been pioneered by Hugh of St Victor. Under God's plan for mankind, unfolding through sacred history, the priesthood had always supplied the leadership of his chosen people: initially, as revealed in the Old Testament, then, in fulfilled fashion, in his church, ruled over by his vicar. In this pronouncedly providential and ecclesiological vision of politics, the dualism of function of each of the powers existed within the one body, the Church, under the control of its one head, the pope. The generalisation received specific exemplification in a second line of thought which Innocent III explained in meticulous detail: the constitutional relationship of empire and papacy. The function of choosing an emperor belonged to the electoral college of the German princes. But its constitutional right to exercise that function had been conferred on it by the papal act of translating the empire from Greeks to Germans, in Charlemagne's time, when the former had shown themselves incapable of fulfilling the work for which it had been established: protection of the Roman Church. It was for the pope to verify that any election had been legally conducted (Innocent III deliberately modelled the procedure on the canonical pattern for the appointment of bishops) and to scrutinise the suitability of their choice, exercising a right of veto on any candidate found wanting. If the candidate were confirmed as emperor-elect, he became emperor when anointed and crowned by the pope, and received his sword from him. Ecclesiology, history, constitutional law and liturgical symbolism led inescapably to one conclusion.

The conclusion that unquestionably the pope had two swords was rapidly drawn by the decretalists of the early thirteenth century and it was they who were responsible for the *glossa ordinaria* acceptance of two swords doctrine. Innocent III's decretals about the empire are lengthy and nuanced.[30] The decretalists summarised their message tersely: though the empire is said to

---

30. Especially important are: *In Genesi* (*Reg. Innocentii III super negotio Romani imperii* no.18); *Venerabilem* (*Decretales* 1.6.34).

proceed'' from God alone, yet the emperor receives the exercise of the sword from the Church,

For there is one body of the Church and therefore it ought to have only one head. Also, the Lord himself used both swords . . . but it was Peter alone that he made his vicar on earth, therefore he left him both swords. Further, Moses had both swords and his successor is the pope. Moreover, the pope is the emperor's judge because he confirms him, consecrates and crowns him and can depose him.[31]

Dualism, in the hierocratic logic, is only meaningful in the context of a single, papally-headed society, for which dual headship would be deformity. A body with two heads was a monster.[32] There was no place, in this logic, for an autonomous lay authority.

III

As the last citation shows, the two swords theory as standardised by the canonists was in part a general theory of the relations of the powers and in part a specific theory of the relations of empire and papacy. The latter could not be an exact microcosm of the former, though commentators kept trying to make it so, because the empire–papacy connection was a unique one, a special relationship, with features fundamentally different from the papacy's relations with other lay powers. Innocent III had defined this *specialis coniunctio* with two adverbs: the empire related to the papacy *principaliter* (in its origin, referring particularly to its translation from Greeks to Germans, and to the coronation ceremony) and *finaliter* (in its end or purpose, which was the protection of the Roman Church).[33] Consequently the papacy had a right (it was argued) to oversee the conduct of

31. Text in n. 28 above, where the *glossa ordinaria* is correct in attributing the formulation to Alanus and Tancred.

32. Hostiensis: 'nec unum corpus nisi unum caput . . . igitur opinionem contrariam monstruosam' (*Apparatus* 4.17.13 s.v. *plenitudinem potestatis*); *idem*: 'Cum enim unum corpus simus in Christo, pro monstro esset quod duo capita haberemus, ut supra de offic. iud. ord. quoniam [1.31.14]. Hoc etiam expressim innuitur, 96 dis. Constantinus' (*Summa* 4.17 n.9). Whence to *Unam sanctam*: 'Igitur ecclesiae unius et unicae unum corpus, unum caput, non duo capita quasi monstrum, Christus videlicet, et Christi vicarius Petrus, Petrique successor, dicente Domino ipsi Petro: "*Pasce oves meas*"' (John 21.17).

33. What became the standard decretalist interpretation of the *Translation of Empire* was adopted by Hostiensis from Tancred: 'Legitur in cronicis quod cum ecclesia romana opprimeretur ab arstulpho rege lombardorum, petiit auxilium a Constantino et eius filio Leone imperatoribus constantinopolitanis, et cum nollent patrocinari ecclesie Stephanus papa secundus natione romanus transtulit imperium in Karolum magnum qui fuerat filius Pipini quem Zacarias predecessor eius substituerat Childerico regi francorum quem deposuerat, sicut legitur xv. q. vi. alius [15 q.6 c.3] et translatio illa facta est anno domini ccccccclxxvi; qui Karolus coronatus est a Leone papa iii, elapsis post hoc xv. annos. T [ancredus].' *Apparatus* 1.6.34 s.v. *a Grecis*.

imperial elections and to veto unsuitable choices. It followed inevitably that those who became unsuitable after initial approval and subsequent coronation could be judged by the pope, deposed for sufficiently grave and incorrigible misconduct and the college of electors instructed to choose a replacement. The two swords allegory sat well to this sort of constitutional relationship.

It was not, however, a reading of Luke 22.38 that Roman emperors readily accepted. Indeed it seems that the first strictly political usage of the text of any significance was that of Henry IV designed to buttress dualism and protect the autonomy of kingship against the encroachments of Gregory VII. It was again to this scriptural authority that the Germans were to have recourse at Besançon in October 1157. The supporters of Frederick Barbarossa threatened papal legates with violence in defence of the honour and dignity of the empire against alleged papal usurpation in the claim that the pope conferred the empire as a *beneficium* or fief. The maladroitness of Adrian IV's vocabulary was compounded when one of the legates, possibly the future Alexander III, asked: 'From whom, then, does the emperor have the empire, if not from the pope?' Frederick's lawyers produced a vigorous restatement of Henry IV's dualism. The autonomy of the empire, its freedom from direct subordination to the Roman Church was emphatically asserted. The imperial crown came from God alone through the election of the princes. This was what God had demonstrated in the symbolism of the two swords shown to him by the apostles. Whoever claimed that the emperor had received the imperial crown as a *beneficium* from the pope thus contradicted God's plan for the world. That plan had been revealed both in the division of powers implicit in Christ's saying that there should be two swords and in Peter's teaching that everyone should be subject to the king and his officials (1 Pet. 2.13–14). Such a claimant 'stood accused of falsehood'.[34] Such indignant bluster, however, did not prevent Barbarossa's grandson becoming emperor on Innocent III's terms nor save him when Innocent IV decided that he had violated them.

The deposition of Emperor Frederick II at the council of Lyons in 1245 was at once the papacy's most spectacular political action and the implementation of the hierocratic logic in its plenitude. Two swords theories were manufactured to promote or repel the claim that the papacy

---

34. 'Cumque per electionem principum a solo Deo regnum et imperium nostrum sit, qui in passione Christi filii sui duobus gladiis necessariis regendum orbem subiecit, cumque Petrus apostolus hac doctrina mundum informaverit: "Deum timete, regem honorificate" [1 Pet. 2.17], quicunque nos imperialem coronam pro beneficio a domno papa suscepisse dixerit, divinae institutioni et doctrinae Petri contrarius est, et mendacii reus erit.' *MGH Const.* 1 n.165 p. 231.

could, or could not, confer or withdraw the imperial authority. But the claim itself developed from a logic much wider than any single scriptural allegory. The image expressed the logic; it did not in itself prove it.

It was a logic which began with the principle that the head of the Church had the power to expel a person from the Christian community.[35] To Peter had been given the power of binding and loosing in heaven and on earth, supreme judicial authority over the whole body of the faithful. A necessary part of that jurisdiction was the power of judging whether or not an individual had so conducted himself as to forfeit his membership of the society whose charge had been confided to Peter. The primary effect of excommunication was spiritual. It cut off the guilty from the sacramental and liturgical life of the Church. But there were important secondary consequences of a social nature. The individual's expulsion was to be marked by the public disapproval of the community and he was to be prevented from contaminating others. He was to be ostracised and isolated, treated, in the expression well-known from Bracton, as a spiritual leper. Dignity of office, height of rank, splendour of majesty allowed no exemption from this sacerdotal power of judgement and sanction. If a ruler suffered major excommunication, he was to be shunned by his ministers and officials and he was to be refused obedience. In societies where the oath was of such prominence in manifesting the obedience of subject to ruler, the overt declaration that ostracisation was being ordered was the subjects' release from their oaths of obedience.

Gratian and the twelfth-century decretists in his wake, discussed this release in the context of the replacement of the last of the Merovingians by Charlemagne's father. A ninth-century precedent was not without its importance. But of more impact on contemporary thinking was Innocent III's practical demonstration of papal power to release subjects from their obedience. In the aftermath of the Albigensian crusade, the fourth Lateran council approved the transfer of the lands of Raymond VI, count of Toulouse, to Simon of Montfort. In effect, count Raymond had been deposed for the crime of harbouring heretics and his territories were adjudged forfeit to another who had proved his fidelity to the faith. The papal action was generalised into formal legal definition in c.3 *Excommunicamus* of the council's decrees. Secular rulers who proved persistently neglectful in purging their lands of heretics and defiant of excommunication by their local bishops were to be denounced to the pope who would declare their vassals absolved from fealty and their lands forfeit

35. Hageneder 1957–8.

to the orthodox in faith.[36] The fate of Raymond VI proved, as the early decretalist glosses show, a powerful reinforcement of the deposition logic.

Even more so did the fate of Emperor Frederick II, victim of Innocent IV and the first council of Lyons. The deposition decree declared that it was Frederick's own persistence in impenitence which had rendered him unfit to be Holy Roman Emperor and king of Sicily and that it was God himself who had cast him out of the Christian community and deprived him of all honour and dignity. The papal sentence, its authority based on the power of binding and loosing, was simply a public declaration of God's judgement. All Frederick's subjects were absolved from their oaths of allegiance, all were forbidden under pain of excommunication to obey him or hold him as emperor or king. The imperial electors were instructed to select a successor. The task of finding a new king of Sicily, the pope reserved for himself.[37]

Innocent IV, in his capacity as private doctor of canon law was to write a commentary on the deposition decree he had promulgated as pope. Its most striking feature was a disquisition on the decree's emphasis on the papal judge as God's mouthpiece. Just as Christ had had power when he was on earth, Innocent argued, to impose sentences on kings and emperors and any other sort of ruler had he so wished, so he had empowered his vicar with the same jurisdiction. Christ himself had meant his people to be subject to the rule of one overriding authority with discretionary power to act for the common good of the whole, a ruler whose responsibilities included power to judge and punish the political conduct of Christendom's lay rulers.[38] Frederick had been guilty of four very serious crimes (perjury, violation of the peace, sacrilege, suspicion of heresy), had reduced the clergy and laity of Sicily to beggary and servitude and had persistently refused to repent. Deprivation of office was the inevitable consequence of such defiance of morality and spiritual sanction.[39]

This logic was of course denied by Frederick II. As against 'the government of one person' (*regimen unius personae*) postulated by Innocent IV as the basic constitutional principle of the Christian community, the

---

36. Definitive text of *Excommunicamus* in García y García 1981, pp. 47–51. J. Teutonicus: '*uasallos ab eius fidelitate denunciet absolutos*: Sic ergo papa potest omnes iudices siue duces siue comites deponere propter heresim et etiam propter alias iniquitates, ut xv. q. vi. Alius, nam et transfert dignitatem de loco ad locum ut extra. iii. de elect. Venerabilem.' *Ibid.*, p. 189.

37. Text of the decree *Ad apostolicae dignitatis* (17 July 1245) in *Conciliorum oecumenicorum decreta*, ed. Alberigo *et al.* 1960, pp. 254–9. Analysis, Wolter and Holstein 1966, pp. 104–12.

38. On Innocent IV's theory of the relationship of the powers, Carlyle 1903–36, vol. v, pp. 319–24; Cantini 1961; Watt 1965a, pp. 66–70; Tierney 1965.

39. Hostiensis supplies important evidence for opinion about the deposing power at the first council of Lyons, Watt 1965b. Other aspects in Peters 1970, pp. 135–69.

emperor did little more than fall back on the classic dualist position of Henry IV and Frederick I, that human society should be governed by two autonomous authorities. The two swords allegory dictated a co-ordination and co-operation of the powers and decreed the supremacy of the temporal in its own sphere. The 'eternal provision' for mankind established two types of government by which human frailty was to be supported and disciplined. The fullness of sacerdotal power in spiritual matters granted to the pope was no more, in essence, than that same power to inflict spiritual punishment for sin as had the humblest priest. Frederick professed his belief in papal possession of the keys as an article of faith. Nevertheless, he argued, it was not of faith that it constituted a power to depose emperors: 'nowhere can it be found commanded in either divine or human law that [a pope] can transfer empires at will or punish kings temporally by depriving them of their kingdoms, or judge temporal rulers at all'. Granted also that it was for the pope to consecrate and crown an emperor, nevertheless this right no more gave him the power to depose emperors than it gave the right to depose to those prelates who in other countries consecrated and crowned their rulers.[40]

Frederick's propaganda against Gregory IX and Innocent IV tended to concentrate more on papal character deficiencies than on principles of papal government. It is perhaps surprising that the controversy did not stimulate an outburst of pro-imperial political writing. Dante had ample justification for complaining, more than half a century later, at the beginning of his *Monarchia*, that the theory of Empire had been neglected. German apologists of imperial dualism, a thoroughly respectable intellectual position, as Ricardus Anglicus had demonstrated from the leading school of canon law, were few and undistinguished. Jordan of Osnabrück avoided the issue of empire–papacy relations; Engelbert of Admont posited a relationship of simple co-ordination but shied away from any extended exposition of it. Other Germans went far towards accepting the gist of the papal position. Alexander of Roes accepted the substance of the papal view of the Translation of Empire theory and of the depositions of Childeric III and Frederick II; the *Schwabenspiegel* accepted the hierocratic reading of the two

---

40. Frederick professed his belief in the fullness of papal power in spiritual matters 'ut quod in terra ligaverit sit ligatum in celis, et quod solverit sit solutum, nusquam tamen legitur divina sibi vel humana lege concessum quod transferre pro libito possit imperia aut de puniendis temporaliter in privacione regnorum regibus aut terre principibus iudicare . . . Nam licet ad eum de iure et more maiorum consecracio nostra pertineat, non magis ad ipsum privacio seu remocio pertinet quam ad quoslibet regnorum prelatos, qui reges suos, prout assolet, consecrant et inungunt.' *MGH Const.* II no. 262, p. 362. On Frederick's opposition more generally, Ullmann 1960b.

swords text; Rudolf of Habsburg in the first opportunist step of the most successful dynasty in European history accepted with his electors in 1279 the papal theory of the imperial constitution.[41] In Italy, the civilian lawyers certainly kept alive the classic imperial dualist position. But they were content to leave it undeveloped in the bald summaries that the literary genre of the marginal gloss demanded.[42] Fullblooded counter-attacks on the triumphant hierocracy with reasoned expositions of the imperial ideology had to wait for Dante and Marsilius of Padua, in days when imperial power had been emasculated.

IV

The two swords theory, in its hierocratic interpretation, was well-known in England. It is to be found well-ventilated in the glosses of English decretists written in English manuscripts at the turn of the twelfth century and in early decretalist writing as it reached England from Bologna. Its Bernardine version was professed by Adam Marsh and so, we may take it, was current in the theology faculty of the university of Oxford: the temporal sword was to be exercised *ad nutum*, at the command of the priest.[43] It received a particularly eloquent formulation from Bishop Robert Grosseteste.[44] He anticipated that grand historical vision of Innocent IV, noted earlier, envisaging God's enduring purpose for his chosen people, first of Israelites, then of Christians, that it should be headed by one priest-ruler. Moses, Joshua and his successors down to Christ himself, then his vicars, wielded supreme authority over God's people, exercising the authority of both

---

41. Rivière 1926, pp. 308–19; Lecler 1931, pp. 327–30, 335–6.
42. *Authentica, Nov. VI*: 'Administrationes et iurisdictiones pape et principis distincte sunt. *Prefatio.* Maxima quidem in omnibus sunt dona Dei, a superna collata clementia, sacerdotium et imperium: illud quidem diuinis ministrans, hoc autem humanis presidens ac diligentiam exhibens, ex uno eodem principio utraque procedentia humanam exornant vitam. [Gloss] *maxima.* Vere est maxima quia ex his duobus totus regitur mundus. Unde illud: *Ecce gladii duo hic,* secundum unum intellectum. Alii dicunt quod duo testamenta significant.' *Collatio Ia, t.vi. n.6, Quomodo oporteat episcopos et ceteros clericos ad ordinationes perduci.*
43. Marsh 1858 *Ep.* 246, pp. 436–7. The letter contains a long quotation from Bernard's *De consideratione* and concludes: 'ille sacerdotis, is militis manu, sed sane ad nutum sacerdotis et iussu imperatoris. Est igitur uterque ecclesie, sed verbalis ad usum, ferreus ad nutum.'
44. Grosseteste 1861, *Ep.* 23, p. 91: 'Debent quoque principes seculi nosse quod uterque gladius, tam materialis videlicet quam spiritalis, gladius est Petri; sed spiritali gladio utuntur principes ecclesie qui vicem Petri et locum Petri tenent, per semetipsos; materiali autem gladio utuntur principes ecclesie per manum et ministerium principum secularium, qui ad nutum et dispositionem principum ecclesie gladium, quem portant, debent evaginare et in locum suum remittere [with a reference to Rom. 13.4].'

swords (*uterque gladius*) and of both laws (*utraque lex*).[45] The powers were distinguished, as the allegory indicated, but their essential unity was preserved within the authority of the one sacerdotal monarchy. And this by divine decree:

I consider that it was the lord Jesus Christ himself who demonstrated and commanded the division of the functions of each of the two swords and of the two laws between temporal and ecclesiastical rulers, yet with the oneness of each sword and each law retained in the charge of the rulers of the church.[46]

But what was the relevance of this highly abstract principle for the relationship in practice of the English monarchy to the *ecclesia anglicana*?

Grosseteste's first excursus on two swords theory came in a letter to William Ralegh, the celebrated royal judge who was later to become, with some difficulty, bishop of Winchester. Grosseteste was trying to persuade William to use his influence to persuade the king and his council to adopt the ecclesiastical law principle that the subsequent marriage of the parents legitimated children born before the marriage. In 1236 the bishop had fallen foul of the civil power by refusing to answer to the standard royal writ which ordered ecclesiastical judges to certify as to the married state of persons concerned in property cases in the lay tribunal where exception of bastardy was being argued. It is not altogether clear whether Grosseteste's objection was to being instructed to provide the required information, which was to put the ecclesiastical court in the subordinate position of being ordered to do something by its theoretical inferior, or to participating in a procedure which involved a principle which canon law found defective, for common law did not recognise legitimation *per subsequens matrimonium*. The letter to Ralegh is a lengthy exposition of arguments drawn from the Bible, philosophy, civil and canon law to prove the correctness of the ecclesiastical doctrine and to convince the judge that he was obliged in conscience to work to have the common law brought into line with the canon law. Ralegh slyly hinted at the absurdity of changing the custom of England to fit Old Testament principles. But the real core of Grosseteste's argument was something simpler. The law of the Church, in this issue

---

45. 'Quod autem uterque gladius, utraque pax, utraque lex sit principaliter principum ecclesiae, liquet non solum ex sacrorum scriptorum expositionibus, sed ex antiquorum principum populi Dei a Deo dispositis actionibus. Moyses enim constitutus a Deo princeps populi Israelitici, in omnibus habens typum praelatorum ecclesiae, utroque gladio, utraque lex, in utraque pace populum sibi commissum per seipsum regebat' *ibid.*, p. 92.

46. 'Divisionem autem duorum gladiorum actuum et duarum legum in principes seculi et principes ecclesiae, unitatem tantum potestatis utriusque gladii et utriusque legis penes principes ecclesie retentam, puto monstrasse et ordinasse ipsum Dominum Jesum Christum' *ibid.*, p. 93.

defined by Alexander III in two decretals,[47] should be obeyed just because it was the law of the church and thereby superior to any lay law, which should follow it. The relationship of temporal law and ecclesiastical law was the relationship of the two swords: distinguished in operation but united in the priesthood so that 'the laws of princes which contradict the decrees of Roman pontiffs are of no validity'.[48] If the secular prince goes against divine or ecclesiastical laws in the exercise of his sword or in the constitution of his law, he is to be regarded as disobedient to Christ. Grosseteste's two swords doctrine, expressive of the principle of the superiority of the spiritual, found practical expression in the demand that where canon law has a clear ruling, civil law has no alternative but to follow suit.[49]

Bracton records the upshot in a famous passage: 'the bishops having asked the king and magnates to consent that those born before marriage should in all respects be as legitimate as those born after. And all the earls and barons as many as there were, answered with one voice that they did not wish to change the laws of England which had hitherto been used and approved.'[50] Maitland thought of this reaction that 'perhaps we do well to treat this as an outburst of nationality and conservatism'.[51] Maybe. But it was also symbolic of English rejection of hierocracy and of that reliance on the primacy of English custom which was the constant in the specifically English experience of the relationship of the powers. All thirteenth-century kings, barons and royal judges would no doubt have agreed with Grosseteste and the episcopate that secular laws which contradicted divine law should be corrected. But they were not prepared to agree that canon law should be equated with divine law just because the clergy said it should be, nor to go along with the suggestion that the pope knew best when it came to drawing up the rules for succession to landed property in England.

Grosseteste's was the commanding influence when the episcopate as a whole shaped into petition-form its resentment of the burdens allegedly laid on churchmen by the civil power; the crown was to remedy their grievances in return for grant of taxation. One cause they espoused, and for

---

47. *Decretales* 4.17.1, 6.
48. 'Constitutiones quoque principum contra canones et decreta praesulum Romanorum nullius sint momenti.' Grosseteste 1861, *Ep.* 23, p. 89. The text is a quotation from *Decretum* D.10 c.4.
49. 'Obtemperare igitur oportet leges principum seculi legibus divinis, et ecclesiasticis non repugnare; quod si gladio aut legis constitutione repugnat princeps secularis Christo aut ecclesiae, inobediens invenitur Patri suo Christo qui eum genuit verbo veritatis, et matri suae quae eum peperit de sacro fonte baptismatis.' Grosseteste 1861, *Ep.* 23, p. 93.
50. '. . . sed rogabant [omnes episcopi] regem et magnates quod ad hoc consensum praeberent, quod nati ante matrimonium quoad omnia legitimi esse possent sicut illi qui post. Et omnes comites et barones quotquot fuerunt una voce responderunt quod noluerunt leges Angliae mutare, quae usque ad tempus illud usitatae fuerunt et approbatae.' *De legibus* IV, p. 296.
51. Pollock and Maitland 1898, vol. I, p. 189.

which Grosseteste attempted theoretical justification, was already well lost: that the clergy should be exempt from all lay jurisdiction except in cases involving lay fee. Again, Grosseteste's defence, stripped of its ample rhetoric, amounted to a simple deduction from the superiority of the spiritual: no mere custom should prevail against the canons. But English custom did. No need was felt to provide theoretical justification.

Grosseteste defended another lost cause which is nevertheless worth looking at for the light it throws on the respective ways, hierocratic and dualist, of looking at a major issue of principle. In 1239, the English episcopate laid before the cardinal-legate Otto twenty-nine specific articles of complaint against the lay power's alleged infringement of liberty of the Church. One clause demanded that the decision as to whether a particular case was ecclesiastical or lay should not be that of secular judges.[52] Clearly this was a crucial matter. If, for hierocrats, the superiority of the spiritual meant anything in practical terms it meant that whenever there was doubt as to whether a case was spiritual or temporal, the decisive voice should be ecclesiastical. To hold otherwise was to leave the lay power in command of the frontier dividing the jurisdictions and thus able at will to redraw it.

Grosseteste based his rejection of this principle of the supremacy of the temporal on his two swords theory. Both swords belonged to the clergy and thus both laws and, therefore, though in different ways, all judgements, civil and ecclesiastical. The ecclesiastical it controlled *per administrationem*, the temporal *per auctoritatem et per doctrinam*. It exercised this latter doctrinal authority when it had to be decided in doubtful cases which tribunal should have the administration. Expanding the argument, he appealed to scripture, 'a difficult and doubtful matter in judgement shall come to the priest of the Levitical race and to the judges that shall be at that time' (his paraphrase of Deut. 17.8, 9), and to Innocent III's citation of the passage in his decretal *Per venerabilem* (4.17.13).[53]

---

52. The legate was asked to persuade the king that twenty-nine current practices were to be abandoned as against ecclesiastical liberty. The sixth read: 'Item, quod per solos iudices seculares non determinetur de aliqua causa utrum debeat dici ecclesiastica vel secularis': Powicke and Cheney 1964, p. 281.

53. 'Potestas vero iudiciaria iudicis ecclesiastici extendat se etiam in secularia, cum, ut supra dictum est [at p. 218], omne iudicium per auctoritatem et per doctrinam sit ecclesiae, licet non omne per ministerium. Is igitur, cuius potestas extendit se tantum in alterum et minus, iudicabit utrumque. Nec erit potestas secularis "iudex et divisor" [Luke 12.14] inter ecclesiam et seculum, sed iudex ecclesiasticus qui praeest ecclesiae et seculo.' The Deuteronomy and *Per venerabilem* passages follow, Grosseteste 1861, *Ep.* 72 pp. 220–1. The text concludes with the summary: 'quod iudices seculares graviter peccant cum in foro suo determinare praesumunt quae causa sit ecclesiastica et quae secularis, quando ad utrum forum pertineat vertitur in dubium,' *ibid.*, p. 231.

Divine law-codes old and new notwithstanding, the common law view of the matter prevailed. Bracton caught well its easy assurance in the power of the crown and its confidence in the rectitude of English custom:

And though in spiritual matters as in temporal [each] ought to decide whether jurisdiction is his or not, in order to ascertain whether the person ought to appear or not, nevertheless, lest the ecclesiastical judge, putting his sickle into another's harvest, presume against the crown and royal dignity, as with respect to lay fee or chattels, when he receives a prohibition from the king he ought in every case to stay proceedings, at least until in the king's court it is settled to whom jurisdiction belongs. For if an ecclesiastical judge could decide whether the jurisdiction was his, he would proceed in every case without distinction, despite the royal prohibition. He must stay proceedings altogether or when attached, come or send, so that, the plea having been examined in the royal court, he desist or proceed by counsel to the [royal] court. If he does not do so, let him be punished with the appropriate penalty.[54]

This was what happened in practice as episcopal *gravamina* testify.[55] The power of the crown with its coercive writ of prohibition was not to be shaken by a papal legate, the bench of bishops and one of the leading intellectuals of thirteenth-century Christendom. Such strength reveals how little earlier papal efforts to shape English customs to a more acceptably hierocratic model had affected the substance of royal control over the relations of the powers.

The two great Church–State crises of medieval England, the confrontations of Henry II and Archbishop Thomas Becket and of King John and Pope Innocent III, both accidental creations of personality and circumstance rather than of any great inevitable clash of principle, did not significantly weaken royal dominance of ecclesiastical jurisdiction. It is true that both

54. 'Et quamvis in temporalibus sicut in spiritualibus aestimare deberet rex vel iustitiarius suus an sua sit iurisdictio vel non, ut sciri possit an summonitus venire debeat an non, tamen si iudex ecclesiasticus falcem ponens in messem alienam aliquid praesumpserit contra coronam et dignitatem regiam, sicut de laico feodo vel de catallis, cum prohibitione a rege susceperit, supersedere debet in omni casu, saltem donec constiterit in curia regia ad quem pertineat iurisdictio, quia si iudex ecclesiasticus aestimare posset an sua esset iurisdictio, sic in omni casu indifferenter procederet non obstante regia prohibitione. Debet igitur vel omnino supersedere vel cum attachiatus fuerit venire vel mittere, quod examinato placito in curia regia de consilio curiae supersedeat vel procedat, quod si non fecerit, poena debita puniatur ut supra.' *De legibus* IV, p. 282.

55. As, for example, the complaints of the clergy at the Canterbury provincial council held in London in 1257: 'Item in quibus omnibus casibus et similibus, si iudex ecclesiasticus contra prohibitionem regiam procedat, attachiatur. Comparens coram iustitiariis, compellitur iudex exhibere acta sua ut per ea decernant utrum negotium pertineat ad forum ecclesiasticum vel seculare. Et si videatur eis quod pertineat ad forum regium, querelatur iudex; si neget, indicitur ei purgatio per iudicem secularem, ad testimonium duorum vilissimorum ribaldorum. Et si purgare se noluerit, incarceratur donec iustitiariis sacramentum prestiterit corporale quod non processit contra prohibitionem; et si facere noluerit, in carcere retinetur. Similiter actor, si sequatur.' Powicke and Cheney 1964, p. 544.

kings were forced to make concessions. Henry II conceded 'benefit of clergy' so that the trial and punishment of felonious clerks was a matter for the church court. But the crown preserved a significant measure of control. Proceedings against the accused clergyman began in the royal court, with outlawry the penalty for failure to present himself for accusation. Before he was relinquished to the ecclesiastical court, the royal court rigorously scrutinised the validity of his claim to clerical status. It made sure, too, that the bishop's commissary who appeared to claim the cleric for the ecclesiastical court had been properly authorised. The lay court decided whether or not there was a charge to be answered to. If there were, the trial took place before the ecclesiastical judge. Technically, no doubt, the accused had not been tried in the lay court, but the ecclesiastical judge and any possible compurgator already knew that a lay jury thought the man guilty. The lay power closely supervised that the ecclesiastical court had followed its own procedure of purgation exactly. If the accused were found guilty in the ecclesiastical court, his chattels were forfeit to the crown. Indeed they were forfeit to the crown on his being relinquished to the ecclesiastical judge and were only released to one cleared of the charge by grace and favour and payment of a fine.[56] Every stage, therefore, was carefully monitored to make it clear that the *privilegium fori* was privilege granted by the crown.

For the rest, however, Henry vindicated all the important principles of English jurisdictional custom set out in the Constitutions of Clarendon: that, benefit of clergy and a few minor issues apart, 'the clerk was protected by and subject to the same rules of temporal law which guarded and governed the layman',[57] that all questions touching the possession and ownership of land, including advowsons of churches and land granted to churches in alms, were reserved most strictly to the royal jurisdiction; that the application of spiritual penalties to tenants-in-chief, royal officials and crown demesne subjects should be carefully controlled. It was no coincidence that the writ of prohibition with all its potentiality for full control over the operation of the ecclesiastical court made its appearance at this time. And all this gained without recourse to political theory; Henry II produced no theory of royal power. Probably, as has been suggested, he did not even have one.[58]

56. Pollock and Maitland 1898, vol. I, pp. 439–57; Cheney 1936.
57. Pollock and Maitland 1898, vol. I, p. 439.
58. Smalley 1973, p. 238: 'It emerged from the muddle of anti-Becket propaganda that Henry II had no coherent theory of royal power to oppose Becket's defence of the Church, or preferred not to state it, if he had one.'

John's brush with Innocent III brought him over four years of personal excommunication and over five years of interdict on England as a whole.[59] Fear of French invasion and unrest among his officials and barons forced him to make peace with the pope. His climb-down brought him significant favours from Innocent III: condemnation of French invasion plans, condemnation of *Magna Carta*, suspension of Innocent's own choice as archbishop of Canterbury, the Stephen Langton whom John had rejected and thereby incurred excommunication, a veto on the appointment of Langton's brother to York because of John's suspicions of him and, finally, at the fourth Lateran council, excommunication and interdict for all baronial leaders of the rebellion and their aiders and abettors, with an interdict for the city of London. These diplomatic gains remind us that hierocracy was there to be exploited by kings as well as defied, resisted or ignored.

For papal support, John made two concessions. The first was the surrender of the kingdoms of England and Ireland to papal suzerainty. England remained a papal fief until parliament abolished the relationship in 1366. If, as Cheney has suggested, Innocent III intended to 'claim direct power in political as well as ecclesiastical matters'[60] over his new vassal state, the pretension was never actualised either by him or his successors. The second concession, the charter guaranteeing free elections, was a matter of more consequence. Indeed it has been claimed that by it, 'State-churchism in England was annihilated'.[61]

The twelfth clause of the Constitutions of Clarendon had laid down procedure for the conduct of episcopal elections and of elections of abbots of religious houses on the king's demesne. It contained the injunction that such elections were to be made in the king's chapel by clergy present because the king had summoned them. The king's personal presence seems to be assumed. In any event, his assent to the choice was a necessary part of the procedure. This procedure was modified in an important way in 1214. Elections were now to be transferred from the king's chapel to the chapter houses of cathedrals and monasteries and they could take place according to the canonical rules soon to be updated in the legislation of Lateran IV. But just as Henry II was able to qualify his concessions concerning procedures envisaged by the Constitutions of Clarendon, so John was able to preserve important elements of their clause 12. Though the crown was to be no

---

59. Definitively analysed by Cheney 1976.   60. Cheney 1976, p. 337.
61. Tillmann 1980, p. 84. Richardson and Sayles 1963, p. 357, are nearer the mark: 'John was not conceding anything more than words . . . The concession of free election was quite illusory.'

longer in such an all-commanding position in the making of prelates as previously, there remained to it at least a platform for decisive intervention. Electors were obliged to give formal notice of vacancy and were forbidden to proceed to an election until they had been given royal permission to do so. This procedure gave the king an opportunity of making known the name of any candidate he might have in mind and to bring to bear any informal pressure he might wish to exercise. With the requirement of his consent to the elect, he had effectually a veto on any candidate whose loyalty was suspect. And the taking of the temporalities into the king's hand during vacancy could be exploited in circumstances of dispute and, more importantly still, the threat of confiscation during tenure gave the crown a sanction on episcopal conduct whose value it was not slow to appreciate. Coercion *per baroniam* was not just an occasional expedient but became established, as will be seen, as a routine legal procedure.

Thus John's concessions in the charter of free election were much less substantial in actuality than full hierocratic theory, the demand for removal of all royal participation, would have hoped for. In fact, John and Innocent III had produced an eminently sensible compromise, a classic example of dualism in action. The agreed procedure recognised the two-fold status of the bishop, both pastor of souls and tenant-in-chief of the crown and the respective legitimate interests of both powers in his appointment. By and large, despite an occasional spectacularly protracted wrangle and not infrequent episcopal complaints of undue prolongation of vacancies by the crown, the system worked well in the thirteenth century, producing conscientious bishops who were also, in the formula of the royal licence to elect, loyal and useful to the kingdom.

Dualism, English style, which is to say it was effectively dualism at the king's command, emerged relatively unscathed from its two most important challenges. Thereafter the will for the extremes of confrontation was lacking. Royal tempers were lost, churchmen wrung their hands, but there was to be no second Becket, no repeat interdict. By and large the powers achieved a harmonious *modus vivendi* under the authority of the crown.[62] Unquestionably the most striking example of the co-operative harmony of the two powers in England is the procedure known traditionally as caption of excommunicates.[63] In what became from the early thirteenth century an established routine procedure, the crown placed itself as a police arm at the disposal of bishops acting in their capacity as

62. Jones 1966, 1969, 1970; Donahue 1974; Adams and Donahue 1978–9, pp. 97–103.
63. Logan 1968.

ecclesiastical judges. A bishop faced with an accused who had been excommunicated for persistent disobedience to attend his court could call on the help of the civil power to compel him to appear. On signification of the facts to the royal chancery, the appropriate sheriff would be instructed to arrest and detain the excommunicate until he made his peace with his episcopal accuser. The procedure was the classic implementation of a truism known to all canonists from the rubric to a text of Isidore: 'What priests are powerless to accomplish by exhortation, the force of discipline may exact by fear.'[64]

The reality of such co-operation did not make it any the less true that in the thirteenth century 'there is always a brisk border warfare simmering'[65] between the two jurisdictions. The episcopate, on the whole led by able and spiritual men, did not lack energy and ingenuity in standing up for their view of liberty of the Church. The drawing up of long lists of their objections to royal practices in the form of *gravamina* and the attempt to link their remedy with granting of taxation and the observance of *Magna Carta*'s guarantee of the Church's liberties are evidence enough of that. These tactics brought concessions, clarifications and assurances of correction of admitted malpractices. But these were palliatives of the system. They did not diminish the royal control of it. Significantly, it was the royal writ *Circumspecte agatis* with its supplement that the clergy were happy to promote to statute status as the authoritative definition of the competence of the ecclesiastical courts.

The chief instrument with which the crown commanded the frontier between the jurisdictions and decided where the boundary should be drawn was the writ of prohibition.[66] Henry II had devised it, and with experience successive kings strengthened and diversified the prohibitory procedure. The writ in question was a royal command that under threat of sanction proceedings in the ecclesiastical court should be stayed until the crown decided where jurisdiction lay – the procedure stated by Bracton in the passage quoted earlier. Writs might originate with the king and council or from royal judges, for it was routine for justices on general eyre to search out abuses of ecclesiastical jurisdiction. But they were available also to private individuals, including clergy; in effect, therefore, to any litigant who hoped to gain advantage thereby. The persistent unpopularity of the writ of prohibition with ecclesiastical judges testified to its effectuality, until gratefully they accepted *Circumspecte agatis* as a guarantee against the

---

64. 23 q.5 c.20: 'Quod sacerdotes efficere docendo non ualent disciplinae terrore potestas extorqueat.'
65. Pollock and Maitland 1898, vol. I, p. 479.   66. Flahiff 1944, 1945; Helmholz 1976.

arbitrary issuing of such writs and, even more gratefully, the procedure of consultation which allowed appeal against them when there was reason for challenging the validity of a writ.

There were other ways in which the lay power could and did coerce. Both Bracton and Grosseteste spoke of *coercio propter baroniam*.[67] The episcopal barony or the *temporalia* of a see could be confiscated to pressurise a bishop who was considered to have stepped out of line. Such action might therefore be taken quite arbitrarily; but it could also be part of routine procedure. It was the sanction employed to force bishops to compel their clergy to appear in lay courts or to pay fines imposed by royal justices. It was of course much resented by the bishops but their protests availed them little. The ultimate lay weapon against the clergy was brought to bear by Edward I. Faced in 1296 with clerical refusal to pay taxes to help finance his wars, he combined the sanction of confiscation of temporalities with withdrawal from the un-cooperative of the protection of the common law: he outlawed them. Later, his grudge long harboured, he procured from the sycophantic Clement V the suspension and exile of the archbishop of Canterbury who had so honourably led the opposition.[68]

Physical force, or the threat of it, unquestionably played a major role in the assertion of the royal supremacy. But it would be a serious error to see the clergy's submission to the royal will as simply the response to force. Dualism at the king's command was not wrung from a cowed clergy. Perhaps it was as much their creation as the king's. Several considerations suggest this. The most fundamental of these is social: the homogeneity of the English ruling class. A network of family connection, where the sons and brothers of royal officials were bishops, where bishops were royal ministers, judges and civil servants, where royal and aristocratic patronage greatly facilitated the ready movement of men from lay to ecclesiastical service and *vice versa*, formed its own community of interest. The social and governmental order had thus a built-in inclination to a spirit of compromise and co-operation in both spheres. Within this homogeneous ruling class, churchmen were allowed to discover the very real advantages of co-operation with the lay power: the protection of the law in general terms

---

67. Bracton: 'Sed numquid capietur aliquis ad mandatum iudicum delegatorum nec archiadiaconi vel alterius iudicis inferioris, quia rex in episcopis coertionem habet propter baroniam.' *De legibus* IV, p. 327; Grosseteste (the context is patronage to benefices; if a bishop refuses to institute the cleric presented by the lay patron): 'praesentator impetrat a curia regis ut episcopus citetur per vicecomitem, et tandem compellatur per baroniam suam quod veniat responsurus coram iustitiariis domini regis'. 1861, *Ep.* 72, p. 205.   68. Denton 1980, pp. 107–30, 231–5.

and, more specifically, such privileges as benefit of clergy, relative freedom of elections, caption of excommunicates, a safeguard and a not inconsiderable area of ecclesiastical jurisdiction. Politically, the higher clergy, the lords spiritual in their parliamentary capacity, and in their convocations, had a formidable potential for influencing royal policy not least for bargaining about their liberties and the extent to which they were to be taxed.

V

The canonists and theologians of Paris and of the other French universities continued to discuss whether or not the pope held both swords because such discussions were part and parcel of a legal or theological education.[69] It was of some significance that the two swords doctrine remained a *quaestio*, a matter for regular scholarly debate, for this academic exercise kept alive the dissenting tradition typified by such earlier canonists as Ricardus Anglicus. But there was little doubt either as to where orthodoxy lay or as to the language in which it was best expressed. Aquinas, graduating in theology at Paris, voiced common opinion in his *Commentary on the Sentences*. Faced with the Lombard's assertion that 'the Church of God knows no other sword than the spiritual', he postulated 'what Bernard said to Pope Eugenius, namely that the pope has both swords', adding Bernard's own refinement as expressed in the *De consideratione*: 'It must be said that the church [i.e. the clergy] has only the spiritual sword in the context of what it exercises itself by its own hand. But it has also the temporal sword; at its command (*nutu*) it must be drawn, as Bernard said.'[70] Thus the Bernardine formula held sway in the schools. It could hardly be otherwise when the papal curia itself professed the same doctrine, often in the same words, no matter how cautiously it might choose to express it in particular diplomatic circumstances.

The French monarchy shared the curia's point of view to the extent that it was prepared to co-operate with the spiritual power. Its co-operation in the suppression of heresy is the most striking illustration of that willingness. But it was no more disposed to accept the hierocratic interpretation of co-operative dualism than was the English monarchy. Joinville has an anecdote which makes very clear how firmly under royal control were the

---

69. Good examples from the beginning of the thirteenth century (Simon of Tournai, Robert Courson, Stephen Langton) have been published by Baldwin 1970 vol. II, pp. 110–11 with commentary vol. I, pp. 163–7.   70. *In IV Sent.*, d.37, exp. text.

circumstances in which the secular arm should come to the assistance of the ecclesiastical power. The issue in question was what in England was called caption of excommunicates. The whole French episcopate had complained strongly to Louis IX that its sentences of excommunication were being nullified through lack of royal co-operation in enforcing them. The bishops therefore demanded of the king that he should order his officials and judges to compel all those who had been under the ban for a year and a day to answer to their ecclesiastical judge. Louis replied that he would willingly do so, always providing that the civil authority was given the full facts so that it might be judged whether the sentence passed in the ecclesiastical court was just or not. The bishops indignantly rejected the notion that their judgements should be subjected to lay assessment, arguing that the whole procedure should be under their sole control. In other words, demanding that the material sword should act at their *nutus*. But Louis withheld his co-operation. He cited a case of a man excommunicated in a French ecclesiastical court who had his sentence quashed at the papal curia, thereby demonstrating the fallibility of the judge. Therefore, argued the king, if he did not scrutinise such possibly erroneous ecclesiastical sentences, before lending his aid, 'he might be acting contrary to God's law and justice'.[71] In other words, even in the area of divine law – domain *par excellence* of the priesthood – he was not prepared to give way to sacerdotal ruling without exercising his independent judgement in a matter which concerned the common good of the kingdom.

This moral of Joinville's instructive anecdote translates easily into juridical doctrine. Beaumanoir, as acceptable a spokesman of the Capetian view of monarchy as Bracton is of the Angevin, was just as uncompromising as his English counterpart in asserting that it was the king who decided how the two powers should relate and co-operate. Certainly each sword should assist the other in the ways appropriate to its proper sphere and function. And especially must the temporal sword be available to guard holy church in her every need. It was, therefore, perfectly in order, for example, in a testamentary case, for the temporal power, at the request of the ecclesiastical judge, to seize property which had been bequeathed in order to force the executor of the will to do his duty. But this request was not to be interpreted as a command. It must not be thought, Beaumanoir stressed, that the temporal sword was exercised at the *commandement* of the spiritual power. It was called into action only at its *supplicacion*; in the

---

71. Joinville, *Histoire de S. Louis* §§ XXI, CXXXV.

custom of France, such exercise of the royal power in the service of the ecclesiastical, was only *par grace*.[72]

The 'custom of France' with its definition of the boundary between the two jurisdictions and the nature of the co-operation between them was ordinarily well under the control of the monarchy. The episcopate could be outspoken – Joinville's anecdote told how the bishops accused Louis IX, of all people, of dishonouring Christendom – as could their brothers in England. But, as in the neighbouring kingdom, their protests left the system of royal control substantially intact. Beaumanoir, no less than Bracton, articulated a two swords theory which expressed accurately the realities of the relationship between the two powers: co-operative dualism at the king's command. The Capetians controlled the *ecclesia gallicana* whilst rarely allowing their overruling of the hierocratic interpretation of two swords theory to provoke head-on clashes with the papacy. And, for its part, the papacy was anxious to avoid conflict. Preservation of a harmonious relationship with the French crown, in the general context of the suppression of heresy and the promotion of the crusade, was the cornerstone of papal diplomacy throughout the thirteenth century.

Franco-papal harmony came under considerable strain, however, at the turn of the century when Boniface VIII called into action every piece in the hierocratic armoury in an attempt, as he saw it, to reduce the king to filial obedience. The Capetian defied him and though less well-supported with polemical firepower, easily defended the 'custom of France' and the heights of command long occupied by his dynasty. This celebrated confrontation has always been accorded by historians a special significance in the evolution of the relationship of Church and State. G. de Lagarde was not far wide of the mark in his assessment of this significance:

In fact, while the supporters of the Holy See lost their way in defending for the first time an abstract system which corresponded neither to the past history of the Church nor to its future needs, the advocates of the 'prince' with singular success identified the fundamental claims of the modern State when confronted by religious society: sovereignty over property and persons, exclusive exercise of justice, absolute autonomy in legislation, and even (the claim is still confused) control over the spiritual life of the nation. Thus they sketch the earliest efforts of the State to recover the fullness of its personality.[73]

72. Beaumanoir, *Coutumes de Beauvaisis*: 'Nepourquant la justice laie ne fet pas ceste contrainte au commandement de la justice de Sainte Eglise, mes a sa supplicacion, car de nule riens qui touche cas de justice temporel, la justice laie n'est tenue a obéir au commandement de la justice espirituel, selonc nostre coustume, se n'est par grace. Mes la grace ne doit pas estre refusée de l'une justice a l'autre, quant ele est requise benignement.' Carlyle 1903–36, vol. v, pp. 361–3.
73. Lagarde 1948a, p. 258.

A theology untutored by experience challenged a political theory well-grounded in a nation's established political system.

Boniface VIII personally, his curia collectively and his loyal theologians and canonists, produced a hierocratic dossier of unprecedented proportions and ingenuity, whose general trend was to assail or abandon every moderating or qualifying tenet about papal omnipotence suggested by past theory and experience. The pope himself 'reminded' French ambassadors that his predecessors had deposed three French kings and threatened to dismiss their king like an errant stable-lad.[74] In *Ausculta fili*, pope and cardinals summoned the French hierarchy to Rome to investigate the whole conduct of the king's government.[75] Henry of Cremona forced every canon of Gratian's *Decretum* and every political decretal thereafter to maximum support of papal authority.[76] Giles of Rome produced a lengthy and exceptionally emphatic restatement of the Bernardine two swords doctrine and devoted a third of his *On Ecclesiastical Power* to an immoderate refutation of those elements in existing canonical and political opinion which militated against his main thesis, that the pope held a plenitude of power *sine pondere, numero et mensura*.[77] James of Viterbo constructed a specifically ecclesiological logic in his *On Christian Government* to establish the same position, in the same phrase.[78] It is in this treatise especially that is caught the authentic hierocratic note of this period: 'It is indeed well said that the vicar of Christ has fullness of power, because the whole of that power to rule which Christ has given to the church, priestly and royal, spiritual and temporal, is held by the pope, vicar of Christ.'[79] In these theories, where society is equated with the *ecclesia*, the autonomy proper to the temporal order is suffocated by the primary authority of the spiritual and lost to the demands of an all-embracing Christian ministry.

---

74. Dupuy 1655, p. 79.
75. Full analysis and partial translation in Digard 1936, pp. 89–92.
76. *De potestate papae* ed. Scholz 1903.
77. The final chapter of the *De ecclesiastica potestate* is headed: 'Quod in ecclesia est tanta potestatis plenitudo, quod eius posse est sine pondere, numero et mensura.' And it concludes: 'Ecclesia quidem est timenda et mandata eius sunt observanda, sive summus pontifex, qui tenet apicem ecclesie et qui potest dici ecclesia, est timendus et sua mandata sunt observanda, quia potestas eius est spiritualis, celestis et divina, et est sine pondere, numero et mensura.' 3.12, ed. Scholz 1929, pp. 206, 209.
78. 'Merito ergo in summo pontifice dicitur existere potestatis plenitudo. Unde et propter hoc dicitur esse potestas eius sine numero, sine pondere et sine mensura, quod sic potest intelligi.' *De regimine christiano*, ed. Arquillière 1926, p. 273.
79. 'Verumtamen dicitur Christi vicarius habere plenitudinem potestatis: quia tota potentia gubernativa que a Christo communicata est ecclesie, sacerdotalis et regalis, spiritualis et temporalis, est in summo pontifice Christi vicario. Tanta vero potestas communicata est ecclesie quanta erat oportuna ad salutem fidelium; quare in vicario Christi tota illa potentia est, que ad hominum salutem procurandam requiritur.' *Ibid.*, p. 272.

Such views were not confined to academic theology, remote from the realities of Franco-papal diplomacy. When the French protested, in Rome, that the pope was asking the king of France to acknowledge that he held his kingdom from the Church, this was strenuously denied.[80] But Cardinal Matthew of Aquasparta, in the presence of the pope, who explicitly concurred with his spokesman's views, expounded a general theory of sacerdotal preeminence which did not differ in substance from that of Giles of Rome or James of Viterbo: 'Thus in the church which is the ship of Christ and Peter, there must be one rector and one head whose command all are obliged to obey. And he who has the plenitude of power ought to be the lord of all temporalities and spiritualities.'[81] This principle has its relevance in a dualistic context:

There are indeed two jurisdictions, spiritual and temporal. The pope holds in principle (*principaliter*) spiritual jurisdiction and that was given by Christ to Peter and to the popes his successors. The emperor and other kings have temporal jurisdiction, yet the pope has cognisance and judgement of all temporal causes by reason of sin (*ratione peccati*) . . . Hence temporal jurisdiction belongs to the pope, who is vicar of Christ and Peter . . . by right (*de iure*) . . . but does not pertain to him as to action and exercise, as shown by what was said to Peter: 'Put up the sword into the scabbard' [cf. John 18.11].[82]

The cardinal's apologia was essentially a gloss on *Ausculta fili*. But it was equally a preview, as was Giles of Rome's *On Ecclesiastical Power* (especially I.2–5), of *Unam sanctam* wherein the curia sought to compress the full hierocratic logic into its basic principles.

Unam sanctam was the culmination of an ideology that had been given its first recension by Hugh of St Victor, as outlined in the beginning of this chapter: two powers inscribed within the one corporate society of Christians. The spiritual power institutes the temporal power and judges it if it errs. It incorporated too both the doctrinal content and terminology of St Bernard's two swords allegory, as reworked by Giles of Rome. Above

---

80. By Boniface VIII himself, in the words cited in n. 2 above.
81. 'Sic in ecclesia, quae sit navis Christi et Petri, debet esse unicus rector et unum caput, ad cuius preceptum omnes tenentur obedire. Et ille debet esse dominus omnium temporalium et spiritualium, qui habet plenitudinem potestatis . . .' *Sermo de potestate papae*, ed. Gal 1962, p. 187.
82. 'Sunt enim duae iurisdictiones: spiritualis et temporalis. Iurisdictionem spiritualem principaliter habet summus pontifex, et illa fuit tradita a Christo Petro et summis pontificibus, successoribus eius; iurisdictionem temporalem habeant imperator et alii reges, tamen de omni temporali habet cognoscere summus pontifex et iudicare ratione peccati. Unde dico quod iurisdictio temporalis potest considerari vel prout competit alicui ratione actus et usus, vel prout competit summo pontifici, qui est vicarius Christi et Petri, de iure; unde qui dicit contrarium, impingit in illum articulum: "Iudicaturus est vivos et mortuos"; et in illum etiam predictum: "Sanctorum communionem". Sed iurisdictio temporalis quantum ad usum et quantum ad exsecutionem actus non competit ei; unde dictum est Petro: "Converte gladium in vaginam"' *ibid.*, pp. 189–90.

all, it is what might be called a Christological political logic: the pope, in unshared headship, rules the Christian community as vicar of Christ. He has therefore such power as the general good of souls requires, his judgement of what constitutes that good is absolute, and therefore obedience to what he decides is essential, for that good is necessary for salvation. This jurisdiction covers every aspect of morality and thus kingship and the temporal order are not exempt from it.[83] *Unam sanctam* is a more explicit and official version of Aquinas' principle that to the pope 'vicar of Christ, all kings of the Christian people should be subject, as if to our lord Jesus Christ himself'.[84]

The French took *Unam sanctam* sufficiently seriously to extract from Clement V, some four years after its promulgation, an assurance that it contained nothing prejudicial to the king, the kingdom and the French people. The pope duly emphasised that he wished it to be understood that the French church, king, kingdom and people remained 'in the same state' in relation to the papacy as they had been before *Unam sanctam*.[85] No doubt this formula of compromise left many questions unanswered and open to each party to interpret as it would precisely what that same state was. But the course of the dispute had shown how the French understood it.

They took their stand on that dualism which Capetian practice had established. The king professed himself a true and devoted son of the Holy See, attentive to such pastoral admonitions as it chose to make for the good of his soul. But such *ratione peccati* authority carried no political jurisdiction. The *regimen temporalitatis regni* belonged exclusively to the king and there he was sovereign, subject to no superior.[86] This sovereignty extended no less

---

83. *Unam sanctam* should be read with the lengthy gloss of Jean Lemoine in any of the early printed editions of the *Extravagantes Communes* (1.8.1).

84. 'Huius regni ministerium, ut a terrenis essent spiritualia distincta, non terrenis regibus, sed sacerdotibus commissum, et precipue summo sacerdoti, successori Petri, Christi vicario, Romano pontifici, cui omnes reges populi christiani oportet esse subditos, sicut ipsi domino nostro Iesu Christo. Sic enim ei ad quem finis ultimi cura pertinet, subdi debent illi ad quos pertinet cura antecedentium finium et eius imperio dirigi.' *De regno* 1.14. Congar considers this to be Aquinas' 'la formule la plus extrême'. Congar 1970, p. 240.

85. 'Hinc est quod nos regi et regno per definitionem et declarationem bonae memoriae Bonifacii papae viii. praedecessoris nostri quae incipit, unam sanctam, nullum volumus vel intendimus praeiudicium generari. Nec quod per illam rex, regnum, et regnicolae praelibati amplius ecclesiae sint subiecti Romanae, quam antea existebant, sed omnia intelligantur in eodem esse statu quo erant ante definitionem praefatam: tam quantum ad ecclesiam, quam etiam ad regem, regnum et regnicolas superius nominatos.' *Extrav. Comm.* 5.7.2 (*Meruit*).

86. Discourse to papal legates, 20 April 1297: 'Regimen temporalitatis regni sui ad ipsum regem solum et neminem alium pertinere, seque in eo neminem superiorem recognoscere ... super rebus pertinentibus ad temporale regimen regni. Quantum autem ipsius regis tangit animam et ad spiritualitatem attinet, idem rex ... paratus est monitionibus et praeceptis sedis apostolicae devote et humiliter obedire, in quantum tenetur et debet, et tanquam verus et devotus filius sedis ipsius et sanctae matris ecclesiae reverentiam observare.' Dupuy 1655, p. 28; Rivière 1926, pp. 101–2.

over the clergy than the laity. The Knight of the *Disputation between a Knight and a Clerk* put the official point of view with characteristic severity:

Curb your tongue, sir clerk, and acknowledge that the king, in right of his royal power, is supreme over the laws, customs and liberties granted to you clergy and that he may add to them or take away from them or amend them according as equity and reason or the advice of his magnates counsels.[87]

It was just such a principle that informed the replies made by Philip the Fair to each of the pope's specific complaints of alleged French violation of ecclesiastical liberty. In the jurisdiction allowed to ecclesiastical courts, in royal rights over ecclesiastical properties and revenues and in collation to benefices, the king took his stand firmly on 'the custom of St Louis and his predecessors'.[88] Throughout the whole conflict, the French upheld 'the custom of France' and resisted what the baronage, alarmed by hierocratic language which suggested that the king of France had power in his kingdom conferred on him by the pope, called 'mauvaises et outrageuses nouvelletez'.[89]

They were not content, however, simply to defend the autonomy of the temporal power and the subjection of the clergy to it. Against *Unam sanctam*'s claim that the supreme spiritual power was immune from human judgement, the French proposed to put Boniface VIII on trial before a general council and actually attempted to arrest him in his Anagni residence. The charges levelled against the pope are scarcely credible. But as a procedure, the projected course of action was not indefensible. Its justification lay in a double line of argumentation, neither line new in itself, but now fused together in a uniquely forcible way.

The first of these was taken from the canonists. They had for long argued that there was an exception to the ordinary rule, reiterated in *Unam sanctam*, that a pope could be judged only by God. Gratian's *Decretum* contained a text, purportedly of St Boniface, which apparently allowed human judgement of a pope who had fallen into heresy. On the basis of this authority, canonists argued that a pope guilty of heresy was accountable to the Church at large and could be deposed. A breach once made in papal immunity, it could be widened. The *glossa ordinaria* on the *Decretum* went on to argue that a pope could be tried for any notorious crime which

---

87. 'Et ideo domine clerice linguam uestram coercete et agnoscite regem legibus, consuetudinibus et privilegiis uestris, et libertatibus datis, regia potestate praeesse, posse addere, posse minuere quaelibet, aequitate et ratione consultis, aut cum suis proceribus, sicut uisum fuerit, temperare.' Ed. Goldast 1611, p. 687.
88. Characteristically expressed in his replies to articles put to him by Boniface VIII, well analysed by Digard 1936, vol. II, pp. 143–5.   89. Dupuy 1655, pp. 60–2; Rivière 1926, p. 107.

constituted a public scandal when he had shown himself incorrigible.[90] When canonists considered ways and means of getting rid of an heretical or incorrigibly criminous pope, they generally agreed that the proper agent was a general council which canonists regarded as the ordinary mechanism for the discussion of important problems of unusual difficulty and for the resolving of crises. They tended to be vague, however, as to the actual procedure whereby a general council might be summoned in these circumstances, a tricky question, when by definition a general council was one adjudged such by the pope who alone could summon it. The French were to exploit the canonist argument about trying a heretical and criminal pope; they were to provide their own answer to the problem of summoning a general council to conduct such a trial.

The process of bringing Boniface VIII to trial was started at a meeting of the king's council in the Louvre held on 12 March 1303. Guillaume de Nogaret opened for the prosecution, headlining his speech with prophetic words of St Peter which he saw fulfilled in his days: 'There were also false prophets among the people even as there shall be among you, lying teachers' (2 Pet. 2.1). Boniface was the lying teacher now among God's people – manifest heretic, usurper of the chair of Peter, simoniac, blasphemer, destroyer of churches, incorrigible public sinner – the very personification of that abomination of desolation of the Temple of which Daniel had spoken (Dan. 9.27). Nogaret undertook to prove these charges at the general council before which he demanded Boniface be arraigned. In the meantime, he should be suspended from office immediately and held under close arrest, a vicar of the Roman Church being appointed until a new head of the Church could be chosen.

Where the canonists were vague as to the procedure for summoning the general council before which an heretical or criminous clerk was to be tried, Nogaret was quite specific. He called on Philip to act like the angel who confronted Balaam with a drawn sword (Num. 22.31) and give the orders to prelates and all concerned to assemble in general council 'to condemn this infamous brigand and provide the church with a legitimate pastor'. Nogaret gave reasons why it was for the king to take the initiative: it was the function of Christian kingship to defend the Church when it was in danger; it was a duty especially incumbent on the kings of France.[91] This double theme, of kingship as religious office and of the special dynastic obligation to fulfil it, runs through all the justifications for royal action against

90. D.40 c.6, s.v. *a fide devius*. Cf. Tierney 1955a, pp. 60–7.
91. Dupuy 1655, pp. 56–9. Digard 1936, vol. II, pp. 156–7.

Boniface VIII, not least in those made by Philip himself. Kings were divinely appointed to uphold and spread the faith and to defend the Church, he argued, and his royal house was renowned for its defence of truth. Christian kings must defend the Church – the coronation oath bound them to it. The dynastic pride of the *reges christianissimi*, newly enhanced by the recent canonisation of Louis IX, ensured Philip would not shirk his duty to protect the Roman Church from its invader.

It was on 14 June 1303 at an assembly of prelates and barons that Philip the Fair made public his determination to bring Boniface VIII before a general council. On this occasion, five archbishops and twenty-one bishops with an assortment of other senior clergy associated themselves with this request. With some help from royal pressure, they were to be followed by all sections of French opinion. An early supporter of Philip's proposed action was the university of Paris. There is some evidence that Nogaret had invited the university to debate whether or not the pope held jurisdiction of the temporal sword in France. No collective response is known, but individual Parisian theologians joined in the current debate and contributed significantly to the literature of the theory of the relationship of the two powers. Two of these works are of especial interest: the *Quaestio in utramque partem*, of unknown authorship and the *On Royal and Papal Power* written by the Dominican John of Paris.

The treatises have much in common, in aim, in content, in tone. Both command an easy mastery of the *quaestio* technique in a comprehensive marshalling of all the authorities, philosophical, juridical and especially scriptural, which schoolmen considered relevant for the methodical examination of the principle of dualism of the powers, their co-operation and the political implications of the superiority of the spiritual power. They are pro-French without being blatantly partisan in producing a rigorous critique of hierocracy and a powerful defence of the autonomy of the temporal. Despite their French sympathies, these writers remain academics, searchers after truth, rather than royal propagandists. Indeed a good case can be made for the view that both authors were seeking, and went far towards achieving, a *via media* between the claims of papacy and monarchy.

The *Quaestio* accumulated evidence and opinion from many sources that the powers were distinct and that the pope enjoyed no predominance in the temporal order. The author was at particular pains to defend the autonomy of the king of France in his own kingdom and to deny that he derived his power from the papacy. The case for dualism, argued with a solidity that can only be suggested in a short summary, proceeded along three main lines.[92] The first came from the political thought of the ancient world. Aristotle and Cicero in particular established the intrinsically natural and ethical origin and function of government; there was no need, therefore, for any sacerdotal validation. The second derived from the experience of the Church gained in the long history of its relationship with lay authority; that practical acquaintance with the relevant problems was reflected in canon law, especially in Gratian's *Decretum*. The third, the most important, came from scripture; inevitably, as the word of God, the ultimate authority.

It was, then, from this last source that the author took his most telling argument. God had created man in a two-fold nature, soul and body, and this duality involved him in a two-fold way of life (*duplex vita*), each with its appropriate societal context (*duplex civilitas*), each regulated by an appropriate power ('two swords'). That God had intended duality of jurisdictions was shown in Luke 22.38. St Paul had indicated the role of each: the one 'beareth not the sword in vain. For he is God's minister' (Rom. 13.4); the other denoted 'the sword of the spirit, which is the word of God' (Eph. 6.17). God gives his minister the sword without recourse to intermediaries and expects him to exercise it on his own responsibility. Since the apostles used only the sword of the spirit, so their successors should follow their example. Scripture said nothing of their use of the material swords, except in the context of Peter's cutting off the ear of the servant of the high priest. Christ's command that he desist was one forbidding him, and thus his successors, the use of the temporal sword.[93] Christ, the model for all, had further lessons for popes: his flight from wordly ambition when the people wanted to make him king, his refusal to act as judge in temporal matters, his command to his apostles that they should render to Caesar what was his.[94]

92. More fully analysed, Watt 1967, pp. 420–7, 431–5.

93. 'Ad utriusque civilitatis regimen, Deus gladios ordinavit, duas iurisdiciones distinctas et differentes ad invicem, sicut exponunt sancti illud Luce XXII: "ecce gladii duo hic", et respondit Dominus: "satis est!". Materiali gladio utuntur principes sicut ait Apostolus, ad Rom. XIII: "princeps non sine causa gladium portat, Dei enim minister, et vindex in iram ei qui malum facit"; de spirituali gladio dicit idem Apostolus, Ephes. VI: "galeam assumite et gladium spiritus quod est verbum Dei". Gladio spirituali utebantur apostoli, materiali vero nunquam usi esse leguntur, nisi dicatur quod imminente Domini passione Petrus cum haberet gladium exemit et unius auriculam amputavit. Distincte sunt igitur hec potestates nec debent se mutuo perturbare, quia sicut princeps non debet de spiritualibus intromittere se, ita nec pontifex debet in temporalibus se immiscere, nec iuridicionem temporalem assumere, nisi in certis casibus determinatis a iure, sicut dicetur.' Ed. Vinay 1939, p. 108.

94. 'Cum igitur Christus dominus hac potestate uti noluerit sed oblatam refugerit, exemplo suo evidenter ostendit et evidencia facti docuit vicarium suum talem potestatem refugere non ambire, nec sibi imperatoriam maiestatem aut dignitatem regiam vendicare. Ecce Christus Ihesus, rex regum et dominus dominancium, regale prefugit dominium et fastuosum fastigium recusavit: quomodo igitur, qua racione vel auctoritate, vicarius eius vendicabit sibi culmen vel nomen regie dignitatis.' *Ibid.*, p. 110; p. 96 for the Matthew 22.19 reference.

Philosophical and historical arguments reinforced what was essentially the classic dualist position, no doubt now well-known in scholastic circles, after many decades of debating the two swords *quaestio*. The author covered the ground more thoroughly and methodically than, say, Ricardus Anglicus, but his only novelty, perhaps, was to sharpen its relevance to France and to introduce a dash of Aristotle into the argument. It is significant that in the last analysis, this re-presentation of a traditional position was scarcely less successful than its predecessors in making its dualism absolute, that is to say, in freeing the temporal completely from any vestige of sacerdotal authority. The author, having made his case for dualism, then went on to allow a subjection of the king of France to that authority, *incidenter et casualiter*. Even such a committed champion of dualism could not escape hierocracy altogether. This emerges very clearly from the most important issue of all, the papal power to depose kings. The author rejected any suggestion that a pope had a direct power of deposition. Nevertheless, he had an indirect or 'incidental' power: 'in a case where action against a prince is allowable, the pope can release vassals from their oath of fidelity, or rather, he can declare them to be released, in a case, for example, of heresy or persistent defiance of the Roman Church'.[95] It is difficult to envisage such a conclusion being acceptable to Philip the Fair whose defiance of Boniface VIII was such a thorn in the flesh of that irascible pontiff. Nor in the preservation of his king from hierocratic sanction (in the theory of the matter) did John of Paris do much better. John too was a trenchant critic of all the major hierocratic arguments. He too produced a reasoned and comprehensive defence of dualism. He shared his colleague's view (and indeed drew on his treatise) that the spiritual power possessed no direct power in the temporal order, did not possess both swords and was not the intermediary through whom the king of France received his power from God. Yet he also allowed the pope a role in the deposition of kings, albeit an indirect one. If a ruler, he argued, were an incorrigible heretic, paying no heed to excommunication, the pope might himself initiate such action among the ruler's subjects as might be expected to lead to his deposition. He was very explicit as to how this might be done. The pope could excommunicate all those who continued to obey a king who by his misdeeds had forfeited the right to rule and to his subjects' loyalty.[96] This

95. '. . . in casu in quo potest agere contra principem, potest etiam absolvere vassallos a iuramento fidelitatis, vel pocius, absolutos declarare, utpote racione heresis vel contumacie contra Romanam ecclesiam'. *Ibid.*, p. 133.
96. 'Dico etiam "nisi per accidens", quia si esset princeps haereticus et incorrigibilis et contemptor ecclesiasticae censurae, possit papa aliquid facere in populo unde ille privaretur honore saeculari et

was not exactly what Philip the Fair wanted to hear from a Parisian theologian.

In one very important respect, however, John of Paris can be considered of greater service to his king than the author of the *Quaestio*. John was a known supporter of Philip the Fair's proposal that Boniface be summoned before a general council for he put his signature to a royal document urging this. In his treatise (it cannot be decided whether it was written before or after Nogaret's Louvre address of 12 March 1303) he provided a rationale for the proposed course of action. He was not concerned with the specific charges so much as with the general principles involved.

One of the most important of these was papal immunity from human judgement, an established principle which *Unam sanctam* reiterated. As has been seen, the canonists already allowed an exception to that rule in the case of an heretical or incorrigibly criminal pope. John of Paris certainly exploited that loop-hole. But his main argument was rather different. Given the especially divine origin of papal power, did it not follow that it could only be taken away by God? The argument had been given recent prominence by those who opposed the abdication of Celestine V in 1294. John of Paris took over the refutation of it given by Giles of Rome in his *On Papal Resignation* but extended it to include papal deposition. A distinction was made. Certainly the papacy in itself came from God alone. But the decision as to which particular person should be chosen as pope is a human one; a pope is made by choice of the electors and the consent of the elect. What has been conferred by human agreement can be dissolved in the same way: by abdication, on the decision of the individual (when for good cause he withdraws his consent previously given), by deposition, on the decision of the whole Church (when for good cause it withdraws its consent previously given). It was the Church as a whole which chose the pope: the college of cardinals was simply its agent, acting on its behalf. What the whole Church has conferred it may withdraw, its will expressed either in a general council or even by the college of cardinals: 'the body whose consent in the place of the whole church makes a pope might, conversely, unmake him'. [97]

There must of course be reasonable cause. 'No one is chosen to be pope

---

deponeretur a populo, et hoc faceret papa in crimine ecclesiastico cuius cognitio ad papam pertinet, excommunicando omnes qui ei ut domino oboedirent, et sic populus ipsum deponeret et papa per accidens.' *De potestate regia et papali*, XIII, ed. Bleienstein 1969, p. 138, English translation of the treatise, Watt 1971.

97. '. . . quia ex quo consensus eorum facit papam loco ecclesiae, videtur similiter quod potest ipsum deponere, et si quidem fuerit causa rationabilis et sufficiens, deponunt eum meritorie. Si vero non fuerint sufficiens, peccant.' XXIV, *ibid.*, p. 202.

for any reason other than the common good of the Church. The purpose of his rulership is the common benefit.' Anything, therefore, which works against the common good, 'anything which is a scandal to the Church or anything which disquiets the Church or disunites the Lord's flock' suffices.[98] John came down to particularities of obvious relevance to the contemporary situation. Suppose there were some doubt as to whether a particular individual had been canonically elected, what should be done about it? John's solution to the problem was to have the person of the elect and the conduct of the election examined 'by learned men and others who were involved'. If anything seriously amiss was uncovered, the wrongfully elected person must be advised to withdraw. What if he refused? Then 'he can be taken captive, a general council called and the case laid before it. If in these circumstances he proves obstinate or violent, he should be removed even with the aid of the secular arm, lest the sacraments of the Church be profaned.'[99]

John referred to another situation whose relevance to the Franco–papal quarrel needs no emphasis. Suppose a pope announced it was heresy to maintain a certain opinion about which the learned differ and he did this without consulting a general council. To declare, for example, that it was heresy to deny the temporal subjection to the pope of the king of France.[100] Or proclaim as an article of faith that the pope held both swords. And this without considerable preliminary discussion by experts and without holding a general council. John argued that to introduce doctrinal novelties of this sort without their acceptance by the whole Church (i.e. in general council: 'the pope with council is greater than the pope alone') would be gravely wrong.[101]

---

98. '. . . non eligitur aliquis in papam nisi propter bonum commune ecclesiae et gregis dominici. Ad hoc enim praeest ut prosit. Si ergo postquam fuerit in papatu invenerit se seu inveniatur totaliter ineptus et inutilis vel superveniat impedimentum, ut insania vel aliquid consimile, debet petere cessionem a populo vel a collegio cardinalium quod in tali casu est loco totius populi. Et ideo perpenditur mollities animi vel ineptitudo scandalum ecclesiae vel quod ipse turbet ecclesiam seu quod dividat gregem Domini faciens divisiones et admonitus non desistat, etiam compellendus est ad cessionem . . .'. xxiv, *ibid.*, pp. 200–1.

99. 'Si vero circa personam vel electionem summi pontificis, post discussionem diligentem a litteratis et ab illis quorum interest factam, aliquid inveniretur legitimum contra statum, non esset dissimulandum, sed monendus esset cedere, et si nollet, posset excipi et generale concilium peti et ad ipsum concilium appellari. Immo in tali casu deberet si pertinax inveniretur cum violentia, et advocato brachio seculari, a sede removeri, ne profanarentur ecclesiae sacramenta.' xxii, *ibid.*, pp. 192–3.

100. xxii, *ibid.*, p. 195.

101. '. . . nam papam habere utrumque gladium non continetur in sacra scriptura quae est regula fidei . . . cum fides christiana sit catholica et universalis, non potest summus pontifex hoc ponere sub fide sine concilio generali . . . eo quod orbis maior est urbe et papa cum concilio maior est papa solo, XCIII D., Legimus' (*Decretum*, D.93 c.24). xx, *ibid.*, pp. 184–5.

It is thus clear that John, without labouring the point, is a conciliarist for whom recourse to a general council would be the acceptable way of dealing with a major crisis such as the alleged illegal election, heresy and public scandal of Boniface VIII. When, however, his text is questioned further as to what he had in mind when he spoke of 'the aid of the secular arm' in this context, it seems that he condoned lay action independently of a general council. Considering what he described as 'abuse of the spiritual sword' – conferring benefices simoniacally, misusing church property, violating the rights of other clergy, false teaching in faith and morals, are given as examples of such abuse – John produced an interesting new variant of the two swords theory. To remedy such abuses of papal power recourse should be had, in the first instance, to the college of cardinals who, 'standing in the place of the whole clergy', should admonish the errant pope. Should he, however, prove incorrigible and the cardinals ineffectual and there is grave danger to the Church in delay, a ruler might intervene: 'For it is in this way two swords are bound to lend help to each other in that common charity which unites the members of the Church.' John approved as a precedent for the implementation of this principle Emperor Henry III's successful intervention in 1046 in the infamous wrangle as to who should be pope:

The prince acting with moderation may resist the violence of the papal sword with his own sword. In this he does not act against the pope as pope but against an enemy of himself and of society, just as Aod the Israelite who slew Eglon king of Moab . . . because he oppressed God's people in harsh servitude, was not considered to have killed a ruler but a wicked man who was an enemy [cf. Judges 3.16–22]. This was not an action against the church but for it . . . So too the emperor Henry going to Rome deposed by imperial and canonical sanction Benedict IX and two others whose contentions for the papacy scandalised the church, and made Clement II pope.[102]

Not for the first or the last time, we are reminded of the importance of ecclesiastical history in the shaping of medieval politico-ecclesiology.

---

102. 'Si tamen periculum rei publicae sit in mora, ut scilicet quod trahitur populus ad malam opinionem et est periculum de rebellione et papa commoveat populum indebite per abusum gladii spiritualis, ut etiam non speratur quod desistat aliter, puto quod in hoc casu ecclesia contra papam deberet moveri et agere contra ipsum. Princeps etiam violentiam gladii papae posset repellere per gladium suum cum moderamine, nec ageret contra papam ut papa est, sed contra hostem suum et hostem rei publicae, sicut Ahyot Judaeus qui Eglon regem Moab interfecit sagitta infixa in femore eius, eo quod gravi servitute populum Dei premebat, non est reputatus interfecisse rectorem, licet malum, sed hostem. Sic enim populus commendabiliter zelo fidei commotus Constantinum papam, qui ecclesiae scandalum erat, oculis privavit et deposuit. Sic etiam Henricus imperator Romam vadens Benedictum IX et duos alios qui contentionibus suis scandalizabant ecclesiam, imperiali et catholica censura deposuit et Clementem II Romanae ecclesiae papam constituit, ut legitur in Chronicis Romanorum.' xxii, ibid., p. 196.

VI

Two swords theories of every emphasis and nuance were well-ventilated in Italy.[103] Hierocratic versions[104] reigned triumphant in the papal curia and among its loyal theologians and canonists; *Unam sanctam* gave them a new fillip. On the other hand, the professors of civil law and writers dependent on them remained faithful to a dualist interpretation.[105] So too did the two leading Italian champions of dualism, Dante and Marsilius of Padua, the writers who above all others represent the specifically Italian contribution to the medieval debate about the relationship of the spiritual and temporal powers. It was with them that the traditional imperial dualist position found its most eloquent and comprehensive defenders. It was from them that papal conduct and the hierocratic logic received its most blistering and radical criticism. Both were convinced of the existence of a catastrophic incongruity between the commands and counsels of the Gospel and the conduct of papal government.[106] Both were convinced too that the essential cause of Italy's wretched political condition was the usurpation of imperial power by the papacy. This conviction was animated by a love of Italy and a corresponding hatred of those responsible for its desolation.[107] Both believed themselves to be specially charged with the identification and denunciation of the papacy as destroyer of peace.[108] This consciousness of mission, at once evangelical and patriotic, gave their writing a passion not found elsewhere in medieval theorising about the relationship of ecclesiastical to temporal power.

A full study of Dante's thinking on Empire and Papacy would begin with the *Convivio* which contains the outline of an argument developed fully in the *Monarchia*, continue with the political *Epistolae* which demonstrate especially his emotional commitment to the Roman Empire and climax with the *Commedia*. His doctrine of Empire is consistent throughout all these four very different types of writing. There is no criticism of the papacy in the *Convivio*, nor in the *Epistolae*, where his dualism is notably respectful

103. Lecler 1932.
104. On Augustinus Triumphus and others, Wilks 1963, pp. 261–2. On hierocratic theory generally, McCready 1973, 1974, 1975.
105. But most emphatically, even obsessively, Ockham: e.g. *Breviloquium*, v.3. (on the invalidity of the mystical sense of Luke 22.38) and v.5 ('Per illa verba: "Ecce duo gladii hic" non potest probari, imperium esse a papa'). 106. Leff 1976, pp. 130–9.
107. Dante, *Purgatorio* 6; *Defensor Pacis*, 1.1.2, 6; 2.26.19, 20.
108. Most poignantly through the mouth of St Peter himself: '"E tu, figliuol, che per lo mortal pondo/ ancor giù tornerai, apri la bocca, / e non asconder quel ch'io non ascondo".' *Paradiso* 27.64–6; Marsilius: 'Quoniam ut indubitanter videre videor, *desuper mihi datum est* . . .' (1.19.13); '. . . tamquam veritatis preco . . .' (2.25.18).

of papal authority. Book III of the *Monarchia*,[109] however, is a sustained attack on hierocracy, aimed especially at those whose exaggerations and misunderstandings of the nature of papal power were motivated by zeal for religion rather than pride or malice. The *Commedia* broadens and personalises criticism of papal government. Boniface VIII, Clement V and John XXII come in for especially vicious attack. Their faults were not simply those of usurping imperial power, though that is condemned and blamed for the incessant strife which was destroying Italy. Condemnation of the contemporary papacy's political stance was only one aspect of Dante's denunciation of the depravity of the papal pastorate as a whole: greed for wealth, nepotism, simony, abuse of the keys are charges added to that of greed for power.

Dante's view of Empire, previewed in the *Convivio* and underpinning much of the political theory of the *Commedia*, received its fullest exposition in the *Monarchia*. It hinged on three fundamental theses, each in the treatise the subject of a book. The first argued that the only guarantee of peace and justice for the Christian world lay in the establishment of unity under one single ruler. The second argued that under God's providence this role had been assigned to the Roman Emperor, even from its origins in pre-Christian times, and given special confirmation of it after the Messiah in sign of its right to rule the world had chosen to live, work and die under its sovereignty. The third thesis postulated that this single universal rulership was given by God directly to each emperor, without mediation by way of the papacy and was exercised independently of any jurisdictional control by the head of the Church. This argument, expounded in Book III of the *Monarchia* gave the principle of imperial *dualitas* its first systematic apologia.

The *Monarchia* has its faults. It is naive in its optimism that because the monarch, as the superior of all other temporal rulers, was left with nothing more to conquer he would be immune from cupidity and hence could not fail to be a just ruler (1.11.13). It is credulous in its argument that Roman military superiority over all rivals was proof of God's endorsement of its world leadership (2.8.9.). It is bizarre in its theology with its argument that the sin of Adam would not have been expiated if the Roman Empire where Christ died had not been based on right (2.12). It is under-researched in that its attempts to refute hierocratic arguments (3.4–15) are elementary as compared with professional theologians such as John of Paris and Remigio de' Girolami or indeed as compared with those very canonists whom Dante affected to despise for their lack of theological and philosophical expertise.

---

109. Excellent analysis by Maccarrone 1955–6.

It is incomplete, even confused, in that its conclusion allows a certain subordination of emperor to pope, apparently a significant qualification of the dualist case, without providing any precise indication of what this subordination meant in practice (3.16). Nevertheless, there is an undeniable classic quality about the ecclesiological principles on which Dante's dualism rested: the demonstration of the weakness of the theological and historical foundations supporting any clerical claim to confer political authority on an emperor (3.14); the reminder that Christ, exemplar of all pastors, specifically renounced earthly power and that the exercise of temporal power by his priests was contrary to the nature of the kingdom he himself had chosen to rule (3.15); the reworking of the patristic and early papal emphasis on Christ's intention when he divided the powers – precisely to save men from the pride and corruption which followed when spiritual and temporal power were concentrated in one authority (3.16).

The *Monarchia* did not pass unnoticed by papalists. Cardinal Bertrand de Pouget, papal legate in Lombardy in 1329, ordered it to be burnt and would have added Dante's bones to the pyre if he could have had his way. The Dominican theologian Guido Vernani of Rimini wrote a *Refutatio* of it which put forward a counter-argument to all the theses Dante had propounded in each of the three books of the *Monarchia*. Vernani's treatise affords a valuable insight into the developed hierocratic logic, making crystal clear the fundamental importance to it of two theses in particular. The first explained the characteristic relationship of the dualism of the powers to the unitary nature of Christian society, already adumbrated by Hugh of St Victor. Guido Vernani, seeking to refute Dante's arguments for the necessity of a *curator orbis* who should be the emperor (3.16), argued that the only authority whom God had appointed 'keeper of the world' was the pope. All the arguments for the emperor's headship of the world, Vernani argued, applied *a fortiori* to the pope:

To speak briefly and summarily, all the arguments which [Dante] put forward in the first part of his treatise which have any vestige of truth can be applied truly to no other monarch, nor can they ever be so applied, except to the lord Jesus Christ. But since he departed from the sight of men and ascended bodily into heaven, lest his body, which is the Church, should remain without a head, he left behind him on earth as his general vicar, the apostle Peter, and each of his legitimate successors who in Christ's place is the true and legitimate monarch to whom all are held to obedience as to the lord Jesus Christ, as is said specifically by Cyril, doctor of the Greeks, as cited by blessed Thomas Aquinas in his book *Against the Errors of the Greeks*. The monarch of the world, therefore, is the high priest of the Christians, general vicar of Jesus Christ; and if all men obeyed him in accordance with the Gospel law laid down by Christ there would be in the world the most perfect

monarchy. Nor shall there ever be in the world a true monarch other than him . . .
and no other power is necessary for men.[110]

The nature of the power exercised by the papal monarch, definition of
which formed the second fundamental thesis of the logic, derived from an
exegesis of Matthew 16.19. Dante had argued (*Monarchia* 3.8) that though
the power of the keys conferred by Christ on Peter gave his papal successors
power to continue what had been entrusted to the leader of the apostles, the
office to which he had been appointed did not mean jurisdiction in the
political sphere. Spiritual fatherhood should not evolve into monarchy
unless it be, like Christ's own kingship, 'not of this world' (John 18.36). To
this argument, Guido Vernani replied with an adaptation of a distinction
much used by contemporary theologians when discussing the power of the
keys, that is, the nature of sacerdotal jurisdiction. They distinguished
between an internal and an external forum. In the former, the priest's power
of the keys was exercised privately, secretly, on the consciences of
individuals in the sacrament of penance. In the latter, it was exercised
openly, publicly, imposing sanctions of excommunication and other
punishments after judicial process. Vernani drew out the full hierocratic
potential of this distinction:

the power of the keys is an effect of ordination to the priesthood and is conferred at
ordination so that it may be used in the forum of the conscience when absolving the
contrite who has confessed his sins and binding him to a penance to make
satisfaction for them. And this power was given generally to Peter and the other
apostles when Christ said to them all: 'Receive ye the Holy Ghost. Whose sins you
shall forgive, they are forgiven etc.' [John 20.22–3]. The other is the power of
jurisdiction by which the ecclesiastical judge in the exterior forum binds with and
looses from the bond of excommunication or binds in condemning and looses in
declaring innocence. This power given generally over the whole Church without
distinction was accepted by Peter from Christ, as is shown in John 21 when he was
told, 'Feed my sheep' [John 21.17]. On which text the gloss states: 'To feed the sheep
is to strengthen those who believe in Christ lest they fall away from the faith, to

110. 'Et sic breviter et summatim omnes rationes quas ponit in prima parte sui tractatus, habentes
aliquam speciem veritatis, in nullo alio monarcha possunt, nec unquam potuerunt, veraciter
inveniri, nisi in domino Iesu Christo. Sed, quoniam ipse discessit a conspectu hominum et
corporaliter ascendit in celum, ne corpus eius quod est ecclesia sine capite remaneret, in terra suum
generalem vicarium dereliquit, scilicet Petrum apostolum et quemlibet eius legitimum
successorem, qui loco Christi est verus et legitimus monarcha cui omnes oboedire tenentur sicut
domino Iesu Christo, sicut expresse dicit Cyrillus doctor Graecorum [*recte* Ps.-Cyril], et allegat hoc
beatus Thomas de Aquino in libro suo quem fecit *Contra errores Grecorum*. Monarcha ergo
mundi est summus pontifex christianorum, generalis vicarius Iesu Christi, cui si omnes homines
secundum legem evangelicam a Christo traditam obedirent, esset in mundo perfectissima
monarchia. Nec unquam fuit in mundo monarcha verus aliquis preter eum . . . .' I, Käpelli 1938,
p. 129.

provide their subjects with material help where there is need, to set before them examples of virtue through preaching, to resist adversaries, to correct the errant.' From which it appears that Christ gave Peter and his successors the power of judicial correction over all the sheep. The pope can therefore correct the emperor who is of the sheep of Christ. Hence it has been decided by councils that every Christian is subject to him and can be corrected by him. And if he who is corrected proves incorrigible, not only ought he to be excommunicated, but even deposed and deprived of all honour and dignity; thus the power of the keys in both fora, the secret and the external, extends by reason of sin not only to spiritual matters but also the temporal. Hence the Church of God may justly expel not only heretics but also schismatics and all the contumacious, take away their property, reduce them to servitude and lawfully impose every manner of penalty on these three categories of offender, except that of capital punishment.[111]

It is not for any especial originality of substance that these texts have been presented here *in extenso*. They formulate succinctly what had become the standard hierocratic defence as doctrine hardened in the political controversies of the early decades of the fourteenth century. There is no doubt that in practice the papal curia often tempered such authoritarian rigour in a world where dualism was the norm and hierocracy was readily ignored or defied or even scoffed at. But the potentialities of the logic were fully appreciated and even feared by some contemporaries, especially as they were manifested in papal policies towards the Holy Roman Empire. After Dante's death in 1321, it was most particularly Marsilius of Padua who understood these best and denounced them most passionately and comprehensively. His *The*

---

111. 'Item dicit quod illud verbum Christi: "Quodcumque solveris super terram etc.," non intelligitur nisi de his que subiacent potestati clavium; unde addit quod papa non potest solvere leges et decreta imperatorum. Ad hoc videtur dicendum quod potestas clavium consequitur ordinem sacerdotalem et simul cum ordine confertur sacerdoti, ut utatur ea in foro conscientie in absolvendo peccatorem, contritum et confessum a peccatis ipsius et ligando ipsum ad penam satisfactoriam pro peccatis. Et ista potestas fuit collata Petro et aliis apostolis equaliter, Ioh. 20, quando Christus dixit omnibus: "Accipite spiritum sanctum, quorum remiseritis peccata remittuntur eis etc." Alia est potestas iurisdictionis per quam iudex ecclesiasticus in foro exteriori ligat vinculo excommunicationis et solvit etiam ab eodem, vel ligat condemnando et solvit innocentem ostendendo. Hanc autem potestatem generaliter quoad totam ecclesiam sine aliqua distinctione accepit Petrus a Christo, Ioh. 21, ubi dictum est ei: "Pasce oves meas". Ubi dicit Glossa: "Pascere oves est credentes in Christo, ne a fide deficiant, confortare, terrena subsidia, si necesse est, subditis providere, exempla virtutum cum verbo predicationis impendere, adversariis obsistere, errantes subditos corrigere". Ex quo patet quod Christus dedit Petro et successoribus Petri potestatem iudicarie correctionis super omnes oves eius. Papa ergo potest corrigere imperatorem qui est de ovibus Christi. Unde etiam determinatum est per concilia quod omnis homo christianus est eius subditus et ab eo corrigendus. Et si est incorrigibilis, non solum est excommunicandus, sed etiam deponendus et omni honore ac dignitate privandus, ita quod potestas clavium in utroque foro, occulto et extrinseco, ratione delicti non solum ad spiritualia sed etiam ad temporalia se extendit. Unde ecclesia Dei non solum hereticos sed etiam schismaticos et omnino contumaces cum iustitia exigit, privat bonis, addicit eos capientium servituti et omnes penas, preter penam sanguinis, omnibus predictis licet ei imponere.' III, *ibid.*, pp. 141–2.

Defender of Peace (1324) was the most thorough and original treatise on the relations of the powers written by a medieval analyst.

Historians have sometimes been apt to make heavy weather of this book, descrying in it complexities and subtleties more perhaps of their own making than the author's. Certainly Marsilius was at pains to define very clearly for his readers his general and particular aims in writing and if his book tends to be prolix and repetitious, it is nonetheless carefully articulated by a meticulous cross-reference system. It is true that the book's relationship to future political theory, its alleged modernity, is complex and highly debatable. But read on his own terms, Marsilius appears as both a vitriolic critic of the papacy of his own day and as a radical analyst of the papal office as such.[112] He proclaimed himself frequently and unambiguously as the champion of Ludwig of Bavaria, aspirant to the office of Holy Roman Emperor. He directed his scorching polemic on specific hierocratic pronouncements of Boniface VIII (*Unam sanctam* was the summation of all he hated most and was an explicitly designated principal target),[113] Clement V and John XXII. His treatise, then, is a tract for the times, focusing on specific contemporary issues and intended to inspire remedial political action. He marshals much the same basic materials as, say, John of Paris – Aristotle on government and society is normative; the New Testament with the standard commentaries is the main source (necessarily, since the problem is essentially ecclesiological); some additional material drawn from twelfth- and thirteenth-century writers long accepted in the schools as authoritative. The nature of the quarrel, yet another in the series of Empire versus Papacy, is familiar enough and so too the matter of the argument. But from it all there emerged a work of true originality. For Marsilius put the axe to the root of hierocratic logic: he denied the divine origin of the papal office. Christ had not chosen Peter and even less so his successors, to be heads of his Church. The headship exercised by the bishops of Rome was of purely human origin, established if not by historical accident at least in purely historical circumstances in which Church members had accepted Roman headship for reasons of piety, and had allowed it to continue for administrative convenience and to establish itself as agreed customary practice. This demotion of the vicariate of Christ is at the heart of the Marsilian logic and was startlingly new in the medieval

---

112. There are three major, and very different, assessments of Marsilius: Lagarde 1948b, 1956–70, vol. III; Gewirth 1951.1956; Quillet 1970a.
113. As containing papal political doctrine, 'cunctisque civiliter viventibus praeiudicialissimam omnium excogitabilium falsorum'. 2.20.8, ed. Scholz 1932–3, p. 398.

debate on the relations of the powers. It is of course true that the divine origin of the papacy had been denied by others before him. But Marsilius was no product of a Waldensian or Catharist or other heretical sect. He was a man of the establishment or near to it: a former rector of the university of Paris, whose papal provision to a canonry of Padua had been promoted by two powerful cardinals.

There is a crucial difference between Marsilius and Dante who otherwise have much in common as defenders of traditional imperial dualism and denouncers of the corruption of the contemporary papacy. Dante retained his belief in the divine headship of the Church. He based his censure of contemporary popes on the distinction between the office of the papacy, duly acknowledged as the vicariate of Christ, and the persons of those who abused it with their corrupt government. Marsilius by contrast attacked the office itself, asserting that its authority was 'not given immediately by God but rather by the decision and will of men, just like any other office in society' (1.19.6).[114] It was necessary for the congregation of believers in Christ to have a leader. If it had come about that this was the bishop of Rome, it was that body itself which had established and endorsed it, not the direct decree of Christ who alone was the Church's foundation and head.

Marsilius chose to call his book *The Defender of Peace*, he tells us, because it examined how civil peace is made and broken (3.3). The civil peace of Italy has been shattered and its inhabitants brought under 'the harsh yoke of the tyrant' (1.1.2). There is a single and unique cause of the misery which has overtaken Italy and the empire and which is creeping insidiously into the foundations of other kingdoms and, if not checked, will subvert them too (2.26.19). Neither Aristotle nor any other philosopher of his time who had also investigated the causes of political disharmony could have unearthed this particular cause, for it was a product of the specifically Christian era (1.1.7; 1.19.3,4). It was Marsilius' divinely commanded task as 'herald of truth' to unmask this cause (1.19.13). He identifies it very precisely as the assumption by the bishop of Rome of 'universal coercive jurisdiction over the whole world' based on the vicariate of Christ and now, in his day, subsumed under the all-embracing term 'plenitude of power'. Thus the 'singular cause' of contemporary civil strife, which Marsilius sees it as his sole purpose to unmask and destroy, emerges in this formulation:

---

114. '. . . quoniam non fit hoc per Deum immediate, sed per hominum voluntatem et mentem, quemadmodum officia cetera civitatis'. 1.19.6, *ibid.*, p. 130. Marsilius referred his readers to 2.15.17 for more extended examination of the matter.

The meaning of this title [plenitude of power] for the bishops of Rome is that just as Christ possessed plenitude of power and jurisdiction over all kings, princes, communities, groups and individuals, so equally those who call themselves vicars of Christ and of St Peter have this same plenitude of coercive jurisdiction, unlimited by any human law.[115]

Marsilius saw the coerciveness of this plenitude of power and jurisdiction manifested most radically in two papal claims. The first was the two swords doctrine; in Marsilius' formulation: 'no ruler can lawfully exercise that coercive jurisdiction which they call the *temporal sword* without or against their consent or command'. The second was the deposing power: 'the authority to grant and withdraw all temporal kings and governments from kings and rulers who disobey their orders' (2.22.20). On the authority of *Unam sanctam* – 'of all imaginable lies, the most harmful to all who live in civil society' (2.20.8) – belief in this doctrine was allegedly necessary for salvation (2.22.20).[116]

The detailed critical analysis of what he had identified as the unique cause of political disharmony, Marsilius reserved for five lengthy chapters on the plenitude of power. These chapters (2.22–6), almost a treatise within a treatise but closely bound by cross-references to all other parts of *The Defender of Peace*, distil the essence of his whole argument. In them, he traced how 'gradually and secretly' the primacy of the first bishop of Rome established on the basis of reverence for the martyred Peter and Paul, continued for reasons of expediency and, after Constantine I, exercised under the jurisdiction of the Roman Emperor, was converted into a tyranny. These chapters are a review of how that tyranny had been exercised in both ecclesiastical and civil affairs. Foreshadowing Luther, Marsilius recalled a personal visit to the papal court to recount with disgust

---

115. 'Est igitur huius tituli sensus apud Romanos episcopos, quod sicut Christus plenitudinem potestatis et iurisdiccionis habuit supra reges omnes, principes, communitates, collegia et singulares personas, sic et ipsi, qui Christi et beati Petri se dicunt vicarios, hanc habeant plenitudinem coactive iurisdiccionis, humana lege nulla determinatam.' 1.19.9, *ibid.*, p. 132.

116. 'Quibus eciam ipsorum moderniores [i.e. popes] excessibus non contenti, suis expresserunt epistolis sive decretis, auctoritatem sive iurisdiccionem coactivam, quam vocant ipsi *gladium temporalem*, preter aut contra ipsorum consensum sive dictamen licite valeat exercere; preter autem contrarium facientes principantes et populos excommunicacionis vel interdicti sentencie vocaliter pronunciando subiectos. Asserunt enim se solos in mundo Christi vicarios, qui fuit *rex regum et dominus dominancium*; hec latenter intendentes per eum quem sibi debitum dicunt titulum *plenitudinis potestatis*. Propter quod eciam ad suam auctoritatem pertinere omnia mundi regna et principatus conferre ac auferre licite posse regibus et ceteris principantibus ipsorum mandata transgredientibus, quamvis impia sint secundum veritatem et illicita sepe. Hoc autem inter ceteros Romanos episcopos, non minus temerarie quam preiudicialiter et contra scripture sensum literalem, metaphoricis eius exposicionibus innisus Octavus Bonifacius intantum expressit et asseruit, ut hanc Romanis episcopis deberi potestatem decreverit ab omnibus credendum et confitendum esse *de necessitate salutis* eterne.' 2.22.20, *ibid.*, pp. 439–40.

what he found in that 'land of misery and darkness, where the shadow of death and no order, but everlasting horror dwelleth' (Job 11.22). The total corruption of the clergy from cardinalate through the episcopate to the lower clergy is attributed to the 'plenitude of power', the doctrine justifying papal monarchy. A parallel sweep through the recent history of Italy and the Holy Roman Empire revealed similar devastation in civil affairs. Pope John XXII's policy towards Ludwig of Bavaria received a long chapter to itself to demonstrate that the pope's arrogation of the 'temporal sword' by right of the plenitude of power was false, evil and a threat to all other rulers of Christendom (2.26).

These chapters, then, in the first place, sought to demonstrate how the manifestly evil deeds of the papal monarchy proved the essential falsity of the doctrine on which its exercise was based. They were, secondly, a refutation of that doctrine and a substitution for it, 'after long, diligent and painstaking examination and study of the Scriptures' of one, he claimed, which was authentically Christian.

Before he turned to the New Testament, however, Marsilius looked to the axioms of political philosophy which the 'established testimonies of eternal truth' would confirm (1.1.8). The first Discourse of *The Defender* established as its central proposition that it is of the intrinsic nature of political communities that ultimate power rests with the whole body of the citizens, by whose authority alone can lawful government be established or disestablished. It is the community itself which is, in Gewirth's phrase, 'the exclusive legitimating principle of the coercive power'[117] which government exercises. This basic principle Marsilius fashioned from reminiscences of Aristotelian philosophy, the *lex regia* doctrine of Roman law deriving the emperor's power from the people, the electoral college of the Holy Roman Empire and the practical workings of Italian urban institutions. It had a corollary: 'The supreme government in a city or kingdom must be only one in number' (3.2.11; cf. 1.17).

The implications of this premise were revolutionary. With it, Marsilius left the world of Dantean dualism – the logic of co-ordinate powers, combined with respect for the autonomy of the spiritual power and conceding to it a certain superiority – and approached that of Hobbes, for whom: '*Temporal* and *spiritual* government are but two words brought into the world to make men see double and mistake their lawful sovereign.'[118] The whole intent of *The Defender* is to ensure that the clergy make no

117. Gewirth 1956, p.xxxviii.
118. *Leviathan*, ed. M. Oakeshott, Basil Blackwell, 1946, p. 306.

mistake as to who is their lawful sovereign: 'the ruler by authority of the legislator [i.e. the whole body of the citizens] has jurisdiction over all bishops, priests and clergy, lest political society be destroyed by the existence of an unordered multiplicity of governments' (2.8.9; 3.2.15).[119]

Reason having established these principles, revelation came to confirm them. The Gospel related how Christ himself, in word and deed, 'sought to remove himself from any type of earthly rulership, wishing always to subject himself to the coercive jurisdiction of temporal authority' (2.4.13).[120] Christ's apostles followed his example and ordered their followers, in turn, to hold the same view. The most authoritative teachers read the scriptures in this same way.[121] Bishops, then, have been forbidden the power of coercive jurisdiction and have been instructed to subject themselves to the civil power which alone has been entrusted with the community's authority to exercise such jurisdiction. They are pastors not judges. A bishop or priest 'must teach and exhort people in the present life, censure and rebuke the sinner and frighten him by a judgement or prediction of future glory or eternal damnation, but he must not coerce' (2.10.2).[122] Thus the pope is simply a teacher of souls, a physician, not a coercive judge or ruler (cf. 2.30.1). Reason and revelation, philosophy and theology integrated to announce the same message (cf. 2.30.2; 2.9.2–9).

With the correct identification of the lawful sovereign, Marsilius removed pope and clergy from jurisdiction in civil affairs. There was a second consequence of this identification: the lawful sovereign was also the sole authority in ecclesiastical affairs, beginning with the definition of articles of faith and the determination of disputed interpretations of the Bible. The lawful sovereign, the whole body of the citizens (*universitas civium*) reappears as the whole body of the faithful (*universitas fidelium*) or, more pertinently, as the general council of believers (*generale concilium credentium*).

Three steps went into the making of Marsilian conciliar theory, generally

119. '. . . iurisdiccionem in episcopos seu presbyteros et clericos omnes legislatoris auctoritate principantem habere, ne principatuum eciam pluralitate inordinata policiam solvi contingat.' 2.8.9, ed. Scholz 1932–3, 230, with a reference to 1.17.
120. 'Ex adductis itaque veritatibus evangelicis ac sanctorum et aliorum approbatorum doctorum interpretacionibus earum apparere debet omnibus evidenter, 'Christum seipsum exclusisse seu excludere voluisse, tam sermone quam opere, ab omni principatu seu regimine, iudicio seu coactiva potestate mundana, ipsumque seipsum principibus et seculi potestatibus coactiva iurisdiccione voluisse subiectum.' 2.4.13, *ibid.*, p.177. 121. 2.5 *in toto*.
122. 'Per reliquum vero iudicem, pastorem scilicet, episcopum seu presbyterum, docendus et exhortandus est homo in vita presenti, arguendus, corripiendus peccator atque terrendus iudicio seu prognostico future glorie vel dampnacionis eterne, nequaquam vero cogendus, ut ex priori capitulo palam.' 2.10.2, *ibid.*, p. 247.

recognised as the most comprehensive such theory before the period of the Great Schism. The first concerned the nature of communities as such: it is only the community itself which can provide adequate safeguard against decision-making being usurped by a particular part of it, liable simply by its own limited nature to be misled 'by ignorance or malice, cupidity or ambition or some other vicious emotion' (2.20.6). The community itself, in other words, is its own best guardian. Marsilius found this axiom strikingly manifested in the practice of the primitive Church. The apostles (who were all equal) solved their problems by the 'method of common deliberation' (2.16.5). The Acts of the Apostles, in particular, showed the model of church government as communal. And it is this model which the general council emulates for the *universitas fidelium*: 'the congregation of the believers or the general council truly represents by succession the congregation of the apostles and elders and the other believers of that time' (2.19.2).[123] The third step in the logic again offered a parallel between the *universitas civium* and the *universitas fidelium*. In the one, so in the other, a link had to be forged between community and ruler; the general council must be related to one who has authority to summon it and enforce its decisions by coercive jurisdiction. To make this relationship, Marsilius again had recourse to the history of the Church. From the primitive Church he moved to the early Church; from the Acts, he moved to the *Codex* of (Pseudo-) Isidore. There he found the history of emperor-dominated general councils, assemblies of bishops summoned by imperial command, their canons enforced by imperial decree.[124] He even unearthed evidence that 'Roman bishops in ancient times begged the emperors to give them rules and laws' (2.21.6). Such should hold no less in the fourteenth century than in the age of Nicea, Constantinople, Ephesus and Chalcedon. Ludwig of Bavaria was to be seen as a Constantine *redivivus*, a new Theodosius. Marsilius had constructed a logic of caesaropapism in direct and conscious opposition to the hierocratic logic of *Unam sanctam*.

No doubt Ludwig of Bavaria was miscast for the role Marsilius had written for him. But Marsilius knew of, and esteemed, Philip the Fair's resistance to *Unam sanctam* (2.20.9; 2.21.9). Here was a sovereign more in the Marsilian mould – prepared to take on the responsibility for the general welfare of Christendom, to call a general council to try a pope, to insist on

123. 'Cum igitur fidelium congregacio seu concilium generale per successionem vere representet congregacionem apostolorum et seniorum ac reliquorum tunc fidelium, in determinandis scripture sensibus dubiis, in quibus maxime periculum eterne damnacionis induceret error, verisimile, quinimo certum est, deliberacioni universalis concilii spiritus sancti dirigentis et revelantis adesse virtutem.' 2.19.2, *ibid.*, p. 385.   124. See especially, 2.21.

continuing the trial even after the accused pope's death. Guillaume de Nogaret and Marsilius of Padua made a harmonious blend in the ideology of fourteenth-century monarchy, as is amply demonstrated in the *Somnium viridarii*.[125] Whence, reinforced by fifteenth-century conciliarism, to fully fledged Gallicanism.

At about the same time as the *Somnium* was being written, Wyclif was producing a specifically English model of caesaropapism. Apparently uninfluenced by Marsilius, his sovereign developed from the traditional position of God's vicar as known to the common law tradition. But Wyclif's vicar of God was invested with more power than the more dualistically minded Bracton had granted. For he is a king with authority to reform a clergy he has shorn of all coercive power, protective privilege and property. As Pollard observed, 'in dealing with the King's relation to the National Church, if Wyclif does not assign to him the position of its Supreme Head, the tendency of his arguments is all in this direction'.[126] But it was not so much Wyclif who was the morning star of the supreme headship as Marsilius. It was the *Defensor Pacis* which Henry VIII commanded to be translated into English and which influenced Thomas Cromwell.[127]

Such developments, however, did little to diminish the papacy's stubborn adherence to hierocracy. This tenacity is best epitomised by the repromulgation on the eve of the Reformation at the fifth Lateran council of *Unam sanctam*. And hierocracy's capacity to do grave damage where it was intended 'to link God's faithful people by the bond of mutual charity in the unity of the Spirit' was never to be more clearly demonstrated than with Pius V's *Regnans in excelsis*, the recourse to traditional deposition theory against Elizabeth I.

This chapter has argued that by the beginning of the fourteenth century the theorists of the relations of the powers had produced two different models: hierocracy and caesaropapism. Each was a logic which rejected any theory predicating a dualism of two autonomous authorities existing co-ordinately in human society. Each was a theory wherein a unity was founded upon the supremacy of one or other of the powers. Each, to continue to use the allegory which has done much to unify the argument here, postulated one

125. Quillet 1977.   126. Wyclif, *De officio regis*, p. xxvii.
127. Elton 1956: 'Though perfect proof is lacking, it does not seem too much to claim that as far as Cromwell was a theorist he was a conscious follower of Marsilius.' In October 1535, the whole community of the London Charterhouse refused to read the *Defensor Pacis*, which William Marshall, its translator, had distributed among them, Dowling 1984, p. 54.

authority to control both swords. Dualism of the type delineated by A.J. Carlyle as quoted at the beginning of this essay, did not wholly disappear. But it is suggested here that it was not that logic which was most characteristic of the later middle ages, nor the one which proved influential when the relationship of the two powers was redrawn in early modern Europe.

15
LAW

I LAW, LEGISLATIVE AUTHORITY, AND THEORIES OF GOVERNMENT, 1150–1300

The will of the prince and the law

In the middle of the twelfth century, Gratian completed his *Concordia discordantium canonum* – a 'Concord of Discordant Canons', later called simply the *Decretum* – and, unlike most earlier compilers of canonical collections, he began with a series of texts and comments on the various sources and types of law. Gratian did more than gather texts together; he unified and explained them, and in some cases he rejected the authority of some as being out-of-date or superfluous. The *Decretum* was the first collection of the high Middle Ages in which the compiler commented on the texts he brought together. It was an important step in medieval jurisprudence.

Gratian made a general statement about law at the beginning of the *Decretum*: 'The human race is ruled by two things: natural law and custom.'[1]

He followed this definition with discussion of the types of human law: unwritten custom, civil law, the law of a city or a people, and the different types of laws in classical Roman law. A few pages later, he ended his treatment of legislation by defining how a law was validated: 'Laws are established through promulgation and validated when they are approved by the acceptance of the people.'[2] Gratian's treatment of law was in the mainstream of legal thought in the twelfth century. But he presented only raw, unassimilated ideas. He thought that the source of law might be a prince or the time-honoured customs of people. He conceived of law as hierarchical; divine and natural law were superior to and took precedence over human law. Law was not, however, to be narrowly defined as an act limited to a certain time and place. It was formed by the collective actions of a society, and it was the duty of the prince to protect the customs of his subjects.

---

1. Gratian (1879), *Decretum*, D.1 a.c.1: 'Humanum genus duobus regitur, naturali videlicet iure et moribus.' On Gratian and his work see Chodorow 1972.
2. *Ibid.*, D.4 a.c.4: 'Leges instituuntur, cum promulgantur, firmantur, cum moribus utentium approbantur.'

The revival of legal studies in the late eleventh century shaped Gratian's understanding of law and its sources. After the rediscovery of Justinian's *Digest*, jurists examined the source of legislative authority in society and the relationship of the monarch to old law. They read texts in the *Digest* describing the emperor's supreme legislative authority in the Roman state, but were uncertain how to reconcile a monarch's legislative authority with the powerful tradition of customary law. The twelfth-century civilians divided over the issue whether custom could abrogate law. At the beginning of the twelfth century Irnerius wrote that established custom should be preserved, particularly if it was not contrary to reason and did not contradict law.[3] Although custom could be a valid source of law, he also noted that custom could not abrogate the decrees of the prince. 'Today', he said, 'all power [of law-making] has been transferred to the emperor.'[4] In the early thirteenth century Azo argued for a more latitudinarian view of custom's legal force. Custom, he maintained, makes, abrogates, and interprets law. A custom that preceded a contrary law was invalid, but a custom arising after a law had been established could abrogate written law.[5] A few legists even noted that the creation of new law was a natural function of society. 'Nature creates many new things daily', wrote Johannes Bassianus, 'and for new situations new responsibility is needed.'[6] However, most civilians also affirmed that new laws should be promulgated only when circumstances demanded change. They defined law as being the will of the prince, promulgated for just and necessary reasons, and tempered by custom that could represent the will of the people.

Gratian's *Decretum* established the science of canon law in the schools, and the canonists who taught the following generations of law students expanded Gratian's and the civilians' definitions with more precise terminology. By the end of the twelfth century, the canonists had created the term *ius positivum*, or positive law, to describe law promulgated by a human legislator. The term remains a fundamental legal concept. They also established a typology of legislation and elaborated a sophisticated analysis

---

3. Brynteson 1966, p. 432, n. 57.
4. Calasso 1957, p. 90, gloss to *Dig.* 1.3.32: 'Sed quia hodie potestas translata est in imperatorem, nihil faceret desuetudo populi.'
5. Azo (1557), *Summa aurea*, fol. 224r, title, 'Quae sit longa consuetudo' (*Cod.* 8.53): 'Consuetudo sit conditrix legis, abrogatrix, et interpretatrix . . . Sed distingue, utrum lex sequatur consuetudinem cui ipsa est contraria, an praecedat. Si lex sequatur, quia que posterior est, derogat consuetudini que praecessit. Alioquin legi consuetudo derogat.'
6. Brynteson 1966, p. 434, n. 68: 'Quia natura deproperat semper novas edere formas, ut C. de vet. iur. enucl. l.ii. Set quia [*Cod.* 1.17.2.18], propterea Deus de coelis imperatorem constituit in terris, ut leges adaptet secundum naturae varietatem.'

of the relationship of the prince to the law. Classical Roman law was not particularly helpful for understanding the limitations of legislative authority. The passages in Roman law touching upon the emperor's right to legislate were open to contradictory interpretations. A text from Justinian's Code, *Digna vox* (*Cod.* 1.14.4) stated that although the emperor is the source of all law, he should conduct his actions according to the law. This was repeated at *Cod.* 6.23.3. These two texts seem to sustain the idea of a limited, constitutional monarch whose actions must conform to the rules of the legal system. In contrast, other texts in the *Digest* stressed the illimitability of the emperor's authority and his absolute power. In *Dig.* 1.4.1, the Roman jurist Ulpian declared that 'what pleases the prince has the force of law', which underlined a similar point he made in another text, 'the prince is not bound by the law' (*Dig.* 1.3.31).

These texts were not intractable. In the hands of skilled lawyers, they could be used to fashion systems of constitutional or of absolute monarchy. In the beginning the lawyers had difficulty assimilating these texts of Roman law into their thought because they did not always have a clear understanding of the complex issues underlying them. Further, their assumptions about monarchical authority were taken primarily from Germanic law and feudal customs, which emphasised the contractual relationship between the people and the monarch and which laid down the king's sacred duty to defend the laws and customs of the land. In this system of thought, law must be reasonable and just. A prince could not exercise his office arbitrarily. A monarch could legislate, but his authority was circumscribed by a restrictive web of ideas which demanded that there be a need for new law and that the people consent to new law, either by approving it formally or by accepting it through use.

To reconcile these conflicting ideas, the lawyers had to solve two problems: to understand and define the sources and function of law in society, and to integrate three systems of thought, Roman, Christian, and Germanic. Perhaps their most difficult task was to accommodate a conception of kingship that rested on divine foundations, derived in part from Roman and in part from Christian thought, with Germanic and feudal kingship, which based its claim to legitimacy on the relationship of the king to his barons and people.

Ernst Kantorowicz described a part of the problem in the title of his classic book, *The King's Two Bodies* (1957). Germanic custom subjected the prince to the law and limited his authority to govern without the consent of his subjects. Christian thought and classical jurisprudence and philosophy stressed the divine origins of kingship and the sacral nature of political authority. Kantorowicz demonstrated that this tension in the thought of the lawyers led them to distinguish between the prince's private body that was subject to the law and his public body that was not.

The law itself could be said to have had two bodies. Germanic conceptions focused on its immutability, while classical thought stressed the origins of law in the will of the prince, 'what pleases the prince has the force of law'. In the early thirteenth century, the canonists began to understand that the will of the prince could be separated from the content of law. The canonists and not the Roman lawyers first grappled with this problem. This is not surprising. The problem was central to the evolving legal system that they studied. Canon law was constantly changing in response to a monarch, the pope, who was inexorably expanding his authority, and the canonists fashioned new theories of government to define his position. They became the first lawyers in the western tradition to establish law as an essential element of political theory.

The papacy had always maintained that its authority and primacy rested on divine foundations established by Christ. Pope Innocent III (1198–1216) added a new dimension to papal power early in his pontificate when he issued the decretal *Quanto personam*, in which he stated that only the pope could sever the matrimonial bond between a bishop and his church. This papal authority, he argued, was not human but divine.

God, not man, separates a bishop from his church because the Roman pontiff dissolves the bond between them by divine rather than human authority, carefully considering the need for and usefulness of each translation. The pope has this authority because he does not exercise the office of man, but that of the true God on earth.[7]

Innocent anticipated a later distinction between the pope's ordinary authority and the special powers that he possessed as vicar of Christ.

Between 1210 and 1215, one of the most creative canonists of his generation, Laurentius Hispanus, glossed Innocent's words with rhetorical and legal brilliance:

Hence [the pope] is said to have a divine will. O, how great is the power of the prince. He changes the nature of things by applying the essences of one thing to another . . . he can make iniquity from justice by correcting any canon or law; for

---

7. Innocent III (1964–79), *Register*, vol. I, no. 335, p. 496: 'Non enim homo sed Deus separat, quod Romanus pontifex, qui non puri hominis sed veri Dei vicem gerit in terris, ecclesiarum necessitate vel utilitate pensata, non humana sed divina potius auctoritate dissolvit.'

in these things his will is held to be reason . . . He is held, nevertheless, to shape this power to the public good.[8]

Although the florid language of the gloss obscures Laurentius' thought for the modern reader, his commentary on *Quanto personam* contains a series of paradoxical definitions of papal authority that are carefully calculated to make his readers – trained jurists or law students – ponder the juridical basis of legislative authority.

Laurentius had the gift of placing old problems in new settings. He broke sharply with traditional definitions of legislative power by describing the prince's right to alter the meanings of legal terms as 'changing the nature of things', and followed this statement with the most revolutionary idea of the gloss: the prince can make iniquitous law, for his will is held to be reason (a quotation from Juvenal's *Satires* 6.223).

Germanic and earlier learned conceptions of law confused the content of law – that law must be just and reasonable – with the source of law, the will of the prince. Before Laurentius, canonists had accepted the idea that a law could not be valid unless it embodied reason. Huguccio of Pisa, the most important canonist of the twelfth century, saw no contradiction in the notion that a legislator's will could be rendered nugatory by forces outside his power:

But cannot the clergy of the people be compelled to do what the prince wills since the pope has the fullness of power, and all power is given to the prince? I believe they can if they deviate from reason or the faith, otherwise not. Again, can the pope promulgate something without or contrary to the will of his cardinals or the emperor against the will of his barons? I think not, if he can have their assent; otherwise he can, provided that it was not contrary to reason and the Old and New Testaments.[9]

Huguccio simply could not imagine that law could be valid unless it was reasonable. By separating the monarch's will from reason, Laurentius located the source of legislative authority in the will of the prince and laid the intellectual groundwork for a new conception of authority in which the prince or the state might exercise power 'unreasonably' but legally. His was an important step in the development of political thought.

8. Pennington 1984, pp. 17–19.
9. Tierney 1977, p. 75; Pennington 1984, pp. 21–2. Huguccio, D.4 p.c. 3 v. *abrogate*, Admont 7, fol. 6vb: 'Set nonne clerus uel populus posset compelli ut impleret quod papa uel princeps uult, cum papa habeat plenitudinem potestatis, et omnis potestas sit in principe collata? Credo quod posset si a ratione uel fide uellet deuiare, ut di. lxii. Docendus [c. 2] alias non deberet. Item posset papa, preter uel contra uoluntatem suorum cardinalium aliquid statuere, uel imperator preter uel contra uoluntatem suorum baronum? Respon. Non deberet si eorum consensum posset habere. Alias posset, dummodo non sit contrarium rationi uel ueteri uel nouo testamento.'

Laurentius did not advocate a monarch endowed with absolute or arbitrary authority. His thought was constitutional; his prince limited. His definitions of legislative authority could be applied to any legislator, constitutional or not. He underlined his abhorrence of arbitrary monarchical power in the last words of his gloss: 'He is bound, nevertheless, to shape this power to the public good.'

Lawyers shaped and reshaped Laurentius' gloss over the next four centuries and *Pro ratione voluntas* became a short-hand description of the source of legislation, even though some were slow to appreciate the subtlety and precision of Laurentius' thought. When the English jurist who composed the book we call 'Bracton' wrote about the king's will and the law in the mid-thirteenth century, he clearly did not understand the thought of the jurists. He relied on older, more comfortable, patterns of thought and was repelled by the idea that the king's will could be law: 'The king must not be under man but under God and the law, because law makes the king; let him therefore bestow upon the law what the law bestows upon him, namely rule and power, for there is no king (*rex*) where will (*voluntas*) rules rather than law (*lex*).'[10] 'Bracton' turned canonistic thought on its head. The canonists defined the authority of the prince to change law, separating his will from the 'morality' of the law, but at the same time stressed the obligation of the prince to subject himself to the law. 'Bracton' could not separate the two ideas, and he underscored the unity of the law and the prince. Law made his prince; therefore the king could only make law that respected the integrity of the legal system and recognised the limitations that law imposed on his sovereignty.

When Thomas Aquinas described the essence of law in his *Summa theologiae*, he asked the question to which Laurentius had given currency: was law in some way part of reason? In his formulation of the objections to such a conclusion, Aquinas paraphrased Juvenal's maxim and quoted Roman law: 'Therefore law does not seem to be a part of reason, but is derived from the will, and because of this the jurist says: "what pleases the prince has the force of law".'[11] Although Aquinas understood the thought of the jurists much better than 'Bracton', he too could not accept the

---

10. Bracton (1968), *De legibus* vol. II, p. 33 (fol. 5b): 'Ipse autem rex non debet esse sub homine sed sub deo et sub lege, quia lex facit regem. Attribuat igitur rex legi, quod lex attribuat ei, videlicet dominationem et potestatem. Non est enim rex ubi dominatur voluntas et non rex.' On Bracton's thought see Tierney 1963b, pp. 295–317.
11. *Summa theologiae* 1.2 q.90.1: 'Ergo lex non pertinet ad rationem, sed magis ad voluntatem: secundum quod etiam iurisperitus dicit: "Quod placuit principi, legis habet vigorem."'

elegance of their definition. To conclude that law and reason could be separated, even as a purely legal definition, was not possible:

Law is a certain rule and measure . . . First, as in that which measures and rules, and since this is a characteristic of reason, in this way law is in reason alone . . . Reason has its power of moving from the will . . . but in order that the will has the reason of law in those things that it commands, it is necessary that it be informed by some reason. And in this way the will of the prince can be said to have the force of law; otherwise the will of the prince would be a sin rather than law.[12]

The canonists would not have quibbled with Aquinas' theory of legislation; it contained many of their own ideas. And when they separated reason from the will of the prince, they carefully explained under what circumstances this was true. But the future development of legislative theory rested on the canonists' locating the ultimate source of authority in the will of the prince. This was a necessary step before a theory of sovereignty could evolve that was untrammelled by morality, reason, and age-old customs.

Definitions and limitations
of sovereignty

Roman law provided the jurists of the twelfth and thirteenth centuries with many definitions of sovereignty, but the classical Roman jurisconsults had never analysed legislative authority, jurisdiction, or delegated power in any systematic way. The jurists needed to work out a coherent theory for themselves. It was a complicated task that was not made any easier by received notions of Germanic law, which emphasised the sanctity of law and the ruler's responsibility to preserve law and custom.

We find the fullest discussion of these questions again in the works of the canonists. They faced a complicated set of problems posed by special features of the church's constitution. The founder of the church's hierarchy was Christ himself. The pope was His representative on earth and was entrusted with the governance of His earthly kingdom. But, just as secular kings and monarchs were limited by the customs and laws of their realms, the pope also had to exercise his authority within a set of constitutional assumptions, which the canonists called the *status ecclesiae*, the state of the

---

12. *Ibid.*: 'Lex quaedam regula est et mensura . . . Uno modo, sicut in mensurante et regulante. Et quia hoc est proprium rationis, ideo per hunc modum lex est in ratione sola . . . ratio habet vim movendi a voluntate . . . Sed voluntas de his quae imperantur, ad hoc quod legis rationem habeat, oportet quod sit aliqua ratione regulata. Et hoc modo intelligitur quod voluntas principis habet vigorem legis; alioquin voluntas principis magis esset iniquitas quam lex.'

church. The canonists acknowledged that the pope's will could create law and that sometimes his legislative will might even be unreasonable; but still there were some limits that the pope could not transgress. He could not alter or disturb the church's structure, just as he could not arbitrarily change the doctrines and laws of the church established in Apostolic times. These were, along with the New Testament, the church's 'customs of the realm'. Further, an important sense of the 'folk', not derived from or dependent upon Germanic notions, permeated Christian thought. Brian Tierney has written: 'Early Christian texts are filled with a sense of community. They tell of community meetings, community sharing, community participation in decisions, and above all they reflect a strong belief that the consensus of Christian people indicates the guidance of the Holy Spirit at work in the church.'[13] Finally the pope himself had to conform to high standards of morality and had to preserve the doctrinal purity of Christian beliefs. All of these elements that informed papal monarchy created problems of interpretation for the canonists when they examined the powers of the pope and the authority of his office.

Definitions of sovereignty

The Roman jurisconsult Ulpian contributed the two most important phrases that defined a prince's power during the Middle Ages: 'what pleases the prince has the force of law' (*Dig.* 1.4.1) and 'the prince is not bound by the law' (*Dig.* 1.3.31). When the thirteenth-century glossator, Accursius, wrote a commentary to *Dig.* 1.3.31 in his Ordinary Gloss to Justinian's codification, he affirmed the authority of the prince to change both the laws of his predecesors and his own earlier legislation. To this Accursius added that the prince should subject himself to the law through his will. In his *Summa Codicis*, Placentinus put this common assumption of the legists very elegantly: 'The emperor says that the laws ought to be observed, by his subjects through necessity, by princes through their will. And the emperor recommends this: '*Digna vox*, etc.' he says' (*Cod.* 1.14.4).[14] Accursius interpreted the phrase 'the prince is not bound by the laws' to mean that the prince may abrogate old legislation by enacting new measures and that the decrees of earlier monarchs did not bind him. The lawyers commonly expressed the same idea with the maxim 'an equal cannot have authority

13. Tierney 1982, p. 14.
14. Placentinus (1536), *Summa Codicis*, p. 17, title, 'De legibus et constitutionibus' (*Cod.* 1.14): 'Inquit imperator leges observari debere a subiectis ex necessitate, a principibus ex voluntate; hocque imperator dicit suadendo, Digna vox etc.'

over an equal' (*par in parem imperium non habet*). Accursius saw Ulpian's definitions as principles of legislative authority and did not think that either maxim justified arbitrary or unconstitutional exercise of princely authority.[15]

The classical Roman lawyers defined the emperor's authority to legislate, command, and judge as *imperium* or *potestas*. Ulpian had written that according to the *Lex Regia* the Roman people conferred all the emperor's *imperium* and power on him (*Dig.* 1.14.1). Placentinus and most other jurists accepted the idea that the Roman people bestowed legislative authority upon the emperor, but a few thought that the people could revoke this grant. Azo wrote that 'the people did not completely abdicate their power, for what is once transferred may be taken back'.[16] At the end of the twelfth century, a debate may have taken place between Azo and another civilian over the emperor's *imperium*. According to tradition, the Emperor Henry VI asked Azo who possessed *merum imperium*, pure imperium, that is, the highest authority in government. Azo responded that the prince and other higher magistrates have *merum imperium*, not just the prince alone. The prince, therefore, cannot revoke the authority of higher magistrates. What Azo actually wrote in his *Summa Codicis* is not so straightforward. He did contend that the prince and other high magistrates (but not municipal magistrates) have *merum imperium*, but did not claim that their powers were irrevocable.[17]

According to classical Roman law, the emperor's sovereignty encompassed all lesser kings, princes, and magistrates. As Johannes Teutonicus wrote in his gloss that was incorporated later into the Ordinary Gloss to the *Decretals of Gregory IX*: 'The emperor is over all kings . . . and all nations are under him . . . He is the lord of the world . . . and no king may gain an exemption from his authority, because no prescription can run against him in this case.'[18] By the high Middle Ages, Johannes' gloss no longer described the reality of Europe's political system. In his famous decretal, *Per venerabilem* (1202), Pope Innocent III stated that the king of France

15. Tierney 1963a, pp. 378–400.
16. Azo (1557), *Summa aurea*, fol. 7v, title, 'De legibus et constitutionibus' (*Cod.* 1.14): 'Dicitur enim translata, id est concessa, non quod populus omnino a se abdicaverit eam . . . nam et olim transtulerat, sed tamen postea revocavit.'
17. Gilmore 1941, pp. 18–19; see in general the discussion in Calasso 1957, pp. 83–123.
18. Johannes Teutonicus (1981), *Apparatus* to 3 Comp. 1.6.19 (x 1.6.34), p. 84: 'Est autem imperator iste super omnes reges . . . et omnes nationes sub eo sunt . . . Ipse enim est dominus mundi . . . Nec aliquis regum potuit prescribere exemptionem, cum non habeat in hoc locum prescriptio.' Tancred copied this gloss into his Ordinary Gloss to Innocent's collection and later Bernardus Parmensis placed it into his *Apparatus* to the decretals of Gregory IX.

recognised no superior in temporal affairs. After this decretal had been included in collections of canon law, lawyers gave juridical precision to Innocent's assertion. Some said that national kings were not subject to the emperor *de facto*, but were so *de iure*, while others insisted that kings were also completely independent of imperial authority. By the mid-thirteenth century jurists commonly defined the kings' untrammelled sovereignty with the maxim 'rex in regno suo imperator est' (a king is emperor in his kingdom).[19] Legally, therefore, kings exercised the same sovereignty as the emperor.

The canonists incorporated Roman legal definitions of sovereignty into older ecclesiastical traditions, and during the course of the twelfth century, they described the pope's authority over the church as being his *plenitudo potestatis*, fullness of power, with increasing frequency. The term dates back to the early Middle Ages but had lain dormant until the flowering of canonical jurisprudence in the twelfth century. At first, *plenitudo potestatis* did not define only papal authority. Archbishops were sometimes characterised as having fullness of power or *plenitudo pontificalis officii* after they accepted their pallium.

There was one sharp difference between Roman and canonical jurisprudence in discussions of sovereignty. In contrast to the classical and medieval legists, the canonists did not think that papal *plenitudo potestatis* could have been granted by the Christian people. The pope received his authority from God. At the same time another similar, but legally quite distinct, technical term came into common usage: *plena potestas*, full power. The jurists used the term, or sometimes *libera potestas*, unlimited power, which was closely related to *plena potestas*, to define unrestricted grants of authority – within the specific provisions of a mandate – to a procurator or representative. The jurists borrowed *plena potestas* from Roman private law, and it normally meant delegated jurisdiction or authority granted to a person or persons who represented a client. As we shall see, the term played an important role in the development of corporate theory. However, in the twelfth and early thirteenth centuries, *plenitudo potestatis* and *plena potestas* were sometimes confused. Pope Innocent III, for example, called his authority *plena potestas* when he clearly meant *plenitudo potestatis*. In the later Middle Ages, *plenitudo potestatis* became a general description of ecclesiastical and secular monarchical authority.

At first the canonists defined papal fullness of power by comparing it to

19. See Post 1964, pp. 453–93. Azo was one of the first lawyers to formulate this maxim describing the independence of royal authority; see Ullmann 1979a, pp. 361–4. Cf. pp. 466–7 below.

episcopal authority. Johannes Teutonicus (c. 1216) gave a classic definition in the Ordinary Gloss to Gratian's *Decretum*: 'The authority of the pope is without limits, that of other bishops is limited because they are called to a share of the responsibility (*pars sollicitudinis*) not to the fullness of power.'[20] In this comparison, the canonists recognised that the pope's jurisdiction extended throughout the church, while a bishop's was limited to his diocese. An anonymous canonist (c. 1215) probably came closest to explaining exactly what the canonists meant when they attributed fullness of power to the pope: 'I believe that his is a special power: that if the pope should so order, any action can be taken in any church, since the church is one . . . and he is the pastor of the entire church, others having been called to a share of responsibility.'[21] This jurist described papal *plenitudo potestatis* as the pope's overriding authority within the church, his power as judge and administrator, and his role as pastor of the entire church.

In addition to papal fullness of power, the canonists added a rich treasure of terms to the vocabulary of sovereignty. The pope was the ordinary judge of all, *iudex ordinarius omnium*, the living law, *lex animata* (from Roman law), and the supreme legislator who had all laws within his breast, *omne ius habet in pectore suo* (another phrase from Roman law). These formulations and maxims elevated papal authority rhetorically, defining any monarch's judicial and legislative authority, whether it be absolute or constitutional.

Although the lawyers of the early thirteenth century were content to use *plenitudo potestatis* as a term to describe the supreme authority of the pope – and also that of the emperor by the late twelfth century – Henricus de Segusio, better known as Hostiensis, pushed canonistic political thought in new and fertile directions. He polished and refined the concept of *plenitudo potestatis* and added two new ideas to canonistic definitions of sovereignty.

First, he made some of the early rhetoric of sovereignty more precise by coining the phrase *suppletio defectuum* to describe the pope's authority to correct any deficiency of law or fact.[22] Laurentius Hispanus had written: 'the pope changes the nature of things by applying the essences of one thing to another . . . he can make iniquity from justice'. Later Johannes

20. Pennington 1984, p. 59–63. Johannes Teutonicus, D.11 c.2 v. *plena auctoritate*: 'Papae auctoritas plena est, aliorum episcoporum semiplena est, quia ipsi sunt in partem sollicitudinis vocati non in plenitudinem potestatis, ut 2 q.6 Decreto et Qui se scit.' On 'plenitudo potestatis' see Watt 1965a, pp. 75–106.
21. Pennington 1984, p. 63. Gloss to introductory letter of 3 Comp. v. *seruus*, Paris B.N. 3932, fol. 103r (Bamberg, Staatsbibl. can. 19, fol. 116v): 'Istud tamen in eo speciale credo quod eo stipulante potest adquiri actio cuilibet ecclesie, cum una sit ecclesia, ut di. xxii. Quamuis, et ipse sit pastor in solidum, aliis in partem sollicitudinis uocatis.'
22. Watt 1965b, pp. 161–87 discusses Hostiensis' use of 'plenitudo potestatis'.

Teutonicus added: 'He can make something out of nothing' (*de nichilo facit aliquid*).[23] The cross-references in their glosses make clear that the two lawyers meant to define the pope's authority to remedy legal problems, errors, and procedural mistakes or deficiencies that might render an otherwise just case nugatory.

Hostiensis minted the term *suppletio defectuum*, but the metal was mined from a letter of Pope Innocent III, who was the most profound and inventive of all the medieval popes when he turned his attention to the topic of papal sovereignty. Innocent's most significant contribution to the panoply of ideas surrounding *plenitudo potestatis* was his often repeated assertion that the pope actually exercised divine authority in some cases and derived this extraordinary power from his office of vicar of Christ. No earlier pope had distinguished between the pope's human and his heavenly power. Innocent's formulation was incorporated into the codes of canon law where Hostiensis read it. On the basis of Innocent's distinction, he created two new definitions of sovereign power: *potestas absoluta et ordinata*, absolute and ordinary power.

With these two terms clarifying *plenitudo potestatis*, Hostiensis, as Laurentius Hispanus had done earlier, moved legal thought further away from the rudimentary notions of law and kingship in Germanic and feudal law. He refined Innocent III's thought by specifying that *potestas ordinata* encompassed the pope's authority to act according to positive law, while *potestas absoluta* permitted him to exercise extraordinary power derived from the pope's vicarship of Christ. Most importantly, absolute power could be used to justify papal actions whose validity had been long debated in the schools. Hostiensis argued that the pope's absolute authority allowed him to legislate in matters touching non-consummated marriages and to dispense from vows, even the religious vow of chastity. Although the pope could not exercise this power indiscriminately or without cause, he was 'above the law' in these matters.[24]

Hostiensis' *potestas absoluta et ordinata* had a long and distinguished career in political thought. Later theologians and polemicists attributed the same powers to secular monarchs, although in the process of transmission to the

---

23. Johannes Teutonicus (1981), *Apparatus* to 3 Comp. 5.2.3, p. 43.
24. Pennington 1984, pp. 65–73; Hostiensis may have borrowed his terminology from the theologians' discussions of God's absolute and ordained powers; see Oakley 1979, pp. 143–5. Alexander of Hales seems to have been the first theologian to use the term (c. 1240). Later, Albertus Magnus (c. 1260) (in a doubtful work) and Aquinas in his *Summa theologiae* (c. 1270), adopted it. In theology, nonetheless, the concept predates the terminology. For the latest summing up of the place of 'absolute power' in political theory of the medieval and early modern periods, see Oakley 1984b, pp. 93–118.

secular sphere, the prince's absolute power justified actions that violated the rights of subjects and long-standing customs. Together with Laurentius Hispanus' *pro ratione voluntas, potestas absoluta* paved the way for more sophisticated ideas of sovereignty. If a sovereign's will was the source of law and not restricted by the strictures of reason and morality, and if, under certain circumstances, a monarch could promulgate and act contrary to standards of justice and the precepts of reason – even though in the Middle Ages these acts were always justified because of the common good or because of great necessity – all the necessary elements were in place for what later would be called 'reason of state'. By the thirteenth century, medieval lawyers had little difficulty in justifying actions of monarchs that were contrary to law, custom, and individual private rights.

Limitations of sovereignty

The canon lawyers of the twelfth century constructed a complex doctrine of papal sovereignty. The predominant thrust of canonical jurisprudence between 1150 and 1190 was to describe the absolute authority of the pope to govern the church and to sit as its supreme judge. The canonists fashioned these doctrines of papal authority in circumstances that seemed to demand strong monarchical rule. They did not reject earlier ideas of kingship but emphasised the pope's rights rather than his limitations. Influenced in large part by the constitutional position of the emperor in Roman law and stimulated by the reform efforts of the popes from the eleventh century on, efforts that demanded strong centralised judicial and legislative authority, the canonists strove to explain the chaotic and varied practices they found in the texts preserved by Gratian in his *Decretum*, texts that reflected the vagaries of a thousand years of ecclesiastical history. They focused on two points: the pope's power to change old law and promulgate new and his omnicompetent, supreme judicial authority. During the last half of the twelfth century, the number of cases appealed to Rome increased with remarkable rapidity, and a clear doctrine of papal judicial authority was needed to define the entire appellate process within the church. All roads began to lead to Rome, but they had to be paved with legal explanations and rules. We have already seen some of the results of these developments: the pope had fullness of power, he was the judge of all, and he could be judged by no one.

Even those decretists who described papal authority in the most exalted terms always acknowledged that the pope had limitations imposed on him by the unwritten constitution of the church, the *status ecclesiae*, and the liability of the pope to err.[25] The state of the church limited the pope's power to alter or abuse the structure of the church and to change or dispense from basic Christian doctrines, which they called the 'articles of the faith'. Since several texts in Gratian's *Decretum* revealed that earlier popes had erred in their faith or committed serious crimes, the canonists were keenly aware that the issue of judging a sinning, wayward pope was not moot. They had, however, great difficulty constructing a legal procedure through which a pope could be brought to judgement. In the end, by locating the ultimate source of authority within the entire church, which they defined as the 'congregation of the faithful', or a general council, or, more rarely, the college of cardinals, they granted these collective bodies of the church the right to judge the pope.

Huguccio of Pisa's solution to the problem was typical. He argued that the pope did not preserve in his own person Christ's promise that the church would not err; rather the purity of the faith would be preserved by the entire church or by the Roman church, i.e. the pope and cardinals. But how was the pope to be judged when he could be judged by no one? And for which crimes might the pope be liable? Huguccio's answers were complicated. He happily envisioned a future pope committing an interesting assortment of crimes: stealing, fornication, simony, concubinage, even fornicating on the altar of a church. The pope could be accused and condemned for these crimes if they were public and notorious, and if the pope were contumacious. Such crimes, observed Huguccio dryly, were just like heresies if they were public and repeated frequently. The pope could, of course, be condemned if he were a heretic.

Huguccio did not construct, however, a completely satisfying system for bringing a straying pope to justice. The pope's crimes had to be contumacious and well-known; his heresy had to be an old one – he could not be accused of a novel heresy or of secret crimes. Consequently Huguccio does not seem to have envisioned a tribunal actually trying a pope, but an indignant and powerful public outcry deposing him without judicial formalities. The pope was really self-condemned and self-deposed before any public action, for, as Huguccio put it, 'a heretic is less than any Catholic'.

A generation later the canonists were not nearly as careful about how they formulated the process through which a pope might be judged. Johannes Teutonicus disagreed with Huguccio that the pope could not be

25. For a thorough study of papal fallibility see Tierney 1955a, pp. 37–45, and 1972, pp. 31–44.

accused and condemned for secret crimes; he did not distinguish between old and new heresies. It may be – although the evidence is not clear – that Johannes thought a general council could judge an erring pope. Generally, the thirteenth-century canonists were far less sensitive to protecting papal immunity from judgement than were their twelfth-century predecessors. Teutonicus' opinions were preserved in his Ordinary Gloss to the *Decretum*, which provided material for almost every thinker of the later Middle Ages who was concerned with the problem of papal sovereignty.

The civilians also placed limitations on the emperor by declaring that property rights of subjects derived from natural law or *ius gentium* and by limiting the right of the emperor to alienate imperial lands. Most of the fathers of the church and many classical philosophers held that private property was not characteristic of man's natural state but was created through his sin and avarice. Some twelfth-century glossators, however, stressed the naturalness of property rights and found their origins in natural law. Accursius canonised this view in his Ordinary Gloss to the *Digest*, and it was accepted by most later civilians.[26] By attributing private property rights to natural law, the jurists could claim that the prince should not infringe upon rights that did not derive from his sovereign authority.

The jurists also limited the unrestrained exercise of royal and imperial sovereignty through a doctrine of inalienability that prohibited alienation of rights attached to the office of the prince. This development grew out of Roman, feudal, and canonical theories of office and offers a telling example of how these systems could blend together to create constitutional doctrines.[27] The attention of the Roman lawyers was drawn to inalienability through their discussions of the Donation of Constantine. The emperor had granted imperial rights to the church, and his grant – a falsification of the late eighth or early ninth century – was included in Gratian's *Decretum*. During the twelfth century, there was little discussion of the rights of the emperor to make grants injurious to the imperial office. However, in the early thirteenth century, Pope Honorius III declared in his decretal, *Intellecto*, that the king of Hungary could not make alienations prejudicing his kingdom and against the honour of his crown, even if he had earlier sworn an oath to do so. The king had, Honorius pointed out, also sworn to preserve the rights of his kingdom and the honour of his crown (*iura regni sui et honorem coronae illibata servare*). *Intellecto* established the doctrine of inalienability in canon law, and the canonists promptly applied the principle

26. Post 1964, pp. 542–6.   27. Post 1967, pp. 493–512.

to ecclesiastical prelates as well as to princes.[28] At almost the same time, Accursius concluded that the Donation of Constantine was not legally valid, for the emperor should not damage the rights of future emperors.[29] Through the doctrine of inalienability, the jurists emphasised the limitations a monarch's office placed on his sovereignty and stressed the role of the king as guardian (or to use the technical terminology of the lawyers, tutor), not lord, of his realm.[30]

Perhaps the most complex issue the modern historian of political theory faces is to determine whether the canonists limited or curbed papal sovereignty in more mundane matters. When Tancred wrote in his gloss to Innocent III's decretal, *Quanto personam*, that 'no one may say to him, "why do you do this?"' he struck a very different tone from the conception of kingship found, for example, in Bracton.

The canonists created a powerful paradigm of sovereignty that left the more primitive assumptions of Germanic and feudal law far behind. Still, a number of factors hindered their developing a theory of absolute monarchy patterned after the Roman emperor of their law books. First, and most importantly, although many popes and curial officials were products of the law schools, the relationship between the papacy and the law schools was not close. The interpreters of law at Bologna and elsewhere were not papal appointees and did not need papal approval of their published work. They were not dependent on the papacy for their authority or positions. While expounding decretal law to their students, they interpreted it with a finely honed independent and critical sense that did not simply accept the doctrines of new papal decretals obediently.

Their teaching and thought created another source of law, a *ratio iuris*, that provided a check to papal absolutism. Legal maxims were characteristic of their thought, being touchstones of legal rectitude and proper practice. Lawyers learned these maxims and invented new ones in the schools, and they became fundamental pieces of their intellectual baggage. Maxims were scattered throughout the commentaries of the jurists and in the decretals of the popes. They provided a filter through which legislation was strained and its validity tested. Many of the maxims were taken from Roman law, although some of them did not have general validity in Justinian's

---

28. Riesenberg 1956, pp. 113–44; Sweeney 1975, pp. 234–9.
29. Maffei 1969, pp. 65–9.
30. Walter Ullmann has stressed the importance of Roman law doctrines of tutorship for medieval definitions of kingship. A convenient summary of his views can be found in Ullmann 1975b, pp. 58–9.

codification, but were meant to govern specific cases. For example, the most famous medieval maxim – *Quod omnes tangit ab omnibus approbari debet* – was only applied to wards and guardians in Roman law, but during the Middle Ages it supported a theory of consent that was a basic element of corporate theory and representative government. The jurists often used these maxims effectively when they wished to blunt the force of a piece of legislation.

The hierarchical state of the church was also a limitation on papal sovereignty. Christ had appointed Peter as the head of the church, but had also established the episcopate. The church could be conceived as a collection of rights and privileges inhering in individual offices. Even the pope could not alter or disturb this divinely ordained system of government. The pope might depose one bishop, but not all. He could allow one monk to marry, but a papal dispensation permitting all monks to abandon their vows of chastity was unthinkable. Further, the old Christian sense of community stressed the role of the ruler as shepherd of his flock and protector of their interests. A favourite quotation of Pope Innocent III, Jeremiah 1.10 – 'I place you over peoples and kingdoms to root up and destroy, to disperse and scatter, to build and plant' – gave equal weight to the idea of the pope as protector of traditions and as reformer of ecclesiastical customs and practices.

Hostiensis, perhaps, best reconciled the claims of papal monarchy with the medieval sense of community and collegiality. On the one hand, he supported papal leadership of the church without reservation, coined new and vital terms to describe papal jurisdiction, and granted the pope wide-ranging authority to grant dispensations that a twelfth-century decretist like Huguccio would have found quite unpalatable. Yet he also granted unusually extensive responsibilities to the Roman cardinals. It may not be stretching the evidence too far to say that he advocated a collegial church, with the pope and cardinals constituting the ruling body. The cardinals, he wrote, shared the responsibility for the state of the church and participated in papal fullness of power. He supported his claims with arguments taken from Roman constitutional and canonistic corporate law. The cardinals were part of the body of the lord pope, he continued, and the pope ought not to settle any difficult matter without their counsel.[31] In more prosaic matters, he rejected the clear and unambiguous wording of a decree of the Fourth Lateran Council which took away the right of the bishops to grant dispensations for pluralists in their dioceses. Hostiensis even wrote that a

31. Tierney 1976, pp. 401–9; Watt 1980, pp. 99–113.

bishop could refuse to obey a direct papal mandate if it violated his conscience.[32]

While Hostiensis was not completely representative of late thirteenth-century canonists, he certainly was the most significant. His thought had great influence on later lawyers. Most canonists acknowledged the responsibility of the pope to rule for the common good of the church, but they were willing to limit his authority in only the most extreme circumstances: heresy and serious, oft-repeated crimes. Even so, the staunchest advocates of papal authority among the canonists stopped well short of granting the pope unbridled power. He was bound by the state of the church and the frailty of his humanity.

It is revealing to contrast the discussions of the canonists over the authority and sovereignty of the ruler to the descriptions of monarchy found in other contemporary legal sources. The Emperor Frederick II issued the Constitutions of Melfi in 1231 – also known as the *Liber Augustalis* – and in the prologue to his collection he included a description of monarchical authority. The prince, he or the drafter of his constitutions wrote, is an instrument of God whose duty it is to establish laws, promote justice, and correct and chastise the iniquitous:

Thus we, whom God has elevated beyond any hope man might have cherished to the pinnacle of the Roman empire and to the singular honour of all other kingdoms at the right hand of divine power, desire to render to God a two fold payment for the talents given to us, out of reverence for Jesus Christ, from whom we have received all we have.[33]

In the constitution from the same collection on the observance of justice, Frederick compared his position to that of the Roman emperors:

It is not without great forethought and well-considered planning that the Quirites [Roman citizens] conferred the right (*ius*) and imperium of establishing laws on the Roman prince by the *Lex Regia*. Thus the source of justice might proceed from the same person by whom justice is defended, who ruled through the authority established by Caesar.[34]

These descriptions of princely authority in the *Liber Augustalis* are steeped in the language of Christian theological and Roman legal thought. The prince

---

32. Pennington 1984, pp. 132–4.
33. *Liber Augustalis* (1973), prologue: 'Nos itaque, quos ad imperii Romani fastigia et aliorum regnorum insignia sola divinae potentiae dextera praeter spem hominum sublimavit, volentes duplicata talenta nobis credita reddere Deo vivo in reverentiam Jesu Christi, a quo cuncta suscepimus . . .'.
34. *Ibid.* 1.31: 'Non sine grandi consilio et deliberatione perpensa condendae legis ius et imperium in Romanum principem Regia lege transtulerunt Quirites, ut ab eodem, qui commisso sibi Caesareae fortunae suffragio per potentiam populis imperabat, prodiret origo iustitiae, a quo eiusdem defensio procedebat.' See Kantorowicz 1957, pp. 97–107 for a discussion of this law.

is established by God; his rule is sanctioned by God; he derives his authority from the people; he rules for the good of the people and out of reverence for God; he is responsible for the health and well-being of society.

Thomas Aquinas also emphasised the necessity and the naturalness of monarchical rule. The opening paragraphs of his *De regimine principum* describe man as a 'social and political animal' whose natural and necessary state is to live in a 'society of many'. If men did not live together in groups ruled by someone who protected the common good, society would fall into chaos: 'The idea of king implies that there is one man who is chief and that he is a shepherd seeking the common good of the multitude and not his own.'[35] In addition to the Christian tradition, the writings of Aristotle and Avicenna influenced Aquinas, but he also drew many of his examples from the writings of Livy, Cicero, and other Roman authors.

Although at first glance these passages taken from the *Liber Augustalis* and Aquinas may seem quite foreign to the technical discussions of the jurists, there are many points of similarity. The main work of the lawyers from 1150 to 1300 was to create a satisfying legal description of princely authority. They borrowed maxims from Roman law, they coined new definitions of judicial and legislative authority, and they underlined, perhaps naturally, the prince's power rather than his limitations. It was, nevertheless, his authority that needed defining. Aquinas is often used as an exemplar of medieval political thought, and indeed he is. However, he never dealt with the technical questions of sovereignty in his work, and consequently his more general descriptions of monarchical power are more heuristic than exact. His is a limited monarch, but limited in rather vague and undefined ways.

The lawyers had already, before Aquinas, established definitions of monarchical government, the responsibility of the prince to rule for the common good, and, most importantly, the precise relationship of the prince and the law. Their thought enabled some later thinkers to develop, paradoxically, coherent theories of absolute monarchy – by eliminating the limitations of the canonists on monarchical authority – and of constitutional government – by stressing the legal relationship of the ruler and his subjects and a prince's responsibility to rule well and wisely.

---

35. *De regimine*, I.2: 'Ex quo manifeste ostenditur quod de ratione regis est quod sit unus, qui praesit, et quod sit pastor commune multitudinis bonum, et non suum commodum quaerens.'

Theories of government

Monarchy was not the only system of government the twelfth- and thirteenth-century jurists knew, but it was the only system they treated seriously and extensively. The lawyers wrote about monarchy imbued with what modern historians have described as 'medieval constitutionalism'. The ruler, nobility, clergy, and people were part of a *societas Christiana* that encompassed all Christian Europe. Each person belonged to a variety of other groups, some local, others more extended. The tendency, natural of people during this period to form collective organisations, led to significant developments in law. The lawyers described the relationships within these groups, particularly between the head of a community and its members, but also the relationship of one group to another and to central authority. For example, the canonists dealt continuously with the legal problems that could be solved only by defining the legal status of the bishop and his chapter of canons, the corporation representing the local church. They formulated procedures and rules regulating how the local church could be summoned to court, whether a canon could bring suit against his own chapter or bishop, how decisions were to be made within the chapter, whether a bishop could overrule all the other members of the chapter, and what constituted a majority in an election and in other matters touching the collective will of the prelate and canons.

The jurists called such a group a *universitas* or, in English, a corporation. *Universitas* was a term borrowed from classical Roman law where it described associations of persons in both public and private law. Much of medieval corporate theory was based on Roman terminology and definitions. The jurists expanded the scope and importance of Roman law corporate theory remarkably quickly. At the beginning of the twelfth century the author of the *Questiones de iuris subtilitatibus* defined the 'people' as a *universitas*.[36] Within the church, each *universitas* possessed a distinctive juridical personality shaped by local customs and the history of the institution. Through their detailed and complex analyses of corporation law, the jurists fashioned a doctrine of community, that is they defined the

---

36. *Questiones de iuris subtilitatibus* (1894a), p. 88: 'Universitas, id est populus, hoc habet officium singulis scilicet hominibus quasi membris providere.' Opinions differ about the authorship of this *summa*, but no one still maintains that it is Irnerius' work. Ginevra Zanetti reedited this work in 1958. For a fuller discussion of the relationship of the corporation and individual members of it, see A. Black, below pp. 598–604.

proper relationship between the head of the corporation and its members. The model of the microcosm was then used to define the macrocosm: the entire church, city states, and the secular state. Brian Tierney has described the work of the canonists: 'The decretalists themselves, down to Innocent IV, certainly had no intention of providing arguments for critics of papal sovereignty; but in fact a more detailed analysis of the structure of corporate groups was precisely what was necessary to provide a sounder juristic basis for the rather vague "constitutional" ideas that occur in decretist works.'[37] It is necessary for an understanding of political thought of the twelfth and thirteenth centuries to look closely at the rules the lawyers made to govern corporations: the theories of election and of jurisdiction they shaped to describe the juridical workings of them and the theory of representation they created to enable a corporation to be represented in court, before the king, or in business affairs.

Corporate theory and representation

The bishop and his cathedral chapter constituted the most important corporate group within the church, and the canonists lavished much effort and ingenuity on its constitutional structure. The jurists called this body an *ecclesia*. The bishop's constitutional position in his *ecclesia* could be viewed from two different and contrary perspectives. He could be the sole ruler of his church, or he might share his authority with his canons. Gratian had included texts in his *Decretum* requiring a bishop to act with the consent or counsel of his chapter. The canonists expanded Gratian's brief exposition and gathered material touching this issue under several different titles in the legal collections of the late twelfth and thirteenth centuries. The most important were 'Concerning those things which a prelate may do without the consent of his chapter' and 'Concerning those things which a greater part of the chapter may do' (X 3.10 and 3.11). The papal decretals and conciliar canons under these titles established that a bishop could not alienate property, present clerics, or make other important decisions within the church without the advice, consent, and, as some texts in the collections specified, the 'subscription' of the canons. These chapters made it almost impossible for any canonist to conclude that a prelate alone possessed jurisdiction over all matters in his diocese. The jurists perceived an important difference between the constitutional position of a bishop in his diocese and the model of rulership that they found in Roman law, where the

37. Tierney 1955a, p. 96. The best survey of medieval corporate theory is Michaud-Quantin 1970.

emperor derived his authority from the people, but the people had no share in the exercise of his authority.

Roman law's absolutist model attracted some canonists. Pope Innocent IV wrote in his commentary (c. 1250) to the decretals of Pope Gregory IX that 'rectors who govern corporations have jurisdiction and not the corporations. Some say that a corporation may exercise jurisdiction without rectors, but I do not believe it.'[38] Few jurists agreed with Innocent's starkly simple analysis of corporate authority; even Innocent did not apply his theoretical model to ecclesiastical corporations. There were really two basic theories of corporate structure among medieval jurists – one derived mainly from Roman law, the other mainly from canon law – and they could result in different political theories. The following discussion focuses on the more complex and fertile canonistic model.

These questions arose most frequently when the distribution of church property was discussed or when a corporation was involved in litigation. The canonists formulated rules governing the rights of bishops and canons to grant prebends or to present clerics to churches. Depending on local custom, a prelate and his chapter might act together or separately. Consequently, the jurists made a distinction between a prelate who sat in his chapter as prelate or as canon, that is, between a prelate who acted as head of his corporation, and one who acted as a member of it. Hostiensis determined that when the affairs of a chapter touched only the rights of the canons, the bishop could sit as canon and his voice was then equal to that of any other member. If in those matters the chapter acted negligently, all rights of jurisdiction devolved to the bishop. If the bishop exercised authority that was his alone, he did so as a prelate, and in this case his voice was equal to that of all the other members of the corporation taken together. The bishop could achieve a majority in the chapter with the vote of only one other canon, in medieval electoral terminology, the *maior et sanior pars*. Hostiensis, however, clearly stated that a bishop must have more than simply his and one other vote when important matters touching the state of the church were transacted. Then, even though he sat in chapter as prelate, he had to have the consent of the chapter, which meant its *maior pars*.

These discussions of corporations had a two-fold importance for the development of political theory. First, the jurists became accustomed to describing complicated relationships between the head and members of a

38. Tierney 1955a, p. 107. Innocent IV to X 1.2.8 v. *sedis*: 'Et est notandum quod rectores assumpti ab universitatibus habent iurisdictionem et non ipsae universitates. Aliqui tamen dicunt quod ipsae universitates deficientibus rectoribus possunt exercere iurisdictionem, sicut rectores, quod non credo.'

group. Each had rights and duties, and corporate theory preserved these distinctions. Most importantly, the lawyers never concluded that the prelate could simply ignore the customs and constitution of the corporation. Secondly, these concepts were easily applied to larger groups, both ecclesiastical and secular. Corporate theory satisfied the Germanic sense of contract between a ruler and his people and described the legal position of an archbishop in his province, a pope in his curia or council, or a king in his kingdom or sitting in his representative assembly.

As the lawyers explored corporate theory, they delved into the juridical personality of the group. By the beginning of the thirteenth century, it became apparent that if a bishop and his chapter represented a church, the bishop or some other delegated person, often called rather indifferently a procurator, syndic, or advocate, could carry out the affairs of a corporation in court and their actions could be binding on the entire group. Such a delegate was said to have *plena potestas* or *generalis et libera administratio* (full power or general and unrestricted administration), and he could sell, buy, lease, make contracts, and represent his client in court; the only limitations placed on him were that he could not violate the terms of his mandate and could not act fraudulently to the detriment of his client.

An ancillary problem, but one of real significance, was the juridical position of a prelate who represented his church and acted without their consent. The canonists borrowed the doctrine of tutorship from Roman law and applied it to prelates. A gloss of Johannes Teutonicus illustrates their thought:

Note that a prelate is convened in the name of the church, as is stated here, although he is part of the church . . . and this is so because the church is in the prelate . . . but the bishop is not always included in the name of the church . . . Whoever wishes to convene the church ought to name the prelate because if one names the church, it may ask for a delay by naming the prelate . . . and if anything is done without the authority of the prelate, it is totally invalid . . . If there is a dispute between the prelate and his church, a superior prelate should appoint a curator . . . Is a prelate always obligated to seek a mandate from his church in all matters? No, just as a tutor must not if he is properly appointed . . . And the same is true of a prelate if he has lawful administration . . . Because prelates may be compared to tutors.[39]

39. Johannes Teutonicus (1981), *Apparatus* to 3 Comp. 1.2.11 v. *ad conventus*, pp. 21–2: 'Nota quod prelatus conuenitur nomine conuentus ut hic dicitur, licet ipse sit pars conuentus . . . set hoc ideo est quia ecclesia est in ipso prelato . . . Set non semper nomine ecclesie intelligitur episcopus . . . Qui ergo uult ecclesiam conuenire, debet conuenire ipsum prelatum, quia si conueniret ipsam ecclesiam, posset ecclesia petere indutias nominando prelatum . . . et si aliquid fieret sine auctoritate prelati, totum retractaretur . . . Si autem dissensio inter prelatum et ecclesiam adeatur superior, et ille constituet curatorem ad litem . . . Set numquid prelatus tenetur cauere de rato? Non uidetur, sicut nec tutor, si constet de tutore . . . Idem uidetur de prelato cum ipse habeat legitimam administrationem . . . Item quia prelati comparantur tutoribus.'

Canonistic doctrines of counsel, consent, and representation achieved maturity in the middle of the thirteenth century. Hostiensis formulated a sophisticated theory of counsel and consent that protected the rights of the members of a corporation. He is often cited as an example of a lawyer who fostered collegiality within the church, and his corporate theory supports this characterisation.

Hostiensis wrote that a bishop did not have to have the consent of his chapter if he carried out the ordinary business of the church. However, in all matters that touched the rights of the chapter – particularly the alienation of property – the bishop must always have the approval of his chapter. If the bishop did anything detrimental to the church, his actions were void, and he could be held accountable.[40]

From the early thirteenth century, the canonists commonly maintained that during an episcopal vacancy, the rights of jurisdiction devolved to the chapter in matters affecting their collective rights. Although the jurists differed considerably over which rights could or could not be exercised, in principle they almost all agreed that the 'headless' corporation could act in a wide range of matters. Their discussions centred on the rights of the canons to confer prebends; by the fourteenth century, canon law, supported by papal decrees, recognised the right of chapters to exercise jurisdiction during an episcopal vacancy.

Canonistic corporate theory gradually defined the relationship of the head to its members. The doctrine was complex, but flexible. It recognised the authority of the prelate, but also protected the rights of members. When these theories were applied to the whole church – as they were in the later Middle Ages, particularly during the Great Schism – and to secular kingdoms, they were ready instruments of constitutional, limited government. Perhaps no other canonistic doctrine was as important for constitutional thought, and canonistic corporate theory provided a needed counterweight to the equally powerful theories of monarchical rule also developed by the jurists. In the end, even papal *plenitudo potestatis* could be bridled if the authority of the pope within the church were compared to that of a bishop in his chapter.

Corporate theory and the mixed constitution

Canonistic corporate theory described an intricate relationship between the head of a *universitas* and its members. It also provided a theoretical model for another theory of government that gained currency once again in the

40. Tierney 1955a, pp. 122–4.

middle of the thirteenth century and would enjoy immense popularity in the centuries that followed: Aristotle's mixed constitution.[41] Aristotle noted that monarchy, aristocracy, and democracy all had virtues and vices. He concluded, therefore, that the best system of government would provide for all classes of society: the rich, the 'middle class', and the poor. A perfect constitution would balance conflicting interests and produce a stable government. His theory of 'mixed government' was adopted and expanded by many thinkers of the ancient world, especially Polybius and Cicero.

In the second half of the thirteenth century, Thomas Aquinas discovered Aristotle's mixed constitution in the government of ancient Israel, creating both a precedent for the philosopher's system and a justification of its correctness. Moses and his successors, observed Thomas, ruled according to a mixed constitution established by divine law. Moses was a king. The seventy-two elders were elected because of their ability, and they represented aristocracy. Democracy was a part of the constitution because the elders were elected by all the people.[42] Aquinas' interpretation of the Israelites' government became a paradigm of constitutional government that remained important until the nineteenth century.

At the beginning of the fourteenth century, John of Paris combined corporate theory and Aquinas' mixed constitution and applied it to the government of the church. In his treatise on papal and royal authority, John compared the position of the pope within the church to that of a bishop to his chapter. In this respect, he accepted a constitutional structure for the church based on canonistic corporate theory. Following Aquinas, he also argued that a 'mixed government' (*regimen mixtum*) was better than pure monarchy. The best form of ecclesiastical government would be a system in which many were elected from the entire church, with some coming from each province, to serve under the pope. Then everyone would have a part in the church's government.[43]

Neither Thomas Aquinas nor John of Paris did more than provide a general description of the mixed constitution. They did not discuss what the proper distribution of authority should be within a monarchy or the

---

41. This section is dependent upon Tierney 1982, pp. 87–92.

42. *Summa theologiae* 1.2 q.105.1: 'Et hoc fuit institutum secundum legem divinam. Nam Moyses et eius successores gubernabant populum quasi singulariter omnibus principantes, quod est quaedam species regni. Eligebantur autem septuaginta duo seniores secundum virtutem . . . et hoc erat aristocraticum. Sed democraticum erat quod isti de omni populo eligebantur.' See Kayser and Lettieri 1982, who, however, underestimate the importance of Aquinas for later thinkers.

43. John of Paris (1969), p. 175, (*De potestate regia et papali*, chap. 19): 'Sic certe esset optimum regimen ecclesiae, si sub uno papa eligerentur plures ab omni provincia et de omni provincia, ut sic in regimine ecclesiae omnes aliquo modo haberent partem suam.'

church. In particular, they simply omitted any analysis of the relationship of the king or pope to the aristocracy (the college of cardinals in the church), i.e. was the king's authority greater than, equal to, or less than that of the aristocracy. Nevertheless, these questions of substance would be broached a century later in the debates of the Great Schism.

Theories of election and jurisdiction

There is a large literature discussing ecclesiastical elections in which the canonists thoroughly examined the nature of governmental office and jurisdiction. During the twelfth century, due largely to the success of the Gregorian Reform movement in freeing ecclesiastical elections from lay control, election became the standard method of selection within the church. The cathedral chapter was recognised as the body competent to elect a bishop, and from the middle of the eleventh century, the college of cardinals had the sole responsibility of electing the pope. Some sort of electoral procedure was even required for the provisioning of benefices.

Through their study of elections, the jurists analysed the electoral body, the office of the elect, and the jurisdictional powers and rights the candidate received at the various stages of an election. An election was also a corporate act, in which the corporation bestowed the right of governance upon the elect. Once the electoral body had been defined, all members of that body had full rights of participation. The most famous of all medieval legal maxims, 'what touches all must be approved by all' (*Quod omnes tangit ab omnibus approbari debet*) established the rights of the electoral body to take part in all matters of importance, and at the same time, bestowed legitimacy on their actions. It was a principle of canon law that a bishop must be freely chosen by the clergy and never be forced on an unwilling flock. Although these concepts were not new to the twelfth and thirteenth centuries, it was only then that they were sharply defined. If we had only the electoral treatises of the canonists, we would still have a clear picture of this aspect of medieval political theory.

Ecclesiastical elections created a tension within the church. Christ established the structure and constitution of the church. He ordained that prelates govern their flocks, and there seemed little room in the church's hierarchy for the rights of those subject to divinely ordered papal and epi-scopal offices. Ecclesiastical elections were, however, a constant reminder that offices within the church had to have the approval of the lower clergy and that jurisdiction and authority could be granted from below as well as from above. Consequently, as the canonists examined the juridical status of a candidate elect, they were confronted by the question what rights an electoral body bestowed upon an elect. In the mid-twelfth century, Rufinus, a canonist at Bologna, provided the first answers.

It is customarily asked whether one who has been confirmed in an election possesses such full authority that he has the right, before his episcopal anointment, to depose clerics just like a consecrated bishop. We, however, say that he should have full power with respect to administration but not with respect to the authority of his dignity. And, therefore, with the right of full administration he can suspend others from administration of offices or orders . . . On the other hand, he who does not yet have the plenitude of authority – which certainly comes only from consecration – cannot depose.[44]

Rufinus drew a preliminary distinction, albeit not fully formed, between the jurisdictional power of the episcopal office, which was received upon election, and what later jurists would call a bishop's powers of orders, or sacramental powers, which could only be granted by a higher authority. After Rufinus, the canonists concurred that a bishop-elect had a part of his authority from his election, and his subsequent consecration then gave him the full exercise of his office.

The canonists quite rapidly explored the ramifications of this distinction. Alanus Anglicus argued that an election bestowed a 'right' upon a bishop that he should be confirmed by a higher authority in his office: 'From his election a bishop obtains a certain right . . . and from that right he can demand confirmation, and thus, in consequence, the episcopate and the power of administering . . . Once received, therefore, the confirmation bestows on him, so to speak, the possession of ecclesiastical property.'[45] Subsequently, the canonists distinguished between a right and the exercise of a right and also carefully defined the right a candidate-elect received from his election. In the early thirteenth century, an anonymous lawyer writing in France noted that a bishop-elect had a *ius ad rem petendam*, which might be translated as 'to have a right to something' and after his consecration

---

44. Benson 1968, p. 58, n. 4 (Benson's translation). Rufinus to D.23 c.1 v. *tamen sicut verus papa*: 'Solet queri, si in electione confirmatus ante episcopalem unctionem usque adeo plenam auctoritatem possideat, ut quemadmodum episcopus consecratus deponere clericos valeat. Sed dicimus quod plenam potestatem habeat quoad administrationem non autem quoad dignitatis auctoritatem, et ideo iure plene administrationis potest aliquos ab administratione procurationum vel ordinum suspendere – quod tamen non sine presentia capituli sui, cui capitulo episcopo mortuo licet itidem facere. Deponere autem, id est exauctorare non potest qui plenitudinem auctoritatis nondum habet, quam ex sola consecratione est certissimum evenire.'

45. *Ibid.* p. 137, n. 8 (Benson's translation). Alanus to 1 Comp. 1.4.18 v. *non habeat facultatem*: 'Per electionem tamen ius est sibi acquisitum in ipso episcopatu . . . Et ex illo iure potest petere confirmationem et ita per consequens episcopatum et administrandi potestatem . . . Confirmatio igitur habita tribuit ei quasi possessionem rerum ecclesiasticarum.'

acquired a *ius in re*, 'to have a secure right over something'. Robert Benson has observed that these two concepts 'played a significant role in the legal thought of the Middle Ages, and, indeed, far more than mere technical terms, they were major concepts for the canonists and Romanists, and feudal lawyers of that period'.[46] These technical terms supported the rights of the electoral body; although the church may have been a divinely ordained monarchy, many governmental rights were conferred by election, and the corporate body that performed the election bestowed real authority on its choice. The jurists believed that all power ultimately came from God, but at an early stage they were capable of formulating the theory that power came from God through the people. In c. 1210 Laurentius Hispanus wrote that the emperor received his power from the people:

> The empire differs from the papacy because the emperor has his jurisdiction from the people, but the Roman church or pope is raised to power by the voice of the Lord and not by synodal statutes . . . Whence it can be said that the emperor can be deposed by the people, but the college of cardinals may not depose the pope.[47]

Of course this theory later became a common element of sixteenth-century political thought.

The mechanism of election itself also fell under the scrutiny of the lawyers, and they explored the problem of what constituted a majority, the *maior pars*, and how the electors could legally represent the *universitas*. Huguccio had defined a majority as being two of the three elements that should be considered in counting votes from an election: the three elements were number, zeal, and authority. When two of these were in concord, their will should prevail. By the early thirteenth century, a more 'democratic' view emerged. Johannes Teutonicus commented that Huguccio's principles were wrong: 'Number always prevails over zeal and authority, unless it only slightly exceeds them; then I would combine either zeal or authority with number . . . and dignity should not be considered unless the electors were evenly divided.'[48] Johannes defined the *maior pars* as the largest number of electors and most thirteenth-century canonists

---

46. *Ibid.*, p. 142, and Landau 1975, pp. 165–70.
47. Laurentius Hispanus to 3 Comp. 1.5.1. (X 1.7.1) v. *Cum ex illo generali priuilegio*, Admont 55, fol. 108v (Karlsruhe Aug. XL, fol. 127v): 'In hoc differt imperium quoad iurisdictionem a papatu, quia imperator a populo habuit iurisdictionem . . . set ecclesia Romana uel papa nullis sinodocis statutis set uocem domini prelatus est ut hic et xxi. di. Quamuis [D.21 c.3]. Vnde dici posset imperatorem deponi posse a populo set papa non a cetu cardinalium.'
48. Johannes Teutonicus (1981), *Apparatus* to 3 Comp. 1.6.7 v. *solum plures*, p. 59: 'Numerus preualet zelo et auctoritati, nisi numerus in modico excederet, tunc conferrem zelum uel auctoritatem cum numero . . . Nec enim recurrendum est ad dignitatem, nisi cum par numerus est hinc inde.'

agreed. The *maior pars* of the cathedral chapter constituted the majority of the canons: 'If the canons litigate among themselves, where the *maior pars* lies, they may call themselves the chapter.'[49]

The concept of the *maior pars* representing the community became a fundamental principle of late medieval political theory. Canonistic electoral theory was applied to the whole church – and constituted an important element of conciliar thought – and to the secular state. Bracton, for example, as early as the middle of the thirteenth century, wrote that the *maior pars* of the magnates and prelates represented the realm when they transacted matters touching the common good and the affairs of the realm.[50]

Just as the *Lex Regia* turned the eyes of the legists towards the problem of origins, the canonists' study of electoral theory posed the question whether the community bestowed jurisdiction through election or through some other mechanism or whether it simply consented to have jurisdiction exercised upon it. Even though the canonists and civilians examined jurisdiction in its various forms in great detail, at first they did not explore its origins. There are several reasons why the question did not interest them. First, although they viewed the world as being hierarchical, they did not conclude that all jurisdiction and authority flowed from above. Germanic ideas of custom, the rights of the people, feudal and Germanic notions of reciprocal rights and obligations between lords and vassals combined to remind the jurists that society was a complicated organism for which simple definitions did not apply.

The papacy presented a special and difficult problem to the canonists. They contrasted the authority of the pope to that of the bishops. The pope, they thought, received his *plenitudo potestatis* immediately upon his election by the college of cardinals. The pope had fullness of power, but the bishops, they thought, had a share of the responsibility, *pars sollicitudinis*. Although this formulation might have led them to conclude that all authority and jurisdiction was derived or delegated from the pope, they never did so before the middle of the thirteenth century. The canonists, however, were not the first to raise the question; it became crucial during the secular-mendicant controversy that began in the 1250s. This dispute revolved around issues that may seem unimportant. The mendicants defended the right of the pope to grant privileges to the friars, exempting them

---

49. *Ibid.* to 3 Comp. 1.6.6 v. *capituli accesserunt*, p. 54: 'Nota quod si canonici agunt inter se, tamen ubi est maior pars, illi se possunt nominare capitulum.'   50. Post 1964, p. 199.

completely from episcopal jurisdiction. A Franciscan, Thomas of York (1256), was the first to claim that the pope's fullness of power was the source of all jurisdiction within the church and that episcopal jurisdiction was simply delegated. The bishops had no legal right to complain about papal privileges given to the mendicants, he concluded, since episcopal jurisdiction was completely dependent upon papal grants. Thomas began a vitriolic debate that lasted for over fifty years. Neither side won – the question remains open today – but lawyers and theologians could no longer discuss the constitution of the church without describing the origins of jurisdiction.

The secular-mendicant controversy occupies a central place in the development of western political thought. As a result of it, the conceptual framework of monarchical authority and power was permanently altered. Earlier constitutional discussions of monarchical power centred on the inviolable rights of subjects, the necessity of the monarch to conform to the customs and laws of the realm, and, within the church, the rights and privileges of prelates and corporate bodies. By shifting the discussion from 'rights' of subjects to the origins of jurisdiction and political authority, mendicant theologians cleared the way for an irresistible emphasis upon the all-encompassing and pervasive authority of the prince. By accepting the premise that all jurisdiction was derived or delegated from the prince, they removed a difficult obstacle of medieval constitutional thought to absolute monarchy. Nevertheless, older ideas continued to flourish alongside new theories. The claim of the bishops to an authority that was not delegated by the pope prevented the mendicants' views from sweeping the field and anticipated later theories concerning the rights of 'inferior magistrates' so prominent in early modern constitutional thought.

II LAW, SOVEREIGNTY AND CORPORATION THEORY, 1300–1450

The period from the late thirteenth century to the mid-fifteenth occupies a particularly important position in the history of the juristic contribution to political thought, because in it there emerged the school of the Commentators, which was the culmination of medieval civilian jurisprudence, and as such was to exert a profound influence on early modern political thought. These years also produced major canonists building on the achievements of the thirteenth century. Juristic theory deeply influenced political ideas in three areas in particular. First, jurists developed further the theme of the relationship between positive law and the overall normative structure within which they considered human law and government operated: that is to say, the relationship between the will of the law-makers (whether emperor, pope, king, *signore*, or people) and the limitations posed by fundamental laws. The other two aspects relate to the jurists' response to the contemporary political phenomenon of the emerging territorial state. They consolidated theories of territorial sovereignty, in the case of kingdoms developing further theories which had originated towards the end of the twelfth century, and in that of city-republics producing innovations in juristic terms. Furthermore they made crucial advances in corporation theory producing thereby a specifically juristic contribution to the emergence of the idea of the state.

The normative context of human law and government

The role of fundamental norms

That these jurists should have accepted such a normative structure was only to be expected: it was, after all, a basic presupposition of the juristic tradition[1] and of medieval thought about law and society with, as we shall see, the possible and notorious exception of the views of Marsilius of Padua. Thus in all juristic works divine law, natural law, and the *ius gentium*

---

1. The most extensive modern treatment is Cortese 1962–4.

provided necessary criteria according to which human positive law could
be judged. These fundamental laws simply could not be abolished by
human enactments: indeed, human laws which opposed them simply were
not valid. These higher norms were considered binding ultimately because
God was seen as the creator of the natural world and of man. Although the
civilians sometimes retained Ulpian's distinction between the natural law
and the *ius gentium*, they normally followed Gaius in considering the *ius
gentium* as a form of natural law in the sense of being specific applications of
it derived through the operation of natural reason.[2] Indeed all jurists laid
great stress on the role of reason both in the composition of law itself and in
the function of the law-maker. As Baldus said, the exercise of supreme
power should itself be subject to reason: 'The *princeps* is a rational creature
possessing supreme power, but insofar as he is rational he should obey
reason.'[3] In making reason the link between man, natural law, and the
eternal law of God, Baldus was clearly revealing the Thomist influence
which was extremely strong amongst fourteenth-century jurists.

Manifestly, given these limitations, no ruler could be considered truly
absolute. Thus the concept of *princeps legibus solutus* retained its established
meaning of freedom from human positive law alone. It was solely within
this sphere that a form of limited absolutism was possible. In conformity
with *l. Digna vox* (C.1.14.4) the submission of the *princeps* to human laws
remained purely voluntary, a well-worn theme[4] to which Baldus made a
refreshingly clear contribution: 'The supreme and absolute power of the
princeps is not under the law, and therefore this law [i.e. *l. Digna vox*] applies
to his ordinary power not his absolute power.'[5] The distinction between
potestas absoluta and *potestas ordinaria* or *ordinata* had been used by Hostiensis
in relation to papal plenitude of power and was also well-established in

2. *Ius naturale* could also be considered as that governing the primeval state of nature preceding the era
   of the *ius gentium*: 'Iure naturali primaevo non statuitur sed per instinctum naturalem iure
   introductum gentes bene aliquid instituerunt quod ius gentium appellatur', Jacobus de Ravannis ad
   Inst., 1.2, 2, n. 1: 1577.
3. 'Princeps est creatura rationabilis habens potestatem supremam, sed inquantum est rationabilis
   debet obedire rationi', Cons. III.277: 1491, fol. 84r (= Cons. I.327, n. 2: 1575, fol. 101r). But Baldus
   also adheres to the commonplace that to obey reason is no infringement of liberty: 'Nam non minus
   est liber quia obediat rationi . . . Immo summa libertas est rationi servire', *Consilium* on the Great
   Schism (ad C.6,34). For Baldus' political thought in general see Canning 1987.
4. Out of a host of examples, see Cynus ad C.1.14.4, n. 2–3: 1578, fols. 25v–26r, 'Dico ergo quod
   imperator est solutus legibus de necessitate; tamen de honestate ipse vult ligari legibus, quia honor
   reputatur vinculum sacri iuris et utilitas ipsius'; and Bartolus, *ibid.*, n. 1: 1577, fol. 27v, 'Fateor quod
   ipse [i.e. princeps] est solutus legibus, tamen aequum et dignum est quod legibus vivat, ita loquitur
   hic, unde ipse submittit se legibus de voluntate, non de necessitate.'
5. 'Suprema et absoluta potestas principis non est sub lege, unde lex ista habet respectum ad potestatem
   ordinariam non ad potestatem absolutam', ad C.1.14.4: 1498a, fol. 50r–v.

thirteenth- and fourteenth-century theological and political writings.[6] In adopting this distinction Baldus sought to differentiate that aspect of the power of the *princeps* which appeared in the ordinary day-to-day exercise of his jurisdiction from the aspect of ultimate and absolute sovereignty which provided the fundamental and underlying guarantee of the structure of positive law.

Yet the ruler's freedom of action was not restricted to the area of positive law. The jurists did not take an unsophisticated view of the relationship between the law-maker's will and higher norms. Thus the ruler could derogate from higher norms *ex causa*, that is, when applying these norms in practice to particular cases, he could interpret them extremely freely and in such a way that he might appear to have denied their specific effects without being understood to have thereby abolished their general principles, a process analogous to casuistry in theological terms.[7] A classic juristic distinction was made between the Mosaic law's prohibition of killing and the validity of judicial execution. This capacity for derogation was accorded to monarchs and sovereign peoples (by those jurists, like Bartolus, Baldus, and Paulus de Castro, who accepted this latter concept). There were limits, however, to this process: as Cynus de Pistoia, for instance, said, some parts of the *ius divinum*, such as the prohibition of the marriage between a man and his mother simply could not be the subject of derogation.[8] It was, however, possible to accept that such derogation did not infringe the integrity of higher norms by seeing the *causa* involved in it as the practical application of reason. Yet the initiative clearly lay with the ruler, and to modern eyes this use of *causa* could be seen as undermining the normative structure, because who but the ruler, monarch, or sovereign people was to determine the validity of the *causa*? Amongst late medieval jurists, however, normative limitations were taken very seriously, as was the ruler's voluntary submission to the positive law.

The role of will

It was, however, the counterpoint and tension between this normative structure and the voluntarist aspect of positive law existing within it that proved to be a fundamental theme in fourteenth- and fifteenth-century jurisprudence. What was particularly notable about juristic thought was the attention given to the role of will in the creation of law – either in the form of the ruler's *voluntas* or the people's consent. This is already clear from the

6. See pp. 435–6 above.
7. C.1.19.7 provided a major *locus* for juristic discussion of this process. See Cortese 1962, vol. I, p. 111, for Azo's contribution on this point. 8. Ad C.1.19.7, n. 10: 1578, fol. 36r.

question of derogation; and most importantly, as we shall see, will emerged as the generator of territorial sovereignty. Highly important implications resulted from the jurists' concentration on will as the constitutive element in positive law.

If the *princeps*, the model for the secular ruler, is considered, there is a formidable mass of evidence suggesting a conception of a truly sovereign will. The implications of the attribution of *plenitudo potestatis* to the *princeps* and other monarchs were further explored; but most notable was the elaboration of the well-established formula, 'in principe pro ratione voluntas', which was universally known and underlay a major statement in the gloss of Accursius.[9] The two main aspects of law as the product of will and of reason were thus combined, but in such a way as to recognise the superiority of the ruler's will, which became its own justification. This trend culminated in Baldus' definition, 'Plenitude of power is, however, a plenitude of will subject to no necessity and limited by no rules of public law':[10] as a definition of sovereign will this on the face of it left nothing to be desired.

Furthermore Jacobus Butrigarius (a teacher of Bartolus) and Baldus moved considerably nearer a less limited absolutism by seriously undermining the strength of the *ius gentium* in the crucial area of subjects' property rights. It was the jurists' *communis opinio* that such rights (harking back to the twelfth-century dispute between Bulgarus and Martinus) were not derived from the *princeps* but were the product of *ius gentium* (or natural law understood in the sense of *ius gentium*), and that the *princeps* could, therefore, only remove or transfer private property *cum causa*. Petrus de Bellapertica and Cynus had accepted that, whereas the *princeps* had no right in law to remove his subjects' property *sine causa*, there was in practice no way of preventing him: he could do this *de facto*, but, as Cynus said, he sinned in so doing.[11] Jacobus Butrigarius went far further by maintaining that the *princeps* through the exercise of his imperial will alone could remove his

---

9. '*Ex aliqua causa*. Magna et iusta causa est eius voluntas', ad D.48.19.4: 1497, fol. 246r. Cf. p. 428 above.

10. 'Est autem plenitudo potestatis arbitrii plenitudo nulli necessitati subiecta nullisque iuris publici regulis limitata', ad C.3.34.2: 1498a, fol. 190v; cf. *idem* ad X.1.2.1, n. 30: 1551, fol. 12r, 'Plenitudini potestatis nihil resistit, nam omnem legem positivam superat, et sufficit in principe pro ratione voluntas.'

11. See Petrus de Bellapertica ad Inst. 1.2, n. 67: 1586, p. 108, 'Et ideo dico princeps de iure (non dico de potestate sua cum sit legibus solutus, ut [D.1.3.31]) non potest mihi rem auferre sine causa'; Cynus ad C.1.19.7, n. 12: 1578, fol. 36v, 'Aut imperator vult mihi auferre rem meam cum causa rationabili, aut sine causa . . . Secundo casu, scilicet, quando vult mihi tollere dominium rei meae sine aliqua causa de mundo, si quaeratur utrum possit de facto, non est dubium. Sed utrum possit de iure, et de potestate sibi per iura concessa, in veritate non potest . . . negari tamen non potest quod si mihi rem meam auferat sine causa quod ipse peccat.'

subjects' property *sine causa*.[12] Bartolus, however, expressly rejected this view on the grounds that, whereas Jacobus was treating imperial power and the laws guaranteeing property rights as being on the same level, the emperor's jurisdiction in this question as in others was hedged about by the requirements of justice, to achieve which God had instituted the imperial authority: a classic statement of the location of the emperor's power within the structure of higher norms.[13] Baldus nevertheless chose to follow Jacobus: in depriving subjects of their property 'any reason which so moves the emperor is cause enough'[14] – that is to say, he interpreted the requirement of a cause not according to objective standards of right but according to the subjective will of the *princeps*, a crystal-clear definition of unrestricted absolute power in this respect. The cause had in short been subsumed in the will. But, it should be noted, Baldus applied this freedom of will only to the emperor: in the immediate continuation of his commentary on this passage (C.1.19.7) he expressly excluded *populi* from the exercise of such unrestricted power.[15]

A balanced view is, however, especially necessary in interpreting the role of will. The jurists indeed admitted a large area of legal activity within which they considered a presumption of the good faith of the *princeps* could

12. 'Item opponitur quod imperator non possit quem privare de dominio rei suae, ut [C.1.19.2]. Sol. potest ex causa, ut hic favore publicae utilitatis, sine causa non potest, ut ibi. Immo puto quod ubicunque princeps non errat in facto et refert ibi contra ius aliquid, quod valeat rescriptum, nam quod ipse non possit aliquem privare re sua non est ex defectu potestatis suae, sed ideo quia dixit se nolle hoc facere. Vbicunque ergo ipse vult, dummodo non sit error in facto, tenet rescriptum, et videtur tollere legem derogatoriam, quae contra hoc est, cum scire omne praesumatur', ad D.1.14.3, n. 12: 1606, p. 37.

13. 'Dominus Iacobus Butrigarius dicebat simpliciter quod princeps potest auferre mihi dominium rei meae sine aliqua causa. Nam eius potestas et potestas istarum legum quae hoc prohibent procedunt a pari potentia; ergo sicut potest istas leges tollere, ergo eodem modo possit dare alteri dominium rei meae sine causa. Quod puto non esse verum, nam princeps non posset facere unam legem quae contineret unum inhonestum vel iniustum. Nam est contra substantiam legis: nam lex est sanctio sancta iubens honesta et prohibens contraria, ut [D.1.3.2]. Eodem modo si vellet auferre mihi dominium rei meae iniuste non posset, quia princeps habet iurisdictionem a deo, ut in auth. "Quomodo oporteat episcopos" [Nov., 6] in prin. Sed deus non dedit ei iurisdictionem peccandi, nec auferendi alienum indebite, ergo etc.', ad C.1.22.6, n. 2: 1577, fol. 35v.

14. 'Quaerunt doctores nunquid imperator potest rescribere contra ius gentium. Glossa videtur dicere quod non; unde per rescriptum principis non potest alicui sine causa auferri dominium, sed cum aliquali bene potest [D.40.11.3; D.21.2.11; D.31.1.78, 1; D.6.1.15]; et habetur pro causa quaelibet ratio motiva ipsius principis', ad C.1.19.7: 1498a, fol. 63r. This view of Baldus became well-known: see Philippus Decius' prominent inclusion of it in his discussion of this whole question (ad X.1.2.7, n. 98–9: 1575, fol. 26r). Cf. Baldus ad C.7.37.3: 1498a, fol. 201v: 'Bona verum singularium personarum non sunt principis . . . de his tamen imperator disponere potest ex potestate absoluta ut de propriis . . . et *maxime* causa subsistente' – a just cause is desirable but not essential.

15. 'Secus est in statuto populi, quia non debet inesse causa motiva, sed debet inesse causa probabilis et condigna, alias non valet.'

be made. Yet, in making the presumption of a just cause on the part of the *princeps* where one was not specified, in for instance the case of an imperial rescript infringing the general provisions of higher norms, they by no means absolved him from the requirement to have in fact a just cause. The *princeps* in such cases was presumed to be willing what was objectively just; it was not considered that whatever he willed was *ipso facto* just simply because he willed it. Thus when Cynus maintained that imperial rescripts contrary to the mutable part of the *ius divinum*, the natural law, and the *ius gentium* made without specified just cause were valid 'quoad observantiam', he did not mean that such rescripts necessarily constituted valid derogations from such higher norms, but only that his subjects must presume that their superior was acting with just cause, and obey. Cynus made it clear that this only applied when there could be a just cause: an obviously unjust rescript would be a different matter.[16] Although there was thus a strong presumption in favour of the *princeps*, which meant that his freedom of action and will was thereby considerably enhanced, the jurists maintained as their general position that the *princeps* through his will alone and without just cause could not derogate from higher norms. It was only positive law that he could change without needing any cause or reason save his own will. Only in that sphere could he act in an untrammelled manner and sweep away existing laws by measures issued 'non obstante lege'. The views of Jacobus Butrigarius and Baldus on property rights remained exceptions.[17]

Nevertheless the extent to which civilians accorded considerable freedom of action to the will of the *princeps* did not go uncriticised in canonist circles. Panormitanus, for instance, rejected the argument that a just cause could be presumed in rescripts *contra ius divinum* or *contra ius*

16. 'Vltimo ut sciatur quando rescriptum principis tenet et quando non, ita distinguatis . . . Aut directo est contra ius, et tunc aut contra ius divinum aut contra ius gentium vel naturale . . . Si est contra ius divinum refert, aut ius divinum est perpetuum, infallibile, id est, quod habet perpetuam causam prohibitionis, verbi gratia, ut filius contrahat matrimonium cum matre vel sorore . . . et hoc casu non valet . . . Aut est tale ius divinum quod ex causa potest immutari, tunc refert, aut scribit cum iusta causa aut sine causa. Si quidem scribit cum iusta causa, ut quia vere homicidam mandat occidi, tunc tollit omnimodo ius divinum; si autem scribat sine causa, tunc aut quaeris utrum valeat quantum ad tollendum ius divinum, et non valet, aut quaeris utrum valeat quantum ad observantiam, dico quod sic, quia praesumere debemus de causa, ex quo causa subsistente fieri potest. Secundo casu quando rescribit contra ius gentium vel naturale, tunc refert, aut facit ex causa rationabili, et tunc tollit . . . aut facit sine causa, tunc non valet quantum ad hoc, ut tollat ius naturale vel gentium, sed valet quantum ad observantiam', ad C.1.22.6, n. 7: 1578, fol. 40r.

17. Cortese (1964, vol. II, pp. 226–7) considers that Raphael Fulgosius made the most extreme juristic statement, holding the *princeps* to be freed from the natural law and the *ius gentium* (Cons. 143, n. 3: 1577, fol. 202v). A close reading, however, reveals that Fulgosius did not take this view in this *consilium*.

naturale.[18] He also even went so far as to say, 'Where there is no legitimate cause for contravening the positive law, the *princeps* sins in violating it',[19] a view which directly contradicted the civilian conception of the nature of the absolute power of the *princeps*. The point, however, remains that, whatever divergences and nuances of opinion existed in juristic treatments of the relationship of positive law to higher norms, throughout the vast bulk of jurisprudential writings the argument was always carried on within a context which assumed an overall structure of higher norms: there could for these jurists be no truly positivist theory of law.

Marsilius of Padua, the one fourteenth-century writer who produced a theory of law which can appear positivist, had no influence on juristic conceptions of law. There has in any case been a serious difference of opinion amongst modern scholars as to whether Marsilius was indeed a thorough-going positivist.[20] Marsilius did not reject the existence of a normative structure as such. He made, however, a very clear distinction between the status of human law and that of higher norms. In considering human law as existing within a strictly this-worldly political perspective, he concentrated on human will and the attribute of coerciveness as the constitutive elements of such law. Indeed, it was only human law understood in these terms that Marsilius was willing to consider as being, properly speaking, law at all: other norms might share the name of law but in the context of this world were not in content truly law.[21] This applied in particular to divine law which he accepted as valid but only possessed of effect in the world to come.[22] Natural law he left to one side, rejecting the medieval tradition of considering it as a form of higher norm, and treated it instead as a kind of positive law (the general principles deducible from the laws of men).[23] It is misleading, however, to conclude that Marsilius adopted a purely positivist approach to human law. His view was that the human legislator would in the vast majority of cases enact laws suitable to

---

18. 'Non praesumatur causa inquantum vult [princeps saecularis] statuere contra ius divinum, quia non debet inferior violare statutum superioris sine causa aperta', ad X.1.2.7, n. 10: 1605, fol. 21r; 'Quando dubitatur an subsit causa auferendi quae mihi competunt de iure naturali, et tunc Cynus et communiter legistae tenent quod praesumitur pro principe quod iusta causa fuit motus . . . Hoc dictum videtur satis durum, et nullo iure aperte probatur . . . tamen in practica servaretur. Limitarem tamen istud dictum multipliciter. Primo ut non procedat, cum ipse princeps sit obligatus in his quae sunt de iure naturali puta ex suo contractu, alias de facili posset evacuare omnem contractum cum eo firmatum', *ibid.*, n. 14, fol. 21v.

19. 'Vbi non subest legitima causa veniendi contra ius positivum, princeps peccat illud violando', *ibid.*, n. 17, fol. 21v.

20. For the argument that Marsilius was a positivist see, for instance, Gewirth 1951, vol. I, pp. 134–6. For criticism of Gewirth's interpretation see Quillet 1970a, pp. 135 and 139.

21. *Defensor pacis*, 1.10.4.   22. *Ibid.*, 1.10.3.   23. *Ibid.*, 2.12.7.

the nature of the people and attuned to the realisation of the ends of the natural state, itself the product of natural reason: that is to say, peace and the good life.[24] He was, however, willing if necessary to accept the validity of objectively unjust laws.[25] Thus for Marsilius the essence of human law is positivist, the product of coercive command, but its content usually either has a moral quality or is morally indifferent. His overriding aim was to produce for human law an economical definition which would leave the determination of secular law in lay hands alone: through ignoring natural law in the traditional sense, locating the effects of divine law in the next world, and denying the validity of ecclesiastical jurisdiction itself, he felt he had removed the grounds upon which the clergy could claim to interfere in secular law and government. His attitude placed Marsilius apart from other late medieval writers including his fellow refugee at Lewis IV's court, William of Ockham, who, although he too sought to desacralise secular authority and law and to stress the spiritual aspects of ecclesiastical authority, nevertheless accepted in a traditional sense the structure of divine law, natural law, and reason as standards by which to assess positive law and government.[26]

The role of feudal custom

The normative limitations on the exercise of government and jurisdiction were not exhausted by the categories already discussed: late medieval jurists also treated feudal custom as existing on what was tantamount to the same fundamental normative level. It came to be accepted that feudal relationships, unknown of course in the *Corpus Iuris Civilis*, were the product of nature as the force for change in human life. Baldus in what came to be accepted as a truly influential commentary on the *Libri feudorum* considered that feudal custom amounted to nothing less than a day-to-day revelation of the natural law, [27] an aspect of the long-established juristic theme that custom was second nature (a derivation ultimately from Aristotle and Cicero).[28] This reveals how deeply ingrained feudal conceptions had become. The civilian, Guido de Suzaria (d. c. 1290), in a famous *quaestio*, now lost but also reported by Cynus, had established what became the *communis opinio* of the

---

24. *Ibid.*, 1.13.2.　25. *Ibid.*, 1.10.5.
26. See McGrade 1974, pp. 185, 190, 196, 211–12; Leff 1975, pp. 622–3; and Lewis 1954, vol. I, pp. 29 and 80–5.
27. 'Nam princeps est subiectus consuetudinibus feudorum tanquam sit ius naturale istius posterioris inventionis, quia ius naturale quotidie nascitur', ad Feud., 2.7: 1495b, fol. 36r.
28. Aristotle, *Nicomachean Ethics*, 7.10; Cicero, *De finibus bonorum et malorum*, 5.74. For the influence of the Aristotelian passage on medieval juristic thought see Kirshner 1979, pp. 193–4, and for that of the Ciceronian see Cortese 1964, vol. II, pp. 161–2.

Commentators, namely that the *princeps* was bound by his contracts and privileges which were guaranteed by the natural law and the *ius gentium*.[29] Amongst the Commentators the prime form that such contracts and privileges took was feudal: as Baldus said of the emperor in this connection, 'God subjected the laws to him, but he did not subject contracts to him.'[30] Furthermore the *princeps* was bound by his predecessors' feudal contracts and privileges, because these were not purely personal but made by virtue of the imperial office.[31] Feudal custom thus performed its function of protecting the rights of the subject against the ruler's whim: Baldus most notably accorded to the subjects' feudal rights a protection which he denied to their other property rights. Feudal custom therefore appeared as a fundamental ethical norm, and one which severely limited the sovereignty of the *princeps*.

The rights of the community

The remaining form of limitation on the exercise of the ruler's will was not on the same fundamental level as those already discussed, but was treated by fourteenth- and fifteenth-century jurists as having the status of a universally valid norm: the rights of the community, the *iura imperii* or *iura regni*. These jurists elaborated the established view of the role of the emperor or king as being an office or dignity with a specific function: the preservation or well-being of the empire or kingdom. This view recognised, therefore, the inalienability of the basic rights of the community which the ruler governed.[32] Canonist opinions were particularly important in the development of the idea of the ruler as procurator whose duty was not to damage the interests of the community in his care.[33] The ruler's duty of protection was institutionalised in the coronation oath, for the discussion of which Honorius III's decretal, *Intellecto* (X.2.24.33), remained the *locus classicus*.[34]

29. Cynus ad C.1.14.4, n. 7: 1578, fol. 26r. But see Cortese 1962, vol. I, pp. 155–9, for the argument that the text of the *quaestio* can be reconstructed. For a trenchant later expression of the *communis opinio* see Paulus de Castro, Cons. 1.318, n. 5: 1582, fol. 168r, 'Communiter doctores tradunt quod ibi etiam princeps contractum initum cum subdito tenetur servare et non potest venire contra de iure, etiam ex suprema potestate, quia faceret contra ius naturale primaevum, seu legem naturae . . . tale ius gentium seu naturale princeps ex suprema etiam potestate non potest tollere.'
30. 'Deus subiecit ei leges, sed non subiecit ei contractus', ad Feud., 1.7: 1495b, fol. 17v.
31. 'Licet princeps non ligetur lege legis, ligatur lege conventionis [C.1.14.4] per Cynum et [D.2.1.14]; ipse dico non successor, quia contractus principis non transit in successorem, quia successor non habet ab eo causam . . . quia ius non transit ad successorem, sed de novo creatur per electionem [X.3.5.25]. Et hoc verum nisi faciat ea quae sunt de natura vel consuetudine sui officii, sicut est infeudare', Baldus ad D.1.4.1, n. 2–3: 1616, fol. 26v.
32. Civilian discussions of the Donation of Constantine treat at great length the problem of the alienation of imperial rights involved in it.
33. See Tierney 1955a, pp. 117–27; also pp. 445–7 above.   34. See pp. 438–9 above.

Particular stress was given to the king's tutorial role, which neatly expressed his duty to conserve the kingdom's inalienable rights. Amongst the fourteenth-century civilians there can be no doubt that Baldus' treatment of kingship and its duties was the most profound and influential: for him the fundamental reason justifying the *iura regni* was that the kingdom was an immortal entity composed of free men possessing the capacity derived from the *ius gentium* to elect their ruler.[35] The individual and mortal king held his kingdom in trust for future generations.

The enforceability of the normative structure

The jurists, therefore, made a commitment to rulership as moral in execution and to the state as a body of right. Tyranny whether by the monarch or the people was universally condemned as infringing the *utilitas publica* which government was considered to have been instituted to achieve. Bartolus' exhaustive tract, *De tyranno*, was the major juristic contribution to this subject and ranks as one of the main treatments of the medieval period. But could the normative structure be enforced, or was it just a theoretical construction? Were the normative limitations merely pious hopes, or did the jurists consider that rulers could actually be controlled? There is evidence in their writings both for the sanctioning of resistance to the tyrant on the grounds that his rule is invalid and for pragmatic acceptance of a tyrannical regime for the fear of the possible disturbances involved in trying to remove him. No legal problem was seen in the removal of a tyrannical *signore* by his oppressed subjects. In the case of a king, however, greater circumspection appears: Baldus, for instance, accepted that a people could expel its king for tyranny, but that he still retained his royal dignity, that is his office.[36] Resistance against the emperor on the grounds of his tyrannical behaviour could be justified on rational

35. 'Rex non potest alienare populum suum nec dare ei alium regem, quia populus est liber, licet sit sub rege', ad D.V., Proem ad v. 'Quoniam': 1498b, fol. 1v; 'Quaeritur an hodie provincia possit sibi eligere regem? Et videtur quod non, nam provinciae sunt sub naturali dominio imperatoris, ergo non possunt conferre alicui merum imperium, in auth. "De defensoribus civitatum" § "interim" [Nov., 15, 1]. Sed tu dic, quod sic, si est talis provincia quae non subsit imperatori, ut Hispania. Nam si dominus Castellae deficeret in totum regnicolae possent sibi eligere regem de iure gentium, ut hic. Nunquid ergo iurisdictiones fuerunt introductae de iure gentium? Dic quod sic, quia rex significat se habere iurisdictionem; cum ergo de iure gentium fuerint reges, ergo et iurisdictiones', ad D.1.1.5: 1498b, fol. 7r. For the kingdom as an immortal entity see Cons. I.359: 1490 (= Cons. III.159: 1575), discussed below p. 475.

36. 'Quaeritur an regem propter iniustitias suas intollerabiles et facientem tyrannica subditi possint expellere? Et videtur quod sic . . . cum malus rex tyrannus sit . . . Contrarium est verum, quia subditi non possunt derogare iuri superioris; unde licet de facto expellant, tamen superior non amittit dignitatem suam', ad D.1.1.5: 1498b, fol. 7r.

grounds.[37] Baldus also accepted that the emperor could justifiably take up armed resistance against the pope if the latter broke the bond of feudal faith existing between them.[38] Those jurists who accepted the claim of the pope to ultimate superiority over the emperor supported the papal power to depose him for just cause. Although the emperor's role in suppressing tyranny remained basic amongst the civilians, those Commentators who accepted the sovereignty of some Italian cities did not put forward any practical means of controlling such cities' infringements of the normative structure: the emperor would be unable to curb them since, as these jurists considered, such cities had obtained their sovereignty precisely because of imperial absence and impotence. Amongst canonists and some but by no means all civilians, a form of universal power of judgement was reserved to the pope *ratione peccati*;[39] but for these civilians any such papal intervention in secular matters outside the lands of the church would be rare indeed and the product of an extreme crisis. Clearly juristic thought could only offer a limited enforceability for higher norms; but the jurists nevertheless considered such norms to have real value even if in practice they were usually unenforceable – a view far removed from any positivist theory rejecting the existence of norms which cannot be enforced.

The juristic theory of territorial sovereignty

Kings

Jurists first developed a theory of territorial sovereignty to accommodate emerging territorial monarchies. Indeed, late thirteenth- and fourteenth-century jurists were in this respect elaborating a theme which had been established from the end of the twelfth century and developed throughout the thirteenth by canonists and civilians in terms of the well-established conceptions of the sovereign king who does not recognise a superior in temporal matters, and who within his kingdom is the emperor of his kingdom.[40]

---

37. 'Notandum est ergo quod originalis intentio creationis imperii fuit bonum et utilitas rei publicae non privatae, puta Caroli imperatoris. Ergo si imperator in respublicas saeviret, excutere ab eo iugum tantae servitutis non esset contrarium rationi naturali', Baldus, Cons. III.283: 1491, fol. 88r (= Cons. I.333: 1575).

38. 'Et est alia ratio quia ecclesia debet vasallo vicem, et de suo imperio non potest eum [imperatorem] laedere. Immo papa se facit alienum a potestate si talem iustitiam non reddit imperatori qui iuravit fidelitatem . . . Et imperator potest se defendere cum exercitu suo', De pace Constantie, ad v. 'In nomine Christi membrum': 1495a, fol. 94v.

39. Cynus' reservations on this point were well-known: 'Ecclesia sibi usurpavit ratione peccati totam iurisdictionem', ad Auth., 'Clericus' (ad C.1.3.33), n. 1–2: 1578, fol. 18v.

40. These two conceptions were in origin distinct although they were soon very often combined: see Ullmann 1979a, p. 188 n. 48; also pp. 432–3 above.

To consider first the civilians in our period, there existed concerning the status of kings two traditions which were differentiated by their attitude towards the emperor. The first denied the universal sovereignty of the emperor, and through treating independent monarchies as being essentially on a par with the territorially restricted empire advocated thereby a plurality of territorially sovereign powers. The major expression of this view was to be found in the works of Neapolitan jurists, notably Marinus da Caramanico (d. 1288) and Andreas de Isernia (d. 1316). Oldradus da Ponte, who taught law at Padua, also maintained this thesis in his famous *Consilium*, 69, in which he justified King Robert of Naples' rejection of imperial overlordship. The kings of Sicily claimed in any case that their kingdom was outside the empire on the grounds that it was a papal fief, and had been won back from Islam by conquest. These jurists did not however consider that the kings' status as papal vassals resulted in any real infringement of royal sovereignty within the kingdom itself, but rather, with the Sicilian monarchy primarily in mind, produced a theory of territorial sovereignty which to a considerable extent possessed a wide application suitable for justifying the independence of kings in general. The fundamental and universal norm of the *ius gentium* was used to justify the sovereignty of kings within their kingdoms. Thus Marinus envisaged for the world a political history in which 'long before the empire and the Roman race from of old, that is from the *ius gentium* which emerged with the human race itself, kingdoms were recognised and founded'.[41] Indeed, he considered that the Romans had no universal right to empire because they had established their dominion through force of arms, so that the empire was essentially a merely *de facto* power: hence, with the contemporary shrinking of the empire's geographical extent, kingdoms were regaining their original rights under the *ius gentium*.[42] Oldradus denied that the Roman emperor was *de iure* lord of the world on the grounds that the Roman people, lacking themselves any just title to dominion over other nations, could not through the *lex regia* legally transfer any such authority to the emperor.[43] Indeed, he considered that the *ius gentium*, being a form of natural law, gave kings a juster title than that of emperors who derived

---

41. 'Longe ante imperium et romanorum genus ex antiquo, scilicet iure gentium quod cum ipso humano genere proditum est, fuerunt regna cognita, condita', *Super libro constitutionum*, Proem, 17 (ed. Calasso 1957, p. 196).

42. *Ibid.*, pp. 196–7.

43. 'Videndum est ergo qualiter [imperator] acquisivit dominium. Et ipse allegat quod habet causam a populo qui ei concessit, et in eum transtulit omnem imperii potestatem . . . Respondetur sic quod populus non potuit plus iuris conferre in eum quam habuit . . . sed populus non habuit de iure dominium super alias nationes, ergo nec ipse', Cons. 69, n. 7: 1550, fol. 24v.

theirs only from Roman civil law.[44] Marinus was willing to attribute to the
king of Sicily within his kingdom all the legal rights and powers which the
princeps possessed under Roman law, but he did this not on the basis of any
pretensions by the emperor, but insofar as it had been accepted by the
custom of the Sicilian people and given effect by the will of the Sicilian
monarchy which expressly appropriated elements from Roman law in the
Liber constitutionum.[45] The pro-Neapolitan *ius gentium* argument was clearly
a contribution to the theme of the *rex qui superiorem non recognoscit*.
For jurists who accepted that in some sense the emperor possessed universal
jurisdiction the other current formula for royal sovereignty, *rex in regno suo
est imperator regni sui*, essentially envisaged that the king enjoyed within his
kingdom the powers which the emperor possessed within the empire as a
whole – that is to say, it involved the notion of a still widespread rather than
restricted empire. Since the pro-Neapolitan argument denied such an
interpretation of the Roman empire, these jurists cannot strictly speaking be
seen as contributing to that interpretation of the formula: for them the
world was composed of a plurality of kingdoms with the empire being but
one territorial body amongst several. Thus Andreas de Isernia did indeed
attribute to a king in his kingdom the same power as the emperor possessed
in the empire; but he meant by this that a kingdom and the empire were in
essence the same kind of territorial body, and that the world had therefore
returned to its pristine condition before the conquests of Rome:

With cause another king will be able to do in his kingdom what the emperor can in
the land of the empire, which is small these days. In Italy he possesses only
Lombardy, and not all of that, and part of Tuscany; the rest belongs to the church of
Rome, like the kingdom of Sicily also. The first lords were kings as Sallust says . . .
The provinces therefore (which have a king) have returned to the pristine form of
having kings, which is easily done. Free kings have as much in their kingdoms as the
emperor in the empire.[46]

The other tradition among the civilians presented a complete contrast: it
was that of the mainstream French and Italian Commentators. They

---

44. 'De iure naturali primaevo, nec sunt regna nec imperium . . . De iure gentium quod etiam naturale
vocatur . . . de iure isto per occupationem distincta sunt dominia, et regna condita [D.1.1.5]. Et sic
cum de iure isto sint reges, et imperatores solum fuerunt de iure civili, quia per populum romanum,
ut infra patebit reges iustiorem titulum habent, cum a iure quodammodo naturali (quod divina
providentia constitutum est) semper firmum atque immutabile perseverat', *ibid.*, n. 5, fol. 24r.
45. Ed. Calasso 1957, 19, pp. 198–9.
46. 'Cum causa rex alius poterit in regno suo quod imperator potest in terra imperii, quae hodie modica
est. In Italia non habet nisi Lombardiam, et illam non totam, et partem Thusciae; et alia sunt ecclesiae
Romanae, sicut et regnum Siciliae. Primi domini fuerunt reges, ut dicit Sallustius . . . Redditae ergo
sunt provinciae (quae regem habent) formae pristinae habendi reges, quod de facili fit [D.2.14.27].
Liberi reges tantum habent in regnis suis quantum imperator in imperio', ad Feud., 2.56, n. 2: 1579,
fol. 286r.

retained the conviction that the emperor as *dominus mundi* possessed a *de iure* universal sovereignty. It was thus very difficult for them to accommodate the existence of territorially sovereign kings. The view of these jurists should therefore be seen as being distinct from that of the thirteenth- and early fourteenth-century publicists who, denying imperial sovereignty over France, had elaborated a theory of the *de iure* sovereignty of the French king in particular.

The early Commentators did not develop a theory of the sovereignty of kings, because they considered them to have, in comparison with the emperor, a merely *de facto* power. Sovereignty remained an essentially *de iure* authority. The only possible exceptions are Johannes de Blanosco and Guilelmus de Cuneo: it can be argued (but not conclusively) that they accorded to the king of France at any rate a *de iure* independence from the emperor.[47] The major jurists, however, of the School of Orleans, Jacobus de Ravannis and Petrus de Bellapertica, were only willing to attribute a *de facto* independence to the king of France. As Jacobus de Ravannis memorably said, 'Some say that France is exempted from the empire. This is impossible *de iure*. You have it in C.1.27.2, 2 that France is subject to the empire . . . If the king of France does not recognise this I do not care.'[48] Similarly, Cynus de Pistoia, who played a key role in familiarising Italian universities with the jurisprudence of the School of Orleans, followed Petrus de Bellapertica in allowing only a *de facto* independence to those who did not recognise the emperor's authority and thus showed themselves unworthy of his laws: the emperor would not demean himself by trying to impose his rule on such people, and thereby making his laws a laughing-stock.[49]

With Bartolus and Baldus, however, a great change of view emerged. It was fundamental to the structure of Bartolus' political thought that, while

---

47. See Meijers 1956–73, vol. III, pp. 192–3, and especially Guilelmus de Cuneo ad D.1.11.1, fol. 11v (Bodleian MS, Can. Misc. 472), 'Dico quod omnes tribuni erant sub rege Romano sicut omnes reges sunt hodie sub imperatore excepto rege Franciae qui non habet superiorem.'

48. 'Quidam dicunt quod Francia exempta est ab imperio; hoc est impossibile de iure. Et quod Francia sit subdita imperio habes . . . [C.1.27.2, 2]. Si hoc non recognoscit rex Franciae, de hoc non curo', ad D.V., Proem, fol. 2r, MS Leiden, d'Ablaing 2 (as quoted in Meijers 1956–73, vol. III, p. 192). C.1.27.2, 2 provides the *locus classicus* for the argument that the French and Spanish kings are subject to the emperor.

49. This was their understanding of the first words of *l. Cunctos populos* (C.1.1.1) – 'Cunctos populos, quos clementiae nostrae regit imperium' (*Codex*, ed. Venice, 1498, fol. 3r) – which invited the application of the *de iure–de facto* distinction to the relationship between the emperor and lesser rulers. Was 'quos' to be taken *declarative* thus signifying that all peoples were under the emperor's rule, or was it to be understood *restrictive* indicating that only his subjects were? Petrus (n. 3: 1571, p. 8) and Cynus (n. 3: 1578, fol. 1v) thus maintained that, whereas the emperor was *de iure* lord of the world, he had intended 'quos' to be taken in a restrictive *de facto* sense.

the emperor retained a genuine *de iure* sovereignty within the *terrae imperii*, other powers which in practice did not recognise a superior could obtain true sovereignty on a purely *de facto* basis. Bartolus in short recognised the facts of political life: such *de facto* authority was no longer mere power without legitimacy. Bartolus, as we shall see, developed this view with Italian city-republics primarily in mind. Despite his major discussion of certain aspects of monarchy in his tract, *De regimine civitatis*, he gave relatively little attention to kingship in the rest of his works. In consequence it was left to Baldus to apply to kings the Bartolist justification of *de facto* sovereignty. Baldus recognised that through custom, the prime expression of political reality, some kings were not subject to the emperor: thus he maintained that, whereas there still remained a *de iure* universal empire, it was in fact no longer whole because there were gaps in the spread of the emperor's jurisdiction where the sovereignty of territorial monarchies was operative.[50] There was in short a hierarchy of sovereignty, a seeming paradox which accurately reflected fourteenth-century conditions as viewed from Italy: north of the papal patrimony the emperor was accepted as an ultimate legitimising authority by bodies which were in practical terms sovereign. The purest expression of Baldus' *de facto* argument was his acceptance that in the fourteenth century free peoples could on the basis of the *ius gentium* still elect their monarchs. This is not to deny that both Bartolus and Baldus also accepted the theocratic aspect of kingship;[51] but it was their recognition of the fact of sovereign monarchies that was crucial.

In terms of canon law our period saw a major development as regards the theme of territorial sovereignty. Clement V's bull, *Pastoralis cura* (Clem., 2.11.2), which was issued in 1313, supported Robert of Naples' claims to independence against the imperial pretensions of Henry VII. Oldradus, who was acting as a legal advisor at the *curia* at Avignon, was highly influential in the drafting of this bull.[52] In *Pastoralis cura* Clement

---

50. 'Respondeo omnes sunt subiecti [imperatori] de iure, et merito; sed non omnes sunt subiecti de consuetudine; et peccant sicut Francigenae et multi alii reges . . . et licet regnum Francorum non sit de Romano imperio, tamen non sequitur, ergo imperium non est universale, nam aliud est dicere universale, aliud integrum', ad Feud., 2.53: 1495b, fol. 74r.

51. 'Omnis rex aut immediate a deo eligitur aut ab electoribus inspiciente deo . . . Et ex hoc nota quod regimen quod est per electionem est magis divinum quam illud quod est per successionem . . . Et ideo electio principis qui est rex universalis fit per electionem praelatorum et principum; non autem vadit per successionem . . . "Hoc" enim "imperium deus de caelo constituit" . . . Reges vero particulares sunt magis ex constitutione hominum, ut [D.1.1.5]', Bartolus, *De regimine civitatis* (ed. Quaglioni 1983, p. 166). See also Baldus ad X.1.29.38, n. 5: 1551, fol. 141r, 'Vbi tamen est rex ibi puto prius regem adeundum, cum in regno suo in temporalibus sit vicarius dei' (this passage concerns appeals from secular to ecclesiastical jurisdiction).

52. His Cons. 43 which considered general principles relative to Robert's case was requested by cardinals and is considered to have formed part of the basis for *Pastoralis cura*: Will 1917, pp. 20–51. Oldradus here concentrated on the position of the king who was 'non subditus imperatori'.

considered the kingdom of Sicily to lie outside the territory of the Roman empire, and thus held that Robert was free from imperial sovereignty insofar as he was king of Sicily. Thus the empire was treated as a geographically restricted territory: the emperor himself possessed a territorially limited sovereignty. Admittedly Clement stressed the king of Sicily's subjection to the Roman church: this can therefore be seen as an aspect of the theme of the hierarchy of sovereignty. What however was crucial was that the king, being considered to be free from any subordination to the emperor, had no secular superior. *Pastoralis cura* constituted the clear (one might say the official) abandonment of the high medieval papal conception of the universality of the Roman empire. The origins of the papal willingness to accept a territorially limited Roman empire can be traced back to *Per venerabilem* (X.4.17.13) in the light of which such a view could be seen as an implied corollary of recognising the fact of the French king's sovereignty in secular matters; *Pastoralis cura* however drew the full implications of this view of the empire and expressed it in a permanent form. Nevertheless the period between Innocent III and Clement V did not see a uniform canonist rejection of the universal sovereignty of the emperor. In the mid-thirteenth century, for instance, whereas Innocent IV maintained that the king of France was *de iure* independent of the emperor, Bernard of Parma held that the king was only so *de facto*.[53] Similarly, Boniface VIII in the midst of his dispute with Philip IV in turning to the emperor-elect, Albrecht I, had expressed opinions favouring the universality of the empire.[54]

Cities

A juristic theory of the sovereignty of city-republics was relatively late in emerging. It was the achievement of Bartolus to produce it, and his thesis, together with Baldus' creative treatment of this theme, constituted a major contribution to late medieval theories of popular sovereignty.

In treating Italian cities the Glossators had not developed a theory of the

---

53. Innocent IV ad X.4.17.13, n. 3, ad v. 'cum rex ipse superiorem in temporalibus minime recognoscat' (1570, fol. 481r), 'De facto, nam de iure subest imperatori Romano, ut quidam dicunt, nos contra, imo pape'; and Bernard of Parma, *ibid.*, 'De facto, de iure tamen subest Romano imperio' (as quoted in Meijers 1956–73, vol. IV, p. 213 n. 24). See above p. 363.

54. 'Vnde haec nota et dicta sunt quod vicarius Ihesu Christi et successor Petri potestatem imperii a Graecis transtulit in Germanos, ut ipsi Germani, id est septem principes quattuor laici et tres clerici, possint eligere regem Romanorum, qui est promovendus in imperatorem et monarcham omnium regum et principum terrenorum. Nec insurgat hic superbia Gallicana, quae dicit quod non recognoscit superiorem. Mentiuntur quia de iure sunt et esse debent sub rege Romano et imperatore . . . Iste enim rex [Romanus] praecellens super omnes reges et nullus est ab eo exemptus', *MGH*, *Leges* IV, *Const.* IV, 1, pp. 139–40.

sovereignty of independent city-republics: for them sovereignty remained with the cities' superior, the emperor. That some Italian cities did not recognise a superior had, however, been admitted by some Commentators before Bartolus: by Jacobus de Ravannis and Oldradus.[55] Furthermore, as we have seen, Petrus de Bellapertica and Cynus had referred generally but without approbation to *populi* who did not recognise the emperor's sovereignty. The canonist tradition, however, although it accorded considerable effectiveness to the law-making of cities, had not produced a theory of the sovereignty of cities to match its theory of the sovereignty of kings. The furthest that a canonist had been prepared to go is illustrated by Hostiensis who simply accepted, but certainly did not justify, Lombard cities' non-recognition of the emperor.[56]

It was Bartolus' achievement to take the leap to justifying the sovereignty of independent city-republics. He was able to do this because he fully appreciated the effectiveness of popular consent. He accepted that the will of the people could be a complete alternative to that of a superior. Developing the work of earlier Commentators Bartolus drew the full conclusions from the identification of consent as the constitutive element of both the people's customs and its statutes. His argument began from customary law. Custom, he held, being the expression of popular consent did not require a superior's authorisation. Since, however, custom as the product of the people's tacit consent, and statute as the product of its express consent, were of equal force (*paris potentiae*), the people's statutes also did not in consequence require the authorisation of a superior.[57] The exercise of consent in law-making led therefore to this measure of autonomy. Bartolus then took, however, the further crucial step of considering that the exercise of the people's consent could lead to the non-recognition of a superior, a fundamental sign of sovereignty. He considered that the *civitas quae superiorem non recognoscit* would be in the position of a free people, a *populus liber*. Bartolus then took the step for which he is most famous: he attributed

---

55. Jacobus de Ravannis ad C.7.33.12: 1519, fol. 344v, 'Hodie, vacante imperio, civitates regunt se ipsas; et una civitas regit se ipsam nec habet superiorem'; and Oldradus, Cons. 69, n. 6: 1550, fol. 23v, 'Sed si ius cuiuslibet civitatis consideremus, de illo non est dubium, quia multae civitates et reges fecerunt leges et constitutiones quod non subessent imperatori.'

56. 'Vnde et haec iura collegiorum, sive corporum, vigent in civitatibus potissime Lombardiae, quae etsi dominum habeant, ipsum tamen non, ut expediret reipublicae, recognoscunt, sicut nec rex Franciae', ad X.1.31.3: 1512, fol. 147r.

57. 'Quando populus habet omnem iurisdictionem potest facere statutum non expectata superioris auctoritate . . . Et quod isto casu non expectetur superioris auctoritas patet exemplo consuetudinis, quae inducitur ex tacito consensu populi et aequiparatur statuto in quo constat quod non requiritur superioris auctoritas', ad D.1.1.9, n. 4: 1577, fol. 9v; and 'Tacitus et expressus consensus aequiparantur et sunt paris potentiae', ad D.1.3.32, n. 4: 1577, fol. 17r.

to the independent city-*populus* within its territory the jurisdictional powers which the emperor possessed within the empire as a whole – it was a *civitas sibi princeps*.[58] Within Roman law terms this was the clearest way of showing the sovereignty of such cities, and was clearly an adaptation of the formula, *rex in regno suo est imperator regni sui*. Bartolus' concept was by no means an obvious one, because the city was a corporate entity whereas the transposition between king and emperor was straightforward since sovereignty in both cases inhered in the person of the ruler.

Bartolus' whole argument from consent was a prime example of his acceptance of the full legitimacy of *de facto* jurisdiction. His theory of the sovereignty of independent cities should, however, be seen in the context of that overall view which he shared with Baldus: the hierarchy of sovereignty. Cities indeed possessed a genuine sovereignty within their territories, but it was not the highest form, which in the *terrae imperii* was in secular matters possessed ultimately by the emperor, and in the *terrae ecclesiae* was in both secular and spiritual matters enjoyed by the pope (a view clearly accommodating the contention of *Pastoralis cura* that imperial jurisdiction in Italy was territorially confined). Furthermore according to Bartolus there existed side by side with cities' *de facto* sovereignty, gained through the exercise of consent, the parallel valid structure of *de jure* jurisdictional rights derived from imperial or papal concession. Bartolus, accepting the realities of Italian political conditions, considered the emperor to be a distant and ultimate legitimising authority; towards the end of Bartolus' life, however, imperial power became to some extent real in Italy during the visit of Charles IV in 1355. In the same period some attempt was made to reestablish papal power in the patrimony from 1353 onwards under Cardinal Albornoz. In the end, as is shown in his commentary on Henry VII's constitution, *Ad reprimendum*, which he produced after Charles IV's visit, Bartolus came to adopt a pro-papal and hierocratic interpretation of the relationship between papal and imperial authority, one by-product of which view was that he considered that the pope had an advantage in that he could cite in the *terrae imperii* whereas the emperor could not in the *terrae ecclesiae*.[59]

Baldus' theory of the sovereignty of independent cities can only be appreciated when seen in relationship to Bartolus'. Baldus certainly adopted

---

58. See, for instance, Bartolus ad D.4.4.3, n. 1: 1577, fol. 133r, 'Per statuta civitatum non possit concedi minoribus administratio bonorum suorum, quia hoc princeps reservavit sibi . . . Civitates tamen quae principem non recognoscunt in dominum et sic earum populus liber est . . . possent hoc forte statuere, quia ipsamet civitas sibi princeps est.' For similar passages from Bartolus see Woolf 1913, pp. 155–8.   59. Ad v. 'Per edictum': 1497, fol. 5r.

Bartolus' argument from consent, but appears to have had an even clearer understanding of the role of the people's will in the non-recognition of a superior: he saw that logically sovereignty in the Italian context could only derive from a *de facto* exercise of will rejecting the superior, and could not be derived from *de iure* concession by the superior.[60] Bartolus in comparison seems to have been a little less rigorous on this question, because on a couple of occasions he referred to cities' non-recognition of a superior 'de iure vel de facto'.[61] In another respect, however, Baldus appears more circumspect than Bartolus, in that he did not baldly describe the sovereign city as *sibi princeps* but as being in the emperor's place (*vice principis*).[62] After all, Bartolus' formula was strictly speaking elliptical because the people was not actually the *princeps*. Baldus did not mean that such cities were imperial vicars, but that in the *de facto* gaps in imperial jurisdiction such cities replaced the *princeps* as the bearers of sovereignty. If, however, the emperor were to be physically present in the city's territory, the gap would be closed up, and then, according to Baldus, the emperor's authorisation of city-statutes would be required: in this sense the emperor remained the ultimate sovereign.[63] But in normal circumstances this argument was irrelevant, because for Baldus the sovereignty of cities was the practical result of the emperor's political weakness and prolonged absence from Italy.

Where, however, Baldus clearly went beyond Bartolus' approach was in

---

60. Baldus does not refer to cities' *de iure* non-recognition of a superior. Typical of his approach is: 'Sed ut dixi civitates quae realiter superiores non recognoscunt et infiscant sibi regalia hoc habent de consuetudine et minime mutanda videntur quae consuetudinem certam semper habuerunt, supra [D.1.3.23]. Equanimiter tolleremus, quia non ipsi facimus. Sed de iure constat potestatem soli principi reservatam a civitatibus esse exemptam [C.10.32.19 & C.4.62.2] . . . Sed olim erat princeps auctoritatem et utilitatem publicae rei prospiciens; nunc vero non eadem fides est in principe nec in subditis, perempto enim seu mortificato nimis uno extremorum aliud extremum pati necesse est', ad D.1.8. Rubr: 1498b, fol. 36r.

61. 'Nota glossam quae dicit quod bona vacantia non applicantur alteri civitati sed fisco. Et verum dicit in civitatibus quae recognoscunt superiorem; sed in his quae non recognoscunt superiorem de iure vel de facto ut civitates Tusciae est ipsamet civitas fiscus. Vocatur enim populus liber', ad D.5.3.20,7, n. 2: 1577, fol. 167v; and 'Quaero utrum pro delictis civitas possit accipere bona? Glossa dicit quod non . . . Secus puto in civitatibus quae de iure vel de facto hodie non recognoscunt superiorem, et sic populus est liber', ad C.10.10.1, n. 7: 1577, fol. 8r.

62. 'Quaero quae aetas requiritur in iudicibus ordinariis, qui non sunt domini iurisdictionis sed administrationis? Respondeo, cum eligatur ab imperatore sufficit quaelibet aetas . . . Idem si eligatur a populo vice imperatoris, quia in territorio suo princeps est', ad X.1.29.41, n. 3: 1551, fol. 143; he says of independent Italian cities exercising originally imperial rights that they are peoples which 'vicem ergo et imaginem principis habent', Cons. II.49: 1490 (= Cons., IV.52: 1575); 'Civitas enim francha a superis concedere potest franchisiam inferis, quia vicem principis in suo gerit solio', Cons., V.406, n. 6: 1575, fol. 107r; and 'Ego quaero nunquid imperator possit facere statutum quod malefidei possessor praescribat? Quidam dicunt quod sic in suo foro . . . et idem possunt civitates quae habent fiscalia seu regalia, quia in suo territorio vice principis funguntur', ad X.1.2.13, n. 3: 1551, fol. 28v.   63. Ad C.1.14.8: 1498a, fol. 54v.

exploring more profoundly the source of human political association and government. Although Baldus was not the first jurist to have adopted the term, 'political man',[64] he does appear to have been the first to use the concept of an avowedly natural and this-worldly political dimension for man's activities: a view for which he was of course indebted ultimately to Aristotle.[65] This provided a philosophical context particularly suited to the *de facto* argument, which essentially accepted the political facts of man's life in this world. According to Baldus natural reason in the form of its product, the *ius gentium*, not only brought city-*populi* into existence, but endowed them with autonomous powers of self-government without the need for the authorisation of a superior: the foundation upon which the argument for their sovereignty could be built.[66]

Corporation theory and the territorial state

Fourteenth-century jurists, however, went beyond theories of territorial sovereignty: through their application of corporation theory to independent cities and kingdoms they made major and quite distinctive contributions to the development of the concept of the territorial state itself. Corporation theory permitted them to define more closely the nature of these territorial entities and to explore their structure of government.

The main contribution was made by Commentators who produced a complex conception of the city or kingdom seen as a corporation: it was at one and the same time a body composed of a plurality of human beings and an abstract unitary entity perceptible only by the intellect.[67] This was a clear

---

64. Amongst the early Commentators there developed a tradition of using the term, 'homo politicus', to indicate the subject-matter of jurisprudence: this appeared in the strikingly similar passages in the following jurists' commentaries on the Proem to the *Digestum vetus* – Guilelmus de Cuneo (Bodleian MS, Can. Misc. 472, fol. 1v – considerable variations are to be found in the text edited in Brandi 1892, p. 111), Cynus (Rome MS Urb. Lat. 172, fol. 8r, and Berlin MS Savigny 22, fol. 11v), and Albericus de Rosciate (n. 12: 1585, fol. 2v).

65. 'Tertio modo [homo] potest considerari prout est quoddam corpus civile seu politicum . . . Sed si consideratur in congregatione tunc homo naturalis efficeretur politicus, et ex multis aggregatis fit populus', ad C.7.53.5: 1498c, fol. 236r. Cf. *idem* ad D.1.3.2: 1498b, fol. 13v, 'Nota ibi, "naturalia et civilia", quod homo naturaliter est animal civile; et lex similis debet esse homini bene composito et civili': he adopts William of Moerbeke's translation of Aristotle's famous passage (ed. Susemihl 1872, p. 7).

66. 'Nota ergo quod populi possunt sibi facere statuta . . . Modo restat videre numquid in tali statuto requiratur auctoritas superioris. Et videtur quod non quia populi sunt de iure gentium ergo regimen populi est de iure gentium, ut supra [D.1.1.5]. Sed regimen non potest esse sine legibus et statutis. Ergo eo ipso quod populus habet esse habet per consequens regimen in suo esse, sicut omne animal regitur a suo spiritu proprio et anima', ad D.1.1.9: 1498b, fol. 9r.

67. For full details see Canning 1980a, pp. 12–14.

advance on the thought of the Glossators who had almost universally identified the corporation with its members, as, for instance, Accursius' famous formulation reveals: 'the corporation is nothing other than the men who are there'.[68] The Commentators, however, saw these human components not as mere isolated individuals (*singuli*), but as corporate men (that is, men seen specifically as united in a corporate whole): a view anticipated to some extent by Johannes Bassianus and Azo. The source for the idea of the corporation as an abstract entity can be found in the works of the Decretalists, certainly from Innocent IV onwards.[69] Commentators who identified the territorially sovereign city or kingdom as an abstract entity distinct from its members or government were, in taking this view, making a crucial contribution to the development of what is generally understood to be a hall-mark of the early modern concept of the state. Baldus, for instance, commenting on Accursius' definition of the corporation neatly showed how the two aspects of the city-*populus* as a corporation combined: it was a collection of men into a unitary entity understandable only by the intellect, a definition embracing both the abstraction and the men who formed the material basis for this abstraction.[70] The city-*populus* as a corporation acted through the medium of its physical members. Furthermore the city or kingdom viewed as a corporation was held to be immortal and in this way quite distinct from its human components.

By the constructive use of legal fiction these territorial states, conceived as abstract corporational entities, were understood to be endowed with legal personality: that is to say, these states as legal persons had legal existence and capacity distinct from those of their members. The Commentators thus developed Innocent IV's formulation that the corporation was a *persona ficta*.[71] Thirteenth-century jurists had invented the use of the term, *persona*, to denote a legal person: *persona* in that sense cannot be found in the *Corpus Iuris Civilis*, although Augustinian theological usage anticipated it somewhat in the identification of Christ as the *persona ecclesiae*.[72]

68. 'Universitas nil aliud est nisi homines qui ibi sunt', ad D.3.4.7: 1497, fol. 63v.

69. For Johannes Bassianus see Ullmann 1948b, pp. 80–1; and see Azo, *Summa aurea* ad C.3.13, n. 7: 1557, fol. 47r, 'Dat iurisdictionem ordinariam universorum consensus . . . Privatorum autem singulorum duorum vel trium, vel etiam plurium ex quibus non constituitur universitas, vel civitatis, vel castri, vel villae, vel burgi, vel gratia professionis, vel negotiationis consensus non instituit, nec facit iudicem.' For the Decretalists see above pp. 444–9; Paradisi 1973, pp. 120–2.

70. 'Nec obstat quod glossa dicit in [D.3.4.7] quod populus non est aliud quam homines, quia debet intelligi de hominibus collective assumptis, unde homines separati non faciunt populum, unde populus proprie non est homines, sed hominum collectio in unum corpus misticum et abstractive sumptum, cuius significatio est inventa per intellectum', ad C.7.53.5: 1498c, fol. 236r.

71. See Canning 1980a, pp. 15–24. 72. See Wilks 1963, p. 24, and 1972a, p. 258.

Bartolus gave the clearest treatment of the structure of government of the city-republics conceived as corporations: the general assembly of the people was understood to elect a council which acted as the governing body of the city, and in turn elected the city's officers.[73] Thus in his memorable phrase, 'The council represents the mind of the people.'[74] For both Bartolus and Baldus the abstract city-*populus* was deemed to consent and act through the instrumentality of its mortal members organised in a structure of councils and representative elected officials.[75] It was Baldus who produced the strikingly effective treatment of the government of sovereign kingdoms as corporations. For him the *regnum* could be identified with its members ('the nations and peoples of the kingdom themselves collectively are the kingdom'),[76] but it also, in the form of the *universitas* or *respublica regni*, possessed an abstract and perpetual aspect, which was distinct from them. This immortal corporation of the kingdom established an abstract and thus also undying royal office or *dignitas* which was operated by each individual as ruler in succession. This was a classic formulation of the theory of 'the king's two bodies': Baldus thus considered that the king housed two completely different kinds of person – his human mortal person and an abstract legal person (his *dignitas*). As Baldus said, 'The person of the king is the organ and instrument of that intellectual and public person; and that intellectual and public person is that which is the principal source of action.'[77] The king was therefore given the role of acting on behalf of the legal persons, the royal office and ultimately the kingdom itself.

Clearly in considering the territorial state as a corporation Commentators were making a specifically juristic contribution to political thought. Bartolus considered that civilians and philosophers had radically different approaches to the nature of groups, and that the legal fiction of the corporation had a specific and purely juristic function.[78] Bartolus was surely right in his judgement. The dissemination of Aristotelian ideas of the

---

73. The best modern discussion is Ullmann 1962, pp. 716–23.
74. 'Consilium repraesentat mentem populi', ad D.1.3.32, n. 10: 1577, fol. 17v.
75. See Canning 1980a, pp. 27–31.
76. 'Ipsae gentes regni et ipsi populi collective regnum sunt', Cons. 1.359: 1490, fol. 109v (= Cons. III.159: 1575).
77. 'Persona regis est organum et instrumentum illius personae intellectualis et publicae; et illa persona intellectualis et publica est illa quae principaliter fundat actus', *ibid.* This *consilium* provides all these details concerning the corporational theory of the kingdom and kingship. But see also Cons. 1.417: 1490, fol. 129r (= Cons. III.217, 1575); and Cons. 1.322: 1490, fol. 98r (= Cons. III.121, 1575); and his commentaries ad C.6.51.1,6 (1498c, fol. 152v), C.7.55.1 and C.7.61.3 (fol. 252v).
78. 'An universitas sit aliud quam homines universitatis? Quidam dicunt quod non, ut no. [D.3.4.7, 1], et [D.47.22.1] in fine, et hoc tenent omnes philosophi et canonistae, qui tenent, quod totum non differt realiter a suis partibus. Veritas est, quod si quidem loquamur realiter vere et proprie, ipsi dicunt verum. Nam nil aliud est universitas scholarium quam scholares; sed secundum fictionem

state had tended to result in an identification of the state with its members. Aquinas, for instance, had adopted this view: thus when he said, 'In civil matters all those who belong to one community are considered as if one body, and the whole community as if one man',[79] he did not mean to establish the community as an entity distinct from its members. It has, however, been argued that Marsilius considered the *universitas civium* to be a corporate entity distinct from individual citizens, but that he derived this view directly from juristic sources.[80] Ockham, in contrast, expressly rejected the jurists' *persona ficta* concept, because for him any group was identified with the human beings who composed it.[81]

The application of corporational concepts thus completed juristic theories of the territorial state in our period. Clearly considerable differences of juristic approach existed reflecting the variety of fourteenth- and fifteenth-century political conditions. For the reasons indicated these jurists can validly be considered to have enunciated theories of territorially sovereign states, although it should also be clear that in the strictest terms the sovereignty of such states was limited, not only because of the overall normative structure, but also because of the independence of ecclesiastical jurisdiction and the privileges of the clergy which all jurists in this period to a greater or lesser degree accepted, a vast subject outside the scope of this study.

iuris ipsi non dicunt verum. Nam universitas repraesentat unam personam, quae est aliud a scholaribus seu ab hominibus universitatis [D.46.1.22], quod apparet quia recedentibus omnibus istis scholaribus et aliis redeuntibus eadem tamen universitas est. Item mortuis omnibus de populo et aliis subrogatis idem est populus, et sic aliud est universitas quam personae quae faciunt universitatem secundum iuris fictionem, quia est quaedam persona repraesentata', ad D.48.19.16, 10, n. 3–4: 1577, fol. 200r.

79. 'In civilibus qui sunt unius communitatis reputantur quasi unum corpus, et tota communitas quasi unus homo', *Summa theologiae*, 1a 2ae, 81, 1.

80. See Wilks 1972a, especially pp. 254–6. For a rejection of this argument see Walther 1976, p. 162 n. 179.

81. See *Tractatus contra Benedictum*, c.8: 1956, p. 189.

16
GOVERNMENT

Sources

In order to discuss medieval theories of government one must first locate
them. There are very few medieval works whose avowed aim was the
examination in conceptual terms of current governmental problems.
Therefore the bulk of material has to be extracted from works that had
another purpose. But this at once creates uncomfortable choices. The
sources conventionally used by historians of political philosophy differ both
from those on which constitutional historians habitually draw and from
those appropriate for the investigation of medieval man's unspoken
assumptions about government. Yet all three have some claim to reveal the
'real' political thought of the age. And past studies suggest that they do not
blend easily.

Because it would be folly, in the space available, to attempt a complete
approach to the subject, this discussion will be limited both geographically
and conceptually to the examination of certain academic and official texts
on government produced in England and France between 1150 and 1450.
Concentration on England and France is justified by their strong cultural
and political ties throughout the later middle ages, and by a large stock of
common experience. Although by the end of the period their political
systems were often contrasted, they nevertheless remained more like each
other than either was like the Empire, Italy or Spain. The emergence of
powerful vernacular traditions, the loosening of the link between Paris and
Oxford universities, the growing sense of national identity, could not
totally erase the past they had shared.

The limit on texts chosen means abandoning the search for common
assumptions on government, as revealed in rituals, art or vernacular
literature. The spotlight is on what educated men chose to commit to paper,
and on its meaning within its historical background. Any political historian
will rapidly see that, if the problem had been tackled from the other end,
from the political facts to the underlying theories, the final structure,
though having many common components and even one or two identical

features, would have taken a very different shape. A political philosopher, on the other hand, will find the building far too concrete, huddling low on the earth, its bricks irritatingly commonplace.

Conceptualising about government did not come naturally to medieval men. They needed to be prodded into it by the requirements of an academic programme, by pastoral needs, by sudden passion or by the pressures of their employment in royal bureaucracy. To examine their ideas in a vacuum would be almost impossible, so disjointed are they, so much dominated by the literary context within which they were articulated – academic treatise, sermon, exhortation, propaganda or official pronouncement. The sorts of material used for illustration in this chapter can be roughly divided into two categories: the speculations of university-trained intellectuals, and the documents produced as an offshoot of the political process.

The first category comprises the vision of secular government conceived by theologians like John of Paris and William of Ockham in the course of their reflections on church–state conflict; *quodlibetic* discussions in the Paris theology faculty; Aquinas' political writings; commentaries on Aristotle's *Ethics* and *Politics*. Most of this work is highly abstract; its concern is with the validating principles of secular government rather than with its form; and the academic context dictates rather more of its content than is habitually allowed when it is excerpted for text-books of medieval political thought. This category also includes the means by which university-trained intellectuals often popularised at least a portion of their political ideas, the 'Mirrors of Princes' and the sermons. These sources will occupy a sizeable portion of this chapter because, though simplified, usually exhortatory and often crude, they commanded wide attention in their own day, and sometimes came near to bridging the gap between philosophical principle and contemporary political fact which is the sphere of political thought.

The second category is more heterogeneous. Perhaps its single most important constituent is the work of customary and common lawyers – Beaumanoir, Glanvill, Bracton,[1] Fleta and, on a more political plane, Fortescue – who strove to systematise, explain and defend the legal systems they knew, which could not be done without some political thinking. Then there are the avowedly publicist pieces, both defending and attacking royal government. Lastly, there are the one or two treatises on specific political issues – Christine de Pisan's *Livre de la paix*, or Oresme's *De moneta*.

---

1. In using the traditional titles 'Glanvill' and 'Bracton', there is no intention of attributing authorship to the king's justices of those names.

Each of these kinds of material has often been examined – and strictly speaking perhaps only should be examined – in its own right, with its problems of interpretation highlighted, its own developing tradition traced. To draw on all these genres for illustration inevitably involves a scissors-and-paste approach, with no certainty that the final outcome will not illuminate rather the mind of its rash proponent than the ideas of the time. But equally, intense specialisation is necessarily myopic. And there is consolation to be found in the fact that most medieval political thinkers were themselves adept practitioners of the art of pastiche. They would have understood the attempt.

States

The first difficulty that faces a modern reader of medieval political literature is the absence of a precise abstract noun to convey 'state', an indispensable concept to all modern political thinking. It was not until the end of the fifteenth century that *status* was first used with its modern connotation.[2] Before that, authors had the choice of *res publica* (necessarily vaguer and a less rich concept than in the time of Cicero), *regnum* (easily manageable, but with several different connotations[3]) or *civitas* (derived from Aristotle but liable to confuse in a world in which city government was usually a subordinate part of the political whole). All could, but need not, denote that combination of a precise territorial area with a form of political organisation which 'state' implies for us.

Political organisation was usually conceived in a surprisingly simple and conservative form. Surprisingly, because the chief feature of English and French government in these three centuries was the appearance and rapid development of bureaucratic administration, both central and local. Yet this has left little trace among theorists. Only Peter of Auvergne, in his *Quaestiones* on Aristotle's *Politics*, appreciating the importance of magistracies in Aristotle's thinking, envisaged an administrative unity composed of a supreme magistrate assisted by numbers of independent but subordinate judges and magistrates, binding by their activities the nobles and people into a whole.[4] Incongruously, he supported this picture not by contemporary experience, but by reference to Proclus' unity-plurality theme, known from *De Causis*, which was fashioned to explain relationships in the pantheon of pagan gods. Peter's highly academic *Quaestiones*

2. Guenée 1967, pp. 17–18.   3. Wood 1967, pp. 22–3.
4. Paris Nat. Lat. 16089, fols. 299v–300r.

(unlike his literal commentary) were not widely known. Other commentators on the *Politics* made little use of Aristotle's magistrates and judges to provide an institutional framework. For most of them, political relations were best discussed in personal terms.

So they, like most other political writers, concentrated on political organisation within its time-honoured unit, the people. Buridan, in his commentary on the *Politics*, revamped the traditional Ciceronian definition of *res publica* with an Aristotelian term, defining it as 'a people joined by consent in the law and in the common utility'.[5] Here he found an abstract way of expressing what was in other men's minds when they used the famous organic image of the body politic to which all medieval intellectuals were drawn like pins to a magnet. (Christine de Pisan's *Livre du corps de policie*[6] was the most long-winded and popular exposition of what had, since John of Salisbury's time, become the standard cliché.) It mattered to its later medieval users that the mutual inter-dependence of the parts of the body militated against tyranny as much as against rebellion. The subordination of the parts to the whole, clearly implied in any use of the image, could be vividly stated:

Depraved is the part that does not conform with its whole, and useless and quasi-paralytic a limb that refuses to support its body. Laymen or cleric, nobleman or man of low birth, whoever refuses to come to the support of his head and his body, that is, the lord king and the kingdom of France and lastly of himself, proves to be a non-conforming part and a useless and quasi-paralytic limb.[7]

Jean de Terre Rouge, in his tract *Contra rebelles suorum regum*, took the analogy further by arguing that the supporters of the duke of Burgundy were but putrefying members of the French body politic, and that they ought therefore to be amputated for the health of the whole.[8] In pictorial terms, it was rather harder to apply the image as a means of subordinating the head; but it could be done. In 1327, Bishop Stratford preached before the assembly convened to ratify Edward II's deposition, on the text *caput meum doleo* – my head pains me. After listing Edward's failings, he called on his hearers for support in the radical step just taken. The body was to provide itself with a new head.[9] Flexibility of application, therefore, as well as vividness, explained the popularity of organic imagery.

---

5. Ed. Turner 1640, p. 248.   6. Ed. Lucas 1967.
7. Dupuy 1655, p. 21; quoted Kantorowicz 1957, p. 258: 'Et quia turpis est pars, quae suo non congruit universo, et membrum inutile et quasi paralyticum, quod corpori suo subsidium ferre recusat, quicumque, sive clerici sive laici sive nobiles sive ignobiles, qui capiti suo vel corpori, hoc est domino regi et regno, imo etiam sibimet auxilium ferre recusant, semetipsos partes incongruas et membra inutilia et quasi paralytica esse demonstrant.'
8. Ed. Bonnaud 1526, fol. 51r.   9. Fryde 1979, p. 199.

Its drawback remained the old one, that it could be applied to any cohesive group of people, whatever the nature of their bond. Therefore the more scholarly of its users were anxious to find some means of defining more closely a people as a unit of political organisation, to give the term relevance to what they knew by experience. Inevitably, they cast their glance backward to the classical past. Although at first Aristotle's city state looked an unpromising model, his opinion that the natural political unit was one in which self-sufficiency could be attained was swiftly appreciated. Giles of Rome in *De regimine principum* opened a fruitful discussion by pointing out that, if a city could provide for a man's needs, a kingdom could cope even better, especially with defence. A kingdom therefore constituted the ideal unit.[10] There was a problem here in that Giles' argument might be taken one step further, to favour the subordination of kingdoms to a larger entity – in traditional terms, the Empire. Dante was not the only thinker to see in one world community the perfect means of keeping peace. To combat imperialist claims, John of Paris contended that, since coercive jurisdiction was a necessary characteristic of all rule, practical considerations ruled out universal monarchy, because it could not but be ineffective in coercion far from its nucleus of power.[11] He added the general principle that differences in climate and physical make-up would be better accommodated in a diversity of states. Later, Nicole Oresme, fighting partly against imperialist pretensions, but also and with greater heat against the English claim to the throne of France, took John's point to its natural conclusion in his commentary on the *Politics*, when he argued that geographical, racial, temperamental and customary differences between people were enduring features of society; any kingdom which attempted to transcend these natural boundaries was therefore unnatural.[12] This contention implies a rather more modern view of a nation-state than might perhaps be expected in a fourteenth-century writer. A land with geographically marked limits, inhabited by a people of common language, custom and temperament, was now clearly recognised as the proper political unit. The theoretical difficulties that had clouded perception of states were now removed.

In practice, the intertwining of a politically organised community with a defined territorial area had already occurred. In England, where geographical frontiers (except in the north) were long-established, where the theoretical unity of the realm went back to the mid-tenth century, the concept of an English nation to the eighth, the centralisation of Henry I and

10. III.i.5: 1556, fol. 243r.   11. *De potestate regia et papali*, iii: 1942, pp. 180–1.
12. Ed. Menut 1970, p. 291.

Henry II supplied the missing ingredient. By the twelfth century, a state might be thought to exist. In the minority of Henry III, the body politic achieved a clearer form in the *communitas regni*, that group of the politically significant – king, prelates, barons – which represented the people as a whole, and which achieved institutional focus in the regular meetings of the Great Council, later to be expanded into Parliament. In France, the process occurred later. Prepared for by the conquests of Philip Augustus and Louis VIII, a sense of French cohesion grew throughout the thirteenth century, acquiring new force and territorial definition in the reign of Philip the Fair.[13] The simultaneous subordination, in theory at least, of the feudal principalities to the kingdom in matters of law, and the expansion of royal bureaucracy within the demesne, provided the sinews that bound the whole together. The body politic was envisaged in the conjunction of king and three Estates, the aristocratic warriors, the clergy and the common people. From the second half of the fourteenth century onwards, this body politic could have institutional focus in the Estates, but they were never necessary to its being.

Simple states therefore antedated both the vocabulary for describing them and a satisfactory conceptual framework in which they could be discussed. As with so many other aspects of medieval political thought, it took time for the intellectuals to appreciate what had happened, to pick out some organic bodies from others, to fix on what proved to have been the significant developments in recent experience. And, as had been said, they never in the middle ages appreciated fully the bureaucratic or administrative developments of their own time.

Kingship

Theories

A political community cannot be conceived without its means of resolving internal frictions, its directive force. As dispenser of justice and represser of evil, the medieval ruler had coercive jurisdiction over his people; as guide to the end for which the state was ordained, he disposed of moral authority which could command obedience. The first aspect of the ruler's rule had been that to which Gregorian reformers had attempted to confine kings: it remained central to the thinking of papal propagandists, and of such very different writers as William of Ockham[14] and Fortescue. The second

13. Guenée 1967.   14. McGrade 1974, p. 127.

aspect, standard opinion in Carolingian times, enjoyed a revival under the influence of Aristotelian teleology. *Gubernare* – to steer – joined *regere* and *imperare* as verbs to describe royal authority. 'To rule is to lead something to its appointed end'[15] – Giles of Orleans neatly expressed the standard Aristotelian view. Ruling acquired once more its positive moral function, the identification and fostering of the common good, a function which the good ruler automatically fulfilled for his people, in which the grateful subject equally automatically concurred and assisted. St Thomas Aquinas dwelled on this theme in his *De Regno: ad regem Cypri*[16] and it became a commonplace in sermons and exhortations addressed to kings.

It was assumed that the function of the ruler demanded unity in operation: 'It is clear that that which is itself a unity can more easily produce unity than that which is plurality.'[17] But there was no logical reason which required that the ruler be a king rather than a group of men. Yet a constitution without a king was of little practical interest to French and English thinkers, who found it easy to defend their prejudice. The analogy between God's rule in the universe and the king's rule on earth sprang easily to the minds of pious men,[18] as did the whole medieval tradition of the king as God's vicar.[19] There was philosophical support in Aristotle's statement (*Ethics* VIII, 10, 1160b) that monarchy was the best form of government. Besides, a king could be fitted neatly into the organic image, usually, following John of Salisbury, as the head, occasionally as the heart[20] and at least once as the arm[21] of the body politic. Their identification of rulers with kings strongly disposed medieval writers to take a Platonic line in political thought, to see the character of the state as determined by that of its ruler. (This principle was clearly enunciated by Philip the Fair's lawyers in 1289.[22]) Rulership became, above all, an ethical act. A king aimed to become virtue personified.

The consequences can be seen in Giles of Rome's *De regimine principum*, which was written for the young Philip the Fair, probably between 1277 and 1279. Giles' blend of the traditional 'Mirror of Princes' style with maxims from Cicero and Isidore, the new Aristotelian ethical and political

---

15. Paris Nat. Lat. 16089, fol. 216v: commentary on Aristotle's *Ethics*.
16. Also known as *De regimine principum*.
17. Ed. Spiazzi 1954a, p. 259: 'Manifestum est autem quod unitatem magis efficere potest quod est per se unum, quam plures.'
18. Aquinas, *Summa theologiae* I, qu. 103, art. 3. *De regno* ed. Spiazzi 1954, p. 272.
19. See eg. Rivière 1926, appendix VI, pp. 435–40.
20. Peter of Auvergne *Quaestiones*, fol. 299v.   21. P.S. Lewis 1965, p. 107.
22. Digard 1936, vol. II, p. 265: 'Innuit ratio civilis et naturalis quod qualitas status membrorum est a qualitate status capitis regulariter praesumenda.'

teaching, and a smattering of Roman law, swept the board. It enjoyed wide circulation in Latin among the learned, was translated into all the major vernaculars of western Europe,[23] and, even more significantly, it penetrated into the libraries of men in government.[24]

In Giles' eyes regal regimes, where the will of the ruler dominates, are fundamentally different from political regimes, in which the ruler is constrained by human laws and conventions. Political regimes, because they involve an element of constraint, are less natural and therefore less good than regal ones (II.ii.3: 1556, fol. 173v; III.ii.3: 1556, fol. 270r and v). Within the latter category, true monarchy is sharply distinguished from despotism by the fact that the despot rules in his own interest, while the king rules for the good of his people. It is this that gives legitimacy to royal rule and permits the king's subjects to serve him willingly, to obey him freely (III.ii.6–7: 1556, fols. 276r–277r). To carry out his appointed tasks, the king must be the guardian of justice (III.ii.1: 1556, fol. 267r), and therefore have control of coercive jurisdiction (III.ii.27: 1556, fols. 311v–312r). More importantly, he must dictate the norms of society; the king is the archer, the people the arrow he directs to its appropriate end (III.ii.8: 1556, fol. 278v). This task he performs by establishing good laws for his people; so essential is his legislative function to his office that 'The law is a sort of inanimate ruler; the ruler is a kind of living law' (I.ii.12: 1556, fol. 48r).[25] Nevertheless in legislating he must take counsel (III.ii.19: 1556, fols. 298v–299r); after this his laws will accord with the natural law, with the common good and with the character of his people (III.ii.6: 1556, fols. 309v–10r). In so far as their dictates embody natural law, the laws will bind the king (III.ii.29: 1556, fol. 315r); but since their character is universal, while the king in his capacity of judge deals with particulars, he must be above the laws in order to tailor them to circumstances and act with equity (III.ii.29: 1556, fol. 315v).

Since the king is completely just, he can be trusted with much power (III.ii.3: 1556, fol. 270r; III.ii.11: 1556, fol. 291r). All privilege and honour derive from him (III.ii.15: 1556, fols. 290v–1r); the choice of councillors is his (though Giles warns against lawyers) (III.ii.18: 1556, fols. 295v–7r; II.ii.8: 1556, fol. 183v). His duties are to keep peace at home (III.ii.1: 1556, fol. 266v), to defend against foreign enemies (III.ii.8: 1556, fol. 279v), to encourage learning (III.ii.8: 1556, fol. 278v), to prevent sedition among his magnates (III.ii.15: 1556, fol. 290v), to make himself loved by his people

23. Berges 1938, pp. 320–8.   24. Jones 1968, p. 144.
25. I.ii.12: 1556, fol. 48r: 'Lex est quidam inanimatus princeps; princeps vero est quaedam animata lex.' Cf. Aristotle *Politics* III, 13, 1284a, and Carlyle 1903–36, vol. I, p. 69.

(III.ii.36: 1556, fol. 326v) and to fulfil his religious obligations (III.ii.9: 1556, fol. 281v). In a nutshell, in his qualities, powers and duties, the king is *quasi semideus* (III.ii.15: 1556, fol. 291v).

What are we to make of this? Obviously there is an element of the utopian. Giles' kingdom would have something in common with Philippe de Mézières' orchard of peace:

These people lived so happily together that they never seemed to grow old. All tyranny and harsh rule was banished from the garden, though there was a king who stood for authority and the common good, and he was so loved and looked up to that he might have been the father of each and all.[26]

But Giles' ideal king – a mixture of the Roman lawyers' 'public person' and the Aristotelian supremely virtuous ruler – was created for a practical purpose: to galvanise the young heir to the French throne, the future Philip IV, into recognition of his heavy responsibilities. Giles' moral lesson to him was that 'No one rules rightfully unless subject to the dictates of right reason'[27] (III.ii.29: 1556, fol. 314v), a conclusion which perhaps rang somewhat threateningly in the ears of its earliest audience.

Even apart from its popularity, it would be unwise to dismiss the *De regimine principum* as a piece of utopianism untypical of its age. What strikes the modern reader as serious imprudence – Giles' belief that the just prince's powers should be unlimited – was echoed by other writers. And if Christine de Pisan, Jean de Terre Rouge and Jean Juvenal des Ursins may all have known Giles' work, other writers arrived at the same conclusion independently. Buridan in his commentary on the *Politics* pointed out that since the king's power was for the common good and for his subjects' good, it should not be limited.[28] William of Ockham, though he certainly shared Aristotle's doubt that there were men of sufficient virtue for the post in his own day, nevertheless expanded at length the concept of the supremely good ruler ruling by will alone, described as a 'right and well-balanced' (*recta et temperata*) constitution.[29] Neither comment was simply a gloss on the Aristotelian text; each suggests agreement with the principle. And for Walter Burley at least, Aristotle's *pambasileus* was no mere abstraction; he existed in the person of King Edward III of England, through whose

---

26. Ed. Coopland 1975, p. 54: 'Les habitants du dit vergier en si grant joye vivoient l'un avec l'autre, qu'il leur sembloit qu'il n'en veillissoient point. Toute tyrannie et crueuse seignourie estoient banies du vergier, et toutesfoiz il y avait un seigneur et roy du dit vergier qui representoit la seigneurie et la chose publique des dessusdiz habitants, et estoit tant amez et reveraument doubtez, comme s'il fust pere a chascun habitant.'

27. III.ii.29: 1556, fol. 314v: 'Nullus recte principatur nisi agat ut recta ratio dictat.'

28. Ed. Turner 1640, p. 186.   29. Ed. Goldast 1614, pp. 794–5.

goodness social harmony prevailed to such an extent that 'It seems to each man that he rules in and with the king.'[30] Rarely was the medieval notion of representation more clearly expressed.

If many thought it was safe to confer power on the just king, others considered it also desirable, because in the strength of the king lay the protection of his subjects. Glanvill gave sonorous expression to a widely held view of the king as the people's shield.

> Not only must royal power be furnished with arms against rebels and nations which rise up against the king and the realm, but it is also fitting that it should be adorned with laws for the government of the subject and peaceful peoples; so that in times of both peace and war our glorious king may so successfully perform his office that crushing the pride of the unbridled and ungovernable with the right hand of strength and tempering justice for the humble and meek with the rod of equity, he may both be always victorious in wars with his enemies and also show himself continually impartial in dealing with his subjects.[31]

Here the influence of Justinian's rescript is clear.

Glanvill's words were closely linked to the tradition which saw the king above all as a legislator, a view of increasing relevance in western Europe during the late twelfth and thirteenth centuries, as kings moved to define and shape customary law. Like the Roman lawyers, practising English and French lawyers derived the right to legislate from the duty of keeping the peace: 'None dare contravene a royal ordinance made for the sake of peace', declared the author of the *Dialogus de scaccario*[32] in the reign of Henry II. Across the Channel, more than a century later, Beaumanoir saw much the same connection.[33] From it, he inferred that since the power to make decrees derived from the people's needs, it must be limited by them: therefore royal decrees must have reasonable cause, be for the common profit, be the product of extensive counsel and contravene neither God's will nor good habits.[34] Beaumanoir's terminology, the context of his discussion, was very different from Giles'; yet the two views were remarkably similar.

---

30. MS Oxford, Balliol College, 95, fol. 184r: 'videtur [cui libet] quod in rege et cum rege conregnat'.
31. Ed. Hall 1965, p. 1: 'Regiam potestatem non solum armis contra rebelles et gentes sibi regnoque insurgentes oportet esse decoratam, sed et legibus ad subditos et populos pacificos regendos decet esse ornatam, ut utraque tempora, pacis scilicet et belli, gloriosus rex noster ita feliciter transigat, ut effrenatorum et indomitorum dextra fortitudinis elidendo superbiam et humilem et mansuetorum equitatis virga moderando iusticiam, tam in hostibus debellandis semper victoriosus existat quam in subditis tractandis equalis iugiter appareat.'
32. Ed. Johnson, Carter and Greenway 1983, p. 101: 'Nec enim est qui regiae constitutioni, quae pro bono pacis fit, obviare praesumat.'
33. Ed. Salmon 1899–1900, sections 1043, 1510. See Wood 1967, p. 131.
34. Ed. Salmon 1899–1900, section 1515.

If the king of the lawyers was a legislator, could he be bound by law? On this, Bracton had much to say, though his words are hard to interpret. Like Giles, he emphasised the reciprocal relationship between king and law: 'The king must not be under any man, but under God and under the law, because law makes the king. Let him therefore bestow upon the law what the law bestows on him, namely rule and power. For there is no *rex* where will rules rather than *lex*.'[35] He went on to emphasise that no man could lawfully coerce the king – against whom no writs ran – but that the king had a duty to bridle his own discretion, to accept the law as an obligation laid on him by God. Again, the wording is different from Giles', the tone is more theological; besides there is the clear implication that the king is bound to the whole of the law, not just to that part which is directly based on divine and natural law (for the significance of this see below pp. 505–6). But like Giles, Bracton believed that kings could dispense from the law[36] and could improve, though not nullify, existing laws.[37] Both Giles and Bracton were close to Aquinas' view that the ruler, although not free from the directive power of the law in the judgement of God, was free from its coercive restraint, and above the law in the sense that he could change or dispense from it.[38]

The dispensing power that meant so much to Giles and Aquinas was largely justified in terms of *epieikeia*, the Aristotelian virtue (Nicomachean Ethics v,10, 1137b) by which law could be corrected if inequitable in a particular case. Commentators on the *Ethics* saw it as a resort of natural law to remedy the deficiencies of positive law;[39] since it could be assumed that the intention of the legislator was the common good, if, in a particular case, adherence to the letter of the law would be harmful, the ruler could override it in the interests of preserving the spirit. So *epieikeia* accommodated, in the more legalistic later middle ages, that flexibility of judicial process which had strikingly characterised earlier feudal society. And now that its use was restricted to the ruler, the case for resort to royal judgement was powerfully reinforced.

But if the king could appeal to natural law and the common good over the head of positive law in certain circumstances when acting as judge, had he similar freedom in other fields? Beaumanoir was in no doubt that the king could override normal rules in emergencies – famine, war or even the

35. Ed. Thorne 1968, vol. II, p. 33: 'Ipse autem rex non debet esse sub homine sed sub deo et sub lege, quia lex facit regem. Attribuat igitur rex legi, quod lex attribuat ei, videlicet dominationem et potestatem. Non est enim rex ubi dominatur voluntas et non lex.' See also p. 484 above.
36. *Ibid.*, vol. II, p. 306.   37. *Ibid.*, vol. II, p. 21.
38. *Summa theologiae* I IIae, qu. 96, art. 5.   39. Paris Nat. Lat. 16110, fol. 263r.

erection of important public buildings.[40] In canon law and in an extension
of *epieikeia* lay the origins of *necessitas* – necessity knows no law – which
provided kings with grounds for imposing unaccustomed taxes or
unusually heavy services. The doctrine was to have a long and distinguished
future. But its medieval exponents, unlike Machiavelli, always maintained
the extraordinary character of emergency powers: abuse was both irrational
and sinful.

For those who discussed it, government by the perfect prince was
quodammodo quid divinum (*De regimine principum* III.ii.7: 1556, fol. 277r), in
some way divine. What pleased this prince had the force of law,[41] because
he could not will anything that was not rational and useful. His discretion
was unlimited because there was complete confidence that it would be used
only for the common good. If it ceased to be so, then he was no longer king
in the true meaning of the word. As a consequence it was possible to argue,
as Wyclif did,[42] that a king of this kind was more tightly bound to his
people than they to him.

Applications

As an image, the perfect prince had immediate visual appeal. To
intellectuals, its attraction lay in its blending of legal and philosophical
traditions, and in its compatibility with the Christian tradition of the king as
God's vicar. Yet common sense might suggest that such an ideal could have
had little practical significance. That men of action could exploit a theory
which assumed that kings were rational by definition – or, to put the same
point differently, which saw the king's conscience as an effective bridle on
his misuse of unlimited power – would seem as inherently improbable as
that the same men might equate their king with a long-dead Roman
emperor. Yet those who were prepared to do both were not merely ivory-
tower academics or flatterers at court.

In France, the identification of the perfect prince with the successors of St
Louis was a vital constituent in the political cement with which royal
propagandists and preachers strove to bind the infant French nation.
Admittedly, the academic tradition here was only one thread in a rich cloth
of myth and reinterpreted history, created by the St Denis historiographers
and by the Joachite prophets,[43] as also by lesser men who recited the royal
healing miracles, or dwelled on the Trojan origins of the royal house, or

40. Ed. Salmon 1899–1900, section 1510.   41. Ulpian. See pp. 46, 431–2 above.
42. Ed. Pollard and Sayle 1887, p. 79.
43. Spiegel 1977; Guenée 1964, pp. 347–50; Reeves 1969, pp. 320–31.

honoured Clovis as the first Christian king and St Louis as his worthy successor. Nevertheless, works like Christine de Pisan's *Livre des fais et bonnes moeurs du sage roy Charles V*[44] enriched popular conceptions by presenting Charles as the ideal. Because she wrote not only to provide a model for future kings, but also to raise public morale at a time of crisis, Christine purveyed the courtly ethic to a wider readership.

Kings were happy to exploit these traditions on their own behalf. Philip the Fair's lawyers spoke of the king as being above human statutes, although bound to respect equality between Christians, justice and equity.[45] Charles V especially understood the value of identifying himself with the philosopher's prince; by patronage of scholars, enthusiastic legislation and lavish counsel-taking, he projected a relentlessly paternalistic image. It was characteristic that his reforming ordinance of 1379 should declare his intention of protecting his subjects from grief and oppression and relieving their injuries.[46] On top of this, he fleshed out the notion of the prince as *quasi semideus* by claiming the 'religious order of royalty' which Carolingian and Ottonian emperors had taken for granted, but which their successors had played down in response to ecclesiastical pressure. And if the king restricted himself to this, some at least of his subjects imputed sanctity to him.[47] By breaching conventional barriers between the sacred and the secular, Charles took his appropriate place at the head of the French nation, earlier extolled by Philip the Fair's lawyers as the chosen of God, the new race of Israel.[48] The holy king and the holy nation together were seen as forming a 'mystic body politic', a counterpart for the church, traditionally thought of as a 'mystic body'.[49] Reinvigorated and sanctified in this way, France and its king could return to the war with England, determined to wipe out the defeats of Crécy (1346) and Poitiers (1356).

The corollary of elevating kingship was requiring the subjects to submit. On the whole, French intellectuals accepted this. Even the moderate Gerson declared that to resist the king was to resist the divine ordinance.[50] But while Christine de Pisan put powerful religious sanction against any form of disloyalty or disobedience,[51] Jean de Terre Rouge, writing at a time of critical danger for the crown, insisted that infidelity be firmly punished on this earth by the action of men. All disobedience or rebellion was from thenceforth to be considered the crime of *lèse majesté*.[52]

44. Ed. Solenden 1936, 1940.   45. Digard 1936, vol. II, p. 261.
46. *Ordonnances des Roys de France*, vol. VI, pp. 442–3.
47. Bloch 1973, pp. 80, 122–3. Cazelles 1982, p. 570.   48. Strayer 1971, pp. 306–14.
49. Kantorowicz 1957, pp. 218–20.   50. Ed. Glorieux 1968, p. 1140.
51. Ed. Willard 1958, book III, ch. 10.   52. Ed. Bonnaud 1526, fol. 74v.

The philosopher's and preacher's righteous monarch moved in parallel with the Roman lawyers' *princeps*, the emperor reincarnate, the public person. This figure constituted a persuasive model for the royal advocates who defended the king's interests by assimilating him with the Roman emperor as and when they found it convenient for their purposes. Quoting from Roman law, they strove to give substance to the more concrete aspect of the perfect prince, his great authority. From their adept juggling with their sources, there emerged a royal *superioritas* which touched on the modern doctrine of sovereignty (though it was often used comparatively rather than absolutely). It boiled down to the twin ideas that there was no right of appeal beyond the king in matters of law; and that, within the kingdom, no one could legitimately dispute his control over temporalities.[53] Ironically, since many of the advocates' victories were won at the expense of the papacy, it was a papal decree – *Per Venerabilem* of 1202 – that offered a jumping-off point in their offensive. Unbothered by the context of Pope Innocent III's words, or by the subtle distinctions with which canonists had interpreted it, the *gens du roi* fastened on the phrase 'Since that king recognises no superior in his temporalities . . .',[54] to assert the jurisdictional independence of the king of France from the emperor, to deny the papal claim to tax the clergy and (most importantly) to establish that the nature of royal power was decisively different from that wielded by any other count or duke within the realm of France. Philip the Fair's battle cry in 1297:

The control of the temporalities of his realm belongs to the king alone and to no one else. He recognises no one as his superior in it, and in things pertaining to the temporal administration of the realm he is not bound, nor does he propose, to subordinate or subject himself in any manner whatsoever to any living man[55]

was the start of a relentless pushing of theory to its limits. Its implications were spelled out by Plaisians in the Gevaudan case of 1305:

Everything which lies within the frontiers of his kingdom belongs to the lord king, at least in respect of protection and high justice and lordship and even in respect of the proprietorship of each and every thing which the lord king can give, receive and consume for the sake of the public good and for the defence of the realm.[56]

53. David 1954, p. 69; Strayer 1971, p. 261.
54. 'Cum rex ipse superiorem in temporalibus non recognoscat . . . .
55. Dupuy 1655 *preuves*, pp. 27–8: 'Regimen temporalitatis regni sui ad ipsum Regem solum et neminem alium pertinere, neque in eo neminem superiorem recognoscere, nec habere, nec se intendere supponere vel subiicere modo quocumque viventi alicui, super rebus pertinentibus ad temporale regimen regni.'
56. Strayer 1970, p. 44 n. 125: 'Omnia quae sunt intra fines regni sui sint domini Regis, saltim quoad protectionem et altam jurisdictionem et dominationem et etiam quantum ad proprietatem

An abstract *superioritas* had here been translated into a theory of almost irresistible power.

Plaisians' claim represented the extreme. Usually the king and his advocates were satisfied with very much less – with incontrovertible authority, not overweening power. Of course the two were not easily separated. When the royal advocate in 1491 stated that the king's authority was greater than his advocates could express, the point of the argument was to prevent discussion over the royal prerogative.[57] Authority thus protected growing power. But no medieval king of France could have entertained a Hobbesian view of sovereignty, for the simple reason that in the three centuries which spanned the reigns of Philip Augustus, St Louis, Philip the Fair, Charles V and Charles VII, the weakness of the French crown was striking. That this was evident at the time was seen in the bishop of Mende's advocate's dry reply to one of Plaisians' more extravagant claims: 'Whether the lord king is emperor in his kingdom or not, whether he can command land, sea and the elements, and whether if he orders it the elements will be calmed, are questions best left to the royal advocate.'[58] To coerce his great men into obedience was rarely either possible or expedient; normally the king had to negotiate on much more down-to-earth terms than his advocates' speeches would suggest. Yet the gap between theory and practice did not mean that theory was valueless. The regular repetition of claims to supreme authority contributed at least some flesh to the skeleton. And when, by the end of the Hundred Years War, authority was joined by greater power, the basic elements had been provided for Bodin's theme.

As to the relevance of the more philosophical aspects of perfect kingship to the facts of life, what matters to the historian is how far Charles V's views penetrated into the popular consciousness or coincided with the opinions of a wider political circle. On this, clear evidence is lacking. The most vocal protagonists of perfect kingship wrote after the battle of Poitiers or during the Anglo-Burgundian struggles, when anyone might be forgiven for regarding blind adherence to a semi-divine monarch as the sole means of avoiding disaster. Even so, men like Gerson and Commynes did not subscribe to it. Yet the fact that the image proved enduring is surely suggestive of its sentimental appeal.

omnium singularum rerum . . . quas dominus Rex donare, recipere et consumere potest, ex causa publicae utilitatis et defensionis regni sui.'

57. P.S. Lewis 1968, p. 35.

58. Strayer 1971, p. 301 n. 2: 'Porro utrum dominus rex sit imperator in regno suo vel non, et utrum possit imperare terrae et mari et elementis et si obtemperarent ipsa elementa si eisdem imperaret, responsio advocato regis relinquatur.'

Since Fortescue's time, the perfect prince and his regal regime has been thought of as non-English. Yet although the prevailing political climate was different, there was a significant current of opinion in England that held French views, even on the king as healer and quasi-priest;[59] and these beliefs were enhanced by the ancient coronation ceremony. While all kings were happy to make capital out of these traditions, there were dangers in enunciating the more philosophical aspects of untrammelled kingship. According to the *Song of Lewes* (1264), admittedly a far from unbiased source, Henry III annoyed his subjects by voicing the opinion that complete freedom of choice was intrinsic to royal power.[60] Richard II's alleged belief that 'the law is in the breast or mouth of the king'[61] formed one of the grounds for his deposition. In abdicating, Richard was forced to renounce 'the royal dignity, the majesty, the crown, also the lordship and power, rule and governance, administration, empire, jurisdiction and the name, honour, regality and highness of the king',[62] a formula which may suggest that his opponents uneasily shared at least some elements of his elevated vision of kingship.

The legal aspects of sovereignty were best exploited, not by failures like Henry III and Richard II, but by Edward I, the father of the English Parliament – though admittedly he chose to enforce his sovereignty principally at the expense of his neighbours, the Welsh and the Scots. The Statute of Wales, which imposed English law upon the conquered country, showed him as an imperious legislator. His claim to overlordship in Scotland was couched in terms like those used by Philip the Fair's lawyers.[63] And in proceeding against David of Wales and William Wallace Edward reinterpreted treason – once simple plotting to kill, or killing, the king – to cover rebellion or warring against the king.[64] When this change in the law was applied within England, the king was raised to a legal category far above that of his lords, since his person and interests were now protected by terrible sanctions; while the ancient baronial right of *diffidatio* (renunciation of allegiance) now stood to be equated with rebellion. The savagery of fourteenth-century politics owed much to this change.

Though the fourteenth and fifteenth centuries saw the rapid development of Parliament, there were still elements of unfettered royal prerogative in the English legal system, as Fortescue admitted. In *De natura legis naturae*, he specified as rights which no king should abandon discretion

59. Bloch 1973, pp. 56–61, 122–3.   60. Ed. Kingsford 1890, lines 489–92.
61. Chrimes and Brown 1961, p. 189.   62. Chrimes 1936, p. 6.   63. Stones 1965, p. 108.
64. Bellamy 1970, pp. 23–58.

(particularly in criminal matters), equity, the dispensing power and the special emergency powers.[65] Here he conformed both with learned opinion and with the facts of life, as the existence of the prerogative courts made plain. Not all Englishmen were hostile to prerogative. The poet Langland exhibited some warmth for kingship above the law as the proper remedy for aristocratic ambition and for the corruption of common law;[66] and after the Wars of the Roses a wider public concurred. But the political problem lay in the integration of these extraordinary royal rights into a system largely based on other principles. While many agreed with Wyclif that 'Although . . . the king may dispense with the execution of the law in a particular case, as if superior to his own law, he may never do so unless reason so requires',[67] consensus on what reason did require was harder to achieve.

Tyranny and resistance

To return to theory: since untrammelled kingship is justified by the supremely virtuous character of the ruler, does an imperfect prince forfeit his right to rule? Academics, permitted by their craft to indulge in black-and-white thinking, often equated a backslider with a tyrant, so destroying his moral, though not necessarily his legal, right to rule. But how was tyranny to be defined? The charge was by no means confined to secular rulers; Grosseteste employed it against the Archbishop of Canterbury, Jean Petit against the duke of Orleans, Jean de Terre Rouge against the duke of Burgundy. Tyranny was sometimes carefully distinguished from despotism, as by Ockham and Buridan; usually it was seen as the same thing. Oresme offered three different ways of recognising it: a tyrant might be one who altered the coinage;[68] one who ruled over unwilling freemen as if they were slaves;[69] or one who aspired to possess greater power than that wielded by all the people of his realm put together.[70] Jean Petit equated tyranny with treason.[71] Gerson's despairing cry that the charge was so vague it could be levelled against anyone[72] was the simple truth. The shudder 'tyrant!' produced in its audience was too handy an ally for the offence to be clearly defined.

Because the tyrant's rule was in his own interest, not that of his subjects,

65. Ed. Clermont 1869, vol. I, pp.28–30.   66. Baldwin 1981, pp. 15–20.
67. Ed. Pollard and Sayle 1887, p. 57. 'Quamvis autem rex dispensare potest in casu cum executione legis tanquam superior lege sua, tamen numquam nisi quando dispensabilitatis ratio hoc requirit.'
68. Ed. Johnson 1956, p. 47.   69. *Ibid.*, p. 42; ed. Menut 1970, p. 52.
70. Ed. Menut 1970, p. 241; Johnson 1956, p. 24.   71. Coville 1974, p. 212.
72. Ed. Glorieux 1963, p. 423.

he forfeited the right to unthinking obedience – though Aquinas pointed out that tyrannical law could still command some obligation in so far as it shared characteristics with ordinary law.[73] The Aristotelian message that tyranny was the most unstable of regimes fell on willing ears, because it simply reinforced everything on which preachers had been insisting since the Carolingian period: kings could not afford to take chances; tyranny was dangerous.[74] But the knottier problem was whether Aristotle, in saying that tyrants would be overthrown, meant to imply that they *should* be. Peter of Auvergne's influential literal commentary on the *Politics* suggested that he did. According to Peter, where there was just cause and sufficient strength to carry it out, it might even be sinful to refrain from rebellion.[75]

But how could this be reconciled with the traditional patristic teaching that resistance was justified only as an alternative to breaking the divine law? The patristic view had adherents all through the middle ages, and was given a more up-to-date form in the later fourteenth century in Wyclif's *De officio regis*.[76] The dilemma was serious. Aquinas avoided it in *De regno* by postulating that where the tyrant was not the supreme power in the state, he could be removed by his superior.[77] In *Summa theologiae*[78] he faced the issue more squarely: his conclusion was that the overthrow of tyrannical government might be accomplished without mortal sin – of which the tyrant himself was guilty – provided that the consequences of the overthrow were more favourable to the community than the continuance of tyranny. These highly circumspect words offered little easy comfort to potential rebels, since they required the outcome of rebellion to be predicted before the question of moral justification could be tackled. Yet *coups d'état* were not completely condemned. The same chink of light might be detected in Gerson's sermon *vivat rex*.[79] As Gerson saw it, subjects had a duty to obey their king: normally, resistance was not just seditious but sacrilegious. Yet, though the proper way to combat tyranny was by persuasion, in the last resort perhaps it might be met with force. Since there was a mean between dissimulation and sedition, subjects had some rights.

The caution with which overthrowing governments was discussed meant that tyrannicide met with almost universal disapproval, despite the backing it derived from Cicero and John of Salisbury. Wyclif admittedly mentioned it among the rights of liegemen,[80] but in a work arguing in the

---

73. *Summa theologiae* I IIae, qu. 92, art. 4.   74. Aquinas, ed. Spiazzi 1954a, pp. 270–2.
75. Ed. Spiazzi 1951, 714, p. 247.   76. Ed. Pollard and Sayle 1887, pp. 9–22.
77. Ed. Spiazzi 1954a, p. 264.   78. IIa IIae qu. 42, art. 2.
79. Ed. Glorieux 1968, pp. 1137–85.   80. Ed. Pollard and Sayle 1887, p. 201.

main for complete submission. Only Jean Petit and Jean de Terre Rouge embraced it, and they against dukes not against the king. Besides, their aim in defending tyrannicide was to prevent further revenge killing, not to incite others to murder. Even so, Jean Petit's assertion that assassination could be laudable met with Gerson's outspoken denunciation, largely because Petit encouraged individuals to act outside the processes of law.[81]

The concept of tyranny was employed above all in exhortatory literature as a means of persuading kings of their duty. Predicting unpleasant consequences on earth and thereafter for those who slipped from the paths of justice was the chief preoccupation of the high-minded. Oresme was merely unusually pointed in his reference to Jean II when, totally condemning alteration of the coinage, he declared:

Whoever . . . should in any way induce the lords of France to such tyrannical government, would expose the realm to great danger and pave the way to its end. For neither has the noble offspring of the French kings learned to be tyrannous nor the people of Gaul to be servile; therefore, if the royal house decline from its ancient virtue, it will certainly lose the kingdom.[82]

Jean Juvenal des Ursins elaborated the theme in his sermon *Loquar in Tribulatione* by holding the king responsible for the tyrannical acts of his servants.[83] So the king became not only the victim of his own self-seeking but also of royal weakness, of his inability to control his ministers. It was a harsh doctrine. The effect of such preaching on royal behaviour cannot be measured, since there is no means of establishing how kings would have comported themselves in its absence. But it has been argued that they were sensitive to it.[84]

To denounce tyrannical behaviour is a long step from condemning a king as a tyrant, far less invoking sanctions against him for lapsing into that state. In practice, the French never took this step. (Jean de Terre Rouge's tract suggests that it may have been contemplated in 1419.[85]) The English, when they deposed Edward II and Richard II, scrupulously refrained from employing tyranny as the justification in the official documents which explained it (though there were certainly accusations of tyranny in unofficial sources). And, needless to say, tyrannicide was not invoked to

81. Coville 1974, p. 446; ed. Glorieux 1963, p. 423.
82. Ed. Johnson 1956, p. 47: 'Quicumque ergo dominos Franciae ad huiusmodi regimen tyrannicum quoquo modo traherent, ipsi regnum magno discrimini exponerent, et ad terminum praepararent. Neque enim regum Franciae generosa propago tyrannizare didicit, nec serviliter subici populus gallicus consuevit. Ideo, si regia proles a pristina virtute degeneret, proculdubio regnum perdet.'
83. Ed. P.S. Lewis 1978, p. 312. See P.S. Lewis 1965, pp. 116–17.
84. Brown 1972. 85. Ed. Bonnaud 1526, fol. 17r.

cover the murder of either king; the terrible deeds were hurried over in silence. So the highly circumspect teaching of academics on resistance to tyranny was not of much importance to men of action.

In practice, the commonest justification for overthrowing a government in this period was the age-old one, that another claimant to the throne had a better title. This allegation left the royal position intact, confining the dispute simply to the question of its proper holder. So Edward III's claim to the French throne provided Robert d'Artois and Jean de Montfort with a means of expressing their grievances against the house of Valois; Richard of York's claim to the English throne in 1459 marked the disintegration of loyalty to Henry VI and his ministers. The only scope for propagandists here lay in phrasing their lord's justification in cogent or emotive language.

But there was another, newer ground for resistance which owed more to the intellectuals. When the image of the perfect prince, the public person, was projected against that of the king in the flesh, human weaknesses became all too plain. The contrast provided baronial opponents with a case for deposing kings in the interests of preserving kingship. So, in 1327, Isabella and Mortimer forced the abdication of Edward II on grounds of his 'insufficiency' to govern;[86] seventy-two years later, Richard II's *inhabilitas et insufficientia* was cited in the commission of abdication.[87] In order to prevent theorising about who was competent to make such judgements (though see below, p. 517) Edward and Richard were both forced or persuaded to concur in the decision. The neatness of this solution to a political problem lay in its avoidance of extremism. A charge of tyranny would certainly not have received the kings' assent, and might well have proved counter-productive by dividing baronial opinion. Even so, the events of 1399 were so contentious that future English insurgents eschewed the precedent. Interestingly, the French version of the same doctrine, employed by Charles VI in his attempt to disinherit his son for incapacity, was seen to be abortive when it ran into the powerful opposition of Jean de Terre Rouge and his adherents.[88] Distinguishing between the king as he was and the king as he ought to be went out of favour after this. But the English stand of 1327 had its impact on political philosophy in the writings of William of Ockham (see below, p. 517).

Theoretically, a better means of dealing with royal inadequacy would have lain in an elective monarchy. All those who considered the question philosophically could see that, in principle, election (in the sense of free choice) was more likely than inheritance to produce a man of the calibre

86. Chrimes and Brown 1961, p. 37.   87. *Ibid*, p. 185.   88. Ed. Bonnaud 1526, fol. 16v.

needed for the job.[89] However, experience of imperial elections moved almost all of them to prefer hereditary succession; a preference justified by a series of largely unconvincing abstract arguments, the most cogent of which was perhaps that it was conducive to the subjects' continuing obedience. Few followed the path of Godfrey of Fontaines in asserting that no hereditary monarch could legitimately claim the powers of Aristotle's *pambasileus*.[90] The consequences of his belief will concern us below (p. 514).

In practice, hereditary succession was not a clear-cut issue. When the good fortune which had nurtured heirs for the Capetian dynasty for three centuries finally died out in 1316, the accessions which followed necessarily involved an element of election, since title was contested. Nicole Oresme took account of this in contending in the 1370s that the best system of promotion to kingship was an initial election, followed by succession within the family, according to customary rules.[91] His argument was carefully framed to boost the Valois, who could purport to have been elected, against the English, whose succession would have breached what Oresme regarded as a customary rule, the exclusion of women from the throne. The rather different circumstances in which Jean de Terre Rouge wrote half a century later led him to stress the prevention of irregularities in hereditary succession within the chosen family: because primogenital succession was so deeply rooted in the custom of France, so firmly accepted by the three Estates, it could not legitimately be interrupted.[92] Jean's view consorted well with the sacrosanct character which now clothed the French monarch. So, after the brief instability of the early fourteenth century, the net effect of the Hundred Years War was to create a new rigidity in French succession laws, a deeper concern with legitimacy, with the rights of blood. Only the acclamation of the people at the coronation survived as a reminder that election had once had some significance.

The English succession was clearly less stable than the French in the later middle ages. Yet from the minority of Henry III, hereditary primogenital succession was upheld as the rule of the kingdom with a consistency at variance with the facts. The most conspicuous interruption in succession, the accession of Henry IV, was managed so as to minimise the strain on conventional theories; this later laid the Lancastrian line open to challenge on the ground of legitimacy because Henry, in steadfastly refusing election, had insisted on designation by God as his title.[93] The potential for elective

---

89. Dunbabin 1965, pp. 68–9.   90. Ed. Hoffmans 1932, p. 76.   91. Ed. Menut 1970, p. 109.
92. Ed. Bonnaud 1526, fols. 17–18. But for Gerson's different treatment of this, see below pp. 517–18.
93. Wilkinson 1939, p. 231.

monarchy, evident in Stephen's accession and upheld in Hubert Walter's sermon at John's coronation, was never developed. Each departure from hereditary succession was justified individually, without modifying the general theory. From the baronial point of view, the drawback to elective monarchy was that it demanded from them a clear view on a man's competence to rule before there was an opportunity to judge by experience. They preferred *ad hoc* remedies to such responsibility.

Kingdoms

The discussion thus far has been focused with laser-beam intensity on the king's noble character, on account of the bulk of the literature devoted to the topic and the coherence with which it was discussed. It was, after all, the simplest way of solving political problems, and one fully backed by the Platonic tradition; it accorded with the conviction that politics was a branch of ethics; it had dramatic appeal; and the king's servants, at least, were paid to propound it. Besides, though it seems with hindsight more than a little simplistic in approach, it was partially justified in that, even in an increasingly bureaucratic administrative system, the king's personality remained a decisive force for good or ill. Yet more thoughtful men, and those deeply involved in political life, realised that the king could not properly be isolated from the rest of the body politic, that no human individual could bear the weight of responsibility assigned to him. A broader view of political life must be taken. But in abandoning the simple approach, medieval thinkers also lost the clear answer. Their thinking on more difficult problems has the character of ordinary light – it is diffuse, spreads widely, is blocked by obstacles, casts shadows and merges into obscurity. As a consequence, it is hard to describe.

Crown

The first of the wider contexts within which the king was viewed was that of the crown. This abstraction, originating from a distinction between the king's private lands and those of the fisc, came to encompass all those royal rights and powers which were inherited and must be passed on intact to the next generation. Because 'crown' characterised the enduring nature of monarchy, it was associated with the realm as a whole, in the phrase *corona regni*, in common use by the mid–twelfth century. This association bestowed on the crown an emotional leverage greater than that which most individual kings could command, as Philip Augustus recognised when, in a letter to the chapter of Rheims appealing for military aid against the Flemish in 1197, he asked for assistance *tum pro capite nostro, tum pro corona regni defendenda* (for the defence of my person and of the crown of the kingdom).[94] The later thirteenth-century poet Richier went so far as to claim that Frenchmen ought to love and adore the crown as much as holy relics; those who died on its behalf would by this very death be saved.[95]

As the lawyers saw it, 'crown' was a bundle of rights, the royal prerogative, royal jurisdictional rights, financial powers, as well as lands and wealth, which must be maintained intact against the claims of any other party, and even against the foolish liberality of the king himself. *Fleta* (c.1290?) recounted the significant legend that in 1275 the kings of Christendom met at Montpellier, to declare that prescription was to be invalid against royal rights, and that previous alienations made by rulers in prejudice of royal rights and crown lands were also to be held invalid.[96] This legend provided a foundation on which to build a distinctive notion of royal – as opposed to seigneurial – power. Clearly, the restriction on alienation seriously limited crown patronage (though it did not apply to all regalian rights or all royal lands); yet the principle of inalienability could be an excellent royal ally. Henry III used it in the Dictum of Kenilworth, clause 6, to resume all rights and pleas lost to the crown during the period 1258–65. Charles V similarly extricated himself from the limits to his jurisdiction imposed in the Treaty of Bretigny. And imprescriptibility was a necessary step on the path to jurisdictional sovereignty.

Yet the more lawyers exalted the crown's legal attributes, the more they subordinated king to crown. In France this became evident in the early fifteenth century, with Jean de Terre Rouge's argument (framed to protect the dauphin against Charles VI's Burgundian and English alliance) that individual kings were mere usufructuaries of crown property, with far fewer rights over it than ordinary heirs to patrimonial inheritance.[97] Kings were thus in the process of being hedged by what the sixteenth century was to term 'fundamental laws'. It is nonetheless significant that the restrictions were meaningful only in relation to crown rights and resources. And if there was a watchdog to enforce them, it was *Parlement*, the king's own ministers; yet even *Parlement*'s powers in the matter were open to question. Jean Juvenal des Ursins advised his brother, the new chancellor, that if the

94. Ed. Delaborde, Petit-Dutaillis and Monicat 1943, vol. II, no. 566, pp. 115–6. Quoted Kantorowicz 1957, p. 340.   95. Bloch 1973, p. 141.
96. Ed. Richardson and Sayles 1953–72 vol. III, p. 12. See Riesenberg 1956, p. 4.
97. Ed. Bonnaud 1526, fols. 10, 11.

king required him to seal a letter alienating the royal demesne, he might prevaricate or cajole, but in the last resort must fulfil the king's order.[98] There was still some way to go before *Parlement's* clear 1489 declaration that king and council were subject to its authority.

In England, the matter had a different dimension. Although political advantage dictated much inconsistency in the use of the term 'crown', even kings were willing to concede that crown rights might be the proper concern of the *communitas regni*. Edward I stated to the pope that he 'was bound by oath to do nothing that touches the diadem of this realm without having resorted to the counsel of the prelates and magnates'.[99] And Bishop Grandisson gave more constitutional expression to the doctrine when he declared that: 'The substance of the nature of the crown is found chiefly in the person of the king as head and the peers as members . . . and especially of the prelates.'[100]

Herein lies a main theme of English constitutional history, a contributing factor to the political conflicts of the later middle ages. For if the *communitas regni* had a legitimate interest in the crown, could it force an unwilling king to take cognisance of that interest? This was the question which lay, at least formally, at the heart of the 1311 conflict. The Ordainers justified their limitation on royal power in these terms: 'Through evil and deceptive counsel our lord the king and all his subjects are dishonoured in all lands and in addition the crown is in many respects reduced and dismembered.'[101] Edward II, in his moment of triumph after the Battle of Boroughbridge, hastened to rebut the claim that the magnates might on their own initiative defend the crown by declaring in the Statute of York of 1322:

After this any manner of ordinances or provisions made at any time by the subjects of our lord the king or of his heirs by whatever authority, concerning the royal power of our lord the king or of his heirs or against the estate of our said lord the king or of his heirs or against the estate of the crown, shall be null and of no sort of validity or force.[102]

There were two ways of looking at this issue: as the Ordainers saw it, they were only acting to subordinate an erring king to the obligations imposed

---

98. Ed. P.S. Lewis 1978, p. 446.   99. Kantorowicz 1957, p. 362.

100. Ed. Hingston-Randulph 1897, vol. II, p. 840: 'Que la substance de la nature de la corone est principaument en la persone le Roi come teste, et en les Piers de la Terre come membres . . . et nomeement des prelats.'

101. Chrimes and Brown 1961, p. 11: 'Par mauvais consail et deceivaunt nostre seigneur le roi et touz les soens sont en totes terres deshoneurez et estre de la coronnement des pointz abaissee et demembree.'

102. *Ibid.*, p. 32: 'Desore james en nul temps nule manere des ordenaunces ne purveaunces faites par les suggetz nostre seignur le roi ou de ses heirs, ou contre lestat de la coronne, soient nulles et de nule manere de value ne de force.'

by the crown; but in so doing they risked the accusation that they had separated the king from the crown. In fact, the baronial opposition to Gaveston *had* committed this fault in 1308, when it made the famous protestation that since vassals owed allegiance to the crown, not to the king, they might on occasion constrain the king.[103] Later the magnates scrupulously refrained from such dangerous words. Yet all baronial oppositions from the beginning of the fourteenth century laid themselves open to the charge of 'accroachment' of royal power, a charge which only made sense when the crown was seen as a bundle of inherited sovereign rights and powers open to usurpation. Accroachment, however, could also be twisted to include usurpation of royal rights by favourites, which crime the Lords Appellant in 1386 identified with treason. The political ramifications of the belief that the crown was in some sense public property brought about a sharp reaction at the end of the century. When Bishop Stafford addressed the Parliament in 1397 on the text 'One king shall be lord of them all', he thundered that 'the power of the king lay simply and wholly in the king, and they who usurped it or plotted against it were worthy of the penalities of the law'.[104] And the Lancastrians, after their coup, were as anxious as Richard had been to stress the personal nature of royal power.

Though the conflicts which surrounded 'crown' were central to English political history, nonetheless the concept of royal powers as in some sense a public possession solidly reinforced the structure of the English state, giving it a co-ordination which was lacking in France.

Counsel

A second way of broadening the perspective on monarchy, and one which followed logically from the first, was to see the king and his councillors as together constituting the ruling body: for it was the public character of royal authority which necessitated counsel at every stage in the political process, especially in the acts of legislation and taxation. Even thinkers like Giles of Rome, who stressed the king's unlimited discretion, insisted on counsel, so that the king could be sure of acting aright. Christine, in her heroic portrait of Charles V, accounted it to the king for righteousness that, as an act of grace, he took counsel even from the townsmen and the poor.[105] To the modern mind, Charles' action merely underlines the propagandist element in counsel-taking; it was something to be seen to be indulging in,

103. *Ibid.*, p.30.
104. Rolls of Parliament 3, p. 347, quoted A. Tuck 1973, pp. 187–8.
105. Ed. Solenden 1940, vol. II, p. 28.

rather than something which was measured by results. Of others than Charles the Bold of Burgundy, it might be said that 'he willingly listened to [his counsellors'] deliberations but, after hearing everything, he followed his own opinion which was usually contrary to what had been advised'.[106] Gerson attempted to close this loophole by his insistence that the king must actually act upon his councillors' advice.[107]

Giles of Rome's assumption that the king would be free to choose his own councillors was a normally accepted principle which was subject to a few radical challenges. The author of the *Song of Lewes*, who regarded evil councillors as enemies of the realm, defended the imposition of a baronial council on Henry III thus: 'Since the governance of the realm is the safety or ruin of all, it matters whose is the guardianship of the realm, just as it is on the sea, all things are confounded if fools are in command.'[108] But it was to be centuries before it was accepted that the public interest was so great as to exclude royal choice. Rather, impeachment (developed in the Good Parliament in 1376) put into the hands of Parliament a weapon for submitting to trial and punishing such of the king's servants as seemed most harmful to the realm. Royal choice thus became temporarily subject to veto.

In France, the Estates General of 1356 demanded more than the powers the Good Parliament attained two decades later. But the failure of Etienne Marcel and Robert le Coq left a lack of institutional means for subjecting the king's choices to public scrutiny. There were, of course, still the old ways of trying to exert influence: exhortation – Gerson's tract for the education of the dauphin spoke at length on the characteristics desirable in councillors,[109] as did *Vivat rex*; criticism – Pierre Dubois dared give vent (in a work intended to ingratiate himself) to outspoken denunciation of recent council action;[110] disillusioned revelation – Jean Juvenal's sermon *A, A, A, Nescio loqui*[111] publicised relentlessly the defects of the system. It may be that these methods usually proved adequate. But the extrusion of Philip the Fair's councillors on his death pointed to widespread exasperation.

The counsel of the French Estates largely related to methods of taxation.

---

106. Vaughan 1975, p. 79.   107. Ed. Glorieux 1968, p. 1164.
108. Ed. Kingsford 1890, lines 809–12:

> Nam cum gubernatio regnis et cunctorum
> Salus vel perditio, multum refert quorum
> Sit regni custodia; sicut est in navi
> Confunduntur omnia si praesint ignavi . . .

109. Thomas 1930, p. 47; ed. Glorieux 1968, p. 1165.
110. Ed. Langlois 1891, pp. 115, 117.   111. Ed. P.S. Lewis 1978, pp. 443–51.

When it went beyond this – most notably in the great reforming period of 1355–8 – the Estates' capacity to inflict their will on the ruler was checked by dissension among the delegates or by failure to raise the taxes which were the necessary *quid pro quo*.[112] As a consequence, the counsel the king of France was obliged to heed was usually only that of his council, the men of his choice. Oresme and Gerson, the two thinkers who went furthest in encouraging the king to widen the range of his councillors, to delegate aspects of sovereignty more widely, both took as their model Theopompus, the king of whom Aristotle recounted that, in order to preserve his power, he had shared it (*Politics* v.1313a). When Oresme advised the consultation of office-holders and the principal citizens, or Gerson proposed submitting on occasion to the judgement of *Parlement*,[113] they were respectfully suggesting an act of prudence, towards which there could be no constraint. The English king, on the other hand, had beyond the councillors of his own choice the *consiliarii nati*, his magnates, whom he could not afford to ignore when he needed money. That had been the lesson of 1258–65. When the magnates were incorporated within the House of Lords, their individual voices blended into a chorus that came close to deafening the king. To resist brought major political conflict – as in 1386. Yet the magnates' counsel could be invaluable to English kings, in peace as in war, because they provided the strong arm of the body politic.

In modern terms, for a king to defer to the counsel of others, whether voluntarily or under constraint, is to change the nature of the constitution. When Henry IV had Archbishop Arundel declare to the Parliament of 1399 that 'It was the king's will to be counselled and governed by the honourable wise and discreet persons of his kingdom and by their common counsel and assent to do his best for the governance of himself and his realm',[114] he was promising limited monarchy. In effect, he was conceding the case, made a century and a half earlier in the *Song of Lewes* (1264), that untrammelled monarchy was the prerogative of God alone; mortal men needed help in carrying the burden.[115] Had medieval intellectuals been more willing to ponder their own experience, they might have integrated this aspect of power-sharing into the frequently enunciated, but little explored, desire for a constitution which embraced monarchy, aristocracy and democracy

112. Cazelles 1982, pp. 274–317.
113. Ed. Menut 1970, p. 274; ed. Glorieux 1968, p. 1159.
114. Chrimes and Brown 1961, p. 194: 'Qil est la volunte du roy destre conseillez et governez par les honurables, sages, et discretes persones de soun roialme, et par lour commune conseil et assent faire le meulx pur la governance de luy et de son roialme.'
115. Ed. Kingsford 1890, lines 641–54.

(see pp. 565–6 below). But the vagueness of their institutional thinking, combined with the fact that contemporary institutions, though potentially formidable, were still fluid, explains their failure. They found it easy to distinguish constitutions from one another by reference to their legislative body (see p. 508 below), much harder to pinpoint the role of counsel.

Law

A third broad context in which the king could be seen was that of the law. There were inconsistencies in almost all writings on the subject. But those who perceived royal power within the framework of law viewed its attributes rather differently from those who portrayed the royal legal functions in isolation. All, even the most ardent royalists, held that the king was bound by divine and natural law, and by human law in so far as it specified the precepts of divine or natural law; also that he should act in conformity with positive law when it served the common good. But the implications of such subordination were rather different in works which did not take as a constant the rational quality of the ruler's will, or which devoted care to elucidating the nature of law. It is one of the paradoxes of medieval thought that while all (or almost all if Marsilius is excluded) thinkers regarded law as an objective yardstick against which human actions could be measured, those who tried to describe it produced rather varying views of its nature and content. So the subject of authority limited by law lent itself to numerous individual interpretations.

To take divine law first, all were agreed that it found its expression in the Scripture. However, the accumulated weight of centuries of theological and canonistic scholarship made its interpretation a matter for experts only. Even the straightforward commandment 'Thou shalt not kill' could only be understood, or circumvented, within the whole corpus of just war theories. War propaganda was therefore at its most effective when it came from the mouths of priests, as both Philip the Fair[116] and Edward III[117] understood. But this highlighted a royal dilemma: a layman could hardly be competent in his own right to judge the extent of divine approval for his actions. The papal claim that the pope was responsible to God for royal behaviour *ratione peccati*, and the corollary drawn by fourteenth-century hierocratic writers that royal power derived from papal, made sense. It could only be answered by making national churches – and indeed local universities – repositories of divine wisdom to be pitted against the pope's. Here lay the origins of Gallicanism as preached by Philip the Fair's lawyers, and of its English

116. Leclercq 1945.   117. See Hewitt 1966, pp. 161–3.

counterpart, advocated by Wyclif, but also by more orthodox figures.

A king who breached divine law automatically forfeited his subjects' obedience. Henry II's hasty penance after Becket's murder indicated that excommunication was a potent threat to his position. But this went some way to explaining the notable reluctance of later medieval popes to use so dangerous a weapon against kings. The church in the fourteenth and fifteenth centuries had no desire to rock the foundations of secular authority, lest anarchy rebound on itself. Conversely, Lollardy taught kings to beware of novel interpretations of divine law as weapons in battles with the clergy. For though Wyclif's use of lordship and proprietorship founded on grace (see chapter 19) constituted a radical argument for the taxation of the clergy, it bore within it the seeds of a threat to the crown. As William Wodeford said: 'The people could lawfully remove the possessions of kings, dukes and their lay superiors whenever they habitually offended.'[118] The savagery with which Lollardy was suppressed was a measure of the fear it inspired. Its philosophical challenge on the nature of lordship received at least some answer in Gerson's *De vita spirituali animae*.[119]

Because natural law was defined in different ways, the limitations it imposed on legitimate secular authority were hazy. It has been argued that Aquinas came close to conferring the status of natural law on expediency.[120] In any case, his emphasis on the common good as an extrapolation from natural law lent new intellectual coherence to, but did not change, the old argument that the king's duty was derived from and limited by its function, the guardianship of the people's good. Commonly, the subordination of secular authority to natural law was interpreted to mean that the king should be governed by reason. This could have revolutionary implications. The English barons in 1308 flirted with the view that they were competent to force reasonable behaviour on the king; by 1321, they regarded their earlier opinion as so dangerous that they imputed it to their enemy Despenser, in order to blacken his name.[121] Gerson, on the other hand, denied that in subjecting himself to reason, 'the sovereign lordship, the sovereign dignity, honour, nobility and simplicity', the king would, in fact, be submitting to his people; but he did imply that he should submit to the University of Paris, which best knew what reason was.[122]

On the binding character of human positive law, the divergences of opinion were open. The contention – most clearly expressed by Aquinas – that the king could not be held beneath the restraining power of the law

118. Aston 1960, p.9.   119. Ed. Glorieux 1962, pp. 113–202.   120. E. Lewis 1940.
121. Chrimes and Brown 1961, pp. 5, 40.   122. Ed. Glorieux 1968, p. 116.

because he controlled coercion, was widely rejected in thirteenth-century England. To ascribe to the king a monopoly of coercion (a notion palpably out of line with the facts in medieval France) was an oversimplification in England, where royal jurisdiction depended upon co-operation for its enforcement in the shires; and the deduction drawn by Aquinas from this misleading premise ran counter to English experience. The barons of 1215 who drew up Magna Carta – a firm statement of laws to which in future the king was to be subject – introduced a sanction in clause 61. Though clause 61 failed in its immediate objective, it set a powerful precedent. When Simon de Montfort and his followers had defeated Henry III in battle in 1264, the author of the *Song of Lewes* expounded the view that if the king broke the law or attempted to harm his people, the community of the realm had a duty to constrain him. Nor should the king resent this constraint; it was in fact true freedom: 'Whoever is truly king is truly free, if he rules himself and his kingdom rightly; let him know that all things are lawful for him which are fitted for ruling the kingdom, but not for destroying it',[123] and 'It is commonly said "as the king wills, the law goes;" truth will otherwise, for the law stands, the king falls.'[124] The claim that the magnates had a right to bridle the king was found also in the *addicio de cartis* in Bracton[125] and in Fleta.[126] The Lords Appellant made more extreme claims in 1386.[127] But the erosion of *diffidatio* (see p. 492 above) sapped arrogance during the fourteenth century. The fear of being convicted as rebels led the magnates normally to concentrate on limiting royal power by negotiation rather than by force.

Both in England and in France, Giles of Rome's view that 'laws are laid down by the prince and established by princely authority'[128] was disputed. Bracton regarded the magnates, the council of the realm, as having an

---

123. Ed. Kingsford 1890, lines 693–7:

> Sed quis vere fuerit rex, est liber vere
> Si se recte rexerit regnumque; licere
> Sibi sciat omnia quae regno regendo
> Sunt-convenientia, sed non destruendo.

124. *Ibid.*, lines 871–3:

> Dicitur vulgariter: ut rex vult, lex vadit;
> Veritas vult aliter, nam lex stat, rex cadit.

125. Ed. Thorne 1968, vol. II, p. 110.
126. Ed. Richardson and Sayles 1953–72, vol. II, pp. 36–7.
127. Chrimes and Brown 1961, p. 132.
128. *De regimine principum*, I.ii.10: 1556, fol. 44v: 'Leges autem traduntur ab ipso Principe et sunt traditae . . . imperio principis, cuius est leges facere.'

essential .role in legislation.[129] Aquinas was struck by the two-edged implication of the Roman law tag 'What pleases the prince has the force of law since, by the *lex regia* which was enacted concerning his empire, the people confers upon him all its authority and power.' He deduced that law-making could be the function either of the people as a whole or of the public person who represented the people.[130] But if legislation by the community as a whole was a possibility, at once the ruler's sacrifice in accepting the directive force of law attained new significance: the king was bound to obey something he might not have created. Where Aquinas simply stated possibility, Oresme argued for a certainty. Drawing on Marsilius' *Defensor pacis*, he declared roundly that legislative power was necessarily vested in the people as a whole, since they alone could judge the common good; therefore the act of the Romans in resigning that power to Augustus was illegitimate, even 'bestial'.[131] For other nations to follow the Roman example would therefore be wrong.

Oresme's view of legislation was roughly compatible with the English constitutional position in the later middle ages, because Parliament was regarded as the indispensable forum for the production of statute law; and Commons' petitions formed the basis of most legislation by the middle of the fourteenth century. It consorted less well with the French position in public law at least, since *Parlement* was not usually seen as representing the community as a whole, and the Estates had no rights in legislation. Oresme may have hoped to widen the range of participants in the legislative process – elsewhere he argued for some popular participation in sovereignty.[132] But whatever his intention on this point, he did mean to assert that the king was under obligation to a law which was not merely his own creation.

The point reached by Oresme, following Marsilius, drawing on Roman law and Aristotelian utility, was arrived at independently by Fortescue as a result of his experience in the English law courts: 'The statutes of England . . . are made, not only by the prince's will, but also by the assent of the whole realm, so they cannot be injurious to the people nor fail to secure their advantage.'[133] The only difference in point of view was Fortescue's insistence on the king's role; in England, legislation was a joint-stock enterprise. Fortescue was, however, as sure as Marsilius that, though the ruler might err in the search for the common good, the people as a whole

129. Ed. Thorne 1968, vol. II, p. 21; 1977, vol. IV, p. 285.
130. *Summa theologiae* Ia IIae, qu. 90, art. 3.   131. Ed. Menut 1970, pp. 137–8.   132. *Ibid.*, p. 274.
133. Ed. Chrimes 1949, p. 41: 'Sed non sic Angliae statuta oriri possunt, dum nedum principis voluntate sed et totius regni assensu ipsa conduntur, quo populi laesuram illam efficere nequeunt vel non eorum commodum procurare.'

could not, because it was theirs. At last there was justification in abstract terms for the step taken as early as 1308, when the barons required Edward II to swear, as part of his coronation oath, to uphold 'the just laws and customs . . . which the community of the realm shall have chosen'.[134]

The difference between Aquinas' and Fortescue's views on legislation was a reflection of two hundred years of state development as well as of a radically different approach. For Aquinas, the common good was a clearly visible objective; therefore he could afford to be indifferent as to the person of the legislator. But also, because he was certain that the inequity of unjust laws would be uncontroversial, he thought it safe to argue that unjust law had no power to bind the consciences of subjects (though they ought to obey if scandal or disorder would result from their refusal).[135] Fortescue, on the other hand, by taking it for granted that the proper process of law-making could not but result in the common good, was able to assume obedience to the law, both from subject and from king.[136] He realised, of course, that kings might resent this bridle but, in an unconscious echo of the *Song of Lewes*, he called on them to understand that their position was not weakened but strengthened by this restraint, for a ruler over free men was always more powerful than one who ruled only over slaves.[137]

The joint-stock character of law-making was so significant in Fortescue's mind that he defined the whole constitutional position of England in its light: it was *dominium politicum et regale* (a political and royal lordship), and therefore unequivocally better than the French *dominium regale*.[138] In making this distinction, he conformed with definitions of royal and political constitutions drawn up by John of Paris at the beginning of the fourteenth century.[139] So both for Englishmen and for Frenchmen, it was the nature of the legislative process that chiefly distinguished constitutions.

Custom

If legislation was the most obvious, it was not the only way in which law was made during the later middle ages. The alternative, custom, was necessarily formed and adhered to or rejected by the people at large. But although intellectuals recognised this, many experienced difficulty in integrating it into their systems of thought. Giles of Rome, in *De regimine principum*, maintained Aristotle's self-contradictory point of view by

134. Chrimes and Brown 1961, pp. 4–5: 'Les leys et les custumes droitureles les quiels la communaute de vostre roiaume aura esleu.' 135. *Summa theologiae* Ia IIae, qu. 96, art. 4.
136. Ed. Chrimes 1949, p. 81. 137. *Ibid.*, p. 81.
138. *Ibid.*, p. 33; ed. Plummer 1885, pp. 111–16.
139. *De potestate regia et papali*, xvii: 1942, p. 228.

arguing on the one hand that custom was almost natural,[140] and therefore by implication binding, and on the other that because many old laws were no longer just, they ought in principle to be changed unless expedience dictated their preservation.[141] Illogical this might be, but it came close to expressing French policy on the matter. For after the brief intrusion of Philip Augustus and St Louis into the realm of substantive law, the French kings allowed custom (or in the south Roman law, treated as if it were custom) to prevail in private law. So while royal ordinances might cover the demesne, administration, public affairs or royal cases (an elastic category), contract, family questions and rights of possession were left to their traditional ways.[142] The fourteenth-century *Avis au Roys* stated that good law is adapted 'to the region, the *pays*, the customs, the people for whom it is made'.[143] Beaumanoir saw it as the king's duty to preserve those customs which had been proved, either by long use or by judgement in a law court.[144] In handling an appeal from a far-flung part of the kingdom, *Parlement* was expected to decide it according to the custom of the locality, not according to that of 'France'.[145] In this respect the king was very much under the law, a law he had had no part in creating.

In fact, the system left a larger role for royal intervention than Beaumanoir anticipated. Because *Parlement* was expected to judge according to the custom of the *pays*, there was pressure to commit that custom to writing (though the process was very slow). A written statement of custom automatically lost that flexibility which had been the hallmark of customary law in the twelfth and thirteenth centuries; and it also highlighted the illogicality or indeed injustice of many local customs. In response, by the end of the thirteenth century, the right to abrogate 'bad' custom was attached to the royal prerogative. Thus the king could escape the shackles theoretically imposed on his legal sovereignty.[146] On the other hand, his last-resort powers of avoidance should not be seen as decisive in determining the extent of his legal authority. The existence of private customary law meant that, even if the king took the final decisions in a small minority of cases, most ordinary decisions in substantive law were outside royal control.

The political significance of this was that royal sovereignty could come smack up against prescriptive rights, real or invented. As Beaumanoir put it, each baron was sovereign in his barony, even though the king was

140. III.ii.5: 1556, fol. 273v.   141. III.ii.31: 1556, fol. 318.   142. Langmuir 1970, pp. 284–6.
143. Ourliac and de Malafosse 1968, vol. III, p. 1: 'à la region, aux pays, aux moeurs, aux gens pour lesquels elle est faite . . .'.
144. Ed. Salmon 1899–1900, section 683.   145. *Ibid.*, 1780.   146. Chaplais 1963, p. 463.

sovereign over all.[147] To the king's claim that all lay jurisdiction was held either directly or indirectly of him,[148] English dukes of Gascony from John onwards pleaded history in defence of their independence. The late fourteenth-century counts of Armagnac followed suit by alleging that the land of Armagnac predated France, and therefore should not be subordinate to it. But the most impressive of these arguments was perhaps that produced by the count of Brittany's advocate in 1463:

Whereas, from time immemorial, we and our predecessors, kings, dukes and princes of Brittany, who have never recognized and do not recognize anyone as the creator, institutor or sovereign lord of our name and principality, save for God Almighty, have the rights and are entitled, by virtue of our royal and sovereign privileges, to institue and hold a sovereign court of Parlement.[149]

Here a case based on prescription was fortified by a Roman-law-inspired claim to sovereignty as dramatic in its terms as any propounded by a royal advocate. The king of France regarded his barons' sovereignty as circumscribed by his own, and therefore only legitimate to the extent that he chose to make it so. The great lords, on the other hand, saw their powers as defined by inherited right and family custom. In practice the outcome of conflicts like these was determined by the political balance of power in France, not by abstract principle. The ultimate royal victory was long delayed.

In England, too, custom formed an integral part of law, as Glanvill and Bracton were at pains to point out. Prescriptive rights could be colourfully claimed, as by Gilbert of Gloucester (or the Earl of Warenne) in a famous episode: when challenged to declare by what warrant he wielded jurisdiction, he waved aloft an old rusty sword, crying 'Here, my lords, is my warrant!' to show that his claim was rooted in his ancestors' conquests and in long use.[150] The processes of parliamentary legislation on the one hand and law based on precedent on the other, while in origin intended simply to state custom or to expand it, in fact came to supersede it. By the *Quo Warranto* Statute of 1290, Edward I recognised the legitimacy of claims like Gloucester's, but prevented new ones from arising. Through such applications of the common law, the king of England had potentially greater control over his subjects' rights than had the king of France.[151] But

---

147. Ed. Salmon 1899–1900, section 1043. Wood 1967, p. 144.
148. Ed. Salmon 1899–1900, section 322.
149. Pocquet du Haut-Jussé 1971, p. 207, quoting from M. Planiol, *Très ancienne coutume de Bretagne* 1896, p. 453.
150. Walter of Guisborough 1957, p. 216: see Lapsley 1951, p. 36.
151. Miller 1952, pp. 128–9.

on the other hand, the common law was rarely left in royal hands. No legislation was the English king's alone – Parliament was essential to the process after the early fourteenth century; and case law was made in local courts staffed by sheriffs, coroners or justices of the peace (who were usually local men, not delegates from Westminister), as well as in the central courts. Fortescue appreciated the common law as the people's law, as guarantor of their rights: 'Ruled by laws that they themselves desire, they freely enjoy their properties and are despoiled neither by their own king nor any other.'[152]

Prescriptive rights were strengthened by a widespread but not yet very well-developed belief in natural rights. That men ought to be free and that they ought to have safe possession of their goods slowly took shape as philosophical truths during the fourteenth century. William of Ockham, by locating freedom within what he called 'second mode' natural law, established it as a necessary part of the best state. Because freedom was part of the law which rational men would observe if not subjected to other pressures, states needed substantial justification to depart from it.[153] From different assumptions, the natural right to property was articulated by John of Paris and then by Ockham's opponents in the course of the poverty conflict (see chapter 19). Both rights were brought together by Gerson in his *De vita spirituali animae,* in what has been hailed as the first true natural rights theory:[154]

There is a natural *dominium* as a gift from God, by which every creature has a *ius* directly from God to take inferior things into its own use for its own preservation. Each has this *ius* as a result of a fair and irrevocable justice, maintained in its original purity, or a natural integrity . . . To this *dominium* the *dominium* of liberty can also be assimilated, which is an unrestrained *facultas* given by God.[155]

If natural rights were slow in finding adequate philosophical expression, they were understood to exist and translated into royal duties before Gerson's day. Ockham deduced from natural freedom the consequence that a king ruling by will alone was prevented from using his subjects' lives or goods[156] for his own advantage. Oresme, from a vague right to property based in divine law, concluded that 'A Prince should not enlarge his

152. Ed. Chrimes 1949, p. 24: 'Quare populus eius libere fruitur bonis suis legibus quas cupit regulatus, nec per regem suum aut quemvis alium depilatur.'
153. McGrade 1974, pp. 179–81.   154. Tuck 1979, p. 27. But see Tierney 1983.
155. Ed. Glorieux 1962, p. 145: 'Erit igitur naturale dominium donum Dei quo creatura jus habet immediate a Deo assumere res alias inferiores in sui usum et conservationem, pluribus competens ex aequo et inabdicabile servata originali justitia seu integritate naturali . . . Ad hoc dominium spectare potest dominium libertatis quae est facultas quaedam libere resultans ex dono Dei . . .'.
156. Ed. Goldast 1614, p. 794.

dominion over his subjects, should not overtax them or seize their goods, should allow or grant them liberties, and should not interfere with them or use his plenary powers, but only a power regulated by law and custom.'[157] But if subjects could transpose their rights into royal duties, kings could deflect those duties back on to the subjects. So that they might perform adequately their task of protecting their subjects' lives, liberties and goods against all other parties – a task which in practice constituted the chief pillar of the people's reverence for their king – the French and English monarchs of the later middle ages demanded sacrifices of lesser rights in the interests of the greater. Occasionally this meant willingness to die for the defence of the realm;[158] far more commonly, it meant the acceptance of taxation.

Because taxation involved an infringement of prescriptive and natural rights, it could not occur without the subjects' consent – which in any case was essential on practical grounds. The Roman law tag *quod omnes tangit ab omnibus debet approbari* (what touches all should be approved by all) came swiftly to mind as a means of expressing the principle (though the question of how far beyond this taxation was affected by Roman law is still a matter of earnest debate among historians). In England, the minority of Henry III saw the *communitas regni* assent in grants of subsidy to the regency government; by 1295, the representation of shires and boroughs in this act of assent was formalised. In the 1320s, the author of the *Modus Tenendi Parliamentum*[159] was contending that the knights of the shire had a louder voice in the act of consent than the magnates, since they represented the whole realm, while the magnates spoke only for themselves. The implications of representation were now well understood. By accepting the principles of consent and representation, the localities of England had turned the *communitas regni* from a baronial club into an assembly which expressed the will of all tax-payers, hence of the political nation as a whole. Since king and people negotiated within the same frame of reference, thereafter only taxation of the clergy re-opened the question of rights. For the laity, each demand for a subsidy began a strictly political battle; neither side had recourse to fundamental questioning of the system.

In France it was different. There the sudden great financial needs of Philip IV fell on a kingdom not wholly prepared to understand his demands,

---

157. Ed. Johnson 1956, p. 45: 'Quod princeps non multum amplificet dominium supra subditos, exactiones captiones non faciat, libertates eis dimittat aut concedat, nec eos impediat, neque utatur plenitudine potestatis sed potentia legibus et consuetudinibus limitata vel regulata.'
158. Henry of Ghent, Quodlibet 15. See Lagarde 1943.
159. Ed. Pronay and Taylor 1980, p. 89. I am indebted to Dr J. Maddicott's help here on *communitas regni*.

perhaps because Philip overstated his case. Most of the king's subjects would have agreed reluctantly with Aquinas: 'It sometimes happens that princes have insufficient revenues to defend the land and for other things which they may reasonably take upon themselves. In such a case it is just that their subjects contribute the means whereby their common good be ensured.'[160] But Philip's lawyers did not confine themselves to this. Plaisians' claim of royal proprietorship over all goods in the kingdom (see p. 490 above) was not unique; Oresme indignantly rebutted the Roman-law-derived idea that in an emergency all things belonged to the prince.[161] As controversial was the question of who decided what constituted an emergency. The influential theologian Godfrey of Fontaines in 1294 denounced false emergencies, urging resistance by subjects if the king imposed taxation without evident necessity.[162] In his insistence that the crown should clearly demonstrate the grounds for taxation, Godfrey touched on the central theme in French taxation history, counsel as a necessary preliminary step. There was not a great leap from here to Oresme's argument that the community was the legitimate judge of emergency.[163] Peter of Auvergne in 1296 declared that if the emergency for which the tax had been ordained was over before the tax-collectors appeared, then the people were not bound to pay; the tax should be abolished.[164] And Dubois between 1305 and 1307 roundly condemned the expedient of asking for more than was strictly necessary.[165] All in all, the anxiety of French intellectuals about possible abuses in the system meant that royal obligations to the tax-payer were defined quite closely.

Because French thinkers stressed the need for all tax-payers to understand why the money was required,[166] their demand could only be satisfied by dialogue. *Quod omnes tangit* was interpreted as necessitating widespread acquiescence in the ground for taxation, rather than bargaining on the amount. This had the unexpected long-term consequence of creating local institutions too various and cumbersome to survive. There were sound pragmatic reasons for the failure of the French Estates.[167] But the development of arbitrary taxation by 1439 was also assisted during the Lancastrian campaigns in France by the fact that the emergencies which

160. Ed. Spiazzi 1954a, p. 251: 'Contingit tamen aliquanto quod principes non habent sufficientes reditus ad custodiam terrae et ad alia quae imminent rationabiliter principibus expetenda et in tali casu iustum est ut subditi exhibeant unde possit communis eorum utilitas procurari.'
161. Ed. Johnson 1956, p. 45. 162. Ed. Hoffmans 1932, pp. 76–8. 163. Ed. Johnson 1956, p. 39.
164. Brown 1972, pp. 585–7. 165. Ed. Langlois 1891, pp. 116–17.
166. Godfrey of Fontaines, ed. Hoffmanns 1932, p. 76; in general see Henneman 1971, 1976.
167. P.S. Lewis 1962.

justified taxation needed no explanation. There was, after all, little point in insisting on the right to widespread and localised consultation when urgent action was manifestly imperative. So the institutional means for the expression of consent to taxation fell into abeyance.

The rights of the people have thus far been seen in terms of the limitations they imposed upon royal power, since that has been the topic of discussion. But it would be misleading to end without emphasising that the royal duty to protect subjects' rights against attack from third parties was the bulwark of medieval monarchy. The meteoric rise of the English and French kings in the second half of the twelfth century was owed principally to their acceptance of their subjects' view of justice, to their willingness to put legal sanction behind rights. Though on occasion when their subjects' claims created political problems, kings might produce maxims redolent of arrogant sovereignty, they had no intention whatever of denying the range of principles from which their opponents argued.

Medieval views on taxation and law-making clearly presupposed subjects with wills and interests of their own. On certain issues, kings realised they could proceed no further without obtaining co-operation; and intellectuals rapidly absorbed this realisation into their thinking. Godfrey of Fontaines gave cogent expression to the doctrine of consent he descried beneath popular objection to imagined emergencies. As he saw it, no hereditary king could rightfully claim to rule by will alone, since that was reserved for the best men, which hereditary succession did not guarantee; therefore hereditary kings were required to live according to the law.

When therefore any man rules over other freemen, not slaves, and only enjoys the right to rule by virtue of the whole community either electing or instituting or accepting him and consenting in his rule, his dominion can only be for the common good and the common utility. And therefore he has no right to impose anything burdensome or binding on them unless it meets with their consent. For as free men they ought to obey willingly, not under compulsion.[168]

In fact, Godfrey's concern was narrow. But in order to make his point, he had elaborated the theme that popular consent was indispensable to legitimate royal action. Did he mean it? His words raise the question of

---

168. Ed. Hoffmans 1932, p. 76: 'Quando ergo aliquis principatur aliquibus ut liberis non ut servis, nec habet ius principandi nisi virtute totius communitatis vel ipsum eligentis vel instituentis vel ipsum acceptantis et in ipsum consentientis, principatus eius non debet esse nisi propter bonum commune et propter communem utilitatem. Et ideo non debet aliquid imponere communitati quod sit eis in gravamen et nexum, nisi hoc procedat de consensu subditorum, qui in quantum liberi debent non coacte sed voluntarie obedire.'

whether the view that government rests on the consent of the governed can be fairly ascribed to later medieval thinkers.

An obvious way of investigating this is to consider whether social contract was meaningful in medieval thought. While a search for myths of institution yields rich results, not all theories of the state's origin in convention had as their aim either the limitation of the ruler's authority or his subjection to some form of popular scrutiny. For medieval Aristotelians, a measure of institution could be integrated without strain into a general theory of natural origins, on the line that Aristotle himself suggested when he remarked that, though the state arose from men's fundamental instincts, nevertheless the man who first instituted it deserved praise (*Politics* 1253a29). Convention might therefore be merely the actualisation of inherent human potential, as it seemed to Oresme.[169] Averroes' oft-quoted gloss on the *Ethics* VIII, 'The king exists by the will of the people, but when he is king it is natural that he should rule',[170] pointed to a rather different view of institution from that favoured in the seventeenth century.

All medieval authors took it for granted that legitimate authority was grounded in the people. Ironically, this train of thought is clearer in the writings of those who, like Giles of Rome or Christine de Pisan, favoured untrammelled monarchy, than in more 'constitutional' thinkers. It was, after all, the necessary corollary of organic thought that government emerged from the needs of the whole people, and was simply an answer to those needs; authority which transcended these bounds was illegitimate. But for Giles and Christine, the people was not in any sense the judge of its own needs, far less the arbiter of how those needs should be satisfied. Very different implications could be drawn from their fundamental premise by any author prepared to allow the subjects discretion; for him a myth of institution could signal belief in the people as a rational, responsible element in the state.

Fortescue's social contract was set among the legendary Trojan predecessors of English kings; agreement to establish royal government went back to the reign of Brutus. This at once threw the weight of ages behind the political arrangements of fifteenth-century England. Having described the contract, he drew the moral:

169. Quillet 1977, p. 157.
170. See, e.g., John of Paris, *De potestate regia et papali*, xix: 1942, p. 235: 'Rex est a populi voluntate, sed, cum est rex, ut dominetur est naturale.' Compare with Ockham: McGrade 1974, pp. 106–7.

You have here, Prince, the form of institution of the political kingdom whence you can estimate the power which the king can exercise in regard of the law and the subjects of such a realm. For a king of this sort is obliged to protect the law, the subjects and their bodies and goods, and he has power to this end issuing from the people, so that it is not permissible for him to rule his people with any other power.[171]

At once the limitation inherent in all organic thinking achieved explicit form: power existed for a purpose, and that purpose limited its proper use. But Fortescue's subjects were conscious participants in the arrangement; it was their law, their lives and property which were to be protected. The implication was that this was the sole purpose of government. No longer were kings free to steer their subjects towards a goal thought to be in their best interests; the end of the state was established at its institution. Fortescue's state bore a marked relation to the one Locke conceived two centuries later.

Yet Fortescue's aim in writing *De laudibus legum Anglie* was to appeal to the conscience of the king, to have him voluntarily accept his limited role in society. Except for the, admittedly large, constitutional limitation that he could not legislate or tax without the consent of Parliament, Fortescue's king was left untrammelled in the exercise of power. A solider financial position, a better constituted council, were appropriate remedies for the ills of the kingdom,[172] not more popular control. What happened if the king were foolish enough not to preserve the laws, lives and property of his subjects, was left untouched. For Fortescue, the contract by which government was instituted was perhaps to be compared with the contract of marriage in his own day; it established what ought to be the nature of relations between the participants; it did not allow for divorce.

Other versions of kingship originating in contract were less precise about the aims of government, much clearer about the people's right to terminate the agreement. Jean de Meun's *Roman de la Rose*, a poem redolent of the learning of the Paris arts faculty in the later thirteenth century, offered a rumbustious and disrespectful account of a peasant community which, impelled by greed to amass possessions, appointed the largest and toughest of their number as ruler, with the sole purpose of protecting their goods, for as long as it suited them to have him.[173] Here, then, rulership was a trust,

---

171. Ed. Chrimes 1949, p. 33: 'Habes, ex hoc iam, princeps, institutionis regni politici formam, ex qua metiri poteris potestatem, quam rex eius in legem ipsius aut subditos valeat exercere; ad tutelam namque legis subditorum ac eorum corporum et bonorum res huiusmodi rectus est, et ad hanc potestatem a populo effluxam ipse habet, quo ei non licet potestate alia suo populo dominari.'
172. Ed. Plummer 1885, pp. 120–53.   173. Lines 5301–15; 9609–12; quoted Paré 1941, p. 178.

revocable by the people at will. The full-blooded way in which Jean insisted on revocability contrasted with the more cautious, more academic, treatment of social contract as trust in the theological writings of Duns Scotus.[174] But both saw the continuing consent of the people as a necessary constituent of government. For them, social contract was like marriage in a modern secular state.

In either Fortescue's or Jean de Meun's contracts, consent conferred legitimacy on the action of government, and was therefore an indispensable foundation of the whole governmental system. But not all later medieval contracts carried with them this significance. For example, Ockham three times in his writings mentioned the people's right to depose its rulers.[175] Yet he conceived of this right as an extraordinary one, a violation of law which, like royal *necessitas*, was only justified by quite exceptional circumstances. Because the people had this last-ditch right, their consent was always meaningful; but popular sovereignty in ordinary times was far from his thoughts. The line between Ockhamist philosophy and the constitutional thought of fourteenth-century England is here a very thin one. For the political manoeuvres of 1327 and 1399 were clearly designed to prove that the people as a whole had co-operated in, agreed and acclaimed the depositions of Edward II and Richard II.[176] The English barons subscribed to the view that, in the last resort, deposition must derive its validity from the whole community. Yet these two extraordinary actions were not intended to undermine basic assumptions about royal power (though it may be conceded that in the long term they did); and popular sovereignty was alien to the magnates' wishes. In theory, Edward III and Henry IV governed with all the rights that their predecessors had enjoyed; if Henry IV chose to conciliate potential opponents, that was an act of grace not a recognition that he ruled by virtue of popular will.

In France, the people's right to depose kings was normally discussed only in the context of rebutting papal claims to be able to do so. John of Paris, for example, was forced to interpret the deposition of the last Merovingian king as an act of the magnates which the pope merely recognised.[177] Robert le Coq tried to exploit this idea in a political context in 1356, but his failure disgraced the argument. Gerson later produced a more subtle interpretation of popular rights with his opinion that, since the king of France's hereditary claim was upheld by custom, it was based on popular consent; hence the

174. Gandillac 1956, pp. 345–8. Cf. pp. 536–7 below.
175. McGrade 1982, p. 754; 1974, pp. 104–7.   176. Wilkinson 1939.
177. *De potestate regia et papali*, xiv: 1942, p. 219.

people could, by law, refuse the right of inheritance to an heir guilty of blatantly evil deeds.[178] Both John of Paris and Gerson were here going beyond the academic defence of overthrowing tyrannical kings, in concentrating rather on popular rights than on royal crimes, and in allowing for processes which would not be interpreted as rebellion. Neither opinion had practical significance. And Gerson's at least allowed for popular action only in very circumscribed conditions.

From what has been said, it might be concluded that, while many intellectuals believed popular consent strengthened government, only a minority thought it fundamental in that it conferred legitimacy. But what did they mean by consent? As with all medieval political terms it was a highly plastic concept. The Latin word *consensus* could have its modern English connotation as well as the meaning of consent. In the former sense, it could be expressed without any conscious act on the part of the people. Oresme understood this when he allowed the king, in an emergency, to alter the coinage with the passive consent of the people,[179] which in practice meant little more than their acquiescence in *force majeure*. Consensus was thought to lie behind all the operations of customary law, because, if the people had disapproved, they would have changed the custom. This was what Gerson meant when he declared the king of France held the realm by title of hereditary succession out of the original consent of his subjects.[180] It was tautologous to argue that government rested on the consent of the people if consent was expressed in this way, since all it meant was that government existed. Yet the formulation could still legitimate withdrawal of obedience.

Expressed consent could either be in person or through representatives. Consent by representation could mean little or much. Should the representative be the ruler, as Aquinas allowed, then consent meant acquiescence in his rule. Where the representative was a member of the Estates or of the English Parliament, his consent was symbolic: his *plena potestas* (full powers) received from the locality did not constitute a mandate; he was not answerable to his constituents when he returned home. In France, his power to bind his locality was always disputed. If the system worked in England, if the consent of the representatives in Parliament was seen as the consent of the whole people, this was largely because the bargaining power that this conferred on the House of Commons was recognised as advantageous by the gentry in the shires and by the leading

178. Ed. Glorieux 1962, p. 151.   179. Ed. Johnson 1956, p. 39.   180. Ed. Glorieux 1962, p. 151.

townsmen. They would have concurred in Gerson's understanding of popular consent: '*quod omnes tangit ab omnibus debet approbari*: by "all", understand by the weightier and saner counsel of all'.[181] In medieval England and France, the people was usually interpreted as meaning its leading citizens, its privileged elite.

Though the consent of the people could be whittled down to their mindless acquiescence in government, it could mean much more. For those who attended the English Parliament, either as representatives or in their own right, their personal consent to taxation or legislation was of crucial significance to the government, since without it there was no means of collecting taxes or of passing laws. The co-operation of the ruling classes in the shires was a *sine qua non* of governmental action; that co-operation could not be obtained without formal consent. At times in the fourteenth and fifteenth centuries, kings were forced to bargain hard to get it; at other times, it was given willingly. Here is the substance of English political history. Yet active consent to taxation and legislation, however significant a development, still meant far less than active consent to government as a whole. If the English Parliament in fact often obtained much wider rights of supervision over royal administration and justice, these were short-term gains. In practice, as well as in theory, there was still a long way to go before it would be recognised that popular consent was essential for the whole range of governmental activities. The implications of Jean de Meun's myth were far from being realised.

181. Thomas 1930, p. 47.

17

COMMUNITY

I COMMUNITY, COUNSEL AND REPRESENTATION

The lack of precision in the medieval political vocabulary and the great diversity of literary genres involved in studying it make it far from easy to provide a full explanation of community, council, representation and constitution over the three hundred years from 1150 to 1450. In addition to that, the words themselves can refer to widely varying social and political realities. It is only very recently that law, ethics and politics have come to be considered independently of each other: the middle ages had no such divisions. Roman law and canon law are used with a liberal disregard for the texts and their original purpose which would be almost inconceivable today, and one result of this is that one may well come across material of prime importance to the subject under consideration here mentioned in passing in a theological commentary on some quite different topic. Medieval thinkers, in other words, tended to see human social and political affairs as one part of a whole, to think of man himself in relation to the world, to his fellow-men, and to God. There was some attempt, following the Latin-speaking West's rediscovery of Aristotle, to unify terms and ideas under his influence: that is precisely the significance of the 'commentaries' on Aristotle, particularly those on the *Politics* and the *Nichomachean Ethics*. These must be understood as commentaries in the broad sense, for in fact one finds Aristotle's thought in treatises which, while not pure commentaries, use his ideas at least as much as the formal commentaries, if not more. The most powerful influence on vocabulary, however, comes not from Aristotle but from the bible and the Church, for medieval political thinking was immersed in a total ethical and religious view of the world, so that there is a constant danger of making anachronistic interpretations. The term 'representation' for example cannot be taken in its modern sense, neither can 'council'; 'constitution' even less. In fact, the meaning of these words has changed so radically in the course of their long evolution, that we face the risk of misunderstanding them altogether.

The first thing to remember in order to understand the range of practical and theoretical uses these expressions were put to, and the realities they referred to, is the central importance of the idea of justice and the judicial function in the middle ages. Community is a term which includes both governors and governed, and the concepts of council and representation developed in the context of the administration of justice, and they are bound up with the constitutional forms that govern the whole body of society.

Politics, in brief, cannot be seen as a separate sphere of thought, even if we agree that its development is in the direction of the gradual emancipation that has been seen by some as a sort of 'birth of the lay mind'.[1] In any case, the words community, council and representation reflect an organic – even organicist – vision of society, in which communication between men is unproblematic because the individual is not taken into account in the overall analysis. This is the explanation of the supreme importance of the idea of community which dominates all social and political organisation.

Community

Historical background

Without going into the semantics of 'community', it is significant that the word is hardly ever used in the sense of collectivity, a social group whose members have something in common, in the treatises on philosophy and political theology that were written in the early middle ages. Generally speaking, authors of that period follow St Augustine in using terms taken from Roman law, such as *populus*, *respublica* or *civitas*, to refer to men united in pursuit of a common aim. A significant example of this occurs in Jonas of Orleans' treatise *De institutione regia*,[2] in which the word *communitas* scarcely appears; instead he uses the phrase *populus Dei* (which I shall have more to say about) to refer to the subjects of a king, or sometimes the term *subjecti*. When he uses *civitas*, it is in the Augustinian sense. The idea of *commune* is everywhere in the works of Cicero, particularly in the *De legibus* and the *De republica*; the term *communitas* itself occurs frequently in the *De officiis*. And Cicero's model, of course, is the Roman republic. The word *communitas* does not have a precise connotation. Cicero defines the republic as the affair of the people (*res publica, res populi*: Book 1, Chapter 25), and *populus* he defines as 'not a gathering of men grouped together anyhow' (*non omnis coetus quoquo modo congregatus*) but as a multitude of men associated with each other by their adherence to one law and by a

1. Lagarde 1956–70.   2. Reviron (ed.) 1930, vol. 1.

community of interest (*coetus multitudinis iuris consensu et utilitatis communione sociatus*). Clearly the idea of that which is common is present in the word *communio*. Elsewhere Cicero defines the people as *coetus multitudinis*, a grouped multitude, while the *civitas* is *constitutio populi*, an 'organised people'. He therefore makes a connection between *multitudo*, the great number, *iuris consensus*, or agreement to submit to the law, and *communio utilitatis*, the common interest. In *De legibus* he uses the word *communio* for the 'society' formed by man and God together, as 'right reason is common to both . . . those who share law must also share justice'.[3] Community here is a community of reason (*ratio communis*). From the sixth to the ninth century *communitas*, strictly speaking, means 'meetings of collectivities of a public nature',[4] and this is the sense in which the word comes to be generally used in the middle ages: 'it refers to a body of individuals who, by their common action based on the existence of bonds between them, constitute a more or less institutionalised group',[5] but also one that varies in size and which may or may not be based on a particular territory. In other words, *communitas* is the word which refers to that basic concrete social reality which is established with the growth of politics, particularly in instances where the development of the political ideas of the community has been influenced by Roman and canon law. *Communitas*, *universitas*, *corpus*, *civitas* and less commonly *societas* come to refer to what we might generically call the social group.

Community and commune

'*Communitas* generally refers to the whole population of a town, whether it is a commune or not', writes Petit-Dutaillis.[6] A commune, technically speaking, is certainly a community; but this does not mean that the reverse is always true, although the commune and the whole communal movement that characterises social and political development from the eleventh to the thirteenth century are an integral part of the history of community and the medieval awareness of it. Narrowly defined, a commune is an association on the basis of an oath: 'Commune means exactly the same as a common oath.'[7] The existence of the oath is the commune's defining characteristic; essentially it is the incarnation of *institutio pacis*, that is its purpose is primarily a defensive one.

---

3. *De legibus*, I.vii.23: 'inter quos autem ratio, inter eosdem etiam recta ratio communis est . . . inter quos porro est communio legis, inter eos communio iuris est'. For *commune* and *communitas* in *De officiis*, cf. I.xl–xlv.139–61; and for the distinction between *commune* and *privatum*, I.v–vii.18, 20–1.
4. Michaud-Quantin 1970, p. 148.   5. *Ibid.*
6. Petit-Dutaillis 1947, pp. 32, 293 n. 64.   7. *Ibid.*, p. 35.

A brief survey of the way the communal movement developed during the second half of the middle ages, without going into too much detail, may shed some light on community in its proper sense. In France, for example, the communes originally provided a force in society on which monarchical power relied during the process of centralisation, but their existence was jeopardised from the moment they could be seen as antagonistic forces. At the same time they were no longer being established in response to a pressingly urgent need, but taking their place as part of a carefully defined juridical system: as soon as communes were regarded as having a juridical personality on the model of the moral person autonomous collectivities were deemed to possess under Roman law, they were provided with *ius communitatis et collegii*, that is, with a privilege. Thus Beaumanoir in his *Coutumes de Beauvaisis* 'draws a clear distinction, using a juridical criterion, between communities based on communes' and other towns.

In the fourteenth century the original communes were joined or replaced by other types of communities, particularly confraternities, craft corporations and communities, colleges, Hanse and guilds, which were primarily professional associations, whose members were normally referred to as sworn members or jurors. As these new types of association integrate or fuse with the old municipal system, or sometimes set up in competition with it, the commune tends always to find itself too rigid to adapt and the old form disappears.

Was there an analogous development of the commune in the different regions of the Latin West? The situation appears to have been different where there was no centralised power, as in the Empire, and more particularly in Italy where communes developed with striking success. The Commune of Padua is an example.[8] The *Sacramentum comunancie Populi paduani* uses the formula *ad honorem et statum civitatis padue et comunis*.[9] The term *comunancia* used here includes within itself both *civitas* and *populus*. The text also mentions the *universus populus*, and *comunis status civitatis padue*: the *comunancia*, that is the community, is here the whole body of the citizens of Padua, or those who are of the *comunancia*, or whose names are entered in the book of the *comunancia*, to the exclusion of all foreigners or outsiders. It is clear how little exactness of vocabulary there is for describing the inhabitants of a commune, and in practice there is not very much difference between *comunancia* (or *comunanza*), *universus populus*, *civitas* and *societas*. At all events, although the influence of Roman law on the medieval conception of the corporation or *universitas* is considerable, the term *communitas* itself –

8. *Statuti* 1873.   9. *Ibid.*, p. 148.

as distinct from *corpus, societas* and *collegium* – does not seem to belong in its vocabulary. Yet paradoxically *communitas* comes to mean not just groups of varying importance depending on their size but to refer to 'the fact that those who constitute them do not enter into a special institutional system within the whole body they constitute'.[10]

In France we find both communes in the proper sense of collectivities which have been granted a commune charter and, also, towns known as 'bonne villes' which do not have anything of that sort. So *communitas* can as easily refer to a juridically organised body as to a multitude, a collectivity with no precise unity either of composition or juxtaposition. *Communitas* does not, therefore, refer to a person, in the Roman law sense. Canon law, on the other hand, uses it to mean ecclesiastical collectivities: the Church itself is a community, *congregatio fidelium, corpus christianorum*, with its own organisational structures. In the Pauline tradition and in the strict theological sense community refers to 'the close union between man and his fellows and between man and God',[11] of course, but it still comes back to having the means in common to achieve that union. In St Paul's writings *koinonia* is based in a transcendent way on the life of the Trinity, but it is a human community nonetheless even if it is not purely so. The very definition of the Church as *koinonia* includes a vertical dimension of union between each believer and God as well as a horizontal dimension of brotherhood with all the other believers who make up the Church. This kind of structure, including within itself both a basic unity and a multiplicity, becomes the pattern for all forms of organisation of religious life, yet without precluding a hierarchical element which (it is worth emphasising) to some extent contradicts the vertical relation with the life of the Trinity. This communitarian model of the Church was not established without a certain amount of tension, one of the deepest sources of this being the monk's or anchorite's enclosure of himself in solitude, wanting no other relationship except union with God. Despite this, however, western monasticism rapidly adopted the form of communities, either under Benedictine rule or some other system. Some commentators have even talked about 'monastic democracy' in the case, for instance, of the Cistercians, where the role of the assembly was of fundamental importance, as will be apparent from the analysis below of the development of the idea of representation in the second half of the fourteenth century.[12] One only has

---

10. *Ibid.*, p. 148.
11. *Dictionnaire de spiritualité* 1976, s.v. *koinonia, communauté, communion*, pp. 1745ff.
12. Moulin 1978, pp. 191ff. Cf. pp. 544–72 below.

to read the Rule of St Benedict to recognise that the community was the model for the monks' communal existence, or to read St Bernard to see that he thought that the religious life could only be lived within a system based on community. In other words, the Church traditions had for a long time shown a preference for evangelical life which took the form of communal existence inside a monastery, or within a religious group; this might be either in relation to the monastic experience itself, with its requirement that all goods should be held in common, or in relation to the mendicant orders, or to any other community that formed part of the Church. And the rapid increase in the number of brotherhoods and confraternities and similar groupings among laymen provides additional confirmation of the inescapable attraction of this way of life.

The point to remember from this hasty sketch is that the emergence of the idea of community, and its persistence in a variety of forms, political and otherwise, does not just give rise to an awareness of belonging to a group, of whatever size; it also creates a desire on the part of the group's members to come together in order to organise and govern themselves. In this creative social ferment they manage to escape from the split between governors and governed by inventing a number of centres of power the intention of which is to divide it up and escape from the limitations imposed by the centralised possession of power on the part of lay or religious seigneurs or even a king. Medieval communities want to govern themselves; their social organisation is part of the process of redistributing political power; they want to take control of their destiny, not necessarily by rebelling against higher authority but often, on the contrary, by treating with it on an equal footing, and sometimes by lending it their support.

This rapid expansion in the number of forms of social existence, and this release of power into a growing number of collective authorities, may seem no more than the demand for what medieval authors like Ockham referred to as *iura et libertates*. But each group or collectivity tends to define itself as possessing juridical status, most often resulting from an agreement of individual wills; the basic purpose of the 'communities' is to have their collective freedom recognised, with the power of dispensing justice and exercising control over their own activities. And so the idea of community is a response to the new forms of social life in which the crucial issue is not the insistence on the rights of individuals but the definition of individuals precisely in terms of their participation in the collective entity: it is this that justifies an individual's existence and his social, political and legal rights.

At the doctrinal level it is almost impossible to over-estimate the significance of the rediscovery of Aristotle in the development of these ideas, as witness the numerous commentaries on the *Politics* in particular, and an analysis of some of them will contribute to a clearer understanding of the doctrinal dimension of the medieval communitarian reality in the second half of the middle ages.

The doctrinal dimension

In William of Moerbeke's translation of Aristotle *communitas* is the translation of the Greek *koinonia*: it refers to the civil community constituted by the city. In the context of the *Politics*, the *polis* is a species of the genus *koinonia*: 'Now since we see that every city exists as a kind of community, and that every community has been established for the sake of some good . . . this is the case with what is called city and with every political community.'[13] Aristotle sees the origins of *koinonia* in a number of different groups such as couples like man and wife, master and slave, and in the family and the village, but also companions in arms, members of the same tribe and, of course, the city.[14] The bond that creates *koinonia* is either interest or *suzèn*, the two elements corresponding word for word with Aristotle's two forms of friendship.[15] Briefly, the concept of *koinonia* involves the following elements: a plurality of participants, with a common aim pursued by common action, with full differentiation between its members but without any relations of subjection or domination on the basis of it.[16] Yet as Gauthier points out in his commentary on the *Nichomachean Ethics* 'it is impossible to find an exact definition of what he means by *koinonia* anywhere in Aristotle's work'.[17] Characteristically the same imprecision recurs in medieval political thought, but so do the basic elements of *koinonia* outlined above: that it is an association of individuals whose distinguishing criterion seems to be the *to koinon*, 'something in common' to the members of the group, none of whom is a tool at the disposal of any other; and this demonstrates the extent to which the Aristotelian community is a place of freedom among equals within the group, and the importance of its purpose, the common interest, *to koinon sumphéron*, or the common good, *to koinon agathon*, which the group's members pursue by common action, *to koinon ergon*.

13. Michaud-Quantin (ed.) 1961, p. 3: 'Quoniam autem omnem civitatem videmus communitatem quandam existentem, et omnem communitatem boni alicuius gratia institutam . . . ipsa autem est quae vocatur civitas et omnis communitas politica.'
14. *Politics* I, 1252 a 24–1252 b 31; *Nicomachean Ethics* VIII, 1160 a 9–30; *Eudemian Ethics* VIII, 1241 b 24ff.
15. *Nicomachean Ethics* VIII, 1159 b 24–1162 b 29; IX, 1171 b 29–1172 a 14.
16. *Politics* I, 1252 a 26; *Eudemian Ethics* VIII, 1241 b 17.
17. Gauthier and Jolif (eds.) 1958–9, vol. II, pt 2, p. 696.

The *Translatio vetus* uses the word *communitas* less frequently than *civitas*: by comparing the occurrences it becomes clear that, as in Aristotle's original text, the translation too uses *communitas* to refer to the male–female, master–slave groups, the *domus*; the city is the *communitas perfecta*, a community by nature;[18] but every social group that has some common interest or activity is a community, so the *koinonia politikè* would appear to be the equivalent of *civitas*.

These are the concepts of the social group that provided medieval thinkers with their essential principles, which responded particularly clearly to political society as it was developing at the time, to the fragmentation and division of authority, while at the same time confirming the existence of two successive types of community, the first governed by blood relationships, and a second type, those that were later called historical societies, governed by political power. The chief lesson medieval thinkers learned from Aristotelian ideas was that these two elements, nature and art, were the two dimensions of human society.

A very few examples will be enough to illustrate this: St Thomas Aquinas in his commentary on the *Politics*, for instance, writes that just as human reason constructs ships out of wood and houses out of stone, so in the same way it arranges communities for the unity of men,[19] the most perfect form of which is the city, which he refers to as a self-sufficient community. The examination of the perfect community comes under the heading of political science, Aquinas establishing the need for it by explaining that although it is a practical science it comes under the science of morality rather than one of the mechanical genera. That is why political science is the most worthy and important of the practical sciences. Its object is the rational study of the city, the 'ideal type' of all human communities, which are measured by reference to it. Every community in fact is established for a certain good; in addition to that, every community is a totality, *quoddam totum*.[20] There is also the phrase *communitas civitatis*,[21] which is defined as *naturalis*.[22] The relationship between *communitas* and *civitas* is in terms of purpose: 'But the city is the end of the aforesaid communities', that is, of the *domus* and the *vicus*, but it stems from these two original communities: 'since the city takes its origin from the aforesaid communities, which are natural'.[23] All communities therefore

18. *Politics* I, 1252 b 9 and Michaud-Quantin (ed.) 1961, p. 4 (52 b 7); 1252 b 16 and Michaud-Quantin (ed.) 1961, p. 4 (52 b 10, 14); 1252 b 29 and Michaud-Quantin (ed.) 1961, p. 5 (52 b 29): 'Ex pluribus autem vicis communitas perfecta civitas, jam omnis habens terminum per se sufficientiae, ut consequens dicere, facta quidem igitur vivendi gratia, existens autem gratia bene vivendi.'
19. Spiazzi (ed.) 1951, p. 1.   20. *Ibid.*, p. 6, § 11.   21. *Ibid.*, p. 17, § 17.   22. *Ibid.*, p. 10, § 32.
23. *Ibid.*, p. 10, § 32: 'Sed civitas est finis praedictarum communitatum . . . cum civitas generetur ex praemissis communitatibus, quae sunt naturales . . .'.

are natural. The city is also defined as a *congregatio hominum*[24] or a *quaedam civium multitudo*,[25] when it is considered from the point of view of the citizens. It is also, in the familiar phrase, *communitas liberorum*. As the city is a *multitudo diversorum* its *unitas* and *communitas* are established by means of well-founded laws. In other words, the law provides the constitutive unity and community of the city. Reiterating Aristotle's criticism of Plato's proposals for community of wives and children, Aquinas demonstrates very clearly the opposition – as well as the complementarity – between that sort of community and the unity of the city, from which it can be seen that a community of that sort, or any sort of community, is not necessarily a unity, and that community of goods does not necessarily contribute to the unity of the city; indeed, community of that sort goes against the very structure of the city, since it makes it impossible to separate the multitude in its diversity from the members that constitute it. Aristotle's division of the city into parts, which is broadly adopted by all the commentators on the *Politics*, corresponds closely to the changes that were being brought about in society itself by the dismantling of monolithic structures, and by giving each section of the city a function appropriate to it. A society that by nature was corporative and associative could not fail to find reassurance for its aims in the Aristotelian model which made it intelligible in theoretical terms. Aquinas is no exception: a city of the kind Socrates wanted to establish, with separate parts and different functions, like those of the husbandman or the artisan, could not exist if there was community of goods, for in a united city the parts composing it must be *quasi duas civitates sibi contrarias*, since everyone pursuing his own activity and owning his own goods must be able to exchange them with others in such a way that there is no conflict of activities and so that the parts of the city form a harmonious unity out of the complementary actions and functions they perform. *Communitas* lies at the heart of the aporia of the one and the many, or the problem of reducing multiplicity to unity: it is what makes unity, in one form or another, possible; but it is not itself unity. It refers rather to *socialitas*, man's social dimension, his aptitude for living in society, than to any specific political reality. Because it is natural it exists by the very fact of man's *impetus naturalis*, for there is a natural impulse in man towards society, just as there is a natural impulse towards the virtues.[26] As the virtues are acquired by education so the city is established by human art and skill. The most

24. *Ibid.*, p. 11, § 34.
25. *Ibid.*, pp. 121–2, § 350: 'Civitas autem est quoddam totum constitutum ex civibus sicut ex partibus, cum civitas nihil aliud sit, quam quaedam civium multitudo.'   26. *Ibid.*, p. 12, § 40.

important thing is the vital human need to communicate, as the *De regimine principum* confirms: 'Man therefore is more inclined than any other animal to communicate with others.'[27] Community represents the total absence of 'war between men', and the complete negation of individual 'solitude': in modern terms, it is sociability. In Lachance's formulation: 'Sociability seen at the moment when it comes fully into being appears as an instinct that in its scope and its force transcends all the system of political society.'[28] 'The social and political state stems from the will of nature . . . in essence, man is part of one multitude or another.'[29] In other words Aquinas sees community as the centre from which all the institutional forms of political organisation are to grow. It does not take any supernatural dimension for its foundations, which are entirely human. It derives its autonomy and its rationality from within itself. It is designed by nature for ethical life and the achievement of the common good.

At the other end of this chain of influence is the vernacular commentary on Aristotle's *Politics* by Nicole Oresme, bishop of Lisieux, which, being written in the late fourteenth century, provides a second reference point for the analysis of doctrines about community. The *Livre de Politiques*, translated from the Latin in 1371, is not just one of the earliest works of political philosophy in French, it also includes a series of glosses following the order of Aristotle's text and designed to explain the translation or to illustrate it with comments and examples which now provide vivid evidence about the social and political structure of life at that time. As far as community is concerned, Oresme seems not to challenge its natural origins, remaining in this respect close to the Aristotelian position. Although there is no exact definition of community in the *Livre des Politiques*, Oresme does differentiate it from the city proper as being 'part of it and under it'.[30] In this sense, the union of man and woman creates a natural community which is also a voluntary one, for marriage is essentially a contractual association. In the same way village communities easily establish relations between neighbours which are also natural. But there are also urban communities, and they should really be called cities as 'a city is composed of a number of streets', as Oresme translates the Latin *vicus*. The city is itself the place of 'natural communication'. 'All partial communities tend naturally, by way of generation, towards the city community, which is complete community.

---

27. Spiazzi (ed.) 1954c, p. 258 (§ 743): 'Magis igitur homo est communicativus alteri quam quodcumque aliud animal.'
28. Lachance 1964, p. 218.   29. *Ibid.*, p. 228 and n. 48: *In Eth.* lect. 1 n. 4.
30. Menut (ed.) 1970, p. 45 (fol. 5 a): 'étant partie de elle et sous elle'.

And therefore it is natural.' In other words, 'communication is the natural purpose of the city' as man 'is naturally civic' (*est naturellement chose civile*), 'ordained by nature to live in civic community'.[31] The city therefore is 'community of men'. To show how well-founded his argument is, Oresme chooses a counter-example: the opposite of communication is excommunication and 'according to canon law this is very severe punishment. And it is a sign that political communication is very natural and fitting for human beings.'[32] After all, did not God himself say, in Genesis, that 'It is not good that man should be alone'?[33]

The city, furthermore, is an organic community, 'for just as a hand cannot truly be a hand if it is not part of a man, so a man is not properly a man if he is not part of a community'. There are, of course, some solitary contemplatives who live away from communities and yet are self-sufficient, not needing help from anybody, 'as some hermits do'; but this does not mean that 'all [men]' have any the less 'natural inclination towards civic communication' and, Oresme adds, 'this is completed by human skill', by which he means that it is human reason, rooted in nature but transcending it, which provides the necessary organisation and discipline for man's original sociability. It is justice or law that perfects the natural community and makes a true political organism out of it. Yet the way Oresme uses the word city indicates his reservations and uncertainties: he uses it as a theoretical concept by means of which he can bring together the problems of man's common life, but he also uses it in the sense of town, even of kingdom. And while he follows Aristotle in rejecting the territorial criterion as a definition, he says that it must be taken into account nonetheless. For him a city is, first and foremost, an episcopal town; but it is also 'a great multitude of houses or habitations, adjacent or near to each other, in one place'. He also uses it to mean a kingdom which in sum, as he says, is 'like a great city'. Even 'the glorious company of Paradise is called a city', he writes, and we can see in this Augustine's two cities showing through under the Aristotelianism. But the Church is a city too, for it is 'the multitude of those who are, or have been, or will be of the catholic communion in the faith of Jesus Christ'. The clergy can thus be seen as a city as they have their

---

31. *Ibid.*, p. 48 (fol. 7 b–c): 'Par voie de generaeion toutes communités partiales tendent par nature à communité de cité, qui est communité parfaite. Et donc elle est naturelle . . . communiquer en cité est fin naturelle, car l'homme est naturellement chose civile . . . ordené de nature à vivre en communité civile.'

32. *Ibid.*, p. 49 (fol. 8 a): 'selon les droits canons, ce est très grand paine, et ce est signe que communication politique est très naturelle et très convenable à humaine créature'.

33. Genesis 2:18.

own distinct government. This institutionalised body has 'governance distribution and disposal of certain possessions and certain public offices (*honorabletés*)'.[34]

When he is dealing with community in the strict sense, then, Oresme prefers to use the term multitude in order to qualify it, as for example here: 'When a small multitude of people who live together communally starts to grow and becomes larger and larger . . . as soon as it reaches a size at which it is able to support itself and live well, that is when it can satisfy all its own requirements, that is when it becomes a city, and not before.'[35] This self-sufficiency is the touchstone for the 'very best size (*quantité*) for a city'. 'The smallest size for a city is that at which a multitude can be self-sufficient: smaller than that it would not be sufficient'; but, he adds, 'it is not a matter of being three or four men short, for one cannot be so mathematically precise as that in this sort of subject'.[36] He solves the problem of the unity of the city by opting for plurality, that is, for diversity and difference. He does not approve of the reduction of all cities to a single unity, as the supporters of the Empire try to do. It must be considered that 'the multitude of all men is not a body or thing that can be ordered under the command of one man'. The kingdom of France, in other words, is not subject to the authority of the emperor: the king is 'emperor in his own kingdom'.

As well as the commentaries properly so called on Aristotle's *Politics*, there is another source of information about the doctrinal aspects of *communitas*, the literary genre of 'treatises On Power' which, for the most part, were written as polemical responses to events in the conflict between the temporal and spiritual powers. Examples are the *De potestate regia et papali* of John of Paris, Dante's *Monarchia* and the *Defensor pacis* of Marsilius of Padua.

34. Menut (ed.) 1970, pp. 119–20 (fols. 78 b–79 b): 'Je di donques que aucunes foix est prinse cité pour une grande multitude de hostelz ou habitacions qui sont prochaines ou ensemble en un lieu . . . tout un royalme ou un pais est une grande cité . . . Item, la glorieuse compagnie de Paradis est appellée cité . . . Item, la multitude de ceuls qui sont ou ont esté ou seront de la communication catholique en la foy de Jhesus Crist peut estre dite cité . . . ceulz quo nous appellons gens de Eglise sont comme une cité; car ils ont une policie quant a la gubernacion, distribucion et ordenance d'aucunes possessions et d'aucunes honorabletés publiques.'

35. Menut (ed.) 1970, p. 289 (fol. 246 d): 'Quant une petite multitude de gens qui communient ensemble procède en cressant et est faicte plus grande et après encore plus grande . . . si tost comme elle vient à telle quantité que elle est par soi suffisante pour vivre bien, ce est à dire quant l'en y peut trouver tout ce qui fault, adonques est-elle premièrement cité, et devant non.'

36. *Ibid.*, p. 289 (fol. 247 c): 'La plus petite quantité de cité est de multitude par soi suffisante laquelle, si elle estoit mendre, ne serait pas par soi suffisante; elle ne doit pas etre dite mendre pour trois hommes ou pour quatre, car l'en ne doit pas prendre en ceste matière mesure mathématique ou précise.'

John of Paris's treatise[37] dates of course from the beginning of the fourteenth century and was written in response to the dispute that had arisen between Boniface VIII and the king of France, Philip the Fair. Like the author of the *Rex pacificus*,[38] John defends a certain amount of independence for the temporal power, in this case the power of the king of France. His model of the political community is the *regnum*, that is to say the *regimen multitudinis perfecte ad commune bonum ordinatum ab uno*. The members of the kingdom constitute a *multitudo* the *telos* of which is the good or common interest.[39] Men are united by what they have in common. Although he basically uses the Aristotelian and Thomist formulations, John lays more stress on the problem of the unity of the kingdom than on the community of interest of its members which can be taken for granted in his perspective.

In both the *Convivio* and the *Monarchia* Dante is concerned to examine, from the Aristotelian point of view throughout, the *civilitas humana* which is the union of different individual societies, particularly the *communitates perfectae*.[40] The *humana civilitas* is ordained for the purpose of furthering the life of happiness, which nobody can achieve without the help of others. It is the property of human nature to be sociable, and this precedes any concrete political organisation.[41]. Taking this as his starting-point, Dante proceeds with great originality to argue for a universal human society, *societas humani generis*, the community of the entire human race, under the authority of a universal monarch.[42] However, he does not overlook the fact that, as he himself says,[43] 'nations, kingdoms and cities have different ways of life, and different laws are required to govern them'. Yet it is to give these various sorts of communities common rules that Dante argues the need for a single universal monarchy, as one monarch is better able than a number of rulers to secure and protect what is common to all. He makes it clear that he regards the Roman Empire as the only historical figure of a political society that would encompass the whole human race. Such a universal community will be both natural and rational; it is neither established nor created by anything other than man's natural tendency to live communally with his fellows in the pursuit of a common aim, the highest form of which is the human happiness that comes from wisdom.

37. Leclercq (ed.) 1942; Bleienstein (ed.) 1969; Watt (transl.) 1971.
38. Cf. Quillet 1977, pp. 42ff.   39. Leclercq (ed.) 1942 p. 176.
40. *Convivio*, iv.iv.1; *Monarchia*, i.ii, iii.
41. *Convivio*, iv.xxv.1: 'poi che noi non potemo perfetta vita avere senza amici, si come ne l'ottavo de l'Etica vuole Aristotile'; also i.i.8: 'però che ciascuno uomo a ciascuno uomo naturalmente è amico . . .'.   42. *Monarchia*, i.xiv.
43. *Monarchia*, i.xiv.5: 'habent namque nationes, reges et civitates inter se proprietates, quae legibus differentibus regulari oportet . . .'.

The political community, in short, develops out of this natural tendency: there is no need to search for any foundation outside that. This emphasis on the natural and rational character of the political community and therefore on its autonomy finds one of its most radical expressions in the work of Marsilius of Padua.[44]

At the beginning of the *Defensor pacis*, Marsilius writes in praise of peace, claiming that 'Individual brethren, and in even greater degree groups and communities are obliged to help one another, both from the feeling of supernatural love and from the bond or law of human society.'[45] Communities are thus characterised both in terms of a human, juridical bond, and the bond of love that transcends human values. Whatever Marsilius' rhetorical purpose may be here, the fact remains that the accent is not placed on the innate naturalness of the bond, but on the brotherhood of men living together, which is essentially an ethical value, although the stoic aspect of this primary sense does not, of course, mean that there is no natural bond. It is also interesting that he uses the word *collegium*, with its canon law associations probably uppermost. In Chapter 3 of the first part of *Defensor Pacis* ('on the origin of the civil community'), Marsilius remains faithful to the Aristotelian tradition, tracing the origins and development of the perfect community, or city, after the manner of Aristotle in the *Politics*, although, it can be argued, also showing the influence of Averroism and even of the thought of al-Farabi.[46] He defines the perfect community as the association of men who join together to arrange for all their needs to be met by the allocation of specific tasks to every part of the city and, most importantly, to ensure the rule of justice. Among these needs, it is to be remarked, is that of achieving the good life – in other words, civil happiness, happiness to be enjoyed in this world as well as in the world to come. It is in this perspective that Marsilius justifies the existence of the priesthood in the city, whose task is to minister to man's desire to seek salvation in this world and, by the same token, to find celestial bliss in the next.[47]

Marsilius refers to the perfect community either as being the whole body of the citizens (*universitas civium*), or as the 'weightier part' (*pars valentior*)[48] – an aspect to be considered later in connection with representation.

The community itself has a natural foundation, made explicit by the mutual agreement of wills, and it achieves the status of *city* through reason

---

44. Previté-Orton (ed.) 1928; Scholz (ed.) 1932–3; Gewirth (transl.) 1951 and 1956, vol. II.

45. *Defensor pacis*, I.i.4: 'singuli fratres, atque magis collegia et communitates se invicem iuvare tenentur, tam supernae caritatis affectu, quam vinculo sive iure societatis humanae.'

46. Cf. Quillet 1979.   47. *Defensor pacis*, I.v *passim*.   48. *Ibid.*, I.xii, xiii *passim*.

and art. The basic datum is 'the natural desire of man to live in society':[49] as for the result, the existence of the community rests, in the final analysis, upon the will, not of all its members, but of the citizens who constitute it.

A possible ambiguity in the simultaneous assertion of a natural desire for life in society and of the mutual agreement of wills has led some historians in discussing Marsilius' thought to advance the hypothesis that a contract is involved.[50] But in fact it can be shown that it is artificial to see a dilemma between naturalism and voluntarism in this context.[51] The city is, of course, the result of a voluntary association of men, but this only expresses their natural tendency to group themselves together. The perfect civil community, in my reading of Marsilius, is a natural entity, as it is in the works of those predecessors of his – Aquinas, Giles of Rome, John of Paris, for example – in the Aristotelian tradition. Marsilius, it is true, does not use the often repeated formula of man as a political animal; but even if we take as typical the argument designed to justify the existence and responsibilities of the priesthood in the city by using the Augustinian vision of the state as *remedium peccati*,[52] all his arguments about the constitution of the perfect community still derive in all their essential elements from Aristotelian naturalism. It is, again, true that the *universitas civium*, which is the key concept from chapter 12 of the first part of *Defensor pacis* onwards, and the *pars valentior* as well, is also the *universitas fidelium*, and it is difficult to see how the community of the faithful can be founded in nature, except by recourse to the artifice of metaphor and analogy: 'Understood in another sense, the truest and most fitting of all in regard to the first application of the term or the intention of those who first applied it, though not now so familiar or in accordance with modern usage', the Church is 'the whole body of the faithful who believe in and invoke the name of Christ, and all the parts of this whole body in any community, even the household'.[53] Marsilius therefore does not see the Church as a community in the real sense; it is the *corpus mysticum*, the famous canonist metaphor, the specific meaning of which varies from instance to instance. Yet he does use the term 'perfect' to qualify a community of the faithful whose prince is also faithful.[54] No matter how perfect a civil community may be in terms of a purely

---

49. *Ibid.*, I.xiii.2.   50. Cf. Quillet 1970a, pp. 93–9, and Grignaschi 1955.
51. Quillet 1970a, p. 81.   52. *Defensor pacis*, I.i.6.
53. *Ibid.*, II.ii.3: 'Rursum, secundum aliam significationem dicitur hoc nomen *ecclesia*, et omnium verissime et propriissime secundum primam impositionem huius nominis seu intentionem primorum imponentium, licet non ita famose seu secundum modernum usum, de universitate fidelium credentium et invocantium nomen Christi, et de huius universitatis partibus omnibus in quacumque communitate, etiam domestica.'   54. *Ibid.*, II.xvii.15; II.xxv.3.

Aristotelian definition, if the prince is not one of the faithful then the community cannot be perfect in that its ruling institutions will not be able to respond adequately to the second fundamental desire of man in society, the search for salvation in the hope of finding celestial bliss in the world to come. Such a desire can only be satisfied in the perfect community of the faithful governed by a faithful prince, since the Christian ministry alone is true, and only the Christian faith possesses the truth and the right knowledge of God.[55] What in fact makes the political community really a perfect community – and this, it seems, has not always been sufficiently emphasised by interpreters of Marsilius' thought – is attaining the status of a community of the faithful, of faithful citizens, the whole body of whom, the *universitas*, or the weightier part of them, or the political authority delegated by them to the government of whatever sort, which is the same thing, is Christian; because a community of that sort can respond to the need to live and to live well, that is to say, to the need for earthly happiness and the search for bliss in the next world. The perfect community thus means the political body of citizens who are also believers.

In this community Marsilius explains that there is a distinction to be drawn between the 'plebeian multitude'[56] and the parts of the state 'in the strict sense', to wit, the priests, the army and the judges, who are the notables; the multitude encompasses the peasants and artisans, the people who in the Italian cities were categorised as the *popolo minuto*, while Marsilius' *honorabilitas* corresponds to the *popolo grosso*.

Marsilius' doctrine of the community is thus not very far removed from the traditional organicist conception derived from Aristotle. He shares with his predecessors an imprecise terminology when it comes to referring to the community: it may be the *populus*, the *multitudo sive populus*, the *universa multitudo*, the *tota* or the *subjecta multitudo*. But whichever word he uses the meaning is always more or less the same: a community is a multitude ordered into a unity, of whatever sort, whose aim and purpose is to achieve peace and tranquillity for the whole social body, as that is the necessary condition for human social existence. By its nature the political community is essentially ethical, and as such responds to the needs of man defined as someone who communicates with his fellows; it constitutes a totality out of which and within the context of which the individual emerges.

Marsilius of Padua, it was observed, does not use Aristotle's concept of the political animal *expressis verbis*, preferring to emphasise the means

55. *Ibid.*,I.v.13. 56. *Ibid.*,I.v.I.

human reason has of establishing the community. Duns Scotus, approaching the question from a quite different set of perspectives, is also dissatisfied with that concept, which he regards as inadequate to deal with the practical problems raised by man's adaptation to the demands of the public interest. His view of political society is Augustinian, with the state as *remedium peccati*, and he thus describes the community as a result of a pact which men, free by nature, reach among themselves despite their fall, to form a political body so that they can live in the least bad conditions possible in a *communitas humana* defined as a 'suitable disposition of equal and unequal persons'. An arrangement of this sort is not absolutely natural, partly because of sin, which has corrupted nature, and partly because of the finite and contingent character of human beings, the fragility of the union of body and soul and the freedom enjoyed by human beings, the *ultima solitudo*, able to abide by or deny the prompting of right reason. There is clearly much less sense of dependence on or respect for Aristotle in this perspective, and the theological and metaphysical point of view is very different from, say, that of Aquinas. As well as the paternal authority which is natural, there is in addition the social pact. Men come together in civil communities in order to combine their separate *dominia* (such as that of the father). The civil community is thus the product of a convention. Men, strangers to one another (once free from paternal authority), come together to enter into a *pactum subjectionis*. The new bond that unites them is by definition external to the family. This suggests a genuine will for association, since none of the constituent parties was bound beforehand to obey any other. In other words, the *viatores* of this world are called to govern a community whose basis is contingent, certainly, but they must do so in accordance with an order aimed at minimising injustice and maximising utility, with due regard for persons and for the rules of strict equity. From this point view, consent and election are the *ultima ratio* of political society. Beyond the individuals and the fulfilment, on these lines, of the community, Duns Scotus is concerned to elaborate the notion of personality: *personalitas est negatio communicationis*[57] – 'personality is the denial of communication', in the sense that its separate existence is not like that of a member of a totality. Its liberty precludes any kind of natural dependence: 'Personality requires an ultimate solitude – the negation of any dependence, actual or potential, in regard to any person of another nature.'[58] The political community, in this

---

57. Gandillac 1968, p. 685 and n. 7, which refers to *Ordinatio* III, d. 1, q.1, n.17.
58. Lagarde 1956–70, vol. II, p. 237; and *Opus oxoniense* III, d. 1, q. 1, n. 6 and 17: 'Ad personalitatem requiritur ultima solitudo, sive negatio dependentiae actualis et aptitudinalis ad personam alterius naturae.'

perspective, is a *communitas aggregationis*, its unity entirely composite.

This position, indications of which are scattered at different points in Duns Scotus' theological works, seems to run counter to the essentially corporatist societies described above. There is usually a connection made between the development of urban institutions and the development of political Aristotelianism, particularly in relation to the 'natural' character of civil communities, and the predominance of the whole community over the individuals who compose it. With Duns Scotus, and even more with Ockham, the connection becomes problematic, and the definition of the political community is no longer derived from the natural sociability of man. Yet this does not necessarily mean that the social philosophy of the *Venerabilis Inceptor* is out of touch with the political realities of the time. As has been pointed out, after all, the medieval world teemed with associations, leagues, colleges and fraternities, all jealous of their rights and freedoms. However it must be realised that the spirit of these diverse 'communities' was leading them in the direction of Aristotelian interpretations of the meaning of life in society and that the doctrines of Duns Scotus and Ockham, with their stress on the individual, could not but be at variance with this tendency. Ockham's notion of the political community, to put it briefly, and without going into the detail of his moral and political ideas, is that it is constituted by the whole body of individuals who compose it, whether in the case of the entire human race, *universitas mortalium*, one city, *una civitas*, a group, *unum collegium*, or more broadly the *connexio inter omnes mortales*.[59]

This sort of perspective is bound up with a vision of the world within which the logical category of *relatio* is only a word 'signifying a number of absolutes, or to put it another way, it is a plurality of absolutes in the same way as a people is a plurality of men and no single man is a people'.[60] The notion of the unity of a community thus becomes rather circumscribed. In one sense it can mean a degree of order, so long as by order is understood nothing more than a particular arrangement of elements or absolutes; but there can be no talk of unity except in an improper sense of the term: 'Something is said to be one improperly and loosely, as when a kingdom is said to be one, or a people, or the world is said to be one.'[61]

59. Sikes, Bennett and Offler (eds.) 1940– , vol. I, pp. 14–15 and 39–41 (*Octo quaestiones*, q. I, c. 1 and 9); also *Dialogus* III, tr. 2, l. 1, c. 1, and l. 3, c. 17 and 22.
60. Baudry 1958, pp. 232ff; Ockham, *In I Sent.*, d. 30, q. 1; *Quodlibet* VI, q. 15. 'Relatio est . . . tantum intentio vel conceptum in anima importans plura absoluta vel est plura absoluta, sicut populus est plures homines et nullus homo est populus.'
61. Baudry 1958, p. 175: 'Aliquid est unum improprie et large, sicut regnum dicitur unum, vel populus unum et mundus unum.'

The structure of society is therefore constituted by a network of arrangements and agreements of which the ultimate aim is the maintenance of order and peace. It is the people, defined as an aggregate of individuals, who have the power to establish institutions: natural freedoms must not be suspended nor even curtailed against the wishes of those who possess them; there is thus respect for the customs and freedoms of the intermediary bodies 'through which were expressed historically (for fourteenth-century man) the fundamental rights of those free, rational individuals who, socially speaking, are the only ones to have any real existence'.[62]

These are the theoretical reasons why, in the political dimension of his thought, William of Ockham exemplifies both the defence of the Empire, which he conceives as the whole body of mortals ruled by a single prince – which ties up with Dante's universalist notions of the human race – and the assertion of the *jura et libertates* of particular groups, thus paradoxically bringing together what may be termed the two antagonistic tendencies in medieval political thought: the concern for universality on the one hand, and on the other, a profound awareness of sub-groups as making up the web of human social existence. This had a significant consequence for the definition of political authority which Ockham and followers of his like Pierre d'Ailly brought to light: whatever form political authority may take, it resides first and fundamentally in the community as a whole, whether it be civil or ecclesiastical. Political institutions, civil or ecclesiastical, fulfil the same role in political philosophy as do general ideas in speculative philosophy: they have no existence or purpose except with reference to the multitude which constitutes them.[63]

By the end of the fourteenth century and the beginning of the fifteenth theorists had to deal with the political community from more or less fixed viewpoints, in particular that of the kingdom. The persistence of the communitarian vision of society, however, led them now to speak of the 'community of the realm'. A long process of evolution, which there is no need to describe here, had culminated in the emergence of distinct national entities, particularly in France and England. By looking at some of the usages of 'community' in vernacular treatises, sermons and literary works, an attempt will be made to show that while the doctrinal arguments continued, so did the perenniality of a communitarian vision of man's social existence.

62. Gandillac 1956, p. 473.   63. Quillet 1974b, p. 353.

In this respect the teachings of Jean Gerson are particularly important. His sermon *Vivat rex*, especially,[64] lays great emphasis on the fundamentally organic nature of the kingdom: in it, he develops three dimensions of life, 'living corporeally, living civically and politically, and living spiritually and everlastingly', devoting most attention to the second of these, which he calls 'civil, political or universal life'. This second aspect of the king's life, for it is in him that all three meet, is 'permanent'; civil life 'is maintained in the union and unity of lord and people in one lawful and just order'. Its purpose is the common good. This is why it is governed by moral philosophy, 'ethics, economics and politics, which the arts and the law deal with'. In the 'considerations' that follow, Gerson questions the basis of this second aspect of life, to wit, its unity, the order that presides over the diversity of its parts. The bond that unites the king's subjects is a bond of love; order is maintained by the exercise of the four cardinal virtues, prudence, temperance ('attrempance'), fortitude and justice. Such a life, not only the corporeal dimension 'but civil and mystical', is comparable to an organism because the subjects of the king are 'like the body having different members for the different estates and offices of the kingdom'. Throughout, Gerson unflaggingly emphasises the close mutual dependence of the prince and his subjects: 'since a king cannot long endure or rationally live without subjects, nor subjects without a king, agreement is necessary'. In other words, the king cannot exist without his subjects; he is a part – the principal part – of the community.

Ernst Kantorowicz has analysed and described the transition of the idea of *corpus mysticum* from reference to the Church to its secular use as a description of the state, the kingdom or to the political community in general. All that is needed here in this connection is to say that the glorification of regal power provided late medieval political thinkers with an opportunity to breathe new life into the organicist metaphor that John of Salisbury had used in the twelfth century to refer to the *corpus quoddam reipublice*, now become the community of the realm. The very idea of political community is thus – as in Gerson's work – connected with the mystical character previously conferred upon the Church; the *communitas mortaliam* is, in a way, coeternal to the Church, and being in reality entirely subject to time, it can find a means of escape from that domination by becoming an intellectual and mystical fact, and a juridical and moral person, all at the same time. The model of the kingdom was to facilitate the visible incarnation of the community in the king's person, or in his 'two bodies', or,

64. Glorieux (ed.) 1968.

to use Gerson's formulation, in his three lives, the first of which corresponds to the sublunary state of creation, bound to decay – the life of the body – the second transcending that fate in the perpetuity of an eternal present – the political life – while the third is the true spiritual life, totally outside time. This appears to be a rather strange interpretation of the Aristotelian doctrine of the eternity of the world, for while Aristotle did in fact put forward an argument of that sort at the level of *phusis* he seems never to have extended it to apply to the political sphere, which he sees as the realm of change and destruction. While one might say that one of Aristotle's central preoccupations in the *Politics* is with knowing how to avoid revolutions, or with ensuring that constitutions degenerate as little as possible, this clearly reflects his sense that nothing is in fact more vulnerable to change than the political domain. The late medieval political thinkers seem to have followed an exactly opposite train of reasoning, by doing their utmost to attribute a kind of 'aeviternity' to the political community, modelled on the Church to some extent, but principally derived from the teachings of Aristotelian physics.

To conclude this hasty sketch of the vernacular literature, we may consider one of the themes closest to the heart of Philippe de Mézières, author of the *Songe du Vieil Pèlerin*[65] and tutor to the future Charles VI, previously Chancellor to the king of Cyprus and, most important of all, one of the circle of Charles V the Wise at the end of the fourteenth century. He advocates a form of collaboration between the various 'estates' of the political community for the smooth running of the kingdom, as we shall see when we deal with the problems of representation, but he also presents a view of the kingdom in its total sense as being for the practical pursuit of the 'common good', something which is not the concern of the king or his councillors alone, but of all orders of society at their own appropriate level. Authority still resides fully in the person of the king, there is no doubt about that: but there is also no doubt that Philippe de Mézières' emphasis falls on the kingdom as a whole. This is borne out by the evidence of the two allegories which he uses to describe political society.

The first, briefly, is the chess board, an allegory he develops in Book III of the *Songe du Vieil Pèlerin*. The game itself was fashionable at Charles V's court, and the king himself possessed copies of French translations of the work of Jacques de Cessoles in his 'library'. The chess board represents the kingdom of France, and the city itself, which must follows the rules of its progress if it is to endure. Even more significant is the allegory of the ship of

65. Coopland (ed.) 1969; and cf. Quillet 1984, pp. 119ff.

France, 'gracious and sovereign', whose various parts and different roles Philippe describes at length. It consists of 'four triple hierarchies of the twelve orders or singular estates of the kingdom of France', each of which is examined in turn. Burgesses, merchants, tradesmen and labourers, officers of the courts, lawyers and all the 'offices' of the city are described minutely and criticised severely, especially the lawyers towards whom Philippe feels particular animosity, in the familiar French tradition of hostility to red tape. Nor is the seigneurial hierarchy spared criticism: it comprises 'the king, the princes of the royal house and the great lords, the knightly order and the ordinary nobles and captains of the realm'. Thus the knights are badly educated nowadays, he says, and their values are out of date. And the great lords are flatterers who misuse their influence on 'the king's innocent majesty'. Meanwhile the people in the lowest rank, the 'common people' taken as a whole, suffer the varied ills that war and taxation bring with them.

The description is long and detailed, but all that need concern us here is the way the symbolism of the social body is worked into various allegorical figures, one of which, reverting to the traditional tripartite division of the 'estates', rests on a metaphorical representation of the Trinity itself. The clergy thus become the symbolic figure of the Father, the people – '*gros et menu*' – become the Son, and the nobles become the Holy Spirit. The fatherhood of the Church is then justified because by its administration of the sacraments it sustains the life of the soul, both of the people and of the nobles. The Son symbolises the people because by their labour and the 'sweat of their body' they provide bread and the life of the body just as Christ provides the bread of life with his own body. The nobles stand for the Holy Spirit, which is 'ardent love proceeding from the Father and the Son'. In the same way, the lives of the nobles 'must be converted into love' and proceed from the Church and the people, the former for the life of the soul, the latter for the life of the body. Kings, princes, barons and knights are thus 'taken for the person of the Holy Spirit'.

The other figure which it is interesting to examine is that of the ship. There is of course a long tradition of ships being used to represent the social body, but although it is not a new idea Philippe de Mézières's description is particularly eloquent. The ship is large, lofty, splendid and stately; its name is *Gracious* and *Sovereign*. It is built of cedarwood, which does not rot in the water, and it has three levels. On the poop there is a royal palace, supported by another smaller palace; at the wheel is a castle for defence and, if necessary, for attack. Around these buildings are grouped all sorts of dwellings and offices 'for all manner of people of all trades and professions, for husbandmen in various kinds of tillage', not forgetting merchants and burgesses. The important thing is that the ship has two doorways, one at the prow, the other at the poop, through which the three levels can communicate.

Philippe also describes the ship's inhabitants, and here the whole structure of the kingdom unfolds before us. And so the ship goes on its way towards its final destination, the holy city of Jerusalem. As it sails on, keeping close inshore to avoid the perils of the open sea in accordance with contemporary practice, it has various unpleasant encounters, as when it meets the *Unneighbourly Ship*, recognisable as England. 'Once one of the XVII ships, called *Unneighbourly*, collided against the sovereign ship with such force that it carried off the six castles on the gracious ship's right side.'[66]

In her treatise *Le livre du corps de policie*, Christine de Pisan takes up, in an almost literal way, the symbolism of the social body that John of Salisbury had used in his *Policraticus*, which was translated into French in 1372 by Denis Foulechat, one of Charles V's translators. There are three parts to Christine's work, the first addressed to princes, the second to nobles and knights and the third to the 'university' of all the people, as she puts it. For her, as for her predecessors, the king is the head of the body – the 'Chief', the understanding, with the knights as the arms and hands, and the people symbolised by the legs and the feet. If the king is 'the head of the living image of the body of the state', nobles and knights are the arms and the hands. Each is responsible for the order established by God, and must maintain himself in the state where birth has placed him – 'that is to say, the nobles as nobles should, the common people likewise in the place appropriate to them, and all alike related to the one body of the same state, so as to live together in peace and justice as they should'.

The 'totality of the common people' is symbolised by the legs and feet of the social body, so that the latter may be 'living, complete, and healthy'. The continued health of the social body, in fact, like that of the human body, requires the harmonious co-operation of all its parts:

for as the body of a man is not whole but defective and deformed when it lacks any of its members, so the body of the state cannot be complete, whole, or healthy unless all the orders [of society] are well joined and united together so that they can succour and help one another, each fulfilling the function allotted to it; for these different functions, when everything is considered, are established and should

---

66. Coopland (ed.) 1969, vol. I, pp. 537, 462ff, 507, 524ff, 533ff, 453ff; and for the 'quatre ordres, par maiiere de gerarchies triples' cf. pp. 447–8.

operate only for the preservation of the whole, just as the members of the human body help to govern and nourish the body as a whole.

The 'whole body of the people' is itself differentiated into a number of estates, harmony among which is a function of the harmony that must exist between them and the other orders of society. The burgesses, whose 'lineage has been long established in the cities', who have 'a proper name, a surname, and bear arms of ancient date', are the mediators between the 'common' (*menu*) people and the princes: they play a fundamental role in the body of the state, for they are merchants, and the merchant estate 'is most necessary', since 'the royal and princely estates and likewise the polity of cities and of countries could by no means do without' their assistance.[67]

It is clear then that the concept of political community continues to figure in vernacular literature, and is adopted with striking unanimity by most of the political thinkers of the period. A final example of this may be taken from the *De Concordantia Catholica* of Nicholas of Cusa,[68] written in 1433, during the council of Basel, one of its aims being to bring about a reconciliation among the various opposing factions. The theme of concord naturally goes far beyond these purely temporal and political considerations: concord is ultimately the 'deep divine harmony of the Church (*profunda divina ecclesiae harmonia*) – the Church here being one of the most general figures of human society; concord is the agreement of differences, it being understood that, in principle, unity is the first consideration:

This is why every creature in its own way comes gradually, by a natural effluence, to bear a diminishing resemblance [to the primary being]; and it is, so to speak, as a shadow or figure or similitude of the higher nature which precedes it that the lower nature finds its place in the scale, until the multiplication of lower and less noble beings exhausts the radiance of life-giving nature. At this final point the process of multiplication comes to a halt, for the radiance, having reached the lowest point at which it can sustain its own existence, has nothing left to communicate; and thus the lowest being in this hierarchy ends in shadow.[69]

Communication, the means by which beings relate to one another, is the key word in this definition. There is no need to go into the detail of Nicholas' doctrine, but the idea of concord itself implies a recognition of the

---

67. Lucas (ed.) 1967, pp. 1–3, 103, 104, 166–7, 183ff, 191–2.
68. Kallen (ed.) 1959–68 (*Nicholai de Cusa Opera Omnia*, vol, xiv).
69. 1.ii.9: 'Unde suo modo naturali fluxu gradatim minus similitudinis gerunt et quasi in umbra, figura seu similitudine praecellentis altioris naturae disponit inferior gradatim, quousque multiplicatio versus inferius et ignobilius ita in radio deficit vitalis naturae, quod absque multiplicatione amplius quiescat in ultimo puncto, ita parum habens virtutis, quod tantum sibi sufficit et non amplius communicare potest, et sic ultimum illius ordinis in umbra terminatur.'

bond between created beings, and between them and their creator. This recognition is fundamental to Nicholas of Cusa's philosophy and governs the whole of his outlook on the political community. In fact in Book III of *De Concordantia* he argues that 'provided from the outset with reason, to set them apart from other animals, men understood by reasoning that companionship and community were extremely useful, and indeed necessary for their survival, and for the purpose of living itself, and so they came together by natural instinct and, living together in that way, built villages and towns'. He follows Aristotle and the commentators in describing man as 'a political and civil animal, who tends naturally to live the life of a citizen',[70] but he places his emphasis not only on a sort of *pactum subiectionis* such as was elaborated by Duns Scotus, but also on a real consensus, implying a kind of 'continued contract' between the members of a political community and the authority that they establish, 'for if men have equal power and equal freedom by nature, the only way to establish the true and well-ordered power of a single ruler must be by election and consensus on the part of the others'. Quoting Gratian's *Decretum*, he adds, 'It is clear that, since human society, by means of a universal contract voluntarily agrees to obey its kings . . . the ruler himself must be elected.'[71]

It is not necessary to emphasise here how much Nicholas of Cusa was influenced by the political ideas of Marsilius of Padua.[72] What is worth noting in conclusion is that Nicholas gives the society of the human race a universalist dimension which is interesting in that he goes beyond the notion of a specific community, and defines the universal society (in the *De Pace fidei*[73]) as the society of all believers, or, as Gandillac puts it,[74] as the manifestation of the 'community of minds', anticipating the formulations Leibniz was to use in his attempt to create a 'religious organisation of the earth'. Nicholas of Cusa sees a concord between natural groups which provides a basis and sanction for the progressive development of a 'universal

70. III, Prooemium, 269–70: 'Homines vero ratione prae cunctis animalibus dotati a principio consoliditatem et communionem suae conservationi ac etiam fini, propter quem quisque est, multum conferre, immo necessarium rationabili discursu intelligentes, naturali instinctu se univere ac sic cohabitantes villagia urbesque construxere . . . Videmus enim hominem animal esse politicum et civile et naturaliter ad civilitatem inclinari.'
71. I.xiv.127: 'Nam si natura aeque potentes et aeque liberi homines sunt, vera et ordinata potestas unius communis aeque potentis naturaliter non nisi electione et consensu aliorum constitui potest, sicut etiam lex ex consensu constituitur, 2 di. *Lex*, 8 di. *Quae contra* . . . Ecce, quia pacto generali convenit humana societas velle regibus oboedire, tunc . . . in vero regiminis ordine ipsius rectoris electio fieri debet . . .'.
72. Quillet 1970b.
73. Klibansky and Bascour (eds.) 1960 (*Nicolai de Cusa Opera Omnia*, vol. VII).
74. Gandillac 1941, p. 442; and cf. Gandillac 1953.

commonwealth' as the utopian conclusion of an ecumenism whose theoretical foundations he propounded with a boldness that goes well beyond Dante's anticipatory ideas in the *Monarchia*.

Counsel and councils

Terminology: doctrinal origins

One of the most important aspects of communal life in the middle ages is reflected in the widespread use of the terms 'counsel' and 'council'. It is therefore necessary to make a brief excursion into their semantic field before going on to analyse their content. Counsel means a decision, a deliberation, advice, plan or opinion; the reference is thus to practical wisdom, to action, whether by one or a number of individuals or by one or a number of groups. It is essentially an ethical concept, which has both Greek and biblical origins. *Euboulia* is primarily a warrior virtue, the characteristic of a good general, but it also has a peacetime connotation, when it becomes the virtue practised in connection with everyday affairs in the 'councils' of the city, such as the *ekklesia* at Athens. It is therefore also a political virtue, which allows the members of the assembly to govern the city wisely. There is, finally, the sense of a private virtue, which, as it were, enables a man to exercise self-control. For Aristotle, *euboulia*, good counsel, 'is a sort of deliberation' which includes a 'right principle' consisting in 'attaining a good end', or in other words, 'the right principle that consists in finding that which is of use for the purpose of which wisdom is a true apperception'.[75] The term also has a long pedigree in the realm of theology where it is one of the Gifts of the Holy Spirit: this reaches back to the bible, and a long Christian tradition of commentary on the relevant verses in Isaiah.[76] St Thomas Aquinas, for instance, regards counsel, *boulè*, as to some extent symbiotic with Aristotle's prudence: 'It is proper to the rational creature to be moved through the research of reason to perform any particular action, and this research is called counsel.'[77] It is prudence that enables us to offer good counsel to ourselves and others. Because of the contingent nature of the events of this world, and because human reason is unable to understand them in their

---

75. *Nicomachean Ethics* VI, 1142 b 16.
76. Isaiah 11: 2: 'And the spirit of the Lord shall rest upon him, the spirit of wisdom and understanding, the spirit of counsel and might, the spirit of knowledge and of the fear of the Lord.'
77. *Summa Theologiae* IIa IIae, q. 52, art. 1: 'Est autem proprium rationali creaturae quod per inquisitionem mentis moveatur ad aliquid agendum; quae quidem inquisitio consilium dicitur . . .'.

singularity, 'man needs the guidance of God in taking counsel, just as in human affairs 'those who are unable to take counsel for themselves need to seek counsel from those who are wiser'.[78] It may be objected that in the hierarchy of the acts of prudence counsel is the least exalted, being placed beneath judgement and commandment: but Aquinas challenges this classification and, setting the gift of counsel beside the 'powers' which move the human soul, he defines it as that which 'helps' (*adjuvans*) prudence and perfects it (*perficiens*).

A final comment on the philosophical and theological status of counsel: it is generally distinguished from precept by the criterion *de necessitate salutis*. This is an important distinction, particularly in Marsilius of Padua's *Defensor pacis*, because that is how the extent of the prince's coercive power is delimited.[79] Taking that as his starting-point, Marsilius defines coercive law as that which is 'a coercive precept with appropriate punishment or recompense to be received in this world'.[80] Counsel, on the other hand, comes into the domain of what Marsilius calls 'permitted acts', acts which are not subject to penal constraint, and is seen as an act 'meritorious according to divine law'.[81] Thus supreme or meritorious poverty comes under counsel rather than precept. It is easy to see how counsel as it operates at the individual human level, in the framework of moral action and practical wisdom, is a prefiguration of its role in political thought, where it becomes the prerequisite of judgement and thus of the very commands and precepts that give rise to action. Thus the notion of counsel pervades an analysis of prudence, an integral, if not the most important, part. And if it is true that, as Aristotle said, prudence is the virtue appropriate to a prince, that it is architectonic, its natural purpose must be to command, or in other words, to govern. This then shows us the theoretical level counsel operates at, and how its metonymy occurs: at first the word refers to an act of human reason and will, and then becomes incarnate, so to speak, in the person or persons who pronounce it. This ties up with the other fundamental aspect of counsel, its interpersonal aspect, its social and political importance, and its connections with justice and the art of government.

78. *Ibid.*, q. 51, art. 1, *ad* 1: 'Sed quia humana ratio non potest comprehendere singularia et contingentia quae occurrere possunt . . . ideo indiget homo in inquisitione consilii dirigi a Deo . . . sicut etiam in rebus humanis, qui sibi ipsis non sufficiunt in inquisitione consilii a superioribus consilium requirunt.'
79. Quillet 1970a, pp. 153ff.
80. *Defensor pacis*, I.x.4: 'praeceptum coactivum per poenam aut praemium in praesenti saeculo distribuenda'.
81. *Ibid.*, II.xii.4: 'Horum . . . permissorum proprie, non obligantium scilicet, quaedam sunt meritoria secundum Legem Divinam et vocantur consilia'.

From counsel to council: the political dimension

Michaud-Quantin has pointed out[82] that there is a problem involved in distinguishing between *concilium* and *consilium* when they refer to a group or a gathering of people; it is difficult to place any reliance on the writing in manuscripts, in addition to which there is, according to J.F. Niermayer, 'a long history of confusion' between *consilium* and *concilium* when the word means an assembly.[83] It is also important, as Kantorowicz emphasises apropos the relationship between the king and the law, to be aware of the distinction in English between counsel and council; it is a distinction that also occurs in French, where 'conseil' in the broad sense refers to all the members of which the council is composed, while 'concile', although it has assumed a technical sense in the ecclesiastical sphere, is not really etymologically similar.[84] However that may be, and considering only the term *consilium*, it should be borne in mind that in Rome the Senate was the '*consilium publicum* of magistrates who govern the commonwealth'. Moreover, as J. Devisse has pointed out,[85] *consilium* is a classic word in the vocabulary of canon law. Hincmar of Rheims uses *consilium* to mean *consultatio*, and Gregory the Great notes that it is quite right that 'preachers are called counsellors, since they give their audiences the counsel they need for life'.

The council (as a group, rather than the deliberation or counsel itself) is a constant factor in religious life. In the medieval sense, first of all, it was understood in terms of the collectivity, and seldom had to do with the exercise of authority; the council had powers of deliberation, not of decision. This is true of religious communities, as for example in the Benedictine order, where the Rule provided for the superior to have a small group of councillors around him for the purposes of consultation, these to be drawn, of course, from among the 'wisest' in the community. This type of relationship between a community and its ruler is taken over into lay organisation, and in England and France a permanent royal council (*curia regis*) soon makes its appearance, composed of ordinary councillors. One of the characteristic features of these councils is that they are instituted by the king, who himself chooses the members. They act as the king's high court of justice and as the supreme political council. The council is principally a service, much more of a duty than a right. Article 14 of the Magna Carta for instance defines the Great Council in such a way that for an aid to be validly

82. Michaud-Quantin 1970, pp. 135ff.   83. *Ibid.*, pp. 135–6.
84. Kantorowicz 1957, pp. 151–3 and n. 187 (p. 152).   85. Devisse 1968.

agreed, the archbishops, bishops, abbots, earls and principal barons of the kingdom had to be summoned by name. All other direct vassals of the king had to be summoned through the intermediary of the sheriff, and at least forty days in advance. The composition of those assemblies, of course, was strictly feudal.[86]

Generally speaking the king, both in the Anglo-Norman and in the Capetian monarchy, governs with the assistance of the counsel of his faithful subjects: from this point of view *curia* and *consilium* mean much the same thing. The councils have both political and judicial jurisdiction, without however having powers of delegation or authority of their own. The Great Council, composed of legists, nobles and dignitaries of the Church, comes to have a separate existence from the close or privy council in France at the beginning of the fourteenth century, and without going into the organisational detail it needs to be emphasised that these consultative organs are an indispensable auxiliary to the power of the king, despite the fact that they have no real autonomy and exist at his discretion, summoned whenever they are needed without any regularity. What is important here is that they represent an awareness of the need to govern 'by means of the counsel of many wise men, both laymen and clerics'. In Gerson's words, 'How much sense has one single man? Wherefore the wise man says: do everything by counsel and you will never repent.' Gerson puts the emphasis on the need for the counsel offered to the king to be sincere: he criticises councillors who want to further their own interests through flattery, but he also criticises the prince who refuses to listen to good advice, even if he does not happen to like it: 'the seigneur must not only ask for counsel, he must believe it and act on it, and keep it secret, so that the decision can be put into practice without any interference . . . Secrecy is the best and most powerful defence against misfortune in the state.' He adds a graphic illustration of this: 'Quintus Fabius Maximus once said that if his own shirt knew the secret of his plan against Hannibal, he would throw it away.' Councillors therefore need to be wise, men who 'fear God and conscience, and who place the common good before their own profit, as otherwise they will not speak truth without fear or favour'.

It is interesting that Gerson believes that councillors should be recruited from all the orders of the kingdom: 'It would seem very expedient for the principal parts of the kingdom to be called and heard, nobles, clerics and burgesses alike', not out of any 'democratic' concern, but because their

86. Pasquet 1914; and for more recent interpretations cf., e.g., Davies and Denton (eds.) 1981; Fryde and Miller (eds.) 1970.

experience gives them concrete knowledge of the kingdom's difficulties, and they are thus more likely to offer judicious and practical counsel: otherwise 'the life [of the kingdom] shrinks to its heart' (that is, it must not be limited to the life of the heart, which as we know symbolises the king, or the king and great seigneurs). Finally, still on the same theme, Gerson compares a king who lacks 'prudent counsel' to a 'head on a body that has no eyes, ears or nose'.[87]

Gerson's recommendations and his teachings about the council are a particularly characteristic illustration of the usage of 'conseil' in late fourteenth-century France. Although it does not yet have the institutional character that it is easy to attribute to it anachronistically, it does have a moral value and expresses, even implicitly, the sense of obligation which requires the king to consult if not all his subjects, then either members of all three estates or at least men of prudence and experience. This was what Nicole Oresme put forward, mainly in the *Livre de Politiques*, but also in the *Livre de Ethiques d'Aristote*: thus in the former he sets out various rules which the king must observe in respect of his councillors and which seem to him to be indispensable to the proper functioning of the kingdom, which the king cannot attend to entirely on his own. The prince must not surround himself with councillors who 'are accustomed to lie', scriptural confirmation for which advice comes from the Book of Proverbs, nor with men who care nothing for the common good, being preoccupied with their own interests. Men of this sort, who in Oresme's eyes are necessarily men of high rank, must be 'men of great prudence and wisdom' (*expers*), and they must not be young, as young men lack experience. There is no requirement for these councillors to be particularly eloquent or accomplished, it being enough that 'they be outstanding in goodness and prudence'. When choosing his councillors, the king should be guided by the Holy Spirit which gives him

---

87. Glorieux (ed.) 1968, pp. 1164–6: 'Le seigneur n'en doibt pas tant seulement demander conseil mais le croire et l'executer et le tenir secret . . . Qu'est-ce du sens d'ung homme seul? Pour ce dit et commande le saige, fai tout par conseil et jamais ne t'en repentiras . . Secret est le plus fort et le meilleur remede contre tout adversite de la chose publique . . . Quintus Fabius Maximus disoit que se sa chemise savoit son secret contre Hannibal, il la getteroit dehors . . .

'Tels doibvent estre appelles es conseulz qui doubtent Dieu et conscience, et qui mettent le bien commun devant leur propre prouffit, car aultrement ja ne diront verite sans crainte ou sans faveur . . .

'. . . il sembleroit tres expediant que dez principalez partie du royaulme fussent aucuns appelles et oyz, tant nobles comme clers et bourgois, pour exposer franchement le miserable estat de leur pays; car trop mieulx le scavent . . . par experience, que ne font ceulx qui sont tout aise en leur estat a Paris ou est toute la gresse du royaulme et ou la vie se retrait au coeur.

'Car roy sans le prudent conseil est comme le chief en ung corps sans yeulz, sans oreillez et sans nez.'

the gift of counsel, as it says in Ecclesiastes.[88] Generally speaking, in a 'very good policy' the 'counselling part' is one of the three main parts of the government of the state. The tasks of this 'part' of the city are numerous and important, and include the arrangement of alliances, the legislative function and discussions about the common good, all of which have to be debated in public council.[89]

The same teachings are stated in his glosses on the *Nichomachean Ethics* in connection with *euboulia* (or good counsel) in the analysis of human action. From this perspective, Oresme examines the content and purpose of counsel, which is concerned, not with the purpose of the action, but with the means of achieving that purpose, concerned with feasibilities: 'with things that can often happen and which are far from certain and of importance, for small things do not require counsel'.

Describing the manner and method of giving counsel, Oresme establishes the protocol of the efficient councillor, as it were:

and thus it appears that in counselling the first necessity is to establish the end that is required, such as the peace of the city or the country in time of war. Then one must think, search and discover the shortest means to that end, which might mean negotiating with the enemy, or fighting them, or so to order and rule one's country as to prevent the enemy from doing any harm. Then one must choose by good judgement one of these means, such as fighting them. Then one must counsel how this should be done, and when, and by whom, and in what numbers. Then they must be chosen, and armed, trained, and so on to the point where the decision has to be put into practice, such as finding money or making arms or any other demands consequent upon the deliberations, and proceeding further in procuring and pursuing the known end by the means agreed upon.[90]

This kind of analysis of Aristotle's *Ethics* rather suggests that this was the method Nicole Oresme himself used when he was one of the councillors of Charles V the Wise. In practice, however, as far as the king's council in the second half of the fourteenth century in France is concerned, its function is a 'service'. It has to inform the prince about the 'state of the kingdom'. As one historian of the reigns of John II the Good and Charles V has said, the council 'is a meter of political activity and a means of research'; as such, and as a reflection of the 'public opinion' of the time, it is a 'very flexible instrument' with a shifting composition, and ill-defined responsibilities. R. Cazelles, in fact, has collected the lists of letters patent for a specific period – here between 1345 and 1365 – 'which has made it possible to tabulate the

88. Menut (ed.) 1970, pp. 329–30 (fols. 285c–286a).
89. *Ibid.*, p. 193 (fol. 153 dff).   90. Menut (ed.) 1940, pp. 188ff and 348ff.

council's activity, the frequency of its sessions and the people who attended'. On the basis of these figures it is possible to say that the council was capable of meeting frequently, as in 1357, when there were 108 councils, and later, after the coronation of Charles V, much less frequently, with only fifteen in 1365. But then 1357 was the year of what is usually called the Paris revolution; the French king had been taken prisoner after the defeat at Poitiers in 1356, and the Dauphin, devoid of resources, had to try to collect enough money to pay the ransom demanded for his father's freedom. Study of the statistics thus indicates that the need to summon the council was not nearly so urgently felt once Charles V was able to exercise his royal power to the full. Under these circumstances it is hard to describe the council as a true organ of government, although on many occasions it did have a number of important responsibilities.[91]

Another member of Charles V's entourage, also tutor to the Dauphin, the future Charles VI, Philippe de Mézières, emphasises what might be called the ethical and religious aspect of the king's council. The council is mentioned frequently in the *Songe du Vieil Pèlerin*, especially in the course of the 'moral chess board' allegory which Philippe develops as a way of expressing his conception of the office of the king. The vivid description of a royal council here is extremely interesting: Queen Truth reminds her royal interlocutor that the Holy Spirit must always be present during the deliberations, and recommends him to appoint to his council 'a secular person equipped with knowledge of divine, civil and moral laws, a man of honest life, not greedy for promotion or wealth. He should know the world and the good customs of this kingdom of Gaul. He should not be obstinate, but he should be bold in God and prepared to stand for truth and speak it without fear of any man. He should be paid at the same rate as other members of the council.' The function of this *prud'homme* was to be very similar to that of the *procureur* in the Parlement; it would be his job to defend the royal interests, if necessary by arguing against the ordinary councillors; he would be able to oppose the 'prelates and clerks' who composed the regular council members; similarly, he would take part in discussion of the lay members' proposals. The queen goes on to say that her proposal has many advantages, as royal councillors are generally

so burdened with a multitude of matters, not slight or unimportant ones but substantial, perilous and weighty issues, and they are further complicated by personal interests, enmities and oppositions . . . that it is hardly surprising if the councillors, thus burdened and perplexed, are divided among themselves, some

91. Cazelles 1982.

taking one side and some the other, both believing they are acting for the best; or if they sometimes fail to choose the better part in the royal council, for it is written that when a man's mind is occupied with a number of matters he will not be able to bring his whole judgement to bear on specific issues.

Philippe de Mézières evinces considerable distrust of councillors, criticising their behaviour, accusing both clerics and laymen of looking after their own interests rather than those of the king and the public good. He sees the '*procureur* of divine goodness', as he calls the member of the council responsible for ensuring the propriety of its discussions and the integrity of its decisions, as a figure analogous to 'the good counsellor of David' and concludes, 'It is good to have such a councillor in the royal council.'[92]

It is quite clear from these few examples that the council is an acknowledged fact. It is composed of the body of councillors, *sapientes, boni homines prudentes*, it is a more or less broad assembly, close to the authority of the law, whose basic purpose is to formulate opinion, although without actually taking decisions. It is interesting now to compare that with the kind of council found in the towns of northern Italy, as being particularly characteristic of communal organisation.

Here it seems the council as assembly, as the municipal institution, had a much more decisive role to play. The members of the various bodies which administered the city with the *podestà* and consuls were known as *consiliarii*. In Padua, the basic organ of government was the Grand Council (*Consilium*

---

92. Coopland (ed.) 1969, vol. II, pp. 332–7: 'Cy traict la royne Verite du vie point du tiers quartier du moral eschequier.

'"... es tous tes grans consaulx royaulx ... l'aide du Saint Esperit ... soit appellee ...

'"... il est expedient ... que a ton grant et secret conseil tu ayes communement une personne d'estat seculier et bien fonde es drois divins, civilz et moraulx, qui soit appreuve d'onneste vie, qui ne tende pas aux honneurs et richesses ... bien expert es choses mondaines et es bonnes coustumes du royaume de Gaule, et sans obstinacion, qui soit hardiz en Dieu et appareilliez en tous cas de dire verite, sans doubter autre que Dieu, et qui ait ses gaiges ordonnez comme un de ceulx du conseil.

'"... de cestui pru dhomme ... l'office sera tel: ... tout ainsi que que en parlement ... tu as ton procureur ... tout ainsi par une similitude assez convenable, le vaillant homme susdit et propose sera procureur especial de la divine bonte; c'est assavoir que en ton grant conseil royal . . sus aucune forme apparant de bonne conclusion, qui ne sera pas a aucuns bien sonant en son effect ... selon Dieu, selon bonne police et selon bonnes murs ... le dit advocat preudomme ... puisse et doye meureement et hardiement comtredire au dit cas ...

'"... les conseilliers royaulx generalement . . aujourdui en parlement et ailleurs sont si chargiez de multitude de causes, non pas petites ne legieres, mais grandes, perilleuses et pesantes, qui sont si entrelaciees de faveurs, d'inimitez, et de contradicions ... que ce n'est pas grant merveille se les conseilliers, ansi chargiez et aucunesfoiz rempliz de perplexite, les uns donans faveur a une cause et les autres au contrayre, cuidans bien faire, se es elections des consaulx royaulx aucunesfoiz ilz faillent a eslire la meilleur partie, car il est escript que la pensee de l'omme en plusieurs choses generalement occupee, es jugemens particuliers, n'a pas le sens entier.

'"... cestui procureur ou advocat de la divine bonte ... sera appelle aussi le bon conseillier de David ... Bon fait avoir un tel counseillier en son conseil royal."'

majus) but unlike the assemblies already examined this represented the whole body of the citizens. Now the *Consilium majus* is the equivalent of what Marsilius of Padua in the *Defensor pacis* calls the *pars valentior civium*, the 'weightier part' of the citizens, the preponderant part both qualitatively and quantitatively.[93] From the end of the thirteenth century, the Grand Council was composed of 1,000 members. Only citizens entered in the city's *estimo* for at least fifty pounds could take part. The Grand Council's principal task was legislative, but it also elected the *podestà*, which was entrusted with executive responsibility. The comparison, or to be more precise the correspondence, between this kind of institution and Marsilius' formulations is too well-known to need restatement here. It is perfectly clear that the way the council was appointed, its composition, and its functions are all very different from the way the council developed in the monarchies of England and France.

When the word council is used in this last sense, of an assembly, a group who form the community's permanent administration – whether it is a municipal institution dealing with the area controlled by one town, or whether, as in the monarchies, it is a whole body of members appointed by a higher authority – it brings with it the problem of the distinction between *communis consensus*, common consent, according to which the decision reached must follow the opinion expressed, and the *commune consilium*, where the general opinion expressed by council members was taken into consideration but without any obligation on the part of the superior power to act in accordance with it.[94] Yet the two expressions gradually come to mean the same thing, or at least to be treated as the same, so that the council assumes a special value as voicing the opinion of the people who will be affected by the authority's decision. It is in this context that the *sapientes*, who were originally chosen for their own abilities, find themselves expressing the general opinion on behalf of those affected by the practical consequences of the decision. In other words, they become representatives of the citizens as a whole, but without ever having been given any specific mandate from them. Then by a gradual process of assimilation they come to represent particular interest groups. There is a similar broadening of the meaning of *sapiens*, which comes to refer both to the experts and to people with experience of this or that social or political problem, as a result of which, as Gerson (and before him Philippe de Mézières) pointed out, men from the three orders of society were drawn into the council to give

93. Quillet 1970a, pp. 23ff, 93ff; Gewirth 1951 and 1956, vol. I, pp. 23ff.; *Defensor pacis*, I.xii.3,4,5.
94. Michaud-Quantin 1970, p. 138 n. 60.

authoritative opinions on issues that concerned them directly. Thus Gerson, writing about the reform of the kingdom in *Vivat rex*, says among other things that

it would seem very expedient for the principal parts of the kingdom to be called and heard, nobles, clerics and burgesses alike, to explain the wretched state of their country in full; for those who have seen and experienced these things know them better than those who live comfortably in Paris . . . Things seen and felt have more force than those that are merely heresay.[95]

In this example, which is only one among many, we can perhaps see the beginning of the process that culminates in the emergence of the idea of representation.

Representation and delegation

Medieval terminology is as ill-defined when it comes to the different senses of representation as anywhere else, as a result of the complex intertwining of notions of morality, politics and law. For the sake of simplicity the discussion here deals only with the senses of delegation and proxy, and not with the symbolic, allegorical and metaphorical meanings of the word, even though these do have interesting political connotations.

First, the contribution of law to the development of the idea of representation: representation originally had a rather narrow legal sense.[96] The representative, *actor, syndic, procurator*,[97] usually nominated in accordance with established legal procedures, acts in the place of the group by whom he is mandated, either in his own discretion or according to rule. Here representation is a procedural matter: Roman law, as is well known, included a set of conditions governing its theory and practice. When it has to do with an individual, the problem is relatively easy; with collectivities, the same principle is involved but at a different level. A community is represented by a *syndic* when it is represented as a moral person, as laid down in the *Digest*.[98] Where an *actor* deals with affairs of all kinds, a *syndic* is involved solely in judicial matters. Then there is a further distinction, between the syndic and the procurator: the latter represents an individual, the former a community, but with the difference that the procurator speaks

95. Glorieux (ed.) 1968, p. 1165: 'il sembleroit tres expedient que dez principalez partie du royaulme fussent aucuns appeles et oyz, tant nobles comme clers et bourgois, pour exposer franchement le miserable estat de leur pays; car trop mieulx la savent par veue d'oel et par experience, que ne font ceulz qui sont tout aise en leur ostel a Paris . . . Plus mouvent choses veuez et sentuez que seulement oyez.' 96. Quillet 1971, p. 187. 97. Post 1964.
98. Michaud-Quantin 1970, p. 306; *Digest*, 2, 7, 25; 35, 1, 96; 50, 1, 14.

in the name of the person he represents, while the syndic appears in his own name, whether or not he has been mandated by the community.

Canon law's contribution to the development of the idea of representation is essentially contained in the declaration *Quod omnes tangit*, and its concrete applications. There is a substantial body of work devoted to this theme, so it is only necessary to mention its main characteristics and how it operated in different sorts of communities; but it is worth examining, as it was made the subject of numerous expositions in political thought proper. First, as Post rightly emphasises,[99] it is impossible to talk about representation in the full sense in connection with the texts of canon law because of the ambiguity that lies at the heart of 'power' in the Church, whether that of an abbot or a general chapter of any other body; and this ambiguity reflects Ullmann's distinction between 'descending' power, in which power is seen as coming from God, as in St Paul's famous formulation, and being distributed hierarchically between the different orders, and an 'ascending' theme, in which power is derived from the 'base' and then chooses, as its preferred method of distribution, representation.[100] Ullmann's distinction is a very interesting one, and it has helped to clarify some of the complex issues that surround the nature of power in the middle ages; yet it is not entirely adequate. Temporal power as well as spiritual power claims to have a divine origin and, what is more, there are plenty of examples of representation in canon law, as well as in Roman law and its medieval institutions, even to the extent that one historian has talked about 'democracy' in the administration of religious communities (although that is probably stretching the term too far).[101] Post is therefore right to say that it is not possible to use the word representation in its real sense in connection with the *Decretum*, because the only kind of representation that is truly worthy of the name is divine delegation; however, the successive interventions of the papacy – Innocent III's in *Pastoralis cura*, and Alexander III's in other texts – ended in reconciling the demands of the 'descending theme' with the most important aspect of the 'ascendant theme', the active participation of constituents, by means of election and delegation, in the conduct of affairs by those they have mandated. This is the point at which the canonical maxim 'What concerns all must be approved by all' finds its full expression. It is also the reason for the importance of *consensus*. The whole issue becomes more complicated when it is realised that this maxim was originally a procedural rule in the *Code*,[102] which was adapted to the

---

99. Post, cit. Michaud-Quantin 1970, p. 310 and n. 15.   100. Cf. esp. Ullmann 1978, *passim*.
101. Moulin 1978, pp. 191–208.   102. Michaud-Quantin 1970, p. 273; *Code*, 5, 59, 5, § 2.

canonic texts to meet the demands of the situation. It becomes yet more complicated when we realise that the rule of unanimity implicit in the famous maxim contradicts the rule of the majority. For there has to be a choice: either one looks for unanimous approval, in which case consent can be understood in the absolute sense; or else there is an agreement to follow the opinion or decision of the majority, in which case the notion of *consensus* must inevitably be limited, not to mention all the 'adjustments' the concept of majority is subject to. What is at stake is the whole concept of community, according to whether it is seen as an association of individuals or as an organically constituted body. On the second of these views, it is almost impossible to be unaware of the hierarchical implications which in theory and in practice lead to a preference for the idea of majority over unanimity, and the majority in this context is not simply a matter of quantity but is also viewed in terms of quality, which is precisely what is expressed by the phrase *major et sanior pars*. The main difficulty the representative principle had to cope with was the possibility of disagreement among the electors which would take away the whole point of representation itself. Obviously a crisis in the history of community occurs at this moment when there is a shift from a unanimist conception of the collective will to a majoritarian one, a shift which occurs, in essence, as a concession to the rule *Quod omnes tangit*. Yet there is a question whether unanimity is really a necessary basis for action. There seems to be a contradiction here between the actual idea of representation, which presupposes a small number who act for and on behalf of the majority, and the idea of unanimity which presupposes that anybody can act with full knowledge without having recourse to representation. If all the electors are in agreement then clearly their mandated representatives only have an executive function to perform. Yet the idea of representation as delegation does not seem to have been reduced to carrying out executive tasks: far from it. Nor should we think of these notions of unanimity, and majority, and *consensus*, purely as legal terms: in reality they were deeply impregnated with ethical and religious values, especially in the realm of canon law. At the beginning of this section it was mentioned that the counsellor was seen both as the *bonus vir*, the *sapiens*, and as the representative of a lay or religious collectivity: it is here that the two elements converge. Any analysis of the concepts of unanimity and majority in fact involves the whole problem of who the electors are and what procedures they adopt. Whether we are looking at royal councils, seigneurial councils, commune councils or at ecclesiastical assemblies, election (in the sense of choice, without its modern connotations) is at the heart of the question. And of course representation means something rather different, viewed *a parte post*, if it includes the power to make decisions, instead of merely putting decisions into practice. M.V. Clarke argued[103] that the idea of representation includes the idea of the substitution of a part for the whole, with all its connotations both symbolic and otherwise. She went on to claim that for it to be properly political the representatives, besides fulfilling certain other basic conditions, must be more than merely members of a deputation or delegation empowered to act *hic et nunc* on a specific issue. The real purpose of bodies such as these, if they are to be political, must be to make or change the laws. It is paradoxical that this practice starts in ecclesiastical institutions and spreads out from there to the purely temporal structures of society, particularly in the light of the Church's belief in the divine origin of power. In other words, it is clear that the link between the formation of the idea of community and the notion of representation is entirely bound up with the problem of how the collective will should be expressed. The adoption of the majoritarian system was the only possible outcome, but some qualifications need to be noted.

The *Digest* contained a number of rules which determined the concept of majority: 'That which the major part of the city does is considered as if it had in fact been done by all.'[104] The use of 'as if' here reveals the conventional character of the rule, and its application created difficult problems such as deciding what the quorum of the majority should be. There is no need to go into the different ways the problem was resolved, the direct and indirect methods, or, in the latter case, the use of the vote. In this connection there are interesting details to be found in the *Statuti* of the Italian cities.[105] In the institutions of the Church, the myth of unanimity diminishes in importance at about the same rate as their formal structures developed: in fact the elaboration of the doctrine of the *major et sanior pars* marks its disappearance.[106] What is interesting about this formulation is that to some extent it implies the notion of the theoretical consent of everybody; it also lessens the difficulties caused by representatives disagreeing among themselves. The canonical doctrine enshrined in the phrase combines the requirements of arithmetic with the moral and religious ones which are more difficult to evaluate, being judged by criteria such as zeal, authority and the rational

103. Clarke 1936 (repr. 1964), pp. 278ff.
104. Michaud-Quantin 1970, p. 273 and n. 9; *Digest*, 41, 2, 1, § ult.; 4, 8, 19, § *principaliter*.
105. *Statuti* 1873; and cf. Ullmann 1962.
106. The literature on this topic is extensive: see the indications given in Quillet 1971; Michaud-Quantin 1970; Lagarde 1956–70, vol. v.

nature of the opinion or decision agreed upon. The arithmetical criterion loses its importance in this perspective, since an arithmetical minority can turn into a majority in terms of the *major et sanior pars*. The significance of this is, in the end, that, whatever form it may take, it should be a decision, or an action or a choice which represents the whole – that is to say, the community; and this is to arrive finally at an agreement (*concordia*) and thus to dispel that conflict whose threatening shadow – constantly reborn (to change the metaphor) from its ashes – the whole endeavour, at once speculative and practical, seeks to eliminate.

It was only with the work of Marsilius of Padua in the fourteenth century that the idea of representation came to occupy a prominent place in political thought. Reference has already been made to his definition of the community as the *universitas civium*, the whole body of citizens, or its 'weightier part' (*pars valentior*).[107] Here, fully developed, is the specifically political practice of the idea of representation identified by Clarke: the power to make, change and revoke laws. Not that Marsilius was entirely innovatory in this respect, as thinkers and theologians had found the theoretical foundations of popular sovereignty in Aristotle's *Politics* from the time his political ideas began to spread, while the Roman *Lex Regia* stated that the prince held his authority by delegation of concession of the people, the ultimate source of sovereignty.[108] Yet although Marsilius is not strictly an innovator in this area, he is the first to coin the phrase *legislator humanus*, which taken in the context of the whole of the *Defensor pacis* rather than just the *Prima pars* is the exact counterpart of the *legislator divinus*, the custodian and ultimate source of power, who is set over and above the *legislator humanus* and the power he holds.[109]

The *legislator humanus* is the people, or the *universitas civium*: it is they who legislate at the human level. In the *Defensor minor* Marsilius actually uses the words of the *Lex Regia* to define it.[110] There is no need to dwell on the precise significance of the theme of popular sovereignty in Marsilius' work, except to say that it almost always takes the form of representation by delegation, and it is this aspect which is of concern to us. The very definition of the principle of representation is bound up with the notion of the human legislator.

The legislator, or the primary and proper efficient cause of the law, is the people or the whole body of the citizens, or the weightier part thereof, through its election or will expressed by words in the general assembly of the citizens, commanding or

---

107. Cf. pp. 533–7 above, and *Defensor pacis*, i.ix, xii, xiii *passim*.
108. Cf. Quillet 1970a and the works cited there.
109. Cf. *Defensor pacis*, i.xiiff.   110. c. XII: Jeudy and Quillet (eds.) 1979, pp. 254–5.

determining that something be done or omitted with regard to human civil acts, under a temporal pain or punishment.[111]

The theme of consent is very clearly expressed here, that of representation follows on from the very notion of *pars valentior*, and the fundamental nature of popular power lies at the root of both. What we need to examine now is the distribution of authority, or in other words the way representation works politically, which as we have seen means in terms of legislation.

A legislator of this sort may act as such directly or he may expressly delegate one or a number of other people to be responsible. There could be as many of these delegations as the legislator wished, as long as it was established that the individual or individuals mandated were only acting on the authority of the chief legislator. Thus the legislator, or the whole body of citizens, elects prudent men, on whom the job of drafting the laws devolves. These men are to be 'the representatives of the whole body of the citizens, and of their authority': they will be a body of magistrates, *vicem et auctoritatem universitatis civium repraesentantes*.[112] In this way, human power operates at all levels of political life by means of representation. This is confirmed by the doctrine of *valentior pars*, a formulation which echoes canon law's *major et sanior pars* in taking account of the actual realities of representation and of its links with the original statement of the popular source of sovereignty: *pars valentior . . . totam universitatem repraesentat*.[113] From this standpoint, the election of *prudentes* remains subordinate to their competence, but it is the people, who elect them, who are the judges of their competence. Representation in its symbolic sense does not figure here at all: the word is used in its full sense. For if the people is indeed the whole body of citizens, a citizen in the political community is 'one who participates in the government or the deliberative or judicial function, in accordance with his rank'.[114] This is the level at which Aristotle's influence on Marsilius is most marked: he uses the Aristotelian argument that the multitude is a better judge than a small number.[115] But for Marsilius this 'multitude' is not simply any group (as it had been for his predecessors – St Thomas, Peter of Auvergne, and, first of all, Albert the Great): here once more the definition

---

111. *Defensor pacis*, I.xii.3: '*legislatorem seu causam legis effectivam primam et propriam esse populum seu civium universitatem, aut eius valentiorem partem per suam electionem seu voluntatem in generali civium congregatione per sermonem expressam, praecipientem seu determinantem aliquid fieri vel omitti circa civiles actus hominum sub poena vel supplicio temporali*'.

112. *Ibid.*, I.xiii.8; and cf. Quillet 1971, pp. 119ff.

113. *Defensor pacis*, I.xii.5: '*pars valentior . . . totam universitatem repraesentat*'.

114. *Ibid.*, I.xii.4: '*Civem autem dico . . . eum qui participat in communitate civili, principatu aut consiliativo vel iudicativo secundum gradum suum.*'   115. *Politics*, III, 1281 b–1282 a.

of the political community provides the key to understanding the doctrine of representation and of the *valentior pars*. The community, as we have seen, is the people or the whole body of the citizens. But only those with specific political responsibilities are defined as citizens. It is not to be supposed that the numerical majority of members of the community are in that position, especially if women and children are excluded from that totality, and if the definition of a citizen is matched by particularly strict rules of membership – rules based on rank, position, function and so on. Leaving aside slaves, where does this leave the *banausi*? So while the *valentior pars* may be both qualitative and quantitative, even quantitative in this context does not mean simply the largest number. The 'people' have to be separated into the *vulgus*, sunk in their daily work, and the *honorabilitas*, which also includes the priests, although they do not play any part in government or council. When we remember that the rest of the citizens have to be of 'a certain rank' we can also exclude all the artisans and the peasants. In fact there is only a small number of citizens remaining who satisfy the criteria for membership of the *pars valentior*. Yet although this might appear to be a disguised return to an oligarchical system (disguised, because Marsilius severely condemns such systems in the name of democratic principles) oligarchy is in fact judged by other criteria. Nor is it really admissible to see the *valentior pars* as a symbol of the people: it is in fact the very opposite of that, its constituent body. The quantitative criterion should be clear enough now not to be misleading: *mutatis mutandis*, it is an adaptation of the *major et sanior pars*. In any event, Marsilius does not seem very interested in the arithmetical aspect of the constitution of the *valentior pars*, frequently saying that it can be 'one or many'. This is why, by successive stages of delegation, the representative principle and its workings enable Marsilius to describe the prince himelf as *pars valentior*, since it is the whole people which is expressed through him. If the prince is an Emperor, the *valentior pars* quite legitimately becomes the seven Electors, without contradicting the theoretical foundations of popular sovereignty. The prince, or the Emperor, can use the authority of a delegation from the legislator to assert his power; if his power is absolute, that is precisely because it comes from such a delegation. Hence in *Defensor minor*, for instance, one comes across phrases like 'There is, similarly, according to human law, a legislator – to wit, the whole body of citizens or its weightier part, or again the supreme Roman prince who is called emperor.'[116]

---

116. XII.9: Jeudy and Quillet (eds.) 1979, p. 280: 'Est etiam similiter secundum legem humanam legislator, ut civium universitas aut eius pars valentior, vel Romanus princeps summus imperator vocatus.'

At the centre of Marsilius' doctrine of the *valentior pars*, then, lies the idea of representation by delegation; and the form he prefers is that of the elective monarchy, to which he devotes many pages of the *Defensor pacis*. Obviously he did not find the concept of popular sovereignty in the least incompatible with the unity, or even the unicity, of power.

When these principles are applied to the Church, the most innovatory aspect of Marsilius' thought lies in his attempt to define the General Council and set it in opposition to the *plentitudo potestatis* of the papacy. The conciliar theme, in fact, is entirely centred upon the idea of consent and representation. The Church is the body of the faithful (*universitas fidelium*); the council is composed of members who represent it. The same process which leads to the representation of the whole body of citizens by their 'weightier part', whichever form that takes, reappears in the representation of the whole body of the faithful by their 'weightier part'.[117] As *congregatio fidelium*, the Church is represented by the General Council: this is representation by delegation again. The council is composed of elected priests and laymen, who are mandated by the members of the universal Church to settle questions about matters of faith. The rights of the faithful of the universal Church are thus entrusted to the 'weightier part' of the council. In the event of disagreement among the members of the 'weightier part' then it is the *major et sanior pars* which prevails, for Marsilius has no hesitation about borrowing the formulation from canon law and using it on several occasions.[118]

The reason for this similarity in procedure between political and religious communities is that by considering the Church as *corpus mysticum*, or as a moral person, it is possible to apply the same rules to it: the legislator thus becomes the 'faithful human legislator', and the same political structures enable the *pars valentior* of the faithful to represent the whole body of the faithful citizens. Political society, therefore, considered as a *persona ficta*, as *populus*, provides a set of rules which can also be applied to the Church, so that the representative principle, along with consent and election, can play its full part in the constitution of the General Council. Just as the *universitas civium* delegates its authority to the *pars valentior*, so the *universitas fidelium* entrusts its rights to the *pars valentior* of the faithful.

William of Ockham's conception of community has already been touched upon: the same nominalist standpoint colours his idea of representation.

117. *Defensor pacis*, II.xx.2, and cf. Quillet 1971, p. 195.
118. *Defensor pacis*, II.vi.12–13; II.xvii.5–6; and cf. Quillet 1971, p. 196.

Ockham rejects the notion of collective personality or the artificial moral person: he has similar reservations about representation. He asks what reality outside the soul it corresponds to. No body of people, whether political, or religious, or even the Church itself, can be an artificial person, he writes in the context of the dispute on evangelical poverty, in reply to the arguments put forward by John XXII, in the *Opus nonaginta dierum*:

For if the Order of Friars Minor is a represented and imaginary person, then by the same argument the Church and *any community* whatever must be a represented and imaginary person, which is absurd: for that which is merely represented and imaginary is a creature of fantasy and has no being in anything outside the mind. But the Church is no creature of fantasy with no existence outside the mind, therefore it is not represented and imaginary. The argument can be confirmed on the following lines: either the Church exists outside the mind, or it exists only in the mind, or it is a composite being, partly in the mind and partly outside it. First, then, if it exists only in the mind, or if it is a composite being partly in the mind and partly outside it, then it cannot have any reality or jurisdiction; and to say this of the Church is impious and blasphemous. On the other hand, however, if the Church exists outside the mind, then it is either one thing or several; and whether it be one thing or several it is not a represented and imaginary person, nor by the same argument is the Order of Friars Minor such a person.[119]

For Ockham, in fact, *repraesentare* is essentially part of the process of knowledge: 'To represent is to be that by which something is known, as something is known in the process of cognition.' In this sense, God represents all things, because his essence is the knowledge of all things. But he represents them only to himself, since he alone knows himself. In a secondary sense, the image represents that which it depicts; and in the third sense *repraesentare* means that which causes knowledge as an object does. Consequently the *repraesentativum* is that which, once known, can, as a partial cause, evoke the memory of a known thing, for example its image or trace. Also Ockham thinks of the *fictum* as a mental representation of

---

119. Sikes, Bennett and Offler (eds.) 1940–, vol. II, p. 568 (*Opus nonaginta dierum*, ch. 62): 'Quia si Ordo Fratrum minorum est persona repraesentata et imaginaria, eadem ratione ecclesia et quaelibet communitas esset persona repraesentata et imaginaria, quod est absurdum, quod enim est tantum repraesentatum et imaginarium est fantasticum, et non est in re extra animam. Sed ecclesia non est quid fantasticum non existens extra animam, ergo non est persona repraesentata et imaginaria. Confirmatur: Quia aut ecclesia est extra animam, aut in anima tantum, aut aliquid compositum ex ente in anima et ente extra animam. Si est in anima tantum, vel aliquid compositum ex ente in anima et ente extra animam, ergo nullum reale nec iurisdictionem realem potest habere: quae dicere de ecclesia est impium et blasphemum. Si autem ecclesia est extra animam vel ergo est una res, vel plures: et sive sit una sive plures, non est persona repraesentata et imaginaria. Ecclesia ergo non est persona repraesentata et imaginaria; et eadem ratione ordo Fratrum Minorum non est persona repraesentata et imaginaria.'

something that exists, or that can exist, although in the *Dialogue* he draws a distinction between *fictum* and *figmentum*, the latter referring to the mental representation of an impossible thing such as a chimera.[120]

Given, then, that the idea of representation implies a conception of the whole and its parts, since it is a process which in one way or another involves taking the part for the whole, it becomes clear why Ockham regards this notion of the whole as metaphorical, and therefore improper: 'In another sense it is taken to mean something that is common to a number of other things, as the genus is said to be a whole with respect to the species and the species with respect to its individual members.'[121] It is therefore always incorrect to speak of the whole of a community. Two separate senses of the word 'part' need to be distinguished: the first sense refers to the essential part, the essence of a whole, without which the whole could not exist; the other is the integrant part. But whereas the first cannot constitute a complete being when it is separated from the whole, the integrant part, despite being incomplete as a part, can nevertheless be an *ens completum* because it can exist on its own in the genus even when separated from the whole.[122] The parts of a community clearly come under the heading of integrant parts, which makes is difficult to see how they could, without absurdity, be taken for the whole. This view is confirmed in Ockham's commentary on the first book of the *Sentences*: in response to the question whether the universal is really separate from the individual thing, he concludes his comment as follows:

Accordingly my answer to the question is that there is not in the individual some universal nature which is really distinct from the contracting difference [or principle of individuation], for no such nature could be located there unless it were an essential of the individual itself; but there is always a proportionality between the whole and the part, such that if the whole is singular and not common, every part is likewise singular proportionally, for one part cannot be more singular than another. Either, therefore, no part of the individual is singular or every part is; but the former alternative is false, therefore every part is singular.

And finally, on the same topic, but as concerns the relation of the part and the whole: 'but between whole and part, as between subject and accident [since the integrant part of a being cannot be its essential part] there is proportionality such that if one is singular so will the other be: therefore

120. Baudry 1958, pp. 93, 234; Ockham, *Quodlibet* IV, q. 3, and *In I Sent.*, d. 3, q. 9 B.
121. Baudry 1958, p. 272; Ockham, *Summa Logicae* I, c. 35: 'Aliter accipitur pro aliquo communi ad multa sicut genus dicitur totum respectu specierum et species, respectu individuorum.'
122. Baudry 1958, p. 188; Ockham, *Quodlibet* IV and *Expositio Aurea*, fols. 17b, 37 d.

every such thing is singular and consequently not universal'.[123] In other words, the accidental, or integrant part cannot be taken for the whole.

This set of attitudes would prevent the 'invincible doctor' from accepting, for instance, Marsilius' conception of representation, and the notions both of *pars valentior*, and of *major et sanior pars*. 'The whole principle of legal substitution, and the transmission of sovereignty that results from representation, is completely contradicted' as Lagarde puts it; 'Collegial structure adds nothing to the reality of things'.[124]

Is Ockham's philosophy therefore totally opposed to representation by delegation? There seems to be a constant tension in his work between that and the theme of unanimous consent required by his individualist perspective, and supported by his literal interpretation of *Quod omnes tangit*, to the point where Bartolus himself responds to his criticism of the conception of the community as a moral or fictitious person, and its implications, by saying: 'The philosophers tell us there is no real difference between the whole and its parts, and this is true in the proper sense of actual reality; nonetheless we believe it is essential for us jurists to sustain the juridic fiction which treats the *universitas* as a reality quite distinct from its individual members.'[125]

Ockham exposes the limits of this sort of substitution, but without rejecting the idea of representation, which seemed to him to be well enough suited to the normal exercise of political and religious power. He does not question the representativeness of any particular organ, such as Emperor, Pope or General Council, but he argues that they are subordinate to the consent of those concerned, taken individually, as autonomous persons enjoying specific rights and freedoms. Duns Scotus had stressed the importance of *consensus* and *electio* in the delegation of political authority, as an agreement reached between strangers (by which he meant people belonging to different families) can only perform its constitutive role if it expresses the mutual consent of everybody.[126] And Ockham's 'elucidations', whatever else, do emphasise the ambiguities in the idea of representation by delegation and in the majority principle, and the

123. Brown and Gál (eds.) 1970, pp. 158–9 (d. 2, q. 5): 'Ideo dico ad quaestionem quod in individuo non est aliqua natura universalis realiter distincta a differentia contrahente, quia non posset ibi poni talis natura nisi esset pars essentialis ipsius individui: sed semper inter totum et partem est proportio, ita quod si totum sit singulare non commune, quaelibet pars eodem modo est singularis proportionaliter, quia una pars non potest plus esse singularis quam alia: igitur vel nulla pars individui est singularis vel quaelibet; sed non nulla, igitur quaelibet . . . sed inter totum et partem, similiter inter subjectum et suum accidens . . . est talis proportio quod, si unum sit singulare reliquum erit singulare: igitur omnis talis res est vere singularis et per consequens non est universalis.'   124. Lagarde 1937, p. 444.   125. *Ibid.*, p. 451 and n. 1.
126. Gandillac 1968, p. 707.

unavoidable difficulties involved in the unanimity of *consensus*. That emphasis reveals the perplexities involved in the sharing and distribution of power at the end of the middle ages. It shows too that there was, in the platonic sense, a 'mixing' between the wisdom of councillors or representatives or lawmakers with their capacity to represent the whole body of citizens, as if it went without saying that it is the best who are appointed to represent all the members of social group. What is involved here is not so much a movement towards 'populism' as an indication that the ethical ideal, which sees political society in moral terms, still permeates the discourse, even though that discourse, inaugurated by Marsilius of Padua, may now be regarded as properly 'political' in character.

Nicole Oresme's position on these issues is interesting. Strongly influenced by Marsilius, he sees the multitude as the foundation of political power; he also insists that it must be a 'reasonable multitude'. And he does not hesitate to say that royal power 'must be less than that of the whole multitude, or its weightier part'.[127] The power itself is controlled by laws, and one of the council's functions is to ensure that the power is kept within reasonable limits. That he does go as far as to say that councillors represent the reasonable multitude, the whole body of the citizens, can be seen from a number of his glosses on the *Politics*. As for example in Book VI, where he comments on the institution of the Ephors: first he explains that it is an institution in a regime where the multitude controls the 'sovereignty of the polity', not just any multitude, as in 'democracy', 'but the multitude and universal congregation of all the princes or officers and principal citizens' which, as such, 'has sovereign dominion'. This multitude corresponds to the *universitas civium* of Marsilius, or to his *valentior pars*, and to illustrate what he means, adds that 'such an arrangement is somewhat like the general assembly of the masters of the university of Paris'. Council here is being used in the sense mentioned above (pp. 545–55), of an elected assembly which acts through representation by delegation and, in theory at least, on the basis of the unanimous consent of the citizens. Yet for all this we know that Oresme shows a marked preference for what he terms 'royal polity', that is, royal government: however he does not hesitate to assert that 'perhaps it is expedient for the reasonable multitude, or part of it, to have this power'; royal power, in other words, whatever its origin (and he is quick to state his preference for an elective monarchy in other parts of his work), must be 'counselled' by a reasonable multitude, meeting in an assembly or in council. But he goes further than this when he makes 'the king and his close

---

127. Menut (ed.) 1970, p. 274 (fol. 231 d): 'Item, . . . la puissance du roi . . . doit estre mendre que celle de toute la multitude ou de la plus vaillant partie.' Quillet 1977, p. 126.

council . . . a small part of this multitude'. This is clearly far removed from any notion of royal absolutism, and nothing appalled Oresme more than government by a tyrant who prevented the functioning of the assemblies appointed by the reasonable multitude. The reason for describing the 'king and his close council' as 'a small part of this multitude' is that they work for the common good, as does the multitude which 'knows best how to consider and order everything that is good for the public realm'. Oresme sees in this an illustration of the principle of *Quod omnes tangit*: 'And also, that which is done and approved by all is stronger and more stable, more acceptable and more agreeable to the community, and provides less opportunity for murmur or rebellion than there might otherwise be.' These principles were to be applied equally to the government of the Church, which is why the pope's power should not be tyrannical, and should not exceed that of the General Council.

The next question concerns how and when such a multitude should be assembled. It could, for example, be summoned for a period as the need arose, as the councils were, or at all events at regular intervals; it could be summoned both by those whose office or function it was, and by those who composed the council; to which Oresme adds that 'in an aristocracy and a kingdom the chief princes have the power to call these people together, and they must do so whenever circumstances require it and it is possible, or when the time for one falls due.' Finally, perhaps to moderate the impact of his proposals, he explains: 'I say all this without insistence, except that it seems to me to follow from the teachings of Aristotle.'[128]

---

128. Menut (ed.) 1970, p. 274 (fols. 231 c–232 b): 'Il me semble que en ceste maniere .ii. choses sont a considerer: une est quele chose doit avoir ou a qui appartient la souveraineté de la policie; l'autre est posé que ce est la multitude, par qui et comment elle doit estre assemblée . . . Et en democratie la multitude populaire tient la souveraineté . . . Mes en commune policie et en aristocracie la multitude non pas la populaire mais la multitude et congregation universele de tous les princeys ou offices et des principalz citoiens a la souveraine domination et la correction ou alteracion des particuliers princeys ou offices et le ressort ou cognoissance des tres grandes questions, et a elle appartient la reformation de la policie, et composer ou muer ou approuver ou accepter les loys . . . Et tele chose est aucunement semblable a l'assemblee general des Maistres de l'Etude de Paris. Et quant est en policie royal encor par aventure est il expedient que tele multitude raisonnable ou partie de elle ait ceste puissance . . . car toute ceste multitude de laquel le roy et son familier conseil sunt une petite parties sait miex considerer et ordener tout ce qui est bon pour la chose publique. Et aussi, ce que tous funt et approuvent est plus ferme et plus estable, plus acceptable et plus aggreable a la communite, et donne moins de occasion de murmures ou de rebellion que se il estoient autrement . . .

'Quant au secunt point comment ceste multitude doit estre assemblée . . . aucune foiz en aristocracie et en royalme, les principalz princes ont puissance de faire ceste congregation, et la doivent faire toutes foiz que les cas le requierent et il est possible ou quant il sunt requis duement. Et tout ce je dis sans affermer, fors en tant qu'il me semble que l'en devroit ainsi dire selon la doctrine de Aristote.'

Oresme puts forward similar arguments in his long discussion of the advantages and disadvantages of hereditary and elective monarchy: his own position, in which many distinctions are drawn, would take too long to expound here. For present purposes it may suffice to mention one of the arguments used to prove the superiority of elective monarchy. The former 'is made by the better part of the whole community, expressly or by tacit consent, or by custom'.[129] This is Marsilius' argument, repeated almost word for word.

Oresme is clearly well aware of the real issues that underlie the idea of representation by delegation, and of the problems raised by the interpretation of the 'dominant part' and unanimous consent; his preference for royalty does not prevent him from mentioning the notion of *major et sanior pars* in connection with the law of 'democracies', as well as the practice of drawing lots in cases where opinion in the assembly is evenly divided. On the first issue, the *major et sanior pars*, which he translates as 'the greater and sounder part', Oresme's interpretation is that it is not in any way majoritarian, and in this he is directly following canonistic tradition. On the second, the case of open conflict between equally divided parts of an assembly in a 'democratic' regime, he comments on Aristotle's recommendation that lots should be drawn, and compares that to 'a game of odds and evens, or the method of choosing a twelfth night Bean King'. A royal government is much to be preferred, because in circumstances like that one can 'refer the problem to the sovereign prince'. It is possible, however, to imagine a situation even then when 'the laws appear contradictory, the councillors cannot reach agreement, and the king is perplexed': and in that situation drawing lots is the only answer, as Roman law and the 'holy Doctors' both attest, as the evils that arise out of discord, such as sedition, disturbances and corruption in the '*policie*' are thus avoided.

Oresme's doctrines demonstrate very clearly the ideal asymptotic convergence between the representative system in its proper sense and the predominance accorded to wisdom: his representatives must be *boni viri*, and the prince must be the most excellent of them all, and yet they are simultaneously, and without contradiction, representatives of the 'people', the 'reasonable multitude'. The method of their appointment has to take account of both aspects, and reconcile consent, election and the common good. This is the perspective in which the doctrines of council must be seen,

---

129. *Ibid.*, p. 109 (fols. 65 c–66 a): 'Item, election de lignage quant a ce est faicte ou fu faicte par la meilleur partie de toute la communité expressement ou par consentement taisible ou par coutume.' Cf. Marsilius, *Defensor pacis*, i.xvi.

and the various forms of representation and delegation, as they gradually came to take shape at the end of the middle ages under the twofold influence of Aristotelianism and of Roman law and canonical literature. This is without doubt because for most of the theorists the principle of representation did not in any way imply the rule of the majority, as Pierre d'Ailly and Jean Gerson can still point out at the turn of the century, both in terms of political power, and the representativeness of the council.

It only remains to consider how far this is still true of the political and ecclesiological thought of Nicholas of Cusa. In this context, the preface to Book III of his *De Concordantia Catholica* is very clear:

> And thus by a kind of instinct the authority of the wise and the subjection of those who lack wisdom come harmoniously together by virtue of the common laws, of which the wise themselves are the principal authors, guardians and executors, while all the others concur in this and consent to it by voluntary submission.[130]

Thus from the outset the basic conditions of political representation are established.

> But law must be made by all those who are to be bound by it, or by the greater part in virtue of election by the rest; for it is intended to promote the common good, and that which touches all should be approved by all, and a common decision is taken only by the consent of all or of the greater part.[131]

This is admittedly a somewhat heterogeneous text, as it takes over Marsilius' doctrines of representation, consent and delegation, but also links them closely with a concern for the common good: the consent of everybody is fundamental, of course, but is it not primarily the justification of the voluntary subjection of all to a few or to a single man? In any event, the 'wise' or the virtuous are the people who make the laws, in accordance with natural law, which is a concept that occupies a central place in Nicholas of Cusa's framework. The crux of his doctrine lies in the harmony which must exist between the wise men who legislate for the common good and the people who give their consent. The whole of Book II of the *De Concordantia* develops the central thesis of *consensus*, and the *electio* which is its corollary, and does so in the context of religious institutions. There are

---

130. III, Prooemium, 275: 'Et sic naturali quodam instinctu praesidentia sapientum et subiectio insipientum redacta ad concordiam exsistit per communes leges, quarum ipsi sapientes maxime auctores, conservatores et executores exsistunt, aliorum omnium ad hoc per voluntariam subiectionem concurrente assensu.'
131. III, Prooemium, 276: 'Legis autem latio per eos omnes, qui per eam stringi debent, aut maiorem partem aliorum electione fieri debet, quoniam ad commune conferre debet, et quod omnes tangit, ab omnibus approbari debet, et communis diffinitio ex omnium consensu aut maioris partis solum elicitur.'

other works, or parts of works, of his, however, which display a much more traditional approach to this area, such as Chapter xiv of Book ii, where he writes:

Every ordinance is rooted in natural law, and if that law is violated the ordinance cannot be valid . . . From this it follows that, since natural law is naturally inherent in reason, every law is of the same nature and origin with man. That is why we choose the wisest and most outstanding men as our rulers, so that they, endowed as they are with wisdom and prudence in their unclouded reason, will enact just laws . . . That is why those who are most outstanding in reason are the lords and rulers of the rest, but not by means of coercive law or judgment enforced upon unwilling subjects.[132].

Election and the consent of subjects, in other words, is based upon the ethical criterion of wisdom and prudence. Men submit voluntarily by a sort of implicit or explicit *recognition* of the superiority of the wise over the others, not by constraint. By submitting in this way they give those who govern the power to command, 'a power which prevents subjects from doing evil, and directs their freedom towards the good by fear of punishment'. The power to command obliges subjects to be virtuous, and punishes them where necessary. This power, Nicholas adds, 'is founded upon concord alone and the consensus of the subjects'.[133] Yet if it is true that 'men naturally possess equal power and equal freedom' the real power of a prince or a law must necessarily be different from, or at least not equivalent to, the power possessed by those who chose them. Nicholas of Cusa is more concerned here with the *agreement* that must exist among men than with the *equality* of their freedom or power. The primary task is to find agreement, and this cannot be achieved except in the form of consent, unanimity and election. As has frequently been pointed out, this involves a contract, but one still within the limits of *pactum subjectionis* rather than *pactum associationis*. It is a solution which would not have been rejected by Aristotle: consent is given to the general good, and to those who are meant to incarnate it, in a well-ordered *politeia*.

Nicholas uses the idea of representation itself at different levels and in

132. II.xiv.127: 'Omnis constitutio radicatur in iure naturali, et si ei contradicit, constitutio valida esse nequit . . . Unde cum ius naturale naturaliter rationi insit, tunc connata est omnis lex homini in radice sua. Ideo sapientiores et praestantiores aliis rectores eliguntur, ut ipsi in sua naturali clara ratione sapientia et prudentia praedita iustas leges eliciant . . . Ex quo evenit quod ratione vigentes sunt naturaliter aliorum domini et rectores, sed non per legem coercivam aut iudicium, quod redditur in invitum.'

133. *Ibid.*: 'Unde cum natura omnes sint liberi, tunc omnis principatus, sive consistat in lege scripta sive viva apud principem, per quem principatum coercentur a malis subditi et eorum regulatur libertas ad bonum metu poenarum, est a sola concordantia et consensu subiectivo.' Cf. the continuation of this passage in n. 71 above.

varying degrees: arguably the whole of his thought is concerned with it, in the sense that any reality is the 'figure' of a higher reality and bears its impression. This is the indispensable foundation of concord, and a necessary presupposition of a hierarchical universe, and we should bear in mind that it is the main sense of representation for Nicholas of Cusa. His use of the concept politically is the same in all major respects as Marsilius of Padua's. It does seem, however, at least in the *De Concordantia Catholica*, that the two different senses of symbolic and delegate representation interpenetrate one another somewhat. Between *petra* and *Petrus* for instance Nicholas sees 'several degrees of representation and signs, from the representation and the least clear figure to the stone which is the truth, passing through less uncertain and truer intermediaries'. This clearly involves the idea of symbolic representation. But he adds at once that the Church, which is one, 'can only be represented and signified by an assembly which is one.' Obviously some idea of delegate representation is involved here, yet it seems to be impossible to dissociate it completely from symbolic representation, which introduces some degree of ambiguity. 'From that and from the foregoing it manifestly follows that anybody who rules over others *figures* the collectivity of his subordinates.' And further on he writes: 'Whence also it follows clearly that the more particular the ruling position is, the clearer and the less ambiguous the representative character assumed by the ruler will be.'[134]

In the preface to Book III of the *De Concordantia*, he proposes a set of reforms designed to restore the grandeur of the Empire, and in these too the theme of representation is central: first, as we have seen in relation to laws laid down 'either by all those they affect or by the greater part of them'; and second at the level of government, in that his preference is for an elective monarchy:

in order that the best man, by the will of all and serving the common interest, may at all times rule over the state, there is no better arrangement than to provide on each occasion for election by all or by the greater part or at least by those leading men who represent all the subjects with their consent.[135]

---

134. II.xviii.158: '. . . inter petram et Petrum sunt plures graduationes repraesentationum et significationum, quousque in petram deveniatur a confusissima repraesentatione et figura usque in veritatem per media certiora et veriora. unam autem ecclesiam significare et repraesentare non potest nisi unus aut una congregatio'; and II.xviii.163: 'Ex hiis et superius tactis manifestum est, quia quisque praesidens figurata generalitate subditos figurat . . . Deinde etiam est ex hoc manifestum quod quanto particularior est praesidentia, tanto certior repraesentatio, quae apud ipsum praesidentem est et minus confusa.'

135. III, Prooemium, 283: 'ut optimus omnium voluntate ad commune conferens praesit rei publicae semper, non est melior quisquam statuendi modus quam per novam electionem omnium aut maioris partis vel saltem eorum procerum, qui omnium vices ex consensu habent'.

This is a sort of equivalent to Marsilius' *pars valentior*, embodied historically in the form of the imperial electors.

Among the practical measures he recommends, Nicholas includes the need for the prince 'to hold a daily council made up of delegates from all parts of the subject provinces, elected with the consent of his universal council'. Counsel and council have the same meaning for Nicholas of Cusa because of the way representation by delegation works:

> the prince should have accomplished men from all those subject to him, elected for this purpose from every part of his kingdom, to assist the king in daily council. These councillors are to represent all the inhabitants of the realm . . . They must continually defend the public good of those whom they represent; they must give their advice and act as the due means whereby the king may govern and influence his subjects.[136]

In order to bring the recommended reform into effect, one of the first measures the Emperor should take is the establishment of an annual assembly and the appointment of judges throughout the provinces. And in each one there should be three judges, drawn from the three estates: clergy, nobles and the people. In the event of disagreement, the majority opinion should prevail.[137]

In the general economy of the *De Concordantia*, the theme of representation is only one of the forms taken by harmony 'that by which the Universal Church agrees in one and in many, in one Lord and many subjects. And from the only prince of peace, whose harmony is infinite, flows the sweet harmony of concord, by degree and succession, to all the subordinate, united members, so that the one God is all in all.'[138] Everything in the universe represents, in its way, *secundum gradum suum*, unity; if it is true that human society, the highest figure of which is the *Ecclesia coniecturalis*, includes within itself structures and institutions which are both religious and political, the latter modelled on the former, the working of representation by delegation will enable the different orders or members who compose the one body, the *corpus mysticum*, of the Church, to function harmoniously

---

136. III.xii.378: 'Habere quippe debet princeps ex omnibus de subiectis viros perfectos ad hoc de omni parte regni electos, qui in cotidiano consilio assint regi. Tales quippe consiliarii vicem gerere debent omnium regnicolarum . . . Et hii tales consiliarii eorum, quos repraesentant, bonum publicum debent continue defensare et avizare et medium proportionatum esse, per quod rex gubernet et influat sibi subiectis . . . Debent quidem isti consiliarii in universali congretatione regni concorditer ad hoc deputari . . .'.

137. Cf. III.xxxii.508 and xxxv.519 (for the annual assembly); III.xxxiii.510–11 (for the appointment of judges).

138. I.i.4: 'Concordantia enim est id, ratione cuius ecclesia catholica in uno et in pluribus concordat, in uno domino et pluribus subditis. Et ab uno infinitae concordantiae rege pacifico fluit illa dulcis concordantialis harmonia spiritualis gradatim et seriatim in cuncta membra subiecta et unita, ut sit unus deus omnia in omnibus.' See also Haubst 1971 and 1972; Gandillac 1972.

together. The *De Concordantia* concludes with a grand metaphor which portrays it as a living organism, the very life of which depends on the harmony of its members. The 'ecclesiastical republic' has the priesthood as its soul and the Empire as its body, its organs are minutely described and its functions harmoniously divided; it is perhaps the last representation of the *respublica christiana* on the medieval pattern. Representation by delegation plays an important part in the hierarchy of resemblances; yet the Church, defined as *corpus mysticum*, has only a distant similarity to the *Ecclesia ipsa*: it is only a sign, a conjectural approach, and in this perspective representation is only a figure of the 'filiation' to which the people of the faithful aspire. Empire and Church are figures, representations of a community which is now no longer the Aristotelian *politeia*: it is a *universitas fidelium* 'founded on the theological virtues'.

II THE CONCILIAR MOVEMENT

The conciliar movement of the late fourteenth and early fifteenth centuries was an attempt to modify and limit papal control over the Church by means of general councils. It was sparked off by the disputed papal election of 1378, when, following the return of the papacy from Avignon to Rome, French cardinals rejected the election of the Italian Urban VI, on canonical grounds, and elected Clement VII as anti-pope. The movement was also a response to growng centralisation of church administration and justice, to perceived abuses of power by the (in fact rather weak) papacy in exile at Avignon (1305–77) and to the widespread desire for church reform. There was, further, a latent contradiction in church tradition between the doctrinal authority of councils and the jurisdictional primacy of Rome. The movement was led mostly by Frenchmen and Germans; it evoked little response in Italy. Conciliarism was a moderate programme in comparison with the aspirations of men like Marsilius, Wyclif or Hus, who wanted national or state churches, and who saw whole aspects of Catholic tradition, especially papal authority, as fundamentally opposed to scripture or to reason. But it also reflected a shift in religious sentiment from universality to nationality, and a sense that religious matters could legitimately be debated, at least by all educated clergy. In the event, the pope–council conflict affected considerably the structure of medieval Christendom. What emerged as the practical alternative to papal centralisation was devolution of power to secular rulers and nation-states. During the schisms of 1378–1417 and 1437–49, ecclesiastical policy and the allegiance of clergy and peoples were to a great extent determined by princes, foreshadowing *cuius regio, eius religio*. In 1418, and again in 1447–50, matters were settled by concordats between the papacy and the various secular powers. The 'Christian republic' had become a very loose confederation.

In arguing that the council is above the pope, conciliarists relied principally on scripture, the early fathers and canon law; they drew extensively upon church history, especially the ecumenical councils. Like Wyclif and the Hussites, they appealed to the practice of the apostles and the primitive church, and sometimes from canon law to scripture.[1] Scripture and history showed that the position of Peter and of his successors was that of *primus inter pares*, that doctrinal disputes were settled by councils, that popes had erred and that the Church ought to be governed by fraternal consultation. But conciliarists also used history in new ways, to show relativity or development in church practices: some aspects of the Church's constitution could legitimately be changed to suit the time, or as a result of 'experience'.[2] Heimerich van de Velde saw the Church as an organism, growing over time from one constitutional form to another.[3] Most conciliar argument was theological and applied primarily to the Church. But the questions at issue were constitutional in nature: conciliarists readily drew arguments from secular politics and sometimes formulated their propositions as general truths about political structures. Conciliarism was a significant chapter in the history of western constitutionalism.[4]

Personalities and events

Conciliarism may be divided into three phases: (i) 1378–83, when its advocates drew extensively on Marsiglio and, especially, Ockham; (ii) 1408–18, when a quasi-patristic doctrine of power-sharing between pope and bishops-in-council was dominant; (iii) 1432–50, when unlimited sovereignty was claimed for an internally democratic council. The first group of tracts was produced by Paris University masters, notably Conrad of Gelnhausen, Henry of Langenstein and Pierre d'Ailly, justifying emergency convocation of a council and its authority over the rival papal claimants. Europe became divided into separate 'obediences'. From 1383 to 1398 France enforced obedience to the Clementine papacy; then the king 'withdrew obedience', urging both claimants to resign, and for a period France was administered ecclesiastically by local and national synods largely under royal control. In 1408 groups of cardinals withdrew from both *curiae* and called a general council at Pisa (1409). This deposed the two claimants

---

1. E.g. Gerson, ed. Glorieux 1966d, p. 227. Cf. Black 1979, pp. 61–2, 128; Krämer 1980, p. 361. Crowder 1977 gives a selection of translated conciliar documents.
2. Langenstein, *Consilium Pacis*, ed. Hardt 1697, p. 47; Scholz 1926; Ragusa, *De auctoritate conciliorum*, fols. 187–97, 212–20; Segovia, *Historia*, ed. Stehlin 1857–1935, vol. II, pp. 129–30, 135, 213–15. Cf. Black 1979, pp. 108, 132–3.   3. Black 1970b.
4. Oakley 1962 and 1969; Rueger 1964. Tierney (1982, p. 87) suggests that 'perhaps we shall eventually learn to see civic humanism and conciliarism as two alternative rhetorical strategies through which the communal ethos of the Middle Ages was transmitted to the modern world'.

and elected a new pope, but with little support; there were now three obediences. The efforts of the Emperor Sigismund led to the Council of Constance (1414–18), which gained general recognition: it deposed two claimants, received the resignation of the third and finally elected Martin V, a forceful Italian. Unity was achieved, but not reform. The period from 1408 to 1418 produced a spate of conciliar propaganda, and important works by Dietrich of Niem, Pierre d'Ailly, Jean Gerson and Franciscus Zabarella. Their teachings were widely influential. Constance issued two decisive constitutional decrees: *Haec sancta* (1415) declared that a general council was superior to a pope in matters of doctrine, schism and reform;[5] and *Frequens* (1417) stated that henceforward councils must meet at stipulated regular intervals.[6]

In accordance with *Frequens*, a council met at Pavia-Siena in 1423–4 – abortively – and another at Basel in 1431. This latter won widespread secular and ecclesiastical support, partly because of Pope Eugenius IV's tactless intransigence and the determination of a group of conciliarists from Paris University, but also because it gave the German Emperor and princes a forum for negotiation with the Bohemian Hussites, whose armies, inspired by radical religious zeal, had proved irresistible. Basel promptly admitted clergy of all ranks on an equal basis, set up its own rival judicial and administrative machinery and unleashed a torrent of reform decrees on taxation, benefices and the whole range of church government. The dominant majority asserted the sovereignty of the council in uncompromising terms, and gradually alienated many prelates and princes; the council became divided along national lines. In 1437 Eugenius adroitly transferred the council to Ferrara (then to Florence); schism was renewed. The rulers of France and Germany held back and adopted neutrality for several years. Thanks to papal diplomacy, they moved from compromise to settlement with Rome. People wearied of a seemingly sterile dispute. A new set of concordats divided power over ecclesiastical appointment and taxation between the papacy and the states. The Council of Basle produced a host of minor theorists, notably Nicholas de Tudeschis, Andreas Escobar and Johannes de Ragusa; its stance was typified in the occasionally original works of Juan de Segovia; and it produced one work of profound importance, Nicholas of Cusa's *De Concordantia Catholica* (1432–3), probably the most interesting of all conciliar tracts.

5. Mansi 1759–98, vol. XXVII, p. 590. Cf. Franzen and Müller (eds.) 1964, pp. 98ff, 113ff, 214ff.
6. Mansi 1759–98, vol. XXVII, p. 590.

Representation

How could a council be called without papal consent? What authority had it over papal claimants? Throughout, the main problem was to justify conciliar action against a recalcitrant pope. The conciliarists invoked 'equity' (*epieikeia*): positive law needs to be supplemented by natural justice, which justifies emergency means to the self-evidently desirable goal of unity.[7] D'Ailly argued that the Church, when its unity was threatened, had the power 'not only on the authority of Christ but also by common right' to assemble itself. Just as any organism under threat 'naturally draws together all its members', so 'any civil body or civil community or rightly ordered polity' can assemble itself in emergency.[8]

Two major interdependent constitutional doctrines were developed: the Church is superior to the pope, and that Church is represented by a general council. Some held that these applied only in an emergency, others that they were constitutional norms of the Church. Canonically, the simplest way to prove that a general council represented the Church was to argue that bishops or cardinals were collectively superior to the pope; this was the main argument of moderates like Gerson. But many conciliarists preferred to locate ultimate authority in 'the Church', and then to derive it to the council; partly because bishops and cardinals were slow to act, partly because sacred texts ascribed authority to the Church, partly because this corresponded to their own moral convictions. If a pope persisted in schism, behaved scandalously or undermined the well-being of the Church, he could be judged and deposed by a council, acting on the authority of the whole Church, as his superior. This was the crucial doctrine developed in response to the Great Schism. Precedents could be quoted from canon law, church history and the New Testament, but so could counter-precedents; hence the need to formulate the juridical supremacy of the council in terms of philosophical theology and political theory.

The argument progressed on two lines. Some early conciliarists adopted Ockham's view of the Church as a collection of individuals, grouped in parishes, which elected a provincial council, which in turn elected representatives to a general council.[9] Most, however, favoured a theory of

---

7. Cf. Ullmann 1948a, pp. 179–83; Morrall 1960, pp. 83–5. But see Oakley 1981, p. 797.
8. *Propositiones Utiles*, ed. Martène and Durand 1733, col. 910: 'Non solum auctoritate Christi, sed etiam communi iure naturali . . . Corpus naturale . . . naturaliter congregat membra . . . Similique modo quodlibet corpus civile seu civilis communitas vel politia rite ordinata, adeoque corpus spirituale seu mysticum ecclesiae christianae . . .'. Cf. Gerson, ed. Glorieux 1966b, p. 134; 1966c, p. 137.   9. Cameron 1952, pp. 15, 26, 37. Cf. Ockham, *Dialogus*, ed. Goldast 1614, p. 603.

'virtual representation': the only way the Church could in practice exercise its authority was through a general council consisting of its leading members. 'The pope, cardinals and other prelates are *in virtute* equivalent to the whole clergy and represent *in effectu* the whole ecclesiastical polity . . . In what concerns faith and related matters, they all collectively represent the whole corporation of faithful.'[10] Later it was also argued that the whole Church was 'virtually' present in a council because its members represented different districts, religious orders and types of learning (theology and canon law), or even because they excelled 'in virtue and power'. A meritocratic tendency was noticeable at Basel, which replaced episcopacy with virtue and learning as qualifications for council membership; 'doctors' were ascribed special authority in matters of faith.[11]

Church or community sovereignty

Conciliarists based the sovereignty of the Church primarily on theology: the Church, as the mystical union of the faithful in Christ, is the immediate recipient of divine authority. But this argument merged with contemporary secular notions of community sovereignty; the general implications were more prominent in some conciliarists than others, but were mentioned by nearly all. It was chiefly at this point that conciliarism became a political theory.

The most systematic available statement of community sovereignty was that of Marsilius, who had stated as general norms the legislative sovereignty of 'the corporation of citizens' and the final authority of 'the corporation of the faithful' in doctrinal and ecclesiastical matters. He used the same arguments for both points: the whole is greater than the part, the majority do not err.[12] Langenstein used a moderate version of this doctrine when he stated that power to elect the pope 'lies primarily with the corporation of the faithful bishops', but if necessary may revert 'to the rest of the faithful', particularly 'the corporation of priests'.[13] Similarly Niem, who used Marsilius extensively, argued that 'the catholic church', consisting of all Christians (Greeks, Latins, barbarians, men and women, rich and poor), had greater authority than 'the apostolic church',

10. Anon., *De Papae*, ed. Finke 1923, p. 701.
11. See Black 1970a, pp. 15–22; Black 1979, pp. 44, 111.
12. *Defensor pacis*, I.xxi.5; I.xiii.4; II.xix–xx. Cf. pp. 558–61 above.
13. *Consilium Pacis*, ed. Hardt 1697, pp. 34–5: 'Potestas constituendi papam primarie residet apud universitatem episcoporum fidelium . . . Si omnes episcopi mortui essent . . . forte universitas sacerdotum consentiente populo eligere possunt primo unum de sacerdotibus.'

comprising pope, bishops and clergy.[14] Marsilius, however, was a condemned heretic, much of whose teaching was anathema to conciliarists. The point could be argued in other ways.

Zabarella framed communal church sovereignty in the language of canon law. In the Church, as in any lesser corporation, certain powers belong uniquely to the whole. 'When it is said that the pope has fullness of power, this should be understood of him, not alone, but as head of the corporation, in such a way that this power is in the corporation itself as in its foundation, and in the pope as principal executive, through whom this power is deployed.'[15] Tierney has shown that conciliarists could reach their desired conclusion simply by applying standard corporation theory, as stated by canonists for cathedral chapters and other ecclesiastical colleges, to the universal Church.[16] A great many of them did this, and Tierney's thesis goes far towards explaining the genesis and character of conciliarism. But Zabarella also used an argument which smacked of Marsilius:

Philosophers also say that the government of the state resides with the assembly of citizens, or its weightier part, a view taken from the third book of Aristotle's *Politics* . . . So too the government of the universal Church, in a papal vacancy, resides with the universal Church itself, which is represented in a general council, and, when the council assembles, with the more powerful part of the council.[17]

Tudeschi repeated Zabarella's argument from corporation theory, concluding that 'the general council represents the whole Church with regard to its total power, because the whole ecclesiastical power is in the Church as in its foundation'.[18] For secular support, he turned to Venice: if the Doge errs, 'he is resisted by the city, and if necessary deposed; for the foundation of jurisdiction is in the body of the city, and in the Doge as its principal executive'.[19] Thus the main *canonist* argument for church sovereignty ended up (if it had not begun) as a general political norm.

Terms like 'corporation of the realm' (*universitas regni*) had been applied to barons and estates; conciliar theory established a crucial link between this language and the right actually to *judge and depose a king* in the community's

---

14. *De modis*, ed. Heimpel 1933, pp. 70–2, 87–8; cf. Sigmund 1962.
15. *De Schismate*, ed. Schard 1566, p. 703 (cf. Tierney 1955a, pp. 220–37, esp. p. 225): 'Id quod dicitur quod papa habet plenitudinem potestatis debet intelligi non solus, sed tanquam caput universitatis ita quod potestas est in ipsa universitate tanquam in fundamento, et in papa tanquam principali ministro per quem haec potestas explicitur.'   16. Tierney 1955a, esp. pp. 106ff.
17. *De Schismate*, ed. Schard 1566, p. 688: cit. Tierney 1955a, p. 223.
18. Memorandum (1442) (*Deutsche Reichstagsakten* 16: 483 (hereafter *DRTA*)): 'Ipsum concilium generale representat totam ecclesiam quoad totalem suam potestatem, quia tota potestas ecclesiastica est in ecclesia tanquam in fundamento.'   19. *DRTA*, 16:521.

name. The council's authority to depose a pope for heresy, schism, scandal or simple maladministration (based partly on views of canonists) was repeated by one conciliarist after another: the papacy could become vacant 'through natural or civil death'.[20] The whole strategy of conciliarism focused on this point. But conciliarists seldom explicitly carried the argument for deposition into the secular sphere. The language they used for the Church, however, was often (as we shall see) general in character – not least, the term *universitas* itself. And, when Basel deposed Eugenius IV (1439), some argued that kings too are subject to the whole people and can be 'banned or thrown out for maladministration or tyranny'.[21]

Some conciliarists, on the other hand, propounded a theory of *mixed government* for the Church. D'Ailly and Gerson described its constitution as a mixture of monarchy (the pope), aristocracy (the cardinals) and polity or timocracy (the council).[22] In the 1450s Segovia stated a version of parliamentary monarchy. The conciliar constitution is 'monarchy veering towards aristocracy'; in a true monarchy, the king rules by law and benefits from regular consultation with wise men and estates. Thus subjects obey more readily, and laws are more speedily executed. 'In every state governed by royal rule . . . general assemblies are frequently held'; this 'does not obscure but glorifies' royal government.[23] But the conciliarists of Constance and Basel did not want things to get out of hand; they never countenanced action by 'the Church' other than through the council; indeed their theory of representation, which made the council the sole channel for community action, headed off any such idea.

In 1416–17, in what superficially appear as statements of mixed government, d'Ailly and Gerson in fact reduced community sovereignty to an abstraction. D'Ailly (October 1416) argued that, since 'actions pertain to individuals', fullness of jurisdiction belongs, properly speaking, to the pope alone 'as in the subject receiving it and exercising it ministerially'; to the Church 'figuratively and . . . equivocally . . . as in its object, as an effect is said to "be in" its cause'; and to the council 'representatively . . . as in an

20. Gerson, ed. Glorieux 1966d, pp. 222–3 ('per mortem naturalem aut civilem'); 1966e, pp. 286–7.
21. Piccolomini, *De Gestis*, ed. Hay and Smith 1967, pp. 28–33; Segovia, *Historia*, ed. Stehlin 1857–1935, vol. ii, p. 261.
22. D'Ailly, *Tractatus de Ecclesiastica Potestate*, ed. Dupin 1706, pp. 946, 957: Gerson, ed. Glorieux 1966d, pp. 247–8.
23. *Amplificatio* 1935, pp. 707–12 (cit. Black 1970a, pp. 144–8): 'In omni politia quae regali dirigitur principatu, hoc idem observatur, ut saepe teneantur curiae generales.' Cf. *De Magna Auctoritate Episcoporum*, cit. Black 1970a, pp. 156–61.

exemplar that represents it and directs it regularly'.[24] Gerson (February 1417) ascribed fullness of power 'essentially (*formaliter*) and subjectively' to the pope, and 'materially or relatively' to Church and council; the council could decide who exercised supreme power as pope, and could prescribe 'the regulation of its use, if perchance it is found to have been abused'.[25] The explanation for Gerson's apparently pro-papal language here is that he was responding to d'Ailly, who, at this stage, was moving towards curialism (some said he had papal ambitions). Gerson was trying to salvage the principle of conciliar supremacy – to which he was unreservedly committed – while competing with d'Ailly for support from moderates at Constance.

During Basel, however, Gerson's formulation was inverted to make the *council* the primary recipient, and the pope the derivative recipient, of Christ's authority. The theory of mixed government was now replaced almost wholly by one of community sovereignty. But here again communal sovereignty was essentially an abstraction; it was never intended to give any independent authority to the Church at large. Rather, the church community was the source, for analytical purposes only, of that unlimited jurisdiction which belonged to the *Church-in-council*, with the pope as its merely executive servant (*primus minister*). The council has *fullness of power* (*plenitudo potestatis*) over the pope and all Christians, including secular rulers. This reflected the difference, in constitutional theory and practice, between Constance and Basel. According to the men of Basel, the council convened itself through decrees like *Frequens*, determined its own membership, chairmanship and procedure and, as the decree *De stabilimento concilii* (15 February 1432) put it, 'It has not been, is not and will not in future be right or possible for the council to be dissolved, transferred

24. *Tract. de Eccl. Pot.*, ed. Dupin 1706, pp. 950–1: 'Haec plenitudo jurisdictionis, proprie loquendo, solum residet in . . . summo pontifice . . . quia proprie aliqua potestas plene dicitur esse in aliquo, quia illam potest generaliter exercere, et ministeraliter in omnes dispensare: hoc autem est in solo papa, et non proprie in aliqua communitate, quia secundum Philosophum actiones sunt suppositorum . . . Huiusmodi plenitudo potestatis, tropice et alio modo equivoce, est in universali ecclesia, et in concilio generali ipsam representante. Pro cuius declaratione sciendum est, quod . . . aliquid dicitur tripliciter esse in alio: primo, tanquam in subiecto, sicut virtus est in anima, et accidens in substantia subiective; secundo modo, tanquam in obiecto, sicut aliquis effectus dicitur esse in sua causa vel in suo fine, quia in illum tendit tanquam in suum obiectum finale; tertio modo, tanquam in exemplo, ut res dicitur esse in speculo, vel aliqua doctrina in libro, quia ibi est representative. Primo ergo modo, plenitudo potestatis est in papa, tanquam in subiecto ipsam recipiente et ministerialiter exercente; secundo, est in universali ecclesia, tanquam in obiecto ipsam causaliter et finaliter continente; tertio, est in generali concilio, tanquam in exemplo ipsam representante et regulariter dirigente.'
25. Ed. Glorieux 1966d, p. 232. Cf. Posthumus-Meyjes 1963, pp. 229–38; Tierney 1975.

. . . or prorogued . . . by any person', including the pope.[26] The council could not only determine matters of faith and general ecclesiastical legislation, but if necessary could (as Basel did) take over the papacy's judicial and administrative functions.[27] The council thus appropriated the traditional jurisdictional primacy of Rome.

The fullest elaboration of general principles of constitutional right was achieved by Nicholas of Cusa and Juan de Segovia: one a canonist turned philosopher, the other a theologian turned historian. Segovia stated the Basilean theory of the unitary and unlimited sovereignty of the Church as a general political norm. For this he used, first, the language of corporations and, secondly, that of contemporary city-states. He made the collegiate model into a norm of 'political and natural reason' by universalising the distinction between the corporation as a whole and its individual members. A ruler 'somehow loses his individual unity and dons the united community, so as to be said to wear or represent the person not of one but of many'. He is sovereign over individuals separately, but subject to them collectively, i.e. in general assembly. Segovia here stated a subtle view of representation and community sovereignty. The ruler's authority depends upon his judgement being 'presumed to conform to the will of all over whom he presides for the benefit of the republic and themselves'.

But if it happens that this whole community assembles together, and its assertions and wishes contradict those of the president, since truth is preferred to fiction, the community will deservedly prevail. For the truth is that this community is many persons, and the fiction is that this president, who is really one person, is said to be many by representation.[28]

---

26. Mansi 1759–98, vol. XXIX, pp. 21–2; and cf. vols. V–VI, pp. 178–80.
27. Black 1979, pp. 50–1, 54–7; Krämer 1980, pp. 12ff.
28. Segovia, *Tractatus de Conciliorum et Ecclesiae Auctoritate* (1439), fol. 224r–v: 'Qui enim praeest multitudini in virtute, dummodo eiusdem ordinis sit, licet singulos, non tamen excedit universos . . . Patet in duce exercitus, vel in praesidente cuiuslibet alterius multitudinis. Ratio autem huius est quoniam qui praeest multorum regimini, si debite habet praeesse, desinit esse privata, et efficitur persona publica, et *perdit quodammodo solitariam unitatem et induit unitam multitudinem*, ut iam non unius sed dicitur gestare sive representare personam multorum . . . Sed si contingat totam illam multitudinem in unum congregari et asserere vel optare aliquid, econtra autem ipse praesidens dicat, quia ipsa veritas praefertur fictioni, ipsa multitudo merito superabit. *Veritas enim est hanc multitudinem esse multas personas, fictio autem quod ipse praesidens, qui unicam personam vere, multas autem esse dicitur repraesentative* . . . Auctoritas praesidentis in praesentia totius multitudinis [fol. 224 v] non sicut primo censetur habere vigorem, propterea cum praesumitur iudicium suum esse conforme intentioni omnium quibus praesidet ad reipublicae et ipsorum utilitatem. Et haec est summa potestas concessa cuilibet praesidenti, vid. id quod sibi videtur debere, omnibus credi quod sit de intentione omnium, qui pro tunc in diversis locis separatim existunt.' Re-phrased in *Amplificatio*, 1935, pp. 720–1 (cf. Black 1979, pp. 162–6, with full translation).

Segovia's 'will of all (*intentio omnium*)', as a universal volition for the common good subjectively recognised as such by the people, is actually analogous to the modern 'general will'.

During and after his long experience of conciliar leadership and diplomatic conflict, Segovia elaborated further this notion of power and authority as based on a legitimate fiction of reasonable trust, conditional upon a ruler's retaining his subjects' confidence. The reason why the council is to be universally obeyed is that society and polity logically presuppose mutual trust among men.[29] People's *experience* establishes the authority of philosophers and kings; 'authority is the greater the more it is believed that someone is least capable of erring from the truth'.[30] Governmental office is a phenomenon of the mind (*ens rationis*).[31]

Secondly, using a civic model, Segovia deliberately reversed Gerson's abstract formula on fullness of power, to make papal power *derive from* the sovereignty of the community. 'Supreme power . . . exists first in the community itself [sc. the Church]; then in the rulers and magistrates, or consulate and senate [sc. the council] . . . and subsequently in the executive or *podesta*, *dictator* or governor.' He thus emphasised the inalienability of sovereignty from the community 'as its own passion or innate *virtus*, inseparable from it': the community 'never abdicates its power . . . [which] belongs to it irretrievably'. The power of consulate and ruler is delegated.[32] But actually, despite this apparent commitment to community sovereignty, Segovia always maintained that the whole Church exercised its authority exclusively through the council, which he made (in a tolerably modern sense) the sovereign body in the Church.[33] Here he faithfully reflected the views of the majority at Basel.

Nicholas of Cusa and consent

Conciliarists also proved their case by the well-established principle of consent. 'The consent of the faithful' had since the early Church been invoked as a sign of doctrinal truth,[34] and secular governments recognised the need for consent in some form. Canon law prescribed that bishops must be elected by the clergy with the consent of the laity; consent of the

---

29. *Historia*, ed. Stehlin 1857–1935, vol. III, p. 572, and *DRTA* 15:652 (cit. Black 1970a, pp. 30–1).
30. *Amplificatio*, 1935, pp. 843–6 (cit. Black 1970a, pp. 152–4), esp. p. 845: 'Tanto maior est auctoritas, quanto plus creditur minime aberrare posse eum a veritate.'
31. *Amplificatio*, 1935, pp. 851–7 (cit. Black 1970a, pp. 154–5).
32. *Amplificatio*, 1935, pp. 802–3 (cit. Black 1970a, pp. 150–2). Cf. Black 1979, pp. 172–5.
33. Cf. Black 1979, pp. 188–90. 34. Cf. Grossi 1958.

members was required for certain acts of an ecclesiastical college. The Roman-law text 'let what touches all be approved by all' had been used both in the Church and by secular advocates of baronial or parliamentary participation in legislation and taxation.[35] The conciliarists of 1378–83 used this text to prove that a disputed papal election must be decided by a general council.[36] Nicholas of Cusa, one of the most original philosophical theologians of the late middle ages, combined the canonist notion of consent with the Christian-Neoplatonic notion of cosmic 'harmonious concord';[37] on this basis he worked out both a theory of conciliar supremacy in the Church and a theory of just authority for all polities. The Church is 'a composite whole' with priesthood as soul and empire as body;[38] Book I of *De Concordantia Catholica* deals with the Church as a whole, Book II with the clergy and the general church council, Book III with the Empire. In this organic view, the same principles must apply to ecclesiastical and secular polity, as Cusa makes abundantly clear. A German, born near Trier, he saw Church and Empire, clergy and laity, as interlocking parts of Christian society, the rationale of which he based on canon law, cosmology and natural right. His argument for the Church, based especially on the early ecumenical councils, was generalised for all forms of human authority, as a postulate of reason and nature.

Ecclesiastical and secular laws, conciliar authority and all governmental power are based upon consent, which binds together willing subjects and legitimate rulers. First, 'the force of law subsists in the subjective concordance of those whom it obliges[39] . . . Canon laws have their roots in natural right'.[40] Secondly, power to make church laws resides in the 'common consent' of a council: 'against this conclusion no prescription or custom carries weight, any more than they do against divine and natural justice, from which this conclusion derives'.[41] Within the council, liberty of speech and 'oneness of spirit (*unanimitas*)' are more important than large numbers.[42] The council must be an 'orderly assembly'; to represent the

---

35. *Codex* 5.59.5; cf. Post 1964, pp. 163–240. Cf. p. 512 above.
36. Gelnhausen, *Ep. Concordiae*, ed. Bliemetzrieder 1910, p. 122.
37. *De Concordantia Catholica*, ed. Kallen 1959–68, I Pref. p. 4; cf. Sigmund 1963, pp. 39–118, and above pp. 569–72.
38. *De Concordantia Catholica*, ed. Kallen 1959–68, I Pref., p. 3.
39. *Ibid.*, II.xii, p. 145: 'Vigor legis ex concordantia subiectionali eorum, qui per eam ligantur, subsistit.'
40. *Ibid.*, II.xiv, p. 164: 'canones radices habent in naturali iure'.
41. *Ibid.*, II.xi, p. 144: 'canonum statuendorum auctoritas non solum dependet a papa, sed a communi consensu. Et contra hanc conclusionem nulla praescriptio vel consuetudo valere potest, sicut nec contra ius divinum et naturale, a quo ista conclusio dependet'.
42. *Ibid.*, II.iii, pp. 101–3: 'non est numerus adeo necessarius sicut libertas et unanimitas'. Cf. Sigmund 1963, p. 181.

universal Church, it must include the pope and other patriarchs. This granted, the coherent judgement of a council overrides an individual pope.[43] The authority and inerrancy of 'the Roman see' refer not to the pope alone but to the patriarchal synod of the West, unfortunately equivalent – because of the Eastern schism – to the present general council.[44] Thirdly, administrative power 'is constituted partly by subjective consent' and confirmed by divine authority. Indeed, divine authorisation and popular consent entail each other. Sacramental and ruling powers are God-given, but those exercising them have to be elected; office is divinely ordained, its tenure determined by the subjects. Thus papal jurisdiction derives from 'divine privilege and election'.[45] The priesthood takes its form or essence from God, its 'moving, growing, feeling power' from the 'potency of matter in the subjects through voluntary subjection'. He concludes: 'it is beautiful to contemplate how in the people all powers, spiritual and temporal, are latent in potency'.[46]

In terms of human agency, then, all legitimate power is elective: 'So that in concord one body may be composed out of subjects and president, reason, natural law and divine law all require mutual consent, which we rightly understand to consist in election by all and consent by the one chosen, as in the spiritual marriage between Christ and the Church.'[47] This electoral principle operates from parish priests to the pope.[48] It would follow that a general council is, directly or indirectly, elected. These principles of consent and election are not confined to the Church, however, but extend to all types of government. Since law is based on natural justice, implicitly known to all men, and since 'all men by nature are free', the natural form of government is by those 'powerful in reason', not coercing unwilling subjects, but chosen by election and ruling by consent. 'Thus all sovereignty . . . exists solely by concord and subjective consent. For, if men by nature are equally strong and equally free, the true and ordained power of one, by nature no stronger than the rest, can only be constituted by the

43. *De Concordantia Catholica*, ed. Kallen 1959–68, II.xviii, p. 194.
44. *Ibid.*, I.xiv, xvii; II.v, vii.
45. *Ibid.*, II.xiii, p. 153: 'maioritas autem administrationis . . . ex consensu subiectionali partim constituitur . . . Non nego tamen divinam potestatem concurrere auctorizantem et confirmantem . . . Ex quibus patet iurisdictionem in Romano pontifice ita constitui ex divino privilegio et electione.'
46. *Ibid.*, II.xix, pp. 204–5: 'motivam, vegetativam et sensitivam potestatem, quae potestas exit de potentia materiae subditorum per voluntariam subiectionem . . . Et pulchra est haec speculatio, quomodo in populo omnes potestates tam spirituales in potentia latent quam etiam temporales'.
47. *Ibid.*, II.xviii, p. 200.   48. *Ibid.*, II.xviii, pp. 200–1.

election and consent of the others.'[49] The natural form of govenment for states is, therefore, a wise and virtuous aristocracy based on popular consent; just as the greater part of the clergy will not err in faith, so 'the greater part of the people's citizens or heroes will not defect . . . from the right way' (Cusa had by this time read Marsiglio).[50] Cusa applied the same principles to the Empire as to the clergy: the emperor must make laws by consent in a 'universal council'; such Diets are to be held regularly, once or twice a year, with freedom of speech; and their laws bind the emperor.[51] Cusa's thought, governed by the idea of harmony, was conciliatory and moderate. Never a majoritarian, and offended by partisan extremism at Basel, he eventually supported the pope, on the grounds that the 'notable part' of the council and important secular powers had dissented from its decisions. His later ecclesiology was, in effect, papalist.[52]

Nevertheless, the leaders of conciliarist opinion at Constance and Basel gave most weight to theological arguments. Time and again, they emphasised the mystical unity of the Church, of the body of Christ directed by one Holy Spirit, as a basis for ascribing sovereignty to it.[53] They commonly drew a distinction between the unity of the Church, which enabled it to act as one, and the looser unity of secular polities, which, they granted, required the unifying force of kingship.[54] According to Gerson, the conciliar assembly gives a formal or essential unity to the Church, which can then act effectively as superior over any 'part' of 'the Church considered dispersedly', including the pope.[55] Segovia, in a doctrinal summary officially adopted by Basel (1434), said that power of self-government resided in the Church 'as in some functional whole' and 'in all the powers together, by virtue of the one soul'.[56] Organic theory was thus developed

---

49. *Ibid.*, II.xiv, pp. 162–3: 'Omnis constitutio radicatur in iure naturali, et si ei contradicit, constitutio valida esse nequit . . . Unde cum ius naturale naturaliter rationi insit, tunc connata est omnis lex homini in radice sua . . . Ex quo evenit quod ratione vigentes sunt naturaliter aliorum domini et rectores, sed non per legem coercivam aut iudicium, quod redditur in invitum. Unde cum natura omnes sint liberi, tunc omnis principatus . . . est a sola concordantia et consensu subiectivo. Nam si natura aeque potentes et aeque liberi homines sunt, vera et ordinata potestas unius communis [?] aeque potentis naturaliter non nisi electione et consensu aliorum constitui potest.'
50. *Ibid.*, III. Pref., pp. 314–21 at pp. 314, 317–18: 'maior pars populi civium aut heroicorum a recta via . . . non deficiet . . . Impossibile est civitatem aristocratizantem, i.e. secundum virtutem per sapientiores aliorum consensu ad communem utilitatem gubernatam, non bene disponi.' Cf. Sigmund 1962. 51. *De Concordantia Catholica*, ed. Kallen 1959–68, III.xii, xxv, xxxviii.
52. Sigmund 1963, pp. 236ff, 266. 53. Cf. Krämer 1980, p. 362; Oakley 1981.
54. Gerson, ed. Glorieux 1966b, pp. 131–2; 1966d, p. 247; Segovia, *Tract. super Presid.*, ed. Ladner 1968, pp. 63–4; Cracow University 1442, p. 489.
55. Ed. Glorieux 1966d, p. 217. Cf. Anon., *De Papae*, ed. Finke 1923, p. 702.
56. *Tract super Presid.*, ed. Ladner 1968, pp. 37–8. Cf. *DRTA* 17:367.

into social holism, the most explicit statement of which came from Velde. Just as the limbs of a body 'are joined up to one root principle of life, which is the heart . . . so all the members of the Church are co-ordinated in one original or root principle of mystical life, which is Christ'.[57] The church is a *substantia*, an 'essential and notional *collectio*';[58] its unity is spiritual and therefore real.

But this existential unity was not only a metaphysical fact. It sprang directly from Christ's precept of mutual love and the fraternal character of the Church; and it was actually observable in conciliar proceedings, when participants developed a common mind through discussion. The New-Testament value of fraternal love was invoked specifically in defence of Basel's equalitarian system of voting by simple majority. Escobar argued that, since all Christians are brothers, they should have 'an equal voice' in church affairs; there should be 'one charity, one will, one intention in the council'.[59] According to Segovia, the Basel committees enabled men of different nationality and status to come together, pool their knowledge, and produce a common outlook. Instead of superiors and subordinates, there was here 'one intermediate status'.[60] Through being 'almost daily forced into each other's company, there is born true love for persons of all nationalities . . . so that, coming together with a certain delight, they explore more wisely the true and common good'.[61] It is only when men listen to one another actually speaking that they can understand the good of the Church.[62] Freedom of debate was essential if the Holy Spirit was to operate thus in a council.[63]

Actually, however, the conciliarists understood conciliar representation, community sovereignty and values like wisdom and fraternity rather narrowly; the beneficiaries were chiefly university clergy rather than the educated laity. The conciliar movement succeeded in reuniting the Western Church in 1417, but failed in its reformist and constitutionalist aims. These could only be achieved through lay support, and most conciliarists remained committed clericalists. The conciliarist contribution to later constitutionalism lay in a more systematic exploration of arguments for

---

57. Velde, *De Eccl. Pot.*, fol. 89v: 'Omnia membra ecclesiae coordinantur ad unum originale seu radicale vitae misticae principium, quod est Christus.'
58. *Ibid.*, fol. 159r: 'essentialis et notionalis collectio'; and 161r: 'In una divina et humana conveniant potentia essentiali . . . substantialiter, notionaliter seu causaliter instaurata'. Cf. Black 1979, pp. 64–8.   59. *Gub. Conc.*, ed. Hardt 1700, p. 265.
60. *Historia*, ed. Stehlin 1857–1935, vol. II, p. 274.   61. *Ibid.*, pp. 133–4.
62. Segovia, *Amplificatio*, 1935, pp. 727–8. Cf. Black 1979, pp. 185–6.
63. Segovia, *Historia* ed. Stehlin 1857–1935, vol. II, pp. 130–2, vol. III, pp. 531–2, 603, 605.

representative government, and especially for the community's power to remove a bad monarch. On these subjects conciliarist writings were a major source of precedent and, occasionally, inspiration for men of the sixteenth and seventeenth centuries.[64] Since the Church was the most ancient, elaborate, bureaucratic and theoretically coherent monarchy in Europe, the principal carrier of Roman-imperial absolutism, an attack on papal prerogatives had widespread significance. But in 1450 the cause seemed lost. The immediate future lay with monarchy, bureaucratic or parliamentary, the principles of which the papalist Juan de Torquemada had expounded, in reply to conciliarism, with an elaborate coherence which few if any of his opponents could match.

64. Oakley 1962 and 1969; Rueger 1964.

18

THE INDIVIDUAL AND SOCIETY

We tend to think of the Middle Ages as a communal or even collectivist epoch, in which there was a sense of 'the real personality of the group',[1] 'absorption of the individual by the community',[2] in which – to go back to Burckhardt – 'man was conscious of himself only as a member of a race, people, party, family, or corporation – only through some general category'.[3] A quite recent study of medieval social language assumes the existence of a 'communitarian' ethos.[4] The distinction between modern individualism and medieval collectivism goes back, through Tönnies and Durkheim, to Romanticism and the Enlightenment. The pioneer of the study of medieval political thought, Otto von Gierke (1841–1921), believed that, in towns, gilds and other 'chosen groups', individuals submitted willingly to communal norms and identified themselves morally with the group, in the tradition of Germanic *Genossenschaft* (fellowship). But now the picture is changing. A variety of social structures and of attitudes to the individual is beginning to emerge. 'The idea of a fixed society, neatly parcelled into categories by rigid, impassable barriers, is *parfaitement inexacte*'.[5] Chronicles composed by monks and friars, who believed men ought to value community, and works by officials anxious to promote civic harmony, cannot be taken at face value.[6] The actual evidence produced by Gierke turns out, on inspection, to be slender indeed: phrases such as 'the consent and will of the city'[7] no more prove the existence of a collectivist attitude than do modern phrases such as 'the spirit of the Labour (or Conservative) party' or 'the will of the electorate'.

Different explanations have been offered for the rise of individualism in Europe: the classical Renaissance (Burckhardt), Ockham's nominalism (Lagarde), Aristotelian naturalism (Ullmann).[8] It would appear, however,

1. Gierke 1868, pp. 310–12, 327, 359, 383, 405–6. See in general Lewis 1954, ch. 4.
2. Ullmann 1967, pp. 32, 43.
3. Burckhardt 1955 (1st edn 1860), p. 81; cf. Lukes 1973, pp. 23–5.
4. Michaud-Quantin 1970, pp. 341–3.   5. Heers 1973, pp. 295–6.
6. Cf. Brandt 1954, pp. 55–8, 68.   7. Gierke 1873, pp. 780, 822; Gierke 1881, p. 790.
8. Burckhardt 1955, p. 81; Lagarde 1946a; Ullmann 1974, pp. 295, 303–4. Cf. Wilks 1963, pp. 20–1, 93–4.

that a profound change in social attitudes began around 1100 when, as Brown puts it, 'the supernatural, which had tended to be treated as the main source of the objectified values of the group, came to be regarded as the preserve par excellence of . . . intensely personal feeling'.[9] The Investiture Controversy was one factor which sparked off – not for the first time in human history – a transition from tribalism and social collectivism to greater individual self-awareness, and a more self-conscious relationship between individual and community. Morris, who locates 'the discovery of the individual' in the twelfth century, remarks that

It is at once obvious that the Western view of the value of the individual owed a great deal to Christianity. A sense of individual identity and value is implicit in belief in a God who has called each man by his name, who has sought him out as a shepherd seeks his lost sheep.[10]

Furthermore, an economic and entrepreneurial individualism was inherent in the development of commerce and capitalism from the twelfth century onwards; 'the strong economic individual was everything'.[11] Economic changes began to replace the feudal system and traditional communities with a money economy and social mobility. At the same time there was a development of 'consciously chosen community'[12] (for instance, the craft gilds). In fact people were related to many different kinds of group: universal and local Church, kingdom, feudal domain, city, village, gild, confraternity, family. This very multiplicity told against the absorption of the individual into any one group. There was no single, all-pervasive, over-arching 'society', but a wide variety of compulsory and voluntary groups, and a corresponding variety of sentiments about social bonds and societal authority. Different intellectual traditions – Neoplatonic, Aristotelian and humanist, theological and juristic, realist and nominalist – produced divergent views on the individual and society.

Forms of society

Rural social patterns varied in different parts of Europe, depending upon the balance struck between 'the weight of communal or collective restraints' and 'the individualism of the landowning peasants'.[13] The free-floating relationship between lord and follower, warrior and band (*comitatus*), which marked early Germanic society, had hardened into hereditary feudal ties. Yet these were still conceived as personal bonds between vassal and

9. Brown 1982, pp. 305, 325.   10. Morris 1972, p. 10.
11. F. Rörig on Lübeck, cit. Brandt 1954, p. 63; cf. Martines 1979, p. 108; Harvey 1950, pp. 39–41, on the attitudes of architects and masons.   12. Bynum 1980, p. 17.   13. Heers 1973, p. 89.

chief; and the ideal of chosen fellowship might reappear when opportunity arose, as in the Crusades. The horizontal ties between vassals holding land from a lord did not necessarily produce a strong sense of community. What counted were personal honour and the sanctity of the pledged word between lord and man. Feudal society left the way open for the formation of other social bonds. The vast majority of people were deeply enmeshed in *family* relationships, which affected agriculture, trade and government. Land ownership and social status being largely hereditary, what mattered was the position one held in a particular family. Family clans and their alliances left their mark on commercial partnerships and urban structures;[14] royal and noble lineage influenced emerging state patterns. The economic strength of family ties depended partly upon whether property was vested in the extended family or in the individual peasant or householder. In the latter case social and economic individualism could more easily arise, with individual ownership, connubial freedom and nuclear families. Even in country areas, there was sometimes a remarkable degree of individual mobility and occupational freedom.[15]

Gilds (*confratriae, gildoniae*) were originally artificial brotherhoods for mutual protection, based on Germanic custom and the oath of mutual aid.[16] Sometimes whole villages organised themselves as 'confraternities'.[17] Craft gilds, which proliferated all over Europe in the twelfth and thirteenth centuries, were a development of this tradition. They spoke of their 'eternal brotherhood'.[18] Jurists, however, held that membership must be open and voluntary; they acknowledged the right of gilds ('personal colleges') to exist as voluntary associations, thus affirming in embryonic form the principle of freedom of association.[19]

Crop rotation, seasonal labour and the use of ploughs and pasture were sometimes organised communally by the village. The type of community known as *commune* (*Gemeinde*)[20] or sworn territorial association spread rapidly over Europe from c. 1100, and produced the first self-governing towns since classical times. The commune asserted its rights against lord or bishop, including corporate ownership and use of land and forest. A distinctive type of social identity thus arose, based (once again) upon the mutual or collective oath between formal equals – the horizontal equivalent of the feudal oath. 'All belonging to the friendship of the *villa* have affirmed

14. Heers 1974.   15. Macfarlane 1978; Le Roy Ladurie 1980.
16. Wilda 1831; Coornaert 1947.   17. Duparc 1975; Heers 1973, pp. 305–6, 322–31.
18. *Codex Dipl. Lubec.*, vol. VII, p. 731 (seafarers' gild c. 1401).   19. Black 1984, p. 21.
20. Michaud-Quantin 1970, pp. 153–6.

by faith and *sacramentum* that one will aid another as his brother in what is useful and honest.'[21] Such groups, whether rural or urban, regarded themselves as quasi-voluntary associations proclaimed by their members' will, given binding form by oath. By adopting the legal term *universitas* (corporation),[22] villages and, especially, towns asserted their right to own corporate property and to be recognised as corporate persons in law.

In towns and gilds, the individual asserted his rights against outsiders by his very membership, which gave him his 'liberty' and defined his socio-economic position. In this context, therefore, it would make little sense to talk of the individual having claims *against* the community; the latter upheld *his* claims. Thus *'territorial immunity* was the basic meaning of liberty throughout the early Middle Ages';[23] or, as John of Viterbo (c. 1250) put it, *'civitas* means the citizens' liberty, the inhabitants' immunity'.[24] The communal movement helped form a distinctive sense of community, which was later reflected in some political theory.

From early times, shared language and law gave some sense of national identity regardless of political affiliation; one was Italian, Jewish, etc. This varied greatly in intensity. States like England or Burgundy developed a sense of community largely in contradistinction to outsiders, especially in war, but often somewhat fleetingly. Over and above these, the 'universal Church' or Latin Christendom was perceived as a spiritual and juridical unity, with common religious and moral beliefs and practices. The 'individual' was related to 'society' at many different levels.

Mentalities

The relationship between individual and society as such was seldom discussed by theorists or mentioned in medieval sources generally; it was not seen as a special problem. There was a rich supply of medieval Latin words for society (*societas, communitas, corpus, universitas, multitudo, congregatio, collectio, coetus, collegium*),[25] but no word for 'individual'.[26] Nevertheless, evidence about attitudes and views can be obtained indirectly: by considering, first, the general currency of ideas, and, secondly, statements on related topics, such as the organic analogy.

21. 'Omnes autem ad amicitiam pertinentes villae per fidem et sacramentum firmaverunt quod unus subveniat alteri tamquam fratri suo in utili et honesto': Aire in Artois, cit. Wilda 1831, p. 148. Cf. Bloch 1961, pp. 354–5; Michaud-Quantin 1970, pp. 233–46.
22. Below, p. 598; cf. Michaud-Quantin 1970, pp. 47–53.   23. Harding 1980, pp. 424–42.
24. *De Regimine Civitatum*, c.2, p. 218.   25. Michaud-Quantin 1970 *passim*. Cf. pp. 521ff above.
26. *Persona singularis* was a term used by scholastics; otherwise one was *civis, fidelis*, etc.

In the prevailing view of things, God was the ground and destiny of all being. The created universe (it was thought) is a single whole in relation to God, who governs and pervades it as a harmonious unity. It is a complex diversity of interacting parts; interdependence and mutual aid are manifested throughout. God being three 'persons' in one 'substance', there are already social relations within Him Who is the pattern for all being and especially man. The purpose of God's creation was to extend the community of love, which requires the autonomous wills of several persons. Fundamental discord entered the universe when rational beings disobeyed God. There are now two basic 'societies', the just and the unjust, each (once again) an utterly coherent society, in which tension between individual and group is meaningless; tension exists, rather, *between* the two societies. The fundamental question for medieval man was which of these two societies one belonged to. Attention was primarily focused upon the relation between each individual and *God*.

God and the created cosmos were the exemplar for all human societies, and the society of the faithful comprises the ultimate human society. Any true society of rational beings requires subjective unity of wills. Yet 'the body of Christ' was no mere metaphor; in the mystery of the Church all the faithful were collectively identified with Christ. This was indeed a real, over-arching entity, existing prior to its individual human components and conceptually distinct from them. Theology emphasised both the communion of divine love and the individual's personal relation with Christ. Since it is through their very act of being what they are by faith that individuals are incorporated, they would not be the same individuals if separated from the body. On the other hand, each individual remains uniquely himself ('not confused in substance but concordant in wills'). There is diversity of functions within the Church: as St Paul said, some are called to teach, others to heal and so on.[27] Discord and division of wills, however, were *ex hypothesi* excluded. All this provided the ultimate rationale of the *organic analogy*, and determined its meaning. There was an intrinsic connection between medieval cosmology and the organic view of society.[28] In Catholic tradition, the visible Church, being the extension in time and space of the invisible, shared all its essential features. It was one: apparent division meant that some party was schismatic. It was diverse: different individuals performed organically related functions within it. This was the basis for the

27. 1 Cor. 12:12–14, 18–21; Eph.4:12, 16.
28. Chroust 1947; Wulf 1920, pp. 354–6; E. Lewis 1938; Ullmann 1967, pp. 40–3. Cf. John of Salisbury, *Policraticus*, IV.i (ed. Webb 1909, vol. I, pp. 235–6)

general medieval notion of social and political structures. The 'members' of this body were ranks or groups: individuals only entered the picture as occupants of certain 'offices' performing appropriate 'duties (*officia*)': bishops, kings, labourers. Once again, the individual as such did not confront society.

Kingdom, lordship and city (each including both clergy and laity) followed the cosmic pattern as 'bodies' with 'members'. All human groups operate on this organic principle of 'a variety of persons distributed through a variety of functions (*officia*) . . . just as the variety of limbs through their diverse functions preserves the strength of the body and manifests its beauty'.[29] The relation between members is both paternalist and altruistic. Each best promotes his own interest by promoting that of others, 'so that all are as members mutually of one another'.[30] Again, individuals as such did not have claims on this basis. But the parts (clergy, king, nobility and so on) might have claims. A bishop or baron opposing a royal command could appeal to his status as bishop or baron, but not as an individual. Diversity of vocations was considered legitimate and necessary: 'men proceed by diverse means to their intended goal, as the very diversity of human concerns and activities shows'.[31] Among the manual crafts this was underpinned by the gild system. The organic analogy was an exquisite means for legitimising social hierarchy and the economic division of labour.

There were, on the other hand, powerful forces making for the dignity, liberty and rights of the individual. The Germanic (and feudal) warrior insisted on his freedom from restraint;[32] and the personal character of feudal ties meant that individual claims could be based upon the specific sworn obligation of lord and man to uphold each other's 'rights' (*iura*), notably of person and property. The feudal oath, having defined such obligations, implied that, these apart, a man walks freely provided he observes the common law. The right to one's property and to trial by peers were, from Magna Carta (1215) onwards, a prominent feature of English law and politics.[33] The Roman-law tradition was developed in a similar direction. 'It is among the men who rediscovered the Digest and created the medieval science of Roman law in the twelfth century that we must look to find the first modern rights theory.' Jurists identified ownership (*dominium*) as a

---

29. 'Varietas personarum per varia officia distributa . . . sicut varietas membrorum per diversa officia et robur corporis servat et pulchritudinem repraesentat': Johannes Andreae on x.1.33.1, cit. Gierke 1868, p. 310. Cf. Kantorowicz 1957.
30. 'Ut singula sint quasi aliorum ad invicem membra': John of Salisbury, *Policraticus*, vi.20 (ed. Webb 1909, vol. ii, pp. 58–9).   31. Aquinas, *De Regimine Principum*, i.i.
32. S. Painter, cit. Ullmann 1967, p. 98.   33. Cf. Ullmann 1967, pp. 63ff, 97–9.

right (*ius*) which the owner 'can claim against all men'.[34] Roman law sanctioned the privacy of the home (*domus*). This was also expressed in the common proverb 'The house is the burgher's stronghold':[35] as John of Viterbo said, 'since the home is each person's safest refuge . . . no one should be taken thence against their will'.[36] Finally, the development of commerce and credit, and the formation of urban communes under whose 'rights, liberties and customs' the runaway serf might claim freedom from his lord, coincided with increasing social and geographical mobility. Commerce and personal mobility depended partly upon the ability to transfer property legitimately; this was facilitated by the location of property, including land, in the sphere of the individual's autonomous discretion.[37]

During the twelfth century, devotion and ethics were increasingly internalised, with emphasis on the personal relationship between Christ and the believer, and on the moral significance of intention.[38] 'The attention of the faithful was fixed less on the destiny of the Church than on the destiny of each believer.'[39] There was a development of emotional and erotic self-awareness and self-expression, and an opening towards self-knowledge and personal development, which seems to have affected the very notion of personality. In the troubadours' romantic love and the ideal of friendship among higher clergy and *literati*, intimate human relationships acquired cosmic value; there was a 'birth of self-consciousness through love'.[40]

Social and intellectual factors combined to make personal liberty a supreme moral ideal. On this subject Cicero and St Paul spoke with one voice. The status of liberty from sin acquired by baptism could of course be regarded as a purely inward condition, but at least it applied equally to all, including women and infants. The common man began to be recognised; the outlandish variety of human expressions found a place in church sculptural ornaments. The precise and basic socio-economic meaning that personal liberty could have for the ordinary individual is suggested in an agreement drawn up between the Teutonic Knights and the Prussians in 1249 by a papal legate. As 'legitimate persons' (provided they accept the Roman faith), the Prussians are to have 'complete personal liberty': freedom to marry, enter religion, sue in court, sell or bequeath land, buy and sell movable goods. Wives must not be bought, sold or inherited.[41] Again, a

---

34. Tuck 1979, pp. 13–14.   35. 'Das Haus ist des Bürghers Feste': cit. Blecher 1975, p. 285.
36. *De Regimine Civitatum*, c.2, p. 218, quoting *Digest* 2.4. and 21.
37. Werveke 1963, pp. 21, 40; Martines 1979, p. 108; and cf. pp. 607–11 below.
38. Morris 1972, pp. 17, 64–6, 73, 142–4.   39. Lubac, cit. Morris 1972, p. 146.
40. Morris 1972, pp. 107–20 at p. 118.
41. Philippi (ed.) 1882, pp. 159–61. Cf. Grundmann 1957; Merzbacher 1970; Harding 1980.

moralist like John of Salisbury would insist that liberty is essential to the development of virtue.[42] Personal eccentricity was not noticeably discouraged, and political dissent was relatively common.

But in the crucial area of religion the medieval view of liberty was severely restricted. Christian society was less tolerant than Islamic. The unbaptised, such as Jews, though permitted to practise their religion, were on various occasions subject to both official and unofficial persecution. The baptised were held to be morally obliged to accept Catholic doctrine and legally subject to the church hierarchy; consequently, heretics and schismatics were treated with the utmost severity. The Church regarded heresy as we regard crime; indeed it was the ultimate crime against Christian society. And, from the twelfth century onward, heresies sprang up as regularly as they were suppressed. It would not be inappropriate to regard heresy, since it affected cultural fundamentals, as the ultimate expression of individual self-determination. Some heresies were forms of Manichaeanism, others were approximations to what would later emerge as Protestantism:[43] according to both views, the church hierarchy, liturgy and sacramental system contradicted scripture, which by implication was open to individual interpretation. The heretical sects necessarily endorsed the principle of individual choice in religion. But, except for the Brethren of the Free Spirit,[44] they were not notably individualist in any further sense. Rather, they took the principle of the chosen group and of freedom of association into the spiritual sphere. As Moore puts it, the 'most sinister habit of heretics' in churchmen's eyes was 'that of forming conventicles . . . by private arrangement'; sect membership provided 'a new solidarity'.[45] Several sects preached communism.

While the relation between individual and society was seldom explicitly discussed, a good deal was implied about it in connection with the organic analogy, the common good, love of one's country (*patria*), and citizenship as friendship. These ideals were proclaimed in popular idiom, official ideology and formal philosophy. In the factious Italian city-states, the organic analogy and devotion to the common good were employed as rhetorical devices against partisanship.[46] In these sophisticated polities, 'party (*pars*)' was still considered illegitimate; when a group acquired power it presented itself as sole representative of the whole.[47] As regards the *common good*, E. Lewis denies that the medieval emphasis upon this implied

42. *Policraticus*, vii.25 (ed. Webb 1909, vol. ii, pp. 217–18).
43. Leff 1967; Cohn 1970; Moore 1977.   44. Cohn 1970, pp. 148–86.
45. Moore 1977, p. 272; cf. Cohn 1970, p. 13.   46. Rubinstein 1958.   47. Peters 1977.

social holism, but rather 'a tendency to conceive all political units, including the Church, as organizations of individuals aiming at the ethical and spiritual fulfilment of individual human destiny, and having no purpose apart from the common end of their individual members'.[48] 'Common good' certainly included the good of individuals. But it also referred to collective goods which would benefit all indiscriminately, such as internal and external peace, and the prosperity of the realm. It meant the promotion of common interests, the integrity of one's territory and the preservation of common assets. There was much emphasis on the subordination of individual to communal need. Aquinas justified the execution of criminals on the ground that 'the good of the community is greater and godlier than that of one person'.[49] Remigio de' Girolami expressed this more positively: 'let the citizen, however poor in himself, strive to make his commune flourish, for in this way he himself will flourish'.[50] Individuals might own property, but in time of emergency the community had a claim upon them and their property. Death for one's country was an act of supreme virtue.[51] Common good also meant maintenance of procedures or facilities, such as common law and sound coinage, which make normal relationships and orderly exchange possible. These were preeminently a ruler's concern: the criterion of 'common good' meant that he should maintain social order, and employ public power and resources for the community, not for personal or partisan gain. Aquinas was not untypical in making common good the bench-mark of valid law and government. In Italian city-states, 'common good (*bonum commune*)' was sometimes equated with 'the good of the Commune (*bonum Communis*)',[52] meaning, again, political conditions under which men could live amicably – notably, legal and fiscal impartiality. It *could* therefore refer to collective goods, without, however, implying that society was a real whole *apart from* its members.

The organic analogy and the common-good argument, as they appear in both everyday sentiment and scholastic philosophy, consistently emphasised societal harmony and unity. This is also found in current terms for social bonding – *unio, communio, commune* (sc. town), *amicitia, fraternitas*[53] – terms which connote a spontaneous fellowship of mutual aid and love, rather than inert acceptance of customary bonds. Indeed the common good was regularly linked to the Christian virtue of *caritas*

48. E. Lewis 1938, p. 875.   49. *De Regimine Principum*, I.xi.
50. Cit. Minio-Paluello 1956, p. 69.   51. Kantorowicz 1957, pp. 232ff.
52. Rubinstein 1958, p. 185.   53. Michaud-Quantin 1970, pp. 147ff, 179ff.

(altruistic love). This found social expression in the confraternities and gilds, and political expression in the early communes and in the ideology of patriotism. As Ptolemy of Lucca (writing c. 1300–5) said, *caritas* 'puts what is common before what is individual (*communia propriis* . . .)'; 'love of country is rooted in charity'.[54] Brunetto Latini explained (c. 1260) that in communes government is based upon love and friendship, which exclude domination and vengeance.[55]

Christian love as unity of wills, the gild practice of 'friendship' as support of fellows in quarrels with outsiders, the Aristotelian notion of citizenship as a diluted type of friendship and the Stoic doctrine of man's natural sociability, were all fused together in the application of love and friendship to political bonds. Political society was necessary for man to realise his God-given natural drive towards mutual aid and affection. Henry of Ghent (c. 1279), discussing the *civitas* as man's highest natural condition, said that it involved

men living together in civil society and communion; for this could not exist unless bound together by supreme friendship, in which each considered the other as a second self, by supreme charity, by which each of them loved the other as himself, and by supreme benevolence, by which each of them wished for the other what he wished for himself.[56]

The Dominican Remigio de' Girolami, writing on Florentine affairs in 1302–4, further developed the ideal of citizenship as love; and here he did affirm the *integration* of individual citizen into *civitas*. Civic disasters deprive the citizens' lives of meaning, for (he said) 'destruction of the city leaves the citizen a mere stone', and 'if you are not a citizen you are not a man'. As 'rational parts' of the state, citizens comprise 'the totality of an integral whole (*totalitas totius integralis*)', based upon 'the union or conjunction of hearts, that is of wills willing the same thing'. He seems to have applied the spiritual ideal of ecstatic love to the civic bond: the city is a 'whole which the parts love more than themselves and to which they are more closely joined than to themselves'.[57] Such a view of society was characteristically medieval and entirely *sui generis*: the civic bond ought to be strong and intense, but it is voluntary and therefore fragile.

54. *De Regimine Principum*, iv.iv, p. 71, and cit. Rubinstein 1958, p. 185.
55. *Livres dou Tresor*, pp. 211–12, 392.
56. Cit. Lagarde 1956–70, vol. ii, p. 178; cf. John of Salisbury, *Metalogicon*, ed. Webb 1929, pp. 6–8.
57. *De Bono Pacis* ed. Davis 1959, pp. 128–9; Minio-Paluello 1956, pp. 60, 64–6, 68–9; Davis 1960, pp. 668–9. Cf. Godfrey of Fontaines, *Quodlibet* xiv, q. 3, pp. 340–1; Duby 1980.

Scholastic and juristic thought

The scholastics and jurists occasionally discussed the relation between society and the individual explicitly, and in a surprisingly modern way. They were concerned not with the degree of self-determination individuals have or ought to have, so much as with the type of entity or structure a society may be said to be. Medieval jurists maintained a clear working distinction, based on Roman law and dictated by the kinds of problem they were expected to resolve, between an association (*universitas*) and its individual members (*singuli*); they distinguished between the powers, liabilities and possessions belonging to the whole, and those belonging to individuals. In the case of property, they made a further distinction between what belonged to members collectively (*ut universi*) and what belonged to them severally (*ut singuli*); on the former category a majority could decide (as on corporate property), on the latter decisions must be unanimous.[58] *Universitas* being also a generic term for society, much of their discussion could apply to bodies that were not technically colleges. Pillius and Bassianus, writing in the late twelfth century, formulated the first modern European definitions of association. Pillius said: 'A college is as it were a conjunction or collection of several persons in one body: this is described by the general term "association (*universitas*)", and also "body"; and in common speech we call it "fellowship (*consortium*)" or "school".'[59] Bassianus was more explicit:

An association (*universitas*) is 'a collection of several bodies distinct from each other, with one name specially assigned to them'. I said 'several' to note that association differs from individuals and species (e.g. ox and Socrates, as logicians say), which bring together not several bodies but several parts of a [single] thing. 'Distinct from each other' is added to distinguish the integral whole (which contains several things not separate but joined together, e.g. a box or cart) from an association. 'Specially assigned to them' is put in to make it clear that the word 'man', though it signifies several bodies, is not an association, because in that case no special [name] is assigned to any person or persons.[60]

The Gloss, on the other hand, simply observed that corporation and individuals are legally and conceptually distinct: the present inhabitants' death does not mean that 'the people dies, because others are substituted in their place', just as, when you stop talking, your voice still exists.[61]

58. Cf. Michaud-Quantin 1970, pp. 271–84.
59. *Summa Codicis* on *Codex* 11.17.1: cit. Michaud-Quantin 1970, p. 27.
60. *Summa Digesti* on *Digest* 41.3.30: cit. Michaud-Quantin 1970, p. 28.
61. Accursius, Gl. *competit* ad *Digest* 47.22.1.

The essentially pragmatic discourse of the early jurists was taken on to a more abstract plane after the mid-thirteenth century. Later jurists embarked on far-ranging generalities about the ontological and epistemological relation between association and individuals, albeit always geared to specifically legal questions. The teaching of Innocent IV (d. 1254) was a watershed. In 1245 he proscribed collective excommunication, and his legal commentaries explained why: a corporation (chapter, people, tribe, etc.) cannot commit a wrong because 'these are names of law and not of persons' – '"chapter" is a mental term, an incorporeal thing'.[62] For certain less crucial purposes, none the less, (such as oaths), a college may be 'pretended to be one person (*fingatur una persona*)' and therefore act through a representative. Although sin and crime cannot be ascribed to collectivities, civil offences can: punishment should be confined to interdict, confiscation or dissolution.[63] It is probably fair to say that Innocent's teaching was based on the Christian doctrine of personal responsibility. It became normative for most jurists and dealt a further blow to social holism. It clearly suggested an individualist view of moral and legal responsibility, and of social entities. Jurists thereafter tended to say that society and individual are different kinds of whole. Personality can only properly be predicated of rational individuals; a group is but 'a representative person'.[64] The earlier working distinction had become a conceptual and ontological one.

After the rediscovery of Aristotle, scholastics became interested in the nature of social entities both from a philosophical and from a political angle. They discussed what kind of thing a society is, and what kind of unity it has; and their answers often had implications for the relation between community and ruler. Aquinas expressed two views about social entities.[65] His more holistic statements sprang from the Aristotelian notion of the *polis* as the proper environment for truly human activity; for Aquinas the 'parts' of society are not offices or functional groups, but individuals. Greco-Roman influence prompted Aquinas and other scholastics to isolate family

---

62. 'Universitas autem non potest excommunicari, quia impossibile est quod universitas delinquat, quia universitas, sicut est capitulum, populus, gens et huiusmodi, nomina sunt iuris et non personarum; et ideo non cadit in eam excommunicatio': on x.5.39.53, fol. 231r. 'Capitulum, quod est nomen intellectuale et res incorporalis, nihil facere potest nisi per membra sua': on *Sext* 5.11.5.
63. On x.2.20.57 and x.5.3.30, fol. 206v, and x.5.39.53, fol. 231r. Cf. Michaud-Quantin 1970, pp. 329–36.
64. 'Et ista, universitas, collegium, corpus, dicuntur unum non simpliciter sed aggregatione . . . et ob hoc nullum horum est vera persona, quae est rei rationabilis individua substantia': Johannes Andreae on *Sext* 3.4.16. Cf. Gierke 1881, pp. 279–85; Feenstra 1956, pp. 428–9.
65. Gilby 1958, p. 241, says: '[Aquinas] spoke in two parts, as a theologian for the supremacy of the person, as a social philosopher for the supremacy of the community.'

and state (*civitas*) as the natural human groupings, leaving intermediate corporations, such as gilds and estates, out of the philosophical picture.[66] Aquinas spoke of individual and community in terms of 'part' and 'whole', and insisted upon the duty of the part to shape itself to the 'good of the whole'. The implication was that men are what they are in virtue of their membership of the state, and that their good is therefore relative to that of the community. Political society enables men to 'live well' both materially and morally, and men can only be good individuals if they accommodate themselves to the common good. Since every man is part of the state, it is impossible for any man to be good unless he is well proportioned to the good of the whole; and the whole can only be well constituted out of parts that are proportioned to it.[67] Here Aquinas expressed the idea of civic virtue without implying any connection with political participation. He not only made the common good the criterion of all political conduct, but insisted that it differs essentially from the individual good.[68] Pursuing this line of thought, Dante conceived of the whole human race as a single polity, precisely on the ground that it has a common natural goal: the actualisation of mind through thought and action 'is constitutive of the species'.[69]

But Aquinas also insisted that the political community does not absorb the whole man: 'man is not related to the political community as to his whole being and everything that is his, and therefore not all his actions need be classified as praiseworthy or blameworthy in relation to the political community'.[70] He eventually stated a nuanced view of the relationship between individual and society, based upon his understanding of political society as such:

This whole, such as a civil society (*civilis multitudo*) or domestic family, has only unity of order, so as not to be one *simpliciter*. Therefore, the part of this whole can have a task (*operatio*) which is not that of the whole, just as a soldier in an army has a task which is not that of the whole army. None the less, the whole itself also has a task which is proper to the whole but not to any of its parts, such as the charge of the whole army.[71]

66. Aquinas, *In Decem Libros Ethicorum* 1.1.1, p. 3 (ed. d'Entrèves 1948, p. 190); Lagarde 1956–70, vol. II, p. 172; Gierke 1900, pp. 97–100.
67. 'Cum igitur quilibet homo sit pars civitatis, impossibile est quod aliquis homo sit bonus nisi sit bene proportionatus bono communi; nec totum potest bene consistere nisi ex partibus sibi proportionatis': *Summa Theologiae* 1a/IIae.92.1 ad 3.
68. *Summa Theologiae* IIa IIae 58.7 (ed. d'Entrèves 1948, p. 164). Cf. Godfrey of Fontaines in Lagarde 1956–70, vol II, p. 174.   69. *Monarchia* 1.3.4 and 1.4.5.
70. *Summa Theologiae* Ia IIae 21.4.ad 3 (ed. d'Entrèves 1948, p. 108). Cf. Gilby 1958, p. 239.
71. *In Decem Libros Ethicorum* 1.1.1, p.3 (ed. d'Entrèves 1948, p. 190).

What this passage means is that, quite apart from the non-political activities of man, citizens perform their social and political tasks both individually and collectively. 'Unity of order' appears as a category *sui generis*, the peculiar feature of *human* society. Society is certainly not, for Aquinas, either an integral or a universal whole: here he agreed with Bassianus. If Aquinas had pursued the organic analogy at this point, he might have ended up by classifying society as a 'functional whole *(totum potentiale)*'.[72] But he did not do so explicitly, and he handled the organic analogy with notable restraint; it connotes 'a resemblance . . . not an exact correspondence or identity' between Church and organism.[73] His defence of Innocent IV's ban on corporate excommunication was consonant with this line of thought.[74]

It would appear that Innocent IV's view of corporations as 'names of law' combined with the development of philosophical nominalism to produce in the later Middle Ages an academic consensus that *social entities have no reality apart from the individual human beings that compose them.* The debate over universals and particulars, species and individual, 'humanity' and 'Peter', was always liable to have repercussions in sociological thought. But medieval philosophers did not always aim at consistency outside their own field; and the Church was one social entity which continued to be personified even by men who professed philosophical nominalism. Statements about the nature of society were used eclectically in political debate, in which the desired conclusion often determined which arguments were employed.[75] Philosophical realism continued to find supporters.

In the case of William of Ockham, the leading nominalist, the claim that he was 'the father of the theory of natural rights', and that 'the foundations of modern individualism can be traced back to [his] speculations about the nature of existence',[76] must be treated with reserve. In his controversy with the papacy, Ockham emphasised the autonomy of each individual believer, and 'called on every Christian individual to take action against papal heresy'.[77] On the other hand, his support of Ludwig der Bayern led him, so far as the Empire was concerned, 'to qualify the liberty of the individual subject out of existence'.[78] In defending the Spiritual Franciscan cause, Ockham made general statements which clarified the nature of private property as something approximating to a personal right. Before the Fall

---

72. Cf. *Summa Theologiae* I.77.1 ad 1; Gilby 1958, pp. 251–6.
73. *Summa Theologiae* III.8.1 *concl.* and ad 2, and III.8.3; cf. *Summa Theologiae* Ia IIae 81.1.
74. Eschmann 1946.   75. Cf. Black 1980, pp. 154ff; Zuckerman 1975.
76. Lagarde 1946b, p. 162, and Stein and Shand 1974, p. 185; cf. Tuck 1979, p. 22.
77. McGrade 1974, p. 76.   78. Leff 1975, p. 643.

property was communal, but thereafter 'the power of appropriating temporal goods to a person, persons or college has been granted by God to the human race':[79] existing property rights have divine as well as human sanction. Private ownership entails freedom of action under the law: men may handle their property 'in any way not prohibited by natural law'.[80] But it appears that Ockham produced neither a general theory of human rights nor a general theory of the nature of social entities. The extent to which his political views were related to his logic and epistemology has indeed been vigorously disputed, and the balance of opinion seems to be that there was rather little connection between them.[81] However much nominalism contributed later to an individualist view of society, Ockham was not a systematic social theorist, and he did not expound a nominalist theory of society or politics.

Both Marsilius and Bartolus stated their positions rather more explicitly. Marsilius distinguished between 'parts' in the sense of functional – or, perhaps, territorial – groupings (*officia*) and the individual members (*supposita*) of such groupings. A city or kingdom's 'unity of order' entailed no actual unity but derived exclusively from the will of the parts to stand in a common relationship to something which is actually one, namely the principate. The 'parts' (in both senses) remain separate entities with their own activities. 'Rome, Mainz and other communities are a single kingdom or empire, but only in the sense that each is ordered through their will to a single principate . . . So too the men of one city or province are called one city or kingdom because they consent to (*volunt*) one principate.'[82] His notion of society was clearly voluntarist.

Bartolus gave an interesting explanation of the jurists' fiction-theory of groups. He insisted that law is a category *sui generis*, distinct from both everyday reality and philosophical concepts. It is perfectly true that, 'speaking really [sc. of actual things], truly and properly', an association is, as the philosophers and canonists claim, nothing other than the people in it.

But according to the fiction of the law they do not speak the truth. For a university stands for one person, which is something other than its scholars . . . Again, when all members of a people die and others replace them, the people is the same . . . and thus an association is something other than the persons composing it, according to the fiction of the law.[83]

---

79. Cit. Lagarde 1946b, p. 181n. Cf. above, pp. 511, 537. 80. Cit. Lagarde 1946b, p. 204n.
81. McGrade 1974, pp. 30–9; Gewirth 1961; Leff 1975, p. 643. 82. *Defensor Pacis* I.xvii.11.
83. 'Debemus videre primo an universitas sit aliud quam homines universitatis. Quidam dicunt quod non . . . et hoc tenent omnes philosophi et canonistae, qui tenent quod totum non differt realiter a suis partibus. Veritas est quod, siquidem loquamur realiter, vere et proprie, ipsi dicunt verum; nam

Bartolus insisted that this was a frame of reference peculiar to the civil (Roman) law: 'this is fiction put in the place of reality, as we jurists do put it'. Civil unity is 'artificial' and 'imagined'.[84] He differed from Innocent IV in holding that groups could commit certain crimes: murder, rape, theft can only be assigned to individuals, but treason and heresy (like legislation and taxation) are acts assignable to collectivities. Punishment should wherever possible fall only on consenting individuals; collective punishment must be restricted to fines or dissolution of the corporation.[85] In this way, medieval jurisprudence arrived by its own route at a nominalist (or, we might say, methodologically individualist) notion of society. Group personality is a legal device, a useful artifice, a mental construction; reality consists solely of individuals.

The dominant philosophy of nominalism emphasised the essential arbitrariness of God, and held that the observed regularities of natural and human phenomena are the result of contingent circumstance rather than innate tendencies. Consequently, some philosophers emphasised, as Marsilius had done, the will of groups – individuals or all members together – as the cause and constituent force of society.[86] This was an analytical argument rather than a statement about how society arose historically; it did not mean that men could have willed solitude or anarchism, nor that individuals today may opt out of society or disobey rulers. Men like Ockham and D'Ailly were careful to leave the parameters of political allegiance essentially undisturbed by their philosophical innovations. Their 'voluntarism' did not imply that existing states were voluntary associations, nor that constitutionalism or popular sovereignty were necessarily better founded than monarchy. Rather, on the one hand, voluntarism encouraged people to attach greater importance to the 'will of the prince' as a constituent force in society and as the basis for law. On the other hand, it could enhance the moral standing of corporate and personal 'liberties, customs and rights'.[87] There were circumstances in which the authoritarian

---

nil aliud est universitas scholarium quam scholares. Sed secundum fictionem iuris ipsi non dicunt verum. Nam universitas repraesentat unam personam, quae est aliud a scholaribus . . . quia mortuis omnibus de populo, et aliis subrogatis, idem est populus . . . et sic aliud est universitas quam personae quae faciunt universitatem, secundum iuris fictionem, quia est quaedam persona repraesentata . . . proprie [universitas] non est persona . . . tamen hoc est fictum positum pro vero, sicut ponimus nos juristae': on *Digest* 48.19.16(10), fol. 200r/a. Cf. Tudeschis: 'Secundum veritatem collegium non est aliud a singulis de collegio, sed secundum iurisdictionem aliud collegium, aliud singuli . . . hoc corpus non est verum sed fictum et representatum . . . sed istud corpus habetur pro vero quoad multos iuris effectus': on x.5.3.30, fols. 98v–99r.

84. 'Tota civitas est una persona et unus homo artificialis et imaginatus': *De Regimine Civitatis*, p. 80.
85. Bartolus on *Digest* 48.19.16(10), fol. 200r/a.
86. Cf. Oakley 1964.   87. Cf. Oakley 1964, pp. 187–92; Lagarde 1946b, pp. 178n., 208–10.

state and individual liberty might find common ground, notably in attacking feudal, ecclesiastical, communal and gild privileges and restrictions.

In the fifteenth century, social theory was frequently the handmaid of political ideology. Supporters of monarchy or absolute rule, and especially of papal supremacy in the Church, used nominalist arguments to deny that one could meaningfully assert the sovereignty of the Church or the community as a whole, because, they argued, such societal wholes have no existential reality. Rather, societal unity depends upon subordination to a prince, who may therefore most appropriately be regarded as full sovereign.[88] On the other hand, parliament was called 'the mystical body of the realm', and the conciliarists, as apologists for community sovereignty in the Church, frequently alluded to the existential reality of the Church-as-a-whole, even though some of them were nominalists and their opponents Thomists. Such communal sovereignty was sometimes said to derive from the unique spiritual unity of the Church. The realist philosopher Heimerich van de Velde (1395–1460) vigorously supported the corporate sovereignty of the Church on social-holist grounds. The Church, he said, is an essential as well as an intelligible unity (*essentialis et notionalis collectio*); it is the *substantia, natura, species* of all Christians, and exists of itself prior to and separate from the incorporation and differentiation of its individual members. Organic theory here became no metaphor but a statement of underlying reality: the Church's essence is a spiritual principle to which individuals are related as accidents to substance.[89]

The early Renaissance

In Burckhardt's words, it was in thirteenth-century Italy that 'man became a spiritual *individual*, and recognised himself as such . . . Italy began to swarm with individuality; the ban laid on the human personality was dissolved'.[90] The issue was not as clear-cut as Burckhardt supposed. Indeed, the 'energetic, individualist drive for fulfilment' took place in the context of 'a plea for a renewal of a theological grace':[91] the *Summa Theologica* of St Antonino of Florence (1389–1459) contained among its titles *On the Wonderful Nobility of the Soul* (I.12), *On the Essence and Excellence of Man* (I.53), *How the Soul is Drawn by God and yet Remains Free* (I.55).

88. E.g. Torquemada, *Summa De Ecclesia* II.71, fol. 195v; cf. Aquinas, *De Regimine Principum* I.xv. But see Zuckermann 1975.   89. Black 1979, pp. 58–84; cf. above, p. 586.
90. Burckhardt 1955, p. 81.   91. Trinkaus 1970, vol. I, pp. xx–xxi; cf. Bolgar 1958, pp. 240–4.

Nevertheless, 'the dignity of man' was also now asserted in the name of the individual simply as a human being, and no longer inexorably placed in the theological context of salvation-history.

The self-development of the individual was now elevated into a principal duty and goal in life. Not only should one conform to a generic pattern of virtue, whether Stoic, Aristotelian or Christian; one should also develop those unique qualities that differentiate each individual from others. It was an artistic ideal, emphasising the aesthetic qualities of virtue as beauty of soul and inventiveness of spirit. While energy, industry, exercise of talent, active business (*negotium*) were more vigorously emphasised than in scholastic thought, the contemplative life was by no means ruled out; indeed there was a cult of solitude. The scholar or artist, though working in solitude, conceived himself through his vocation to be in direct contact with human society and the republic of letters. As Bolgar says of Petrarch, 'the boldest flights of his histrionic genius were reserved for the part he best loved to play, the role of the famous author sitting at his desk, withdrawn from the world, but conscious of the devoted attention of a million admirers'.[92] The artist and 'intellectual' were given a new and commanding position in society. This was a meritocratic view of mankind and of human society; it was an ideology for exceptional characters, especially for 'talented boys from poor families'.[93] Nobility comes from personal qualities and achievements rather than birth; thus equality of opportunity is essential. 'Perhaps the most notable characteristic of the new Renaissance order was the high value given to individual effort and the consequent emphasis placed upon the distinction which was to reward such effort.'[94]

This programme was most clearly articulated by Leonardo Bruni. He expounded an ethic of talent and hard work, devoted not to gain or economic pursuits, but to literary excellence and public service – a Ciceronian ideal. He emphasised civic virtue: the citizen pursues 'honour', in the sense of both fame and public office, by service to the community. Bruni wrote of political effort much as a modern soothsayer might of economic initiative:

Human nature is such that when the path to greatness and honours lies open, men more easily raise themselves up; but, if it is closed, they sit back listlessly . . .[95]

[At Florence] the hope of acquiring honour and raising oneself up is equal for all, provided they have industry, talent, a proven and serious way of life. Our city

92. Bolgar 1958, p. 248; cf. Trinkaus 1970, vol. I, pp. 282–3.   93. Martines 1979, p. 277.
94. Bolgar 1958, p. 245; cf. Skinner 1978, vol. I, pp. 81–2.
95. Cit. Baron 1966, pp. 427–8, 559–60.

requires virtue and probity in its citizens. It deems anyone who has these qualities sufficiently qualified to run the state . . . And it is amazing how when the opportunity and ability to acquire and achieve honours is provided to a free people, it serves to stimulate the talents of citizens. When hope of honour is manifest, men exert themselves and raise themselves up.[96]

Humanists writing under despotic governments, however, cultivated privacy as a human ideal.[97] By retiring into private life, a man could excel by devoting himself to 'business (*negotium*)' in the economic sphere, and to philosophy and literature (a lay version of the contemplative ideal).

Classical philosophy, as transmitted by both Aristotle and Cicero, taught that the principal social bond among men is the *polis* or *civitas*. The Renaissance completed the Christian-Aristotelian emphasis upon the family, on the one hand, and the state, on the other. Corporations and the communal tradition were pushed intellectually into the background. In Germany, self-governing crafts and semi-autonomous towns had a long life ahead of them. But in England and France corporate allegiances would soon be subordinated to the national state apparatus, with its bonds of bureaucracy, law, language and culture.

In the study of any remote culture, evidence must override speculation. The idea of medieval European society as collectivist or totalitarian is a myth; the only evidence for it is certain late medieval pro-papal propaganda, written at a time when the papacy was declining.[98] There was, on the other hand, a strong sense of community, especially at the local level. Legal and economic individualism was common among most classes; the literate upper class developed a strong sense of individual personality. The balance between communal sentiment (relating to town, village, gild) and individual sentiment was tilted more towards the communal than today, but on the other hand there was far less nationalism. The Renaissance and the Reformation served to elevate both the individual and the nation-state.

96. 'Spes vero honoris adipiscendi ac se attollendi omnibus par est, modo industria adsit, modo ingenium et vivendi ratio quaedam probata et gravis. Virtutem enim probitatemque in cive suo civitas nostra requirit. Cuicunque haec adsint, eum satis generosum putat ad rempublicam gubernandam . . . Atque haec honorum adipiscendorum facultas potestasque libero populo haec assequendae proposita, mirabile quantum valet ad ingenia civium excitanda. Ostensa enim honoris spe, erigunt se homines atque attollunt': *Oratio*, ed. Baluze 1680, pp. 230–2. Cf. Baron 1966, pp. 191ff; Skinner 1978, vol. I, pp. 74–81.
97. Burckhardt 1955, pp. 82–3.
98. Wilks 1963.

19
PROPERTY AND POVERTY

Between the eleventh century and the fourteenth the economy of Latin Christendom underwent fundamental and rapid transformations. There is, it is true, scholarly debate as to the direction and pace of economic development; but some points are clear enough. The population increased threefold, urban centres attracted an increasingly mobile populace and there was a massive minting of money. At a time when feudal society still flourished, there was a concomitant development of the basic structures of pre-industrial society, most of which had taken shape by 1300, so that many towns were to retain their essential appearance until the nineteenth century.[1] While feudal tenure was still widespread, especially in France, England and the Empire, it appears that in England, by 1300, such tenures were becoming more like private property, transferred by sale as well as, more traditionally, by inheritance. What was formerly seen by historians as the area of 'classic feudalism' has shrunk somewhat, for regional studies in France and the Low Countries have shown that even by the mid-eleventh century allodial holdings, independent of vassalage, constituted the principal form of property. Allods meant that real estate was more mobile than an extensively feudalised society would permit.[2] More generally, the commercial revolution of this period produced a market economy centred on towns; and the agriculture which was still the main activity of medieval men and women became organised for that economy.[3] The desire for new land and for the more efficient exploitation of the land led to massive reclamation projects, to the assessment of property by reference to rental income instead of service and produce, and to the increasing importance of bankers and credit transactions.[4] Credit and payment techniques in general improved during the twelfth and thirteenth centuries so that turnover became more rapid and the volume of money was increased. It is with such factors as these – with elements in the economic process which defied or

1. Little 1978.   2. Witt 1971, pp. 965–88; Verriest 1959 and 1946.   3. Lis and Soly 1979.
4. Lopez 1971; Herlihy 1958.

transformed traditional feudal relations, rather than with 'classic feudalism' itself – that the discussion here is concerned.

In eleventh-century Tuscan cities, as elsewhere somewhat later, second-line nobles (*valvassores*) became part of the expanded feudal elite. Commercial families and the old aristocracy blended together so as to obscure the distinction between rural and urban power bases; and, especially in Italy, there is evidence for a widespread intrusion of the nobility into the legal and administrative professions. The increasing use of money and the development of an elaborate structure of financial credit in the new market economy, especially conspicuous in towns, gave rise to impersonal transactions unaffected by considerations of the status of buyer and seller; and this helped to produce a mentality in which the seed of capitalism was sown, thereby generating attitudes to property that were to survive into and beyond the early modern era. The distinctive spiritualities of the period between the eleventh and late fourteenth century were also, in part, responses and adjustments to this social and economic change: the laity became more involved in church reform.[5] The distinctive political and legal theory and practice of this period, the very survival of the political communities of Europe as they emerged in the twelfth and thirteenth centuries, point to the role of money and financial sophistication in the development of civic-spirited, abstract social ties, replacing the earlier mentality based on kinship and blood relationships.[6]

Any discussion of the evolution of concepts of property in this period must deal with some of the ways in which the abstract ties of credit and a faith in the durability of financial relations gained primacy in the public mind even while feudal rights and obligations persisted. In eleventh-century Tuscany there developed a harsh critique of ecclesiastical institutions that accepted gifts in return for spiritual benefits. This can be seen as an offshoot of the Gregorian Reform movement which inspired monasteries to be freer from the world of power, arms and gifts; priests and monks were inspired to be free of the taint of simony, thereby enforcing spiritual authority as autonomous and abstract. It has recently been argued that the reform movement and a pious laity affected by it, challenged a system of values and social relationships structurally dependent on gift and literal exchange.[7] A growing belief that interpersonal relationships could be predicated of abstract ties was reflected in the renewed use of Roman law categories on the part of the Holy Roman Emperor and his allies and the

5. Little 1975, pp. 11–26; Le Goff 1970; Bolton 1983; Violante 1974.
6. Becker 1981; Goody 1983; Mollat 1974.   7. Becker 1981.

parallel development of canon law categories by a reformed papacy. A collective Christian set of interests and a collective set of civic, universal interests were enshrined both in the Roman and church law compendia and their commentaries. Ecclesiastical canon law developed to encompass ever widening jurisdiction in men's lives as did civil law. The nuclear family replaced the extended family solidarity.[8] Marriage achieved sacramental status; dowries became real contracts; wills became true contracts of alienation with the right of *usufruct* at the end of the eleventh century. Notarial formulae came into vogue to guarantee universal legitimacy. The two laws generally classified human behaviour and reified obligation through written formulae in a more mobile, increasingly literate and pious lay society. Roman law projected a vision of legal· order that was more stable, autonomous and more universal than the clannish, localised laws of an earlier period. In business as in law, the shift was away from voluntary and amiable transactions ruled by the principle of *convenientia*, that resulted in pacts publicly verified through witnesses and iconic documents enshrining benefactions, towards more impartial legal norms. This was related to a renewed and realised notion of Empire on the part of the Hohenstaufen and an extension of power over local communities through an extension of a more universal tribunal that was fuelled by credit transactions and taxation in money. Ancient imperialism and republicanism were revived in theory, made explicit in revived Roman law, and previously unexplored libraries were examined to reveal ancient texts to justify papal or imperial attempts at consolidation of power. Illegitimacy was censured, ecclesiastical concubinage was condemned, and, in general, a pious laity intervened in the reform of the local churches. Collective contracts between landlords and peasant communities evolved into communal rural statutes in favour of the survival of the community. Communal assemblies were charged with administering parish properties. Twelfth-century Lombard communes corporatively owned and claimed customary rights in pastures, fishing, mills, ovens, banks, food-markets and houses built on public streets. The possibility of living an authentic Christian life whilst remaining of the world (and therefore, not retreating to the monastic cloister) was gaining force, and one observes the shift in legal justifications for private, public and corporate ownership of property. Some of the first juridical texts to define the status of the laity, Gratian's *De matrimonio* and his collection of ecclesiastical law, the *Decretum* (c. 1140), described men as righteously married, tillers of the soil, capable of

8. Goody 1983; Violante 1953.

adjudication amongst themselves, and with the rights to pursue their own affairs as possessors and users of worldly goods.[9] On the subject of economic policy, city authorities and larger states came to be seen as the appropriate regulators. In effect, Empire and papacy, the two major forces behind the two collected bodies of law, Roman and canon, began to realise more fully in practice their two competing theoretical jurisdictions over Christian lives.

Through the minting of coins and the lending of money at interest, the European commercial revolution came to maturity well in advance of either the concept or reality of the state.[10] It is a commonplace of medieval textbook history that the keystone of feudal government was the personal agreement between a lord and a vassal to exchange, mutually, protection of a gift of land for counsel and military support and incidents in kind. By at least the early twelfth century on the continent, early thirteenth century in England, the personal agreement between two consenting parties to the feudal contract was beginning to be replaced by money payment. The encroachment of a profit economy on government is apparent in the development of a salaried bureaucracy of lawyers, administrators and publicists. Those who moved into the cities from the surrounding countryside adopted a single function as a means to earn their way, raising problems concerning the moral probity of some of the urban professions. Simultaneously bourgeois professions like the lawyer, doctor, administrator were both pursued and also scorned.[11] If the major vice had once been pride it was now seen to be joined by avarice,[12] and numerous lay religious movements emerged whose members attempted to live as voluntary paupers, confronting a moneyed economy with a challenge to all coercive power and to the impersonality of financial credit. They rejected the daily materialist world in favour of a return to what was interpreted to be a primitive church community living without ties either to money or material goods and property. An age of finance was producing on the one hand a revived *contemptus mundi*, and on the other the opportunities for pious laymen to be involved in urban society, creating new forms of religious expression for those laymen who needed to be reassured that making money was indeed a Christian activity. The early thirteenth-century debates over the legitimacy of the activities of judges, notaries,

9. Dist. 1 c. 7.   10. Bisson 1979.
11. Baldwin 1970; Le Goff 1963, pp. 46–7; Baldwin 1959; Little 1978.
12. Damiani, *Laus eremeticae vitae, PL* CXLV, 247–8; *Opusculum* XII, iv, *PL* CXLV, 255; *Ep.* I, 15, *PL* CXLIV, 234; *Ep.* III, 2, *PL* CXLIV, 289; *Contra clericos regulares proprietarios*, VI, *PL*, 490; Little 1971.

merchants, teachers, prepared the way for the justification of these professions by the end of the century. As we shall see, the new mendicant orders of the thirteenth century made a unique contribution to the already elaborate theological and legal justification of property and wealth. The friars became some of the major voices in scholasticism, treating issues close to the heart of their own recent foundations: the role of private property, the just price, the nature of money, the morality of professional fees, commercial profit, business partnerships and usury.[13] The moral and intellectual problem of the legitimacy of private property had not been raised in this way since the patristic period. Private property was justified for the convenience and utility of men.

The tradition of Roman law was invoked, as was the newly translated corpus of Aristotle's writing, to elaborate on the naturalness of ownership and the necessity of private property as an instrument of the good life and the ordered society. The notion of lordship (*dominium*), the various forms of use of property that one might rent or lease for money, and the notion of private property as a distinguishing characteristic of the individual who was seen to be a rational, rights-bearing *persona* with certain capacities regarding the goods of his world, issued from a situation in which the status of buyer or seller was increasingly coming to be of no consequence in the transaction.

Property and Roman law: the classical position, its revival and modification

In this environment it is not surprising that Roman law had both a theoretical and practical role to play. According to classical Roman private law, which pertains to persons, things and actions, the *ius rerum* is the law of patrimonial rights, all those rights known to the law which are looked on as capable of being estimated in money.[14] Institutionally a *res* is some element of wealth, an asset with a legally guaranteeable value; it is an economic conception. Justinian speaks of *res corporales* as physical, material objects, and the notion of lordship or *dominium* is treated not as an abstract right but as ownership of corporeal things,[15] although there is also a range of inferior modes of ownership like *usucapio, mancipatio, possessio, dos, tutela, dominium bonitarum*.[16] Informal transfers of land were possible in the time of Gaius so that a *dominus* could lose all practical interest in the land he sold without

---

13. Above n. 11. McLaughlin 1939, pp. 81–147; McLaughlin 1940, pp. 1–22; Noonan 1957; Gilchrist 1969; Roover 1971; Le Goff 1960, pp. 417–33.
14. Buckland 1975, pp. 181–2. 15. *Ibid.*, p. 185.
16. *Ibid.*, pp. 187–8. Inferior modes of ownership, pp. 194–6; *occupatio*, pp 205–6; *bona fide possessor*, p. 224; *traditio*, p. 227; *usucapio*, p. 242; *usufruct*, p. 270.

formally transferring *dominium*; only by a lapse of time did *dominium* also pass to the purchaser although in the mean time all practical rights in the land were transferred to the buyer. *Dominium* in classical Roman law was an ultimate right,[17] one was an owner in perpetuity, even if this meant the *dominium* had no practical content. But by Justinian's time the distinction between *dominium* and its inferior modes began to be relaxed, and the classification of modes of acquisition of *dominium* grew more ambiguous and confused. Civil law modes of acquisition included *usus* – acquisition by use; *usufruct* was the inalienable right to enjoy the property of another and take the fruits therefrom, a right separate from ownership.[18] But since the usufructuary was bound to return the thing (land) in good condition there could be no *usufruct* of perishable goods. As we shall see, this would cause thirteenth- and fourteenth-century Franciscans serious problems since they wished to maintain their status as mere users, even of consumables, arguing that consumables were somehow still not owned by them. Furthermore, that *possessio* and *usus* could be seen as distinct from ownership (*dominium*) in classical Roman law set a standard for mendicant attitudes to property in the thirteenth and fourteenth centuries. The papacy became, according to a legal fiction, the *dominus* of what the Franciscans, owning nothing, had the right to use.

West Roman Vulgar law,[19] practised during the period of Diocletian to Justinian saw a number of alterations in classical Roman law that were incorporated into the Roman portions of various barbarian legal codes and thus passed as legacies to the later middle ages. Especially in the field of property and obligations there were numerous changes. The classical notion of *dominium* as a complete and positive mastery over a thing quite distinct from possession, and having its own legal remedy, disappeared in the post-classical period. Limited *dominium*, especially *usufruct*, came to be treated as that form of *dominium* which was to be regarded as the best right to possession, without separate remedies for owners and possessors. The nature of the distinction between *dominium* (defined as property or ownership considered as title) and possession (as practical enjoyment) was central to the development of medieval canon and civil law attitudes applied to contemporary situations of the twelfth through fourteenth centuries.[20]

Italian Roman jurists habitually translated *dominium* by the word *signoria*, and meant thereby that the feudal lord had the ultimate right to a thing

---

17. I.e. that which has no right behind it. It may be a *nudum ius* with no practical content. Buckland 1975, p. 188. 18. *Ibid.*, p. 270. 19. Watson 1968; E. Levy 1951; Wieacker 1961.
20. Gaudemet 1979.

which was, in effect, a minimum right left over when the rights of his vassals were removed.[21] Customary law (in England, the common law, where *seisin* was akin to possession) appears to have drawn upon Roman law categories to classify and justify the slow evolution of customary practices throughout Latin Christendom, practices that were often alien to Roman civil law.[22] And where they could, lawyers drew upon the various and often ambiguous Roman categories (which they none the less saw as constituting a universal jurisprudence) to arrange what had become a hierarchy of actions descending from the purely proprietary to the purely possessory, the latter having become a matter of degree. Feudal practices and the expanding use of money valuations combined to produce a situation in which two persons could dispute over who had the best right, the *maius ius* of *seisin* in a property; by the later middle ages the question was not simply which of the two was the owner (*dominus*).[23]

English lawyers during the second half of the twelfth century were introduced to Justinian's Roman law by Master Vacarius, and even where the English common law or ecclesiastical canon law was seen as more specifically authoritative in individual cases, Roman civil law principles and structures fundamentally moulded the other two laws.[24] By the 1250s royal jurisdiction over freehold land was extensive, and Bracton's arrangement of remedies and procedures in the king's court point to a compromise between Justinian and earlier custom as in Glanvill.[25] And Bracton draws on his extensive knowledge of learned, academic Roman law and glosses, incorporating lengthy extracts. From Azo he gets much of his account of the original division of things and the natural modes of acquiring them.

Azo (c. 1200) had distinguished between property that was natural and that which belonged to civil law or the law of nations. Other civilians, however, denied that there was any property that was an institution of natural law; rather it belonged to the *ius gentium* and *ius civile*, to convention. Likewise, in Roman law texts, some ways of alienating property were based on civil law, others on the law of nature. In Gaius' *Institutes* we learn that natural ways of acquiring title to property include tradition, occupation, the capture of an enemy's property, accession, etc. But then in the *Digest*, excerpts from Gaius' works say that acquisition of ownership comes only through the civil law or the law of nations, both of which base themselves

21. Buckland and McNair 1952, pp. 65–6.   22. J. Ph. Lévy 1976.
23. Buckland and McNair 1952, p. 67.   24. Stein 1969; Stein 1975, pp. 119–38.
25. Bracton, *De legibus et consuetudinibus Angliae*, ed. Thorne 1968–77; Barton 1971.

on natural reason. Acquisition by tradition, occupation, etc., is attributed here to the law of nations. Other jurists in the *Digest* vacillate between stating that by the law of nature all things are held in common, or that some things are naturally private; some modes of acquisition belong to the *ius gentium* and are natural, while others belong to the conventional, positive civil law. The *Institutes* of Justinian merely repeat the ambiguities of the *Digest*. Various medieval legal theorists chose one position or another to serve their purposes.

There are essentially two views one finds in civilian texts dealing with *dominium* and *possessio* of the thirteenth century: either a distinction is made between *dominium* as a passive mastery over property and the *ius* or active right to use this property; or there is a failure to make this distinction so that *dominium* is the same thing as *ius*. In practical terms thirteenth-century law appears to have begun to protect users. Early glossators of the Roman law distinguished between *dominium* and *usufruct* as they found it in classical Roman law. But the Bolognese glossator Accursius (1220–30) argued that there was a *dominium utile* which described what a usufructuary possessed, while *dominium directum* described what a superior lord possessed. *Dominium utile* was to be taken as any *ius in re*, any right which could be defended against all other men and it could be transferred or alienated by the possessor to others.[26] This is distinct from classical Roman law which said that alienation of the right of *usufructus* was not possible.

Bartolus in the fourteenth century indicated that users *de facto* had extensive rights akin to *dominium* over their property recognised in law. The debate in the thirteenth and fourteenth centuries consequently tried to determine whether these rights of users were conventional creations of social life and the civil government and its laws, or whether a conflation of *dominium* with *possessio* and *usus* was a characteristic of men prior to governments. Do men have rights over things before government gives them such rights by recognising them as possessors in law? Is property natural to man or is property only natural to man after the Fall?

The early church fathers accepted a theory that private property was a result of Adam's Fall and expulsion from the Garden. Arguments from Ambrose and Augustine, where property divisions were to be seen as the fruits of sin, as conventional creations of the state, instituted to keep the peace, were taken over by canonists and civilians who could not resolve the contradiction between those who held that all was common by nature and that there was no private property from nature, and those who argued that

26. Meynial 1908, p. 419.

some modes of property acquisition were indeed natural. Alexander of Hales in the thirteenth century would argue that property was 'natural' only to Fallen Man.[27] And that there was a frequent conflation of *dominium* and *possessio*, of lordship and use, further confused the issue. Before we observe how significant thinkers of our period came down on one side or another, resolving the questions of the origins of private property and its use in favour of whatever publicist position they were inclined to adopt, we should observe what in practice was occurring during the thirteenth century. There were extraordinary changes in attitudes to customary feudal obligations and notions of holding land and alienating it, and much legal theory reflected this. Taking the case of England we can tell the following story about property.

Feudal to capitalist dominium *and* possessio.

Reconstructing the feudal component in the structure of English society around 1200, from Glanvill and plea rolls of Richard I and John, we confront the formulaic, rule-bound expression of a customary, feudal and rule-bound practice of twelfth-century human relationships between diverse ranks. The unspoken relationship behind court cases is seigniorial and the underlying question has to do with entitlement – to hold land, to expect services, in what was a mutual contract between lord and vassal. Side by side with the king's court was the feudal lord's court, the royal justice trying to reinforce the feudal system by making certain that lords were not abusing their side of the feudal bargain. Royal justice was not meant to replace seigniorial jurisdiction but provide a sanction against its abuse. But through the records we see a waning of this dialectical mutuality of lord and vassal so characteristic of feudalism. According to Milsom, by the end of the thirteenth century land tenure is drained of much of this mutuality, and tenements and dues appear as independent properties in most regions, fixed by an external, centralised legal system, that of the king. The seigniorial order was rapidly destroyed as a result of what some have called a juristic accident – the development of central royal government (through the writ of *novel disseisin*). Although some would argue that Milsom's description is too sweeping a generalisation, and that feudal obligations still existed, however difficult to quantify, there is little doubt that at the end of the thirteenth century courts were dealing with rights *in rem*, rights good against the world; in the earlier feudal world rights as individual possessions

27. *Summa fratris Alexandri*, 1948, vol. IV, p. 348.

were a nonsense, and it was tenures rather than property rights that were being protected in earlier courts. Feudal *theory* became increasingly anachronistic as the centuries passed. By 1290 an objective enforcement was to override customary lordship and mutual service, with seigniorial courts having become agents of royal law in practice. The picture is now two-sided rather than mutual: a tenant makes his claim to his right to his tenement (*possessio*); the lord makes his claim to his right of dues (*dominium*). Each is an independent property, each passes from hand to hand without reference to the other. The tenant or possessor *de facto* owns his land and the lord has a residual 'servitude' over the land, a *ius in re aliena*. Although much land still changed hands by inheritance, by the end of the thirteenth century, *dominium* increasingly was seen as independent property and no longer a relative, interdependent thing. By the end of the thirteenth century, Latin Christendom could be characterised as a congeries of communities of equal owners disputing abstract rights over property; and although lords were left with fixed economic rights over property the land belonged to the tenant. What was once a right to hold land of a lord in return for feudal dues had turned into the right of ownership acquired by money. The lord could no longer prevent alienation of his lands by his tenants who became 'owners' of the property; the alienator was, however, forced out of the relationship and the grantee substituted for him and, as the new owner, owed nominal 'services' (income) to the lord. The monetary evaluation of land supplanted customary relationships so that the fee simple became an estate whose ownership was an article of commerce. The legal framework in England had changed from a feudal to a national, common law about land. Freehold land came to be what it is for us, an object of property, capable of alienation with the lord's rights being merely economic, but irrelevant to the conveyance of the land. Possessors or tenants were owners, in England and on the continent, and their individual rights were defensible before the law.[28]

Property and canon law

When Gratian came to collect the discordant canons of early church councils along with the several theories of property espoused by church fathers, he was faced with selecting those documents that had survived the Dark Ages and were to be revived and regarded as living law. He saw the juridical church as distinct from the evangelical experience so important to

28. Milsom 1976; Milsom 1969.

the radical, reforming laity of the time. His *Decretum* provides us with the prevailing assumptions concerning the proper distribution, control and social obligations of property in the twelfth century.[29] The opening pages raise the problem of the natural law in relation to private property and it was his ambiguous presentation of the natural law that provided problems for future canonists whose task it was to unravel the tangle in this textbook of church law. Canonists generally accepted the contemporary structures of property relationships as both necessary and just, a system in which individual property rights were acknowledged and attended by corresponding obligations. Not only individual Christians but also the Church as an institution were substantial property holders. Canonists were faced with framing an acceptable doctrine of property that was consistent with early church legislation. But they also dealt with the criticism of contemporary radicals who favoured a poor church living along what they believed to be apostolic lines. The *Decretum* collected arguments of church fathers who defended the virtuous use of wealth but it also included citations from those who were violently opposed to the abuses of wealth, implying thereby a condemnation of private property often in favour of a primitive communism as described in Acts 4: 32–5. According to some venerated texts, private property seemed contrary to the law of nature. Believing that in the creation God implanted in the nature of things as well as in man's nature, principles of rational conduct that were perpetually binding and immutable, Gratian notes that the human race is ruled by two norms, natural law and custom. The first is that which is contained in the Old Testament (Tobias) and the Gospels, by which everyone is commanded to do to others that which he wishes done to himself, and each is forbidden to do to others what he would not have done to himself.[30] This natural law is common to all nations, held everywhere instinctually rather than by positive legal enactment, and it sanctions the coming together of men and women, procreation, the common possession of all things, the liberty of all, the acquisition of whatever may be taken by air, land or sea, the restitution of goods or money loaned, the use of force to repel force.[31] It is by natural law that all things are common to all men. But the laws of custom and legal enactment enable men to say 'this is mine'. Citing Augustine, who argued that private property was a creation of imperial law and was not a characteristic of natural man before the Fall, the *Decretum* notes that the human laws that permit us to say 'this house is mine' are laws of emperors and kings of the world, laws that are distributed by God by means of earthly rulers.[32] However, if any customary or written law is found to be contrary to natural law, it must be considered null and void. Here was a problem: if all was originally common according to natural law, then it could be the case that positive law establishing private property ran contrary to the natural law and private property rights were null and void. If every man by natural law had the right to help himself to secure his needs then how could private property be justly maintained?

And yet there were many instances in the Bible which showed private property to be acceptable. What then was to be understood by the expression 'natural law'?[33] Some saw it as describing those original primitive conditions in which men lived when they were as yet untouched by civilisation's conventions. Others used it to describe psychological and physical characteristics of men no matter what environment in which they found themselves. Gratian included both senses of natural law. In failing to distinguish between conditions of primitive society and conditions proper to human society which satisfied intellectual, psychological and spiritual human needs, he offered a problem for canonists that was never fully resolved in our period.

The *Summa Parisiensis* (c. 1159)[34] noted that when a community of property is said to be prescribed by the divine law, it should be interpreted to mean that, in the beginning, the primeval institution was communal property. Rufinus (mid-twelfth century)[35] argued that some parts of the natural law (commands and prohibitions) were indeed immutable, but other parts were mere *demonstrationes*, having nothing morally binding about them. The community of property was not morally binding. The natural law of common property was merely a description of the early state of society and was not meant to be taken as a command for all times. The two most influential decretists, Huguccio and Johannes Teutonicus put forward a different solution. Natural law, equated with rational judgement, tells us that all things are common, to be shared in times of necessity with those in need.[36] Natural reason teaches us that we should retain for ourselves only necessities and thereafter distribute what is left to neighbours in need. This passed into Johannes Teutonicus' *Glossa Ordinaria*.[37] According to our rational, natural instinct we know that all things are

32. Dist. 8 c. 1. 33. Weigand 1967.
34. *The Summa Parisiensis on the Decretum Gratiani*, ed. McLaughlin 1952, ad Dist. 8. c. 1.
35. *Die Summa Decretorum des Magister Rufinus*, ed. Singer 1902, ad Dist, 1, p. 7.
36. Cited in Lottin 1931, p. 110; Tierney 1959, p. 146 n. 17.
37. Dist. 47 c. 8; Johannes Teutonicus, *Apparatus ad Compilationem Quartam*, MS 17, Gonville and Caius College, Cambridge, Gl. Ord. ad Dist. 1. c. 7.

common in that they are to be shared in time of necessity. Here Johannes drew upon classical Roman law saying that in time of need all things were common. This was, however, an abstract rendering of a law that, as we have already seen, spoke in corporeal rather than abstract terms about property rights.

The *Decretum* also provided patristic texts that dealt with the right to own property as well as with its appropriate use.[38] Ambrose discussed the duty of the rich to help the poor, questioning whether the rich had a right to own property at all divorced from this obligation of charity.[39] Johannes Teutonicus avoided the implication that communal ownership was a norm, and explained Ambrose's text by saying that private property is not denied; rather what is denied is the right of anyone to appropriate to himself more than suffices for his own needs. Thus, in times of necessity any surplus wealth is to be regarded as common property to be shared by all those in need.[40] Thereafter the term 'superfluities' was discussed and some of the major debates concerning almsgiving either as a duty or as a voluntary virtuous act developed from here. If canonists accepted that superfluous property belonged to the poor in need, they none the less never developed arguments concerning private property with egalitarian implications.[41] And they took into account that superfluity of wealth was to be measured according to what was considered decent and fitting to one's status in society. In a wider sense they cited Roman law in agreement that 'it is expedient for the commonwealth (*res publica*) that a man should not use his property badly'.[42]

Confronting contemporary radical pious opinions (Patarini,[43] Humiliati,[44] Poor Men of Lyons, etc.) which doubted that there was any virtue or necessity in the church owning property, canonists defined prelates and bishops as *trustees* rather than owners, acting on behalf of the real owner. Who was the real owner of church property? Gratian had said, under the influence of Roman law, that a cleric could own private property but that if he did so he could not also draw income from the Church.[45] Later canonists disagreed. Johannes Teutonicus argued that any cleric could own property unless he had taken a vow of poverty. If, however, a wealthy cleric accepted an ecclesiastical income from avaricious motives he was guilty of sin. Although there was a growing belief in the thirteenth century that a

38. Dist. 47. c. 8.   39. St Ambrose, *PL* xvii, 613–14.
40. Gl. Ord. ad Dist. 86 c. 18. possumus &c.   41. Tierney 1959, p. 37.
42. Gl. Ord. ad Dist. 47. c. 8 s.v. *Aliena*.   43. Violante 1955.   44. Bolton 1975, pp. 52–9.
45. *Decretum* c. 12 q.1 *post* c. 24; Tierney 1959, p. 39.

priest did have a right to receive compensation for his services to the Church, he was not considered the owner of the church property he merely administered. Some argued that a corporate group of clerics or a cathedral chapter could be an owner, but ultimate ownership of church goods inhered in God or in the poor.[46] The position developed that true *dominium* or ownership of church property could only inhere in the whole collective body of clergy. Innocent IV went further and referred to the Church as the mystical body of Christ so that the Church's property belonged to the whole Christian community.[47] Hostiensis amplified Innocent's arguments and stated that *dominium* in fact rests with the *congregatio fidelium*. The poor and needy were to be supported from the goods of the Church for they had a *right* to this support from the common property of the Church. On this view the use of church property on behalf of the poor was not charity but an established legal use of public property whose purpose was the maintenance of the common welfare and especially the sustenance of the needy poor.[48] If in the thirteenth century this was enshrined in canon law, expanding the jurisdiction of the Church over all Christians in need, it was a conception that had already proved to be an issue for churchmen in the early twelfth century who were confronted with the ambiguities of the Gregorian Reform regarding wealth. Gerhoh of Reichersberg (1093–1169) increasingly insisted that the idea of the Church renouncing its wealth would weaken it irremediably, preventing it from fulfilling its duties to the poor. He decided that the Church was to persevere and increase its patrimony by whatever means, although revenues should be more equitably distributed with priority to the poor. And he accorded a privileged place to the voluntary poor, the canons regular, the new order to which he himself belonged. The clergy, he said, should be deprived of all personal property but the Church must be rich to support its voluntarily poor members.[49]

Overlapping jurisdictions

What is clear so far is that by the thirteenth century with the immense growth of papal governmental activity promoted by the Gregorian Reform, by papal leadership of the Crusades and by the papal revival of legal studies to suit its needs, canon lawyers were defining a power of

46. Glosses *Ecce Vicit Leo*, MS. o. 5. 17, Trinity College, Cambridge, and *Glossa Palatina* (1210), MS. o. 10.2, Trinity College, Cambridge, *ad* c. 12 q. 1 c. 13; Tierney 1955a, pp. 118–19.
47. *Commentaria ad* x. 2. 12. 4.
48. Tierney 1959, pp. 42–3; Hostiensis, *Summa Aurea super Titulis Decretalium*, 1612.
49. Gerhoh of Reichersberg, cited in Vauchez 1970, p. 1570.

ecclesiastical jurisdiction that was distinct from the domain of the individual's interior intention. They spoke as well of the ecclesiastical power of jurisdiction in the public sphere over material goods and of *dominium*, the *potestas jurisdictionis in foro exteriori*. If *dominium* of the Church's property rested with the whole Christian community where clerics were stewards who administered temporal goods, then this came very close to saying that the Church possessed a coercive power like that pertaining to a public authority, directed to the common good of the faithful.[50] The question of *dominium* and the role of the Church in administering wealth and property was providing arguments for the Church possessing truly governmental powers, an argument that developed the much earlier Gelasian view concerning the relationship between royal power and priestly authority. The debate between *sacerdotium* and *regnum* and the conflict of jurisdictions was to reach its height in the confrontation between Philip the Fair of France and Boniface VIII at the turn into the fourteenth century. Although Innocent IV had declared that 'the jurisdictions of pope and emperor were distinct',[51] at the turn of the fourteenth century Boniface VIII was to declare that 'the papacy has universal coercive power and that *imperium* depends upon the Church'.[52] The question of *dominium* was to become one of the exercise of political authority. Pierre de Flotte, emissary of Philip the Fair, was able to reply to Boniface's 'we have universal power' with: 'certainly, my lord, but yours is verbal whilst ours is real'.[53]

Aquinas on property

Drawing on this mass of civil and canon law as well as on the newly translated *Politics* of Aristotle, Thomas Aquinas developed a magisterial and synthetic theory of property in his *Summa Theologiae*.[54] His was not merely a theoretical exposition of property rights, presenting the canonical and civilian state of play in the mid-thirteenth century; it was also an eclectic presentation of the century-long battle between the mendicant orders and the seculars within the ecclesiastical community, and Aquinas as a

---

50. Oakley 1979, pp. 27–8.   51. *De iudiciis, capitulo 'Novit'*, c. 13, X (2.1).

52. *Unam Sanctam*: 'papa utramque gladii habeat potestatem et ab ecclesia imperium dependeat': Text no. 5382 in *Register*; H. Denifle, *Specimina palaeographica ex Vaticani tabularii Romanorum pontificum registris selecta* (Rome, 1888), p. 44 and Table xlvi.

53. 'Utique domine, sed vestra est verbalis, nostra autem realis': *Acta inter Bonifacium VIII, Benedictum XI, Clementem V et Philippum Pulchrum Regem Christianum* (1614), fol. 164v. Cf. pp. 546–7 above.

54. Parel 1979; Aquinas, *Summa Theologiae*, ed. Spiazzi 1951.

Dominican was directly concerned with the outcome of this discussion. The juridical aspect of the question of property was, for him, rooted in the metaphysics of Greek, Roman and patristic thought, in which, more generally, material goods were taken to be means to a higher end for man, to be used rather than enjoyed in their own right.

Through his reason man is a master of what is within himself and also he has mastery, *dominium*, over other things, not by commanding but by using them.[55] His capacity for reason makes man a person, which is the most perfect thing in all nature.[56] His goal is twofold: in this life it is felicity, in the next, it is beatitude. Material goods are subordinated to higher ends. Riches, honour, glory, bodily well-being and sensory pleasures are not the ultimate end of human life.[57] Thus man's desire for material goods has only instrumental value, as a *bonum utile*, a means conducive to an end which transcends any use to which property may be put. Property is a means to this end rather than the end in itself. And it is in the very nature of material things, in their transitoriness, that they are unable to satisfy human desires completely. The place of private property is therefore within the larger consideration of material things, and Aquinas asks whether it is natural for man to possess exterior material things, distinguishing between the nature of material things and the use to which they are put. Man has no *dominium* over the nature of material things for only God has such *dominium*. But man has a natural *dominium* over the use of material things to his benefit.[58] Initially then, *dominium* is taken to be that indeterminate capacity, that authority which reason has over its own acts, over the acts of the human mind and will. This extends to material things as well. Possession is a specification, a determination of *dominium*, extended to material goods.[59] Man therefore, was created with *dominium naturale* in this wider sense which did not specify the mode of possession, be it private or in common. Possessions were originally required to be for the use of all mankind. Private property is not wrong but it is a mode of possession that has only conventional justification (*ius gentium*), and the primary recognition of the purpose of property is its use for men in pursuance of higher ends. Man is described as having the capacity to care for and exchange material goods and it is permitted that he possess things as his own. Human affairs are more efficiently organised when each has his own responsibility over his own things for there would be chaos if everyone cared for everything. Men live together more peaceably when each has what suits his own taste; quarrels would erupt were they to

---

55. Aquinas, *Summa Theologiae* I q. 96 a. 2.   56. *Ibid.*, q. 29 a. 3.   57. *Ibid.*, I II q. 2 a. 1–8.
58. *Ibid.*, II II q. 66 a. 1.   59. *Ibid.*,

hold things in common without distinction.[60] But natural law does not specify how private property should be arrived at and therefore historical institutions determine distribution; private possessions are not contrary to natural law but are inventions of reason. They are human additions to natural principles.

Dominium naturale provides for a primary right of use which takes precedence over the power to acquire and exchange private property, the latter being only a secondary right. And when there is a superfluity of private goods, there can be no justification for its being maintained as private; natural law teaches that this surplus is due to the poor. Man's needs have to be met by such material goods that suffice to living and a surplus can only be justified in terms of its social use.[61] Thus, wherever necessity exists, it is permitted to expropriate a surplus held privately by another without being considered a thief, whether one expropriates this secretly or openly. In extreme necessity a starving man may take what is necessary to free himself from certain death. Furthermore, private owners do indeed have freedom to acquire and exchange as they wish, but when the common welfare is at stake, the civil law is obliged to activate the natural law principle of the primacy of use over ownership, and civil law must regulate property in the interest of the society as a whole.

Turning to the vexed issue of the different kinds of use of things, especially of consumables, Aquinas argues that when things are used through consumption, what has been exchanged is the ownership of the consumables as well as their use. Franciscan apologists argued, in contrast, for the separation of use and *dominium* in consumables. But where the use of a thing can be distinguished from its ownership (house, land), then a rent may be offered for use without the concomitant transfer of *dominium* or ownership. Money is a consumable, but it is not, according to Aquinas, saleable. When there is a lending of money, what is transferred is both its use and *dominium*. Usury violates the justice of selling what is not saleable because in charging interest on a loan you are charging for something you no longer own and whose increase in value comes through the use made of the money by others. This does not mean that men ought not to seek shares of profit in some investment in a trading or manufacturing company, and, of course, renting land is legitimate. Profit in trade and commerce is to be had privately but it too must be governed by his principle of the primacy of social use for superfluities. There is a kind of natural business which has a social purpose other than the pure self-assertion through the accumulation

60. *Ibid.*, a. 2.   61. *Ibid.*, a. 7.

of private property and wealth. Such natural business is moderate, and its purpose is the maintenance of life rather than the accumulation of profit for its own sake.[62]

Aquinas is therefore not against profit that is socially beneficial and he goes well beyond Aristotle in his positive attitude to business activities whose proper purpose is the making of a moderate profit to support a family, the poor, or to contribute to the public good. But nothing is exercised here without due reason and limits. Property is not an end in itself nor is the right to it unlimited. Men live in a world created by and for their fallen natures and they are prey to the vice of avarice and immoderate accumulation. Avarice can become so dominant in a man's character that money can replace his true end, felicity. Avarice is the immoderate appetite for temporal things which have a measurable valuation.[63] A society in which money transactions have increased the possibility of monetary misuse increases the range of avarice. There are fools, he notes, who believe in only those goods which can be acquired by money.[64] Avarice dehumanises man, reversing the right order of things so that men enjoy rather than merely use their possessions. It is of utmost importance, then, that men develop an inner freedom from avarice, an internal control that is more significant than external legal regulations of property. Men must obey their desire for natural wealth which is terminated when natural needs are satisfied. Without this internal freedom social disorder becomes the norm and men take things that rightfully belong to others.[65] The inordinate desire for money and property is the root of all evil. When the accumulation of property becomes the end of human existence, then avarice subverts the moral and social order creating a situation in which men are incurably dehumanised. The use of money and property must be guided by the virtue of liberality, whereby the quantity given is of little consequence in comparison to the attitude of the giver. Liberality creates in man that attitude of indifference towards one's own possessions, creating an inner freedom which alone allows them use rather than the enjoyment of material goods. This liberality is the founding virtue of a good society.[66] It inspires justice in the social forum where there is respect for the property of others and the obligation of fairness in property exchange. Only with justice can the rule of equality prevail over every public consideration of ownership. And only a good government can maintain just property relations, directing its authority towards the common good. The good law-

62. *Ibid.*, q. 77 a. 4.   63. *Ibid.*, 1 q. 63 a. 2 *ad* 2; 11 11 q. 78 a. 2.   64. *Ibid.*, 1 11 q. 2 *ad* 1 and 3.
65. *Ibid.*, 11 11 q. 118 a. 1 *ad* 2 and a. 8.   66. *Ibid.*, q. 117 a. 6.

giver, then, following Aristotle, has the responsibility for justly regulating private property for the common good. We are no longer in a society of lords and vassals but in one of kings and subjects where there is an acceptance as a proper concern of royal government and its courts of the whole field of torts.

Definitions of 'the poor'[67]

The poor may be defined, in a period when agriculture is the dominant means of subsistence, as those who do not possess a minimum of arable land sufficient to support a family; a family of four, say, in the thirteenth century required 4 hectares. It appears that in our period the spread of a money economy and commutation of labour services into rents in money helped only a minority of wealthy peasants. Fixed land rents, facilities for borrowing, the sale of franchises contributed instead to a differentiation and polarisation amongst an already differentiated peasantry, enmeshing the less well-off who did not move to towns in a web of debts, binding them in effective slavery to the economy of urban centres or to their better-off neighbours.[68] Although the population between 1000 and 1300 grew faster in towns than in the countryside, the vast bulk of the European population lived in the country. But it was the towns which determined the course of economic development through the rise of commercial capitalism based on a rural economy whose agrarian production increased substantially. Whilst feudal landlords became increasingly involved in the expanded market and urbanisation, the increasing production for this market disrupted the peasantry and accelerated the social differentiation between rich and poor. This process has been described as 'the proletarianization of a steadily increasing number of people alienated from the land'.[69]

Furthermore, until the fourteenth century, merchants and entrepreneurs remained two distinct groups, and a growing tension between artisans and a merchant patriciate became evident by the end of the thirteenth century. At the same time the bulk of the rural population lived in penury: around 1300, between 40% and 60% of the European peasantry had insufficient land to maintain a family; they survived by wage labour and contributed to the increasing numbers of shifting, landless paupers in search of work – a quest which often led them into towns. The fourteenth century saw a growth in pauperisation amongst the urban masses who were not integrated into

67. Mollat 1974 and 1978; Bosl 1974; Bosl, Graus and Devisse 1974; Goglin 1976.
68. Duby 1966, pp. 25–33.   69. Lis and Soly 1982, pp. 1–25.

confrèries and *corps de métiers*, which led to frequent eruptions of urban violence.[70]

The vocabulary of the social categories used by canonists and moralists in the thirteenth century reveals perhaps the most fundamental of contemporary oppositions in the pair *dominus/servus*.[71] The *servus* is a part of society, he submits to a certain number of obligations and possesses rights limited by those who act as master or *dominus*. The *dominus* is the proprietor, the possessor of land and of *servi* attached to the property, and he draws revenues from the exploitation of both. This *dominus* possesses *dominium* which is essentially an economic capacity. The Dominican Raymond of Penyafort in his *Summa de casibus poenitentiae* suggested that if by chance a landholder was unable to draw profit from his lands it was advisable that he at least collect symbolic rents from his dependents as a sign of their subjection and to avoid the situation in which his proprietorial rights might seem purely theoretical (*inanis*).[72] The *dominus* was also he who possessed jurisdiction, authority to govern, to establish justice, to levy taxes in return for maintaining the security of his *subditi*, and to wage war within established limits.

Poverty is a relative notion, determined by what is taken to be privation and the needs of men in different contexts. In Carolingian times the *dominus* was a *potens* in contrast to the *pauper*, the man with authority in relation to the dependent impotent.[73] The latter had originally no rights, no weapons, was often unfree and laboured for survival. His *pauper* status was only in part ascribed to economic circumstances. *Paupertas* could be a normal way of life and church alms the normal means of subsistence within a gift economy. Gradually, poverty came to be a synonym for drifting and uprootedness. Then the reform movements of the twelfth and thirteenth centuries brought another change. When the poverty of Christ and the Apostles was emphasised by reforming lay groups and spiritual ascetics like the Patarini, the Poor Men of Lyons, the Humiliati and others, the pauper was no longer taken to be the embodiment of original and personal sin but the living example of the spiritually powerful, unattached to material goods, the object of charity and mercy, the *imitatio christi*. By the thirteenth century men voluntarily chose to be poor.[74] When money could buy freedom from servile work, many of the pious fled from money. A dilemma emerged between what appeared to be the evangelical requirement of poverty and

70. Chevalier 1982, pp. 18–44.   71. Michaud-Quantin 1973, pp. 73–86.
72. Raymond of Penyafort, *Summa de casibus poenitentiae*, 1601 vol. II, pp. 5, 15.
73. Bosl 1963, pp. 68–87.   74. Manteuffel 1970 (1963); Vauchez 1970, pp. 1566–73.

the social necessity to combat an increasingly evident indigence and misery. The reform movements and city life redefined the status of the pauper.

The term *miserabiles personae* was used, in the *Decretum* and thereafter, to designate precisely a category of persons recommended to judicial benevolence, whom the clergy would represent in cases where this was normally forbidden. Included here were widows, orphans and the poor who had not the means to pay for the maintenance of their rights in an age when lawyers' costs were beyond them. *Miserabiles personae* were those deprived of protection of the family, whose freedom and material poverty left them solitary and on the edge of survival. Paupers, according to canon law, were those who passively received alms as a right. In a society which recognised authority in degrees, the weight in social relations of different functional groups placed the poor man at the very bottom as he who has no authority. Hostiensis affirmed that one cannot accept the testimony of the poor man because, according to Roman law, he is not the equal of those more powerful. Contrasting with this social category were the rich, *divites*, those who were obliged to give alms. By the twelfth century *nobiles/ ignobiles*, *divites/pauperes*, *civis/pauper* expressed a relative superiority which came to be measured primarily in terms of material possession and money or the lack thereof. The social meaning included rights–bearing, civic capacity and its opposite.[75] One gave material aid in proportion to the social status of the person who found himself in poverty, so that alms itself was an obligation that admitted of degrees. These social categories and the advocacy in the twelfth and thirteenth centuries of voluntary poverty and mendicancy depended on the fiscal resources of an expanding urban economy and on the perception of a growing social disparity consequent on this economic development. There is, of course, a close connection between the economic changes we have been discussing and the development of charitable institutions established by municipal authorities as civic measures of social control.

Shifting attitudes to poverty

Augustine had spoken of the poor without resources who could scarcely procure what they needed to live on and who needed charitable aid to such a degree as no longer to possess any shame in begging. Thus by the fifth century we already have a sketch for a reprobatory judgement on the poor

75. Couvreur 1961; Michaud-Quantin 1973. *Miserabiles personae* in commentaries on *Decretum*, Dist. 87, 88; Gl. Ord. c. 15. q. 2 c. 1.

man who has been reduced to begging and who feels no shame. It remained important throughout our period that the worthy poor be those who were ashamed of their poverty. St Ambrose spoke of how important it was to recognise the shame of those in need and that perfect liberality was therefore secretly given.[76] Although no one should be ashamed of having once been rich and now being poor, the shame (*verecundia*) of the poor does comprise a part of the circumstance which should guide the giver's perfect liberality. Alms was explicitly linked with the embarrassment of downward social mobility.[77] 'Look for the man who is ashamed of being found and remain silent when you give. All the needy have a right to mercy but compassion is the stronger towards those who were rich and noble and who misfortune has thrown into extreme misery.' Drawing on Matthew VI, 3 and Psalm XL, 2 the tradition of giving alms was based on preferring those who were ashamed to receive it. In the eleventh century the reformer Peter Damian presented a picture of the worthy poor man who was often of knightly status, who did not know how to beg to survive, who suffered embarrassment as well as hunger, preferred to die than beg publicly and who thereby merited most to receive secret alms.[78]

Throughout the twelfth century one observes two strands of thought developing regarding the worthy poor, and Gratian includes both: the notion of selective charity pertaining to the original status of the poor, and an unselective principle which defines the poor as those simply in extreme need.[79] There is no discussion of the aptitude or the physical incapacity for work, but it is significant that work was considered a humbling experience and that monastic rules (Augustine's *De opere monarchorum* and the *Benedictine Rule*) exhorted monks to work with their hands, 'for the monk is a pauper, possessing nothing and working to live'. Augustine observed however, that those who, prior to their monastic vocation, had received a 'soft' education and could not bear heavy physical work would receive exemptions. This could never be the case, he noted, for those monks who previously were slaves and then freed, or peasants and artisans.[80] During and after the Gregorian Reform when numerous groups chose to live communally and work, many members originally coming from those social groups for whom labouring had been out of the question, it became part of the voluntarily poor ethos to beg, work and live by merely using rather than owning material goods, in imitation of what was believed to

---

76. St Ambrose, *De officiis ministrorum*, I, PL XVI, 71–4, 130–1.   77. Ricci 1983, pp. 158–77.
78. Damiani, *De eleemosyna*, PL CXLV, 214.   79. Tierney 1958–9, pp. 362–3; Tierney 1959.
80. St Augustine, *De opere monachorum, liber unus*, PL XL, 547–82.

have been the evangelical life of Christ and the Apostles. Stephen of Muret, founder of what eventually became the Order of Grandmont in the time of Gregory VII, established a rule whereby rents were refused as was control over churches, no land was held outside their enclosure; they did all their own work, possessed neither flocks nor books nor buildings and were not in competition with the local clergy:[81] St Francis would later speak in his rule of living by labouring, according to merit and work rather than rank and status.[82] Attitudes to time and work had begun to change so that by the thirteenth century work for all men was a rehabilitated concept in the sense that labouring was not only a tragic result of Adam's sin, but a means to salvation for all. A distinction was drawn between manual labour and intellectual work, the former remaining despised but for some all the more appropriate as a means to imitating the apostolic life.

When worldly social values were systematically stood on their head by St Francis[83] in the early thirteenth century, the question of the valid poor, the valid mendicant, the voluntary assumption of powerlessness in all senses came under intense scrutiny. The Franciscans typified the real change in attitudes to poverty that had developed rapidly from the mid-twelfth century when a growing population, increasingly conscious of social stratification, experienced the transformation of agrarian structures, the development of a money economy and urbanisation. Only then was the pauper a major social phenomenon, materially deprived. Until the twelfth century the disinherited, the ill, the old, the indigent were not a marginal group and they survived through the charity of the parish and the monastery. Before the twelfth century the shameful poor, real though they once were, were used primarily as moral and religious examples drawn from scriptural and patristic sources. But a new economic poverty emerged in our period. Only by the thirteenth century could theft in the case of extreme necessity be morally condoned. And new social opportunities stimulated the widespread poor relief that had come to be seen as an obligation placed on the property-holding and money-making groups.[84] The ideals of St Francis and the attempts to put them into widespread practice throughout the thirteenth and fourteenth centuries caused major social disruptions and reevaluations of practical attitudes to property and poverty. The consequences of the debate within the Franciscan order and

81. Witters 1974, p. 183. 82. Le Goff 1973. 83. Esser 1975, pp. 60–70.
84. Some of the contemporary and practical considerations concerning the question of poverty were discussed by Aquinas, *Summa Theologiae* II II q. 144 a. 2 and q. 32 a. 10, and in his *Quaestio de eleemosyna*.

between the order and its opponents throughout the thirteenth and fourteenth centuries were to be felt into the early modern period when notions of *dominium* and its opposite would penetrate debates on the nature of sovereignty in Church and state.

Reform movements and poverty

The rise of diverse religious orders and movements in the twelfth century is best described as a reformation. There is a noticeable coherent line of church reform from the Italian hermits of the eleventh century to the early generations of the friars.[85] A new emphasis was placed on the interpretation of the Gospels and the Acts of the Apostles as codes of behaviour to be imitated through literal observance. Scripture was to be the Rule for the laity as monastic *Regulae* were to be observed by the cloistered. The new lay piety stressed the observance of material poverty, disdaining those values of the increasingly sophisticated market economy that required the impersonality of money transactions. The very handling of money was rejected. Withdrawal and contemplation, fundamental to the ideals of the older monastic orders, were replaced by an engaged ministry to the faithful, an active apostolate that recognised the need for preaching.[86] It must be said that many of the older monastic orders were actively involved in the market economy. There was a large audience for preaching in those who were no longer satisfied with a religious life practised vicariously on their behalf by monks. The process of adjusting the religious life to social and economic change was consciouly undertaken with the papal establishment of the friars. The Fourth Lateran Council of 1215 prohibited the establishment of any further orders. This was the culmination of lay reform movements of the twelfth century like the Patarini whose initial impetus derived from the desire to dignify and purify the already existing clergy and to restore the *forma* of the *Ecclesia primitiva*. This developed into a desire for personal poverty amongst lay groups. The Humiliati of Lombardy are a case in point: their Tertiaries may be regarded as having set the tone for the mendicant orders a few years later.[87]

85. Manselli 1969; Bolton 1983.
86. Peter Damian, *Contra intemperantes clericos*, PL cxlv, and *Contra clericos regulares proprietarios*, PL cxlv.
87. Bolton 1975, pp. 52–9.

St Francis and the Franciscans[88]

Francis grew up as the son of a cloth merchant in the flourishing town of Assisi, where new money joined with this religious lay ferment. Although his own writings avoid reference to social hierarchies, never using terms like *vassallus* or *vavassor*, his biographers speak in terms of his youthful nobility; prior to his conversion he is described not as a greedy merchant but as generous like the nobility. In his own writings we can observe an attempt to efface feudal and capitalist hierarchies of status, an attempt to level social degrees by means of a vocabulary that raised to spiritual prominence all the social inferiors of the day. Francis called himself *servus, rusticus, mercenarius, inutilis, subditus, idiota, minor*, calling upon his followers to associate with and be considered poor, feeble, vagabonds, beggars, labourers, unlettered, the powerless and the dispossessed. The touchstone of his understanding of poverty was begging, and he rejected the shame that was conventionally associated with this demeaning posture. His social ideal was the reconstituted family in which fraternal love imitated the artificial family of the Apostles and Christ, without hierarchy except when he saw himself as Father, to be obeyed in love rather than fear. They were to possess nothing of their own, not even the knowledge of the educated which was itself treated as a commodity evaluated in money. The social vocabulary of Francis and his early followers reflects the transitional phase between feudal and capitalist relations, but rejects the castes, orders, classes of both in favour of a concept of a universally poor and levelled society of the materially impotent.

A first revision of Francis' Rule of 1209, the *Regula Prima* of 1221, has no legal standing, but it does survive and allows us to examine his attitudes to property and poverty before these views would be reformulated with the help of juristically minded brethren and a cardinal protector who would become pope. It must be said that Francis' intentions were not always clear, either to his order or to those outside, and a decisive standard of measurement for his mind is wanting.[89] There is no contemporary document we can select as a completely reliable guide. The Rule of 1221 is perhaps best seen as a series of Admonitions to his followers:[90]

---

88. Lambert 1961; Brooke 1959; Moorman 1940 and 1968.   89. Esser 1949.
90. *Regula Prima* (1221), in Francis of Assisi, ed. Esser 1978; also in Francis of Assisi, ed. Habig 1973, with English transl.

The friars are to have no property; Franciscan candidates should sell all possessions and give the money to the poor; friars may not meddle in the candidates' property affairs; no one is to be called 'prior' for there is no distinction amongst friars minor; they may not accept positions of authority in houses of their employers; friars who have a trade should remain at it; their payment is never in money; otherwise they seek alms; they may not claim ownership of any place. In general, they should have neither use nor regard for money, considering it as dust.

The Rule of 1221 gives the impression that Francis wished the friars to sever all ties with the commercial system of the world. When he uses legal and commercial terms, *hereditas*, *commercium*, *mutuum*, they lose their customary meaning and take on a significance drawn from the spiritual values he wished to stress. Both *denarius* and *pecunia*, money tokens and all forms of wealth, are to be eschewed. Here is a total withdrawal from the world of buying and selling replaced by a contact with the economic world of the most tenuous kind. But the Rule of 1223, the *Regula Bullata*,[91] modified the relations between friars and the economic world. It permitted intermediaries, allowing for the accumulation of a surplus of material goods at least as a possibility which became an inevitability. Although Francis' strict attitudes to the renunciation of all property survived into the *Regula Bullata*, it remained unclear whether he intended the renunciation of all common as well as all individual property. If contact with money was still restricted, there was added a clause that for the necessities of the sick and clothing of the other friars, ministers were to have recourse to spiritual friends. But there is no reference to words like *dominium* or *usus*, words that would be put in his mouth by his biographers like Celano and which would loom so large in the history of the order.

In his Admonitions, what is clearly condemned is the action of brethren arrogating to themselves as an individual corporation any goods which should remain the common property of all men. He was against the principle of exclusion implied in private property rights. The money prohibition was absolute, money being considered as something unnatural and associated inextricably with worldly avarice. If he died without clarifying the legal aspects of the friars' relation to property, he none the less clearly condemned the property-owning mentality. This would become a sticking point when the order did achieve some measure of economic security. It is still debated whether he intended the order to be totally divested of all property rights, if only because in his own lifetime the issue of

91. *Regula Bullata*, in *Regula Fratrum Minorum*, in *Seraphicae Legislationis, textus originales* (Quaracchi, 1897), pp. 36–47, including Honorius III's Bull *Solet annuere* (1223), also in Francis of Assisi, ed. Esser 1978.

common *dominium* was of slight importance. 'No reserves of property' was not the same thing as 'not having rights to property'. Whatever his intentions, and these would be elucidated by radical and conservative followers throughout the next centuries, it is clear that from the practical point of view his ideal was so extreme that it was nearly impossible for the developing order to follow it strictly.

One of the major dilemmas was the order's interpretation of Christ's and the Apostles' poverty: the friars refused property in temporal goods because they believed themselves to be imitating Christ. But the question was in fact an exegetical one. Did Christ and the Apostles possess goods and was one imitating them in refusing *dominium* and *possessio*? Was extreme voluntary poverty the highest state of perfection? What was the nature of property ownership and was it possible to divorce use from ownership? And is the divorce of use and ownership what Francis intended? Extreme poverty was clearly an encumbrance to successive popes, and along with members of the order itself, the Franciscan Rule's interpretation evolved to establish a life for Franciscans far from the primitive life apparently envisaged by Francis. Even in Francis' own lifetime Honorius III began the process of exempting the order from the control of local ecclesiastics, opening the way to their role in pastoral care previously exercised only by the secular clergy. In *Quo Elongati* (1230),[92] Gregory IX extended the functions of the spiritual friend by allowing him to have recourse to goods considered imminent necessities, and a further official was introduced who could receive money, the *nuntius*, who was defined as an agent of the *almsgiver* rather than of the friars. As the friars became more dependent on alms it became inconvenient for these to be given in kind alone.

But when movable goods were given to the order who was it that held *dominium* over such property if it was true that Franciscans could have no corporate ownership? The legal language of *Quo Elongati* answered vaguely that the friars, in not being able to alienate goods and having to ask permission of the cardinal protector, were therefore, not owners. Gregory said that the friars were not to have either individual or common *proprietas*, but that they might have *usus* of utensils, books, moveables permitted them, leaving all property rights to the donor. An administrative system had replaced the strict, literal observance of the Rule. Building programmes proceeded throughout the 1240s and the faithful were encouraged to contribute to Franciscan convents. Friars were then permitted to supple-

92. Text in Gregory IX, ed. Grundmann 1961. See also Eubel 1898–1904, vol. I; Brooke 1959, pp. 130–3.

ment their alms by taking restitution money: fines paid by usurers or sums illicitly gained where the owners remained unknown. The Franciscan *studium* at Bologna was thus financed. So many problems of interpretation of the *Regula Bullata* arose that learned commentaries were requested on difficult points from Franciscan scholars of the various provinces. The province of France sent back the *Expositio Quatuor Magistrorum* (Alexander of Hales, John of Rupella, Robert of Bascia and Odo Rigaldus are believed to have been the authors (1241)).[93] Chapter four discussed the provision of material needs according to the *forma paupertatis*. In chapter six they used the vocabulary of law and business to discuss friars and money. Their attitudes and terminology became authoritative. They sought appropriate solutions to property problems of the Rule in Roman law, citing the *Digest* and the Glossators with which they were familiar, although their references to the meaning of wealth, *pecunia 'secundum iura'* are never indicated. Here we see the language of *emere, vendere, locare, mutuare, commutare* defined.

It was clear that different styles of life were arising within the order and discourse on the Rule and on papal 'clarification' were ways to judge the admissibility of differing interpretations of Francis' intentions. Innocent IV (1245) further relaxed strict adherence to the Rule as interpreted in *Quo elongati* with a statement in *Ordinem vestrum*. Intermediaries now could not only buy necessities but superiors could use these agents to take money alms and any commodities offered. Now the *nuntius* was not only an agent of the almsgiver, as before, but could also act on behalf of the friars: the office of *amicus spiritualis* and *nuntius* merged into one official who handled both expenditure and alms. Although benefactors retained *dominium* over major items of property, it was unclear who owned moveables. Innocent agreed to receive all *dominium* of those goods that were used by the Franciscans into the domain of St Peter. The legal fiction of the pope as *dominus, in ius et proprietatem beati Petri*, separated from the Franciscans as simple users, was born. Innocent IV (*Quanto studiosius*, 1247) further relaxed the mechanism whereby application to alienate goods had to be made to the cardinal protector of the order; the friars could now appoint procurators acting nominally on behalf of the *dominus*, the pope, but who were in effect at the disposal of the order. *Ordinem vestrum* and *Quanto studiosius* created a bitter split in the order. And it is here that the strand of apocalyptic biblical exegesis, whose origins were in the biblical commentaries of the late twelfth century renegade Cistercian Joachim of Flora, rose to the surface.

For some time there had been an undercurrent, more or less explicit,

93. *Expositio quatuor magistrorum super regulam fratrum minorum* (1241–2), ed. Oliger 1950.

amongst Franciscans, that theirs was an elect body of spiritual men who, Joachim had predicted, were to usher in the last age of world history.[94] This order of monks was called to descend from contemplation to action in the sixth age of history which was fast rushing to its close at the end of the twelfth century. In his *Expositio in Apocalypsim*, Joachim described two new orders, one to preach in the world, the other in operation in the seventh and last age; the latter was in perfect imitation of the life of the Son of Man.[95] Characteristic of Joachim's many more radical followers amongst the Franciscans (who instead of awaiting the new order in the last age of history claimed to be that order) was their belief that the degree and nature of their humility and poverty was a sign of their perfection and election. Gerard of Borgo San Donnino tried to answer the question of Francis' historical significance by taking over Joachim's elaborate progressive trinitarian notion of the world's history, and saw Francis as initiating the last age. The secular masters at the University of Paris jumped at this opportunity to discredit the mendicants who had so successfully moved into university positions, and mounted an attack not only on Joachim but on the Franciscans' understanding of their Rule and its injunction to live according to evangelical poverty. William of St Amour and Gerard of Abbeville wrote vitriolic tracts which created havoc in the order, causing the mendicants temporarily to lose their privileges.[96] A commission was set up to examine the works of Gerard of Borgo San Donnino and Joachim. Franciscan intellectuals were thus forced to develop a defence and a coherent theory of absolute poverty, and Bonaventure's *Apologia Pauperum* (1269)[97] became their classic exposition.

Bonaventure defined poverty as living by what was not one's own. This meant that Franciscans renounced voluntarily all title to possession and they abdicated all ownership, possession, usufruct, leaving only the obligation to use what was necessary to stay alive, which was termed *simplex usus facti*. Simple use was a natural duty imposed on all creatures to maintain their lives; but this did not imply that they also had rights of any kind in things. Hugh of Digne, more radical than Bonaventure, was in effect the forerunner of these ideas. The original renunciation of material goods had become, by the 1260s, a renunciation of ownership, *dominium* and *possessio*, but not *usus*. It is, said Bonaventure, the

94. Coleman 1982, pp. 1–23; Reeves 1969.
95. Joachim of Fiore, *Expositio in Apocalypsim*, 1527, fols. 83r, fol. 175v–176r; Reeves 1969.
96. Dufeil 1975, pp. 241–2; Faral 1950–1.
97. St Bonaventure, *Apologia Pauperum* in *Opera Omnia*, vol. VIII (Quaracchi, 1898), pp. 233–330.

nature of evangelical poverty to renounce earthly possession in respect of *dominium* and *proprietas*, and not to reject *usus* utterly but to restrain it.[98] He clarified the situation further by describing a fourfold gradation of *dominium, possessio, usus* and *simplex usus facti*, which would be taken over as official doctrine in Nicholas III's bull of 1279: *Exiit qui seminat*.[99] The notion of restraining the use of material goods was to lead to the even more radical doctrine maintained by Peter John Olivi and those extremists later called the Spirituals as the doctrine of *usus pauper*. Bonaventure argued that *dominium* was capable of renunciation in two ways because *dominium* is possessed both individually and in common. The renunciation of both individual and common *dominium*, based on the life of Christ and the Apostles, was the pattern of Franciscan poverty, a poverty imposed on the Apostles by Christ but not forced upon the Church. Penurious poverty, lack of possessions, rejection of money and other movable goods, served as a certain sign of perfection. It would be absurd to claim that the present possessionate way of living was to be preferred to the life of Christ and the Apostles. And the Franciscans were closer to imitating Christ's perfection than were others, because they renounced, as Christ did, the capacity to possess temporal goods.[100]

With this classic statement, Bonaventure was able to balance the two wings of the Franciscans in a kind of equilibrium for twenty years. Apart from the distinctive interpretation of scriptural references to the economic aspects of the life of Christ and the Apostles, Bonaventure was also drawing upon a distinctive and questionable use of civil law. In brief, *dominium* (as we saw earlier) could, in fact, be separated from possession, but could possession be separated from use where consumables were concerned? Roman law noted that the *usufructus* shall not be separated in perpetuity from *proprietas* lest the holder be deprived of temporal benefit which it is the nature of *proprietas* to convey.[101] What possible value to the papacy as *dominus* could Franciscan property and goods given for Franciscan use be? The Franciscan claim to a total renunciation of *dominium* and *possessio* was a nonsense.

Radical Franciscans like Peter John Olivi[102] countered by arguing that the indispensable condition of the Franciscan poverty vow was the

98. *Ibid.*, c. vii para 3, pp. 272–3.
99. *Exiit qui seminat* (1279) in *Seraphicae Legislationis, textus originalis* (Quaracchi, 1897), pp. 181–227; *Registres de Nicolas III* (1277–80), ed. Gay 1916, pp. 232–41.
100. St Bonaventure, *Apologia Pauperum*, c. ix, p. 289.
101. *Corpus Iuris Civilis*, I, Institutiones, ed. Krueger 1928, p. 13.
102. Gieben 1968; Hödl 1958; Alverny 1928.

irrevocable bond to a life of penury where use was strictly limited to the most basic of human needs: ragged habits, no shoes, no horse-riding, and the practice of begging. The intention to live according to a minimum of needs was insufficient: it was the practice of abject poverty that counted. Anything less was seen as a betrayal of Francis' original intentions. He set this argument within the Joachite cosmic struggle between the forces of Christ and Antichrist.

Olivi's views[103] were incorporated into Nicholas III's attempt to clear up once and for all the practical interpretation of the Rule in his *Exiit qui seminat* (1279), especially with regard to outside critics. Nicholas dogmatically affirmed that a renunciation of *proprietas* of all things (*abdicatio proprietatis hujusmodi omnium rerum tam in speciali quam etiam in communi*), individually and in common, for God, *is* evangelical and worthy of merit. It was taught by Christ as a *via perfectionis* through his example. Thus in distinguishing *dominium, proprietas,* from *possessio, usufructus, ius iutendi* and *simplex usus facti,* Nicholas insisted that it was appropriate for the order, whose founder was inspired by the testimonial of the trinity, to have only *simplex usus facti* of certain necessary temporal goods, and their use was revocable at the will of the donor. Drawing on the language of Bonaventure, on Olivi and on the *Expositio Quatuor Magistri,* Nicholas seemed to go much further than the more conservative element in the order, which accepted that the vow of poverty was really only a renunciation of *dominium* alone. Nicholas did not, however, adopt the radical scheme of history of the Joachites, nor did he designate the Franciscans as the perfect men of the final age with a clear historical mission. As a consequence, the more conservative Franciscan Conventuals closed ranks as did the rigorists who came to be known as the Spirituals in the fourteenth century.

The university response to poverty–property disputes

The debate between the seculars and mendicants over poverty intensified discussions concerning proper attitudes to property and *dominium* in its extended sense of sovereignty. This spilled over into university quodlibetal sessions. University masters in theology participated in *quodlibets,* the *determinatio* of which was reserved to the master to present his views on issues that his wide-ranging public audience raised from the floor of the debating chamber. The *quodlibets* of Giles of Rome, an Augustinian, and Godfrey of Fontaines,[104] a secular, in the 1280s and 90s treat of

---

103. Ed. Flood 1972; Burr 1975, pp. 71–8.   104. Lejeune 1958–62, pp. 1215–61.

contemporary political issues and current ethical or doctrinal problems, one of which was the notion of *dominium*. And it is not surprising that one finds *quodlibets* that ask whether the church would best be ruled by a good lawyer rather than by a theologian.[105] Here the meaning of legal terms such as *dominium* (lordship), property, possession and use of material goods and the respective realms of jurisdiction over such goods of lay and clerical powers were disputed. The *quodlibets* of Godfrey of Fontaines are specially illuminating for their frequent attention to problems of property rights of different social groups: can a religious who has taken a vow to own nothing arrogate to himself a steady income of alms?[106] What is the nature of the mendicant 'use' as opposed to personal or communal ownership? Is the pope to be seen as head of the church but, regarding material possession, only steward of communal church property? Godfrey also treated problems of illegal financial gain and debt.[107] His *quodlibet* 13, q.5 *responsio*, setting out the nature of ecclesiastical and papal relationships to material goods, incorporating canon and civil law developments, would be adopted by the Dominican John of Paris early in the fourteenth century.

When John wrote his justly famous *De potestate regia et papali*[108] in 1302, he was contributing to a wider controversy between Philip IV, the Fair, of France and Pope Boniface VIII.[109] Ostensibly the issue was the debate between *sacerdotium* and *regnum* which sought to determine the spheres of sovereignty on the parts of secular and ecclesiastical powers. John has often been seen as a moderate, establishing a *via media* that recognised two powers but separated ecclesiastical from secular jurisdiction: with regards to the respective internal structures of each hierarchy, with regard to their respective powers over property, and with regard to the separate moral influence of each power. But he is far more radical than his *via media* implies when he elaborated his notions of *dominium in rebus* and *jurisdictio*.[110] John incorporates the opinion of Godfrey of Fontaines on *dominium* in his chapters six and seven, to produce a clear distinction between church and lay rights to *dominium*. He defines *dominium* as only referring to things, *dominium in rebus*. The pope is not a true *dominus* but merely an

105. Godfrey of Fontaines, *Quodlibet* x (1293) q. 18 (ed. Hoffmans, *P.B.*, 4). *Utrum per unum bonum iuristam melius possit regi ecclesia quam per theologum*: Glorieux 1925b, p. 162.
106. *Quodlibet* x q. 16 (ed. Hoffmans, *P.B.*, 4). Ms Paris BN Lat. 14311 fols 123–5.
107. *Quodlibet* VIII q. 11 (ed. Hoffmans, *P.B.*, 4, p. 116) and *Quodlibet* XI q. 8 (ed. Hoffmans, *P.B.*, 5, p. 42); *Quodlibet* XII q. 1 (ed. Hoffmans, *P.B.*, 5, p. 169); *Quodlibet* XIV q. 1 (ed. Hoffmans, *P.B.*, 5, p. 304); *Quaestiones ordinariae*, III (ed. Hoffmans, *P.B.*, 14, p. 134).
108. *De potestate regia et papali*, ed. Bleienstein 1969; *On Royal and Papal Power*, transl. Watt 1971; Leclercq 1942.
109. Tierney 1955a, p. 161; Ullmann 1976, pp. 58–87.   110. Coleman 1983b.

administrator of collective church goods.[111] These goods were given to ecclesiastical communities rather than to individuals, so that no one person has proprietary right or lordship over them. The intention of those who gave property to the church was not to transfer proprietary right and lordship to Christ: these things are his already. The transfer was to Christ's ministers. The pope may not, therefore, treat collective church property as his own, and only where the welfare of the whole church requires it may he deprive anyone. If the pope does not act in good faith and should he betray the trust of his stewardship, he must make restitution from his own patrimony. Furthermore, regarding lay property the pope does not even have stewardship. Lay property is not granted to the community as a whole, but is, rather, acquired by individual people through their own skill, labour and diligence.[112] Only individuals have *ius* and *dominium* over their own property. The individual alone administers, disposes, holds or alienates his property so long as he injures no one else.[113] There is *no* common head to administer this individually acquired and owned property: not even the prince has lordship or administration of it. It is only when civil peace is disturbed through disagreements over possession, that a ruler is thereafter established to act only as arbiter and judge in property disputes.[114]

John argues further that Christ's royal power is not of the temporal order. His kingdom is not of this world and therefore his royalty is spiritual. As incarnate Man/God, Christ acts as mediator, exercising in the world a spiritual royalty. Considered with respect to his humanity alone Christ is not a temporal king over goods possessed by men, be they Christian or not. He voluntarily took on human nature, accepting poverty and other human deficiencies without contracting sin. In his terrestrial life Christ did not exercise *dominium* or temporal jurisdiction over lay goods; he reigns in and over the hearts of the faithful but not over their possessions. Whatever

---

111. Cap. vi: 'quod [summus pontifex] non sit verus dominus exteriorum bonorum sed dispensator simpliciter vel in casu' (Bleienstein 1969, p. 91).

112. Cap. vii: 'Ad quod declarandum considerandum est quod exteriora bona laicorum non sunt collata communitati sicut bona ecclesiastica, sed sunt acquisita a singulis personis arte, labore vel industria propria, et personae singulares ut singulares sunt, habent in ipsis ius et potestatem et verum dominium' (Bleienstein 1969, p. 94).

113. *Ibid.*: 'et potest quilibet de suo ordinare, disponere, dispensare, retinere, alienare pro libito sine alterius iniuria, cum sit dominus' (Bleienstein 1969, p. 94).

114. *Ibid.*: 'Verum quia ob talis bona exteriora contingit interdum pacem communem turbari dum aliquis quod est alterius usurpat, qui etiam interdum homines quae sunt nimis amantes ea non communicant prout necessitati vel utilitati patriae expedit, ideo positus est princeps a populo qui in talibus praeest ut iudex decernens iustum et iniustum, et ut vindex iniuriarum, et ut mensura in accipiendo bona a singulis secundum proportionem pro necessitate vel utilitate communi' (Bleienstein 1969, p. 97).

imperfections Christ had, as described in Scripture, he adopted in order to ransom us back. Having assumed human nature he also took on voluntarily hunger, thirst, death and poverty.[115]

Both John of Paris and Godfrey of Fontaines were responding in the legal language of property rights, drawing on contemporary events as well as on civil and canon law theory to counter the views expressed by the Augustinian Giles of Rome, who argued from a more theological base concerning the plenitude of papal power in matters of *dominium* and rights over material goods. The contrast between Giles' *De ecclesiastica potestate*[116] and John of Paris' *De potestate regia et papali* epitomised the two major tracks along which the debate would run throughout the fourteenth century between the respective sovereignties of church and state regarding *dominium*.

John of Paris, the anonymous authors of the *Quaestio in utramque partem* and the *Rex pacificus*,[117] Marsilius of Padua, Augustinus Triumphus, Alvarus Pelagius, James of Viterbo, William of Ockham, Richard FitzRalph, John Wyclif and various conciliarists would contribute to the genre *de potestate regia et papali*, specifying *dominium* as property rights, *ius in rem*. At one end of the spectrum, legitimate property rights were seen as created by governments or through recognition by the church of men's pacts with men (Giles of Rome). At the other end, legitimate rights in things were acquired by men prior to the establishment of governments and issued from men's natural capacities to labour for their requirements in a world created for their common use. Civil law was taken to be either a formalisation of property rights and *dominium* acquired through one's labour, or an institution that gave men such rights, which did not exist before. In many of these tracts the secular ruler and his subjects, defined as property-owning individuals, were established as autonomous in relation to the Church. For John of Paris, the most radical of all these early fourteenth-century theorists, men already had individual property rights prior to the establishment of government; and government then transformed these into positive legal rights as its main service to the individual.

John XXII versus the radical Franciscans: Ockham

Amongst the Franciscan Spirituals like Ubertino da Casale at the beginning of the fourteenth century, the poverty position of *usus pauper*, non-

115. Leclercq 1942, pp. 102–3.
116. Giles of Rome, *De ecclesiastica potestate*, ed. Scholz 1929, Cap. II.
117. Ed. Vinay 1939; Kuiters 1958; Watt 1967. On *Rex pacificus*, Saenger 1981.

possession and sparseness in use became hardened into something more than a mere legal theory. They wished to exemplify an attitude and practice of disdain for the material world beyond the direst of necessities, and they said that no pope had the power to dispense from gospel vows. Consequently, the Spirituals were persecuted and Olivi's writings met with a concerted effort to get them out of the life of the order, culminating in their condemnation by John XXII in 1326.

A series of documents issued from the papacy between 1321 and 1323 ended with a dogmatic definition in *Cum inter nonnullos*.[118] John argued that a pope had the right to alter edicts of his predecessors at will; and he began with *Exiit qui seminat*, which accepted that Franciscans could renounce all the rights of civil law and maintain only *simplex usus facti* in their goods. John also rejected *Ordinem vestrum* and its establishment of the legal fiction that the papacy was *dominus* of Franciscan property. He refused to accept this *dominium* over goods which might come to the order in the future and refused to appoint procurators. He argued that the notion of papal *dominium* was nonsensical if, as was the case, the Franciscans under certain circumstances had the right to give, sell and exchange goods normally held by the pope. And as to consumables: 'what sane man could believe that it was the intention of so great a father to preserve to the Roman Church the dominion over one egg, one bean, or one crust of bread, which are often given to the brothers?' Furthermore, the claim that Christ and the Apostles had totally renounced *dominium* was untrue because such renunciation was impossible. John studied the civil law definitions of *usufruct, ius utendi, simplex usus facti* regarding consumables, affirming that the use of a consumable object implied the right of its use. He says nothing about the natural-law precept that allowed men to have use without positive rights in a thing in extreme necessity; he appears to have accepted this. Thomas Aquinas' views, far more moderate, as we have seen, than those of the Franciscans, were preferred, and Aquinas was canonised. John deemed it heretical to say and believe that Christ and the Apostles had nothing either privately or in common, for this contradicted holy scripture, which asserts that they did have some things. It was also deemed heretical to say that Christ and the Apostles had no right of use in those things, no right of selling, giving or exchanging them, for scripture testified that they could have done so. In effect, the Franciscans had misunderstood the civil law. But had they? We have seen that classical Roman law did separate *possessio, usus* and *usufruct* (except in consumables) as distinct from *dominium*. But Roman

118. *Cum inter nonnullos*, *Extra. Joann.* XXII, 14.4, Freidberg, *Corpus Iuris Civilis*, II, pp. 1229–30; Eubel 1898–1904, vol. v, pp. 256–9.

law had also evolved, as we have seen, where *dominium* was collapsed into *possessio*. None the less, John made his final pronouncement in *Quia vir reprobus* (1328)[119] that perfection was now commensurate with possessory rights because without rights there could be no justice.

As a result of these dogmatic definitions from 1323 onwards, a group of Franciscans led by the Minister General of the order, Michael of Cesena, revolted and joined the papally unconsecrated Holy Roman Emperor Louis of Bavaria. From his court at Munich the Franciscan William of Ockham attacked John's theses in the *Opus nonaginta dierum* (1332),[120] a work of overwhelming erudition dealing with the legal terms *dominium, usufruct* and *simplex ususfacti* amidst scriptural exegesis. He followed up these themes in his *Epistola ad fratres minores*, his *Breviloquium*, the *Octo questiones* and the *Dialogus* (1338?).[121] Elaborating on the wider concern for the location of political and juristic power (*potentia*), Ockham wished to define what sort of entity could have power and what was its relation to *dominium*. He demonstrated that distinct individuals have powers of various kinds prior to any political structure or arrangement giving them such powers. Men had two kinds of *dominium*, corresponding to the situations before and after the Fall. Each *dominium* was possessed in common by the species and naturally. Prelapsarian *dominium* was a miraculous power to command all creatures but was not property-ownership. The world was given by God to mankind in common. Man's nature was improved after the Fall by God giving fallen men a second kind of natural *dominium* in the form of natural common powers to appropriate temporal goods as individual appropriators and he gave them the power to set up governments to secure these rights. In the *Opus nonaginta dierum* he distinguished pre-and post-lapsarian conditions, defining *ius poli* (as used in *Exiit qui seminat*) as a natural equity conforming to right reason and independent of positive laws. He also defined *ius fori*, or positive law, which need not conform to right reason or divine law. Under the category of the *ius poli* he included man's right to sufficient goods for his survival. He then argued that the Franciscans were in fact fulfilling the initial natural obligation to maintain their existence and were exercising the *ius poli*. But since *dominium* and *possessio* resulted from the Fall and governments were established as a result of Adam's sin, the power of exercising dominion over men and their property was exclusively that of

---

119. *Quia vir reprobus,* in Eubel 1898–1904, vol. v, pp. 408–49.
120. William of Ockham, *Opus nonaginta dierum,* in *Opera Politica,* I, ed. Sikes and Bennett 1940.
121. *Epistola ad fratres minores,* in *Ibid.,* III, 6; *Dialogus,* in *Monarchia Sancti Romani Imperii,* II, ed. Goldast 1614; Kölmel 1962; Damiata 1978–9; McGrade 1980, pp. 149–65.

temporal rulers. The Franciscan ideal was therefore broadened into an attack on the very foundations of the church's claim to a plenitude of power in the spiritual and temporal affairs of Christendom.

The legally-minded pope John had said something more than that *dominium* was the same as *ius*. In arguing for *dominium/possessio* as an active right in something he implied, (like John of Paris), that rights in things entailed specific duties of others that determined how men ought to behave towards possessors of rights. *Dominium* had become *de facto* private rights of individuals defensible in law against all others. And like John of Paris, the pope argued that natural men, prior to governments, had *dominium* over *temporalia* so that property was natural to men, sustained by divine law and unavoidable. God's *dominium* over the earth was conceptually the same as man's *dominium* over his earthly goods. But in the tradition of Boniface VIII and Giles of Rome, he also argued that such active rights needed church sanction to be realised, whereas John of Paris invoked the secular monarch as the defender and transformer rather than creator of these rights.

Marsilius *on* dominium

Theoretical tracts were only one of many ways to counter the papal claims of plenitude of power, and Marsilius of Padua wrote one of the most radical, not only in defence of *imperium* but also in defence of the Franciscan notion of poverty which he applied to the situation of the whole church.[122] Although Marsilius was chiefly concerned with his native *Italicum regnum*, in the *Defensor pacis* he developed a political doctrine to which he attributed universal validity against the claims of John XXII. He maintained a distinction between *dominium* and *usus* against what he says is often common practice, admitting that it is more common to use the term *dominium* to mean both the principal power to lay claim to something rightfully acquired (in accordance with 'right' taken to mean a coercive command or prohibition of the human legislator), and the use or *usufruct* of the thing.[123] He also notes that possession does more commonly mean both abstract incorporeal ownership and the actual corporeal handling of the thing or its use.[124] But he wishes to put his clearly defined terms, *dominium*, *ius*, *possessio*, *proprium*, to a narrower, more polemical use which argues for the temporal disendowment of the whole church through defining it as

---

122. Marsilius of Padua, *Defensor pacis*, ed. Previté-Orton 1928; *Defensor minor: De translatione imperii*, ed. Jeudy and Quillet 1979.   123. *Defensor pacis*, II, xii (13) and (14).   124. *Ibid.*, II, xii (19).

incapable of *dominium* in its own right.[125] Marsilius had taken the Franciscan example and universalised it regarding the whole church and its relation to temporal goods.

Church and state powers over property: FitzRalph and Wyclif

Throughout the fourteenth century assemblies of clergy and laity met to debate the relations between the two powers without resolution. By mid-century the concept of the public good which was in the care of the monarch inspired new reflections on the notion of the state and its relation to *dominium* and jurisdiction over *temporalia*. Dialogues proliferated between knights and clerics to define the rights and powers of the two jurisdictions and to coordinate these, continuing into the conciliar epoch.[126] By mid-century the place of mendicancy and poverty in the church flared up once again at the papal court at Avignon and the campaign of Richard FitzRalph[127] against the mendicant orders gave rise to a radical doctrine of *dominium* and its relationship to grace. This would be the inspiration of Wyclif's doctrine, not unlike that of Marsilius, to disendow the church entirely, which issued from his belief that all property was held from God and thus from the king who was, by grace, God's vicar. Objecting to the clergy assuming lay offices, Wyclif argued that ecclesiastical possessions were derived from the king as patron and could be reduced when necessary. His thesis would influence Jan Hus and Jerome of Prague in the fifteenth century.

FitzRalph's *De pauperie salvatoris* (1356)[128] subjected the Franciscan poverty doctrine to minute analysis; his earlier sermons focused on the issue of secular and mendicant pastoral jurisdiction.[129] Once again he raised the tangled questions concerning the nature of property and discussed whether its use could be divorced from ownership. He argued that the friar who engaged in pastoral activity, especially in preaching, thereby ensuring a regular means of subsistence, was violating his vow of poverty. Denying that voluntary poverty was meritorious, FitzRalph went on to argue for a new theory of *dominium* whereby all lordship, ownership and jurisdiction was founded in God's grace to the individual soul. Those who commit grave sin are deprived of just *dominium*, ecclesiastical or temporal. But he

125. *Ibid.*, II, xiv (18) and (22).   126. Black 1979.
127. Walsh 1981; Dawson 1983; Walsh 1975.
128. Richard FitzRalph, *De pauperie salvatoris*, ed. Lane Poole, 1890, books I–IV, as appendix to Wyclif's *De dominio divino*; ed. Brock 1954, books V–VII.   129. Gwynn 1937; Coleman 1984.

never suggested that either the church or the secular powers should deprive such sinners of actual proprietorship as Wyclif was to do.

Just civil lordship requires divine sanction. Thus, before the Fall all temporal possessions were held in common; private property was introduced as a result of sin. But the just are in a state of grace whereby at least theoretically they continue to share equal dominion over all things. FitzRalph does recognise a limitation placed on original lordship by legally sanctioned private property so that he appears to be arguing for a double legitimation: sanction by God and sanction by men's laws. When he comes to discuss Franciscan absolute poverty he distinguishes five degrees, the strictest of which is the abdication of all secondary rights of use, of all civil lordship, where only original lordship which was common to all in a state of grace was to be preserved. This original or natural lordship whereby possessions were held only by the common natural right of use was epitomised by the teaching and practice of Christ and the Apostles. Christ had restored the original situation in which distinctions of property after the Fall were reversed and he recreated with his Apostles the community of all things. But it is impossible to take this as a model for contemporary society. The mendicant poverty of the Franciscans cannot be equated with the lifestyle of Christ and the Apostles.

FitzRalph summarised the conclusions of his *De pauperie salvatoris* in a series of sermons preached publicly in London,[130] and as a consequence, the friars led a party to Avignon to accuse him of heresy.[131] The confrontation dragged on without conclusion until his death in 1360. Thereafter it continued to trouble the university of Paris during the 1360s and Oxford in the 1370s as a result of Wyclif taking FitzRalph's doctrine of *dominium* and grace further.

Wyclif came to Oxford and by 1354 had distinguished himself in logic and in theological dispute. Quite early on he became involved in the political issues that were to cause him to formulate a radical position regarding the unjustified possessions of property by ecclesiastical authorities.[132] In 1371 Parliament heard arguments in favour of the removal of clerical administration and its replacement by laymen more in touch with the nation's needs in time of war: the wealth of the church should contribute

---

130. Four such sermons are printed at the end of FitzRalph's *Summa in Quaestionibus Armenorum* (Paris, 1511), including assertions that voluntary poverty was neither of Christ's example nor of present obligation; that mendicancy had no warrant in scripture or primitive tradition.
131. *Appellatio* of the London Greyfriars. MS 64. 4. 2, fol. 4. Sidney Sussex College, Cambridge.
132. McFarlane 1952; Wilks 1965, pp. 220–36; Daly 1973, pp. 177–87.

to a larger extent to the war against France. Wyclif was present to hear two Austin friars argue that it was justifiable to seize ecclesiastical property for the common good. Churchmen were rebuked for being unpatriotic possessioners. It was argued that what pious laymen had given the church could, *in extremis*, be lawfully taken back by their heirs in the interests of self-preservation. The clergy was reminded of its obligations to the state, to national taxation, and advised of the right of the king to appoint to vacant benefices. Wyclif appears to have been employed by John of Gaunt and the widow of the Black Prince to make it clear to the papacy that in time of war the English clergy could not afford papal taxation. He composed tracts of a highly political if theoretical nature making the case for the secular government's right to despoil the wealthy clergy. He refuted the clerical argument of long standing that the church's spiritual authority, being higher than that of the state, granted her immunity from secular interference in her property. Wyclif adopted FitzRalph's arguments, citing long passages of the *De pauperie salvatoris* in his own writings, that true *dominium* came from God's grace to possessioners and that the man who failed in his service to God as *dominus* by falling into mortal sin forfeited his rights. Seeing secular government as the instrument of all reform, Wyclif argued further that the state could deprive the undeserving possessioners of their secular power and wealth. God is the *dominus capitalis* who has delegated his powers to the king or prince, and in so far as the king derives his just power from the grace of God, only secular lordship is justified in the world. Wyclif's full thesis on *dominium* appeared in 1378 (*De officio regis, De potestate papae, De dominio divino, De civili dominio*), and the papacy lost little time in condemning it, unsuccessfully. Only when he wrote down his unorthodox views on the eucharist was he effectively silenced and edicts passed against his writings and his followers.

It is clear that Wyclif's was, above all, a political movement concerned with a great renewal and reform of Christian life which could only come about through a restructuring of society. Doctrinal reform would follow, and Wyclif conceived of a new age, in which tyrant priests would be dispossessed and forcibly returned to an apostolic church, a vision that had informed the apocalyptic writings of radical Franciscans. Property ownership was not itself evil but a possessionate clergy was a misinterpretation of its spiritual function, a perversion of the very nature of true dominion. He saw an end to the separation of church and state jurisdictions over temporal goods, and argued that only the king should head the commonwealth of the righteous, the *communitas iustorum*. The king's law was the final arbiter, and this would be made clear if Scripture were placed in the hands of the laity, especially lay lords. Holy writ should be defended by lay lords for the church comprised not only the prelates but included members of the whole congregation of the faithful who were imbued with grace, and predestined to salvation. However unjust, the king was vicar of God and above all human laws. If necessary he was obliged to reform the church, correcting the worldly pursuit of the clergy for honours and offices, punish their simony and remove them from temporal dominion. The clergy were to live in an apostolic manner surviving on tithes and alms offered by the faithful.[133] It is not surprising that pope Gregory XI saw Wyclif as an heir to Marsilius of Padua.

Wyclif combined theological, political and popular radicalism in a unified programme of reform that appealed beyond university circles, and his followers, the Lollards, merely expanded in the vernacular on the more scholarly presentation of his complaints against the contemporary *ordo* of church and state. They publicised his views in a more manageable form to an increasingly literate laity. Although some Lollards went considerably beyond Wyclif's teachings he helped to inspire such offshoots of his theories by supporting if not actually initiating wandering 'poor priests' to educate the laity in the nature of the proposed new reform of society. His ideas were not bounded by the school room and he was consequently perceived as a danger. Although the Lollards and Wyclif were not responsible for the 'peasants' revolt' of 1381–2, their opponents suggested their culpability. This is only one of many instances where the scholarly debates over property and poverty reached beyond the literate and educated groups, inspiring lay movements to reassess their social conditions and their piety. The debate would pass into the fifteenth century and beyond amongst groups of high and low degree.

If there is an outstanding theme related to property and poverty in this period, it is the gradual development of arguments which clarify the twofold nature of the individual: his power over his own and his responsibility for his fellows in so far as they partake of the common good. By the fourteenth century the concern for the individual was expressed in theological and political works by means of arguments demonstrating that individuals have powers or capacities of various kinds before anyone or any political or ecclesiastical arrangement gives these to them. This reflected a *de facto* situation throughout Europe. By the end of the century *dominium* in its

133. Wilks 1965.

narrower sense, as *dominium in rebus*, had become a *ius in re*, any right to some material thing like land defensible against all others, transferable and capable of alienation by the possessor – a situation that depended on a profit economy. Men were described in political theory, in legal treatises, in political poetry and prose, in polemic and ephemera, as individuals controlling their lives by being in some way responsible for the material as well as the spiritual aspects of their existence.[134] The debate over *dominium* and property would not end here; it would continue to echo, even more emphatically but in a new key, in seventeenth-century England.[135]

134. Coleman 1981.   135. Tierney 1980, pp. 167–82.

CONCLUSION

Only the briefest of notes is either appropriate or necessary by way of conclusion to a book of this kind. Yet there are questions which will naturally be asked and which it is necessary to consider even if they cannot be completely or definitively answered. There are questions, already touched on in the Introduction, as to method and approach – questions which may perhaps be encapsulated in the question whether these pages have reflected any significant change or development in the histriography of the subject. It can perhaps be claimed that there is evidence of such a shift, both in the range of the evidence considered and in at least some of the perspectives in which it has been analysed. One illustration of both points may be found in the thoroughness with which ecclesiological concepts have been considered, whether in the Carolingian and post-Carolingian period or in the context of fifteenth-century conciliarism – the latter in particular a case in which earlier historians would have taken a more narrowly 'political' view of the material. Again – a not unrelated point – it is surely the case that the evidence of canon law has taken a much more prominent place here than would have been the case even in the early decades of this century. This is not to say that the canonists were neglected in earlier account: Carlyle, for example, drew extensively on canonistic sources, and devoted the greater part of his second volume to 'the political theory of the canon law' from the ninth to the thirteenth century. Yet it was precisely in the preface to that volume that Carlyle acknowledged the disadvantage under which he had laboured from lack of access to 'the mass of unprinted material, especially in the canon law of the twelfth century.'[1] Over recent decades, however, the work of such scholars as Walter Ullmann, Stephan Kuttner, and Brian Tierney among many others has transformed this situation; and that transformation is one of the changes reflected in the pages of this volume.

Similar points could be made in respect of the now immense mass of scholarly work on medieval philosophy, even though that work has not, for

1. Carlyle 1903–36, vol. II, p. viii.

the most part, concentrated primarily on the political or even the moral theory of the scholastics.[2] This has clearly, for example, added new dimensions to our understanding of Ockham's political ideas, however complex the relationship between those ideas and Ockham's general philosophical position may seem to remain. Again, a tendency in the study of the medieval period – as indeed of other periods too – to move from predominantly political history to a history more fully aware of interconnected social, cultural and economic factors is one reason why the political ideas examined above have so often been sought in a broader context of ideas about communities in general.

There is also, however, a legitimate question to be asked about the chronological range of the book as well as about the scope of its subject-matter. A line has been drawn in the middle of the fifteenth century. Can this be defended? History does not abound in unmistakable final curtains like that which descended upon the eastern empire of Byzantium in 1453: and in the west there is no mid-fifteenth-century event of comparable decisiveness which might be seen as marking an end or a beginning in any aspect of political thinking. If, for example, we say – as we might – that the conciliar movement in the western Church ended with the final dissolution, in 1449, of the Council of Basel–Lausanne and the 'Little Schism' it had precipitated, the fact remains that conciliarist *ideas* (and even in some measure policies based upon them) retained their importance and relevance well into the next century and even beyond.[3] It is no doubt true that the last major thinker considered in these pages is Nicholas of Cusa, who lived until 1464, but whose creative thinking had all been done two or three decades earlier. And many would agree that for the next political thinker of notable originality we have to wait for Machiavelli, who was not born until five years after Nicholas' death. On the other hand, if anything has emerged from this survey it is surely that a comprehensive study of political ideas cannot restrict itself to the contributions of 'great thinkers'; and our notional dividing-line of 1450 is spanned by a diversity of writers and sources still essentially concerned with the problems examined above and analysing them in the language and with the conceptual equipment of 'medieval' society. It has not been possible, and it would have been absurd to attempt, to exclude such sources rigidly from consideration here: so that Fortescue, for example, duly appears in the course of Chapter 16, since his

---

2. Cf. *The Cambridge History of Later Medieval Philosophy*, Cambridge University Press, 1982, where some 130 pages out of 850 or so are devoted to 'Ethics' and 'Politics'.
3. See Oakley 1981, with comprehensive review of sources and secondary literature.

ideas, though deployed to meet specific situations in the 1460's, reflect and illustrate patterns of thought belonging emphatically to the period with which Part V of this volume is concerned.

It could no doubt be argued indeed, that it is not the elasticity of the 1450 limit that is open to criticism but rather the attempt to operate within such a limit at all. Historians of medieval political thought have sometimes interpreted their terms of reference as extending down to the end of the sixteenth century (Carlyle, d'Entrèves) – or even later. Brian Tierney, for one, has pointed to issues for debate and analysis which he sees as extending over a period from the mid-twelfth to the mid-seventeenth century;[4] and, though doubtless less convincingly, John Locke has been represented as having been, at the end of the seventeenth century, largely content in his political thinking with 'the solutions of St Thomas Aquinas'.

Must we conclude then that there is no more to be said in justification of ending this survey in the mid-fifteenth century than the somewhat limp observation that, after all, a book must end somewhere? The answer surely is that something more, and more to the point, can in fact be said. It is of course true that many of the medieval themes and 'traditions' of thought analysed above persist with considerable vitality into the later fifteenth century and beyond. It is also true, however, that they survive increasingly in a situation of co-existence with other, newer (and no doubt at the same time older) ways of thinking. The co-existence of what, for convenience and brevity, we may loosely designate as 'scholasticism' and 'humanism' was at times easier and more peaceful than has sometimes been supposed. Yet there was a fundamental divergence which inevitably led to hostility; and just as the great institutions of medieval society – the papacy, the empire, the 'feudal monarchies', the canon and civil laws – survived only in changed forms, so medieval political ideas survived to play a part in changed circumstances and were themselves changed in the process. The new forces that were at work were not, of course, simply or absolutely new. Humanism itself, after all, must be traced to beginnings at least as far back as the mid-fourteenth century; and the great, the revolutionary changes in religious and ecclesiastical life which were to provide, precisely, the context into which many medieval ideas about society and authority were to survive, have themselves been seen as the product of an 'age of reform' extending from the mid-thirteenth to the mid-sixteenth century.[5] When all

---

4. Tierney 1982.
5. S. Ozment *The Age of Reform 1250–1550: An Intellectual and Religious History of Late Medieval and Reformation Europe*, Yale University Press, 1980.

this is said and acknowledged, however, when it is recognised that the 'new' was not entirely new, while the 'old' was not yet, or for many decades, a spent force, the sense of change survives. It is neither mistaken nor misleading to suggest that somewhere around the middle of the fifteenth century we can detect enough of a decisive shift in the patterns of intellectual life to justify the claim that the principal movements of 'medieval political thought' as it has been analysed in these pages were drawing to a significant close.

BIOGRAPHIES

NOTES ON MEDIEVAL AUTHORS

These notes have no function more ambitious than that of identifying and locating chronologically the authors who are their subjects. In many cases the notes are 'biographical' in only the most skeletal sense; and even where substantial information is available it is provided here in outline form. Notes on some particularly important anonymous and pseudonymous writings have been included. The vexed question of referring to medieval authors by Christian names or surnames has been dealt with pragmatically, at the cost of uniformity, in the hope of maximising ease of access: cross-references are provided for these and other variations. The Bibliography, to which reference is made or implied in most of the notes, expands the short titles used in references here.

ABBO OF FLEURY
c. 945–1004. Abbot of Fleury from 987; defended monastic exemption against bishop Arnulf of Orleans 991; canonist and polemicist.
TEXTS: *Epistolae*, PL 139: 417ff; *Canones*, PL 139: 473ff.

ABELARD, PETER
1079–c. 1142. Educated at Loches or Tours and at Laon; taught dialectic and theology at Melun and Paris; abbot of St Gildas de Rhuys and founder of the Paraclete; briefly a monk at St Denis; condemned for heresy at Soissons 1121 and at Sens 1140; pupils included John of Salisbury and Arnold of Brescia, Abelard's foremost critic was Bernard of Clairvaux.
TEXTS: *see* Bibliography, part IV.
SECONDARY LITERATURE: Jolivet 1966; Luscombe 1966; Gregory 1974, 1975b; Verger and Jolivet 1982.

ABUBACER: *see* IBN TUFAIL

ACCURSIUS, FRANCISCUS (Accorso)
c. 1191–1263. Taught Roman law at Bologna; author of the Ordinary Gloss on the *Corpus Iuris Civilis* (c. 1230).
TEXTS: *Apparatus* to *Corpus Iuris Civilis*, Lyon, 1575, and many other editions between 1468 and 1627; *see also* Bibliography, part V.
SECONDARY LITERATURE: Landsberg, Ernst (1883). *Die Glosse des Accursius und ihre Lehre von Eigenthum, rechts- und dogmengeschichtliche Untersuchung*, A. Brockhaus; Kantorowicz, Hermann (1929). 'Accursio e la sua biblioteca', *Rivista di storia del diritto italiano* 2:35–62, 193–212; Genzmer, E. (1945). 'Zur Lebensgeschichte des Accursius', *Festschrift für Leopold Wenger, Münchener Beiträge zur Papyrusforschung und antiken rechtsgeschichte* 35:223–41; Fiorelli, Piero (1960). 'Accorso', *Dizionario biografico degli Italiani* 1:116–21; Tierney 1963a.

ADALBERO OF LAON

Bishop of Laon from 977 to c. 1030.
TEXT: *see* Bibliography, part IV.
SECONDARY LITERATURE: Coolidge 1965; Duby 1980.

ADAM MARSH: *see* MARSH, ADAM

ADELARD OF BATH
fl. early twelfth century.
TEXTS: *see* Bibliography, part IV.
SECONDARY LITERATURE: Haskins 1927; Bliemetzrieder 1935.

ADMONT, ENGELBERT OF: *see* ENGELBERT OF ADMONT

AEGIDIUS ROMANUS: *see* GILES OF ROME

AGAPETUS
fl. first half of sixth century. Deacon of St Sophia, Constantinople; author of Ἔκθεσις κεφαλαίων παραινετικῶν (Exposition of Heads of Advice or Counsel) addressed to the Emperor Justinian.
TEXT: *PG* 86, 1:1164–86.

AGOBARD OF LYONS, ST
b. c. 769; d. 6 June 840. Archbishop of Lyons 816; exiled for participation in revolt of sons of Louis the Pious; polemicist.
TEXTS: *De privilegio et iure sacerdotii*, PL 104:127ff; *Epistola ad clericos et monachos Lugdunenses de modo regiminis ecclesiastici*, PL 104:189ff; *De dispensatione ecclesiasticarum rerum*, PL 104:227ff; *De comparatione regiminis ecclesiastici et politici*, PL 104:291ff; and *see* Bibliography, part IV.

AGOSTINO TRIONFO OF ANCONA: *see* AUGUSTINUS TRIUMPHUS

AILLY, PIERRE D' (Petrus de Alliaco)
1352–1420. Leading philosophical theologian of nominalist school at University of Paris, chancellor 1389–95; advocated conciliar solution to the Great Schism 1379–83, then supported Avignonese popes till 1408; a moderate conciliarist 1408–17 and a leading figure at the councils of Pisa and Constance: cardinal 1411.
TEXTS: *see* Bibliography, part V.
SECONDARY LITERATURE: Oakley 1964; *LTK* 8:329–30.

ALAN OF LILLE
c. 1128–1202/3. Studied at Paris, taught there and at Montpellier; preached against the Cathar heretics in the south of France; some time before his death entered the abbey of Citeaux, where he died.
TEXTS: *see* Bibliography, part IV.
SECONDARY LITERATURE: Walsh 1977; Wilks 1977; Evans 1983.

ALANUS ANGLICUS
fl. 1190–1215. Taught canon law at Bologna.
TEXTS: *Summa Decretorum*, 1st recension (1192), Seo de Orgel, Bibl. Capitular. 113; 2nd recession (1205), Paris, Bibliothèque Mazarine, 1318; *Apparatus* to *Compilatio prima*,

Karlsruhe, Landesbibl. Aug. XL: *Collectio decretalium*, Vercelli, Cath. Chap. 89 (2nd recension).
SECONDARY LITERATURE: Stickler, Alfons M. (1959). 'Alanus Anglicus als Verteidiger des monarchischen Papsttums', *Salesianum* 21:346–406; Kuttner, Stephan (1953). 'The Collection of Alanus: A Concordance of its two Recensions', *Rivista di storia del diritto italiano* 26:37–53.

ALBERT THE GREAT, ST (Albertus Magnus)

b. c. 1200; d. 1280. Studied at Padua, where he joined the Dominican order in 1223; taught theology in Germany; went to Paris in the 1240s, became Master of Sacred Theology 1245; teaching at Cologne, 1249, where Thomas Aquinas was among his pupils; provincial of the Dominicans in Germany 1254; bishop of Regensburg 1260–2, then returned to Cologne for the rest of his life.
TEXTS: *Opera omnia*, ed. Jammy, P., Lyon, 1651; ed. Borgnet, A., 1890–9; ed. Geyer, B. *et al.*, 1951– ; *Politicorum Aristotelis commentarii*, Borgnet edn 8; *Super Ethica*, Borgnet edn 7.
SECONDARY LITERATURE: Grabmann 1941; Dunbabin 1965, 1982; Weisheipl 1980.

ALCUIN

c. 730–804. Of Northumbrian noble family; educated at York, where he was master of the cathedral school in 767; joined Charlemagne's court circle in 782; abbot of St Martin, Tours, 796; wrote extensively on grammar, logic, theology, morals, liturgy; revised text of the Bible.
TEXTS: *Epistolae*, *MGH Epp.* 4; and *see* Bibliography, part IV.
SECONDARY LITERATURE: Anton 1968, pp. 84–131; Godman 1982; Wallace-Hadrill 1983, pp. 205–16.

ALEXANDER OF HALES

c. 1185–1245. Born in Gloucestershire, he studied in Paris and later became a Franciscan. His *Summa* was one of the first works of the Latin west to be based on a full knowledge of the philosophy of Aristotle.
TEXTS: *see* Bibliography, part V.
SECONDARY LITERATURE: Gossmann, E. (1964). *Metaphysik und Heilsgeschichte: eine theologische Untersuchung der Summa Halensis*, Hueber; Barnes 1982.

ALFANUS OF SALERNO

b. 1015/20; d. 1085. Friend and fellow monk of Desiderius of Monte Cassino; archbishop of Salerno from 1958 and strong supporter of Gregory VII; author and translator of medical works; poet.
TEXTS: *see* Bibliography, part IV.

AL-FĀRĀBI

d. 950. Studied and taught at Baghdad.
TEXTS: *see* Bibliography, part IV.
SECONDARY LITERATURE: Dieterici 1900; Salman 1940; Strauss 1945; Walzer 1967, pp. 652–66; Maḥdi 1972, pp. 182–202; Maḥdi 1975.

ALFRED

849–99. Son of West Saxon king Aethelwulf (839–58); king of Wessex from 871; patron of scholars, seeking revival of literacy, both Latin and vernacular; author or inspirer of Old English versions (with original prefaces and interpolations) of Boethius, *De Consolatione Philosophiae*, Crosius, *Historia adversus Paganos*, Gregory the Great, *Regula Pastoralis*, etc.

ALVARUS PELAGIUS (Alvaro Pelayo, Alvaro Pais)
c. 1275–1349. Studied canon and civil law at Bologna, became a Franciscan in 1306, and was involved in the poverty controversy. From 1330 to 1332 he was papal penitentiary at Avignon. In 1333 he became bishop of Silves in Portugal, but his relations with the king were uneasy and he spent the last years of his life in retirement at Seville. His most important work, *De statu et planctu ecclesiae*, was written during his Avignon period and revised between 1335 and 1340. His *Speculum regis* was written for Alfonso XI of Castile.
TEXTS: *see* Bibliography, part V.
SECONDARY LITERATURE: Iung 1931; Wilks 1963; Sousa Costa 1966; A. García y García (1973). 'Pelayo o Pelagio, Alvaro', in *Diccionario de Historia Ecclésiastica de España*, Istituto Enrique Florez, Consejo Superior de Investigaciones Cientifícas, vol. III, pp. 1954–5.

AMBROSE, ST, OF MILAN
c. 334/40–97. Son of a praetorian prefect, held the office of *consularis* (governor) in province of Aemilia-Liguria; became bishop of Milan in 374; in close contact with court of western emperors in Milan and with Theodosius I on his visits to Italy; influential not only in Milan but in the western church at large; well-educated, with a knowledge of Greek, author of theological works, scriptural commentaries, sermons and letters.
TEXTS: *see* Bibliography, part III.
SECONDARY LITERATURE: Palanque 1933; Dudden 1935; Campenhausen 1949.

AMBROSIASTER
fl. c. 380. Anonymous author (given this name by Erasmus) of a set of commentaries on the epistles of St Paul; almost certainly the author of a set of questions on the Old and New Testaments and, less probably, of a collection of legal material.
TEXTS: *see* Bibliography, part III.
SECONDARY LITERATURE: Souter, A. (1905). 'A Study in Ambrosiaster', *Cambridge Texts and Studies* VII/4; Souter, A. (1927). *The Earliest Latin Commentaries on the Epistles of St Paul*, Clarendon Press; Heggelbacher 1959.

ANDREAE, JOHANNES: *see* JOHANNES ANDREAE

ANDREAS DE ISERNIA
b. c. 1316. Professor of law, University of Naples and a luminary of the Neapolitan school of jurists.
TEXTS: *In usus feudorum commentaria* (composed c. 1300), Venice, 1514, and Lyon, 1579; *lectura* on the *Liber constitutionum* of Frederick II (composed after 1305).
SECONDARY LITERATURE: Palumbo 1886; Calasso 1961.

ANONYMOUS OF HERSFELD
fl. 1090. Monk of Hersfeld; polemicist.
TEXT: *see* Bibliography, part IV.
SECONDARY LITERATURE: Zafarana 1966.

ANONYMOUS OF YORK: *see* NORMAN ANONYMOUS

ANSELM OF LAON
d. 1117. Taught at Laon with his brother Ralph from end of eleventh century; a major influence in the composition of the *Glossa ordinaria* on the whole of the Bible and in the preparation of collections of theological 'sentences'; conventionally regarded as one of the founders of scholasticism.

TEXTS: the corpus of Anselm's writings is not yet established; but see Lottin 1959, where many texts are discussed and edited. See also Landgraf 1973.
SECONDARY LITERATURE: Flint 1976; Smalley 1983, esp. pp. ix–x, 49–51.

ANSELM II OF LUCA
1036–86. Bishop of Lucca from 1075; designated by Gregory VII as his successor; canonist and exegete.
TEXTS: *see* Bibliography, part IV.

ANTONY IV
d. 1397. Patriarch of Constantinople 1389–90, 1391–7.
TEXT: letter to Basil I of Moscow, ed. Miklosich, P. and Müller, J. (1860–90). *Acta et diplomata graeca medii aevi* 2:188–92.

APOCAUCUS, JOHN
c. 1150–c. 1235. Bishop of Naupactus in Aetolia; letter-writer and canonist.
TEXTS: some works ed. Vasilievskij, V.G. (1896). 'Epirotica saeculi XIII', *Vizantijskij Vremennik* 3:241–99; for the rest see Nicol, D.M. (1957). *The Despotate of Epiros*, Basil Blackwell, Appendix 2, pp. 217–19; Stiernon, L. (1959). 'Les Origines du Despotat d'Epire', *Revue des études byzantines* 17:90–126; Bees-Seferlis, E. (1976). 'Unedierte Schriftstücke aus der Kanzlei des Johannes Apokaukos', *Byzantinisch–neugriechische Jahrbücher* 21:Appendix, 1–243.

AQUINAS, THOMAS, ST
c. 1225–74. Educated at Monte Cassino from 1231, then at University of Naples, 1239–44, where in the latter year he joined the Dominicans; studied in Paris 1245–8, moved to Cologne where he studied and taught under Albert the Great 1248–52; returned to Paris where he became master of theology in 1256 and taught until 1259; in Italy 1259–68 he wrote the first part of the *Summa theologiae*; in Paris for the last five years of his life, writing the second part of the *Summa* and most of his Aristotelian commentaries – some of which, however, like the third part of the *Summa* were unfinished when he died on his way to the Council of Lyons.
TEXTS: *see* Bibliography, part V.
SECONDARY LITERATURE: Eschmann 1958; Gilby 1958; Ullmann 1960a; Fitzgerald 1979; Congar 1983.

ARNOLD OF BRESCIA
Excommunicated by Eugenius III in 1148 for rejecting the temporal dominion of the pope and executed in 1155 by the imperial authority of Frederick Barbarossa for supporting a Roman republic. Cf. Otto of Freising, *Gesta Friderici* II.xxviii; John of Salisbury, *Historia Pontificalis* c. xxxi.

ATHANASIUS I
c. 1230/5–c. 1320. Patriarch of Constantinople 1289–93, 1303–9; ascetic, letter-writer, church reformer.
TEXTS: letters, ed. Talbot, A.–M.M. (1975), *The Correspondence of Athanasius I Patriarch of Constantinople. Letters to the Emperor Andronicus II, Members of the Imperial Family, and Officials*, Dumbarton Oaks Texts 3 (=Corpus Fontium Hist. Byz. 7), Dumbarton Oaks, Washington DC.

ATTO OF VERCELLI

c. 885–961. Bishop, theologian, canonist, reformer.

TEXTS: *De pressuris ecclesiasticis, PL* 134:51ff.; *Expositio in Epistolas Pauli, PL* 134:125ff.

AUGUSTINE, ST, OF HIPPO

354–430. Born of middle-class family at Thagaste, North Africa. Completed his early studies at Carthage and entered upon a teaching career. Moved to Italy and after a brief stay in Rome taught rhetoric at Milan. In 386 he came under the influence of Ambrose, whose preaching he had heard, had contacts with a circle of Christian neo-Platonists and read translations of neo-Platonist literature. During 386–7 he abandoned the Manichaean religion he had adopted in Africa and, after a period of reflection and discussion with friends, was baptised as a Christian in 387. Returned to Africa in 388, *via* Ostia (where his mother died). Ordained priest (391) and lived in community until his consecration as bishop of Hippo in 395, first to assist then to succeed the aged bishop Valerius. Involved in controversy with pagans, Manichaeans, Donatists, Pelagians; author of some (early) philosophical discussions, numerous theological works, many of them polemical, letters, sermons, and the autobiographical *Confessions*.

TEXTS: *see* Bibliography, part III.

SECONDARY LITERATURE: Bonner, G. (1963). *St Augustine of Hippo: Life and Controversies*, Westminster Press; Brown, P.R.L. (1967). *Augustine of Hippo: A Biography*, Faber and Faber; University of California Press; Marrou, H.I. (1938; with *Retractatio* 1949). *Saint Augustine et la fin de la culture antique*, E. de Boccard; Deane 1963; Markus 1970.

AUGUSTINUS TRIUMPHUS (Agostino Trionfo of Ancona)

b. c. 1270/3; d. 1328. An Austin friar, he studied in Paris from 1297 to 1300 and later lectured on the *Sentences* there before becoming lector in the Augustinian school at Padua. Master of Theology in Paris 1313–15; chaplain to Charles the son of Robert of Anjou, king of Naples and Sicily, 1322.

TEXTS: *Summa de potestate ecclesiastica*, Rome, 1479, 1582; *Tractus brevis de duplici potestate prelatorum et laicorum*, ed. in Scholz 1903.

SECONDARY LITERATURE: Ministeri, B. (1953). *De Vita et Operibus Augustini de Ancona*, O.E.S.A., *Analecta Augustiniana* 31:7–56, 148–262; Wilks 1963.

AUVERGNE, PETER OF: *see* PETER OF AUVERGNE

AVEMPACE: *see* IBN BAJJA

AVERROES (Ibn Rushd)

1126–98. Lived most of his life in Spain under the Almohads, and in Marrakesh. Tried to restore authentic Aristotelian thought. His works were much more respected by Hebrew than by Arabic scholars. In 1195 he was accused of heresy and exiled, but was restored before his death. His commentaries on Aristotle became widely known in the west during the thirteenth century.

TEXTS: *see* Bibliography, part IV.

SECONDARY LITERATURE: Vaux 1937; Alonso 1947; Gauthier 1948; Wolfson 1973c.

AVICENNA: *see* IBN SINA

AZO (Azzo, Azzone)

fl. 1198–1230. Taught Roman law at Bologna.

TEXTS: *see* Bibliography, part V.

SECONDARY LITERATURE: Kantorowicz, E.H. and Buckland, W. (1938). *Studies in the Glossators of the Roman Law*, Cambridge University Press (reprinted Scientia Verlag, 1969); Landsberg, E. (1889). 'Das Madrider Manuscript von Azos Quaestiones', *Zeitschrift der Savigny-Stiftung für Rechtsgeschichte*, Röm. Abt. 10:145–6; Genzmer, E. (1957). 'Gli Apparati di Azzone al Digestum 50.17.1', *Annali di storia del diritto* 1:7–11; Fiorelli, P. (1962). 'Azzone', *Dizionario biografico degli Italiani* 4:774–81.

BALDUS DE UBALDIS (Baldus de Perusio, Baldo degli Ubaldi)

c. 1327–1400. Studied at Perugia and possibly Pisa: Roman law under Bartolus and others; canon law under Federicus Petruccius. Date of doctorate unknown. From 1351 professor of law at Perugia; Pisa probably 1357–8; Florence 1359–64; Perugia 1365–76; Padua 1376–9; Perugia 1379–90; Pavia 1390–1400. Pupils included Pierre Roger de Beaufort (Pope Gregory XI) and the jurists Petrus de Ancharano, Paulus de Castro. Held public offices in Perugia and served on diplomatic missions. After Bartolus' death (1357) he was the most celebrated jurist in Europe.

TEXTS: *see* Bibliography, part V.

SECONDARY LITERATURE: Baldus de Ubaldis 1901; Curcio 1937; Horn 1967 and 1968; Wahl 1968, 1970, 1974 and 1977; Kirshner 1974 and 1979; Quaglioni 1980; Canning 1980a, 1980b, 1983 and 1987.

BALSAMON, THEODORE

fl. second half of twelfth century. Deacon and archivist of St Sophia, Constantinople; Patriarch of Antioch 1185–91, though resident at Constantinople. Canon lawyer and commentator, especially on the *Nomocanon in 14 Titles*.

TEXTS: in *PG* 137, 138; Rhalles, G.A. and Potles, M. (1852–4). Σύνταγμα τῶν θείων καὶ ἱερῶν κανόνων, pp. 1–4.

SECONDARY LITERATURE: Beck 1959, pp. 657–8.

BARTOLUS OF SASSOFERRATO (Bartolo da Sassoferrato)

1313/14–57. Studied under Cynus de Pistoia at Perugia, then at Bologna: *baccalaureus* 1333, doctor 1334. Assessor at Todi 1336; magistrate at Pisa and professor of law there 1339. From 1343 until his death taught at Perugia. With his pupil Baldus the most famous jurist in the school of commentators on Roman law.

TEXTS: *see* Bibliography, part V.

SECONDARY LITERATURE: Woolf 1913; Van de Kamp 1936; *Bartolo da Sassoferrato* 1962 (esp. articles by Baskiewicz, D. and by Ullmann, W.); Kirshner 1973.

BASSIANUS, JOHANNES

fl. 1175–97. Student of Bulgarus: taught Roman law at Bologna.

TEXTS: *see* Bibliography, part V.

SECONDARY LITERATURE: Kantorowicz, E.H. and Buckland, W. (1938). *Studies in the Glossators of the Roman Law*, Cambridge University Press (reprinted Scientia Verlag, 1969): Gualazzini, U. (1965). 'Bassiano', *Dizionario biografico degli Italiani* 7:140–2.

BEAUMANOIR, PHILIPPE DE RÉMI, SIRE DE

c. 1250–96. *Bailli* of Clermont 1279; king's service 1284. Asked by Robert of Artois to produce *Coutumes de Beauvaisis*. Also wrote poetry.

TEXT: *see* Bibliography, part V.

BECKET, ST THOMAS

1118(?)–70. Studied at Paris under Robert of Melun; c. 1141 joined household of Archbishop

Theobald of Canterbury, who sent him to study law at Bologna and Auxerre. Archdeacon of Canterbury 1154. Henry II made him chancellor of the realm in 1155. Archbishop of Canterbury 1162. Rejected the Constitutions of Clarendon in 1164, and his subsequent quarrel with the king, especially his claim that criminous clerks were not answerable to the royal courts of justice, provoked a crisis in relationships of crown, church and papacy. Assassinated in Canterbury Cathedral 1170. For sources, *see* Bibliography, part IV.
SECONDARY LITERATURE: Foreville 1943; Knowles 1951, 1970; Smalley 1973.

BELLAPERTICA, PETRUS DE (Pierre de Belleperche)
d. 1308. With Jacobus de Ravannis, the major luminary of the school of early commentators at Orleans, pioneering the application to jurisprudence of developed scholastic method. Through Cynus de Pistoia Bellapertica had a great influence on Italian jurisprudence. He taught at Toulouse and at Orleans and was royal chancellor at the time of his death.
TEXTS: *Lectura institutionum*, Paris, 1512; *Quaestiones et distinctiones*, Lyon, 1517; *Tractatus de Feudis*, Lyon, 1517; and *see* Bibliography, part V.
SECONDARY LITERATURE: Savigny 1834–51, vol. VI, pp. 27–33; Meijers 1956–73, vol. III, pp. 95ff; Weimar 1967; Gordon 1974.

BERNARD, ST, OF CLAIRVAUX
1090–1153. Entered the monastery of Citeaux 1112; from 1115 until his death abbot of the new foundation of Clairvaux. Became a formidable influence in the affairs of Europe, both secular and ecclesiastical.
TEXTS: *see* Bibliography, part IV.
SECONDARY LITERATURE: Vacandard 1920; Gilson 1940; *Mélanges Saint Bernard* 1953; *Saint Bernard théologien* 1953; Delhaye 1957; Maccarone 1959; Leclercq 1962, 1966, 1969; Jacqueline 1952, 1965; Kennan 1967; Evans 1983.

BERNARD OF PARMA
d. 1266. Born in the late twelfth or early thirteenth century, he studied at Bologna, where he was a canon and papal chaplain in 1247. His major work was his gloss on the decretals of Gregory IX, which was very influential.
SECONDARY LITERATURE: Kuttner, S. and Smalley, B. (1945). 'The Glossa Ordinaria to the Gregorian Decretals', *English Historical Review* 60:97–105; Abbondanza, R., in *Dizionario biografico degli Italiani* 9:276–9. Ourliac, P., in *Dictionnaire de droit canonique* 2:781–2.

BERNARD SILVESTRIS
fl. c. 1130–60. Taught at Tours; a friend of Thierry of Chartres, to whom he dedicated his *Cosmographia*.
TEXTS: *see* Bibliography, part IV.
SECONDARY LITERATURE: Gilson 1928; Stock 1972.

BERNOLD OF CONSTANCE
c. 1050–1100. Canon of Constance; monk of St Blasien and Schaffhausen. Historian, canonist, liturgist, polemicist: supporter of Gregory VII.
TEXTS: *see* Bibliography, part IV.
SECONDARY LITERATURE: Mirbt 1894; Grabmann 1909–11, vol. I, pp. 234–9; Robinson 1978b.

BLEMMYDES, NICEPHORUS
c. 1197–c. 1272. Byzantine scholar and monk. Tutor of the Emperor Theodore II Lascaris at Nicaea. Abbot of a monastery near Ephesus.
TEXTS: In *PG* 142; *Curriculum vitae et carmina*, ed. Heisenberg, A. (1896), Leipzig; and *see* Bibliography, part II.

BONIFACE-WINFRID, ST
c. 675–754. Missionary in Thuringia, Frisia, Hessen; archbishop of Mainz 748.
TEXTS: *MGH Epp.* 3:252ff; *MGH Epistolae selectae* 1.

BONIFACE VIII (Benedict Gaetani)
c. 1235–1303. Canon law graduate of Bologna; entered papal service 1264; cardinal 1281. Elected pope 1294 following abdication of Celestine V. His pontificate was overshadowed by his controversy with Philip IV of France, culminating in the seizure of the pope in his Anagni residence, which hastened his death. The *Liber Sextus Decretalium* was the lasting monument of a distinguished legislator, while his *Unam sanctam* is the most celebrated statement of the high principles of the papal interpretation of the relationship between the spiritual and temporal powers.
TEXTS: *see* Bibliography, part V.
SECONDARY LITERATURE: Le Bras 1951; Ullmann 1976.

BONIZO OF SUTRI (Bonitho, Bonitus)
c. 1045–c. 1090. Bishop of Sutri c. 1078; anti-bishop of Piacenza; canonist and polemicist.
TEXTS: *Liber ad amicum, MGH Libelli* 1:571ff; and *see* Bibliography, part IV.

BRACTON, HENRY DE
d. 1268. A royal justice under Henry III of England, but no longer believed to be the author of *De legibus et consuetudinibus Angliae* (for which see Bibliography, part V, under 'Bracton').

BRUNETTO LATINI: *see* LATINI, BRUNETTO

BRUNI, LEONARDO, OF ARETINO (Aretinus)
1369–1444. Classical-humanist scholar, author, leader of Italian Renaissance thought, publicist for the Florentine republic, of which he was chancellor 1427–44.
TEXTS: *see* Bibliography, part V.
SECONDARY LITERATURE: Baron 1966, pp. 58–65, 191–265; Skinner 1978, vol. I, pp. 72–84.

BRUNO OF SEGNI, ST
1040/50–1123. Bishop of Segni; abbot of Monte Cassino; adviser of Pope Urban II; exegete, theologian, polemicist.
TEXTS: *PL* 164–5; *MGH Libelli* 2:546ff.
SECONDARY LITERATURE: Grégoire 1965.

BURCHARD OF WORMS
c. 965–1025. Bishop of Worms 1000–25; canonist.
TEXTS: *PL* 140:499ff.

BURIDAN, JEAN
b. 1295/1300; d. after 1358. MA of Paris c. 1320 and lectured in the arts faculty there; rector of the university 1328, 1340. His pupils included Nicole Oresme.
TEXTS: *see* Bibliography, part V.
SECONDARY LITERATURE: Grignaschi 1960; Dunbabin 1982, pp. 735–7.

BURLEY, WALTER (Burleigh)
c. 1275–1344/5. MA and fellow of Merton College by 1301. Ordained 1309 and was studying theology in Paris before 1310. Master of theology c. 1320–2, fellow of the Sorbonne by 1324. Edward III's envoy to the papal court at Avignon 1327. Clerk in the bishop of Durham's household 1333, in the royal household 1336. Especially notable for his

logical works, he was also the author of an important commentary on Aristotle's *Politics*, surviving in a number of MSS.
TEXTS: *see* Bibliography, part V.
SECONDARY LITERATURE: Daly 1969.

BUTRIGARIUS, JACOBUS
c. 1274–1348. Major teacher of law at Bologna, where Bartolus was among his pupils.
TEXTS: *see* Bibliography, part V.
SECONDARY LITERATURE: Savigny 1834–51, vol. VI.

CAPPUCCI, JACOPO: *see* JAMES OF VITERBO

CECAUMENUS
fl. mid-eleventh century. Byzantine soldier and writer; author of a military handbook (*Strategikon*) addressed to his son.
TEXTS: *see* Bibliography, part II.

CHOMATIANOS, DEMETRIOS
fl. first half of thirteenth century. Archbishop of Ochrida 1217–35. Canon lawyer, jurist, theologian.
TEXTS: ed. Pitra, J.B. (1891). *Analecta sacra et classica spicilegio Solesmensi parata*, vol. VI, Rome.

CHRISTINE DE PISAN
1365–1430. Born in Venice, daughter of Thomas Pizzano, with whom she moved in 1369 to France, where her father was astrologer and physician to Charles V. Christine married Etienne de Castel in 1379 but ten years later was widowed with three children. In 1418 she retired to an abbey, possibly at Poissy. Her copious writings covered many subjects.
TEXTS: *see* Bibliography, part V.
SECONDARY LITERATURE: Pinet, M.-J. (1927). *Christine de Pisan (1364–1430): Etude biographique et littéraire*, Bibliothèque du XVe siècle 35; Solente, S. (1964). 'Christine de Pisan', *Dictionnaire des lettres française*, Le Moyen Age, pp. 183–7.

CINO DA PISTOIA: *see* CYNUS

COLLECTIO ANSELMO DEDICATA
Canonical collection addressed to archbishop Anselm II of Milan (882–96).
TEXTS: partial edn in Besse 1959.

COLLECTIO IN LXXIV TITULOS DIGESTA
Diversorum patrum sententiae. The earliest canonical collection of the eleventh-century papal reform movement, dated variously between 1050 and 1075; attributed by Michel 1943 to Humbert of Silva Candida (q.v.).
TEXTS: *see* Bibliography, part IV.

COLONNA, EGIDIO: *see* GILES OF ROME

CONRAD OF GELNHAUSEN: *see* GELNHAUSEN, CONRAD OF

CONSTANTINE PORPHYROGENITUS
905–59. Byzantine emperor from 912 as Constantine VII. Historian, scholar, antiquarian and patron of arts and letters. Author or compiler of three major works.

TEXTS: *see* Bibliography, part II.
SECONDARY LITERATURE: Toynbee 1973.

COSMAS INDICOPLEUSTES
fl. mid-sixth century. Byzantine traveller, geographer and theologian. Reputed author of the anonymous *Christian Topography*.
TEXTS: ed. Wolska-Canus, W. (1968, 1970, 1973), *Cosmas Indicopleustès, Topographie Chrétienne*, 3 vols. (Sources chrétiennes, 141, 159, 197), Editions du Cerf.
SECONDARY LITERATURE: Wolska, W. (1962). *La Topographie Chrétienne de Cosmas Indicopleustès. Théologie et science au VIe siècle*, Presses Universitaires de France.

CUNEO, GUILELMUS DE: *see* GUILELMUS DE CUNEO

CUSA, NICHOLAS OF (Cues, Kues, Cusanus)
1401–64. Philosopher and theologian, from Kues near Trier. At school in Deventer with the Brethren of the Common Life, he then studied first at Heidelberg and then Padua, where he was trained in canon law. Ordained priest, he became archdeacon of Liège. At the council of Basel from 1431 to 1437 he supported the conciliarist cause, but he had changed his view by 1439, and acted as papal legate in Germany between 1440 and 1447. Cardinal in 1448 he became bishop of Brixen in 1450, acting on the pope's behalf in 1451 for the reform of monastic houses in Germany and the Low Countries.
TEXTS: *see* Bibliography, part V.
SECONDARY LITERATURE: Vansteenberghe, E. (1920). *Le Cardinal Nicolas de Cues*, Champion; Gandillac 1941, 1953, 1969, 1972, 1983; Sigmund 1963; *LTK* 7:988–91.

CYNUS DE PISTOIA (Cino)
1270–1336/7. Studied at Bologna and in France, where he was greatly influenced by Jacobus de Ravannis and, especially, Petrus de Bellapertica. He introduced from France into Italy the scholastic techniques of the early commentators and himself became a most influential jurist, with Bartolus among his pupils at Perugia. Also a major vernacular Italian poet and a friend of Dante. Originally a Ghibelline (he was Henry VII's assessor at Rome in 1310), he moved at the end of his life to a pro-papal position.
TEXTS: *see* Bibliography, part V.
SECONDARY LITERATURE: Savigny 1834–51, vol. VI; Chiappelli 1881, 1911; Maffei 1960, 1963; Bowsky 1967; Gordon 1974.

DANTE ALIGHIERI
1265–1321. Born in Florence, where he entered public life in 1295, but was driven into exile after the Black Guelfs seized power in 1301 and was never to return. Between 1310 and 1313 his political hopes were fixed upon the Emperor Henry VII; and *Monarchia*, though the precise date of its composition remains uncertain, reflects this 'imperialist' position. The *Commedia*, begun probably before 1310, was completed only shortly before Dante's death.
TEXTS: *see* Bibliography, part V.
SECONDARY LITERATURE: Passerin d'Entréves 1952; Limentani 1965; Chiavacci Leonardi 1977; Foster 1977, ch. 9; Holmes 1980a, 1980b.

DENIS THE (PSEUDO-) AREOPAGITE, ST (Dionysius Areopagita)
Various identifications of this pseudonym have been proposed, including Peter the Fuller, Patriarch of Antioch 471–88. Denis' writings include four treatises and ten letters, exploring the ways in which by knowledge of God the intelligence (both human and angelic) are deified and united. The two treatises on Hierarchy (Angelical and Ecclesiastical) moulded

Christian neo–Platonic ideas of authority, and much medieval reflection on the structure of the church militant and the correspondences between the orders of temporal and of spiritual authority was directly inspired by Denis' writings, which had been translated into Latin by the year 835.

TEXTS: *Dionysiaca* (1937). *Recueil donnant l'ensemble des traductions latines des ouvrages attribués à Denys l'Aréopage*, 2 vols., Desclée; de Brouwer; and *see* Bibliography, part III.
SECONDARY LITERATURE: Roques, R. (1954). *L'univers dionysien: structure hiérarchique du monde selon le pseudo-Denys* (Théologie 29); Congar 1961.

DESCHAMPS, EUSTACHE (Morel)

1346–1407. Served Charles V as *huissier d'armes* from c. 1372 and was *bailli* of Valois; from 1389 to 1404 royal *bailli* of Senlis. Noted chiefly for his copious and satirical poetical writings.
TEXTS: *Oeuvres complètes* (1874–1904), 11 vols., Société des anciens textes français.
SECONDARY LITERATURE: Raynaud, G. (1904). *Eustache Deschamps, sa vie, ses oeuvres, son temps: étude historique et littéraire sur la deuxième moitié du XIVe siècle*, Firmin Didot.

DEUSDEDIT

c. 1040–1100. Cardinal priest *in Eudoxia*; canonist.
TEXTS: *see* Bibliography, part IV.

DIETRICH OF NIEM: *see* NIEM, DIETRICH VON

DUNS SCOTUS, JOHANNES

c. 1265–1308. A Franciscan, he studied and taught at Oxford, Cambridge and Paris (where he was regent master in the theology faculty in 1305). He moved to Cologne in 1307.
TEXTS: *see* Bibliography, part V.
SECONDARY LITERATURE: Gandillac 1956 and 1968.

EGIDIO COLONNA: *see* GILES OF ROME

EIKE VON REPGAU (Repkau, Repgow, Reppichau)

fl. between 1180 and 1233. Author of the *Sachsenspiegel* (Mirror of the Saxons) and of the Saxon Universal Chronicle. Free vassal of count Hoyer von Falkenstein. The *Sachsenspiegel* is one of the most influential law-books of the Middle Ages: the original draft was written in Latin between 1220 and 1224 and translated into German within two or three years. Essentially concerned with German customary law, it shows traces of canonistic influence: its two parts deal with *Landrecht* and *Lehnrecht*. *Sächische Weltchronik*, compiled c. 1230–1, is less original.
TEXTS: *Werke* (1842–4, 1861). Ed. Homeyer, C.G.; *MGH Deutsche Chroniken* (1877), vol. II, ed. Waitz, G.; *Sachsenspiegel* (1937, 1956), ed. Schwerin, Cl. v., Thienne, H.
SECONDARY LITERATURE: Merzbacher 1970.

EINHARD

c. 770–840. Born in the Rhineland of a noble Frankish family; craftsman and scholar at Charlemagne's court from the 790s and an important political figure in the last part of the reign and the early years of Louis the Pious. Author, c. 806, of the epic poem *Karolus Magnus et Leo Papa*. Left the court for religious life at his own foundation of Seligenstadt (Hesse), where he wrote, in 830, *Translatio* of St Marcellinus and Peter and, about the same time, *Vita Karoli Magni*.
TEXTS: *see* Bibliography, part IV.
SECONDARY LITERATURE: Buchner, M. (1922). *Einhard's Kunstler- und Gelehrtenleben*, K.

Schroeder; Ganshof, F.L. (1951). 'Einhard', *Bibliothèque d'Humanisme et Renaissance* 13:217–30; Beumann 1962.

ENGELBERT OF ADMONT

c. 1250–1331. A Benedictine, he studied at Prague and at Padua. He was a prolific writer and a man of notably extensive and varied learning. His *De ortu et fine Romani Imperii* advocated the restoration of the empire as a defence against Anti-Christ, while the *De regimine principum* was an analysis, drawing heavily on Aristotelian concepts, of the temporal state.
TEXTS: *see* Bibliography, part V.
SECONDARY LITERATURE: Posch 1920; Fowler 1947; *LTK* 3:876–7.

ESCOBAR, ANDREAS (DE) (Andrés Diaz, Didace)

1367–1437. Portuguese Benedictine, most of whose career was spent in the papal penitentiary: his *Lumen confessorum*, a work on penance, was written in 1429. He attended the council of Constance and represented Eugenius IV in negotiations with the council of Basel. He was bishop of various sees – from 1428 until his death the titular see of Megara – and was abbot of a Benedictine house in the Oporto diocese from 1432. His *Gubernaculum conciliorum* was written in 1434–5.
TEXT: *see* Bibliography, part V.
SECONDARY LITERATURE: Walters 1901; Black 1979, ch. 5.

EUSEBIUS PAMPHILI

263–339. Bishop of Caeserea. The first and the foremost apologist of Constantine the Great and the Christian Roman Empire. Church historian, biographer, biblical commentator, orator.
TEXTS: *Triakontaeterikos* (1902). Ed. Heikel, I.A., *Eusebius Werke*, vol. 1 (Die griechischen christlichen Schriftsteller der ersten Jahrhunderts, 7), J.C. Hinrichs'sche Buchhandlung; trans. Drake, H.A. (1967). *In Praise of Constantine. A Historical Study and New Translation of Eusebius' Tricennial Orations*, University of California Press. *Vita Constantini* (1975). Ed. Winkelman, F, *Eusebius Werke*, vol. 1 (Die griechischen christlichen Schriftsteller der ersten Jahrhunderts), Akademie-Verlag.

FALSE DECRETALS: *see* PSEUDO-ISIDOREAN DECRETALS

FITZRALPH, RICHARD

c. 1300–60. Born at Dundalk, educated at Oxford, where he was fellow of Balliol before 1325 and chancellor in 1333; chancellor of Lincoln 1334; dean of Lichfield 1337; archishop of Armagh 1347. At the papal court in Avignon in 1349 (one of several sojourns there) he became involved in the negotiations with the Armenian church: hence his *Summa in Questionibus Armeniorum*. Subsequently his main controversial activity was directed against the mendicant orders on the issue of poverty: hence *De pauperie salvatoris*.
TEXTS: *see* Bibliography, part V.
SECONDARY LITERATURE: Betts 1969; Walsh 1981; Dawson 1983; Coleman 1984.

FONTAINES, GODFREY OF: *see* GODFREY OF FONTAINES

FORTESCUE, SIR JOHN

c. 1394–c. 1476. Chief justice of the king's bench under Henry VI. Adhered to the Lancastrian cause, in defence of which he wrote, until its final defeat in 1471.
TEXTS: *see* Bibliography, part V.
SECONDARY LITERATURE: Chrimes 1936; Burns 1985.

FRANÇOIS DE MEYRONNES, *see* MEYRONNES, FRANÇOIS DE

FULBERT OF CHARTRES
c. 970–1028. Born in Italy, he may have studied in Rheims under Gerbert of Aurillac. As a theologian, he made the school of Chartres famous and was the most influential teacher there until he became bishop of Chartres in 1006.
TEXTS: *see* Bibliography, part IV.
SECONDARY LITERATURE: Behrends, F. (1981). 'Fulbert de Chartres', *Dictionnaire d'Histoire et de géographie ecclésiastique*, ed. Aubert, R. Lecouzey et Ané, 19:333–6.

GAETANI, BENEDICT: *see* BONIFACE VIII

GALBERT OF BRUGES
fl. c. 1100–50. A Flemish cleric in the service of the counts of Flanders; author of a diary covering events in Flanders between the death of Count Charles the Good and the accession of Count Thierry of Alsace (1127–8).
TEXT: *see* Bibliography, part IV.

GELASIUS I
Pope from 492 to 496. Of uncertain origin, a member of the Roman clergy who had risen to a position of importance and influence under his predecessors Simplicius I and Felix III. Upheld Chalcedonian teaching during the Acacian schism and defended the authority of the Roman see against the court and see of Constantinople. Author of a christological treatise, a number of short tractates concerning the current controversies and a large number of letters on various subjects.
TEXTS: *see* Bibliography, part III.
SECONDARY LITERATURE: Caspar 1933, pp. 10–81; Ullmann 1981.

GELNHAUSEN, CONRAD OF
c. 1320–90. Canonist; lectured at Paris and Heidelberg; between 1379 and 1383 advocated a conciliar solution to the schism.
TEXTS: *see* Bibliography, part V.
SECONDARY LITERATURE: *LTK* 6:463:4.

GERARD OF CAMBRAI
Bishop of Cambrai-Arras from 1012 to 1051. Previously a pupil of Gerbert of Aurillac at Rheims and chaplain to the Emperor Henry II. In 1025 at the synod of Arras he faced the heretical followers of a certain Gandulph. He was related to Adalbero of Laon, with whom he corresponded.
TEXT: *see* Bibliography, part IV.
SECONDARY LITERATURE: Morembert 1982.

GERHOH OF REICHERSBERG
1093–1169. Studied at Moosburg, Freising and Hildesheim; 'scholasticus' at Augsburg, 1119; an Augustinian canon at Rottenbuch in 1124 and provost of the Augustinian canons at Reichersberg from 1132. A vigorous advocate of reform as well as a critic of contemporary errors in theology. His prolific controversial writings include *De investigatione Antichristi* (c. 1161) in which he defined the relationship between papal and imperial power.
TEXTS: *see* Bibliography, part IV.
SECONDARY LITERATURE: Beinert 1973; Classen 1960, 1967; Lazzarino del Grosso 1973, 1974; Methuen 1959.

GERSON, JEAN (Charlier de)
1363–1429. Theologian; born in Champagne, pupil of Pierre d'Ailly at Paris, where he himself became chancellor of the university in 1395. A conciliarist from the early 1400s, he worked strenuously for reunion and reform of the church, especially at the councils of Pisa and Constance. He wrote, besides mystical and pastoral works, a large number of ecclesiological tracts, notably *De auctoritate concilii* (1408), *De unitate Ecclesiae* (1409) *De ecclesiastica potestate* (1417).
TEXTS: *see* Bibliography, part V.
SECONDARY LITERATURE: Morrall 1960; Posthumus-Meyjes 1963; Pascoe 1973; *LTK* 5:1036–7.

GILES OF ROME (Aegidius Romanus, Egidio Colonna)
c. 1243–1316. Joined the Hermits of St Augustine when he was fourteen and was sent to Paris, where he completed his arts studies in 1266. In the theology faculty he was probably a pupil of Aquinas from 1269 to 1272. Involved in the controversy over the condemned propositions of 1277, he left Paris for Italy. It seems unlikely that he was, as is sometimes said, tutor to the Dauphin, later Philip IV (the Fair), to whom his *De regimine principum* is dedicated; but he had returned to Paris by 1285 and taught theology there, as the Augustinians' first regent master, until 1291. He was general of his order from 1292 to 1295, when he was appointed archbishop of Bourges by Boniface VIII, with whom he was closely associated: Giles' *De ecclesiastica potestate* is a strong assertion of the hierocratic position.
TEXTS: *see* Bibliography, part V.
SECONDARY LITERATURE: Scholz 1903; Bruni, G. (1936). *Le opere di Egidio Romano*, Olschki; Vinay 1939; Kuiters 1958; Ullmann 1976; Quaglioni 1978.

GIROLAMI, REMIGIO DE'
d. 1319. Dominican theologian, probably taught by Aquinas; lectured at the Dominican school in Florence and wrote *De bono communi* (1302), *De bono pacis* (1304).
TEXTS: *see* Bibliography, part V; also Minio-Paluello 1956 for extracts from *De bono communi*.
SECONDARY LITERATURE: Davis 1960; Skinner 1978, vol. I, pp. 52, 55–9.

GLANVILL, RANULF DE
d. 1190. Royal justice; justiciar to Henry II from 1180. He may have been the author of the *Tractatus de legibus et consuetudinibus Angliae*, commonly cited by his name, but the attribution is doubtful.
TEXT: *see* Bibliography, part IV.

GODFREY OF FONTAINES (Godefroid de Fontaines)
c. 1250–c. 1306/9. Arts student at Paris in the early 1270s; from 1274 at least studied theology under Henry of Ghent and Gervais of Mt St Elias. Master in the theology faculty 1285–1298/9 and again c. 1303/4.
TEXTS: *see* Bibliography, part V.
SECONDARY LITERATURE: Lagarde 1943–5; Lagarde 1956–70, vol. II; Lejeune 1958–62; Wippel, J.F. (1981). *The Metaphysical Thought of Godfrey of Fontaines: A Study in Late Thirteenth-Century Philosophy*, Catholic University of America Press.

GOTTSCHALK OF AACHEN
b. 1010/20; fl. 1071–1104. Writer of charters and letters for the Emperor Henry IV and author of sermons, treatises and sequences.
TEXTS: *see* Bibliography, part IV.
SECONDARY LITERATURE: Erdmann and Gladiss 1939.

GRATIAN OF BOLOGNA
Camaldolese monk and canonist: little is known of his life. His chief work the *Decretum* (*Concordia discordantium canonum*) was completed c. 1140 and was the culmination of attempts to shape the materials of canon law into a system and provide a basis for its study and application. It became the standard textbook of the subject in the schools.
TEXT: *see* Bibliography, part IV.
SECONDARY LITERATURE: Vetulani 1946–7; Kuttner 1948a, 1948b, 1953 (repr. 1983), 1976; Rambaud-Buhot 1953, 1957; Hubrecht 1955; Fransen 1956; Chodorow 1972; Noonan, J.T. (1979). 'Gratian Slept Here: The Changing Identity of the Father of the Systematic Study of Canon Law', *Traditio* 35:145–72.

GREGORY I (St Gregory the Great)
c. 540–604. Born of a Roman family distinguished in both civil and ecclesiastical office. Educated in Rome, where he held civic office (probably city prefect in 573). Retired into monastic life in a community he established on his own family property in Rome. Deacon of the Roman church in 578/9 and its representative (*apocrisiarius*) at Constantinople until 585/6. After a further period of monastic life and study he was elected in 590 to succeed Pelagius II as pope, at a time of acute suffering following plague and war in Italy. HIs letters concern the life of the church throughout Europe, especially Italy, and he took a deep interest in the Germanic kingdoms, including England, to which he sent a mission in 596–7 under Augustus. Author of scriptural commentaries, homilies, the *Dialogues*, and the *Rule of Pastoral Care*.
TEXTS: *see* Bibliography, part III.
SECONDARY LITERATURE: Dudden 1905; Caspar 1933, pp. 305–514; Dagens, C. (1977). *Saint Grégoire le Grand: culture et expérience chrétiennes*, Etudes Augustiniennes, Paris; Markus 1983b, chaps. x–xv.

GREGORY VII, ST (Hildebrand)
c. 1030–85. Archdeacon of the Roman church and papal legate; reforming pope 1073–85.
TEXTS: *see* Bibliography, part IV.
SECONDARY LITERATURE: Hofmann 1933; Kuttner 1947.

GROSSETESTE, ROBERT
c. 1168–1253. D. Theol. by 1214, but whether of Oxford or Paris is uncertain; probably the first chancellor of Oxford; lector to the English Franciscans c. 1232–5; bishop of Lincoln from 1235. A prolific and important writer in scriptural exegesis, pastoral theology, philosophy and the natural sciences. An uncompromising defender of the principle of papal primacy, though critical of some aspects of its exercise. A strong champion of the 'the liberty of the church' and of the rights of his see. His views on royal and ecclesiastical jurisdiction are found most typically in his *Epistolae*.
TEXTS: *see* Bibliography, part V.
SECONDARY LITERATURE: Pantin 1955; Tierney 1955b; McEvoy 1982.

GUIBERT OF NOGENT
1053–1124. Born at Clermont; monk of Flay, 1066; abbot of Nogent-sous-Coucy (diocese of Laon) from 1104. Author of *Gesta Dei per Francos* and *De vita sua*.
TEXTS: *see* Bibliography, part IV.

GUIDO DE SUZARIA
d. c. 1290. Law professor at Padua and Bologna; taught Jacobus de Arena and Guido de Baisio. Served Charles of Anjou but opposed execution of Conradin. Famous for a *quaestio*,

now lost but referred to by Cynus (ad C.1.14.4) on the obligation of *princeps* to adhere to his contracts and privileges.

TEXTS: MSS only of commentaries on *Digest* and *Code*; published tracts *De ordine causarum, De instrumento guarentigiato, Super causarum ordinatione.*
SECONDARY LITERATURE: Savigny 1850, vol. V; Nitschke 1956.

GUIDO VERNANUS: *see* VERNANI, GUIDO

GUILELMUS DE CUNEO (Guillaume de Cunh)
d. 1335. A major luminary of the law school at Toulouse. His works had a considerable influence on those of Baldus.
TEXTS: *see* Bibliography, part V.
SECONDARY LITERATURE: Fournier 1921; Meijers 1956–73, vol. III.

GUILLAUME DE PLAISIANS
d. 1313. Advocate; counsellor of Philip IV.
SECONDARY LITERATURE: Strayer 1970.

HEIMERICUS DE CAMPO: *see* VELDE, HEIMERICH VAN DE

HENRICUS DE SEGUSIO: *see* HOSTIENSIS

HENRY OF LANGENSTEIN: *see* LANGENSTEIN, HENRY OF

HENRY OF LAUSANNE
d. sometime after 1145. An itinerant preacher in France over a period of thirty years and an advocate of the idea of voluntary poverty.
SECONDARY LITERATURE: Manselli 1953; Wakefield and Evans 1969, pp. 107–17; Moore 1977, pp. 82–114.

HERBERT OF BOSHAM
c. 1120–c. 1194. Studied at Paris under Peter Lombard, c. 1150, and perhaps also at St Victor under Andrew. A biblical scholar, he edited Peter Lombard's *Gloss* on St Paul besides commenting on the *Hebraica*. Entered Henry II's service while Becket was chancellor and went to Canterbury when Becket became archbishop. His advice had considerable weight with Becket, whose life he recorded from 1162 till the archbishop's death.
TEXTS: *see* Bibliography, part IV.
SECONDARY LITERATURE: Smalley 1973, pp. 59–86.

HILDEBRAND: *see* GREGORY VII

HILDEGARD OF BINGEN
1098–1179. Became a Benedictine abbess in 1136 and established a convent at Rupertsberg near Bingen c. 1150 and another near Rüdesheim c. 1165. A visionary, who exerted considerable influence on her contemporaries and correspondents, including the Emperor Frederick Barbarossa. Her *Scivias* contains twenty-six visions, including prophecies of disaster.
TEXTS: *see* Bibliography, part IV.
SECONDARY LITERATURE: Liebeschütz 1930; Widmer 1955.

HINCMAR OF RHEIMS

c. 805/6–81. Born into a noble Frankish family, he became a monk at St Denis, probably a child oblate. Spent some years at Louis the Pious' court in the 820s, and again after 834. Became archbishop of Rheims through the patronage of Charles the Bald in 845. Learned in Roman and canon law, and a prolific author on law (*De divortio Lotharii*, 860); politics (*De ordine palatii*, 882); history (*Annals of St Bertin* from 861 to 882); and hagiography (*Vita Remigii*, c. 880). His interests ranged from pastoral care and diocesan administration to drafting legislation and composing royal consecration rites. Played a leading political role throughout the reign of Charles the Bald.

TEXTS: *see* Bibliography, part IV.
SECONDARY LITERATURE: Devisse 1975–6; Nelson 1977a; Wallace-Hadrill 1983, pp. 292–303.

HONORIUS AUGUSTODUNENSIS

c. 1080/90–c. 1156. A prolific writer of popular theological works, of whose life little is known. Influenced by St Anselm of Canterbury, he may have lived for a time in England and in south Germany. His best known work is the *Elucidarium*, a survey of Christian teaching. He also wrote on topics arising from church reform during his lifetime.

TEXTS: *see* Bibliography, part IV.
SECONDARY LITERATURE: Endres 1906; Flint 1972, 1977; Goetz 1978.

HOSTIENSIS (Henricus de Segusio)

d. 1271. Born at Susa; elected bishop of Sisteron, 1244; archbishop of Embrun, 1250; cardinal-bishop of Ostia, 1262. Taught canon law at Paris and perhaps at Bologna.

TEXTS: *Summa aurea* (1586), Venice; *In primum – quintum decretalium librum commentaria* (1581), Venice (repr. Bottega d'Erasmo, 1965); *Apparatus in Novellam Innocentii quarti* (1581), Venice; and *see* Bibliography, part V.
SECONDARY LITERATURE: Watt 1965c, 1980; Tierney 1976; Gallagher, C. (1978). *Canon Law and the Christian Community: The Role of Law in the Church According to the Summa Aurea of Cardinal Hostiensis*, Università Gregoriana Editrice; Pennington 1984.

HRABANUS MAURUS: *see* RABANUS MAURUS

HUGH OF ST VICTOR

c. 1098–1142. The most important of a celebrated group of theologians in the Augustinian abbey of St Victor in the twelfth century. Perhaps from the Low Countries, he entered St Victor c. 1115 and taught there for most of his life. Of his numerous and wide-ranging works the most important is *De sacramentis christianae fidei*, a synthesis of Christian theology showing an appreciation of historical development.

TEXTS: *see* Bibliography, part IV.
SECONDARY LITERATURE: Baron 1957, 1963; Eynde 1960.

HUGUCCIO (Uguccione)

fl. 1180–1210. Taught canon law at Bologna; Bishop of Ferrara 1191.

TEXTS: *Summa decretorum* (1180–91): Admont, Stiftsbibl. 7 and Vatican City, Bibliotheca Apostolica Vaticana lat. 2280 (other MSS listed *Traditio* 11, 1955, 441–4); *Liber derivationum* (1198–1205?): MSS listed by Marigo, A. (1936), *I codici manoscritti delle 'Derivationes' di Uguccione Pisano*, Istituto di Studi Romani; *De dubio accentu, Agiographia, Expositio de symbolo apostolorum*, ed. Cremascoli, G. (1978), Biblioteca degli studi Medievali, 10, Centro Italiano di Studi sull'Alto Medioevo.
SECONDARY LITERATURE: Stickler 1947; Corrado, L. (1956). 'La vita e l'opera di Uguccione da

Pisa, decretista', *Studia Gratiana* 4:39–120; Catalano 1959; Ríos Fernández, M. (1961–6). 'El primado del romano pontifice en el pensamiento de Huguccio de Pisa decretista', *Compostellanum* 6:47–97; Lenherr, T. (1981), 'Der Begriff "executio" in der Summa Decretorum des Huguccio', *Archiv für katholisches Kirchenrecht* 150:5–44, 392–420.

HUMBERT OF SILVA CANDIDA
1000–61. A monk of the Lotharingian monastery of Moyenmoutier, he became cardinal of Silva Candida in 1050 and acted as legate and counsellor of the reforming popes. His *Adversus Simoniacos* is one of the principal denunciations of the simony the Roman reformers sought to eradicate. He was also in charge of the mission to Constantinople in 1054 which led to the schism between the eastern and western churches.
TEXTS: *see* Bibliography, part IV.
SECONDARY LITERATURE: Michel 1924–30, 1943, 1947, 1953; Gilchrist 1962–3.

IBN BAJJA (Avempace)
d. 1138. An Arab philosopher who lived in Spain. His works became known in the west chiefly through Averroes.
TEXT: *see* Bibliography, part IV.
SECONDARY LITERATURE: Dunlop 1945; Rosenthal 1951; Dunlop, D.M. (1971). 'Ibn Badjdja', in *Encyclopaedia of Islam*, new edn, Brill, 3:728–9.

IBN RUSHD: *see* AVERROES

IBN SINA (Avicenna)
980–1037. Arab philosopher and physician, who devoted his whole life to writing poetic, scientific and philosophical works which drew upon a wide range of Aristotelian and neoplatonist sources. Several of these works became known in the west in Hebrew and in Latin from the twelfth century onwards and constituted one of the most important channels through which the pervasive influence of Aristotle affected medieval scholastic thought.
TEXTS: *see* Bibliography, part IV.
SECONDARY LITERATURE: Alverny 1957, 1982; Corbin 1960; Goichon 1951, 1959.

IBN ṬUFAIL (Abubacer)
Arab philosopher and physician, born in Spain in the early twelfth century. Served the Almohad rulers and was acquainted with Ibn Rushd, who succeeded him as court physician. Died at Marrakush in 1185.
TEXT: *see* Bibliography, part IV.
SECONDARY LITERATURE: Gauthier 1909, 1936.

INNOCENT III (Lotario dei Conti di Segni)
c. 1160–1216. Studied theology at Paris and law at Bologna. Elected pope in 1198.
TEXTS: *see* Bibliography, part V.
SECONDARY LITERATURE: Cheney 1976; Laufs, M. (1980). *Politik und Recht bei Innocenz III*, Böhlau; Imkamp, W. (1983). *Das Kirchenbild Innocenz' III*, Hiersemann; Pennington 1984.

INNOCENT IV (Sinibaldo Fieschi)
c. 1200–54. Taught canon law at Bologna; lawyer at the papal curia from 1226; cardinal 1227; pope 1243–54. His pontificate was notable politically for his contest with Frederick II, deposed at the first Council of Lyons in 1245, and for his successful campaign to prevent further Hohenstaufen reigns. His celebrated *Apparatus in V Libros Decretalium* was completed

shortly after 1245. He wrote commentaries, as a private doctor, on legislation he had promulgated as pope, including an authoritative commentary on the Lyons deposition decree.

TEXTS: *see* Bibliography, part V.

SECONDARY LITERATURE: Puttkamer, G. von (1930). *Papst Innocenz IV* (Universitas-Archiv, 30), Helios Verlag; Pacaut 1960; Cantini 1961; Black 1984.

INNOCENT V (Pierre de Tarentaise)

c. 1224–76. Dominican theologian who taught in Paris 1259–64 and 1267–9; archbishop of Lyons 1272; cardinal 1273; elected pope on 21 January 1276 but died on the following day.

TEXT: *In quattuor libros Sententarium commentaria* (1649–52), Toulouse (reprinted Gregg, 1964).

SECONDARY LITERATURE: Laurent, M.H. (1947). *Le bienheureux Innocent V. Pierre de Tarentaise et son temps* (Studi e Testi 129), Vatican City.

IRNERIUS OF BOLOGNA

d. 1130. The chief contributor to the revival of the study of Roman law at Bologna. He also wrote theological sentences and was a supporter of the imperialist party during the papal schisms of 1118.

TEXTS: *see* Bibliography, part IV.

SECONDARY LITERATURE: Fitting 1888; Grabmann 1909–11, vol. II, pp. 131–5; Kantorowicz 1938; Calasso 1954; Spagnesi 1970.

ISERNIA, ANDREAS DE: *see* ANDREAS DE ISERNIA

ISIDORE OF SEVILLE, ST

c. 560–636. Family probably of Greek origin. Educated by his brother Leander, whom he succeeded as metropolitan bishop of Seville c. 600. Presided at the second Council of Seville (619) and the fourth Council of Toledo (633) – the first provincial, the second plenary, but both of great importance. Close to three Visigothic kings between 612 and 636, especially Sisebut (612–21), a learned man, who commissioned Isidore's *Etymologiae* and to whom the *De Natura Rerum* was dedicated. Often called the 'Schoolmaster of the Middle Ages', principally because the *Etymologiae* was so widely read. Formally canonised in 1598 and declared Doctor of the Church in 1722.

TEXTS: *see* Bibliography, part III.

SECONDARY LITERATURE: Romero, J.L. (1947). 'San Isidoro de Sevilla. Su Pensamiento Históricopolítico y sus Relaciones con la Historia Visigoda', Cuadernos de Historia de Espana 8:5–71; Ewig 1956a, pp. 30–4; Fontaine, J. (1959). *Isidore de Séville et la Culture Classique dans L'Espagne Wisigothique*, Etudes Augustiniennes; Borst, A. (1966). 'Das Bild der Geschichte in der Enzyklopädie Isidors von Seville', *Deutsches Archiv für Erforschung des Mittelalters* 22:1–62 Anton 1968, pp. 55–60; Ullmann 1970 (*see* Bibliography, part IV), pp. 28–31; Löwe 1973, pp. 40–6; Diesner 1978; Reydellet 1981, pp. 505–97; Teillet 1984, pp. 463–501.

ISIDORUS MERCATOR: *see* PSEUDO-ISIDOREAN DECRETALS

IVO OF CHARTRES, ST

c. 1040–1115. The leading theologian-canonist at the beginning of the twelfth century; bishop of Chartres from 1090. His opposition to the adulterous plans of Philip I of France led to his imprisonment in 1092. In the investiture struggle he successfully distinguished the issues in dispute. His treatises, including the *Decretum* (1095) and the *Panormia*, in which he evolved principles for the study of canon law, were of great importance until the time of Gratian of Bologna.

TEXTS: *see* Bibliography, part IV.
SECONDARY LITERATURE: Fournier and Le Bras 1931–2, vol. II, pp. 55–114; Sprandel 1962; Jacqueline 1965.

JACOBUS BUTRIGARIUS: *see* BUTRIGARIUS, JACOBUS

JACOBUS DE RAVANNIS: *see* RAVANNIS, JACOBUS DE

JAMES OF VITERBO (Jacopo Cappucci)
c. 1260–1307/8. Studied in Paris from at least 1281 and taught in the theology faculty there. He dedicated his *De regimine christiano* to Boniface VIII in 1301–2. Archbishop of Benevento 1302, later of Naples.
TEXT: *see* Bibliography, part V.
SECONDARY LITERATURE: Arquillière, H.-X. (1926). *Le plus ancien traité de l'Eglise. Jacques de Viterbe, De regimine christiano (1301–1302). Etude des sources et édition critique*, Gabriel Beauchesne.

JEAN DE MEUNG (Jean Clopinel or Chopinel)
fl. 1250–82. Born at Meung sur Loire; clerk of the arts faculty in the University of Paris, where he had a house in the Rue St Jacques. Author of a lengthy continuation of the *Roman de la Rose*, written between 1225 and 1240 by Guillaume de Lorris. Jean's poem was enormously popular and survives in numerous MSS: it was one of the first works to be printed in France.
TEXT: ed. Langlois, E. (1914–24), 5 vols., Société des Anciens Textes Francais.
SECONDARY LITERATURE: Paré 1941; Paré, G. (1947). *Les idées et les lettres au XIIIe siècle*, Université de Montréal.

JEAN PETIT
d. 1411. Doctor of theology and master of the university of Paris; counsellor of John the Fearless of Burgundy, who instigated the assassination of his rival, the duke of Orleans, on 23 November 1407. Jean defended this as justifiable tyrannicide; but this position, initially censured by the archbishop of Paris as well as by the university, was eventually condemned formally by the Council of Constance in 1415, the initiative in the process being taken by Jean Gerson.
SECONDARY LITERATURE: Coville 1974.

JEAN QUIDORT: *see* JOHN OF PARIS

JEAN DE TERRE ROUGE (de Terrevermeille; Johannes de Terra Rubea)
fl. at the turn of the fourteenth and fifteenth centuries. Doctor of law and *avocat* of the *senechaussé* of Beaucaire. His *Contra rebelles suorum regum* was written in 1419.
TEXT: *see* Bibliography, part V.
SECONDARY LITERATURE: Giesey 1961; Barbey 1983.

JEAN JUVENAL DES URSINS
1388–1473. Bishop of Beauvais 1432; bishop of Laon 1444; archbishop of Rheims 1449.
TEXTS: *see* Bibliography, part V.
SECONDARY LITERATURE: Lewis 1965, 1968.

JOACHIM OF FIORE

1145–1202. Mystical and prophetic writer from Calabria. After a period as abbot of the Cistercian monastery at Curazzo, he received papal permission to found a stricter order at San Giovanni dei Fiore. He applied minute scriptural study to the interpretation of history, in which he identified three ages corresponding to the Father, the Son and the Holy Spirit. He prophesied the coming of the third age in the year 1260. His ideas were widely influential, especially among the Spiritual Franciscans and Fraticelli, but became closely associated with revolutionary and heretical views.

TEXTS: *see* Bibliography, part IV.

SECONDARY LITERATURE: Reeves 1969, 1976; Reeves and Hirsch-Reich 1972.

JOHANNES ANDREAE

c. 1270–1348. Celebrated jurist known as *fons et tuba iuris.* A layman, from a poor and humble background, he studied under Guido de Baysio among others at Bologna, where he subsequently taught both canon and civil law, though it was as a canonist that he was chiefly notable. He was a friend of Cynus de Pistoia and of Petrarch.

TEXTS: *see* Bibliography, part V.

SECONDARY LITERATURE: Savigny 1834–51, vol. VI, pp. 98–125: *Dictionnaire de droit canonique,* vol. VI, pp. 89–92.

JOHANNES BASSIANUS: *see* BASSIANUS, JOHANNES

JOHANNES MONACHUS: *see* LEMOINE, JEAN

JOHANNES DE SEGOVIA: *see* SEGOVIA, JUAN DE

JOHANNES TEUTONICUS

fl. 1210–45. Taught canon law at Bologna; *scholasticus* (1220), dean (1235), and provost (1241) in Halberstadt.

TEXTS: Ordinary Gloss to Gratian's *Decretum* (as revised by Bartholomaeus Brixiensis) (1582), Rome, and many other edns; *Apparatus* to *Compilatio tertia* (1981), ed. Pennington, K. (*see* Bibliography, part V); *Apparatus* to Fourth Lateran Constitutions (1981), ed. García y García, A., Biblioteca Apostolica Vaticana; *Apparatus* to *Compilatio quarta* (1576; reprinted in Agostín's *Opera omnia,* Lucca (1769)); gloss to *Arbor Consanguinitatis et Affinitatis* (1982), ed. García y García, A., *Zeitschrift der Savigny-Stiftung für Rechtsgeschichte* Kan. Abt. 68:153–85; *Quaestiones* (partial edn) (1983), ed. Fransen, G., *Bulletin of Medieval Canon Law* 13:39–47; *Consilium* (1970), ed. Pennington, K., *Traditio* 26:435–40.

SECONDARY LITERATURE: Kuttner, S. (1946). 'Johannes Teutonicus, das vierte Laterankonzil, und die Compilatio quarta', *Miscellena Giovanni Mercati* (Studi e Testi 125), Biblioteca Apostolica Vaticana; Kurtner, S. (1974). 'Johannes Teutonicus', *Neue Deutsche Biographie* 10:571–3; Stelzer, W. (1982). 'Johannes Teutonicus', *Die deutsche Literatur des Mittelalters: Verfasserlexikon* 4:777–83; Pennington, K. (1983). 'Johannes Teutonicus and Papal Legates', *Archivum Historiae Pontificiae* 21:183–94.

JOHANNES DE TURRECREMATA: *see* TORQUEMADA, JUAN DE

JOHN VIII

Pope from 872 to 882. One of the few early popes of whose register parts have survived.

TEXT: *Epistolae* in *MGH Epp.* 7:1–272.

SECONDARY LITERATURE: Lohrmann, D. (1968). *Das Register Papst Johannes VIII,* Max Niemeyer Verlag.

JOHN OF DAMASCUS, ST
c. 675–754. Byzantine theologian and monk of the monastery of St Saba in Palestine. Principal apologist for the veneration of icons during the iconoclast regime. Author of the *Fountain of Knowledge*, a very influential dogmatic work, as well as of treatises against the iconoclasts.
TEXTS: *PG* 94–6.
SECONDARY LITERATURE: Beck 1959, pp. 300ff, 476–7.

JOHN OF MANTUA
fl. 1081/3. Grammarian and theologian.
TEXT: *see* Bibliography, part IV.

JOHN OF PARIS (Jean Quidort)
c. 1240–1306. Dominican theologian, who taught, after studying, in Paris, where he became one of the outstanding teachers of his generation. He wrote extensively, dealing with natural philosophy and metaphysics as well as theology and politics, and defending the Thomist position against the attacks to which it was subjected in the decades after Aquinas' death. His first major work, the *Commentary on the Sentences* dates from the mid-1280s. Fifteen years or so later he wrote *De potestate regia et papali* as a contribution to the dispute between Philip the Fair and Boniface VIII and supported the petition of the French clergy seeking the arraignment of Boniface before a general council.
TEXTS: *see* Bibliography, part V.
SECONDARY LITERATURE: Leclercq 1942; Watt 1965a; Coleman 1983b, 1985.

JOHN OF SALISBURY
c. 1115/20–80. Born at Salisbury, studied at Paris from 1136 and entered the service of archbishop Theobald of Canterbury in 1148. Later he also served the papacy and, after Theobald's death in 1161, served under the new archbishop, Thomas Becket, whom he championed in exile during the dispute with Henry II. Bishop of Chartres from 1176. His writings include a defence of the liberal arts (*Metalogicon*, completed 1159); the *Policraticus* (1159) dealing with statesmanship and court life; a memoir of his time in the papal service (*Historia pontificalis*); and many letters.
TEXTS: *see* Bibliography, part IV.
SECONDARY LITERATURE: Liebeschütz 1950, 1968; Rota 1953/4; Elrington 1954; Momigliano 1955; Desideri 1958; Massey 1967; Rouse 1967; Martin 1968, 1969; Eberenz 1969; Sheerin 1969; Miczka 1970; Ullmann 1975, 1978; Kerner 1976, 1977, 1979; Garfagnini 1977; Laarhoven 1977a, 1977b; Linder 1977a, 1977b; Turk 1977; Guth 1978; Struve 1978; Wilks 1984.

JONAS OF ORLEANS
c. 780–842/3. Bishop of Orleans from 818. His ideas on the place of the laity in the church and on the ecclesiastical hierarchy, expressed in the tracts *De institutione laicali* and *De institutione regia*, were influential at the important Council of Paris in 829.
TEXTS: *see* Bibliography, part IV.
SECONDARY LITERATURE: Delaruelle 1955; Anton 1968, 212ff, 373–5.

JUSTINIAN I
482–565. Byzantine emperor from 527. Under his authority Roman law was codified in the form in which it was studied and applied in the west from its recovery in the twelfth century onward.
TEXTS: *Novellae* in the Berlin edn of the *Corpus juris civilis* (1912).

SECONDARY LITERATURE: Bury, J.B. (1923). *A History of the Later Roman Empire from the Death of Theodosius to the Death of Justinian*, vol. II, St Martin's Press; Browning, R. (1971). *Justinian and Theodora*, Weidenfeld and Nicolson.

LAMPERT OF HERSFELD

c. 1025–c. 1085. Monk of Hersfeld (Hesse). His support for Cluniac monastic reform and opposition to Henry IV led to his expulsion by his fellow-monks. His political bias and the influence of Sallust are both reflected in his world history, the *Annales* written c. 1077–9.
TEXTS: *see* Bibliography, part IV.

LANGENSTEIN, HENRY OF

1325–97. Eminent German theologian, who taught at Paris and Vienna. From 1378 to 1383 he advocated a conciliar solution to the schism.
TEXT: *see* Bibliography, part V.
SECONDARY LITERATURE: Ullmann 1948a, 176ff; *LTK* 5:190–1.

LATINI, BRUNETTO

1220–c. 1294. Notary and chancellor to the commune of Florence, where he was a notable public and literary figure until 1260 and after 1266. He spent the intervening years in exile in France, where he wrote his principal works, the allegorical *Tesoretto* and the encyclopaedic *Li livres dou Tresor*.
TEXT: *see* Bibliography, part V.
SECONDARY LITERATURE: Conini, G. (1960). *Poeti del Duecento*, vol. II, pp. 169–284, Milan.

LAURENTIUS HISPANUS

fl. 1200–48. Taught canon law at Bologna; bishop of Orense from 1218.
TEXTS: glosses to Gratian's *Decretum* in the *Apparatus* to *Glossa Palatina* (1210–15), Vatican City, Biblioteca Apostolica Vaticana, Palatina lat. 658 and Salzberg, St Peter's Archabbey, a.xii.9; *Apparatus* to *Compilatio tertia* (1210–16), Admont, Stiftsbibl. 55 and Karlruhe, Landesbibl. Aug. XL.
SECONDARY LITERATURE: García y García, A. (1956). *Laurentius Hispanus: Datos biográficos y estudio crítico de sus obras*, Consejo Superior de Investigaciones Científicas; Nörr, K.W. (1961). 'Der Apparat des Laurentius zur Compilatio tertia', *Traditio* 17:542–3; Stickler, A.M. (1966). 'Il decretista Laurentius Hispanus', *Studia Gratiana* 9:461–549.

LEMOINE, JEAN (Johannes Monachus)

c. 1250–1313. Trained as a canonist at Paris and began his career as a jurist in the papal curia; promoted cardinal by Celestine V in 1294. He founded a college bearing his name in Paris. Boniface VIII employed him as his emissary during the controversy with Philip IV. He wrote an important commentary on the *Liber Sextus Decretalium* and numerous glosses on the *Extravagantes* of Boniface VIII and Benedict XI: among these the extended commentary on *Unam sanctam* is outstanding.
TEXTS: *see* Bibliography, Part v.
SECONDARY LITERATURE: van Hove 1945; Ullmann 1948a, pp. 204–8; Tierney 1955a.

LUCAS DE PENNA (Luca da Penne)

d. c. 1390. Born at Penne in the Abruzzo, he became doctor of law at Naples in 1345 and was a practitioner as well as a private teacher of the subject. In his commentary on the Code he drew on an extensive range of learning besides displaying considerable independence of judgement on political issues.
TEXT: *see* Bibliography, part V.
SECONDARY LITERATURE: Ullmann 1946a.

LUPOLD OF BEBENBURG

c. 1297–1363. Studied at Bologna between 1314 and 1322. At various dates he was provost of Erfurt and of Bingen, and canon of Würzburg, Mainz and (1339) Bamberg, where he became bishop in 1353. In his *Tractatus de juribus regni et imperii*, which dates from 1340, he defended the authority of the emperor with specific reference to Germany and with extensive use of historical precedents.

TEXT: *see* Bibliography, part V.

SECONDARY LITERATURE: Most 1941; *LTK* 6:1218.

MAIMONIDES, MOSES

1135–1204. Jewish philosopher born in Cordova. During the anti-Jewish persecution of 1149 he fled to Morocco, then to Palestine and finally to Egypt. Some of his works are in Hebrew, including his commentary on the *Mishnah* (1168) and his Mishneh Torah (c. 1180), a Talmudic code. His other works are in Arabic, including his most important treatise, the *Guide of the Perplexed* (119). He ought to harmonise reason and faith by reconciling Jewish revelation with the philosophy of Aristotle; and his work had great influence on western scholastic thinkers from the thirteenth century onwards.

TEXTS: *see* Bibliography, part IV.

SECONDARY LITERATURE: Rosenblatt 1927; Strauss 1935, 1936, 1953; Silver 1965; Rosenthal 1971; Lerner 1972; Wolfson 1973a, 1973b; Twersky 1980.

MAKREMBOLITES, ALEXIUS

fl. mid-fourteenth century. Byzantine author and theorist.

TEXTS: ed. Ševčenko, I. (1960). 'Alexios Makrembolites and his "Dialogue between the Rich and the Poor"', *Zbornik Radova Vizatološkog Institut*, Belgrade, 6:187–228.

MANEGOLD OF LAUTENBACH

b. c. 1045. Entered the monastery of Lautenbach after 1080 and remained there until its destruction by the supporters of Henry IV. From at least 1094 he was Provost of the Augustinian abbey of Marbach in Alsace. He died between 1103 and 1119. Manegold's *Liber contra Wolfelmum* and *Liber ad Gebehardum* were written at about the time of the death of Gregory VII in 1085. Like others at the time Manegold denounced the study of pagan philosophy, especially that of Macrobius; but he also accused students of such ideas as being opponents of the pope and supporters of the emperor. The last two chapters of the *Liber contra Wolfelmum* are concerned with the investiture conflict, while the *Liber ad Gebehardum* attacks the imperialists and Henry IV.

TEXTS: *see* Bibliography, part IV.

SECONDARY LITERATURE: Hartmann 1970; Fuhrmann 1975.

MARINUS DA CARAMANICO

d. 1288. Major jurist of the school of Naples.

TEXT: *Glossa ordinaria* to the *Constitutiones regni Siciliae* of Frederick II (composed by 1282), Naples, 1773 (Proem ed. in Calasso 1957, pp. 179ff).

SECONDARY LITERATURE: Calasso 1930; Nuzzo 1940.

MARSH, ADAM

d. 1258? Studied theology under Grosseteste at Oxford and remained his lifelong friend and correspondent, sharing his intellectual interests though not matching his scholarly output. He became a Franciscan in 1232–3. Prominent in public life, notably as friend and counsellor of Simon de Montfort. His most notable 'political treatise' is perhaps the address to the pope drafted at the request of Boniface of Savoy for use when Henry III took the cross in 1250.

TEXT: *see* Bibliography, part V.

SECONDARY LITERATURE: Knowles 1948.

MARSILIUS OF PADUA (Menandrinus; Marsilio/Marsiglio dei Mainardini)
1275/80–1342/3. Born and educated in Padua, where he trained as a physician; but he had migrated to Paris by 1312–13, when he was rector of the university there. Returning to Italy and practising medicine, he served at various times Matteo Visconti in Milan and Can Grande della Scala in Verona. He had returned to Paris by 1319 and spent the next six or seven years there, probably teaching in the arts faculty and writing his most important work, the *Defensor pacis*, which was completed in 1324. When its authorship became known, Marsilius sought the protection of Lewis the Bavarian, at whose Munich court he had arrived by 1326, together with John of Jandun, whose close associate he had been in Paris and who has sometimes been seen as part-author of the *Defensor*. The book was condemned as heritical by John XXII in 1327. During Lewis' Italian expedition of 1327–30 Marsilius accompanied the would-be emperor and played a prominent part in the short-lived regime established by Lewis in Rome itself. He spent the rest of his life at the Bavarian court, where he wrote his later works, the *Defensor minor* and the *De iurisdictione imperatoris in causis matrimonialibus*.
TEXTS: *see* Bibliography, part V.
SECONDARY LITERATURE: Gewirth 1951 and 1956; Lagarde 1956–70, vol. III; Quillet 1964, 1970a, 1970b, 1979, 1980; Wilks 1972a.

METOCHITES, THEODORE
d. 1332. Grand Logothete and friend of the Byzantine Emperor Andronicus II. Philosopher, rhetorician, essayist, letter-writer, astronomer, commentator on Aristotle and patron of the arts.
TEXTS (essays): Eds. Müller, C.G. and Kiessling, T. (1821). *Theodori Metochitae Miscellanea philosophica et historica*, Munich; (poems) ed. Teru, M. (1890). *Dichtungen des Grosslogotheten Theodoros Metochites*, Potsdam Gymnasium Programm; also Guilland 1959, pp. 177–205.
SECONDARY LITERATURE: Beck, H.-G. (1952). *Theodoros Metochites. Die Krise des byzantinischen Weltbildes im 14. Jahrhundert*, Munich; Ševčenko, I. (1975). 'Theodore Metochites, the Chora and the Intellectual Trends of His Time', in ed. Underwood, P.A., *The Kariye Djami* vol. IV *Studies in the Art of the Kariye Djami and Its Intellectual Background*, Routledge and Kegan Paul; Princeton University Press.

MEYRONNES, FRANÇOIS DE (Francis of Mayron)
d. c. 1328. A Franciscan philosopher and theologian, who had studied at Paris, where he gained his *licencia docendi* in 1323. His political doctrine, which may be contrasted with that of Dante, was expressed in his *Quaestio de subjectione*, *De principatu regni Siciliae* – he supported the Sicilian claim of Robert the Wise, king of Naples (1309–43) – *De principatu temporali*, and *Quaestio de obedientia*.
TEXTS: *see* Bibliography, part V.
SECONDARY LITERATURE: Langlois 1927; Roth 1936.

MÉZIÈRES, PHILIPPE DE
1327–1405. Chancellor of the kingdom of Cyprus 1358–9; counsellor of Charles V of France; author of several works, of which the most important is *Le Songe du Vieil Pélerin*.
TEXTS: *see* Bibliography, part V.
SECONDARY LITERATURE: Jorga, N. (1896). *Philippe de Mézières, 1327–1405, et la croisade au XIVe siècle*, Bibliothèque de l'Ecole des Hautes Etudes; Bell, D.M. (1955). *Etude sur le 'Songe du Vieil Pèlerin de Philippe de Mézières (1327–1405)*, Geneva; Quillet 1981.

MODOIN OF AUTUN
fl. first half of ninth century. Poet, bishop of Autun from 815, last mentioned in 840. A member of Charlemagne's 'academy', where he called himself Naso. He glorified the emperor as a prince of peace in poems imitating Virgil.

TEXT: *Nasonis Muaduvini Ecloga, MGH Poetae* 1:382–93 (1881).
SECONDARY LITERATURE: Godman 1985.

MOSES MAIMONIDES: *see* MAIMONIDES

NICHOLAS I
Pope 858–67.
TEXTS: *MGH Epp.* 6:257ff.

NICHOLAS OF CUSA: *see* CUSA, NICHOLAS OF

NICOLE ORESME: *see* ORESME, NICOLE

NIEM, DEITRICH VON (Theodoricus; Dietrich von Nieheim)
c. 1340–1418. Curial official and conciliar publicist; a strong critic of the Roman curia and
supporter of the imperial role in the church. He wrote a number of works, including *Nemis
unionis* (1408) and *De modis uniendi ac reformandi ecclesiam in concilio generali* (1410).
TEXTS: *see* Bibliography, part V.
SECONDARY LITERATURE: Heimpel 1932; Cameron 1952; Sigmund 1962; *LTK* 3:386.

NITHARD
d. 844. Son of Charlemagne's daughter Bertha and her lover Angilbert (a scholar and abbot
of St Riquier), b. shortly before 800. Remained a layman, but highly educated in both
scripture and classical texts. Sided with Charles the Bald when conflict broke out in 840
among the sons of Louis the Pious. Commissioned in 841 to write the *Histories*, justifying
Charles' cause, he retired to St Riquier, where he completed the work early in 843. He was
killed in battle in the following year.
TEXT: *see* Bibliography, part IV.
SECONDARY LITERATURE: Wehlen 1970; Nelson 1985.

NORMAN ANONYMOUS
fl. c. 1100. Also known as the author of the York tracts (*Tractatus Eboracenses*). This was the
title given by H. Böhmer to the thirty-one tracts in Cambridge, Corpus Christi College MS
415, of which he edited six in *MGH Libelli de Lite* 3:642–87. Böhmer wrongly attributed
these tracts to archbishop Gerard of York.
TEXT: *see* Bibliography, part IV.
SECONDARY LITERATURE: Funk 1935; Lapparent 1946; Williams 1951; Nineham 1963; Pellens
1965.

OBERTUS DE ORTO (Oberto dell'Orto)
fl. 133–58. Milanese jurist, consul of his city and imperial judge under the Emperor Lothair
(1133–7). He expounded feudal law on the basis of his experience in the Milanese court. In
the form of two letters to his son, a student at Bologna, he wrote, c. 1154–8, the first
systematic survey of Lombard feudal customs – the modes of acquisition of fiefs, the forms
and effects of homage and the rules of inheritance. His work was the first nucleus of the *Libri
Feudorum* and was preserved in successive redactions.
TEXT: printed as an appendix in early editions of the *Corpus Iuris Civilis*.
SECONDARY LITERATURE: Lehmann, K. (1896). *Das langobardische Lehensrecht*, Dietrich.

OCKHAM, WILLIAM (OF) (Occam)
c. 1280/5–1349. Franciscan theologian and philosopher, probably born at Ockham in
Surrey. He taught at Oxford, lecturing c. 1317–19 on the *Sentences*. In 1323 fifty-six extracts

from his writings were submitted for censure to the pope at Avignon, where Ockham was summoned while the case was considered. Though not formally condemned, he defected to the court of Lewis the Bavarian together with Michael of Cesena, the Minister General of the Franciscans, whose ally Ockham had become in the controversy with John XXII over the issue of apostolic poverty. He spent the remainder of his life as a vehemently anti-papal publicist and polemicist. His work as a theologian and logician made him one of the most influential writers of the later Middle Ages, as the presiding genius of the 'nominalists'. He died, after seeking reconciliation to the church, probably a victim of the Black Death.
TEXTS: *see* Bibliography, part V.
SECONDARY LITERATURE: Hofer, J. (1913). 'Biographische Studien über Wilhelm von Ockham, O.F.M.', *Archivum Franciscanum Historicum* 6:209–33, 439–65, 654–65; Lagarde 1937, 1956–70 (vols. IV–VI), 1960; Hamman 1942, 1950; Boehmer 1943; Scholz 1944; Baudry 1949, 1958; Bayley 1949; Gandillac 1956, pp. 417–73; Tierney 1954; Vasoli 1954, Grignaschi 1957, 1970; Brampton 1960, 1966; Oakley 1961; Villey 1964; Miethke 1969; McGrade 1974.

OLDRADUS DA PONTE
d. 1335. Professor of law at Padua (perhaps also at Siena and Bologna). A canonist as well as a civilian, he entered the papal service at Avignon.
TEXTS: *see* Bibliography, part V.
SECONDARY LITERATURE: Will 1917: Meijers 1956–73, vol. IV, pp. 190–6.

OLIVI, PETER JOHN
1248–98. Theologian and philosopher; deeply involved, as a leader of the Spiritual Franciscans, in the poverty controversy.
TEXTS: *see* Bibliography, part V.
SECONDARY LITERATURE: Partee 1960; Burr 1975, 1976.

ORESME, NICOLE
d. 1382. Born in Normandy; theology student at Paris 1348 (college of Navarre). Dean of Notre Dame, Rouen 1364; bishop of Lisieux 1377. Close friend and adviser of Charles V (1364–80). Oresme wrote on a wide range of subjects, in Franch as well as Latin, and translated into French a number of Aristotelian and other texts.
TEXTS: *see* Bibliography, part V.
SECONDARY LITERATURE: Quillet 1984; Babbitt 1985.

OTTO OF FREISING
c. 1114/15–58. Son of the margrave of Austria, uncle of Frederick Barbarossa. Studied in Paris, then became a Cistercian at Morimond c. 1132. Abbot of Morimond c. 1136; bishop of Freising from 1138. Wrote *Chronica sive Historia de duabus civitatibus* 1143–6 and *Gesta Friderici* 1156–8.
TEXTS: *see* Bibliography, part IV.
SECONDARY LITERATURE: Hofmeister 1911–12; Brezzi 1939; Koch 1953; Folz 1958; *Otto von Freising* 1958; Lammers 1961, 1977; Goetz 1984.

PANORMITANUS (Nicholas de Tudeschis)
1386–1445. The most important canonist of his time. Born at Catania, he studied at Bologna and Padua (under Franciscus Zabarella). Taught at Bologna, Parma, Siena and Florence. Took part in the papal delegation to the Council of Basel in 1431. Archbishop of Palermo (whence the designation Panormitanus) 1435. Ambassador to Basel of Alfonso V of Aragon (I of Sicily; 1416–58). Became a consiliarist.
TEXTS: *see* Bibliography, part V.
SECONDARY LITERATURE: *Dictionnaire de droit canonique*; Nörr 1964; Black 1979, pp. 92–105.

PENNA, LUCAS DE: *see* LUCAS DE PENNA

PETER ABELARD: *see* ABELARD, PETER

PETER OF AUVERGNE (Pierre Crocq)
d. 1304. Disciple of Thomas Aquinas, several of whose works he completed. Rector of the University of Paris 1275, Master of Theology by 1296 when he became a canon of Notre Dame, Paris; bishop of Clermont 1302.
TEXTS: *see* Bibliography, part V.
SECONDARY LITERATURE: Hocedez, E. (1933). 'La vie et les oeuvres de Pierre d'Auvergne', *Gregorianum* 14:3–36; Grech, G.M. (1964). 'Recent bibliography on Peter of Auvergne', *Angelicum* 41:446–9.

PETER THE CHANTER
d. 1197. Teacher of theology in Paris from at least 1173 and precentor of Notre Dame there from 1183; dean of Rheims 1197. His teaching concentrated especially on pastoral and sacramental issues and on moral reform.
TEXTS: *see* Bibliography, part IV.
SECONDARY LITERATURE: Baldwin 1970.

PETER DAMIAN, ST (Damiani)
1007–72. After teaching at Ravenna (his birthplace) and Parma, he entered the monastery of Fonte Avellana (prior 1043) and lived an austere life as a hermit. As a reformer he attacked clerical marriage and simony. He became, under papal pressure, cardinal-bishop of Ostia in 1057 and was frequently employed as legate. With Humbert of Silva Candida he was at the head of the pre-Hildebrandine reform movement. He retired to Fonte Avellana two years before his death.
TEXTS: *see* Bibliography, part IV.
SECONDARY LITERATURE: Dressler 1954.

PETER JOHN OLIVI: *see* OLIVI, PETER JOHN

PETER LOMBARD
c. 1100–60. Born in Lombardy, he studied at Rheims and came to Paris c. 1134 to teach theology in the cathedral school. Bishop of Paris 1159. His commentaries on the Psalms (written before 1148) became standard works; and his *Four Books of Sentences* (1155–8) established themselves as the principal theological work taught in medieval schools and universities.
TEXTS: *see* Bibliography, part IV.
SECONDARY LITERATURE: *Repertorium commentariorum* 1947; de Ghellinck 1948; Brady, I., in Peter Lombard 1971–81, vol. I, part I.

PETRUS DE ALLIACO: *see* AILLY, PIERRE D'

PETRUS DE BELLAPERTICA: *see* BELLAPERTICA, PETRUS DE

PHILIPPE DE MÉZIÈRES: *see* MÉZIÈRES, PHILIPPE DE

PHILOTHEUS KOKKINOS
c. 1300–76. Patriarch of Constantinople 1353–4, 1364–76. Theologian and hagiographer.
TEXTS: *PG* 150–1; speeches and sermons, ed. Psevtongas, B.S. (1979, 1981). Φιλοθέου Κόκκινου Πατριάρχου Κωνσταντινουπόλεως 'Έργα 3, Λόγοι καὶ 'Ὁμιλίες, Aristotelian

University of Thessaloniki, Theological School; new edn (1981), Centre of Byzantine Studies, Thessaloniki.

PHOTIUS
c. 820–c. 893. Patriarch of Constantinople 858–67, 877–86. Scholar, statesman, lexicographer, theologian and commentator on classical and scriptural texts. His patriarchate marked a stage in the schism between the churches of Rome and Constantinople.
TEXTS: *PG* 101–4 (including some works probably wrongly ascribed to Photius).
SECONDARY LITERATURE: Dvornik, F. (1948). *The Photian Schism. History and Legend*, Cambridge University Press; Beck 1959, pp. 520–5.

PILLIUS (Pillio)
d. after 1207. Born near Bologna, where he studied and taught civil law before moving c. 1190 to Modena. He continued the *Summa* of Placentinus and was also one of the earliest glossators of the feudal law.
SECONDARY LITERATURE: Savigny 1834–51, vol. IV, pp. 312ff.

PISAN, CHRISTINE DE: *see* CHRISTINE DE PISAN

PLACENTINUS
d. 1192. Born in Piacenza, studied with Bulgarus at Bologna, where he himself taught, as well as at Mantua and at Piacenza, before migrating to Montpellier, where he died. One of the outstanding jurists of his generation. His *Summa Codicis* was particularly notable.
TEXT: *see* Bibliography, part V.
SECONDARY LITERATURE: Tourtoulon 1896; Lefebvre, C., 'Placentin', *Dictionnaire de droit canonique* 7:1–10.

PLAISIANS, GUILLAUME DE: *see* GUILLAUME DE PLAISIANS

PLETHON, GEORGE GEMISTOS
d. 1432, at an advanced age. Byzantine philosopher and Platonist; social and political reformer; attended the Council of Florence in 1438–9, but lived and taught mostly at Mistra in the Peloponnese.
TEXTS: *see* Bibliography, part II.
SECONDARY LITERATURE: Masai, F. (1956). *Pléthon at le platonisme de Mistra*, Paris; Nikolaos, T.S. (1974). *Αἱ περὶ πολιτείας καὶ δικαίου ἰδέαι τοῦ Γ. Πλήθωνος Γεμιστοῦ* (Byzantine Texts and Studies, 13), Centre for Byzantine Studies, Thessaloniki; Medvedev, I.P. (1976). *Vizantijskij Gumanism XIV-XV vv.*, Academy of Sciences USSR, Historical Institute, Leningrad.

PSEUDO-ISIDOREAN DECRETALS (False Decretals; Isidorus Mercator)
Collection of papal letters, forged and genuine, and authentic conciliar canons, perhaps compiled in the circle of the deposed archbishop Ebo of Rheims (816–41).
TEXT: *see* Bibliography, part IV, under *Decretales*.
SECONDARY LITERATURE: Fuhrmann 1972–4.

PULLEN, ROBERT: *see* ROBERT PULLEN

QUIDORT, JEAN: *see* JOHN OF PARIS

RABANUS MAURUS (Hrabanus; Rhabanus; Raban Maur)
780–856. Master of the school of Fulda; archbishop of Mainz from 847. Exegete, homilist, encyclopaedist.
TEXTS: *see* Bibliography, part IV.
SECONDARY LITERATURE: Carlyle 1903–36, vol. I: as index (under *Hrabanus*).

RAGUSA, JOHANNES DE (Ragusio; Jan Stojkovic)
d. 1443. Born in Dubrovnik, he became a Dominican and studied theology in Paris. A leading member of the University of Paris delegation at the Council of Pavia–Siena and prominent from the first at Basel, where he strongly defended the majority conciliarist position.
TEXTS: *see* Bibliography, part V.
SECONDARY LITERATURE: Thils 1940; Krchnák 1960; Brandmüller 1968; Black 1979, pp. 106–9.

RAVANNIS, JACOBUS DE (Jacques de Révigny)
d. 1296. A major luminary of the juristic school of Orleans, he also taught at Toulouse, and was later auditor of the Rota. Instrumental in introducing developed scholastic method into jurisprudence.
TEXTS: *see* Bibliography, part V.
SECONDARY LITERATURE: Boulet-Sautel 1962; Chevrier 1968; Bezemer 1981.

RAYMOND OF PENYAFORT, ST (Ramon de Penyafort, Peñafort, Pennaforte)
c. 1180–1275. Catalan canon lawyer. After studying, and teaching philosophy, at Barcelona, he went to study law at Bologna sometime between 1210 and 1220. He entered the Dominican order in 1222 after his return to Barcelona. Called to Rome by Gregory IX in 1230, he presided over the commission which compiled the *Liber Extra* (the authoritative collection of decretals promulgated by the pope in 1234). Returning to Catalonia, Raymond was confessor to Jaume I of Aragon (1213–76) and prominent in the activities of the Dominican order, of which he was master-general from 1238 to 1240. Thomas Aquinas wrote his *Summa contra Gentiles* at Raymond's insistence. He was canonised in 1601.
TEXTS: *see* Bibliography, part V.
SECONDARY LITERATURE: Balmé, F. and Paban, C., eds. (1900), *Raymundiana* (Monumenta Historica Ordinis Predicatorum 4 and 6), In domo generalitia; *Dictionnaire de droit canonique* 7:461ff; Barnes 1982.

REMIGIO DE' GIROLAMI: *see* GIROLAMI, REMIGIO DE'

ROBERT GROSSETESTE: *see* GROSSETESTE, ROBERT

ROBERT OF MELUN
d. 1167. Born in England, studied at Paris; succeeded Abelard as master of the school in Mont St Geneviève, where his pupils included Thomas Becket and John of Salisbury. From 1142 taught at Melun. Bishop of Hereford from 1163.
TEXTS: *see* Bibliography, part IV.
SECONDARY LITERATURE: Knowles 1951, pp. 28–30; Smalley 1973, pp. 51–8.

ROBERT PULLEN
d. 1146. Teacher of theology at Oxford and archdeacon of Rochester in 1133; later taught theology in Paris. His pupils included John of Salisbury. Called to Rome and created cardinal

1143–4; c. 1144 appointed chancellor of the Roman church.
TEXT: *see* Bibliography, part IV.
SECONDARY LITERATURE: Courtney 1954; Smalley 1973, pp. 39–50.

RUFINUS
fl. 1150–91. Taught canon law at Bologna; bishop of Assisi c. 1157; archbishop of Sorrento c. 1180.
TEXTS: *Summa decretorum* 1902 (*see* Bibliography, part V); *De bono pacis*, PL 150:1591–1638.
SECONDARY LITERATURE: Morin, G. (1928). 'Le discours d'ouverture du Concile général du Lateran (1179) et l'oeuvre littéraire de maître Rufin, évêque d'Assisi', *Atti della Pontificia accademia Roman di archeologia*, 3rd ser. *Memorie* 2:113–33; Congar 1957; Benson, R. (1961). 'Rufin', *Dictionnaire de droit canonique* 7:779–84; Benson 1968, chap. 3.

RUPERT OF DEUTZ
c. 1075–1129. Entered abbey of St Laurent c. 1082 as an oblate, professed monk c. 1091. In 1902 exiled for three years with his abbot during the investiture contest. Refused to be ordained priest, c. 1105–8, because his bishop was excommunicated. Fled to Siegburg 1116–17 after attacks on his eucharistic doctrines. Abbot of Deutz from 1120. Much concerned in his writings with the history of salvation.
TEXTS: *see* Bibliography, part IV.
SECONDARY LITERATURE: Magrassi 1959; Van Engen 1983.

SCOTUS, JOHANNES DUNS: *see* DUNS SCOTUS, JOHANNES

SEGOVIA, JUAN DE
1386–1458. Theologian from Castile; in 1432 represented University of Salamanca at council of Basel, where he rose to a position of doctrinal and personal eminence. From 1449 he lived in honorific retirement, writing between that date and 1453 his *De magna auctoritate episcoporum in concilio generali* and his most important work, the *Historia actorum generalis synodi Basiliensis*, incorporating the massive *Amplificatio* of his speech at the diet of Mainz in 1441. In his last years he was much concerned with the problem of Islam.
TEXTS: *see* Bibliography, part V.
SECONDARY LITERATURE: Black 1979, pp. 118–93; Krämer 1980, pp. 207–55; *LTK* 5:101–2.

SOMNIUM VIRIDARII (*Le Songe du Vergier*)
Written in 1376 at the command of Charles V of France and translated into French two years later. While the Latin text emphasised the need for ecclesiastical and lay collaboration, the French version developed the theme of temporal sovereignty much more strongly.
TEXTS: *see* Bibliography, part V.
SECONDARY LITERATURE: Merzbacher 1956; Royer 1969; Quillet 1977.

SUGER OF ST DENIS
c. 1080/1–1151. A child–oblate at St Denis, he became abbot there in 1122. A lifelong friend and counsellor of Louis VI, a *Life* of whom is his main work: it exalts the French monarchy and seeks to strengthen its association with St Denis. Suger also wrote on church-building and manorial administration.
TEXT: *see* Bibliography, part IV.
SECONDARY LITERATURE: Spiegel 1975.

TANCRED (Tancredus)
fl. 1185–1235. Taught canon law at Bologna, where he was also canon and archdeacon. His

Apparatus to *Compilationes prima, secunda, tertia* were received as the Ordinary Glosses in the schools.
TEXTS: *Apparatus,* as above, Vatican City, Biblioteca Apostolica Vaticana lat. 1377 (other MSS listed in Kuttner 1937, for which *see* Bibliography, part IV); *Ordo iudiciarius* (1842) ed. Bergmann, F., Vandenhoeck and Ruprecht.
SECONDARY LITERATURE: Schulte, J.F. von (1875). *Die Geschichte der Quellen un Literatur des canonischen Rechts,* F. Enke (repr. Akademische Druck -u. Verlagsanstalt, 1956), vol. I, pp. 199–205.

THEMISTIUS
c. 317–88. Pagan orator and philosopher; lived at Constantinople, then at Rome; much admired by Emperors Constantinius, Julian, Jovian, Gratian and Theodosius I.
TEXTS: *Themistii Orationes Quae Supersunt* (1965, 1971), ed. Schenkel, H. and Downey, G., 2 vols., Teubner.

THEODORE OF STUDIUS, ST
759–826. Abbot of the monastery of Studius, Constantinople. Monastic reformer, leader of the anti-iconoclastic movement in the early ninth century, for which he was three times exiled. Theologian, hagiographer, hymn-writer and poet.
TEXTS: Qorks *PG* 99; poems: Theodorus Studites, *Jamben auf verschiedene Gegenstände* (1968), ed. Speck, P. (Supplementa Byzantina 1), W. de Gruyter.

THEOPHYLACT OF OCHRIDA
d. c. 1108. Pupil of Michael Psellus; deacon of St Sophia, Constantinople, and teacher of rhetoric. Archbishop of Bulgaria, with seat at Ochrida, c. 1090.
TEXTS: works: *PG* 123–6; secular works other than letters: ed. Gautier, P. (1983), *Theophylacte d'Achrida: Discours, Traités Poésies* (Corpus Fontium Hist. Byz. 16/1), Pournaras, Thessaloniki.
SECONDARY LITERATURE: Beck 1959, pp. 649–51; Hunger 1978, vol. I, pp. 161–2.

THOMAS AQUINAS, ST: *see* AQUINAS, THOMAS, ST

THOMAS MAGISTER
fl. first half of the fourteenth century. Byzantine philologist, orator, and letter-writer, who taught in Thessaloniki and Constantinople. Monk Theodulus.
TEXTS: speeches and letters: *PG* 145; Lenz, F.W. (1963). *Fünf Reden Thomas Magisters,* Leiden.

TORQUEMADA, JUAN DE (Turrecremata, Johannes de)
1388–1468. Dominican theologian, canonist and diplomat; studied at Paris; supported Eugenius IV against the Council of Basel; created cardinal 1439. Chief works, *Summa de Ecclesia* (c. 1440–50); *Commentarium super toto Decreto* (c. 1455–68).
TEXTS: *Commentarium,* Venice, 1578; and *see* Bibliography, part V.
SECONDARY LITERATURE: Black 1970a; Black 1979; *LTK* 5:1093–4.

TUDESCHIS, NICHOLAS DE: *see* PANORMITANUS

UGUCCIONE: *see* HUGUCCIO

VELDE, HEIMERICH VAN DE (Heimericus de Campo)
1395–1460. Theologian and realist philosopher, born in the Netherlands. Taught at University of Cologne, where Nicholas of Cusa was one of his pupils, 1425–6. From 1432 to

1435 he represented the university at the Council of Basel, maintaining a conciliarist position until 1435. Thereafter taught at Louvain.

TEXT: *see* Bibliography, part V.

SECONDARY LITERATURE: Black 1970b; Black 1979, pp. 58–84.

VERNANI, GUIDO

d. c. 1348. Born in or near Rimini, where he entered the Dominican order. Between 1310 and 1320 he was *lector* in the Dominican *studium* at Bologna, but he had returned to San Cataldo at Rimini by the mid-1320s. Apart from the attack on Dante's *Monarchia* for which he is chiefly remembered he wrote commentaries on Aristotle's *Ethics*, *Rhetoric* and *De Anima*. His treatise *De potestate Summi Pontificis* and a commentary on the bull *Unam sanctum* were written c. 1327 during the conflict between John XXII and Lewis the Bavarian.

TEXT: *see* Bibliography, part V.

SECONDARY LITERATURE: T. Käppeli in Vernani 1938; N. Matteini in Vernani 1958.

VITAL DU FOUR (Vitalis de Furno)

c. 1260–1327. Franciscan friar and cardinal. Wrote *Speculum morale totius sacrae scripturae*, *De rerum principio* and *Quaestiones disputatae* (on the problem of knowledge).

TEXT: *see* Bibliography, part V.

VITERBO, JAMES OF: *see* JAMES OF VITERBO

WALTER BURLEY: *see* BURLEY, WALTER

WIDUKIND OF CORVEY

b. c. 925, d. after 976. Monk, probably child-oblate, at Corvey (Saxony). Only surviving work, *Rerum Saxonicarum Libri III*, written c. 965 and dedicated to Matilda, mother of the German king Otto I (966–73): it reflects the Saxon view of contemporary history.

TEXT: *see* Bibliography, part IV.

SECONDARY LITERATURE: Beumann 1950; Erdmann 1951; Leyser 1979.

WILLIAM OF CONCHES (Gulielmus de Conchis)

c. 1080–c. 1154. A pupil of Bernard of Chartres and tutor of prince Henry, later Henry II of England. An important commentator and philosopher with strong interests in natural science as well as in the arts of the *trivium*.

TEXTS: *see* Bibliography, part IV.

SECONDARY LITERATURE: Parent 1938; Gregory 1955; Elford 1983.

WILLIAM OF MALMESBURY

c. 1090–c. 1143. Historian, scholar and monk of Malmesbury for most of his life. The chief historian of his generation in England, he provided a broad survey of English history from Bede to his own day.

TEXTS: *see* Bibliography, part IV.

WILLIAM (OF) OCKHAM: *see* OCKHAM, WILLIAM (OF)

WIPO

c. 1000–after 1046. Born in Burgundy. Chaplain to king Henry III of Germany (1039–56), for whom he wrote a 'mirror of princes'. His chief surviving work is *Gesta Chuonradi Imperatoris* (Henry's father), written in the early 1040s.

TEXT: *see* Bibliography, part IV.

WYCLIF, JOHN
d. 1384. Date of birth unknown and little known of his early life. Merton College, Oxford 1358; master of Balliol 1360; later Queen's, and warden of Canterbury Hall. By 1372 doctor of theology and leading master in that faculty. In 1374 he was sent to Bruges to negotiate with papal ambassadors on matters of ecclesiastical finance. Entered the service of John of Gaunt. Until early 1370s his writings were non-controversial; but thereafter his attention turned increasingly to political controversy and theological doctrines of a highly controversial character, which became the basis of Lollardy. By the time of his death a number of his views had been censured, but the most systematic condemnation came posthumously, at the Council of Constance in 1415.
TEXTS: *see* Bibliography, part V.
SECONDARY LITERATURE: McFarlane 1952; Wilks 1972b.

YORK TRACTS (*Tractatus Eboracenses*): *see* NORMAN ANONYMOUS

ZABARELLA, FRANCISCUS (DE)
c. 1339–1417. Italian canonist; leading pro-conciliar figure at Councils of Pisa and Constance; helped to draft the decree *Haec sancta* (1415); cardinal 1411. Wrote famous *Super quinque libris decretalium commentaria*, which incorporates (on x.1.6.6) his *Tractatus de Schismate*.
TEXTS: *Commentaria*, Venice, 1602; and *see* Bibliography, part V.
SECONDARY LITERATURE: Ullmann 1948a, pp. 191–231; Tierney 1955a, pp. 220ff; *LTK* 10:1295–6.

BIBLIOGRAPHY

Note: The bibliography is intended primarily to provide detailed references for works cited in the text and notes, though its scope is not limited to these works. It has been divided in accordance with the principal divisions of the book, and subdivided between primary and secondary sources under each heading. Cross-references to the main entry have been provided for works cited in more than one part or chapter; but works listed in the relatively short 'General' section have not been mentioned elsewhere. Publishers' names rather than places of publication have generally been provided, except in the case of early printed books.

GENERAL WORKS

Black, A. (1984). *Guilds and Civil Society in European Political Thought from the Twelfth Century to the Present*, Methuen

Carlyle, R.W. and A.J. (1903–36). *A History of Medieval Political Theory in the West*, 6 vols., William Blackwood and Sons (last repr. 1970)

Gierke, O. von (1868). *Das deutsche Genossenschaftsrecht*, vol. I: *Rechtsgeschichte der deutschen Genossenschaft*, Weidmannsche Buchhandlung; repr. 1954, Akademische Druck- u. Verlagsanstalt

(1873). *Das deutsche Genossenschaftsrecht*, vol. II: *Geschichte der deutschen Körperschaftsbegriff*, Weidmannsche Buchhandlung; repr. 1954, Akademische Druck- u. Verlagsanstalt

(1881). *Das deutsche Genossenschaftsrecht*, vol. III: *Die Staats- und Korporationslehre des Altertums und des Mittelalters und ihre Aufnahme in Deutschland*, Weidmannsche Buchhandlung; repr. 1954, Akademische Druck- u. Verlagsanstalt

(1900). *Political Theories of the Middle Age*, transl. by F.W. Maitland, from Gierke 1881, pp. 501–640, Cambridge University Press

Kantorowicz, E.H. (1957). *The King's Two Bodies: A Study in Medieval Political Theology*, Princeton University Press

Koelmel, W. (1970). *Regimen christianum. Weg und Ergebnisse des Gewaltenverhältnisses und des Erwaltenverständnisses, 8. bis. 14. Jahrhundert*, W. de Gruyter

Lerner, R. and Maḥdi, M., eds. (1963). *Medieval Political Philosophy. A Sourcebook*, Free Press of Glencoe; Collier-Macmillan; Cornell University Press

Lewis, E. (1954). *Medieval Political Ideas*, 2 vols., Routledge and Kegan Paul (2nd edn 1974)

Lexicon für Theologie und Kirche (1957–65). Ed. M. Buchberger *et al.*, Herder

McIlwain (1932). *The Growth of Political Thought in the West from the Greeks to the End of the Middle Ages*, Macmillan

Michaud-Quantin, P. (1970). *Universitas: Expressions du mouvement communautaire dans le moyen-âge latin* (L'Eglise et l'Etat au Moyen Age 15), J. Vrin

Morrall, J.B. (1971). *Political Thought in Medieval Times*, 3rd edn, Hutchinson

Passerin d'Entrèves, A. (1939). *The Mediaeval Contribution to Political Thought. Thomas Aquinas. Marsilius of Padua. Richard Hooker*, Oxford University Press; repr. 1959

(1970). *Per la storia del pensiero politico medioevale*, G. Giappichelli

Post, G. (1964). *Studies in Medieval Legal Thought*, Princeton University Press

Quillet, J. (1971). *Les clefs du pouvoir au moyen âge*, Flammarion

Smalley, B., ed. (1965). *Trends in Medieval Political Thought*, Basil Blackwell

Tierney, B. and Linehan, P., eds. (1980). *Authority and Power: Studies in Medieval Law and Government Presented to Walter Ullmann on his Seventieth Birthday*, Cambridge University Press.

Ullmann, W. (1967). *The Individual and Society in the Middle Ages*, Methuen

(1975a). *A History of Political Thought: The Middle Ages*, 3rd edn, Penguin Books (first published 1965; 2nd edn 1970)

(1975b). *Law and Politics in the Middle Ages: An Introduction to the Sources of Medieval Political Ideas* (The Sources of History: Studies in the Uses of Historical Evidence), The Sources of History, Ltd; Cambridge University Press; Cornell University Press

(1978). *Principles of Government and Politics in the Middle Ages*, 4th edn, Methuen (first published 1961; 2nd edn 1966; 3rd edn 1974)

I FOUNDATIONS

Note: given the essentially preliminary character of the chapters in this part of the book, the bibliographical indications are necessarily limited in scope, and some items belonging here chronologically have been listed rather under the sections where they have been specifically cited. In regard to primary sources it should be noted that the Latin texts of Aristotle which became available in the west in the thirteenth century have been listed under section V below.

Primary sources

Chapter 1

For scriptural texts, it may be noted that a convenient edition of the Latin Bible, influential on the political thought of the medieval west, is *Biblia Sacra iuxta Vulgatam Clemetinam*, ed. A. Colunga and L. Turrado, 6th edn (Biblioteca de autores cristianos 14), La editorial catolica, SA 1982.

The patristic texts are, besides other later editions, mostly available in *PG* and *PL*. For general bibliographical guides see

Gerard, M. (1974). *Clavis Petrum Graecorum*
Dekkers, E. (1961). *Clavis Patrum Latinorum*

Chapter 2

Most of the authors mentioned, with the notable exception of Themistius' speeches, can be read in the Loeb dual language editions. For the fragments of 'Diotogenes' and 'Ecphantus' see Goodenough 1928 under *Secondary sources* below; and for a useful selection of Hellenistic and later material, including some Themistius, Barker 1955, also listed below.

Chapter 3

The standard modern text of Justinian's *Corpus Iuris* is the 'Berlin stereotype' edition:

I. *Institutiones*, ed. P. Krüger; *Digesta*, ed. T. Mommsen and P. Kreuger, 19th edn, 1966
II. *Codex*, ed. P. Krüger, 13th edn, 1963
III. *Novellae*, ed. R. Schöll and G. Kroll, 8th edn, 1963

Secondary sources

Aalders, G.J.D. (1969). '*ΝΟΜΟΣ ΕΜΨΥΧΟΣ*', in *Politeia und Respublica, Gedenkschrift R. Stark, Palingenesis* 4:315–29, Franz Steiner Verlag
Athanassiadi-Fowden, P. (1981). *Julian and Hellenism*, Clarendon Press
Barker, E. (1955). *From Alexander to Constantine*, Clarendon Press
Barnes, T.D. (1981). *Constantine and Eusebius*, Harvard University Press

Baynes, N.H. (1955). 'Eusebius and the Christian Empire', in Baynes 1955 (*see* section II below)

Berkhof, H. (1947). *Kirche und Kaiser. Eine Untersuchung der Entstiehung der byzantinischen und der theokratischen Staatsauffassung im vierten Jahrhundert*, Evangelischer Verlag

Brown. P.R.L. (1982). *Society and the Holy in Late Antiquity*, Faber and Faber

Buckland, W.W. (1975). *A Text-Book of Roman Law from Augustus to Justinian*, 3rd edn, ed. P. Stein, Cambridge University Press

Cadoux, C.J. (1925). *The Early Church and the World*, T. and T. Clark

Charlesworth. M.P. (1937). 'The Virtues of a Roman Emperor. Propaganda as the Creation of Belief', *Proceedings of the British Academy* 23:105–33

Combès, C. (1927). *See* section III below

Crawford, M.H. (1978). *The Roman Republic*, Fontana/Collins

Dagron, G. (1968). *L'empire romain d'Orient au IVème siècle et les institutions politiques de l'hellénisme: le témoignage de Thémistion* (Travaux et Mémoirs, Centre de Recherche d'Histoire et Civilisation Byzantines) 3:1–242, Centre Nationale de la Recherche Scientifique, Paris

Dawson, J.P. (1968). *The Oracles of the Law*, ch. 2 'The Heritage of Roman Law', University of Michigan Law School

Deane, H.A. (1963). *See* section III below

Dihle, A. (1973). 'Zum Streit um den Altar der Viktoria', in *Humanitas und Christianitas. Festschrift Waszink*, North-Holland, pp. 81–97

Duchrow, U. (1983). *Christenheit und Weltverantwortung: Traditionsgeschichte und systematische Struktur der Zweireichslehre*, 2nd edn, Klett-Cotta

Dvornik, F. (1955). 'The Emperor Julian's "Reactionary" Ideas on Kingship', in *Late Classical and Medieval Studies in Honor of A.M. Friend*, Princeton University Press
(1966). *Early Christian and Byzantine Political Philosophy: Origin and Background*, 2 vols. (Dumbarton Oaks Studies 9), Dumbarton Oaks Center for Byzantine Studies

Ehrhardt, A.A.T. (1959). *Politische Metaphysik von Solon bis Augustin*, J.C.B. Mohr

Festugière, A.J. (1951). 'Les inscriptions d'Asoka et l'Idéal du roi hellénistique', *Recherches de science religieuse* 39:32–57

Goodenough, E.R. (1928). 'The Political Philosophy of Hellenistic Kingship', *Yearbook of Classical Studies* 1:53–102

Greenslade, S.L. (1954). *See* section III below

Greeven, H. (1935). *Das Hauptproblem der Socialethik in der neuen Stoa und in Urchristentum*, C. Bertelsmann

Gülzow, H. (1969). *Christentum und Sklaverei*, Rudolf Habelt

Hadot, P. (1971). 'Fürstenspiegel', *Reallexikon für Antike und Christentum* 61:555–632

Harnack, A. von (1924). *Die mission und Ausbreitung des Christentums*, 4th edn, J.C. Hinrichs

Hengel, M. (1974). *Property and Riches in the Early Church*, SCM Press; Porpoise Press

Honoré, T. (1978). *Tribonian*, Duckworth

Joolwicz, H.F. and Nicholson, B. (1972). *Historical Introduction to the Study of Roman Law*, 3rd edn, Cambridge University Press

Jones, C.P. (1971). *Plutarch and Rome*, Clarendon Press
(1978). *The Roman World of Dio Chrysostom*, Harvard University Press

Kantorowicz, E.H. (1952). 'Kaiser Friedrich II und das Königsbild des Hellenismus', in *Varia Variorum. Festschrift für Karl Reinhardt*, Böhlau Verlag, pp. 169–93

Karayannopoulos, J. (1956). 'Der frühbyzantinischer Kaiser', *Byzantinische Zeitschrift* 49:369–84

Klein, M. (1972). *Der Streit um den Viktoriaaltar* (Texte und Forschung 7),
 Wissenschaftliche Buchgesellschaft
Long, A.A. (1974). *Hellenistic Philosophy*, Duckworth
Morino, C. (1969). *See* section III below
Murphy, F.X. (1967). *Politics and the Early Christian Church*, Desclée; de Brouwer
Nicholas, B. (1962). *Introduction to Roman Law*, Clarendon Press
Obolensky, D. (1971). *See* section II below
Palanque, J.R. (1933). *See* section III below
Peterson, E. (1935). *Der Monotheismus als politisches Problem*, Jakob Regner; repr. in
 Peterson, E. (1961). *Theologische Traktate*, Kösel-Verlag, pp. 45–147
Ste Croix, G.E.M. de (1981). *The Class Struggle in the Ancient Greek World*, Duckworth
Schubart, W. (1937). 'Das hellenistische Königsideal nach Inschriften und Papyri',
 Archiv für Papyrusforschung 12:1–26
Setton, K.M. (1941). *Christian Attitudes towards the Emperor in the Fourth Century*,
 Columbia University Press; P.S. King and Son
Sinclair, T.A. (1951). *A History of Greek Political Thought*, Routledge
Stein, P. (1968). *Regulae iuris: From Juristic Rules to Legal Maxims*, Edinburgh University
 Press
Steinwenter, A. (1946). *See* section II below
Thesleff, H., ed. (1965). *The Pythagorean Texts*, Acta Academiae Aboensis 30.1
Walbank, F.W. (1957). *A Historical Commentary on Polybius I*, Clarendon Press
Watson, G. (1971). 'The Natural Law and Stoicism', in A.A. Long (ed.) *Problems in
 Stoicism*, Athlone Press
Wirszubski, Ch. (1950). *Libertas as a Political Idea at Rome during the Late Republic and
 Early Principate*, Cambridge University Press

II BYZANTIUM

Primary Sources

Blemmydes, Nicephorus (1906). Ἀνδριὰς βασιλικός, in E. Emminger (ed.) *Studien zu den griechischen Fürstenspiegeln*, vol. 1: *Zum 'Ανδριὰς βασιλικὸς des Nikephoros Blemmydes*, Program Maximilians-Gymnasium, München

Cecaumenus (1896). *Strategicon*, in B. Wassiliewsky and V. Jernstedt (eds.) *Cecaumeni Strategicon et incerti scriptoris de officiis regiis libellus*, St Petersburg

(1972). *Strategicon*, in G.G. Litavrin (ed.) *Sočinenie vizantijskogo polkovodca XI veka*, Moscow.

Cinnamus, John (1836). *Historia*, ed. A. Meineke (*Corpus script. hist. Byz.*)

Comnena, Anna (1937–45). *Alexiad*, ed. B. Leib, 3 vols. (Collection Byzantine-Budé), Les Belles Lettres

Constantine Porphyrogenitus De Administrando Imperio, vol. 1 (1967). Ed. Gy. Moravcsik and R.J.H. Jenkins (Corpus Fontium Historiae Byzantinae 1), Dumbarton Oaks Center for Byzantine Studies

Corpus scriptorum historiae Byzantinae (1828–97). E. Weber, Bonn

Ecloga Legum Leonis et Constantini (1931). In J. and P. Zepos, *Jus graeco-romanum*, vol II, pp. 3–62

Epanagoge (1931). In J. and P. Zepos, *Jus graeco-romanum*, vol. II, pp. 229–368

Lambros, Sp. P. (1912–30). Παλαιολόγεια καὶ Πελοποννησιακά, 4 vols., Athens

Leo Diaconus (1828) *History*, ed. C.B. Haase (*Corpus script. hist. Byz.*)

Leo Grammaticus (1842). *Chronographia*, ed. I. Bekker (*Corpus script. hist. Byz.*)

Liudprand of Cremona (1915). *Antapodosis: Relatio de Legatione Constantinopolitana*, ed. I. Bekker, *MGH SS rerum Germanicarum in usum scholarum*

Mansi, J.D. (1759–98). *Sacrorum conciliorum nova et amplissima collectio*, 31 vols., Florence; Venice

Mazaris (1975). *Mazaris' Journey to Hades*, ed. J.N. Barry, M.J. Share, A. Smithies and L.G. Westerink (Arethusa Monographs 5), Department of Classics, State University of New York at Buffalo

Migne, J.P. (1857–66). *Patrologiae cursus completus. Series graeco-latina*, 161 vols., Paris

Miklosich, F. and Müller, J., eds. (1860–90). *Acta et Diplomata graeca medii aevi sacra et profana*, 6 vols., Vienna

Pachymeres, George (1835). *De Michaele et Andronico Palaeologis*, ed. I. Bekker (*Corpus script. hist. Byz.*)

Philopatris (1967). Ed. M.D. Mcleod, *Lucian* 8 (Loeb Classical Library), William Heinemann and Harvard University Press

Plethon, George Gemistos (1858). *Treatise on the Laws*, in C. Alexandre (ed.) *Pléthon, Traité des Lois*, Firmin Didot

Procopius (1906). *Anecdota (Secret History)*, in J. Haury (ed.) *Procopii Caesariensis Opera Omnia*, Teubner; trans. by G.A. Williamson (1966), Penguin Books

Pseudo-Kodinos (1966). *Traité des Offices*, ed. J. Verpeaux, Centre Nationale de la Recherche Scientifique, Paris

Rhalles, G.A. and Potles, M. (1852–9). Σύνταγμα τῶν θείων καὶ ἱερῶν κανόνων, 6 vols., Athens

Symeonis Thessalonicensis Archiepiscopi Opera Omnia (1866). PG 155

Syropoulos, Sylvester (1971). *Les 'Mémoires' du Grand Ecclésiarque de l'Eglise de Constantinople Sylvestre Syropoulos sur le Concile de Florence (1438–1439)*, ed. V. Laurent, Institut français d'Etudes Byzantines, Centre Nationale de la Recherche Scientifique

Theophanes Continuatus (1838), *Chronographia*, ed. I. Bekker (*Corpus script. hist. Byz.*)

Timarion (1860). *Analekten der mittel- und neugriechischer Literatur*, ed. A. Ellison, 4:41–86

(1974). *Pseudo-Luciano, Timarione*, ed. R. Romano (Testo critico, traduzione, commentario e lessico. Byzantina et neo-hellenica neapolitana 2), Università di Napoli, Cattedra di Filologia Byzantina

Zachariae von Lingenthal, K.E. (1856–84). *Jus graeco-romanum*, 7 vols., Leipzig

Zepos, J. and P. (1931). *Jus graeco-romanum*, 8 vols., Academy of Athens

Secondary sources

Ahrweiler, Hélène (1975). *L'idéologie politique de l'empire byzantin*, Presses Universitaires de France

Alexander, P.J. (1962). 'The Strength of Empire and Capital as Seen through Byzantine Eyes', *Speculum* 37:339–57

(1963). 'The Donation of Constantine and Its Earliest Use against the Western Empire', *Zbornik Radova Vizantološkog Instituta* 8 (= *Mélanges G. Ostrogorsky* 1):11–26

Alföldi, A. (1948). *The Conversion of Constantine and Pagan Rome*, Clarendon Press

Anastos, M.V. (1978). 'Byzantine Political Theory: Its Classical Precedents and Legal Embodiment', in Sp. Vryonis, Jr (ed.) *The 'Past' in Medieval and Modern Greek Culture* (= *Byzantina kai Metabyzantina* 1), Undena Publications, pp. 13–53

Barker, E. (1957). *Social and Political Thought in Byzantium from Justinian I to the Last Palaeologus*, Clarendon Press

Barnes, T.D. (1981). *See* section I above

Baynes, N.H. (1929). *Constantine the Great and the Christian Church*, The British Academy (2nd edn by H. Chadwick 1972, Oxford University Press)

(1955). *Byzantine Studies and Other Essays*, Athlone Press

Baynes, N.H. and Moss, H. St. L.B., eds. (1948). *Byzantium. An Introduction to East Roman Civilization*, Clarendon Press

Beck, H.-G. (1959). *Kirche und theologische Literatur im byzantinischen Reich*, C.H. Beck'sche Verlagsbuchhandlung

(1960). 'Reichsidee und nationale Politik im spätbyzantinischen Stadt', *Byzantinische Zeitschrift* 53:86–94; repr. in Beck 1972, no. VI.

(1966). *Senat und Volk von Konstantinopel. Probleme der byzantinischen Verfassungsgeschichte* (Bayerische Akademie der Wissenschaften, philosoph.-historische Klasse, Sitzungsberichte, 6), Bayerische Akademie der Wissenschaften; repr. in Beck 1972, no. XII

(1970). *Res Publica Romana. Vom Staatsdenken der Byzantiner* (Bayerische Akademie der Wissenschaften, philosoph.-historische Klasse, Sitzungsberichte, 2), Bayerische Akademie der Wissenschaften

(1972). *Ideen und Realitaeten in Byzanz*, Variorum Reprints

(1978). *Das Byzantinische Jahrtausend*, C.H. Beck'sche Verlagsbuchhandlung (Oscar Beck)

(1981). *Nomos, Kanon und Staatsraison in Byzanz* (Österreichische Akademie der Wissenschaften, philosoph.-historische Klasse, Sitzungsberichte, 384), Österreichische Akademie der Wissenschaften

Bréhier, L. (1948). *'ΙΕΡΕΥΣ ΚΑΙ ΒΑΣΙΛΕΥΣ'*, *Mémorial Louis Petit. Mélanges d'histoire et d'archéologie byzantines* (Archives de l'Orient chrétien 1: Bucharest), pp. 41–5

(1969, 1970). *Le monde byzantin*, vol. I: *Vie et mort de Byzance*, vol. II: *Les institutions de l'empire byzantin*, vol. III: *La civilisation byzantine* (Evolution de l'Humanité 32), 2nd edn, Albin Michel

Browning, R. (1966). *Notes on Byzantine Prooimia* (Wiener Byzantinische Studien 1: Supplement), Böhlaus Nachfolger

(1975). *Byzantium and Bulgaria. A Comparative Study across the Early Medieval Frontier*, Temple Smith

Bury, J.B. (1910). *The Constitution of the Later Roman Empire* (Creighton Memorial Lecture), Cambridge University Press

Cambridge Medieval History, vol. IV: *The Byzantine Empire*, Part 1 (1966), Part 2 (1967). ed. J.M. Hussey, D.M. Nicol, G. Cowan, Cambridge University Press

Cameron, Averil (1983). 'Eusebius of Caesarea and the Rethinking of History', in E. Gabba (ed.) *Tria Corda. Scritti in onore di Arnaldo Momigliano* (Biblioteca di Athenaeum 1), Como, pp. 71–88

Christophilopoulou, Aikaterine (1949). Ἡ σύγκλητος εἰς τὸ Βυζαντινὸν κράτος (Ἐπετηρὶς τοῦ Ἀρχείου τῆς ἱστορίας τοῦ ἑλληνικοῦ λαοῦ τῆς Ἀκαδημίας Ἀθηνῶν, 2), Academy of Athens

(1956). Ἐκλογή, ἀναγόρευσις καὶ στέψις τοῦ Βυζαντινοῦ αὐτοκράτορος (Πραγματεῖαι τῆς Ἀκαδημίας Ἀθηνῶν, 22.2), Academy of Athens

Dagron, G. (1974). *Naissance d'une capitale. Constantinople et ses institutions de 330 à 451*, Presses Universitaires de France

De Decker, D. and Dupuis-Masay, G. (1980). 'L' "épiscopat" de l'empereur Constantin', *Byzantion* 50:118–57

Dölger, F. (1937). 'Rom in der Gedankenwelt der Byzantiner', *Zeitschrift für Kirchengeschichte* 56: 1–42; repr. in Dölger 1953, pp. 70–115

(1938–9). 'Die Kaiserurkunde als Ausdruck ihrer politischen Anschauungen', *Historische Zeitschrift* 159:229–50; repr. in Dölger 1953, pp. 9–33

(1940). 'Die "Familie der Könige" im Mittelalter', *Historisches Jahrbuch* 60:397–420; repr. in Dölger 1953, pp. 34–69

(1953). *Byzanz und die europäische Staatenwelt. Ausgewählte Vorträge und Aufsätze*, Buch-Kunstverlag Ettal

(1956). *Byzantinische Diplomatik*, Buch-Kunstverlag Ettal

(1961). *ΠΑΡΑΣΠΟΡΑ*. 30 *Aufsätze zur Geschichte, Kultur und Sprache des byzantinischen Reiches*, Buch-Kuntsverlag Ettal

Dölger, F. and Karayannopoulos, J. (1968). *Byzantinische Urkundenlehre. Erster Abschnitt: Die Kaiserurkunden*, C.H. Beck'sche Verlagsbuchhandlung

Drake, H.A. (1976). *In Praise of Constantine. A Historical Study and New Translation of Eusebius' Tricennial Orations*, University of California Press

Dvornik, F. (1966). *See section I above.*

Ensslin, W. (1967). 'The Government and Administration of the Byzantine Empire', in *Cambridge Medieval History*, vol. IV, 2, pp. 1–53

Fenster, E. (1968). *Laudes Constantinopolitanae* (Miscellanea Byzantina Monacensia 9)

Geanakoplos, D.J. (1966). 'Church and State in the Byzantine Empire: A Reconsideration of the Problem of Caesaropapism', in D.J. Geanakoplos *Byzantine East and Latin West: Two Worlds of Christendom in Middle Ages and Renaissance*, Basil Blackwell

Grabar, A. (1936). *L'empereur dans l'art byzantin. Recherches sur l'art officiel de l'Empire de l'Orient*, Strasbourg; repr. 1971, Variorum Reprints

Grierson, P. (1981). 'The Carolingian Empire in the Eyes of Byzantium', *Settimane di Studio del Centro Italiano di Studi sull'Alto Medioevo* 27:885–918

Guilland, R. (1947). 'Le droit divin à Byzance', *Eos* 42:142–68; repr. in Guilland 1959, pp. 207–30

(1954). 'La destinée des empereurs de Byzance', Ἐπετηρὶς τῆς Ἑταιρείας Βυζαντινῶν Σουδῶν 24:37–66; repr. in Guilland 1959, pp. 1–32

(1959). *Etudes Byzantines*, Presses Universitaires de France

Heisenberg, A. (1905). 'Kaiser Johannes Batatzes der Barmherzige', *Byzantinische Zeitschrift* 14:193–235

Henry, P. (1967). 'A Mirror for Justinian: The *Ekthesis* of Agapetus Diaconus', *Greek, Roman and Byzantine Studies* 8:281–308

Hunger, H. (1964). *Prooimion. Elemente der byzantinischen Kaiseridee in den Arengen der Urkunden* (Wiener Byzantinische Studien 1)

(1978). *Die hochsprachliche profane Literatur der Byzantiner*, vols. I–II, C.H. Beck'sche Verlagsbuchhandlung

(1982). 'State and Society in Byzantium', *Proceedings of the Royal Irish Academy* 82, C, 8:197–209

Karayannopoulos, I.E. (1970). 'Ἡπολιτικὴ θεωρία τῶν Βυζαντινῶν', *Byzantina* 2:39–61

Laurent, V. (1955). 'Les droits de l'empereur en matière ecclésiastique: l'accord de 1380/82', *Revue des études byzantines* 13:5–20

McCormack, Sabine G. (1981). *Art and Ceremony in Late Antiquity*, University of California Press

Michel, A. (1959). *Die Kaisermacht in der Oskirche (843–1204)*, Wissenschaftliche Buchgesellschaft

Moss, H. St L.B. (1966). 'The Formation of the East Roman Empire', in *Cambridge Medieval History*, vol. IV, I, pp. 1–41

Nelson, Janet L. (1976). 'Symbols in Context: Rulers' Inauguration Rituals in Byzantium and the West in the Early Middle Ages', in *Studies in Church History*, vol. XIII: *The Orthodox Churches and the West*, ed. D. Baker, Basil Blackwell, pp. 97–119

Nicol, D.M. (1967). 'The Byzantine View of Western Europe', *Greek, Roman and Byzantine Studies* 8:315–39; repr. in Nicol 1972, no. 1

(1972) *Byzantium: Its Ecclesiastical History and Relations with the Western World*, Variorum Reprints

(1976). 'Kaisersalbung. The Unction of Emperors in Late Byzantine Coronation Ritual', *Byzantine and Modern Greek Studies* 2:37–52

(1979). *Church and Society in the Last Centuries of Byzantium*, Cambridge University Press

Obolensky, D. (1971). *The Byzantine Commonwealth. Eastern Europe, 500–1453*, Weidenfeld and Nicolson

Ohnsorge, W. (1947). *Das Zweikaiser-problem im früheren Mittelalter. Die Bedeutung des byzantinischen Reiches für die Entwicklung der Staatsidee in Europa*, August Lax

(1958). *Abendland und Byzanz. Gesammelte Aufsätze zur Geschichte der byzantinisch-abendländischen Beziehungen und des Kaisertums*, Böhlaus Nachfolger

Ostrogorsky, G. (1935). 'Avtokrator i Samodržac', *Glas Srpske Akademije* 165:95–187

(1936). 'Die byzantinische Staatenhierarchie', *Seminarium Kondakovianum* 8:95–187

(1956). 'The Byzantine Empire and the Hierarchical World Order', *Slavonic and East European Review* 35:1–14

(1968). *History of the Byzantine State*, transl. by J. Hussey, Basil Blackwell

Raybaud, L.-P. (1968) *Le gouvernement et l'administration centrale de l'empire byzantin sous les premiers Paléologues (1258–1354)* (Société d'Histoire du Droit), Sirey

Runciman, S. (1933). *Byzantine Civilisation*, Edward Arnold

(1975). *Byzantine Style and Civilisation*, Penguin Books

(1977). *The Byzantine Theocracy*, Cambridge University Press

Scheltema, H.J. (1967). 'Byzantine Law', in *Cambridge Medieval History*, vol. IV, 2, pp. 55–77

Sickel, W. (1898). 'Das byzantinische Krönungsrecht bis zum 10. Jahrhundert', *Byzantinische Zeitschrift* 7:511–57

Simon, D. (1984). 'Princeps legibus solutus. Die Stellung des byzantinischen Kaisers zum Gesetz', in *Gedächtnissschrift für Wolfgang Kunkel*, ed. D. Nörr and D. Simon, Vittorio Klostermann GmbH, pp. 450–92

Steinwenter, A. (1946). '*ΝΟΜΟΣ ΕΜΨΥΧΟΣ*. Zur Geschichte einer politischen Theorie', *Anzeiger der Akademie der Wissenschaften in Wien*, philosoph.-historische Klasse, 83:250–68.

Straub, J. (1957). 'Kaiser Konstantin als '*ἐπίσκοπος τῶν 'ἐκτός*', *Studia Patristica* 1:678–95

(1967) 'Konstantin als *κοινὸς 'ἐπίσκοπος*', *Dumbarton Oaks Papers* 21:37–55

Tatakis, B. (1959). *La philosophie byzantine* (Histoire de philosophie, fascicule supplémentaire, 2), Presses Universitaires de France

Tinnefeld, F.H. (1971). *Kategorien der Kaiserkritik in der byzantinischen Historiographie von Prokop bis Niketas Choniates*, Wilhelm Fink Verlag

Toynbee, A. (1973). *Constantine Porphyrogenitus and his World*, Oxford University Press

Treitinger, O. (1938). *Die oströmische Kaiser- und Reichsidee nach ihrer Gestaltung im höfischen Zeremoniell. Vom oströmischen Staats- und Reichsgedanken*, W. Bierdermann; repr. 1956, H. Gentner

Voigt, K. (1936). *Staat und Kirche von Konstantin dem Grossen bis zum Ende der Karolingerzeit*, Kohlhammer

Vryonis, Sp. (1982). 'Byzantine Imperial Authority: Theory and Practice in the Eleventh Century', in G. Makdisi, S. Sourdel and Janine Sourdel-Thomine, *La notion d'autorité au moyen âge. Islam, Byzance, Occident*, Presses Universitaires de France, pp. 141–61

Zakythinos, D.A. (1932, 1953, 1975). *Le Despotat grec de Morée*, vol. I: *Histoire politique*, vol. II: *Vie et Institutions*, revised and expanded edn by C. Maltézou, Variorum Reprints

III BEGINNINGS: c. 350–c. 750

Primary sources
Note: Where more than one edition is cited, the date given is usually that of the most recent.

Ambrose, St (1845). *De officiis ministrorum*, PL 16:23ff
    (1897). *De Abraham*, ed. Schenkl, *CSEL* 32/1; PL 14:419ff
    (1897b). *De apologia prophetae David*, ed. Schenkl, *CSEL* 32/2; PL 14:851
    (1897c). *De fuga saeculi*, ed. Schenkl, *CSEL* 32/2; PL 14:569
    (1897d). *De Tobia*, ed. Schenkl, *CSEL* 32/2; PL 14:759ff
    (1897e). *Exameron [Hexaemeron]*, ed. Schenkl, *CSEL* 32; PL 14:123ff
    (1913). *Expositio de psalmo cxviii*, ed. Petschenig, *CSEL* 62; PL 15:1197ff
    (1919). *Explanatio super psalmos xii*, ed. Petschenig *CSEL* 64; PL 14:921ff
    (1955). *De obitu Theodosii*, ed. Faller, *CSEL* 73; PL 16:1385ff
    (1957). *Expositio Evangelii secundum Lucam*, ed. Adriaen, *CC* 14; *CSEL* 32/4; PL 15:1527ff
    (1982). *Epistulae*, ed. Faller and Zelzer, *CSEL* 82/1–3; PL 16:876ff
Ambrosiaster (1908). *Quaestiones veteris et novi testamenti*, ed. Souter, *CSEL* 50; PL 35:2207ff
    (1966–9). *Commentarius in xiii epistulas Paulinas*, ed. Vogels, *CSEL* 81; PL 17:45ff
Ammianus Marcellinus (1937). *Rerum Gestarum Libri qui supersunt*, ed. J.C. Rolfe, Loeb
Anonymous Valesianus (1872). In *MGH AA* IX:7–11, 306–28
Augustine, St, of Hippo (1845). *Sermones*, PL 38–9
    (1891). *Contra Faustum Manichaeum*, ed. Zycha, *CSEL* 25/1; PL 42:207ff
    (1894). *De Genesi ad litteram*, ed. Zycha, *CSEL* 28/1; PL 34:245
    (1895–1923). *Epistulae*, ed. Goldbacher, *CSEL* 34/1, 34/2, 44, 57, 58; PL 33:61ff
    (1902). *Retractationes*, ed. Knöll, *CSEL* 36; PL 32:583ff
    (1910). *Contra Gaudentium*, ed. Petschenig, *CSEL* 53; PL 43:707ff
    (1955). *De civitate Dei*, ed. Dombart and Kalb, *CC* 47–8; PL 41:13ff
    (1956). *Enarrationes in Psalmos*, ed. Dekkers and Fraipont, *CC* 38–40; PL 36:67ff
    (1962a). *De doctrina christiana*, ed. Martin, *CC* 32; PL 34:15ff
    (1962b). *De vera religione*, ed. Daur, *CC* 32; PL 34:121ff
    (1964). *De catechizandis rudibus*, ed. Bauer, *CC* 46; PL 40:309ff
    (1968). *De Trinitate*, ed. Mountain and Glorie, *CSEL* 50; PL 42:819ff
    (1970a). *De libero arbitrio*, ed. Green, *CC* 29; *CSEL* 74; PL 32:1221ff
    (1970b). *De ordine*, ed. Green, *CC* 29; *CSEL* 63; PL 32:905ff
Avitus (1893). *Epistulae, Homiliae, Carmina*, in *MGH AA* VI/ii
Bede (1969). *Historia Ecclesiastica Gentis Anglorum*, in B. Colgrave and R.A.B. Mynors (eds) *Bede's Ecclesiastical History of the English People*, Clarendon Press
Boethius, Anicius Manlius Severinus (1882, 1860). *Opera Omnia*, PL 63, 64

Cassiodorus (1894). *Variae*, in *MGH AA* XII

(1937). *Cassiodori Senatoris Institutiones*, ed. R.A.B. Mynors, Clarendon Press

Denis the (Pseudo-) Areopagita (1970). *La Hiérarchie céleste*, ed. R. Roques, G. Heil and M. de Gandillac, 2nd edn (Sources chrétiennes no. 58 bis), Editions du Cerf

Dionysiaca (1937). *Recueil donnant l'ensemble des traductions latines des ouvrages attribués au Denys l'Aréopage* . . ., 2 vols., desclée; de Brouwer

Ennodius (1885). *Opera*, in *MGH AA* VII

Epistolae Austrasiacae (1982). In *MGH AA* III:110–53

Fredegar (1982). *Chronicarum Libri Quattuor*, in Wolfram, ed., 1982 (q.v.)

Gelasius I (1868). *Epistulae*, ed. A. Thiel, *Epistulae Romanorum pontificum*, 287ff; *PL* 59:13ff

Gregory I, St (1849). *Regula pastoralis*, *PL* 77:13ff

(1971). *Homiliae in Ezechielem*, ed. Adriaen, *CC* 142; *PL* 76:785ff

(1972–). *Moralia in Job*, ed. Adriaen, *CC* 143, 143A, (143B); *PL* 75:515–76:782

(1978–80). *Dialogi*, ed. De Vogüé, *SC* 251, 260, 265; ed. Moricca (1924); *PL* 77:148ff

(1982). *Registrum epistolarum*, ed. Norberg, *CC* 140, 140A (also ed. Ewald and Hartmann *MGH Epp.* 1–2, 1891–9)

Gregory of Tours (1977). *Historiarum Libri Decem* (Freiherr vom Stein-Gedächtnisausgabe 2 and 3), Wissenschaftliche Buchgesellschaft

Haddan, A.W. and Stubbs, W., eds. (1871). *Councils and Ecclesiastical Documents Relating to Great Britain and Ireland*, vol. III, Clarendon Press

Isidore of Seville (1850a). *Differentiae*, *PL* 83:9–98

(1850b). *Allegoriae Quaedam Sacrae Scripturae*, *PL* 83:97–130

(1850c). *Quaestiones in Vetus Testamentum*, *PL* 83:207–424

(1850d). *De Fide Catholica contra Judaeos*, *PL* 83:449–538

(1850e). *Sententiae*, *PL* 83:537–738

(1850f). *De Ecclesiasticis Officiis*, *PL* 83:737–826

(1894). *Historia Gothorum, Wandalorum, Sueborum*, in *MGH AA* XI:268–303

(1911). *Etymologiarum sive Originum libri XX*, 2 vols., ed. W.M. Lindsay (Scriptorum Classicorum Bibliotheca Oxoniensis), Clarendon Press

Jerome (1845), *Libri duo adversus Iovinianum*, *PL* 23:211–338

John of Biclar (1894). *Chronica*, in *MGH AA* XX:207–20

Jordanes (1882). *Romana et Getica*, in *MGH AA* V/i

Macrobius (1952). *Commentary on the Dream of Scipio*, transl. with an introduction and notes by W.H. Stahl (Records of Civilization, Sources and Studies 48), Columbia University Press

(1963). *Saturnalia* and *Commentarii in Somnium Scipionis commentarii*, ed. J. Willis (Bibliotheca Scriptorum Graecorum et Romanorum Teubneriana), Teubner

Orosius (1889). *Historiarum Adversum Paganos Libri VII*, Teubner

Paul the Deacon (1878). *Historia Langobardorum*, in *MGH SS Rerum Langobardicarum et Italicarum Saec. VI–IX* 12–187

Rau, R. (ed.) (1968). *Briefe des Bonifatius; Willibalds Leben des Bonifatius* (Freiherr vom Stein-Gedächtnisausgabe 4b), Wissenschaftliche Buchgesellschaft

Sidonius Apollinaris (1887). *Epistulae et Carmina*, in *MGH AA* VIII:1–264

Tacitus (1938). *De Origine et Situ Germanorum*, Clarendon Press

Thiel, A., ed. (1867). *Epistolae Romanorum Pontificum Genuinae*, vol. I, Edward Peter

Venantius Fortunatus (1881). *Opera Poetica*, in *MGH AA* IV/i

Victor of Vita (1879). *Historia Persecutionis*, in *MGH AA* III/i:1–58

Wolfram, H., ed. (1982). *Quellen zur Geschichte des 7. und 8. Jahrhunderts* (Freiherr vom Stein-Gedächtnisausgabe 4a), Wissenschaftliche Buchgesellschaft

Secondary sources

Anton, H.H. (1968). *Fürstenspiegel und Herrscherethos in der Karolingerzeit* (Bonner Historische Forschungen 32), Ludwig Röhrscheid Verlag

Arcari, P.M. (1968). *Idee e sentimenti politichi dell'Alto Medioevo*, Giuffrè

Arquillière, H.X. (1934). *L'Augustinisme politique*, J. Vrin

Barrow, R.H. (1950). *Introduction to St Augustine: The City of God*, Faber and Faber

Bathory, P.D. (1981). *Political Theory as Public Confession: The Social and Political Thought of St Augustine of Hippo*, Transaction

Baynes, N.H. (1962). *The Political Ideas of Saint Augustine's De civitate Dei*, Historical Association

Berkhof, H. (1947). *See section I above*

Brown, P. (1961). 'Religious Dissent in the Later Roman Empire: The Case of North Africa', *History* 46:83–101; repr. in Brown 1972, pp. 237–59

(1963). 'Saint Augustine', in Smalley 1965 (see 'General DD works'); repr. in Brown 1972, pp. 25–45, and Markus 1972a, pp. 311–35

(1964). 'St Augustine's Attitude to Religious Coercion', *Journal of Roman Studies* 54:107–16; repr. in Brown 1972, pp. 260–78

(1972). *Religion and Society in the Age of Saint Augustine*, Faber and Faber

Bund, Konrad (1979). *Thronsturz und Herrscherabsetzung im Frühmittelalter* (Bonner Historische Forschungen 4), Ludwig Röhrscheid Verlag

Campenhausen, H. von (1949). *Ambrosius von Mailand als Kirchenpolitiker*, W. de Gruyter

Caspar, E. (1933). *Geschichte des Papsttums*, vol. II, J.C.B. Mohr

Chaney, William A. (1970). *The Cult of Kingship in Anglo-Saxon England*, Manchester University Press

Claude, D. (1971). *Adel, Kirche und Königtum im Westgotenreich* (Voträge und Forschungen 8), Jan Thorbecke Verlag

(1978). 'Universale und partikulare Züge in der Politik Theoderichs', *Francia* 6:19–58

Combès, G. (1927). *La doctrine politique de saint Augustin*, Les petits fils de Plon et Nourrit

Courcelle, P. (1964). *Histoire Littéraire des Grandes Invasions Germaniques*, 3rd edn, Etudes Augustiniennes

Courtois, C. (1964). *Les Vandales et l'Afrique*, Scientia Verlag (repr. of 1955 Paris edn)

Cranz, F.E. (1950). '*De Civitate Dei* xv.2 and Augustine's Idea of a Christian Society', *Speculum* 25:215–25; repr. in Markus 1972a, pp. 404–21

(1952). 'Kingdom and Polity in Eusebius of Caesarea', *Harvard Theological Review* 45:47–66

(1954). 'The Development of Augustine's Ideas on Society before the Donatist Controversy', *Harvard Theological Review* 47:255–316; repr. in Markus 1972a, pp. 336–403

Dagens, C. (1970). 'La fin des temps et l'Eglise selon Saint Grégoire le Grand', *Recherches de science religieuse* 58:273–88

Deane, H.A. (1963). *The Political and Social Ideas of St Augustine*, Columbia University Press

Diesner, H.J. (1963). *Kirche und Staat im spätrömischen Reich. Aufsätze zur spätantike und geschichte der alten Kirche*, Evangelische Verlagsanstalt

(1966). *Das Vandalenreich: Aufstieg und Untergang* (Urban Bücher, Die wissenschaftliche Taschenbuchreihe 95), Kohlhammer

(1978). *Isidor von Sevilla und das westgotische Spanien* (Occidens 2), Spee-Verlag

*

Dudden, F.H. (1905). *Gregory the Great. His Place in History and Thought*, 2 vols., Longmans, Green and Co.
(1935). *The Life and Times of St Ambrose*, 2 vols., Oxford University Press
Dvornik, F. (1966). *See* section I above
Erdmann, C. (1951). *Forschungen zur politischen Ideenwelt des Frühmittelalters*, Akademie-Verlag
Ewig, E. (1956a). 'Zum christlichen Königsgedanken im Frühmittelalter', in Mayer 1956 (q.v.)
(1956b). 'Das Bild Constantins des Grossen in den ersten Jahrhunderten des abendländischen Mittelalters', *Historisches Jahrbuch* 75:1–46
Figgis, J.N., (1921). *The Political Aspects of St Augustine's 'City of God'*, Longmans, Green and Co.
Fischer, E.H. (1950). 'Gregor der Grosse und Byzana: ein Beitrag zur Geschichte der päpstlichen Politik', *Zeitschrift für Rechtsgeschichte, Kanonistische Abteil* 36:15–144
Folz, R. (1953). *L'Idée d'Empire en Occident du Ve au XIVe Siècle*, Aubier, Editions Montaigne (Eng. transl. *The Concept of Empire in Western Europe from the Fifth to the Fourteenth Century* (1969), Edward Arnold)
Fortin, E.L. (1972). *Political Idealism and Christianity in the Thought of St Augustine* (The Saint Augustine lecture, 1971). Augustinian Institute, Villanova University
Gaudemet, J. (1976). 'Droit séculier et droit de l'Eglise chez Ambroise', in G. Lazzati (ed.), *Ambrosius episcopus* (Studia patristica mediolanensia 6), 1:286–315
Graus, F. (1965). *Volk, Herrscher und Heiliger im Reich der Merowinger*, Nakladatelství Československé Akademie Věd
Greenslade, S.L. (1954). *Church and State from Constantine to Theodosius*, SCM Press
Grierson, P. (1941). 'Election and Inheritance in Early Germanic Kingship', *Cambridge Historical Journal* 7:1–22
Hartigan, R.S. (1966). 'Saint Augustine on War and Killing: The Problem of the Innocent', *Journal of the History of Ideas* 27:195–204
Heggelbacher, O. (1959). *Vom römischen zum christlichen Recht. Iuristische Elemente in den Schriften des sog. Ambrosiaster*, Universitätsverlag Freiburg
Hill, C. (1979). 'Classical and Christian Traditions in Some Writings of Saint Ambrose of Milan', unpublished Oxford University D.Phil. thesis
Höfler, O. (1956). 'Der Sakralcharakter des germanischen Königtums', in Mayer 1956 (q.v.)
James, E. (ed.) (1980). *Visigothic Spain: New Approaches*, Clarendon Press
King, P.D. (1972). *Law and Society in the Visigothic Kingdom* (Cambridge Studies in Medieval Life and Thought, Third Series, 5), Cambridge University Press
(1980). 'The Alleged Territoriality of Visigothic Law', in Tierney and Linehan 1980, pp. 1–11 (*see* General works)
Lamirande, E. (1975). *Church, State and Toleration. An Intriguing Change of Mind in Saint Augustine* (The Saint Augustine Lecture, 1974), Augustinian Institute, Villanova University
Lohse, B. (1960). 'Augustins Wandlung in seiner Beurteilung des Staates', *Studia Patristica* 6:447–75
Löwe, H. (1973). *Von Cassiodor zu Dante*, W. de Gruyter
Maes, B. (1967). *La loi naturelle selon S. Ambroise* (Anal. Greg. 162), Presse Universaire Grégorienne
Markus, R.A. (1965). 'Two Conceptions of Political Authority: Augustine, *De civitate Dei* XIX.14–15 and Some Thirteenth Century Interpretations', *Journal of Theological Studies*, New Series, 16:68–100; partly repr. Markus 1970, pp. 197–230

(1970). *Saeculum: History and Society in the Theology of Saint Augustine*, Cambridge University Press

(1972a). *Augustine: A Collection of Critical Essays* (Modern Studies in Philosophy), Anchor Books, Doubleday and Co.

(1972b). 'Christianity and Dissent in Roman North Africa: Changing Perspectives in Recent Work', in *Studies in Church History*. vol. IX: *Schism, Heresy and Religious Protest*, ed. D. Baker, Cambridge University Press, pp. 21–30; repr. in Markus 1983c, n. VIII

(1981). 'Gregory the Great's Europe', *Transactions of the Royal Historical Society*, 5th ser., 31:21–36; repr. in Markus 1983c, n. XV

(1983a). 'Saint Augustine's Views on the Just War', *Studies in Church History* 20:1–13

(1983b). *From Augustine to Gregory the Great* (Collected Studies Series 169), Variorum Reprints

(1985). 'The Sacred and the Secular: From Augustine to Gregory the Great', *Journal of Theological Studies* n.s. 36: 84–96.

(1986). 'Gregory the Great's *Rector* and His Genesis', in J. Fontaine, R. Gillet and S. Pellistrandi (eds.), *Grégoire le Grand* (Colloques Internationaux du Centre de la Recherche Scientifique, Chantilly, 1982. Paris), pp. 137–46.

Mayer, Th., ed. (1956). *Das Königtum. Seine geistigen und rechtlichen Grundlagen* (Vorträge und Forschungen 3), Jan Thorbecke Verlag

Michel, A. (1933). 'Der Kampf um das politische oder petrinische Prinzip der Kirchenführung', in A. Grillmeier (ed.), *Das Konzil von Chalkedon*, 2:491–562, Echter Verlag

Morino, C. (1969). *Church and State in the Teaching of St Ambrose*, Catholic University of America Press

Morrison, K.F. (1964). *Rome and the City of God. An Essay concerning the Relationships of Empire and Church in the Fourth Century* (Transactions of the American Philosophical Society, New Series, 54 pt 1)

Palanque, J.R. (1933). *S. Ambroise et l'empire romain*, E. de Beccard

Peterson, E. (1935, 1961). *See* section I above

Reydellet, M. (1981). *La Royauté dans la Littérature Latine de Sidoine Apollinaire à Isidore de Séville* (Bibliothèque des Ecoles Françaises d'Athènes et de Rome 243), Ecole Française de Rome

Roques R. (1954). *L'univers dionysien. Structure hiérarchique du monde selon le pseudo-Denys* (Théologie 29), Aubier

Russell, F.H. (1975). *The Just War in the Middle Ages* (Cambridge Studies in Medieval Life and Thought, Third Series, 8), Cambridge University Press

Schilling, O. (1910). *Dies Staats- und Soziallehre des hl. Augustinus*, Herder

(1914). *Naturrecht und Staat nach der Lehre der alten Kirche* (Görres-Gesellschaft, Veröffentlichungen der Sektion für Rechts- und Sozialwissenschaft 24)

Schlesinger, W. (1956). 'Über germanisches Heerkönigtum', in Mayer 1956 (q.v.)

See, K. von (1972). *Kontinuitätstheorie und Sakraltheorie in der Germanenforschung*, Athenäum

Stengel, E.E. (1965). *Abhandlungen und Untersuchungen zur Geschichte des Kaisergedankens im Mittelalter*, Böhlau Verlag

Straub, J.A. (1939). *Vom Herrscherideal der Spätantike*, Kohlhammer

(1954). 'Augustins Sorge um die *regeneratio imperii*: das *Imperium Romanum* als *civitas terrena*', *Historisches Jahrbuch* 73:36–60; repr. in Straub, J.A. (1972). *Regeneratio imperii*, Wissenschaftliche Buchgesellschaft, pp. 271–95

Suerbaum, W. (1977). *Vom antiken zum frühmittelalterlichen Staatsbegriff. Über Verwen-*

dung und Bedeutung von Res Publica, Regnum, Imperium und Status von Cicero bis Jordanis, 3rd edn, Aschendorffsche Verlagsbuchhandlung

Teillet, S. (1984). *Des Goths à la Nation Gothique. Les Origines de l'Idée de Nation en Occident du Ve au VIIe Siècle* (Collection d'Etudes Anciennes), Les Belles Lettres

Thompson, E.A. (1966). *The Visigoths in the Time of Ulfila*, Clarendon Press

Ullmann, W. (1963). 'The Bible and Principles of Government in the Middle Ages', *Settimane di Studio del Centro Italiano di Studi sull'Alto Medioevo* 10:181–227 (also in Ullmann 1975c)

(1975c). *The Church and the Law in the Earlier Middle Ages*, Variorum Reprints

(1981). *Gelasius I. Das Papsttum an der Wende des Spätantike zum Mittelalter* (Päpste und Papsttum 18), Hiersemann

Vollrath-Reichelt, H. (1971). *Königsgedanke und Königtum bei den Angelsachsen bis zur Mitte des 9. Jahhunderts.* (Kölner Historische Abhandlungen 19), Böhlau Verlag

Wallace-Hadrill, J.M. (1962). *The Long-haired Kings*, Methuen

(1971). *Early Germanic Kingship in England and on the Continent*, Clarendon Press

Wenskus, R. (1961). *Stammesbildung und Verfassung. Das Werden der frühmittelalterlichen Gentes*, Böhlau Verlag

Wolfram, H., ed. (1967). *Intitulatio, i: Lateinische Königs- und Fürstentitel bis zum Ende des 8. Jahrhunderts* (MIÖG Ergänzungsband 21), Böhlaus Nachfolger

(1970). 'The Shaping of the Early Medieval Kingdom', *Viator* 1:1–20

Wormald, P. (1977). '*Lex Scripta* and *Verbum Regis*: Legislation and Germanic Kingship, from Euric to Cnut', in P.H. Sawyer and I.N. Wood (eds.) *Early Medieval Kingship*, pub. by the editors

Wormald, P. et al., eds. (1983). *Ideal and Reality in Frankish and Anglo-Saxon Society*, Basil Blackwell

IV FORMATION: c. 750–c. 1150

Primary sources

Abelard, Peter (1849, 1859). *Opera*, ed. V. Cousin, 2 vols., Aug. Durans
    (1855). *Opera, PL* 178
    (1969). *Theologia Christiana*, in E.M. Buyaert (ed.) *Petri Abelardi opera theologica*, vol.
    II, *CC*, Continuatio medievalis 12
    (1970). *Dialogus inter Philosophum, Iudaeum et Christianum*, ed. T.R. Friedrich,
    Frommann Verlag (Günther Holzboog)
    (1971). *Peter Abelard*, ed. D.E. Luscombe, with introd., English transl. and notes
    (Oxford Medieval Texts), Clarendon Press
Actus pontificum Cenomannis (1901). In G. Busson (ed.) *Actus pontificum Cenomannis in*
    urbe degentium (Archives historiques de Maine 2)
Adalbero of Laon (1979). *Carmen ad Rotbertum regem*, in C. Carozzi (ed.) *Adalbéron de*
    Laon. Poème au roi Robert (Les Classiques de l'histoire de France au moyen âge 32),
    Les Belles Lettres, with a French trans.
Adelard of Bath (1903). *De eodem et diverso*, ed. H. Willner, (Beiträge zur geschichte der
    Philosophie des Mittelalters 4.1), Aschendorff
    (1934). *Quaestiones naturales*, ed. M. Müller (Beiträge zur Geschichte der Philosophie
    und Theologie des Mittelalters 31.2), Aschendorff
Adso of Montierender (1976). *De ortu et tempore Antichristi*, ed. D. Verhelst, *CC*,
    Continuatio mediaevalis 45
Agobard of Lyons (1951). *Opera, PL* 104:29–251
    (1887). *Libri duo pro filiis et contra Iudith uxorem Ludovici Pii*, ed. G. Waitz, *MGH SS*
    15:274–9
    (1899). *Epistolae*, ed. E. Dümmler, *MGH Epp.* 5:150–239
Alan of Lille (1855). *Opera, PL* 210
    (1908). *The Complaint of Nature . . .*, transl. from the Latin by D.M. Moffat (Yale
    Studies in English, ed. A.S. Cook, 36), H. Holt and Company
    (1955). *Anticlaudianus*, ed. R. Bossuat, J. Vrin
    (1965). *Hierarchia*, in M.T. d'Alverny (ed.) *Alain de Lille. Textes inédits* (Etudes de
    philosophie médiévale, ed. E. Gilson), J. Vrin, pp. 219–35
    (1973). *Anticlaudianus*, transl. into English by J.J. Sheridan, *Alan of Lille.*
    Anticlaudianus or The Good and Perfect Man (Medieval Sources in Translation 14),
    Pontifical Institute of Mediaeval Studies, Toronto
    (1978). *De Planctu naturae*, ed. N.M. Häring, 'Alan of Lille, De Planctu naturae',
    Studi medievali, 3rd series, 19:797–879
Alcuin (1982). *The Bishops, Kings and Saints of York*, ed. and trans. by P. Godman,
    Oxford University Press
Alfanus of Salerno (1917). *Nemesii episcopi Premnon physicon . . . a N. Alfano*
    archiepiscopo Salerni in latinum translatus, ed. C. Burkhard, Teubner

(1974). *I Carmi di Alfano 1, arcivescovo di Salerno*, ed. A. Lentini and F. Avagliano (Miscellanea Cassinese 38), Monte Cassino

Al-Fārābī (1895). *Principles of the Views of the Citizens of the Excellent State*, ed. F. Dieterici, as *Alfarabi's Abhandlung. Der Musterstaat* (Arabic text), E.J. Brill: German transl. by F. Dieterici, *Der Musterstaat von Alfārābī*, E.J. Brill, 1900; a French transl. by R.P. Jaussen and others was published at Cairo in 1949. For English transl. see Al-Fārābī (1985).

(1943). *De Platonis philosophia*, ed. F. Rosenthal and R. Walzer (Corpus Platonicum Medii Aevi, ed. R. Klibansky, Plato Arabus 2), Warburg Institute

(1952). *Compendium Legum Platonis*, ed. with Latin transl. by F. Gabrieli (Corpus Platonicum Medii Aevi, ed. R. Klibansky, Plato Arabus 3), Warburg Institute (Al-Fārābī's authorship has been challenged)

(1953). *Catalogus scientiarum*, in Ángel González Palencia (ed.) *Alfārābī: Catálogo de las ciencias*, with Spanish transl., 2nd edn, Madrid, Consejo Superior de Investigaciones Científicas, Patronato Menédez y Pelayo – Instituto 'Miguel Asín'

(1954). *De scientiis*, in P. Manuel Alonso Alonso (ed.) *Domingo Gundisalvo: De scientiis*, with Spanish transl., Madrid–Granada, Consejo Superior de Investigaciones Científicas, Patronato Menéndez y Pelayo – Instituto 'Miguel Asín'

(1961). *Fusūl al-Mandanī (Aphorisms of the Statesman)*, ed. with English transl. by D.M. Dunlop, Cambridge University Press

(1962). *Al Fārābī's Philosophy of Plato and Aristotle*, transl. with an introd. by M. Mahdi, Free Press of Glencoe

(1963). *On Political Government*, English transl. in Lerner and Mahdi 1963, pp. 39ff (*see* General works)

(1985). *Abū Nasr al-Fārābī's Mabādiʾ Ārāʾ Ahl Al-Madīna Al-Fādila (On the Perfect State)*, revised text with introd. transl. and commentary by R. Walzer, Clarendon Press

Amalarius (1899). *Epistolae*, ed. E. Dümmler, *MGH Epp.* 5:240–74

Angilbert (1881), *Carmina*, ed. E. Dümmler, *MGH Poetae* 1:355–81

Annales Bertiniani (1883). Ed. G. Waitz, *MGH SS rerum Germanicarum in usum scholarum*

(1964). Ed. F. Grat, J. Vielliard and S. Clémencet, Librairie C. Klincksieck, Librairie de la Société de l'Histoire de France

Annales Fuldenses (1891). Ed. F. Kurze, *MGH SS rerum Germanicarum in usum scholarum* 7

Annales Laureshamenses (1826). *MGH SS* 1:19–39

Annales Regni Francorum inde ab a. 741 usque ad a. 829 qui dicuntur Annales Laurissenses Maiores et Einhardi (1895). Ed. F. Kurze, *MGH SS rerum Germanicarum in usum scholarum* 6

Annals of Lorsch, *see Annales Laureshamenses*

Anonymous of Hersfeld (1892). *Liber de unitate ecclesiae conservanda*, *MGH Libelli* 2:173–284

Anonymous of York/Rouen, *see* Norman Anonymous

Anselm II of Lucca (1906–15). *Anselm Episcopi Lucensis Collectio canonum, una cum collectione minore*, ed. F. Thaner, Libraria Academica Wagneriana

(1965). *Sermo Anselmi episcopi de caritate*, ed. E. Pásztor, 'Motivi dell' ecclesiologia di Anselmo di Lucca. In margine a un sermone inedito', *Bullettino dell' Istituto storico italiano per il medio evo e Archivio Muratoriano* 77:96–104

Avempace, *see* Ibn Bajja

Averroes (1949–). *Commentaries on Aristotle*, ed. H.A. Wolfson *et al.*, Mediaeval Academy of America

(1956). *Averroes' Commentary on Plato's Republic*, ed. and transl. by E.I.J. Rosenthal, Cambridge University Press

(1974). *On Plato's Republic*, transl. by R. Lerner, Cornell University Press

Avicenna, *see* Ibn Sina

Becket, St Thomas (1875–85). *Materials for the History of Thomas Becket, Archbishop of Canterbury*, ed. J.C. Robertson and J.B. Sheppard (Rerum Britannicarum Medii Aevi), 7 vols., Longman

Benedictionals of Freising (1974), Ed. R. Amiet (Henry Bradshaw Society 88), British Legion Press, Maidstone

Bernard of Clairvaux (1957–77). *Opera omnia*, ed. J. Leclercq, H.M. Rochais and C.H. Talbot, 8 vols., Editiones Cistercienses

(1963a). *De consideratione*, in Bernard of Clairvaux 1957–77, vol. III

(1963b). *Liber ad milites templi de laude novae militiae*, in Bernard of Clairvaux 1957–77, vol. III

Bernard Silvestris (1973). *The Cosmographia*, transl. with introd. and notes by Winthrop Wetherbee, Columbia University Press

(1978). *Cosmographia*, ed. with an introd. and notes by P. Dronke (Textus Minores 53), E.J. Brill

Bernold of Constance (1878). *Opera*, PL 148:1057–272

(1892). *Libellus*, ed. F. Thaner, MGH *Libelli* 2:168

(1937). *De veritate corporis et sanguinis Domini*, ed. H. Weisweiler, in 'Die vollständige Kampfschrift Bernolds von St. Blasien gegen Berengar', *Scholastik* 12:58ff

Bigelow, M.M. (1879). *Placita Anglo-Normannica: Law Cases from William I. to Richard I. Preserved in Historical Records*, Sampson Low, Marston, Searle and Rivington

Bonizo of Sutri (1930). *Liber de vita christiana*, ed. E. Perels (Texte zur Geschichte der römischen und kanonischen Rechts im Mittelalter 1), Weidmann

Capitularia regum Francorum (1883). Ed. A. Boretius and V. Krause, MGH *Legum Sectio* II: 1–2

Chanson de Roland (1957). *The Song of Roland: A New Translation by Dorothy L. Sayers* (Penguin Classics 175), Penguin Books

(1969). *La Chanson de Roland: texte établi d'après le manuscrit d'Oxford*, ed. G. Moignet (with a modern French transl. which was separately reissued in 1970), Editions Bordas; Larousse

(1971). *La Chanson de Roland: edizione critica*, ed. C. Segre, Riccardo Ricciardi

Clausula de Pippino rege (1885). Ed. B. Krusch, MGH SS *rerum merovingicarum* 1:15–16

Codex Carolinus (1892). Ed. W. Gundlach, MGH *Epp. KA* I

Collectio in LXXIV titulos digesta (1973). In J.T. Gilchrist (ed.) *Diversorum patrum sententiae sive Collectio in LXXIV titulos digesta* (Monumenta Iuris Canonici, series B: Corpus Collectionum, 1), Vatican City

Constitutions of Clarendon, 1164 (1921). In W. Stubbs (ed.) *Select Charters and Other Illustrations of English Constitutional History* (9th edn revised throughout by H.W.C. Davis), Clarendon Press, pp. 161–7

Constitutum Constantini (1968). *Das Constitutum Constantini (Konstantinische Schenkung)*, MGH *Fontes iuris Germanici Antiqui* 10

Continuator of Fredegar (1960). *Chronicle*, ed. J.M. Wallace-Hadrill, Nelson

Corpus Iuris Canonici (1879–81). Ed. A. Friedberg, 2 vols., Tauchnitz

Cosmas of Prague (1923). *Chronica Bogmorum*, ed. B. Bretholz, MGH SS *rerum Germanicarum in usum scholarum* 6

Coustant, P. (1721). *Epistolae Romanorum Pontificum . . . a s. Clemente usque ad Innocentium III*, vol. I: *Ab anno Christi 67 ad annum 40* (no more published), Paris

Decretales Pseudo-Isidorianae (1863). *Decretals Pseudo-Isidorianae et Capitula Angilramni*, ed. P. Hinschius, Tauchnitz.

Deusdedit (1892). *Libellus contra invasores et symoniacos et reliquos scismaticos*, ed. E. Sackur, *MGH Libelli* 2:292–365

(1905). *Collectio canonum*, in V. Wolf von Glanvell (ed.) *Die Kanonessammlung des Kardinals Deusdedit*, vol. i, F. Schöningh

Dhuoda (1975). *Manuel pour mon fils*, ed. P. Riché, Sources chrétiennes, Paris

Dilcher, H. (1973). *Constitutiones Regni Siciliae. Faksimiledruck mit einer Einleitung*, Glashütten, Detlev Auvermann (Mittelalterliche Gesetzbücher europäischer Länder, dir. by A. Wolf, VI), Glashütten, Detlev Auvermann

Donation of Constantine, see Constitutum Constantini

Einhard (1911). *Vita Karoli Magni*, ed. O. Holder-Egger. *MGH SS rerum Germanicarum in usum scholarum* 25

Erchanbert (1829). *Breviarium regum francorum*, ed. G. Pertz, *MGH SS* 2:327–8

Ermold (1932). *Carmen in honorem Pippini regis*, and *In honorem Hludowici*, in E. Faral (ed.) *Poème sur Louis le Pieux et épîtres au roi Pépin* (Les Classiques de l'histoire de France an moyen âge 14), Les Belles Lettres

Espinas, G. (1934–43). *Recueil de documents relatifs à l'histoire du droit municipal en France des origines à la Révolution. Artois*, 3 vols (Société d'Histoire du Droit), Sirey

Flodoard (1881). *Historia Remensis Ecclesiae*, ed. I. Heller and G. Waitz, *MGH SS* 13

Fulbert of Chartres (1976). *The Letters and Poems of Fulbert of Chartres*, ed. F. Behrends (Oxford Medieval Texts), Clarendon Press

Galbert of Bruges (1891). *De multro, traditione et occisione gloriosi Karoli comitis Flandriarum*, ed. H. Pirenne, Picard

Gallus Anonymus (1952), *Chronica et Gesta Ducum sive Principum Polonorum*, ed. K. Maleczyński (Monumenta Poloniac-Historica, nova series ii,ii), Cracow

Gelasian Sacramentary (1958). In L.C. Mohlberg (ed.) *Liber Sacramentorum Romanae Ecclesiae Ordinis Anni Circuli* (Rerum Ecclesiasticarum Documenta, Series Maior Foutes iv) Rome

Gelasius I (1868). *See* section III

Geoffrey of Monmouth (1929). *Historia Regum Britanniae*, ed. Acton Griscom, Longmans Green and Co.

Gerard of Cambrai (1953). *Acta synodi Atrebatensis in Manichaeos, PL* 142:1269–312

Gerhoh of Reichersberg (1854–5). *Opera. PL* 193–4

(1875). *Gerhohi Reichersbergensis praepositi opera hactenus inedita*, ed. F. Scheibelberger, vol. i, M. Quirein

(1897). *Opera*, ed. E. Sackur, *MGH Libelli* 3:131–525

(1955–6). *Opera inedita*, ed. D. Van den Eynde (Spicilegium Pontificii Athenaei Antoniani viii–x)

(1974). *Letter to Pope Hadrian on the Novelties of the Day*, ed. N.M. Häring (Studies and Texts 24), Pontifical Institute of Mediaeval Studies, Toronto

Gesta episcoporum cameracensium (1846). Ed. L.C. Bethmann, *MGH SS* 7:393–525

Gesta episcoporum Cenomannensium (1723). In J. Mabillon (ed.) *Vetera Analecta*, Paris

Gesta Stephani (1976). Ed. and transl. by K.R. Potter with new introd. and notes by R.H.C. Davis, Oxford University Press

Giles of Rome (1929). *See* section V

Glanvill (1965). In G.D.G. Hall (ed.) *Tractatus de legibus et consuetudinibus regni Angliae qui Glanvilla vocatur*, Nelson

Gottschalk of Aachen (1937). *Die Briefe Heinrichs IV.*, ed. C. Erdman (*MGH Deutsches Mittelalter. Kritische Studientexte des Reichsinstituts für ältere deutsche Geschichtskunde* 1). Hiersmann

Graphia aureae urbis Romae (1946). In R. Valentini and G. Zucchetti (eds.) *Codice topografico della città di Roma*, vol. III (Fonti per la storia d'Italia 90), Tipografia del Senato, pp. 67–110

(1969). In P.E. Schramm (ed.) *Kaiser, Könige und Päpste. Gesammelte Aufsätze zur Geschichte des Mittelalters*, 5 vols. (1968–71), Hiersemann, here vol. III, p. 313–53

Gratian of Bologna (1879). *Concordia discordantium canonum* (or *Decretum Magistri Gratiani*), in *Corpus Iuris Canonici* 1879–81, vol. I

Gregory VII (1901). Liturgical text, *In die resurrectionis*, ed. G. Morin, *Revue Bénédictine* 18:179

(1932). *Letters, a Selection*, transl. into English by E. Emerton (Records of Civilisation, Sources and Studies, 14), Columbia University Press

(1955). *Registrum*, ed. E. Caspar, in *MGH Epp. selectae* 2 (parts 1 and 2), 2nd edn (1st edn 1920–3)

(1972). *The 'Epistolae vagantes' of Pope Gregory VII*, ed. and transl. by H.E.J. Cowdrey (Oxford Medieval Texts), Clarendon Press

Grim, Edward (1876). *Vita Sancti Thomae*, in Becket 1875–85, vol. II, pp. 353–450

Guibert of Nogent (1879). *Gesta Dei per Francos* (Recueil des Historiens des Croisades, Historiens occidentaux, 4), Académie des Inscriptions et Belles-Lettres, pp. 113–263

(1907). *De vita sua*, in G. Bourgin (ed.) *Guibert de Nogent. Histoire de sa vie (1053–1124)* (Collection de textes pour servir à l'étude et à l'enseignement de l'histoire 40), Picard

Haddan, A.W. and Stubbs, W., eds. (1871). *See* section III

Helmold of Bosau (1937). *Cronica Slavorum*, ed. B. Schmeidler, *MGH SS rerum Germanicarum in usum scholarum* 32:1–218

Henry of Huntingdon (1879). *Historia Anglorum*, ed. T. Arnold (Rerum Britannicarum Medii Aevi), Longman

Herbert of Bosham (1877). *Vita Sancti Thomae*, in Becket 1875–85, vol. II, pp. 155–534

(1881–2). *Epistolae*, in Becket 1875–85, vols. I–VI

Hildegard of Bingen (1855). *Opera*, PL 197

(1978). *Scivias*, ed. A. Fürkötter and A. Carlevaris, CC, Continuatio mediaevalis 43–43A

Hincmar of Rheims (1852a). *De Regis Persona et regio ministerio*, PL 125:833–56

(1852b). *De Divortio Lotharii Regis et Tetbergae Reginae*, PL 125:619–772

(1980). *De Ordine Palatii*, ed. T. Gross, and R. Schieffer, *MGH Fontes iuris Germanici Antiqui in usum scholarum separatum editi* 3 (with a German translation)

Honorius Augustodunensis (1895). *Opera*, PL 172

(1897). *Libelli*, ed. L. Dieterich, *MGH Libelli* 3:29–80

Hrabanus Maurus, *see* Rabanus Maurus

Hugh of St Victor (1854a). *Opera*, PL 175–7

(1854b). *Expositio in Hierarchiam Coelestem S. Dionysii Areopagitae*, in Hugh St Victor 1854a, PL 175:923–1154

(1939). *Didascalicon de studio legendi, a Critical Text*, ed. C.H. Buttimer (Catholic University of America, Studies in Medieval and Renaissance Latin, 10), The Catholic University.

(1961). *The Didascalicon of Hugh of St Victor: A Medieval Guide to the Arts*, transl. into English by J. Taylor (University Records of Civilization, Sources and Studies, 64), Columbia University Press

Humbert of Silva Candida (1882). *Opera*, PL 143:929–1218

(1891). *Libri III adversus simoniacos*, ed. F. Thaner, *MGH Libelli* 1:95–253

Ibn Bajja (1946). *El régimen del solitario*, ed. M. Asín Palacios, Madrid–Granada, Consejo

Superior de Investigaciones Científicas Instituto Miguel Asín, Escuelas de Estudios éabes de Madrid y Granada

Ibn Rushd, *see* Averroes

Ibn Sina (1495). *Metaphysica sive ejus prima philosophia*, Venice
  (1953). *Le Récit de Hayy ibn Yaqzan*, ed. H. Corbin (Collection UNESCO d'ouvres représentatives. Série persane), Tehran, Commission des monuments nationaux de l'Iran

Ibn Ṭufail (1674). (*Ḥayy ibn yagẓán*). *An Account of the Oriental Philosophy Showing particularly, the Profound Wisdom of Hai Ebn Yokdan . . . out of the Arabic Translated into Latine, by E. Pocock and now faithfully out of his Latine, Translated into English* [London]

Irnerius of Bologna. *Liber divinarum sententiarum*, unprinted MS Milan, Bibl. Ambrosiana Y 43 sup.
  (1894b). *Summa codicis*, ed. H. Fitting, J. Guttentag
  (1958). *Questiones de iuris subtilitatibus*, ed. G. Zanetti, La Nuova Italia Editrice

Ivo of Chartres. *Collectio Tripertita*, inedited
  (1889). *Opera*, PL 161–2
  (1949). *Letters*, part ed. with a French transl. by J. Leclercq, *Correspondence*, vol. I (1090–1098) (Les Classiques de l'histoire de France au moyen âge 22), Les Belles Lettres

Joachim of Fiore (1519). *Liber concordie noui ac veteris Testamenti*, per Simonem de Luere
  (1527). *Expositio . . . in Apocalipsim . . . Cui adiecta sunt eiusdem Psalterium decem cordarum*, F. Bindon and M. Pasyn
  (1953). *Liber Figurarum*, 2 vols., 2nd edn, L. Tondelli and B.M. Hirsch-Reich, Società editrice internazionale

John of Mantua (1973). *In Cantica Canticorum et de Sancta Maria Tractatus ad Comitissam Matildam*, ed. B. Bischoff and B. Taeger (Spicilegium Friburgense 19), Universitätsverlag Freiburg Schweiz

John of Paris (1942). See section V below

John of Salisbury (1909). *Policraticus*, ed. C.C.J Webb, 2 vols., Clarendon Press
  (1927). *The Statesman's Book of John of Salisbury; 4th, 5th and 6th Books and Selections from the 7th and 8th Books of the 'Policraticus'*, trans. into English by J. Dickinson, Knopf
  (1929). *Metalogicon*, ed. C.C.J. Webb, Clarendon Press
  (1938). *Frivolities of Courtiers and Footprints of Philosophers. A Translation of the First, Second and Third Books and Selections from the Seventh and Eighth Books of the 'Policraticus' of John of Salisbury*, J.B. Pike, University of Minnesota Press; Oxford University Press
  (1954). *Entheticus*, in C.R. Elrington (ed.) *John of Salisbury's 'Entheticus de dogmate philosophorum'*, unpublished London University MA thesis
  (1955). *The Metalogicon of John of Salisbury. A Twelfth-Century Defense of the Verbal and Logical Arts of the Trivium*, transl. with an introd. and notes by D.D. McGarry, University of California Press
  (1955–79). *The Letters of John of Salisbury*, vol. I: *The Early Letters (1153–1161)* ed. W.J. Millor and H.E. Butler, revised by C.N.L. Brooke, Nelson; vol. II: *The Later Letters 1163–1180*, ed. W.J. Millor and C.N.L. Brooke, Clarendon Press
  (1956). *Historia pontificalis*, in M. Chibnall (ed.) *John of Salisbury's Memoirs of the Papal Court* (Latin text and English transl.), Nelson
  (1969a). *Entheticus*, in D.J. Sheerin (ed.) *John of Salisbury's 'Entheticus de Dogmate Philosophorum': Critical Text and Introduction*, unpublished University of North Carolina at Chapel Hill PhD thesis

(1969b). *Le 'Policraticus' de Jean de Salisbury, traduit par Denis Foulechat en 1372, Livres I–II*, ed. with an introd. by C. Brucker, Roneo Copy, Nancy
(1975). *Entheticus*, ed. R.E. Pepin, in 'The *Entheticus* of John of Salisbury: A Critical Text', *Traditio* 31:127–93
(1984). *Policraticus*, ed. M. Angel, with Spanish transl. by M. Alcalá (Clásicos para una Biblioteca Contemporánea. Pensiamento. Serie dirigada por J.M.P. Prendes), Editora Nacional
Jonas of Orleans (1851). *De institutione laicali*, *PL* 106:121–78
(1930). *De institutione regia*, ed. J. Reviron (L'Eglise et l'état au moyen âge 1), J. Vrin
Kaiserchronik (1892). Ed. E. Schröder, *MGH SS qui vernacula lingua usi sunt* 1
Lampert of Hersfeld (1894). *Annales*, ed. O. Holder-Egger, *MGH SS rerum Germanicarum in usum scholarum* 38:1–304
Lehmann, A. (1896). *Das Langobardische Lehnrecht*, Dieterich
Leo III (1899). *Epistolae*, ed. K. Hampe, *MGH Epp.* 5:85–104
Levillain, L. (1926). *Actes de Pépin I et Pepin II rois d'Aquitaine (814–848)*, Imprimerie Nationale, Paris
Lex Salica. 100-Titel Text (1969). Ed. K.A. Eckhardt, *MGH Leges* 4/ii
Libellus de diversis ordinibus et professionibus qui sunt in aecclesia (1972). Ed. G. Constable and B. Smith (Oxford Medieval Texts), Clarendon Press
Liber de unitate ecclesiae conservanda (1892). Ed. W. Schwenkenbecher, *MGH Libelli* 2:173–284
Liebermann, F. (1898–1916). *Die Gesetze der Angelsachsen*, 3 vols., Max Niemeyer
Liutprand of Cremona (1915). *Relatio de Legatione Constantinopolitana*, in *Liutprandi Opera*, ed. J. Becker, *MGH SS rerum Germanicarum in usum scholarum* 41:115–212
Ludwigslied (1892). Ed. K. Müllenhof and W. Scherer, *Denkmäler deutscher Poesie und Prosa aus dem VIII–XII Jahrhundert*, Weidmannsche Buchhandlung
Maimonides, Moses (1856–66). *Le guide des égarés; traité de théologie et de philosophie par Moïse ben Maimoun, dit Maïmonide*, ed. S. Munk, A. Franck
(1934–5). *Letter to Samuel ibn Tibbon*, ed. A. Marx, in *Jewish Quarterly Review*, New Series, 25:378–80
(1938). *Millot ha-Higgayon*, Maimonides' Treatise on Logic (*Maḳālah fisināaʿt al-manṭiḳ*), the original Arabic and three Hebrew translations critically edited on the basis of manuscripts and early editions, and transl. into English by Israel Efros, American Academy for Jewish Research
(1963). *Moreh Nĕḇuḵum* (*The Guide of the Perplexed*), transl. by S. Pines, with an introductory essay by L. Strauss, University of Chicago Press
Manegold of Lautenbach (1891). *Liber ad Gebehardum*, ed. K. Francke, *MGH Libelli* 1:300–430
(1972). *Liber contra Wolfelmum*, ed. W. Hartmann (*MGH Quellen zur Geistesgeschichte des Mittelalters* 8), Böhlaus Nachfolger Modoin of Autun (1880). *Egloga*, *MGH Poetae* 1:382–92
Missale Francorum (1957). Ed. L.C. Mohlberg (Rerum Ecclesiasticarum Documenta, Series Maior, Fontes II). Rome
Mommsen, T.E. and Morrison, K.F., eds. (1962). *Imperial Lives and Letters of the Eleventh Century* (Records of Civilisation: Texts and Studies LXVII), Columbia University Press
Moralium dogma philosophorum (1929). In J. Holmberg (ed.) *Das Moral. dog.philos. des Guillaume de Conches, latienisch, altfranzösisch und mittelniederfränkisch* (Arbeten utgivna med understöd av Vilhelm Ekmans universitetsfond, Uppsala, 37), Almqvist & Wiksell

Nithard (1926). *Historiarum Libri IV*, ed. with French transl. by P. Lauer, *Histoire des fils de Louis le Pieux*, Les Belles Lettres

Norman Anonymous (1897). Part ed. under the title *Tractatus Eboracenses* by H. Böhmer, in *MGH Libelli* 3:642–87

(1966). *Die Texte des Normannischen Anonymous*, ed. K. Pellens (Veröffentlichungen) des Instituts für Europäische Geschichte Mainz (42), Franz Steiner Verlag

See also Williams 1951

Notker the Stammerer (1959). *Gesta Karoli*, ed. H.F. Haefele, *MGH SS rerum Germanicarum* n.s. 13

Orderic Vitalis (1969–80). *Historia ecclesiastica*, ed. M. Chibnall, 6 vols., Clarendon Press

Ordines coronationis Imperialis (1960). Ed. R. Elze, *MGH Fontes Iuris Germanici Antiqui* 9

Otto of Freising (1912a). *Chronica sive Historia de Duabus Civitatibus*, ed. A. Hofmeister, *MGH SS rerum Germanicarum in usum scholarum* 45

(1912b). *Gesta Friderici I, Imperatoris*, ed. G. Waitz, *Ottonis et Rahewini Gesta Friderici I. Imperatoris*, 3rd series, *MGH SS rerum Germanicarum in usum scholarum* 46

(1928). *The Two Cities. A chronicle of Universal History to the Year 1146 A.D.*, English transl. by C.C. Mierow (Records of Civilization, Sources and Studies), Columbia University Press

(1953). *The Deeds of Frederick Barbarossa by Otto of Freising and his Continuator, Rahewin*, English transl. by C.C. Mierow (Records of Civilization, Sources and Studies 49), Columbia University Press

(1965). In Schmale, F.J. (ed.) *Ottonis Episcopi Frisingensis et Rahewini Gesta Friderici, seu rectius Cronica*, with German transl. (Ausgewählte Quellen zur deutschen Geschichte des Mittelalters 17), Deutscher Verlag der Wissenschaften

Peter the Chanter (1855). *Verbum abbreviatum*, short version in *PL* 205:1–554; long version in MSS Paris, Bibliothèque Sainte-Geneviève 250, Bibliothèque Mazarine 772 and Vatican Reginensis lat. 106

(1954 *et seq*). *Summa de sacramentis et animae consilliis*, ed. J.-A. Dugauquier (Analecta mediaevalia Namurcensia, 4, 7, 11, 16, 21 etc.), Editions Nauwelaerts

Peter Damian (1867). *Opera*, *PL* 144–5

Peter Lombard (1879–80). *Opera*, *PL* 191–2

(1971–81). *Sentiniae in IV Libris distinctae*, 2 vols., 3rd edn (Spicilegium Bonaventurianum 4–5), Editiones Collegii S. Bonaventurae ad Claras Aquas

Pontificale Romano-Germanicum (1963). Ed. C. Vogel and R. Elze, 2 vols. (Studi e Testi 226), Biblioteca Apostolica Vaticana

Powell, J.M. (1971). *The Liber Augustalis*, Syracuse University Press, Syracuse, NY

Pseudo-Cyprian (1910). *De XII abusivis saeculi*, ex. S. Hellmann (Texte und Untersuchungen zur Geschichte der altchristlichen Literatur 34), Leipzig

Rabanus Maurus (1851). *De clericorum institutione*, *PL* 107:293ff

(1899). *Epistolae*, *MGH Epp.* 5

Regino of Prüm (1826). *Chronicon*, *MGH SS* 1:537–612

(1890). *Chronicon*, ed. F. Kurze, *MGH SS rerum Germanicarum in usum scholarum* 50

Richer (1877). *Historiarum Libri IV*, ed. G. Waitz, *MGH SS rerum Germanicarum in usum scholarum*

Robert of Melun (1932). *Quaestiones de divina pagina*, in R.J. Martin (ed.) *Ouvres de Robert de Melun*, 1 (Spicilegium Sacrum Lovaniense 13), Louvain

(1938). *Quaestiones de epistolis Pauli*, in R.J. Martin (ed.) *Ouvres de Robert de Melun*, vol. II (Spicilegium Sacrum Lovaniense 18), Louvain

(1947, 1952). *Sententiae*, in R.J. Martin (ed.) *Oeuvres de Robert de Melun*, vol. III, i, and (with R.M. Gallet) vol. III, ii (Spicilegium Sacrum Lovaniense 21 and 25), Louvain

Robert Pullen (1854). *Sententiarum libri octo*, PL 186:639–1010

Rupert of Deutz (1967). *Liber de divinis officiis*, ed. H. Haacke, CC, Continuatio mediaevalis 7

(1969). *Commentaria in Evangelium Sancti Johannis*, ed. H. Haacke, CC, Continuatio mediaevalis 9

(1970). *De victoria verbi dei*, ed. H. Haacke (*MGH Quellen zur Geistesgeschichte des Mittelalters* 5), Böhlaus Nachfolger

(1971–2). *De sancta trinitate et operibus eius*, ed. H. Haacke, CC, Continuatio mediaevalis 21–4

(1974). *Commentaria in Canticum Canticorum*, ed. H. Haacke, CC, Continuato mediaevalis 26

(1979). *De gloria filii hominis*, ed. H. Haacke, CC, Continuatio mediaevalis 29

Sedulius Scottus (1851). *Liber de rectoribus christianis*, PL 103:291–332

(1906). *Liber de rectoribus christianis*, ed. S. Hellmann (Quellen und Untersuchungen zur lateinischen Philologie des Mittelalters 1, 1), Munich

Smaragdus (1851). *Via regia*, PL 102:931–70

Song of Roland. See Chanson de Roland

Stubbs, W. (1913). *Select Charters and Other Illustrations of English Constitutional History from the Earliest Times to the Reign of Edward the First*, 9th edn, Clarendon Press

Suger (1949). *Vie de Louis VI le Gros*, ed. H. Waquet, Les Belles Lettres

Tessier, G. (1943–55). *Recueil des Actes de Charles II le Chauve*, 3 vols., Imprimerie Nationale, Paris

Theodulph of Orleans (1881). *Carmina*, ed. E. Dümmler *MGH Poetae* 1:437–581

Thorpe, L. (1969). *Einhard and Notker the Stammerer. Two Lives of Charlemagne*, Penguin Books

Tractatus Eboracenses, *see* Norman Anonymous

Vercauteren, F. (1938). *Actes des Comtes de Flandre 1071–1128* (Commission Royale d'Histoire, Recueil des Actes des Princes Belges), Royal Academy, Brussels

Verhulst, A. and Gysseling, M., eds. (1962). *Le compte général de 1187, connu sous le nom de 'Gros Brief' et les institutions financières du comté de Flandre au XIIe siècle* (Académie Royale des Sciences. Commission Royale d'Histoire)

Vita Lebuini antiqua (1934). Ed. A. Hofmeister, *MGH SS* 30/2:789–95

Waszink, J.A., ed. (1962). *Plato. Timaeus a Calcidio translatus commentarioque instructus*. *Plato Latinus*, ed. R. Klibansky, 4. *Corpus Platonicum Medii Aevi*, ed. R. Klibansky, Warburg Institute and E.J. Brill

Widukind (1935). *Rerum gestarum Saxonicarum Libri Tres*, ed. P. Hirsch and H.-E. Lohmann, *MGH SS rerum Germanicarum in usum scholarum* 60

Will, C.J.C., ed. (1861). *Acta et Scripta quae de controversiis ecclesiae Graecae et Latinae saeculo undecimo composita extant*, N.G. Elwert

William of Conches (1567). *Dragmaticon*, ed. G. Gratarolus, under the title *Dialogus de Substantiis Physicis . . . confectus a Wuilhelmo Aneponymo philosopho . . .*, Iosias Rihelius

(1862, 1895). *Philosophia mundi*, printed among the works of Bede (1862) in PL 90:1127–78 and those of Honorius Augustodunensis (1895) in PL 171:39–102

(1938). Ed. J.M. Parent, *La doctrine de la création dans l'école de Chartres; études et textes* (Publications de l'institut d'études médiévals d'Ottowa 8), J. Vrin

(1965). *Glosae super Platonem*, ed. E. Jeaneau (Textes philosophiques du moyen âge 13), J. Vrin

(1980). *Philosophia mundi*, ed. and transl. into German by G. Maurach, with the assistance of H. Telle, University of South Africa, Pretoria (Book 1 in this edition was first published separately in 1974 in the series of Studia, vol. 15)

William of Malmesbury (1870). *De gestis pontificum Anglorum*, ed. N.E.S.A. Hamilton
    (Rerum Britannicarum Medii Aevi Scriptores), Longman
    (1887, 1889). *De gestis regum Anglorum libri quinque*, 2 vols., ed. W. Stubbs (Rerum
    Britannicarum Medii Aevi Scriptores), Eyre and Spottiswoode
    (1955). *Historia Novella*, ed. and transl. into English by K.R. Potter, Nelson
Wipo (1915). *Gesta Chuonradi*, ed. H. Bresslau, *MGH SS rerum Germanicarum in usum
    scholarum* 61:1–62
Wright, F.A. (1930) *The Works of Liutprand of Cremona*, Routledge
Wulfstan of York (1959). *Die 'Institutes of Polity, Civil and Ecclesiastical'. Ein Werk
    Erzbischof Wulfstans von York*, ed. K. Jọst (Schweizer Anglistische Arbeiten Bd.
    47), A. Francke
York Tracts, see Norman Anonymous
Zeumer, K. (1886). *Formulae merovingici et karolini aevi*, *MGH Libelli* 5

Secondary sources

Affeldt W. (1969a). *Die weltliche Gewalt in der Paulus-Exegese. Rom. 13, 1–7 in den
    Römerbriefkommentaren der lateinischen Kirche bis zum Ende des 13. Jahrhunderts*
    (Forschungen zur Kirchen- und Dogmengeschichte 22), Vandenhoeck und
    Ruprecht
    (1969b). 'Königserhebung Pippins und Unslösbarkeit des Eides im *Liber de unitate
    ecclesiae conservanda*', *Deutsches Archiv* 25:313–46
    (1972). 'Das Problem der Mitwirkung des Adels an politischen Entscheidungsprozessen
    in Frankenreich des 8. Jahrhunderts', in *Festschrift für H. Herzfeld*,
    W. de Gruyter
    (1980). 'Untersuchungen zur Königserhebung Pippins', *Frühmittelalterliche Studien*
    14:95–187
Alonso, M. (1947). *Teologia de Averroes*, Consejo superior de investigaciones scientíficas,
    Instituto 'Miguel Asín', escuelas de estudios Arabes de Madrid y Granada
Alverny, M.-T. d' (1957). 'Les traductions d'Avicenne (Moyen Age et Renaissance)',
    in *Avicenna nella storia della cultura medioevale* (Academia nazionale dei Lincei, Anno
    CCCLIV, Problemi attuali di scienza e di cultura, Quaderno 40, pp. 71–87), G. Bardi
    (1982). 'Translations and Translators', in R.L. Benson and G. Constable (eds.)
    Renaissance and Rewnewal in the Twelfth Century, Harvard University Press;
    Clarendon Press
Angenendt, A. (1973). 'Tanfe und Politik im frühen Mittelalter', *Frühmittelalterliche
    Studien* 7:43–68
    (1980). 'Das geistliche Bundnis der Päpste mit den Karolingern', *Historisches Jahrbuch*
    100:1–94
    (1982). 'Rex et sacerdos. Zur Genese der Königssalbung', in N. Kamp and J. Wollasch
    (eds.) *Tradition als Historische Kraft. Interdisziplinäre Forschungen zur Geschichte des
    früheren Mittelalters*, W. de Gruyter
Anton, H.H. (1968). *Fürstenspiegel und Herrscherethos in der Karlingerzeit* (Bonner
    Historische Forschungen 32), Ludwig Röhrscheid Verlag
    (1979). 'Zum politischen Konzept Karolingischer Synoden und zur Karolingischen
    Brudergemeinschaft', *Historisches Jahrbuch* 99:55–132
Appelt, H. (1967). *Die Kaiseridee Friedrichs Barbarossas* (Österreichische Akademie der
    Wissenschaften, philosoph.-historische Klasse, Sitzungsberichte, 252, 4),
    Osterreichische Akademie der Wissenschaften
Arquillière, H.X. (1947). 'Origines de la théorie des deux glaives', *Studi Gregoriani* 1:501–21
    (1955). *See* section III above

Autenrieth, J. (1958). 'Bernold von Konstanz und die erweiterte 74-Titelsammlung',
	Deutsches Archiv 14:375ff
Badawi, A. (1972). *Histoire de la philosophie en Islam* (Etudes de philosophie médiévale
	60), J. Vrin
Bak, J.M. (1973). 'Medieval Symbology of the State: Percy E. Schramm's
	Contribution', *Viator* 4:33–63
Baker, J.H. (1979). *An Introduction to English Legal History*, 2nd edn, Butterworths
Baldwin, J.W. (1970). *Masters, Princes and Merchants. The Social Views of Peter the
	Chanter and His Circle*, 2 vols., Princeton University Press
Barlow, F. (1980). 'The King's Evil', *English Historical Review* 95:3–27
Baron, R. (1957). *Sciences et sagesse chez Hugues de Saint-Victor*, P. Lethielleux
	(1963). *Etudes sur Hugues de Saint-Victor*, Desclée; de Brouwer
Barraclough, G. (1950). *The Mediaeval Empire, Ideal and Reality*, Historical Association
Barzillay, P. (1964). 'The *Entheticus de dogmate philosophorum* of John of Salisbury',
	Mediaevalia et Humanistica 16:11–29
Batiffol, P. (1938). *Cathedra Petri. Etudes d'Histoire ancienne de l'Eglise*, Editions du Cerf
Beinert W. (1973). *Die Kirche, Gottes Heil in der Welt. Die Lehre von der Kirche nach den
	Schriften des Rupert von Deutz, Honorius Augustodunensis und Gerhoch von
	Reichersberg, Ein Beitrag zur Ekklesiologie des 12. Jahrhunderts* (Beiträge zur
	Geschichte der Philosophie und Theologie des Mittelalters, n.s. 13), Aschendorf
Bellomo, M. (1977). *Società e Istituzioni in Italia tra Medioevo ed Età Moderna*, Editrice
	Giannotta
Benson R.L. (1982). 'Political *Renovatio*: Two Models from Roman Antiquity', in R.L.
	Benson and G. Constable (eds.) *Renaissance and Renewal in the Twelfth Century*,
	Harvard University Press; Clarendon Press
Besse, J.-C. (1959). 'Anselmo dedicata. Etudes et texte', *Revue de Droit canonique* 9:207ff
	(1961/2). 'La suprématie romaine dans la collection "Anselmo dedicata" à travers
	quelques textes conciliaires', *L'Année canonique* 8:67ff
Besta, E. (1869). *L'opera di Irnerio. Contributo alla storia del diritto romano*, 2 vols., E.
	Loescher
Beumann, H. (1950). *Widukind von Korvei*, Böhlau Verlag
	(1956). 'Zur Entwicklung transpersonaler Staatsvorstelungen', in *Das Königtum*
	(Vorträge und Forschungen 3): 185–224
	(1958). '*Nomen imperatoris*. Studien zur Kaiseridee Karls des Grossen', *Historische
	Zeitschrift* 185:515–49
	(1962). *Ideengeschichtliche Studien zu Einhard und anderen Geschichtsschreibern des rüheren
	Mittelalters*, Wissenschaftlicht Buchgesellschaft
	(1981a). '*Unitas ecclesiae – unitas imperii – unitas regni*. Von der imperiaten
	Reichseinheitsidee zur Einheit der *regna*', *Settimane di Studio del Centro Italiano di
	Studi sull'Alto Medioevo* 27, ii:531–71
	(1981b). 'Der deutsche König als *Romanorum rex*', *Sitzungsberichte der
	Wissenschaftlichen Gesellschaft an der J.W. Goethe-Universität, Frankfurt-am-Main
	18, 2)*, Franz Steiner Verlag
Beumer, J. (1953). 'Das Kirchenbild in der Schriftkommentaren Bedas des
	Ehrwürdigen', *Scholastik* 28:40ff
Bibliographie générale de l'Ordre Cistercien. Saint Bernard (1979). H. Rochais and E.
	Manning, *Bibliographie de Saint Bernard*, vol. I, La Documentation Cistercienne
Bishop, T.A.M. (1961). *Scriptores Regis*, Clarendon Press
Bisson, Th. N. (1978). 'The Problem of Feudal Monarchy: Aragon, Catalonia, and
	France', *Speculum* 53:460–78
Bliemetzrieder, F.P. (1933). 'L'oeuvre d'Anselme de Laon et la littérature théolegique

contemporaine, I. Honorius von Autun', *Recherches de théologie ancienne et médiévale* 5:275–91

(1935). *Adelhard von Bath*. M. Hueber

Bloch H. (1982). 'The New Fascination with Ancient Rome', in R.L. Benson and G. Constable (eds.) *Renaissance and Renewal in the Twelfth Century*, Harvard University Press; Clarendon Press, pp. 615–36

Bloch, M. (1924). *Les rois thaumaturges: Etude sur le caractère surnaturel attribué à la puissance royale particulièrement en France et en Angleterre* (Publications de la faculté de l'Université de Strasbourg, fasc. 19); Eng. transl. Anderson, J.E. (1973). *The Royal Touch: Sacred Monarchy and Scrofula in England and France*, Routledge and Kegan Paul

(1939–40). *La société féodale*, vol. I: *La formation des liens de dépendance*, vol. II: *Les classes et le gouvernement des hommes* (Evolution de l'Humanité 24), Albun Michel

(1961). *Feudal Society*, Routledge and Kegan Paul

(1967). 'The Empire and the Idea of Empire under the Hohenstaufen', in *Land and Work in Medieval Europe. Selected Papers by Marc Bloch*, Routledge and Kegan Paul

Bongert, Y. (1949). *Recherches sur les cours laiques du Xe au XIIIe siècle*, A. and J. Picard

(1970). 'Vers la formation d'un pouvoir législatif royal (fin Xe-début XIIIe siècle)', *Etudes offertes à Jean Macqueron*, Faculté de Droit et des Sciences Economiques d'Aix-en-Provence

Bonnassie, P. (1969). 'Les conventions féodales dans la Catalogne du XIe siècle', in *Les structures sociales de l'Aquitaine, du Languedoc et de l'Espagne au premiere âge féodal* (Colloques Internationaux du Centre National de la Recherche Scientifique: Sciences Humaines), Editions du Centre National de la Recherche Scientifique, Paris.

Bonnaud-Delamare, R. (1939). *L'idée de Paix à l'Époque Carolingienne*, Domat-Montchrestien

(1957). 'Les institutions de paix dans la province ecclésiatique de Reims au XIe siècle', *Bulletin philologique et historique du comité des travaux historiques et scientifiques. Années 1955 et 1956*:113–200

Bosl, K. (1963). 'Herrscher und Beherrschte im deutschen Reich des 10–12. Jahrhunderts', (Bayerische Akademie der Wissenschaften, philosoph.-historische Klasse, Sitzungsberichte, 2), Bayerische Akademie der Wissenschaften

(1974). 'Leitbilder und Wertvorstellungen des Adels von der Merowinger zeit bis zur Höhe der feudalen Gesellschaft', (Bayerische Akademie der Wissenschaften, philosoph.-hist. Klasse, Sitzungsberichte, 5), Bayerische Akademie der Wissenschaften

Bouman, C.A. (1957). *Sacring and Crowning. The Development of the Latin Ritual for the Anointing of Kings and the Coronation of an Emperor before the Eleventh Century*, J.B. Wolters

Bournazel, E. (1975). *Le gouvernement capétien au XIIe siècle 1108–1180. Structures sociales et mutations institutionnelles*, Presses Universitaires de France

Boussard, J. (1964). 'La diversité et les traits particuliers du régime féodal dans l'Empire Plantagenêt', *Annali della Fondazione Italiana per la Storia amministrativa* 1:157–82

Bouton, J. de la Croix (1958). *Bibliographie Bernardine 1891–1957* (Commission d'historie de l'Ordre de Cîteaux: Etudes et documents 5), P. Lethielleux

Boutruche, R. (1968–70). *Seigneurie et Féodalité*, vol. I: *Le premier âge des liens d'homme à homme*, vol. II: *L'apogée (XIe–XIIIe siècles)*, (Collection Historique, dir. P. Lemerle), Aubier

Brancoli-Busdraghi, (1965). *La formazione storica del feudo lombardo come diritto reale*, (Quaderni di 'Studi Senesi' 11), Giuffrè

Brandileone, F. (1884). *Il diritto romano nelle leggi normanne e sueve del Regno di Sicilia*

(Nuova Collezione di Opere Giuridiche 21), Fratelli Bocca

Brezzi, P. (1939), 'Ottone di Frisinga', *Bullettino dell'Istituto Storico Italiano per il Medio Evo e Archivio Muratoriano*, 54:130–328

Brown, E.A.R. (1974). 'The Tyranny of a Construct: Feudalism and Historians of Medieval Europe', *American Historical Review* 79:1063–88

Brown, R.A. (1973). *Origins of English Feudalism* (Series: Historical Problems: Studies and Documents, ed. G.R. Elton, 19), George Allen and Unwin

Brunner, H. (1928). *Deutsche Rechtsgeschichte*, 2 vols., 2nd edn, Duncker and Humblot

Brunner, K. (1973). 'Der Fränkische fürstentitel im neunten und zehnten Jahrhundert', in Wolfram, ed., 1967 (*see* section III).

(1979). *Oppositionelle Gruppen im Karolingerreich* (Veröffentlichungen des Instituts für Österreichische Geschichtsforschung 25)

Bullough, D. (1975). '*Imagines Regum* and Their Significance in the Early Medieval West', in *Studies in Memory of David Talbot Rice*, Edinburgh University Press

Bund, K. (1979). *Thronsturz und Herrscheralsetzung im frühmittelalter* (Bonner Historische Forschungen 44), Ludwig Röhrscheid Verlag

Büttner, H. (1956). 'An den Anfängen des abendlandischen Staatsgedankens: die Königerhebung Pippins' in *Das Königtum* (Vorträge und Forschungen 3):155–67

Calasso, F. (1954), *Medio Evo del Diritto*, vol. I: *Le Fonte*, Giuffrè

Cam, H. (1940). 'The Decline and Fall of English Feudalism', *History* 25:216–33

Campbell, J. (1975). 'Observations on English Government from the Tenth to the Twelfth Century', *Transactions of the Royal Historical Society*, 5th ser., 25:39–54

(1980). 'The Significance of the Anglo-Norman State in the Administrative History of Western Europe', in W. Paravicini and K.F. Werner (eds.) *Histoire comparée de l'administration (IVe–XVIIe siècles)*, Beiheft der *Francia* 9:117–34

Carabie, R. (1943). *La propriété foncière dans le très ancien droit normand (Xe–XIIIe siècles)*, vol. I: *La propriété domaniale* (Bibliothèque d'Histoire du Droit Normand. 2e série: Etudes, t. v), R. Bigot

Caravale, M. (1966). *Il Regno Normanno di Sicilia* (Ius Nostrum: Studi e testi istituto di storia del diritto italiano dell' università di Roma 10), Giuffrè

Carozzi, C. (1978). 'Les fondements de la tripartition sociale chez Adalbéron de Laon', *Annales – Economies, Sociétés, Civilisations* 33:683–702

(1981). 'Le roi et la liturgie chez Helgaud de Fleury', in E. Patlagean and P. Riché (eds.) *Hagiographie, Cultures et Sociétés IVe–XIIe siècles*, Etudes Augustiniennes

Caspar, E. (1933). 'Papst Gregor II. und der Bilderstreit', *Zeitschrift für Kirchengeschichte* 52:72ff

Cheney, C.R. (1956). *From Becket to Langton. English Church Government 1170–1213*, Manchester University Press

Chodorow, S. (1972). *Christian Political Theory and Church Politics in the Mid Twelfth Century: The Ecclesiology of Gratian's 'Decretum'* (Center for Medieval and Renaissance Studies, University of California at Los Angeles Publications 5), University of California Press

Classen, P. (1951). '*Romanum gubernans imperium*: zur Vorgeschichte der Kaisertitulator Karls des Grossen', *Deutsches Archiv* 9:103–21

(1960). *Gerhoch von Reichersberg. Eine Biographie mit einem Anhang über die Quellen, ihre handschriftliche Überlieferung und ihre Chronologie*, Steiner Verlag

(1963). 'Die Verträge von Verfdun und Coulaines 843 als politischen Grundlagen des Westfränkischen Reiches', *Historische Zeitschrift* 196:1–35

(1964). '*Corona Imperii*. Die Krone als Inbegriff des römisch-deutschen Reich im 12. Jht.', in *Festschrift P.E. Schramm* Franz Steiner Verlag

(1965). 'Karl der Grosse, das Papsttum und Byzanz', in W. Braunfels (ed.) *Karl der*

Grosse: Lebenswerk und Nachleben, vol. I, Schwann, pp. 587ff

(1967). 'Aus der Werkstatt Gerhochs von Reichersberg. Studien zur Entstehung und Ueberlieferung von Briefen, Briefsammlungen und Widmungen', *Deutsches Archiv* 23:31–92

(1972). 'Karl der Grosse und die Thronfolge im Frankenreich' in *Festschrift für H. Heimpel*, III, Vandenhoeck und Ruprecht

(1981). Comments in discussion of Werner 1981, pp. 209–12

(1982). '*Res gestae*, Universal History, Apocalypse', in R.L. Benson and G. Constable (eds.) *Renaissance and Renewal in the Twelfth Century*, Harvard University Press; Clarendon Press

(1983). *Ausgewählte Aufsätze von Peter Classen*, Jan Thorbecke Verlag

Clercq, C. de (1936). *La Législation religieuse franque de Clovis à Charlemagne*, Bureaux du Recueil, Bibliothèque de l'Université de Louvain

Congar Y.M.-J. (1953). 'L'Ecclésiologie de S. Bernard', *S. Bernard théologien. Actes du Congrès de Dijon, 15–19 Septembre 1953* (Analecta Sacri Ordinis Cisterciensis 9), pp. 136–90

(1955). 'Die Ekklesiologie des Heiligen Bernhard', in J. Lortz (ed.). *Bernard von Clairvaux, Mönch und Mystiker. Internationaler Bernhardkongress, Mainz, 1953*, Franz Steiner Verlag

(1968a). *L'Ecclésiologie du haut moyen âge*, Editions du Cerf

(1968b). 'Les laics et l'ecclésiologie des "ordines" chez les théologiens des XIe et XIIe siècles', in *I Laici nella 'Societas Christiana' dei secoli XI e XII* (Miscellanea del Centro di Studi Medioevali 5), Milan

(1970), *L'Eglise. De saint Augustin à l'époque moderne* (Histoire des dogmes, 3: Christologie – Sotériologie – Mariologie, fasc. 3), Editions du Cerf

Conrad, H. (1962). *Deutsche Rechtsgeschichte*, vol. I: *Frühzeit und Mittelalter*, 2nd edn, F. Müller Verlag

Constable G. (1977). 'The Structure of Medieval Society According to the *Dictatores* of the Twelfth Century', in K. Pennington and R. Somerville (eds.) *Law, Church and Society: Essays in Honour of Stephen Kuttner* (The Middle Ages Series), University of Pennsylvania Press, pp. 253–67

(1982). 'Renewal and Reform in Religious Life. Concepts and Realities', in R.L. Benson, and G. Constable (eds.) *Renaissance and Renewal in the Twelfth Century*, Harvard University Press; Clarendon Press

Coolidge, R.T. (1965). 'Adalbero, Bishop of Laon', *Studies in Medieval and Renaissance History* 2:1–114

Corbin, H. (1960). *Avicenna and the Visionary Recital*, transl. from the French by W.R. Trask, Routledge and Kegan Paul (includes transl. of Avicenna's *Risalat Ḥayy ibn Yaqẓān*)

(1964). *Histoire de la philosophie islamique*, vol. I: *Des origines jusqu'à la mort d'Averroes* (1198) (Collection Idées), Gallimard

Courtney, F. (1954). *Cardinal Robert Pullen. An English Theologian of the Twelfth Century* (Analecta Gregoriana 64: Series Facultatis Theologicae, sectio A: n.10), Apud Aedes Universitatis Gregorianae

Cowdrey, H.E.J. (1968). 'The Papacy, the Patarenes and the Church of Milan', *Transactions of the Royal Historical Society*, 5th series, 18:25ff

(1981). 'The Anglo-Norman *Laudes Regiae*', *Viator* 12:39–78

Cristiani, M. (1978). *Dall' unanimitas all' universitas: da Alcuino a Giovanni Eriugena: lineamenti ideologici e ferminologia politica della cultura del secolo IX* (Istituto storico per il medio evo, studi storici, fasc. 100–2), Rome

Critchley, J.S. (1978). *Feudalism*, George Allen and Unwin

Dahlhaus-Berg, E. (1975). *Nova Antiquitas et Antiqua Novitas. Typologische Exegese und isidorianisches Geschichtsbild bei Theodulf von Orléans* (Kölner Historische Abhandlungen 23), Böhlau Verlag

David, M. (1954). *La Souveraineté et les Limites Juridiques du Pouvoir Monarchique du IXe au XVe siècle*, Librairie Dalloz

DeAragon, R. (1982). 'The Growth of Secure Inheritance in Anglo-Norman England', *Journal of Medieval History* 8:381–92

De Ghellinck, J. (1948). *Le mouvement théologique du XIIe siècle*, 2nd edn, De Tempel

De Gryse, L.M. (1976). 'Some Observations on the Origin of the Flemish Bailiff (Bailli): The Reign of Philip of Alsace', *Viator. Medieval and Renaissance Studies* 7:243–94

Delaruelle, E. (1955). 'Jonas d'Orléans et le moralisme carolingien', *Bulletin de la littérature ecclésiastique* 55:129ff, 221ff

Delhaye, P. (1947). 'L'organisation scolaire au XIIe siècle', *Traditio* 5:211–68

(1948). 'La place de l'éthique parmi les disciplines scientifiques au XIIe siècle', in *Miscellanea moralia in honorem exemii Domini Arthur Jansen* (Bibliotheca Ephemeridum theologicarum Lovaniensium, series i, vol. 2), Editions Nauwerlaerts; J. Duculot

(1949). 'L'enseignement de la philosophie morale au XIIe siècle', *Medieval Studies* 11:77–99

(1957). *Le problème de la conscience morale chez S. Bernard* (Analecta Mediaevalia Namurcensia 9), Editions Godenne

(1958). '"Grammatica" et "Ethica" au XIIe siècle', *Recherches de théologie ancienne et médiévale* 25:59–110

Deshman, R. (1976). 'Christus Rex et magi reges: Kingship and Christology in Ottonian and Anglo-Saxon Art', *Frühmittelalterliche Studien* 10:375–405

(1980). 'The Exalted Servant: The Ruler Theology of the Prayerbook of Charles the Bald', *Viator* 11:385–417

Desideri, S. (1958). *La "Institutio Traiani"* (Università di Genova, Facoltà di Lettere: Pubblicazioni dell'Istituto di filologia classica 12), Tivoli, Istituto de filologia classica

Devisse, J. (1975–6). *Hincmar Archevêque de Reims 845–882*, 3 vols., Droz

Dewick, E.S., ed. (1899). *The Coronation Book of Charles V of France*, Henry Bradshaw Society 16

Dhondt, J. (1943). *Korte geschiedenis van het ontstaan van het graafschap Vlaanderen*, Manteau

(1948). *Etudes sur la naissance des principautés territoriales en France (IXe–Xe siècle)* (Rijksuniversiteit te Gent. Werken Fac. Letteren, 102), De Tempel

Dieterici, F. (1900). *Der Musterstaat von Alfārābī. Aus dem arabischen übertragen*, E.J. Brill

(1904). *Die Staatsleitung von Alfārābī. Deutsche Bearbeitung mit einer Einleitung 'Ueber das Wesen der arabischen Philosophie'*, Aus dem Nachlasse des . . . Dr. F. Dieterici herausgegeben . . . von Dr. P. Brönnle, Leiden

Dilcher, H. (1975). *Die sizilische Gesetzgebung Kaiser Friedrichs II. Quellen der Constitutionen von Melfi und ihrer Novellen*, (Studien und Quellen zur Welt Kaiser Friedrichs II, III), Böhlau Verlag

Dod, B.G. (1982). 'Aristotles latinus', in N. Kretzmann, A. Kenny, J. Pinborg (eds.) *The Cambridge History of Later Medieval Philosophy from the Rediscovery of Aristotle to the Disintegration of Scholasticism 1100–1600*, Cambridge Univeristy Press

Dressler, F. (1954). *Petrus Damiani. Leben und Werk* (Studia Anselmiana 34), Herder

Duby, G. (1953). *La société aux XIe et XIIe siècles dans la région mâconnaise* (Bibliothèque Générale de l'Ecole Pratique des Hautes Etudes, VIe Section), Librairie Armand Colin

(1967). *Adolescence de la chrétienté occidentale 980–1140*, Editions d'Art Albert Skira
(1978). *Les trois ordres ou l'imaginaire du féodalisme*, Gallimard
(1980). *The Three Orders: Feudal Society Imagined*, transl. from the French by A.
  Goldhammer, University of Chicago Press
Duchrow, U. (1970). *Christenheit und Weltverantwortung. Traditionsgeschichte und
  systematische Struktur der Zweireichelehre* (Forschungen und Berichte der
  Evangelischen Studiengemeinschaft 25), Ernest Klett Verlag
Duggan, A. (1980). *Thomas Becket: A Textual History of His Letters*, Clarendon Press
Duggan, C. (1962). 'The Becket Dispute and Criminous Clerks', *Bulletin of the Institute
  of Historical Research* 35:1–28
Dunlop, D.M. (1945). 'Ibn Bājjah's Tadbīru 'l-muta-wahhid (Rule of the Solitary)'.
  Journal of the Royal Asiatic Society, 61–81
Dürig, W. (1958). 'Der theologische Ausgangspunkt der mittelalterlichen liturgischen
  Auffassung vom Herrscher als *Vicarius Dei*', *Historisches Jahrbuch* 77:176–87
Dvornik, F. (1949). *The Making of Central and Eastern Europe*, The Polish Research
  Centre Ltd, London
Eberenz, James H. (1969). *The Concept of Sovereignty in Four Medieval Philosophers: John
  of Salisbury, St Thomas Aquinas, Egidius Colonna and Marsillius of Padua* (Catholic
  University of America, Philosophical Studies 232), University Microfilms
Eberhardt, O. (1977). *Via regia Der Fürstenspiegel Smaragds von St Mihiel und seine
  literarische Gattung* (Münstersche Mittelalterschriften 28)
Ehler, S.Z. and Morrall, J.B., eds. (1954). *Church and State through the Centuries*, Burns
  and Oates
Ehlers, J. (1976). 'Karolingische Tradition und frühes Nationalbewusstsein in
  Frankreich', *Francia* 4:213–35
(1978). 'Die *Historia Francorum Senonensis* und der Aufstieg des Hauses Capet', *Journal
  of Medieval History* 4:1–25
Eichmann, E. (1909). *Acht und Bann im Reichsrecht des Mittelalters*, Görres-Gesellschaft
(1912). *Kirche und Staat 1. (750–1122) Quellen zur kirchlichen Rechtsgeschichte und zur
  Kirchenrecht*, Görres-Gesellschaft
Elford, D.J. (1983). 'Developments in the Natural Philosophy of William of Conches:
  A Study of his *Dragmaticon* and a Consideration of its Relationship to the
  Philosophia', Cambridge University PhD thesis
Elrington, C.R. (1954). 'John of Salisbury's "Entheticus de dogmate philosophorum"',
  London University MA thesis
Endres, J.A. (1906). *Honorius Augustodunensis Beitrag zur Geschichte des geistigen Lebens im
  12. Jahrhundert*, Kösel-Verlag
English, B. (1979). *The Lords of Holderness 1086–1260. A Study in Feudal Society*, Oxford
  University Press
Ensslin, W. (1955). 'Auctoritas und Potestas. Zur Zweigewaldenlehre des Papstes
  Gelasius I.', *Historisches Jahrbuch* 74:661ff
Erdmann, C. (1932). 'Der Heidenkrieg in der Liturgie und die Kaiserkrönung Ottos I.',
  Mitteilungen des Österreichischen Instituts für Geschichtsforschung 46:129ff
(1935). *Die Entstehung des Kreuzzugsgedankens*, repr. 1965
(1951). *See* section III above
Erdmann, C. and Gladiss, D. von (1939). 'Gottschalk von Aachen im Dienste Heinrichs
  IV.', *Deutsches Archiv* 3:115–74
*L'Eremitismo in occidente nei secoli XI e XII. Atti della seconda Settimana internazionale di
  studio. Mendola, 30 agosto – 6 settembre 1962* (1965). (Miscellanea del Centro di Studi
  Medioevali 4: Pubblicazione dell'Università Cattolica del Sacro Cuore Contributi
  – Serie Terza, Varia-4), Società editrice Vita e Pensiero
Evans, G.R. (1983). *Alan of Lille*, Cambridge University Press

(1983). *The Mind of St. Bernard of Clairvaux*, Oxford University Press

Evergates, T. (1975). *Feudal Society in the Bailliage of Troyes under the Counts of Champagne, 1152–1284*, The Johns Hopkins University Press

Ewig, E. (1956). 'Zum christlichen Königsgedanken im Frühmittelalter', in *Das Königtum* (Vorträge und Forschungen 3):7–73

(1981). 'Überlegungen zu den Merowingischen und Karolingischen Teilungen', *Settimane di Studio del Centro Italiano di Studi sull'Alto Medioevo* 27, i:225–53

Eynde, D. van den (1957). *L'oeuvre littéraire de Géroch de Reichersberg* (Spicilegium Pontificii Athenaei Antoniani 11), Apud Pontificum Athenaeum Antonianum

(1960). *Essai sur la succession et la date des écrits de Hugues de Saint-Victor* (Spicilegium Pontificii Athenaei Antoniani 13), Apud Pontificium Athenaeum Antonianum

Feine, H.E. (1964; 1972). *Kirchliche Rechtsbeschichte. Die Katholische Kirche*, 4th and 5th edns, Böhlau Verlag

Fichtenau, H. (1957). *Arenga* (Mitteilungen des Instituts für Österreichische Geschichtsforschung, Erganzungsband 18) Böhlau Verlag

Finberg, H.P.R. (1974). *The Formation of England 550–1042* (The Paladin History of England), Hart-Davis, MacGibbon

Fischer, B. (1934). 'Die Entwicklung des Instituts der Defensoren in der Römischen Kirche', *Ephemerides Liturgicae* 48:443ff

Fisher, D.J.V. (1973). *The Anglo-Saxon Age c. 400–1042* (A History of England in Eleven Volumes, ed. W.N. Medlicott), Longman

Fitting. H. (1888). *Die Anfänge der Rechtsschule zu Bologna*, J. Guttentag; transl. into French by Leseur, P. (1888). *Les commencements de l'école de droit de Bologne*, A. Rousseau

Fleckenstein, J. (1953). *Die Bildungsreform Karls des Grossen als Verwirklichung der 'norma rectitudinis'*, Albert

(1966). *Die Hofkapelle der deutschen Könige*, vol. II: *Die Hofkapelle im Rahmen der ottonisch-salischen Reichskirche* (MGH 16/2), Hiersemann

Fliche, A. (1946). 'La valeur historique de la collection canonique d'Anselme de Lucques', in *Miscellanea Historica in honorem Alberti de Meyer* 1:348ff

Flint, V.I.J. (1972). 'The Chronology of the Works of Honorius Augustodunensis', *Revue Bénédictine* 82:215–42

(1976). 'The "School of Laon": A Reconstruction', *Recherches de théologie ancienne et médiéval* 43:89–110

(1977), 'The Place and Purpose of the Works of Honorius Augustodunensis', *Revue Bénédictine* 87:97–127

Flori, J. (1982). 'La chevalerie selon Jean de Salisbury (nature, fonction, idéologie)', *Revue d'histoire ecclésiastique* 77, 1–2:35–77

Folliet, J. (1954). 'Les trois catégories de chrétiens. Survie d'un thème augustinien', *L'Année théologique augustinienne* 14:82ff

Folz, R. (1953). *See* section III above

(1958). 'Otton de Friesing, témoin de quelques controverses intellectuelles de son temps', *Bulletin de la Société historique et archéologique de Langres* 13:70–89

(1964). *Le Couronnement impérial de Charlemagne*, Gallimard (English transl. by J. E. Anderson (1974). *The Coronation of Charlemagne*, Routledge and Kegan Paul)

(1969). *See* section III above

(1972). *De l'Antiquité au Monde Médiéval* (Peuples et Civilisations V), with the coll. of A. Guillou, L. Musset and D. Sourdel, Presses Universitaires de France

Foreville, R. (1943). *L'Eglise et la royauté en Angleterre sous Henri II Plantagenet, 1154–1189*, Bloud and Gay

Fortin, E.L. (1981). *Dissidence et philosophie au moyen âge Dante et ses antécédents* (Cahiers d'études médiévales 6), Bellarmin; J. Vrin

Fournier, P. (1901). 'Observations sur diverses recensions de la Collection Canonique d'Anselme de Lucques', *Annales de l'Université de Grenoble* 13:427ff
(1911). 'Le Décret de Burchard de Worms. See caractères, son influence', *Revue d'histoire ecclésiastique* 12:451ff
(1912). 'L'origine de la Collectio Anselmo dedicata', in *Etudes d'Histoire juridique offertes a Paul Frédéric Girard . . . par ses élèves*, vol. 1, P. Geuthner, pp. 475–92
(1920). 'Les collections canoniques romaines de l'époque de Grégoire VII', *Mémoires de l'Institut National de France. Académie des Inscriptions et Belles-lettres* 41:327ff
Fournier, P. and Le Bras, G. (1931–2). *Histoire des collections canoniques en Occident depuis les Fausses décrétales jusqu'au Décret de Gratien*, 2 vols. (Société d'Histoire du Droit), Sirey
Fourquin, G. (1970). *Seigneurie et Féodalité au Moyen Age*, Presses Universitaires de France
Fransen, G. (1956). 'La date du décret de Gratien', *Revue d'histoire ecclésiastique* 51:521–31
Fried, J. (1982). 'Der Karolingische Herrschaftsverband im 9. Jh. zwischen "Kirche" und "Königshaus"', *Historische Zeitschrift* 235:1–43
Frugoni, A. (1954). *Arnaldo da Brescia nelle fonti del secolo XII* (Istituto storico italiano per il Medio Evo. Studi storici 8–9), Nella sede dell'Istituto
Fuchs, V. (1930). *Der Ordinationstitel von seiner Entstehung bis auf Innozenz III.* (Kanonische Studien und Texte 4), K. Schroeder
Fuhrmann, H. (1959). 'Konstantinische Schenkung und Sylvesterlegende in neuer Sicht', *Deutsches Archiv* 15:523–40
(1966). 'Konstantinische Schenkung und obendländisches Kaisertum', *Deutsches Archiv* 22:63–178
(1972–4). *Einfluss und Verbrietung der pseudoisidorischen Fälschungen*, 3 vols. (*MGH* 24), Hiersemann
(1975). '"Volkssouveränität" und "Herrschaftsvertrag" bei Manegold von Lantenbach', in *Festschrift für H. Krause*, Böhlau Verlag
Funk, P. (1935). 'Der fragliche Anonymous von York', *Historisches Jahrbuch* 55:251–76
Funkenstein, A. (1965). *Heilsplan und natürliche Entwicklung. Formen der Gegenwartsbestimmung im Geschichtsdenken des hohen Mittelalters* (Sammlung dialog. 5), Nymphenburger Verlagshandlung
Gagnér, S. (1960). *Studien zur Ideengeschichte der Gesetzgebung* (Acta Universitatis Upsaliensis: Studia Iuridica Upsaliensia 1), Almqvist and Wiksell
Ganshof, F.L. (1944). *Vlaanderen onder de eerste graven*, Standard
(1949). *The Imperial Coronation of Charlemagne. Theories and Facts* (The David Murray Lecture no. 16), Glasgow University
(1958a). 'L'immunité dans la monarchie franque', in *Recueils de la Société Jean Bodin*, vol. 1: *Les liens de vassalité et les immunités*, 2nd ed, Librairie Encyclopédique, Brussels
(1958b). *Recherches sur les Capitulaires* (Société d'Histoire du Droit), Sirey (first published in the *Revue historique de droit français et étranger* of 1957)
(1960). 'L'église et le pouvoir royal dans la monarchie franque sous Pépin III et Charlemagne', *Settimane di Studio del Centro Italiano di Studi sull'Alto Medioevo* 7:95–141
(1970). *The Middle Ages. A History of International Relations*, Harper and Row
(1971). *The Carolingians and the Frankish Monarchy*, Longman
(1982). *Qu'est-ce que la féodalité?* 5th edn, Tallandier (transl. by Grierson, P. (1964). *Feudalism*, 3rd edn, Longman)
Ganshof, F.L. and Van Caenegem, R.C. (1972). *Les institutions féodo-vassaliques* (Introduction bibliographique à l'histoire du droit et à l'ethnologie juridique, dir.

J. Gilissen, B/8, Editions de l'Institut de Sociologie, Université Libre de Bruxelles

Garaud, M. (1964). *Les châtelains de Poitou et l'avènement du régime féodal XIe et XIIe siècles* (Mémoires de la Société des Antiquaires de l'Ouest, 4e s., t. VIII), Société des Antiquaires de l'Ouest, Poitiers

Garfagnini, G.C. (1977). 'Legittima *potestas* e tirannide nel *Policraticus* di Giovanni di Salisbury. Riflessioni sulla sensibilita di un "clericus" per i problemi storico-politici', *Critica storica* 14:575–610

Gastaldelli, F. (1983). *Wilhelmus Lucensis. Comentum in tertiam Ierarchiam Dionisii que est De Divinis Nominibus* (Introduzione e testo critico. Unione Accademica Nazionale. Corpus Philosophorum Medii Aevi. Testi e Studi 3), L.S. Olschki

Gaudemet J. (1965). 'Le droit romain dans la pratique et chez les docteurs aux XIe et XIIe siècles', *Cahiers de civilisation médiévale* 8:365–80

(1983). 'Les collections canoniques, miroir de la vie sociale', in *Mélanges en l'honneur de Jacques Ellul*, Presses Universitaires de France, pp. 243–53

Gauthier, L. (1909). *Ibn Thofaïl, sa vie, ses oeuvres* (Publications de l'Ecole des lettres d'Alger: Bulletin de correspondence africaine 42), E. Leroux

(1936). *Hayy ben Yaqdhân; roman philosophique d'Ibn Thofaïl* (Texte arabe avec les variantes des manuscrits et de plusieurs éditions et traduction française), 2nd edn, Beyrouth, Imprimerie catholique

(1948). *Ibn Rochd (Averroes)*, Presses Universitaires de France

Gellinek, C. (1971). *Die Deutsche Kaiserchronik. Erzähltechnik und Kritik*, Athenäum

Genicot, L. (1982). *L'Economie rurale Namuroise au Bas Moyen Age*, vol. III: *Les hommes – le commun* (Université de Louvain. Recueil de travaux d'histoire et de philologie, 6e s., fasc. 25), Editions Nauwelaerts

Gilchrist, J.T. (1962–3). 'Humbert of Silva Candida and the Political Concept of *Ecclesia* in the Eleventh Century Reform Movement', *Journal of Religious History* 2:13–28

Gillingham, J.B. (1971). *The Kingdom of Germany in the High Middle Ages*, Historical Association

Gilson, E. (1928). 'La cosmogonie de Bernardus Silvestris', *Archives d'histoire doctrinale et littéraire du Moyen Age* 3:5–24

(1940). *The Mystical Theology of Saint Bernard*, transl. A.H.C. Downes, Sheed and Ward

Giordanengo, G. (1981). 'Le droit féodal dans les pays de droit écrit. L'exemple de la Provence et du Dauphiné. XIIe–début XIVe siècle', Montpellier, Law Faculty (thesis)

Godman, P. (1982). *Alcuin. The Bishops, Kings and Saints of York*, Clarendon Press

(1985). *Poetry of the Carolingian Renaissance*, Duckworth

Goetz, H.-W. (1978). 'Die "Summa Gloria". Ein Beitrag zu den politischen Vorstellungen des Honorius Augustodunensis', *Zeitschrift für Kirchengeschichte* 89:307ff

(1981). *Strukturen der spätkarolingischen Epoche im Spiegel der Vorstellungen eines zeitgenössischen Mönchs. Eine Interpretation der 'Gesta Karoli' Notkers von St. Gallen*, Rufolf Habelt

(1984). *Das Geschichtsbild Ottos von Freising. Ein Beitrag zur historischen Vorstellungswelt und zur Geschichte des 12. Jahrhunderts* (Archiv für Kulturgeschichte, Beiheft 19), Böhlau Verlag

Goez, W. (1958). *Translatio imperii: Ein Beitrag zur Geschichte des Geschichtsdenkens und der politischen Theorien im Mittelalter und in der frühen Neuzeit*, J.C.B. Mohr

Goichon, A.M. (1951). *La philosophie d'Avicenne et son influence en Europe médiévale* (Forlong Lectures, 1940. Deuxième édition revue et augmentée), Adrien-Maisonneuve

(1959). *Le récit de Ḥayy ibn Yaqẓān commenté par des textes d'Avicenne* (French transl. with a commentary), Desclée; de Brouwer

Grabe, N. (1973). 'Die Zweistaatenlehre bei Otto von Freising und Augustin. Ein Vergleich', *Cistercienserchronik* 80:34–70

Grabmann, M. (1909–11). *Die Geschichte der scholastischen Methode*, 2 vols., Herder; repr. 1957, Wissenschaftliche Buchgesellschaft

(1926–56). 'Kaiser Friedrich II. und sein Verhältnis zur aristotelischen und arabischen Philosophie', in *idem, Mittelalterliches Geistesleben. Abhandlungen zur Geschichte der Scholastik und Mystik*, vol. II, M. Hueber, ch. 5, pp. 103–37

Grandclaude, M. (1923). *Etude critique sur les livres des Assises de Jérusalem*, Jouve et Cie

Gransden, A. (1974). *Historical Writing in England, c. 550–c. 1307*, Routledge and Kegan Paul

Grassotti, H. (1969). *Las instituciones feudo-vasalláticas en León y Castilla*, vol. I: *El vasallaje*. vol II: *La recompensa vasallática*, Centro Italiano di Studi sull'Alto Medioevo

(1982). 'Autolimitaciones del poder real en León y Castilla desde las primeras leyes territoriales de 1020 a la carta magna leonesa de 1188', in *Diritto e potere nella storia europea: Atti in onore di Bruno Paradisi*, vol. I, L.S. Olschki

Graus, F. (1959). 'Über die sogenannte germanische Treue', *Historia* 1:71–121

Green, D. (1965). *The Carolingian Lord*, Cambridge University Press

Grégoire, R. (1965). *Bruno de Segni: exégète médiéval et théologien monastique*, Centro Italiano di Studi sull'Alto Medioevo 3

Gregory, T. (1955). *Anima mundi: la filosofia di Guglielmo di Conches e la scuola di Chartres* (Pubblicazioni dell'Istituto di filosofia dell' Università di Roma 3), G.C. Sansoni

(1958). *Platonismo medievale: Studi e ricerche* (Istituto storico italiano per il Medio Evo. Studi storici, fasc. 26/27), G. Bardi

(1966). 'L'idea di natura nella filosofia medievale prima dell'ingresso della filosofia di Aristotele: Il secolo XII', in *La filosofia della natura nel Medioevo. Atti del terzo congresso internazionale di filosofia medioevale, Passo della Mendola (Trento) – 31 agosto – 5 settembre 1964*, Società editrice Vita e Pensiero, pp. 27–65

(1974). 'Abélard et Platon', in E.M. Buytaert (ed.). *Peter Abelard. Proceedings of the International Conference, Louvain. May 10–12, 1971* (Mediaevalia Lovaniensia, Series I, Studia 2), Leuven University Press. pp. 38–64

(1975a). 'La nouvelle idée de nature et de savoir scientifique au XIIe siècle', in J.E. Murdoch and E.D. Sylla (eds.) *The Cultural Context of Medieval Learning* (Boston Studies in the Philosophy of Science, 26. Synthese Library, 76), Reidel

(1975b). 'Considérations sur Ratio et Natura chez Abelard', *Pierre Abelard. Pierre le Vénérable. Les courants philosophiques, littéraires et artistiques en occident au milieu du XIIe siècle. Abbaye de Cluny, 2 au 9 juillet 1972* (Colloques internationaux du Centre nationale de la recherche scientifique 546), Editions du Centre National de la Recherche Scientifique, Paris pp. 568–81

Grierson, P. (1981). *See* section II above

Guterman, S.L. (1972). *From Personal to Territorial Law. Aspects of the History and Structure of the Western Legal-Constitutional Tradition*. Scarecrow Press

Guth, K. (1978). *Johannes von Salisbury (1115/20–80) Studien zur Kirchen-, Kultur- und Socialgeschichte Westeuropas in 12. Jahrhundert* (Münchener Theologische Studien: 1, Historische Abteilung, 20), Sankt Ottilien:Eos-Verlag

Hägermann, D. (1975). 'Reichseinheit und Reichsteilung Bemerkungen zur *Divisio regnorum* von 806 und zur *Ordinatio Imperii* von 817', *Historisches Jahrbuch* 95:278–307

Hallam, E. (1982). 'Royal Burial and the Cult of Kingship in France and England, 1060–1330', *Journal of Medieval History* 8:359–80

Haller, J. (1962). *Das Papsttum. Idee und Wirklichkeit*, 2nd edn, vol. II, Port Verlag

Halphen, L. (1947). *Charlemagne et l'Empire Carolingien*, Albin Michel; repr. with up-to-date bibliography 1968, Albin Michel
  (1950a). 'La lettre d'Eudes II de Blois au roi Robert', in L. Halphen, *A travers l'Histoire du Moyen Age*, Presses Universitaires de France
  (1950b). 'La place de la royauté dans le système féodal', in L. Halphen, *A travers l'Histoire du Moyen Age*, Presses Universitaires de France
Hannig, J. (1982). *Consensus Fidelium. Frühfeudale Interpretationen des Verhältnisses von Königtum und Adel am Beispiel des Frankenreiches* (Monographien zur Geschichte des Mittelalters 27) Hiersemann
Harmer, F.E. (1952). *Anglo-Saxon Writs*, Manchester University Press
Hartmann, W. (1970). 'Manegold von Lautenbach und die Anfänge der Frühscholastik', *Deutsches Archiv* 26:47–149
  (1975). Beziehungen des Normannischen Anonymus zu frühscholastischen Bildungszentren', *Deutsches Archiv* 31:108–43
Haselbach, I. (1970). *Aufstieg und Herrschaft der Karlinger in der Darstellung der sogenannten Annales Mettenses Priores* (Historische Studien 412), Matthiesen Verlag
Haskins, C.H. (1927). *Studies in the History of Mediaeval Science*, 2nd edn, Harvard University Press
Helbig. H. (1951). 'Fideles Dei et regis', *Archiv für Kirchengeschichte* 33:275–306
Herlihy, D.J., ed. (1970). *The History of Feudalism*, Harper and Row
Hoffmann, H. (1964a). Gottesfriede und Treuga Dei (*MGH* 20), Hiersemann
  (1964b). 'Die beiden Schwerter im hohen Mittelalter', *Deutsches Archiv* 20:78–114
Hofmann, K. (1933). *Der 'Dictatus Papae' Gregors VII. Eine rechtsgeschichtliche Erklärung*, F. Schöningh
Hofmeister, A. (1911–12). 'Studien über Otto von Freising', *Neues Archiv der Gesellschaft für ältere deutsche Geschichtskunde*, 37:99–161, 633–768
Hollister, C.W. (1968). 'The "Feudal Revolution"', *American Historical Review* 73:708–23
Holt, J.C. (1972). 'Politics and Property in Early Medieval England', *Past and Present* 57:3–52
  (1982). 'Feudal Society and the Family in Early Medieval England, I: The Revolution of 1066', *Transactions of the Royal Historical Society*, 5 series, 32:193–212
Hoyt, R.S. and Chodorow, S. (1976). *Europe in the Middle Ages*, 3rd edn, Harcourt Brace Jovanovich
Hubrecht, G. (1955). 'La "juste guerre" dans le Décret de Gratien', *Studia Gratiana* 3:161–77
Hyman, A. and Walsh, J.J. (1973). *Philosophy in the Middle Ages. The Christian, Islamic and Jewish Traditions*, Hackett Publications
Ius Romanum Medii Aevi (1961–) (Auspice Collegio Antiqui Iuris studiis prouehendis. Société d'histoire des droits de l'antiquité), Giuffrè
Jacqueline, B. (1952). 'Saint Bernard et le droit romain', *Revue historique de droit français et étranger* 30:223–8
  (1965). 'Yves de Chartres et Saint-Bernard', *Etudes d'histoire du droit canonique dédiées à Gabriel Le Bras*, 2 vols., here vol. I, pp. 179–84, Sirey
Jamison, E. (1968). 'The Career of Judex Tarentinus magne curie magister justiciarius and the Emergence of the Sicilian regalis magna curia under William I and the Regency of Margaret of Navarre, 1156–72', *Proceedings of the British Academy* 53:289–343
Jarnut, J. (1982). 'Wer hat Pippin 751 zum König gesalbt?', *Frühmittelalterliche Studien* 16:45–57
Jäschke, K.-U. (1975). *Burgenbau und Landesverteidigung um 900*, Jan Thorbecke Verlag

Jaussen, R.P. *et al.* (1949). *Al-Fārābī. Idées des habitants de la cité vertueuse*, French transl. (Publications de l'Institut français d'archéologie orientale. Textes et traductions d'auteurs orientaux 9), La Caire: Imprimerie de l'Institut français d'archéologie orientale

Joliffe, J.E.A. (1963). *Angevin Kingship*, A. and C. Black

Jolivet, J. (1966). 'Elements du concept de nature chez Abélard', *La filosofia della natura nel Medioevo. Atti del terzo congresso internazionale di filosofia medievale. Passo della Mendola (Trento) – 31 agosto–5 settembre 1964*, Società editrice Vita e Pensiero, pp. 297–304

Jones, M. (1982). '"Bons Bretons et Bons Francoys": The Language and Meaning of Treason in Later Medieval France', *Transactions of the Royal Historical Society*, 5th series, 32:91–112

Jordan, E. (1921). 'Dante et saint Bernard', *Bulletin du Jubilé [de Dante Alighieri]*, Librairie de l'Art catholique

Jordan, K. (1958). 'Das Reformpapsttum und die abendländische Staatenwelt', *Welt als Geschichte* 18:122ff

Kahl, H.-D. (1955). 'Compellere intrare. Die Wendenpolitik Bruns von Querfurt im Lichte hochmittelalterlichen Missions- und Völkerrechts', *Zeitschrift für Ostforschung* 4:161ff, 360ff

Kahles, W. (1960). *Geschichte als Liturgie: Die Geschichtstheologie des Rupertus von Deutz*, Aschendorff

Kaiser, R. (1983). 'Selbsthilfe und Gewaltmonopol', *Frühmittelalterliche Studien* 17:55–72

Kantorowicz, E.H. (1952). '*Deus per naturam, Deus per gratiam*: A Note on Mediaeval Political Theology', *Harvard Theological Review* 45:253–77

(1958). *Laudes Regiae. A Study in Liturgical Acclamations and Medieval Ruler Worship* (University of California Publications in History 33), University of California Press (2nd edn; first published 1946)

(1961). 'Kingship under the Impact of Scientific Jurisprudence', in M. Clagett, G. Post and R. Reynolds (eds.) *Twelfth-Century Europe and the Foundations of Modern Society*, University of Wisconsin Press

Kantorowicz, H.U. (1938). *Studies in the Glossators of the Roman Law. Newly Discovered Writings of the Twelfth Century*, ed. and explained . . . with the collaboration of W.W. Buckland, Cambridge University Press

Keen, M.H. (1984). *Chivalry*, Yale University Press

Keller, H. (1976). 'Die Entstehung der italienischen Stadtkommunen als Problem der Sozialgeschichte', *Frühmittelalterliche Studien* 10:169–211

(1982). 'Reichsstruktur und Herrschaftsauffassung in ottonisch-frankischer Zeit', *Frühmittelalterliche Studien* 16:74–128

Kelley, D.R. (1964). 'De origine feudorum: the Beginnings of an Historical Problem', *Speculum* 39:207–28

Kemp, E.W. (1948). *Canonization and Authority in the West*, Clarendon Press

Kennan, E. (1967). 'The *De Consideratione* of St. Bernard of Clairvaux and the Papacy in the Mid-Twelfth Century: A Review of Scholarship', *Traditio* 23:73–115

Kern, F. (1919). 'Recht und verfassung im Mittelalter', *Historische Zeitschrift* 24:1–79

(1954). *Gottesgnadentum und Widerstandsrecht im früheren Mittelalter* 2nd rev. edn, R. Buchner, Böhlau Verlag (1st edn 1914, transl., with Kern 1919, by Chrimes, S.B. (1939). *Kingship and Law in the Middle Ages*, Basil Blackwell)

Kerner, M. (1976). 'Zur Entstehungsgeschichte der Institutio Traiani', *Deutsches Archiv* 32:558–71

(1977). *Johannes von Salisbury und die logische Struktur seines Policraticus*, Franz Steiner Verlag

732 *Bibliography*

(1979). 'Natur und Gesellschaft bei Johannes von Salisbury' in A. Zimmermann (ed.) *Soziale Ordnungen im Selbstverständnis des Mittelalters* (Miscellanea Mediaevalia. Veröffentlichungen des Thomas-Instituts der Universität zu Köln, Band 12/1), W. de Gruyter

Keynes, S. and Lapidge, M. (1983). *Alfred the Great: Asser's Life of Alfred and Other Contemporary Sources*, Penguin

Knabe, L. (1936). *Die gelasianische Zweigewaltentheorie bis zum Ende des Investiturstreits* (Historische Studien 292), E. Ebering

Knowles, D. (1951). *The Episcopal Colleagues of Archbishop Thomas Becket* (Ford Lectures, 1949), Cambridge University Press

(1970). *Thomas Becket*, A. and C. Black

Köbler, G. (1971). *Lateinisch- alt hoch deutsches Wörterbuch*, Musterschmidt Verlag

Koch, J. (1953). 'Die Grundlagen der Geschichts philosophie Ottos von Freising', in W. Dürig and B. Panzram (eds.) *Studien zur historischen Theologie. Festgabe für Franz Xavier Seppelt*, Zink; also published (1953) as vol. 1/2 of the *Münchener Theologische Zeitschrift*

Kolb, H. (1971). 'Himmlisches und irdisches Gericht im Karolingischer Theologie', *Frühmittelalterliche Studien* 5:284–303

Krause, H. (1965). 'Königtum und Rechtsordnung in der Zeit der sächsischen und salischen Herrscher', *Zeitschrift der Savigny-Stiftung für Rechtsgeschichte. Germanistische Abteilung* 82:1–98

Kula, W. (1970). *Théorie économique du système féodal* (Civilisations et Sociétés 15), Mouton

Kuttner S. (1936). 'Sur les origines du terme "droit positif"', *Revue historique du droit français et étranger* 15:728–40

(1937). *Repertorium der kanonistik (1140–1234), Prodromus corporis glossarum*, vol. 1 (Studi e testi 71), Biblioteca Apostolica Vaticano

(1947). 'Liber Canonicus. A note on "Dictatus papae" c. 17'. *Studi Gregoriani* 2:387ff

(1948a). 'De Gratiani opere noviter edendo', *Apollinaris* 21:118–28

(1948b). 'The Father of the Science of Canon Law', *The Jurist* 1:2–19

(1953). 'Graziano: l'uomo e l'opera', *Studia Gratiana* 1:15–29; repr. in Kuttner, S. (1983). *Gratian and the Schools of Law 1140–1234*, Variorum Reprints

(1976). 'Gratian and Plato', in *Church and Government in the Middle Ages* (Essays presented to C.R. Cheney on his 70th Birthday and edited by C.N.L. Brooke *et al.*), Cambridge University Press

Laarhoven, J. van (1977a), 'Iustitia bij John of Salisbury: Proeve van een terminologische statistiek', *Nederlands Archief voor Kerkgeschiedenis* 58, 1:16–37

(1977b). 'Die tirannie verdrijven. John of Salisbury als revolutionnair', in *Geloof en Revolutie. Kerkhistorische kanttekeningen bij een actueel vraagstuk, aangeboden aan prof. dr. W.F. Dankbaar*, pp. 21–50, T. Bolland

Ladner, G.D. (1956). 'Two Gregorian Letters on the Sources and Nature of Gregory VII's Reform Ideology', *Studi Gregoriani* 5:221–42

(1968). *Theologie und Politik vor dem Investiturstreit*, 2nd edn, Wissenschaftliche Buchgesellschaft

(1982). 'Terms and Ideas of Renewal', in R.L. Benson and G. Constable (eds.) *Renaissance and Renewal in the Twelfth Century*, Harvard University Press; Clarendon Press

Lammers, W., ed. (1961). *Geschichtsdenken und Geschichtsbild im Mittelalter. Ausgewählte Aufsätze und Arbeiten aus den Jahren 1933 bis 1959* (Wege der Forschung 21), Wissenschaftliche Buchgesellschaft

(1973). 'Ein Karolingisches Bildprogramm in der *Aula regia* von Ingelheim', in

Festschrift für H. Heimpel. vol. III, Vandenhoech and Ruprecht

(1977). *Weltgeschichte und Zeitgeschichte bei Otto von Freising* (Sitzungsberichte der Wissenschaftlichen Gesellschaft an der Johann Wolfgang Goethe-Universität Frankfurt am Main, Bd. 14, Nr. 3) Franz Steiner Verlag

La Monte, J.L. (1932). *Feudal Monarchy in the Latin Kingdom of Jerusalem*, Medieval Academy of America

Landgraf, A.M. (1973). *Introduction à l'histoire de la littérature théologique de la scolastique naissante*, transl. A.M. Landry and L.B. Geiger (Université de Montreal. Publications de l'Institut d'études médiévales 32)

Lapparent, P. de (1946). 'Un précurseur de la Réforme anglaise: l'Anonyme d'York', *Archives d'histoire doctrinale et littéraire du Moyen Age* 15:149–68

Lazzarino del Grosso, A. (1973). *Armüt und Reichtum im Denken Gerhohs von Reichersberg* (Zeitschrift für bayerische Landesgeschichte. Reihe B. Beiheft 4), Beck

(1974). *Società e potere nella Germania del XII secolo. Gerhoch di Reichersberg* (Il Pensiero politico, Biblioteca 6), L.S. Olschki

Le Bras, G., Lefebvre, Ch., Rambaud, J. (1965). *L'Age classique, 1140–1378. Sources et théories du droit* (Histoire du Droit et des Institutions de l'Eglise en Occident, ed. G. Le Bras, 7), Sirey

Lecler, J. (1931). 'L'argument des deux glaives (Luc. XXII, 38) dans les controverses politiques du moyen age', *Recherches de science religieuse* 21:312ff

Leclercq, J. (1962, 1966, 1969). *Recueil d'études sur S. Bernard et ses écrits*, 3 vols., Edizioni di Storia e Letteratura

Le Gentil, P. (1969). *The Chanson de Roland* (transl. by Frances F Beer from *La 'Chanson de Roland'*, 2nd edn, Harier, 1967), Harvard University Press

Lehmann, P. (1956)., 'Nachrichten und Gerüchte von der Überlieferung der libri sex Ciceronis *de re publica*', *Studi Italiani di filologia classica* 27/28:202–15

Lemarignier, J.-F. (1951). 'La dislocation du "pagus" et le problème des "consuetudines" (Xe–XIe siècles)', in *Mélanges d'histoire du moyen âge dédiés à la mémoire de Louis Halphen*, Presses Universitaires de France

(1965). *Le gouvernement royal aux premiers temps capétiens (987–1108)*, A. and J. Picard

(1970). *La France médiévale: Institutions et société* (Collection U. Série 'Histoire médiévale' dir. G. Duby), Librairie Armand Colin

Lemosse, M. (1946). 'La Lèse-Majesté dans la monarchie franque', *Revue du Moyen Age latin* 2:5–24

Lentini, A. (1960). 'Alfano', in *Dizionario biografico degli italiani* (Istituto della Enciclopedia Italiana), 2:253–7

Lerner, R. (1972). 'Maimonides', in L. Strauss and J. Cropsey (eds.) *History of Political Philosophy*, 2nd ed, Rand McNally College Publishing Company, pp. 203–22

Levison, W. (1951). 'Die mittelalterliche Lehre von den beiden Schwerten', *Deutsches Archiv* 9:14–42

Lewis, N.B. (1958). 'The Last Medieval Summons of the English Feudal Levy, 13 June 1385', *English Historical Review*, 73:1–26

Leyser, K.J. (1965). 'The Polemics of the Papal Revolution', in B. Smalley (ed.) *Trends in Medieval Political Thought*, Basil Blackwell

(1975). 'Frederick Barbarossa, Henry II and the Hand of St James', *English Historical Review* 90:481–506

(1979). *Rule and Conflict in an Early Medieval Society. Ottonian Saxony*, Edward Arnold

(1981). 'Ottonian Government', *English Historical Review* 96:721–53

(1982). *Medieval Germany and Its Neighbours, 900–1250*, Hambledon Press

(1983). 'Die Ottonen und Wessex', *Frühmittelalterliche Studien* 17:73–97

Liebeschütz, H. (1930). *Das allegorische Weltbild der heiligen Hildegard von Bingen* (Studien der Bibliothek Warburg 16), Teubner

(1950). *Medieval Humanism in the Life and Writings of John Salisbury* (Studies of the Warburg Institute 17), Warburg Institute, University of London; repr. 1968, Kraus Reprint

(1968). 'Chartres und Bologna. Naturbegriff und Staatsidee bei Johannes von Salisbury', *Archiv für Kulturgeschichte* 50:3–32

Linder, A. (1977a). 'The Knowledge of John of Salisbury in the Late Middle Ages', *Studi medievali*, 3rd series, 18/2:315–66

(1977b). 'John of Salisbury's *Policraticus* in Thirteenth-Century England: The Evidence of MS Cambridge Corpus Christi College 469', *Journal of the Warburg and Courtauld Institutes* 40:276–82

Lot, F. and Fawtier, R. (1958). *Histoire des institutions françaises au moyen âge*, vol. II: *Institutions royales*, Presses Universitaires de France

Lottin, O. (1931). *Le droit naturel chez Saint Thomas d'Aquin et ses prédécesseurs*, 2nd edn, C. Beyaert

(1959). *Psychologie et morale aux XIIe et XIIIe siècles 5: Problèmes d'histoire littéraire. L'école d'Anselme de Laon et de Guillaume de Champeaux*, J. Duculot

Louis, R. (1946). *De l'histoire à la legende: Girart comte de Vienne*, 3 vols., l'Imprimerie Moderne

(1956). 'L'Epopée française et carolingienne', *Caloquios de Roncesvalles 1955* (Publication de la facultad de filosofia y Letras Universidad de Saragossa), II, 18:327–460

Loyn, H. and Percival, J. (1975). *The Reign of Charlemagne*, Edward Arnold

Lubac, Henri de (1949). *Corpus Mysticum: L'Eucharistie et l'Eglise au moyen âge*, Aubier

Luscombe, D.E. (1966). 'Nature in the Thought of Peter Abelard', *La filosofia della natura nel Medioevo. Atti del terzo congresso internazionale di filosofia medioevale. Passo della Mendola (Trento) – 31 agosto–5 settembre 1964*, Società editrice Vita e Pensiero, p. 314–19

Lyon, B. (1951). 'The Money Fief under the English Kings 1066–1485', *English Historical Review* 66:161–93

(1980). *A Constitutional and Legal History of Medieval England*. 2nd edn, W.W. Norton

Lyon, B. and Verhulst, A. (1967). *Medieval Finance. A Comparison of Financial Institutions in Northwestern Europe* (Rijksuniversiteit Gent. Werken Fac. Letteren 143), De Tempel

Maassen, F. (1870). *Geschichte der Quellen und Literatur des kanonischen Rechts*, Graz

Maccarrone M. (1959). *Papato e Impero: della elezione di Federico I alla morte di Adriano IV (1152–9)* (Lateranum. Nova Series An. xxv, N. 1–4), Facultas Theologica Pontificiae Universitatis Lateranensis

(1960). 'La Dottrina del Primato papale dal IV all' VIII secolo nelle relazioni con le Chiese occidentali', *Settimane di Studio del Centro Italiano di Studi sull'Alto Medioevo* 7

McGinn, B. (1979). *Visions of the End. Apocalyptic Traditions in the Middle Ages* (Records of Civilisation. Sources and Studies, 96), Columbia University Press

McKitterick, R. (1977). *The Frankish Church and the Carolingian Reforms, 789–895*, Royal Historical Society

Magnou, E. (1964). 'Note sur le sens du mot *fevum* en Septimanie et dans la marche d'Espagne à la fin du Xe et au début du XIe siècle', *Annales du Midi* 76:141–52

Magnou-Nortier, E. (1968). 'Fidélité et féodalité méridionales d'après les serments de fidélité (Xe-début XIIe siècle)', in *Les structures sociales de l'Aquitaine, du Languedoc et de l'Espagne au premier âge féodal* (Colloques Internationaux du CNRS. Sciences Humaines), Editions du Centre National de la Recherche Scientifique

(1969). 'Fidélité et féodalité méridionales d'après les serments de fidélité (Xe-début XIIe siècle)', in *Les structures sociales de l'Aquitaine, du Languedoc et de l'Espagne au premier âge féodal* (Colloques Internationaux du CNRS. Sciences Humaines), Editions du Centre National de Recherche Scientifique

(1976). *Foi et fidelité: recherches sur l'évolution des liens personnels chez les Francs du VIIe an IXE siècle*, Association des publications de l'Université de Toulouse-Le Mirail

Magrassi, M. (1959). *Teologia e storia nel pensiero di Ruperto di Deutz* (Studia Urbaniana 2), Pontificia Universitas de Propaganda Fide

Maḥdi, M. (1972). 'Alfarabi', in L. Strauss and J. Cropsey, (eds.) *History of Political Philosophy*, 2nd edn, Rand McNally College Publishing Company, pp. 182–202

(1974). 'Islamic Theology and Philosophy', *The New Encyclopaedia Britannica* (Macropaedia 9), 15th edn, Encyclopaedia Britannica Inc., pp. 1012–25

(1975). 'Science, Philosophy and Religion in Alfarabi's Enumeration of the Sciences', in J.E. Murdoch and E.D. Sylla (eds.) *The Cultural Context of Medieval Learning* (Boston Studies in the Philosophy of Science, 26. Synthese Library, 76), Reidel

Manitius, Max (1923). *Geschichte der lateinischen Literatur des Mittelalters*, 3 vols. (Handbuch der Altertumswissenschaft 9), Beck

Manselli, R. (1953). 'Il monaco Enrico e la sua eresia', *Bullettino dell' Istituto Storico Italiano per il Medio Evo* 45:1–63

Marongiu, A. (1964). 'A Model State in the Middle Ages: The Norman and Swabian Kingdom of Sicily', *Comparative Studies in Society and History* 6:307–20

Marot, H. (1965). 'Décentralisation structurelle et Primauté dans l'Eglise ancienne', *Concilium* 7:19ff

Marshall, L.E. (1979). 'The Identity of the "New Man" in the *Anticlaudianus* of Alan of Lille', *Viator* 10:77–94

Martin, J. (1968). 'John of Salisbury and the Classics', Harvard University PhD thesis

(1969). Summary of dissertation in *Harvard Studies in Classical Philology*, 73:319–21

Martini, E. (1963). 'Alcune considerazioni sulla dottrina Gelasiana', *Bulletino dell' Istituto Storico Italiano per il Medio Evo* 75:7ff

Massey, H.J. (1967). 'John of Salisbury: Some Aspects of his Political Philosophy', *Classica et Mediaevalia* 28:357–72

Mayer, T. (1956). 'Staatsauffassung in der Karolingerzeit', in *Das Königtum* (Vorträge und Forschungen 3):169–83

Mayer-Pfannholz, A. (1941). 'Der Wandel des Kirchenbildes in der Geschichte', *Theologie und Glaube* 33:22ff

Mélanges Saint Bernard. XXIVe Congrès de l'Association bourguignonne des sociétés savantes (8e Centenaire de la mort de saint Bernard) (1953). Association des Amis de Saint Bernard, Dijon, M. l'abbé Marilier

Ménager, L.R. (1959). 'L'institution monarchique dans les états normands d'Italie', *Cahiers de Civilisation Médiévale* 2:303–31

(1969). 'La législation sud-italienne sous la domination normande', *Settimane di Studio del Centro Italiano di Studi sull' Alto Medioevo* 16

Methuen, E. (1959). *Kirche und Heilsgeschichte bei Gerhoh von Reichersberg* (Studien und Texte zur Geistesgeschichte des Mittelalters 6), E.J. Brill

Meyer, O. (1935). 'Überlieferung und Verbrietung des Dekrets des Bischofs Burchard von Worms', *Zeitschrift der Savigny-Stiftung für Rechtsgeschichte, Kanonistische Abteilung* 24:141ff

(1950). 'Zur Geschichte des Wortes Staat', *Welt als Geschichte* 10:229–39

Miccoli, G. (1966). 'Le ordinazioni simoniache nel pensiero di Gregorio VII. Un capitolo della dottrina del primato?', in G. Miccoli, *Chiesa Gregoriana*, La Nuovo Italia; Società tipografica editrice bolognese

Michel, A. (1924–30). *Humbert und Kerullarios: Quellen und Studien zum Schisma des XI.*

Jahrhunderts, 2 vols. (Quellen und Forschungen aus dem Gebiete der Geschichte 21 and 23), F. Schöningh

(1943). *Die Sentenzen des Kardinals Humbert, das erste Rechtsbuch der päpstlichen Reform* (Schriften des Reichsinstituts für ältere deutsche Geschichtskunde 7), Hiersemann

(1947). 'Die folgenschweren Ideen des Kardinal Humbert und ihr Einfluss auf Gregor VII.', *Studi Gregoriani* 1:65ff

(1953). 'Humbert von Silva Candida (+ 1061) bei Gratian', *Studi Gratiana* 1:83ff

Miczka, G. (1970). *Das Bild der Kirche bei Johannes von Salisbury* (Bonner historische Forschungen 34), Ludwig Röhrscheid Verlag

Milsom, S.F.C. (1976). *The Legal Framework of English Feudalism* (The Maitland Lecture, 1972), Cambridge University Press

(1981). *Historical Foundations of the Common Law*, 2nd edn, Butterworths

Mirbt, K. (1894). *Die Publizistik im Zeitalter Gregors VII.*, J.C. Hinrichs; repr. 1965, Zentral-Antiquariat der Deutschen Demokratischen Republik

Mitteis, H. (1933). *Lehnrecht und Staatsgewalt*, Böhlau Verlag

(1940). *Der Staat des hohen Mittelalters. Grundlinien einer vergleichenden, verfassungsgeschichte des Lehnzeitalters* Böhlaus Nachfolger (English transl. 1975, North-Holland)

Mohlberg, K. and Baumstark, A. (1927). *Die älteste erreichbare Gestalt des Liber sacramentorum anni circuli* (Liturgeigeschichtliche Quellen 11/12), Aschendorff

Momigliano, A. (1955). 'Notes on Petrarch, John of Salisbury and the *Institutio Traiani*', in *idem, Contributo alla storia degli studi classici*. (Storia e letteratura 47), Edizioni di Storia e Letteratura

Monti, G.M. (1940). 'Il testo e la storia esterna delle Assise Normanne', in *Studi di storia e diritto in onore di C. Calisse*, Giuffrè; rev. repr. in Monti, G.M. (1945). *Lo stato normanno-svevo. Lineamenti e ricerche* (Regia Deputazione di Storia Patria per le Puglie. Documenti e monografie 26), Trani, Vecchi Ed.

Moore, R.I. (1977). *The Origins of European Dissent*, Allen Lane

Mor, C.G. (1935). 'La recezione del diritto romano nelle collezioni canoniche dei secoli IX–XI in Italia e oltr' Alpe', *Acta Congressus Iuridici Internationalis . . . 1934* 2:281ff

Morembert, T. de (1982). 'Gérard I, évêque de Cambrai', in *Dictionnaire de biographie française*, ed. M. Prevost and R. d'Amat (Letouzey et Ané), 15:1200–1

Morrison, K.F. (1964). *The Two Kingdoms. Ecclesiology in Carolingian Political Thought*, Princeton University Press

(1980). 'Otto of Freising's Quest for the Hermeneutic Circle', *Speculum* 55:207–36

(1981). '"*Unum ex multis*": Hincmar of Rheims' Medical and Aesthetic Rationales for Unification', *Settimane di Studio di Centro Italiano di Studi sull'Alto Medioevo* 27, ii:583–712

Müller-Mertens, E. (1970). *Regnum Teutonicum*, Böhlaus Nachfolger

Munier, C. (1957). 'Les sources patristiques du Droit de l'Eglise du VIIIe au XIIe siècle', dissertation, Mulhausen

(1966). 'Nouvelles recherches sur l'Hispana chronologique', *Revue des Sciences religieuses* 40:400ff

Myers, H.A. (1971). 'Kingship in "The Book of Emperors"', *Traditio* 27:205–30

(1982). *Medieval Kingship*, Nelson Hall

Nelson, J.L. (1975). 'Ritual and Reality in the Early Medieval *Ordines*', *Studies in Church History* 11:41–51

(1977a). 'Kingship, Law and Liturgy in the Political Thought of Hincmar of Rheims', *English Historical Review* 92:241–79

(1977b). 'Inauguration rituals', in P. Sawyer and I.N. Wood (eds.) *Early Medieval Kingship*, University of Leeds

(1977c). 'On the Limits of the Carolingian Renaissance', *Studies in Church History* 14:61–9

(1982). 'The Rites of the Conqueror', *Proceedings of the Battle Conference* 4:117–32, 210–21

(1983a). 'Legislation and Consensus in the Reign of Charles the Bald', in P. Wormald (ed.) *Ideal and Reality in Frankish and Anglo-Saxon Society. Studies Presented to J.M. Wallace-Hadrill*, Basil Blackwell

(1983b). 'The Church's Military Service in the Ninth Century: A Contemporary Comparative View?', *Studies in Church History* 20:15–30

(1985). 'Public "Histories" and Private History in the Work of Nithard', *Speculum* 60:251–93

(1986). *Politics and Ritual in Early Medieval Europe*, Hambledon Press.

Niermeyer, J. (1976). *Mediae Latinitatis Lexicon Minus*, E.J. Brill

Nineham, R. (1963). 'The So-Called Anonymous of York', *Journal of Ecclesiastical History* 14:31–45

Noble, T.F.X. (1976). 'The Monastic Ideal as a Model for Empire: The Case of Louis the Pious', *Revue Bénédictine* 86:235–50

(1984). *The Republic of St Peter. The Birth of the Papal State, 680–825*, University of Pennsylvania Press

Nothdurft, K.D. (1963). *Studien zum Einfluss Senecas auf die Philosophie und Theologie des Zwölften Jahrhunderts* (Studien und Texte zur Geistesgeschichte des Mittelalters 7), E.J. Brill

Odegaard, C.E. (1941). 'Carolingian Oaths of Fidelity', *Speculum* 16:284–96

(1945). 'The Concept of Royal Power in Carolingian Oaths of Fidelity', *Speculum* 20:279–89

Ohly, F. (1958). *Hohelied-Studien. Grundzüge einer Geschichte der Hoheliedauslegung des Abendlandes bis zum 1200*, Franz Steiner Verlag

Olivier-Martin, F. (1938). 'Le roi de France et les mauvaises coutumes au moyen âge', *Zeitschrift der Savigny-Stiftung für Rechtsgeschichte. Germanistische Abteilung* 58:108–37

Otto von Freising, 1158–1958 (1958). *Analecta Sacri Ordinis Cisterciensis* (Editiones Cistercienses, annus 14. fasc. 3/4 Jul./Dec. 1958)

Ourliac, P. (1980). Review of Fuhrmann 1972–4, *Francia* 8:787–90

Pacaut, M. (1964). *Louis VII et son royaume* (Bibliothèque générale de l'Ecole Pratique des Hautes Etudes, VIe Section), SEVPEN

Packard, S.R. (1973). *12th Century Europe. An Interpretive Essay*, University of Massachusetts Press

Palmer, J.J.N. (1968). 'The Last Summons of the Feudal Army in England (1385)', *English Historical Review* 83:771–75

Panzer, K. (1880). *Wido von Ferrara, de scismate Hildebrandi* (Historische Studien 2). Veit

Paradisi, B. (1962).*Storia del diritto romano. Le fonti dal secolo X fino alle soglie dell'eta bolognese*, vol. 1: *Le fonti del diritto nell'epoca bolognese*, Liguori Editore

Parent, J.M. (1938). *La doctrine de la création dans l'école de Chartres. Etude et textes* (Publications de l'Institut d'Etudes Médiévales d'Ottowa 8), J. Vrin

Patlagean, E. (1974). 'Les armes et la cité à Rome du VIIème au IXème siècle, et le modèle europeén des trois fonctions sociales', *Mélanges de l'Ecole française de Rome* 86, i:25–62; repr. in Patlagean, E. (1981). *Structure sociale, famille, chrétienté à Byzance, IVe–XIe siècle*, Variorum Reprints, ch. 2

Pellens, K. (1965). 'The Tracts of the Norman Anonymous: CCCC 415', *Transactions of the Cambridge Bibliographical Society*, 4, ii:155–65

Penndorf, U. (1974). *Das Problem der 'Reichseinheitsidee' nach der Teilung von Verdun (843)* (Münchner Beiträge zur Mediävistik und Renaissance-Forschung 20), Arbeo-Gesellschaft

Pennington, B. (1973). *Bernard of Clairvaux. Studies Presented to Dom Jean Leclercq*, Cistercian Publications

Pepin, R.E. (1975). 'The "Entheticus" of John of Salisbury: A Critical Text', *Traditio*, 31:127–93

Peters, E. (1970). *The Shadow King. Rex Inutilis in Medieval Law and Literature, 751–1327*, Yale University Press

Peters, F.E. (1968a). *Aristoteles Arabus: The Oriental Translations and Commentaries on the Aristotelian Corpus* (Monographs on Mediterranean Antiquity 2), E.J. Brill

(1968b). *Aristotle and the Arabs. The Aristotelian Tradition in Islam* (New York University Studies in Near Eastern Civilization 1), New York University Press

Petit-Dutaillis, C. (1933). *La monarchie féodale en France et en Angleterre (Xe–XIIIe siècle)* (Evolution de l'Humanité XLI), La Renaissance du Livre; repr. with up-to-date bibliography, 1971, Albin Michel

Petot, P. (1927). 'L'hommage servile. Essai sur la nature juridique de l'hommage', *Revue historique de droit français et étranger*, 4th series, 6:68–107

Pirenne, H. (1939). *Mohammed and Charlemagne*, George Allen and Unwin

Planiol, M. (1887). 'L'assise au comte Geffroi. Etude sur les successions féodales en Bretagne', *Nouvelle revue historique du droit français et étranger* 11:117–62, 652–708

Plumpe, J.C. (1943). *Mater Ecclesiae. An Inquiry into the Concept of the Church as Mother in Early Christianity*, Catholic University of America Press

Poly, J.-P. (1976). *La Provence et la société féodale. Contribution à l'étude des structures dites féodales dans le Midi*, Bordas

Poly, J.-P. and Bournazel, E. (1980). *La Mutation Féodale Xe–XIIe siècles* (Nouvelle Clio 16), Presses Universitaires de France

Prawer, J. (1969). *Histoire du Royaume latin de Jérusalem*, Centre National de la Recherche Scientifique

Prinz, F. (1971). *Klerus und Krieg im früheren Mittelalter* (Monographien zur Geschichte des Mittelalters 2), Hiersemann

Prosdocimi, L. (1965). 'Chierici e laici nella società occidentale del secolo XII. A proposito di Decr. Grat. C.12 q.1 c.7: "Duo sunt genera Christianorum"', in *Proceedings of the Second International Congress of Medieval Canon Law, Boston 1963*, Biblioteca Apostolica Vaticana

Rahner, H. (1947). 'Navicula Petri', *Zeitschrift für katholische Theologie* 69:1ff

Rambaud-Buhot, J. (1953). 'Le *corpus iuris civilis* dans le décret de Gratien', *Bibliothèque de l'Ecole des Chartres* 111:54–64

(1957). 'Le décret de Gratien et le droit romain', *Revue historique de droit françgis et étranger* 35:290–300

Reeves, M. (1969). *The Influence of Prophecy in the Later Middle Ages. A Study in Joachimism*, Clarendon Press

(1976). *Joachim of Fiore and the Prophetic Future*, Society for the Promotion of Christian Knowledge

Reeves, M. and Hirsch-Reich, B. (1972). *The 'Figurae' of Joachim of Fiore* (Oxford-Warburg Studies), Clarendon Press

Repertorium Biblicum Medii Aevi (1940–80), ed. F. Stegmüller, 11 vols. (Consejo Superior de Investigaciones Científicas. Instituto Francisco Suárez), Gráficas Marina

Repertorium commentariorum in Sententias Petri Lombardi (1947). Ed. F. Stegmüller, 2 vols., F. Schöningh

Reuter, T., ed. (1979). *The Medieval Nobility*, North-Holland

Rexroth, K.H. (1978). 'Volkssprache und werdendes Volksbewusstsein', in H. Beumann and W. Schröder (eds.) *Aspekte der Nationenbildung im Mittelalter* (= Nationes 1), Jan Thorbecke Verlag

Reydellet, M. (1981). *La Royauté dans la littérature latine de Sidoine Apollinaire à Isidore de Seville*, Ecole Française de Rome, Palais Farnèse

Reynolds, L.D. (1965). *The Medieval Tradition of Seneca's Letters* (Oxford Classical and Philosophical Monographs), Oxford University Press

Reynolds, S. (1984). *Kingdoms and Communities in Western Europe, 900–1300*, Oxford University Press

Richard, J. (1968). 'Le château dans la structure féodale de la France de l'Est au XIIème siècle', in *Probleme des 12. Jahrhunderts. Reichenau-Vorträge 1965–67* (Vorträge und Forschungen 12), Jan Thorbecke Verlag

Richards, J. (1979). *The Popes and the Papacy in the Early Middle Ages, 476–752*, Routledge and Kegan Paul

Riché, P. (1972). 'L'enseignement et la culture des laics dans l'Occident pré-carolingien', *Settimane di Studio del Centro Italiano di Studi sull'Alto Medioevo* 19, i:231–53
ed. (1975). Introduction to Dhuoda, *Manuel pour mon fils*, Sources chrétiennes, Paris
(1976). 'Les représentations du palais dans les textes littéraires du haut moyen âge', *Francia* 4:161–71

Riché, P. and Tate, G. (1974). *Textes et Documents d'Histoire du Moyen Age Ve–Xe siècles*, Société d'Edition d'Enseignement Supérieur, Paris

Riedlinger, H. (1958). *Die Makellosigkeit der Kirche in den lateinischen Hoheliedkommentaren des Mittelalters* (Beiträge zur Geschichte der Philosophie und Theologie des Mittelalters 38.3), Aschendorff Verlagbuchhandlung

Rippe, G. (1975). 'Feudum sine Fidelitate. Formes féodales et structures sociales dans la région de Padoue à l'époque de la première ère communale (1131–1236)', *Mélanges de l'Ecole Françoise de Rome. Moyen Age et Temps Modernes* 87:187–239
(1979). 'Commune urbaine et féodalité en Italie du Nord: l'exemple de Padoue (Xe s.-1237)', *Mélanges de l'Ecole Française de Rome. Moyen Age et Temps Modernes* 91:659–97

Rivière, J. (1925). 'In partem sollicitudinis: évolution d'une formule pontificale', *Revue des sciences religieuses* 5:210ff

Robinson, I.S. (1978a). '"Periculosus Homo": Pope Gregory VII and Episcopal Authority', *Viator* 9:103ff
(1978b). 'Zur Arbeitsweise Bernolds von Konstanz und seines Kreises', *Deutsches Archiv* 34:51ff
(1978c). 'Bernold von St. Blasien', *Die deutsche Literatur des Mittelalters. Verfasserlexikon* 1:795ff
(1979). 'Pope Gregory VII, the Princes and the *Pactum*, 1077–80', *Economic History Review* 94:721ff
(1982). 'Zur Entstehung des Privilegium Maius Leonis VIII papae', *Deutsches Archiv* 38:26ff

Rosenblatt, S. (1927). *The High Ways to Perfection of Abraham Maimonides*. vol. I, Columbia University Press; (1938) vol. II, Johns Hopkins University Press

Rosenthal, E.I.J. (1951). 'The Place of Politics in the Philosophy of Ibn Bajja', *Islamic Culture* 25: 187–211
(1958). *Political thought in Medieval Islam*, Cambridge University Press
(1971). 'Maimonides' Conception of State and Society', in *idem, Studia Semitica*, vol. I, Cambridge University Press, pp. 275–89

Rota, A. (1953/4). 'L'influsso civilistico nella concezione dello stato di Giovanni Salisberiense', *Rivista di storia del diritto italiano* 26/7:209–26

Rouse, R. and M.A. (1967). 'John of Salisbury and the Doctrine of Tyrannicide', *Speculum* 42:693–709

Ryan, J.J. (1947). 'Saint Peter Damian and the Sermons of Nicholas of Clairvaux: A Clarification', *Medieval Studies* 9:151–61

(1956). *Saint Peter Damiani and His Canonical Sources*, Pontifical Institute of Mediaeval Studies 2, Toronto

Saint Bernard théologien (1953). *Actes du Congrès de Dijon 15–19 Septembre 1953*, (Analecta Sacri Ordinis Cisterciensis 9, iii–iv), Editiones Cistercienses

Salman, D.H. (1939). 'The Medieval Latin Translations of Alfarabi's Works', *The New Scholasticism* 13:245–61

(1940). 'Le "Liber exercitationis ad viam felicitatis" d'Alfarabi', *Recherches de théologie ancienne et médiévale* 12:33–48

Sánchez Albornoz, C. (1969). 'Conséquences de la reconquête et du repeuplement sur les institutions féodo-vassaliques de Léon et di Castille', in *Les structures sociales de l'Aquitaine, du Languedoc et de l'Espagne au premier âge féodal*, Centre National de la Recherche Scientifique (Colloques Internationaux du CNRS. Sciences Humaines), Editions du Centre National de la Recherche Scientifique

Schaller, D. (1976). 'Das Aachener Epos für Karl den Kaiser', *Frühmittelalterliche Studien* 10:134–68

Scheibe, F.-C. (1959). 'Alcuin und die Briefe Karls des Grossen', *Deutsches Archiv* 15:181–93

Schieffer, R. (1981). *Die Entstehung des päpstlichen Investiturverbots für den deutschen König* (MGH 28), Hiersemann

(1982). 'Ludwig "der Frome". Zur Entstehung eines Karlingischen Herrscherbeinamens', *Frühmittelalterliche Studien* 16:58–73

Schieffer, T. (1957). 'Die Krise des Karolingischen Imperiums', in *Festschrift für G. Kallen*, Peter Hanstein

Schlesinger, W. (1958). 'Kaisertum und Reichsteilung. Zur *Divisio regnorum* von 806', in *Festgabe für Hans Herzfeld*, Duncker and Humblot; repr. in Schlesinger 1963

(1963). *Beiträge zur deutschen Verfassungsgeschichte des Mittelalters*, 2 vols., Vandenhoeck and Ruprecht

Schmidlin, J. (1905). 'Die Eschatologie Ottos von Freising', *Zeitschrift für katholische Theologie* 29:445–81

(1906). *Die geschichtsphilosophie und kirchenpolitische Weltanschauung Ottos von Freising*, Herder

Schmidt, R. (1961). 'Königsumritt und Huldigung in ottonisch-salischer Zeit', *Vorträge und Forschungen* 6:97–233

Schmidt-Wiegand, R. (1977). 'Eid und Gelöbnis im Mittelalterlichen Recht', in P. Classen (ed.) *Recht und Schrift im Mittelalter* (Vorträge und Forschungen 23), Jan Thorbecke Verlag

Schminck, C.U. (1969). *Crimen laesae maiestatis. Das politische Strafrecht Siziliens nach den Assisen von Ariano (1140) und den Konstitutionen von Melfi (1231)* (Untersuchungen zur deutschen Staats- und Rechtsgeschichte, N.F. 124), Scientia Verlag

Schneidmüller, B. (1979). *Karolingische Tradition und frühes französisches Königtum*, Franz Steiner Verlag

Scholz, B.S. (1970). *Carolingian Chronicles: Royal Frankish Annals and Nithard's Histories*, University of Michigan Press

Schramm, P.E. (1928). *Die deutschen Kaiser und Könige in Bildern ihrer Zeit*, vol. 1: *Bis zur Mitte des 12 Jahrhunderts (751–1152)* (Veröffentlichungen der Forschungsinstitut an der Universität Leipzig)

(1929; 1957; 1962). *Kaiser, Rom und Renovatio. Studien und Texte zur Geschichte des römischen Erneuerungsgedankens vom Ende des karolinischen Reiches biszum Investiturstreit*, 2 vols., 1st, 2nd, 3rd edns, Teubner

(1947). 'Sacerdotium und Regnum im Austausch ihrer Vorrechte: "imitatio imperii" und "imitatio sacerdotii"'. Eine geschichtliche Skizze zur Beleuchtung des "Dictatus papae" Gregors VII.', *Studi Gregoriani* 2:403ff

(1950). 'Das Kastilische Königtum und Kaisertum wahrend der Reconquista (11 Jahrhundert bis 1252)', in *Festschrift für G. Ritter*, J.C.B. Mohr

(1960). *Der König von Frankreich. Das Wesen der Monarchie vom 9. zum 16. Jahrhundert*, 2nd edn, Böhlaus Nachfolger

(1968). *Kaiser, Könige und Päpste*, 4 vols., Hiersemann

Schramm, P.E. and Mütherich, F. (1962). *Denkmale der deutschen Könige und Kaiser* (Veröffentlichungen des Zentralinstitut für Kunstgeschichte in München 2), Prestel-Verlag

(1983). *Die deutschen Kaiser und Könige*, rev. edn of Schramm 1928, Prestel Verlag

Sheerin, D.J. (1969). 'John of Salisbury's *Entheticus de Dogmate Philosophorum*: Critical Text and Introduction', University of North Carolina at Chapel Hill PhD thesis

Silver, D.J. (1965). *Maimonidean Criticism and the Maimonidean Controversy, 1180–1240*, E.J. Brill

Slicher van Bath, B.H. (1974). 'Feudo-vazallitische verhoudingen en agrarische maatschappijstructuur', *Bijdragen en Mededelingen voor de Geschiendenis der Nederlanden* 89:225–40

Smalley, B. (1960). *English Friars and Antiquity in the Early Fourteenth Century*, Basil Blackwell

(1973). *The Becket Conflict and the Schools. A Study of Intellectuals in Politics*, Basil Blackwell

(1981). *Studies in Medieval Thought and Learning from Abelard to Wycliff*, Hambledon Press

(1983). *The Study of the Bible in the Middle Ages*, 3rd edn, Basil Blackwell (1st edn 1952)

Southern, R.W. (1953). *The Making of the Middle Ages*, Hutchinson

Spagnesi, E. (1970). *Wernerius Bononiensis Judex. La figura storica d'Irnerio* (Accademia toscana di scienze e lettere La Colombaria. Studi 16), L.S. Olschki

Spiegel, G. (1975). 'The Cult of St Denys and Capetian Kingship', *Journal of Medieval History* 1:43–69

Sprandel, R. (1962). *Ivo von Chartres und seine Stellung in der Kirchengeschichte* (Pariser historische Studien 1), Hiersemann

(1975). *Verfassung und Gesellschaft im Mittelalter*, F. Schöningh

Stafford, P. (1981). 'The King's Wife in Wessex 800–1066', *Past and Present* 91:3–27

(1983). *Queens, Concubines, and Dowagers. The King's Wife in the Early Middle Ages*, University of Georgia

Staubach, N. (1983). 'Germanisches Königtum und lateinische Literatur', *Frühmittelalterliche Studién* 17:1–54

Stenton, F.M. (1932). *The First Century of English Feudalism 1066–1166* (Ford Lectures 1929), Clarendon Press

Stickler, A.M. (1942). 'De ecclesiae potestate coactiva materiali apud magistrum Gratianum', *Salesianum* 4:2–23, 97–119

(1944). 'De potestate gladii materialis ecclesiae secundum *Quaestiones Bambergenses* ineditas', *Salesianum* 6:113–40

(1947a). 'Der Schwerterbegriff bei Huguccio', *Ephemerides iuris canonici* 3:201–42

(1947b). 'Il potere coattivo materiale della Chiesa nella Riforma Gregoriana secondo Anselmo di Lucca', *Studi Gregoriani* 2:235–85

(1948a). 'Il *gladius* nel Registro di Gregorio VII', *Studi Gregoriani* 3:89–103

(1948b). 'Magistri Gratiani sententia de potestate ecclesiae in statum', *Apollinaris* 21:36–111

(1951). 'Il "gladius" negli atti dei concili e dei RR. Pontefici sino a Graziano e Bernardo di Clairvaux', *Salesianum* 13:414ff

(1953). 'Sacerdotium et Regnum nei decretisti e primi decretalisti: Considerazioni metodologiche di ricerca e testi', *Salesianum* 15:572–612

(1954a). 'Sacerdozio e regno nelle nuove ricerche attorno ai secoli XII e XIII nei decretisti e decretalisti fino alle decretali di Gregorio IX', in *Sacerdozio e regno da Gregorio VII a Bonifacio VIII. Studi presentati alla Sezione storica del Congresso della Pontificia Università gregoriana, 13–17 ottobre 1953* (Miscellanea Historiae Pontificiae 18), Pontificia Università gregoriana, pp. 1–26

(1954b). 'Imperator vicarius Papae', *Mitteilungen des Instituts für Österreichische Geschichtsforschung* 62:165–212

Stock, B. (1972). *Myth and Science in the Twelfth Century*, Princeton University Press

Stoclet, A. (1980). 'La "clausula de unctione Pippini regis": mises au point nouvelles hypothèses', *Francia* 8:1–42

Stollberg, G. (1973). *Die soziale Stellung der intellektuelen Obsersicht im England des 12. Jahrhunderts* (Historische Studien 427), Mathiesen Verlag

Strand, B. (1980). *Kvinner och män i Gesta Danorum* (Kvinnohistoriskt arkiv 18) (with English summary), Viktoria Bokförlag

Strauss, L. (1935). *Philosophie und Gesetz. Beiträge zum Verfständnis Maimunis und seiner Vorläufer*, Schocken Verlag

(1936). 'Quelques remarques sur la Science Politique de Maïmonide et de Fārābī', *Revue des études juives* 100 bis:1–37

(1945). 'Fārābī's Plato', in *Louis Ginzberg Jubilee Volume*, American Academy for Jewish Research, pp. 357–93

(1953). 'Maimonides' Statement on Political Science', *Proceedings of the American Academy for Jewish Research* 22:115–30

Strayer, J.R. (1961). 'The Development of Feudal Institutions', in M. Clagett, G. Post and R. Reynolds (eds.) *Twelfth-Century Europe and the Foundations of Modern Society*, University of Wisconsin Press

(1965). *Feudalism*, O. Van Nostrand Co. (Anvil original)

(1967). 'The Two Levels of Feudalism', in R.S. Hoyt (ed.) *Life and Thought in the Early Middle Ages*, University of Minnesota Press; repr. in Strayer 1971, pp. 63–76

(1971). 'The Two Levels of Feudalism', in J.R. Strayer, *Medieval Statecraft and the Perspectives of History*, Princeton University Press

Struve, T. (1978). *Die Entwicklung der organologischen Staatsaufassung im Mittelalter* 16), Hiersemann

Studia Gratiana post Octava Decreti Saecularia auctore Consilio Commemorationi Gratianae Instruendae edita (1953–   ) (Institutum Iuridicum Universitatis Studiorum Bononiensis), vol. III published by Institutum Gratianum, vol. X published by Libreria Ateneo Salesiano

Suerbaum, W. (1961). *Vom antiken zum frühmittelalterlichen Staatsbegriff*, Aschendorff

Szövérffy, J. (1957). *Irisches Erzählgut im Abenland. Studien zur vergleichenden Volkskunde und Mittelalterforschung*, E. Schmidt

Tabacco, G. (1960). 'La dissoluzione medievale dello stato nella recente storiografia', *Studi Medievali* 1:397–446

Tabuteau, E.Z. (1982). 'Definitions of Feudal Military Obligations in Eleventh-Century Normandy' in M.S. Arnold, T.A. Green, S.A. Scully and S.D. White (eds.) *On the Laws and Customs of England, Essays in Honor of Samuel E. Thorn*, University of North Carolina Press

Tellenbach, G. (1934/5). 'Römischer und christlicher Reichsgedanke in der Liturgie des frühen Mittelalters', (Heidelberger Akademie der Wissenschaften, philosoph.-historische Klasse, Sitzungsbereichte), Heidelberger Akademie der Wissenschaften (1941). 'Die Unteilbarkeit des Reiches. Ein Beitrag zur Enstehungsgeschichte Deutschlands und Frankreichs', *Historische Zeitschrift* 163:20ff

(1979). 'Die geistige und politischen Grundlagen der Karolingischen Thronfolge. Zugleich eine Studie über kollektive Willensbildung und kollektiven Handeln im 9. Jht.', *Frühmittelalterliche Studien* 13:184–302

Tessier, G. (1962). *Diplomatique royale française*, Picard

Théry, G. (1932–7). *Etudes dionysiennes*, vol. I, J. Vrin

(1933). 'Scot Erigène, traducteur de Denys', *Bulletin du Cange* 8:185ff

Tierney, B. (1963). '*Natura id est Deus*: A Case of Juristic Pantheism?' *Journal of the History of Ideas* 24:307–22; repr. with unaltered pagination in Tierney, B. (1979). *Church, Law and Constitutional Thought in the Middle Ages*, Variorum Reprints 7

(1964). *The Crisis of Church and State 1050–1300*, Prentice-Hall

Töpfer, B. (1974). '*Reges Provinciales*. Ein Beitrag zur staufischen Reichsideologie unter Kaiser Friedrich I.', *Zeitschrift für Geschichtswissenschaft* 22:1348–58

Toubert, P. (1973). *Les structures du Latium médiéval. Le Latium méridional et la Sabine du IXe siècle à la fin du XIIe siècle* (Bibliothèque des Ecoles Françaises d'Athènes et de Rome, Fasc. 221), Ecole Française de Rome

Turk, E. (1977). *Nugae curialium. Le règne d'Henri II Plantagenêt (1145–1189) et l'éthique politique*, Préface d'A. Vernet (Centre de Recherches d'Histoire et de Philologie de la IVe Section de l'Ecole pratique des Hautes Etudes. Hautes études médiévales et modernes 28), Librarie Droz

Twersky, I. (1980). *Introduction to the Code of Maimonides ('Mishneh Torah')*, Yale University Press

Uhlig, C. (1973). *Hofkritik im England des Mittelalters und der Renaissance. Studien zu einem Gemeinplatz der europäischen Moralistik* (Quellen und Forschungen zur Sprach- und Kulturgeschichte der germanischen Völker. Neue Folge 56), W. de Gruyter

Ullmann, W. (1953). 'The Origins of the *Ottonianum*', *Cambridge Historical Journal* 9:114ff

(1960). 'Leo I and the Theme of Papal Primacy', *JTS* 11:25ff

(1962). *See* under Ullmann 1955, section V below

(1964). 'Der Souveränitätsgedanke in den Krönungsordines', in *Festscrift für P.E. Schramm*, Franz Steiner Verlag

(1966). *Papst und König. Grundlagen des Papsttums und der englischen Verfassung im Mittelalter* (Salzburger Universitätsschriften. Dike: Schriften zu Recht und Politik 3), Verlag Anton Pustet

(1969). *The Carolingian Renaissance and the Idea of Kingship*, Methuen

(1970). *The Growth of Papal Government in the Middle Ages*, 3rd edn, Methuen (first published 1955; 2nd edn 1962)

(1975c). *The Church and the Law in the Earlier Middle Ages. Selected Essays*: art. xv: 'The Influence of John of Salisbury on Medieval Italian Jurists', pp. 383–92 (repr. with original pagination from *English Historical Review* (1944),59), Variorum Reprints

(1978). 'John of Salisbury's *Policraticus* in the Later Middle Ages', in K. Hauck and H. Mordek (eds.), *Geschichtsschreibung und geistiges Leben im Mittelalter. Festschrift für Heinz Löwe zum 65. Geburtstag*, Böhlau Verlag

(1979). 'Roman Public Law and Medieval Monarchy: Norman Rulership in Sicily', in W. de Vos *et al.* (eds.) *Acta Iuridica: Essays in Honour of Ben Beinart*, vol. III, Cape Town

(1981). *Gelasius I.* (Päpste und Papsttum 18), Hiersemann

744 *Bibliography*

Vacandard, E. (1920). *Vie de Saint Bernard, abbé de Clairvaux*, Librairie Victor Lecoffre

Valdeavellano, L.G. de (1963). 'Las instituciones feudales en España', in F.L. Ganshof (ed.) *El Feudalismo*, Ediciones Ariel

Vallentin, B. (1908). 'Der Engelstaat zur mittelalterlichen Anschauung vom Staate (bis auf Thomas von Aquino)', in K. Breysig, F. Wolters, B. Vallentin and F. Andreae (eds.) *Grundrisse und Bausteine zur Staats- und zur Geschichtslehre zusammengetragen zu den Ehren Gustav Schmollers*, G. Bondi, pp. 41–120

Van Caenegem, R.C. (1973). *The Birth of the English Common Law*, Cambridge University Press

(1976). 'Public Prosecution of Crime in Twelfth-Century England', in C.N.L. Brooke, D.E. Luscombe, G.H. Martin and D. Owen (eds.) *Church and Government in the Middle Ages. Essays presented to C.R. Cheney*, Cambridge University Press

Van Caenegem, R.C. and Ganshof, F.L. (1978). *Guide to the Sources of Medieval History*, North-Holland

Van de Kieft, C. (1974), 'De feodale maatschappij der Middeleeuwen', *Bijdragen en Mededelingen voor de Geschiedenis der Nederlanden* 89:193–211

Van Engen, J.H. (1983). *Rupert of Deutz* (Publications of the UCLA Center for Medieval and Renaissance Studies 18), University of California Press

Van Winter, J.M. (1967). *'Uxorem de militari ordine sibi imparem'*, in *Miscellanea Mediaevalia in memoriam J.F. Niermoyer*, J.B. Wolters

Vaux, R. de (1937). 'La première entrée d'Averroës chez les latins', *Revue des sciences philosophiques et theologiques*, 22:193–245

Verger, J. and Jolivet, J. (1982). *Bernard–Abélard ou le cloître et l'école* (Douze hommes dans l'histoire de l'église. Collection dirigée par J.-R. Armogathe), Fayard-Mame

Vetulani, A. (1946–7). 'Gratien et le droit romain', *Revue historique de droit français et étranger* 24/25:11–49

Vlasto, A. (1970). *The Entry of the Slavs into Christendom*, Cambridge University Press

Vollrath, H. (1974). 'Kaisertum und Patriziat in den Anfängen des Investiturstreits', *Zeitschrift für Kirchengeschichte* 85:11ff

Von Giesebrecht, W. (1881). *Geschichte der deutschen Kaiserzeit*, vol. II, 5th edn, Duncker & Humblot

Waas, A. (1966). 'Karls des Grossen frommigkeit', *Historische Zeitschrift* 203:265–79

Wakefield, W.L. and Evans, A.P. (1969). *Heresies of the High Middle Ages* (Records of Civilization, Sources and Studies 81), Columbia University Press

Wallace-Hadrill, J.M. (1965). 'The Via Regia of the Carolingian Age', in B. Smalley (ed.) *Trends in Medieval Political Thought*, Basil Blackwell

(1983). *The Frankish Church*, Oxford University Press

Walsh, P.G. (1977). 'Alan of Lille as a Renaissance Figure', in *Studies in Church History*, vol. XIV: *Renaissance and Renewal in Christian History*, ed. D. Baker, Basil Blackwell, pp. 117–35

Walzer, R. (1945). 'Arabic Transmission of Greek Thought to Medieval Europe', *Bulletin of the John Rylands Library* 29:160–83

(1962). *Greek into Arabic. Essays on Islamic Philosophy* (Oriental Studies 1), Bruno Cassirer

(1967). 'Early Islamic Philosophy', in A.H. Armstrong (ed.) *The Cambridge History of Later Greek and Early Medieval Philosophy*, Cambridge University Press, pp. 643–69

Weber, M. (1978). *Economy and Society. An Outline of Interpretative Sociology*, ed. G. Roth and C. Wittich, 2 vols., University of California Press

Wehlen, N. (1970). *Geschichtsschreibung und Staatsauffassung im Zeitalter Ludwigs des Frommen* (Historische Studien 418), Matthiesen Verlag

Weinacht, P.L. (1968). *Staat. Studien zur Bedeutungsgeschichte des Wortes von den Anfängen bis zum 19. Jahrhundert*, Duncker and Humbolt

Werner, K.F. (1952). 'Andreas von Marchiennes und die Geschichtsschreibung von Anchiun und Marchiennes in der zweiten Hälfte des 12. Jahrhunderts', *Deutsches Archiv* 9:402–64

(1959). 'Untersuchungen zur Frühzeit des französischen Fürstentums (9.–10. Jht.); IV', *Die Welt als Geschichte* 19:146–93

(1965). 'Bedeutende Adelsfamilien im Reich Karls des Grossen', in W. Braunfels (ed.) *Karl der Grosse. Lebenswerk und Nachleben*, vol. I, Schwann (English transl. in Reuter 1979)

(1968). 'Königtum und Fürstentum im französischen 12. Jahrhundert', *Vorträge und Forschungen* 12:177–225 (English transl. in Reuter 1979)

(1976). 'Le rôle de l'aristocratie dans la christianisation du Nord-Est de la Gaule', in *La Christianisation des pays entre Loire et Rhin, IVe–VIIe siècles*, Actes du colloque de Nanterre, *Revue d'Histoire de l'Église de France* 62:45–73

(1979). 'Gauzlin von Saint-Denis und die westfränkische Reichsteilung von Amiens (März 880)', *Deutsches Archiv* 35:395–462

(1980a). 'Missus–*marchio*–comes. Entre l'administration centrale et l'administration locale de l'empire carolingien', in W. Paravicini and K.F. Werner (eds.) *Histoire comparée de l'administration (IVe–XVIIIe siècles)*, Beiheft der *Francia* 9:191–239

(1980b). 'L'Empire carolingien et le saint empire', in M. Duverger (ed.) *Le Concept d'empire*, Presses Universitaires de France

(1981). 'La genèse des duchés en France et en Allemagne', *Settimane di Studio del Centro Italiano di Studi sull'Alto Medioevo* 27:175–207

Wickham, C. (1982). *Early Medieval Italy. Central Power and Local Society 400–1000*, Macmillan

Widmer, B. (1955). *Heilsordnung und Zeitgesehen in der Mystik Hildegards von Bingen* (Basler Beiträge zur Geschichtswissenschaft 52) Helbing and Lichtenhahn

Wilks, M. (1977). 'Alan of Lille and the New Man', in *Studies in Church History*, vol. XIV: *Renaissance and Renewal in Christian History*, ed. D. Baker, Basil Blackwell, pp. 137–57

ed. (1984). *The World of John of Salisbury* (*Studies in Church History*, Subsidia 3), published for the Ecclesiastical History Society by Basil Blackwell

Williams, G.H. (1951). *The Norman Anonymous of 1100 A.D. Toward the Identification and Evaluation of the So-Called Anonymous of York* (Harvard Theological Studies 18), Harvard University Press

Wilmart, A. (1920). 'Les Allegories sur l'Ecriture attribuées à Rhaban Maur', *Revue Bénédictine* 32:47ff

Wolf, A. (1973). 'Die Gesetzgebung der entstehenden Territorialstaaten', in H. Coing (ed.) *Handbuch der Quellen und Literatur der neueren europäischen Privatrechtsgeschichte*, vol. I: *Mittelalter (1100–1500)*, C.H. Beck'sche Verlagsbuchhandlung

Wolfram, H. (1963). *Splendor Imperii* (Mitteilungen des Instituts für Österreichische Geschichtsforschung, Erganzungsband 20), Böhlau Verlag

(1967). *Intitulatio I. Lateinische Königs- und Fürstentitel bis zum Ende des 8. Jahrhunderts* (Mitteilungen des Instituts für Österreichische Geschichtsforschung, Erganzungsband 21), Böhlau Verlag

Wolfson, H.A. (1973a). 'The Classification of Sciences in Medieval Jewish Philosophy', in I. Twersky and G.H. Williams (eds.) *Studies in the History of Philosophy and Religion*, vol. I, Harvard University Press, pp. 493–550

(1973b). 'Note on Maimonides' Classification of the Sciences', in I. Twersky and G.H. Williams (eds.) *Studies in the History of Philosophy and Religion*, vol. I, Harvard University Press, pp. 551–60

(1973c). 'Plan for the Publication of a Corpus Commentariorum Averrois in Aristotelem', in I. Twersky and G.H. Williams (eds.) *Studies in the History of Philosophy and Religion*, vol. I, Harvard University Press, pp. 430–54

Wollasch, J. (1957). 'Eine adlige familie des frühen Mittelalters', *Archiv für Kulturgeschichte* 39:150–88

Woody, K.M. (1970). '*Sagena piscatoris*: Peter Damiani and the Papal Election Decree of 1059', *Viator* 1:33ff

Wormald, P. (1978). 'Aethelred the Lawmaker', in D. Hall (ed.) *Ethelred the Unready: Papers from the Millenary conference*, Oxford, British Archaeological Reports, British Series LIX

  (1983). 'Bede, the *Bretwaldas* and the Origins of the *gens Anglorum*', in P. Wormald (ed.) *Ideal and Reality in Frankish and Anglo-Saxon Society*, Basil Blackwell

Wright, R. (1982). *Late Latin and Early Romance in Spain and Carolingian France*, Francis Cairns

Wurm, H. (1939). *Studien und Texte zur Dekretalensammlung des Dionysius Exiguus*, L. Röhrscheid

Yver, J. (1969). 'Les premières institutions du duché de Normandie', *Settimane di Studio del Centro Italiano di Studi sull'Alto Medioevo* 16

  (1971). 'Le "Très Ancien Coutumier" de Normandie, miroir de la législation ducale? Contribution à l'étude de l'ordre public normand à la fin du XIIe siècle', *Revue d'Histoire du Droit* 39:333–74

Zafarana, Z. (1966). 'Ricerche sul *Liber de unitate ecclesiae conservanda*', *Studi medievali*, 3rd series, 7:617ff

Zecchino, O. (1980). *Le Assise di Ruggiero*, vol. II: *Problemi di storia delle fonti e di diritto penale*, Pubblicazioni della Facoltà Giuridica dell' Università di Napoli

Ziegler, A.K. (1941–2). 'Pope Gelasius and His Teaching on the Relation of Church and State', *Catholic Historical Review* 27:412ff

V DEVELOPMENT: c. 1150–c. 1450

Primary sources

Accursius (1497). *Glossa Ordinaria* in *Corpus Juris Civilis*, Venice
    (1575). *Glossa ordinaria*, Antwerp
Adam Marsh, *see* Marsh, Adam
Adams, N. and Donahue, C. (1978–9). *Select Cases from the Ecclesiastical Courts of the*
    Province of Canterbury c. 1200–1301, Selden Society 95
Admont, Engelbert of, *see* Engelbert of Admont
Aegidius Romanus, *see* Giles of Rome
Ailly, Pierre d' (1706). *Tractatus de Ecclesiastica Potestate*, ed. L. Dupin, *Gersonii Opera*,
    vol. II, Antwerp, pp. 925–60
    (1733). *Propositiones Utiles*, in E. Martène and V. Durand (eds.) *Veterum Scriptorum*
    . . . *Amplissima Collectio*, vol. VII, Paris, cols. 909–11; transl. by F. Oakley in
    Church History (1960), 29:398–403
Albericus de Rosciate (1585). *In primam digesti veteris partem commentarii*, Venice
    (anastatic reproduction, 1974, Arnaldo Forni Editore)
Alexander of Hales (1924–48). *Summa fratris Alexandri*, Quaracchi
Alvarus Pelagius (1517). *De planctu Ecclesiae Libri* II, Lyon
    (1955). *Speculum regis*, in M. Pinto de Meneses (ed.) *Espelho dos Reis por Álvaro Pais*,
    Instituto de Alta Cultura, Lisbon
Andreae, Johannes, *see* Johannes Andreae
Andreas de Isernia (1579). *In usus feudorum commentaria*, Lyon
Anon. (1923). *De Papae et Concilii Auctoritate*, in H. Finke (ed.), *Acta Concilii*
    Constantiensis, vol. II, Regensbergschen Verlagsbuchhandlung, pp. 701–3
Antonino of Florence, St (1740). *Summa Theologica*, 4 vols., Verona (reprint 1959,
    Akademische Druck- und Verlaganstalt)
Aquinas, St Thomas (1948). *Selected Political Writings*, ed. J.G. Dawson and A.P.
    d'Entrèves, Basil Blackwell
    (1949). *Opuscula Omnia necnon Opera Minora*, vol. I: *Opera Philosophica*, ed. J. Perrier,
    P. Lethielleux
    (1951). *In octo libros Politicorum Expositio*, ed. R.M. Spiazzi, Marietti
    (1952–62). *Summa theologiae*, 4 vols., Marietti
    (1954a). *Opuscula philosophica*, ed. R.M. Spiazzi, Marietti
    (1954b). *De regimine Iudaeorum ad ducissam Brabantiae*, in Aquinas 1954a, pp. 249–52
    (1954c). *De regimine principum ad regem Cypri*, in Aquinas 1954a, pp. 257–80
    (1962). *Summa Theologiae*, Editiones Pantinae Alba
    (1964). *In Decem Libros Ethicorum Aristotelis ad Nicomachum Expositio*, ed. R.M.
    Spiazzi, 3rd edn, Marietti
    (1964–80). *Summa Theologiae*, ed. T. Gilby *et al.*, 61 vols., Blackfriars; Eyre and
    Spottiswoode; McGraw-Hill

Aristotle (1562–74). *Opera cum Averrois commentariis*, Venice
  (1872). *Aristotelis Politicorum libri octo. Cum vetusta translatione Gulielmi de Moerbeka*, ed. F. Susemihl, Teubner
  (1961). *Politica*, Libri I–II, II, *Translatio prior imperfecta*, ed. P. Michaud-Quantin (*Aristoteles Latinus*, 29, 1), Desclée; de Brouwer
  (1972–4). *Ethica Nicomachea*, ed. R.A. Gauthier (*Aristoteles Latinus*, 26, 3), E.J. Brill; Desclée; de Brouwer
Azo (1557). *Summa aurea ad Codicem, Tres Libros Codicis, Institutiones, Digestum vetus, Informatiatum, Digestum novum, Authenticarum Collationes IX*, Lyon (repr. Minerva 1968)
  (1568). *Brocardica aurea*, Naples
  (1581). *Lectura Azzonis*, Paris
  (1888a). *Die Quaestiones des Azo*, ed. E. Landsberg, J.C.B. Mohr
  (1888b). *Un consulte d'Azione dell' anno 1205*, ed. L. Chiapelli and L. Zdekauer, Bracali
Baldus de Ubaldis (1490–1). *Consilia*, I–V, Brescia
  (1495a). *Commentarium super pace constantie*, Pavia
  (1495b). *Super usibus feudorum interpretatio*, Pavia
  ([1498a]). *Commentaria super I–V libris codicis* [Lyon]
  (1498b). *Lectura super prima et secunda parte digesti veteris* [Lyon]
  ([1498c]). *Lectura in VI–IX libros codicis* [Lyon]
  (1551). *Super decretalibus*, Lyon
  (1575). *Consilia*, I–V, Venice (Anastatic reproduction, 1971, Bottega d'Erasmo)
  (1616). *In primam digesti veteris partem commentaria*, Venice
  (1901). *L'opera di Baldo, per cura dell' Università di Perugia*, Perugia: Tipi della Unione cooperativa
Bartolus of Sassoferrato (1497). *Super Constitutione 'Ad reprimendum'*, in *Corpus Iuris Civilis*, Venice 1497–8
  (1523). *Commentaria in Authenticum*, Lyon
  (1577). *Opera omnia*, Turin
  (1588). *Opera omnia*, Basel
  (1976). *Tractatus de Regimine Civitatis*, ed. D. Quaglioni, *Pensiero Politico* 9:70–93
  (1983). *De regimine civitatis*, in D. Quaglioni, *Politica e diritto nel trecento italiano: il 'De tyranno' di Bartolo da Sassoferrato (1314–1357), con l'edizione critica dei trattati 'De Guelphis et Gebellinis', 'De regimine civitatis' e 'De tyranno'*, Pensiero Politico, bibliotheca 11
Bassianus, Johannes (1954). *Abor actionum*, ed. A. Brinz, Junge
  (1925). *Die Summa 'Quicunque vult'*, ed. L. Wahrmund, Universitätsverlag Wagner (repr. Scientia Verlag. 1962)
Beaumanoir, Philippe de (1899–1900). *Coutumes de Beauvaisis*, ed. A. Salmon, 2 vols., Picard
Bebenburg, Lupold von, *see* Lupold of Bebenburg
Bellapertica, Petrus de (1571). *Repetitiones in aliquot divi Iustiniani imperatoris codicis leges*, Frankfurt (anastatic reproduction, 1968, Arnaldo Forni Editore)
  (1586). *Lectura institutionum*, Lyon (anastatic reproduction, 1972, Arnaldo Forni Editore)
Bernard of Clairvaux, St (1963). *See* section IV above
Bonaventure, St (1898). *Apologia Pauperum* in *Opera Omnia*, vol. VIII, Quaracchi
Boniface VIII (1907–35). *Les registres de Boniface VIII*, ed. G. Digard, M. Faucon, A. Thomas and R. Fawtier, 4 vols., Bibliothèque des Ecoles Françaises d'Athènes et de Rome, sér. 2, t. 4

Bracton (1968–77). *De legibus et consuetudinibus Angliae*, ed. S. Thorne, Harvard
   University Press
Bruni, Leonardo (Aretino) (1680). *Oratio in Funere Nannis Strozae*, in S. Baluze (ed.),
   Miscellanea, 3:226–48, Paris
   (1968). *Laudatio Florentinae Urbis*, in H. Baron, *From Petrarch to Leonardo Bruni*,
   Chicago University Press, pp. 232–63
Buridan, Jean (1513). *Quaestiones super decem libros Ethicorum*, Paris (Minerva repr. 1968)
   (1640). *Quaestiones in octo libros Politicorum Aristotelis*, ed. W. Turner, Oxford
   (1942). *Quaestiones super libros quattuor de caelo et mundo*, ed. E.A. Moody, Mediaeval
   Academy of America
Burley, Walter. *In libros Politicorum*, MS Oxford, Balliol College 95, fols. 161r–191r
Butrigarius, Jacobus (1606). *In primam et secundam veteris digesti partem*, Rome (anastatic
   reproduction, 1978, Arnaldo Forni Editore)
Chrimes, S.B. and Brown, A.L. (1961). *Select Documents of English Constitutional
   History, 1307–1485*, Adam and Charles Black
Christine de Pisan (1936, 1940). *Le livre des fais et bonnes moeurs du sage roy Charles V*,
   ed. S. Solenden, 2 vols., Librairie Ancienne Honoré Champion
   (1958). *Livre de la paix*, ed. C.C. Willard, Mouton
   (1967). *Le livre du corps de policie*, ed. R.H. Lucas, Droz
Codex Diplomaticus Lubecensis: Lübeckisches Urkundenbuch (1889). Lübeck
Colonna, Egidio, *see* Giles of Rome
Conciliorum oecumenicorum decreta (1960). Ed. J. Alberigo *et al.*, Fribourg; Rome
Conrad of Gelnhausen, *see* Gelnhausen, Conrad of
Corpus Iuris Canonici (1879–81). *See* section IV above
Cracow University. *Consilium* (1442). In C. Egasse du Boulay (ed.) *Historia Universitatis
   Parisiensis*, Paris (1665–73), 5:479–515
Cuneo, Gulielmus de, *see* Gulielmus de Cuneo
Cusa, Nicholas of (1959–68). *De Concordantia Catholica*, ed. G. Kallen, in *Nicolai Cusani
   Opera Omnia*, vol. XIV, Felix Meiner
   (1960). *De pace fidei cum epistula ad Joannem de Segobia*, ed. R. Klibansky and H.
   Bascour in *Nicolai Cusani Opera Omnia*, vol. VII, Felix Meiner
Cynus de Pistoia (1578). *In codicem et aliquot titulos digesti veteris doctissima commentaria*,
   Frankfurt (anastatic reproduction, 1964, Bottega d'Erasmo)
Dante Alighieri (1950). *Monarchia*, ed. G. Vinay, G.C. Sansoni
   (1965). *Monarchia*, ed. P.G. Ricci, Mondadori
   (1966). *Dantis Alighierii Epistolae*, ed. P. Toynbee, Oxford University Press
   (1970, 1973, 1975). *The Divine Comedy*, transl. with a commentary by C.S.
   Singleton, 6 vols. (Bollinger Series LXXX), Princeton University Press
Deusdedit (1892). *See* section IV above
Deutsche Reichstagsakten (1957, 1963). Ed. hist. Komm. Bayer. Akad. d. Wiss., vols. XVI
   and XVII, Vandenhoeck und Ruprecht
Dialogus de Scaccario (1950). ed. C. Johnson, Nelson
   (1983). ed. C. Johnson, F.E.L. Carter and D.E. Greenway, Clarendon Press
Dietrich of Niem, *see* Niem, Dietrich von
Disputatio inter clericum et militem (1611). In Goldast, M. (1611–14), vol. I, pp. 13–18
   (mistakenly attributed to William of Ockham)
Dubois, Pierre (1891). *De Recuperatione Terre Sancte*, ed. C.V. Langlois, Picard
Duns Scotus, John (1639). *Opera omnia*, ed. L. Wadding, 12 vols., Lyon (George Gins
   reprint 1968)
   (1950–). *Opera omnia*, ed. G. Balič, Vatican City
Dupuy, Pierre (1655). *Histoire du différend d'entre le pape Boniface VIII et Philippe le Bel*,
   Paris (reissue Tucson, Arizona, 1963)

Engelbert of Admont (1614). *De Ortu, Progressu et Fine Regnorum, et praecipue Regni seu Imperii Romani*, in M. Goldast, *Politica imperialia sive discursus politici*, Frankfurt, pp. 754–73
  (1725). *De regimine principum*, ed. I.G. Hufnagel, Ratisbon
Escobar, Andreas (1700). *Gubernaculum Conciliorum*, in H. von der Hardt (ed.) *Magnum Oecumenicum Constantiense Concilium*, vol. VI, pp. 139–334, Frankfurt; Leipzig
Eubel, K., ed. (1898–1904). *Bullarium Franciscanum, sive Romanorum Pontificum constitutiones, epistolae, diplomata tribus ordinibus minorum* (originally ed. J.H. Sharalea, Rome, 1759), Typis Sacrae Congregationis de Propaganda Fide ed. (1908) *Epitome Bullarii Franciscani*, Quarrachi
Expositio quatuor magistrorum (1950). *Expositio quatuor magistrorum super regulam fratrum minorum (1241–42)*, ed. L. Oliger, Edizioni di Storia e Letteratura, Rome
FitzRalph, Richard (1511). *Summa in Quaestionibus Armenorum*, Paris
  (1890). *Unusquisque* (sermon); *De pauperie salvatoris* (books I–IV with summary of V–VII), in R. Lane Poole (ed.) *Iohannis Wycliffe De dominio divino libri tres*, Wyclif Society
  (1954). *De pauperie salvatoris*, books V–VII, ed. R. Brock, University of Colorado, Boulder, unpublished PhD dissertation
(FitzRalph, Richard). *Appellatio* of London Greyfriars, MS 64.4.2, fol. 4, Sidney Sussex College, Cambridge (this records information regarding FitzRalph's allegedly erroneous opinions on twenty-one points)
Fleta (1953–72). Ed. H.G. Richardson and G.O. Sayles, vols. II and III (Publications of the Selden Society, 72, 89), Bernard Quaritch
Fontaines, Godfrey of, *see* Godfrey of Fontaines
Fortescue, Sir John (1869). *De natura legis naturae*, in Thomas Fortescue (Lord Clermont) (ed.). *The Works of Sir John Fortescue*, vol. I, pp. 63–333, privately printed
  (1885). *The Governance of England: Otherwise Called the Difference between an Absolute and a Limited Monarchy*, ed. C. Plummer, Oxford University Press
  (1949). *De laudibus legum Anglie*, ed. S.B. Chrimes, Cambridge University Press
Francis of Assisi, St (1973). Ed. M. Habig, *St Francis of Assisi, Writings and Early Biographies. English Omnibus of the Sources for the Life of St Francis*, Franciscan Herald Press
  (1976), Ed. K. Esser, O.F.M., *Die Opuscula des hl. Franziskus von Assisi* (Spicilegium Bonaventuriana XIII), Collegium S. Bonaventurae ad Claras Aquas
  (1978). Ed. K. Esser, O.F.M., *Opuscula Sancti Patris Francisci Assisiensis* (Bibliotheca Franciscana Ascetica Medii Aevi XII), Collegium S. Bonaventurae ad Claras Aquas
François de Meyronnes, *see* Meyronnes, François de
Gelnhausen, Conrad of (1910). *Epistola Concordiae*, in F. Bliemetzrieder (ed.) *Literarische Polemik zur Beginnung der Grossen Abendländischen Schismas* (Publikationen des Österreichischen Historischen Instituts im Rom 1), Tempsky-Freytag (repr. Johnson Reprint Corp., 1967)
Gerson, Jean (1952). *De potestate ecclesiastica*, transl. in Cameron 1952, pp. 115–88
  (1953). *De unitate ecclesiae*, transl. by J.K. Cameron in Spinka 1953, pp. 140–8
  (1958). *De auctoritate concilii*, ed. Z. Rueger, in *Revue d'Histoire ecclésiastique* 53:775–95
  (1961–). *Ouvres complètes*, 9 vols., ed. P. Glorieux, Desclée; de Brouwer
  (1962). *De vita spirituali animae*, in Gerson 1961– , vol. III, pp. 113–202
  (1963). *Oportet haereses esse*, in Gerson 1961– , vol. V, pp. 420–35
  (1966a). *De auctoritate concilii*, in Gerson 1961– , vol. VI, pp. 114–23
  (1966b). *Propositio facta coram Anglis*, in Gerson 1961– , vol. VI, pp. 125–35
  (1966c). *Tractatus de unitate Ecclesiae*, in Gerson 1961– , vol. VI, pp. 136–45

(1966d). *De potestate Ecclesiae*, in Gerson 1961– , vol. vi, pp. 210–50
(1966e). *An liceat in causis fidei a Papa appellare?*, in Gerson 1961– , vol. vi, pp. 283–90
(1968). *Vivat rex (Pour la réforme du royaume)*, in Gerson 1961– , vol. vii (2), pp. 1137–85
Giles of Orleans, *Quaestiones in libros Ethicorum*, MS Paris Nat. Lat. 16039, fols. 105r–233v
Giles of Rome (1556). *De regimine principum*, Rome
(1929). *De ecclesiastica potestate*, ed. R. Scholz, Böhlau Verlag (Aalen reprint 1961)
Girolami, Remigio de' (1959). *De Bono Pacis*, in C.T. Davis, 'Remigio de' Girolami and Dante: A Comparison of their Conceptions of Peace', *Studi Danteschi* 36:123–36
'Glanvil' (1965). See section IV above
Godfrey of Fontaines (1904–35). *Quodlibets: i–iv*, ed. M. de Wulf and A. Pelzer (*Philosophes Belges*, 2, 1904); v–vii, ed. M. de Wulf, and J. Hoffmans (*PB*, 3, 1914); viii–x, ed. J. Hoffmans (*PB*, 4, 1924, 1931); xi–xiv, ed. J. Hoffmans (*PB*, 5, 1932–5), Institut Supérieur de Philosophie, Université de Louvain
Goldast, M., ed. (1611–14). *Monarchia S. Romani Imperii, siue Tractatus de Iurisdictione Imperiali seu Regia, et Pontificia seu Sacerdotali*, 3 vols., Frankfurt
Grandisson, Reg. (1897). *The Register of John de Grandisson, Bishop of Exeter A.D. 1327–1369*, ed. F.C. Hingston-Randulph, 3 vols., G. Bell and Sons
Gratian (1879). See section IV above
Gregory IX, Pope (1961). 'Quo elongati' (1230), ed. H. Grundmann, *Archivum Franciscanum Historicum* 54:20–5
Grosseteste, Robert (1861). *Epistolae*, ed. H.R. Luard, Rolls Ser. London
(1971). *De Tyrannide*, ed. S. Gieben, *Collectanea Franciscana* 41
Guilelmus de Cuneo. *Lectura super Digeste veteri*, Bodleian Library, Oxford, MS Can. Misc. 472
(1513). *Lectura super Codicem*, Lyon
Heimericus de Campo, see Velde, Heimerich van de
Henry of Langenstein, see Langenstein, Henry of
Hostiensis (1512). *Lectura in V decretalium libros*, Paris
(1612). *Summa Aurea super Titulis Decretalium*, Coliniae
Hugh of Digne (1912). *De finibus paupertatis*, ed. C. Florovsky, *Archivum Franciscanum Historicum* 5:277–90
Hugh of St Victor (1854). See section IV above
Huguccio. For MSS of his works, see 'Biographies', above p. 672
Innocent III (1947). *Regestum super negotio Romani Imperii*, ed. F. Kempf, Pontificia Università Gregoriana
(1964–79). *Die Register Innocenz' III.*, ed. O. Hageneder and A. Haidacher et al., 2 vols., Böhlau Verlag
Innocent IV (1570). *Super libros quinque decretalium*, Frankfurt
(1581). *In Quinque Libros Decretalium Commentarium*, Turin
Irnerius of Bologna. See section IV above
Isernia, Andreas de, see Andreas de Isernia
James of Viterbo (1926). *Le plus ancien traité de l'église, Jacques de Viterbo, De regimine christiano (1301–2)* ed. H.X. Arquillière, Gabriel Beauchesne
Jean de Terre Rouge (1526). *Contra rebelles suorum regum*, ed. J. Bonaud, Paris
Jean Juvenal des Ursins (1978). *Ecrits politiques*, vol. I, ed. P.S. Lewis, La société de l'histoire de France: Librairie C. Klincksieck
Joachim of Fiore (1527). See section IV above
Johannes Andreae (1504). *Novella* (on the *Liber Sextus*), Venice
(1550). *Commentaria in Sextum*, Lyons

Johannes Bassianus, *see* Bassianus, Johannes
Johannes Duns Scotus, *see* Duns Scotus, Johannes
Johannes Monachus, *see* Lemoine, Jean
Johannes Teutonicus (1981). *Apparatus glossarum in Compilationem tertiam*, ed. K.
    Pennington (*Monumenta Iuris canonici*, Series A, vol. 3), Biblioteca Apostolica
    Vaticana
John of Paris (1942). *De potestate regia et papali*, ed. J. Leclercq, in *Jean de Paris et
    l'écclesiologie du xiiie siècle*, J. Vrin, pp. 173–260
    (1969). *De potestate regia et papali, Johannes Quidort von Paris Über königliche und
    päpstliche Gewalt*, ed. F. Bleienstein (Textkritische Edition mit deutscher
    Übersetzung), Klett
    (1971). *On Royal and Papal Power*, transl. by J.A. Watt, Pontifical Institute of
    Mediaeval Studies, Toronto
John of Salisbury (1909). *See* section IV above
    (1929). *See* section IV above
John of Viterbo (1901). *Liber de Regimine Civitatum*, ed. C. Salvemini in A. Guardentius
    (ed.), *Bibliotheca Juridica Medii Aevi: Scripta Anecdota Glossatorum*, vol. III, pp. 217–
    80, Monti
Joinville, Jean, sire de (1906). *Histoire de S. Louis*, ed. N. de Wailly, Hachette
Jonas of Orleans (1930). *See* section IV, above
Langenstein, Henry of (1697). *Consilium Pacis de Unione ac Reformatione Ecclesiae in
    Concilio Universali Quaerenda*, in H.v.d. Hardt (ed.) *Magnum Oecumenicum
    Constantiense Concilium*, vol. II, pp. 2–61, Frankfurt; Leipzig; transl. Cameron 1952,
    part 2, pp. 1–92 (abridged in Spinka 1953, pp. 106–39)
Latini, Brunetto (1948). *Li livres dou Tresor* (University of California Publications:
    Modern Philology 22), University of California Press
Legendae S. Francisci Assisiensis, saec. XIII et XIV conscriptae (1926–41). in *Analecta
    Franciocana* 10, Quaracchi
Lemoine, Jean (1561). *Glossa ordinaria ad Extravagantium communium*, Paris
    (1585). *Apparatus super Decretales*, Venice
Lewes, Song of (1890). ed. C.L. Kingsford, Clarendon Press
Liber Augustalis (1973). In H. Conrad *et al.* (eds.) *Die Konstitutionen Friedrichs II. von
    Hohenstaufen für sein Königreich Sizilien*, Böhlau Verlag
Lucas de Penna (1597). *Commentarium in Tres Libros*, Lyon
Lupold of Bebenburg (1566). *Tractatus de juribus regni et imperii*, in S. Schard (ed.) *De
    jurisdictione, auctoritate et praeeminentia imperiali ac potestate ecclesiastica*, Basel, pp.
    328–409
Mansi, J.D. (1759–98). *See* section II above
Marsh, Adam (1858). *Epistolae, Monumenta Franciscana*, ed. J.S. Brewer, Rolls Ser.
    London
Marsilius of Padua (1928). *Defensor pacis*, ed. C.W. Previté–Orton, Cambridge
    University Press
    (1932–3). *Defensor pacis* ed. R. Scholz, *MGH Fontes iuris Germanici antiqui* 7
    (1968). *Le défenseur de la paix*, ed. J. Quillet, J. Vrin
    (1979). *Oeuvres mineures: Defensor minor; De translatione imperii*, ed. C. Jeudy and J.
    Quillet, Editions du Centre National de la Recherche Scientifique, Paris
Matthew of Aquasparta (1962). 'Sermo de potestate papae' in G. Gal (ed.). *Sermones de
    S. Francisco, de S. Antonio et de S. Clara. Bibliotheca Franciscana Ascetica Medii Aevi*
    10:176–190
Meinsterlin, Sigmund (1864). *Chronik der Reichstadt Nürnberg*, in D. Kerler and M.
    Lexer (eds.) *Chroniken der Städte vom 14. bis ins 16. Jahrhundert*, vol. III (Historische

Kommission bei der Bayerische Akademie der Wissenschaften), S. Hirzel, pp. 32–256 (reprint, Vandenhoeck und Ruprecht, 1961)

Meyronnes, François de (1940–2). P. de Lapparent, 'L'oeuvre politique de François de Meyronnes, ses rapports avec celle de Dante', *Archives d'histoire doctrinale et littéraire du moyen âge* 13 (15ème–17ème annes):5–151

(1954). J. Barbet, 'Le Prologue du Commentaire dionysien de François de Meyronnes, O.F.M.', *Archives d'histoire doctrinale et littéraire du moyen age* 21 (29ème année):183–91

(1961). J. Barbet, *François de Meyronnes – Pierre Roger, Disputatio 1320–1321* (Textes philosophiques du moyen âge 9), J. Vrin

Mézières, Philippe de (1969). *Le Songe du Vieil Pèlerin*, ed G.W. Coopland, 2 vols., Cambridge University Press

(1975). *Letter to King Richard II: A Plea Made in 1395 for peace between England and France*, ed. G.W. Coopland, Liverpool University Press

Nicholas III (1897). *Exiit qui seminat* (1279), in *Seraphicae Legislationis textus originales*, Quaracchi

(1916). *Registres de Nicholas III 1277–1280: recueil des bulles de ce pape*, ed. J. Gay, Bibliothèque des Ecoles Françaises d'Athènes et de Rome, sér. 2, t. 14

Niem, Dietrich von (1933). *De modis uniendi ac reformandi ecclesiam*, in H. Heimpel (ed.) *Dietrich von Niem Dialog über Union und Reform der Kirche, 1410*, Teubner (transl. Cameron 1952, pp. 226–348; abridged Spinka 1953, pp. 149–74)

Ockham, William of (1491). *Quodlibeta septem*, Strasbourg (repr. Louvain 1962)

(1614). *Dialogus*, in M. Goldast (ed.) *Monarchia*, vol. II, pp. 392–957, Frankfurt

(1940–). *Guillelmi de Ockham Opera Politica*, ed. J.G. Sikes, R.F. Bennett and H.S. Offler, Manchester University Press

(1944). *Breviloquium*, in R. Scholz (ed.) *Wilhelm von Ockham als politischer Denker und sein Breviloquium de principatu tyrannico* (Schriften des Reichsinstituts für ältere deutsche Geschichtskunde 8), Hiersemann

(1951). *Summa logicae*, ed. P. Boehmer, 2 vols., Franciscan Institute

(1956). *Tractatus contra Benedictum*, ed. H.S. Offler, in Ockham 1940– , vol. III, pp. 157–322

(1970). *Scriptum in librum primum Sententiarum, Ordinatio; Distinctiones II–III*, ed. S. Brown and G. Gál (in *Opera philosophica et theologica*, 1967–), Franciscan Institute, University of St Bonaventure

(1974a). *Octo quaestiones de potestate papae*, ed. H.S. Offler in Ockham 1940– , vol. I (2nd edn), pp. 1–277

(1974b). *An princeps pro suo succurse, scilicet guerrae possit recipere bona ecclesiarum etiam invito Papa*, ed. H.S. Offler, in Ockham 1940– , vol. I (2nd edn), pp. 219–67

(1974c). *Consultatio de causa matrimoniali*, ed. H.S. Offler, in Ockham 1940– , vol. I (2nd edn), pp. 269–86

(1974, 1963). *Opus nonaginta dierum*, ed. H.S. Offler and J.G. Sikes, in Ockham 1940– , vol. I (2nd edn), pp. 287–368, and vol. II

(1979) *Opera philosophica et theologica* ed. G.I. Etzkorn and F. Kelly, St Bonaventure, New York

Oldradus da Ponte (1550). *Consilia*, Lyon

Olivi, Peter John (1966). *Quaestiones de perfectione evangelica*, Q.5, *Studi Franciscani* 63:88–108

(1972). *Peter Olivi's Rule Commentary, Edition and Presentation*, ed. D. Flood, Franz Steiner Verlag

Ordonnances des Roys de France de la Troisième race (1791). Ed. D.F. Sécousse, vol. VI, Paris

Oresme, Nicole (1940). *Le Livre de Ethiques d'Aristote*, ed. A.D. Menut, G.E. Stechert and Co.

(1956). *De moneta*, ed. C. Johnson, Nelson

(1970). *Le livre de Politiques d'Aristote*, ed. A.D. Menut, Transactions of the American Philosophical Society

Panormitanus (1571). *Commentarium in Primum-Quintum Decretalium Librum*, 7 vols., Venice

(1957). Memorandum (1442: *incipit* 'Quoniam veritas verborum'; also known as *Tractatus de Concilio Basiliensi*), *Deutsche Reichstagsakten* 16:439–538

(1605). *Commentaria in V decretalium libros*, Venice

Paulus de Castro (1582). *Consilia*, Frankfurt

Peckham, John (1910). *Fratris Johannis Pecham Tractatus tres de paupertate*, ed. A.G. Little et al., British Society of Franciscan Studies

Peter of Auvergne. *Quaestiones in libros Politicorum*, Paris Nat. Lat. 16089 fols. 274r–319r

(1951). Continuation of Aquinas, *In octo libros Politicorum expositio*, ed. R.M. Spiazzi, Marietti

(1967). G.M. Grech (ed.) *The Commentary of Peter of Auvergne on Aristotle's Politics*, Pontifical Institute of Mediaeval Studies, Toronto

Peter Damian, *see* section IV above

Petrus de Bellapertica, *see* Bellapertica, Petrus de

Philip Augustus (1943). *Recueil des Actes de Philippe Auguste*, vol. II, ed. H. Delaborde, C. Petit-Dutaillis and J. Monicat, Académie des Inscriptions et Belles-Lettres

Philippi, ed. (1882). *Preussisches Urkundenbuch*, vol. I, part I (Scientia repr. 1961)

Philippus Decius (1575). *In decretales commentaria*, Turin

Piccolomini, Aeneas Sylvius (1967). *De Gestis Concilii Basiliensis Commentariorum Libri II*, ed. D. Hay and W.K. Smith, Oxford University Press

Pisan, Christine de, *see* Christine de Pisan

Placentinus (1536). *Summa Codicis*, Mainz (repr. Bottega d'Erasmo, 1962)

Powicke, F.M. and Cheney, C.R. (1964). *Councils and Synods, with Other Documents Relating to the English Church*, 2 vols., Clarendon Press

Pronay, N. and Taylor, J., eds. (1980). *Parliamentary Texts of the Later Middle Ages*, Clarendon Press

Ptolemy of Lucca (1949). Continuation of *De regimine principum*, in Aquinas 1949, pp. 270–426

Quidort, Jean, *see* John of Paris

Ragusa, Johannes de. *Tractatus de ecclesia*, Basel Universitätsbibliothek, MS A.I.29, fols. 302–432

De auctoritate conciliorum et de modo celebratione eorum, Basel Universitätsbibliothek. MS A.I.17, fols. 134–297

Raphael Fulgosius (1577). *Consilia*, Venice

Ravannis, Jacobus de (1519). *Lectura super prima et secunda parte codicis* (wrongly attributed to Petrus de Bellapertica by the sixteenth-century editor), Paris

(1577). *Super institutionibus commentaria*, Turin (wrongly attributed to Bartolus in the latter's collected works)

Raymond of Penyafort (1601). *Summa de casibus poenitientiae*, Rome

(1945). *Opera omnia*, ed. J. Rius i Serra, University of Barcelona

Regula Fratrum Minorum (1897). In *Seraphicae Legislationis, textus originales*, Quaracchi

Remigio de' Girolami, *see* Girolami, Remigio de'

Rufinus (1902). *Die Summa Decretorum des Magister Rufinus*, ed. H. Singer, F. Schöningh

Scholz, R. (1914). *Unbekannte Kirchenpolitische Streitschriften aus der Zeit Luduigo des Bayern (1327–54)*, vol. II (Texte), Loescher

Scotus, Johannes Duns, *see* Duns Scotus, Johannes

Segovia, Juan de. *De Magna Auctoritate Episcoporum in Synodo Generali*, Basel Universitätsbibliothek, MS B.V.15

    Tractatus de Conciliorum et Ecclesiae Auctoritate (1439). Codices Vaticani Latini 4039, fols. 192r–232v; extracts printed in Black 1970a, pp. 141–4 (under alternative title *Decem Advisamenta*)

    (1857–1935). *Historia Gestorum Generalis Synodi Basiliensis*, ed. C. Stehlin, *Monumenta Conciliorum Generalium Seculi XV*, vols. II–III, Vienna; Basel

    (1935). *Amplificatio Disputationis*, in Segovia 1857–1935, vol. III, pp. 695–941

    (1968). *Tractatus super Presidentia in Concilio Basiliensi*, ed. P. Ladner, *Zeitschrift für schweizerische Kirchengeschichte* 62:31–113

Somnium Viridarii (1611). In M. Goldast, *Monarchia* 1:58–229, Hanover

Songe du Vergier (1982). M. Schnerb-Lièvre, *Le songe du vergier édité d'après le manuscrit royal 19 C IV de la British Library*, 2 vols. (*Sources d'histoire médiévale*), Editions du Centre National de la Recherche Scientifique

Spinka, M., ed. (1953). *Advocates of Reform from Wyclif to Erasmus* (Library of Christian Classics 14), SCM

Statuti del Comune di Padova del secolo XII all'Anno 1285 (1873). Ed. A. Gloria, Padua

Summa Parisiensis (1952). T.P. McLaughlin (ed.), *The Summa Parisiensis on the Decretum Gratiani*, Pontifical Institute of Mediaeval Studies, Toronto

Thomas Aquinas, St̄, *see* Aquinas

Torquemada (Turrecremata), Juan de (1561). *Summa de Ecclesia*, Venice

Tudeschis, Nicholas de, *see* Panormitanus

Velde, Heimerich van de (Heimericus de Campo). *De Ecclesiastica Potestate* (1433–4), Cusanus-Bibliothek, Bernkastel-Kues, Cod. Cus. 106, fols. 89r–194r

Vernani, Guido (1938). *Tractatus de reprobatione monarchie composite a Dante*, ed. T. Käppeli, O.P., 'Der Dantegegner Guido Vernani, O.P. von Rimini', *Quellen und Forschungen aus Italienischen Archiven und Bibliotheken* 28:107–46

    (1958). *Tractatus de reprobatione Monarchiae compositae a Dante*, ed. N. Matteini, *Il piu antico oppositore politico de Dante: Guido Vernani da Rimini* (*Il Pensiero Medioevale*, ser. 1, vol. 6), Antonio Milani

Vital du Four (1513). *Speculum morale totius sacre scripture a . . . Iohanne Vitali . . . alphabetico ordine perutile editum. . .*, Impressus Iohānē moylin alias de cábray

Walter Burley, *see* Burley, Walter

Walter of Guisborough (1957). *The Chronicle of Walter of Guisborough*, ed. H. Rothwell (Camden Third Series 89), Royal Historical Society

Woodford, William, O.F.M. *Defensorium Mendicantis*, Magdalen College, Oxford, MS 75

Wyclif, John (1885). *Tractatus de Civili Dominio*, ed. R. Lane Poole, Wyclif Society

    (1887). *Tractatus de Officio Regis*, ed. A.W. Pollard and C. Sayle, Wyclif Society

    (1890). *De Dominio Divino Libri Tres*, ed. R. Lane Poole, Wyclif Society

Zabarella, Franciscus (1566). *Tractatus de Schismate*, in S. Schard (ed.), *De jurisdictione, auctoritate et praeeminentia imperii ac potestate ecclesiastica*, pp. 688–711, Basel

Secondary sources

Alverny, M.-T. d' (1928). 'Les écrits théologiques concernant la pauvreté évangélique depuis Pierre Jean Olieu jusqu'à la bulle "Cum inter nonnullos"', *Revue d'histoire Franciscaine* 5:218–21

Arquillière, H.X. (1911). 'L'origine des théories conciliaires', *Séances et travaux de l'Académie des Sciences morales et politiques*, 175:573–86

Aston, M.E. (1960). 'Lollardy and Sedition', *Past and Present* 17:1–44
Aubert, F. (1897). *Histoire du Parlement de Paris de l'origine à François Ier (1250–1515)*, 2 vols., Picard
Babbit, S.M. (1985). 'Oresme's *Livre de Politiques* and the France of Charles V', *Transactions of the American Philosophical Society*, 75, 1
Baldwin, A. (1981). *The Theme of Government in Piers Plowman*, D.S. Brewer
Baldwin, J.W. (1959). 'The Medieval Theories of the Just Price: Romanists, Canonists and Theologians in the Twelfth and Thirteenth Centuries', *Transactions of the American Philosophical Society*, New Series, 49, 4
  (1970). *See* section IV above
Barbey, J. (1983). *La Fonction royale: essence et légitimité d'après les 'Tractatus' de Jean de Terrevermeille*, Nouvelles Editions Latines
Barnes, J. (1982). 'The Just War', in *Cambridge History of Later Medieval Philosophy*, Cambridge University Press, pp. 771–84
Baron, H. (1966). *The Crisis of the Early Italian Renaissance. Civic Humanism and Republican Liberty in an Age of Classicism and Tyranny*, rev. edn, Princeton University Press
Bartolo da Sassoferrato – studi e documenti per il VI centenario (1962). 2 vols., ed. D. Segoloni, Università degli Studi, Perugia
Barton, J.L. (1965). 'The Medieval Use', *Law Quarterly Review* 81:562–9
  (1971). *Roman Law in England* (Ius romanum medii aevi, Société d'hist. des droits de l'antiquité, pars v, 13a), Giuffrè
Baskiewicz, J. (1962). 'Quelques remarques sur la conception de dominium mundi dans l'oeuvre de Bartolus', in *Bartolo da Sassoferrato 1962*, vol. II, pp. 9–25
Batany, J., Contamine, P., Guenée, B., Le Goff, J., eds. (1973). 'Plan pour l'étude historique du vocabulaire social de l'occident médiéval', in D. Roche and C.E. Labrousse (eds.) *Ordres et classes, colloque d'histoire sociale*, Mouton
Baudry, L. (1949). *Guillaume d'Occam: sa vie, ses oeuvres, ses idées sociales et politiques*, J. Vrin
  (1958). *Lexique philosophique de Guillaume d'Ockham*, P. Lethielleux
Bayley, C.C. (1949). 'Pivotal Concepts in the Political Philosophy of William of Ockham', *Journal of the History of Ideas* 10:199–218
Becker, M. (1981). *Medieval Italy, Constraints and Creativity*, Indiana University Press
Bellamy, J.G. (1970). *The Law of Treason in England in the Middle Ages*, Cambridge University Press
Benson, R.L. (1968). *The Bishop-Elect: A Study in Medieval Ecclesiastical Office*, Princeton University Press
Berges, W. (1938). *Die Fürstenspiegel des hohen und Späten Mittelalters*, Hiersemann
Betts, R.R. (1969). 'Richard FitzRalph, Archbishop of Armagh, and the Doctrine of Dominion', in *Essays in Church History*, Athlone Press, pp. 160–75
Bezemer, C.H. (1981). 'A repetitio by Jacques de Révigny on the Creation of the *ius gentuim*', *Tijdschrift voor Rechts geschiedenis* 49:287–321
Bisson, T. (1979). *Conservation of Coinage: Monetary Exploitation and Its Restraint in France, Catalonia and Aragon (c. AD 100–c. 1225)*, Clarendon Press
Black, A. (1970a). *Monarchy and Community: Political Ideas in the Later Conciliar Controversy 1430–1450* (Cambridge Studies in Medieval Life and Thought, Third Series, 2), Cambridge University Press
  (1970b). 'Heimericus de Campo: The Council and History, *Annuarium Historiae Conciliorum* 2:78–86
  (1979). *Council and Commune: The Conciliar Movement and the Fifteenth-Century Heritage*, Burns and Oates

(1980). 'Society and the Individual from the Middle Ages to Rousseau: Philosophy, Jurisprudence and Constitutional Theory', *History of Political Thought* 1:145–66

(1984). *Guilds and Civil Society in European Political Thought from the Twelfth Century to the Present*, Methuen

Blecher, M. (1975). 'Aspects of Privacy in the Civil Law', *Tijdschrift voor Rechtsgeschiedenis* 43:279–96

Bloch, M. (1933). 'Liberté et servitude personnelle au Moyen Age', *Anuario de historia del derecho español* 10:93–115

(1947). 'Comment finit l'esclavage antique', *Annales, Economie, Sociétés, Civilisations* 2:30–44

(1961). *See* section IV above

(1973). *The Royal Touch: Sacred Monarchy and Scrofula in England and France*, transl. by J.E. Anderson, Routledge and Kegan Paul

Boehmer, P. (1943). 'Ockham's Political Ideas', *Review of Politics* 5:462–87

Bolgar, R.R. (1958). *The Classical Heritage and Its Beneficiaries*, Cambridge University Press

Bolton, B.M. (1972). 'Tradition and Temerity: Papal Attitudes to Deviants 1159–1216', in *Studies in Church History*, vol. IX: *Schism, Heresy and Religious Protest*, ed. D. Baker, Cambridge University Press

(1975). 'The Poverty of the Humiliati', in D. Flood (ed.) *Poverty in the Middle Ages*, Dietrich-Coelde Verlag, pp. 52–9

(1983). *The Medieval Reformation*, Edward Arnold

Bonolis, L.G. (1908). *Questioni di diritto internazionale in alcuni consigli inediti di Baldo degli Ubaldi. Testo e commento*, Enrico Spoerri Libraio-Editore

Bosl, K. (1963). 'Potens und Pauper: Begriffsgeschichtliche Studien zur Gesellschaftlichen Differenzierung im frühen Mittelalten und zum "Pauperismus" des Hochmittelalters', in *Alteuropa und die Moderne Gesellschaft, Festschrift für Otto Brunner*, Vandenhoeck und Ruprecht, pp. 60–87

(1965). 'Der geistige Widerstand am Hofe Ludwigs des Bayern gegen die Kurie: die Politische Ideenwelt um die wende vom 13-/14- Jahrhundert und ihr historiches milieu in Europa', in Th. Mayer (ed.) *Die Welt zur Zeit des Konstanzer Konzils* (Vorträge und Forschungen 9), Thorbecke

(1974). *Das Problem der Armut in der hochmittelalterlichen Gesellschaft*, Österreichische Akademie der Wissenschaften

Bosl, K., Graus, F. and Devisse, J., eds. (1974). *La concecione della povertà nel medioevo*, Bologna

Boulet-Sautel, M. (1962). 'Le concept de souveraineté chez Jacques de Révigny', *Actes du Congrès d' Orleans*, Imprimerie du Bourdon-Blanc, pp. 15–27.

Bowsky, W.M. (1967). 'A New Consilium of Cino of Pistoia (1324): Citizenship, Residence and Taxation', *Speculum* 42:431–41

Brampton, C.K. (1960). 'Traditions Relating to the Death of William of Ockham', *Archivum Franciscanum Historicum* 53:30–8

(1966). 'Personalities in the Process against Ockham at Avignon, 1324–1326', *Franciscan Studies*, New Series, 25:4–25

Brandi, B. (1892). *Notizie intorno a Guillelmus de Cunio*, Forzani E. Tipografi del Senato

Brandmüller, W. (1968). *Das Konzil von Oaivia-Siena 1423–1424*, 2 vols., Aschendorff

Brandt, A. (1954). *Geist und Politik in der Lübeckischen Geschichte*, Verlag Max Schmidt-Römhild

Brooke, R.B. (1959). *Early Franciscan Government: Elias to Bonaventure*, Cambridge University Press

Brown, E. (1972). '"Cessante causa" and the Taxes of the Last Capetians: The Political

Applications of a Philosophical Maxim', *Studia Gratiana*, Post Scripta, 15:565–87
(1973). 'Taxation and Morality in the Thirteenth and Fourteenth Centuries: Conscience and Political Power and the Kings of France', *French Studies* 8:1–28
Brown, P.R.L. (1982). *See* section I above
Brynteson, William E. (1966). 'Roman Law and Legislation in the Middle Ages', *Speculum* 41:420–37
Buckland, W.W. (1975). *See* section I above
Buckland, W.W. and McNair, A.D. (1952). *Roman Law and Common Law: A Comparison in Outline*, rev. 2nd edn, ed. F.H. Lawson, Cambridge University Press
Buisson, L. (1958). *Potestas et Caritas: die päpstliche Gewalt im Spätmittelalter*, Böhlau Verlag
Buckhardt, J. (1955). *The Civilization of the Renaissance in Italy: An Essay*, transl. by S. Middlemore, Phaidon Press
Burns, J.H. (1985). 'Fortescue and the Political Theory of *dominium*', *Historical Journal* 28:777–97
Burr, D. (1975). 'Poverty as a Constituent Element in Olivi's Thought', in M. Flood (ed.), *Poverty in the Middle Ages*, Dietrich-Coelde Verlag, pp. 11–26
(1976). 'The Persecution of Peter Olivi', *Transactions of the American Philosophical Society*, n.s., 66, 5
Bynum, C.W. (1980). 'Did the Twelfth Century Discover the Individual?', *Journal of Ecclesiastical History* 31:1–17
Calasso, F. (1930). 'Origini italiane della formola "Rex in regno suo est imperator"', *Rivista di storia del diritto italiano* 3:213–59
(1954). *Medio Evo del Dritto*, vol. I: *Le Fonti*, Giuffrè
(1957). *I glossatori e la teoria della sovranità: Studio di diritto comune pubblico*, 3rd edn, Giuffrè
(1961). 'Andrea d' Isernia', in *Dizionario biografico degli Italiani* 3:100–3
(1964). 'Bartolo da Sassoferrato', in *Dizionario biografico degli Italiani* 6:640–69
Cameron, J.K. (1952). 'Conciliarism in Theory and Practice, from the Outbreak of the Schism till the End of the Council of Constance', Hartford, Conn., dissertation
Campitelli, A. and Liotta, F. (1962). 'Notizia del Ms. Vat. Lat. 8069', *Annali di storia del diritto*, 6:387–406
Canning, J.P. (1980a). 'The Corporation in the Political Thought of the Italian Jurists of the Thirteenth and Fourteenth Centuries', *History of Political Thought* 1, 1:9–32
(1980b). 'A Fourteenth-Century Contribution to the Theory of Citizenship: Political Man and the Problem of Created Citizenship in the Thought of Baldus de Ubaldis', in B. Tierney and P.A. Linehan (eds.) *Authority and Power: Studies on Medieval Law and Government Presented to Walter Ullmann on His Seventieth Birthday*, Cambridge University Press, pp. 197–212
(1983). 'Ideas of the State in Thirteenth and Fourteenth-Century Commentators on the Roman Law', *Transactions of the Royal Historical Society*, 5th series, 33:1–27
(1987). *The Political Thought of Baldus de Ubaldis* (Cambridge Studies in Medieval Life and Thought, Fourth Series, 6), Cambridge University Press
Cantini, J.A. (1961). 'De autonomia judicis saecularis et de Romani pontificis plenitudine potestatis in temporalibus secundum Innocentium IV', *Salesianum* 3:407–80
Casamassima, E. (1971). *Codices operum Bartoli de Sassoferrato recensiti: iter Germanicum*, L.S. Olschki
Catalano, G. (1959). *Imperio, regno e sacerdozio nel pensiero di Uguccio da Pisa*, Giuffrè
Cazelles, R. (1982). *Société Politique, Noblesse et Couronne sous Jean le Bon et Charles V*, Librairie Droz

Chaplais, P. (1963). 'La souveraineté du roi de France et le pouvoir législatif en Guyenne au début du xive siècle', *Le Moyen Age* 69:449–69

Cheney, C.R. (1936). 'The Punishment of Felonious Clerks', *English Historical Review* 51:215–36

(1976). *Pope Innocent III and England*, Hiersemann

Chenu, M.D. (1940). 'Arts mécaniques et oeuvres serviles', *Revue des sciences philosophiques et théologiques* 29:313–15

Chevalier, B. (1982). 'Corporations, conflits politiques et paix sociale en France aux XIVe et XVe siècles', *Revue historique* 268:18–44

Chevrier, G. (1968). 'Jacques de Révigny et la Glose d'Accurse', *Atti Studi Accursiani* 3:979–1004

Chiappelli, L. (1881). *Vita e opere giuridiche de Cino da Pistoia con molti documenti inediti*, Pistoia: Officina tipografia cooperativa

(1911). *Nuove ricerche su Cino da Pistoia con testi inediti*, Pistoia: Officina tipografica cooperativa

Chiavacci Leonardi, A.M. (1977). 'La "Monarchia" di Dante alla luce della "Commedia"', *Studi medievali*, 3rd series, 18:147–83

Chodorow, S. (1972). See section IV above

Chrimes, S.B. (1936). *English Constitutional Ideas in the Fifteenth Century*, Cambridge University Press

Chroust, A.H. (1947). 'The Corporate Idea and the Body Politic in the Middle Ages', *Review of Politics* 9:423–52

Clarke, M.V. (1936). *Medieval Representation and Consent: A Study of Early Parliaments in England and Ireland, with special reference to the Modus Tenendi Parlamentum*, Oxford University Press; repr. 1964

Clasen, S. (1964). 'Die Armut als Beruf: Franziskus von Assisi', *Miscellanea Mediaevalia* 3:73–85

Cohn, V. (1970). *The Pursuit of the Millennium: Revolutionary Millenarians and mystical Anarchists of the Middle Ages*, 3rd edn, Paladin

Coleman, J. (1981). *English Literature in History, 1350–1400: Medieval Readers and Writers*, Hutchinson

(1982). 'The Continuity of Utopian Thought in the Middle Ages: A Reassessment', *Vivarium* 20:1–23

(1983a). 'English Culture in the Fourteenth Century', in P. Boitani (ed.) *Chaucer and the Italian Trecento*, Cambridge University Press

(1983b). 'Medieval Discussions of Property: *Ratio* and *Dominium* According to John of Paris and Marsilius of Padua', *History of Political Thought* 4:209–28

(1984). 'FitzRalph's Antimendicant *proposeio* (1350) and the Politics of the Papal Court at Avignon', *Journal of Ecclesiastical History* 35:1–15

(1985). '*Dominium* in Thirteenth and Fourteenth-century Political Thought and Its Seventeenth-Century Heirs: John of Paris and Locke', *Political Studies* 33:73–100

Congar, Y.M.-J. (1957). 'Maître Rufin et son De bono pacis', *Revue des sciences philosophiques et théologiques* 41:428–44

(1958). 'Quod omnes tangit ab omnibus tractari et approbari debet', *Revue historique de droit français et étranger*, 4e sér., 36:210–59

(1961). 'Aspects ecclésiologiques de la quaérelle entre mendiants et séculiers dans la seconde moitié du XIIIe siècle et le début du XIVe siècle', *Archives d'histoire doctrinale et littéraire du moyen âge*, 36ème année:35–151

(1970). *L'Eglise. De saint Augustin a l'époque moderne*, Editions du Cerf

(1983). *Thomas d'Aquin: sa vision de théologie et de l'Eglise*, Variorum Reprints

Coornaert, E. (1947). 'Les ghildes mediévales (Ve–XIVe siècles): définition-évolution', *Revue Historique* 199:22–55, 208–43

Cortese, E. (1962–4). *La norma giuridica: spunti teorici nel diritto comune classico*, 2 vols., Giuffrè

Couvreur, G. (1961). *Les pauvres, ont-ils des droits? Recherche sur le vol en cas d'extrême nécessité depuis le concordat de Gratien (1140) jusqu'à Guillaume d'Auxerre (1231)*, Presses de l'Université Grégorienne; Editions SOS

Coville, A. (1974). *Jean Petit: la question du tyrannicide au commencement du XVe siècle*, Slatkins Reprints

Cranz, F.E. (1940). 'Aristotelianism in Medieval Political Theory: A Study of the Reception of the Politics', Harvard University Graduate School, summaries of theses

Crook, J. (1976). 'Classical Roman Law, the Sale of Land', in M.I. Finley (ed.) *Studies in Roman Property*, Cambridge University Press, pp. 71–83

Crowder, C.M.D. (1977). *Unity, Heresy and Reform, 1378–1460: The Conciliar Response to the Great Schism*, Edward Arnold

Curcio, C. (1937). 'La politica di Baldo', *Rivista internazionale di filosofia del diritto* 17:113–39

Curschmann, F. (1900). *Hungersnöte im Mittelalter*, R.G. Trübner

Daly, L.J. (1969). 'Some Notes on Walter Burley's Commentary on the Politics', in T.A. Sandquist and M.R. Powicke, (eds.), *Essays in Medieval History Presented to Bertie Wilkinson*, Toronto University Press, pp. 270ff

(1973). 'Wyclif's Political Theory: A Century of Study' (bibliography), *Medievalia et Humanistica* (new series) 4:177–87

Damas, A.R. (1964). *Pensiamento politico de Hostiensis* (Institutum Historicum Iuris Canonici Studia Textus Historiae Juris Canonici 3), Pas-Verlag

Damiata, M. (1978–9). *Guglielmo d'Ockham: povertà e potere*, 2 vols., Biblioteca di studi francescani, Florence

D'Amelio, G. (1972). 'Il Dictionarium iuris di Jacques de Révigny', *Tijdschrift voor Rechtsgeschiedenis* 40:43–72

David, M. (1954). *La souveraineté et les limites juridiques du pouvoir monarchique du xie au xve siècles* (Annales, fac. de droit et de sci. pol. de Strasbourg 1), Librairie Dalloz

(1962). 'Le contenu de l'hégémonie impériale dans la doctrine de Bartole', in *Bartolo da Sassoferrato 1962*, vol. II, pp. 201–16

Davies, R.G. and Denton, J.H., eds. (1981). *The English Parliament in the Middle Ages*, Manchester University Press

Davis, C.T. (1960). 'An Early Florentine Political Theorist: Fra Remigio de' Girolami', *Proceedings of the American Philosophical Society* 104:662–76

Dawson, J.D. (1983). 'Richard FitzRalph and the Fourteenth-Century Poverty Controversies', *Journal of Ecclesiastical History* 34:315–44

Denton, J.H. (1980). *Robert Winchelsey and the Crown 1294–1313: A Study in the Defence of Ecclesiastical Liberty*, Cambridge University Press

Devisse, J. (1968). 'Essai sur l'histoire d'une expression qui a fait fortune: *Consilium et auxilium* au IXe siècle', *Le Moyen Age* 74:179–205

Digard, G. (1936). *Philippe de Bel et le Saint-Siège de 1285 a 1304*, 2 vols., Sirey

Dolcini, C. (1977). *Il Pensiero Politico di Michele da Cesena 1328–1338*, Faenza-Fratelli Lega

Dolezalek, G. (1972). *Verzeichnis der Handschriften zum römanischen Recht bis 1600. Materialsammlung, System und Programm für elektronische Datenverarbeitung*, Max-Planck-Institut für europäische Rechtsgeschichte

Donahue, C., Jnr (1974). 'Roman Canon Law in the Medieval English Church: Stubbs vs. Maitland Re-Examined after 75 Years in the Light of Some Records from the Church Courts', *Michigan Law Review* 72:647–716

Dowling, M. (1984). 'Humanist Support for Katherine of Aragon', *Bulletin of the Institute of Historical Research* 57:46–55

Doyle, E., OFM (1973). 'William Woodford's *De dominio civili clericorum* against John Wyclif', *Archivum Franciscanum Historicum* 66:49–109

Duby, G. (1966). 'Les pauvres des campagnes dans l'occident médiéval jusqu'an XIIIe siècle', *Revue d'historie de l'Eglise de France* 52:25–33

(1970). *See* section IV above

(1980). *See* section IV above

Dufeil, M.-M. (1975). 'Un universitaire parisien réactionnaire vers 1250: G. de Saint-Amour', *Actes du 95e congrès national des Sociétés savantes, 1970*, 1:241–2

Dunbabin, J. (1965). 'Aristotle in the Schools', in Smalley 1965 (*see* General works), pp. 65–85

(1982). 'The Reception and Interpretation of Aristotle's *Politics*', in N. Kretzmann, A. Kenny and J. Pinborg (eds.) *Cambridge History of Later Medieval Philosophy*, Cambridge University Press, pp. 723–37

Duparc, P. (1975). 'Confraternities of the Holy Spirit and Village Communities in the Middle Ages', in F.L. Cheyette (ed.) *Lordship and Community in Medieval Europe*, Holt, Rinehart and Winston, Inc., pp. 341–56

Elton, G.R. (1956). 'The Political Creed of Thomas Cromwell', *Transactions of the Royal Historical Society*, 5th series, 6:69–92

Eschmann, I. Th. (1946). 'Studies on the Notion of Society in St Thomas Aquinas: I. St Thomas and the Decretal of Innocent IV *Romanae Ecclesiae*', *Medieval Studies* 8:1–42

(1947). 'Studies on the Notion of Society in St Thomas Aquinas: II. Thomistic Social Philosophy and the Theology of Original Sin', *Medieval Studies* 9:19–55

(1958). 'St Thomas and the Two Powers', *Medieval Studies* 20:179–205

Esser, K. (1949). *Das Testament des Heiligen Franziskus von Assisi, eine Untersuchung über seine Echheit und seine Bedeutung*, Aschendorff

(1975). 'Die Armutsanfassung des Hl. Franziskus', in D. Flood (ed.), *Poverty in the Middle Ages*, Dietrich-Coelde-Verlag, pp. 60–70

Faral, E., ed. (1950–1). 'Les *responsiones* de Guillaume de Saint-Amour', *Archives d'Histoire Doctrinale et Littéraire du Moyen Age* 25–6:337–94

Feenstra, R. (1956). 'L'Histoire des Fondations à propos de quelques Etudes Récentes', *Tijdschrift voor Rechtsgeschiedenis* 24:381–448

(1972). 'Quaestiones de materia feudorum de Jacques de Révigny', *Studi senesi* 21:379ff

(1980). 'Droit romain du moyen age (1100–1500)', in Gilissen 1964–

Fiumi, F. (1901). 'Alcune ricerche sui manoscritti delle opere di Baldo degli Ubaldi nelle principali biblioteche d'Italia', in Baldus de Ubaldis 1901, pp. 397–406

Fitzgerald, L.P. (1979). 'St Thomas Aquinas and the Two Powers', *Angelicum* 36:515–56

Flahiff, G.B. (1944, 1945). 'The Writ of Prohibition to Courts Christian in the Thirteenth Century', *Medieval Studies* 6:266–313; 7:229–90

Foster, K. (1977). *The Two Dantes and Other Studies*, Darton, Longman and Todd

Fournier, P. (1921). 'Guillaume de Cunh, légiste', *Histoire littéraire de France* 35:361–85

Fowler, G.B. (1947). *The Intellectual Interests of Engelbert of Admont*, Columbia University Press

Franzen, A. and Müller, W., eds. (1964). *Das Konzil von Konstanz, Beiträge zu seiner Geschichte und Theologie*, Herder

Fryde, E.B. and Miller, E., eds. (1970). *Historical Studies of the English Parliament*, vol. 1, Cambridge University Press

Fryde, N. (1979). *The Tyranny and Fall of Edward II, 1321–1326*, Cambridge University Press

Gadamer, H.G. (1965). *Wahrheit und Methode*, J.C.B. Mohr

Gandillac, M. de (1941). *La philosophie de Nicolas de Cues*, Aubier; Editions Montaigne
  (1953). *Nikolaus von Kues*, Schwann
  (1956). *Le mouvement doctrinal du xie au xive siècle*, livre III, 'Le xive siècle', in A. Fliche and E. Jarry (eds.) *Histoire de l'Eglise depuis les origines jusqu'à nos jours*, vol. XIII, Bloud et Gay, pp. 331–473
  (1968). 'Loi naturelle et fondements de l'ordre social selon les principes du Bienheureux Duns Scot', in *De Doctrina Iohannis Duns Scoti, Studia Scholastico-Scotica* 2:683–784
  (1969). 'Le *De Concordantia Catholica* de Nicolas de Cues', *Revue d'histoire ecclésiastique* 64:418–23
  (1972). 'Nicolas du Cues et l'oecuménisme', *Revue d'histoire ecclésiastique* 68:443–54
  (1983). 'Nicolas de Cues, théoricien des "Droits de l'homme"', in *Pascua Mediaevalia: Studies voor Prof. Dr. J.M. de Smet* (Mediaevalia Lovanensia, series 1, Studia, 10), Universitaire Pers Leuven, pp. 181–3

García, A. (1973). *Codices operum Bartoli de Sassoferrato recensiti: iter Hispanicum*, L.S. Olschki

García y García, A. (1981). *Constitutiones concilii quarti Lateranensis una cum commentariis glossatorum* (Mon, Iuris Canonici Series A: Corpus Glossatorum 2), Bibliotheca Apostolica Vaticana

Gaudemet, J. (1974). *Le droit privé romain*, Librairie Armand Colin
  (1979). *La formation du droit séculier et du droit de L'Eglise aux IVe et Ve siècles*, 2nd edn (Publications de l'institut de droit romain 15), Sirey

Gauthier, R.A. and Jolif, J.Y. (1958–9). *L'Ethique à Nicomaque*, 2 vols., 2nd edn, Editions Nauwelaerts; Béatrice Nauwelaerts

Geremek, B. (1969). *Le salariat dans l'artisanat parisien aux XIIIe–XVe siècles*, Mouton
  (1973). 'Renfermement des pauvres en Italie (XIVe–XVIIe s)', in *Mélanges en l'honneur de Fernand Braudel*, vol. 1, Privat

Gewirth, A. (1951, 1956). *Marsilius of Padua – the Defender of Peace*, 2 vols., Macmillan
  (1961). 'Philosophy and Political Thought in the Fourteenth Century', in F. Utley (ed.) *The Forward Movement of the Fourteenth Century*, Ohio State University Press

Gieben, S. (1968). 'Bibliographia Oliviana (1885–1967)', *Collectanea Franciscana* 38:167–95

Giesey, R.E. (1961). 'The Juristic Basis of Dynastic Right to the French Throne', *Transactions of the American Philosophical Society*, n.s., 51, 5

Gilby, T. (1958). *Principality and Polity: Aquinas and the Rise of State Theory in the West*, Longmans

Gilchrist, J. (1969). *The Church and Economic Activity in the Middle Ages*, Macmillan

Gilissen, J., ed. (1964–). *L'Introduction bibliographique à l'histoire du droit et à l'ethnologie juridique*, 8 vols., Editions de l'Institut de sociologie, Université libre de Bruxelles
  (1982). *La Coutume* (Typologie des sources du Moyen Age occidental, BREPOLS, Turnhaut, Belgium, fasc. 41)

Gilmore, Myron P. (1941). *Argument from Roman Law in Political Thought 1200–1600* (Harvard Historical Monographs 15), Harvard University Press

Glorieux, P. (1925a). 'Prélats français contre religieux mendiants (1281–90)', *Revue d'histoire de l'église de France*, 11:309–31, 471–95
  (1925b). *La littérature quodlibétique de 1260 à 1320*, Kain

Goglin, J.-L. (1976). *Les misérables dans l'occident médiéval*, Editions du Seuil
Goody, J. (1983). *The development of the Family and Marriage in Europe*, Cambridge University Press
Gordon, W.M. (1974). 'Cinus and Pierre de Belleperche', in A. Watson (ed.) *Daube noster: Essays in Legal History for David Daube*, Scottish Academic Press
Grabmann, M. (1941). 'Die mittelalterlichen Kommentare zur Politik des Aristoteles', (Bayerische Akademie der Wissenschaften, philosoph.-historische Klasse, Sitzungsberichte, 10), Bayerische Akademie der Wissenschaften
Grégoire, R. (1971). 'La place de la pauvreté dans la conception et la pratique de la vie monastique médiévale latine', in *Il monachesimo e la riforma ecclesiastica 1049–1122* (Miscellanea del Centro di studi medioevali 6), Publicazione dell'università cattolica del Sacro Cuore, Milan
Griesbach, M.F. (1959). 'John of Paris as a Representative of Thomistic Political Philosophy', in C.J. O'Neill (ed.) *An Etienne Gilson Tribute*, Marquette University Press, pp. 33–50
Grignaschi, M. (1955). 'Le rôle de l'aristotélisme dans le *Defensor Pacis* de Marsile de Padoue', *Revue d'histoire et de philosophie religieuse* 35:301–40
    (1957). 'La limitazione dei poteri del principans in Guglielmo d'Ockham et Marsilio da Padova', Comitato internazionale di scienze storiche: *Atti del 10 Congresso internazionale, Roma 1955*:35–51
    (1960). 'Un commentaire nominaliste de la *Politique* d'Aristote', *Commission Internationale pour l'histoire des assemblées d'états, Ancien pays et assemblées d'états* 19:123–42
    (1970). 'L' interprétation de la Politique dans le *Dialogus* de Guillaume d'Ockham', in *Liber memorialis Georges de Lagarde*, Editions Nauwelaerts; Béatrice Nauwelaerts
Grossi, P. (1958). 'Unanimitas: alle Origine del Concetto della Persona Giuridica nel Diritto Canonica', *Annali di Storia del Diritto* 2:229–331
Grundmann, H. (1935). *Religiöse Bewegungen im Mittelalter*, Emil Ebering
    (1957). 'Freiheit als religiöses, politisches und persönliches Postulat im Mittelalter', *Historischer Zeitschrift* 183:23–53
Guenée, B. (1964). 'L'histoire de l'état en France a la fin du moyen âge vue par les historiens français depuis cent ans', *Révue historique* 232:331–60
    (1967). 'Etat et nation en France au moyen age', *Revue historique* 237:17–30
    (1971). *L'occident aux XIVe et XVe siècles: Les Etats*, Presses Universitaires de France
Guterman, S.L. (1972). *From Personal to Territorial Law, Aspects of the History and Structure of the Western Legal-Constitutional Tradition*, Scarecrow Press
Gwynn, A. (1937). 'The Sermon-Diary of Richard FitzRalph, Archbishop of Armagh', *Proceedings of the Royal Irish Accademy* 44, sect. c:1–57
Habig, M., ed. (1973). *St Francis of Assisi, Writings and Early Biographies, English Omnibus of the Sources for the Life of St Francis*, 3rd rev. edn, Franciscan Herald Press
Hageneder, O. (1957–8). 'Exkommunikation und Thronfolgeverlust bei Innozenz III', *Römische Historische Mitteilungen* 2:9–50
Hamman, A. (1942). *La doctrine de l'église et de l'état chez Occam: étude sur le 'Breviloquium'*, Editions Franciscaines
    (1950). 'La doctrine de l'église et de l'état d'après le *Breviloquium* d'Occam', *Franziskanische Studien* 32:135–41
Harding, A. (1980). 'Political Liberty in the Middle Ages', *Speculum* 55:423–43
Harrison Thomson, S. (1940). *The Writings of Robert Grosseteste, Bishop of Lincoln, 1235–1253*, Cambridge University Press
    (1947). 'Walter Burley's Commentary on the Politics of Aristotle', in *Mélanges A.*

Pelzer (Université de Louvain: Recueil de travaux d'histoire et de philosophie, 3/ 26), Louvain, pp. 577ff

Harvey, J. (1950). *The Gothic World 1100–1600: A Survey of Architecture and Art*, Batsford

Haubst, R. (1956). *Die Christologie des Nikolaus von Kues*, Herder

(1971). 'Nikolaus von Kues als Promotor des Ökumene', *Mitteilungen und Forschungsbeiträge der Cusanus-Gesellschaft*, 9, Matthias-Grünewald-Verlag

(1972). 'Wort und Leitidee des "Repraesentatio" bei Nikolaus von Kues', in *Der Begriff des Repraesentatio im Mittelalter, Miscellanea Mediaevalia* 8:139–62

(1975). 'Nikolaus von Kues in der Geschichte des Erkenntnisproblems', *Mitteilungen und Forschungsbeiträge der Cusanus-Gesellschaft*, 11, Mathias-Grünewald-Verlag

Hecker, N. (1981). *Bettelorden und Bürgertum, Konflikt und Kooperation in deutschen Städter des Spätmittelalters* (European University Studies, Series 23, Theology, vol. 146), Peter D. Lang

Heers, J. (1973). *L'Occident aux XIVe et XVe siècles: aspects économiques et sociaux* (Nouvelle Clio 23), Presses Universitaires de France

(1974). *Le clan familiale au moyen âge: étude sur les structures politiques et sociales des milieux urbains*, Presses Universitaires, de France (transl. Herbert, B. (1977). *Family Clans in Europe in the Middle Ages* (Selected Studies 4), North-Holland)

Heimpel, H. (1932). *Dietrich von Niem (c. 1340–1418)*, Regensbergschen Verlagsbuchhandlung

Helmholz, R.M. (1976). 'Writs of Prohibition and Ecclesiastical Sanctions in the English Courts-Christian', *Minnesota Law Review* 60:1011–33

Henneman, J.B. (1971). *Royal taxation in Fourteenth-Century France: The Development of War Financing 1322–1356*, Princeton University Press

(1976). *Royal Taxation in Fourteenth-Century France: The Captivity and Ransom of John II 1356–70* (American Philosophical Society Memoirs 116)

Herlihy, D. (1958). *Pisa in the Early Renaissance: A Study of Urban growth* (Yale Historical Publications, Miscellany, LXVIII), Yale University Press

Hewitt, H.J. (1966). *The Organization of War under Edward III*, Manchester University Press; Barnes and Noble

Highfield, J.R.L. and Jeffs, R., eds. (1981). *The Crown and Local Communities in England and France in the Fifteenth Century*, Alan Sutton

Hödl, L. (1958). *Die Lehre des Petris Johannis Olivi OFM von der Universalgewalt des Papstes* (Mitteil. d. Grabmann-Institut d. Univ. München 1), Hueber

Hoffmann, H. (1964). 'Die beiden Schwerter im hohen Mittelalter', *Deutsches Archiv* 20:77–114

Holmes, G. (1980a). *Dante* (Past Masters), Oxford University Press

(1980b). 'Dante and the Popes', in C. Grayson (ed.), *The World of Dante: Essays on Dante and His Times*, Clarendon Press, pp. 18–43

Horn. N (1967). 'Philosophie in der Jurisprudenz der Kommentatoren: Baldus philosophus', *Ius commune*, Veröffentlichungen des Max-Planck-Instituts für europäische Rechtsgeschichte, Frankfurt-am-Main, 1:104–49

(1968). *Aequitas in den Lehren des Baldus* (Forschungen zur neueren Privatrechtsgeschichte 11), Böhlau

Hudson, A. (1972). 'A Lollard Compilation and the Dissemination of Wycliffite Thought', *Journal of Theological Studies*, 23, 1:65–81

ed. (1978). *English Wycliffite Writings*, Cambridge University Press

(1984). *John Wyclif and His Influence in England* (catalogue of commemorative exhibition, Lambeth Palace Library, 4 June–27 July 1984), Lambeth Palace Library, London

Immink, P.W. (1973). *La liberté et la peine. Etude sur la transformation de la liberté en occident avant le XIIe siècle*, Van Gorcum

Iung, N. (1931). *Un franciscain, théologien du pouvoir pontifical au XIVe siècle: Alvaro Pelayo, évêque et pénitencier de Jean XXII* (L'église et l'état au moyen âge 3), J. Vrin

Jacqueline, B. (1953). 'Le pouvoir pontificale selon saint Bernard. L'argument des deux glaives', *L'année canonique* 2:197–201

Jaher, F.C., ed. (1973). *The Rich, the Well-Born and the Powerful, Elites and Upper Classes in History*, University of Illinois Press

Jones, R.H. (1965). *The Royal Rule of Richard II*, Basil Blackwell
    (1968) *The Royal Policy of Richard II: Absolutism in the Later Middle Ages*, Basil Blackwell

Jones, W.R. (1966). 'Bishops, Politics and the Two Laws: The *Gravamina* of the English Clergy, 1237 to 1399', *Speculum* 41:209–45
    (1969). 'The Two Laws in England: The Later Middle Ages', *A Journal of Church and State* 11:111–31
    (1970). 'Relations of the Two Jurisdictions: Conflict and Cooperation in England during the Thirteenth and Fourteenth Centuries', *Studies in Medieval and Renaissance History* 7:77–211

Kallen, G. (1942). 'Die politische Theorie im philosophischen System des Nikolaus von Kues', *Historische Zeitschrift* 165:246ff

Kayser, J.R. and Lettieri, R.J. (1982). 'Aquinas's *Regimen bene commixtum* and the Medieval Critique of Classical Republicanism', *The Thomist* 46:195–220

Kennan, E. (1967). 'The "De consideratione" of St Bernard of Clairvaux and the Papacy in the Mid-Twelfth Century: A Review of Scholarship', *Traditio* 23:73–115

Kirshner, J. (1972). 'Messer Francesco di Bicci degli Albergotti d'Arezzo, Citizen of Florence (1350–1376)', *Bulletin of Medieval Canon Law*, New Series, 2:84–90
    (1973). '"Civitas sibi faciat civem": Bartolus of Sassoferrato's Doctrine of the Making of a Citizen', *Speculum* 48:694–713
    (1974). '"Ars imitatur naturam": a *consilium* of Baldus on Naturalization in Florence', *Viator* 5:289–331
    (1979). 'Between Nature and Culture: An Opinion of Baldus of Perugia on Venetian Citizenship as Second Nature', *Journal of Medieval and Renaissance Studies* 9, 2:179–208

Kölmel, W. (1962). *Wilhelm Ockham und seine Kirchenpolitischen Schriften*, Ludgerus Verlag Wingen

Knowles, D. (1948). *The Religious Orders in England*, vol. 1, Cambridge University Press

Krämer, W. (1980). *Konsens und Rezeption: Verfassungsprinzipien der Kirche im Basler Konziliarismus*, Aschendorff

Krchnák, A. (1960). *De vita et operibus Joannis de Ragusio*, Facultas Theologica Universitatis Lateranensis

Kuiters, R. (1957–8). 'Was bedeuten die Ausdrücke "directa" und "indirecta potestas papae in temporalibus" bei Aegidius von Rom, Jakobus von Viterbo und Johannes von Paris?', *Archiv für Katholisches Kirchenrecht* 128:99–105
    (1958). 'Aegidius Romanus and the Authorship of *in utramque partem* and *de ecclesiastica potestate*', *Augustiniana* 8:267–80

Lachance, L. (1964). *L'humanisme politique de St Thomas d'Aquin*, Editions Sirey; Editions du Lévrier

Lagarde, G. de (1937). 'L'idée de représentation dans les oeuvres de Guillaume d'Ockham', in *Album Helen Cam: Etudes présentées à la commission internationale pour l'histoire des Assemblées d'Etats, Bulletin of the Committee of Historical Sciences* 9:425–51

(1943). 'Individualisme et corporatisme au moyen âge', in *L'organisation corporative du moyen âge à la fin de l'ancien régime* (*Etudes présentées a la commission internationale pour l'histoire des assemblées d'états* 7: *Université de Louvain, Recuil de travaux d'histoire et de philologie,* 3/18), Louvain

(1943–5). 'La philosophie sociale de Henri de Gand et de Godefroid de Fontaines', *Archives d'histoire doctrinale et littéraire du moyen âge* 14:73–142

(1946a). *La naissance de l'esprit laïque au déclin du moyen âge,* vol. V: *Bases de départ de L'Ockhamisme,* Editions Béatrice

(1946b). *La naissance de l'esprit laïque au déclin du moyen âge,* vol. VI: *L'Ockhamisme: La morale et le droit,* Editions Béatrice

(1948a). *La naissance de l'esprit laïque au déclin du moyen âge,* vol. I: *Bilan du XIIIe siècle,* 2nd edn, Presses Universitaires de France

(1948b). *La naissance de l'esprit laïque au déclin du moyen age,* vol. II: *Marsile de Padoue ou le premier théoricien de l'Etat laïque,* 2nd edn, Presses Universitaires de France

(1955). 'Les théories représentatives des XIVe et XVe siècles et l'Eglise', *Actes du Xe Congrès International des Sciences Historiques,* 65–75

(1956–70). *La naissance de l'esprit laique au déclin du moyen âge,* 5 vols., Editions Nauwelaerts; Béatrice Nauwelaerts

(1960). 'Ockham et le concile générale', in *Album Helen Maud Cam,* Universitaires de Louvain, pp. 83–94

Lambert, M. (1961). *Franciscan Poverty: The Doctrine of Absolute Poverty of Christ and the Apostles in the Franciscan Order 1210–1323,* Society for the Promotion of Christian Knowledge

Landau, P. (1975). *Ius patronatus: Studien zur Entwicklung des Patronats im Dekretalenrecht und der Kanonistik des 12. und 13. Jahrhunderts,* Böhlau Verlag

Langlois, C. (1927). 'François de Meyronnes, Frère mineur', *Histoire littéraire de la France* 36:305–42

Langmuir, G. (1970). 'Community and Legal Change in Capetian France', *French Historical Studies* 6:275–86

Lapparent, P. de (1940–2).' L'oeuvre politique de François de Meyronnes, ses rapports avec celle de Dante', *Archives d'histoire doctrinale et littéraire du moyen âge,* 15ème–17ème années, 13:5–151

Lapsley, G.T. (1951). *Crown, Community and Parliament in the Later Middle Ages: Studies in English Constitutional History,* ed. H.M. Cam and G. Barraclough (Studies in Medieval History VI), Basil Blackwell

Le Bras, G. (1951). 'Boniface VIII, symphoniste et modérateur', in *Mélanges Louis Halphen,* Presses Universitaires de France, pp. 383–94

Lecler, J. (1931). 'L'argument des deux glaives (Luc XXII. 38) dans les controverses politiques du moyen âge: ses origines et son dévelopment', *Recherches de science religieuse* 21:299–339

(1932). 'L'argument des deux glaives (Luc XXII. 38): Critique et déclin (XIVe–XVIe Siècle)', *Recherches de science religieuse* 22:151–77

Leclercq, J. (1942). *Jean de Paris et l'Eclésiologie du XIIIe siècle,* J. Vrin

(1945). 'Un sermon prononcé pendant la Guerre de Flandre,' *Révue du moyen âge Latin* 1:165–72

Lefebvre, M. (1975). 'Private Property According to St Thomas and Recent Papal Encyclicals', in *Aquinas 1964–80,* vol. XXXVIII, pp. 275–83

Leff, G. (1967). *Heresy in the Later Middle Ages: the Relation of Heterodoxy to Dissent c. 1250–1450,* 2 vols., Manchester University Press

(1975). *William of Ockham: The Metamorphosis of Scholastic Discourse,* Manchester University Press

(1976). *The Dissolution of the Medieval Outlook. An Essay on Intellectual and Spiritual Change in the Fourteenth Century*, Harper Torchbooks

(1980). 'The Franciscan Concept of Man', in A. Williams (ed.) *Prophecy of Millenarianism, Essays in Honour of Marjorie Reeves*, Longmans, pp. 217–37

Legendre, P. (1964). *La pénétration du droit romain dans le droit canonique de Gratian à Innocent IV (1140–1254)*, Imprimerie Jouvre

Le Goff, J. (1960). 'Temps de l'Eglise et temps du marchand', *Annales (Economies, Sociétés, Civilisations)* 15:417–33

(1963). 'Métiers licites et métiers illicites dans l'occident médiévale: études historiques', *Annales de l'Ecole des Hautes Etudes de Gand* 5:46–7

(1970). 'Ordres mendiants et urbanisation dans la France médiévale', *Annales, économies, sociétés, civilisations* 25:924–46

(1973). 'Le vocabulaire des catégories sociales chez saint François d'Assise et ses biographes du XIIIe siècle', in D. Roche and C.E. Labrousse (eds.) *Ordres et classes, colloque d'histoire sociale 1967*, Mouton, pp. 93–123

Leguai, A. (1976). 'Les troubles urbains dans le nord de la France à la fin du XIIIe s. et au début du XIVe s', *Revue d'histoire économique et sociale* 54:281–303

Lejeune, J. (1958–62). 'De Godefroid de Fontaines à la paix de Fexhe (1316)', *Annuaire d'Histoire Liègoise* 6, 13:1215–61

Le Patourel, J. (1965). 'The King and the Princes in Fourteenth Century France', in J. Hale, R. Highfield and B. Smalley (eds.) *Europe in the Late Middle Ages*, Faber and Faber, pp. 155–83

Le Roy Ladurie, E. (1980). *Montaillou: Cathars and Catholics in a French Village 1294–1324*, transl. by B. Bray, Penguin Books

Lesnick, D. (1977–8). 'Dominican Preaching and the Creation of Capitalist Ideology in Late Medieval Florence', *Memorie Domenicane*, New Series, 8–9:199–247

Levison, W. (1952). *See* section IV above

Levy, E. (1951). *West Roman Vulgar Law, the Law of Property*, American Philosophical Society

Lévy, J. Ph. (1957). 'La pénétration du droit savant dans les coutumiers angevins et bretons au moyen âge', *Tijdschrift voor Rechtsgeschiedenis* 25:1–53

(1976). *Le droit Romain en Anjou, Bretagne, Poitou d'après les coutumiers* (Ius romanum medii aevi, pars v, 4b, societeé d'histoire des droits de l'antiquite), Giuffrè

Lewis, E. (1938). 'Organic Tendencies in Medieval Political Thought', *American Political Science Review*, 32:849–76

(1940). 'Natural law and Expediency in Medieval Political Theory', *Ethics* 50:144–63

Lewis, P.S. (1962). 'The failure of the French medieval estates', *Past and Present* 23:3–24

(1965). 'Jean Juvenal des Ursins and the Common Literary Attitude towards Tyranny', *Medium Aevum* 34:103–21

(1968). *Later Medieval France: The Polity*, Macmillan

Limentani, U. (1965). 'Dante's Political Thought', in U. Limentani (ed.), *The Mind of Dante*, Cambridge University Press, pp. 113–37

Lis, C. and Soly, H. (1979). *Poverty and Capitalism in Pre-Industrial Europe*, Harvester Press; republished 1982

Little, L.K. (1971). 'Pride Goes before Avarice: Social Change and the Vices in Latin Christendom', *American Historical Review* 76:27–9

(1975). 'Evangelical Poverty, the New Money Economy and Violence', in D. Flood (ed.) *Poverty in the Middle Ages*, Dietrich-Coelde Verlag

(1978). *Religious Poverty and the Profit Economy in Medieval Europe*, Elek

Logan, F.D. (1968). *Excommunication and the Secular Arm in Medieval England. A Study in Legal Procedure from the Thirteenth to the Sixteenth Century* (Studies and Texts 15),

Pontifical Institute of Mediaeval Studies, Toronto

Lopez, R.S. (1971). *The Commercial Revolution of the Middle Ages*, Prentice-Hall

Lottin, O. (1931). *Le droit naturel chez saint Thomas et ses prédécesseurs*, C. Beyaert

Lubac, H. de (1949). *Corpus mysticum: l'Euchariste et l'Eglise au Moyen Age*, Aubier

Lukes, S. (1973). *Individualism*, Basil Blackwell

Lyon, B. (1957–8). 'Medieval Real Estate Developments and Freedom', *American Historical Review* 63:47–61

Maccarrone, M. (1952). *Vicarius Christi: Storia del titolo papale*, Facultas Theologica Pontificii Athenaei Lateranensis

(1955–6). 'Il terzo Libro della Monarchia', *Studi danteschi* 33:1–142

McCready, William D. (1973). 'Papal *plenitudo potestatis* and the Source of Temporal Authority in Late Medieval Hierocratic Theory', *Speculum* 48:654–74

(1974). 'The Problem of the Empire in Augustinus Triumphus and Late Medieval Papal Hierocratic Theory', *Traditio* 30:325–49

(1975). 'Papalists and Anti-Papalists: Aspects of the Church–State Controversy in the Later Middle Ages', *Viator* 6:241–73

ed. (1982). *The Theory of Papal Monarchy in the Fourteenth Century* (Studies and Texts 56), Pontifical Institute of Mediaeval Studies, Toronto

McEvoy, J.J. (1982). *The Philosophy of Robert Grosseteste*, Oxford University Press

MacFarlane, A. (1978). *The Origins of English Individualism: The Family, Property and Social Transition*, Basil Blackwell

McFarlane, K.B. (1952). *John Wycliffe and the Beginnings of English Nonconformity*, English Universities Press

(1973). *The Nobility of Later Medieval England, the Ford lectures 1953 and Related Studies*, Clarendon Press

McGrade, A.S. (1974). *The Political Thought of William of Ockham. Personal and Institutional Principles* (Cambridge Studies in Medieval Life and Thought, Third Series, 7), Cambridge University Press

(1980). 'Ockham and the Birth of Individual Rights', in B. Tierney and P. Linehan (eds.), *Authority and power. Studies on Medieval Law and Government Presented to Walter Ullmann on His Seventieth Birthday*, Cambridge University Press

(1982). 'Rights, Natural Rights and the Philosophy of Law', in N. Kretzmann, A. Kenny and J. Pinborg (eds.), *Cambridge History of Later Medieval Philosophy*, Cambridge University Press, pp. 738–56

McKeon, R. (1938). 'The Development of the Concept of Property in Political Philosophy: A Study of the Background of the Constitution', *Ethics* 48:297–366

McLaughlin, T.P. (1939). 'The Teaching of the Canonists on Usury', *Mediaeval Studies* 1:81–147

(1940). 'The Teaching of the Canonists on Usury', *Mediaeval Studies* 1:1–22

Macpherson, C.B., ed. (1978). *Property, Mainstream and Critical Positions*, University of Toronto Press

Maffei, D. (1960). 'Cino da Pistoia e il "Constitutum Constantini"', *Annali dell' Università Macerata* 26:100ff

(1963). *La 'Lectura super Digesto veteri' di Cino da Pastoia. Studio sui MSS Savigny 22 e Urb. Lat. 172*, Giuffrè

(1967). 'Il giudice testimone e una "quaestio" di Jacques de Révigny (MS Bon. Coll. Hisp. 82)', *Tijdschrift voor Rechtsgeschiedenis* 35:54–76

(1969). *La donazione di Costantino nei giuristi medievali*, Giuffrè

Manselli, R. (1969). 'Evangelismo e Poverta', in *Poverta e ricchezza nella spiritualità dei secoli XI et XII* (80 convegno del Centro di studi sulla spiritualità medievale), Todi

(1975). *La Religion populaire au moyen âge: Problèmes de methode et d'histoire*, Institut d'études médiévales Albert-le-Grand, Montreal

Manteuffel, T. (1970). *Naissance d'une hérésie: les adeptes de la pauvreté volontaire au moyen âge*, Mouton (French transl. by A. Posner of Polish edn, 1963)

Marongiu, A. (1968). 'The Theory of Democracy and Consent in the Fourteenth Century', in F.L. Cheyette (ed.), *Lordship and Community in Mediaeval Europe*, Holt, Rinehart and Winston, Inc., pp. 404–21

Martin, C. (1949). 'The Commentaries on the Politics of Aristotle in the Late Thirteenth and Fourteenth Centuries, with Reference to the Thought and Political Life of the Time', unpublished Oxford University DPhil thesis

(1951). 'Some Medieval Commentaries on Aristotle's *Politics*', *History* 36:29–44

Martines, L. (1979). *Power and Imagination: City-States in Renaissance Italy*, Knopf

Mathes, F.A. O.S.A. (1968, 1969). 'The Poverty Movement and the Augustinian Hermits', *Analecta Augustiniana* 31:5–154; 32:5–116

Meijers, E.M. (1956–73). *Etudes d'histoire du droit*, 4 vols. (Leidse juridische reeks. dl. 5–8), Universitaire Pers, Leiden

(1959). 'Les glossateurs et le droit féodal', in Meijers 1956–73, vol. III, pp. 261ff

(1966). 'Le soi-disant "jus ad rem"', in Meijers 1956–73, vol. IV, pp. 475–89

Merzbacher, F. (1956). 'Das Somnium viridarii von 1376 als Spiegel des gallikanischen Staatskirchenrechts', *Zeitschrift der Savigny-Stiftung für Rechtsgeschichte 73. Kanonistische Abteilung* 42:55–72

(1970). 'Die Bedeutung von Freiheit und Unfreiheit im weltlichen und kirchlichen Recht des deutschen Mittelalters', *Historisches Jahrbuch* 90:257–83

Meynial, E. (1908). 'Notes sur la formation de la théorie du Domaine Divisé', in *Mélanges Fitting*, vol. II, Larose et Tenin

Michaud-Quantin, P. (1962). 'Collectivités médiévales et institutions antiques', *Antike und Orient im Mittelalter, Miscellanea Mediaevalia* 1:239–52

(1970). *See* General works above

(1973). 'Le vocabulaire des catégories sociales chez les canonistes et les moralistes du XIIIe siècle', in D. Roche and C.E. Labrousse (eds.) *Ordres et classes, colloque d'histoire sociale 1967*, Mouton, pp. 73–86

Miethke, J. (1969). *Ockhams Weg zur Sozialphilosophie*, W. de Gruyter

(1972). 'Repräsentation und Delegation in den politische Schriften Wilhelms von Ockham', *Miscellanea Mediaevalia* 8:163–85

(1974). 'Zeitbezug und Gegenwarts-bewusstsein in der politische Theorie der ersten hälfte des 14. Jahrhunderts', *Miscellanea Mediaevalia* 9:262–92

Miller, E. (1952). 'The State and Landed Interest in Thirteenth Century France and England', *Transactions of the Royal Historical Society*, 5th series, 2:109–29

Milsom, S.F.C. (1969; 2nd edn 1981). *See* section IV above

(1976). *See* section IV above

Minio-Paluello, L. (1956). 'Remigio Girolami's *De Bono Communi*: Florence at the Time of Dante's Banishment and the Philosopher's Answer to the Crisis', *Italian Studies* 11:56–71

Mochi Onory, S. (1951). *Fonti canonistiche dell'idea moderna dello stato; imperium spirituale, iurisdictio divisa, sovranità* (Pubblicazioni dell'Università cattolica del Sacro Cuore, nuova ser. 38), Società editrice 'Vita e Pensiero'

Mollat, M. (1970). 'Les pauvres et la société médiévale', section médiéval du XIIIe Congrès International des sciences historiques, Moscow

(ed. (1974). *Etudes sur l'histoire de la pauvreté* (Moyen âge – XVIe siècle) 2 vols., Publications de la Sorbonne, Paris

(1975). 'Hospitalité et assistance au début du XIIIe siècle', in D. Flood (ed.) *Poverty in the Middle Ages*, Dietrich-Coelde Verlag, pp. 37–51

(1978). *Les pauvres au Moyen Age*, Hachette

Monti, G.M. (1942). *Le 'Questiones' e i 'Consilia'* (Orbis romanus; biblioteca di testi medievali a cura dell' Università cattolica del Sacro Cuore 13), Società editrice 'Vita e Pensiero'

Moody, E. (1967). 'Ockham, Buridan and Nicholas of Autrecourt', *Franciscan Studies* 7:133–59

Moore, R.I. (1977). *The Origins of European Dissent*, Allan Lane

Moorman, J. (1940). *The Sources of the Life of St Francis of Assisi*, Manchester University Press

(1968). *A History of the Franciscan Order from Its Origins to the Year 1517*, Clarendon Press

Morrall, J. (1960). *Gerson and the Great Schism*, Manchester University Press

Morris, C. (1972). *The Discovery of the Individual 1050–1200*, Society for the Promotion of Christian Knowledge

Most, R. (1941). 'Der Reichsgedanke des Lupolds von Bebenburg', *Deutsche Archiv* 4:444–55

Moulin, L. (1970). 'Les Eglises comme institutions politiques; l'Assemblée, autorité souveraine dans l'Ordre des Chartreux', *Respublica, Revue de l'Institut belge de science politique* 12:7–76

(1978). *La vie quotidienne des réligieux au Moyen-Age, Xe–XVe siècles*, Hachette

Muldoon, J. (1966). '*Extra ecclesiam non est imperium*. The Canonists and the Legitimacy of Secular Power', *Studia Gratiana* 9:551–80

(1971). 'Boniface VIII's Forty Years of Experience in the Law', *The Jurist* 31:449–77

Nitschke, A. (1956). 'Der Prozess gegen Konradin', *Zeitschrift der Savigny-Stiftung für Rechtsgeschichte*, Kanonistische Abteilung 42:25ff

Noonan, J.T. (1957). *The Scholastic Analysis of Usury*, Harvard University Press

Nörr, K.W. (1964). *Kirche und Konzil bei Nicolaus de Tudeschis (Panormitanus)* (*Forschungen zur Kirchlichen Rechtsgeschichte und zum Kirchenrecht* 4), Böhlau Verlag

Nuzzo, V. (1940). *La sovranità e le leggi del regno di Sicilia nella glossa alle costituzione di Marino da Caramanico*, Benevento

Oakley, F. (1961). 'Medieval Theories of Natural Law: William of Ockham and the Significance of the Voluntarist Tradition', *Natural Law Forum* 6:65–83; repr. in Oakley 1984a

(1962). 'On the Road from Constance to 1688', *Journal of British Studies* 1:1–32; repr. in Oakley 1984a

(1964). *The Political Thought of Pierre d'Ailly: The Voluntarist Tradition* (Yale Historical Publications Miscellany 81), Yale University Press

(1969). 'Figgis, Constance and the Divines of Paris', *American Historical Review* 75:368–86; repr. in Oakley 1984a

(1979). *The Western Church in the Later Middle Ages*. Cornell University Press

(1981). 'Natural Law, the *Corpus Mysticum*, and Consent in Conciliar Thought from John of Paris to Mathias Ugonis', *Speculum* 56:786–810; repr. in Oakley 1984a

(1984a). *Natural Law, Conciliarism and Consent in the Late Middle Ages*, Variorum Reprints

(1984b). *Omnipotence, Covenant, and Order: An Excursion in the History of Ideas from Abelard to Leibniz*, Cornell University Press

Oberman, H. and Trinkaus, C., eds. (1974). *The Pursuit of Holiness in Late Medieval and Renaissance Religion* (Papers from the University of Michigan Conference. 1972), E.J. Brill

Olivier-Martin, F. (1938). *L'organisation corporative de la France d'Ancien Régime*, Editions Sirey

(1948). *Histoire du droit français des origines à la Révolution*, Domat Montchrètien

Ourliac, P. and Malafosse, J. de (1968). *Histoire du droit privé*, vol. III, Presses Universitaires de France

Pacaut, M. (1960). 'L'Autorité pontificale selon Innocent IV', *Moyen Age* 66:85–119
Palumbo, L. (1886). *Andrea d' Isernia*, Tipografia e stereotipia della Regia Università, Napoli
Pantin, W.A. (1955). 'Grosseteste's Relations with the Papacy and with the Crown', in D.A. Callus (ed.) *Robert Grosseteste, Scholar and Bishop*, Clarendon Press
Paradisi, B. (1973). 'Il pensiero politico dei giuristi medievali' in L. Firpo (ed.) *Storia delle idee politiche, economiche e sociale*, vol. II, Unione tipografico-editrice torinese
Paré, G. (1941). *Le Roman de la Rose et la scholastique courtoise*, Publications de l'Institut d'Etudes Médiévales d'Ottawa 3
Parel, A. (1979). 'Aquinas' Theory of Property', in A. Parel and T. Flanagan (eds.) *Theories of Property, Aristotle to the Present*, Wilfred Laurier University Press, The Calgary Institute for the Humanities.
Partee, C. (1960). 'Peter John Olivi: Historical and Doctrinal Study', *Franciscan Studies* 20:215–60
Pascoe, L.B. (1973). *Jean Gerson: Principles of Church Reform* (Studies in Medieval and Reformation Thought 7), E.J. Brill
Pasquet, D. (1914). *Essai sur les origines de la Chambre des Communes*, Librairie Armand Colin
Passerin d'Entrèves, A. (1952). *Dante as a Political Thinker*, Clarendon Press
Paul, J. (1966). 'Les franciscains et la pauvreté au XIIIe et XIVe siècles', *Revue d'histoire de l'Eglise de France* 52:33–7
Pennington, K. (1977). 'Pope Innocent III's Views on Church and State: A Gloss to *Per venerabilem*', in K. Pennington and C. Somerville (eds.) *Law, Church and Society: Essays in Honor of Stephen Kuttner*, Pennsylvania University Press, pp. 49–67
    (1984). *Pope and Bishops: A Study of the Papal Monarchy in the Twelfth and Thirteenth Centuries*, Pennsylvania University Press
Peters, E.M. (1970). *The Shadow King; Rex Inutilis in Medieval Law and Literature, 751–1327*, Yale University Press
    (1977). '*Pars parte*: Dante and an Urban Contribution to Political Thought', in H. Miskimin, D. Herlihy and A. Udovitch (eds.), *The Medieval City*, Yale University Press
Petit-Dutaillis, C. (1947). *Les communes françaises, caractère et évolution des origines au XVIIIe siècle*, Albin Michel; reissued in L'Evolution de l'Humanité, 25 (English transl. of Part I by J. Vickers (1978). *The French Communes in the Middle Ages*, North-Holland)
Pocquet du Haut-Jussé, (1971). 'A Political Concept of Louis XI: Subjection instead of Vassalage', in P.S. Lewis (ed.), *The Recovery of France in the Fifteenth Century*, Macmillan
Pollock, F. and Maitland, F.W. (1898). *The History of English Law before the Time of Edward I*, 2 vols., Cambridge University Press
Posch, A. (1920). *Die staats- und kirchenpolitische Tätigkeit Engelberts von Admont*, F. Schöningh
Post, G. (1964). *Studies in Medieval Legal Thought: Public Law and the State, 1100–1322*, Princeton University Press
    (1967). 'Early Medieval Ecclesiastical and Secular Sources of *Iura Illibata-Illaesa* in the Inalienability Clause of the Coronation Oath', in *Collectanea Stephen Kuttner* I (Studia Gratiana 11), Institutum Gratianum
Posthumes-Meyjes, G.H.M. (1963). *Jean Gerson: zijn kerkpolitiek en ecclesiolozie*, Martinus Nijhoff
Quaglioni, D. (1978). '"Regimen ad populum" e "regimen regis" in Egidio Romano e Bartolo de Sassofarrato', in *Bullettino dell' Istituto Storico per il medio evo e Archivio Muratoriano* 87:201–28

(1980). 'Un "Tractatus de tyranno" il commento di Baldo degli Ubaldi (1327?–1400) alla lex Decernimus, C. De sacrosanctis ecclesiis (C.I.2, 16)', *Il pensiero politico* 13, 1:64–77

Quillet, J. (1964). 'L'organisation de la société humaine selon le Defensor Pacis de Marsile de Padoue', in *Beiträge zum Berufsbewusstsein des mittelalterlichen Menschen*, *Miscellanea Mediaevalia* 3:185–205

(1970a). *La philosophie politique de Marsile de Padoue* (*L'église et l'état au moyen âge* XIV), J. Vrin

(1970b). 'Le "Defensor Pacis" de Marsile de Padoue et le "De concordantia catholica" de Nicolas de Cues', in *Nicolo Cusano agli Inizi del Mondo Moderno*, G.C. Sensoni, pp. 345–58

(1971). '*Universitas populi* et représentation au XIVe siècle', in *Der Begriff des Repraesentatio im Mittelalter*, *Miscellanea Mediaevalia* 8:186–201

(1974a). 'La philosophie politique de Dante', in *Annales de l'Université de Dakar*. Presses Universitaires de France, pp. 219–34

(1974b). 'Les doctrines politiques du Cardinal Pierre d'Ailly', in *Antiqui und Moderni*, *Miscellanea Mediaevalia* 9:345–8

(1977). *La philosophie politique du Songe du Vergier (1378). Sources doctrinales*, J. Vrin

(1979). 'L'aristotélisme de Marsile de Padoue et ses rapports avec l'averroisme', *Medioevo: Rivista di Storia della Filosofia Medievale* 5:81–142

(1980). 'Nouvelles études marsilliennes', *History of Political Thought* 1:391–409

(1981). 'Hermeneutique ou discours allégorique dans "Le Songe du Viel Pèlerin"', *Miscellanea Mediaevalia* 13/2:1084–93

(1984). *Charles V le roi lettré: Essai sur la pensée politique d'un règne*, Librairie Académique Perrin

Reeves, M. (1969). *The Influence of Prophecy in the Later Middle Ages*, Clarendon Press

Ricci, G. (1983). 'Naissance du Pauvre Honteux: entre l'histoire des idées et l'histoire sociale', *Annales, économies, sociétés, civilisations* 38:158–77

Richardson, H.G. and Sayles, G.O. (1963). *The Governance of Mediaeval England from the Conquest to Magna Carta*, Edinburgh University Press

Riesenberg, P.N. (1955). 'Roman Law, Renunciations and Business in the Thirteenth Century', in J.H. Mundy (ed.) *Essays in Medieval Life and Thought, Presented in Honor of Austin Patterson Evans*, Biblo and Tannen

(1956). *Inalienability of Sovereignty in Medieval Political Thought*, Columbia University Press

(1969). 'Civism and Roman Law in Fourteenth-Century Italian Society', *Explorations in Economic History* 7:237–54

Riis, Th., ed. (1981). *Aspects of Poverty in Early Modern Europe*, Alphen

Rivière, J. (1926). *Le problème de l'église et de l'état au temps de Philippe le Bel*, Spicilegium Sacrum Lovaniense

Robson, J.A. (1961). *Wyclif and the Oxford Schools*, Clarendon Press

Roensch, F.J. (1964). *Early Thomistio School*, Priory Press

Roover, R. de (1971). *La pensée économique des scholastiques, doctrines et méthodes*, Institut des études médiévales Albert-le-Grand, Montreal

Roth, B. (1936). *Franz von Mayronis O.F.M. Sein Leben, seine Werke, seine Lehre von Formalunterschied in Gott* (Franziskanische Forschungen 3), Franziskus-druckerei

Royer, J.P. (1969). *L'Eglise et le Royaume de France au XIVe siècle d'après le 'Songe du Vergier' et la jurisprudence du Parlement* (Bibliothèque d'histoire du droit et du droit romain, 15). Librairie générale de droit et de jurisprudence

Rubenstein, N. (1958). 'Political Ideas in Sienese Art: The Frescoes by Ambrogio Lorenzetti and Taddeo di Bartolo', *Journal of the Warburg and Courtauld Institutes* 21:179–207

(1965). 'Marsilius of Padua and Italian Political Thought of His Time', in J. Hale, R. Highfield and B. Smalley (eds.) *Europe in the Late Middle Ages*, Faber, pp. 44–75

Rueger, Z. (1964). 'Gerson, the Conciliar Movement and the Right of Resistance', *Journal of the History of Ideas* 25:467–80

Ryan, J.J. (1956). *Saint Peter Damiani and His Canonical Sources* (Studies and Texts 2), Pontifical Institute of Mediaeval Studies, Toronto

Saenger, P. (1981). 'John of Paris, Principal Author of the *Quaestio de potestate papae (Rex pacificus)*', *Speculum* 56:41–55

Savigny, F.C. von (1834–51). *Geschichte des römischen Rechts im Mittelalter*, 2nd edn, J.C.B. Mohr

Saxl, E. (1956). 'Veritas filia temporis', in *Philosophy and History: Essays Presented to Ernst Cassirer*, Clarendon Press

Schlatter, R.B. (1951). *Private property: The History of an Idea*, Allen and Unwin

Schmitt, J.-C. (1978). *Mort d'une hérésie. L'église et les clercs face aux béghards du Rhin supérieur du XIVe au XVe siècle* (Civilisations et sociétés), Editions de l'Ecole de Hautes études en sciences sociales

Scholz, R. (1903). *Die Publizistik zur Zeit Philipps des Schönen und Bonifaz VIII*, F. Enke
    (1926). 'Eine Geschichte und Kritik der Kirchenverfassung vom Jahre 1406', in A. Brachmann (ed.) *Papsttum und Kaisertum: Forschungen zur Politischen Geschichte und Geisteskultur des Mittelalters*, Verlag der Müncher Drucke
    (1944). *Wilhelm von Ockham als politischer Denker und sein Breviloquim de Principatu Tyrannico* (repr. 1952)

Sheehan, M. (1963). *The Will in Medieval England*, Pontifical Institute of Mediaeval Studies, Toronto

Sigmund, P. (1962). 'The Influence of Marsilius on Fifteenth-Century Conciliarism', *Journal of the History of Ideas* 23:393–402
    (1963). *Nicholas of Cusa and Medieval Political Thought*, Harvard University Press

Skinner, Q. (1978). *The Foundations of Modern Political Thought*, vol. 1: *The Renaissance*, Cambridge University Press

Smalley, B. (1952). *The Study of the Bible in the Middle Ages*, Basil Blackwell
    (1973), *see* section IV above

Sousa Costa, A.D. de (1966). *Estudios sobre Alvaro Pais*, Instituto de Alta Cultura, Lisbon

Spicq, C. (1930). 'L'aumône obligation de justice ou de charité?', *Mélanges Mandonnet* 1:245–64

Spiegel, G. (1977). 'Defence of the Realm: The Evolution of a Capetian Propaganda Slogan', *Journal of Medieval History* 3:115–33

Stein, P. (1969). *Roman Law and English Jurisprudence Yesterday and Today*, Cambridge University Press
    (1975). Rev. 3rd edn of W.W. Buckland, *A Text-Book of Roman Law from Augustus to Justinian*, Cambridge University Press

Stein, P. and Shand, J. (1974). *Legal Values in Western Society*, Edinburgh University Press

Stickler, A.M. (1947). 'Der Schwerterbegriff bei Huguccio', *Ephemerides iuris canonici* 3:201–42
    (1948). 'Magistri Gratiani sententia de potestate ecclesiae in statum', *Apollinaris* 21:36–111
    (1951). 'Il "gladius" negli atti dei concili e dei Romani Pontefici sino a Graziano e Bernardo di Clairvaux', *Salesianum* 13:414–45
    (1953). 'Sacerdotium et Regnum nei Decretisti e Primi Decretalisti', *Salesianum* 15:575–612

Stones, E.L.G. (1965). *Anglo-Scottish Relations 1174–1328*, Nelsons

Strayer, J.B. (1970). *Les gens de justice de Languedoc sous Philippe le Bel*, Association Marc Bloch de Toulouse
  (1971). *Medieval Statecraft and the Perspectives of History*, Princeton University Press
  (1980). *The Reign of Philip the Fair*, Princeton University Press
Sweeney, J.R. (1975). 'The Problem of Inalienability in Innocent III's correspondence with Hungary: A Contribution to the Study of the Historical Genesis of *Intellecto*', *Mediaeval Studies* 37:235–51
Tessier, G. (1938). 'L'activité de la Chancellerie royale au temps de Charles V', *Moyen Age* 48:14–52, 81–113
Thils, G. (1940), 'Le "Tractatus de ecclesia" de Jean de Ragusa', *Angelicum* 17:219–44
Thomas, S. (1930). *Jean de Gerson et l'éducation des Dauphins de France: étude critique suivie du texte de deux de ses opuscules*, Librairie Droz
Thouzellier, C. (1957). 'La pauvreté, arme contre l'albigéisme', *Revue de l'histoire des religions* 151:79–92
Tierney, B. (1953). 'The Canonists and the Medieval State', *Review of Politics* 15:376–88
  (1954). 'Ockham, the Conciliar Theory and the Canonists', *Journal of the History of Ideas* 15:40–70
  (1955a). *Foundations of the Conciliar Theory: The Contribution of the Medieval Canonists from Gratian to the Great Schism*, Cambridge University Press
  (1955b). 'Grosseteste and the Theory of Papal Sovereignty', *Journal of Ecclesiastical History* 6:1–17
  (1958–9). 'The Decretists and the "Deserving Poor"', *Comparative Studies in Society and History*, pp. 362–3
  (1959). *Medieval Poor Law, a Sketch of Canonical Theory and Its Application in England*, University of California Press
  (1963a). '"The Prince is not Bound by the Laws": Accursius and the Origins of the Modern State', *Comparative Studies in Society and History* 5:378–400
  (1963b). 'Bracton on Government', *Speculum* 38:295–317
  (1964). *The Crisis of Church and State 1050–1300*, Prentice-Hall
  (1965). 'The Continuity of Papal Political Theory in the Thirteenth Century. Some Methodological Considerations', *Mediaeval Studies* 27:227–45
  (1972). *Origins of Papal Infallibility 1150–1350: A study on the Concepts of Infallibility, Sovereignty and Tradition in the Middle Ages*, E.J. Brill
  (1975). '"Divided Sovereignty" at Constance: A Problem of Medieval and Early Modern Political Theory', *Annuarium Historiae Conciliorum* 7:238–56
  (1976). 'Hostiensis and Collegiality', in *Proceedings of the Fourth International Congress of Medieval Canon Law*, Biblioteca Apostolica Vaticana
  (1977). '"Only Truth Has Authority": The Problem of "reception" in the Decretists and in Johannes de Turrecremata', in *Law, Church and Society: Essays in Honour of Stephen Kuttner*, University of Pennsylvania Press
  (1979). *Church, Law and Constitutional Thought in the Middle Ages*, Variorum Reprints
  (1980). 'Public Expediency and Natural Law: A Fourteenth Century discussion on the Origins of Government and Property', in B. Tierney and P. Linehan (eds.) *Authority and Power. Studies in Medieval Law and Government Presented to Walter Ullmann on his Seventieth Birthday*, Cambridge University Press, pp. 167–82
  (1982). *Religion, Law, and the Growth of Constitutional Thought (1150–1650)*, Cambridge University Press
  (1983). 'Tuck on Rights: Some Medieval Problems', *History of Political Thought* 4:429–41
Tillmann, H. (1980). *Pope Innocent III*, transl. by W. Bax, North-Holland
Timbal, P.C. (1958–9). *La coutume, source du droit privé français*, Centre National des Recherches Scientifiques

Tourtoulon, P. de (1896). *Placentin, sa vie, ses oeuvres. Etude sur l'enseignement du droit romain au moyen âge dans le midi de la France*, A. Chevalier-Maresq et Cie

(1899). *Etudes sur le droit écrit. Les oeuvres de Jacques de Révigny*, A. Chevalier-Maresq et Cie

Trexler, R.C. (1973). 'Charity and the Defense of Urban Elites in the Italian Communes', in Jaher, ed., 1973

Trinkaus, C. (1970). *In our Image and Likeness: Humanity and Divinity in Italian Humanist Thought*, 2 vols., Constable

Tuck, A. (1973). *Richard II and the English Nobility*, Edward Arnold

Tuck, R. (1979). *Natural Rights Theories, their Origin and Development*, Cambridge University Press

Ullmann, W. (1946a). *The Medieval Idea of Law as Represented by Lucas de Penna: A Study in Fourteenth-Century Legal Scholarship*, Methuen

(1946b). 'A Medieval Document on Papal Theories of Government', *English Historical Review* 61:180–201

(1948a). *Origins of the Great Schism: A Study in Fourteenth-Century Ecclesiastical History*, Burns and Oates (repr. Archon 1972)

(1948b). 'The Delictal Responsibility of Medieval Corporations', *Law Quarterly Review* 64:78–96

(1955). *The Growth of Papal Government in the Middle Ages*, Methuen (2nd edn 1962)

(1960a). *The Medieval Papacy, St Thomas Aquinas and Beyond* (Aquinas Papers 35)

(1960b). 'Some Reflections on the Opposition of Frederick II to the Papacy', *Archivio Storico Pugliese* 13:3–26

(1962). 'De Bartoli sententia: Concilium repraesentat mentem populi', in *Bartolo da Sassoferrato* 2:707–33

(1967). *The Individual and Society in the Middle Ages*, Methuen

(1974). 'Die Bulle Unam Sanctam: Rückblick und Ausblick', *Römische Historische Mitteilungen* 16:45–58

(1976). 'Boniface VIII and his Contemporary Scholarship', *Journal of Theological Studies* 27:58–87

(1979a). 'This Realm of England is an Empire', *The Journal of Ecclesiastical History* 30, 2:175–203

(1979b). 'Arthur's Homage to King John', *English Historical Review* 94:356–64

Valois, N. (1885). *Le gouvernement représentatif en France au XIVx siècle: Etude sur le conseil du roi pendant la captivité de Jean le Bon*, A. Vromant

Vanderjagt, A. (1981). *'Qui sa vertu anoblist': The Concepts of noblesse and chose publique in Burgundian Political Thought*, Krips

Van de Kamp, J.L.J. (1936). *Bartolus de Saxoferrato, 1313–1357: Leven, Werken, Invloed, Beteekenis*, H.N. Paris

Van Hove, A. (1945). *Prolegomena ad Codicem Iuris Canonici*, H. Dessain

Vasoli, C. (1954). 'Il pensiero politico di Guglielmo d'Occam', *Rivista critica di storia della filosofia* 9:232–53

Vauchez, A. (1970). 'La pauvreté volontaire au moyen Age', *Annales, économies, sociétés, civilisations* 25:1566–73

(1978). 'Assistance et charité en occident XIIIe–XVe siècles', in *Domanda e consumi, livelli e strutture*, Florence

Vaughan, R. (1975). *Valois Burgundy*, Allen Lane

Verriest, L. (1946). *Institutions Médiévales*, Union des imprimeries, Mons

(1959). *Noblesse, chevalerie, lignages* (Questions d'histoire des institutions médiévales), published by the author

Villey, M. (1964). 'La genèse du droit subjectif chez Guillaume d'Occam'. *Archives de philosophies du droit* 9:97–127

(1968). *La formation de la Pensée Juridique Moderne*, Montchrétien

Violante, C. (1953). *La società milanese nell' età precomunale*, Istituto italiano per gli studi storici

(1955). *La patria milanese e la riforma ecclesiastica* (Edizioni istituto storico italiano per il medio evo: Studi storici, fasc. 11–13), G. Bardi

(1974). 'Riflessioni sulla povertà nel secolo XI', *Studi sul medioevo cristiano offerti a Raffaello Morghen*, Istituto storico italiano per il medio evo

Vinay, G. (1939). 'Egidio Romano e la considetta Questio in utramque partem', *Bulletino dell'Istituto storico Italiano* 53:43–136

Vismara, G. (1981). 'Le fonti del diritto romano nell' alto medioevo secondo la più recente storiografia (1955–80)', *Studia et Documenta Historiae et Iuris* 47:1–30

Vodola, E.P. (1980). '*Fides et culpa*: The Use of Roman Law in Ecclesiastical Ideology', in B. Tierney and P. Linehan (eds.) *Authority and Power. Studies in Medieval Law and Government Presented to Walter Ullmann on his Seventieth Birthday*, Cambridge University Press, pp. 167–82

Wahl, J.A. (1968). 'Baldus de Ubaldis' Concept of State: A Study in Fourteenth-Century Legal Theory', Unpublished PhD dissertation, University of St Louis

(1970). 'Immortality and Inalienability: Baldus de Ubaldis', *Mediaeval Studies* 32:308–28

(1974). 'Baldus de Ubaldis: A Study in Reluctant Conciliarism', *Manuscripta* 18:21–9

(1977). 'Baldus de Ubaldis and the Foundations of the Nation-State', *Manuscripta* 21, 2:80–96

Walsh, K. (1970, 1971). 'The "De vita evangelica" of Geoffrey Hardeby (d. c. 1385)', *Analecta Augustiniana* 33:151–262; 34:5–83

(1975). 'Archbishop FitzRalph and the Friars at the Papal Court in Avignon, 1357–60', *Traditio* 31:223–45

(1981). *A Fourteenth Century Scholar and Primate: Richard FitzRalph in Oxford, Avignon and Armagh*, Clarendon Press

Walters, L. (1901). *Andreas von Escobar, ein Vertreter der konziliaren Theorie am Anfange des 15. Jahrhunderts*, inaugural dissertation, Münster

Walther, H.G. (1976). *Imperiales Königstum, Konziliarismus und Volkssouveränität. Studien zu den Grenzen des littelalterischen Souveränitätsgedanken*, Wilhelm Fink Verlag

Watson, A. (1968). *The Law of Property in the Later Roman Republic*, Clarendon Press

Watt, J.A. (1965a). *The Theory of Papal Monarchy in the Thirteenth Century. The Contribution of the Canonists*, Fordham University Press

(1965b). 'Medieval Deposition Theory: A Neglected Canonist *Consultatio* from the First Council of Lyons', *Studies in Church History* 2:197–214

(1965c). 'The Use of the term *Plenitudo potestatis* by Hostiensis', in *Proceedings of the Second International Congress of Medieval Canon Law*, Biblioteca Apostolica Vaticana

(1967). 'The Quaestio in utramque partem Reconsidered', *Studia Gratiana* 13:411–54

(1980). 'Hostiensis on *Per venerabilem*: The Role of the College of Cardinals', in B. Tierney and P. Linehan (eds.) *Authority and Power. Studies in Medieval Law and Government Presented to Walter Ullmann on his Seventieth Birthday*, Cambridge University Press, pp. 99–113

Weigand, R. (1967). *Die Naturrechtslehre der Legisten und Dekretisten*, Hueber

Weimar, P. (1967). 'Die Erstausgabe der sogenannten Lectura Institutionum des Pierre de Belleperche', *Tijdschrift voor Rechtsgeschiedenis* 35:284–9

Weisheipl, J.A., ed. (1980). *Albertus Magnus and the Sciences*, Pontifical Institute of Mediaeval Studies, Toronto

Werner, E. (1956). *Pauperes Christi, Studien zur Social-Religiösen Bewegungen im Zeitalter des Reformpapsttums*, Koehler and Amelang

Werveke, H. van (1963). 'The Rise of the Towns', in M. Postan, E. Rich and E. Miller (eds.) *Cambridge Economic History of Europe*, vol. III, Cambridge University Press, pp. 3–41

Wieacker, F. (1961). *Vom römischen Recht; zehn Versuche; neubearb. und erweiterte Aufl.*, Koehler

Wielockx, R. (1980), 'La censure de Gilles de Rome', *Bulletin de philosophie médiévale* 22:87–8

Wilda, W. (1831). *Das Gildewesen im Mittelalter*, Verlag der Rengerschen Buchhandlung (Halle) (repr. Scientia Verlag, 1964)

Wilkinson, B. (1939). 'The Deposition of Richard II and the Accession of Henry IV', *English Historical Review* 54:215–39

Wilks, M.J. (1963). *The Problem of Sovereignty in the Later Middle Ages – The Papal Monarchy with Augustinus Triumphus and the Publicists* (Cambridge Studies in Medieval Life and Thought, 2nd series, 9), Cambridge University Press

(1965). 'Predestination, Property and Power: Wyclif's theory of Dominion and Grace', *Studies in Church History* 2:220–36

(1972a). 'Corporation and Representation in the Defensor Pacis', *Studia Gratiana* 15:253–92

(1972b). 'Reformatio Regni: Wyclif and Hus as Leaders of Religious Protest Movements', in *Studies in Church History* 9:109–30

Will, E. (1917). *Die Gutachten des Oldradus de Ponte zum Prozesse Heinrichs VII. gegen Robert von Neapel*, W. Rothschild

Willibrord, P., OFM Cap. (1960). *Le message spirituel de St François d'Assise dans ses écrits*, Editions Note Dame de la trinité

Witt, R.G. (1971). 'The Landlord and the Economic Revival of the Middle Ages in Northern Europe 1000–1250', *American Historical Review* 76:965–88

Witters, W., OSB (1974). 'Pauvres et pauvreté dans les coutumiers monastiques du moyen âge', in Mollat, ed., 1974, vol. I, pp. 177–215

Wolter, H. and Holstein, H. (1966). *Lyon I et Lyon II (Histoire des conciles oecuméniques 7)*, Editions de l'Orante

Wood, C.T. (1967). 'Regnum Franciae: A Problem in Capetian Administrative Usage', *Traditio* 23:117–43

(1967). *Philip the Fair and Boniface VIII*, Holt, Rinehart and Winston, Inc.

Woolf, C.N.S. (1913). *Bartolus of Sassoferrato – His Position in the History of Medieval Political Thought*, Cambridge University Press

Wright, J.R. (1980). *The Church and the English Crown 1305–1334*, Pontifical Institute of Mediaeval Studies, Toronto.

Wulf, M. de (1920). 'L'Individu et le Groupe dans la Scolastique du XIIIe Siècle', *Revue Néo-Scolasticue de Philosophie* 22:341–57

Zuckermann, C. (1975). 'The Relationship of Theories of Universals to Theories of Church Government in the Middle Ages: A Critique of Previous Views', *Journal of the History of Ideas* 36:579–94

INDEX OF NAMES OF PERSONS

This index is intended to include the names of all persons mentioned in the text and in the Notes on Medieval Authors (the latter distinguished by the abbreviation '(biog.)'. The abbreviation '(bib.)' indicates, for authors of primary source material only, an entry or entries in the Bibliography. References to footnotes (as in '123n') are included only where a note includes a substantive mention of the person in question additional to those in the text. Modern scholars are included only where their work is directly discussed in the text.

INDEX OF SUBJECTS

Figures in bold type refer to chapters, sections, or extended passages devoted to particular subjects or themes.

Index of subjects